REALIDADES 3
Professional Development

Table of Contents

REALIDADES, Research, and the Standards

Topics covered:

▷ **REALIDADES and Research-based Instruction**

▷ **Achieving the Standards with REALIDADES**

REALIDADES is based on the belief that the purpose of learning Spanish is to communicate with the people who speak it and to understand their cultures. **REALIDADES** presents a fresh, exciting approach to Spanish by making language learning real for today's students.

....

REALIDADES and Research-based Instruction

REALIDADES reflects the most current research on how students learn languages and what teachers and materials need to do to help them become proficient language users. Let's take a look at some of the basic premises about language and language learning.

Communication

Communication is an authentic exchange of information for a real purpose between two or more people. By this we mean that people tell each other (through speech or writing) something the other person doesn't already know.

Communicating meaning has several aspects. Students need to listen to and read Spanish in order to interpret intended meanings. Students need to express meaning by conveying their own messages for a purpose and to a real audience. They also need to negotiate meaning through the natural give-and-take involved in under-standing and making oneself understood. Research tells us that classroom activities must provide students practice in interpreting, expressing, and negotiating meaning through extensive and frequent peer interactions.

Throughout REALIDADES, students are engaged in understanding messages, in sending their own messages, and thus in communicating real ideas and real meanings for real purposes.

Comprehensible input

Research states that students learn best when they have ample opportunities to internalize meanings before they have to produce them. In other words, comprehension precedes production. The term "comprehensible input" suggests that learners acquire language by understanding what they hear and read. Students need many opportunities to match what they hear with visual cues (pictures, video, or teacher pantomime) or experiences (physical actions). Reading input should be supported by a close connection between text and visuals. All these strategies for comprehensible input help students associate meaning with forms.

In keeping with this research, *REALIDADES* begins each chapter with a section call *A primera vista*. These four pages of language input give students opportunities to comprehend new language before producing it. The visualized presentation of vocabulary in context, the reading input in the *Videohistoria*, and the listening input in the *A primera vista* video segment provide a wide range of comprehensible input of new language that addresses all students and all learning styles.

Practice activities

Research tells us that students need extensive practice in using their new language to create and convey their own messages. The *Manos a la obra* section provides a wide range of practice activities. New vocabulary and grammar are first practiced in skill-getting activities that provide concrete practice. This basic practice helps to develop accuracy in using the language and prepares students to transition into more communicative tasks. In these transitional activities, students work with a partner or in small groups with information- or opinion-gap activities that are characteristic of real-life communication. Students then continue on to more open-ended, personalized speaking or writing tasks.

> " Communication is an authentic exchange of information for a real purpose between two or more people. "

Meaningful context in language learning

All effective learning is rooted in a meaningful context. We know from research that information is most likely to be retained when it is connected to other information in a meaningful way. Thus, language learning is most successful and retention more likely when we present new language organized into topics or by situations.

REALIDADES is organized into themes. All material in a chapter—vocabulary, grammar, culture— is rooted in a context and used meaningfully. Students engage in communicative tasks that are relevant to their lives. Students work with readings, realia, photography, and art that are authentic to the Spanish-speaking world. The video programs and Internet links show native speakers engaged in real-life situations and experiences.

Understanding grammar

Students learn grammar most effectively when it is presented and practiced in a meaningful context and when it connects to real communication needs. Students also benefit when shown how the patterns of grammar work.

In *REALIDADES*, new structures are foreshadowed through lexical presentation (grammar is presented as vocabulary) in the *A primera vista* language input section. In addition, early vocabulary activities in the *Manos a la obra* section have students work with the grammar lexically. This allows students to see the grammar and work with it in a meaningful context before being formally presented with the rules or paradigms.

Grammar is formally presented with clear explanations and examples. Comparisons between English and Spanish grammar are made whenever possible. Students then practice the grammar concepts in a variety of tasks that range from concrete activities that focus primarily on the structures to more open-ended tasks that focus on communication.

To further facilitate the learning of grammar, *REALIDADES* offers *GramActiva,* a multi-modality approach to grammar that includes grammar videos and hands-on grammar activities. By teaching and practicing grammar through different learning styles, more students will be able to learn grammar.

Building cultural perspectives

The *Standards for Foreign Language Learning* have expanded how culture is taught in today's classroom. We want students to understand the *why* (perspectives) of culture that determines the *what* (products and practices).

The approach to culture in *REALIDADES* not only teaches students the *what* but asks students to explore the *why.* Cultural products, practices, and comparisons are presented throughout *REALIDADES* in features such as *Fondo cultural, La cultura en vivo,* and *Perspectivas del mundo hispano,* and in *REALIDADES 3, Puente a la cultura.* Students read information about cultures that offer different perspectives and they are asked questions that encourage them to think and make observations about cultures.

Strategies for Success

Research shows that effective learners know how to help themselves become successful learners. One way they do this is by using specific problem-solving strategies.

REALIDADES teaches students strategies to be effective communicators whether listening, speaking, reading, or writing. Each reading selection is supported by a reading strategy. Each performance-based task includes a useful strategy that connects to a step-by-step approach that helps students plan, rehearse, and present or publish. Each also includes a rubric so students know how they might be evaluated.

We know more than ever about how foreign languages are learned. *REALIDADES* is based on solid research in second-language acquisition, on accepted theories about the teaching of culture, and on sound pedagogical practices that are common to all disciplines. We are sure that you and your students will find this an exciting, motivating, and enormously successful approach to learning Spanish.

Achieving the Standards with *REALIDADES*

The *Standards for Foreign Language Learning* provide an important and useful framework to guide the teaching and learning of foreign languages. This framework should result in a new generation of language learners prepared to meet the demand for competence in other languages that our nation will face as we move into an increasingly interdependent world.

REALIDADES is written based upon the Standards. This means that instruction used in *REALIDADES* will help students develop the competencies delineated in the *Standards for Foreign Language Learning.* Teachers will find a correlation to the Standards at the beginning of each chapter and with the notes that accompany each activity (if appropriate) in the Teacher's Edition.

Goal 1: Communication

1.1 (Interpersonal): Each chapter provides a wide range of paired and group activities. Students speak with a partner, work in small groups, and interview classmates.

1.2 (Interpretive): *REALIDADES* builds the interpretive listening skill through the Audio Program. This CD program supports activities in the Student Edition (input checks, dictations, listening comprehension, and test preparation) and the *Writing, Audio & Video Workbook.* The Video Program also develops listening through theme-related video segments.

REALIDADES provides extensive support for the interpretive reading skill. Students read throughout the chapter: comprehensible input, practice activities, realia, culture notes, and reading selections. Reading is seamlessly integrated with practice and anchored in real-life contexts. Whenever possible, readings are supported by focused strategies.

1.3 (Presentational): Each chapter features a speaking task and a writing task. Both presentations are supported by strategies and the speaking or writing process, step-by-step support to help students successfully complete the task.

Goal 2: Culture

2.1 (Practices and Perspectives): 2.2 (Products and Perspectives) Each chapter in *REALIDADES* explores a cultural theme through a wide range of practices, products, and perspectives. Students see authentic culture through realia, art, photographs, poetry, and authentic literature. In addition, the unique *Fondo cultural* readings generally include a Standards-based critical thinking question.

Goal 3: Connections

3.1 (Cross-curricular Connections): *REALIDADES* integrates cross-curricular activities within the *Manos a la obra* section. Students make connections to a variety of disciplines through activities that integrate the language of the chapter.

3.2 (Connections to Target Culture): *REALIDADES* exposes students to perspectives only available within the target culture through art, realia, poetry, and literature.

Goal 4: Comparisons

4.1 (Language Comparisons): *REALIDADES* enables students to see comparisons between languages in both the grammar explanations in the text and in a unique section called *Ampliación del lenguaje*. Students learn to look for language connections, to understand how language works, and to integrate these new skills as they continue in their study of Spanish.

4.2 (Cultural Comparisons): *REALIDADES* is rich in cultural comparisons. A unique feature called *Fondo cultural* generally informs students about a cultural product or practice and is followed by a question that challenges students to think critically and make comparisons between cultures.

Goal 5: Communities

5.1 (Outside the Classroom): *REALIDADES* provides informative features called *El español en la comunidad* and *El español en el mundo del trabajo*. These sections help students see how to use Spanish beyond the classroom, in their communities, and in the world of work.

5.2 (Lifelong Learners): For a textbook to help students achieve this goal, it must motivate students to want to communicate and want to learn more about the culture. The core of *REALIDADES*—real language, real culture, real tasks—motivates students. The video programs and other technology support engage learners in ways that may encourage them to continue their exploration of the Spanish language and cultures.

Standards for Foreign Language Learning

Goal 1: Communicate In Languages Other Than English

- Standard 1.1: Students engage in conversation, provide and obtain information, express feelings and emotions, and exchange opinions.
- Standard 1.2: Students understand and interpret written and spoken language on a variety of topics.
- Standard 1.3: Students present information, concepts and ideas to an audience of listeners or readers on a variety of topics.

Goal 2: Gain Knowledge And Understanding Of Other Cultures

- Standard 2.1: Students demonstrate an understanding of the relationship between the practices and perspectives of the culture studied.
- Standard 2.2: Students demonstrate an understanding of the relationship between the products and perspectives of the culture studied.

Goal 3: Connect With Other Disciplines And Acquire Information

- Standard 3.1: Students reinforce and further their knowledge of other disciplines through the foreign language.
- Standard 3.2: Students acquire information and recognize the distinctive viewpoints that are only available through the foreign language and its cultures.

Goal 4: Gain Insight Into The Nature Of Language And Culture

- Standard 4.1: Students demonstrate understanding of the nature of language through comparisons of the language studied and their own.
- Standard 4.2: Students demonstrate understanding of the concept of culture through comparisons of the cultures studied and their own.

Goal 5: Participate In Multilingual Communities At Home And Around The World

- Standard 5.1: Students use the language both within and beyond the school setting.
- Standard 5.2: Students show evidence of becoming life-long learners by using the language for personal enjoyment and enrichment.

Program Organization

Middle School

REALIDADES A and *B* are separate middle school books that meet the needs of the younger learners. Each Student Edition provides the same content of *REALIDADES 1* but has been adapted with new art, photographs, and activities that are age-appropriate for the younger learner. Students completing *REALIDADES B* will make a smooth transition into *REALIDADES 2.*

High School

Each high school Student Edition provides the complete curriculum for one year of instruction. The spiraling of themes and extensive recycling of content allows for smooth articulation between the three levels. Students completing *REALIDADES 3* will have a solid foundation for advanced Spanish study.

REALIDADES is a communication-based five-level series with a full range of printing and technology components that allow teachers to meet the needs of the different students in today's Spanish classroom.

....

REALIDADES A
• Introductory section *Para empezar*
• Themes 1–4

REALIDADES B
• Review section *Para empezar*
• Themes 5–9

REALIDADES 1
• Introductory section *Para empezar*
• Themes 1–9

REALIDADES 2
• Review section *Para empezar*
• Themes 1–9

REALIDADES 3
• Review section *Para empezar*
• Chapters 1–10

Chapter Organization

▶ Temas

REALIDADES 3 is organized around ten thematic chapters that contain two separate vocabulary and grammar sections.

Tema	Capítulo
Para empezar	A. Tu vida diaria B. Días especiales
1: Accomplishments	1: **Días inolvidables**
2: Artistic and Personal Expression	2: **¿Cómo te expresas?**
3: Health and Exercise	3: **¿Qué haces para estar en forma?**
4: Interpersonal Relationships	4: **¿Cómo te llevas con los demás?**
5: The World of Work	5: **Trabajo y comunidad**
6: The Future	6: **¿Qué nos traerá el futuro?**
7: Interpreting the Past	7: **¿Mito o realidad?**
8: Encounters between Cultures	8: **Encuentro entre culturas**
9: Protecting the Environment	9: **Cuidemos nuestro planeta**
10: Rights and Responsibilities	10: **¿Cuáles son tus derechos y deberes?**

▶ Chapters

Each chapter in *REALIDADES* is built around a clear sequence of instruction.

Chapter Section	Pedagogical support
A primera vista 1 y 2	Provides comprehensible language input for the chapter's new vocabulary and grammar within an authentic context. Input includes words, dialogues, narration, visuals, and audio. Students' language production focuses on comprehension and limited production.
Manos a la obra 1 y 2	Provides productive language practice with a variety of concrete, transitional, and open-ended activities. The activities develop all four language skills and focus on relevant language tasks. Many activities build off of authentic documents, *realia*, and photographs.
¡Adelante!	Provides culminating theme-based activities that have students apply what they have learned. The section features a culturally-based reading, listening and picture sequence activities, performance-based speaking and writing tasks, and authentic literature.
Repaso del capítulo	Provides complete support for the end-of-chapter assessment. Two pages summarize what students need to know (vocabulary and grammar). The next two pages outline the proficiency and culture sections of the test by describing the task, providing a practice task, and referring students to chapter activities for review.

Program Organization

Articulation

REALIDADES offers a completely articulated Scope and Sequence across all levels. The recursive themes allow for the recycling, review, and reteaching of vocabulary and grammar.

REALIDADES 1

Tema	Capítulo	
Para empezar	• En la escuela: greetings; introductions; leave-takings; numbers; time; body parts • En la clase: classroom, date, asking for help • El tiempo: weather, seasons	
	A	**B**
1: Mis amigos y yo	**1A ¿Qué te gusta hacer?** **Vocabulary:** activities and expressions for saying what you like and don't like to do **Grammar:** infinitives; making negative statements	**1B ¿Y tú cómo eres?** **Vocabulary:** adjectives and vocabulary to ask about and describe someone's personality **Grammar:** adjectives; definite and indefinite articles; word order
2: La escuela	**2A Tu día en la escuela** **Vocabulary:** classroom items and furniture; parts of the classroom; prepositions of location **Grammar:** subject pronouns; the present tense of -ar verbs	**2B Tu sala de clases** **Vocabulary:** classroom items and furniture; parts of the classroom; prepositions of location **Grammar:** the verb *estar;* plurals of nouns and articles
3: La comida	**3A ¿Desayuno o almuerzo?** **Vocabulary:** foods; beverages; adverbs of frequency; expressions to show surprise **Grammar:** present tense of -er and -ir verbs; *me gusta(n), me encanta(n)*	**3B Para mantener la salud** **Vocabulary:** food; beverages; expressions to discuss health; expressions to discuss preferences, agreement, disagreement, and quantity; adjectives to describe food **Grammar:** the plural of adjectives; the verb *ser*
4: Los pasatiempos	**4A ¿Adónde vas?** **Vocabulary:** leisure activities; places; expressions to tell where and with whom you go; expressions to talk about when things are done **Grammar:** the verb *ir;* interrogative words	**4B ¿Quieres ir conmigo?** **Vocabulary:** leisure activities; feelings; expressions for extending, accepting, and declining invitations; expressions to tell when something happens **Grammar:** *ir + a + infinitive;* the verb *jugar*
5: Fiesta en familia	**5A Una fiesta de cumpleaños** **Vocabulary:** family and parties **Grammar:** the verb *tener;* possessive adjectives	**5B ¡Vamos a un restaurante!** **Vocabulary:** describing people and ordering a meal **Grammar:** the verb *venir;* the verbs *ser* and *estar*
6: La casa	**6A En mi dormitorio** **Vocabulary:** bedroom items; electronic equipment; colors; adjectives to describe things **Grammar:** comparisons and superlatives; stem-changing verbs: *poder* and *dormir*	**6B ¿Cómo es tu casa?** **Vocabulary:** rooms in a house and household chores **Grammar:** affirmative *tú* commands; the present progressive tense
7: De compras	**7A ¿Cuánto cuesta?** **Vocabulary:** clothing; shopping; numbers 200–1,000 **Grammar:** stem-changing verbs: *pensar, querer,* and *preferir;* demonstrative adjectives	**7B ¡Qué regalo!** **Vocabulary:** places to shop; gifts; accessories; buying and selling **Grammar:** preterite of -ar, -car, and -gar verbs; direct object pronouns *lo, la, los, las*
8: Experiencias	**8A De vacaciones** **Vocabulary:** vacation places; activities; modes of transportation **Grammar:** preterite of -er and -ir verbs; preterite of *ir;* the personal *a*	**8B Ayudando en la comunidad** **Vocabulary:** recycling and volunteer work; places in a community **Grammar:** the verb *decir;* indirect object pronouns; preterite of *hacer* and *dar*
9: Medios de comunicación	**9A El cine y la televisión** **Vocabulary:** television shows; movie genres; giving opinions **Grammar:** *acabar de* + infinitive; *gustar* and similar verbs	**9B La tecnología** **Vocabulary:** computers; communication; computer-related activities **Grammar:** the verbs *pedir* and *servir; saber* and *conocer*

REALIDADES A and *B* provide the same Scope and Sequence as *REALIDADES 1.*

REALIDADES A covers the same content as the *Para empezar* section and *Temas* 1–4.

Tema	Capítulo
Para empezar	• En la escuela: greetings; introductions; leave-takings; numbers; time; body parts • En la clase: classroom, date, asking for help • El tiempo: weather, seasons

Tema	Capítulo (A)	Capítulo (B)
1: Mis amigos y yo	**1A ¿Qué te gusta hacer?** **Vocabulary:** activities and expressions for saying what you like and don't like to do **Grammar:** infinitives; making negative statements	**1B ¿Y tú cómo eres?** **Vocabulary:** adjectives and vocabulary to ask about and describe someone's personality **Grammar:** adjectives; definite and indefinite articles; word order
2: La escuela	**2A Tu día en la escuela** **Vocabulary:** classroom items and furniture; parts of the classroom; prepositions of location **Grammar:** subject pronouns; the present tense of *-ar* verbs	**2B Tu sala de clases** **Vocabulary:** classroom items and furniture; parts of the classroom; prepositions of location **Grammar:** the verb *estar;* plurals of nouns and articles
3: La comida	**3A ¿Desayuno o almuerzo?** **Vocabulary:** foods; beverages; adverbs of frequency; expressions to show surprise **Grammar:** present tense of *-er* and *-ir* verbs; *me gusta(n), me encanta(n)*	**3B Para mantener la salud** **Vocabulary:** food; beverages; expressions to discuss health; expressions to discuss preferences, agreement, disagreement, and quantity; adjectives to describe food **Grammar:** the plural of adjectives; the verb *ser*
4: Los pasatiempos	**4A ¿Adónde vas?** **Vocabulary:** leisure activities; places; expressions to tell where and with whom you go; expressions to talk about when things are done **Grammar:** the verb *ir;* interrogative words	**4B ¿Quieres ir conmigo?** **Vocabulary:** leisure activities; feelings; expressions for extending, accepting, and declining invitations; expressions to tell when something happens **Grammar:** *ir + a +* infinitive; the verb *jugar*

REALIDADES B provides a review section called *Para empezar* and continues with *Temas* 5–9.

Tema	Capítulo (A)	Capítulo (B)
5: Fiesta en familia	**5A Una fiesta de cumpleaños** **Vocabulary:** family and parties **Grammar:** the verb *tener;* possessive adjectives	**5B ¡Vamos a un restaurante!** **Vocabulary:** describing people and ordering a meal **Grammar:** the verb *venir;* the verbs *ser* and *estar*
6: La casa	**6A En mi dormitorio** **Vocabulary:** bedroom items; electronic equipment; colors; adjectives to describe things **Grammar:** comparisons and superlatives; stem-changing verbs: *poder* and *dormir*	**6B ¿Cómo es tu casa?** **Vocabulary:** rooms in a house and household chores **Grammar:** affirmative *tú* commands; the present progressive tense
7: De compras	**7A ¿Cuánto cuesta?** **Vocabulary:** clothing; shopping; numbers 200–1,000 **Grammar:** stem-changing verbs: *pensar, querer,* and *preferir;* demonstrative adjectives	**7B ¡Qué regalo!** **Vocabulary:** places to shop; gifts; accessories; buying and selling **Grammar:** preterite of *-ar, -car,* and *-gar* verbs; direct object pronouns *lo, la, los, las*
8: Experiencias	**8A De vacaciones** **Vocabulary:** vacation places; activities; modes of transportation **Grammar:** preterite of *-er* and *-ir* verbs; preterite of *ir;* the personal *a*	**8B Ayudando en la comunidad** **Vocabulary:** recycling and volunteer work; places in a community **Grammar:** the verb *decir;* indirect object pronouns; preterite of *hacer* and *dar*
9: Medios de comunicación	**9A El cine y la televisión** **Vocabulary:** television shows; movie genres; giving opinions **Grammar:** *acabar de* + infinitive; *gustar* and similar verbs	**9B La tecnología** **Vocabulary:** computers; communication; computer-related activities **Grammar:** the verbs *pedir* and *servir; saber* and *conocer*

Program Organization

REALIDADES 2 uses a recursive Scope and Sequence that revisits the themes from *REALIDADES A, B,* or *1.* This natural recycling allows for important review and reteaching. In addition, students expand their vocabulary, grammar, and cultural understanding as they revisit each theme in greater depth.

REALIDADES 2

Tema	Capítulo	
Para empezar	A. ¿Cómo eres tú? *Repaso:* describing people; asking for information; nationalities; adjective agreement; the verb *ser* B. ¿Qué haces? *Repaso:* leisure activities; seasons of the year; regular *-ar, -er,* and *-ir* verbs	

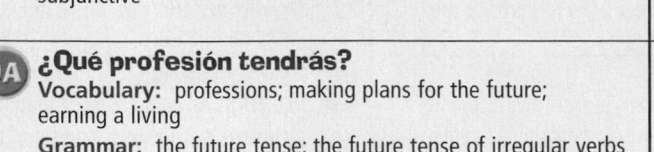

Tema	**A**	**B**
1: Tu día escolar	**1A ¿Qué haces en la escuela?** Vocabulary: classroom items, activities, and rules Grammar: *(Repaso)* stem-changing verbs; affirmative and negative words	**1B ¿Qué haces después de las clases?** Vocabulary: extracurricular activities Grammar: making comparisons; *(Repaso)* the verbs *saber* and *conocer; hace* + time expressions
2: Un evento especial	**2A ¿Cómo te preparas?** Vocabulary: daily routines, getting ready for an event Grammar: reflexive verbs; *(Repaso)* the verbs *ser* and *estar;* possessive adjectives *mío, tuyo, suyo*	**2B ¿Qué ropa compraste?** Vocabulary: shopping vocabulary, prices, money Grammar: *(Repaso)* the preterite of regular verbs; demonstrative adjectives
3: Tú y tu comunidad	**3A ¿Qué hiciste ayer?** Vocabulary: running errands; locations in a downtown; items purchased Grammar: *(Repaso)* direct object pronouns; the irregular preterite of the verbs *ir, ser, hacer, tener, estar, poder*	**3B ¿Cómo se va . . . ?** Vocabulary: places in a city or town; driving terms; modes of transportation Grammar: *(Repaso)* direct object pronouns: *me, te, nos;* irregular affirmative *tú* commands; *(Repaso)* present progressive: irregular forms
4: Recuerdos del pasado	**4A Cuando éramos niños** Vocabulary: toys; play terms; describing children Grammar: the imperfect tense: regular verbs and irregular verbs; *(Repaso)* indirect object pronouns	**4B Celebrando los días festivos** Vocabulary: expression describing etiquette; holiday and family celebrations Grammar: the imperfect tense: describing a situation; reciprocal actions
5: En las noticias	**5A Un acto heroico** Vocabulary: natural disasters; emergencies; rescues; heroes Grammar: the imperfect tense: other uses; the preterite of the verbs *oír, leer, creer,* and *destruir*	**5B Un accidente** Vocabulary: parts of the body; accidents; events in the emergency room Grammar: the irregular preterites: *venir, poner; decir, traer;* the imperfect progressive and preterite
6: La televisión y el cine	**6A ¿Viste el partido en la televisión?** Vocabulary: watching television programs; sporting events Grammar: the preterite of *-ir* stem-changing verbs; other reflexive verbs	**6B ¿Qué película has visto?** Vocabulary: movies; making a movie Grammar: verbs that use indirect objects; the present perfect
7: Buen provecho	**7A ¿Cómo se hace la paella?** Vocabulary: cooking expressions; food; appliances; following a recipe; giving directions in a kitchen Grammar: negative *tú* commands; the impersonal *se*	**7B ¿Te gusta comer al aire libre?** Vocabulary: camping and cookouts; food Grammar: *usted* and *ustedes* commands; uses of *por*
8: Cómo ser un buen turista	**8A Un viaje en avión** Vocabulary: visiting an airport; planning a trip; traveling safely Grammar: the present subjunctive; irregular verbs in the subjunctive	**8B Quiero que disfrutes de tu viaje** Vocabulary: staying in a hotel; appropriate tourist behaviors; traveling in a foreign city Grammar: the present subjunctive with impersonal expressions; the present subjunctive of stem-changing verbs
9: ¿Cómo será el futuro?	**9A ¿Qué profesión tendrás?** Vocabulary: professions; making plans for the future; earning a living Grammar: the future tense; the future tense of irregular verbs	**9B ¿Qué haremos para mejorar el mundo?** Vocabulary: environment; environmental issues and solutions Grammar: the future tense: other irregular verbs; the present subjunctive with expressions of doubt

REALIDADES 3 offers ten thought-provoking thematic chapters that integrate rich vocabulary groups and a thorough presentation of grammar. Chapter activities combine communication, culture, and cross-curricular content with authentic literature and poetry.

REALIDADES 3

Capítulo	Each thematic chapter is divided into two sections. Each of these sections (1 and 2) presents and practices vocabulary and grammar.	
Para empezar	1. Tu vida diaria *Repaso:* daily routines; school life; leisure activities; present tense verbs; reflexive verbs 2. Días especiales *Repaso:* weekend activities; celebrations; special events; verbs like *gustar;* possessive adjectives	
	①	**②**
1: Días inolvidables	**Vocabulary:** hiking objects, activities, and perils; weather **Grammar:** *(Repaso)* preterite verbs with the spelling change *i→y; (Repaso)* preterite of irregular verbs; *(Repaso)* preterite of verbs with the spelling change *e→i* and *o→u*	**Vocabulary:** getting ready for an athletic or academic competition; emotional responses to competition; awards and ceremonies **Grammar:** *(Repaso)* the imperfect; uses of the imperfect
2: ¿Cómo te expresas?	**Vocabulary:** describing art and sculpture; tools for painting; describing what influences art **Grammar:** *(Repaso)* the preterite vs. the imperfect; *estar* + participle	**Vocabulary:** musical instruments; describing dance; describing drama **Grammar:** *(Repaso) ser* and *estar;* verbs with special meanings in the preterite vs. the imperfect
3: ¿Qué haces para estar en forma?	**Vocabulary:** nutrition; illnesses and pains; medicine; habits for good health **Grammar:** *(Repaso)* affirmative *tú* commands; *(Repaso)* affirmative and negatives commands with *Ud.* and *Uds.*	**Vocabulary:** exercises; getting and staying in shape; health advice **Grammar:** *(Repaso)* the subjunctive: regular verbs; *(Repaso)* the subjunctive: irregular verbs; *(Repaso)* the subjunctive with stem changing *-ar* and *-er* verbs
4: ¿Cómo te llevas con los demás?	**Vocabulary:** personality traits; interpersonal behavior; friendship **Grammar:** *(Repaso)* the subjunctive with verbs of emotion; *(Repaso)* the uses of *por* and *para*	**Vocabulary:** expressing and resolving interpersonal problems; interpersonal relationships **Grammar:** commands with *nosotros;* possessive pronouns
5: Trabajo y comunidad	**Vocabulary:** after-school work; describing a job; **Grammar:** *(Repaso)* the present perfect; *(Repaso)* the past perfect	**Vocabulary:** volunteer activities; the benefits and importance of volunteer work **Grammar:** the present perfect subjunctive; demonstrative adjectives and pronouns
6: ¿Qué nos traerá el futuro?	**Vocabulary:** jobs and professions; qualities of a good employee **Grammar:** *(Repaso)* the future; *(Repaso)* the future of probability	**Vocabulary:** technology; inventions; jobs in the future **Grammar:** the future perfect; *(Repaso)* the use of direct and indirect object pronouns
7: ¿Mito o realidad?	**Vocabulary:** archeological terms and activities; describing archeological sites **Grammar:** the present and past subjunctive in expressions of doubt	**Vocabulary:** myths and legends; ancient beliefs; Precolumbian scientific discoveries **Grammar:** the subjunctive in adverbial clauses
8: Encuentro entre culturas	**Vocabulary:** architecture and history of Spain **Grammar:** the conditional	**Vocabulary:** Spain in the Americas; the encounter between Cortés and the Aztecs; family heritage **Grammar:** the past subjunctive; the past subjunctive with *si* clauses
9: Cuidemos nuestro planeta	**Vocabulary:** caring for the environment **Grammar:** present subjunctive with conjunctions (*mientras, tan pronto como,* etc.); relative pronouns *que, quien, lo que*	**Vocabulary:** environmental issues, endangered animals **Grammar:** present subjunctive with other conjunctions (*a menos que, sin que, para que,* etc.)
10: ¿Cuáles son tus derechos y deberes?	**Vocabulary:** rights and responsibilities **Grammar:** the passive voice: *ser* + past participle; the present vs. the past subjunctive	**Vocabulary:** government; the role of government; individual rights **Grammar:** the past perfect subjunctive; the conditional perfect

Program Components

REALIDADES: One program for <u>all</u> your students with complete print and technology support.

Student Print Resources

Practice Workbook	• focused practice for new vocabulary and grammar • end-of-chapter crossword puzzle • end-of-chapter Organizer • go online Web Codes for linking to Web site
Writing, Audio & Video Workbook	• additional writing practice • student response pages for the Audio Program • student response pages for the *A primera vista* video segments

REALIDADES para hispanohablantes
• all-Spanish companion worktext to Student Edition
• grammar explanations in Spanish
• more practice for language mechanics, usage, vocabulary, grammar, reading, and writing

Lecturas para hispanohablantes
• literature anthology for additional reading

Reading and Writing for TAKS Success
• thematic readings practice test-taking skills

Grammar Study Guide
• laminated cards summarize grammar for Spanish 3–4

Student Technology

  **REALIDADES Companion Web Site**	• instant access using Web Codes • tutorial practice for vocabulary and grammar • internet links and activities • end-of-chapter vocabulary and grammar lists • end-of-chapter self-test
 **MindPoint™ Quiz Show CD-ROM**	• interactive game show format for review • competition against computer, a partner, or entire class • detailed report provides instant overview of student performance against chapter objectives
 **Interactive Textbook**	• interactive Student Edition online or on CD-ROM • access to audio and video • interactive activities
 **Downloadable audio files**	• audio for vocabulary, Student Edition activities, and pronunciation for students to download • Web Codes listed in Student Edition

Teacher Transparencies

Vocabulary and Grammar Transparencies
- Maps
- Graphic Organizers
- *A primera vista*
  - *Vocabulario y gramática en contexto*
- *Gramática*
  - verb paradigms and grammar charts
- Realia

Answers on Transparencies
- Student Edition answers
- *Practice Workbook* answers

Fine Art Transparencies
- 72 beautiful transparencies to be used across all five levels
- Accompanying notes and activities

Teacher Print Resources

Teacher's Resource Book
Organized by chapters:
- Input Script
- Video Script
- Audio Script
- *Practice Workbook* Answer Key
- *Writing, Audio & Video Workbook* Answer Key
- Communication Activities on Blackline Masters

- Situation Cards on Blackline Masters
- School-to-Home Letters
- **GramActiva** Blackline Masters
- Vocabulary Clip Art

Teacher Technology

TeacherExpress™ CD-ROM
- Lesson Planner
- Interactive Teacher's Edition
- Teaching Resources
- Vocabulary Clip Art
- Computer Test Bank
- Web Resources

Video Program (VHS or DVD)
- Theme-based videos that connect to the chapter theme

Companion Web Site
- teaching ideas
- links to other resources

Audio Program (14 CDs)
- *A primera vista*
  - *Vocabulario y gramática en contexto*
- Student Edition *Escuchar* Activities
- *En voz alta*
- *Writing, Audio & Video Workbook* Listening Activities
- Listening section of *Examen del capítulo*

Computer Test Bank with CD-ROM
- Variety of questions per chapter
- Create tests and alternate versions

Teacher Assessment

Assessment Program
- for use with students using Student Edition

Assessment Program REALIDADES para hispanohablantes
- for use with heritage learners

Computer Test Bank with CD-ROM
- Variety of questions per chapter
- Create tests and alternate versions

Getting Started

Students get started in *REALIDADES 3* with these colorful reference and introductory sections:

▷ **Mapas**

▷ **Tips for success**

▷ **Para empezar**

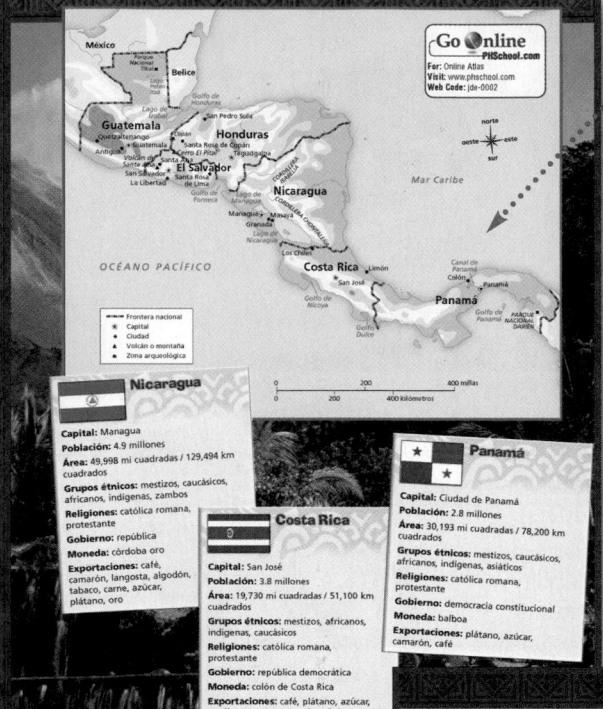

Mapas

Colorful atlas pages support geography skills. Students can go online to learn more about each country.

Tips for success

Students are reminded of study tips as they begin *REALIDADES 3*.

Para empezar

This bridge section provides a basic review of key content from *REALIDADES 2*.

Basic review

The quick review covers concepts from the second year.

A ver si recuerdas

This section helps students review the key vocabulary and grammar learned in first- and second-year Spanish as it relates to the upcoming chapter.

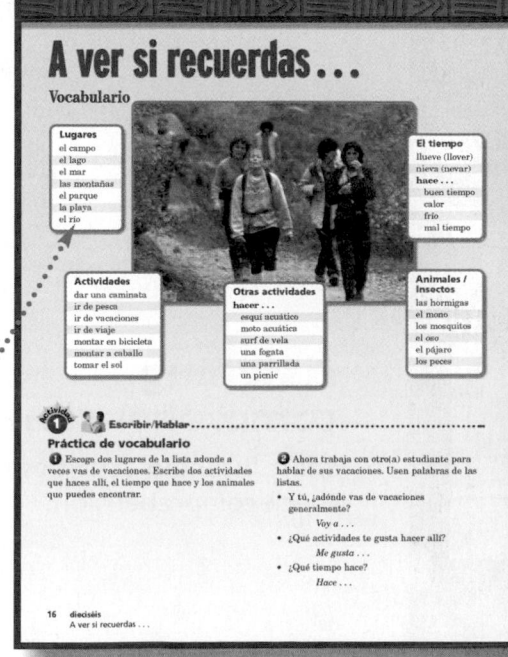

Vocabulary review

Thematic vocabulary is reviewed using a graphic organizer.

Grammar review

Students review and practice key grammar concepts.

Chapter Organization

Chapter Sequence

▶ **A primera vista 1 y 2**

▶ **Manos a la obra 1 y 2**

▶ **¡Adelante!**

▶ **Repaso del capítulo**

▶ Chapter opener *Capítulo 1*

A primera vista 1 y 2

This four-page section gives students a "first look" at the new vocabulary and grammar through comprehensible input that integrates visuals and text. There are two *A primera vista* sections per chapter.

Visualized vocabulary

New words are presented visually and in context.

Language input

Input continues with visuals accompanied by narrative. All new vocabulary words and grammar are highlighted in blue.

Listening comprehension

Short listening activities check comprehension.

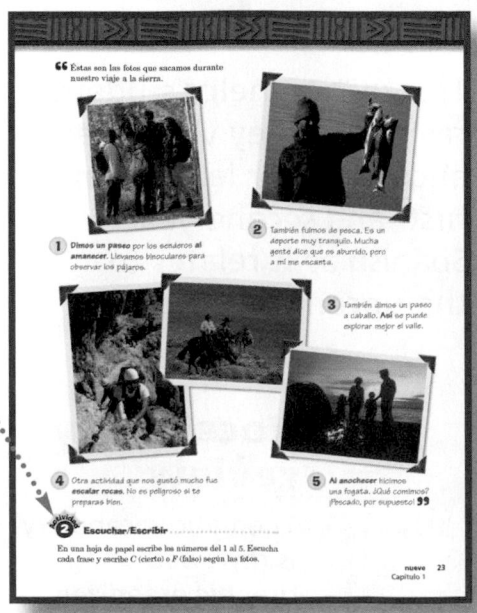

Reading and language input

The input of new vocabulary and grammar continues using longer narratives such as a story, realia, or a dialogue. New content is highlighted in blue.

¡Una aventura desastrosa!

Estrategia
Cause and effect
Identifying cause and effect relationships helps us understand what we are reading.
Look at the pictures. Write the effect for each cause:

Causa — Efecto
A Guille no ve la raíz.
B Aparece un oso.
C El oso ve la mochila.

1 Al amanecer, Guille, Felipe y yo nos levantamos para dar un paseo. **Anduvimos** por dos horas por un sendero. Queríamos ir a La Peña, una roca enorme, perfecta para escalar.

2 De repente, Guille se cayó y dio un grito.
—¿Qué **sucedió**, Guille?
—No vi la raíz del árbol. ¡Ay! Se rompió la brújula.
—¡Qué desastre! Y no tenemos otra. Vamos a **perdernos**.
—Creo que no. Se puede ver La Peña en la distancia. ¡Vamos!

3 **Nos acercamos** al pie de La Peña. Nos **impresionó** mucho porque era muy alta.
—¿Por qué no descansamos **un rato** antes de escalar?
—Buena idea.

4 Una vez allí, nos sentamos. De repente, **apareció** un oso muy grande. ¡Uf, nos **asustó** con lo grande que era!
¡Ay! ¿Qué podemos hacer? ¿Adónde podemos ir? ¿Dónde **nos refugiamos**?

5 Empezamos a correr **hacia** La Peña. No había otro **refugio**. El oso empezó a correr también.
—¡Rápido!
—¡Mira! Hay una roca grande a la izquierda. ¡Vamos allí!
—¡Ay! Perdí la mochila.
—No importa. ¡Corre!

6 Felipe **perdió el equilibrio**, se cayó y se torció el tobillo.
—¡Felipe, te ayudo!
De repente, el oso **dejó de** correr. Vio la mochila y la abrió. Sacó la comida que estaba adentro y se fue con la comida en la boca.

7 ¡Qué mala suerte! Inmediatamente empezó a llover. Vimos unos **relámpagos** y oímos un **trueno** tremendo. Luego, empezó a **caer granizo**. Entonces . . .

8 ¿Cómo crees que terminó la aventura?

Actividad 3 Escribir/Hablar
¿Comprendiste?
1. ¿Por qué querían ir a La Peña los chicos?
2. ¿Qué le pasó a Guille?
3. ¿Qué animal los asustó? ¿Dónde se refugiaron?
4. Imagínate que estás con los chicos cuando aparece el oso. ¿Qué crees que deben hacer?

● **Más práctica**
Practice Workbook 1-3, 1-4
Go Online PHSchool.com
For: Vocabulary practice
Visit: www.phschool.com
Web Code: jsd-0102

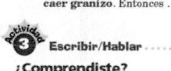

24 diez
A primera vista 1

More practice

Extra practice is available in the *Practice Workbook* and online.

Reading comprehension

Questions check students' comprehension of the story while practicing the new vocabulary and grammar.

La Voz Del Estudiante
Santiago, 23 de septiembre

Nuestros jóvenes maestros

Diez estudiantes de nuestra escuela participaron en el concurso de ajedrez. **Desafortunadamente**, nuestra escuela no ganó el primer premio, pero estamos orgullosos de nuestros representantes.

El poder de las palabras

Felicitaciones a nuestros poetas estudiantiles. La ceremonia de **entrega de premios** tuvo lugar la semana pasada en el teatro de la escuela. Al final de la ceremonia los ganadores estaban muy contentos.

¡Campeonas de básquetbol!

¿Recuerdan cuando el año pasado **eliminaron** a nuestro equipo del campeonato de básquetbol? Pues este año, con mucho **entrenamiento** y esfuerzo, las chicas del equipo de nuestra escuela jugaron **contra** el equipo rival del Liceo San Martín y **vencieron** 68 a 62. ¡Felicitaciones, campeonas!

Actividad 28 Escribir
¿Comprendiste?
1. ¿Qué concurso no ganaron los estudiantes de la escuela?
2. ¿Cómo se sintieron los jóvenes poetas al final de la ceremonia?
3. ¿Qué le pasó el año pasado al equipo de básquetbol de la escuela?
4. ¿Quién perdió este partido de básquetbol?
5. ¿Por qué crees que los estudiantes están orgullosos de sus jugadores de ajedrez?

38 treinta y ocho
A primera vista 2

Manos a la obra 1 y 2

Students "get to work" using the chapter's new vocabulary and grammar. Each chapter has two *Manos a la obra* sections.

Paired practice

Students transition to paired practice activities that focus on the new vocabulary.

Focused practice

Students start with activities that focus on reading, listening, and basic writing.

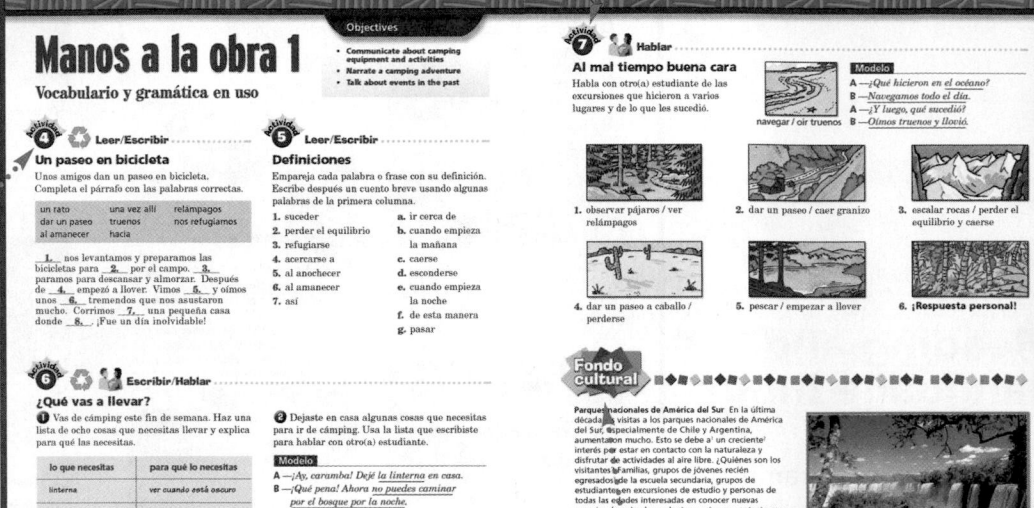

Integrated culture

Cultural notes are embedded throughout the chapter.

Grammar integrated with communication

The complete grammar presentation features clear explanations and examples.

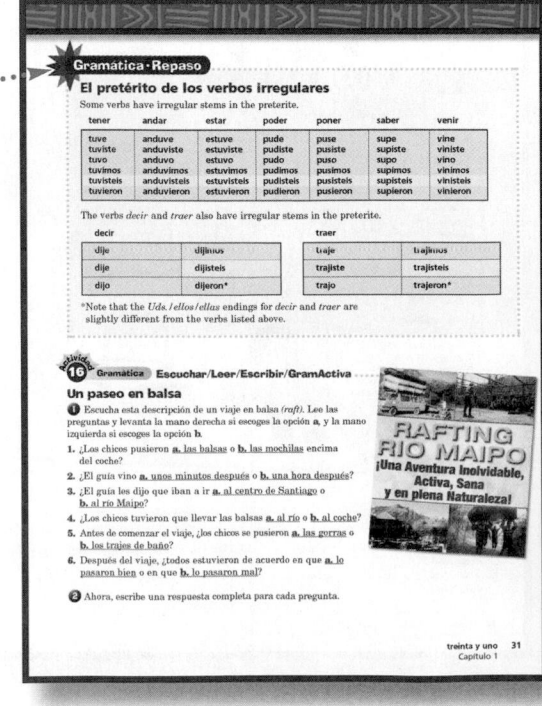

Language and culture

Culture and real experiences are woven throughout the language practice.

Connections to other disciplines

Cross-curricular connections are integrated into the language practice.

Actividad 24 Leer/Escribir

Una caminata por Torres del Paine

Imagínate que fuiste con unos(as) amigos(as) a hacer una excursión como la que se describe en este anuncio turístico. Escribe tres frases para describir lo que pasó en cada actividad.

Modelo

El primer día dimos una caminata muy larga.

VIAJE

Parque Nacional
Torres del Paine

▶ Caminatas de entre 4 a 7 horas por día
▶ Navegar en el lago
▶ Escalar el Glaciar Grey
▶ Montar a caballo por el Valle del Ascencio
▶ Acampar en el exclusivo Ecocamp

Precio: USD $1,130   7 días, 6 noches

Actividad 25 Leer/Escribir

Los Ecocamps de Torres del Paine

Lee el texto sobre el Parque Nacional Torres del Paine y los Ecocamps, y contesta las siguientes preguntas.

El Parque Nacional Torres del Paine, situado en la zona patagónica de Chile, es uno de los lugares más hermosos de nuestro planeta. Los senderos del parque ofrecen vistas magníficas del paisaje patagónico: montañas, bosques, ríos, glaciares, lagos, y abundante flora y fauna. Este parque, remoto y misterioso, atrae a miles de turistas y aventureros de todo el mundo que vienen cada año a hacer caminatas, montar a caballo o navegar. Desafortunadamente, la gran demanda por visitar el parque ha generado problemas serios de impacto ecológico y en la calidad de los servicios turísticos en general.

Una solución a este problema ha sido cambiar los hoteles por "Ecocamps", tiendas de acampar modernas, cómodas y transportables. Los "Ecocamps" permiten a los visitantes estar más cerca de la naturaleza y producen menos basura que los hoteles.

1. ¿Qué tipos de paisajes ofrece el Parque Nacional Torres del Paine?
2. ¿Qué solución ofrecen los Ecocamps para mejorar los problemas de impacto ecológico?
3. ¿Qué crees que puedes hacer tú para ayudar a cuidar lugares como éste?

● **Más práctica**
Practice Workbook 1-7

Go Online PHSchool.com

For: Practice with preterite verbs
Visit: www.phschool.com
Web Code: jed-0105

treinta y cinco   35
Capítulo 1

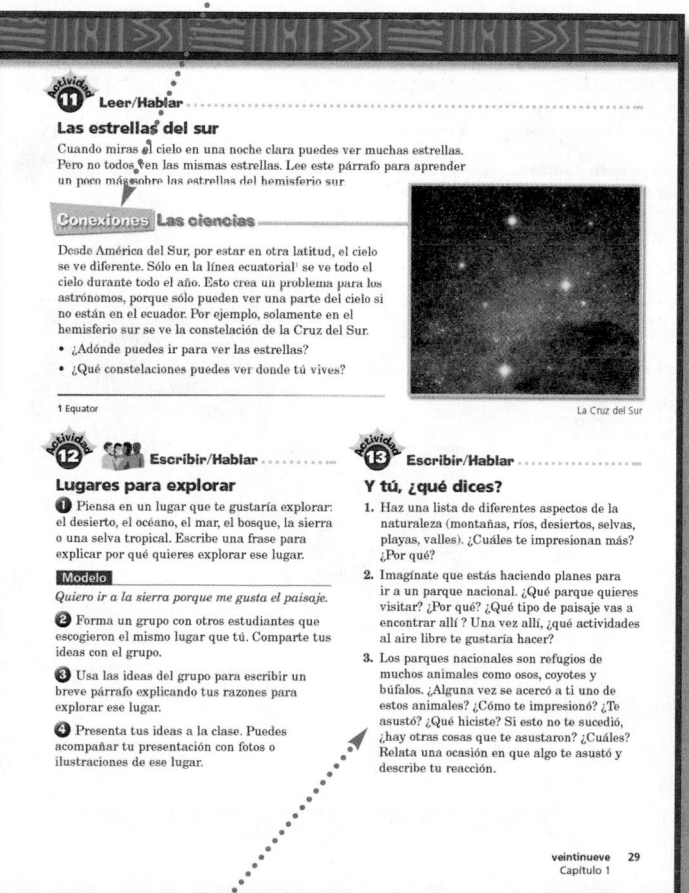

Actividad 11 Leer/Hablar

Las estrellas del sur

Cuando miras el cielo en una noche clara puedes ver muchas estrellas. Pero no todos ven las mismas estrellas. Lee este párrafo para aprender un poco más sobre las estrellas del hemisferio sur.

Conexiones Las ciencias

Desde América del Sur, por estar en otra latitud, el cielo se ve diferente. Sólo en la línea ecuatorial¹ se ve todo el cielo durante todo el año. Esto crea un problema para los astrónomos, porque sólo pueden ver una parte del cielo si no están en el ecuador. Por ejemplo, solamente en el hemisferio sur se ve la constelación de la Cruz del Sur.

• ¿Adónde puedes ir para ver las estrellas?
• ¿Qué constelaciones puedes ver donde tú vives?

1 Equator

La Cruz del Sur

Actividad 12 Escribir/Hablar

Lugares para explorar

❶ Piensa en un lugar que te gustaría explorar: el desierto, el océano, el mar, el bosque, la sierra o una selva tropical. Escribe una frase para explicar por qué quieres explorar ese lugar.

Modelo

Quiero ir a la sierra porque me gusta el paisaje.

❷ Forma un grupo con otros estudiantes que escogieron el mismo lugar que tú. Comparte tus ideas con el grupo.

❸ Usa las ideas del grupo para escribir un breve párrafo explicando tus razones para explorar ese lugar.

❹ Presenta tus ideas a la clase. Puedes acompañar tu presentación con fotos o ilustraciones de ese lugar.

Actividad 13 Escribir/Hablar

Y tú, ¿qué dices?

1. Haz una lista de diferentes aspectos de la naturaleza (montañas, ríos, desiertos, selvas, playas, valles). ¿Cuáles te impresionan más? ¿Por qué?
2. Imagínate que estás haciendo planes para ir a un parque nacional. ¿Qué parque quieres visitar? ¿Por qué? ¿Qué tipo de paisaje vas a encontrar allí? Una vez allí, ¿qué actividades al aire libre te gustaría hacer?
3. Los parques nacionales son refugios de muchos animales como osos, coyotes y búfalos. ¿Alguna vez se acercó a ti uno de estos animales? ¿Cómo te impresionó? ¿Te asustó? ¿Qué hiciste? Si esto no te sucedió, ¿hay otras cosas que te asustaron? ¿Cuáles? Relata una ocasión en que algo te asustó y describe tu reacción.

veintinueve   29
Capítulo 1

Personal responses

The sequence of exercises culminates with personalized speaking and writing tasks.

Integrated poetry and song lyrics

The *En voz alta* section in each chapter features poetry or song lyrics.

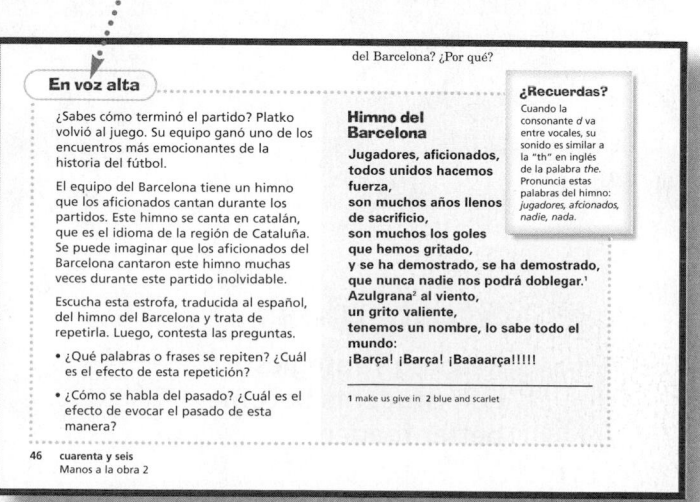

del Barcelona? ¿Por qué?

En voz alta

¿Sabes cómo terminó el partido? Platko volvió al juego. Su equipo ganó uno de los encuentros más emocionantes de la historia del fútbol.

El equipo del Barcelona tiene un himno que los aficionados cantan durante los partidos. Este himno se canta en catalán, que es el idioma de la región de Cataluña. Se puede imaginar que los aficionados del Barcelona cantaron este himno muchas veces durante este partido inolvidable.

Escucha esta estrofa, traducida al español, del himno del Barcelona y trata de repetirla. Luego, contesta las preguntas.

• ¿Qué palabras o frases se repiten? ¿Cuál es el efecto de esta repetición?
• ¿Cómo se habla del pasado? ¿Cuál es el efecto de evocar el pasado de esta manera?

Himno del Barcelona

Jugadores, aficionados,
todos unidos hacemos fuerza,
son muchos años llenos de sacrificio,
son muchos los goles
que hemos gritado,
y se ha demostrado, se ha demostrado,
que nunca nadie nos podrá doblegar.¹
Azulgrana² al viento,
un grito valiente,
tenemos un nombre, lo sabe todo el mundo:
¡Barça! ¡Barça! ¡Baaaarça!!!!!

1 make us give in 2 blue and scarlet

¿Recuerdas?
Cuando la consonante *d* va entre vocales, su sonido es similar a la "th" en inglés de la palabra *the*. Pronuncia estas palabras del himno: *jugadores, aficionados, nadie, nada.*

46   cuarenta y seis
Manos a la obra 2

¡Adelante!

Each chapter culminates with rich and varied activities that feature cultural readings, literature, listening, speaking, and writing.

Building a bridge to culture

High-interest cultural readings deepen cultural perspectives.

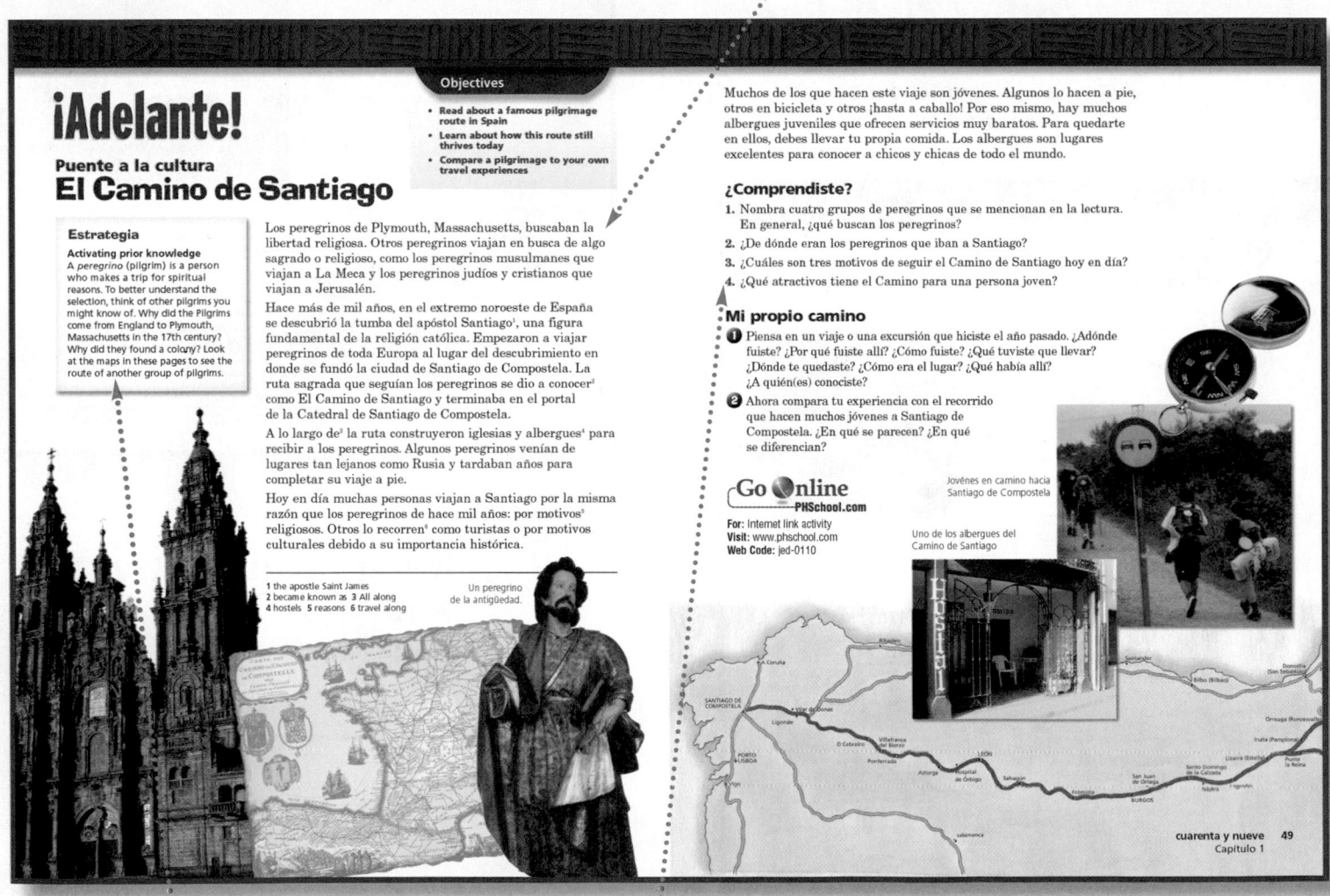

¡Adelante!

Objectives
- Read about a famous pilgrimage route in Spain
- Learn about how this route still thrives today
- Compare a pilgrimage to your own travel experiences

Puente a la cultura
El Camino de Santiago

Estrategia

Activating prior knowledge
A *peregrino* (pilgrim) is a person who makes a trip for spiritual reasons. To better understand the selection, think of other pilgrims you might know of. Why did the Pilgrims come from England to Plymouth, Massachusetts in the 17th century? Why did they found a colony? Look at the maps in these pages to see the route of another group of pilgrims.

Los peregrinos de Plymouth, Massachusetts, buscaban la libertad religiosa. Otros peregrinos viajan en busca de algo sagrado o religioso, como los peregrinos musulmanes que viajan a La Meca y los peregrinos judíos y cristianos que viajan a Jerusalén.

Hace más de mil años, en el extremo noroeste de España se descubrió la tumba del apóstol Santiago[1], una figura fundamental de la religión católica. Empezaron a viajar peregrinos de toda Europa al lugar del descubrimiento en donde se fundó la ciudad de Santiago de Compostela. La ruta sagrada que seguían los peregrinos se dio a conocer[2] como El Camino de Santiago y terminaba en el portal de la Catedral de Santiago de Compostela.

A lo largo de[3] la ruta construyeron iglesias y albergues[4] para recibir a los peregrinos. Algunos peregrinos venían de lugares tan lejanos como Rusia y tardaban años para completar su viaje a pie.

Hoy en día muchas personas viajan a Santiago por la misma razón que los peregrinos de hace mil años: por motivos[5] religiosos. Otros lo recorren[6] como turistas o por motivos culturales debido a su importancia histórica.

1 the apostle Saint James
2 became known as 3 All along
4 hostels 5 reasons 6 travel along

Un peregrino de la antigüedad.

Muchos de los que hacen este viaje son jóvenes. Algunos lo hacen a pie, otros en bicicleta y otros ¡hasta a caballo! Por eso mismo, hay muchos albergues juveniles que ofrecen servicios muy baratos. Para quedarte en ellos, debes llevar tu propia comida. Los albergues son lugares excelentes para conocer a chicos y chicas de todo el mundo.

¿Comprendiste?

1. Nombra cuatro grupos de peregrinos que se mencionan en la lectura. En general, ¿qué buscan los peregrinos?

2. ¿De dónde eran los peregrinos que iban a Santiago?

3. ¿Cuáles son tres motivos de seguir el Camino de Santiago hoy en día?

4. ¿Qué atractivos tiene el Camino para una persona joven?

Mi propio camino

1 Piensa en un viaje o una excursión que hiciste el año pasado. ¿Adónde fuiste? ¿Por qué fuiste allí? ¿Cómo fuiste? ¿Qué tuviste que llevar? ¿Dónde te quedaste? ¿Cómo era el lugar? ¿Qué había allí? ¿A quién(es) conociste?

2 Ahora compara tu experiencia con el recorrido que hacen muchos jóvenes a Santiago de Compostela. ¿En qué se parecen? ¿En qué se diferencian?

Go Online PHSchool.com

For: Internet link activity
Visit: www.phschool.com
Web Code: jed-0110

Jóvenes en camino hacia Santiago de Compostela

Uno de los albergues del Camino de Santiago

cuarenta y nueve 49
Capítulo 1

Strategies

Reading strategies help students become better readers.

Comprehension checks

Follow-up questions check students' comprehension.

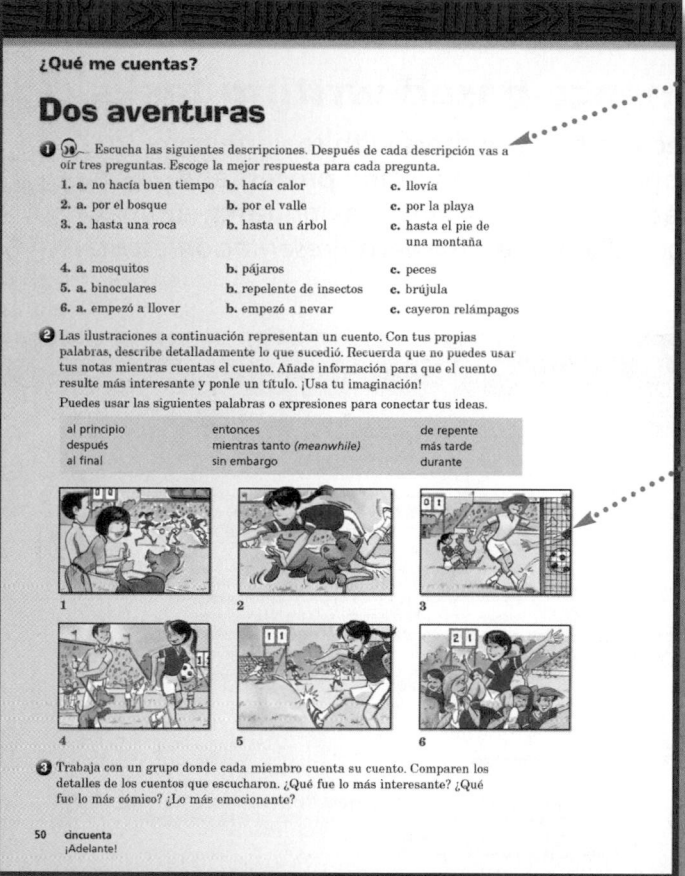

¿Qué me cuentas?

Dos aventuras

1 🔊 Escucha las siguientes descripciones. Después de cada descripción vas a oír tres preguntas. Escoge la mejor respuesta para cada pregunta.

1. a. no hacía buen tiempo b. hacía calor c. llovía
2. a. por el bosque b. por el valle c. por la playa
3. a. hasta una roca b. hasta un árbol c. hasta el pie de una montaña

4. a. mosquitos b. pájaros c. peces
5. a. binoculares b. repelente de insectos c. brújula
6. a. empezó a llover b. empezó a nevar c. cayeron relámpagos

2 Las ilustraciones a continuación representan un cuento. Con tus propias palabras, describe detalladamente lo que sucedió. Recuerda que no puedes usar tus notas mientras cuentas el cuento. Añade información para que el cuento resulte más interesante y ponle un título. ¡Usa tu imaginación!

Puedes usar las siguientes palabras o expresiones para conectar tus ideas.

al principio	entonces	de repente
después	mientras tanto (meanwhile)	más tarde
al final	sin embargo	durante

1 2 3

4 5 6

3 Trabaja con un grupo donde cada miembro cuenta su cuento. Comparen los detalles de los cuentos que escucharon. ¿Qué fue lo más interesante? ¿Qué fue lo más cómico? ¿Lo más emocionante?

50 cincuenta
¡Adelante!

Listening comprehension
Students expand their listening skills.

Speaking using picture sequences
Students expand their speaking skills through story narration.

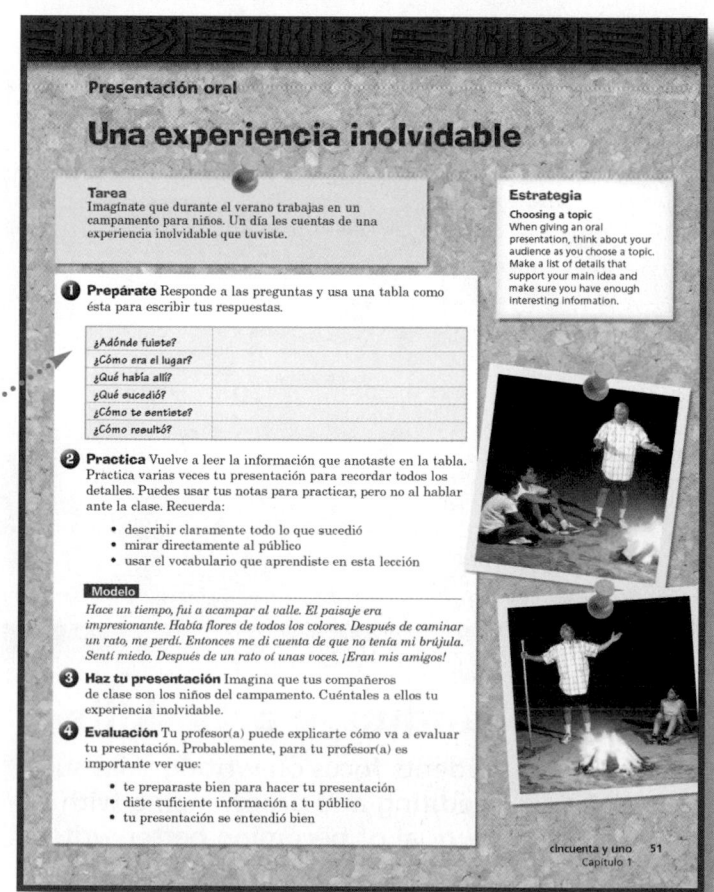

Presentación oral

Una experiencia inolvidable

Tarea
Imagínate que durante el verano trabajas en un campamento para niños. Un día les cuentas de una experiencia inolvidable que tuviste.

Estrategia
Choosing a topic
When giving an oral presentation, think about your audience as you choose a topic. Make a list of details that support your main idea and make sure you have enough interesting information.

1 **Prepárate** Responde a las preguntas y usa una tabla como ésta para escribir tus respuestas.

¿Adónde fuiste?	
¿Cómo era el lugar?	
¿Qué había allí?	
¿Qué sucedió?	
¿Cómo te sentiste?	
¿Cómo resultó?	

2 **Practica** Vuelve a leer la información que anotaste en la tabla. Practica varias veces tu presentación para recordar todos los detalles. Puedes usar tus notas para practicar, pero no al hablar ante la clase. Recuerda:

- describir claramente todo lo que sucedió
- mirar directamente al público
- usar el vocabulario que aprendiste en esta lección

Modelo
Hace un tiempo, fui a acampar al valle. El paisaje era impresionante. Había flores de todos los colores. Después de caminar un rato, me perdí. Entonces me di cuenta de que no tenía mi brújula. Sentí miedo. Después de un rato oí unas voces. ¡Eran mis amigos!

3 **Haz tu presentación** Imagina que tus compañeros de clase son los niños del campamento. Cuéntales a ellos tu experiencia inolvidable.

4 **Evaluación** Tu profesor(a) puede explicarte cómo va a evaluar tu presentación. Probablemente, para tu profesor(a) es importante ver que:

- te preparaste bien para hacer tu presentación
- diste suficiente información a tu público
- tu presentación se entendió bien

cincuenta y uno 51
Capítulo 1

Performance-based speaking task
Real-life speaking tasks are supported by strategies and a step-by-step process that helps all students to be successful. The *Assessment Program* contains the rubric for this task.

Chapter Organization

Performance-based writing tasks

Students become better writers with real-life tasks that are supported with the writing process and focused strategies. As with the speaking tasks, a rubric has been specially written for each *Presentación escrita*.

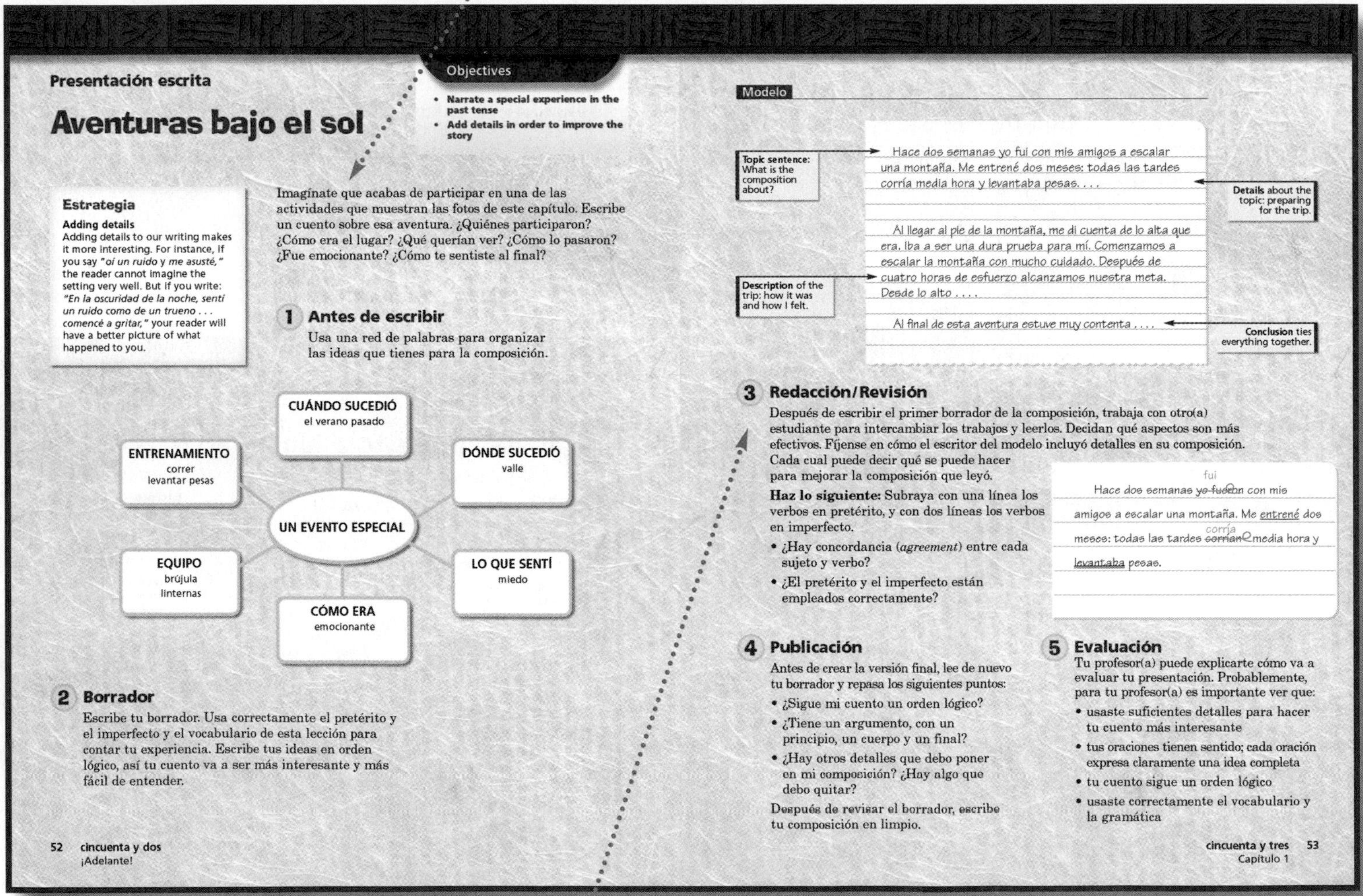

Presentación escrita

Aventuras bajo el sol

Objectives
- Narrate a special experience in the past tense
- Add details in order to improve the story

Estrategia

Adding details
Adding details to our writing makes it more interesting. For instance, if you say "*oí un ruido y me asusté,*" the reader cannot imagine the setting very well. But if you write: "*En la oscuridad de la noche, sentí un ruido como de un trueno . . . comencé a gritar,*" your reader will have a better picture of what happened to you.

Imagínate que acabas de participar en una de las actividades que muestran las fotos de este capítulo. Escribe un cuento sobre esa aventura. ¿Quiénes participaron? ¿Cómo era el lugar? ¿Qué querían ver? ¿Cómo lo pasaron? ¿Fue emocionante? ¿Cómo te sentiste al final?

1 Antes de escribir
Usa una red de palabras para organizar las ideas que tienes para la composición.

CUÁNDO SUCEDIÓ
el verano pasado

ENTRENAMIENTO
correr
levantar pesas

DÓNDE SUCEDIÓ
valle

UN EVENTO ESPECIAL

EQUIPO
brújula
linternas

LO QUE SENTÍ
miedo

CÓMO ERA
emocionante

2 Borrador
Escribe tu borrador. Usa correctamente el pretérito y el imperfecto y el vocabulario de esta lección para contar tu experiencia. Escribe tus ideas en orden lógico, así tu cuento va a ser más interesante y más fácil de entender.

Modelo

Topic sentence: What is the composition about?

Hace dos semanas yo fui con mis amigos a escalar una montaña. Me entrené dos meses: todas las tardes corría media hora y levantaba pesas. . . .

Details about the topic: preparing for the trip.

Description of the trip: how it was and how I felt.

Al llegar al pie de la montaña, me di cuenta de lo alta que era. Iba a ser una dura prueba para mí. Comenzamos a escalar la montaña con mucho cuidado. Después de cuatro horas de esfuerzo alcanzamos nuestra meta. Desde lo alto . . . .

Al final de esta aventura estuve muy contenta . . . .

Conclusion ties everything together.

3 Redacción/Revisión
Después de escribir el primer borrador de la composición, trabaja con otro(a) estudiante para intercambiar los trabajos y leerlos. Decidan qué aspectos son más efectivos. Fíjense en cómo el escritor del modelo incluyó detalles en su composición. Cada cual puede decir qué se puede hacer para mejorar la composición que leyó.

Haz lo siguiente: Subraya con una línea los verbos en pretérito, y con dos líneas los verbos en imperfecto.

- ¿Hay concordancia (*agreement*) entre cada sujeto y verbo?
- ¿El pretérito y el imperfecto están empleados correctamente?

Hace dos semanas yo ~~fueron~~ *fui* con mis amigos a escalar una montaña. Me *entrené* dos meses: todas las tardes ~~corrían~~ *corría* media hora y levantaba pesas.

4 Publicación
Antes de crear la versión final, lee de nuevo tu borrador y repasa los siguientes puntos:
- ¿Sigue mi cuento un orden lógico?
- ¿Tiene un argumento, con un principio, un cuerpo y un final?
- ¿Hay otros detalles que debo poner en mi composición? ¿Hay algo que debo quitar?

Después de revisar el borrador, escribe tu composición en limpio.

5 Evaluación
Tu profesor(a) puede explicarte cómo va a evaluar tu presentación. Probablemente, para tu profesor(a) es importante ver que:
- usaste suficientes detalles para hacer tu cuento más interesante
- tus oraciones tienen sentido; cada oración expresa claramente una idea completa
- tu cuento sigue un orden lógico
- usaste correctamente el vocabulario y la gramática

52 cincuenta y dos
¡Adelante!

cincuenta y tres 53
Capítulo 1

Language arts skills

Students focus on writing skills such as editing and proofreading with the goal of becoming better writers.

Strategy

Reading strategies support comprehension.

Authentic literature

Students read a wide range of authentic literature.

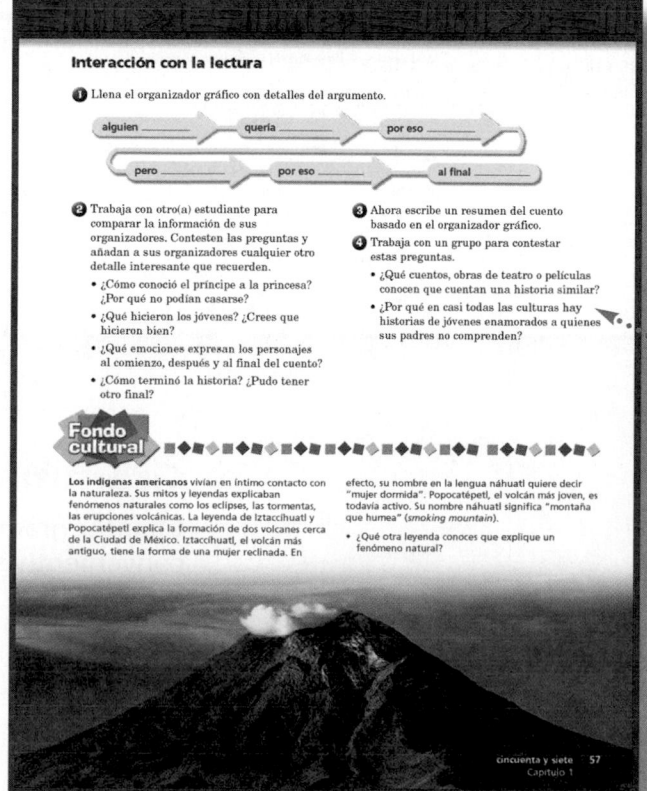

Comprehension checks

A variety of questions check students' comprehension of the literature and their reaction to it.

Chapter Organization

Repaso del capítulo

These four pages provide complete review and preparation for the chapter test.

Repaso del capítulo

Vocabulario y gramática

para hablar de actividades al aire libre

acercarse a	to approach
andar	to walk, to move
dar un paseo	to take a walk, stroll
dejar de	to stop (doing something)
escalar	to climb (a rock or mountain)
perderse	to get lost
refugiarse	to take shelter

para describir la naturaleza

el bosque	wood, forest
el desierto	desert
hermoso, -a	beautiful
la naturaleza	nature
el paisaje	landscape
el refugio	refuge, shelter
la roca	rock
la sierra	sierra, mountain range
el valle	valley

para hablar de cámping

los binoculares	binoculars
la brújula	compass
la linterna	flashlight
el repelente de insectos	insect repellent
el saco de dormir	sleeping bag
la tienda de acampar	tent

para hablar del tiempo

caer granizo	to hail
el granizo	hail
el relámpago	lightning
el trueno	thunder

para indicar que sucede algo

suceder	to occur
tener lugar	to take place

para indicar cuándo sucede algo

al amanecer	at dawn
al anochecer	at dusk
al principio	at the beginning
un rato	a while
una vez allí	once there

para prepararse para un evento deportivo

el entrenamiento	training
entrenarse	to train
hacer un esfuerzo	to make an effort
inscribirse	to register
la inscripción	registration

para hablar de competencias deportivas

alcanzar	to reach
la carrera	race
la ceremonia	ceremony
el certificado	certificate, diploma
contra	against
eliminar	to eliminate
la entrega de premios	awards ceremony
¡Felicitaciones!	Congratulations!
la medalla	medal
obtener	to obtain, get
el / la participante	participant
el / la representante	representative
la meta	goal
salir campeón, campeona	to become the champion
el trofeo	trophy
vencer	to beat

para expresar emociones e impresiones

animado, -a	excited
asustar	to scare
darse cuenta de	to realize
desafortunadamente	unfortunately
desanimado, -a	discouraged
duro, -a	hard
emocionarse	to be moved
estar orgulloso / orgullosa de	to be proud of
impresionar	to impress
pasarlo bien / mal	to have a good / bad time

otras palabras y expresiones

aparecer	to appear
así	this way
hacia	toward
perder el equilibrio	to lose one's balance
sin embargo	however

58 cincuenta y ocho
Repaso del capítulo

el pretérito

destruir *to destroy*

destruí	destruimos
destruiste	destruisteis
destruyó	destruyeron

leer *to read*

leí	leímos
leíste	leísteis
leyó	leyeron

The verbs *creer, oír,* and *caerse* follow the same pattern as *leer.*

tener *to have*

tuve	tuvimos
tuviste	tuvisteis
tuvo	tuvieron

Other verbs that have an irregular stem in the preterite and share the same endings as *tener* are: *andar, estar, poder, poner, venir.*

decir *to tell*

dije	dijimos
dijiste	dijisteis
dijo	dijeron

The verb *traer* follows the same pattern as *decir.*

pedir (i) *to ask for*

pedí	pedimos
pediste	pedisteis
pidió	pidieron

The verbs *sentir, divertirse, preferir, sugerir,* and *vestirse* follow the same pattern as *pedir.*

dormir (u) *to sleep*

dormí	dormimos
dormiste	dormisteis
durmió	durmieron

The verb *morir* follows the same pattern as *dormir.*

el imperfecto

estar (-ar) *to be*

estaba	estábamos
estabas	estábais
estaba	estaban

tener (-er) *to have*

tenía	teníamos
tenías	teníais
tenía	tenían

vivir (-ir) *to live*

vivía	vivíamos
vivías	vivíais
vivía	vivían

ir *to go*

iba	íbamos
ibas	ibais
iba	iban

ser *to be*

era	éramos
eras	erais
era	eran

ver *to see*

veía	veíamos
veías	veíais
veía	veían

The imperfect of *hay* is *había.*

● **Más práctica**
Practice Workbook Organizer 1-13, 1-14

cincuenta y nueve 59
Capítulo 1

Vocabulary list

Chapter vocabulary is listed as language functions and with English translations.

Grammar summary

Chapter grammar is conveniently summarized.

T26 Chapter Organization

Test preparation: Vocabulary and grammar

This page practices new content using an achievement test format.

Chapter Review

To prepare for the test, check to see if you . . .
- know the new vocabulary and grammar
- can perform the tasks on pp. 46 and 47

Go Online
PHSchool.com
For: Test preparation
Visit: www.phschool.com
Web Code: jed-0111

Preparación para el examen

❶ Vocabulario Escribe la letra de la palabra o expresión que mejor complete cada frase. Escribe tus respuestas en una hoja aparte.

1. Me levanté muy temprano, _____, para ir de cámping.
   a. por la tarde
   b. al anochecer
   c. por la noche
   d. al amanecer

2. Cuando fuimos al bosque, Luis trajo _____ porque no había mucha luz.
   a. unos binoculares
   b. una linterna
   c. un repelente de insectos
   d. un saco de dormir

3. El paisaje era impresionante. _____ mucho cuando vi las montañas.
   a. Me cansé
   b. Me asusté
   c. Me emocioné
   d. Me aburrí

4. Cuando gané el campeonato mis padres me dijeron que estaban muy _____ de mis esfuerzos.
   a. orgullosos
   b. desanimados
   c. asustados
   d. tristes

5. Buscamos un refugio porque _____.
   a. perdí el equilibrio
   b. nos eliminaron
   c. comenzó a caer granizo
   d. no dormimos bien.

6. Cuando llegué tarde a casa mis padres me preguntaron: "¿Qué te _____?"
   a. dieron
   b. sucedió
   c. rompiste
   d. pusiste

7. Antes de participar en el campeonato, la chica _____ por tres meses.
   a. se entrenó
   b. se perdió
   c. se divirtió
   d. se durmió

8. Fue un partido muy _____. Todos tuvimos que hacer un gran esfuerzo para ganar.
   a. agitado
   b. fácil
   c. aburrido
   d. duro

❷ Gramática Escribe la letra de la palabra o expresión que mejor complete cada frase. Escribe tus respuestas en una hoja aparte.

1. Leí en el diario que la tormenta _____ muchos árboles.
   a. destruye
   b. destruía
   c. destruyendo
   d. destruyó

2. No puedo creer que te olvidaste la mochila. ¿Por qué no la _____?
   a. trajiste
   b. traen
   c. trajeron
   d. traían

3. _____ la una de la tarde cuando llegamos al campamento.
   a. Fue
   b. Era
   c. Eran
   d. Estaban

4. El sábado pasado, los chicos _____ dos horas por los senderos.
   a. anduvieron
   b. andaban
   c. andan
   d. anduviste

5. Anoche, después del partido, el campeón _____ diez horas porque estaba cansado.
   a. dormía
   b. durmió
   c. está durmiendo
   d. duerme

6. De niña, a menudo yo _____ a los partidos de tenis con mis tíos.
   a. voy
   b. fui
   c. iba
   d. iban

7. El atleta que salió en primer lugar _____ un trofeo.
   a. obtuvo
   b. obtiene
   c. obtenía
   d. obtuviste

8. Generalmente, ¿cómo _____ cuando tu equipo perdía un partido?
   a. te sientes
   b. te sentiste
   c. se sentían
   d. te sentías

En el examen vas a . . .	Éstas son las tareas de práctica que te pueden ser útiles para el examen . . .	Si necesitas repasar . . .
❸ Escuchar Escuchar y comprender la descripción de una excursión a un parque nacional	Un amigo(a) te deja un mensaje por teléfono sobre una excursión que hizo a un parque nacional. (a) ¿Adónde fue? (b) ¿Qué vio? (c) ¿Qué hizo allí? (d) ¿Qué le sucedió? (e) ¿Cómo lo pasó?	**pp. 22–25** *A primera vista 1* **p. 27** Actividad 7 **p. 29** Actividades 12–13 **p. 34** Actividad 22 **p. 35** Actividades 24–25
❹ Leer Leer y comprender un anuncio sobre un concurso	Lee el anuncio que apareció en el periódico de la escuela y decide (a) qué tipo de concurso es (b) cuándo es la inscripción (c) quiénes pueden participar (d) cuándo es la audición (e) qué premio va a obtener el / la ganador(a). **Concurso de Música** Invitamos a todos los estudiantes de tercer y cuarto año a participar en nuestro concurso. **Fecha de inscripción:** 6 de octubre. **Audición:** 9 de octubre. **Primer premio:** dos entradas (tickets) para un concierto en el teatro San Martín	**pp. 36–39** *A primera vista 2* **p. 41** Actividades 33–35
❺ Escribir Escribir un artículo sobre un evento deportivo importante para el periódico de la escuela	Imagina que eres reportero del periódico de la escuela. Tienes que hacer un artículo sobre el último partido del año de un equipo de tu escuela. Tu artículo debe contar (a) quiénes jugaron, (b) dónde y cuándo fue, (c) si hacía buen tiempo, (d) cómo se sentían los jugadores, (e) qué sucedió, (f) cómo se sentían al final, (g) si fue un partido aburrido o emocionante y por qué.	**p. 43** Actividad 37 **p. 44** Actividad 40 **p. 45** Actividad 41
❻ Hablar Hablar sobre una excursión que hizo tu clase	Tu clase fue de excursión a un lugar especial. Cuéntale lo que pasó a un(a) compañero(a) que no pudo ir. Incluye quiénes fueron, adónde fueron, qué había allí, qué tiempo hacía, qué hicieron y cómo lo pasaron.	**p. 50** *¿Qué me cuentas?* **p. 51** *Presentación oral*
❼ Pensar Pensar en los peregrinos de hoy y de ayer	Piensa en el viaje de los peregrinos de Santiago de Compostela hace mil años. ¿Por qué quieren seguir la misma ruta muchos jóvenes hoy en día? ¿Hay lugares aquí en los Estados Unidos como Santiago de Compostela? ¿Cuáles son los motivos de viajar a estos lugares? ¿En qué se parecen? ¿En qué se diferencian?	**pp. 48–49** *Puente a la cultura*

Test preparation: Proficiency and culture

This page prepares students for the proficiency and culture sections of the chapter test. Students are told how they will be tested, what the task might be like, and how to review.

Using the Teacher's Edition

- ▶ **Teaching the Theme**
- ▶ **Planning for Instruction**
- ▶ **Alignment with the Standards for Foreign Language Learning**
- ▶ **Complete Teaching Support**

Teaching the Theme

The Teacher's Edition provides complete planning support for teaching the themes.

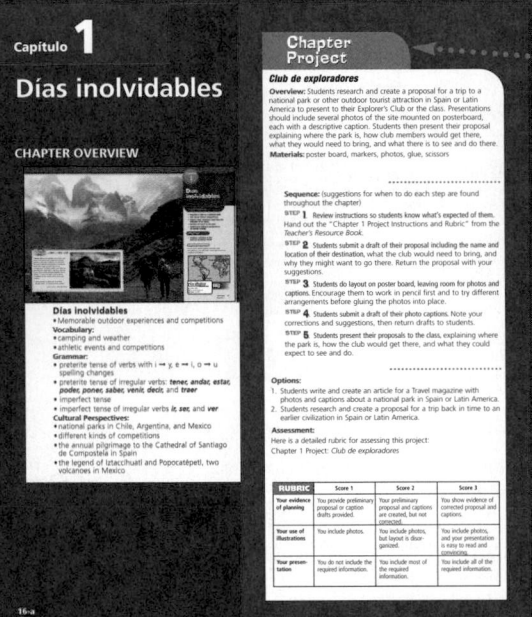

Theme project

Each theme begins with an optional project. The project is divided into manageable steps and includes a rubric.

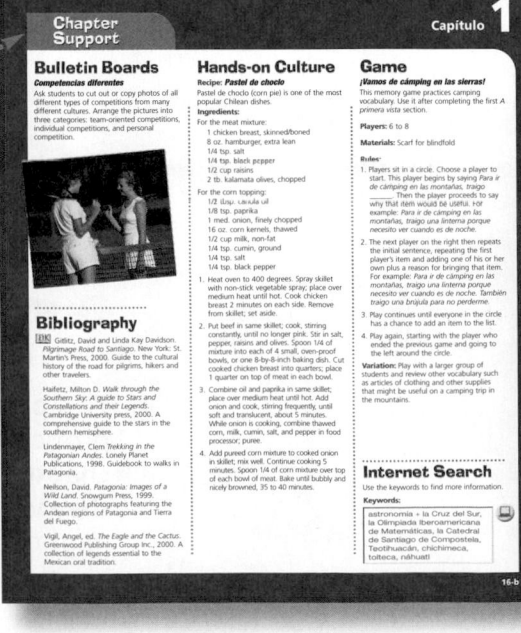

Theme support

Additional support per theme includes bulletin board ideas, games, hands-on culture activities, and teaching resources.

Planning for Instruction

The Teacher's Edition provides six pages of planning support interleaved at the beginning of each chapter.

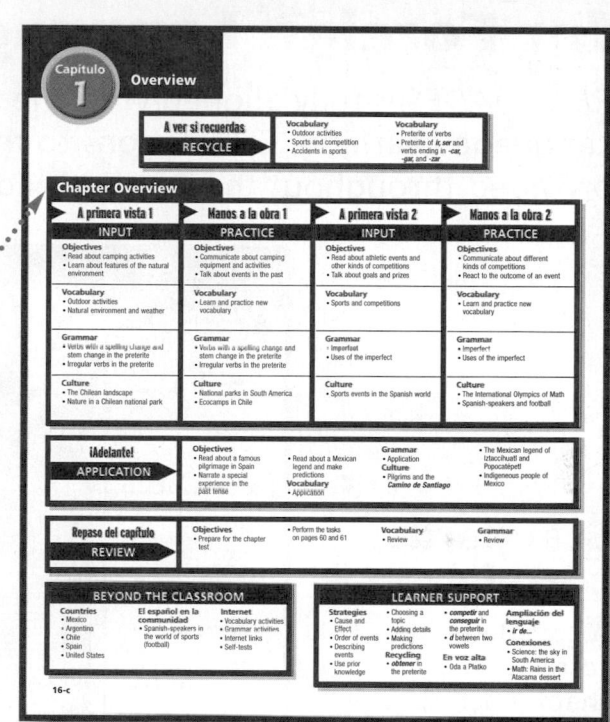

Scope and Sequence

This section gives a quick overview of the chapter sections, objectives, and content.

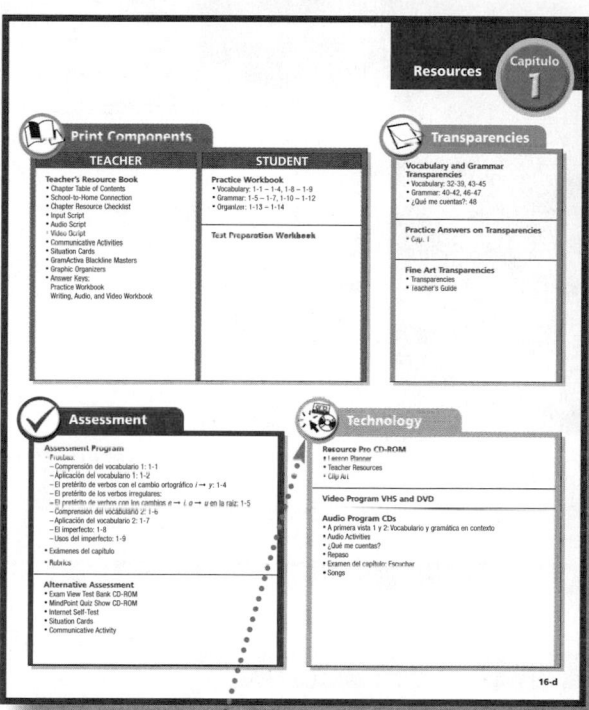

Program Resources

This section shows all the program resources available for this chapter. All resources are conveniently referenced at point of use in the chapter.

Lesson Plans

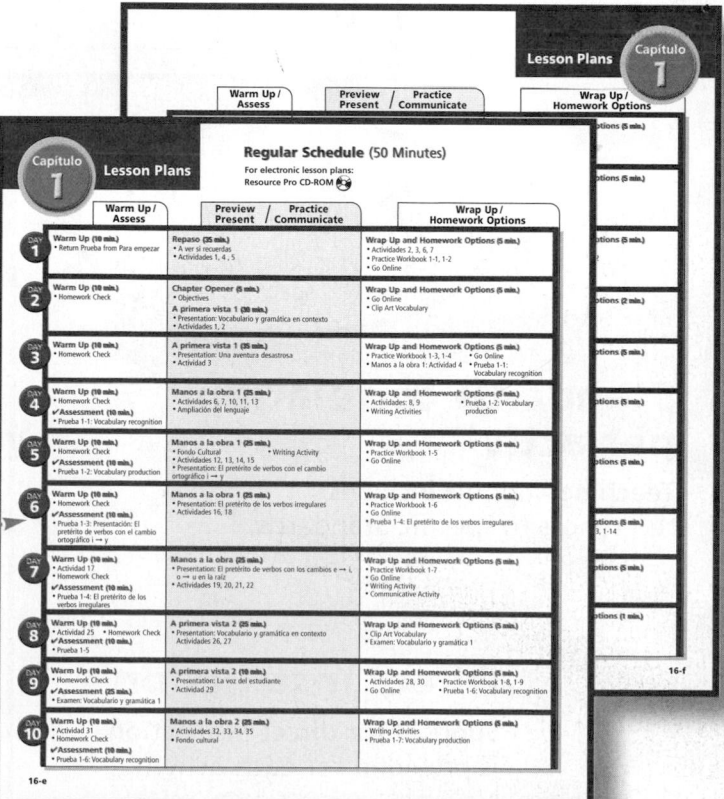

Lesson Plans

Lesson plans are provided for instruction on the regular or block schedule.

Alignment with the Standards for Foreign Language Learning

REALIDADES is fully aligned with the Standards for Foreign Language Learning. Correlations to the Standards are provided throughout the Teacher's Edition.

Standards correlation

A complete correlation of chapter activities to the Standards is provided at the beginning of each chapter.

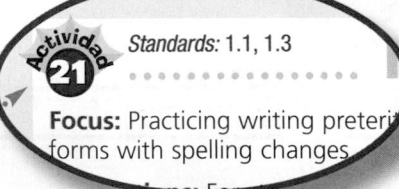

Standards correlation per activity

Teaching support includes references to specific Standards.

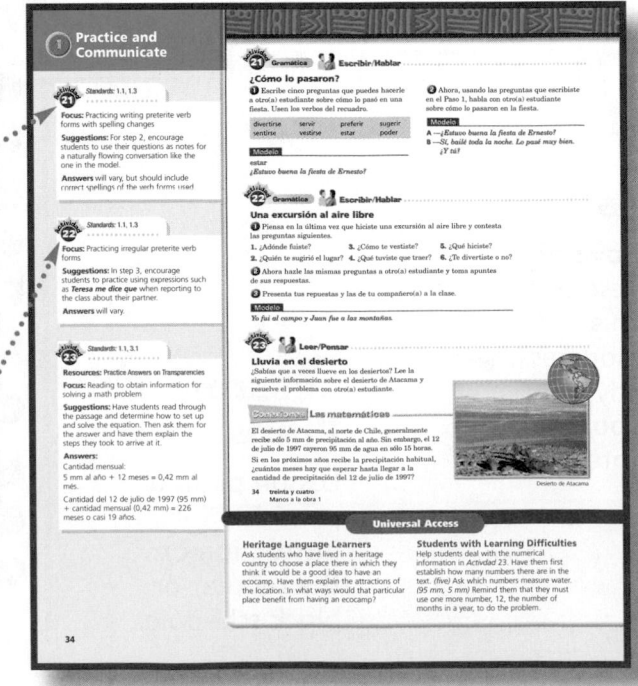

Direct instruction

Support for direct instruction is provided for each activity.

Complete Teaching Support

REALIDADES provides teachers with complete instructional support that can be found in the Teacher's Edition and in the various print and technology resources.

Program Organization

Each chapter provides a well-organized structure, clear student outcomes and goals, and a variety of activities that develop all language skills.

Chapter Objectives

- Describe a visit to a national park
- Talk about school competitions
- Express your emotions regarding the outcome of an event
- Narrate an event in the past
- Understand cultural perspectives on family outings

Assessment

Teachers are provided with multiple print and technology tools that measure student progress in listening, speaking, reading, and writing.

✓ **Assessment**
- Prueba 5A-3: The verb *tener*

Go Online
PHSchool.com
For: Test preparation
Visit: www.phschool.com
Web Code: jed-0111

Presentación oral

Una experiencia inolvidable

Tarea
Imagina que durante el verano trabajas en un campamento para niños. Un día les cuentas de una experiencia inolvidable que tuviste.

1 Prepárate Responde a las preguntas y usa una tabla como ésta para escribir tus respuestas.

Universal Access

REALIDADES provides teaching suggestions to help all students learn Spanish.

Universal Access

Students with Learning Difficulties
Provide photocopies of the invitation for students to use. Preview the *¿Comprendes?* questions with students, and have them highlight pertinent information on photocopies. When students write their *nombre completo,* they might draw a family tree with their parents' and grandparents' names to help them.

Heritage Language Learners
If students have been to a *fiesta de quince años* celebration, ask them to describe it. Who was there? What food was served? What did people do during the celebration? If they can, have them describe the gifts and decorations.

Universal Access

Advanced Learners
Have students create and describe a fictional "royal family" and a fictional country for the family to rule. Encourage them to write humorous stories that will be entertaining when reviewed by the class. Some students may want to illustrate their royal families after writing their descriptions.

Special Education
Matching the silhouette to the photograph may be especially difficult for students with visual problems. Pair students who have strong spatial skills with those who don't.

Instructional Planning and Support

REALIDADES provides complete support for implementing the Standards. The Teacher's Edition, program resources, and Companion Web site provide direct instruction and complete support to implement the program and accompanying resources.

Assessment

Topics covered:

▷ **Assessing Student Progress**

▷ **Purposes of Assessment**

▷ **Forms of Assessment**

▷ **Portfolios and Assessment**

▷ **Self-Assessment**

▷ **Making Assessment Real**

> **❝What do I expect my students to learn? What do I want them to be able to do? How can I assess what I am looking for in student performance?❞**

An assessment program in a second language classroom should be based on the premise that the main purpose of learning a language is to communicate in a meaningful and culturally appropriate way. As you begin to teach a unit of instruction, you might want to start by asking a few key questions: What do I expect my students to learn? What do I want them to be able to do? How can I assess what I am looking for in student performance?

Assessing Student Progress

There are several assessment strategies that will enable students to develop proficiency in a language other than English. This particular list comes from *The Foreign Language Framework for California Public Schools*.[1] These strategies include:

- Have a clear purpose readily communicated to teachers, students, and parents;
- Provide information to guide the teacher in planning instruction;
- Measure how well students perform in reading, writing, listening, and speaking;
- Have clear and concise criteria;
- Include instruments that provide representative samples of what students know and are able to do;
- Integrate the speaking, listening, reading, and writing skills;
- Include a wide range of assessment strategies that allow for a variety of responses;
- Provide students and parents with ongoing information on their progress;
- Allow students to monitor and adjust their individual learning strategies; and
- Employ various forms of assessment.

[1] *The Foreign Language Framework for California Public Schools, Kindergarten Through Grade Twelve (2003), California Department of Education, 38.*

Purposes of Assessment

The following chart outlines the various purposes for assessment:

Purposes of Assessment	
Entry-level assessment	• Analyzes students' ability to communicate as a basis for placing students at an appropriate level in an established foreign language program.
Progress/monitoring assessment	• Gathers evidence about students' progress towards achieving objectives as measured in relation to the stage of the curriculum. • Will occur on an ongoing basis. • May occur at any point in an instructional sequence other than at the end of the course of study.
Summative assessment	• Judges students' achievement at the end of a unit, chapter, or course of study.

Forms of Assessment

Achievement assessment determines what students know by evaluating them on specific, previously learned material, such as the names of items of clothing or the conjugation of -*ar* verbs. They test for discrete bits of information. Achievement tests are used to measure the incremental steps involved in learning a second language—for example, to cover what was taught in a specific chapter. Achievement may be quizzed or tested with some frequency as proof of regular progress for both student and teacher.

Proficiency or **performance-based assessment** measures what students can do with this knowledge and how well they can perform in the language. These tests do not involve testing specific items; rather they are performance-based, checking how well students integrate what they have learned. Their characteristic open-endedness permits students to use what they know to receive or communicate a message, since the emphasis is on communication needs. Proficiency tests address the questions: How well and at what level can the student use the language to receive and express meaningful communication?

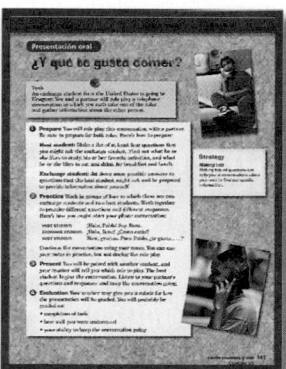
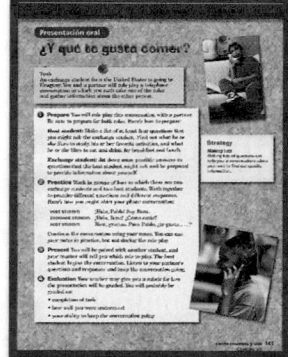

Performance-based speaking task

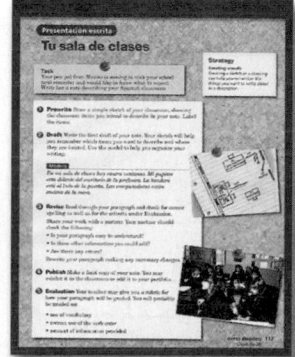

Performance-based writing task

Assessment

Portfolios and Assessment

Portfolios are another form of assessment that can measure student progress and growth. Portfolios contain samples of a student's work collected over time. This enables both the teacher and the student to observe the progress being made. Portfolios provide students the opportunity to examine and reflect upon what they have produced so that they become more involved in improving their work. The portfolio can be useful to determine grade/level placement.

Chapter Assessment in *REALIDADES*

REALIDADES offer a wide variety of options for end-of-unit (chapter) assessment. There are three different Assessment Programs in *REALIDADES* to evaluate the different students in your classroom:

- monolingual students
- students using *REALIDADES para hispanohablantes*

There is also a Placement Test for heritage learners.

Contents of the Portfolio

☐ written work, such as short paragraphs, compositions, short stories, poems, or journals

☐ audio and/or video cassettes of student performance

☐ quizzes and tests

☐ evidence of reading comprehension

☐ evidence of listening comprehension

☐ individual student projects

☐ art work

☐ cultural projects

☐ technology projects and Web research

☐ picture dictionaries

☐ story boards

☐ evidence that language skills were practiced outside the classroom

☐ evidence of contact with Hispanic cultures in the community

☐ evidence of student reflection on his or her own writing or speaking

✓ Teacher Assessment

Assessment Program
- Placement Test
- chapter quizzes and tests
- cumulative tests
- rubrics and portfolio support

Assessment Program: *REALIDADES para hispanohablantes*
- chapter quizzes and tests with directions in Spanish
- cumulative tests with directions in Spanish
- rubrics in Spanish and portfolio support

Placement Test for Heritage Learners
- leveled Placement Tests with audio CD
- vocabulary, grammar, and proficiency assessment

Assessment Resources in *REALIDADES*

The Student Edition, print ancillaries, and technology components offer a wide range of assessment options to be used for different purposes and for both achievement and performance assessments. Teachers are encouraged to pick and choose from the many resources.

Assessment Program

- Placement Test
- Chapter Quizzes
- Chapter Tests
- Chapter Checklist and Self-Assessment
- Cumulative Tests
- Rubrics
- Portfolios
- Review and Remediation

▶ Assessment Resources	Achievement	Proficiency	Self-Assessment
Student Edition			
• *Actividades* (various)	✔	✔	
• *Lectura*		✔	
• *Presentación oral*		✔	
• *Presentación escrita*		✔	
• *Preparación para el examen*	✔	✔	✔
Assessment Program			
• Placement Tests	✔	✔	
• Chapter Quizzes	✔		
• Chapter Tests	✔	✔	
• Cumulative Tests	✔	✔	
• Rubrics		✔	✔
• Portfolio Assessment		✔	✔
• Chapter Checklist and Self-Assessment Worksheet			✔
Teacher Resource Book			
• Communicative Activities		✔	
• Situation Cards		✔	
Technology			
• Interactive Textbook	✔	✔	✔
• Computer Test Bank with CD-ROM	✔	✔	
• MindPoint Quiz Show CD-ROM	✔		✔
• Companion Web site	✔		✔

Making Assessment Real

The Latin root of "assess" is to "sit beside." The goal of our assessment program is indeed a sitting beside the student, encouraging performance to the best of his or her ability in the language. Although learning a language is a complicated endeavor, *REALIDADES* provides students with many opportunities to practice these real-life tasks before their performance is evaluated and graded. Conversely, *REALIDADES* offers a wide range of assessment options that reflect each chapter's communication and culture goals.

Universal Access

Instructional Strategies

▶ **Success in Universal Access**

▶ **Effective Instructional Strategies**

▶ **Planning Instruction for Students with Special Needs**

▶ **Teaching Spanish to Students with Learning Disabilities**

▶ **Teaching Spanish to Students with Special Physical Needs**

▶ **Teaching Spanish to Advanced Learners**

▶ **Teaching Heritage Learners**

The nation is more diverse than ever and this diversity is a significant asset to the strength of our nation. Yet this diversity also places considerable stress on the educational system to effectively accommodate the range of learning needs found in today's classrooms. The range of student needs, interests, motivation, and skill levels often presents heightened challenges to both curriculum and instruction. It should be clearly acknowledged that the individual needs of some students require additional specialized support. However, the goal of a comprehensive Spanish program remains the provision of "universal access" for all students to a communicative and culturally rich program in addition to whatever specialized intervention may be required.

·····················

Success in Universal Access

Universal access occurs when teachers provide curriculum and instruction in ways that allow all learners in the classroom to participate and to achieve the instructional and behavioral goals of general education, as well as of the core curriculum. Success is achieved in classrooms that are heterogeneous, inclusive and that consistently and systematically integrate instructional strategies that are responsive to the needs of all learners with special focus on advanced learners, heritage learners, students with learning difficulties, and students who are eligible for and receiving special education services.

Effective Instructional Strategies

Here are general strategies that deliver effective instruction in a classroom with diverse learners.

• **Clarify the objectives for a chapter.** Students needs to understand the outcomes for which they will be assessed.

• **Provide "thinking time" before students have to talk.** You may want to ask a question and then count to 10 before expecting a response. If a student is struggling, state that you want him/her to think about it, and indicate that you'll be back for the response in a minute. Move on to another student, and then return to the student for his/her response.

- **Write all assignments on the board.** Assignments given both verbally and visually are clearer to all students.

- **Using visuals throughout the lesson.** Present vocabulary visually. Use charts to present grammar. Use video that provides visual support such as vocabulary words highlighted on the screen and grammar videos that visualize grammar patterns. Use graphic organizers whenever possible. Connect communicative tasks to photos, art, and *realia*.

- **Assist in time management.** When requiring students to complete projects, or long-term assignments, provide a calendar that breaks down requirements by due dates. Many students experience significant difficulties in self-managing the time needed to complete complex projects.

- **Build in opportunities for reteaching and practice vocabulary words and grammar.** Students need many opportunities to learn new concepts and need to practice in a variety of formats.

- **Build vocabulary skills by teaching the patterns of language.** Teach the meaning of prefixes, suffixes, and the role of cognates. Point out connections between English, Spanish, and Latin.

- **Consider alternative means for demonstrating understanding.** Think beyond the common modes of reading and writing. Students could present information orally, create a poster or visual representation of work, tape-record their ideas, or act out their understanding.

> **❝**The goal of a comprehensive Spanish program remains the provision of "universal access" for all students to a communicative and culturally rich program in addition to whatever specialized intervention may be required.**❞**

- **Have students begin all work in class.** Prior to class dismissal, check to ensure that each student has a good start and understands what is expected.

- **Consider setting up a homework hotline using voicemail or e-mail.** Homework assignments could be posted and easily accessed by parents and students outside of school hours.

Teaching Today's Students

The strategies presented on these pages provide an overview of instructional strategies that are effective with all learners. Today's students need instruction that enables them to see how learning is relevant, that helps them organize their time and learning, that provides focus on what is important (either within instructional materials or with classroom activities), that provides multiple opportunities to learn utilizing different modalities, and that assures students know what is expected of them whether in the classroom or for homework.

Teaching Spanish to Students with Learning Disabilities

There are many reasons why students may experience difficulties in learning a second language. In general, these difficulties may be characterized by the inability to spell or read well, problems with auditory discrimination and in understanding auditory input, and difficulty with abstract thinking. Research by Ganchow and Sparks (1991) indicates that difficulties with one's first language are a major factor in foreign language learning difficulties.

It is not always evident which students will experience difficulties with learning a second language. Many times these students are bright and outgoing. They may have experienced reading or spelling problems in elementary school, but they have learned to compensate over time. Ask students what problems they may have experienced with their first language, especially in the areas of reading and dictation.

Accommodating Instruction

Students with learning disabilities can develop a level of proficiency in a second language with some modifications to instruction and testing. These learners benefit from a highly structured approach that teaches new content in context and in incremental amounts. Teach, practice, and assess using multi-sensory strategies. Many students benefit when instruction combines seeing, hearing, saying, and writing. For example, a teacher would first show a visual of a word and say it aloud. This is followed by using the new word in context. The teacher then writes the word on the board. Students would say the word aloud with the teacher. They then write it down and say it aloud again. In subsequent days, many students benefit from frequent reviews of learned auditory materials.

Accommodations for Students with Special Needs

Here are suggestions for instruction for students with special needs. For additional support, see the *REALIDADES* Alternate Assessment Program.

Hearing Impairments

- Help students comprehend oral information or instructions. Provide written directions/materials and/or visual cues to support what is presented orally. Face the students when speaking, repeat as needed, and speak clearly. Seat these students in the front of the classroom. Provide outlines of lectures or oral presentations. Have another student take notes and make copies of notes available to all students. Use the audio and video scripts of the *REALIDADES* Audio or Video Program. Utilize the close-captioned version of the Video Program.

- Allow students to refer to their textbooks or to other written materials during oral presentations.

- Limit background noises that may distract students. Avoid seating these students where they may hear extraneous noise.

- Change listening activities and assessments to reading/writing activities. In activities that require aural/oral skills, let students demonstrate skills through alternative responses such as writing.

- Provide access to the audio and video materials. When using *REALIDADES*, students can download all Student Edition audio material from the Companion Web Site. The Interactive Textbook (online or CD-ROM) provides pronunciation support for all vocabulary, access to all Student Edition listening activities, and access to the vocabulary and grammar videos.

Visual perception problems

- Help students access information provided visually. Allow for preferred seating in the front of the class, including providing space for a guide dog, if necessary. Avoid seating students where they will be distracted by extraneous auditory or visual stimuli. Give students additional time to review visual input prior to an oral or written task. Highlight important information by providing key words, visuals, and simple outlines.

- Provide support for accessing printed information. Make sure the print is easy to read. The readings should be designed to maximize readability: easy-to-read font, layout, and design. Teach reading strategies that highlight the visual aspects of a selection: text organization, use of visuals, titles and headers, and the use of color. Provide copies of reading selections with additional support: underline key words/sentences/concepts or magnify the text in duplication.

- Teach, practice, and assess using multi-sensory strategies.

ADHD/ADD

- Provide additional support that enables students to focus. Present information in small "chunks." This includes new content, short instructions or directions, and shorter assignments, or break assignments into steps. Limit extraneous auditory and visual stimulation. Provide visual and written support for aural instructions or input. Repeat and explain (again) as needed. Provide outlines of oral presentations. Support readings with strategies similar to those for students with visual perception problems. Use graphic organizers.

- Verify that students "got it." Check that students are looking at you (eye contact) when providing oral instructions. Ask students to repeat what you just told them. Move closer to students to increase attention. Provide preferential seating that allows you to monitor students' focus and attention. Allow extra wait time when students are responding.

- Provide a variety of different learning activities that reach different learning styles. This will also allow for frequent changes of activities within a class. Provide for hands-on activities, vocabulary clip art, and grammar manipulatives.

- Use technology to provide interactive learning. These students benefit from using interactive textbooks, CD-ROMs, and Web sites.

- Be predictable. Establish a daily routine for managing the classroom and be consistent. Avoid surprises with these students.

- Help students organize themselves and their learning. Ask students to maintain notebooks that are organized by dividers. Provide study guides, summary sheets, and organizers for daily or weekly assignments.

Teaching Spanish to Advanced Learners

REALIDADES 3 offers a wide range of activities that enable advanced learners to expand their language skills and cultural understanding. These include:

Pre-AP* strategies and practice in the ¡Adelante! and Repaso del capítulo sections

Puente a la cultura: rich, cultural readings

¿Qué me cuentas?: extended, contextualized listening comprehension and picture sequence speaking practice

Presentación oral: performance-based speaking activities

Presentación escrita: two-page writing workshop that integrates the writing process and self-editing strategies

Lectura: readings introduce students to a wide range of authentic literature

Repaso del capítulo: thorough summary of vocabulary and grammar

Preparación para el examen: vocabulary and grammar modeled after advanced testing such as the AP* Language Examination plus focused practice for the proficiency sections of the chapter test

Creative and challenging opportunities

- Pick and choose from among the many open-ended activities, theme projects, or Advanced Learners suggestions so students can creatively use Spanish in skits, presentations, discussion groups, and journal or creative writing.

Technology integration

- Have students explore topics on the Internet as allowed. Encourage the use of presentation software, videos, and audio in presentations.

* Advanced Placement Program is a registered trademark of the College Entrance Examination Board, which was not involved in the production of, and does not endorse, this product.

Teaching Heritage Learners

A diverse background

Those who have a home language other than English bring a wider range of language abilities to the classroom. These abilities range from minimal functioning in the language to complete fluency and literacy. It is important for teachers to assess the language skills of the different heritage learners in the classroom. This diversity includes:

- Students who are able to understand the spoken language, but are unable to respond in the language beyond single-word answers.

- Students who are able to understand the language and communicate at a minimal level. These students may be able to read some items, but because of their limited vocabulary, they may not comprehend much information. They may write what they are able to sound out, but errors are evident.

- Students who can speak the language fluently but who have little to no experience with the language in its written form.

- Students who have come to the United States from non-English-speaking countries. They can understand and speak the language fluently; however, their reading and writing skills may be limited due to lack of a formal education in their country of origin.

- Fluent bilingual students who can understand, speak, read, and write another language very well and have possibly received formal instruction in that language in the United States or in another country.

Program goals

Heritage learners bring rich home language experiences to the classroom that can serve as a foundation for learning. Because of their language background, these students have the potential to be bilingual, biliterate, and bicultural. Heritage learners need to be exposed to a program that can improve and maintain the home language. Students need to study the grammar and focus on vocabulary development. Emphasis should be placed on building reading and writing skills. It is important that students develop a sensitivity to, when in a social situation, standard and non-standard language should be employed and comfortably adjust their language accordingly. In addition, students should be exposed to the diverse cultures within the Spanish-speaking community while developing a sense of pride in their own heritage. Heritage learners need to reach a high level of proficiency and accuracy that will ensure success at the advanced level of language study and testing. These students should also be ready to transition into a focused study of Spanish in specific professional areas.

Focus on individual needs

Due to their diverse backgrounds, heritage learners differ greatly in language skills and may need individualized instruction. In many of today's classrooms, teachers encounter classes that contain a mixture of beginning-level students and heritage learners. These groups need different materials, different instructional approaches, and different objectives. Here are several strategies that may be helpful for heritage learners:

- Build upon their background knowledge. Develop instructional units around themes and topics that relate to their life experiences. Encourage students to use these experiences as the foundation for building language skills through vocabulary development, reading, and writing.

- Help students connect aural with written language. If students don't understand a word in a reading, have them read it aloud or ask a friend or teacher to read it aloud. Often they can recognize the word once they hear it. Allow for opportunities for students to follow along as a story is read aloud.

- Use strategies that are effective in a language arts classroom, such as building schema, teaching language-learning strategies, using graphic organizers, and incorporating pre- and post-reading tasks. Use the writing process to develop good writers.

- Encourage students to begin communicating, especially in writing. Have them write down their thoughts in the way they sound to them. Then have students work with the teacher or another student for corrections. Students can also look through textbooks and dictionaries to assist with error correction.

- Maintain high standards. Require students to focus on accuracy and proficient communication. Many heritage learners experience frustration with reading and writing in the home language when they have good aural/oral skills. Building language skills takes time.

Teaching Heritage Learners with *REALIDADES 3*

REALIDADES 3 offers ideal support for teaching heritage learners at the intermediate level of proficiency. The Student Edition, the *REALIDADES para hispanohablantes* all-Spanish worktext, the *Lecturas para hispanohablantes 3* literature anthology, and the varied assessment options offer a rich and varied curriculum. In addition, the pre-AP* support in each chapter of the Student Edition will lay the foundations for success on the AP* Language Examination.

Teaching All Students: Summary

The diverse needs of today's Spanish students pose a challenge to teachers, curriculum developers, and school administrators as they design programs to ensure that all students develop language proficiency. With *REALIDADES,* teachers have at their disposal a variety of materials and strategies to enable them to provide access to Spanish for all learners. Clearly, some students will require additional tutoring and specialized services to reach their full learning potential. However, the activities and materials that accompany *REALIDADES,* coupled with instructional strategies described within this article, constitute a viable framework for reaching and teaching all learners.

Teaching Heritage Learners with *REALIDADES para hispanohablantes*

REALIDADES 3 provides extensive support for teaching heritage learners.

Student Edition
- focused vocabulary and grammar
- integrated language and culture
- extensive reading and writing
- test preparation

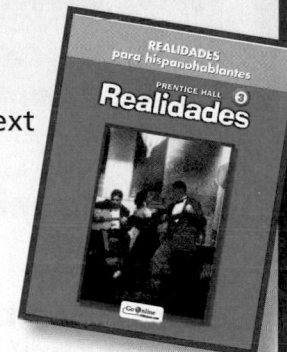

REALIDADES para hispanohablantes
- all-Spanish companion worktext
- all-Spanish grammar explanations
- companion pages for each section of Student Edition
- increased emphasis on reading and writing
- accompanying Teacher's Guide

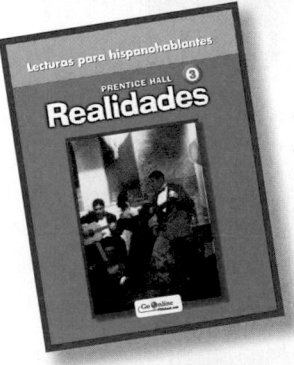

Lecturas para hispanohablantes
- literature anthology for additional readings

Assessment Program: *REALIDADES para hispanohablantes*
- direction lines in Spanish
- complete assessment support
- rubrics in Spanish

Instructional Planning and Support

Topics covered:

Today's Spanish classroom is a vibrant and interactive learning community, integrating language with culture. Teachers are planning for instruction that is communicative, motivating, and real for *all* students. They are incorporating a wide range of strategies, activities, and technology to achieve clearly defined teaching objectives. This section provides an overview of instructional strategies that will help teachers achieve these goals.

·····························

Creating a Communicative Learning Community

A communicative classroom is built upon activities that enable students to use language in meaningful and purposeful ways. One of the challenges is to get students ready, willing, and able to communicate. Here are several strategies that can be built into communicative tasks to help all students be successful.

Teach and use learning strategies

Research states that successful language students use a wide range of learning strategies. In contrast, unsuccessful students employ fewer strategies and tend to give up quickly. Strategies are inherently student-centered and when employed by learners, allow them to become more independent and more successful. Learning strategies enable students to:

- Learn and recall information more efficiently

- Interpret and comprehend language when reading or writing

- Speak more effectively

- Write more effectively

- Take more risks and be more positive

- Work more cooperatively with others

Use activities based upon multiple intelligences

The Multiple Intelligences Theory tells us that students learn in different ways. If new material is presented in a variety of formats, more students will likely learn and be able to demonstrate proficiency with the new material. Howard Gardner in 1983 proposed the theory of Multiple Intelligences in his book, *Frames of Mind*. This theory states that a person has many different ways of acquiring and demonstrating intelligence. Some people remember just about anything if learned to the tune of a jingle or chant, while someone else may be able to grasp an idea, concept, or grammatical point if presented as a graph, chart, or picture.

Gardner presents the notion that there is no "general intelligence," but rather that the mind is organized around distinct functional capacities, which he defines as "intelligences". Though each of the intelligences is developed independently of the others over the course of a lifetime, they usually work together and do not often appear in isolation. Gardner has identified and labeled eight main styles of acquiring and demonstrating knowledge; those eight intelligences are:

- Verbal/Linguistic
- Visual/Spatial
- Bodily/Kinesthetic
- Logical/Mathematical
- Interpersonal/Social
- Intrapersonal/Introspective
- Musical/Rhythmic
- Naturalist

In the Teacher's Edition, you will find frequent specific suggestions for accommodating and teaching to the Multiple Intelligences. This is not meant to be construed as a paradigm for labeling every student in your class. On the contrary, they are presented as tools to help more students access content while recognizing that they are intelligent in many ways and that their overall "intelligence" is based upon the sum of all their intelligences.

Activities that incorporate critical thinking tend to be more interesting for students as they are guided to think differently in ways such as:

- ❑ use or apply
- ❑ illustrate / sketch / diagram
- ❑ compare and contrast
- ❑ analyze
- ❑ categorize
- ❑ create
- ❑ organize / prepare
- ❑ evaluate
- ❑ revise
- ❑ value

Provide activities that require critical thinking

All students learn more effectively when activities help them make connections and see and use information in new and different ways. Critical thinking skills can be used as tools for learning and are easily integrated in a variety of tasks beginning in the first year of language study in both communication and culture activities.

Scaffolded tasks

Step-by-step support builds success.

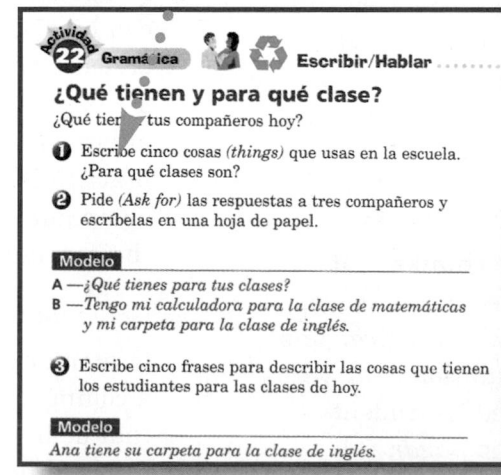

Scaffold communicative tasks

Communicating in a second language is a complicated task. There are mental steps that take place as a student attempts to communicate a message. Activities that help students get through these mental steps allow students to be successful. This "scaffolded" support is provided throughout *REALIDADES*.

For example, in preparing for a speaking task, students think through what they might want to say using a chart. In writing, they might fill out a word web before attempting the first draft. By providing a scaffold that asks students to think, plan, process, and then communicate, more students will become effective communicators.

Instructional Planning and Support

The Role of Grammar in a Communicative Classroom

In a proficiency-based curriculum, vocabulary and grammar are viewed as tools that students need in order to communicate, rather than as ends in themselves.

Input grammar in context

For students to internalize grammar, it needs to be presented in a meaningful context. For example, students can grasp the concept of the preterite more easily if it is presented within a topic, like shopping. As the teacher presents clothing and store vocabulary, she can tell the class what items of clothing she or another person bought, when it was purchased, and how much was paid. As the teacher points to a picture of a sweater on an overhead transparency or clip art or an actual sweater, she begins with comprehensible input that uses the *yo* form of the preterite: *Ayer, yo fui de compras y compré un suéter nuevo. Y pagué veinte dólares. No es mucho, ¿verdad?* Repetition of the input can continue with other articles of clothing, allowing students to easily deduce and internalize the meaning of *compré* and *pagué*. The teacher then begins to ask students questions using *compraste* and *pagaste* and makes summary comments about what is said in the class, drawing other students into the discussion as she introduces other preterite forms. As students begin to internalize these forms and the chapter vocabulary, they begin to make simple statements or ask questions to a partner about shopping for clothing.

Input grammar in small, manageable chunks

Present new grammar in manageable chunks that can be immediately practiced. In the example above, students can use a few preterite forms of *comprar* and *pagar* as they talk about shopping. Additional -*ar* verbs and other preterite forms can be added as students become comfortable using *comprar* and *pagar.*

Input grammar in readings

Grammar input can also take place through reading. As students read sentences, short paragraphs, and dialogues with supporting contextual and visual cues, they can understand new grammatical forms. Through carefully planned out questions asked by their teacher, students can be led to explain grammatical concepts.

Teach what is needed for the immediate communication objectives

Teach students the grammar needed to accomplish the communicative objective. This allows students to learn the concept in context and practice. For example, if you teach *pensar* or *querer* in connection to a theme, don't give students an additional list of all -*ie* stem-changing verbs. Rather, teach additional -*ie* verbs in later chapters as they connect to the themes.

Practice grammar in a variety of activities

Just as there are several ways to provide input, there are many useful methods for practicing grammar. This practice can involve hands-on activities and games that let students manipulate grammatical structures. Grammar practice is effectively integrated into communicative activities such as surveys, Venn diagrams, and paired and group activities. In addition, practice can involve computerized activities on a Web site that allows students to practice grammar again and again at their own pace.

Grammar and communication

Grammar can be successfully integrated in a communicative classroom with activities that deal with grammatical accuracy at different levels. When presented in meaningful contexts, in manageable chunks, and with presentation and practice that incorporate a variety of activities, students will develop increasing accuracy with grammar.

Pair and Group Activities in a Communicative Classroom

Benefits of grouping work

Effective group work develops a friendly and cooperative atmosphere by giving students a chance to get to know each other better. This sense of camaraderie leads to a more relaxed classroom in which students are more willing to talk and to participate. Group work also allows more opportunity for "student talk", thereby increasing the quantity of student practice in the target language.

Grouping options and techniques

The communicative activities in a Spanish classroom allow for a variety of grouping options.

The most common option is random grouping that includes pairing up two students or creating small groups of three to five students. Some possible ways to randomly group students include:

- Count off by going left to right or up and down in rows.
- Place on pieces of paper vocabulary words (English/Spanish), countries/capitals, opposites, colors, or categories that can be matched up in a bag. Have students draw a piece of paper and find their partner(s).
- Order students along a continuum by birthday, height, phone numbers, etc.
- Place numbers or a deck of cards in a hat, bag, or box and have students draw.
- Turn to the student to the left or right, front or back.

Another grouping option is to place students by their ability level. Homogeneous grouping allows students of similar ability to work together. In this case, teachers assign tasks based upon the ability level of the group. Advanced students are given a more challenging task. Other students are given tasks that they can successfully complete. Heterogeneous grouping places students of varying abilities together. This allows for stronger students to help weaker students.

Grouping students by interest level is another option to consider. Students could group themselves for an activity or longer project based upon mutual interest.

Planning and facilitating an effective group activity

- Make sure that the task involves a true exchange of information.
- Think through the language functions and content information to make certain students can complete the task.
- Prepare all materials in advance and anticipate questions.
- Explain the task before the students break up into groups. Be sure to model the task if necessary.
- Determine in advance how students will be evaluated and share that criteria with the class.
- Allow adequate time for the task. Make sure at least three quarters of the students at different ability levels can complete it. Tell students how much time they have and stick to the plan.
- Encourage students to stay on-task by walking around the class and monitoring the groups.
- Build into your grading system a way to include group participation and staying on-task.
- Develop some sort of follow-up upon completion of the task.

Error correction

As students work in groups, they will be making mistakes. Here are strategies that can help students to focus on accuracy while doing group work.

- Listen for common errors while monitoring the class. If the error is one of vocabulary usage or grammar, discuss the error with the class and do some focused practice once the task is completed. If the error is one of meaning (very common in beginning writing), have the class work together to determine how best to express the message.
- If you want to correct an individual student error, correct the student only after he or she has spoken. Restate the student's response using the correction in your restatement.

Integrating Technology in the Classroom

Technology offers teachers and students a wide range of useful, creative, and motivating tools that build language proficiency. The varied learning experiences available through audio, video, CD-ROMs, and the Internet address different learning styles through multi-sensory and interactive tasks.

REALIDADES 3 Video Program

Student Technology in REALIDADES

REALIDADES offers technology-based learning tools.

- **Interactive Textbook** The Student Edition comes alive with interactive learning. The Interactive Textbook provides the same instruction as in the Student Edition but with additional features that include built-in audio, pronunciation practice, video, interactive activities, links to workbook pages, links to the Companion Web Site plus other learning resources. Available online or on CD-ROM.

- **Companion Web Site** The online interactive activities, easily accessed by Web Codes, provide additional practice for vocabulary and grammar, end-of-chapter self-tests, and Internet links.

- **MindPoint™ Quiz Show CD-ROM** The interactive games offer a fun end-of-chapter review while providing students and teachers with detailed reports on how well individual students and/or the class have performed on questions based upon the chapter objectives.

- **Downloadable audio files** Students can download all the Student Edition listening activities to a computer or audio player. The audio activities are easily accessed through Web Codes provided in the front matter of the Student Edition.

Teacher Technology in REALIDADES

- **TeacherExpress™ CD-ROM** Teach, plan, and assess with this interactive Teacher's Edition. The CD-ROM provides instant access to Lesson Planning, Teacher Edition pages, Teaching Resources, Exam*View*™ Computer Test Bank on CD-ROM, Vocabulary Clip Art, and Web Resources.

- **Video Program** The innovative videos on DVD or VHS accompany each chapter.

- **Audio Program** Audio supports the *A primera vista* language input, pronunciation, Student Edition listening activities, audio activities that accompany the *Writing, Audio & Video Activities,* songs, and the listening tasks from the chapter tests.

> **" Technology provides new ways to reach and teach today's learners. "**

- **Exam*View*™ Computer Test Bank on CD-ROM** The Test Bank provides a wide range of questions per chapter. Teachers can create alternate tests.

- **Transparencies** Three different sets of transparencies include Vocabulary and Grammar Transparencies, Answers on Transparencies, Fine Art Transparencies.

Technology in *REALIDADES 3*

REALIDADES 3 provides a complete, state-of-the-art technology package for each chapter at all levels of the program. Technology is integrated into the instruction design of each chapter as follows:

Chapter Section	Chapter Opener	A primera vista	Manos a la obra	¡Adelante!	Repaso del capítulo
Student **Learning Tools**	**Web site** • Atlas **Interactive textbook**	**Web site** • Vocabulary practice **Interactive textbook**	**Web site** • Grammar practice **Interactive textbook**	**Web site** • Internet link and activity **Interactive textbook**	**Web site** • *Vocabulario y gramática* • Self-test **Interactive textbook** **MindPoint™ Quiz Show CD-ROM**
Teacher **Planning**	**TeacherExpress™ CD-ROM** **Web site**	**TeacherExpress™ CD-ROM** **Web site**	**TeacherExpress™ CD-ROM** **Web site**	**TeacherExpress™ CD-ROM** **Web site**	**TeacherExpress™ CD-ROM** **Web site**
Instruction	**Fine Art Transparencies** **Vocabulary and Grammar Transparencies** • Maps	**Vocabulary and Grammar Transparencies** • *Vocabulario y gramática en contexto* **Answers on Transparencies** **Audio Program** • *Vocabulario y gramática en contexto* • *Actividades* • Audio Activities (Writing, Audio & Video Workbook)	**Vocabulary and Grammar Transparencies** • *Gramática* (verbs and charts) • Graphic Organizers **Answers on Transparencies** **Fine Art Transparencies** **Audio Program** • *Actividades* • *En voz alta* • Audio Activities (Writing, Audio & Video Workbook)	**Vocabulary and Grammar Transparencies** • Graphic Organizers **Answers on Transparencies** **Audio Program** • *¿Qué me cuentas?* **Video Program**	**Audio Program** • *Repaso del capítulo (Vocabulario y gramática)* • *Escuchar (Preparación para el examen)*
Assessment					**Computer Test Bank with CD-ROM** **Audio Program** • Listening Assessment

Spanish 3: A Time of Transition

Spanish 3 is a transition time for language study. At this level, students are asked to communicate using more complex language. Their vocabulary groups are expanding and they are learning more grammar. They are transitioning into authentic literature and dealing with broader themes and issues in the classroom. Spanish 3 is the time when students are starting to "put it all together".

Tips for Success at Spanish 3

Here are some tips that are helpful for building a successful Spanish 3 program.

- **Start with Spanish 1 and 2** The key to success in Spanish 3 is a strong language program in the beginning levels. Students in the upper levels of study are most successful when earlier levels have featured thematic instruction with integrated vocabulary, grammar, communication, and culture. Successful learners have learned to use a variety of strategies and advanced organizers for speaking, listening, reading, and writing. They have also explored how language works: cognates, word families, language connections, prefixes, suffixes, and the patterns of grammar.

- **Use themes to organize instruction** Use student-centered themes as the focus for the vocabulary, grammar, culture, and communicative goals in a chapter. The theme provides a unifying and meaningful context for learning and it allows for natural recycling as themes from previous levels can be revisited and explored in greater depth.

- **Develop a strong vocabulary base** Vocabulary, vocabulary, vocabulary. Continue to increase the students' thematic vocabulary. Use graphic organizers such as word webs and activities that integrate previously learned vocabulary in combination with activities that use the new vocabulary. Thematic instruction is ideal for building a strong vocabulary base because it allows for natural recycling. In

addition, at this level, students benefit from activities that help them recognize word families and language patterns.

- **Connect grammar with communication** As the grammar gets more complex, it is important that students see grammar connected to themes and real life applications. Build upon and reinforce grammar that students already know. Provide clear explanations and charts. Provide practice that includes concrete practice, paired activities, realia-based activities, and open-ended speaking and writing tasks.

- **Provide many opportunities for reading** Reading serves many purposes in Spanish 3. It is an excellent tool for language input. It helps students see how language works in context. It increases student's vocabulary base. It opens the door to the world of literature, songs, and poetry. It gives students access to information and perspectives only available through authentic readings. When focusing on the reading skill, it is important to provide pre- and post-reading activities and to teach strategies. Active reading strategies, like the use of graphic organizers, helps them to deal with longer and more complex readings.

- **Explore culture at a deeper level** Integrate culture into the classroom by weaving it into practice activities. Build communicative activities around art and realia. Develop pronunciation skills using song lyrics and poetry. Build bridges to cultural understanding through readings on cultural products, practices, and comparisons. Integrate authentic readings and literature that connect to the theme.

Teaching in the third-year Spanish classroom offers many challenges as students transition into the intermediate level of language. However, it also provides many rewards as teachers see their students begin to put the language together. *REALIDADES 3* provides the support for teachers and students that will build success at Spanish 3.

Professional Resources

- ▷ **Professional Organizations**
- ▷ **Regional Conferences**
- ▷ **Listservs**
- ▷ **Web sites**

National Organizations

These national organizations provide an annual conference and a wide range of teaching support.

The American Council on the Teaching of Foreign Languages (ACTFL)
http://www.actfl.org

American Association of Teachers of Spanish and Portuguese (AATSP)
http://www.aatsp.org

State Organizations

Each state offers the support of a language association. These organizations provide workshops, conferences, job placement, networking opportunities, and updates on state and second language issues. Teachers are encouraged to contact their state organizations and get involved.

Regional Conferences

These regional conferences provide annual conferences and support teacher advocacy in their regions. They can each be reached via their Web sites.

Central States Conference on the Teaching of Foreign Languages
http://www.centralstates.cc

Northeast Conference on the Teaching of Foreign Languages
http://www.dickinson.edu/nectfl

Southern Conference on Language Teaching
http://www.valdosta.edu/scolt

Southwest Conference on the Teaching of Foreign Languages
http://www.swcolt.org

NOTE: Web site addresses are subject to change.

Listservs

The following electronic resources are helpful to language teachers and curriculum developers. To subscribe to a listserv, send a message with no subject line as follows:

    subscribe [name of listserv] your first name your last name

    for example: subscribe **FLTEACH** Abraham Lincoln

FL TEACH: a forum for discussion among foreign language educators

listserv@listserv.acsu.buffalo.edu

SLART-L: focuses on second language acquisition research and teaching

listserv@cunyvm.cuny.edu

IECC: an e-mail listserv that helps teachers find partners for intercultural e-mail classroom connections

iecc-request@stolaf.edu

LLTI: a form to discuss language learning and technology

listserv@dartcms1.dartmouth.edu

http://www.nclrc.org

Web sites

The number of Web sites of interest to foreign language educators is too large to list. Below are some places to begin.

http://www.clta.net/lessons
- excellent source of Web-based activities for the foreign language classroom

http://www.cortland.edu/www/flteach/flteach.html
- allows for keyword searches of the archives of the FLTEACH listserv and provides an extensive number of links with other sites of interest to foreign language teachers

http://www.cal.org/ericcll/
- provides information to foreign language educators in many areas, including publications, study abroad, and links

http://www.elok.com/rendezvous/
- penpal and penfriends service for teachers looking to link with students in other countries

http://www.nclrc.org
- Georgetown University/George Washington University/Center for Applied Linguistics

http://www.educ.iastate.edu/nflrc
- Iowa State University

Bibliography

Assessment

Boyles, Peggy. *"Assessing the Speaking Skill in the Classroom: New Solutions to an Ongoing Problem."* Northeast Conference Reports: Testing, Teaching, and Assessment, ed. Charles R. Hancock. Lincolnwood, IL: National Textbook Company, 1994.

Burke, K., R. Fogarty, and S. Belgard. *The Mindful School: The Portfolio Connection.* Palatine, IL: IRI/Skylight Publishing Inc., 1994.

Cohen, Andrew D. *Assessing Language Ability in the Classroom,* 2nd ed. Boston: Heinle & Heinle, 1994.

Liskin-Gasparro, Judith. *"Assessment: From Content Standards to Student Performance."* National Standards. A Catalyst for Reform, ed. Robert Lafayette. Lincolnwood, IL: National Textbook Company, 1996.

Pettigrew, Frances, and Ghislaine Tulou. *"Performance Assessment for Language Students."* Language Learners of Tomorrow: Process and Promise, ed. Margaret Ann Kassen. Lincolnwood, IL: National Textbook Company, 1999.

Block Scheduling

Blaz, Deborah. *Teaching Foreign Languages on the Block.* Larchmont, NY: Eye on Education, 1998.

Canady, R. L., and M. D. Rettig. *Block Scheduling: A Catalyst for Change in High Schools.* Larchmont, NY: Eye on Education, 1995.

———. Teaching on the Block: *Strategies for Engaging Active Learners.* Larchmont, NY: Eye on Education, 1996.

Culture

Byram, Michael. *Teaching and Assessing Intercultural Competence. Clevedon,* U.K.: Multilingual Matters, 1997.

Fantini, Alvino. *"Comparisons: towards the Development of Intercultural Competence."* Foreign Language Standards: Linking Theory, Research, and Practice, ed. June Phillips. Lincolnwood, IL: National Textbook Co., 1999.

Galloway, Vicki. *"Bridges and Boundaries: Growing the Cross-Cultural Mind."* Language Learners of Tomorrow: Process and Promise. Lincolnwood, IL: National Textbook Co., 1999.

Seelye, H. Ned. *Teaching Culture,* 3rd ed. Lincolnwood, IL: National Textbook Co., 1993.

Curriculum and Instruction

ACTFL Performance Guidelines for K-12 Learners. Yonkers, NY: ACTFL, 1999.

"Challenge for a New Era." Nebraska K-12 Foreign Language Frameworks. Lincoln: Nebraska Department of Education, 1996.

Chamot, Anna U. *"Reading and Writing Processes: Learning Strategies in Immersion Classrooms."* Language Learners of Tomorrow: Process and Promise, ed. Margaret Ann Kassen. Lincolnwood, IL: National Textbook Company, 1999.

Davis, Robert. *"Group Work is NOT Busy Work: Maximizing Success of Group Work in the L2 Classroom."* Foreign Language Annals, Vol. 30 (1997): 265-279.

Foreign Language Framework for California Public Schools Kindergarten Through Grade Twelve. Sacramento: California State Department of Education, 2002

Guntermann, G., ed. *Teaching Spanish with the Five C's: A Blueprint for Success.* New York: Harcourt College Publishers, 2000.

Hall, Joan Kelly. *"The Communication Standards."* Foreign Language Standards: Linking Theory, Research, and Practice, ed. June Phillips. Lincolnwood, IL: National Textbook Co., 1999.

Heining-Boyton, Audrey L., and David B. Heining-Boyton. *"Incorporating Higher-Order Thinking Skills in the Foreign Language Curriculum."* Foreign Languages: Internationalizing the Future, ed. Robert M. Terry. Valdosta, GA: Southern Conference on Language Teaching, 1993.

Jackson, Claire, et al. *Articulation & Achievement: Connecting Standards, Performance, and Assessment in Foreign Language.* New York: College Board of Publications, 1996.

Klee, Carol A. *"Communication as an Organizing Principle in the National Standards: Sociolinguistic Aspects of Spanish Language Teaching."* Hispania. Vol. 81 (2) (1998), pp. 339-351.

Knerr, Jennifer and Charles James. *"Partner Work and Small-Group Work for Cooperative and Communicative Learning."* Focus on the Foreign Language Learner: Priority and Strategies, ed. Lorraine Strasheim. Lincolnwood, IL: National Textbook Company., 1991.

Krashen, Stephen. *Principles and Practice in Second Language Acquisition.* Oxford: Pergamon Press, 1982.

Lafayette, R. C., ed. *National Standards: A Catalyst for Reform.* Lincolnwood, IL: National Textbook Company, 1996.

Met, Myriam, with J. Phillips. *Curriculum Handbook.* Association for Supervision and Curriculum Development, 1999.

———. *"Making Connections."* Foreign Language Standards: Linking Theory, Research, and Practice, ed. June Phillips. Lincolnwood, IL: National Textbook Co., 1999.

National K-12 Foreign Language Resource Center. *"A Guide to Aligning Curriculum with the Standards."* Ames: Iowa State University, 1996.

——. *Bringing the Standards into the Classroom: A Teacher's Guide.* Ames: Iowa State University, 1997.

Standards for Foreign Language Learning in the 21st Century: *Including Chinese, Classical Languages, French, German, Italian, Japanese, Portuguese, Russian, and Spanish.* Lawrence, KS: Allen Press, 1999.

Trayer, Marie. *"Foreign Language Standards: The Nebraska Story."* ACTFL Newsletter, IX: 3 (Spring 1997): 10.

Van Patton, Bill. *"Grammar Teaching for the Acquisition-Rich Classroom."* Foreign Language Annals, Vol. 25 (1993): 435-450).

Zaslow, Brandon. *"Teaching Language for Proficiency: From Theory to Practice (An Instructional Framework)."* Unpublished document. School of Education, University of California, Los Angeles, 2001.

Heritage Learners

Colombi, Cecilia M. and Francisco X. Alarcón, eds. *La enseñanza del español a hispanohablantes: Praxis y teoría.* Boston: Houghton Mifflin Co., 1997.

Miller, Barbara L., and John B. Webb, eds. *Teaching Heritage Language Learners: Voices from the Classroom, ACTFL Series.* Princeton: Princeton University, 2000.

Rodriguez-Pino, Cecilia, and Daniel Villa. *"A Student-Centered Spanish for Native Speakers Program: Theory, Curriculum Design and Outcome Assessment."* Faces in a Crowd: The Individual Learner in Multisection Courses, ed. Carol Klee. Boston: Heinle & Heinle, 1994.

Valdés, Guadalupe. *"The Role of Foreign Language Teaching Profession in Maintaining Non-English Languages in the United States."* Northeast Conference Reports: Languages for a Multicultural World in Transition, ed. H. Byrnes. Lincolnwood, IL: National Textbook Company, 1992.

Methodology

Hadley, Alice Omaggio. *Teaching Language in Context,* 2nd ed. Boston: Heinle & Heinle, 1993.

Hall, Joan Kelly. *Methods for Teaching Foreign Languages: Creating a Community of Learners in the Classroom.* Upper Saddle River, NJ: Merrill Prentice Hall, 2001.

Lee, James, and Bill Van Patten. *Making Communicative Language Teaching Happen.* New York: McGraw Hill, 1995.

Oxford, Rebecca L. *Language Learning Strategies: What Every Teacher Should Know.* New York: Newbury House, 1990.

Shrum, Judith, and Eileen Glisan. *Teacher's Handbook: Contextualized Language Instruction.* Boston: Heinle & Heinle, 1994.

Multiple Intelligences

Armstrong, Thomas. *Awakening Your Child's Natural Genius.* Los Angeles, CA: Heremy P. Tarcher, Inc., 1991.

Armstrong, Thomas. *Multiple Intelligences in the Classroom.* Alexandria, VA: Association for Supervision and Curriculum Development, 1994.

Gardner, Howard. *Frames of Mind: The Theory of Multiple Intelligences.* New York, NY: Basic Books, 1983.

Lazear, David. *Seven Pathways of Learning: Teaching Students and Parents about Multiple Intelligences.* Tuczon, AZ: Zephyr Press, 1994.

Middle School

Raven, Patrick T. and Jo Anne S. Wilson. *"Middle-School Foreign Language: What Is It? What Should It Be?,"* Visions and Reality in Foreign Language Teaching: Where We Are, Where We Are Going, ed. William N. Hatfield. Lincolnwood, IL: National Textbook Company, 1993.

Verkler, Karen W. *"Middle School Philosophy and Second Language Acquisition Theory: Working together for Enhanced Proficiency."* Foreign Language Annals, Vol. 27 (1994): 19-42.

Students with Learning Disabilities

Ganschow, Leonore, and Richard Sparks. *"A Screening Instrument for the Identification of Foreign Language Learning Problems."* Foreign Language Annals, Vol. 24 (1991): 383-398.

——, **and James Javorsky, John Patton, Jane Pohlman, Richard Sparks.** *"Test Comparisons among Students Identified as High-Risk, Low-Risk, and Learning Disabled in High School Foreign Language Courses."* The Modern Language Journal, Vol. 76 (1992): 142-159.

Sax Mabbott, Ann. *"An Exploration of Reading Comprehension, Oral Reading Errors, and Written Errors by Subjects Labeled Learning Disabled."* Foreign Language Annals, Vol. 27 (1994): 294-324.

Sheppard, Marie. *"Proficiency as an Inclusive Orientation: Meeting the Challenge of Diversity."* Reflecting on Proficiency from the Classroom Perspective, ed. June Phillips. Lincolnwood, IL: National Textbook Company, 1993.

Technology

Blyth, C. S. *Untangling the Web.* New York: St. Martin's Press, 1998.

Bush, M.D., R. M. Terry, eds. *Technology-Enhanced Language Learning.* Lincolnwood, IL: National Textbook Company, 1997.

Muyskens, Judith Ann., ed. *New Ways of Learning and Teaching: Focus on Technology and Foreign Language Education.* Boston: Heinle & Heinle, 1997.

Index of Cultural References

The numbers following each entry indicate the pages on which a reference to that topic is made; an *i* following a number indicates that the reference appears on that page in an illustration, photograph, or artwork; an *m* indicates that the reference appears in a map.

Index of Cultural References

PRENTICE HALL
Realidades 3

Peggy Palo Boyles
Oklahoma City, OK

Myriam Met
Rockville, MD

Richard S. Sayers
Longmont, CO

PEARSON
Prentice
Hall

Needham, Massachusetts
Upper Saddle River, New Jersey

PRENTICE HALL ③
Realidades

Realidades authors

Peggy Palo Boyles

During her foreign language career of over thirty years, Peggy Palo Boyles has taught elementary, secondary, and university students in both private and public schools. She currently serves as the Foreign Language/ESL Curriculum Coordinator for the Putnam City Schools in Oklahoma City, OK. She was a member of the ACTFL Performance Guidelines for K–12 Learners task force and served as a Senior Editor for the project. Ms. Boyles is currently President of the National Association of District Supervisors of Foreign Languages (NADSFL). She frequently conducts foreign language workshops for state and national organizations, public school districts, and private schools throughout the country.

Myriam Met

For most of her professional life, Myriam (Mimi) Met has worked in the public schools, starting as a high school teacher in New York City. Other positions include supervisor of language programs in the Cincinnati Public Schools, K–12, and Coordinator of Foreign Languages, K–12, for Montgomery County Public Schools, MD. She is currently deputy director of the National Foreign Language Center, where she is responsible for K–12 language education policy analysis. Dr. Met has served on the Advisory Board for the National Standards in Foreign Language Learning, the task force that developed national standards in Spanish, and co-chaired the Pacesetter Spanish task force for the College Board.

Richard S. Sayers

Rich Sayers has been an educator in world languages for 25 years. He taught Spanish at Niwot High School in Longmont, CO, for 18 years, where he also served as department chair, Teacher on Special Assignment coordinating the district foreign language department, and board member of the Colorado Congress of Foreign Language Teachers. In 1991, Mr. Sayers was selected as one of the Disney Company's Foreign Language Teacher Honorees for the American Teacher Awards. He presently serves as a board member of the Southwest Conference on Language Teaching. Mr. Sayers is Senior National Consultant for Pearson Prentice Hall.

v

Tabla de materias

Para empezar

Go Online
PHSchool.com

For: Online Table of Contents
Visit: www.phschool.com
Web Code: jck-0001

Capítulo 1

Días inolvidables

Objectives

- Describe a visit to a national park
- Talk about school competitions
- Express your emotions regarding the outcome of an event
- Narrate an event in the past
- Understand cultural perspectives on family outings

Video Focus

- Outdoor activities in the Spanish-speaking world

Objectives

- Talk about the arts
- Give an opinion about a work of art
- Relate the arts to your own experience
- Describe how people express themselves

- Narrate events in the past
- Discuss some important artists of the Spanish-speaking world

Video Focus

- Music, dance and art in the Spanish-speaking world

¿Qué haces para estar en forma?

Objectives
- Talk about symptoms and remedies
- Give advice about health and nutrition
- Express how you feel under certain circumstances
- Tell others what to do

- Understand cultural perspectives about health, physical fitness and nutrition

Video Focus
- Maintaining a healthy lifestyle

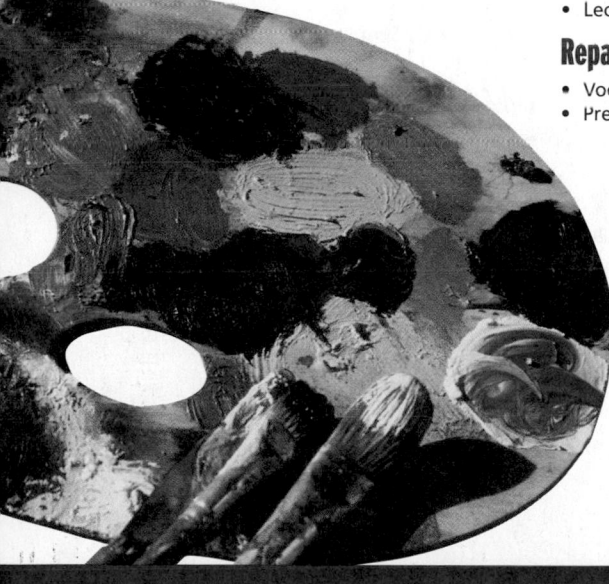

Tabla de materias   ix

4 ¿Cómo te llevas con los demás?

Objectives

- Express how you relate to friends and family
- Explain what is needed to maintain friendships
- Express how you feel under certain circumstances

- Talk about family conflicts and how to resolve them
- Understand cultural perspectives on dealing with friends and family

Video Focus

- Characteristics of friendships and family relationships

Objectives

- Talk about ways of getting a job
- Describe skills and abilities needed to perform a job
- Talk about opportunities for volunteer work in your community
- Explain how you can help your community

- Understand cultural perspectives on dealing with student jobs and volunteer work

Video Focus

- Student volunteer work

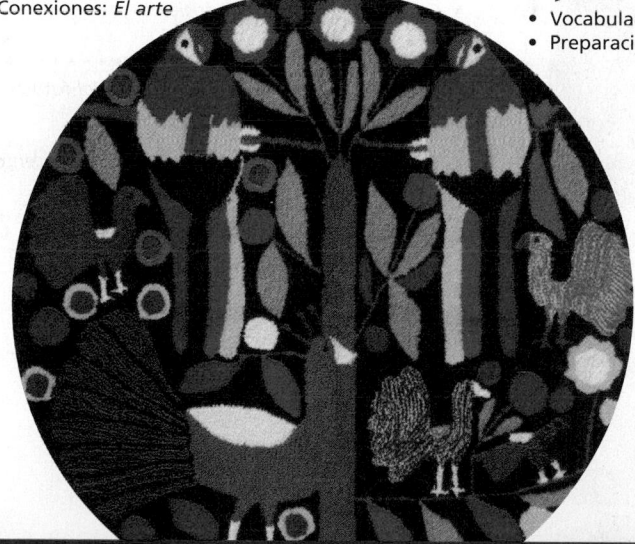

Tabla de materias   **xi**

Capítulo 6
¿Qué nos traerá el futuro?

Objectives
- Talk about careers and professions
- Talk about plans for the future
- Explain the impact of science and technology on our lives

- Understand cultural perspectives on jobs and technology

Video Focus
- The effects of technology on society

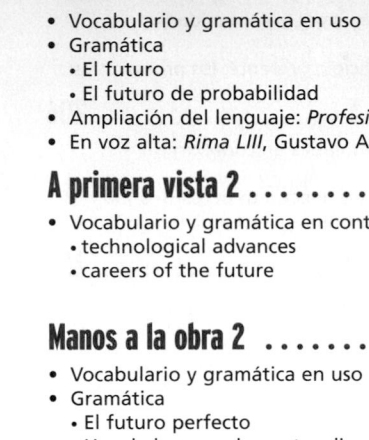

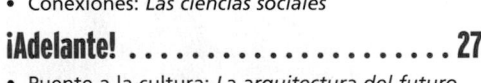

¿Mito o realidad?

Objectives
- Describe what archaeologists do
- Identify and describe some extraordinary phenomena
- Give your opinion about mysterious events
- Talk about the contributions of the Maya and Aztec civilizations

- Compare some myths and legends from the Spanish-speaking world with those of the United States

Video Focus
- Famous archaeological sites in the Spanish-speaking world

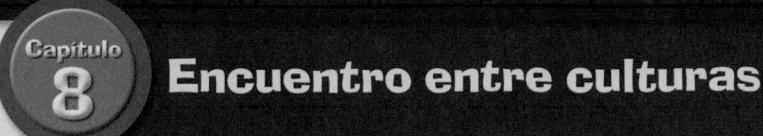

Capítulo 8
Encuentro entre culturas

Objectives

- Describe how different cultures interact
- Talk about the fusion of cultures in Spain before 1492
- Talk about fusion of different cultures in the Americas after the Europeans arrived
- Understand cultural perspectives on dealing with different ethnic groups in the United States

Video Focus

- Cultural diversity in the Spanish-speaking world

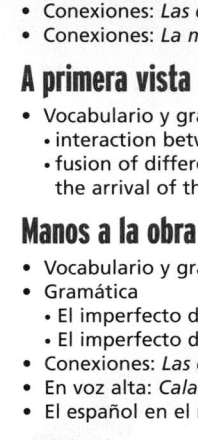

Cuidemos nuestro planeta

Objectives

- Talk about environmental concerns in the community
- Discuss how to solve local and global environmental problems
- Express attitudes and opinions about the environment

- Understand cultural perspectives on dealing with conservation and the environment

Video Focus

- Protecting our natural environment

Tabla de materias **xv**

Capítulo 10 ¿Cuáles son tus derechos y deberes?

Objectives
- Talk about rights and responsibilities at home and in school
- Discuss rights in society guaranteed by the U.S. Constitution
- Talk about the role of government
- Learn what young people think
- about the world problems they face and the solutions they propose
- Understand cultural perspectives on rights and responsibilities

Video Focus
- Human rights education

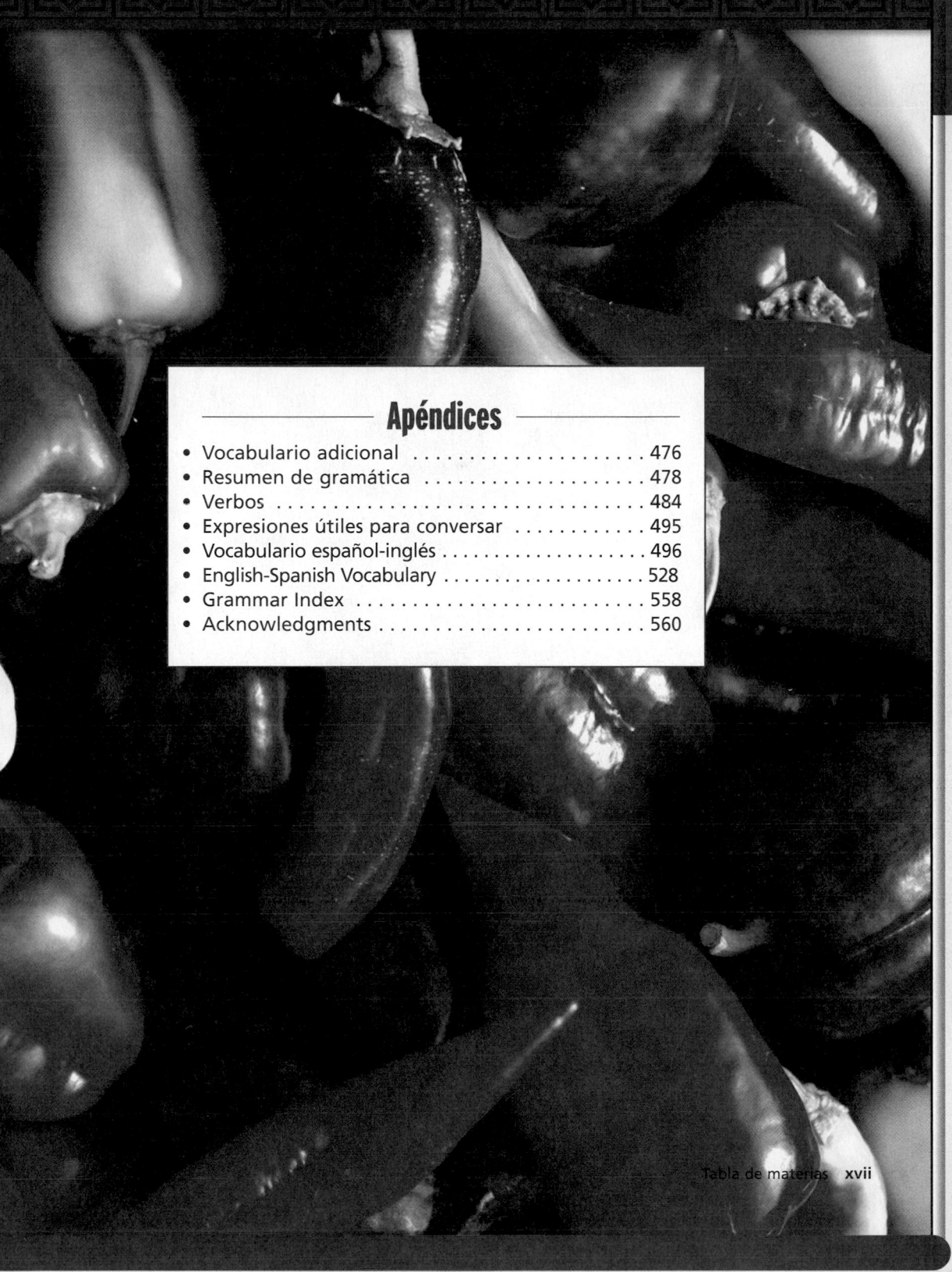

Apéndices

México

Standards:
2.1, 2.2, 3.1, 4.2

Geography

Mexico is the fifth largest country in the Western Hemisphere. Its geography ranges from the rugged mountains of the Sierra Madre Occidental and Sierra Madre Oriental to tropical rain forests, volcanic peaks, and world-renowned beaches.

The central area of the country, a high plateau between the ranges of the Sierra Madre, is dry, with limited rainfall. Most of the population lives in this area. Its hub is México, D.F. (Distrito Federal), the nation's capital. The city is located in a basin known historically as the Valley of Mexico. Earthquakes are not uncommon. In 1985 one of the worst earthquakes in Mexican history shook Mexico City and its environs, causing many deaths and extensive damage.

The central plateau is also home to Mexico's highest peaks and volcanoes, including Popocatépetl and Iztaccíhuatl. Pico de Orizaba is the highest mountain in Mexico at 5,610 meters (18,406 feet).

To the north of the central plateau is the Sierra Tarahumara, or Copper Canyon, the largest canyon system in North America. The climate varies dramatically here. At the rim of the canyons the weather is temperate, with cold winters and mild summers, punctuated by heavy rainfall. Deep below the canyon rims, the climate is tropical, wet, and hot for most of the year.

North of the Sierra Tarahumara is the border with the United States, most of which is formed by the Rio Grande, known in Mexico as the Río Bravo.

To the southwest of Mexico City is Acapulco. Mexican vacationers and tourists from around the world visit the heavily populated city and its tropical ocean beaches. Southeast of the capital, on the Yucatan peninsula, is Cancún. Tourists flock to this area's white sandy beaches and the turquoise waters of the Caribbean.

One of the highlights of southern Mexico is Oaxaca, where the climate is spring-like throughout the year. Here archeological sites dot the landscape, revealing the ancient remains of pre-Columbian settlements.

Morelia, México

Cabo San Lucas, Baja California, México

xviii México

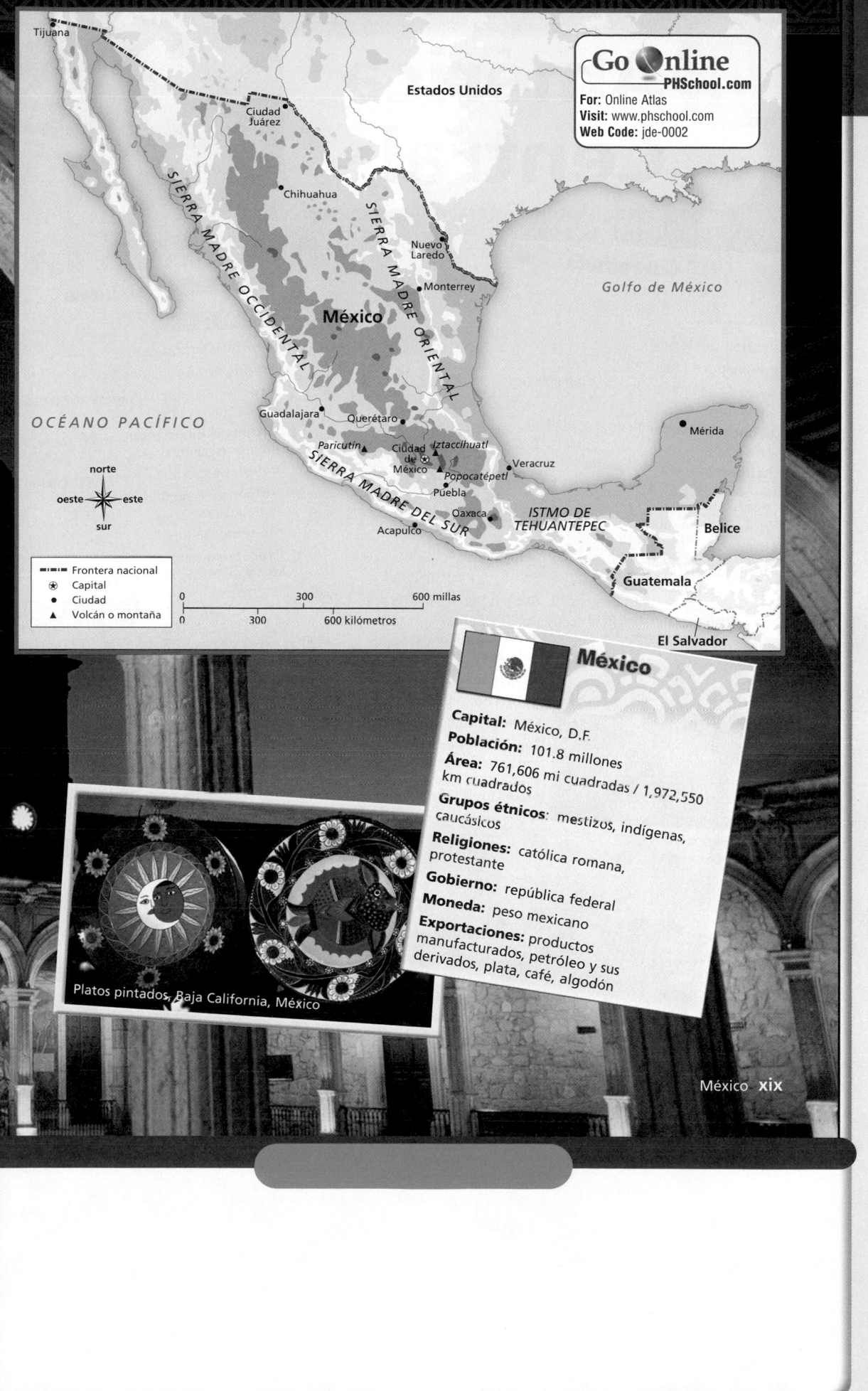

Estados Unidos

Tijuana

Ciudad
Juárez

Chihuahua

Nuevo
Laredo

Monterrey

Golfo de México

SIERRA MADRE OCCIDENTAL

SIERRA MADRE ORIENTAL

México

OCÉANO PACÍFICO

Guadalajara

Querétaro

Mérida

Paricutín

Ciudad
de
México

Iztaccíhuatl

Veracruz

Popocatépetl

Puebla

SIERRA MADRE DEL SUR

Oaxaca

Acapulco

ISTMO DE
TEHUANTEPEC

Belice

Guatemala

El Salvador

norte

oeste — este

sur

- ----- Frontera nacional
- ⊛ Capital
- • Ciudad
- ▲ Volcán o montaña

| 0 | | 300 | | 600 millas |
| 0 | 300 | | 600 kilómetros | |

México

Capital: México, D.F.

Población: 101.8 millones

Área: 761,606 mi cuadradas / 1,972,550 km cuadrados

Grupos étnicos: mestizos, indígenas, caucásicos

Religiones: católica romana, protestante

Gobierno: república federal

Moneda: peso mexicano

Exportaciones: productos manufacturados, petróleo y sus derivados, plata, café, algodón

Platos pintados, Baja California, México

México **xix**

History

1519 Hernán Cortés conquers the Aztec emperor Moctezuma II and establishes the first Spanish settlement in Mexico.

1810 Mexico declares its independence from Spain.

1845 Mexican-American War begins as U.S. troops capture Mexico City in an effort to annex Texas.

1862–1864
French troops, led by Napoleon III, march into Mexico City. Maximilian of Austria is declared Emperor of Mexico.

1867 Mexican forces regain control of the country. Maximilian is assassinated.

1876 Porfirio Díaz becomes president of the Republic and eventual dictator (1876–80, 1884–1911).

1910–1911
The Mexican Revolution begins. Francisco I. Madero becomes president.

1913 Madero is assassinated and civil war breaks out.

1934 The Party of Institutionalized Revolution (PRI) is formed and is in power for the next 60 years.

1968 Over 300 protesters against the government are killed during the Mexico City Olympic games.

1993 The North American Free Trade Agreement (NAFTA) between Canada, the United States, and Mexico is signed.

1994 The Zapatista National Liberation Army (a group of Native American rebels) declares war on the government.

1995–2000
The PRI grip begins to loosen in Mexico with a variety of parties winning provincial elections.

Social Background

Mexico has a diverse population made up of many cultures and customs. The majority of the people are *mestizo,* or a mix of indigenous and European (mostly Spanish) ancestry. Most of the population speaks Spanish as its first language. Indigenous people make up the second largest ethnic group of the population.

América Central

Geography

A series of islands were once scattered between what is now the Caribbean Sea and the Pacific Ocean. Three million years ago (relatively recently in geological terms) they merged to form Central America, a land bridge that links North and South America.

The region is geographically unstable. It is home to at least 14 active volcanoes and experiences frequent earthquakes. Managua, capital of Nicaragua, has been nearly destroyed by earthquakes twice in the last 100 years.

The land is marked by volcanic mountains and **calderas,** lakes that have formed in the volcanic craters. Central America's western coastal plain is fairly narrow, sloping dramatically up to the central mountain region. A less dramatic plateau slopes eastward to the Caribbean.

The climate is diverse, mostly due to a variety of altitudes rather than to topography. There are three major areas. The hottest *(tierra caliente)* is the lowest area, ranging from sea level to an altitude of roughly 915 meters (3,000 feet). The *tierra templada* ranges from 1,830 meters to 3,050 meters (6,000–10,000 feet) and averages temperatures of 65–75° F. The coldest area *(tierra fría)* is the highest and encompasses the mountain peaks.

Water is key to Central American geography. Bordered on east and west by enormous bodies of water, the region also has several rivers and two very large lakes—Lake Nicaragua and Lake Managua. The Panama Canal is a commercial waterway that links the Caribbean and the Pacific. It was constructed at the narrowest point of Central America so that ships carrying goods between distant ports would not have to sail all the way around the southern tip of South America.

The countries of Central America offer a variety of products and resources that are traded worldwide. Honduras and Nicaragua are rich in minerals, including gold and silver. Honduras also has significant deposits of lead, zinc, copper, and iron ore, while Nicaragua offers offshore oil. Bananas and coffee are key to the economies of Costa Rica and Panama, which are the chief exporters of these products to the United States.

Guatemala

Capital: Guatemala
Población: 13 millones
Área: 42,043 mi cuadradas / 108,890 km cuadrados
Grupos étnicos: indígenas, mestizos, caucásicos
Religiones: católica romana, protestante, creencias tradicionales mayas
Gobierno: república democrática constitucional
Moneda: quetzal
Exportaciones: combustibles, maquinaria y equipos de transporte, materiales para construcción, granos

Honduras

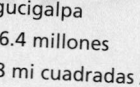

Capital: Tegucigalpa
Población: 6.4 millones
Área: 43,278 mi cuadradas / 112,090 km cuadrados
Grupos étnicos: mestizos, africanos, indígenas, caucásicos
Religiones: católica romana, protestante
Gobierno: república democrática constitucional
Moneda: lempira
Exportaciones: café, plátano, camarón, langosta, carne, cinc, madera

El Salvador

Capital: San Salvador
Población: 6.2 millones
Área: 8,124 mi cuadradas / 21,040 km cuadrados
Grupos étnicos: mestizos, indígenas, caucásicos
Religiones: católica romana, protestante
Gobierno: república
Moneda: colón salvadoreño
Exportaciones: elaboración de productos con materiales fabricados en el extranjero, equipos, café, azúcar, camarón, textiles, productos químicos, electricidad

San Jóse, Costa Rica

Lago Atitlán, Guatemala

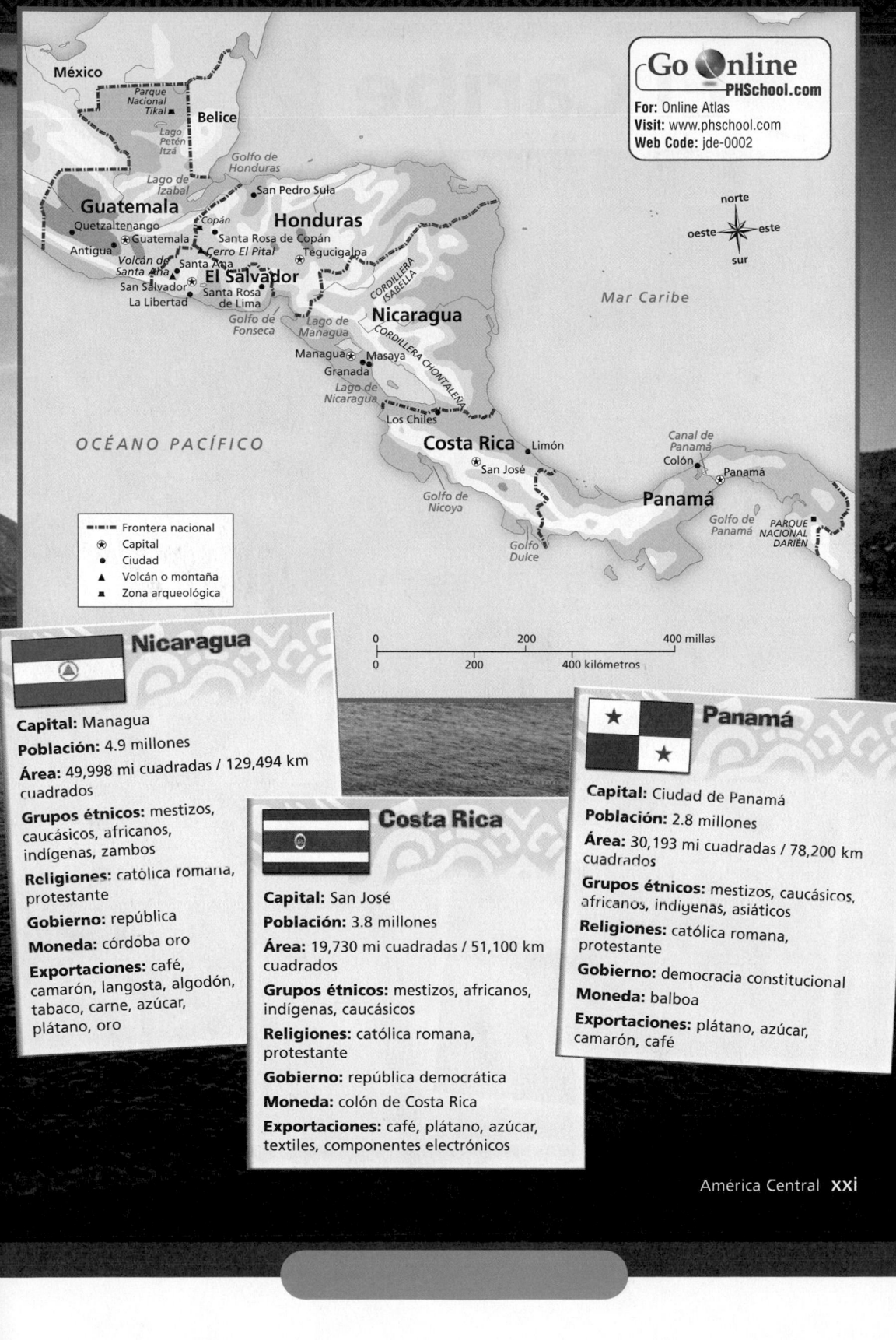

Go Online
PHSchool.com

For: Online Atlas
Visit: www.phschool.com
Web Code: jde-0002

Nicaragua

Capital: Managua

Población: 4.9 millones

Área: 49,998 mi cuadradas / 129,494 km cuadrados

Grupos étnicos: mestizos, caucásicos, africanos, indígenas, zambos

Religiones: católica romana, protestante

Gobierno: república

Moneda: córdoba oro

Exportaciones: café, camarón, langosta, algodón, tabaco, carne, azúcar, plátano, oro

Costa Rica

Capital: San José

Población: 3.8 millones

Área: 19,730 mi cuadradas / 51,100 km cuadrados

Grupos étnicos: mestizos, africanos, indígenas, caucásicos

Religiones: católica romana, protestante

Gobierno: república democrática

Moneda: colón de Costa Rica

Exportaciones: café, plátano, azúcar, textiles, componentes electrónicos

Panamá

Capital: Ciudad de Panamá

Población: 2.8 millones

Área: 30,193 mi cuadradas / 78,200 km cuadrados

Grupos étnicos: mestizos, caucásicos, africanos, indígenas, asiáticos

Religiones: católica romana, protestante

Gobierno: democracia constitucional

Moneda: balboa

Exportaciones: plátano, azúcar, camarón, café

América Central **xxi**

History

1502 On his fourth voyage, Columbus establishes Spain's claim to Central America.

1510–1519 Explorers create and settle colonies. The region is divided into two jurisdictions.

1821–1822 Guatemala, El Salvador, Honduras, Nicaragua, and Costa Rica declare their independence from Spain and create The United Provinces of Central America.

1823 U.S. President James Monroe and Secretary of State John Quincy Adams develop the Monroe Doctrine, warning Europe against intervening in the government or trade of countries in the Western Hemisphere.

1840 Guatemala, Honduras, El Salvador, Nicaragua, and Costa Rica become independent republics.

1855 The Panama Railroad is completed, improving commerce to the Pacific coast ports.

1903 Panama becomes independent from Colombia.

1960 Guatemala, Honduras, El Salvador, and Nicaragua create the Central American Common Market (CACM).

1979 The Sandinistas in Nicaragua overthrow the government of Anastasio Somoza.

1987 Costa Rican president Oscar Arias Sánchez wins the Nobel Peace Prize for creating a peace plan for Central America.

1992 Guatemalan activists Rigoberta Menchú Tum wins the Nobel Peace Prize for her work in Social Justice and ethno-cultural reconciliation. She is the first Native American and the youngest person (33 years old) ever to receive this honor.

1990–present The nations of Central America continue to strive for political stability and economic modernization.

Social Background

The majority of people in America Central are *mestizo,* a mix of Native American and European—mostly Spanish. Though the first language of most of the population is Spanish, in Guatemala 23 dialects of Mayan are also spoken.

El Caribe

Punta Cana, La República Dominicana

Standards:
2.1, 2.2, 3.1

Geography

The Spanish-speaking islands of the Caribbean share common and dramatic geographical features, including a similar topography of mountain ranges and extensive shorelines.

Cuba consists of one main island and several small ones, including la Isla de la Juventud (The Isle of Youth) and four small archipelagos.

Cuba is the largest island in the Caribbean. It is unusual in that three quarters of the country are fertile farmland, where crops such as sugar, tobacco, citrus fruits, and coffee grow in abundance. Cuba's shoreline is home to spectacular beaches, coral reefs, and deep harbors.

The Dominican Republic shares the island of Hispaniola with Creole-speaking Haiti. It, too, has fertile farmland, but the majority of the island consists of mountain ranges. Its most valuable crops are sugar, cocoa, and tobacco.

Puerto Rico's landscape is marked by steep mountains. The Cordillera Central extends from east to west and divides the country into northern and southern regions. The island's mountain peak of El Yunque (The Anvil) attracts tourists throughout the year. The warm, sunny beaches of the coastline are also a major tourist destination. Puerto Rico's economy relies on industry and tourism rather than agriculture. An estimated five million tourists visit the island each year.

The three countries share a similar climate. Generally, the temperatures are moderate to tropical all year round. The mountainous areas receive the most rainfall, while the beaches remain fairly warm and sunny throughout the year.

La Habana, Cuba

xxii El Caribe

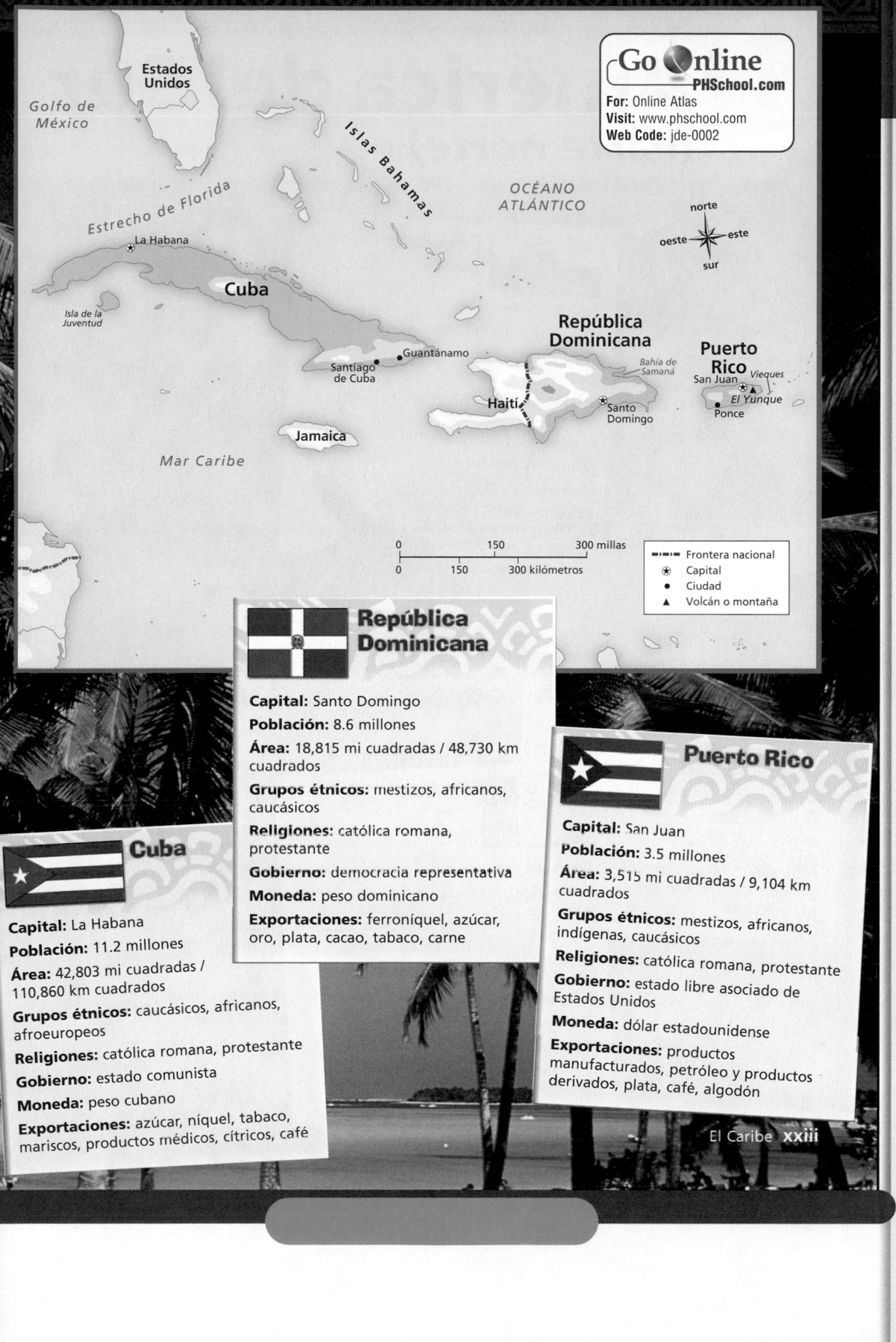

Go Online
PHSchool.com
For: Online Atlas
Visit: www.phschool.com
Web Code: jde-0002

Estados Unidos

Golfo de México

Islas Bahamas

OCÉANO ATLÁNTICO

Estrecho de Florida

La Habana

norte
oeste · este
sur

Cuba

Isla de la Juventud

Santiago de Cuba

Guantánamo

República Dominicana

Bahía de Samaná

Puerto Rico

San Juan · Vieques

Haití

El Yunque
Ponce

Santo Domingo

Jamaica

Mar Caribe

| 0 | 150 | 300 millas |
| 0 | 150 | 300 kilómetros |

Frontera nacional
✴ Capital
● Ciudad
▲ Volcán o montaña

República Dominicana

Capital: Santo Domingo

Población: 8.6 millones

Área: 18,815 mi cuadradas / 48,730 km cuadrados

Grupos étnicos: mestizos, africanos, caucásicos

Religiones: católica romana, protestante

Gobierno: democracia representativa

Moneda: peso dominicano

Exportaciones: ferroníquel, azúcar, oro, plata, cacao, tabaco, carne

Puerto Rico

Capital: San Juan

Población: 3.5 millones

Área: 3,515 mi cuadradas / 9,104 km cuadrados

Grupos étnicos: mestizos, africanos, indígenas, caucásicos

Religiones: católica romana, protestante

Gobierno: estado libre asociado de Estados Unidos

Moneda: dólar estadounidense

Exportaciones: productos manufacturados, petróleo y productos derivados, plata, café, algodón

Cuba

Capital: La Habana

Población: 11.2 millones

Área: 42,803 mi cuadradas / 110,860 km cuadrados

Grupos étnicos: caucásicos, africanos, afroeuropeos

Religiones: católica romana, protestante

Gobierno: estado comunista

Moneda: peso cubano

Exportaciones: azúcar, níquel, tabaco, mariscos, productos médicos, cítricos, café

El Caribe **xxiii**

History

1492 Christopher Columbus explores Hispaniola and Cuba on his first voyage to the Americas.

1493 Puerto Rico is claimed by Spain during Columbus's second voyage.

1496 Santo Domingo, the oldest Spanish settlement in the Western Hemisphere and the capital of the Dominican Republic, is founded.

1898 Puerto Rico is ceded to the U.S. after the Spanish-American War.

1899 Cuba becomes an independent republic under U.S. protection.

1917 Residents of Puerto Rico are granted U.S. citizenship.

1934 Cuba terminates its alliance with the U.S.

1956–1959 Fidel Castro launches the Cuban Revolution. Many Cubans flee to Florida.

1961 The U.S. suspends diplomatic relations with Cuba due to Castro's ties with Communist U.S.S.R.

1996 The Dominican Republic holds its first free elections.

1997 Puerto Rican voters decide to maintain their Commonwealth status.

2002 Castro claims he has 99% of the Cuban electorate's backing to retain its socialist system.

Standards:
2.1, 3.1, 4.1

Geography

The countries of northern South America share dramatic landscapes of high mountains, lush tropical rainforests, and striking coastlines. Yet each country has a unique geography that distinguishes it from its neighbors.

Venezuela is the continent's northernmost nation. Most of its population lives in the northern highlands or the coastal regions, where the capital, Caracas, is located. The rest of the country is divided between the **Llanos,** tropical grasslands, and the Guiana Highlands, a mountainous area comprising over half of the country. The highlands have recently become more populated due to large deposits of iron, manganese, and bauxite that have been discovered there.

Colombia's landscape is divided between east and west by the spectacular Andes Mountains, which extend southward, dividing Ecuador, Peru, and Bolivia as well. Most of the population of Colombia lives in the basins around the Cordillera Oriental. One of the highest ranges of the Andes, the Cordillera's peaks reach to 5,500 meters (18,000 feet). To the east lies a jungle lowland, thinly populated and one of the last minimally explored areas on earth.

Ecuador, named for its location on the Equator, has four distinct geographic regions, including the coastal plain and the Sierra, where the Andes mountains and one of the world's highest volcanoes, Cotopaxi, are found. The Oriente jungle covers almost half the country, while the Galapagos Islands are a series of 15 offshore islands dotted with volcanic peaks.

Peru lies just south of Ecuador and Colombia. Peru's Andean peaks are some of the highest in the world. Huascarán, at 6,768 meters (22,205 feet), is the highest mountain in the country. Earthquakes occur in this part of Peru, and these mountains are virtually impassable. Peru's long coast is dry and wide and is the economic and population center of the country.

Bolivia is nicknamed "Rooftop of the World," because most of the country sits at a high elevation atop the Andes. Most of the people live in the mountains and in the capital cities of La Paz and Sucre.

Ecuador

Capital: Quito

Población: 13.1 millones

Área: 109,483 mi cuadradas / 283,560 km cuadrados

Grupos étnicos: mestizos, indígenas, caucásicos

Religiones: católica romana

Gobierno: república

Moneda: sucre

Exportaciones: petróleo, textiles, plátano, camarón, cacao, azúcar, carne

Colombia

Capital: Bogotá

Población: 40.3 millones

Área: 439,736 mi cuadradas / 1,138,910 km cuadrados

Grupos étnicos: mestizos, caucásicos, africanos, indígenas

Religiones: católica romana

Gobierno: república

Moneda: peso colombiano

Exportaciones: textiles, petróleo y productos derivados, café, oro, esmeraldas, plátano, tabaco, algodón, madera, energía hidroeléctrica

Perú

Capital: Lima

Población: 25 millones

Área: 496,226 mi cuadradas / 1,285,220 km cuadrados

Grupos étnicos: mestizos, indígenas, caucásicos

Religiones: católica romana

Gobierno: república constitucional

Moneda: nuevo sol

Exportaciones: oro, cinc, cobre, pescado y productos de pescado, textiles

Mujer en los Andes, Perú

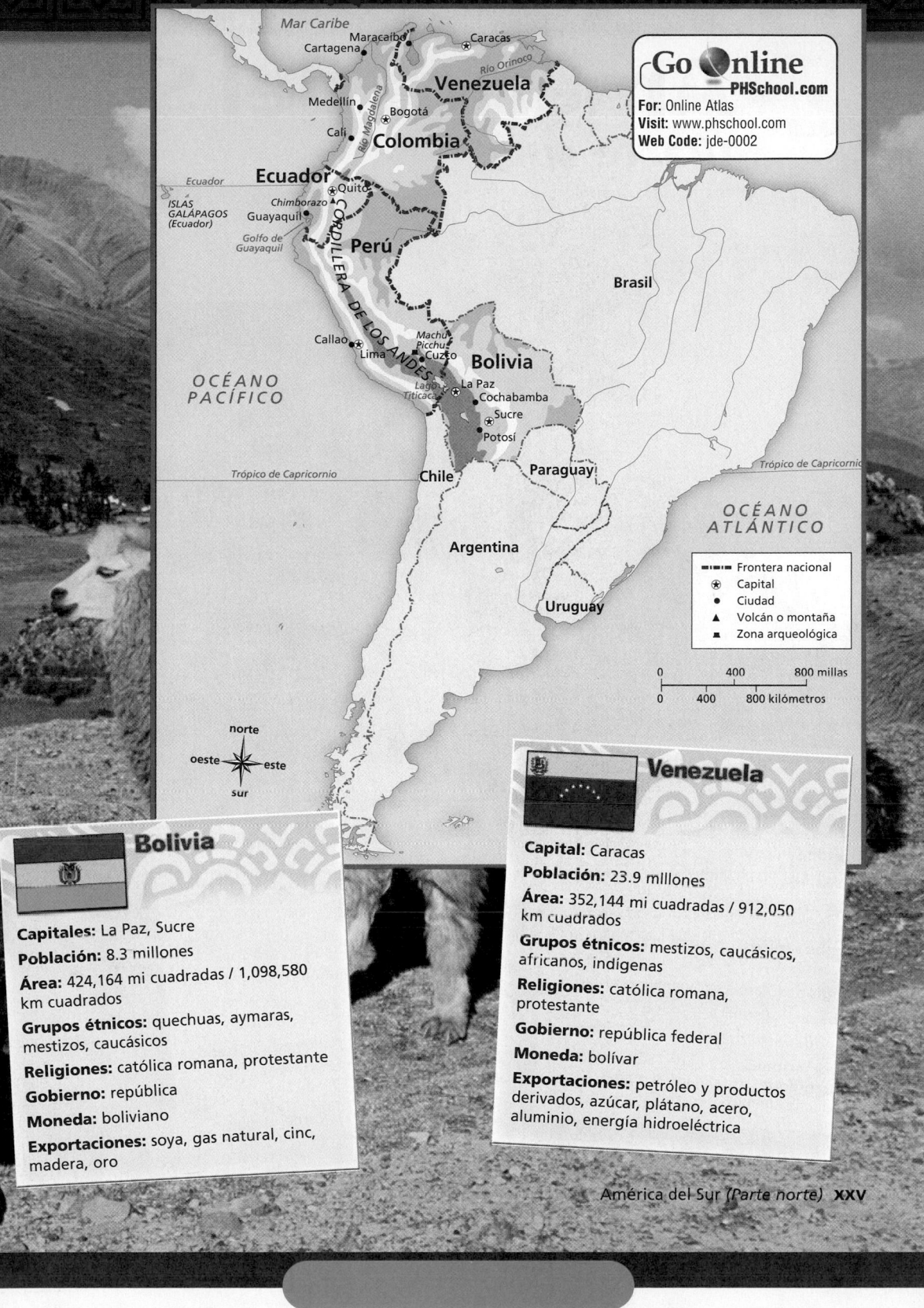

Go Online
PHSchool.com

For: Online Atlas
Visit: www.phschool.com
Web Code: jde-0002

Venezuela del Sur

Mar Caribe
Maracaibo
Cartagena
Caracas
Venezuela
Medellín
Bogotá
Cali
Colombia
Río Orinoco
Ecuador
Quito
ISLAS GALÁPAGOS (Ecuador)
Chimborazo
Guayaquil
Golfo de Guayaquil
Perú
Brasil
Callao
Machu Picchu
Lima
Cuzco
Bolivia
Lago Titicaca
La Paz
Cochabamba
Sucre
Potosí
OCÉANO PACÍFICO
Trópico de Capricornio
Chile
Paraguay
Trópico de Capricornio
OCÉANO ATLÁNTICO
Argentina
Uruguay

Frontera nacional
⊛ Capital
● Ciudad
▲ Volcán o montaña
■ Zona arqueológica

0   400   800 millas
0   400   800 kilómetros

norte
oeste ✦ este
sur

Bolivia

Capitales: La Paz, Sucre

Población: 8.3 millones

Área: 424,164 mi cuadradas / 1,098,580 km cuadrados

Grupos étnicos: quechuas, aymaras, mestizos, caucásicos

Religiones: católica romana, protestante

Gobierno: república

Moneda: boliviano

Exportaciones: soya, gas natural, cinc, madera, oro

Venezuela

Capital: Caracas

Población: 23.9 millones

Área: 352,144 mi cuadradas / 912,050 km cuadrados

Grupos étnicos: mestizos, caucásicos, africanos, indígenas

Religiones: católica romana, protestante

Gobierno: república federal

Moneda: bolívar

Exportaciones: petróleo y productos derivados, azúcar, plátano, acero, aluminio, energía hidroeléctrica

América del Sur (Parte norte) **XXV**

History

1498 Christopher Columbus sights Venezuela on his third voyage.

1502 On his fourth voyage, Columbus explores the Colombian coast.

1532 Francisco Pizarro lands in Peru.

1533 Sebastián de Benalcázar enters Ecuador under the auspices of Pizarro.

1538 Hernando Pizarro, son of Francisco, conquers Bolivian territory.

1811 Venezuela declares its independence from Spain.

1819 Simón Bolívar leads the revolution that unites present-day Colombia and Venezuela as la República de Gran Colombia.

1820 Peru declares its independence from Spain.

1821 Ecuador is liberated from Spain and joins Gran Colombia.

1825 Bolivia declares its independence from Spain.

1830 Ecuador becomes an independent country.

1879 War begins over land disputes between Chile, Peru, and landlocked Bolivia over access to the Pacific.

1970s Ecuador becomes South America's second largest producer of oil.

1980 Peru begins an economic decline that leads to depression.

1994 Under President Alberto Fujimoro, Peru's economy begins to recover.

2000 Fujimoro loses popularity and is forced to flee the country.

2002 Venezuela's controversial president, Hugo Chávez, is ousted from power. Three days later he is reinstated.

Social Background

Bolivia and Peru have very large indigenous populations. The two largest groups are the Quechua, descended from the ancient Incas, and the Aymará. The entire Aymará population of the world—roughly 1.2 million people—live in the area around Lake Titicaca on the border between Peru and Bolivia.

América del Sur
(Parte sur)

Standards:
2.1, 3.1, 4.2

Geography

The southern part of South America has dramatic contrasts between the west coast of Chile and the eastern plains of Uruguay. This part of the world, south of the massive country of Brazil, has fascinating culture, geography, and history.

Chile's footprint is easy to remember. The country is long and extremely narrow, with a rugged desert coastline punctuated by dozens of undersea volcanic peaks that form islands along its southernmost coast. Like its neighbors to the north—Peru, Ecuador, and Colombia—Chile's principal geographic landmark is the Andes Mountains, which extend the entire length of the country. Chile's population is centered in the Central Valley. This area is only 40 to 80 kilometers wide.

Argentina is almost as long as Chile, but it is much wider. It is geographically and topographically quite diverse. Along its western border, it shares the Andes with Chile. Eastward from the Andes is a flat, rolling plain divided into two territories: Gran Chaco, which it shares with neighboring Paraguay, and the Pampas, which are treeless plains that are the center of the country's prosperous agriculture. The southernmost plains are part of Patagonia, a dry, desolate, sparsely inhabited region.

Uruguay is one of the smallest countries of South America. Its landscape offers a sharp contrast to the Andean countries. Due to its relatively uniform elevation, Uruguay has a moderate temperature. Along its Atlantic coast, there are beaches, deep lagoons, and wide sand dunes, which extend almost as much as eight kilometers inland. The economy is based largely on agriculture.

Paraguay, to the northeast of Argentina, is characterized mainly by the Paraná plateau, which is 300–600 meters (1,000–2,000 feet) high. The area slopes gently to the Paraná River and boasts spectacular waterfalls. Paraguay's weather averages 60–80° F year round.

La Boca, Buenos Aires, Argentina

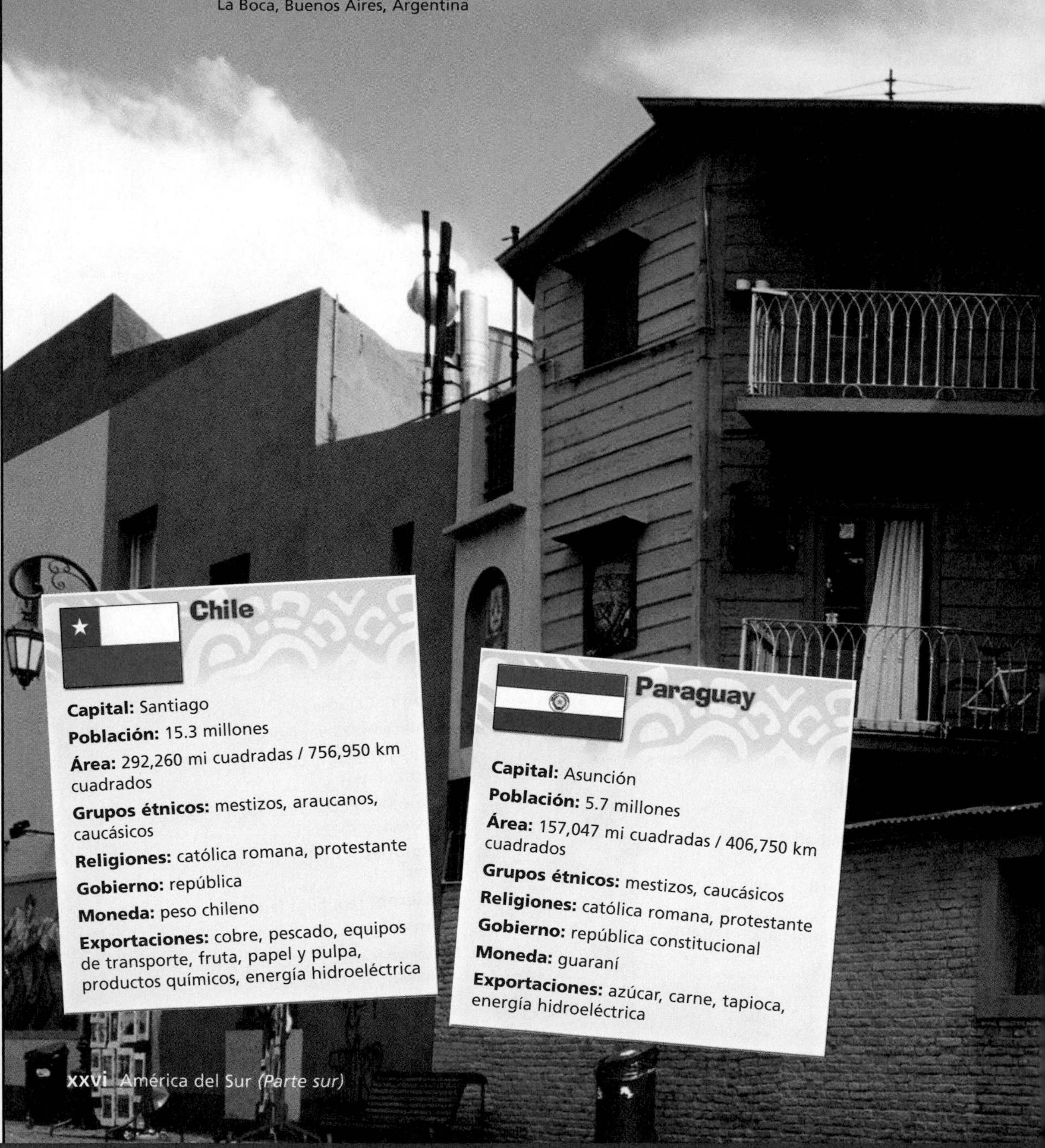

Chile

Capital: Santiago

Población: 15.3 millones

Área: 292,260 mi cuadradas / 756,950 km cuadrados

Grupos étnicos: mestizos, araucanos, caucásicos

Religiones: católica romana, protestante

Gobierno: república

Moneda: peso chileno

Exportaciones: cobre, pescado, equipos de transporte, fruta, papel y pulpa, productos químicos, energía hidroeléctrica

Paraguay

Capital: Asunción

Población: 5.7 millones

Área: 157,047 mi cuadradas / 406,750 km cuadrados

Grupos étnicos: mestizos, caucásicos

Religiones: católica romana, protestante

Gobierno: república constitucional

Moneda: guaraní

Exportaciones: azúcar, carne, tapioca, energía hidroeléctrica

xxvi América del Sur *(Parte sur)*

Go Online
PHSchool.com

For: Online Atlas
Visit: www.phschool.com
Web Code: jde-0002

Uruguay

Capital: Montevideo
Población: 3.3 millones
Área: 68,039 mi cuadradas / 176,220 km cuadrados
Grupos étnicos: caucásicos
Religiones: católica romana, protestante
Gobierno: república constitucional
Moneda: peso uruguayo
Exportaciones: alimentos, vehículos, carne, arroz, maderas

Argentina

Capital: Buenos Aires
Población: 37. 8 millones
Área: 1,068,302 mi cuadradas / 2,766,890 km cuadrados
Grupos étnicos: caucásicos
Religiones: católica romana, protestante, judía
Gobierno: república
Moneda: peso
Exportaciones: carne, aceites comestibles, combustibles y energía, cereales, forraje, vehículos automotores

América del Sur *(Parte sur)* **xxvii**

History

1520 Portuguese explorer Ferdinand Magellan lands in Chile.

1536 Buenos Aires is founded.

1540 Chile becomes colonial vice-regency of Spain.

1624 First permanent Spanish settlement in Uruguay is founded.

1810 Chile breaks ties with Spain.

1811 Paraguay declares independence.

1814 The Spanish governor is driven from Uruguay.

1815 Representatives from various provinces in Argentina declare independence from Spain.

1816 Bernardo O'Higgins is named supreme dictator of Chile.

1828 Uruguay officially becomes an independent nation.

1839 Chile invades Peru for territorial reasons.

1864–1870
After years of growth under President Carlos Antonio López, Paraguay is devastated in a war with the Triple Alliance (Argentina, Brazil, and Uruguay) over borders.

1906 An earthquake devastates the city of Santiago, Chile.

1946 Juan Perón becomes head of state of Argentina.

1955 Perón's government is ousted.

1970 Salvador Allende Gossens is elected president of Chile.

1973 Perón is reinstated as Argentina's president.
Allende of Chile dies during Augusto Pinochet's military coup.

1974 Isabel Perón, third wife of Juan Perón, is elected first woman head of state in the Western Hemisphere.

1990 Pinochet is ousted as president of Chile.

Standards:
2.1, 3.2

Geography

Spain, in the southwest of Europe, occupies most of the Iberian peninsula, which it shares with Portugal. It is surrounded on three sides by the Mediterranean and the Atlantic. The Pyrenees Mountains extend across the northeastern border with France.

The most pronounced topographical feature in Spain is the *Meseta Central,* or Central Plateau, which slopes downward from north to south and east to west. The eastern coastal plain is narrow, broken by rocky mountains that slope directly to the sea. Barcelona is the best harbor on Spain's Mediterranean coast.

Spain is separated from Africa by only 13 kilometers at the Strait of Gibraltar. On the southern coast, the people enjoy a subtropical climate; the coldest it gets is around 57° F. It does not rain often, except in the northern mountains. In fact, along the central plateau, the summers are so dry that droughts are not uncommon.

Spain has many environmental concerns, and has embraced international agreements on air quality, marine dumping, and endangered species protection.

Equatorial Guinea is located in Western Africa between Gabon and Cameroon. It includes a mainland territory, known as Mbini, and several islands, the largest of which is Bioko Island. The entire country is smaller than the state of Maryland.

The mainland is covered with gently rolling forests and woodland. In contrast, Bioko Island was formed by volcanic eruptions and is quite mountainous, with a steep and rocky coast. Inland, the island is made up of fertile volcanic soils.

Equatorial Guinea has a climate similar to that of the Canary Islands (see inset), its Spanish island neighbor off the coast of Morocco. The weather on Bioko is hot and humid, with a rainy season from December through February.

The primary occupation of the country's nearly half million residents is agriculture. In 1995, however, offshore oil deposits were discovered, which could transform the country's economy.

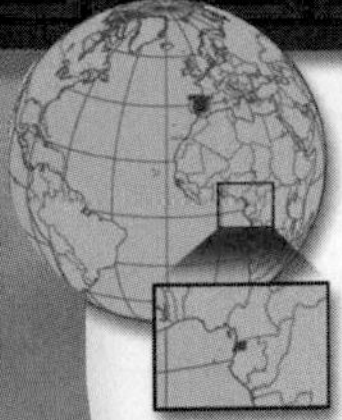

España
Guinea Ecuatorial

El pueblo blanco de Casares, España

España

Capital: Madrid

Población: 40 millones

Área: 194,897 mi cuadradas / 504,782 km cuadrados

Grupos étnicos: europeos

Religiones: católica romana

Gobierno: monarquía parlamentaria

Moneda: euro

Exportaciones: alimentos, maquinaria, vehículos automotores

Museo Guggenheim, Bilbao, España

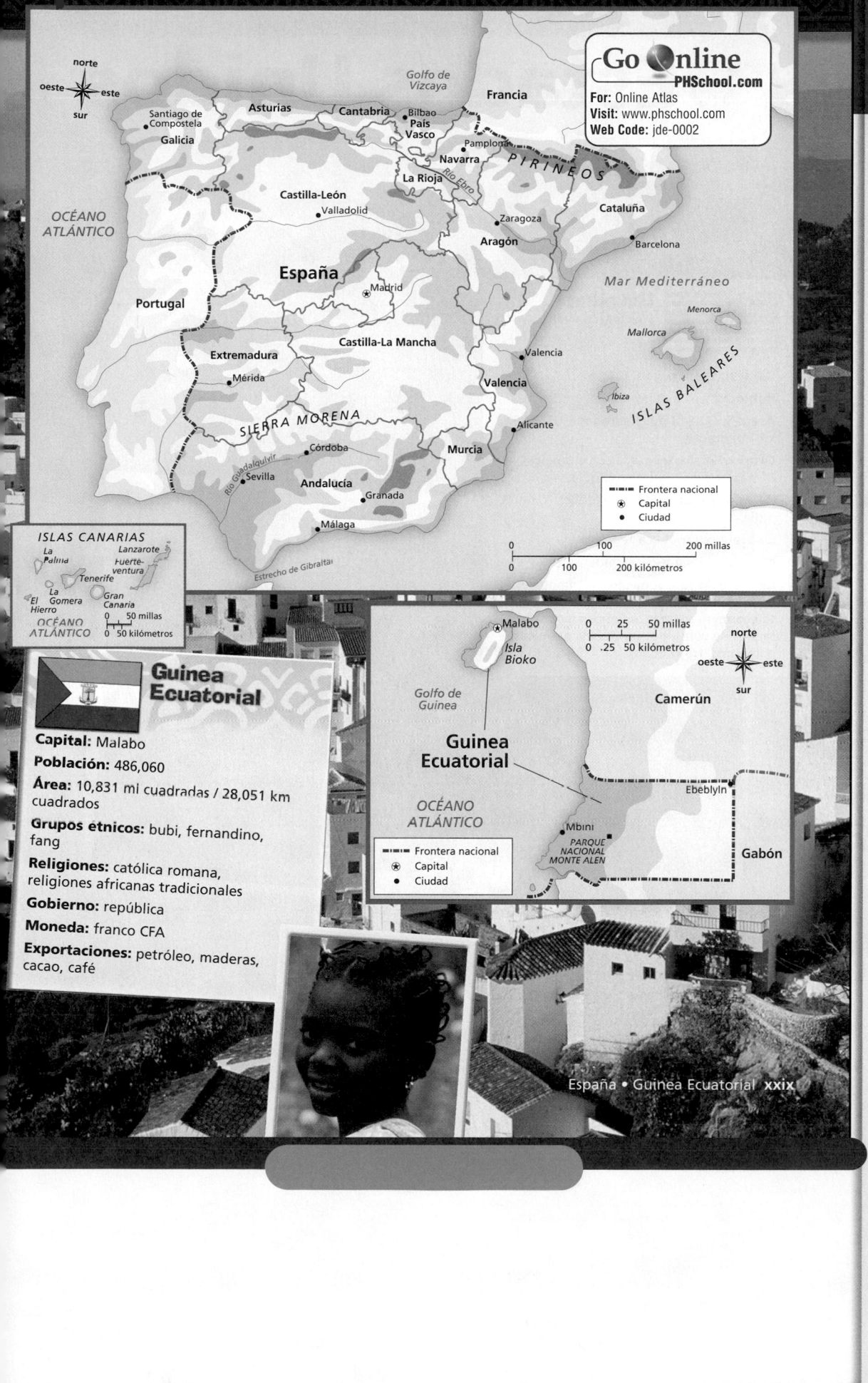

Islas Canarias

La Palma · Lanzarote · Fuerteventura · Tenerife · La Gomera · Gran Canaria · El Hierro

OCÉANO ATLÁNTICO

0 50 millas
0 50 kilómetros

Norte · oeste · este · sur

OCÉANO ATLÁNTICO

Santiago de Compostela · Galicia · Asturias · Cantabria · Bilbao · País Vasco · Pamplona · Navarra · La Rioja · PIRINEOS · Francia · Golfo de Vizcaya

Castilla-León · Valladolid · Aragón · Zaragoza · Cataluña · Barcelona

Portugal · España · Madrid

Extremadura · Mérida · Castilla-La Mancha · Valencia · Valencia · Alicante · Mar Mediterráneo · Menorca · Mallorca · Ibiza · ISLAS BALEARES

SIERRA MORENA · Río Guadalquivir · Córdoba · Sevilla · Andalucía · Granada · Murcia · Málaga

Estrecho de Gibraltar

Frontera nacional
Capital
Ciudad

0 100 200 millas
0 100 200 kilómetros

Guinea Ecuatorial

Capital: Malabo

Población: 486,060

Área: 10,831 mi cuadradas / 28,051 km cuadrados

Grupos étnicos: bubi, fernandino, fang

Religiones: católica romana, religiones africanas tradicionales

Gobierno: república

Moneda: franco CFA

Exportaciones: petróleo, maderas, cacao, café

Malabo · Isla Bioko · Golfo de Guinea · Camerún

Guinea Ecuatorial

OCÉANO ATLÁNTICO

Ebeblyln · Mbini · PARQUE NACIONAL MONTE ALEN · Gabón

0 25 50 millas
0 .25 50 kilómetros

norte · oeste · este · sur

Frontera nacional
Capital
Ciudad

España • Guinea Ecuatorial **xxix**

History

1469 The marriage of Ferdinand and Isabella unites the kingdoms of Aragon and Castille.

1492 Spain is created after Granada falls to Ferdinand and Isabella.

1492 Queen Isabella finances Columbus's first voyage to the Americas.

1519–1580 Spain explores and colonizes throughout the Americas.

1588 The British defeat the Armada, beginning the decline of Spain's hold on large parts of the world.

1826 By 1826, all of the Spanish colonies in the Americas have won their independence.

1898 The Spanish-American War marks the end of the Spanish Empire.

1936–1939 Civil War breaks out. Franco becomes dictator of Spain.

1947 Franco declares Spain a monarchy, but continues to rule.

1955 The United Nations admits Spain as a member.

1975 Franco dies; Juan Carlos I de Borbón becomes king.

1978 A constitution is drafted

Guinea Ecuatorial

1473 Explorer Fernando Poo claims Equatorial Guinea for Portugal.

1778 Portugal relinquishes the area to Spain.

1904 Bioki Island (known as Fernando Poo) and the mainland (known as Río Muni) become known as Spanish Guinea.

1959 Spanish Guinea becomes an official province of Spain.

1963 Spanish Guinea is granted autonomy.

1972 Spanish Guinea becomes an independent country and is renamed Equatorial Guinea.

Social Background

The Bubi were the original inhabitants of the region. The Fang were indigenous to the mainland and, with the Bubi, have migrated to Bioki. The Fernandinos are a mix of Spanish and African people. In Equatorial Guinea, most of the people have Spanish first names and African middle and last names, giving them a total of four names.

Estados Unidos

Jackson Hole, Wyoming

Standards:
2.1, 2.2, 3.1

Geography

The geography of the United States is as diverse as its people.

The United States is made up of fifty states and a number of territories, including Puerto Rico, the U.S. Virgin Islands, American Samoa, and Guam. The states vary in size from the largest (Alaska) at 1,593,438 square km (615,230 square miles) to Rhode Island, which is just 3,188 square km (1,231 square miles).

The United States is mountainous, with the Appalachians in the east and the Rocky Mountains, which run north to south, in the west-central part of the country. In the center of the country lie flat, fertile plains.

Like its geography, the climate varies greatly from region to region. In general, the northern half of the country experiences cold winters and mild summers. The southern coastal areas are semi-tropical, with mild winters and hot, humid summers, while inland areas in the southwest have a desert climate. The southeastern and east central parts of the country also see more violent weather patterns, such as tornados and hurricanes.

The country is rich in natural resources and has a diverse economy that includes industry, agriculture, technology, and financial services. The eastern part of the country includes uninterrupted urban centers extending from Massachusetts to the Carolinas and is home to one third of the nation's largest corporations. Many of the area's cities are also major tourist attractions.

The central U.S. is home to both industry and agriculture. Rich soils, abundant rainfall, and a long growing season offer ideal conditions for its soybean, wheat, corn, and alfalfa crops. Livestock and dairy farms dot the landscape. Manufacturing includes the auto industry, with Ohio and Michigan as its chief centers.

Agriculture, industry, and tourism also dominate the western part of the United States. Wine, cotton, citrus fruits, and vegetables are the region's principal crops. Aircraft manufacturing, computer technology, aerospace technology, and entertainment are all key factors in the region's economy.

Estados Unidos

Capital: Washington, D.C.

Población: 278 millones

Área: 3,717,813 mi cuadradas / 9,629,091 km cuadrados

Grupos étnicos: caucásicos, hispanos, afroamericanos, asiáticos, indígenas

Religiones: protestante, católica romana, judía, musulmana

Gobierno: república federal

Moneda: dólar estadounidense

Exportaciones: vehículos automotores, equipos aeroespaciales, telecomunicaciones, equipos electrónicos, bienes de consumo, productos químicos, alimentos, trigo, maíz

Puente Golden Gate, San Francisco, California

XXX Estados Unidos

Paseo del Río, San Antonio, Texas

Map labels

Frontera nacional
⊛ Capital
• Ciudad

0 300 600 millas
0 300 600 kilómetros

Canadá

Seattle

MONTAÑAS ROCOSAS

GRANDES LLANURAS

Grandes Lagos

Boston

Minneapolis

Detroit
Cleveland
Nueva York

Chicago
Filadelfia

MONTES APALACHES

San Francisco

Denver

Estados Unidos

St. Louis

Washington, D.C.

Los Ángeles
San Diego

Phoenix

OCÉANO ATLÁNTICO

OCÉANO PACÍFICO

Dallas

Atlanta

Río Grande

Houston

México

San Antonio

Golfo de México

Miami

Estrecho de Florida

Trópico de Cáncer

Alaska | Canadá

Mar de Bering

Golfo de Alaska

OCÉANO PACÍFICO

Hawaii

0 250 500 millas
0 250 500 kilómetros

0 50 100 millas
0 100 kilómetros

History

1492 Christopher Columbus is the first European to encounter America.

1497–1620 Explorers from Spain, France, Portugal, and England explore and establish colonies.

1763 Britain defeats France in the French and Indian War and gains control of eastern North America.

1775–1781 The Revolutionary War ends with U.S. independence.

1787 U.S. Constitution is ratified.

1803 Louisiana Purchase doubles the size of the U.S.

1821 U.S. purchases Florida from Spain.

1823 The Monroe Doctrine warns European nations not to interfere in the Western Hemisphere.

1848 U.S. wins the Mexican War and obtains huge areas of land from Texas to California.

1861–1865 U.S. Civil War.

1898 U.S. defeats Spain in the Spanish-American War.

1917 The U.S. joins European allies in fighting World War I.

1941 Japanese attack the U.S. at Pearl Harbor, Hawaii, and U.S. enters World War II.

1945 President Truman orders the use of the atomic bomb against Japan.

1962 U.S.S.R. removes missiles from Cuba, averting war with the U.S.

1969 U.S. astronauts walk on the moon.

2001 Terrorists attack New York (World Trade Center) and Washington (Pentagon).

Social Background

Spanish speakers are rapidly becoming the largest minority group in the United States. Thirty-five million, or 13% of the U.S. population, is considered to be Hispanic. Mexicans make up the majority.

Spanish speakers are active in the workforce, and many of their customs and celebrations are becoming part of mainstream U.S. culture.

Most U.S. citizens of Hispanic origin live in five states—California, Texas, New York, Florida, and Illinois.

Why Study Spanish?

¡Bienvenidos!

Welcome back to **Realidades** 3! Spanish 3 is an exciting year. Throughout the year your Spanish skills will improve as the themes, topics, and language become slightly more complex. In addition, your understanding of the rich cultures in the Spanish-speaking world will increase as you explore the cultural topics in each chapter.

In **Realidades** 3, you'll:
- review vocabulary and grammar
- learn additional vocabulary and grammar
- expand your skills: listening, speaking, reading, and writing
- connect Spanish with science, math, history, and geography
- read about people, places, and traditions from the Spanish-speaking world
- read authentic literature: short stories, poems, autobiographies, legends, and song lyrics
- communicate about what's important to you: friends, relationships, leisure activities, and future plans
- communicate about contemporary topics: health, history, government, the arts, and the environment
- develop a strong foundation for the study of the Spanish language and culture

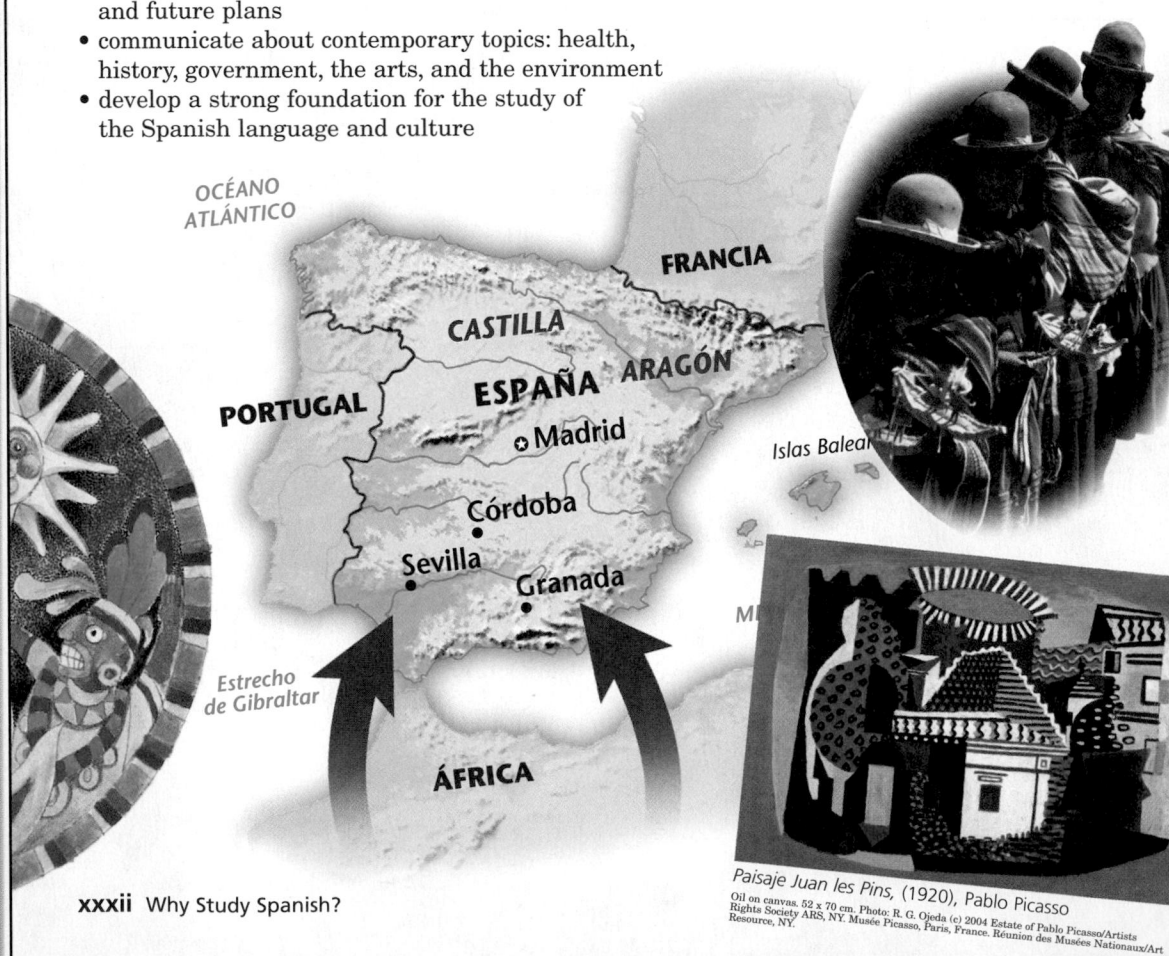

Paisaje Juan les Pins, (1920), Pablo Picasso
Oil on canvas, 52 x 70 cm. Photo: R. G. Ojeda (c) 2004 Estate of Pablo Picasso/Artists Rights Society ARS, NY. Musée Picasso, Paris, France. Réunion des Musées Nationaux/Art Resource, NY.

Study Tips

Go Online
PHSchool.com

For: More tips for studying Spanish
Visit: www.phschool.com
Web Code: jee-0003

Tips for Success!

The goal of Spanish is to communicate! Throughout **Realidades** 3, you'll find a wide range of support to help you communicate more effectively.

• **Para empezar Realidades** 3 begins with a review chapter that focuses on the basics from second year. It is likely you'll remember this vocabulary and grammar. If not, use the textbook activities and the **Go online** links at the Web Site for extra practice.

• **A ver si recuerdas** Each chapter begins with a review section that provides a quick summary of the vocabulary and grammar from first and second year Spanish that connect with the upcoming chapter. This material isn't tested, but it might be something you'll use as you communicate.

• **Grammar Summary and Glossaries** At the end of the book, you'll find grammar and vocabulary reference sections from all levels of **Realidades**. These will be a useful tool as you need to look up information.

• **Go Online** Be sure to use the online activities as a review or extra practice. Be sure to visit the online **Web Code** listed at the top of this page for a wide range of study suggestions.

• **Estrategia** You'll find a wide range of strategies that offer useful study tips. Be sure to use all the different strategies you learned in the previous levels: using cognates, using visuals, using graphic organizers, using prior knowledge, etc. Visit the **Go online** Study Tips **Web Code** for a list of all the strategies you've used in the program.

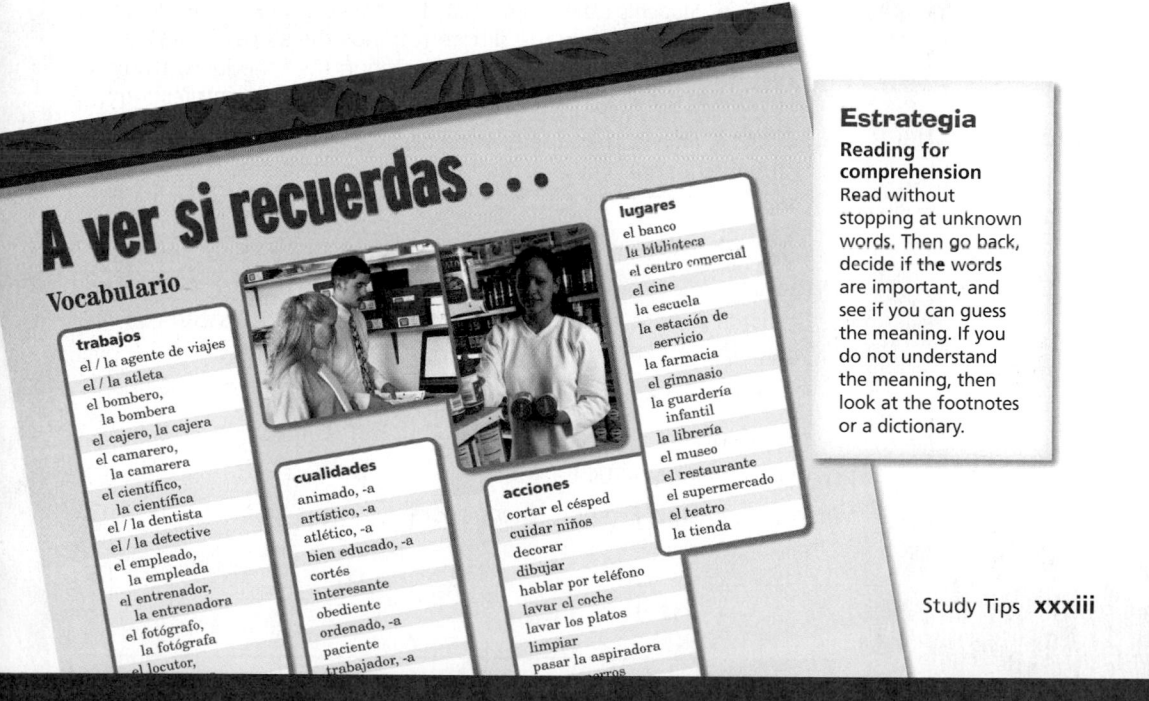

A ver si recuerdas . . .

Vocabulario

trabajos
el / la agente de viajes
el / la atleta
el bombero,
la bombera
el cajero, la cajera
el camarero,
la camarera
el científico,
la científica
el / la dentista
el / la detective
el empleado,
la empleada
el entrenador,
la entrenadora
el fotógrafo,
la fotógrafa
el locutor,

cualidades
animado, -a
artístico, -a
atlético, -a
bien educado, -a
cortés
interesante
obediente
ordenado, -a
paciente
trabajador, -a

acciones
cortar el césped
cuidar niños
decorar
dibujar
hablar por teléfono
lavar el coche
lavar los platos
limpiar
pasar la aspiradora

lugares
el banco
la biblioteca
el centro comercial
el cine
la escuela
la estación de
servicio
la farmacia
el gimnasio
la guardería
infantil
la librería
el museo
el restaurante
el supermercado
el teatro
la tienda

Estrategia
Reading for comprehension
Read without stopping at unknown words. Then go back, decide if the words are important, and see if you can guess the meaning. If you do not understand the meaning, then look at the footnotes or a dictionary.

Study Tips **xxxiii**

Para Empezar

CHAPTER OVERVIEW

 1 Tu vida diaria
* school and non-school daily activities

Vocabulary
* daily activities
* house chores
* errands

Grammar
* present tense of irregular verbs
* present tense of stem-changing verbs
* reflexive verbs

Cultural Perspectives
* daily activities of young people in Spain

 2 Días especiales
* weekend activities and special events and celebrations

Vocabulary
* entertainment
* special events and celebrations
* television and movies
* travel

Grammar
* verbs that conjugate like *gustar*
* possessive adjectives

Cultural Perspectives
* skiing in Bariloche, Argentina

Chapter Project

La entrevista

Overview: Students write a television script for an interview program about all the things a student does everyday from the time he / she wakes up. They also create a time schedule showing all the things the interviewee (a student) does. They then perform the interview and videotape it for the class to view.

Materials: poster board, markers, video camera, videocassette

Sequence: (suggestions for when to do each step appear throughout the unit)

STEP 1. Review instructions so students know what is expected of them. Hand out the "Para empezar Project Instructions and Rubric" from the *Teacher's Resource Book*.

STEP 2. Students write a rough sketch of their interview. They then exchange scripts with a partner for peer editing. Students make corrections based on their partner's comments.

STEP 3. Students create a time schedule on poster board. The time schedule should show the different things the student says he / she does during the day. After completing the schedules, students could add drawings or illustrations to make it more interesting.

STEP 4. Students rehearse their interview with a partner. Partners give students feedback about the content, accuracy, and presentation of the subject.

STEP 5. Students videotape their interview. Show videotapes to the class.

Options:

1. Students present their interviews to the class "live" instead of videotaping them.

2. Students give a presentation of the everyday activities of a student.

Assessment:

Here is a detailed rubric for assessing this project:.

Preliminary Unit Project: *La entrevista*

RUBRIC	Score 1	Score 2	Score 3
Your evidence of planning	You do not include a written draft.	Your draft is written, but not corrected.	You provide evidence of corrected draft.
Your use of illustrations	You do not include a time schedule.	Your time schedule is difficult to read, incomplete, and / or inaccurate.	Your time schedule is easy to read, complete, and accurate.
Your interview presentation	You do not include the majority of the required elements.	You include some of the following: greeting, questions, answers, and descriptions.	You include the following: greeting, questions, answers, and descriptions.

Theme: *Días especiales*

Ask students to cut out, copy or download photos or pictures of special celebrations and holidays in different countries. They can also include photos of family gatherings and parties with friends. Cluster photos or pictures according to the countries they are from.

Bibliography

Harris, Zoe, Suzanne Williams, Yolanda G. Woo. *Piñatas and Smiling Skeletons: Celebrating Mexican Festivals*. Pacific View Press, 1998. Examines the historical background, legends, recipes, crafts and celebrations of a year of special Mexican festivals.

Lomas Garza, Carmen. *In my family / En mi familia*. San Francisco: Children's Book Press, 1996.

Lomas Garza, Carmen. *Making magic windows: Creating Papel Picado / Cut-Paper Art with Carmen Lomas Garza*. San Francisco: Children's Book Press, 1996.

Trenchard, Kathleen. *Mexican Papercutting*. Asheville, N.C.: Lark Books, 1998.

Kindersley, Anabel. *Children Just Like Me: Celebrations*. New York: Dorling Kindersley, 1997. Cultural traditions around the world.

McKay, Susan. *Spain. Festival of the World*. Milwaukee: Gareth Stevens, 1999.

Hands-on Culture

Craft: *Piñata*

A *piñata* is a decorated container filled with candy and toys that is suspended from a height. Children take turns trying to break it open with a stick while blindfolded. The *piñata* is a Mexican custom that has existed for many centuries. Original *piñatas* were made of clay, and then replaced by carboard.

Materials:

medium-sized round balloon
string and scissors
newspapers
white liquid glue and water
old tablespoon for measuring
small bowl for glue
bowl to hold the balloon
brush for glue
tissue paper in assorted colors
wrapped Candy and/or small toys
masking tape (optional)

Steps:

1. Blow up the balloon and tie it with a string. Do not cut the string ends.

2. In a small bowl, dilute six tablespoons of white liquid glue with three tablespoons of water.

3. Tear off small pieces of tissue paper. Brush diluted glue over the balloon, a small section at a time, and paste on the paper pieces. Overlap the pieces and brush more glue on top. Continue to cover the balloon, making large patches of different colors, overlapping them at edges. Hold the balloon in empty bowl while you work so that it won't roll all over the place. Leave a 2" patch uncovered around the knot. Then turn the balloon right side up, knotted end down, and cover the top.

4. Use the string to hang the balloon upside down. Let dry overnight.

5. Paste two more layers of paper pieces on the balloon, letting it dry overnight between each layer.

6. Cut the knotted end off, pull the balloon out and discard it.

7. Fill the piñata with wrapped candies. Paste tissue paper pieces to cover the opening. Let dry.

8. Paint and decorate the piñata.

9. Use the strings to hang up the piñata outside.

Game

Preguntas y respuestas

This game practices making questions and answers, using verbs in the present tense.

Players: the entire class

Materials: 3" x 5" index cards, cut in half, small paper bag

Steps:

1. Give each student two halves of an index card and ask him / her to write a question in the present tense on one half and an answer in the present tense on the other. Questions can be funny, silly, or serious. The answers should include as many details as possible.
   Student 1: ¿Cómo ayudas a tu mamá cuando regresas de la escuela?
   Student 2: Voy al supermercado con ella y la ayudo a cocinar.

2. Place answers in a bag and mix them up.

3. Each student selects a card from the bag without showing it to the classmates.

4. Students decide on a playing order.

5. The first player reads his / her question aloud while students listen to see if the answer is on the card they drew. A student who thinks he / she has the correct answer reads it to the class. If correct, this student reads the next question. An incorrect answer gives another player a chance to read an answer. If, after three tries, no one presents the correct answer, the player who wrote the original question and answer says the correct answer and chooses someone to read the next question.

6. The game is over when all the questions and answers have been matched.

Variation: Instead of questions and answers, students can write the name of an action they do everyday in one half of an index card and the description of it on the other half. You can give them the actions so students don't repeat them.

Internet Research

Use the keywords to find more information.

Keywords:

juventud española, quehaceres, fútbol femenino, encuestas, El señor de los anillos, Miami, Bariloche

Chapter Overview

1 Tu vida diaria

INPUT

Objectives
- talk about school and non-school daily activities
- describe your day before and after school

Vocabulary
- daily activities (school-related and non-school related)
- help around the house
- errands

Grammar
- irregular verbs
- stem-changing verbs in the present tense
- reflexive verbs

Culture
- daily activities of young people

2 Días especiales

PRACTICE

Objectives
- talk about weekend activities
- describe special events and celebrations

Vocabulary
- entertainment
- events, celebrations
- television and movies
- traveling

Grammar
- verbs that conjugate like *gustar*
- possessive adjectives

Culture
- skiing in Bariloche, Argentina

BEYOND THE CLASSROOM

Countries
- Spain
- Venezuela
- Argentina
- Puerto Rico
- United States

Internet
- vocabulary activities
- grammar activities
- Internet links
- self-tests

LEARNER SUPPORT

Strategies
- evaluate your lead to see wether added details might help to generate more interest in your topic

Recycling
- talk about your favorite movies

Print Components

TEACHER

Teacher's Resource Book
- Chapter Table of Contents
- School-to-Home Connection
- Chapter Resource Checklist
- Input Script
- Audio Script
- Communicative Activities
- Situation Cards
- GramActiva Blackline Masters
- Graphic Organizer
- Answer Keys:
  Practice Workbook
  Writing, Audio, and Video Workbook

Realidades para hispanohablantes
Teacher Edition

STUDENT

Practice Workbook
- Part 1: P-1–P-3
- Part 2: P-4–P-5

Writing, Audio & Video Workbook
- Audio: 1–5
- Writing: 6–7

Realidades para hispanohablantes

Transparencies

Vocabulary and Grammar Transparencies
- Vocabulary: 23, 29, 30, 33
- Grammar: 24–27, 31-32

Practice Answers on Transparencies
- Para Empezar

Fine Art Transparencies
- Transparencies
- Teacher's Guide

Assessment

Assessment Program
- Quizzes:
  - Part 1
  - Part 2
- Rubrics

Assessment Program: *Realidades para hispanohablantes*

Technology

TeacherExpress™ CD-ROM
- Lesson Planner
- Teacher Resources
- Clip Art

Audio Program CDs
- Part 1 and 2
- Audio Activities

Regular Schedule (50 Minutes)

For electronic lesson plans:
Resource Pro CD-ROM 💿

	Warm Up / Assess	Preview Present / Practice Communicate	Wrap Up / Homework Options
DAY 1	**Warm Up (10 min.)** • Chapter Opener • Fondo cultural	**Manos a la obra (35 min.)** • Presentation: Tu vida diaria • Actividad 1 • Presentation: Gramática-Repaso • Actividades 3, 4, 5, 6 • Audio Activity 1 • Presentation: Gramática-Repaso	**Wrap Up and Homework Options (5 min.)** • Actividades 2, 7, 8, 9 • Practice Workbook: P-1 • Clip Art Vocabulary
DAY 2	**Warm Up (10 min.)** • Homework Check	**Manos a la obra 1 (45 min.)** • Actividad 10 • Audio Activity 2 • Presentation: Gramática-Repaso • Actividad 11 • Audio Activity 3 • Communicative Activity • Presentation: Días especiales • Actividad 13	**Wrap Up and Homework Options (5 min.)** • Actividad 12 • Practice Workbook P-2, P-3
DAY 3	**Warm Up (10 min.)** • Homework Check	**Manos a la obra 1 (35 min.)** • Actividades 15, 16 • Audio Activity 4 • Presentation: Gramática-Repaso • Actividades 17, 18 • Audio Activity 5	**Wrap Up and Homework Options (5 min.)** • Actividad 14 • Practice Workbook P-4 • Go Online
DAY 4	**Warm Up (10 min.)** • Homework Check	**Manos a la obra 1 (20 min.)** • Presentation: Gramática-Repaso • Actividades 19, 20, 21 **¡Adelante! (15 min.)** • Presentación oral • Fondo cultural • Communicative Activity	**Wrap Up and Homework Options (5 min.)** • Practice Workbook P-5 • Presentación oral • Go Online
DAY 5	**Warm Up (3 min.)** **Assessment (32 min.)** • Presentación oral	**¡Adelante! (14 min.)** • Presentación escrita	**Wrap Up and Homework Options (1 min.)** • Presentación escrita

Block Schedule (90 Minutes)

For electronic lesson plans:
Resource Pro CD-ROM

Lesson Plans

	Warm Up / Assess	Preview Present / Practice Communicate	Wrap Up / Homework Options
DAY 1	**Warm Up** (10 min.) • Chapter Opener • Fondo cultural	**Tu vida diaria** (75 min.) • Presentation: Tu vida diaria • Actividad 1 • Presentation: Gramática-Repaso • Actividades 3, 4, 5, 6 • Audio Activity 1 • Presentation: Gramática-Repaso • Actividades 8, 9, 10 • Audio Activity 2 • Presentation: Gramática-Repaso • Actividad 11 • Audio Activity 3 • Communicative Activity	**Wrap Up and Homework Options** (5 min.) • Actividades 2, 7, 12 • Practice Workbook: P-1, P-2, P-3 • Clip Art Vocabulary
DAY 2	**Warm Up** (10 min.) • Writing Activity 6 • Homework Check	**Días especiales** (60 min.) • Presentation: Días especiales • Actividades 13, 15, 16 • Audio Activity 4 • Presentation: Gramática-Repaso • Actividades 17, 18 • Audio Activity 5 • Presentation: Gramática-Repaso • Actividades 20, 21 **¡Adelante!** (15 min.) • Presentación oral	**Wrap Up and Homework Options** (5 min.) • Go Online • Actividades 14, 19 • Practice Workbook: P-4, P-5 • Presentación oral
DAY 3	**Warm Up** (10 min.) • Writing Activity • Homework Check	**Assessment** (60 min.) • Presentación oral • Presentación escrita	**Wrap Up and Homework Options** (20 min.) • Fondo cultural • Communicative Activity • Go Online

Preview

Standards for Foreign Language Learning: *Para empezar*

- To achieve the goals of the Standards, students will:

Communication

1.1 Interpersonal
- Talk about the activities of Spanish young people
- Talk about daily routines, pastimes, and household chores
- Talk about TV programs, entertainment, special days, and vacations
- Talk about Bariloche, Argentina

1.2 Interpretive
- Read about the activities of Spanish young people
- Read and listen to information about daily routines, pastimes, and household chores
- Read and listen to information about TV programs, entertainment, special days, and vacations
- Read about Bariloche, Argentina
- Read about speech and composition preparation

1.3 Presentational
- Write and present information orally about daily routines, pastimes, and household chores
- Write and present information orally about TV programs, entertainment, special days, and vacations
- Write about activities for visiting foreign students

Culture

2.1 Practices and Perspectives
- Understand lifestyles and values of Spanish and Venezuelan young people
- Understand the vacation practices of Spanish-speaking peoples

2.2 Products and Perspectives
- Learn about the ski resort of Bariloche, Argentina

Connections

3.1 Cross-curricular
- Learn key facts about Spanish youth
- Learn key facts about an Argentine town
- Learn Language Arts Strategies: evaluate your lead

3.2 Target Culture
- Read poetry from Spain by Rafael Alberti
- Learn how indigenous peoples have affected the language of Mexico
- Learn how ancient pilgrimages have shaped travel practices in Spain today

Comparisons

4.1 Language
- Compare the use of Spanish verbs *encantar, gustar, importar,* and *interesar* to that of their English counterparts
- Compare Spanish words to their English counterparts

4.2 Culture
- Compare the activities of young people in Spain to those in the United States

Communities

5.1 Beyond the School
- Link to Web sites from around the Spanish-speaking world

Fondo cultural

Vida diaria de los jóvenes ¿Qué cosas son importantes para los jóvenes de España? Según una encuesta *(survey)*, para los jóvenes españoles son importantes los amigos, la familia, la salud, la libertad¹, las cosas que tienen, el tiempo libre, los estudios, la situación económica y el trabajo. ¿Qué hacen en su tiempo libre? Los días de semana practican deportes, estudian instrumentos musicales o idiomas, escuchan música, ven la televisión o usan la computadora. Los fines de semana salen con sus amigos, van al cine o a bailar.

- ¿Cómo eres similar o diferente de los jóvenes que respondieron a la encuesta?

1 freedom

Universal Access

Personalizing the Theme
Help students focus on favorite activities by saying: *Piensa en la familia, los amigos, la escuela y en tus pasatiempos. ¿Cuáles son las cosas más importantes para ti?* Record students' answers in a graphic organizer such as a concept web. Then rate the activities from most to least important for the whole class.

Heritage Language Learners
Invite students who have lived in heritage countries to talk about activities that were important to them there, and which they can no longer do in the United States. Ask how they spend their time differently in the United States.

Para empezar

Objectives

1 Tu vida diaria

- **Talk about school and non-school daily activities**
- **Describe your day before and after school**

2 Días especiales

- **Talk about weekend activities**
- **Describe special events and celebrations**

Enriching Your Teaching

Planning for Instruction

Resources:

- Teacher Express CD-ROM or Resource Book
  - Teaching resources
  - Lesson Planner
  - Chapter Resource Checklist
  - School-to-Home Connection Letter

Culture Note

Foosball ***(el fútbol de mesa)*** continues to be widely played in Europe. Some of its enduring popularity stems from the fact that soccer itself is by far the number one sport. Worldwide, about two million people regularly play foosball. European competitions have prize monies totaling hundreds of thousands of dollars.

Preview

PE

Chapter Opener

Presentation

This *Para empezar* section is designed to give a quick re-entry into the new school year by allowing students to talk about the things they enjoy doing in and out of school. It reviews fundamental structures such as the present tense of regular and irregular verbs, reflexive verbs, and possessives, as well as vocabulary associated with family, daily routines, telling time, vacations and travel, and describing things and events. Additional review of vocabulary and structures will be woven throughout the book in the *A ver si recuerdas* sections as well as in the regular chapters. Throughout the review, you should feel free to incorporate any favorite activities or materials from *Realidades* 1 and 2 that deal with the same topics or structures.

Suggestions: Introduce yourself to students who don't know you. Provide a brief description of yourself, such as where you are from and some activities that you like to do. Then have students turn to a partner he or she doesn't know, to find out information such as his or her name, what he or she is like, where he or she is from, some favorite activities he or she likes to do, and how often he or she does them. Point out to returning students that they may have forgotten things over the summer, but that with practice, the language they learned last year will come back to them quickly.

Fondo cultural

Standards: 1.1, 1.2, 2.1, 3.1, 4.2

Suggestions: After students read the information silently, guide them to answer the question by saying: *¿Hay cosas que son importantes para los jóvenes españoles que no son importantes para ti? ¿Cuáles son?*

Answers will vary.

Tu vida diaria

Presentation

Standards: 1.2

Resources: Voc. & Gram. Transparencies: 23; Resource Book: Cap. PE, Input Script; Audio Program: CD Cap. PE, Track 1

Focus: Reviewing daily routines and pastimes

Suggestions: After students have read the conversations, focus on the activities mentioned by saying them aloud and having volunteers pantomime the actions.

Standards: 1.1, 1.2

Resources: Practice Answers on Transparencies

Focus: Demonstrating reading comprehension

Suggestions: Have students write down words and phrases to answer the questions. Have them use these notes as they answer orally in complete sentences.

Common Errors: Students may forget to change first-person forms to the third-person when answering. Model correct verb forms as necessary and have students repeat.

Answers:
1. Ana hace la cama, toma el desayuno, pone los libros en la mochila y sale de casa.
2. Su actividad favorita es jugar al fútbol.
3. A veces va al gimnasio con sus amigos.
4. Hace su tarea.
5. Dicen que él cocina muy bien.

Standards: 1.3

Focus: Practicing daily-routine and pastime vocabulary

Suggestions: Encourage students to include details, such as times and descriptive adjectives, in their answers.

Answers will vary.

---

1 Tu vida diaria

Objectives
• Talk about your daily routine
• Discuss school and extracurricular activities

—Hola, Ana. Tengo que escribir un artículo para la revista de la escuela sobre la vida diaria de los estudiantes. ¿Puedes responder a unas preguntas?

—¡Por supuesto!

—¿Qué haces generalmente por la mañana, antes de salir para la escuela?

—Hago la cama, tomo el desayuno, pongo los libros en la mochila y salgo de casa a las 7:30.

—¿Y en tu tiempo libre?

—Juego al fútbol . . . mi actividad favorita.

—Hola Tomás, ¿puedes contestar unas preguntas sobre lo que haces después de la escuela?

—Hmm, . . . A veces voy con mis amigos al gimnasio a hacer ejercicio.

—¿Y cuándo haces la tarea?

—Hago la tarea por la tarde, antes de ayudar a mi mamá con los quehaceres de la casa.

—¿Cómo ayudas a tu mamá?

—Voy al supermercado con ella y la ayudo a cocinar. Me encanta hacer la cena y todos en mi familia dicen que cocino muy bien.

 Leer/Hablar ·

Cada día

Contesta las preguntas sobre Ana y Tomás.

1. ¿Qué hace Ana por la mañana?
2. ¿Cuál es la actividad favorita de Ana?
3. ¿Adónde va a veces Tomás? ¿Con quién?
4. ¿Qué hace Tomás antes de ayudar a su mamá con los quehaceres de la casa?
5. ¿Qué dicen en la familia de Tomás acerca de cómo cocina él?

 Escribir ·

Tu vida diaria

¿Qué haces durante el día? Completa las frases con lo que haces en un día típico.

1. Voy . . .
2. Hago . . .
3. Tomo . . .
4. Juego . . .
5. Pongo . . .
6. Salgo . . .
7. Miro . . .
8. Ayudo . . .
9. Estudio . . .
10. Escucho . . .

Universal Access

Multiple Intelligences

Bodily/Kinesthetic: Have students group themselves, pantomime an action, and conjugate one verb accordingly. For example, one student pantomimes and says: *Yo tomo el desayuno.* Another joins him or her and they say: *Nosotros tomamos el desayuno.* Another addresses them and says: *Uds. toman el desayuno,* and so on.

Advanced Learners

Have students interview a classmate on the subject of his or her daily activities on a typical day. Then ask them to convert the interviewee's answers to the third-person and present an oral report of the person's typical day.

Gramática · Repaso
Verbos irregulares

Remember that some verbs in Spanish are irregular in the first person singular of the present tense. Look at the following examples. Note that other verbs you know that are conjugated like *conocer* are *obedecer*, *ofrecer*, and *parecer*.

conocer	cono**zco**	salir	sal**go**
dar	**doy**	traer	trai**go**
hacer	ha**go**	ver	**veo**
poner	pon**go**	caer	ca**igo**
saber	**sé**		

Also, there are some verbs in Spanish that are irregular in all the persons of the present tense:

ser

soy	somos
eres	sois
es	son

ir

voy	vamos
vas	vais
va	van

decir

digo	decimos
dices	decís
dice	dicen

estar

estoy	estamos
estás	estáis
está	están

oír

oigo	oímos
oyes	oís
oye	oyen

tener

tengo	tenemos
tienes	tenéis
tiene	tienen

 3 Hablar

¿Qué haces tú?

No todas las personas hacen las mismas actividades durante el día. Trabaja con otro(a) estudiante para hablar sobre las actividades que hacen usando los verbos del recuadro. Usen *¿qué?*, *¿cómo?*, *¿cuándo?*, *¿dónde?*, *¿para qué?*, *¿a qué hora?*, *¿por qué?* para hacer las preguntas.

Modelo

A —¿A qué hora <u>desayunas</u>?
B —<u>Yo desayuno</u> a las ocho de la mañana.

comer	ir de compras	tomar el desayuno
estudiar	hacer la tarea	ir a la escuela
ir al gimnasio	hacer/practicar un	llegar
ver la tele	deporte	tomar (lecciones)
salir de paseo	hablar por teléfono	navegar en la Red

tres   3
Para empezar

Practice and Communicate

Gramática · Repaso
Presentation

Resources: Voc. & Gram. Transparencies: 24

Suggestions: Conduct a rapid interchange, moving through the class with questions to which students invent answers on the spot:
—*María, ¿de dónde sales por la mañana?*
—*Salgo de la casa.*
—*Pedro, ¿de dónde sale María?*
—*Sale de la casa.*
—*¿Y tú? ¿De dónde sales por la tarde?*
—*Salgo de la escuela.*
—*Y Pedro, ¿qué pones en la mochila?*
—*Pongo mis libros.*

 3 *Standards:* 1.1

Focus: Practicing verbs that are irregular in the first person

Suggestions: Have students conduct the activity twice, switching roles, so that each partner can practice the first-person forms.

Answers will vary.

Extension: Ask students questions about their partner's activities, and then about their own:
—*Belinda, ¿qué dice Tomás sobre la tarea?*
—*Tomás hace su tarea después de la cena.*
—*¿Y tú? ¿Cuándo haces tu tarea?*
—*Yo hago mi tarea antes de la cena.*

Additional Resources
• Writing, Audio & Video Workbook: Cap. PE, Audio Activity 1, Track 2

Enriching Your Teaching

Culture Note

In most places in Latin America, school sports are not as heavily funded and organized as they are in United States schools. However, this doesn't mean young people there don't play league sports. Rather, sports enthusiasts belong to neighborhood teams sponsored by local merchants or parents' organizations.

Teacher-to-Teacher

Time pair work and group work activities with a kitchen timer. When the alarm sounds, stop the activity, address any questions students may have, and move on. Timed activities will help you greatly in designing and sticking to your lesson plans.

Standards: 1.2

Resources: Audio Program: CD Cap. PE, Track 3; Resource Book: Cap. PE, Audio Script; Practice Answers on Transparencies

Focus: Practicing daily-routine vocabulary

Suggestions: Before playing the *Audio CD* for step 2, ask questions with **quién:** *¿Quién corta el césped?* Have students respond with complete sentences.

Answers:

1.	F	4.	F
2.	F	5.	C
3.	F	6.	F

Actividad 5

Standards: 1.1, 1.3

Focus: Practicing daily-routine vocabulary

Suggestions: Encourage students to use Elena's account in *Actividad 4* as a model for their own accounts of household chores.

Answers will vary.

Actividad 6

Standards: 1.1, 1.3

Focus: Practicing daily-routine vocabulary

Suggestions: Point out to students that they should concentrate on verbs involved in performing the activity, in order to adequately describe it. For *lavar el coche,* for example, suitable verbs might be *llenar* or *usar.*

Answers will vary.

 Actividad 4 **Leer/Escuchar** ....

Elena y su familia

❶ Lee la siguiente descripción de Elena de los quehaceres que hace cada miembro de su familia.

En mi familia todos ayudamos con los quehaceres de la casa. Cada uno de nosotros tiene una tarea específica. Como nuestros horarios son diferentes, nunca estamos todos trabajando al mismo tiempo. Las tareas que tenemos son:

Mamá:
* *preparar el almuerzo*
* *limpiar la cocina y el baño*
* *lavar la ropa*

Papá:
* *hacer el desayuno*
* *cortar el césped*
* *lavar el coche*

Yo:
* *arreglar mi cuarto y hacer la cama*
* *dar de comer al perro*
* *poner la mesa*

Mi hermano mayor:
* *preparar la cena*
* *arreglar su cuarto y hacer la cama*
* *pasar la aspiradora*

Como todos ayudamos con los quehaceres, las tareas se hacen más rápido y tenemos más tiempo libre para salir a pasear o hacer otras actividades.

❷ Escribe los números del 1 al 6 en una hoja. Escucha las frases y escribe *C* si la frase es cierta y *F* si es falsa.

  Actividad 5 **Escribir/Hablar** ....

En tu familia

❶ Escribe una breve descripción sobre quiénes hacen los quehaceres en tu casa y qué hace cada uno. Escribe la información en forma de frase.

❷ Trabaja con un(a) compañero(a) para comparar las descripciones que escribieron. Decidan qué actividades tienen en común y por qué.

 Actividad 6 Gramática **Escribir/Hablar** ....

Tu actividad favorita

❶ Decide cuál es tu actividad favorita del día y descríbela. No digas qué actividad es.

Modelo

Leo mis libros y escribo cosas.

❷ En grupo, cada uno(a) lee su descripción. El resto debe adivinar de qué actividad se trata.

Modelo

Tu actividad favorita es hacer la tarea.

Más práctica ....
Practice Workbook P-1

Go Online
PHSchool.com

For: Practice with vocabulary and irregular verbs
Visit: www.phschool.com
Web Code: jed-0001

4 cuatro
Tu vida diaria

Students with Learning Difficulties

Have students work with partners who are kinesthetic learners. The partners can pantomime doing household chores while students name the chore being pantomimed.

Advanced Learners

Have students with cameras create photo essays of people, preferably their families, doing household chores. Each picture of a chore should be accompanied by a one-sentence caption saying who is doing the chore.

Gramática · Repaso

Presente de los verbos con cambios de raíz

Remember that in Spanish there are three groups of stem-changing verbs. The stem change occurs in all forms except the *nosotros(as)* and *vosotros(as)* forms. Here are the present-tense forms of *perder (ie)*, *poder (ue)* and *pedir (i)*.

perder (e → ie)	
pierdo	perdemos
pierdes	perdéis
pierde	pierden

poder (o → ue)	
puedo	podemos
puedes	podéis
puede	pueden

pedir (e → i)	
pido	pedimos
pides	pedís
pide	piden

Other verbs like *perder* are: *empezar, querer, preferir, pensar, divertirse, despertarse, sentirse, mentir, cerrar, comenzar, entender.*

Other verbs like *poder* are: *jugar (u → ue), contar, costar, encontrar, recordar, volar, dormir, volver, devolver, acostarse, almorzar.*

Other verbs like *pedir* are *servir, repetir, reír, sonreír, seguir, vestirse.*

 **Gramática** **Leer**

Vida deportiva

Lee lo que escribió Carmen sobre su equipo de fútbol. Completa el párrafo con la forma correcta del verbo apropiado en el presente.

Después de la escuela yo __1.__ (*preferir* / *dormir*) ir al club para jugar al fútbol. Mis compañeras y yo __2.__ (*recordar* / *jugar*) bastante bien pero nuestra entrenadora __3.__ (*poder* / *pensar*) que el equipo rival __4.__ (*empezar* / *jugar*) mejor. A veces nosotras __5.__ (*perder* / *servir*) un partido, pero cuando nuestro equipo __6.__ (*poder* / *comenzar*) meter un gol es fabuloso.

 Gramática **Escribir**

Actividades de la semana

Usa los verbos del recuadro para completar las frases según tu experiencia.

servir	querer	perder	jugar
dormir	poder	sentirse	preferir

1. Después de la escuela, mis amigos . . .
2. Para el almuerzo, mi mamá . . .
3. A veces, mis amigos y yo . . .

4. Cuando mi equipo favorito . . .
5. Muchas veces yo . . . pero no . . .

 **Gramática · Repaso**

Presentation

Resources: Voc. & Gram. Transparencies: 25

Suggestions: Ask students to write sentences that contain two verbs from each of the three lists in the *Gramática*. Tell them not to use **nosotros** or **vosotros** forms.

 Standards: 1.2

Resources: Practice Answers on Transparencies

Focus: Practicing verbs with stem changes in the present tense

Suggestions: Remind students to pay attention to the subject of each sentence before they write their answer.

Answers:
1. prefiero
2. jugamos
3. piensa
4. juega
5. perdemos
6. puede

 Standards: 1.3

Focus: Practicing verbs with stem changes in the present tense

Suggestions: Encourage students to refer as often as necessary to the verb conjugations in the *Gramática* while they complete the activity.

Answers will vary.

Additional Resources
• Writing, Audio & Video Workbook: Cap. PE, Audio Activity 2, Track 4

Enriching Your Teaching

Teacher-to-Teacher

Have students get acquainted with the book at the outset of the school year. Make a list of features for students to find as quickly as they can. These might include: maps of the Spanish-speaking world, English-Spanish and Spanish-English vocabulary lists, a *¿Recuerdas?* box, a

Go Online feature, a *Repaso* section, the first *Lectura*, and so on. Have students write down the page numbers of the various features. This could be done as a whole-class activity or as a race between groups of students.

Actividad 9
Standards: 1.2, 1.3

Focus: Practicing review vocabulary and structures via reading and response

Common Errors: Some students may forget to make the spelling changes when they use forms of verbs that have them. Point out that the spelling changes affect the pronunciation of the forms as well. Model correct pronunciation where the spelling changes occur. Have students repeat, or correct their spelling if the error was written.

Suggestions: Help students focus on the content of the reading by having them copy the chart to their own paper before they read.

Answers will vary.

Actividad 10
Standards: 1.3

Focus: Using new vocabulary and structures in sentences

Suggestions: Point out to students that they can skip around when choosing their cues. They don't have to use the cues in a straight, horizontal line.

Answers will vary.

Actividad 9 — Leer/Escribir

Roberto y Lucas

① Imagina que conoces a dos hermanos muy diferentes entre sí *(from each other)*. Observa las fotos y lee el texto que las acompaña.

Roberto y Lucas son hermanos. Ellos son muy diferentes entre sí. Los fines de semana, Roberto empieza el día temprano—duerme solamente hasta las siete de la mañana. A las ocho, juega al fútbol con sus amigos y a las diez vuelve a casa. Lucas prefiere levantarse tarde porque se acuesta muy tarde. No entiende cómo su hermano puede levantarse temprano. A Lucas le gusta tocar la guitarra y escribir canciones. Sonríe mucho cuando escucha música porque le encanta. Cuando Lucas toca la guitarra muy alto *(loudly)*, Roberto se vuelve loco. Lucas se vuelve loco cuando Roberto enciende la luz y lo despierta. A los dos hermanos les gusta ir al cine y navegar en la Red. Los dos son muy amables pero no se entienden muy bien.

② ¿Eres más similar a Roberto o a Lucas? Indica con una X quién hace cada una de estas actividades y si tú también las hace. Luego, escribe un párrafo comparándote a ti mismo con Roberto o Lucas.

Actividad	Roberto	Lucas	Yo
jugar al fútbol			
tocar la guitarra			
sonreír al escuchar música			
preferir levantarse tarde			
encender la luz temprano			

Modelo

Lucas y yo preferimos más escuchar música que hacer deportes.

Actividad 10 — Gramática — Escribir

¿Y qué haces tú?

Imagina que estás en una reunión de amigos y comienzan a hablar de lo que hacen. Escribe frases usando las palabras de las tres columnas.

Modelo

yo / cortarse / el pelo
Yo me corto el pelo todos los meses.

A	B	C
yo	ayudar	autobús
tú	correr	de paseo
Carlos	desayunar	en el parque
nosotros	hacer	quehaceres
ustedes	salir	tarea de la escuela
mis amigos	tomar	temprano / tarde

6   seis
Tu vida diaria

● **Más práctica**
Practice Workbook P-2

Go Online
PHSchool.com

For: Practice with present tense of stem-changing verbs
Visit: www.phschool.com
Web Code: jed-0002

Block Schedule

After students have written their paragraphs, put them in pairs. Have each student exchange paragraphs. The partner is to write six *Cierto/Falso* statements about the information. Each student reads the statements to the partner who will agree or correct the incorrect information.

Universal Access

Students with Learning Difficulties
Help students orientate themselves when using the chart in *Actividad* 9. Slide your finger across the first row of the chart and explain that all the information in that row has to do with playing football. Repeat this procedure for each row of the chart.

Students with Special Needs
Provide hearing-impaired students with a seat near the speakers, or with headphones if possible, whenever conducting recorded listening activities.

Gramática · Repaso

Los verbos reflexivos

To say that people do something to or for themselves, you use reflexive verbs. A reflexive verb has two parts: a reflexive pronoun (*me, te, se, nos, os*) and a verb form. Here are all the present-tense forms of *levantarse*:

me levanto	**nos** levantamos
te levantas	**os** levantáis
se levanta	**se** levantan

Many reflexive verbs in Spanish describe daily routine actions: *acostarse (ue), afeitarse, arreglarse, bañarse, cepillarse, despertarse (ie), ducharse, lavarse, pintarse, ponerse, secarse, vestirse (i)*.

Except for *se*, the reflexive pronouns are the same as the indirect object pronouns. They usually come before the verb, but they may also be attached to an infinitive.

Me lavo la cara.　　　　Voy a **lavarme** la cara.

Remember that with reflexive verbs, you usually use the definite article with parts of the body or articles of clothing.

Me pongo **la** chaqueta.　　Me cepillo **los** dientes.

Escribir

Lo opuesto a ti

Imagina que tienes hermanos(as) muy diferentes a ti. Lo que a ti te gusta hacer, a ellos(as) no. Escribe frases comparándose.

Modelo

secarse el pelo
Mi hermana no se seca el pelo antes de salir de la casa pero yo sí.

1. lavarse la cara
2. cepillarse los dientes
3. vestirse con ropa moderna
4. cortarse el pelo todos los meses
5. despertarse
6. acostarse

Escribir

A las 7:00 . . .

Describe lo que haces cada mañana desde que abres los ojos hasta que sales para ir a la escuela.

Modelo

7:00: Me despierto. 7:05: Me levanto de la cama.

● **Más práctica**
Practice Workbook P-3

For: Practice with reflexive verbs
Visit: www.phschool.com
Web Code: jed-0003

siete　**7**
Para empezar

Enriching Your Teaching

Teacher-to-Teacher
Conduct an information exchange. Prepare a worksheet with students' names in the left column and in the right column a list of daily activities with their times of day, such as **almorzar a la una.** Give each student a slip of paper with a daily activity and time from the right column of the worksheet written on it. Have students complete the worksheet by circulating around the room and asking each other questions about the right column: *¿Tú almuerzas a la una?* The first to match all the names and daily activities on his or her worksheet wins.

Practice and Communicate

 PE

Gramática · Repaso

Presentation

Resources: Voc. & Gram. Transparencies: 26

Suggestions: Use the reflexive verbs in sentences about what you are going to do tomorrow. Have students respond by saying that they perform the action every day. —*Mañana, voy a despertarme a las seis y media.* —*Yo me despierto a las seis y media todos los días.* Pantomime the action for each sentence, and have students do likewise when they respond.

 Standards: 1.3

Resources: Practice Answers on Transparencies

Focus: Practicing reflexive verbs

Suggestions: Point out to students that for this activity, all reflexive pronouns should precede the verb.

Answers: Family members will vary. Students will use the following verb forms (with singular subjects).

1. se lava
2. se cepilla
3. se viste
4. se corta
5. se despierta
6. se acuesta

 Standards: 1.1, 1.3

Focus: Practicing reflexive verbs

Suggestions: Have students prepare by first listing all their morning activities. Suggest that they refer to the *Gramática* for reminders. Then have them convert their list into a final draft that includes the times and complete sentences. As they make their final draft they can include other activities that they may have forgotten in their lists.

Answers will vary.

Additional Resources

• Writing, Audio & Video Workbook: Cap. PE, Audio Activity 3, Track 5

• Writing, Audio & Video Workbook: Cap. PE, Writing Activity 6

• Resource Book: Cap. PE, Communicative Activity BLM

7

Días especiales

Presentation

Standards: 1.2

Resources: Voc. & Gram. Transparencies: 4, 27; Resource Book: Cap. PE, Input Script; Audio Program: CD Cap. PE, Track 6

Focus: Reviewing celebrations and special events

Suggestions: Use *Vocabulary and Grammar Transparency 27* to aid understanding as students read the information. Then show *Vocabulary and Grammar Transparency 4.* Enter the names **Margarita, Laura,** and **Manuel** at the tops of the first three columns. Leave the fourth column empty. Ask guiding questions to elicit information about each of the three people and record students' answers in the appropriate column. For example, if you ask *¿A quién le gustan las celebraciones para los acontecimientos importantes?* students should say **a Manuel.** Under **Manuel** on the chart, write **celebraciones.** Continue until all information for each person is recorded.

Actividad 13

Standards: 1.2, 1.3

Resources: Practice Answers on Transparencies

Focus: Demonstrating reading comprehension

Suggestions: Ask students to answer the questions in complete sentences, using their own words as much as possible.

Answers:

1. El día favorito de Margarita es el día de su cumpleaños. El de Manuel es el día que la familia entera se reúne.
2. Se reúnen para celebrar algún acontecimiento importante, como una boda o una graduación.
3. Se arregla con sus amigas en la casa de una de ellas.
4. Lo mejor para Margarita es pasar la noche bailando con sus amigos.
5. Manuel tiene que cuidar a sus hermanos y primos más pequeños.
6. En los dos días favoritos, la gente baila. También los días se parecen en que pasan sólo una vez al año.

---

2 Días especiales

Objectives
- Talk about special events and activities
- Discuss what you do with your family and friends on these occasions
- Talk about entertainment and sports

Todos los años, la revista *Familia* hace una encuesta. A continuación aparecen algunas de las respuestas más interesantes a la encuesta "¿Cuál es tu día de fiesta favorito?".

Margarita: ▶

"Mi día de fiesta favorito es el día de mi cumpleaños. Siempre hacemos una fiesta. Mis padres y yo decoramos la casa con globos y luces. Mi mamá siempre me prepara un pastel. Pero lo mejor es que todos mis amigos vienen y traen música y nos pasamos la noche bailando. "

◀ **Laura:**

"Lo que más me gusta es el baile de la escuela de fin de año. Me gusta porque puedo charlar con mis amigos y bailar. Además me encanta arreglarme para la fiesta.

Con mis amigas siempre nos reunimos en una de las casas para prepararnos e ir juntas a la fiesta."

Manuel: ▶

"Mi día preferido es el día que la familia entera se reúne para celebrar algún evento importante, como una boda o una graduación. La abuela prepara una gran cena pero todos ayudamos con algo. Yo tengo la tarea de cuidar a mis primos y hermanos más pequeños."

Actividad 13   Leer/Escribir

Los días de fiesta

Contesta las preguntas sobre los jóvenes de la encuesta.

1. ¿Cuál es el día favorito de Margarita? ¿Y el de Manuel?
2. ¿Por qué se reúnen Manuel y sus parientes?
3. ¿Cómo se arregla Laura para la fiesta de fin de año de la escuela?
4. ¿Qué es lo mejor para Margarita?
5. ¿Qué tarea tiene Manuel en las fiestas?
6. ¿Cómo son similares los días favoritos de Margarita y Laura?

8   **ocho**
Días especiales

Universal Access

Heritage Language Learners

Invite students to share information about special days they celebrate with their families. What is the occasion? What activities take place? Are there decorations? Are any special foods prepared?

Students with Learning Difficulties

As students read the information about each person, point to appropriate parts of the accompanying photo to help them associate words and meanings.

Actividad 14 Leer/Escribir/Hablar

Actividades de una joven

1 Lucía participa en una encuesta. Lee la siguiente gráfica que indica cuántas veces Lucía realiza cada actividad.

Actividad	1 a 3 veces por semana	1 vez al mes	1 a 3 veces al año	Nunca
ir a bailar		x		
practicar deportes	x			
ir al cine		x		
ver la televisión	x			
ir de compras	x			
ir a una fiesta de sorpresa			x	
tocar un instrumento musical	x			
celebrar un día especial		x		
reunirse con amigos	x			
ir de vacaciones			x	
tener una cita		x		
ir a una boda				x
hacer un concurso		x		
hacer una audición		x		
ir a un desfile		x		
ver fuegos artificiales				x
hacer un picnic			x	

2 Copia la gráfica y úsala para hacer la encuesta a tres estudiantes.

Modelo

A —¿Cuántas veces al mes o al año vas a bailar?
B —Voy a bailar tres veces al año.

3 Con los resultados que obtengas, escribe cinco frases sobre las actividades de tus compañeros.

Actividad 15 Leer/Escribir

Tu día favorito

1 Piensa en cuál es tu día de fiesta favorito y contesta las siguientes preguntas.

1. ¿Celebras con tu familia o con tus amigos?
2. ¿Te preparas para ese día durante la semana?
3. ¿Qué haces para celebrarlo?
4. ¿Es un día importante para otras personas?

2 Basándote en tus respuestas, escribe un párrafo para describir tu día favorito del año y decir cuál es. Cuenta lo que ocurre ese día.

Actividad 14   *Standards:* 1.1, 1.3

Focus: Practicing vocabulary related to celebrations and special events

Suggestions: Explain that for step 2, students should write the names of each student they interview in the appropriate space, rather than using Xs.

Answers will vary.

Actividad 15   *Standards:* 1.3

Focus: Practicing vocabulary related to celebrations and special events

Suggestions: Remind students about rules for writing effective paragraphs before they complete step 2. Explain, for example, that the first sentence of their paragraph should announce which favorite day they are going to describe.

Answers will vary.

Extension: Invite volunteers to read their completed paragraphs to the class.

Enriching Your Teaching

Culture Note

In Mexico, a girl's fifteenth birthday celebration, her **quinceañera,** is often one of the biggest of her life. (The term **quinceañera** is used to refer to the girl herself, as well as to the celebration.) It is often a huge family affair. Traditionally, this day marks the transition from girlhood to womanhood. Depending on the family, it may begin with a religious celebration, often a Catholic Mass. Urban families might lease a banquet hall and have a formal gala dinner. Rural families might have a more casual celebration, perhaps outdoors, with plenty of food, music, and relaxing fun for everyone.

9

Practice and Communicate

PE

Actividad 16

Standards: 1.2, 1.3

Resources: Voc. & Gram. Transparencies: 28; Practice Answers on Transparencies

Focus: Practicing adjectives

Suggestions: Review some of the adjectives suggested in step 2 before students complete the activity. Use exaggerated gestures and pantomime to clarify the meanings of adjectives such as *horrible, violento, emocionante,* and *artístico.* Meanings of other adjectives can be taught by using them in sentences.

Answers:

Step 1

1. Possibilities include: los personajes, el argumento, la música, los efectos especiales
2. Sandra dice que la película no muestra los personajes tan bien como el libro. También dice que tiene menos detalles que en el libro.
3. A Lucas le gustan los actores y le gusta la imaginación del director. No le gusta el argumento.

Step 2

Answers will vary.

Actividad 16 Leer/Escribir . . . .

Las películas

❶ Una actividad que le gusta hacer a casi todo el mundo es ir al cine. Lee lo que dicen estos jóvenes venezolanos de la película *El señor de los anillos* y contesta las preguntas que siguen.

LAS PELÍCULAS

Película: El señor de los anillos

Es una película impresionante. Me encantan los personajes y el argumento. La música y los efectos especiales son fantásticos. La gente no se aburre de verla. Su director es un genio. *Pedro Rosas, 16 años, Caracas* ★★★★★

La película es interesante pero los actores no me gustan. No muestran (*show*) bien cómo son los personajes del libro. El director no cuenta la historia con detalles y es difícil de entender. La gente que no conoce el libro no puede entender de qué trata. *Sandra Gómez, 17 años, Maracaibo* ★

La película no se parece al libro pero mantiene la misma idea. Me gusta la imaginación del director. Los actores hacen un buen trabajo pero el argumento no me fascina. Recomiendo la película para pasar un buen momento. *Lucas Pérez, 15 años, Valencia* ★★★

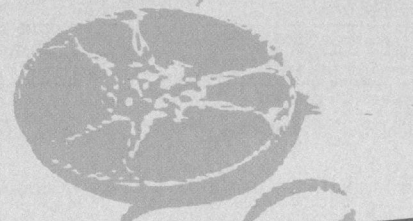

1. Nombra tres cosas que le gustan a Pedro de la película.
2. ¿Qué cree Sandra sobre cómo la película se compara al libro?
3. Nombra una cosa que le gusta y una cosa que no le gusta a Lucas.

❷ Piensa en una película que te gusta mucho o que no te gusta nada. Escribe una descripción de la película. Puedes usar las palabras del recuadro.

inolvidable	despacio(a)
típico(a)	divertido(a)
estupendo(a)	emocionante
bello(a)	exagerado(a)
artístico(a)	horrible
talentoso(a)	violento(a)

¿Recuerdas?

To talk about your favorite movies:
un drama
una comedia
una película de ciencia ficción
una película policiaca
una película romántica
una película de horror

10 diez
Días especiales

Universal Access

Students with Learning Difficulties

Make a set of index cards containing the adjectives in step 2 of *Actividad* 16. Go through the movie section of a local newspaper. Help students match the various adjectives with appropriate movies. Then ask them to make a sentence about each movie using the adjective on the card.

Advanced Learners

Ask students to write their own opinion about a film they have recently seen. Have them use the opinions in *Actividad* 16 as models.

Gramática · Repaso

Verbos que se conjugan como *gustar*

You already know several verbs that always use the indirect object pronouns *me, te, le, nos, os, les:*

encantar	*to love*	importar	*to matter*
gustar	*to like*	interesar	*to be interested in*

These verbs all use the same construction: indirect object pronoun + verb + subject.

Me gusta el fútbol.   ¿**Te interesan** las pinturas?

Remember, in the sentences above, the verb forms *gusta* (singular) and *interesan* (plural) agree with the subjects *fútbol* and *pinturas*. The words *me* and *te* are indirect object pronouns.

Actividad 17   Hablar

Los programas de televisión

¿Qué programas te gustan? Trabaja con un(a) compañero(a) para hablar sobre sus programas favoritos. Usa *gustar, encantar, e interesar.*

Modelo

A—*¿Te interesan los programas de noticias?*
B—*Sí, me interesan mucho. Me gusta saber lo que pasa en el mundo.*
o: *No, no me gustan porque son aburridos.*

Estudiante A

1. los programas educativos
2. los programas de la vida real
3. los programas de dibujos animados
4. los programas de deportes
5. las telenovelas

Estudiante B

¡Respuesta personal!

Actividad 18   Hablar

Programas de deportes

Trabaja con otro(a) estudiante para hacer y contestar preguntas sobre tus deportes favoritos. Usa los verbos *gustar, encantar, importar e interesar.*

Modelo

A — *¿Te gusta jugar al béisbol?*
B — *Sí, me encanta jugar al béisbol.*

● **Más práctica**
Practice Workbook P-4

Go Online
PHSchool.com

For: Practice with vocabulary and verbs like *gustar*
Visit: www.phschool.com
Web Code: jed-0004

once 11
Para empezar

Gramática · Repaso

Presentation

Resources: Voc. & Gram. Transparencies: 29

Suggestions: Have students practice the verbs by talking about things that please, enchant, interest, or matter to them. Remind them that in a sentence such as: *Me gusta el perro*, the subject is **perro**. The construction moves in the opposite direction from the English sentence "I like the dog."

Actividad 17 *Standards:* 1.1

Focus: Practicing verbs like *gustar*

Suggestions: Tell Student B to "bounce" the question back to Student A with a question such as: *¿Y a ti?* or *¿Y qué piensas tú?* This way both students can practice the verbs like *gustar* in a natural, flowing conversation.

Answers will vary.

Actividad 18 *Standards:* 1.1

Focus: Practicing verbs like *gustar*

Suggestions: Suggest that students talk about sports they enjoy watching as well as those they enjoy playing, so they can extend the activity for further practice.

Answers will vary.

Additional Resources

• Writing, Audio & Video Workbook: Cap. PE, Audio Activity 4, Track 7

Enriching Your Teaching

Culture Note

The name **Venezuela** comes from the impression the first Europeans had when they saw houses rising on stilts out of the water of the Sinamaica lagoon near what is now Maracaibo. The houses reminded them of Venice, and so they called the place **Venezuela** or "little Venice." There are still many such houses—more modern versions of them—in the country's delta areas.

Internet Search

Keywords:

Caracas + Venezuela + turismo

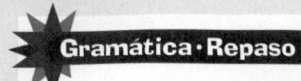
Presentation

Resources: Voc. & Gram. Transparencies: 30

Suggestions: Have students practice the possessive adjectives by describing first their own home, then that of a friend or relative. Ask guiding questions as necessary to elicit the various pronouns: —¿Y cómo es el jardín de tu abuelo? —Su jardín es muy hermoso.

Standards: 1.2

Resources: Practice Answers on Transparencies

Focus: Practicing possessive adjectives

Suggestions: Have students scan the entire postcard first for meaning before they begin to write their answers.

Answers:

1.	mi	6.	mis
2.	nuestro	7.	Mis
3.	nuestros	8.	mi
4.	Nuestro	9.	su
5.	nuestras	10.	sus

Standards: 1.1, 1.2

Resources: Voc. & Gram. Transparency 18 (map)

Suggestions: Before students read the information, show *Vocabulary and Grammar Transparency* 18 and point out the location of Bariloche, Argentina, or have a volunteer do so. It is a bit more than halfway down the length of Argentina, in the Andes Mountains, near the Chilean border.

Answers will vary.

Go Online

The online atlas will provide a more detailed map of Argentina.

Additional Resources

• Writing, Audio & Video Workbook: Cap. PE, Audio Activity 5, Track 8

Gramática · Repaso

Adjetivos posesivos

Remember that possessive adjectives in Spanish agree in gender and number with the nouns they describe. They are placed in front of the noun.

Singular		Plural	
mi, tu, su, nuestro, vuestro	vuelo	mis, tus, sus, nuestros, vuestros	vuelos
mi, tu, su, nuestra, vuestra	maleta	mis, tus, sus, nuestras, vuestras	maletas

Since *su* and *sus* have many meanings, use the prepositional phrase *de* + name/pronoun instead for clarity or emphasis.

Sus pantalones son elegantes.
¿Los pantalones **de ella?**
No, los **de usted.**

Actividad 19 **Gramática** **Leer/Escribir**

¡A esquiar!

Pablo sale mañana para esquiar con su familia en Bariloche, Argentina. Él está muy emocionado *(excited)* y escribe cómo se siente en su diario. Lee lo que escribe y llena los espacios con la forma correcta del adjetivo posesivo apropiado.

Mañana voy con 1._____ familia a esquiar en Bariloche. Estamos un poco nerviosos porque 2._____ vuelo sale muy temprano y todavía tenemos que recoger 3._____ boletos en el aeropuerto. 4._____ agente de viajes nos dice que 5._____ reservaciones están confirmadas, y yo creo lo que ella dice.

Estoy muy emocionado con esquiar. ¡Hace una semana que están hechas 6._____ maletas! 7._____ padres y 8._____ hermana mayor tienen maletas muy grandes a causa de 9._____ ropa. Mi hermano menor también lleva una maleta grande a causa de 10._____ juguetes... ¡tiene muchos!

Fondo cultural

Esquiar en Bariloche Cuando hay nieve, mucha gente aprovecha *(takes advantage)* para practicar su deporte preferido: esquiar. En Bariloche, Argentina, se encuentra uno de los centros de esquí más famosos de Latinoamérica. Esquiadores de todas partes del mundo, tanto profesionales como principiantes *(beginners)*, llegan a este lugar cada año. Aquí pueden disfrutar de modernas pistas de esquí y también de los impresionantes paisajes *(scenery)* que hay a su alrededor. Bariloche es un lugar ideal para hacer deportes y conocer las bellezas naturales que nos ofrece nuestro planeta.

• ¿En qué otros países hispanobablantes es posible esquiar? ¿En qué países hace demasiado calor?

12 doce
Días especiales

Universal Access

Students with Learning Difficulties

Have students work with single objects and pairs of similar objects, such as a pencil and a pair of pencils. Hand the object or objects to various individuals or pairs and ask students to say sentences such as: *Son sus lápices. Son mis lápices. Es mi lápiz. Es tu lápiz.*

Advanced Learners

Have students pretend they are on a trip to a vacation spot of their choice in Spain or Latin America. Ask them to research the place and write a postcard as if they were there, telling about some of its attractions. Tell them to use at least two possessive adjectives.

Actividad 20 Leer/Escribir ....

Días de vacaciones

● Lee esta tarjeta postal que Rosa le escribe a una amiga sobre sus vacaciones de verano.

SALUDOS DE MIAMI

Querida Sara,
¿Cómo estás? Te escribo desde la playa en Miami. ¡Me encanta estar de vacaciones! Todos los días me levanto tarde, desayuno y voy a la playa con mi familia. Mis hermanos y yo nos bañamos en el mar todo el día, y a veces salimos a dar vueltas por la ciudad en nuestras bicicletas. Mi hermano también se encuentra con sus amigos. Todas las noches, después de cenar, voy con mi hermano y sus amigos al cine o a comer helado.

Nuestro hotel también es fantástico. Hay un vendedor que vende artesanías en la playa y me encanta mirar sus aretes de plata. ¡Qué divertido!
Saludos,
Rosa

● Haz una lista de las cosas que hace Rosa en sus vacaciones.

Modelo

Rosa le escribe una tarjeta postal a su amiga.

  Actividad 21 Escribir/Hablar ....

Unas preguntas sobre tus vacaciones

● Piensa en las cosas que haces durante tus vacaciones. En una hoja escribe las respuestas a estas preguntas.

1. ¿Qué haces durante tus vacaciones?
2. ¿Te quedas en la ciudad todo el tiempo?
3. ¿Viajas con tu familia o amigos a algún lugar? ¿Adónde?
4. ¿Qué haces generalmente en un día de vacaciones?
5. ¿A qué hora te levantas? ¿Y a qué hora te acuestas?
6. ¿Qué lugar te gusta más para irte de vacaciones?

● Trabaja con otro(a) estudiante para hablar sobre las vacaciones. Usen las preguntas anteriores como modelo para su conversación. Escriban las respuestas y un párrafo sobre las vacaciones.

 ● **Más práctica** ....

Practice Workbook P-5,
Practice Workbook Organizer P-6

Go Online
PHSchool.com

For: Practice with possessive adjectives
Visit: www.phschool.com
Web Code: jed-0005

Standards: 1.2

Actividad 20

Resources: Voc. & Gram. Transparencies: 31
Focus: Practicing possessive adjectives

Suggestions: Instruct students to mention with whom Rosa does the activities, so they practice using plural possessive adjectives.

Answers will vary.

Standards: 1.1, 1.3

Actividad 21

Focus: Practicing vocabulary related to vacation and travel

Suggestions: Have students who may not go on vacations themselves write about their partner's vacation or that of someone they know.

Answers will vary.

trece **13**
Para empezar

 Enriching Your Teaching

Culture Note

The first European settlers arrived in the area around what is now Bariloche, Argentina in about 1892. They settled along the banks of Lake Nahuel Huapi. They were primarily North Americans and Germans. The founding of the town itself is attributed to a man named Carlos Weitherholdt. He built a house and began regular trade in wool, leather, potatoes, cheese, butter, and other products. He traded mostly with the Chilean town of Puerto Montt, located over the mountains to the west. German influence can still be seen in some of the architecture in the older parts of the town.

Communicate: Speaking

PE

Presentación oral

Presentation

Standards: 1.2, 1.3, 3.1

Focus: Preparing and delivering an oral presentation

Suggestions: Help students decide on which task they will do. Review the four-step approach with them. Review the rubric with the class (see *Assessment* below) to explain how you will grade the performance task. Encourage them to use a graphic organizer, such as a column chart or a concept web in step 1, as an aid to organizing their ideas.

Portfolio

Record students' oral presentations on audiocassette or videotape for inclusion in their portfolios.

✓ Assessment

• Assessment Program: Cap. PE, Rubrics

Give students copies of the rubric before they begin the activity. Go over the descriptions of the different levels of performance. After assessing students, help individuals understand how their performance could be improved.

Presentación oral

Mi vida

Tarea

Imagínate que tienes que hacer una presentación oral en español para graduarte de la escuela. Escoge uno de estos aspectos de tu vida para hablar ante un grupo de estudiantes.

• Un día en la escuela. ¿Qué haces antes de ir a la escuela? ¿Te diviertes en tu escuela? ¿Cómo son tus amigos? ¿Qué actividades haces después de la escuela?

• Tu película o programa de televisión favorito. ¿Quiénes son los personajes del programa o de la película? ¿Qué problemas tienen? ¿Qué hacen para resolverlos?

• Tus vacaciones. ¿A dónde te gusta ir de vacaciones? ¿Vas a ese lugar con tus amigos o tu familia? ¿Qué haces allí?

• El deporte que practicas. ¿Por qué te gusta ese deporte? ¿Con quiénes practicas ese deporte? ¿Dónde lo practicas? ¿Qué se necesita para ser un buen jugador?

1 **Prepárate** Contesta las preguntas o escribe frases y palabras que te van a ayudar a hacer tu presentación ante el grupo.

2 **Practica** Vuelve a leer la información que escribiste y piensa cómo la vas a presentar. Puedes usar tus notas para practicar, pero no al hablar ante la clase. Después, vas a ir al lugar del salón de clases donde están los estudiantes que van a hablar del mismo tema que tú. Contesta las preguntas que te hacen los estudiantes de tu grupo sobre tu presentación.

3 **Haz tu presentación** Habla de tu tema con tu grupo como ayuda para pensar en más ideas. Al final, cada estudiante de cada grupo debe presentar el tema ante la clase.

4 **Evaluación** Tu profesor(a) puede explicarte cómo va a evaluar tu presentación. Probablemente, para tu profesor es importante ver que:

• te preparas bien para hacer tu presentación

• todo lo que dices tiene relación con tu tema

• el público puede entender tu presentación

Enriching Your Teaching

RUBRIC	Score 1	Score 3	Score 5
How well you organize your ideas	You have too few ideas. Your ideas aren't organized.	Some organizational problems make your speech hard to follow.	You organize ideas well, making your speech easy to follow.
How well you use details	You include no details in your speech.	You include one or two interesting details, but need more.	Good use of details makes your speech interesting.
How effectively you deliver your speech	You read your speech and make no eye contact with your audience.	You make some eye contact, and you use some intonation.	Your eye contact is good. Your intonation helps get your message across.

Actividades en mi comunidad

Tarea

Imagínate que tienes que hacer una página Web describiendo las actividades que hacen los jóvenes de tu ciudad. Imagina que la página Web la leen jóvenes de otros países que planean visitar los Estados Unidos y necesitan información sobre las diferentes cosas que pueden hacer en tu ciudad.

Estrategia

Evaluate your lead to see whether added details might help to generate more interest in your topic. Make notes to suggest areas for further development, and jot down ideas that will make the paragraphs and the information more appealing.

1 Antes de escribir Piensa en los siguientes temas para incluir en tu página Web:

- gimnasios
- cines y teatros
- restaurantes
- lugares para bailar

- lugares para hacer amigos
- escuelas de instrumentos musicales, idiomas, computación
- lugares para ir de compras

2 Borrador Escribe tu borrador de la página Web. Usa la información de arriba. Piensa en las ilustraciones que acompañan a la página Web.

3 Redacción/Revisión Trabaja con otro(a) estudiante para intercambiar los borradores de las páginas Web y leerlos. Habla de qué se puede hacer para mejorar el borrador.

- ¿Incluye la página Web información sobre los temas de la sección *Antes de escribir*?
- ¿Usaste la forma correcta de los verbos y adjetivos posesivos?

4 Publicación Revisa otra vez tu borrador y escribe el texto de la página Web en una hoja grande de papel para hacer un póster. Añade fotos o ilustraciones para decorar la página.

5 Evaluación Tu profesor(a) puede explicarte cómo va a evaluar tu presentación. Probablemente, para tu profesor(a) es importante ver que:

- usaste suficiente información en tu página Web
- añadiste detalles interesantes
- usaste correctamente las palabras y la gramática de esta sección

Las actividades de los jóvenes

quince   15
Para empezar

Enriching Your Teaching

RUBRIC	Score 1	Score 3	Score 5
Completion of task	Your Web page is incomplete.	Your Web page is complete, but some parts still need work.	Your Web page is complete and carefully revised.
Effective development	Your topic is undeveloped.	You have some ideas that enhance your topic.	Your ideas are all well developed and enhance your topic.
Grammar, spelling, mechanics	You make many grammar, spelling, and/or mechanics errors.	You make some grammar, spelling, and/or mechanics errors.	You make very few grammar, spelling, or mechanics errors.

Communicate: Writing

Presentación escrita

Presentation

Standards: 1.2, 1.3, 3.1

Focus: Combining review vocabulary and structures in a written presentation

Suggestions: Begin by explaining the criteria you will use to evaluate students' compositions. (See step 5, *Evaluación,* in the Student Edition, and *Assessment* below.)

Direct students' attention to the *Estrategia.* Point out that to evaluate their lead, they can simply ask classmates and other students for their opinions on the activities that they want to include on their Web page. If the people they ask don't think an activity is interesting, they should abandon that idea and think of another activity for their Web page. Point out also that talking with other people this way often generates new and better ideas. Students should write down ideas that they like and try to include them in their Web page.

In step 2, students should concentrate on the general layout of their Web page and fitting in the information they want to include.

In step 3, students should pay closer attention to the written portions of their Web page, in particular to their use of verbs and possessive adjectives.

Evaluation

Steps 4 and 5 overlap. Students will need evaluation by you, their peers, or self-evaluation to fine-tune and polish their drafts.

Portfolio

Keep students' final drafts in their portfolios as a writing sample.

✓ Assessment

- Assessment Program: Cap. PE, Rubrics

Give students copies of the rubric before they begin the activity. Go over the descriptions of the different levels of performance. After assessing students, help individuals understand how their performance could be improved.

Días inolvidables

CHAPTER OVERVIEW

Días inolvidables
- Memorable outdoor experiences and competitions

Vocabulary:
- camping and weather
- athletic events and competitions

Grammar:
- preterite tense of verbs with i → y, e → i, o → u spelling changes
- preterite tense of irregular verbs: *tener, andar, estar, poder, poner, saber, venir, decir,* and *traer*
- imperfect tense
- imperfect tense of irregular verbs *ir, ser,* and *ver*

Cultural Perspectives:
- national parks in Chile, Argentina, and Mexico
- different kinds of competitions
- the annual pilgrimage to the Cathedral of Santiago de Compostela in Spain
- the legend of Iztaccíhuatl and Popocatépetl, two volcanoes in Mexico

Chapter Project

Club de exploradores

Overview: Students research and create a proposal for a trip to a national park or other outdoor tourist attraction in Spain or Latin America to present to their Explorer's Club or the class. Presentations should include several photos of the site mounted on posterboard, each with a descriptive caption. Students then present their proposal explaining where the park is, how club members would get there, what they would need to bring, and what there is to see and do there.

Materials: poster board, markers, photos, glue, scissors

• •

Sequence: (suggestions for when to do each step are found throughout the chapter)

STEP 1. Review instructions so students know what's expected of them. Hand out the "Chapter 1 Project Instructions and Rubric" from the *Teacher's Resource Book.*

STEP 2. Students submit a draft of their proposal including the name and location of their destination, what the club would need to bring, and why they might want to go there. Return the proposal with your suggestions.

STEP 3. Students do layout on poster board, leaving room for photos and captions. Encourage them to work in pencil first and to try different arrangements before gluing the photos into place.

STEP 4. Students submit a draft of their photo captions. Note your corrections and suggestions, then return drafts to students.

STEP 5. Students present their proposals to the class, explaining where the park is, how the club would get there, and what they could expect to see and do.

• •

Options:
1. Students write and create an article for a Travel magazine with photos and captions about a national park in Spain or Latin America.
2. Students research and create a proposal for a trip back in time to an earlier civilization in Spain or Latin America.

Assessment:

Here is a detailed rubric for assessing this project:

Chapter 1 Project: *Club de exploradores*

RUBRIC	Score 1	Score 2	Score 3
Your evidence of planning	You provide preliminary proposal or caption drafts provided.	Your preliminary proposal and captions are created, but not corrected.	You show evidence of corrected proposal and captions.
Your use of illustrations	You include photos.	You include photos, but layout is disorganized.	You include photos, and your presentation is easy to read and convincing.
Your presentation	You do not include the required information.	You include most of the required information.	You include all of the required information.

Bulletin Boards

Competencias diferentes

Ask students to cut out or copy photos of all different types of competitions from many different cultures. Arrange the pictures into three categories: team-oriented competitions, individual competitions, and personal competition.

Bibliography

Gitlitz, David and Linda Kay Davidson. *Pilgrimage Road to Santiago*. New York: St. Martin's Press, 2000. Guide to the cultural history of the road for pilgrims, hikers and other travelers.

Heifetz, Milton D. and Wil Tirion. *A Walk Through the Southern Sky: A Guide to Stars and Constellations and their Legends*. Cambridge University press, 2000. A comprehensive guide to the stars in the southern hemisphere.

Lindenmayer, Clem. *Trekking in the Patagonian Andes*. Lonely Planet Publications, 1998. Guidebook to walks in Patagonia.

Neilson, David. *Patagonia: Images of a Wild Land*. Snowgum Press, 1999. Collection of photographs featuring the Andean regions of Patagonia and Tierra del Fuego.

Vigil, Angel, ed. *The Eagle and the Cactus*. Greenwood Publishing Group Inc., 2000. A collection of legends essential to the Mexican oral tradition.

Hands-on Culture

Recipe: *Pastel de choclo*

Pastel de choclo (corn pie) is one of the most popular Chilean dishes.

Ingredients:

For the meat mixture:
  1 chicken breast, skinned/boned
  8 oz. hamburger, extra lean
  1/4 tsp. salt
  1/4 tsp. black pepper
  1/2 cup raisins
  2 tbsp. kalamata olives, chopped

For the corn topping:
  1/2 tbsp. canola oil
  1/8 tsp. paprika
  1 med. onion, finely chopped
  16 oz. corn kernels, thawed
  1/2 cup milk, non-fat
  1/4 tsp. cumin, ground
  1/4 tsp. salt
  1/4 tsp. black pepper

1. Heat oven to 400 degrees. Spray skillet with non-stick vegetable spray; place over medium heat until hot. Cook chicken breast 2 minutes on each side. Remove from skillet; set aside.

2. Put beef in same skillet; cook, stirring constantly, until no longer pink. Stir in salt, pepper, raisins, and olives. Spoon 1/4 of mixture into each of 4 small, oven-proof bowls, or one 8-by-8-inch baking dish. Cut cooked chicken breast into quarters; place 1 quarter on top of meat in each bowl.

3. Combine oil and paprika in same skillet; place over medium heat until hot. Add onion and cook, stirring frequently, until soft and translucent, about 5 minutes. While onion is cooking, combine thawed corn, milk, cumin, salt, and pepper in food processor; puree.

4. Add pureed corn mixture to cooked onion in skillet; mix well. Continue cooking 5 minutes. Spoon 1/4 of corn mixture over top of each bowl of meat. Bake until bubbly and nicely browned, 35 to 40 minutes.

Game

¡Vamos de cámping en las sierras!

This memory game practices camping vocabulary. Use it after completing the first *A primera vista* section.

Players: 6 to 8

Materials: Scarf for blindfold

Rules:

1. Players sit in a circle. Choose a player to start. This player begins by saying *Para ir de cámping en las montañas, traigo _____*. Then the player proceeds to say why that item would be useful. For example: *Para ir de cámping en las montañas, traigo una linterna porque necesito ver cuando es de noche.*

2. The next player on the right then repeats the initial sentence, repeating the first player's item and adding one of his or her own plus a reason for bringing that item. For example: *Para ir de cámping en las montañas, traigo una linterna porque necesito ver cuando es de noche. También traigo una brújula para no perderme.*

3. Play continues until everyone in the circle has a chance to add an item to the list.

4. Play again, starting with the player who ended the previous game and going to the left around the circle.

Variation: Play with a larger group of students and review other vocabulary such as articles of clothing and other supplies that might be useful on a camping trip in the mountains.

Internet Search

Use the keywords to find more information.

Keywords:

astronomía + la Cruz del Sur, la Olimpiada Iberoamericana de Matemáticas, la Catedral de Santiago de Compostela, Teotihuacán, chichimeca, tolteca, náhuatl

A ver si recuerdas
RECYCLE

Vocabulary
- Outdoor activities
- Sports and competition
- Accidents in sports

Vocabulary
- Preterite of verbs
- Preterite of *ir, ser* and verbs ending in *-car, -gar,* and *-zar*

Chapter Overview

A primera vista 1	Manos a la obra 1	A primera vista 2	Manos a la obra 2
INPUT	**PRACTICE**	**INPUT**	**PRACTICE**
Objectives • Read about camping activities • Discuss features of the natural environment	**Objectives** • Communicate about camping equipment and activities • Talk about events in the past	**Objectives** • Read about athletic events and other kinds of competitions • Talk about goals and prizes	**Objectives** • Communicate about different kinds of competitions • React to the outcome of an event
Vocabulary • Outdoor activities • Natural environment and weather	**Vocabulary** • Practice new vocabulary	**Vocabulary** • Sports and competitions	**Vocabulary** • Practice new vocabulary
Grammar • Verbs with a spelling change and stem change in the preterite • Irregular verbs in the preterite	**Grammar** • Verbs with a spelling change and stem change in the preterite • Irregular verbs in the preterite	**Grammar** • Imperfect • Uses of the imperfect	**Grammar** • Imperfect • Uses of the imperfect
Culture • The Chilean landscape • Nature in a Chilean national park	**Culture** • National parks in South America • Ecocamps in Chile	**Culture** • Sports events in the Spanish world	**Culture** • The International Olympics of Math • Spanish speakers and football

¡Adelante!
APPLICATION

Objectives
- Read about a famous pilgrimage in Spain
- Narrate a special experience in the past tense

- Read about a Mexican legend and make predictions

Vocabulary
- Application

Grammar
- Application

Culture
- Pilgrims and the *Camino de Santiago*

- The Mexican legend of Iztaccíhuatl and Popocatépetl
- Indigeneous people of Mexico

Repaso del capítulo
REVIEW

Objectives
- Prepare for the chapter test

- Perform the tasks on pp. 60 and 61

Vocabulary
- Review

Grammar
- Review

BEYOND THE CLASSROOM

Countries
- Mexico
- Argentina
- Chile
- Spain
- United States

El español en el mundo del trabajo
- Spanish-speakers in the world of sports (football)

Internet
- Vocabulary activities
- Grammar activities
- Internet links
- Self-tests

LEARNER SUPPORT

Strategies
- Cause and effect
- Order of events
- Describing events
- Use prior knowledge

- Choosing a topic
- Adding details
- Making predictions

Recycling
- *obtener* in the preterite

- *competir* and *conseguir* in the preterite
- *d* between two vowels

En voz alta
- *Himno del Barcelona*

Ampliación del lenguaje
- *ir de...*

Conexiones
- Science: The sky in South America
- Math: Rain in the Atacama desert

Print Components

TEACHER

Teacher's Resource Book
- Chapter Table of Contents
- School-to-Home Connection
- Chapter Resource Checklist
- Input Script
- Audio Script
- Video Script
- Communicative Activities
- Situation Cards
- GramActiva Blackline Masters
- Graphic Organizers
- Answer Keys:
  Practice Workbook
  Writing, Audio & Video Workbook

***Realidades para hispanohablantes*
Teacher Edition**

STUDENT

Practice Workbook
- Vocabulary: 1-1 – 1-4, 1-8 – 1-9
- Grammar: 1-5 – 1-7, 1-10 – 1-12
- Organizer: 1-13 – 1-14

Writing, Audio & Video Workbook
- Audio: 1–5
- Writing: 6–13
- Video: 14–17

Reading and Writing for Success
- Chapter 1, Test 28

Realidades para hispanohablantes

Transparencies

Vocabulary and Grammar Transparencies
- Vocabulary: 32–39, 43–45
- Grammar: 40–42, 46–47
- ¿Qué me cuentas?: 48

Practice Answers on Transparencies
- Cap. 1

Fine Art Transparencies
- Transparencies
- Teacher's Guide

Assessment

Assessment Program
- Pruebas:
  - Comprensión del vocabulario 1: 1-1
  - Aplicación del vocabulario 1: 1-2
  - El pretérito de verbos con el cambio ortográfico *i* → *y*: 1-3
  - El pretérito de los verbos irregulares: 1-4
  - El pretérito de verbos con los cambios *e* → *i, o* → *u* en la raíz: 1-5
  - Comprensión del vocabulario 2: 1-6
  - Aplicación del vocabulario 2: 1-7
  - El imperfecto: 1-8
  - Usos del imperfecto: 1-9

- Exámenes del capítulo

- Rubrics

Alternative Assessment
- ExamView Test Bank CD-ROM
- MindPoint Quiz Show CD-ROM
- Internet Self-test
- Situation Cards
- Communicative Activity

Assessment Program: *Realidades para hispanohablantes*

Technology

TeacherExpress™ CD-ROM
- Lesson Planner
- Teacher Resources
- Clip Art

Video Program VHS and DVD

Audio Program CDs
- A primera vista 1 y 2: Vocabulario y gramática en contexto
- Audio Activities
- ¿Qué me cuentas?
- Repaso
- Examen del capítulo: Escuchar

Regular Schedule (50 Minutes)

For electronic lesson plans:
Teacher Express CD-ROM

	Warm-up / Assess	Preview Present / Practice Communicate	Wrap-up / Homework Options
DAY 1	**Warm-up (10 min.)** • Return Prueba from Para empezar	**Repaso (35 min.)** • A ver si recuerdas. . . • Actividades 1, 4 , 5	**Wrap-up and Homework Options (5 min.)** • Actividades 2, 3, 6, 7 • Practice Workbook 1-1, 1-2 • Go Online
DAY 2	**Warm-up (10 min.)** • Homework check	**Chapter Opener (5 min.)** • Objectives **A primera vista 1 (30 min.)** • Presentation: Vocabulario y gramática en contexto • Actividades 1, 2	**Wrap-up and Homework Options (5 min.)** • Go Online • Clip Art Vocabulary
DAY 3	**Warm-up (10 min.)** • Homework check	**A primera vista 1 (35 min.)** • Presentation: Una aventura desastrosa • Actividad 3	**Wrap-up and Homework Options (5 min.)** • Practice Workbook 1-3, 1-4 • Go Online • Manos a la obra 1: Actividad 4 • Prueba 1-1: Vocabulary recognition
DAY 4	**Warm-up (10 min.)** • Homework check ✔**Assessment (10 min.)** • Prueba 1-1: Vocabulary recognition	**Manos a la obra 1 (25 min.)** • Actividades 6, 7, 9, 11 • Ampliación del lenguaje • Audio Activity 1	**Wrap-up and Homework Options (5 min.)** • Actividades: 8, 10 • Prueba 1-2: Vocabulary production • Writing Activity 6
DAY 5	**Warm-up (10 min.)** • Homework check ✔**Assessment (10 min.)** • Prueba 1-2: Vocabulary production	**Manos a la obra 1 (25 min.)** • Fondo cultural • Actividades 12, 13, 14, 15 • Presentation: El pretérito de verbos con el cambio ortográfico *i → y*	**Wrap-up and Homework Options (5 min.)** • Practice Workbook 1-5 • Prueba 1-3: El pretérito de verbos con el cambio ortográfico *i → y* • Go Online • Writing Activity 7
DAY 6	**Warm-up (10 min.)** • Homework check ✔**Assessment (10 min.)** • Prueba 1-3: Presentación: El pretérito de verbos con el cambio ortográfico *i → y*	**Manos a la obra 1 (25 min.)** • Presentation: El pretérito de los verbos irregulares • Actividades 16, 18	**Wrap-up and Homework Options (5 min.)** • Practice Workbook 1-6 • Writing Activity 8 • Go Online • Prueba 1-4: El pretérito de los verbos irregulares
DAY 7	**Warm-up (10 min.)** • Actividad 17 • Homework check ✔**Assessment (10 min.)** • Prueba 1-4: El pretérito de los verbos irregulares	**Manos a la obra (25 min.)** • Presentation: El pretérito de verbos con los cambios *e → i, o → u* en la raíz • Actividades 19, 20, 21, 22, 23, 24 • Audio Activity 2	**Wrap-up and Homework Options (5 min.)** • Practice Workbook 1-7 • Go Online • Writing Activity 9 • Communicative Activity
DAY 8	**Warm-up (10 min.)** • Actividad 25 • Homework check ✔**Assessment (10 min.)** • Prueba 1-5	**A primera vista 2 (25 min.)** • Presentation: Vocabulario y gramática en contexto • Actividades 26, 27	**Wrap-up and Homework Options (5 min.)** • Clip Art Vocabulary • Examen: Vocabulario y gramática 1
DAY 9	**Warm-up (10 min.)** • Homework check ✔**Assessment (25 min.)** • Examen: Vocabulario y gramática 1	**A primera vista 2 (10 min.)** • Presentation: La voz del estudiante • Actividad 29	**Wrap-up and Homework Options (5 min.)** • Actividades 28, 30 • Practice Workbook 1-8, 1-9 • Go Online • Prueba 1-6: Vocabulary recognition
DAY 10	**Warm-up (10 min.)** • Actividad 31 • Homework check ✔**Assessment (10 min.)** • Prueba 1-6: Vocabulary recognition	**Manos a la obra 2 (25 min.)** • Actividades 32, 33, 34, 35 • Fondo cultural • Audio Activity 3	**Wrap-up and Homework Options (5 min.)** • Writing Activity 10 • Prueba 1-7: Vocabulary production

	Warm-up / Assess	Preview Present / Practice Communicate	Wrap-up / Homework Options
DAY 11	**Warm-up (10 min.)** • Activity 11 • Homework check ✔**Assessment (10 min.)** • Prueba 1-7: Vocabulary production	**Manos a la obra 2 (25 min.)** • Presentation: El imperfecto • Actividades 36, 37, 38	**Wrap-up and Homework Options (5 min.)** • Practice Workbook 1-10 • Go Online • Prueba 1-8: El imperfecto
DAY 12	**Warm-up (10 min.)** • Homework check ✔**Assessment (10 min.)** • Prueba 1-8: El imperfecto	**Manos a la obra 2 (25 min.)** • Presentation: Usos del imperfecto • Actividades 39, 40, 41 • El español en el mundo del trabajo	**Wrap-up and Homework Options (5 min.)** • Practice Workbook 1-11, 1-12 • Go Online • Prueba 1-9: El imperfecto • En voz alta
DAY 13	**Warm-up (10 min.)** • Actividad 43 • Homework check ✔**Assessment (10 min.)** • Prueba 1-9: Usos del imperfecto	**Manos a la obra 2 (25 min.)** • Actividades 42, 44 • Audio Activities 4, 5 • Writing Activities 12, 13 • Communicative Activity	**Wrap-up and Homework Options (5 min.)** • Go Online • Examen: Vocabulario y gramática 2
DAY 14	**Warm-up (10 min.)** • Homework check ✔**Assessment (30 min.)** • Examen: Vocabulario y gramática 2	**¡Adelante! (8 min.)** • Presentación oral: Step 1	**Wrap-up and Homework Options (2 min.)** • Presentación oral: Step 2
DAY 15	**Warm-up (10 min.)** • Presentación oral: Step 2	**¡Adelante! (35 min.)** • Presentación oral: Step 3	**Wrap-up and Homework Options (5 min.)** • El Camino de Santiago • Go Online • ¿Comprendiste? • Mi propio camino
DAY 16	**Warm-up (15 min.)** • El Camino de Santiago: ¿Comprendiste? • Homework check	**¡Adelante! (30 min.)** • ¿Qué me cuentas? 1, 2, 3 • View Video	**Wrap-up and Homework Options (5 min.)** • Presentación escrita: Steps 1, 2
DAY 17	**Warm-up (10 min.)** • Homework check	**¡Adelante! (15 min.)** • Presentación escrita: Step 3 **Repaso (20 min.)** • Preparación para el examen: Actividades 3, 6 • MindPoint Quiz Show	**Wrap-up and Homework Options (5 min.)** • Presentación escrita: Step 4 • Fondo cultural
DAY 18	**Warm-up (10 min.)** • Homework check	**¡Adelante! (35 min.)** • Lectura • Interacción con la lectura • Vocabulario y gramática	**Wrap-up and Homework Options (5 min.)** • Practice Workbook: Organizer 1-13, 1-14 • Go Online: Self-test
DAY 19	**Warm-up (20 min.)** • Preparación para el examen: Actividades 1, 2 • Homework check	**Repaso (25 min.)** • Preparación para el examen: Actividades 4, 5, 7 • MindPoint Quiz Show • Other review	**Wrap-up and Homework Options (5 min.)** • Examen del capítulo
DAY 20	**Warm-up (5 min.)** • Answer questions ✔**Assessment (44 min.)** • Examen del capítulo		**Wrap-up and Homework Options (1 min.)** • A ver si recuerdas: Capítulo 2

Block Schedule (90 minutes)

For electronic lesson plans:
Teacher Express CD-ROM

	Warm-up / Assess	Preview Present / Practice Communicate	Wrap-up / Homework Options
DAY 1	**Warm-up (10 min.)** • Return Prueba from Para empezar	**A ver si recuerdas (30 min.)** • Presentation: Vocabulario p. 16 • Actividad 1 • Presentation: Gramática p. 17 • Actividades 2, 3 **A primera vista 1 (35 min.)** • Objectives • Presentation: Vocabulario y gramática en contexto • Actividades 1, 2 **Manos a la obra 1 (10 min.)** • Actividades 4, 5 • Presentation: Vocabulario p. 18 • Actividades 4, 5 • Presentation: Gramática p. 19 • Actividades 6, 7 • Presentation: ¡Una aventura desastrosa! • Actividad 3	**Wrap-up and Homework Options (5 min.)** • Practice Workbook 1-1 to 1-4 • Go Online • Clip Art Vocabulary
DAY 2	**Warm-up (10 min.)** • Vocabulario y gramática en contexto • ¡Una aventura desastrosa! • Homework check ✔**Assessment (10 min.)** • Prueba 1-1: Vocabulary recognition	**Manos a la obra 1 (65 min.)** • Actividades 6, 7, 10, 11, 13 • Ampliación del lenguaje • Fondo cultural • Communicative Activity	**Wrap Up and Homework Options (5 min.)** • Go Online • Writing Activities • Prueba 1-2: Vocabulary production
DAY 3	**Warm-up (10 min.)** • Writing Activity • Homework check **Manos a la obra 1 (20 min.)** • Actividad 12 ✔**Assessment (10 min.)** • Prueba 1-2: Vocabulary production	**Manos a la obra 1 (45 min.)** • Presentation: El pretérito de verbos con el cambio ortográfico $i \rightarrow y$ • Actividades 14, 15 • Presentation: El pretérito de verbos irregulares • Actividades 16, 17, 18 • Actividades 24, 25	**Wrap-up and Homework Options (5 min.)** • Practice Workbook 1-5, 1-6 • Go Online • Pruebas 1-3, 1-4: El pretérito de verbos con el cambio ortográfico $i \rightarrow y$, • El pretérito de verbos irregulares
DAY 4	**Warm-up (10 min.)** • Writing Activity • Homework check ✔**Assessment: (20 min.)** • Pruebas 1-3, 1-4: El pretérito de verbos con el cambio ortográfico $i \rightarrow y$ • El pretérito de verbos irregulares	**Manos a la obra 1 (40 min.)** • Presentation: El pretérito de verbos con los cambios $e \rightarrow i$, $o \rightarrow u$ en la raíz • Actividades 19, 20, 21, 22, 23 • Writing Activity • Communicative Activity **A primera vista 2 (15 min.)** • Presentation: Vocabulario y gramática en contexto • Actividades 26, 27	**Wrap-up and Homework Options (5 min.)** • Practice Workbook 1-7 • Go Online • Prueba 1-5: El pretérito de verbos con los cambios $e \rightarrow i$, $o \rightarrow u$ en la raíz • Examen: Vocabulario y gramática 1
DAY 5	**Warm-up (10 min.)** • Homework check ✔**Assessment Options: (40 min.)** • Prueba 1-5: El pretérito de verbos con los cambios $e \rightarrow i$, $o \rightarrow u$ en la raíz • Examen: Vocabulario y gramática 1	**A primera vista 2 (25 min.)** • Presentation: La voz del estudiante • Actividades 28, 29, 30, 31 **Manos a la obra 2 (10 min.)** • Actividad 32 • Fondo cultural	**Wrap-up and Homework Options (5 min.)** • Practice Workbook 1-8, 1-9 • Go Online • Prueba 1-6: Vocabulary recognition
DAY 6	**Warm-up (10 min.)** • Homework check ✔**Assessment (10 min.)** • Prueba 1-6: Vocabulary recognition	**Manos a la obra 2 (65 min.)** • Actividades 33, 34, 35 • Presentation: El imperfecto • Actividades 36, 37, 38	**Wrap-up and Homework Options (5 min.)** • Practice Workbook 1-10 • Go Online • Pruebas 1-7, 1-8: Vocabulary production, El imperfecto

	Warm-up / Assess	Preview Present / Practice Communicate	Wrap-up / Homework Options
DAY 7	**Warm-up (10 min.)** • Writing Activity • Homework check **Assessment (20 min.)** • Pruebas 1-7, 1-8: Vocabulary production, El imperfecto	**Manos a la obra 2 (40 min.)** • Presentation: Usos del imperfecto • Actividades 39, 40, 41 • El español en el mundo del trabajo **¡Adelante! (15 min.)** • Presentación oral: Steps 1, 2	**Wrap-up and Homework Options (5 min.)** • Presentación oral: Step 2 • Go Online
DAY 8	**Warm-up (15 min.)** • Actividad 43 • Homework check **Assessment (40 min.)** • Presentación oral: Step 3	**Manos a la obra 2 (30 min.)** • En voz alta • Actividades 42, 43, 44 • Communicative Activity	**Wrap-up and Homework Options (5 min.)** • Practice Workbook 1-11, 1-12 • Go Online • Prueba 1-9: Usos del imperfecto • Examen: Vocabulario y gramática 2
DAY 9	**Warm-up (10 min.)** • Writing Activity • Homework check **Assessment Options: (30 min.)** • Prueba 1-9: Usos del imperfecto • Examen: Vocabulario y gramática 2	**¡Adelante! (45 min.)** • El Camino de Santiago • ¿Comprendiste? • ¿Qué me cuentas? 1, 2, 3 • Video • Video Activities • Presentación escrita: Step 1	**Wrap-up and Homework Options (5 min.)** • Presentación escrita: Step 2 • Go Online • Preparación para el examen: Actividades 1, 2
DAY 10	**Warm-up (20 min.)** • Presentación escrita: Step 3 • Homework check	**¡Adelante! (35 min.)** • Lectura • Interacción con la lectura • Fondo cultural **Repaso (30 min.)** • Preparación para el examen: Actividades 3, 6 • MindPoint Quiz • Preparación para el examen: Actividades 4, 5, 7	**Wrap-up and Homework Options (5 min.)** • Presentación escrita: Step 4 • Practice Workbook: Organizer 1-13, 1-14 • Go Online: Self-test • Preparación para el examen: Actividades 4, 5, 7 • Examen del capítulo
DAY 11	**Warm-up (10 min.)** • Homework check **Assessment (45 min.)** • Examen del capítulo	**Theme Game (20 min.)** **A ver si recuerdas – Capítulo 2 (10 min.)** • Presentation: Vocabulario (all) • Presentation: Gramática (all)	**Wrap-up and Homework Options (5 min.)** • A ver si recuerdas – Capítulo 2 • Actividades 1–6

Vocabulario

Standards: 1.1, 1.2

Resources: Voc. & Gram. Transparencies: 32

Suggestions: Show the blank organizer and have students copy it on a sheet of paper. With the book closed, students work in groups of two and list as many words as they can remember in each category.

Actividad 1

Standards: 1.1, 1.3

Focus: Practicing review vocabulary

Suggestions: Remind students to use the word web as a source for ideas. Encourage them to use vocabulary and expressions that they might know which are not on the list.

Common Errors: Following English logic, some students may talk about weather conditions attempting to use *estar* + adjective when *hacer* + noun would more commonly be used in Spanish. Provide repeated models of the *hacer* construction.

Extension: Have students take notes on what their partner says and later use the notes to write a paragraph with complete sentences.

Answers will vary.

A ver si recuerdas...

Vocabulario

Lugares
el campo
el lago
el mar
las montañas
el parque
la playa
el río

El tiempo
llueve (llover)
nieva (nevar)
hace . . .
buen tiempo
calor
frío
mal tiempo

Actividades
dar una caminata
ir de pesca
ir de vacaciones
ir de viaje
montar en bicicleta
montar a caballo
tomar el sol

Otras actividades
hacer . . .
esquí acuático
moto acuática
surf de vela
una fogata
una parrillada
un picnic

Animales / Insectos
las hormigas
el mono
los mosquitos
el oso
el pájaro
los peces

Actividad 1   **Escribir/Hablar** ....

Práctica de vocabulario

1 Escoge dos lugares de la lista adonde a veces vas de vacaciones. Escribe dos actividades que haces allí, el tiempo que hace y los animales que puedes encontrar.

2 Ahora trabaja con otro(a) estudiante para hablar de sus vacaciones. Usen palabras de las listas.

• Y tú, ¿adónde vas de vacaciones generalmente?
Voy a . . .

• ¿Qué actividades te gusta hacer allí?
Me gusta . . .

• ¿Qué tiempo hace?
Hace . . .

Have students break into groups of four. Taking turns, each student has to stand up and pantomine a vocabulary word from the word web. The other students in the group have to guess the word. Alternate students acting out words until all the words have been used or you call time.

Heritage Language Learners
Assign students one or more of the following from the *Actividades* list: **dar un(a), ir de, montar en/a,** or **tomar.** Ask them to think of as many expressions as they can that begin with their assigned word(s), such as **dar una vuelta, ir de compras, montar en bicicleta** or **tomar precauciones.**

Advanced Learners
Have students apply the same expressions to other situations: *¿Adónde vas los fines de semana?*

Gramática · Repaso

El pretérito de los verbos

You use the preterite to talk about things that happened in the past.
Here are the regular preterite forms of verbs ending in *-ar, -er,* and *-ir:*

caminar

caminé	caminamos
caminaste	caminasteis
caminó	caminaron

comer

comí	comimos
comiste	comisteis
comió	comieron

vivir

viví	vivimos
viviste	vivisteis
vivió	vivieron

Here are the preterite forms of the irregular verbs *hacer, dar,* and *ver:*

hacer

hice	hicimos
hiciste	hicisteis
hizo	hicieron

dar

di	dimos
diste	disteis
dio	dieron

ver

vi	vimos
viste	visteis
vio	vieron

 Actividad 2 Leer/Escribir

Práctica de gramática

Carmen describe lo que hizo su familia durante el fin de semana. Completa las siguientes frases con la forma correcta del pretérito de los verbos.

hacer	visitar	correr	dar
pasear	comer	aprender	ver

1. (Yo) _____ a mis abuelos.
2. Mis hermanos _____ en bote.
3. Tú _____ muchas películas.
4. Nosotros _____ a montar a caballo.
5. Mi padre _____ caminatas.
6. Mis primos _____ por la playa.
7. Tú y yo _____ helados.
8. Mi hermana _____ ejercicio.

 Actividad 3 Escribir/Hablar

Práctica de gramática

1 Haz una lista de ocho actividades que tú y otras personas hicieron durante las vacaciones pasadas.

Modelo

Caminé por la playa.
Mi familia y yo hicimos un picnic en el campo.

2 Con otro(a) estudiante hablen de sus vacaciones. Comparen las actividades que hicieron.

Presentation

Resources: Voc. & Gram. Transparencies: 33

Suggestions: Allow students a few minutes to read through the grammar review on their own. Continue by using verbal cues to elicit preterite forms of regular verbs such as **ayer, anoche, la semana pasada,** or **el año pasado.**

 Actividad 2 *Standards:* 1.2

Resources: Practice Answers on Transparencies

Focus: Practicing regular preterite verb forms

Suggestions: After students complete the activity, have them check their answers with a partner.

Common Errors: Students commonly confuse first- and third-person preterite endings. Provide them with this mnemonic device: The first-person endings are **-e** as in the English first-person **"me"** and **-i** as in English first-person **"I."**

Answers:
1. visité
2. pasearon
3. viste
4. aprendimos
5. dio
6. corrieron
7. comimos
8. hizo

 Actividad 3 *Standards:* 1.1, 1.3

Focus: Reviewing regular preterite verb forms

Suggestions: Remind students that they can use the verbs on p. 16 to complete this activity.

Answers will vary.

Extension: Ask students to write a list of activities they did at another time in the past: **ayer en la clase...; el fin de semana pasado....**

Enriching Your Teaching

Teacher-to-Teacher

Have students work in pairs to practice preterite verb forms. Student A cues Student B by asking if he or she is doing something in the present. Student B gives a negative response, adds that he or she did that thing yesterday, and asks Student A another question:

A —¿Hablas con Rita hoy?
B —No, pero hablé con ella ayer.
B —¿Vemos una película en clase hoy?
A —No, pero vimos una película en clase ayer.

Vocabulario

Presentation

Standards: 1.1, 1.2

Resources: Voc. & Gram. Transparencies: 34

Suggestions: Have students use the vocabulary to talk about the photos. Help them expand on their statements with questions such as *¿A cuántos jugadores ves en la foto?* For names of parts of the body, use a picture from a magazine or bring in a doll. Point to various parts of the body and have students name them.

Standards: 1.1, 1.2

Focus: Practicing review vocabulary

Suggestions: Model intonation as necessary and encourage students to speak with intonation that is appropriate for the sentence.

Answers will vary.

Extension: Have each student write two sentences that are similar to the exercise items: one about a positive occurrence and one about a negative one. Then have partners take turns reading and reacting to their sentences.

Standards: 1.2, 1.3

Resources: Practice Answers on Transparencies

Focus: Practicing review vocabulary

Suggestions: Have students check their answers with a partner orally. Reading the items aloud will provide additional pronunciation practice.

Answers:
1. a   2. d   3. b   4. e   5. c

Extension: Invite students who wrote stories to read them aloud. Encourage those who wrote dialogues to act them out with you or a partner.

Vocabulario

Deportes
- correr
- esquiar
- jugar al fútbol
- montar en monopatín
- nadar
- navegar
- patinar

Reacciones
- ¡Fantástico!
- ¡Genial!
- ¡Increíble!
- Lo siento.
- ¡Qué lástima!
- ¡Qué pena!
- ¡Uy!

Acciones
- ganar
- jugar
- participar
- perder
- practicar

El cuerpo
- el brazo
- el codo
- el dedo
- el hueso
- la mano
- la muñeca
- el músculo
- el pie
- la pierna
- la rodilla
- el tobillo

Accidentes
- caerse
- cortarse
- lastimarse
- romperse
- torcerse

Competencias
- el campeón, la campeona
- el campeonato
- la competencia
- competir
- el concurso
- el equipo
- el jugador, la jugadora
- el partido
- el premio
- el tanteo

Actividad 4
  Leer/Hablar ....

Práctica de vocabulario

Trabaja con otro(a) estudiante para leer y reaccionar a los comentarios siguientes.

Modelo

A —Perdimos el partido.
B —*¡Qué lástima!*

1. ¡Ganamos cinco a cero!
2. El jugador se cayó y se lastimó.
3. Me torcí el tobillo.
4. Nuestro equipo quedó campeón.
5. Les metimos tres goles.
6. ¡Perdimos el campeonato!
7. Hoy llovió y no pudimos jugar.

18 **dieciocho**
A ver si recuerdas . . .

Actividad 5
 Leer/Escribir ....

Práctica de vocabulario

Empareja cada definición con la palabra correspondiente. Luego, escribe un diálogo o un cuento usando cuatro de las palabras o expresiones de la segunda columna.

1. una parte del cuerpo que usas para jugar al fútbol
2. un grupo de personas que juegan un partido
3. la persona que siempre gana una competencia
4. lo que dices si te caes
5. un tipo de accidente

a. el pie
b. el campeón / la campeona
c. torcerse la muñeca
d. un equipo
e. ¡uy!

Universal Access

Students with Special Needs
Students with hearing disabilities may not be able to distinguish between the sounds of *-car* and *-gar*, or between *-qué* and *-gué.* Such minimal pairs may require exaggerated emphasis on the first consonant sound.

Students with Learning Difficulties
Using vocabulary clip art, have students sort vocabulary into appropriate categories: *la rodilla* goes in *partes del cuerpo* and so on.

Gramática · Repaso ....

El pretérito de los verbos *ir* y *ser* y de los verbos que terminan en *-car, -gar* y *-zar*

The preterite forms of *ir* and *ser* are exactly the same.

> Carlos **fue** de vacaciones a las montañas. (ir)
> Mi equipo **fue** campeón escolar el año pasado. (ser)

fui	fuimos
fuiste	fuisteis
fue	fueron

Remember that verbs ending in *-car, -gar,* or *-zar* have a spelling change in the *yo* form in the preterite. The other forms of these verbs are regular.

buscar	yo bus**qué**
chocar	yo cho**qué**
practicar	yo practi**qué**
sacar	yo sa**qué**

investigar	yo investi**gué**
navegar	yo nave**gué**
jugar	yo ju**gué**
llegar	yo lle**gué**

almorzar	yo almor**cé**
comenzar	yo comen**cé**
cruzar	yo cru**cé**
empezar	yo empe**cé**

Actividad 6 · Leer/Escribir ....

Práctica de gramática

En una hoja de papel escribe los números del 1 al 8. Completa las siguientes frases sobre el partido de ayer con el pretérito de *ser* o *ir*. Indica si usaste una forma del verbo *ser* o del verbo *ir*.

Modelo

Yo no *fui* al partido ayer. (*Ir*)

1. El partido de fútbol _____ ayer por la noche.
2. Todos los padres _____ al estadio.
3. Tú _____ el mejor jugador del equipo.
4. El partido _____ muy emocionante.
5. Este equipo _____ campeón hace dos años.
6. Durante el partido, nosotros _____ a comprar unas salchichas.
7. El partido duró más de tres horas. _____ muy largo.
8. Después del partido, los campeones _____ a celebrar a un restaurante.

Actividad 7 · Leer/Escribir ....

Práctica de gramática

Luisa no pudo hacer la tarea. Completa esta nota que le escribió a su profesora con la forma correcta del verbo apropiado.

> Estimada Srta. Herrera:
> Perdón, yo no pude hacer la tarea, por eso no la __1.__ (entregar / llegar). Ayer pensaba jugar al tenis pero no __2.__ (caminar / jugar). Por la mañana __3.__ (salir / llegar) al club deportivo. Después __4.__ (buscar / pintar) mi raqueta y la __5.__ (llevar / sacar) del bolso. Cuando yo __6.__ (ganar / empezar) a jugar __7.__ (comenzar / ir) a llover. Entonces __8.__ (cantar / tropezar) y me lastimé la mano. Esta nota la escribió mi hermano.
> Gracias, Luisa

● **Más práctica** ....
Practice Workbook 1-1, 1-2

Go Online
PHSchool.com
For: More review
Visit: www.phschool.com
Web Code: jed-0101

Gramática · Repaso

Presentation

Resources: Voc. & Gram. Transparencies: 35

Suggestions: Assign one verb from the charts to each student and ask them to use their verb in two sentences with two different subjects. Ask students to spell the ending of each verb form.

Actividad 6   *Standards:* 1.2

Resources: Practice Answers on Transparencies

Focus: Practicing preterite verb forms of *ir* and *ser*

Suggestions: Have students read their completed activity items aloud.

Answers:
1. fue/ser
2. fueron/ir
3. fuiste/ser
4. fue/ser
5. fue/ser
6. fuimos/ir
7. Fue/ser
8. fueron/ir

Common errors: Students tend to misspell **fueron**. Remind them there is no **"i"** in **fue** or **fueron**.

Extension: Ask students to use **ser** and **ir** to create and share two additional sentences about yesterday's soccer match.

Actividad 7   *Standards:* 1.2

Resources: Practice Answers on Transparencies

Focus: Reviewing preterite verb forms with spelling changes

Suggestions: Point out the reason for the spelling change in *-car* and *-gar* verbs: it allows the **c** and **g** consonants to retain their "hard" sound before the vowel **e.**

Answers:
1. entregué
2. jugué
3. salí
4. busqué
5. saqué
6. empecé
7. comenzó
8. tropecé

Enriching Your Teaching

Teacher-to-Teacher

It is always a good idea for students to continue to review the irregular preterite forms. Many students find it useful to create a section of their notebooks that contains the conjugations of the more common irregular verbs. They can add to the list throughout the year and it can serve as a convenient reference.

1 Preview

Standards for Foreign Language Learning: *Capítulo 1*

• To achieve the goals of the Standards, students will:

Communication

1.1 Interpersonal

• Talk about national parks, camping, and outdoor vacations
• Talk about competitive events
• Talk about geographic locations
• Talk about weather events
• Talk about fine art
• Talk about a party
• Talk about opinions
• Talk about childhood memories
• Talk about ancient pilgrimages
• Talk about Aztec myths

1.2 Interpretive

• Read and listen to information about national parks, camping, and outdoor vacations
• Read and listen to information about competitive events
• Read about geographic locations
• Read about weather events
• Read about fine art
• Read about a professional translator
• Read about childhood memories
• Read about ancient pilgrimages
• Read about Aztec myths

1.3 Presentational

• Write and present information orally about national parks, camping, and outdoor vacations
• Write and present information orally about competitive events
• Write about geographic locations
• Write about a party
• Write about childhood memories
• Write and present information orally about Aztec myths
• Present information orally about ancient pilgrimages

Culture

2.1 Practices and Perspectives

• Interpret pilgrimages in Spain
• Interpret the effects of Aztec myths in Mexico

2.2 Products and Perspectives

• Discuss Matilde Pérez and her paintings
• Discuss *El Camino de Santiago*
• Discuss the Aztec myths of *Iztaccíhuatl* and *Popocatépetl*

Connections

3.1 Cross-curricular

• Talk about an artist and her work: Matilde Pérez
• Explain Language Arts strategies: cause and effect, describing events, using prior knowledge, choosing a topic, adding details, making predictions
• Use the skill of using graphic organizers
• Describe constellations in the southern hemisphere
• Discuss key facts about Mexico and Spain

3.2 Target Culture

• Read the soccer team anthem, *Himno del Barcelona*
• Discuss how indigenous peoples have affected the language of Mexico
• Discuss how ancient pilgrimages have shaped travel practices in Spain today

Fondo cultural ■◆◇◇■◆■◇■◆

Paisaje chileno Imagínate un lugar que tiene el desierto más árido del mundo, glaciares eternos, volcanes, un inmenso océano y además majestuosas montañas. Pues este lugar no está sólo en tu imaginación. Se llama Chile y sus diversos paisajes han inspirado a famosos artistas. Entre ellos está la pintora Matilde Pérez (1920–), quien escogió el tema de la Cordillera de los Andes para crear este cuadro.

• ¿Qué paisaje es típico de la región donde vives? ¿Y cómo te hace sentir?

Paisaje chileno, Matilde Pérez

20 **veinte**

Universal Access

Personalizing the Theme

Ask students to think about outdoor activities they enjoy participating in with friends and family. Where do they go and what do they do? Does the activity involve any extensive travel? Do students share similar experiences?

Heritage Language Learners

Invite students to talk about the terrain and climate of their heritage countries. Is it flat or mountainous, like the terrain in the photo and the painting? Did they live in a rainy region or a desert? In what ways do the terrain and climate of an area affect the lives of people there?

Capítulo
1

Días inolvidables

Chapter Objectives

- **Describe a visit to a national park**
- **Talk about school competitions**
- **Express your emotions regarding the outcome of an event**
- **Narrate an event in the past**
- **Understand cultural perspectives on family outings**

Video Focus

- **Outdoor activities in the Spanish-speaking world**

Country Connection

As you learn about outdoor activities and competitions, you will make connections to these countries and places.

España

México

Chile

Argentina

Go Online
PHSchool.com

For: Online Atlas
Visit: www.phschool.com
Web Code: jee-0002

DK

veintiuno **21**
Capítulo 1

Preview

Standards for Foreign Language Learning (cont'd)

Comparisons
4.1 Language
- Compare Spanish words to their English counterparts
- Compare Spanish and English commands

4.2 Culture
- Compare ancient Central American ball games to modern ones
- Compare Spanish and Latin American teen magazines and their readership to those in the United States

Communities
5.1 Beyond the School
- Link to Web sites from around the Spanish-speaking world

5.2 Lifelong Learner
- Talk about important facts about healthy lifestyles
- Talk about important facts about scientific studies
- Develop an appreciation for the art of songwriting

Chapter Opener
Presentation

Resources: Voc. & Gram. Transparencies: 14, 18, 20 (maps)

Suggestions: Introduce students to the theme of the chapter and go over the objectives. Use the map transparencies to locate and discuss the countries featured in the chapter.

Fondo cultural *Standards:* 1.1, 1.2, 2.2, 3.1, 4.2
◆■◆✦■◆✦■◆✦■◆✦■◆✦■◆✦■◆

Resources: Fine Art Transparencies; Fine Art Transparencies Teacher's Guide

Suggestions: Tell students that, although Matilde Pérez began painting realistic scenes like the one shown, she later became famous for her abstract art. Ask them to do an Internet search to find out more about her *arte cinética* (kinetic art).
Answers will vary.

Enriching Your Teaching

Planning for Instruction
Resources:
- Teacher Express CD-ROM or Resource Book
  - Teaching resources
  - Lesson Planner
  - Chapter Resource Checklist
  - School-to-Home Connection Letter

Culture Note
Created some 70 million years ago, the Andes are the world's longest mountain range, measuring some 4,500 miles in length. One of the highest ranges in the world, the peaks of the Andes can measure up to 22,000 feet. Aconcagua, the range's highest peak, rises almost 23,000 feet or 7,000 meters.

Teaching with Art
Standards: 1.1

Ask students to write down as many landscape features as they can see in the photo. Then ask: *¿Piensas que el paisaje que se ve en la foto es igual al que se ve en la pintura? ¿En qué se parecen? ¿Cuáles son las diferencias?*

Vocabulario y gramática

Presentation

Standards: 1.1, 1.2

Resources: Voc. & Gram. Transparencies: 36; Resource Book: Cap. 1, Input Script; Audio Program: CD Cap. 1, Tracks 1, 3

Focus: Presenting new vocabulary and using grammar lexically in context

Suggestions: These two pages present new vocabulary and grammar in context using visuals. Each page can be presented separately, but they complement each other. The presentation of new content will continue on the following two pages (pp. 24–25) through the use of a story. Use the *Audio CD* to present new vocabulary. Have students read along as you play it. Ask what each item is used for. Check comprehension by asking questions. See the Input Script in the *Teacher's Resource Book* for examples.

 **Actividad 1** *Standards:* 1.2

Resources: Audio Program: CD Cap. 1, Track 2; Resource Book: Cap. 1, Audio Script; Practice Answers on Transparencies

Focus: Practicing listening comprehension of new vocabulary

Suggestions: Use the *Audio CD* or read the script aloud to students.

Common Errors: Remind students not to try to understand every word they hear during listening comprehension activities. They should let the language "flow through" as a stream.

Answers:

1. lógica
2. ilógica
3. lógica
4. ilógica
5. lógica

Objectives

Read, listen to, and understand information about:
- camping activities
- features of the natural environment

A primera vista 1

Vocabulario y gramática en contexto

Los parques nacionales de Chile ofrecen una gran oportunidad para explorar **la naturaleza**. Todos los años, miles de jóvenes vienen a acampar en **los bosques**, **valles**, montañas, lagos y **desiertos** de este país **hermoso**.

66 Hola, me llamo Fernando y soy chileno. El verano pasado, mi familia y yo fuimos de cámping a **la sierra**. **Lo pasamos bien**. ¡**El paisaje** era impresionante! Como ves, tuvimos que llevar mucho equipo. 99

la linterna

el repelente de insectos

la brújula

los binoculares

la tienda de acampar

el saco de dormir

Actividad 1 Escuchar

Equipo de cámping

En una hoja de papel escribe los números del 1 al 5. Vas a escuchar a unos jóvenes hablar sobre el equipo de cámping. Escucha cada frase y escribe si es lógica o ilógica.

22 veintidós
A primera vista 1

Universal Access

Heritage Language Learners
Invite students to research information they have about camping abroad. They might describe national parks or comment on differences between the camping experience in the United States and in other places.

Students with Learning Disabilities
Remind students that the new vocabulary is presented in blue. Use the visuals and context to determine meaning.

" Éstas son las fotos que sacamos durante nuestro viaje a la sierra.

1 **Dimos un paseo** por los senderos **al amanecer.** Llevamos binoculares para observar los pájaros.

2 También fuimos de pesca. Es un deporte muy tranquilo. Mucha gente dice que es aburrido, pero a mí me encanta.

3 También dimos un paseo a caballo. **Así** se puede explorar mejor el valle.

4 Otra actividad que nos gustó mucho fue **escalar rocas.**

5 Al **anochecer** hicimos una fogata. ¿Qué comimos? ¡Pescado, por supuesto! **"**

Escuchar

El viaje

En una hoja de papel escribe los números del 1 al 5. Escucha cada frase y escribe *C* (cierto) o *F* (falso) según las fotos.

veintitrés **23**
Capítulo 1

Language Input

Actividad 2 *Standards:* 1.2

Resources: Voc. & Gram. Transparencies: 37; Audio Program: CD Cap. 1, Track 4; Resource Book: Cap. 1, Audio Script; Practice Answers on Transparencies

Focus: Practicing listening comprehension of new vocabulary

Suggestions: Use the *Audio CD* or the script. Remind students that this listening activity is based on the vocabulary on p. 23.

Answers:
1. C   4. F
2. C   5. F
3. C

Extension: On the board, copy as models two or three statements from the Audio Script. Have each student write two statements like the models, one true and one false. Ask volunteers to read aloud one of their statements. After each statement, ask another volunteer to determine whether it is **cierto** or **falso**.

Teacher-to-Teacher
Have students create a photo album of a travel experience they have had, complete with photo captions. They can use p. 23 as a model.

Enriching Your Teaching

Culture Note
Ecotourism has become an important industry in Latin America. The beauty and variety of climate, landscape, flora, and fauna found throughout Central and South America make ecotourism an attractive investment for private organizations and governments. In recent years, countries such as Costa Rica, Venezuela, and Brazil have become internationally renowned ecotourism hotspots.

Internet Search
Keywords:

ecoturismo, área recreativa, excursiones de ecología

23

Standards: 1.2, 3.1

Resources: Voc. & Gram. Transparencies: 38–39; Resource Book: Cap. 1, Input Script; Audio Program: CD Cap. 1, Track 5

▶ Rapid Review

On the board, begin a word web with the expression **ir de cámping** at the center. Invite students to share what they know about camping and have them tell about outdoor experiences they have had. Add to the web the camping and outdoors-related vocabulary that students use.

Vocabulario y gramática

Presentation

Standards: 1.2, 3.1

Resources: Voc. & Gram. Transparencies: 38–39; Resource Book: Cap. 1, Input Script; Audio Program: CD Cap. 1, Track 5

Focus: Presenting additional vocabulary; extending presentation of vocabulary and grammar in the context of a story

Suggestions:

Pre-reading: Direct attention to the *Estrategia*. Have students talk about their reasons for writing each **efecto**.

Reading: Have students read along as they listen. Have them look at each of the visuals as they are reading to aid comprehension. Allow them to listen more than once. Model pronunciation of the words in boldface. Check comprehension by asking questions. See the Input Scripts in the *Teacher's Resource Book* for specific questions.

Post-reading: Complete *Actividad* 3 to check comprehension.

Extension: Have students rewrite the story as a third-person narrative.

Block Schedule

Divide students into groups of three. Give each group a number from 1 to 7 that represents a scene in *Una aventura desastrosa*. The group has five minutes to present that scene for the class. They are also to create the scene for panel 8. Have each group present their scene sequentially as the story is retold. Then have each group present panel 8. The class can vote on the most creative ending!

¡Una aventura desastrosa!

Estrategia

Cause and effect
Identifying cause and effect relationships helps us understand what we are reading.
Look at the pictures. Write the effect for each cause:

Causa   Efecto
A Guille no ve la piedra.
B Aparece un oso.
C El oso ve la mochila.

1 Al amanecer, Guille, Felipe y yo nos levantamos para dar un paseo. **Anduvimos** por dos horas por un sendero. Queríamos ir a La Peña, una roca enorme, perfecta para escalar.

2 De repente, Guille se cayó y dio un grito.
—¿Qué **sucedió**, Guille?
—No vi la raíz del árbol. ¡Ay! Se rompió la brújula.
—¡Qué desastre! Y no tenemos otra. Vamos a **perdernos**.
—Creo que no. Se puede ver La Peña en la distancia. ¡Vamos!

3 **Nos acercamos** al pie de La Peña. Nos **impresionó** mucho porque era muy alta.
—¿Por qué no descansamos **un rato** antes de escalar?
—Buena idea.

24 veinticuatro
A primera vista 1

4 **Una vez allí**, nos sentamos. De repente, **apareció** un oso muy grande. ¡Uf, nos **asustó** con lo grande que era!
—¡Ay! ¿Qué podemos hacer? ¿Adónde podemos ir? ¿Dónde **nos refugiamos**?

Universal Access

Students with Special Needs

Help visually impaired students deal with the information on these two pages by asking other volunteers to describe each panel. Remind them to include details about the weather, location, colors, and the expressions on the boys' faces.

Advanced Learners

Have students prepare descriptions of the story in their own words describing as accurately as possible the elements and actions in each picture. Partners then take turns giving their descriptions of the pictures in random order. The listener identifies which picture is being described.

5 Empezamos a correr **hacia** La Peña. No había otro **refugio**. El oso empezó a correr también.

—¡Rápido!

—¡Mira! Hay una roca grande a la izquierda. ¡Vamos allí!

—¡Ay! Perdí la mochila.

—No importa. ¡Corre!

6 Felipe **perdió el equilibrio**, se cayó y se torció el tobillo.

—¡Felipe, te ayudo!

De repente, el oso **dejó de** correr. Vio la mochila y la abrió. Sacó la comida que estaba adentro y se fue con la comida en la boca.

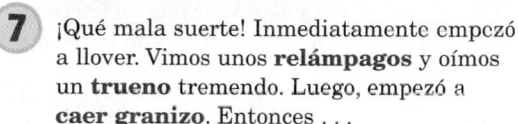

7 ¡Qué mala suerte! Inmediatamente empezó a llover. Vimos unos **relámpagos** y oímos un **trueno** tremendo. Luego, empezó a **caer granizo**. Entonces . . .

8 ¿Cómo crees que terminó la aventura?

● **Más práctica** •••••••••••
Practice Workbook 1-3, 1-4

Go ●**nline**
PHSchool.com

For: Vocabulary practice
Visit: www.phschool.com
Web Code: jed-0102

Actividad 3 **Escribir/Hablar** ••••••••••••••••••••

¿Comprendiste?

1. ¿Por qué querían ir a La Peña los chicos?
2. ¿Qué le pasó a Guille?
3. ¿Qué animal los asustó? ¿Dónde se refugiaron?
4. Imagínate que estás con los chicos cuando aparece el oso. ¿Qué crees que deben hacer?

Enriching Your Teaching

Culture Note

A backpacking trip to the mountains in the southern part of South America would probably include sightings of the guanaco or its cousin the vicuña. These wild herd animals are related to the camel, but smaller. The adult guanaco is approximately three and one-half feet tall at the shoulder. The llama and the alpaca, domestic animals used in the Andes, are descendants of the guanaco.

Internet Search
Keyword: | oso andino |

Actividad 3 *Standards:* 1.1, 1.2, 1.3

Resources: Voc. & Gram. Transparencies: 38–39; Practice Answers on Transparencies

Focus: Demonstrating comprehension of a story

Suggestions: As students answer the questions, have them also supply the number of the picture in which the information for their answer is presented.

Answers:
1. Querían escalar la roca enorme. (panel 1)
2. Guille se cayó y dio un grito. Rompió la brújula. (panel 2)
3. Un oso los asustó. Se refugiaron en una roca grande. (panel 4)
4. Answers will vary.

Extension: Ask students to write down one question they have about the story. This may involve story elements such as plot or characters, or it may be a question about new words or structures. Invite them to take turns reading their questions. As much as possible, allow other students to answer the questions.

Additional Resources
• Resource Book. Cap. 1, Clip Art

✔ **Assessment**
• Prueba 1-1: Vocabulary recognition

Teacher-to-Teacher
Asking students to visualize parts of a story is a good way to help them understand new material. During a second or third presentation, ask students to close their eyes and visualize scenes as they listen. Then ask them to describe what they visualized. Doing this regularly helps students improve their memories by creating mental "corners" or "places" in which to store information.

Chapter Project
Give students copies of the Chapter Project outline and rubric from the *Teacher's Resource Book.* Explain the task to them, and have them perform step 1. (For more information, see p. 16-a.)

Practice and Communicate

Actividad 4
Standards: 1.2

Resources: Practice Answers on Transparencies

Focus: Using new words and expressions in a cloze exercise

Recycle: reflexive pronouns, preterite forms

Suggestions: Refer students to pp. 22–25 for vocabulary.

Answers:
1. Al amanecer
2. dar un paseo
3. Una vez allí
4. un rato
5. relámpagos
6. truenos
7. hacia
8. nos refugiamos

Actividad 5
Standards: 1.2, 1.3

Resources: Practice Answers on Transparencies

Focus: Practicing new vocabulary

Suggestions: Ask students to check their answers with a partner.

Answers:
1. g 2. c 3. d 4. a 5. e 6. b 7. f

Actividad 6
Standards: 1.1, 1.3, 3.1

Resources: Practice Answers on Transparencies

Focus: Practicing new vocabulary

Recycle: expressions with the infinitive

Suggestions: Point out that only seven camping items are pictured. Students must come up with their own eighth item in step 1.

Answers:
tienda de acampar; dormir y descansar
binoculares; ver animales
agua; beber
brújula; no perderme
sartén; cocinar pescado
mochila; llevar cosas
Answers will vary.

Manos a la obra 1
Vocabulario y gramática en uso

Objectives
- **Communicate about camping equipment and activities**
- **Narrate a camping adventure**
- **Talk about events in the past**

Actividad 4 · Leer/Escribir
Un paseo en bicicleta

Unos amigos dan un paseo en bicicleta. Completa el párrafo con las palabras correctas.

un rato	una vez allí	relámpagos
dar un paseo	truenos	nos refugiamos
al amanecer	hacia	

___1.___ nos levantamos y preparamos las bicicletas para ___2.___ por el campo. ___3.___ paramos para descansar y almorzar. Después de ___4.___ empezó a llover. Vimos ___5.___ y oímos unos ___6.___ tremendos que nos asustaron mucho. Corrimos ___7.___ una pequeña casa donde ___8.___. ¡Fue un día inolvidable!

Actividad 5 · Escribir
Definiciones

Empareja cada palabra o frase con su definición. Escribe después un cuento breve usando algunas palabras de la primera columna.

1. suceder
2. perder el equilibrio
3. refugiarse
4. acercarse a
5. al anochecer
6. al amanecer
7. así

a. ir cerca de
b. cuando empieza la mañana
c. caerse
d. esconderse
e. cuando empieza la noche
f. de esta manera
g. pasar

Actividad 6 · Escribir/Hablar

¿Qué vas a llevar?

❶ Vas de cámping este fin de semana. Haz una lista de ocho cosas que necesitas llevar y explica para qué las necesitas.

❷ Dejaste en casa algunas cosas que necesitas para ir de cámping. Usa la lista que escribiste para hablar con otro(a) estudiante.

lo que necesitas	para qué lo necesitas
linterna	ver cuando está oscuro

Modelo
A —¡Ay, caramba! Dejé _la linterna_ en casa.
B —¡Qué pena! Ahora _no puedes caminar_
por el bosque por la noche.

26 veintiséis
Manos a la obra 1

Universal Access

Students with Learning Difficulties
For *Actividad* 4, have students copy the word bank to their papers. As they complete each item, tell them to check off or cross out the item they used from the word bank in order to minimize their choices for the remaining items.

Advanced Learners
Have students use the preterite to write their own paragraph about a real or imagined outdoor experience. Invite them to read their paragraphs aloud in a small group and discuss similarities and differences among their outdoor experiences.

Actividad 7

Hablar

Al mal tiempo buena cara

Habla con otro(a) estudiante de las excursiones que hicieron a varios lugares y de lo que les sucedió.

navegar / oír truenos

Modelo
A —¿Qué hicieron en el océano?
B —Navegamos todo el día.
A —¿Y luego, qué sucedió?
B —Oímos truenos y llovió.

1. observar pájaros / ver relámpagos

2. dar un paseo / caer granizo

3. escalar rocas / perder el equilibrio y caerse

4. dar un paseo a caballo / perderse

5. pescar / empezar a llover

6. ¡Respuesta personal!

Fondo cultural

Parques nacionales de América del Sur En la última década las visitas a los parques nacionales de América del Sur, especialmente de Chile y Argentina, aumentaron mucho. Esto se debe a¹ un creciente² interés por estar en contacto con la naturaleza y disfrutar de actividades al aire libre. ¿Quiénes son los visitantes? Familias, grupos de jóvenes recién egresados³ de la escuela secundaria, grupos de estudiantes en excursiones de estudio y personas de todas las edades interesadas en conocer nuevas especies de animales y plantas y estar en contacto con la naturaleza. La gran variedad de parques nacionales atrae⁴ a todo tipo de gente. En la Argentina hay selvas tropicales en el Parque Nacional Baritú, enormes cataratas⁵ en el Parque Nacional Iguazú y hasta glaciares en el Parque Nacional Perito Moreno.

Las Cataratas del Iguazú en el Parque Nacional Iguazú

• ¿Quiénes visitan los parques nacionales de Chile y Argentina? ¿Por qué?

1 is due to **2** growing **3** graduated **4** attracts **5** waterfalls

---

Ampliación del lenguaje
Presentation
Standards: 1.2, 4.1

Resources: Practice Answers on Transparencies

Suggestions: Ask volunteers to supply the verbs that correspond with the nouns in the second part. Ask other volunteers to use the **ir de...** expressions in complete sentences.

Answers:

comprar	visitar
cazar	viajar

Standards: 1.3

Focus: Writing new vocabulary in context

Suggestions: In addition to using the word or expression in parentheses in a sentence, encourage students to supply an extra detail or two, as the model does.

Answers will vary.

Standards: 1.2, 1.3

Focus: Writing new vocabulary in context

Suggestions: Remind students that paying attention to cause and effect will help them write their e-mail messages.

Answers will vary.

Standards: 1.1, 1.2

Focus: Practicing and demonstrating comprehension of new vocabulary

Suggestions: After students have done their role-play once through with the narration, ask them to do it again and describe what is happening.

Answers will vary.

Ampliación del lenguaje

Ir de . . .

Muchos verbos en español se pueden expresar usando *ir de* más un sustantivo *(noun)* de la misma familia que el verbo. Por ejemplo:

ir de pesca	pescar
ir de paseo	pasear

Como puedes ver, el sustantivo *pesca* y el verbo *pescar* pertenecen a la misma familia de palabras.

¿Puedes adivinar *(guess)* cuáles son los verbos que corresponden a las siguientes expresiones con *ir de . . .* ?

ir de compras

ir de caza *(hunting)*

ir de visita

ir de viaje

Actividad 9 Escribir

¡Fue un desastre!

Acabas de regresar de una excursión de cámping desastrosa. Quieres escribir un mensaje electrónico a un(a) amigo(a) para decirle cómo lo pasaste. Escribe cinco frases para describir tu experiencia. Escoge entre las siguientes palabras y expresiones:

una vez allí	aparecer	dejar de
caer granizo	llover	relámpago
trueno	así	impresionar
perderse	refugiarse	

Modelo

Durante toda la noche cayó granizo sobre la tienda de acampar.

28 **veintiocho**
Manos a la obra 1

Actividad 8 Leer/Escribir

¿Qué pasó?

Imagina lo que pasó en cada situación y escribe una frase usando los verbos entre paréntesis.

Modelo

Fuimos de pesca el sábado. *(perder)*
Perdimos el equilibrio en el bote y nos caímos al agua.

1. Mis padres fueron de paseo. *(acercarse)*
2. Mi hermana fue de compras. *(pasarlo bien)*
3. Fui de viaje con mi familia. *(impresionar)*
4. Fuimos de caza al amanecer. *(asustar)*
5. Mis abuelos fueron de visita. *(perderse)*

Actividad 10 Hablar/Escuchar

Juego

Trabaja con un grupo de cuatro estudiantes y escojan uno de los mensajes electrónicos que escribieron para la Actividad 9. Actúen el mensaje mientras otro grupo cuenta lo que pasó.

Universal Access

Students with Learning Difficulties
Point out to students that **ir de** is very similar to the English expression "to be going." Like that expression, **ir de** is often used to talk about future events. Provide examples, such as: *¿Qué vas a hacer el sábado? Voy de pesca.*

Advanced Learners
Have students work in a group to develop one of the situations from *Actividad 9* into a skit about an outdoor experience. One student can narrate in the past tense, while the others act out the scene(s) and engage in dialogue that uses preterite forms and new vocabulary.

Actividad 11 Leer/Hablar

Las estrellas del sur

Cuando miras el cielo en una noche clara puedes ver muchas estrellas. Pero no todos ven las mismas estrellas. Lee este párrafo para aprender un poco más sobre las estrellas del hemisferio sur.

Conexiones Las ciencias

Desde América del Sur, por estar en otra latitud, el cielo se ve diferente. Sólo en la línea ecuatorial[1] se ve todo el cielo durante todo el año. Esto crea un problema para los astrónomos, porque sólo pueden ver una parte del cielo si no están en el ecuador. Por ejemplo, solamente en el hemisferio sur se ve la constelación de la Cruz del Sur.

• ¿Adónde puedes ir para ver las estrellas?

• ¿Qué constelaciones puedes ver donde tú vives?

[1] Equator

La Cruz del Sur

  Actividad 12 Escribir/Hablar

Lugares para explorar

❶ Piensa en un lugar que te gustaría explorar: el desierto, el océano, el mar, el bosque, la sierra o una selva tropical. Escribe una frase para explicar por qué quieres explorar ese lugar.

Modelo

Quiero ir a la sierra porque me gusta el paisaje.

❷ Forma un grupo con otros estudiantes que escogieron el mismo lugar que tú. Comparte tus ideas con el grupo.

❸ Usa las ideas del grupo para escribir un breve párrafo explicando tus razones para explorar ese lugar.

❹ Presenta tus ideas a la clase. Puedes acompañar tu presentación con fotos o ilustraciones de ese lugar.

 Actividad 13 Escribir/Hablar

Y tú, ¿qué dices?

1. Haz una lista de diferentes aspectos de la naturaleza (montañas, ríos, desiertos, selvas, playas, valles). ¿Cuáles te impresionan más? ¿Por qué?

2. Imagínate que estás haciendo planes para ir a un parque nacional. ¿Qué parque quieres visitar? ¿Por qué? ¿Qué tipo de paisaje vas a encontrar allí ? Una vez allí, ¿qué actividades al aire libre te gustaría hacer?

3. Los parques nacionales son refugios de muchos animales como osos, coyotes y búfalos. ¿Alguna vez se acercó a ti uno de estos animales? ¿Cómo te impresionó? ¿Te asustó? ¿Qué hiciste? Si esto no te sucedió, ¿hay otras cosas que te asustaron? ¿Cuáles? Relata una ocasión en que algo te asustó y describe tu reacción.

veintinueve **29**
Capítulo 1

Practice and Communicate   ①

 Actividad 11 *Standards:* 1.1, 1.2, 3.1

Focus: Reading about the constellations in different latitudes

Suggestions: Point out the cognates *latitud, ecuatorial, hemisferio, astrónomos,* and *constelación.* Remind students that such cognates are a valuable aid to understanding new material.

Answers will vary.

 Actividad 12 *Standards:* 1.1, 1.3, 3.1

Focus: Speaking, listening, and writing to contribute to group reports

Suggestions: Encourage students to use a graphic organizer such as a concept web or a chart to help them develop their group presentation.

Answers will vary.

 Actividad 13 *Standards:* 1.1, 1.2, 1.3, 3.1

Focus: Discussing and writing about personal experiences and opinions

Suggestions: Assign or have students choose one or more of the options, depending on time and ability. Option 3 is the most challenging.

Answers will vary.

Additional Resources

• Writing, Audio & Video Workbook: Cap. 1, Audio Activity 1, Track 6
• Writing, Audio & Video Workbook: Cap. 1, Writing Activity 6
• Resource Book: Cap. 1, Communicative Activity BLM

✓ **Assessment**

• Prueba 1-2: Vocabulary production

 Enriching Your Teaching

Culture Note

The beautiful colored lights of the aurora borealis sometimes appear in the night sky of the Northern Hemisphere. The aurora australis is found in the Southern Hemisphere. Both phenomena occur when electrons and protons from the sun are drawn toward the poles by Earth's magnetic field.

Internet Search

Keywords:

parque nacional, desierto peruano + Atacama, sandboard chileno, Patagonia argentina, selva venezolana

29

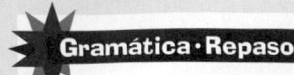

Practice and Communicate

Gramática · Repaso

Presentation

Resources: Voc. & Gram. Transparencies: 40

Suggestions: Point out the *i* to *y* changes in the paradigm. Have students write out the verbs that follow the same pattern.

Actividad 14 *Standards:* 1.2

Resources: Practice Answers on Transparencies

Focus: Practicing verbs with spelling changes in the preterite

Suggestions: Ask volunteers to spell aloud the verb forms they wrote.

Answers:

Step 1

1. dimos	5. oímos	8. Cayó
2. oyó	6. se cayó	9. destruyó
3. creyó	7. empezó	10. corrimos
4. vimos		

Step 2

Answers will vary.

Actividad 15 *Standards:* 1.2

Resources: Audio Program: CD Cap. 1, Track 7; Resource Book: Cap. 1, Audio Script; Practice Answers on Transparencies

Focus: Practicing listening comprehension and writing accuracy

Answers:

Step 1

1. se cayeron	4. leyó
2. oímos	5. creyó
3. destruyó	

Step 2
1. Tres árboles se cayeron.
2. Uno de los árboles destruyó un puente.
3. La hermana no creyó el cuento. Ella no estaba allí.

Additional Resources
• Writing, Audio & Video Workbook: Cap. 1, Writing Activity 7

 Assessment
• *Prueba 1-3: El pretérito de verbos con el cambio ortográfico* i → y

30

 **Gramática · Repaso**

El pretérito de los verbos con el cambio ortográfico *i* → *y*

Verbs ending in *-uir*, such as *destruir*, have a spelling change in the preterite. The *i* becomes *y* in the *Ud. / él / ella* and *Uds. / ellos / ellas* forms.

destruí	destruimos
destruiste	destruisteis
destruyó	destruyeron

Note that the *i* is only accented in the *yo* form.

Other verbs, such as *leer*, *creer*, *oír*, and *caerse*, follow a similar pattern.

leí	leímos
leíste	leísteis
leyó	leyeron

In these verbs, the *i* is always accented.

Actividad 14 **Gramática** **Leer/Escribir/Hablar**

En el bosque

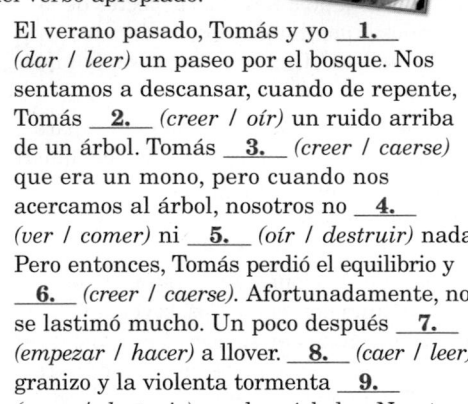

❶ En una hoja de papel escribe los números del 1 al 10. Completa este cuento con el pretérito del verbo apropiado.

El verano pasado, Tomás y yo __1.__ (dar / leer) un paseo por el bosque. Nos sentamos a descansar, cuando de repente, Tomás __2.__ (creer / oír) un ruido arriba de un árbol. Tomás __3.__ (creer / caerse) que era un mono, pero cuando nos acercamos al árbol, nosotros no __4.__ (ver / comer) ni __5.__ (oír / destruir) nada. Pero entonces, Tomás perdió el equilibrio y __6.__ (creer / caerse). Afortunadamente, no se lastimó mucho. Un poco después __7.__ (empezar / hacer) a llover. __8.__ (caer / leer) granizo y la violenta tormenta __9.__ (creer / destruir) muchos árboles. Nosotros __10.__ (correr / vivir) a refugiarnos pero . . .

❷ Ahora, con otro(a) estudiante, escribe un final para el cuento.

Actividad 15 **Gramática** **Escuchar/Leer/Escribir**

Después de la tormenta

❶ En una hoja de papel escribe los números del 1 al 5. Escucha lo que pasó después de una tormenta y escribe los verbos que completan el párrafo.

Ayer, después de la tormenta, __1.__ tres árboles en el parque. Hicieron un ruido tremendo. Nosotros estábamos en el lago, pero lo __2.__ claramente. Uno de los árboles __3.__ un puente. Esta mañana, mi hermana __4.__ la noticia en el periódico. Ella no estaba con nosotros en el lago y no __5.__ el cuento hasta que vio la noticia.

❷ Ahora escribe las respuestas a estas preguntas sobre la tormenta.

1. ¿Cuántos árboles se cayeron?
2. ¿Qué destruyó uno de los árboles?
3. ¿Quién no creyó este cuento? ¿Por qué?

● **Más práctica**
Practice Workbook 1-5

For: Practice with preterite verbs
Visit: www.phschool.com
Web Code: jed-0103

30 treinta
Manos a la obra 1

Universal Access

Heritage Language Learners
Have students review the irregular preterite forms in the *Gramática* on p. 31 in groups. Ask them to work together to think of other words that have irregular preterite forms and write the forms in tables like the one in the *Gramática*. Encourage them to check their spelling using the Student Edition or a dictionary.

Advanced Learners
Have students write five sentences that use verbs with the *i* to *y* change in the preterite. Ask them to read their sentences aloud to a partner. The partner who listens writes down the preterite verb he or she hears in each sentence. Partners can then check their spelling of the preterite verb forms with each other.

El pretérito de los verbos irregulares

Some verbs have irregular stems in the preterite.

tener	andar	estar	poder	poner	saber	venir
tuve	anduve	estuve	pude	puse	supe	vine
tuviste	anduviste	estuviste	pudiste	pusiste	supiste	viniste
tuvo	anduvo	estuvo	pudo	puso	supo	vino
tuvimos	anduvimos	estuvimos	pudimos	pusimos	supimos	vinimos
tuvisteis	anduvisteis	estuvisteis	pudisteis	pusisteis	supisteis	vinisteis
tuvieron	anduvieron	estuvieron	pudieron	pusieron	supieron	vinieron

The verbs *decir* and *traer* also have irregular stems in the preterite.

decir

dije	dijimos
dijiste	dijisteis
dijo	dijeron*

traer

traje	trajimos
trajiste	trajisteis
trajo	trajeron*

*Note that the *Uds./ellos/ellas* endings for *decir* and *traer* are slightly different from the verbs listed above.

Actividad 16 · Gramática · Escuchar/Leer/Escribir/GramActiva

Un paseo en balsa

1 Escucha esta descripción de un viaje en balsa *(raft)*. Lee las preguntas y levanta la mano derecha si escoges la opción **a,** y la mano izquierda si escoges la opción **b.**

1. ¿Los chicos pusieron **a.** las balsas o **b.** las mochilas encima del coche?

2. ¿El guía vino **a.** unos minutos después o **b.** una hora después?

3. ¿El guía les dijo que iban a ir **a.** al centro de Santiago o **b.** al río Maipo?

4. ¿Los chicos tuvieron que llevar las balsas **a.** al río o **b.** al coche?

5. Antes de comenzar el viaje, ¿los chicos se pusieron **a.** las gorras o **b.** los trajes de baño?

6. Después del viaje, ¿todos estuvieron de acuerdo en que **a.** lo pasaron bien o en que **b.** lo pasaron mal?

2 Ahora, escribe una respuesta completa para cada pregunta.

RAFTING RÍO MAIPO
¡Una Aventura Inolvidable, Activa, Sana y en plena Naturaleza!

Enriching Your Teaching

Teacher-to-Teacher

English speakers often wonder why there are two forms of "you" in Spanish. Explain that the answer begins with Latin's second-person plural: **vos.** In the fourth century, the Romans began to use this form as a sign of respect for individuals. The custom carried over to languages that evolved from Latin. (Spanish **vosotros** is a vestige, although it is a plural form.) In the eighteenth century, Spain's upper classes refined rules of address for individuals. **Vos** (a singular form) became **vuestra merced,** which underwent such variations as **vuesarcé** and **ucé** until it became **usted.** This was later used by the nobility with the third-person singular verb forms.

Presentation

Resources: Voc. & Gram. Transparencies: 41

Suggestions: Have students practice listening comprehension of the verb forms by providing them with models that use the forms. Then ask questions in the preterite for students to answer. Point out the irregular stems and the endings they all share.

Actividad 16 *Standards:* 1.2

Resources: Audio Program: CD Cap. 1, Track 8; Resource Book, Cap. 1; Audio Script; Practice Answers on Transparencies

Focus: Practicing listening comprehension and writing accuracy

Suggestions: Have students read through the questions before they hear the audio. Remind students to use verbs in the preterite.

Answers:

Step 1

1. a   2. a   3. b   4. a   5. b   6. a

Step 2

1. Pusieron las balsas encima del coche.
2. Vino unos minutos después.
3. Les dijo que iban a ir al Río Maipo.
4. Tuvieron que llevar las balsas al río.
5. Se pusieron los trajes de baño.
6. Estuvieron de acuerdo en que lo pasaron bien.

Common Errors: Some students regularly forget to use reflexive pronouns. Take advantage of *Actividad* 16 to remind students of how strongly these pronouns can affect meaning. Point out the difference in meaning between **pusieron** in item 1 and **se pusieron** in item 5.

Chapter Project

Students can perform step 2 at this point. Be sure they understand your corrections and suggestions. (For more information, see p. 16-a.)

Practice and Communicate

1

Standards: 1.3

Resources: Practice Answers on Transparencies

Focus: Writing preterite verb forms

Suggestions: Tell students that, besides targeting verb forms, this activity examines their comprehension of the sentence parts that they must put together.

Answers:
1. Yo no pude venir.
2. Nosotros trajimos la comida.
3. Perla se puso el traje de baño.
4. Raúl y Silvia estuvieron muy ocupados.
5. Tú viniste en bicicleta.
6. Todos dijeron "¡Claro que sí!"

Standards: 1.1, 1.2

Focus: Asking and answering questions in the preterite

Recycle: time expressions, daily routines

Suggestions: Tell students they should listen carefully to their partner's question, and answer using the same verb that the question contained.

Answers will vary.

Additional Resources
• Writing, Audio & Video Workbook: Cap. 1, Writing Activity 8

✓ **Assessment**
• Prueba 1-4: *El pretérito de los verbos irregulares*

Actividad 17 **Gramática** **Escribir**

Una invitación a la playa

Carolina invitó a sus amigos a ir con ella a la playa. Describe cómo respondió cada amigo(a) usando el pretérito del verbo entre paréntesis y las palabras apropiadas del recuadro.

Modelo
José *(venir)* / después de un rato.
José *vino después de un rato.*

| el traje de baño | muy ocupados(as) | venir | en bicicleta | la comida | "¡Claro que sí!" |

1. Yo no *(poder)*
2. Nosotros *(traer)*
3. Perla *(ponerse)*
4. Raúl y Silvia *(estar)*
5. Tú *(venir)*
6. Todos *(decir)*

Actividad 18 **Gramática**  **Leer/Hablar**

En el campamento "Amistad"

Los consejeros del campamento "Amistad" hablan de las actividades que hicieron los niños. Trabaja con otro(a) estudiante para hablar del horario. Puedes usar los verbos *andar, estar, poder, poner, venir, tener* y *traer.*

Modelo
A —¿Dónde estuvo Daniel a las 11:00?
B —Estuvo en la piscina.
A —¿Qué tuvo que hacer Julián a la 1:00?
B —Tuvo que servir la comida.

Nombre	9:00 a 10:30	11:00 a 12:30	1:00 a 1:15	3:00 a 5:00	6:00 a 7:00
Daniel	campo de deportes/jugar al fútbol	piscina/traer el traje de baño	comedor/lavar los platos	playa/bucear	sala/usar la computadora
Marta	campo de deportes/jugar al tenis	piscina/traer las toallas	comedor/traer el pan	lago/navegar	sala/poner flores
Estela	campo de deportes/jugar al tenis	bosque/andar por los senderos	comedor/poner la mesa	campo/montar a caballo	jardín/traer los binoculares
Julián	en cama/enfermo	lago/navegar	comedor/servir la comida	playa/nadar	playa/hacer una fogata

Horario del grupo "Los piratas" para el 15 de julio

● **Más práctica**
Practice Workbook 1-6

Go Online
PHSchool.com
For: Practice with preterite verbs
Visit: www.phschool.com
Web Code: jed-0104

Universal Access

Heritage Language Learners
Have students list in chronological order five activities that they did today before they arrived to Spanish class. Have them exchange lists with a partner and check each other's work for errors in spelling or placement of accent marks.

Students with Learning Difficulties
Help students better understand the schedule in *Actividad 18.* Reproduce the schedule on the board with clock faces at the top to show the time periods. Point out that the time gets later as students read from left to right in the schedule.

Gramática · Repaso

El pretérito de los verbos con los cambios e → i, o → u en la raíz

Stem changing -ir verbs in the present tense also have a stem change in the preterite tense. The changes are e → i and o → u and take place in the Ud. / él / ella and Uds. / ellos / ellas forms only.

Here are the preterite forms of *pedir*, *sentir*, and *dormir*:

pedí	pedimos	sentí	sentimos	dormí	dormimos
pediste	pedisteis	sentiste	sentisteis	dormiste	dormisteis
pidió	pidieron	sintió	sintieron	durmió	durmieron

Other verbs like *pedir (i)* and *sentir (i)* are: *divertirse, preferir, sugerir, vestirse*.
Another verb like *dormir (u)* is: *morir*.

 19 Gramática **Leer/Escribir**

¿Qué pasó en el picnic?

La familia Suárez hizo un picnic en la playa. Completa las frases con el pretérito del verbo apropiado.

1. Yo *(preferir / dormir)* dar un paseo por la playa.

2. Mis hermanitos *(morirse / pedir)* de miedo cuando hicieron moto acuática.

3. Fuimos de pesca y *(morirse / divertirse)* mucho.

4. Mamá hizo una fogata y *(sentir / servir)* pescado.

5. Mi hermanita *(pedir / dormir)* más postre.

6. Después de comer mis hermanos y yo *(dormir / servir)* una siesta.

7. Después de nadar en la playa, nosotros *(vestirse / divertirse)* rápidamente y regresamos a casa.

 20 Gramática **Hablar**

¿Cómo lo pasaron?

Una semana después, los hermanos Suárez fueron de cámping por cinco días. Habla con otro(a) estudiante de su experiencia.

Modelo
¿A qué hora? / dormirse
A —¿A qué hora se durmieron?
B —Se durmieron a las siete.

Estudiante A

1. ¿Por dónde? / andar los hermanos

2. ¿Dónde? / dormir los hermanos

3. ¿Qué? / ponerse el hermano menor

4. ¿Qué? / traer los chicos para beber

5. ¿Dónde? / divertirse más

Estudiante B

 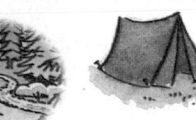  

treinta y tres **33**
Capítulo 1

Practice and Communicate

Actividad 21

Standards: 1.1, 1.3

Focus: Practicing writing preterite verb forms with spelling changes

Suggestions: For step 2, encourage students to use their questions as notes for a naturally flowing conversation like the one in the model.

Answers will vary, but should include correct spellings of the verb forms used.

Actividad 22

Standards: 1.1, 1.3

Focus: Practicing irregular preterite verb forms

Suggestions: In step 3, encourage students to practice using expressions such as *Teresa me dijo que* when reporting to the class about their partner.

Answers will vary.

Actividad 23

Standards: 1.1, 3.1

Resources: Practice Answers on Transparencies

Focus: Reading to obtain information for solving a math problem

Suggestions: Have students read through the passage and determine how to set up and solve the equation. Then ask them for the answer and have them explain the steps they took to arrive at it.

Answers:
Cantidad mensual:
5 mm al año ÷ 12 meses = 0,42 mm al més.

Cantidad del 12 de julio de 1997 (95 mm) ÷ cantidad mensual (0,42 mm) = 226 meses o càsi 19 años.

 **Actividad 21 Gramática** **Escribir/Hablar**

¿Cómo lo pasaron?

1 Escribe cinco preguntas que puedes hacerle a otro(a) estudiante sobre cómo lo pasó en una fiesta. Usen los verbos del recuadro.

divertirse	servir	preferir	sugerir
sentirse	vestirse	estar	poder

Modelo

estar
¿Estuvo buena la fiesta de Ernesto?

2 Ahora, usando las preguntas que escribiste en el Paso 1, habla con otro(a) estudiante sobre cómo lo pasaron en la fiesta.

Modelo

A —*¿Estuvo buena la fiesta de Ernesto?*
B —*Sí, bailé toda la noche. Lo pasé muy bien. ¿Y tú?*

 **Actividad 22 Gramática** **Escribir/Hablar**

Una excursión al aire libre

1 Piensa en la última vez que hiciste una excursión al aire libre y contesta las preguntas siguientes.

1. ¿Adónde fuiste?   **3.** ¿Cómo te vestiste?   **5.** ¿Qué hiciste?

2. ¿Quién te sugirió el lugar?   **4.** ¿Qué tuviste que traer?   **6.** ¿Te divertiste o no?

2 Ahora hazle las mismas preguntas a otro(a) estudiante y toma apuntes de sus respuestas.

3 Presenta tus repuestas y las de tu compañero(a) a la clase.

Modelo

Yo fui al campo y Juan fue a las montañas.

 Actividad 23 **Leer/Pensar/Hablar**

Lluvia en el desierto

¿Sabías que a veces llueve en los desiertos? Lee la siguiente información sobre el desierto de Atacama y resuelve el problema con otro(a) estudiante.

Conexiones | **Las matemáticas**

El desierto de Atacama, al norte de Chile, generalmente recibe sólo 5 mm de precipitación al año. Pero, el 12 de julio de 1997 cayeron 95 mm de agua en sólo 15 horas.

Si en los próximos años recibe la precipitación habitual, ¿cuántos meses hay que esperar hasta llegar a la cantidad de precipitación del 12 de julio de 1997?

Desierto de Atacama

Universal Access

Heritage Language Learners

Ask students who have lived in a heritage country to choose a place there in which it would be a good idea to have an ecocamp. Have them explain the attractions of the location. In what ways would that particular place benefit from having an ecocamp?

Students with Learning Difficulties

Help students deal with the numerical information in *Actividad* 23. Have them first establish how many numbers there are in the text. *(five)* Ask which numbers measure water. *(95 mm, 5 mm)* Remind them that they must use one more number, 12, the number of months in a year, to do the problem.

Actividad 24 · Leer/Escribir

Una caminata por Torres del Paine

Imagínate que fuiste con unos(as) amigos(as) a hacer una excursión como la que se describe en este anuncio turístico. Escribe tres frases para describir lo que pasó en cada actividad.

Modelo
_____

El primer día dimos una caminata muy larga.

VIAJE

Parque Nacional
Torres del Paine

▶ Caminatas de entre 4 a 7 horas por día

▶ Navegar en el lago

▶ Escalar el Glaciar Grey

▶ Montar a caballo por el Valle del Ascencio

▶ Acampar en el exclusivo Ecocamp

Precio: USD $1,130   7 días, 6 noches

Actividad 25 · Leer/Escribir

Los Ecocamps de Torres del Paine

Lee el texto sobre el Parque Nacional Torres del Paine y los Ecocamps y contesta las siguientes preguntas.

El Parque Nacional Torres del Paine, situado en la zona patagónica de Chile, es uno de los lugares más hermosos de nuestro planeta. Los senderos del parque ofrecen vistas magníficas del paisaje patagónico: montañas, bosques, ríos, glaciares, lagos y abundante flora y fauna. Este parque, remoto y misterioso, atrae a miles de turistas y aventureros de todo el mundo que vienen cada año a hacer caminatas, montar a caballo o navegar. Y la gran demanda por visitar el parque ha generado problemas serios de impacto ecológico y en la calidad de los servicios turísticos en general.

Una solución a este problema ha sido cambiar los hoteles por "Ecocamps", tiendas de acampar modernas, cómodas y transportables. Los "Ecocamps" permiten a los visitantes estar más cerca de la naturaleza y producen menos basura que los hoteles.

1. ¿Qué tipos de paisajes ofrece el Parque Nacional Torres del Paine?

2. ¿Qué solución ofrecen los Ecocamps para mejorar los problemas de impacto ecológico?

3. ¿Qué crees que puedes hacer tú para ayudar a cuidar lugares como éste?

● **Más práctica**
Practice Workbook 1-7

PHSchool.com
For: Practice with preterite verbs
Visit: www.phschool.com
Web Code: jed-0105

treinta y cinco **35**
Capítulo 1

Enriching Your Teaching

Culture Note
The Atacama desert extends from the Pacific Ocean to the Andes Mountains. It is 600 miles long and a little less than 100 miles wide in most places. It is the most arid place on Earth—so arid, in fact, that scientists believe it may have a lot in common with Mars. A robot that will be sent to Mars is being tested in the Atacama desert.

Teacher-to-Teacher
Tap into students' passions to fuel language learning. Organize a debate around the topic of national parks, with the two sides being *Nuestros parques nacionales están bien como están* and *Hay que tomar medidas para proteger nuestros parques nacionales.*

35

Vocabulario y gramática

Presentation

Standards: 1.1, 1.2

Resources: Voc. & Gram. Transparencies: 43–44; Resource Book: Cap. 1, Input Script; Audio Program: CD Cap. 1, Tracks 10–11

Focus: Presenting new vocabulary and using grammar lexically in context

Suggestions: Have students read along as you play the *Audio CD* to present the new vocabulary. Model the pronunciation of the new vocabulary words. Have students repeat in chorus. Make sure they read the information on the poster. Check for comprehension by asking questions. See the Input Scripts in the *Teacher's Resource Book* for specific questions.

Standards: 1.2

Resources: Practice Answers on Transparencies

Focus: Practicing listening comprehension of new vocabulary

Suggestions: Remind students to look at the race poster.

Common Errors: Remind students that names of days and months are not capitalized in Spanish.

Answers:
1. 4 de agosto
2. cuatro
3. $1,200
4. 9:30
5. $120

A primera vista 2

Objectives

Read, listen to, and understand information about
- athletic events
- other kinds of competitions
- goals and prizes

Vocabulario y gramática en contexto

—Mira, no sabía que el 4 de agosto es **la carrera** de San Cristóbal. ¿Quieres participar?

—¡Claro! ¿Dónde **tiene lugar**?

—En Ecatepec. No está muy lejos.

—Entonces **me** voy a **inscribir** hoy mismo.

5 KM.

CARRERA ATLÉTICA SAN CRISTÓBAL

El Consejo de Participación Ciudadana en coordinación con el Club de Atletismo los invitan a participar

FECHA: Domingo 4 de agosto
HORA: A partir de las 9:00 A.M.
LUGAR: Explanada del Palacio Municipal de Ecatepec, Edo. de México

INSCRIPCIONES

En deportes "Maxi Diablo" **la inscripción** (Av. Morelos #129 San Cristóbal Centro) teléfono: 555-02-54
Y en la oficina del H.C.P.C. (centro cívico)

Donativo de inscripción: $40.00 (para gastos del evento)

¡Medallas a los primeros 500 participantes!

CATEGORÍAS Y PREMIOS

participantes

	chicos (14 a 18 años) 9:00 horas	chicas (14 a 18 años) 9:30 horas	hombres (mayores de 18 años) 9:00 horas	mujeres (mayores de 18 años) 9:30 horas
1°	$1000.00	$1000.00	$1.200.00	$1.200.00
2°	$700.00	$700.00	$1000.00	$1000.00
3°	$400.00	$400.00	$700.00	$700.00

Leer

¿Qué dice el anuncio?

Lee el anuncio de la carrera atlética y completa las frases.

1. La carrera atlética tiene lugar el *(8 de abril / 4 de agosto)*.

2. Hay *(tres / cuatro)* categorías de participantes.

3. El premio de primer lugar para la categoría de hombres es de *($1200 / $1000)*.

4. La carrera para chicas entre 14 y 18 años tiene lugar a las *(9:00 / 9:30)*.

5. Si quieres participar con dos amigos(as), la inscripción les cuesta *($100.00 / $120.00)*.

Universal Access

Students with Learning Difficulties

Help students interpret the information in the *categorías y premios* part of the poster. Ask volunteers to read each of the categories separately from top to bottom. Point out that the information in each of these vertical sections pertains to one age and gender group.

Advanced Learners

Have students write an interview with the person who came in last in the race. They can use some of the same questions asked of the winner, but challenge them to invent one or two that an interviewer might ask someone who didn't win.

Después de la carrera, una reportera del periódico de la escuela entrevistó a Héctor Díaz, el campeón de la competencia.

el trofeo

1 —**¡Felicitaciones**, Héctor! Ganaste el trofeo. ¿Cómo te sentías antes de la carrera?

—Estaba muy **animado,** porque sabía que podía ganar. Ésa era mi **meta: salir campeón** y **obtener** el trofeo.

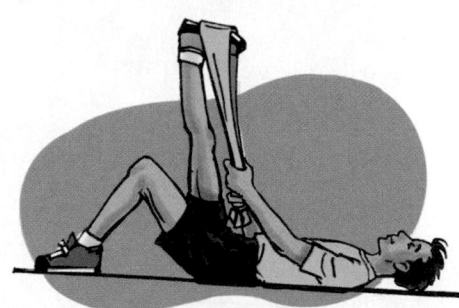

2 —¿Cómo te preparaste?

—**Me di cuenta de** que para **alcanzar** mi meta, debía **hacer un esfuerzo**. Estuve dos meses **entrenándome**. Corría cinco veces por semana. Comía bien y bebía mucho líquido.

la medalla

3 —¿Fue una carrera muy **dura?**

—Sí, **al principio** iba en tercer lugar. **Sin embargo,** no estaba **desanimado.** Hice un esfuerzo y gané. **Me emocioné** mucho al final.

Actividad 27 Escuchar

¿Qué dice el campeón?

Numera una hoja del 1 al 6. Escucha las frases. Escribe *C* (cierto) o *F* (falso) para cada frase.

Certificado

el certificado

treinta y siete **37**
Capítulo 1

Actividad 27 *Standards:* 1.2

Resources: Voc. & Gram. Transparencies: 44; Audio Program: CD Cap. 1, Track 12; Resource Book: Cap. 1, Audio Script; Practice Answers on Transparencies

Focus: Practicing listening comprehension of new vocabulary

Suggestions: Before using the *Audio CD* or the script for this activity, allow students a few minutes to reread p. 37.

Answers:
1. F   2. F   3. F   4. C   5. F   6. F

Extension: Read the script or play the *Audio CD* again. Ask students to correct the false statements.

Chapter Project
Students can perform step 3 at this point. (For more information, see p. 16-a.)

Enriching Your Teaching

Culture Note
Over 500 years ago, the Incas relied on runners to maintain their hold over a huge empire. Runners brought messages and materials along a network of almost 20,000 miles of roads. These men would run for a distance and be relieved by a fresh runner. That way, news could cross the empire in a few days.

Teacher-to-Teacher
For many students, listening comprehension is the most difficult language skill to master. Once you and your students are ready to begin a listening activity, allow students a few seconds of silence in order to mentally prepare themselves. Don't begin until classroom noise and other distractions have settled down.

Vocabulario y gramática

Presentation

Standards: 1.1, 1.2

Resources: Voc. & Gram. Transparencies: 45; Resource Book: Cap. 1, Input Script; Audio Program: CD Cap. 1, Track 13

Focus: Extending presentation of vocabulary and grammar in context

Suggestions:

Pre-reading: Have students use the titles and pictures to predict what each story is about.

Reading: Play the *Audio CD* or read aloud from the script. Have students read along as they listen. Allow them to listen more than once.

Post-reading: Check comprehension by asking questions.

Standards: 1.3

Resources: Practice Answers on Transparencies

Focus: Demonstrating comprehension of school newspaper articles

Suggestions: Have students give the answers orally before writing them. If they have difficulty, rephrase the question, embedding the answer. For item 1, for example, ask: *¿Qué concurso no ganaron los estudiantes: el concurso de ajedrez o el partido de básquetbol?*

Answers:

1. Los estudiantes de la escuela no ganaron el concurso de ajedrez.
2. Los jóvenes poetas estaban muy contentos al final de la ceremonia.
3. El año pasado eliminaron al equipo de básquetbol.
4. Las chicas del equipo del Liceo San Martín perdieron el partido de básquetbol.
5. Answers will vary.

La Voz Del Estudiante

Santiago, 23 de septiembre

Nuestros jóvenes maestros

Diez estudiantes de nuestra escuela participaron en el concurso de ajedrez. **Desafortunadamente**, nuestra escuela no ganó el primer premio, pero **estamos orgullosos** de nuestros **representantes**.

El poder de las palabras

Felicitaciones a nuestros poetas estudiantiles. La **ceremonia** de **entrega de premios** tuvo lugar la semana pasada en el teatro de la escuela. Al final de la ceremonia los ganadores estaban muy contentos.

¡Campeonas de básquetbol!

¿Recuerdan cuando el año pasado **eliminaron** a nuestro equipo del campeonato de básquetbol? Pues este año, con mucho **entrenamiento** y esfuerzo, las chicas del equipo de nuestra escuela jugaron **contra** el equipo rival del Liceo San Martín y **vencieron** 68 a 62. ¡Felicitaciones, campeonas!

 Escribir

¿Comprendiste?

1. ¿Qué concurso no ganaron los estudiantes de la escuela?

2. ¿Cómo se sintieron los jóvenes poetas al final de la ceremonia?

3. ¿Qué le pasó el año pasado al equipo de básquetbol de la escuela?

4. ¿Quién perdió este partido de básquetbol?

5. ¿Por qué crees que los estudiantes están orgullosos de sus jugadores de ajedrez?

38 treinta y ocho
A primera vista 2

Universal Access

Heritage Language Learners

Ask students to think of other information that could be included in one of the articles from *La voz del estudiante.* Encourage them to invent names for teams and individual players, and include details about highlights during an event. Have them rewrite the article incorporating their new information.

Advanced Learners

Invite students to write their own brief articles for a school newspaper. They should report on an actual recent competitive event or awards ceremony at your school. Collaborative efforts can be combined into a Spanish-language school newspaper. Have students place sketches where photos would go.

Escuchar

¡Salimos campeonas!

Escucha las siguientes frases e indica a qué dibujo se refiere cada una. Cada dibujo puede referirse a más de una frase.

Estrategia

Order of events
Trying to determine the order of events in a story will help you understand it better. When you listen to a story in Spanish, pay attention to words such as *antes*, *al principio, durante, después, más tarde,* and *finalmente* to determine the sequence.

1

2

3

Leer/Pensar

Ordena las notas

Imagínate que eres reportero(a) de *La Voz del Estudiante*. Acabas de tomar unas notas sobre el partido de básquetbol, pero tus notas no están en orden. Ordena las frases y escríbelas según la secuencia de los dibujos.

- Durante el partido tuvimos que hacer un gran esfuerzo porque el otro equipo era muy bueno.
- Más tarde, tuvimos un empate de 42 a 42.
- Cuando nos dieron el trofeo, todas nos emocionamos mucho.
- Antes del partido, nuestra entrenadora nos hizo practicar con la pelota.
- Finalmente, pudimos vencer a nuestras rivales 68 a 62.

Hablar

Evalúa las actividades

En el periódico se habla de tres actividades en las que participan los estudiantes. Con un(a) compañero(a), da tu opinión de las actividades. Usa:

Prefiero . . .

No disfruto mucho . . .

No me gusta . . .

Sólo me gusta observar . . .

● **Más práctica**
Practice Workbook 1-8, 1-9

Go Online
PHSchool.com

For: Vocabulary practice
Visit: www.phschool.com
Web Code: jed-0106

treinta y nueve **39**
Capítulo 1

Language Input

 1

Actividad 29

Standards: 1.2, 3.1

Resources: Audio Program: CD Cap. 1, Track 14; Resource Book: Cap. 1, Audio Script; Practice Answers on Transparencies

Focus: Practicing listening comprehension of new vocabulary and structures

Suggestions: Review the *Estrategia* with students before beginning the activity.

Answers:
1.1 2.3 3.2 4.3 5.1 6.2

Actividad 30

Standards: 1.2

Resources: Practice Answers on Transparencies

Focus: Sequencing events to demonstrate comprehension

Suggestions: Encourage students to use the transitions in the *Estrategia* as they sequence the events.

Answers:
Antes del partido, nuestra entrenadora nos hizo practicar con la pelota. Durante el partido tuvimos que hacer un gran esfuerzo porque el otro equipo era muy bueno. Más tarde, tuvimos un empate de 42 a 42. Finalmente, pudimos vencer a nuestras rivales 48 a 46. Cuando nos dieron el trofeo, todas nos emocionamos mucho.

Actividad 31

Standards: 1.1

Focus: Using new vocabulary in context

Suggestions: Remind students that the expressions they are using to begin their sentences introduce statements of opinion.

Answers will vary.

Additional Resources
• Resource Book: Cap. 1, Clip Art

✓ **Assessment**
• Prueba 1-6: Vocabulary recognition

Enriching Your Teaching

Teacher-to-Teacher
After students complete and check *Actividad 29*, ask them to say which elements in each picture helped them decide on the answer. Guide them with questions. For picture number 1, ask: *¿Cómo sabemos que es una sesión de* *entrenamiento y no un partido?* For number 2: *¿Las chicas llevan uniformes? ¿Qué más nos muestra que esto es el partido?* And for number 3: *¿Cómo sabemos que este equipo ganó el partido?*

Practice and Communicate

Actividad 32 Standards: 1.2

Resources: Practice Answers on Transparencies

Focus: Using new words and expressions in a cloze exercise

Suggestions: Encourage students to quickly read over the entire passage first in order to have an idea of what it is about.

Answers:
1. representantes
2. meta
3. Desafortunadamente
4. eliminaron
5. desanimados
6. Sin embargo
7. se dio cuenta
8. alcanzar
9. orgulloso
10. animados

Fondo cultural Standards: 1.2, 3.1, 4.2

Suggestions: Many high-level competitions use the word "Olympic" in their title. Ask students why they think this is so. They might say it's because the Olympic Games are the height of sports competition, because there are participants from many different places, and so on. What are some competitions in which they participate?

Answers will vary.

Block Schedule

Inside-Outside Circles. Have each student write two questions to ask a partner on a sheet of paper or index card that relate to an event or competition. Have students count off by twos. One partner goes to the "inside circle" and faces out. The second partner goes to the "outside circle" and faces in. The partners ask their questions and after about one minute, you call time and everyone moves two spaces. Repeat the questioning.

Manos a la obra 2
Vocabulario y gramática en uso

Objectives
• Communicate about different kinds of competitions
• React to the outcome of a special event
• Review forms and uses of the imperfect tense

Actividad 32 Leer/Escribir

El concurso

Completa los párrafos con las palabras de los recuadros.

| desafortunadamente | eliminaron | desanimados | meta | representantes |

Los **1.** de mi escuela organizaron un concurso de música. Su **2.** era obtener suficiente dinero para construir un nuevo teatro. Todos los padres de la escuela participaron. Vendieron refrescos y galletas. **3.** nuestra banda no llegó a los finales y nos **4.** de la competencia. Todos nos sentimos muy **5.** .

| animados | orgulloso | sin embargo | se dio cuenta | alcanzar |

6. , al día siguiente, tuvimos una gran sorpresa. El director de la escuela **7.** de que con la venta de galletas pudimos **8.** nuestra meta. Después, dijo que estaba muy **9.** de los esfuerzos de nuestro equipo. Esta vez, todos nos sentimos muy **10.** .

Fondo cultural

La Olimpiada Iberoamericana de Matemáticas
Cada año, chicos y chicas de América Latina y España participan en la Olimpiada Iberoamericana de Matemáticas. Es una competencia para jóvenes de escuela secundaria. Las olimpiadas tienen como meta estimular el estudio de las matemáticas y el desarrollo[1] de jóvenes con talento para esta ciencia, a través de[2] la resolución ingeniosa de problemas matemáticos en un tiempo limitado.

¿Dónde y cuándo? La Olimpiada Iberoamericana de Matemáticas tiene lugar cada año en un país diferente de América Latina o en España, en el mes de septiembre. Otros países del mundo también tienen olimpiadas de matemáticas.

• ¿Puedes pensar en una competencia similar en los Estados Unidos?

OLIMPIADA DE MATEMÁTICAS

3x4=12

---

1 development 2 through

Universal Access

Heritage Language Learners
Ask students to research the ***Olimpiada Iberoamericana de Matemáticas*** on the Internet. Have them prepare brief reports in which they share the information they find, such as where the next event will be held and what kinds of events it will involve.

Advanced Learners
Invite students to browse through sports magazines and describe situations and events they see in pictures about competitive events. Encourage them to talk about the events in the past tense.

Actividad 33
Hablar
La entrega de premios

Di qué premios obtuvieron los atletas en la ceremonia de entrega de premios.

Modelo
el atleta que salió en tercer lugar
El atleta que salió en tercer lugar obtuvo una camiseta.

1. el equipo campeón
2. el atleta que ganó la carrera
3. el atleta que salió en segundo lugar
4. todos los participantes
5. los entrenadores

¿Recuerdas?
El verbo *obtener* tiene las mismas terminaciones en el pretérito que *tener*.

Actividad 34
Escuchar/Escribir
El campeonato de tenis

Escucha el reportaje sobre el campeonato de tenis. Luego contesta las preguntas.

1. ¿Cuándo tuvo lugar el campeonato?
2. ¿Cómo fue el partido?
3. ¿Cuándo hizo un gran esfuerzo María?
4. ¿Quién ganó?

5. ¿Qué recibió como premio la campeona?
6. ¿Cómo se sintieron las dos tenistas al final?

Actividad 35

Escribir/Hablar
El festival deportivo

1 Imagina que fuiste a un festival deportivo en el que había partidos de diferentes deportes, comida y premios. Un(a) estudiante te entrevista para aprender un poco más del festival. Contesta sus preguntas.

1. ¿Cuándo y dónde tuvo lugar el festival?
2. ¿Cuánto costó la inscripción?
3. ¿Qué eventos deportivos había?
4. ¿En cuáles participaste tú?
5. ¿Jugaste con un equipo? ¿Contra quién jugaste?
6. ¿Participaste en alguna carrera?
7. ¿Ganaste algún premio? Si es así, ¿qué ganaste?
8. ¿Cómo se sintieron los participantes después de la ceremonia de entrega de premios?
9. ¿Cómo lo pasaste?

2 Trabaja con otro(a) estudiante para hacer y contestar preguntas sobre el festival.

cuarenta y uno **41**
Capítulo 1

Practice and Communicate
 1

Actividad 33
Standards: 1.1

Resources: Practice Answers on Transparencies

Focus: Practicing new vocabulary

Recycle: irregular preterite stems, sports terms

Suggestions: First refer students to the *¿Recuerdas?* before doing the exercise.

Answers:
1. obtuvo un trofeo
2. obtuvo una medalla
3. obtuvo una medalla
4. obtuvieron un certificado
5. obtuvieron flores

Actividad 34
Standards: 1.2, 1.3

Resources: Audio Program: CD Cap. 1, Track 15; Resource Book: Cap. 1, Audio Script; Practice Answers on Transparencies

Focus: Practicing and reviewing new vocabulary and preterite forms

Answers:
1. Tuvo lugar el 25 de agosto.
2. El partido fue muy largo y duro.
3. Hizo un gran esfuerzo en el último set.
4. María ganó el partido.
5. Recibió un trofeo de plata.
6. Se sintieron muy orgullosas.

Actividad 35
Standards: 1.1, 1.2, 1.3

Focus: Practicing new vocabulary and preterite forms

Suggestions: Encourage students to write their answers based on real events.

Answers will vary.

Additional Resources
• Writing, Audio & Video Workbook: Cap. 1, Audio Activity 3, Track 16
• Writing, Audio & Video Workbook: Cap. 1, Writing Activity 10
• Resource Book: Cap. 1, Communicative Activity BLM

✓ Assessment
• Prueba 1-7: Vocabulary production

Enriching Your Teaching

Culture Note
Point out that the suffix **ibero-** is often used in words having to do with Spain and the Spanish-speaking world. **América Latina** is often called **Iberoamérica**, and Spain itself is sometimes still referred to as **Iberia**. These appellations tend to be used by Spaniards rather than Latin Americans. **Iberia** and its variations come from the name the ancient Greeks gave to the peninsula comprising what are now Spain and Portugal (*la Península Ibérica*). The Greeks got the name **Iberia** from a river on the peninsula that they called the Iber River, which many believe to be the Ebro, one of Spain's major rivers.

41

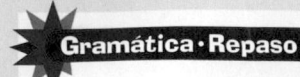

Standards: 1.2

Resources: Practice Answers on Transparencies

Focus: Practicing the imperfect tense in a cloze exercise

Recycle: regular and irregular verbs, imperfect tense

Suggestions: Before students write their answers, ask them to point out expressions in the exercise that are similar to those in the *¿Recuerdas?* above.

Answers:

1. era
2. tenía
3. íbamos
4. leía/sacaba
5. leía/sacaba
6. pedían
7. molestaba
8. devolvían
9. enojaba
10. eran

Gramática·Repaso

El imperfecto

Use the imperfect tense to talk about actions that happened regularly. In English you often say "used to" or "would" to express this idea.

> Todos los meses, mi escuela **organizaba** una carrera. Nuestro equipo nunca **perdía**.

¿Recuerdas?

Expresiones como *generalmente, a menudo, muchas veces, todos los días, siempre* y *nunca* indican el uso del imperfecto.

estar

estaba	estábamos
estabas	estabais
estaba	estaban

tener

tenía	teníamos
tenías	teníais
tenía	tenían

vivir

vivía	vivíamos
vivías	vivíais
vivía	vivían

- Stem-changing verbs do not have a stem change in the imperfect.

  Quería participar en el campeonato pero no **me sentía** bien.

The verbs *ir, ser,* and *ver* are the only irregular verbs in the imperfect. Here are their forms:

ir

iba	íbamos
ibas	ibais
iba	iban

ser

era	éramos
eras	erais
era	eran

ver

veía	veíamos
veías	veíais
veía	veían

- The imperfect form of *hay* is *había* ("there was / were, there used to be").

  Generalmente, no **había** muchos participantes en el campeonato.

 **Gramática** **Leer/Escribir**

Recuerdos de mi niñez

Completa los párrafos con la forma del imperfecto del verbo apropiado de cada recuadro.

ir	tener	ser	leer	sacar

Cuando yo __1.__ niño, me gustaba mucho leer. Yo __2.__ una colección de más de cien libros. Todos los sábados, mi hermana y yo __3.__ a la biblioteca. Generalmente, mi hermana __4.__ libros de historia. Yo, en cambio, __5.__ los libros de aventura.

molestar	devolver	pedir	enojar	ser

A veces, mis amigos me __6.__ prestado un libro. A mí no me __7.__ compartir los libros, pero cuando ellos no los __8.__ , entonces yo me __9.__ mucho. Los libros __10.__ mis mejores amigos.

Universal Access

Students with Learning Difficulties

Some students may need extra help in order to understand verb form paradigms like those in the *Gramática* on this page. Copy some of the paradigms on the board, including the subject pronouns, so students can associate subjects with verb forms.

Advanced Learners

Invite students to prepare and deliver a short presentation in which they practice using the imperfect. They can tell about a situation that occurred regularly in the past, such as a summer camp they attended, a vacation spot their family repeatedly visited, a pastime they engaged in, or a class they attended in grade school.

 **Gramática** **Leer/Hablar** ···········

Campeonatos escolares

Marilú recuerda los deportes y las actividades que hacía de niña en la escuela primaria. Depués de leer su descripción, trabaja con otro(a) estudiante para hacer y contestar preguntas sobre los recuerdos de Marilú.

❝ Cuando yo asistía a la escuela primaria, jugaba con un equipo de fútbol que siempre vencía a los demás. Mis compañeras y yo nos entrenábamos todos los días y nuestros entrenadores nos ayudaban mucho. Nuestros padres siempre nos animaban para alcanzar nuestra meta, que era hacer el mejor esfuerzo posible para ganar.

Un año, salimos campeonas de todo el estado y nos dieron un trofeo.

—¡Felicitaciones campeonas! —nos decían todos durante la entrega de premios. Nos emocionamos mucho. **❞**

Modelo

A —¿Qué deporte jugaba Marilú de niña?
B —Marilú jugaba al fútbol.

 Gramática   **Escribir/Hablar** ···········

¿Qué hacías de niño(a)?

❶ Escribe una descripción de tu vida cuando eras niño(a). Incluye:

- los juegos
- los deportes
- la familia
- los programas de televisión
- la comida
- los(as) amigos(as)

❷ Ahora, pregúntale a otro(a) estudiante si hacía las mismas cosas que tú. Toma notas de sus respuestas.

Modelo

A —De niño(a) yo leía libros de cuentos. ¿Tú también leías libros de cuentos?
B —Sí, a mí me gustaba leer libros de cuentos.

❸ Preséntale a la clase una comparación entre tu vida de niño(a) y la de tu compañero(a).

Modelo

Los dos comíamos cosas dulces. Yo prefería chocolate y él prefería helado.

● **Más práctica** ···········
Practice Workbook 1-10

PHSchool.com
For: Practice with the imperfect
Visit: www.phschool.com
Web Code: jed-0107

cuarenta y tres **43**
Capítulo 1

Enriching Your Teaching

Teacher-to-Teacher
Students enjoy talking about movie or TV characters they know well. Have them choose one such character and prepare a brief description, telling about where the character lived, what he or she was like, what activities he or she regularly did, and what makes this character stand out: *Gandalf era un mago en la historia* El señor de los anillos. *Era muy bueno y siempre luchaba contra el mal. Tenía la barba muy larga y blanca....*

---

 37 *Standards:* 1.1, 1.2

Focus: Practicing the imperfect tense through reading and discussion

Suggestions: Before students work in pairs, ask them to look through Marilú's description for verbs that are in the preterite rather than the imperfect. Discuss the difference between actions that happened at one specific time in the past and those that happened regularly.

Answers will vary.

Extension: Ask students to write their questions about Marilú's description on slips of paper. Place the slips in a hat or other container. Have students take turns drawing one question at a time, reading it aloud, and answering it orally.

 38 *Standards:* 1.1, 1.3

Focus: Practicing the imperfect verb forms in context

Recycle: games and pastimes, food, family members

Suggestions: In step 1, tell students they should write at least one sentence about each of the items. Point out that, as students are interviewing each other in step 2, they should take notes they can use in step 3.

Answers will vary.

Additional Resources
- Writing, Audio & Video Workbook: Cap. 1, Writing Activity 11

 Assessment
- Prueba 1-8: *El imperfecto*

Chapter Project
Students can perform step 4 at this point. Be sure they understand your corrections and suggestions. (For more information, see p. 16-a.)

Gramática·Repaso

Presentation

Resources: Voc. & Gram. Transparencies: 47

Suggestions: Ask volunteers to give additional examples of each use of the imperfect.

Standards: 1.3

Focus: Practicing the imperfect

Recycle: household chores, leisure activities

Suggestions: After students write their sentences, have them share their recollections with the class.

Answers will vary.

Actividad 40

Standards: 1.1, 1.2, 1.3

Focus: Practicing new vocabulary and past tenses through speaking and writing in context

Suggestions: Tell students that the event they choose to talk about with their partners can be real or imaginary. In step 2, encourage students to write in complete sentences in paragraph form.

Answers will vary.

Alternative Assessment: Use the written report from step 2 of *Actividad 40* as an opportunity to assess students' writing skills. Students' oral presentations of their reports can likewise be used to assess speaking skills.

Gramática·Repaso

Usos del imperfecto

You have learned to use the imperfect to describe something that used to take place regularly. You also use the imperfect

- to describe people, places, and situations in the past.
  Hacía mucho calor. El estadio **estaba** lleno. Los espectadores **gritaban**.

- to talk about a past action that was continuous or that kept happening.
  Los atletas **se entrenaban** en el gimnasio.

- to describe the date, time, age, and weather in the past.
  Era el 5 de noviembre. **Eran** las seis de la mañana pero ya **hacía** calor.

 Gramática **Escribir**

Los sábados del pasado

Cuando eras pequeño(a), ¿cómo pasabas los sábados? Usa *ir, ver* o *ser* en cada respuesta.

Modelo

A veces, yo . . .
A veces, yo iba al supermercado con mi mamá.

1. Por las mañanas, mis hermanos y yo . . .
2. Por las tardes, yo . . .
3. Muchas veces, yo . . .
4. Mis padres . . .
5. Los quehaceres . . .
6. Por la tarde, mis amigos . . .

 **Gramática** **Hablar/Escribir**

Entrevista

❶ Entrevista a un(a) compañero(a). Hazle preguntas sobre alguna competencia a la que asistió o en la que participó. Toma notas de sus respuestas.

1. ¿Dónde tuvo lugar la competencia de . . . ?
2. ¿A qué hora era?
3. ¿Cómo era el auditorio / estadio / salón / gimnasio?
4. ¿Quiénes eran los participantes?
5. ¿Quiénes asistieron al evento?
6. ¿Cómo se sintió el público?
7. ¿Qué premios entregaron a los ganadores?
8. ¿Cómo se sentían los ganadores después de recibir sus premios?

❷ Escribe un reportaje basado en las notas de la entrevista que hiciste. Luego, lee tu reportaje a la clase.

Universal Access

Students with Learning Difficulties

Help students better understand the concept of completed actions vs. continuous actions in the past. Have them first focus on a completed action they did earlier in the day: "I ate breakfast." Then ask them to think of something that was happening while they performed that action: "It was raining." Translate their sentences to Spanish.

Advanced Learners

Have students prepare and present brief oral presentations about an important event they experienced in the past. Their presentations should include the imperfect and preterite tenses. They should use the imperfect to "set the scene" of the event and to describe people, places, or things, and the preterite to tell about the event itself.

Actividad 41 Gramática ♻ Leer/Escribir ········

Una atleta olímpica

❶ Completa la biografía de la atleta olímpica Jennifer Rodriguez con el pretérito o el imperfecto del verbo entre paréntesis.

> **¿Recuerdas?**
> Los verbos *competir* y *conseguir* tienen el cambio e → i en el pretérito.

De niña, Jennifer (1976–) __1.__ *(ser)* muy atlética. Ella __2.__ *(ser)* la primera atleta de origen hispanohablante que __3.__ *(ganar)* dos medallas en los Juegos Olímpicos de Invierno en las carreras de patinaje de velocidad.

Cuando __4.__ *(ser)* pequeña, Jennifer __5.__ *(comenzar)* a patinar sobre ruedas. __6.__ *(demostrar)* tanto entusiasmo y agilidad que sus padres __7.__ *(decidir)* inscribirla en clases cuando __8.__ *(tener)* sólo 4 años.

Un año más tarde, Jennifer __9.__ *(competir)* en patinaje artístico y de velocidad y __10.__ *(vencer)* a otros niños de su edad.

En 1996, Jennifer __11.__ *(comenzar)* a practicar el patinaje sobre hielo. En 1998, Jennifer __12.__ *(conseguir)* la cuarta posición en la carrera de 3,000 metros en los Juegos Olímpicos de Invierno, en Nagano.

En los Juegos Olímpicos de Invierno de Salt Lake City, Jennifer __13.__ *(subir)* al podio por primera vez, al obtener dos medallas de bronce en patinaje de velocidad sobre hielo en las categorías de 1,000 y 1,500 metros.

Jennifer Rodriguez

❷ Contesta las preguntas sobre Jennifer Rodriguez.

1. ¿Por qué sus padres inscribieron a Jennifer en clases de patinaje?

2. ¿Por qué crees que Jennifer pudo comenzar a competir sólo años después de comenzar a patinar sobre hielo?

3. ¿Qué características personales crees que ayudaron a Jennifer a triunfar?

4. ¿Qué importancia tienen las medallas olímpicas de Jennifer para otros jóvenes hispanohablantes de los Estados Unidos?

5. ¿Qué edad tenía Jennifer cuando compitió en los Juegos Olímpicos de Invierno en Nagano?

6. ¿Conoces a otros(as) campeones(as) olímpicos(as) de habla hispana? ¿Qué hacen?

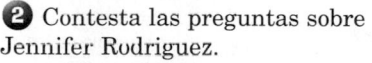

El español en el mundo del trabajo

El español y el fútbol americano

"Hoy en día, muchos latinoamericanos que viven en los Estados Unidos disfrutan del fútbol americano. Algunas cadenas[1] de televisión transmiten sus programas sobre fútbol americano también en español. Mi labor es traducir[2] lo que dicen los jugadores y locutores. Pero ese deporte no se practica mucho en América Latina ni en España, por eso a veces es difícil buscar la palabra que exprese en español la jugada, el error o la regla que no existe en nuestro idioma. Muchas veces hay que inventar la palabra o expresión que necesitamos. Traducir es hacer que dos culturas distintas puedan conversar . . . hasta de deportes."

1 networks 2 translate

cuarenta y cinco 45
Capítulo 1

Enriching Your Teaching

Culture Note

The 1992 Summer Olympics cost the city of Barcelona $10 billion. A quarter of this sum was used to modernize the city, especially the old waterfront area. The Games earned only $3 billion, but the publicity led to an enormous increase in tourism, and the improved roads, housing, and transportation have benefited the citizens.

Internet Search

Keywords:

intérpretes, traducción castellana, trabajar de traductor

Practice and Communicate   ①

Actividad 41   *Standards:* 1.2, 1.3

Resources: Practice Answers on Transparencies

Focus: Practicing the preterite and imperfect tenses in a cloze exercise; writing to demonstrate comprehension of a reading passage

Recycle: sports, personality traits

Suggestions: After students complete the activity on their own, have them take turns reading through it aloud together. Have them give their reasons for choosing the preterite or imperfect. In step 2, point out to students that not all the questions have explicit answers. They must use their critical thinking skills and background knowledge to answer questions 2, 3, 4, and 6.

Answers:

1. era	8. tenía
2. fue	9. compitió
3. ganó	10. venció
4. era	11. comenzó
5. comenzó	12. consiguió
6. Demostró	13. subió
7. decidieron	

Step 2

1. Jennifer demostró mucho entusiasmo y agilidad en patinar sobre ruedas.

2–4. Answers will vary.

5. Tenía 22 años.

6. Answers will vary.

El español en el mundo del trabajo

Presentation

Standards: 1.2, 5.2

Suggestions: Explain that translation *(la traducción)* rests in the domains of reading and writing. Most translators *(los traductores)* read in the foreign language and write the translation in their own language. Interpretation *(la interpretación)* is a more immediate oral activity. Interpreters *(los intérpretes)* listen to the foreign language and speak the interpretation in their own language.

45

Practice and Communicate

Actividad 42

Standards: 1.2, 1.3

Resources: Practice Answers on Transparencies

Focus: Practicing the preterite and imperfect tenses in a cloze exercise

Suggestions: Point out that the information in *En voz alta* continues the story of the same soccer match.

Answers:

Step 1

1. Era	6. eran	11. paró
2. Llovía	7. eran	12. dio
3. hacía	8. comenzó	13. tuvo
4. Era	9. iba	14. llegó
5. Jugaban	10. parecía	15. estaban

Step 2

1. El partido tuvo lugar el 28 de mayo de 1928 en Santander, España.
2–4. Answers will vary.

En voz alta

Presentation

Standards: 1.2, 3.1, 3.2, 5.2

Resources: Audio Program: Cap. 1, Track 17

Suggestions: Have students silently read the information about the famous soccer match and the *Himno del Barcelona.* Ask comprehension questions about the *Himno: ¿Qué dice el himno acerca de la relación entre los jugadores y los aficionados? Según el himno, ¿qué nombre tienen ellos?*

Before having students recite the anthem, direct their attention to the information in the *¿Recuerdas?* Allow them a few minutes to practice with a partner.

Answers will vary.

Chapter Project

Students can perform step 5 at this point. Record their presentations on cassette or videotape for inclusion in their portfolio. (For more information, see p. 16-a.)

Actividad 42 Gramática Leer/Escribir

Un partido inolvidable

1 Completa esta descripción de un famoso partido de fútbol que tuvo lugar en 1928 en Santander, una ciudad en el norte de España, con el pretérito o el imperfecto del verbo entre paréntesis.

___1.___ *(ser)* el 28 de mayo de 1928. ___2.___ *(llover)* y ___3.___ *(hacer)* viento. ___4.___ *(ser)* un día muy especial para Santander. ___5.___ *(jugar)* el Barcelona y La Real Sociedad. Platko y Samitier ___6.___ *(ser)* las grandes estrellas del Barcelona. Las estrellas de la Real ___7.___ *(ser)* Zaldúa y Cholín.

Por fin ___8.___ *(comenzar)* el partido. En un momento en que la Real ___9.___ *(ir)* hacia el área del Barcelona, Cholín avanzó[1] hasta el arco[2]. Cuando el gol ___10.___ *(parecer)* inevitable, el guardameta[3] Platko se arrojó[4]

---

sobre el pie de Cholín y ___11.___ *(parar)* la pelota. Sin embargo, el pie de Cholín ___12.___ *(dar)* contra la cabeza de Platko, quien ___13.___ *(tener)* que salir del campo, con la frente[5] llena de sangre. A los pocos minutos se ___14.___ *(llegar)* al descanso, con un empate de cero a cero. Los aficionados del Barcelona ___15.___ *(estar)* desanimados. ¿Cómo podían ganar el campeonato sin Platko, su gran guardameta?

---

5 forehead

2 Ahora, contesta las preguntas.

1. ¿Dónde y cuándo tuvo lugar el partido?
2. ¿Crees que Platko era valiente? ¿Por qué?
3. ¿Qué pensaban los aficionados del Barcelona sobre Platko? ¿Cómo lo sabes?
4. ¿Alguna vez te sentiste como los aficionados del Barcelona? ¿Por qué?

1 moved forward 2 goal 3 goalkeeper 4 leaped

En voz alta

¿Sabes cómo terminó el partido? Platko volvió al juego. Su equipo ganó uno de los encuentros más emocionantes de la historia del fútbol.

El equipo del Barcelona tiene un himno que los aficionados cantan durante los partidos. Este himno se canta en catalán, que es el idioma de la región de Cataluña. Se puede imaginar que los aficionados del Barcelona cantaron este himno muchas veces durante este partido inolvidable.

Escucha esta estrofa, traducida al español, del himno del Barcelona y trata de repetirla. Luego, contesta las preguntas.

- ¿Qué palabras o frases se repiten? ¿Cuál es el efecto de esta repetición?
- ¿Cómo se habla del pasado? ¿Cuál es el efecto de evocar el pasado de esta manera?

Himno del Barcelona

Jugadores, aficionados,
todos unidos hacemos fuerza,
son muchos años llenos de sacrificio,
son muchos los goles que hemos gritado,
y se ha demostrado, se ha demostrado,
que nunca nadie nos podrá doblegar.[1]
Azulgrana[2] al viento,
un grito valiente,
tenemos un nombre, lo sabe todo el mundo:
¡Barça! ¡Barça! ¡Baaaarça!!!!!

---

1 make us give in 2 blue and scarlet

¿Recuerdas?

Cuando la consonante *d* va entre vocales, su sonido es similar a la "th" en inglés de la palabra *the.* Pronuncia estas palabras del himno: *jugadores, afcionados, nadie, nada.*

46 cuarenta y seis
Manos a la obra 2

Universal Access

Heritage Language Learners

Have students pick a sport and recall the most thrilling game they ever saw, either live or on TV. Ask them to write about the game's most exciting moment or moments and to describe in detail one or two events that made the game so thrilling.

Students with Learning Difficulties

On the board, create a T-chart. Label the left side *pretérito* and the right side *imperfecto.* Write a few examples of one-time, completed actions on the left and longer, "background" actions on the right. Allow students to use the chart as a reference as they complete *Actividad 42.*

Gramática · Escribir

Actividad 43

Una competencia artística

Fuiste a una competencia artística y tuviste que escribir un informe para presentar en tu clase. Usa los dibujos para escribir lo que sucedió. Usa las formas correctas del pretérito y del imperfecto.

Estrategia

Describing events
When you describe a sequence of events, it is useful to write words such as *primero* (first), *luego* (next), *después* (then), *al final* (finally) to describe the order in which these events have occurred.

1.
2.  El Palacio de las Artes
3.
4.
5.

6.
7.
8.
9.
10.

Actividad 44 · Escribir/Hablar

Un cuento en grupo

1 Usa tu imaginación para completar este cuento con cuatro de tus compañeros(as). Traten de incorporar en su cuento el vocabulario y la gramática que aprendieron en este capítulo.

1. Había una vez un(a) . . .
2. Era una persona muy . . . y . . .
3. Vivía en . . . con su(s) . . . y su(s) . . .
4. Siempre le gustaba . . . y . . .
5. Un día, al amanecer, (nombre) fue . . .
6. Era un lugar . . . y . . .
7. De repente, oyó / vio . . .
8. ¡Era un(a) . . . !
9. Cuando el / la . . . se acercó, (nombre) empezó a . . .
10. Pero entonces, se dio cuenta de . . . y . . . a pasear por . . .
11. Al final, (nombre) . . .
12. Fue una aventura muy . . .

2 Trabajen en grupo para leer, comentar y corregir el cuento que escribieron. ¿Usaron el pretérito y el imperfecto correctamente? ¿Incorporaron el vocabulario del capítulo? Añadan más detalles si es necesario.

3 Presenten su cuento a la clase. La clase va a votar por el cuento más imaginativo, el más divertido y el mejor cuento de horror.

● **Más práctica**
Practice Workbook 1-11, 1-12

Go Online
PHSchool.com

For: Practice with the imperfect
Visit: www.phschool.com
Web Code: jed-0108

Practice and Communicate

 1

Actividad 43 · *Standards:* 1.3, 3.1

Resources: Practice Answers on Transparencies

Focus: Combining learned vocabulary and structures in a written presentation

Suggestions: Direct students' attention to the transitions in the *Estrategia*. Before they write, have them practice these and other transitions orally by telling about what they did in Spanish class yesterday and using the sequencing transitions to connect their ideas.

Answers:
Reports will vary, but should include some or all of the following phrases, based on the pictured items:

1. las tres y cuarto
2. El Palacio de las Artes
3. la participante
4. el cantante
5. el pianista
6. entusiasmados
7. aplaudir
8. el trofeo
9. el certificado
10. las seis y media

Actividad 44 · *Standards:* 1.1, 1.2, 1.3

Focus: Combining learned vocabulary and structures in a group-planned story

Suggestions: Remind students that an important component of this activity is that they include in their stories all of the twelve numbered items in the correct order. Explain that this will be a factor in how they evaluate each other's stories in step 3. Their stories should also refer in some way to the picture.

Answers will vary.

Additional Resources

• Writing, Audio & Video Workbook: Cap. 1, Writing Activities 12–13
• Writing, Audio & Video Workbook: Cap. 1, Audio Activity 4–5, Tracks 18–19
• Resource Book: Cap. 1, Communicative Activity BLM

✓ **Assessment**
• Prueba 1-9: *Usos del imperfecto*
• Examen: Vocabulario y gramática 2

Enriching Your Teaching

Teacher-to-Teacher
For *Actividad 44*, give groups the option of presenting their story in the form of a skit with a narrator and actors. Kinesthetic learners will enjoy the skit format. Acting out a scene that a narrator describes in words is similar to TPR and will help reinforce meaning.

Internet Search
To heighten students' awareness of Spain's regional languages, find a bilingual version (Catalan and Spanish) of the *Himno del Barcelona* on the Internet. Write on the board or on a transparency the Catalan version of the stanza on p. 46. Ask students to point out differences and similarities between the Spanish stanza and the Catalan.

Culture

▶ **Rapid Review**
On the board, draw a simple compass rose and use it to review direction words, such as **norte, sur, este, oeste,** and the intermediate points. Point to a place on the compass rose and ask students to say which direction it is.

Country Connection

Presentation

Standards: 3.1

Resources: Voc. & Gram. Transparencies: 20 (map)

Use *Vocabulary & Grammar Transparency* 20 to help students become further acquainted with Spain. Point out that it is comprised of 17 **regiones autónomas,** including **Las Islas Canarias** and **Las Islas Baleares.** Remind students that, besides the **castellano** they are learning, four other languages are spoken in Spain: **vascuence** in **el País Vasco, catalán** in **Cataluña, valenciano** in **la Comunidad Valenciana**, and **gallego** in **Galicia**, the region in which Santiago de Compostela is located.

Puente a la cultura

Presentation

Standards: 1.1, 1.2, 1.3, 2.1, 2.2, 3.1

Focus: Reading to learn about culture

Suggestions:

Pre-reading: Ask a volunteer to read the title of the passage aloud. Read the *Estrategia* aloud together and have students answer the questions. Then go through the pictures that accompany the story. Have students read the captions, describe what they see, and add any background information they may know about pilgrimages to Santiago de Compostela.

Reading: Encourage students to read once through the entire passage silently, without stopping at problem words or to ask questions. Then have them read it again, stopping after each paragraph to address comprehension issues.

Post-reading: Ask the *¿Comprendiste?* questions to check comprehension.

¡Adelante!

Puente a la cultura
El Camino de Santiago

Objectives
- Read about a famous pilgrimage route in Spain
- Learn about how this route still thrives today
- Compare a pilgrimage to your own travel experiences

Estrategia

Activating prior knowledge
A *peregrino* (pilgrim) is a person who makes a trip for spiritual reasons. To better understand the selection, think of other pilgrims you might know of. Why did the Pilgrims come from England to Plymouth, Massachusetts in the 17th century? Why did they found a colony? Look at the maps on these pages to see the route of another group of pilgrims.

Los peregrinos de Plymouth, Massachusetts, buscaban la libertad religiosa. Otros peregrinos viajan en busca de algo sagrado o religioso, como los peregrinos musulmanes que viajan a La Meca y los peregrinos judíos y cristianos que viajan a Jerusalén.

Hace más de mil años, en el extremo noroeste de España se descubrió la tumba del apóstol Santiago[1], una figura fundamental de la religión católica. Empezaron a viajar peregrinos de toda Europa al lugar del descubrimiento en donde se fundó la ciudad de Santiago de Compostela. La ruta sagrada que seguían los peregrinos se dio a conocer[2] como El Camino de Santiago y terminaba en el portal de la Catedral de Santiago de Compostela.

A lo largo de[3] la ruta construyeron iglesias y albergues[4] para recibir a los peregrinos. Algunos peregrinos venían de lugares tan lejanos como Rusia y tardaban años para completar su viaje a pie.

Hoy en día muchas personas viajan a Santiago por la misma razón que los peregrinos de hace mil años: por motivos[5] religiosos. Otros lo recorren[6] como turistas o por motivos culturales debido a su importancia histórica.

1 the apostle Saint James
2 became known as 3 All along
4 hostels 5 reasons 6 travel along

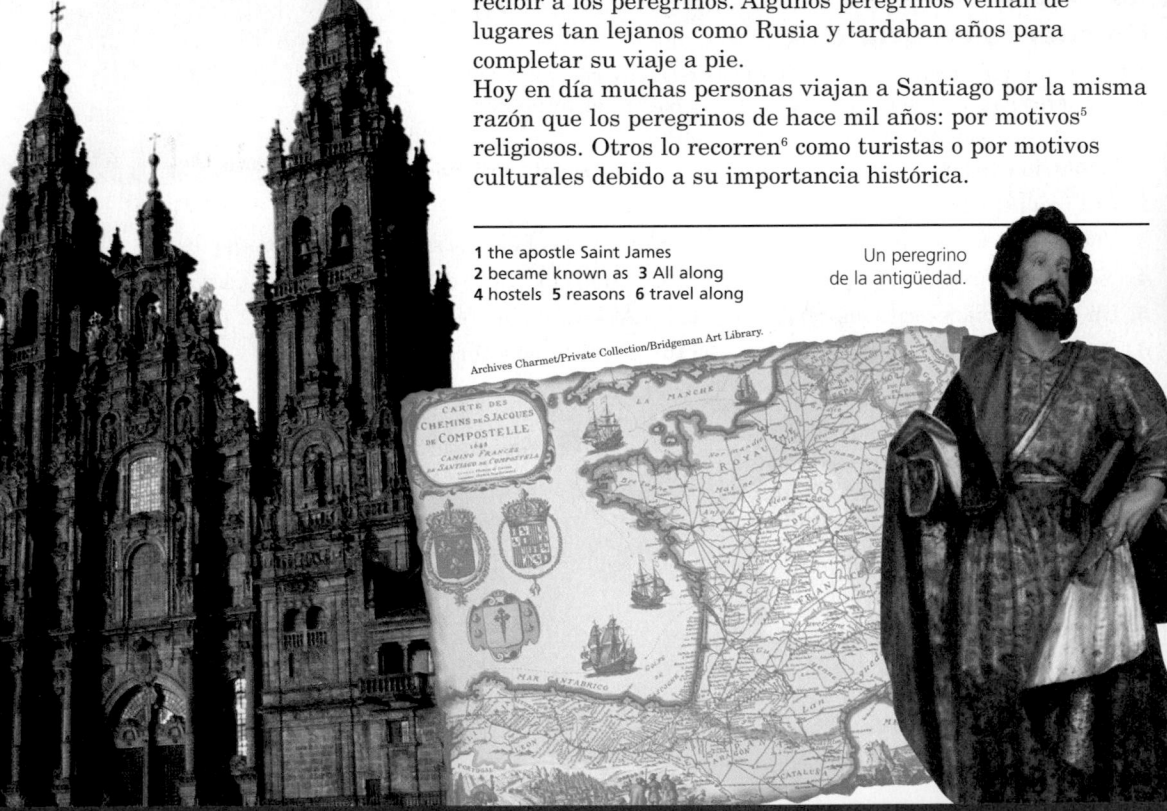

Un peregrino de la antigüedad.

Archives Charmet/Private Collection/Bridgeman Art Library.

CARTE DES CHEMINS de S.JACQUES de COMPOSTELLE

Universal Access

Heritage Language Learners
Ask students to research and report on a pilgrimage that takes place in Latin America or the southwestern United States. They might also report on a major shrine, such as the **Basílica de la Virgen de Guadalupe** in Mexico City.

Advanced Learners
Invite students to research **el Camino de Santiago** and report back to the class. They can look for information such as the names and locations of **albergues juveniles,** the costs and procedures involved when staying there, tour groups, and distances between towns along the pilgrimage.

Muchos de los que hacen este viaje son jóvenes. Algunos lo hacen a pie, otros en bicicleta y otros ¡hasta a caballo! Por eso mismo, hay muchos albergues juveniles que ofrecen servicios muy baratos. Para quedarte en ellos, debes llevar tu propia comida. Los albergues son lugares excelentes para conocer a chicos y chicas de todo el mundo.

¿Comprendiste?

1. Nombra los cuatro grupos de peregrinos que se mencionan en la lectura. En general, ¿qué buscan los peregrinos?
2. ¿De dónde eran los peregrinos que iban a Santiago?
3. ¿Cuáles son tres motivos para seguir el Camino de Santiago hoy en día?
4. ¿Qué atractivos tiene el Camino para una persona joven?

Mi propio camino

❶ Piensa en un viaje o una excursión que hiciste el año pasado. ¿Adónde fuiste? ¿Por qué fuiste allí? ¿Cómo fuiste? ¿Qué tuviste que llevar? ¿Dónde te quedaste? ¿Cómo era el lugar? ¿Qué había allí? ¿A quién(es) conociste?

❷ Ahora compara tu experiencia con el recorrido que hacen muchos jóvenes a Santiago de Compostela. ¿En qué se parecen? ¿En qué se diferencian?

Go Online
PHSchool.com

For: Internet link activity
Visit: www.phschool.com
Web Code: jed-0110

Jovénes en camino hacia
Santiago de Compostela

Uno de los albergues del
Camino de Santiago

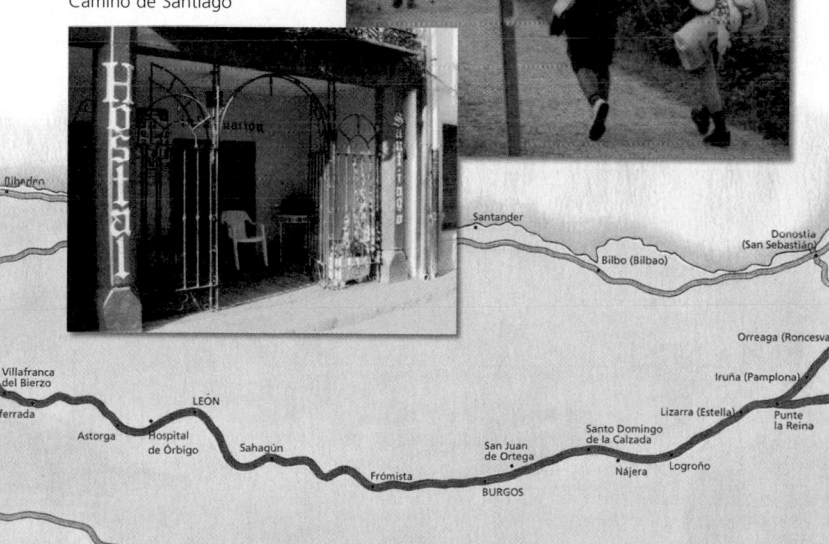

cuarenta y nueve   49
Capítulo 1

¿Qué me cuentas?

Presentation

Standards: 1.1, 1.2, 1.3

Resources: Voc. & Gram. Transparencies: 48; Audio Program: CD Cap. 1, Track 20; Resource Book: Cap. 1, Audio Script; Practice Answers on Transparencies

Focus: Practicing listening comprehension of new vocabulary and structures

Suggestions: For step 1, use the *Audio CD* or read the descriptions aloud. Allow students to hear both descriptions twice through: the first time to write their answers and the second time to check them.

For step 2, help students by pointing out important details in the pictures, such as the changing score and bandage on the girl's knee.

Depending on the size of your class, conduct step 3 as a whole-class activity.

Answers:
Step 1
1. a **2.** b **3.** c **4.** a **5.** b **6.** a

Steps 2–3
Answers will vary.

Extension: As students do step 2, have them also write three multiple-choice questions about their story, like the ones they answered in step 1. Remind them to make their distractors (the incorrect answers) different from the correct answers. Have them ask their questions orally as part of their presentation in step 3.

Dos aventuras

1 Escucha las siguientes descripciones. Después de cada descripción vas a oír tres preguntas. Escoge la mejor respuesta para cada pregunta.

1. **a.** no hacía buen tiempo   **b.** hacía calor   **c.** llovía
2. **a.** por el bosque   **b.** por el valle   **c.** por la playa
3. **a.** hasta una roca   **b.** hasta un árbol   **c.** hasta el pie de una montaña

4. **a.** mosquitos   **b.** pájaros   **c.** peces
5. **a.** binoculares   **b.** repelente de insectos   **c.** brújula
6. **a.** empezó a llover   **b.** empezó a nevar   **c.** cayeron relámpagos

2 Las ilustraciones a continuación representan un cuento. Con tus propias palabras, describe detalladamente lo que sucedió. Recuerda que no puedes usar tus notas mientras cuentas el cuento. Añade información para que el cuento resulte más interesante y ponle un título. ¡Usa tu imaginación!

Puedes usar las siguientes palabras o expresiones para conectar tus ideas.

al principio	entonces	de repente
después	mientras tanto (*meanwhile*)	más tarde
al final	sin embargo	durante

1

2

3

4

5

6

3 Trabaja con un grupo donde cada miembro cuenta su cuento. Comparen los detalles de los cuentos que escucharon. ¿Qué fue lo más interesante? ¿Qué fue lo más cómico? ¿Lo más emocionante?

50   cincuenta
¡Adelante!

Block Schedule

True/False Quiz. Have students work in pairs to create a series of ten statements that are *cierto* or *falso* about the picture sequence. Have them partner with another pair and read their statements. The team has to determine whether the other pair's statements are *cierto* or *falso.*

Universal Access

Heritage Language Learners
After students complete step 2 on p. 50, ask them to think of a sporting or other event they have witnessed that was interrupted by an unexpected incident. Have them tell what happened. Encourage them to use both the preterite and imperfect tenses.

Multiple Intelligences
Visual/Spatial: For step 2 on p. 50, help students think about details that aren't shown in the pictures by visualizing a similar event that they themselves attended. Encourage them to describe sensory images that come with the visualization. Remind them to include information about smells and sounds as well as sights.

Una experiencia inolvidable

Tarea
Imagínate que durante el verano trabajas en un campamento para niños. Un día les cuentas de una experiencia inolvidable que tuviste.

Estrategia
Choosing a topic
When giving an oral presentation, think about your audience as you choose a topic. Make a list of details that support your main idea and make sure you have enough interesting information.

Prepárate Responde a las preguntas y usa una tabla como ésta para escribir tus respuestas.

¿Adónde fuiste?	
¿Cómo era el lugar?	
¿Qué había allí?	
¿Qué sucedió?	
¿Cómo te sentiste?	
¿Cómo terminó?	

Practica Vuelve a leer la información que anotaste en la tabla. Practica varias veces tu presentación para recordar todos los detalles. Puedes usar tus notas para practicar, pero no al hablar ante la clase. Recuerda:

- describir claramente todo lo que sucedió
- mirar directamente al público
- usar el vocabulario que aprendiste en esta lección

Modelo

Hace un tiempo, fui a acampar al valle. El paisaje era impresionante. Había flores de todos los colores. Después de caminar un rato, me perdí. Entonces me di cuenta de que no tenía mi brújula. Sentí miedo. Después de un rato oí unas voces. ¡Eran mis amigos!

Haz tu presentación Imagina que tus compañeros de clase son los niños del campamento. Cuéntales a ellos tu experiencia inolvidable.

Evaluación Tu profesor(a) puede explicarte cómo va a evaluar tu presentación. Probablemente, para tu profesor(a) es importante ver que:

- te preparaste bien para hacer tu presentación
- diste suficiente información a tu público
- tu presentación se entendió bien

cincuenta y uno **51**
Capítulo 1

Presentación oral

Presentation

Standards: 1.1, 1.2, 1.3, 3.1

Resources: Voc. & Gram. Transparencies: 4

Focus: Preparing and delivering an oral presentation

Suggestions: Review the task and the four-step approach with students. Before they write their questions, direct students' attention to the *Estrategia*. Review the rubrics with the class (see Assessment below) to explain how you will grade the performance task. Do a presentation of your own (called an anchor) to model a top-scoring presentation. Have students work through each step of the speaking process.

Portfolio

Record students' oral presentations on audiocassette or videotape for inclusion in their portfolios.

✓ Assessment

- Assessment Program: Cap. 1, Rubrics

Give students copies of the rubric before they begin the activity. Go over the descriptions of the different levels of performance. After assessing students, help individuals understand how their performance could be improved.

Teacher-to-Teacher

Here's a handy tactic that many students may find useful. Record your model presentation on videotape. This way, students can view the model as often as they wish while they prepare and practice their own presentations. Some students show a marked improvement in their presentation skills when they have a readily accessible model to study. Remind them that it is only a model and that their presentations should not include any content taken directly from it.

Enriching Your Teaching

RUBRIC	Score 1	Score 3	Score 5
How well you narrate the event	You don't include narration or have incomplete narration.	You present an idea for narration, but it needs development.	Your narration is well developed and interesting.
How well you use chapter vocabulary	Your chapter vocabulary is absent.	You used one or two chapter vocabulary items.	You used several chapter vocabulary items appropriately.
How effectively you deliver your speech	You have no eye contact with the audience. There is little or no intonation.	You made some eye contact. You used intonation, but not convincingly.	You had good eye contact with the audience. Intonation and gestures made the narration interesting.

Language Arts Connection

Standards: 3.1

Explain to students that the five-step writing process presented on these two pages will be used consistently throughout *Realidades*. Point out that this is the same process they most likely use for writing assignments in their Language Arts classes. They can apply the skills and strategies they learn there to their writing in Spanish and vice versa.

Presentación escrita

Presentation

Standards: 1.3, 3.1

Resources: Voc. & Gram. Transparencies: 5

Focus: Combining learned vocabulary and structures in a written presentation

Suggestions: Explain at the start the criteria you will use to evaluate students' compositions. (See step 5, *Evaluación* and *Assessment* on the next page.)

During step 1, circulate and consult with students. Use questions and suggestions to help them limit their topic. For example, a student will have trouble bringing life to a composition on a topic as broad as **un verano en Chiapas.** Help him or her narrow the topic to one important or interesting incident that happened that summer.

During step 2, direct students' attention to the *Estrategia.* Point out that focusing on details requires them to stretch their vocabulary and grammar skills because they will include more ideas and images in their sentences.

Presentación escrita

Aventuras bajo el sol

Estrategia

Adding details
Adding details to our writing makes it more interesting. For instance, if you say *"oí un ruido y me asusté,"* the reader cannot imagine the setting very well. But if you write: *"En la oscuridad de la noche, sentí un ruido como de un trueno . . . comencé a gritar,"* your reader will have a better picture of what happened to you.

Imagínate que acabas de participar en una de las actividades que muestran las fotos de este capítulo. Escribe un cuento sobre esa aventura. ¿Quiénes participaron? ¿Cómo era el lugar? ¿Qué querían ver? ¿Cómo lo pasaron? ¿Fue emocionante? ¿Cómo te sentiste al final?

1 Antes de escribir

Usa una red de palabras para organizar las ideas que tienes para la composición.

2 Borrador

Escribe tu borrador. Usa correctamente el pretérito y el imperfecto y el vocabulario de esta lección para contar tu experiencia. Escribe tus ideas en orden lógico, así tu cuento va a ser más interesante y más fácil de entender.

52 cincuenta y dos
¡Adelante!

Universal Access

Heritage Language Learners

These students are sometimes used as reference sources by those who are not heritage speakers. This arrangement can be beneficial to both parties, and many heritage language learners are happy to provide help. Set limits, however, to make sure their own work is not unduly interrupted.

Students with Learning Difficulties

To stress the importance of details in a narrative, ask students to "freeze" the action of the characters in their minds, as if they had pressed the "pause" button on a video or DVD. While the characters are frozen tell them to concentrate on the details in the scene, such as clothing and background objects.

Modelo

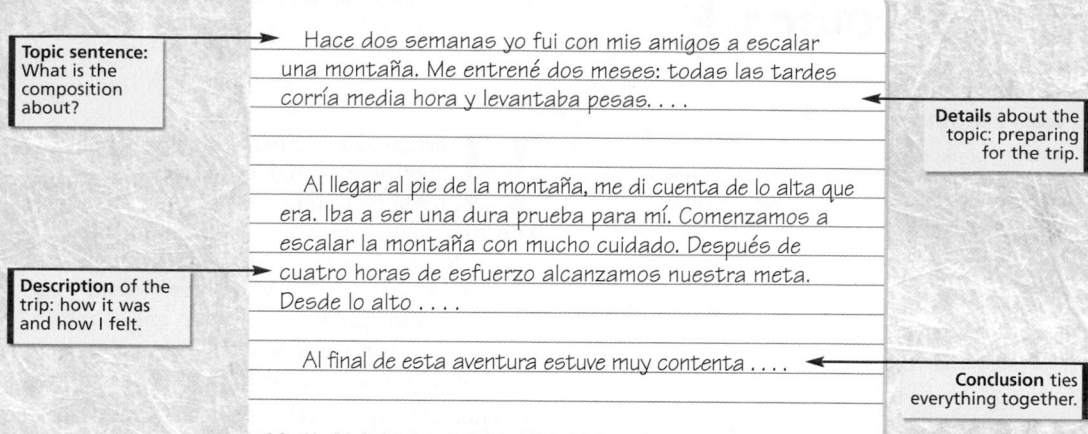

Topic sentence: What is the composition about?

Hace dos semanas yo fui con mis amigos a escalar una montaña. Me entrené dos meses: todas las tardes corría media hora y levantaba pesas. . . .

Details about the topic: preparing for the trip.

Al llegar al pie de la montaña, me di cuenta de lo alta que era. Iba a ser una dura prueba para mí. Comenzamos a escalar la montaña con mucho cuidado. Después de cuatro horas de esfuerzo alcanzamos nuestra meta. Desde lo alto . . . .

Description of the trip: how it was and how I felt.

Al final de esta aventura estuve muy contenta . . . .

Conclusion ties everything together.

3 Redacción/Revisión

Después de escribir el primer borrador de la composición, trabaja con otro(a) estudiante para intercambiar los trabajos y leerlos. Decidan qué aspectos son más efectivos. Fíjense en cómo el escritor del modelo incluyó detalles en su composición. Cada persona puede decir qué se puede hacer para mejorar la composición que leyó.

Haz lo siguiente: Subraya con una línea los verbos en pretérito, y con dos líneas los verbos en imperfecto.

- ¿Hay concordancia *(agreement)* entre cada sujeto y verbo?

- ¿El pretérito y el imperfecto están empleados correctamente?

fui
Hace dos semanas ~~yo fueron~~ con mis

amigos a escalar una montaña. Me <u>entrené</u> dos

corría
meses: todas las tardes ~~corrían~~ media hora y

<u>levantaba</u> pesas.

4 Publicación

Antes de crear la versión final, lee de nuevo tu borrador y repasa los siguientes puntos:

- ¿Sigue mi cuento un orden lógico?

- ¿Tiene un argumento, con un principio, un cuerpo y un final?

- ¿Hay otros detalles que debo poner en mi composición? ¿Hay algo que debo quitar?

Después de revisar el borrador, escribe tu composición en limpio.

5 Evaluación

Tu profesor(a) puede explicarte cómo va a evaluar tu presentación. Probablemente, para tu profesor(a) es importante ver que:

- usaste suficientes detalles para hacer tu cuento más interesante

- tus oraciones tienen sentido; cada oración expresa claramente una idea completa

- tu cuento sigue un orden lógico

- usaste correctamente el vocabulario y la gramática

cincuenta y tres 53
Capítulo 1

Suggestions (Cont'd):
During step 3, encourage students to add details to their writing, focusing on sentence structure and transitions as they work in added details. During their peer consultations, remind them to follow the suggestions shown. Remind them that now is the time to think about a title to give their finished work.

Evaluation: Steps 4 and 5 overlap. Students will need evaluation by you, their peers, or self-evaluation to fine-tune and polish their drafts.

Portfolio

Keep students' final drafts in their portfolios as a writing sample.

✓ **Assessment**
- Assessment Program: Cap. 1, Rubrics

Give students copies of the rubric before they begin the activity. Go over the descriptions of the different levels of performance.

Enriching Your Teaching

RUBRIC	Score 1	Score 3	Score 5
Completion of task	You don't highlight any special event.	Your idea for narration is present but needs development.	Your special event is clearly narrated and made prominent.
Organization and level of detail	Your ideas aren't presented in logical order nor with details.	You have some organizational problems. One or two details are provided.	Your organization is easy to follow. You use good details.
Sentence structure	Your sentences are run-on or are fragmented with many errors.	You use sentences consistently, but with some errors.	Your sentence structure is correct with few errors.

Lectura

Presentation

Standards: 1.2, 1.3, 2.2, 3.1, 3.2, 5.2

Focus: Reading an extended passage

Suggestions:

Pre-reading: Read aloud the title of the passage. Model the pronunciation of the names ***Iztaccíhuatl*** and ***Popocatépetl*** and have students repeat. Ask if anyone knows from what Native American culture these unusual names come. If necessary, explain that they are ***náhuatl*** names. ***Náhuatl*** is the language of the Aztecs. Before the arrival of the conquistadors, the Aztecs had a great civilization that included the area around what is today Mexico City. Tell students they will come across other ***náhuatl*** words as they read the selection.

Ask students to share what they know about the two volcanoes near Mexico city named ***Iztaccíhuatl*** and ***Popocatépetl.*** Tell them they are going to read an Aztec legend that explains how these two mountains were created and got their names.

Before reading, direct students' attention to the *Estrategia* and to the *Al leer* section. Have them answer the questions there and copy the graphic organizer from p. 57.

Block Schedule

After reading the *Lectura,* assign each student a paragraph for which he or she must write four questions. Have students circulate around the class asking and answering the questions related to each of their paragraphs. This should help students comprehend the story in more detail.

Lectura

El Iztaccíhuatl y el Popocatépetl

Objectives

- Read about a Mexican legend
- Make predictions about a story
- Recount the plot of a story

Estrategia

Making predictions
Making predictions about what will happen in a story allows us to focus on what we read and increases our interest in the story.

- Do you know any stories that explain a natural phenomenon?
- Look at the picture of the volcanoes. What do you think this story will explain?

Al leer

El cuento que vas a leer es una leyenda mexicana que relaciona una historia de amor con dos volcanes en México. Copia la gráfica organizadora de la página 57. Mientras lees la selección, llena todos los espacios de la gráfica con la información del cuento.

Mientras lees, presta atención a los siguientes puntos:

- el conflicto entre las dos familias
- la relación entre los personajes principales y la naturaleza

54 cincuenta y cuatro
Lectura

Hace mucho tiempo, en la gran ciudad de Teotihuacán, había un rey tolteca que tenía una hija muy hermosa. El pelo de la princesa era tan negro y suave como una noche de verano, sus ojos eran tan grandes y oscuros como las aguas de un lago secreto y su sonrisa era tan bonita que decían que el sol miraba por las montañas todas las mañanas para ser el primero en verla.

Muchos príncipes ricos y famosos venían de todas partes de la región tolteca para ganar el amor de la princesa, pero ella no se enamoraba de ninguno. El rey, que quería para su hija un esposo rico de buena posición en la sociedad tolteca, ya estaba impaciente. A veces le preguntaba a la princesa qué esperaba.

—No sé —contestaba la muchacha—. Sólo sé que mi esposo va a ser alguien que voy a amar desde el principio y para siempre.

Un día llegó a la ciudad un príncipe chichimeca. Los chichimecas no tenían una civilización tan espléndida como la de los toltecas. Vivían de la caza[1] y la pesca en las montañas. Los toltecas pensaban que los chichimecas vivían como perros, y se reían de ellos.

---

1 hunting

Universal Access

Students with Special Needs

To help the hearing-impaired understand these names, say them aloud slowly several times (note that final *-l* is hardly pronounced): Popocatépetl (poh-poh-ca-TEH-pehtl), Iztaccíhuatl (is-tahs-IH-wahtl), Teotihuacán (tah-oh-tee-hwah-KAHN), chichimeca (chee-chee-MEH-kuh), náhuatl (NAH-wahtl).

Advanced Learners

Invite students to write a narrative about a volcanic eruption from the point of view of a Toltec or Chichimec person. Encourage them to try to portray the emotions such a person might feel at such a moment.

Príncipe chichimeca

El príncipe chichimeca venía para visitar el gran mercado de Teotihuacán, donde vendían hermosísimos objetos de oro, ropa de brillantes colores, animales exóticos y muchas otras cosas.

Ese mismo día, la princesa tolteca estaba en el mercado comprando canastas², telas y alfombras para su palacio. Pasó que, de repente, entre toda la gente y el ruido del mercado, el príncipe y la princesa se fijaron³ uno en el otro. Sin una palabra, desde el principio y para siempre, el príncipe y la princesa se enamoraron.

Los dos sabían muy bien que su amor era prohibido. Cada uno debía casarse con alguien de su pueblo y su clase: la princesa tolteca con un príncipe tolteca y el príncipe chichimeca con una princesa chichimeca.

---

2 large round basket **3** they noticed

Las señoras que acompañaban⁴ a la princesa se dieron cuenta de lo que pasaba, y rápidamente llevaron a la princesa a su palacio. El príncipe también regresó al suyo en las montañas. Trató de olvidar a la bella princesa, pero no pudo.

Después de un tiempo, el príncipe decidió volver a Teotihuacán, a pedir la mano de la princesa. Un día se vistió de su ropa más fina y fue al palacio del rey tolteca. Allí mandó⁵ a sus mensajeros a hablar con el rey para pedirle a su hija como esposa.

Cuando oyó las palabras de los mensajeros del príncipe, el rey tembló⁶ de furia y gritó: —¡Mi hija sólo se va a casar con un príncipe tolteca, nunca con un chichimeca que vive en las montañas como un animal!

---

4 escorted **5** sent **6** shook

Princesa tolteca

cincuenta y cinco   55
Capítulo 1

Enriching Your Teaching

Culture Note

Teotihuacán was home to a culture that flourished from the first century A.D. until the middle of the sixth—before the Toltecs arrived. With 200,000 people, it was one of the largest cities in the entire world. Nevertheless, very little is known about the people who lived there, not even what language they spoke.

Internet Search
Keywords:

leyenda + Popocatépetl, leyenda + azteca, Iztaccíhuatl, Ixtaccíhuatl

---

Suggestions (Cont'd):

Reading: Allow students time to read silently through the entire selection on their own. You might assign this task for homework. Then go back and read the selection again together, either aloud or silently, depending on time.

During the second reading, pause at regular intervals, such as after each paragraph, in order to address any comprehension issues students may bring up. Ask your own comprehension questions to help students focus on the main idea and important details of each section.

Here are some possible questions you might ask about the second paragraph of the passage. Note that some of them are accompanied by a partner question with a lower level of difficulty:

¿Quiénes venían de todas partes de la región tolteca?

¿Por qué venían los príncipes? ¿Venían para ver los volcanes o para ganar el amor de la princesa?

¿La princesa se enamoraba de algún príncipe?

¿Qué quería el rey para su hija? ¿Qué tipo de esposo quería para ella?

Cierto o falso: El rey estaba impaciente porque su hija se enamoró de dos príncipes.

Remind students to fill out their charts as they read the passage.

Teacher-to-Teacher

Try timing students for their initial silent reading of a longer passage. Give them three to four minutes per page, and call out these increments as they read. This forces them to keep moving and to get an overview of the entire passage, including spots that might be problematic, without getting bogged down on any one word or sentence.

Suggestions (Cont'd):

Post-reading: Once students have read and discussed the passage section by section, allow them time for another silent reading. This allows them to apply their prior knowledge about the topic, as well as the information they have learned from class discussion. During a final silent reading, students can approach the passage with more confidence and iron out any final comprehension problems they may have.

Cuando la princesa oyó todo esto, se sintió muy triste. Le tenía mucho respeto a su papá, pero sabía que no podía vivir sin el amor del príncipe chichimeca. Salió de su palacio y se reunió con el príncipe para decirle que sí quería casarse con él. Se fueron a las montañas, y esa noche se casaron.

Al día siguiente, la princesa regresó a Teotihuacán y le dijo a su padre que ya era la esposa del príncipe chichimeca. Le pidió perdón y esperó la comprensión de su padre. Pero el rey estaba furioso: —¿Cómo pudiste hacerme eso? —le preguntó a su hija—. ¡Vete de aquí y no vuelvas nunca! ¡Y no le pidas ni comida ni casa a ningún tolteca, que no te va a dar nada! ¡Lo prohíbo!

Lo mismo le pasó al príncipe cuando volvió a su palacio. Su padre le gritó: —¿Te casaste con una tolteca? ¡Ya no eres mi hijo, ni eres chichimeca! ¡No esperes nunca la ayuda de ningún chichimeca!

Con el corazón muy triste, el príncipe y la princesa se reunieron y empezaron a buscar dónde vivir en las montañas. Nadie los quería ayudar o darles un lugar para descansar y refugiarse de los vientos fríos.

Comían sólo hierbas[7] y frutas, porque el príncipe no tenía nada con qué cazar o pescar. Poco a poco, los esposos se estaban muriendo.

Una noche muy fría y larga, el príncipe se dio cuenta de que pronto se iban a morir los dos. Estaban en un valle pequeño desde donde podían ver la ciudad de Teotihuacán. La princesa pensaba en su casa, y el príncipe la miraba con tristeza y amor, sabiendo lo que pensaba.

—Mi bella princesa —le dijo—, ya nos vamos a morir. Nos vamos a separar ahora en este mundo para estar siempre juntos en el otro. Duerme por última vez en mis brazos esta noche. En la mañana, tú te vas a ir a la montaña más baja que mira sobre tu ciudad, y yo me voy a ir a la montaña más alta que también mira sobre tu ciudad. Allí vamos a descansar, allí te voy a cuidar para siempre y nuestros espíritus[8] van a ser un solo espíritu. Al día siguiente los dos se separaron, y cada uno empezó a subir su montaña. La princesa subió la montaña Iztaccíhuatl y el príncipe subió la montaña Popocatépetl.

Cuando la princesa llegó a la cumbre[9] de su montaña, se durmió y la nieve la cubrió[10]. El príncipe se puso de rodillas, mirando hacia la princesa y la nieve también lo cubrió.

De esta manera podemos ver hoy al príncipe y a la princesa, en la cumbre del Iztaccíhuatl y el Popocatépetl. A veces hay grandes ruidos desde muy dentro del Popocatépetl. Es el príncipe llorando por su princesa.

7 grass **8** spirits, souls **9** summit **10** covered

Universal Access

Students with Learning Difficulties
Help students deal with long reading passages by "jigsawing" the reading process. Divide the passage into sections and have individuals or pairs work on reading comprehension for their assigned section only. Then have students meet and share what they have learned about their section.

Advanced Learners
Mt. Popocatéptl erupted in 1997 and again in 2000. Encourage students to research and report on these eruptions and on the status of the volcano today

Interacción con la lectura

1 Llena el organizador gráfico con detalles del argumento.

alguien _____ → quería _____ → por eso _____

pero _____ → por eso _____ → al final _____

2 Trabaja con otro(a) estudiante para comparar la información de sus organizadores. Contesten las preguntas y añadan a sus organizadores cualquier otro detalle interesante que recuerden.

- ¿Cómo conoció el príncipe a la princesa? ¿Por qué no podían casarse?
- ¿Qué hicieron los jóvenes? ¿Crees que hicieron bien?
- ¿Qué emociones expresan los personajes al comienzo, después y al final del cuento?
- ¿Cómo terminó la historia? ¿Pudo tener otro final?

3 Ahora escribe un resumen del cuento basado en el organizador gráfico.

4 Trabaja con un grupo para contestar estas preguntas.

- ¿Qué cuentos, obras de teatro o películas conocen que cuentan una historia similar?
- ¿Por qué en casi todas las culturas hay historias de jóvenes enamorados a quienes sus padres no comprenden?

Fondo cultural

Los indígenas americanos vivían en íntimo contacto con la naturaleza. Algunos de sus mitos y leyendas explicaban fenómenos naturales como los eclipses, las tormentas, las erupciones volcánicas. La leyenda de Iztaccíhuatl y Popocatépetl explica la formación de dos volcanes cerca de la Ciudad de México. Iztaccíhuatl, el volcán más antiguo, tiene la forma de una mujer reclinada. En efecto, su nombre en la lengua náhuatl quiere decir "mujer dormida". Popocatépetl, el volcán más joven, es todavía activo. Su nombre náhuatl significa "montaña que humea" (smoking mountain).

- ¿Qué otra leyenda conoces que explique un fenómeno natural?

cincuenta y siete 57
Capítulo 1

Enriching Your Teaching

Culture Note

Perhaps the most famous volcano in Mexico is Parícutin. It was born in 1943, when a farmer discovered a crack in his cornfield. Soon ashes covered the area. A year later, the village of San Salvador Parícutin had been overrun by lava. The last eruption was in 1952. By then the volcano had grown to an altitude of 424 meters, or about 1,300 feet.

Internet Search

Keywords:

mitos y leyendas, leyenda indígena, leyenda mexicana

Interacción con la lectura

Resources: Voc. & Gram. Transparencies: 6

Suggestions: This four-step process helps guide students toward better comprehension of the reading passage. It also develops their speaking, listening, and writing skills by using the passage as a vehicle for pair and group discussions and a writing assignment.

Answers:
Step 1
Answers will vary, but should follow a story line somewhat like the following:

La princesa tolteca y el príncipe chichimeca se enamoraron.
Por eso querían casarse.
Pero sus padres prohibieron el matrimonio. Por eso los enamorados tuvieron que buscar dónde vivir.
Al final, subieron a dos montañas para estar cerca el uno del otro, y dormir para siempre cubiertos de nieve.

Steps 2–4
Answers will vary.

Fondo cultural

Standards: 1.1, 1.2, 2.1, 3.1, 4.1

Suggestions: If students have difficulty coming up with legends concerning natural phenomena, ask them if they have ever heard of the following legends: In Greek myth, the Cyclopes—giant, one-eyed monsters—were responsible for giving thunder and lightning to Zeus, the ruler of all the gods. In Navajo lore, Changing Woman is responsible for the creation of light.

Ask these questions about the photo:

¿Por qué tienen los volcanes estos nombres?

¿Qué pueblo antiguo mexicano les puso estos nombres a los volcanes?

¿Desde qué ciudad mexicana se puede ver estos volcanes?

¿Son volcanes activos?

Answers will vary.

Review Activities

Para hablar de actividades al aire libre, cámping y el tiempo/Para describir la naturaleza/Para indicar que sucede algo y cuándo sucede algo: Show a five-minute segment of an adventure film or recorded TV show set in the outdoors. Tell students to open their books to this page. Ask them to think of ways to use as many vocabulary items as they can to talk about what they saw. Play the segment again, pausing frequently to allow students to make their comments. Ask questions to elicit words and expressions they have not yet included in their comments.

Make It a Game: The above review strategy can also be set up as a game. Divide the class into two teams. Choose two students as neutral "readers." After showing the recorded segment, give teams ten minutes to use as many vocabulary items as they can in comments about the segment. Have them write their comments as a single list of sentences. Only accurate and sensible comments count. Collect the two lists, and have the readers take turns reading one comment at a time. Keep a tally. The team that uses the most vocabulary items wins.

Para prepararse para un evento deportivo/Para hablar de competencias deportivas/Para expresar emociones e impresiones

Have pairs of students create comic strips about a character or characters involved in a sporting event. Their strips should include at least one scene each involving training, the event itself, and a victory or awards ceremony. The strips should include narrative lines and speech and/or thought balloons for the characters. Display completed comic strips in the classroom.

Otras palabras y expresiones: Students can use these words and expressions as they do the review activities for the other categories.

Repaso del capítulo

Vocabulario y gramática

para hablar de actividades

acercarse a	to approach
andar	to walk, to move
dar un paseo	to take a walk, stroll
dejar de	to stop (doing something)
escalar	to climb (a rock or mountain)
perderse	to get lost
refugiarse	to take shelter

para describir la naturaleza

el bosque	wood, forest
el desierto	desert
hermoso, -a	beautiful
la naturaleza	nature
el paisaje	landscape
el refugio	refuge, shelter
la roca	rock
la sierra	sierra, mountain range
el valle	valley

para hablar de cámping

los binoculares	binoculars
la brújula	compass
la linterna	flashlight
el repelente de insectos	insect repellent
el saco de dormir	sleeping bag
la tienda de acampar	tent

para hablar del tiempo

caer granizo	to hail
el granizo	hail
el relámpago	lightning
el trueno	thunder

para indicar que sucede algo

suceder	to occur
tener lugar	to take place

para indicar cuándo sucede algo

al amanecer	at dawn
al anochecer	at dusk
al principio	at the beginning
un rato	a while
una vez allí	once there

para prepararse para un evento deportivo

el entrenamiento	training
entrenarse	to train
hacer un esfuerzo	to make an effort
inscribirse	to register
la inscripción	registration

para hablar de competencias deportivas

alcanzar	to reach
la carrera	race
la ceremonia	ceremony
el certificado	certificate, diploma
contra	against
eliminar	to eliminate
la entrega de premios	awards ceremony
¡Felicitaciones!	Congratulations!
la medalla	medal
la meta	goal
obtener	to obtain, get
el / la participante	participant
el / la representante	representative
salir campeón, campeona	to become the champion
el trofeo	trophy
vencer	to beat

para expresar emociones e impresiones

animado, -a	excited
asustar	to scare
darse cuenta de	to realize
desafortunadamente	unfortunately
desanimado, -a	discouraged
duro, -a	hard
emocionarse	to be moved
estar orgulloso / orgullosa de	to be proud of
impresionar	to impress
pasarlo bien / mal	to have a good / bad time

otras palabras y expresiones

aparecer	to appear
así	this way
hacia	toward
perder el equilibrio	to lose one's balance
sin embargo	however

Universal Access

Multiple Intelligences
Verbal/Linguistic: Ask a volunteer with good acting skills to say the items in the *emociones e impresiones* list and exaggerate the corresponding intonation. Have the other students repeat chorally, imitating the intonation.

Students with Learning Difficulties
Given the importance of the element of time when dealing with the past tenses, students may find it easier to retain vocabulary—and use the proper tense—if they add a few words when reviewing the lists of preterite and imperfect verbs. For example: *Yo leí un libro ayer. ¿Qué tiempo hacía ayer?*

el pretérito

destruir *to destroy*

destruí	destruimos
destruiste	destruisteis
destruyó	destruyeron

leer *to read*

leí	leímos
leíste	leísteis
leyó	leyeron

The verbs *creer*, *oír*, and *caerse* follow the same pattern as *leer*.

tener *to have*

tuve	**tuv**imos
tuviste	**tuv**isteis
tuvo	**tuv**ieron

Other verbs that have an irregular stem in the preterite and share the same endings as *tener* are: *andar, estar, poder, poner, venir.*

decir *to tell*

dije	**dij**imos
dijiste	**dij**isteis
dijo	**dij**eron

The verb *traer* follows the same pattern as *decir*.

pedir (i) *to ask for*

pedí	pedimos
pediste	pedisteis
pidió	pidieron

The verbs *sentir, divertirse, preferir, sugerir,* and *vestirse* follow the same pattern as *pedir*.

dormir (u) *to sleep*

dormí	dormimos
dormiste	dormisteis
durmió	durmieron

The verb *morir* follows the same pattern as *dormir*.

el imperfecto

estar (-ar) *to be*

est**aba**	est**ábamos**
est**abas**	est**abais**
est**aba**	est**aban**

tener (-er) *to have*

ten**ía**	ten**íamos**
ten**ías**	ten**íais**
ten**ía**	ten**ían**

vivir (-ir) *to live*

viv**ía**	viv**íamos**
viv**ías**	viv**íais**
viv**ía**	viv**ían**

ir *to go*

iba	íbamos
ibas	ibais
iba	iban

ser *to be*

era	éramos
eras	erais
era	eran

ver *to see*

veía	veíamos
veías	veíais
veía	veían

The imperfect of *hay* is *había*.

● **Más práctica** . . . .
Practice Workbook Organizer 1-13, 1-14

cincuenta y nueve   **59**
Capítulo 1

Enriching Your Teaching

Review

Performance Tasks

Standards: 1.1, 1.2, 1.3, 2.1

Resources: Audio Program: CD Cap. 1, Track 22; Resource Book: Cap. 1, Audio Script; Practice Answers on Transparencies

1. Vocabulario

Suggestions: Encourage students to review the vocabulary from the *A primera vista* sections on pp. 22–25 and 36–38 before they complete the activity.

Answers:

1. d   5. c
2. b   6. b
3. c   7. a
4. a   8. d

2. Gramática

Suggestions: Remind students that the main ideas of the grammar presentations in *Capítulo* 1 were the forms and uses of the preterite and the imperfect.

Answers:

1. d   5. b
2. a   6. c
3. b   7. a
4. a   8. d

Chapter Review

To prepare for the test, check to see if you . . .
- know the new vocabulary and grammar
- can perform the tasks on pp. 46 and 47

Preparación para el examen

1 Vocabulario Escribe la letra de la palabra o expresión que mejor complete cada frase. Escribe tus respuestas en una hoja aparte.

1. Me levanté muy temprano, _____, para ir de cámping.
   a. por la tarde   c. por la noche
   b. al anochecer   d. al amanecer

2. Cuando fuimos al bosque, Luis trajo _____ porque no había mucha luz.
   a. unos binoculares   c. un repelente de insectos
   b. una linterna   d. un saco de dormir

3. El paisaje era impresionante. _____ mucho cuando vi las montañas.
   a. Me cansé   c. Me emocioné
   b. Me asusté   d. Me aburrí

4. Cuando gané el campeonato mis padres me dijeron que estaban muy _____ de mis esfuerzos.
   a. orgullosos   c. asustados
   b. desanimados   d. tristes

5. Buscamos un refugio porque _____.
   a. perdí el equilibrio   c. comenzó a caer granizo
   b. nos eliminaron   d. no dormimos bien.

6. Cuando llegué tarde a casa mis padres me preguntaron: "¿Qué te _____?"
   a. dieron   c. rompiste
   b. sucedió   d. pusiste

7. Antes de participar en el campeonato, la chica _____ por tres meses.
   a. se entrenó   c. se divirtió
   b. se perdió   d. se durmió

8. Fue un partido muy _____. Todos tuvimos que hacer un gran esfuerzo para ganar.
   a. agitado   c. aburrido
   b. fácil   d. duro

2 Gramática Escribe la letra de la palabra o expresión que mejor complete cada frase. Escribe tus respuestas en una hoja aparte.

1. Leí en el diario que la tormenta _____ muchos árboles.
   a. destruye   c. destruyendo
   b. destruía   d. destruyó

2. No puedo creer que te olvidaste la mochila. ¿Por qué no la _____?
   a. trajiste   c. trajeron
   b. traen   d. traían

3. _____ la una de la tarde cuando llegamos al campamento.
   a. Fue   c. Eran
   b. Era   d. Estaban

4. El sábado pasado, los chicos _____ dos horas por los senderos.
   a. anduvieron   c. andan
   b. andaban   d. anduviste

5. Anoche, después del partido, el campeón _____ diez horas porque estaba cansado.
   a. dormía   c. está durmiendo
   b. durmió   d. duerme

6. De niña, a menudo yo _____ a los partidos de tenis con mis tíos.
   a. voy   c. iba
   b. fui   d. iban

7. El atleta que salió en primer lugar _____ un trofeo.
   a. obtuvo   c. obtenía
   b. obtiene   d. obtuviste

8. Generalmente, ¿cómo _____ cuando tu equipo perdía un partido?
   a. te sientes   c. se sentían
   b. te sentiste   d. te sentías

60 sesenta
Preparación para el examen

Universal Access

Students with Learning Difficulties

Before students complete the tasks, have them review the *Vocabulario* on p. 58 and make flashcards for any words that they do not know. Have them use the cards for practice in pairs with partners who are more confident.

Advanced Learners

Ask students to serve as tutors for classmates who are struggling. Give tutors specific targets to work on. Some students may consider these requests an unfair imposition and extra work. Consider these feelings, while at the same time working towards maintaining an atmosphere of cooperation.

60

For: Test preparation
Visit: www.phschool.com
Web Code: jed-0111

En el examen vas a . . .	Éstas son las tareas de práctica que te pueden ser útiles para el examen . . .	Si necesitas repasar . . .
❸ **Escuchar** Escuchar y comprender la descripción de una excursión a un parque nacional	Un amigo(a) te deja un mensaje por teléfono sobre una excursión que hizo a un parque nacional. (a) ¿Adónde fue? (b) ¿Qué vio? (c) ¿Qué hizo allí? (d) ¿Qué le sucedió? (e) ¿Cómo lo pasó?	**pp. 22–25** *A primera vista 1* **p. 27** Actividad 7 **p. 29** Actividades 12–13 **p. 34** Actividad 22 **p. 35** Actividades 24–25
❹ **Hablar** Hablar sobre una excursión que hizo tu clase	Tu clase fue de excursión a un lugar especial. Cuéntale lo que pasó a un(a) compañero(a) que no pudo ir. Incluye quiénes fueron, adónde fueron, qué había allí, qué tiempo hacía, qué hicieron y cómo lo pasaron.	**p. 50** *¿Qué me cuentas?* **p. 51** *Presentación oral*
❺ **Leer** Leer y comprender un anuncio sobre un concurso	Lee el anuncio que apareció en el periódico de la escuela y decide: (a) qué tipo de concurso es; (b) cuándo es la inscripción; (c) quiénes pueden participar; (d) cuándo es la audición; (e) qué premio va a obtener el / la ganador(a). **Concurso de Música** Invitamos a todos los estudiantes de tercer y cuarto año a participar en nuestro concurso. **Fecha de inscripción:** 6 de octubre **Audición:** 9 de octubre **Primer premio:** dos entradas (tickets) para un concierto en el teatro San Martín	**pp. 36–39** *A primera vista 2* **p. 40** *Fondo cultural* **p. 41** Actividades 33–35
❻ **Escribir** Escribir un artículo sobre un evento deportivo importante para el periódico de la escuela	Imagina que eres reportero del periódico de la escuela. Tienes que escribir un artículo sobre el último partido del año de un equipo de tu escuela. Tu artículo debe contar (a) quiénes jugaron, (b) dónde y cuándo fue, (c) si hacía buen tiempo, (d) cómo se sentían los jugadores, (e) qué sucedió, (f) cómo se sentían al final, (g) si fue un partido aburrido o emocionante y por qué.	**p. 43** Actividad 37 **p. 44** Actividad 40 **p. 45** Actividad 41
❼ **Pensar** Pensar en los peregrinos de hoy y de ayer	Piensa en el viaje de los peregrinos de Santiago de Compostela hace mil años. ¿Por qué quieren seguir la misma ruta muchos jóvenes hoy en día? ¿Hay lugares aquí en los Estados Unidos como Santiago de Compostela? ¿Cuáles son los motivos para viajar a estos lugares? ¿En qué se parecen? ¿En qué se diferencian?	**pp. 48–49** *Puente a la cultura*

sesenta y uno **61**
Capítulo 1

3. Escuchar

Suggestions: Use the *Audio CD* or read from the script.

Answers:

a. **Fue al Parque Nacional Torres del Paine.**
b. **Vio valles y montañas altísimas.**
c. **Hizo caminatas y montó a caballo.**
d. **Perdió el equilibrio y se cayó del caballo.**
e. **Lo pasó muy bien.**

4. Leer

Suggestions: Tell students to refer to pp. 22–25 and 36–38 if they have questions about vocabulary in the announcement.

Answers:

a. **Es un concurso de música.**
b. **La inscripción es el 6 de octubre.**
c. **Todos los estudiantes de tercer y cuarto año pueden participar.**
d. **La audición es el 9 de octubre.**
e. **El (la) ganador(a) va a obtener dos entradas para un concierto en el teatro San Martín.**

5. Escribir

Suggestions: Encourage students to put their thoughts in a graphic organizer before writing.

Answers will vary.

6. Hablar

Suggestions: As students take turns telling about their excursions, encourage the listeners to help the speakers by asking questions.

Answers will vary.

7. Pensar

Suggestions: Ask students to write down the answers and be ready to share them with the class.

Answers will vary.

✓ Assessment

- Examen del capítulo: 1
- Audio Program: CD 12, Cap. 1, Track 2
- Assessment Program: *RPH*

Alternative Assessment

- ExamView Test Bank CD-ROM
- Resource Book: Cap 1, Situation Cards
- Resource Book: Cap 1, Communicative Activity BLM

Enriching Your Teaching

Teacher-to-Teacher

Allow students to go through the work they have collected for the chapter and reassess it, revisiting areas in which their performance was weak earlier. Then encourage them to choose the piece of work of which they are most proud and share it in a portfolio study group. By sharing their finest work in groups, students minimize their weaknesses and benefit from each other's strengths.

¿Cómo te expresas?

CHAPTER OVERVIEW

¿Cómo te expresas?
• Different artistic expressions and how to appreciate them

Vocabulary:
• types of art and how to describe them
• music, drama and dance performances

Grammar:
• preterite vs. imperfect
• *estar* + past participle
• *ser* and *estar*
• verbs with different meanings in the imperfect and the preterite

Cultural Perspectives:
• artistic expressions and artists in the Spanish-speaking world
• the art of Mexican artists Diego Rivera and David Alfaro Siqueiros
• the origins of *salsa*
• the Spanish *zarzuela*
• the world of Francisco Goya

Chapter Project

Escultura personal

Overview: Students create their own sculpture that will represent their personality. First they draw a draft and write how the design relates to them. Then they create the sculpture. It might be done with clay, papier-mâché, carved soap, cardboard, or other scrap materials found at home. Have them paint it or decorate it according to their taste. Finally, they give an oral presentation of the piece, explaining how it relates to them or represents them.

Materials: paper, clay, cardboard, soap, paint, markers, scrap materials found at home. Remind students that there are no restrictions on materials, as long as they are safe.

• •

Sequence: (suggestions for when to do each step are found throughout the chapters)

STEP 1. Review instructions so students know what is expected of them. Hand out the "Chapter 2 Project Instructions and Rubric" from the *Teacher's Resource Book*.

STEP 2. On a sheet of paper students draw a rough draft of their sculpture and write a few paragraphs explaining how it relates to their personality. Return their draft and text with suggestions. For vocabulary and grammar practice, ask partners to present their sketches and text to each other.

STEP 3. Students create their sculpture, based on their previous drafts. Encourage them to try different materials for their work and to use as much vocabulary as possible from *Capítulo* 2 in their written text.

STEP 4. Students submit a draft of their text, explaining how the sculpture relates to their personality. Write your corrections and suggestions, then return drafts to students.

STEP 5. Students present their sculpture to the class, using their notes to explain how it relates to them.

Options:
1. Students create a collage to represent aspects of their personality.
2. Students create a brochure about an artist of their choice.

Assessment:
Here is a detailed rubric for assessing this project:
Chapter 2 Project: *Escultura personal*

RUBRIC	Score 1	Score 2	Score 3
Your evidence of planning	You present no draft or written text.	Your draft or text is missing.	You show evidence of a corrected draft.
Your use of materials	You provide little or no decoration.	Your structure or decoration is missing.	Your piece is well done.
Your oral presentation	Your presentation is short and does not relate to the sculpture.	You describe part of the sculpture.	You describe in detail your relationship with the sculpture.

Bulletin Boards

Theme: *Las artes*

Ask students to cut out, draw, or download pictures of artists from different Spanish-speaking countries and of their work. Cluster photos into categories: painting, sculpture, dance, music and literature.

Bibliography

Anderson, Robert. *Artists in Their Time: Salvador Dalí*. New York: Franklin Watts, 2002. Dalí's life and work.

Goldstein, Ernest, and Diego Rivera. *The Journey of Diego Rivera*. Minneapolis: Lerner Publications, 1996. A look at Rivera's art with color prints.

Stewart, Sue and Willie Colón. *Música: The Rhythm of Latin America: Salsa, Rumba, Merengue and More*. Chronicle Books, 1999. Comprehensive guide to the music of Latin America, its history, and the legendary individuals who perform it.

Venezia, Mike. *Getting to know the World's Greatest Artists: Picasso*. Chicago Children's Press, 1994. The life and art of Pablo Picasso.

[DK] Wright, Patricia. *Goya*. Eyewitness Art Series. New York: Dorling Kindersley, 1993. Information on and illustrations of the life and work of Goya.

Hands-on Culture

Craft: *Una máscara de tigre*

In Mexico, the art of making tiger or jaguar masks has its roots in pre-Hispanic theatrical performances. The character of the tiger or jaguar is extremely popular and important in many Mexican festivals and pageants. Tiger masks are typically painted yellow with black spots in keeping with the coloring of the real animal.

Materials: water, white flour (one part flour to one part water), newspaper (uncut), aluminum foil, masking tape, strips of newspaper (about 1 inch wide), acrylic or poster paint, brushes

Directions:

1. Prepare paste by mixing flour and water in a large bowl until it makes a smooth paste.
2. Make a mold by forming a large round or oval shape out of balled-up sheets of dry newspaper. Next, cover the front of this shape with aluminum foil, smoothing it down so it forms to your shape. Use more balled-up newspaper to form facial features on your mold. Attach them to the aluminum foil with masking tape.
3. Dip the newspaper strips, one at a time, into the paste. Lay the coated newspaper on the mold. Smooth out the wrinkles and continue to place coated newspaper strips over the surface until it is completely covered. Continue until you have put 3 to 4 layers of newspaper strips on your mold. Allow the mask to dry for about 24 hours.
4. When the mask is dry, pull the balled-up newspaper out of it. The aluminum foil will remain attached to your mask as a lining. Paint the mask yellow and add black spots. Cut holes for the eyes and mouth.

Internet Search

Use the keywords to find more information.

Keywords:

Diego Rivera, Goya, artes visuales, surrealismo, cubismo, pintura latinoamericana, danza, literatura, poesía, música latina

Game

Veo, veo. ¿Qué ves?

Use this traditional children's game to practice art-related vocabulary in the *Manos a la obra* 1 section.

Players: entire class

Materials: Poster of a painting from a Spanish or Latin American artist. Make sure the painting has sufficient details to elicit the vocabulary learned in *Capítulo 2, A primera vista* 1.

Rules:

1. Students write their names on scraps of paper and place them in a paper bag.
2. Shake the paper bag to mix up the names. Then call on a volunteer to come to the front of the class. The volunteer draws the name of a student from the paper bag, then gives the paper to you.
3. Students take turns asking the volunteer questions in an attempt to guess an object from the painting that the volunteer has chosen.

   Student 1: Veo, veo.

   Student 2: ¿Qué ves?

   Student 1: Una cosa.

   Student 2: ¿De qué color?

   Student 1: Verde.

   Student 2: ¿Está en primer plano?

   Student 1: Sí.

   Student 2: Es una manzana.

   Student 1: Sí.
4. When a student correctly guesses the object in the painting, he or she becomes the new volunteer. Play continues in this manner until every student has had a chance to ask one or two questions.

Variation: Exhibit two paintings representing different art movements in order to provide additional vocabulary practice.

2 Overview

A ver si recuerdas
RECYCLE

Vocabulary
- Art and artists
- Colors and materials
- In the theatre

Grammar
- Agreement and comparison of adjectives
- Comparison of nouns and the superlative

Chapter Overview

A primera vista 1	Manos a la obra 1	A primera vista 2	Manos a la obra 2
INPUT	**PRACTICE**	**INPUT**	**PRACTICE**
Objectives • Talk about different types of art • Discuss art materials	**Objectives** • Talk about art forms and art supplies • Describe a work of art	**Objectives** • Read about performing arts • Read art reviews • Describe how people express themselves	**Objectives** • Talk about different forms of entertainment • Express your opinion about a dance, music, or theatre performance
Vocabulary • Art and artists • Art materials • To describe a work of art	**Vocabulary** • Practice new vocabulary	**Vocabulary** • Performing arts • On stage • Music and dance	**Vocabulary** • Practice new vocabulary
Grammar • Preterite vs. imperfect • Verb *estar* + participle	**Grammar** • Preterite vs. imperfect • Verb *estar* + participle	**Grammar** • *ser* and *estar* • Verbs with different meanings in imperfect and preterite	**Grammar** • *ser* and *estar* • Verbs with different meanings in imperfect and preterite
Culture • Picasso and cubism • Interview ceramist Dina Bursztyn • Artists: Carlos Enríquez, Diego Rivera, Osvaldo Guayasamín	**Culture** • The worlds of Miró and Dalí • Diego Rivera and his art • David Alfaro Siqueiros	**Culture** • Facundo Cabral • Marc Anthony • Museum of Tango	**Culture** • Dancing *salsa* • The *zarzuela*

¡Adelante!
APPLICATION

Objectives
- Read about a famous Spanish painter
- Write an evaluation about a student's audition

• Read part of an autobiography

Vocabulary
- Application

Grammar
- Application

Culture
- The world of Francisco Goya
- Fragment of *Cuando era puertorriqueña*
- Esmeralda Santiago, Puerto Rican writer

Repaso del capítulo
REVIEW

Objectives
- Know the new vocabulary and grammar

• Perform the tasks on p. 8

Vocabulary
- Review

Grammar
- Review

BEYOND THE CLASSROOM

Countries
- Mexico
- Argentina
- Puerto Rico
- Chile
- Spain
- Ecuador
- Cuba
- United States

El español en la communidad
- the *Museo del Barrio*

Internet
- Vocabulary activities
- Grammar activities
- Internet links
- Self-tests

LEARNER SUPPORT

Strategies
- Context clues
- Using illustrations
- Using visuals
- Organizing information
- Categorizing
- Monitoring your reading

Recycling
- Expressions used with verbs in preterite and imperfect
- The letters *b* and *v*

En voz alta
- *Amigos*

Ampliación del lenguaje
- The suffix *-ismo*

Conexiones
- Art and History: Diego Rivera
- Art: Pepón Osorio

62-c

 **Print Components**

TEACHER

Teacher's Resource Book
• Chapter Table of Contents
• School-to-Home Connection
• Chapter Resource Checklist
• Input Script
• Audio Script
• Video Script
• Communicative Activities
• Situation Cards
• GramActiva Blackline Masters
• Graphic Organizers
• Answer Keys:
  Practice Workbook
  Writing, Audio & Video Workbook

Realidades para hispanohablantes
Teacher Edition

STUDENT

Practice Workbook
• Vocabulary: 2-1 – 2-4, 2-8 – 2-9
• Grammar: 2-5 – 2-7, 2-10 – 2-12
• Organizer: 2-13 – 2-14

Writing, Audio & Video Workbook
• Audio: 1–5
• Writing: 6–13
• Video: 14–17

Reading and Writing for Success
• Chapter 2, Test 29

Realidades para hispanohablantes

 **Transparencies**

Vocabulary and Grammar Transparencies
• Vocabulary: 49–56, 59–62
• Grammar: 57–58, 63–64
• ¿Qué me cuentas?: 65

Practice Answers on Tranparencies
• Cap. 2

Fine Art Transparencies
• Transparencies
• Teacher's Guide

 **Assessment**

Assessment Program
• Pruebas
  – Comprensión del vocabulario 1: 2-1
  – Aplicación del vocabulario 1: 2-2
  – Pretérito vs. imperfecto: 2-3
  – *Estar* + participio: 2-4
  – Comprensión del vocabulario 2: 2-5
  – Aplicación del vocabulario 2: 2-6
  – *Ser* y *estar*: 2-7
  – Verbos con distinto sentido en el pretérito y en el imperfecto: 2-8
• Exámenes del capítulo
• Rubrics

Alternative Assessment
• ExamView Test Bank CD-ROM
• MindPoint Quiz Show CD-ROM
• Internet Self-Test
• Situation Cards
• Communicative Activity

Assessment Program: *Realidades para hispanohablantes*

 **Technology**

TeacherExpress™ CD-ROM
• Lesson Planner
• Teacher Resources
• Clip Art

Video Program VHS and DVD

Audio Program CDs
• A primera vista 1 y 2: Vocabulario y gramática en contexto
• Audio Activities
• ¿Qué me cuentas?
• Repaso
• Examen del capítulo: Escuchar

Regular Schedule (50 Minutes)

For electronic lesson plans:
Teacher Express CD-ROM

	Warm-up / Assess	Preview Present / Practice Communicate	Wrap-up / Homework Options
DAY 1	**Warm-up (10 min.)** • Return Examen del capítulo: Capítulo 1	**Repaso (35 min.)** • A ver si recuerdas . . . • Actividad 5	**Wrap-up and Homework Options (5 min.)** • Practice Workbook 2-1, 2-2 • Go Online
DAY 2	**Warm-up (10 min.)** • Homework check	**Chapter Opener (10 min.)** • Objectives • Fondo cultural **A primera vista 1 (25 min.)** • Presentation: Vocabulario y gramática en contexto • Actividades 1, 2	**Wrap-up and Homework Options (5 min.)** • Go Online • Clip Art Vocabulary
DAY 3	**Warm-up (10 min.)** • Homework check	**A primera vista 1 (35 min.)** • Presentation: Entrevista con Dina Bursztyn • Actividad 3 • Presentation: Artistas latinoamericanos • Actividades 4, 5	**Wrap-up and Homework Options (5 min.)** • Practice Workbook 2-3, 2-4 • Manos a la obra 1: Actividad 6 • Go Online • Prueba 2-1: Vocabulary Recognition
DAY 4	**Warm-up (10 min.)** • Homework check ✔**Assessment (10 min.)** • Prueba 2-1: Vocabulary recognition	**Manos a la obra 1 (25 min.)** • Actividades 7, 8, 9, 10 • Ampliación del lenguaje	**Wrap-up and Homework Options (5 min.)** • Actividades 11, 12 • Writing Activities • Prueba 2-2: Vocabulary Recognition
DAY 5	**Warm-up (10 min.)** • Homework check ✔**Assessment (10 min.)** • Prueba 2-2: Vocabulary production	**Manos a la obra 1 (25 min.)** • Actividad 13 • Presentation: Pretérito vs. imperfecto • Actividades 15, 16 • Writing Activity	**Wrap-up and Homework Options (5 min.)** • Practice Workbook 2-5 • Go Online
DAY 6	**Warm-up (10 min.)** • Actividad 14 • Homework check	**Manos a la obra 1 (35 min.)** • Actividades 17, 18 • Communicative Activity • Presentation: *Estar* + participio • Actividad 19	**Wrap-up and Homework Options (5 min.)** • Writing Activity • Prueba 2-3: Pretérito vs. imperfecto
DAY 7	**Warm-up (10 min.)** • Fondo cultural • Homework check ✔**Assessment (10 min.)** • Prueba 2-3: Pretérito vs. imperfecto	**Manos a la obra 1 (25 min.)** • Actividades 20, 21, 22 • El español en la comunidad • Communicative Activity	**Wrap-up and Homework Options (5 min.)** • Practice Workbook 2-6, 2-7 • Go Online • Prueba 2-4: *Estar* + participio
DAY 8	**Warm-up (15 min.)** • Writing Activity • Homework check ✔**Assessment (10 min.)** • Prueba 2-4: *Estar* + participio	**A primera vista 2 (20 min.)** • Presentation: Vocabulario y gramática en contexto • Actividades 23, 24	**Wrap-up and Homework Options (5 min.)** • Clip Art Vocabulary • Examen: Vocabulario y gramática 1
DAY 9	**Warm-up (5 min.)** • Homework check ✔**Assessment (30 min.)** • Examen: Vocabulario y gramática 1	**A primera vista 2 (10 min.)** • Presentation: Espectáculos del mundo latino • Actividad 25	**Wrap-up and Homework Options (5 min.)** • Actividad 26 • Practice Workbook 2-8, 2-9 • Go Online • Prueba 2-5: Vocabulary recognition
DAY 10	**Warm-up (20 min.)** • Actividad 27 • Homework check ✔**Assessment (10 min.)** • Prueba 2-5: Vocabulary recognition	**Manos a la obra 2 (15 min.)** • Actividades 30, 31	**Wrap-up and Homework Options (5 min.)** • Actividades 28, 29 • Prueba 2-6: Vocabulary production

	Warm-up / Assess	Preview / Practice Present / Communicate	Wrap-up / Homework Options
DAY 11	**Warm-up (10 min.)** • Writing Activity • Homework check ✔**Assessment (10 min.)** • Prueba 2-6: Vocabulary production	**Manos a la obra 2 (25 min.)** • Presentation: *Ser* y *estar* • Actividades 32, 33, 34 • Communicative Activity	**Wrap-up and Homework Options (5 min.)** • Actividad 35 • Go Online • Practice Workbook 2-10 • Prueba 2-7: *Ser* y *estar*
DAY 12	**Warm-up (10 min.)** • Writing Activity • Homework check ✔**Assessment (10 min.)** • Prueba 2-7: *Ser* y *estar*	**Manos a la obra 2 (25 min.)** • Presentation: Verbos con • Fondo cultural distinto sentido en el pretérito • En voz alta y en el imperfecto • Actividades 36, 37	**Wrap-up and Homework Options (5 min.)** • Practice Workbook 2-11, 2-12 • Go Online • Prueba 2-8: Verbos con distinto sentido en el pretérito y en el imperfecto
DAY 13	**Warm-up (10 min.)** • Homework check ✔**Assessment (10 min.)** • Prueba 2-8	**Manos a la obra 2 (25 min.)** • Actividades 38, 39 • Fondo cultural • Communicative Activity	**Wrap-up and Homework Options (5 min.)** • Go Online • Examen: Vocabulario y gramática 2
DAY 14	**Warm-up (8 min.)** • Writing Activity ✔**Assessment (30 min.)** • Examen: Vocabulario y gramática 2	**¡Adelante! (10 min.)** • Presentación oral: Steps 1, 2	**Wrap-up and Homework Options (2 min.)** • Presentación oral: Step 2
DAY 15	**Warm-up (10 min.)** • Presentación oral: Step 2	**¡Adelante! (35 min.)** • Presentación oral: Step 3	**Wrap-up and Homework Options (5 min.)** • El mundo de Francisco Goya • ¿Comprendiste? • Go Online
DAY 16	**Warm-up (15 min.)** • El mundo de Francisco Goya: ¿Comprendiste? • Homework check	**¡Adelante! (30 min.)** • Escribe tu opinión • ¿Qué me cuentas? 1, 2, 3 • View Video	**Wrap-up and Homework Options (5 min.)** • Presentación escrita: Steps 1, 2
DAY 17	**Warm-up (10 min.)** • Homework check	**¡Adelante! (15 min.)** • Presentación escrita: Step 3 **Repaso (20 min.)** • Preparación para el examen: Actividades 3, 4 • MindPoint Quiz Show	**Wrap-up and Homework Options (5 min.)** • Presentación escrita: Step 4
DAY 18	**Warm-up (10 min.)** • Homework check	**¡Adelante! (35 min.)** • Lectura • ¿Comprendiste? • Fondo cultural	**Wrap-up and Homework Options (5 min.)** • Practice Workbook: Organizer 2-13, 2-14 • Go Online: Self-test
DAY 19	**Warm-up (20 min.)** • Preparación para el examen: Actividades 1, 2 • Homework check	**Repaso (25 min.)** • Preparación para el examen: Actividades 5, 6, 7 • MindPoint Quiz Show • Other review	**Wrap-up and Homework Options (5 min.)** • Examen del capítulo
DAY 20	**Warm-up (5 min.)** • Answer questions ✔**Assessment (44 min.)** • Examen del capítulo		**Wrap-up and Homework Options (1 min.)** • A ver si recuerdas: Capítulo 3

Block Schedule (90 Minutes)

For electronic lesson plans:
Teacher Express CD-ROM 💿

	Warm-up / Assess	Preview Present / Practice Communicate	Wrap-up / Homework Options
DAY 1	**Warm-up (35 min.)** • Return Examen del capítulo: Capítulo 1 • A ver si recuerdas . . . • Actividad 5 • Homework check	**Chapter Opener (10 min.)** • Objectives • Fondo cultural **A primera vista 1 (30 min.)** • Presentation: Vocabulario y gramática en contexto • Actividades 1, 2 • Presentation: Entrevista con Dina Bursztyn • Actividad 3 • Presentation: Artistas latinoamericanos • Actividades 4, 5 **Manos a la obra 1 (10 min.)** • Actividades 6, 7	**Wrap-up and Homework Options (5 min.)** • Practice Workbook 2-3, 2-4 • Go Online • Clip Art Vocabulary • Prueba 2-1: Vocabulary recognition
DAY 2	**Warm-up (15 min.)** • Actividad 8 • Homework check ✔**Assessment (10 min.)** • Prueba 2-1: Vocabulary recognition	**Manos a la obra 1 (60 min.)** • Actividades 9, 10, 11, 12, 13 • Ampliación del lenguaje • Communicative Activity	**Wrap-up and Homework Options (5 min.)** • Go Online • Writing Activities • Prueba 2-2: Vocabulary production
DAY 3	**Warm-up (15 min.)** • Writing Activity • Homework check ✔**Assessment (10 min.)** • Prueba 2-2: Vocabulary production	**Manos a la obra 1 (60 min.)** • Presentation: Pretérito vs. imperfecto • Actividades 14, 15, 16, 18 • Fondo cultural • Audio and Writing Activities	**Wrap-up and Homework Options (5 min.)** • Practice Workbook 2-5 • Go Online • Prueba 2-3: Pretérito vs. imperfecto
DAY 4	**Warm-up (10 min.)** • Actividad 17 • Homework check ✔**Assessment (10 min.)** • Prueba 2-3: Pretérito vs. imperfecto	**Manos a la obra 1 (50 min.)** • Presentation: *Estar* + participio • Actividades 19, 20, 21, 22 • El español en la comunidad • Communicative Activity **A primera vista 2 (15 min.)** • Presentation: Vocabulario y gramática en contexto • Actividades 23, 24	**Wrap-up and Homework Options (5 min.)** • Practice Workbook 2-6, 2-7 • Go Online • Prueba 2-4: *Estar* + participio • Examen: Vocabulario y gramática 1
DAY 5	**Warm-up (10 min.)** • Writing Activity • Homework check ✔**Assessment Options (40 min.)** • Prueba 2-4: *Estar* + participio • Examen: Vocabulario y gramática 1	**A primera vista 2 (20 min.)** • Presentation: Espectáculos del mundo latino • Actividades 25, 26, 27 **Manos a la obra 2 (15 min.)** • Actividades 30, 31	**Wrap-up and Homework Options (5 min.)** • Practice Workbook 2-8, 2-9 • Go Online • Prueba 2-5: Vocabulary recognition
DAY 6	**Warm-up (20 min.)** • Actividades 28, 29 • Homework check ✔**Assessment (10 min.)** • Prueba 2-5: Vocabulary recognition	**Manos a la obra 2 (55 min.)** • Presentation: *Ser* y *estar* • Actividades 32, 33, 34, 35 • Fondo cultural • En voz alta • Writing Activities	**Wrap-up and Homework Options (5 min.)** • Practice Workbook 2-10 • Go Online • Pruebas 2-6, 2-7: Vocabulary production, *ser* y *estar*

	Warm-up / Assess	Preview Present / Practice Communicate	Wrap-up / Homework Options
DAY 7	**Warm-up (10 min.)** • Homework check ✔**Assessment (20 min.)** • Pruebas 2-6, 2-7: Vocabulary production, *ser* y *estar*	**Manos a la obra 2 (40 min.)** • Presentation: Verbos con distinto sentido en el pretérito y en el imperfecto • Actividades 36, 37, 38, 39 • Fondo cultural **¡Adelante! (15 min.)** • Presentación oral: Steps 1, 2	**Wrap-up and Homework Options (5 min.)** • Presentación oral: Step 2 • Go Online
DAY 8	**Warm-up (10 min.)** • Writing Activity • Homework check ✔**Assessment (40 min.)** • Presentación oral: Step 3	**Manos a la obra 2 (20 min.)** • Communicative Activity **¡Adelante! (15 min.)** • Presentation: El mundo de Francisco Goya	**Wrap-up and Homework Options (5 min.)** • Practice Workbook 2-11, 2-12 • Go Online • Prueba 2-8: Verbos con distinto sentido en el pretérito y en el imperfecto • Examen: Vocabulario y gramática 2
DAY 9	**Warm-up (10 min.)** • Homework check ✔**Assessment Options (30 min.)** • Prueba 2-8: Verbos con distinto sentido en el pretérito y en el imperfecto • Examen: Vocabulario y gramática 2	**¡Adelante! (45 min.)** • El mundo de Francisco Goya • ¿Comprendiste? • Escribe tu opinión • ¿Qué me cuentas? 1, 2, 3 • Presentación escrita: Step 1 • Video • Video Activities	**Wrap-up and Homework Options (5 min.)** • Presentación escrita: Step 2 • Go Online • Preparación para el examen: Actividades 1, 2
DAY 10	**Warm-up (20 min.)** • Presentación escrita: Step 3 • Homework check	**¡Adelante! (35 min.)** • Lectura • ¿Comprendiste? • Fondo cultural **Repaso (30 min.)** • Preparación para el examen: Actividades 3, 4, 6 • MindPoint Quiz	**Wrap-up and Homework Options (5 min.)** • Presentación escrita: Step 4 • Practice Workbook: Organizer 2-13, 2-14 • Go Online: Self-test • Preparación para el examen: Actividades 5, 7 • Examen del capítulo
DAY 11	**Warm-up (30 min.)** • Homework check ✔**Assessment (30 min.)** • Examen del capítulo	**Theme Game (15 min.)** **A ver si recuerdas – Capítulo 3 (10 min.)** • Presentation: Vocabulario • Presentation: Gramática	**Wrap-up and Homework Options (5 min.)** • A ver si recuerdas – Capítulo 3 • Actividades 1–6 • Go Online • Practice Workbook 3-1, 3-2

Vocabulario

Resources: Voc. & Gram. Transparencies: 49; Fine Art Transparencies; Fine Art Transparencies Teacher's Guide

Suggestions: Call out vocabulary items from the six categories in random order. Have a volunteer use the item you call out to make a statement about one or both of the paintings.

Standards: 1.1

Focus: Practicing review vocabulary

Suggestions: For step 1, make sure students choose vocabulary from various categories, rather than just one or two. Point out that the sentence starters in steps 2 and 3 are suggestions. Encourage students to experiment with other ways to incorporate the vocabulary in their paired discussion about the paintings.

Answers will vary.

Extension: During their discussion in pairs, ask students to write down their partner's comments about the paintings. Then have students take turns reporting their partners' comments to the class: *Victoria cree que el cuadro de Picasso es...*

Teaching with Art
Standards: 2.2, 3.1

Resources: Fine Art Transparencies

To guide the discussion of the two paintings, ask: *¿Cuál de los dos cuadros tiene un estilo más realista? ¿Puedes explicar tu respuesta? ¿Qué elementos tienen en común los cuadros? ¿Cuál de los dos cuadros prefieres? ¿Por qué?*

Block Schedule

Have a pair of students pantomime two people with contrasting characteristics. The class should guess what is being portrayed using comparatives, superlatives, and adjective agreement.

62

A ver si recuerdas...

Vocabulario

el arte y los artistas
el / la artista
el cuadro
dibujar
el estilo
la estatua
el museo
pintar
el pintor,
  la pintora

color y luz
amarillo, -a
anaranjado, -a
azul
blanco, -a
claro, -a
gris
marrón
morado, -a
negro, -a
oscuro, -a
pastel
rojo, -a
rosado, -a
verde
vivo, -a

opiniones
a mí también / tampoco
creo que . . .
estoy / no estoy de acuerdo
me parece que . . .
me gusta / no me gusta
no estoy seguro, -a
para mí, ti . . .
¿qué te parece?

materiales
el oro
el papel
la piedra
el plástico
la plata

descripciones
aburrido, -a
bonito, -a
complicado, -a
divertido, -a
exagerado, -a
fascinante
feo, -a
horrible
interesante
mejor
moderno, -a
peor
realista
sencillo, -a
serio, -a
triste

comparaciones
más / menos . . . que
mejor / peor . . . que
tan . . . como

Paisaje Juan les Pins, (1920), Pablo Picasso

Oil on canvas. 52 x 70 cm. Photo: R. G. Ojeda © 2004 Estate of Pablo Picasso/Artists Rights Society ARS, NY. Musée Picasso, Paris, France. Réunion des Musées Nationaux/Art Resource, NY.

Paisaje hondureño de San Antonio de Oriente, (1957), José Antonio Velásquez

Oil on canvas. 26" x 37". Collection of the Art Museum of the Americas. Organization of American States.

 **Escribir/Hablar**...

Práctica de vocabulario

❶ Haz una lista de diez palabras que describan estas obras de arte.

❷ Usa la información que escribiste para describir las pinturas a tu compañero(a). Usa como guía las siguientes preguntas: ¿Cómo son? ¿Qué representan?

El cuadro de . . . es . . .
El cuadro de . . . muestra . . .

❸ Intercambia opiniones con tu compañero(a).

• Pregúntale su opinión.
"¿Cuál de los cuadros . . . ?"

• Expresa tu opinión.
Yo creo que el cuadro de . . . es . . .
No estoy de acuerdo . . . porque . . .

62   sesenta y dos
A ver si recuerdas . . .

Universal Access

Students with Learning Difficulties
Have students create their own visual clues to reinforce new vocabulary. As they choose and list adjectives in *Actividad* 1, encourage them to utilize simple drawings, colored pencils, or colored chalk to help reinforce the meanings of the descriptive words they have chosen.

Advanced Learners
Have students write a paragraph describing the scene in the Picasso painting. Encourage them to study the painting closely in order to find real-world elements that Picasso chose to portray in an unusual way. For example, the wavy lines in the upper right most likely portray the sea. What do they think some of the other shapes and colors represent?

Gramática · Repaso

Concordancia y comparación de adjetivos

Adjectives agree in gender and number with the persons or things they describe. Masculine adjectives usually end in *-o* and feminine adjectives usually end in *-a*.

una estatua **moderna**　　　un cuadro **moderno**

• Adjectives that end in *-e* or in a consonant may be either feminine or masculine.

un cuadro **interesante**　　　una estatua **gris**

• Adjectives that end in *-ista* may be either masculine or feminine.

un dibujo **realista**　　　una pintora **surrealista**

• To form the feminine form of adjectives that end in *-or*, add *-a* at the end.

un niño **trabajador**　　　una niña **trabajadora**

• If an adjective describes a combination of masculine and feminine nouns, the masculine plural ending is used.

Ese cuadro y esa estatua no son **feos**.

To express a comparison of similarity, use *tan* + adjective + *como*.

El cuadro de Picasso es **tan bonito como** el cuadro de Velázquez.

To express a comparison of difference, use *más / menos* + adjective + *que*.

El cuadro de Picasso me parece **más / menos interesante que** el de Velázquez.

• The adjectives *bueno(a), malo(a), viejo(a),* and *joven* have irregular comparative forms. The words *más / menos* are not used.

| bueno(a) | **mejor (que)** | viejo(a) | **mayor (que)** |
| malo(a) | **peor (que)** | joven | **menor (que)** |

Leer/Escribir

Práctica de gramática

Dos amigos fueron al museo. Completa lo que dijeron con la forma correcta de los adjetivos del recuadro.

| complicado | moderno | plástico |
| exagerado | fascinante | |

A —Ayer fui a un museo de arte **1.** y vi unos cuadros **2.** . Me gustaron mucho. Sin embargo, las estatuas de **3.** son **4.** .

B —¿Sí? Pues yo no entiendo el arte moderno. El estilo moderno es **5.** y tienes que pensar para comprenderlo.

Escribir

Práctica de gramática

Usa los siguientes adjetivos para escribir cinco frases que comparen el cuadro de Velásquez con el de Picasso en la página 62. Usa *más / menos ... que* o *tan ... como,* según sea necesario.

| inteligente | moderno | sencillo |
| serio | realista | bonito |

Modelo

El cuadro de Velásquez me parece tan interesante como el cuadro de Picasso.

Enriching Your Teaching

Teacher-to-Teacher

Display several works of art of varying styles and periods. These might be reproductions of paintings or photographs of sculptures, ceramics, or other kinds of art. Ask students to select two works of art to compare and not to reveal their choices to anyone. Have them write sentences describing and comparing the two works of art, but not to mention either of them by name. Invite students to take turns sharing their sentences. Ask the rest of the class to decide which two works of art are being described and compared.

Gramática · Repaso

Presentation

Resources: Voc. & Gram. Transparencies: 50

Suggestions: After students review the *Gramática,* write several different adjectives on the board, one at a time. Point to one adjective and say different nouns. Have students use the adjective to modify each noun, making sure it agrees in gender and number each time.

 Standards: 1.2

Resources: Practice Answers on Transparencies

Focus: Reviewing adjective agreement

Suggestions: Remind students that in noun phrases such as **museo de arte,** they must consider which noun is being modified in order to know which adjective form to use. In this case, since both nouns are masculine, the same adjective form can be used for either noun. But in a noun phrase such as **sala de cuadros,** they must decide whether they are modifying **sala** or **cuadros.**

Answers:
1. moderno
2. fascinantes
3. plástico
4. exageradas
5. complicado

 Standards: 1.3, 2.2

Focus: Reviewing comparison of adjectives

Suggestions: Since students are comparing one **cuadro** with another each time, the adjective forms for the activity will all be masculine singular. This allows students to focus on the constructions **más/menos...que** and **tan...como.**

Answers will vary.

63

▶ Rapid Review

Use the verbs in the *reacciones* section of the vocabulary to help students review the preterite. Assign each student a subject pronoun to work with, such as *nosotros* or *tu amigo y tú.* Have students use their subject and one or more of the verbs to create and share sentences about an entertainment event: *¿Tu amigo y tú se aburrieron en el concierto?*

Vocabulario

Presentation

Standards: 1.1

Resources: Voc. & Gram. Transparencies: 51

Suggestions: Begin by having students use the vocabulary to talk about the photos. Then play *5 preguntas*—a shortened version of 20 Questions. Each student chooses a word or expression and takes a turn at being "it." Other students ask up to five *Sí/No* questions to try to determine what the word is: *¿Es una persona? ¿Esta persona canta?*

Standards: 1.2, 1.3

Resources: Practice Answers on Transparencies

Focus: Practicing review vocabulary

Suggestions: Tell students to look over the complete *mensaje* in step 1 before writing their answers.

Answers:

Step 1

1. argumento	4. actor
2. comedia	5. galán
3. drama	6. aplaudió

Step 2

Answers will vary.

Extension: Help students practice the vocabulary under the *reacciones* and *comentarios* categories. Have them write and read aloud dialogues of two to three lines in which two people talk about an entertainment event. Provide a model like the following:

—*Anoche vi una obra de teatro inolvidable.*

—*¿Sí? ¿Te divertiste?*

—*¡Muchísimo! Después, aplaudí durante cinco minutos con todo el público.*

Vocabulario

en el teatro
la actuación
el argumento
la comedia
el concierto
el drama
los efectos especiales
el ensayo
la escena
la luz
la obra de teatro

en el concierto
el auditorio
la banda
la canción
el coro
la música
la orquesta
la voz

participantes
el actor, la actriz
el bailarín, la bailarina
el / la cantante
el crítico, la crítica
el director, la directora
el galán
el músico, la música
el personaje

actividades
bailar
cantar
ensayar
hacer el papel de . . .
hacer el papel principal
tener éxito
tocar . . .
    la guitarra
    el piano

reacciones
aburrirse
aplaudir
divertirse
dormirse
gritar

comentarios
emocionante
estar basado, -a en . .
flojo, -a
increíble
inolvidable
largo, -a
más o menos
talentoso, -a

4 Leer/Escribir ....

Práctica de vocabulario

1 Completa el siguiente mensaje que te dejó una amiga sobre una noche en el teatro. Usa las palabras del recuadro.

galán	aplaudió	comedia
drama	argumento	actor

Anoche fui al teatro. Desde el principio, el __**1.**__ de la obra me pareció muy divertido. Prefiero ir al teatro a reír con una __**2.**__ que llorar con un __**3.**__. El __**4.**__ que hacía el papel del __**5.**__ tuvo una actuación extraordinaria. Al final, el público __**6.**__ por más de cinco minutos.

2 Usa las palabras del vocabulario para escribir una descripción de estas personas. Trata de incluir información sobre lo que hace la persona y dónde lo hace.

Modelo

un actor
Un actor hace el papel de un personaje en una película o una obra de teatro.

1. un(a) músico(a)   **3.** un(a) cantante

2. un(a) crítico(a)   **4.** un bailarín, una bailarina

64 sesenta y cuatro
A ver si recuerdas . . .

Universal Access

Heritage Language Learners

Have students write a description of a performing arts event that they have seen either in the United States or in their heritage country. Encourage them to use specific descriptive language in order to elaborate on each detail presented. Those who have not recently seen a performing arts event can describe one they would most like to see.

Multiple Intelligences

Musical/Rhythmic: Encourage students to prepare a short selection of music to share with the class. They might play an instrument, sing a song, or bring in a favorite recording. Use these as the basis for the descriptions and comparisons in *Actividad* 6 on p. 65.

Gramática·Repaso

Comparación de sustantivos y el superlativo

To make a comparison or differentiation between two nouns, use *más / menos* + noun + *que*.

> Hoy hay **menos gente que** ayer en el teatro.

To make a comparison between two similar nouns, use: *tanto(a)* + noun + *como*. Since *tanto* is an adjective, it should agree with the noun in both gender (masculine or feminine) and number (singular or plural).

> Hoy hay **tanto público como** ayer en el teatro.
>
> Hoy hay **tantas personas como** ayer en el teatro.

The superlative is used to say something is the "most" or the "least." To express a superlative comparison use: *el / la / los / las* + noun + *más / menos* + adjective.

> **El concierto más emocionante** fue el de ayer.
>
> Para mí, **la obra menos divertida** es "Algún día".

- When *mejor* and *peor* are used as superlatives, the following construction is used: *el / la / los / las* + *mejor(es) / peor(es)* + noun.

> Pienso que Alejandra Ruiz es **la mejor bailarina**.
>
> ¡Ustedes son **los peores cantantes**!

- The preposition *de* is used after the adjective when the superlative comparison occurs within a group or category.

> El concierto de ayer fue **el más emocionante de** todos.

 Hablar

Práctica de gramática

Un(a) compañero(a) y tú van a expresar su opinión sobre los siguientes temas.

Modelo

la mejor película del año
A —*Para ti, ¿cuál fue la mejor película del año?*
B —*Para mí, la mejor película fue "Frida".*

a. el mejor actor de teatro

b. la peor actriz de Hollywood

c. la canción más romántica de este año

d. el baile que les gusta más a los jóvenes

e. el programa de tele más aburrido de la semana

● **Más práctica**
Practice Workbook 2-1, 2-2

 Escribir

Práctica de gramática

Escribe comparaciones entre dos artistas o grupos de música. Usa los siguientes temas.

- número de canciones que grabaron
- talento que tienen
- instrumentos que tocan
- discos compactos que tienen

Modelo

Selena tiene más canciones que Shakira.

For: Vocabulary practice
Visit: www.phschool.com
Web Code: jed-0201

sesenta y cinco **65**
Capítulo 2

Gramática·Repaso

Presentation

Resources: Voc. & Gram. Transparencies: 52

Suggestions: On the board, write the frames for the two constructions:
más/menos + noun + *que*
el/la/los/las + noun + *más/menos* + adj.
Fill the frames with different nouns and adjectives from p. 50 that make sense and have students create sentences using the results: *Hay más público que actores en el teatro. Los bailarines son los más talentosos de todos.*

 Standards: 1.3

Focus: Reviewing noun comparisons

Suggestions: For further practice, have students think of additional categories for their comparisons.

Answers will vary.

 Standards: 1.1

Focus: Reviewing comparatives

Suggestions: Partners might share opinions or discuss their differing opinions. After they have gone through the list together, invite them to share their opinions with the rest of the class.

Answers will vary.

Extension: Ask students to collect the opinions of the class and compile the information in a chart. Consider keeping this chart and bringing it out again a few months from now to see how students' opinions have changed.

Enriching Your Teaching

Teacher-to-Teacher

Ask students to form small groups based on topics in which they share an interest. These might include cars, a particular sport or type of music, computers, or a reading genre. Have them talk about their common interest and create a few comparative and superlative statements about it to share with the class. Other students can ask them to support their opinions, which will often elicit other comparative and superlative statements.

Preview

Standards for Foreign Language Learning: *Capítulo* 2

- To achieve the goals of the Standards, students will:

Communication

1.1 Interpersonal

- Talk about the style, features, tools, and media used in the creation of works of visual, literary, and performing art
- Talk about important artists
- Talk about art museums
- Talk about events in the past

1.2 Interpretive

- Read and listen to information about the style, features, tools, and media used in the creation of works of visual, literary, and performing art
- Read and listen to information about important artists
- Read about the suffix -*ismo*
- Read about a family party
- Read about art museums
- Read arts and entertainment reviews
- Read about events in the past
- Read poetry by Juan Luis Guerra

1.3 Presentational

- Write about the style, features, tools, and media used in the creation of works of visual, literary, and performing art
- Write and present information orally about artists
- Write arts and entertainment reviews and write about their contents
- Present information orally about "the artist of the millennium"
- Write a review of a student audition

Culture

2.1 Practices and Perspectives

- Explain the practices and perspectives of important Latin American and Spanish figures in the visual, literary, and performing arts

2.2 Products and Perspectives

- Discuss the work of important Latin American and Spanish figures in the visual, literary, and performing arts
- Talk about Museo del Barrio and its cultural roots
- Talk about the popular TV show *Sábado Gigante*
- Describe *salsa* music
- Discuss the poetry of Juan Luis Guerra
- Talk about a Spanish version of *When Harry Met Sally*

Connections

3.1 Cross-curricular

- Talk about key facts about the fine arts
- Talk about key facts about the Mexican Revolution
- Talk about key facts about the history of Spain
- Discuss Language Arts strategies: using illustrations, using context clues, using visuals, organizing information, categorizing, monitoring your reading
- Discuss the Language Arts skill of using graphic organizers

3.2 Target Culture

- Read the titles of works of art
- Read a famous slogan from the Mexican Revolution
- Read an advertisement for El Museo del Barrio
- Read about the cultural significance of the term *salsa*
- Read poetry by Juan Luis Guerra
- Read an excerpt from a work by Esmeralda Santiago

Fondo cultural ■◆■◆■◆■◆■◆■◆

Picasso y el cubismo Si observas con atención esta pintura del artista español Pablo Picasso (1881–1973), te vas a dar cuenta de que el artista representa a la modelo, a la izquierda, y al pintor, a la derecha, con formas geométricas. A esta forma de expresión se la conoce como *cubismo*, un movimiento artístico que comenzó en Francia entre 1907 y 1914, y que tuvo una gran importancia en Europa y los Estados Unidos.

- ¿Conoces un artista de los Estados Unidos que usa formas geométricas en sus obras?

El pintor y su modelo, (1928), Pablo Picasso
Oil on canvas. 51 1/8 " x 64 1/4". The Sidney and Harriet Janis Collection. (644.19) © Digital Image. The Museum of Modern Art/Licensed by Scala-Art Resource, NY. © 2004 Estate of Pablo Picasso/Artists Rights Society ARS, New York.

66 sesenta y seis
Capítulo 2

Universal Access

Personalizing the Theme

Invite students to talk about their favorite visual arts genre or artist. Ask: ¿*Cómo descubriste al (a la) artista? ¿Sabes el título de alguna obra suya? ¿Puedes explicar por qué te gusta?* Encourage students to bring in pictures or recordings to share with the class.

Students with Special Needs

Provide visually impaired students with a short oral description of *El pintor y su modelo*. Utilize geometry and vocabulary rich in color to communicate the style of the work. Or, have students use thick paper and cut out some of the forms found in the painting. Arrange the forms so that students can feel the composition of the work.

Capítulo 2

¿Cómo te expresas?

Chapter Objectives

- Talk about the arts
- Give an opinion about a work of art
- Relate the arts to your own experience
- Describe how people express themselves
- Narrate events in the past
- Discuss some important artists of the Spanish-speaking world

Video Focus

- Music, dance and art in the Spanish-speaking world

Country Connection

As you learn about the arts, you will make connections to these countries and places.

Estados Unidos — España
México — Cuba
Puerto Rico
Ecuador
Chile
Argentina

Go Online
PHSchool.com

For: Online Atlas
Visit: www.phschool.com
Web Code: jee-0002

sesenta y siete **67**
Capítulo 2

Preview

②

Standards for Foreign Language Learning (cont'd)

Comparisons
4.1 Language
- Compare Spanish words to their English counterparts
- Compare the use and meanings of Spanish comparatives and superlatives to those in English
- Compare the uses of English and Spanish past tenses

4.2 Culture
- Compare growing up in one culture to growing up in more than one culture

Communities
5.1 Beyond the School
- Link to Web sites from around the Spanish-speaking world

5.2 Lifelong Learner
- Develop an appreciation for artistic role models
- Develop an appreciation for the fine arts
- Recognize sources of artistic inspiration
- Discuss the impact culture has on the formation of personality

Chapter Opener
Presentation

Resources: Voc. & Gram. Transparencies: 14, 16, 17, 18, 20, 22 (maps)

Suggestions: Introduce students to the theme of the chapter and go over the objectives. Point out that they will learn about artists from around the Spanish-speaking world who work in a variety of media and styles.

Fondo cultural *Standards:* 1.1, 1.2, 2.2, 3.1

Resources: Fine Art Transparencies; Fine Art Transparencies Teacher's Guide

Suggestions: Remind students that the painting shows an artist in a studio, painting a model. Have volunteers point to various parts of the painting and say what they think they portray.

Answers will vary, but may include American cubists such as Stuart Davis, Alfred Maurer, or Max Weber.

Enriching Your Teaching

Planning for Instruction
Resources:

- Teacher Express CD-ROM or Resource Book
  - Teaching resources
  - Lesson Planner
  - Chapter Resource Checklist
  - School-to-Home Connection Letter

Culture Note

While Picasso is known as one of the foremost figures of the cubist movement, his early career was characterized by experimentation with many different painting styles. In fact, in Picasso's early work, he portrayed his subject matter in a much more traditional or realistic way.

Vocabulario y gramática

Presentation

Standards: 1.1, 1.2, 2.2, 3.1, 3.2

Resources: Voc. & Gram. Transparencies: 53–54; Resource Book: Cap. 2, Input Script; Audio Program: CD Cap. 2, Tracks 1,3

Focus: Presenting new vocabulary and using grammar lexically in context

Suggestions: Use the Input Script from the *Teacher's Resource Book* as a source of ideas for presentation of new vocabulary and comprehensible input. Use pantomime to clarify the meaning of the adjectives *sentado(a)* and *parado(a).* For objects, use TPR. Name an object on the transparency and ask a volunteer to come and point to it. Point out that *mural, famoso(a), abstracto(a), expresar,* and *representar* are cognates.

 **Actividad 1** *Standards:* 1.2

Resources: Audio Program: CD Cap. 2, Track 2; Resource Book: Cap. 2, Audio Script; Practice Answers on Transparencies

Focus: Practicing listening comprehension of new vocabulary

Suggestions: Before engaging students in the listening activity, give them a few minutes to read over and study p. 68 silently. Then play the *Audio CD* or read the script aloud.

Answers:

1. C	4. C
2. F	5. C
3. F	6. C

A primera vista 1

Vocabulario y gramática en contexto

Objectives

Read, listen to, and understand information about
- different types of art
- art materials

Los estudiantes de la escuela Simón Bolívar de Caracas, Venezuela, querían decorar la cafetería de su escuela. Para esto, decidieron pintar un mural en una pared de la cafetería. Antes de comenzar a pintar, los estudiantes se reunieron en **el taller** de arte para planear lo que querían hacer.

la naturaleza muerta

el mural

sentada   parado

el pincel

la paleta

Los estudiantes miraron muchas **obras de arte** de diferentes pintores y, finalmente, escogieron una del pintor catalán Joan Miró para usarla en el mural. Joan Miró fue un artista **famoso** del **siglo** XX.

Escuchar

¡A pintar!

Escribe los números del 1 al 6 en una hoja de papel. Escucha cada frase y escribe *C* (cierto) o *F* (falso) según las fotos y la información en esta página.

Naturaleza Muerta, (1999), Alfonso Fernández. Oleo sobre lino, 110 x 120 cm.

68   sesenta y ocho
A primera vista 1

Universal Access

Advanced Learners

Ask students to work together to draw and label the floor plan of the art room in your school. Encourage them to include details such as furniture, art supplies, and the various types of art that are currently on display or projects that are in progress. Then have them share the floor plan with the rest of the class. They can point out the various features of the room, tell where each of them works when they are in art class, and talk about art projects they may be currently involved in. Listeners can join in and talk about their own experiences in the art room.

Éstas son algunas de las obras de Miró que los estudiantes miraron cuando estaban buscando un cuadro para su mural.

1 Cuando era joven, Miró pintaba con un estilo realista, como podemos ver en el paisaje *La granja*, de 1922. En este paisaje se ve en primer plano un árbol entre una casa y un establo *(stable)*. Al fondo del cuadro vemos el cielo y la luna.

fondo

primer plano

¹ *La Granja*, (1922), Joan Miró

2 En esta pintura de 1919, el joven Miró hizo su propio **retrato**, es decir, pintó su autorretrato.

la pintura

el autorretrato

² *Autorretrato*, (1919), Joan Miró

3 Más tarde, el estilo de Miró **se vuelve** mucho menos realista, como se ve en este *Interior holandés*, de 1928.

³ *Interior holandés*, (1928), Joan Miró

¹ (c) Archivo Iconográfico, S.A./CORBIS. (c) 2004 Successio Miró/Artists Rights Society ARS, NY.
² Oil on canvas. (c) 2004 Successio Miró/Artists Rights Society ARS, NY. Photo: J.G. Berizzi. Musée Picasso, Paris, France.
³ Oil on canvas. 36 1/8" x 28 3/4". Mrs. Simon Guggenheim Fund. (163.1945). (c) 2004 Successio Miró/Artists Rights Society ARS, NY. The Museum of Modern Art/Licensed by Scala-Art Resource, NY.

4 Cuando ya era un artista famoso, Miró comenzó su obra de **escultor**. Esta **escultura** es **abstracta**, no vemos claramente lo que **representa**, pero sus colores vivos **expresan sentimientos** de alegría.

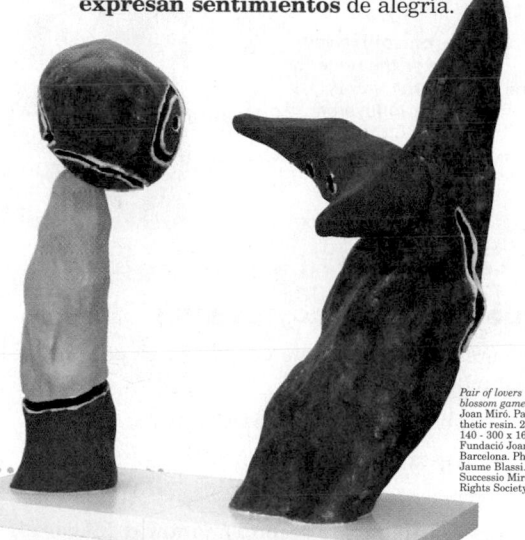

Pair of lovers with almond blossom games, (1975), Joan Miró. Painted synthetic resin. 273 x 127 x 140 - 300 x 160 x 140 cm. Fundació Joan Miró, Barcelona. Photo by Jaume Blassi. (c) 2004 Successio Miró/Artists Rights Society ARS, NY.

Escuchar

El guía del museo

Escucha la descripción que hace un guía de museo de las obras de arte que aparecen en la página. Señala cada obra que describe.

sesenta y nueve   69
Capítulo 2

Language Input   2

Actividad 2   *Standards:* 1.2

Resources: Voc. and Gram. Transparencies: 54; Audio Program: CD Cap. 2, Track 4; Resource Book: Cap. 2, Audio Script; Practice Answers on Transparencies

Focus: Practicing listening comprehension of new vocabulary

Suggestions: Use the *Audio CD* or read the script. Allow students to listen more than once. Pause to monitor students, making sure they are identifying the correct works of art.

Answers:
| 1. 1 | 3. 3 | 5. 4 |
| 2. 3 | 4. 2 | |

Extension: Have students write their own set of four comments, one for each work of art pictured on the page. Then have them work in pairs. One student reads his or her comments aloud while the partner identifies which work of art is being described.

Block Schedule

Have students draw a self-portrait modeled after Miró's or in a different style. Then place students in groups of four or five and have each member of the group ask a question about the self-portrait.

69

Vocabulario y gramática

Presentation

Standards: 1.2, 2.1, 2.2, 3.1, 5.2

Resources: Voc. & Gram. Transparencies: 55; Resource Book: Cap. 2, Input Script; Audio Program: CD Cap. 2, Track 5

Focus: Extending presentation of vocabulary and grammar in the context of an interview

Suggestions:

Pre-reading: Direct students' attention to the *Estrategia*. Remind them that, with the amount of Spanish they now know, they can use context clues as they read, in much the same way as they do in English.

Reading: Allow students time to read the interview silently first. Then play the *Audio CD* or read the interview aloud, with students reading along as they listen. Allow them to listen more than once. Another option after silent reading is to have volunteers take turns reading the parts of the interviewer and Dina Bursztyn.

Post-reading: Complete *Actividad* 3 to check comprehension.

 Actividad 3   *Standards:* 1.2, 1.3

Resources: Practice Answers on Transparencies

Focus: Demonstrating comprehension of the reading passage

Suggestions: Have students share their written answers. Use items 3–5 as a springboard to discussion about art.

Answers:
1. La artista usó barro para hacer la escultura.
2. La tía Fanny influyó mucho en Dina Bursztyn porque pintaba y tenía obras de cerámica en su casa.
3–5. Answers will vary.

Chapter Project

Give students copies of the Chapter Project outline and rubric from the *Teacher's Resource Book*. Explain the task to them, and have them perform step 1. (For more information, see p. 62-a.)

Entrevista con Dina Bursztyn

Dina Bursztyn es una escultora que nació en Mendoza, Argentina, y vive en Nueva York. Escribe poesía y cuentos y trabaja **la cerámica** para hacer murales y esculturas en distintos lugares de la ciudad.

¿Qué material prefiere para expresarse?
"Principalmente el barro[1], pero también me gusta escribir y pintar."

*¿Qué artista la **inspiró**?*
"Mi mayor **fuente de inspiración** fue mi tía Fanny. Ella pintaba y tenía obras de cerámica en su casa. **Influyó** mucho en mí y empecé a moldear[2]. A los cinco años ya llevaba siempre un poco de plastilina[3] en los bolsillos[4]."

¿De qué está hecha esta escultura?
"*Lady Dreams* está hecha de barro."

*¿Qué representa **la figura** de* Lady Dreams?
"Es una suma de **las imágenes** de mis sueños[5]. También hice otras *Ladies*."

*¿Por qué escogió **el tema** de las* Ladies?
"Porque siempre me interesaron los mitos[6] y pensé que necesitaba crear nuevos mitos. Entonces decidí crear mi propia mitología."

---

1 clay **2** to mould **3** modeling clay **4** pockets
5 dreams **6** myths

Nota

The preterite form of the verb *influir* is similar to the preterite of the verb *destruir: influí, influiste, influyó, influyeron.*

Estrategia

Context clues
When you read, try to determine the meaning of words you don't understand by using context clues. Sometimes words in the same sentence or surrounding sentences will give you the meaning of the word you don't know. For example, if you do not know the meaning of the word *barro*, you may determine that it is a material for making sculptures by looking at the context.

Lady Dreams

Dina en su taller

 **Actividad 3**   **Leer/Escribir** ....

Lo que nos dice *Lady Dreams*

1. ¿Qué materiales crees que usó la artista para hacer la escultura *Lady Dreams*?
2. ¿Por qué fue importante la tía Fanny para Dina?
3. ¿Te gusta esta escultura? ¿Por qué?
4. ¿Qué representa *Lady Dreams* para ti?
5. ¿Alguna vez alguien te inspiró a pintar o dibujar algo? Cuenta esa experiencia.

70   setenta
A primera vista 1

Universal Access

Heritage Language Learners

Have students conduct an interview with a Spanish-speaking professional whose work they respect. Encourage them to prepare questions and to record the interview on audiocassette. Invite them to share the interview with the class.

Students with Learning Difficulties

Direct students to read for specific information about each of the artists presented. Have them create a simple chart with the following headings: ***nombre del artista, país, material, tema.*** Then have students fill in the chart with key points found in the reading.

Artistas latinoamericanos

Durante el siglo XX América Latina tuvo numerosos artistas que, **a través de** sus diferentes estilos, expresaron en sus obras la rica cultura de sus países.

1 El pintor cubano Carlos Enríquez vivió en París en los años 20 y recibió la influencia del **movimiento** surrealista. Sus paisajes **muestran** la naturaleza y la luz intensa de los países del Caribe.

Paisaje criollo, (1941), Carlos Enríquez
Oil on composition board. 17 1/2" x 23 5/8". Gift of Dr. C. M. Ramírez Corria. (604.1942). The Museum of Modern Art/Licensed by SCALA/Art Resource, NY.

3 El pintor ecuatoriano Oswaldo Guayasamín mostró en su obra la cultura de los indígenas de América Latina y cómo vivían muchos de ellos.

La madre y el niño, (1989), Oswaldo Guayasamín
Photo Nicolas Osorio Ruiz. Museo Fundación Guayasamín, Quito, Ecuador.

2 El movimiento muralista mexicano muestra un país en el que se mezclan la cultura indígena y la española.

Hombre controlando el universo, (1934), (detalle del mural) Diego Rivera
(c) 2005 Banco de México Diego Rivera & Frida Kahlo Museums Truct. Av. Cinco de Mayo Nu. 2, Col. Centro, Del. Cuauhtemoc 06059, México, D.F. Reproduction authorized by the *Instituto Nacional de Bellas Artes y Literatura.* CORBIS, Inc.

Diego Rivera (en la foto con su esposa, la pintora Frida Kahlo) fue el artista más importante del muralismo mexicano.

Leer/Escuchar

¿De quién es?

Mira las ilustraciones y lee sus descripciones. Luego, escucha las frases y di a qué ilustración se refiere cada una.

Hablar

Mi favorita

Escoge la obra de arte que más te gusta de esta página y descríbesela a otro(a) estudiante. Explícale por qué te gusta más que las otras.

● **Más práctica**
Practice Workbook 2-3, 2-4

Go Online
PHSchool.com

For: Vocabulary practice
Visit: www.phschool.com
Web Code: jed-0202

setenta y uno   **71**
Capítulo 2

Actividad 6

Standards: 1.2, 1.3

Resources: Practice Answers on Transparencies

Focus: Using new words and expressions in sentences

Suggestions: Use the Transparencies to review visualized vocabulary. Leave them on the projector as a visual reference while students work.

Answers:
1. un taller
2. una naturaleza muerta
3. Un siglo
4. inspiración
5. mural

Actividad 7

Standards: 1.1

Resources: Practice Answers on Transparencies

Focus: Practicing new vocabulary

Suggestions: Make sure partners switch roles, so both can practice explaining the uses of the various items.

Answers:
1. A —El pintor usa una paleta y un pincel, ¿no?
   B —Sí, los usa para mezclar los colores.
2. A —Una escultora usa piedra, ¿no?
   B —Sí, la usa para crear una escultura.
3. A —Un(a) poeta usa papel y lápiz, ¿no?
   B —Sí, los usa para escribir sus poesías.
4. A —Un escritor usa una computadora, ¿no?
   B —Sí, la usa para escribir cuentos.

Ampliación del lenguaje

Presentation

Standards: 1.2, 4.1

Resources: Practice Answers on Transparencies

Focus: Understanding the suffix *-ismo*

Suggestions: Ask students to brainstorm other words they have heard that contain the *-ismo* suffix, such as *idealismo* or *modernismo.*

Answers:
impresionismo
realismo

Manos a la obra 1

Vocabulario y gramática en uso

Objectives
- Talk about art forms
- Talk about art supplies
- Describe a work of art
- Review uses of the preterite and imperfect
- Practice *estar* and the past participle

Actividad 6 **Leer/Escribir**

Definiciones

Completa cada frase con una palabra o expresión apropiada del recuadro. Luego, escribe frases usando las palabras del recuadro.

una naturaleza muerta	inspiración	un taller	mural	un siglo

1. Los artistas generalmente trabajan en _____ .
2. Un cuadro que representa objetos, frutas o comida es _____ .
3. _____ son cien años.
4. Un artista necesita _____ para crear su obra.
5. Cuando la pintura se hace en una pared, se llama _____.

Actividad 7 **Hablar**

¿La paleta o el pincel?

En el taller de arte, los estudiantes usan diferentes materiales para crear sus obras. Habla con un(a) compañero(a) para explicar lo que usa cada artista y para qué lo usa.

Modelo

los niños ✂

A —*Los niños usan tijeras, ¿no?*

B —*Sí, las usan para cortar papel.*

Estudiante A
1. pintor
2. escultora
3. poeta
4. escritor

Estudiante B

¡Respuesta personal!

Ampliación del lenguaje

El sufijo *-ismo* se usa para nombrar una doctrina o un movimiento artístico. Para hablar de los pintores que hacen pinturas *románticas*, usamos la palabra *romanticismo*. Otros ejemplos son:

cubo → **cubismo**   futuro → **futurismo**   surreal → **surrealismo**

Completa cada frase.

Un pintor dijo que quería pintar la *impresión* que tenía del paisaje, por eso llamaron al movimiento **1.** . Otros querían pintar la vida *real*, y llamaron a su movimiento **2.** .

Universal Access

Multiple Intelligences
Visual/Spatial: Have students create a painting or drawing in the style of Miró, Picasso, Velázquez, or one of the other artists discussed in the chapter. Use these "original" works of art to supplement partner discussions in *Actividad* 9 on p. 73.

Advanced Learners
Have students prepare and present detailed descriptions of artistic processes such as writing a story, making a ceramic sculpture, painting a mural, or writing a song. Ask them to describe the process step by step. Remind them to use sequencing words such as *primero, segundo, después,* and *finalmente* to help listeners understand their presentations.

Actividad 8 — Leer/Escribir

La inspiración de un joven artista

Lee la siguiente entrevista con el pintor chileno Alfonso Fernández. Después, observa el cuadro de este artista y contesta las preguntas.

¿Qué te gustaba hacer cuando eras joven?
"Desde joven me gustaba dibujar más que salir a bailar. Hasta los 15 años, los temas históricos fueron mi fuente de inspiración."

¿Qué artista influyó en tu obra y por qué?
"Cuando empecé a estudiar arte me inspiré en la obra del famoso pintor español Goya, porque a través de su obra criticó el momento político y cultural en que vivió."

¿De qué época era Goya?
"Goya era del siglo XIX."

¿En qué se parece tu obra a la de Goya?
"Goya, como yo, representó al pueblo *(common people)* en su obra."

¿Qué consejo le puedes dar a un joven artista?
"Es importante expresar tus sentimientos en tu obra."

Naturaleza Muerta,
(1999),
Alfonso Fernández
Oleo sobre lino, 110 x 120 cm.
1999.

1. ¿Qué temas inspiraban a Fernández cuando era joven?

2. Más tarde, ¿qué artista influyó en su arte? ¿Cuándo vivió ese artista? ¿En qué se parecen el arte de ese artista y el de Fernández?

3. ¿Qué cree Fernández que debe hacer un joven artista?

4. ¿Tú te expresas a través del arte? ¿Cómo? ¿A través del dibujo, de la pintura o de la escultura? ¿Cuáles son tus fuentes de inspiración?

Actividad 9 — Hablar

Describe el cuadro

Diego Rodríguez de Silva y Velázquez (1599–1660) fue el pintor de la corte del rey Felipe IV de España. *Las Meninas,* un retrato de la familia real, es su obra maestra. Trabaja con otro(a) estudiante para hablar de los detalles de este cuadro.

Modelo

A —*¿Qué se ve* a la derecha de la niña rubia?
B —*Se ve* la figura de un perro sentado.

Las Meninas, (1656), Diego Velázquez
Oil on canvas (1656). 318 x 270 cm. Inv. 1174. Museo Nacional del Prado, Madrid, Spain (c) Lessing/Art Resource, NY.

Estudiante A

1. en el centro, a la izquierda
2. al fondo, en la puerta
3. en primer plano
4. a la izquierda de la niña rubia
5. en la pared del fondo

Estudiante B

el pintor, parado con los pinceles y la paleta
una niña rubia de pelo largo
un hombre
un cuadro
una joven que le ofrece algo

setenta y tres **73**
Capítulo 2

Practice and Communicate (2)

Actividad 8

Standards: 1.2, 1.3, 2.2, 3.1, 5.2

Resources: Fine Art Transparencies; Fine Art Transparencies Teacher's Guide; Practice Answers on Transparencies

Focus: Using new vocabulary and structures in contextual reading and writing

Suggestions: Remind students to pay attention to Fernández's use of the preterite and imperfect tenses.

Answers:
1. Los temas históricos lo inspiraban.
2. Goya lo influyó más tarde. Goya era del siglo XIX. Los dos artistas representan al pueblo.
3. Debe expresar sus sentimientos en su obra.
4. Answers will vary.

Actividad 9

Standards: 1.1, 2.2, 3.1

Resources: Fine Art Transparencies; Fine Art Transparencies Teacher's Guide; Practice Answers on Transparencies

Focus: Practicing new vocabulary and structures

Suggestions: Have students switch roles in order to practice both questioning and answering. Encourage them to elaborate on the speaking cues they are given.

Answers:
1. A —¿Qué se ve en el centro, a la izquierda?
   B —Se ve al pintor, parado con los pinceles y la paleta.
2. A —...al fondo, en la puerta?
   B —...a un hombre.
3. A —...en primer plano?
   B —...a una niña rubia de pelo largo.
4. A —...a la izquierda de la niña rubia?
   B—...a una joven que le ofrece algo.
5. A —...en la pared del fondo?
   B —Se ve un cuadro (espejo).

Enriching Your Teaching

Culture Note

Even master painters are influenced and inspired by others. Pablo Picasso, for example, was clearly influenced by the work of other Spanish masters. The connection between Picasso's portraits, such as *Lady in Blue,* and the work of Diego de Silva y Velázquez is evident.

Similarly, much of the work during Picasso's Blue Period is reminiscent of the paintings of El Greco in terms of composition and style. The link between Picasso's *Guernica* and Goya's theme of the horror of war is also clear.

73

Actividad 10

Standards: 1.1

Resources: Fine Art Transparencies; Fine Art Transparencies Teacher's Guide

Focus: Using new vocabulary and structures in a guessing game

Suggestions: If possible, have students refer to the transparencies for this activity. Otherwise have them refer to the photos in the student book. Have them look over the questions in *Actividad* 11 before they begin the game.

Answers will vary.

Actividad 11

Standards: 1.2, 1.3, 2.1, 2.2, 3.1, 3.2

Resources: Fine Art Transparencies; Fine Art Transparencies Teacher's Guide; Practice Answers on Transparencies

Focus: Practicing and demonstrating comprehension of new vocabulary and structures

Suggestions: Have students answer the questions in step 2 as a list first, before attempting to organize this information into a written comparison.

Answers

1. Los dos artistas son de España.
2. Pintaron en el siglo XX.
3–6. Answers will vary.
7. Es arte surrealista (abstracto).
8–9. Answers will vary.

Country Connection

Presentation

Standards: 3.1

Ask students to research on the Internet the hometowns of Joan Miró *(Barcelona, Cataluña)* and Salvador Dalí *(Figueras, Cataluña)*. Have them locate these places on a map.

  Actividad 10 — **Hablar** ....

Juego

Escoge una de las obras de arte que se encuentran en las páginas 69 y 71. No se la muestres a tu compañero(a). Tu compañero(a) te va a hacer preguntas como las que están al final de la Actividad 11 y va a intentar adivinar la obra. ¡Después, cambien los papeles!

 Actividad 11 — Leer/Escribir ....

Los mundos de Miró y de Dalí

⬤ Lee este artículo sobre los artistas surrealistas Joan Miró y Salvador Dalí.

El movimiento surrealista empezó poco después de la Primera Guerra Mundial. Los pintores del surrealismo se inspiraban en temas de su propia imaginación. Querían capturar en sus cuadros ideas e imágenes del subconsciente *(subconscious)*, como las que vemos en los sueños. El español Salvador Dalí (1904–1989) fue uno de los pintores más famosos de este grupo. Su cuadro *La persistencia de la memoria*, que aparece en esta página, es un ejemplo del estilo surrealista.

Como muchos otros artistas, el español Joan Miró (1893–1983) se fue a París a principios de los años veinte. Allí lo influyeron los surrealistas, si bien su estilo es más abstracto que el de Salvador Dalí. Además, Miró usa colores vivos y figuras que recuerdan a los dibujos de los niños. Su obra es una fiesta de la imaginación y los colores. Un ejemplo es su cuadro *Interior holandés II*.

⬤ Ahora contesta las siguientes preguntas sobre estos dos artistas y los cuadros de esta página. Usa las respuestas para escribir una comparación de los dos cuadros.

1. ¿De qué país son estos artistas?
2. ¿En qué siglo pintaron?
3. En cada cuadro, ¿qué se ve en primer plano? ¿Qué se ve al fondo?
4. ¿Qué se ve a la izquierda?
5. ¿Qué colores usa más cada artista?
6. ¿Cómo son las figuras, realistas o más abstractas?
7. ¿Qué tipo de arte es?
8. ¿Cómo te hace sentir este arte?
9. ¿Te gusta alguno de los cuadros? ¿Por qué?

La persistencia de la memoria, (1931), Salvador Dalí
Oil on canvas, 9 1/2 x 13 in. (24.1 x 33 cm). Given anonymously. (c) 2004 Salvador Dalí, Gala-Salvador Dalí Foundation/Artists Rights Society (ARS), New York.† A.K.G., Berlin/SuperStock.

Dutch Interior II, (19.. Joan Miró
The Art Archive/Peggy Guggenheim Collection Venice/Dagli Orti (A). (c Successio Miró/Artists Rights Soci NY.

74 setenta y cuatro
Manos a la obra 1

Universal Access

Heritage Language Learners

Students may have spelling difficulty with words involving the letters **b** and **v**. Have them identify words containing these letters. Some examples might include **obra, dibujo, abstracto(a), cubismo,** and **movimiento.** Have students separate the words into two columns and quiz each other on proper spelling.

Students with Learning Difficulties

Before they answer the questions in *Actividad* 11, have students brainstorm a bank of applicable nouns and adjectives to describe each of the paintings presented. Review the meanings of these descriptive words and have students use their word banks when answering the questions.

Leer/Escribir ....

Diego Rivera: arte y revolución

> **Estrategia**
>
> **Using illustrations**
> The details in a painting or illustration can give you clues about the main theme of a text. Observe the painting on the right. What does it tell you about the main theme of this article?

Conexiones **El arte y la historia** ————

Diego Rivera creía que el arte debe ayudar a los campesinos[1] a entender su propia historia. Este panel titulado *Emiliano Zapata* representa a Zapata, el líder de los campesinos durante la Revolución Mexicana. Con el famoso lema[2] "tierra y libertad", Zapata luchó[3] por una reforma agraria a principios del siglo XX.

Diego Rivera pensaba que Zapata era un verdadero héroe de la Revolución. En este panel, que es parte de un mural del Palacio Nacional de la Ciudad de México, vemos a Zapata en primer plano y a sus revolucionarios campesinos detrás de él. En la mano derecha lleva una guadaña[4] y con la mano izquierda sujeta[5] un caballo. A sus pies hay un hombre muerto.

———————————————

1 peasants **2** motto **3** fought **4** scythe **5** restrains

Observa los detalles del panel.

1. ¿Quién es la figura central en esta composición? ¿Cómo está vestido?

2. ¿Qué representa el caballo blanco?

3. ¿Qué representa la guadaña?

La obra del pintor mexicano Diego Rivera (1886–1957) muestra una preocupación por los ideales de la Revolución Mexicana. Lee el siguiente artículo sobre una de las figuras principales de la obra de Rivera y contesta las preguntas.

Emiliano Zapata (panel de un mural), (1931), Diego Rivera
Fresco, 7' 9 3/4" x 6' 2". Abby Aldrich Rockefeller Fund. (1631.1940). Banco de México Diego Rivera & Frida Kahlo Museums Trust. Av. Cinco de Mayo No. 2, Col. Centro, Del. Cuauhtemoc 06059, México, D.F. Reproduction authorized by the *Instituto Nacional de Bellas Artes y Literatura*. (c) The Museum of Modern Art/Licensed by Scala/Art Resource, NY.

4. ¿Qué comunica Rivera con los hombres que están al fondo?

5. ¿Qué representa el hombre muerto a los pies de Zapata?

6. ¿Qué crees que sucedió en esta escena?

 **Escribir/Dibujar/Hablar** ....

Nuestra obra de arte

Trabaja con un(a) compañero(a) para escoger un tema histórico que les gustaría pintar. Escriban una descripción de su pintura. Si es posible, hagan un dibujo de lo que van a pintar. Usen por lo menos tres símbolos *(symbols)* para representar el tema que escogieron. Luego, presenten la descripción a la clase. Incluyan la siguiente información:

- el título
- el tema y por qué lo escogieron
- qué o a quién van a mostrar en primer plano
- qué o a quién van a mostrar al fondo
- qué representan los símbolos que incluyeron

Enriching Your Teaching

Culture Note
In 1920, Diego Rivera traveled to Italy to study the frescoes of the Renaissance. The fresco technique involves painting directly onto plaster that has been freshly applied to a wall. As the plaster dries into a hard surface, the color of the paint becomes fixed. Rivera was especially influenced by the Italian Renaissance painter Giotto.

Internet Search
Keywords:

Emiliano Zapata, Diego Rivera, la Revolución Mexicana

Actividad 12

Standards: 1.2, 1.3, 2.2, 3.1, 3.2 ....

Resources: Fine Art Transparencies; Fine Art Transparencies Teacher's Guide; Practice Answers on Transparencies

Focus: Reading about a historical person and event in the context of a mural painting

Suggestions: Point out to students that carefully studying the panel will help them understand the second paragraph of the reading.

Answers:
1. Es Emiliano Zapata. Está vestido de blanco.
2–6. Answers will vary.

Actividad 13

Standards: 1.1, 1.3 ....

Focus: Discussing, planning, and reporting on a proposed painting about a historical event

Suggestions: Ask students to make their drawings large enough to be visible to everyone when they make their presentations. Point out that they will be using the future tense to tell what they plan to include in their proposed paintings. Ask questions such as: *¿Qué pondrás en primer plano? ¿Y en el fondo? ¿Qué tendrá tu pintura?*

Answers will vary.

Additional Resources
- Writing, Audio & Video Workbook: Cap. 2, Audio Activity 1, Track 8
- Writing, Audio & Video Workbook: Cap. 2, Writing Activity 6
- Resource Book: Cap. 2, Communicative Activity BLM

✓ **Assessment**
- Prueba 2-2: Vocabulary production

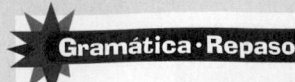
Gramática·Repaso

Presentation

Resources: Voc. & Gram. Transparencies: 57

Suggestions: After presenting the *Gramática* information to students, direct their attention to the *¿Recuerdas?* Ask students to explain why each expression takes the tense that it does. For example, *generalmente* takes the imperfect tense because it introduces either a habitual action in the past or background details in the past. Have them give examples.

Standards: 1.2

Resources: Practice Answers on Transparencies

Focus: Practicing uses of the preterite and imperfect tenses

Suggestions: Remind students that sometimes expressions like those in the *¿Recuerdas?* will help them determine which tense to use.

Answers:

1. tomaba
2. me inscribí
3. fue
4. Eran/llegamos
5. trabajó
6. llevaba
7. visitaban
8. gustaban

Extension: After students have completed the activity, have them compare answers and discuss the reasons for their choices.

Standards: 1.1

Resources: Practice Answers on Transparencies

Focus: Practicing the preterite and imperfect tenses in a guided conversation

Recycle: time expressions, things to do on a trip

Suggestions: Before doing the activity, ask: *Las actividades ocurrieron a una hora específica en el pasado. Por eso, ¿qué tiempo verbal tenemos que usar?* **(el pretérito)**

Gramática·Repaso

Pretérito vs. imperfecto

When speaking about the past, you can use either the preterite or the imperfect, depending on the sentence and the meaning you wish to convey. Compare:

> Este fin de semana **tomé** una clase de cerámica. Cuando **era** niño, **tomaba** clases de escultura.

- Use the preterite to tell about past actions that happened and are complete.

> El sábado, la clase **empezó** a las 10 de la mañana.

- Use the imperfect to tell about habitual actions in the past.

> Cuando **era** niño, las clases **empezaban** a las 5 de la tarde.

- Use the preterite to give a sequence of actions in the past.

> Cuando **llegamos,** la profesora **sacó** su pintura y sus pinceles y **empezó** a pintar.

¿Recuerdas?

Las expresiones como *generalmente*, *a menudo* y *muchas veces* se usan frecuentemente en frases que tienen verbos en imperfecto.

Las expresiones como *ayer, la semana pasada* y *una vez* se usan en frases que llevan verbos en pretérito.

- Use the imperfect to give background details such as time, location, weather, mood, age, and physical and mental descriptions.

> **Eran** las dos de la tarde. **Estábamos** en el parque. **Era** un día de otoño. Todos **estábamos** muy contentos.

- Use the preterite and the imperfect together when an action (preterite) interrupts another that is taking place in the past (imperfect).

> **Estábamos** en el taller cuando **entró** el profesor.

- Use the imperfect when two or more actions are taking place simultaneouly in the past.

> Mientras los niños **pintaban,** el profesor **observaba** las pinturas.

 Gramática **Leer/Escribir**

Una familia de artistas

La familia Gutiérrez, desde que eran niños, participan en muchos proyectos de arte. Completa estas frases con el tiempo verbal correcto.

1. Cuando era niño *(tomé / tomaba)* clases de pintura todas las tardes.

2. Este fin de semana, *(me inscribí / me inscribía)* en un concurso de cerámica.

3. La semana pasada, mi hermano Juan *(fue / iba)* a pintar en la playa.

4. *(Eran / Fueron)* las dos de la tarde cuando nosotros *(llegué / llegamos)* a la clase de escultura.

5. Ayer, mi mamá *(trabajó / trabajaba)* varias horas en un retrato.

6. Todos los años, nuestra tía nos *(llevó / llevaba)* a ver su taller.

7. Generalmente, mis padres *(visitaron / visitaban)* el museo todos los fines de semana.

8. Y a ti, ¿qué te *(gustaban / gustaron)* más de niño(a), las clases de pintura o las clases de música?

Universal Access

Students with Learning Difficulties

Students may have difficulty making the distinction between past actions that have been completed and past actions that are habitual or ongoing. Have students attempt to dramatize the examples in *Actividad* 14. Explain that the examples that are "easier" to act out (because the action is completed) require **el pretérito**.

Advanced Learners

Ask students to prepare a narration about a situation, real or imagined, in the past. It should include a mixture of the preterite and imperfect tenses. Allow them to prepare their narrative either as notes or as a paragraph to be read aloud. Remind them to improve their narrative by using expressions like those in the *¿Recuerdas?*

  **15** **Gramática** **Hablar**

¿Qué pasó en el museo?

Con otro(a) estudiante, hablen de la visita de la clase al museo, la semana pasada.

1. la maestra / ir a comprar los boletos / 11:20
2. ustedes / comenzar la visita / 11:30
3. Juan y Lucía / perderse en el museo / 12:00

Modelo

ustedes / llegar al museo / 11:15
A —¿*Cuándo llegaron al museo?*
B —*Eran las 11:15 cuando llegamos.*

4. la maestra / darse cuenta / 12:20
5. tú / encontrar a Juan y a Lucía / 1:00
6. ustedes / salir del museo / 2:30

 **16** **Gramática** **Escuchar/Escribir/Hablar/GramActiva**

¿Imperfecto o pretérito?

En una hoja de papel, haz una tabla de dos columnas. Escribe "Pretérito" en la columna de la izquierda e "Imperfecto" en la columna de la derecha. Vas a escuchar una historia con los verbos en infinitivo. Cada vez que escuches un verbo, decide si debe ir en pretérito o imperfecto y escríbelo en la columna correcta. Luego, habla con otro(a) estudiante sobre las formas que escogieron.

 17 **Gramática** **Escribir**

Vida de artista: Remedios Varo

Completa esta corta biografía de la artista surrealista Remedios Varo con los verbos entre paréntesis. Usa la forma apropiada del pretérito o del imperfecto.

María de los Remedios Varo y Uranga __1.__ (nacer) el 16 de diciembre de 1908, en Anglés, un pequeño pueblo al norte de Barcelona, España. __2.__ (ser) hija de Rodrigo Varo y de Ignacia Uranga. Su padre __3.__ (ser) ingeniero. __4.__ (construir) canales. A causa de su trabajo, Rodrigo Varo __5.__ (llevar) a su familia por muchas partes de España y del Norte de África.

Desde joven, a Remedios le __6.__ (gustar) pintar. Como otros artistas y escritores españoles de su generación, ella __7.__ (viajar) a París en 1930 en búsqueda de nuevas ideas. Allí __8.__ (encontrar) una fuente de inspiración en el movimiento surrealista. Los surrealistas __9.__ (tratar) de expresar imágenes del subconsciente. En 1936, a causa de la Guerra Civil española, Remedios __10.__ (tener) que buscar refugio en México. Allí, Remedios __11.__ (crear) algunas de las obras más originales de la pintura moderna.

Still life reviving, (1963), Remedios Varo
Collection of Beatriz Varo de Cano, Valencia Spain. Donation of Walter Gruen and Anna Alexandra Varsoviano in memory of Isabel Gruen Varsoviano. Col. Museo de Arte Moderno, INBA-CONACULTA.

setenta y siete 77
Capítulo 2

 Enriching Your Teaching

Culture Note

In Spain and some countries in Latin America, people traditionally use two family names or surnames. The first *apellido* is the father's family name, and the second is the mother's. The two *apellidos* may be separated by *y,* as is the case for Remedios Varo y Uranga, hyphenated, or just used together.

Internet Search
Keywords:

Remedios Varo, Spanish Civil War, Spanish surrealism, Mexican surrealism

---

Practice and Communicate 2

 15 *Standards:* 1.1

(Cont'd)

Answers:
1. A —¿Cuándo fue la maestra a comprar los boletos?
   B —Eran las 11:20 cuando fue.
2. A —¿Cuándo comenzaron ustedes la visita?
   B —Eran las 11:30 cuando comenzamos.
3. A —¿Cuándo se perdieron Juan y Lucía en el museo?
   B —Eran las 12:00 cuando se perdieron.
4. A —¿Cuándo se dio cuenta la maestra?
   B —Eran las 12:20 cuando se dio cuenta.
5. A —¿Cuándo encontraste a Juan y a Lucía?
   B —Era la 1:00 cuando los encontré.
6. A —¿Cuándo salieron ustedes del museo?
   B —Eran las 2:30 cuando salimos.

 16 *Standards:* 1.2

Resources: Audio Program: CD Cap. 2, Track 9; Resource Book: Cap. 2, Audio Script; Practice Answers on Transparencies

Focus: Determining use of the preterite versus the imperfect tense

Suggestions: Use the *Audio CD* or read the script. Allow students to listen more than once.

Answers:

Pretérito	Imperfecto
llegó	iba
llegó	estaba
encontró	Eran
oyó	dormían
vio	

 17 *Standards:* 1.2, 2.2, 3.1

Resources: Fine Art Transparencies; Fine Art Transparencies Teacher's Guide; Practice Answers on Transparencies

Focus: Practicing using the preterite vs. the imperfect tense

Suggestions: Have students read through the entire biography once before writing their answers.

Answers:
1. nació
2. Era
3. era
4. Construía
5. llevó
6. gustaba
7. viajó
8. encontró
9. trataban
10. tuvo
11. creó

77

2

Actividad 18

Standards: 1.1

Resources: Practice Answers on Transparencies

Focus: Practicing using the preterite vs. the imperfect tense

Suggestions: After students answer the questions, encourage them to talk about the picture further by describing the people's clothes.

Answers will vary, but should contain the following tense usage and information.

1. Eran las dos de la tarde.
2. Era probablemente el verano. Hacía buen tiempo y la gente estaba vestida de ropa de verano.
3. Las niñas saltaban a la cuerda cuando llegó la mamá.
4. El perro robó las salchichas porque tenía hambre.
5. Carlos se enojó. Él también tenía hambre.
6. Eva se reía.
7. Luis le sacaba una foto.
8. El policía se acostó debajo de un árbol para tomar una siesta.

Fondo cultural

Standards: 1.1, 1.2, 2.2, 3.1, 5.2

Resources: Fine Art Transparencies; Fine Art Transparencies Teacher's Guide

Suggestions: Remind students that all details in a mural like this one by Siqueiros are present for a reason. As they answer the questions, ask them to elaborate on details with questions such as the following: *¿Por qué muestra el artista a tantas personas en el mural? ¿Qué cosa llevan los hombres en la mano? ¿Piensas que la presencia de las mujeres es importante? ¿Por qué?*

Answers will vary.

Additional Resources

• Writing, Audio & Video Workbook: Cap. 2, Writing Activity 7

Assessment

• Prueba 2-3: *Pretérito vs. imperfecto*

Actividad 18 **Gramática** **Hablar**

Escena en el parque

Contesta las preguntas para describir lo que pasó en el parque.

1. ¿Qué hora era?
2. ¿Qué estación del año crees que era, probablemente? ¿Cómo lo sabes?
3. ¿Qué hacían las niñas cuando llegó la mamá?
4. ¿Quién robó las salchichas? ¿Por qué?
5. ¿Cómo se sentía Carlos? ¿Por qué?
6. ¿Qué hacía Eva?
7. ¿Qué hacía Luis mientras su papá leía?
8. ¿Quién se acostó debajo de un árbol? ¿Por qué?

Fondo cultural

David Alfaro Siqueiros A principios del siglo XX, ocurrían muchos cambios sociales en México. En 1910, terminó el régimen de Porfirio Díaz, quien fue Presidente de México durante 30 años, y comenzó la Revolución Mexicana.

Junto a Rivera y Orozco, David Alfaro Siqueiros (1898–1974) fue uno de los grandes artistas del muralismo mexicano, el movimiento artístico que se inspiró en los ideales de la Revolución.

A través de su obra, Siqueiros nos habla de los tiempos en que vive el país, de los cambios que ocurren. Sus murales nos muestran una nueva realidad en la que los pobres son las figuras centrales de la historia de México. En la obra de Siqueiros, podemos ver un retrato de la Revolución.

• ¿Quiénes crees que son las personas que nos muestra el mural? ¿Cómo los representa Siqueiros?

• ¿Qué nos dice este mural de Siqueiros sobre la Revolución Mexicana?

Del porfirismo a la revolución, (1906–1913), David Alfaro Siqueiros

● **Más práctica**
Practice Workbook 2-5

Go Online
PHSchool.com

For: Practice with preterite and imperfect
Visit: www.phschool.com
Web Code: jed-0203

78 setenta y ocho
Manos a la obra 1

Universal Access

Heritage Language Learners

Have students tell about family gatherings in their heritage country. For what types of events do families typically get together? What foods, decorations, and activities are usually involved?

Students with Learning Difficulties

Before completing the chart in *Actividad* 19 on p. 79, have students brainstorm and list the infinitive forms of verbs that would be applicable to the picture. Then lead them through the process outlined in the *Gramática.* Model, step-by-step, the conversion of each verb into the appropriate past participle form.

Gramática

Estar + participio

Many adjectives in Spanish are actually past participles of verbs. Recall that to form a past participle you add *-ado* to the root of *-ar* verbs and *-ido* to the root of *-er* and *-ir* verbs.

decorar	decorado	conocer	conocido	preferir	preferido

- The past participle is frequently used with *estar* to describe conditions that are the result of a previous action. In those cases, the past participle agrees with the subject in gender and number.

  El pintor **está sentado.**   Las paredes **estaban pintadas.**

- Recall that there are a number of cases in which the past participle is irregular.

abrir: **abierto**	poner: **puesto**	decir: **dicho**	resolver: **resuelto**	escribir: **escrito**
romper: **roto**	hacer: **hecho**	ver: **visto**	morir: **muerto**	volver: **vuelto**

 **19** **Gramática** Escuchar

Retrato de familia

Rosario describe un retrato de una fiesta familiar. ¿Quiénes estaban allí? ¿Cómo estaban? En una hoja de papel, copia la siguiente tabla. Escucha la descripción del retrato y escribe cómo estaban las siguientes personas y cosas.

¿Quién? o ¿Qué?	¿Cómo estaban?
Yo	
Mi padrino	
Mi papá	
Mi tía Luisa	
Mi primo Jorge	
La mesa	
Los refrescos	
Los niños	
Mis primos más pequeños	

Enriching Your Teaching

Culture Note

Like Diego Rivera, David Alfaro Siqueiros was trained in the classic technique of fresco painting. However, Siqueiros was also known for his innovations to the technique. In addition to painting on non-conventional surfaces such as concrete and cement, Siqueiros used non- traditional oil-based paints or airbrushing to cover large areas quickly. In addition to his own painting, Siqueiros taught many other artists. One of his most famous pupils was Jackson Pollock, a painter who went on to develop his own, original technique.

Gramática

Presentation

Resources: Voc. & Gram. Transparencies: 58

Suggestions: Point out that, just as Spanish uses past participles ending in **-ado** or **-ido** as adjectives, English also uses past participles ending in *-ed* and *-en* as adjectives: *a heated room, a typed memo, a driven student, a given answer.*

Actividad 19   *Standards:* 1.2

Resources: Audio Program: CD Cap. 2, Track 10; Resource Book: Cap. 2, Audio Script; Practice Answers on Transparencies

Focus: Practicing listening comprehension

Suggestions: Use the *Audio CD* or the script. Allow students to listen more than once. Remind them to use the picture to help them.

Common Errors: In the *estar* + *participio* construction, students often forget to make the participle agree in number and gender with the subject. Correct this error with visual cues. Hold up two fingers to cue plural. Prepare a pair of flashcards with masculine and feminine symbols to cue gender.

Answers:
1. estaba sentada
2. estaba parado
3. estaba sentado
4. estaba parada
5. estaba vestido de Superman
6. estaba puesta
7. estaban servidos
8. estábamos muy cansados
9. estaban dormidos

Additional Resources
- Writing, Audio & Video Workbook: Cap. 2, Audio Activity 2, Track 11

Chapter Project
Students can perform step 2 at this point. Be sure they understand your corrections and suggestions. (For more information, see p. 62-a.)

Practice and Communicate

Gramática · **Hablar** · · · · · · · · · · · · · · · · · · ·

En el cuarto de la pintora

Una artista te invitó a visitar su taller. Describe la escena que viste cuando llegaste. Usa el participio pasado de los siguients verbos: *abrir, dormir, hacer, romper, esconder, encender, parar.*

Modelo

Cuando llegué a su taller, el niño estaba sentado.

Leer/Escribir ·

Pepón Osorio, artista entre dos culturas

¿Cómo refleja un artista una vida entre dos culturas? Lee este artículo para aprender un poco más sobre la vida y el arte de Pepón Osorio, un artista puertorriqueño. Después contesta las preguntas.

 El arte ——————

Pepón Osorio nació en 1955, en Santurce, Puerto Rico. A los 20 años vino a Nueva York para empezar su carrera de artista. Osorio cree que los artistas deben hacer trabajos que muestren su época y su país de origen. Su obra representa frecuentemente su niñez y adolescencia en Puerto Rico, y su experiencia multicultural como artista puertorriqueño en Nueva York. Dice que los puertorriqueños son multiculturales porque viven en dos culturas, la puertorriqueña y la neoyorkina.

Osorio hace montajes[1] de cosas que encuentra. En *100% Boricua*[2], Osorio mezcla recuerdos turísticos de Nueva York con banderas puertorriqueñas y otros objetos típicos del Caribe.

Su objetivo es reunir los elementos de toda una comunidad en un solo lugar.

—————————————————————

[1] assemblages [2] *Boricua* is a term Puerto Ricans use to describe themselves as natives to the island.

❶ Observa el montaje de Osorio. ¿Cómo es un montaje similar a otras obras de arte? ¿Cómo es diferente?

❷ Ahora vas a planear tu propio montaje. Piensa en varios objetos que representan parte de tu historia. Escribe un corto párrafo describiendo cada objeto y explicando por qué es importante para ti. Dale un título y preséntalo a la clase.

100% Boricua, (1991), Pepón Osorio
Wood, glass, plexiglass, paper, fabric, metal, plastic. 79 3/8 x 33 1/2 x 20 1/2 inches. Collection Walker Art Center, Minneapolis. Gift of the Peter Norton Family Foundation, 1992.

80 ochenta
Manos a la obra 1

Actividad 22 · Leer/Hablar

Una visita a El Museo del Arte

❶ Lee el siguiente anuncio de El Museo del Arte y contesta las preguntas:

• ¿Dónde está El Museo del Arte?

• ¿Qué artistas presenta?

• Observa la foto en el anuncio. ¿De quién crees que es el retrato?

• ¿Qué puedes aprender de los artistas si vas a la exposición?

❷ Trabaja con otro(a) estudiante para representar una visita a un museo. Hablen del museo y de las obras que tiene (autorretratos, esculturas, cerámica). Describan qué es lo que les gusta o no les gusta (tema, forma, colores). Digan cuál es su obra favorita y expliquen por qué.

Frida **Kahlo** Diego **Rivera**
y el Arte Mexicano del Siglo XX

3 de agosto al 18 de noviembre de 2003

• *Sus retratos y autorretratos*

• *Sus fuentes de inspiración*

• *El movimiento que los influyó*

 El Museo del Arte
500 Avenida Juárez

El español en la comunidad

El Museo del Barrio En 1969, un grupo de educadores, artistas y representantes puertorriqueños fundaron El Museo del Barrio en Harlem del Este. Su objetivo era ayudar a mantener la cultura, las tradiciones y el idioma de los puertorriqueños, y en general, de todos los latinoamericanos de Nueva York.

El Museo ha influido en la población hispanohablante de Nueva York gracias a sus programas educativos para la comunidad. Los estudiantes universitarios pueden hacer prácticas *(internships)* en El Museo y ser guías de visitas, ayudar a realizar talleres de orientación sobre arte y ayudar a los maestros de arte a preparar sus clases.

El Museo del Barrio es una de las instituciones culturales de la población hispanohablante más importantes de los Estados Unidos. Sirve de puente de comunicación entre los diferentes grupos latinoamericanos de Nueva York y también entre la cultura hispanohablante y la anglosajona. Ése fue el sueño de sus fundadores.

• Imagínate que vas a trabajar durante el verano en El Museo del Barrio como voluntario(a). ¿Qué trabajo quieres hacer? ¿En qué crees que puedes ayudar?

• Identifica otros ejemplos de instituciones culturales que representen a las comunidades hispanohablantes en los Estados Unidos.

● Más práctica

Practice Workbook 2-6, 2-7

Go Online
PHSchool.com

For: Practice with past participles
Visit: www.phschool.com
Web Code: jed-0205

ochenta y uno **81**
Capítulo 2

Enriching Your Teaching

Culture Note

Across the United States, there are many museums and resources for Spanish and Latin American art. Some examples include the San José Center for Latino Arts, The Florida Museum of Hispanic and Latin American Art in Miami, and the Latino Museum of History, Art and Culture in Los Angeles.

Teacher-to-Teacher

Invite students to set up an exhibit of art from the Spanish-speaking world. Works by the same artists can be downloaded from the Internet, printed, and included in the exhibit. Students can accompany the works with captions, brief explanations, photos, and biographical information about the artists.

Language Input

Vocabulario y gramática

Presentation

Standards: 1.2, 3.1

Resources: Voc. & Gram. Transparencies: 59–60; Resource Book: Cap. 2, Input Script; Audio Program: CD Cap. 2, Track 12

Focus: Presenting new vocabulary and using grammar lexically in context

Suggestions: Use the Input Script from the *Teacher's Resource Book* as a source of ideas for presentation of new vocabulary and comprehensible input. Pantomime to clarify the meaning of words and expressions such as *pararse, exagerar, el aplauso* and *los pasos de una danza.* Use TPR to teach the meaning of visualized vocabulary. Show *Vocabulary & Grammar Transparency* 59 and ask volunteers to point to *la trompeta, el tambor,* and *el micrófono.*

Standards: 1.2

Resources: Audio Program: CD Cap. 2, Track 13; Resource Book: Cap. 2, Audio Script; Practice Answers on Transparencies

Focus: Practicing listening comprehension of new vocabulary

Suggestions: Before engaging students in the listening activity, give them a few minutes to silently read and study the reviews on p. 82. Tell them that the information they will hear refers to the *Semana Cultural* announcement. Then play the *Audio CD* or use the script to read the activity aloud.

Answers:

1. F	4. F
2. F	5. F
3. C	6. F

Block Schedule

Have students work in pairs to write a short review for a cultural event similar to the models shown. Ask students to read them to the class imitating a critic.

A primera vista 2

Vocabulario y gramática en contexto

Objectives

Read, listen to, and understand information about
- music, drama, and dance performances
- art reviews

Aquí tienes algunas **reseñas** que aparecieron en el periódico sobre las actividades de la Semana Cultural.

1 El actor que **actuó** en "Sueño de una noche de verano" y que **interpretó** el papel de Puck fue muy cómico. Al **exagerar** tanto los **gestos, se pareció a** un político. El público se rió mucho.

SEMANA CULTURAL PROGRAMA

"Sueño de una noche de verano"
de William Shakespeare
Teatro Estudiantil
Martes 20, 9:00 p.m.

Conjunto musical "Los Salseros de Hoy"
Miércoles 21, 7:00 p.m.

Taller de danza
Presentación de danza
clásica y moderna
Jueves 23, 8:00 p.m.

Lectura de poemas de autores latinoamericanos
Viernes 24, 6:00 p.m.

2 **El conjunto** de salsa "Los Salseros de Hoy" estuvo sensacional. Interpretó "Burbujas de amor" con **entusiasmo**. Muchos jóvenes bailaron al **ritmo** de las canciones."

el micrófono

la trompeta

el tambor

 **Escuchar** · · · · · · · · · · ·

La semana cultural

Escucha cada frase sobre el programa y levanta una mano si es cierta y dos manos si es falsa.

82 ochenta y dos
A primera vista 2

Universal Access

Students with Learning Difficulties

Use concrete objects and listening samples to reinforce the meaning of new vocabulary. For example, bring in a CD of a *conjunto de salsa* so that students can hear the *ritmo*. Read aloud from a book written by *un(a) poeta*. Encourage students to bring in programs from cultural events that they have attended.

Advanced Learners

Have students work in groups to create a series of narrated pantomimes that use the vocabulary presented on pp. 82–83. Ask them to choose one student in each group as the narrator. The other members act out the actions or scenes that the narrartor describes. Have them present their narrated pantomimes to the class.

82

3 Felicitaciones a los bailarines que **realizaron una interpretación** hermosa del "Lago de los Cisnes". El aplauso del público fue impresionante y muchas personas **se pararon** con entusiasmo.

el aplauso

danza clásica

4 Los jóvenes en el auditorio **se identificaron con** la interpretación de *hip hop* del Grupo de Danza Moderna. Algunos quisieron aprender sus movimientos rápidos y sus **pasos** complicados pero no pudieron.

5 La **poeta** Sandra Cisneros leyó los poemas en voz alta y las palabras **sonaron a** música. Todos queríamos escuchar más.

lectura de **poemas**

el escenario

 Actividad 24 Escuchar/Hablar ······················

Lo que dijo la prensa

Escucha cada fragmento y di a qué reseña se refiere.

 Actividad 24   *Standards:* 1.2
··············

Resources: Voc. & Gram. Transparencies: 59–60; Audio Program: CD Cap. 2, Track 15; Resource Book: Cap. 2, Audio Script; Practice Answers on Transparencies

Focus: Practicing listening comprehension of new vocabulary

Suggestions: Use the *Audio CD* or the script. Allow students to listen more than once. Pause to monitor students, making sure they are identifying the correct review.

Answers:
1. 5
2. 4
3. 2
4. 1
5. 3

Extension: Clarify the meaning of the expression *identificarse con*. Use *Vocabulary & Grammar Transparency* 60 as well as magazine or newspaper ads and pictures that show contrasting types of art, such as ballet vs. salsa, poetry vs. fiction, or classical music vs. hip hop. Show two contrasting art types at once and ask: *¿Con qué danza te identificas?* Students answer with *Me identifico con....*

Teacher-to-Teacher

Encourage students to bring in CD covers, posters, magazines, and ads that demonstrate their own artistic preferences. These can be used as props throughout this chapter to aid in question-and-answer sessions and discussions about the varying types of art and students' responses to them.

Chapter Project

Students can perform step 3 at this point. (For more information, see p. 62-a.)

Enriching Your Teaching

Culture Note

There are many different styles of the dance we call **salsa.** The Puerto Rican Style is known for its footwork; the New York Style shows the influence of disco; the Los Angeles Style is influenced by West Coast Swing. The Cuban Style stresses the "one" and "three" beats of the music, as opposed to the "two" beat, and the rhythms are much faster. For this reason, people sometimes dance Cuban Style solo, rather than with a partner.

Internet Search

Keyword: música salsa

Vocabulario y gramática

Presentation

Standards: 1.2, 2.2, 3.1

Resources: Voc. & Gram. Transparencies: 61–62; Resource Book: Cap. 2, Input Script; Audio Program: CD Cap. 2, Track 16

Focus: Extending presentation of vocabulary and grammar in the context of reviews of the arts

Suggestions:

Pre-reading: Have students read just the titles of the four reviews. Ask them to name the kinds of art that they expect the reviews to be about.

Reading: Allow students time to read the reviews silently first. Then play the *Audio CD* and have students read along as they listen. Allow them to listen more than once.

Post-reading: Ask students to write down two statements about two different cultural events on pp. 84–85. Each statement should tell something that happened at the chosen event or describe how it happened. Have students take turns reading one statement at a time. Listeners identify which event is being talked about:

A: *Este cantante cantó canciones con títulos en inglés.*

B: *Es el concierto de Marc Anthony.*

Then check comprehension by having students complete *Actividades* 26 and 27.

Espectáculos del mundo latino

¿Alguna vez buscaste información sobre **un espectáculo** en una revista, en un periódico o en la Red? Las reseñas te pueden ayudar a encontrar las películas, las obras de teatro y las exposiciones que más te interesan. ¿Qué dicen estas reseñas?

Facundo Cabral cantó en el teatro Metropólitan en México

Facundo Cabral se presentó en el teatro Metropólitan para festejar sus 30 años en la música. Cabral, quien a los 14 años era analfabeto[1], es autor de la **letra** y la **melodía** de sus canciones. En esta ocasión, Cabral cantó "No soy de aquí, ni soy de allá", "Éste es un nuevo día", "América" y muchas más.

1 illiterate

Address: http://www.tangoshow.com/MUSEO/

Museo Vivo del Tango

Museo Vivo del Tango dedicó la semana a la música argentina

El Museo Vivo del Tango en Buenos Aires ofreció un espectáculo original de gran esplendor. Los que más **se destacaron** fueron un cantante y el Tango Ballet, quienes después de actuar, enseñaron a los visitantes los pasos básicos del tango.

Universal Access

Heritage Language Learners
Have students compose two newspaper clips reporting on a favorite artist's exhibition or performance. Explain that one clip would appear in the newspaper before the event, and the other clip would appear after the event. Remind students to keep the time frame consistent whether they are reporting on a future or past event.

Students with Learning Difficulties
Have students preview the sentences in *Actividad* 26 on p. 85 prior to reading *Espectáculos del mundo latino.* After they have read the selection and answered true or false, have them locate and point to the sentence in the reading that proves their answer is correct.

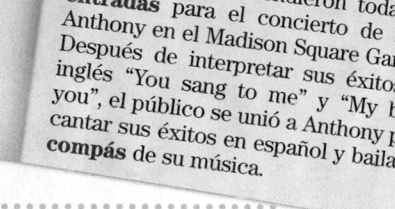

Recuerdan a *Lope de Vega*

La Compañía de Danza Contemporánea de León presentó "Poeta del cielo y de la tierra", basada en la obra de Lope de Vega. Los bailarines representaron con sus movimientos y gestos la obra de este **escritor** español, que se caracteriza por combinar lo trágico y lo cómico.

Marc Anthony

Llenó el Madison Square Garden

Una vez más, se vendieron todas las **entradas** para el concierto de Marc Anthony en el Madison Square Garden. Después de interpretar sus éxitos en inglés "You sang to me" y "My baby you", el público se unió a Anthony para cantar sus éxitos en español y bailar al **compás** de su música.

 Actividad 25 Escuchar/Escribir

El mundo del espectáculo

Escribe los números del 1 al 5 en una hoja de papel. Escucha las siguientes preguntas y escribe la respuesta correcta.

 **Actividad 26** Leer

¿Es cierto?

Lee las frases y escribe *C* (cierto) o *F* (falso) según lo que leíste en "Espectáculos del mundo latino".

1. En el Museo Vivo del Tango, los visitantes aprenden a bailar salsa.

2. Marc Anthony sólo canta canciones en inglés.

3. Facundo Cabral escribe la letra y la melodía de sus canciones.

4. A través de su obra, Lope de Vega combina lo trágico y lo cómico.

 Actividad 27 Escribir

Quisiera ir

Después de leer estas reseñas, escribe una frase para cada una, diciendo por qué sí o por qué no te gustaría ir a ese espectáculo.

● **Más práctica**
Practice Workbook 2-8, 2-9

PHSchool.com
For: Vocabulary practice
Visit: www.phschool.com
Web Code: jed-0206

ochenta y cinco **85**
Capítulo 2

Enriching Your Teaching

Culture Note
Born in France, Carlos Gardel (the "Father of Tango") moved to Argentina as a young child. He went on to become one of the foremost interpreters of the Argentine tango ballad, as well as a motion picture actor. Gardel appeared in many feature films produced for Spanish-speaking audiences, such as the 1934 film *El Tango en Broadway.*

Internet Search
Keywords:

Facundo Cabral, Museo Vivo del Tango, compañía de danza contemporánea, Marc Anthony

---

Language Input ②

 **Actividad 25** *Standards:* 1.2, 1.3

Resources: Voc. & Gram. Transparencies: 61–62; Audio Program: CD Cap. 2, Track 17; Resource Book: CD Cap. 2, Audio Script; Practice Answers on Transparencies

Focus: Demonstrating comprehension of arts reviews

Suggestions: Remind students that answers to the questions they hear are found in the reviews on pp. 84–85.

Answers:
1. Es cantante.
2. Era escritor.
3. Está en Buenos Aires.
4. Se presentó en el Madison Square Garden.
5. El público bailó.

 Actividad 26 *Standards:* 1.2

Resources: Practice Answers on Transparencies

Focus: Demonstrating comprehension of arts reviews

Suggestions: Have students check their answers with a partner and correct the false statements.

Answers:
1. F 2. F 3. C 4. C

 Actividad 27 *Standards:* 1.3

Focus: Expressing personal opinions in writing

Suggestions: Invite students to share and support their opinion with a partner.

Answers will vary.

Additional Resources
• Resource Book: Cap. 2, Clip Art

✓ **Assessment**
• Prueba 2-5: Vocabulary recognition

85

Standards: 1.2, 3.1

28

Resources: Practice Answers on Transparencies

Focus: Categorizing new vocabulary

Suggestions: When checking answers with students, ask them to say why the word they chose does not belong with the others.

Answers:

1. d	4. c
2. a	5. d
3. d	6. c

Standards: 1.2, 2.2

29

Resources: Practice Answers on Transparencies

Focus: Practicing new vocabulary in a cloze activity

Suggestions: Remind students that looking over the entire review first will give them an idea of what it is about and help them select the correct answers.

Answers:

1. se identifica	5. gestos
2. las actuaciones	6. exagera
3. se destacan	7. interpretan
4. cómico	8. actuar

Extension: Invite students to work in groups. Have them choose a popular TV show they all know and make critical comments about it.

Manos a la obra 2

Vocabulario y gramática en uso

Objectives

- Talk about different forms of entertainment
- Express your opinion about a dance, music, or theater performance
- Review uses of *ser* and *estar*
- Practice verbs that have different meanings in the preterite and the imperfect

 **Leer/Escribir**

¡Quita la palabra!

Escribe en una hoja de papel los números del 1 al 6. Para cada grupo de palabras, escribe en la hoja la letra de la palabra que no está relacionada con las otras. Después, haz una lista de las palabras que no están relacionadas con las demás y escribe una frase con cada una.

1.	a. la melodía	b. el ritmo	c. el compás	d. el gesto
2.	a. el poema	b. la danza	c. el paso	d. bailar
3.	a. la actuación	b. el gesto	c. interpretar	d. el conjunto
4.	a. el escenario	b. realizar	c. la entrada	d. la interpretación
5.	a. el escritor	b. el poeta	c. el poema	d. el micrófono
6.	a. el tambor	b. la trompeta	c. el actor	d. el piano

 Leer/Escribir

Una reseña

Loreto Michea, un crítico, escribe sobre el popular programa de tele, *Sábado Gigante*. Completa la reseña con la palabra correcta.

"Sábado Gigante no es sólo un programa familiar. Es un lugar donde la audiencia   **1.**   *(actúa / se identifica)* con otros hispanohablantes, sin importar en qué lugar de América viven. Pero los concursos, la música, el humor,   **2.**   *(los pasos / las actuaciones)* y las entrevistas, no son los elementos del programa que más   **3.**   *(se destacan / se exageran)*. Don Francisco, su presentador, es la clave *(key)*. Es un actor muy   **4.**   *(aburrido / cómico)* y energético que utiliza sus   **5.**   *(libros / gestos)*, su voz y su picardía *(wit)* para divertir al público. Su   **6.**   *(entusiasmo / paso)* es impresionante, y cuando los cantantes   **7.**   *(interpretan / actúan)* las canciones populares o los artistas aparecen en el escenario para   **8.**   *(exagerar / actuar)*, la energiá de don Francisco inspira al público."

Universal Access

Students with Learning Difficulties

Encourage students to bring in examples of their own favorite music CDs. After copying the chart in *Actividad* 31 on p. 87, guide students to take appropriate notes for each of the songs they hear. Have them use these to conduct the partner conversations.

Advanced Learners

Challenge students to write six sentences, one for each item in *Actividad* 28. Each sentence should use all of the words in the row—including the word that does not belong—in a way that makes sense.

Actividad 30

Escribir/Hablar ·

Un espectáculo de flamenco

Imagina que estuviste en el espectáculo de flamenco de la ilustración y describe la escena. Escribe frases en pretérito o imperfecto. Puedes usar las palabras y frases del recuadro. Luego, otro(a) estudiante te va a hacer preguntas sobre lo que escribiste.

el fondo	al frente
al lado	a la izquierda
el micrófono	los bailarines
tocar la guitarra	cantar
el cantante	sentado
parado	el paso
el escenario	

Modelo

A —*Vi un espectáculo en el escenario.*
B —*¿Qué clase de espectáculo fue?*
A —*Fue un espectáculo de flamenco.*

Actividad 31

Escribir/Hablar ·

¡Viva la música!

❶ ¿Cuál es tu disco compacto favorito? ¿Por qué? Piensa en algunas palabras que describan los diferentes elementos de tu canción o disco compacto favorito. En una hoja de papel, dibuja y completa una tabla como la siguiente.

Elemento	Disco compacto/Canción
el compás / el ritmo	
la melodía	
la voz	
los instrumentos	
la letra	
el tema	

Estudiante A

¿Qué te parece . . . ?
¿Cómo suena . . . ?
¿Cómo es . . . ?
¿Qué canción tiene mejor . . . ?

Estudiante B

interesante	largo(a)
original	corto(a)
alegre	alto(a)
aburrido(a)	bajo(a)
tradicional	rápido(a)
	lento(a)

❷ Habla con otro(a) estudiante sobre tu canción o disco compacto favorito. Usa las palabras que escribiste en la tabla.

Modelo

A —*¿Qué te parece la melodía de la primera canción del disco compacto de Shakira?*
B —*La melodía es muy original, me gusta mucho.*
A —*¿Cómo suenan las guitarras en esta canción?*
B —*Suenan demasiado alto, no se oye la voz.*

ochenta y siete **87**
Capítulo 2

Enriching Your Teaching

Culture Note

Flamenco is an art form comprised of three parts: the dance, the song, and the music of the guitar. Flamenco enjoyed its "Golden Age" in the late nineteenth and early twentieth century. During this era, the art was developed in Spain's many **cafés cantantes** or musical cafés.

During the twentieth century, the popularity of flamenco grew, and artists made their way from small cafés to large theaters and concert stages.

Internet Search

Keyword: música flamenca

 Standards: 1.1
Actividad 30
· ·

Focus: Using new vocabulary and structures in a guided conversation

Suggestions: Encourage students to build more than one question-and-answer exchange around each word or expression. Make sure they switch roles, so that all students have a chance to practice both asking and answering.

Answers will vary.

 Standards: 1.1, 3.1
Actividad 31
· ·

Focus: Practicing new vocabulary in a guided conversation

Suggestions: Explain to students that they should choose just one favorite CD or song for the chart and to talk about with their partner.

Common Errors: Some students make the assumption that all Spanish nouns ending in *-a* are feminine. Remind them that many nouns ending in *-a*, such as **el tema, el programa,** and **el problema,** are masculine.

Answers will vary.

Additional Resources

• Writing, Audio & Video Workbook: Cap. 2, Audio Activity 3, Track 17
• Writing, Audio & Video Workbook: Cap. 2, Writing Activity 10

 Assessment

• Prueba 2-6: Vocabulary production

Teacher-to-Teacher

Invite students to share with the class a favorite art work or artist. They might play part of a song, read a poem or a rap, or show a favorite scene from a film, and then tell about it and what it means to them. Aside from any English involved, their presentations should be in Spanish. Then take the assignment one step further: request that they spend equal time showing and telling about an art form or artist from the Spanish-speaking world.

Practice and Communicate

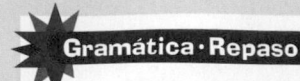

Gramática · Repaso

Presentation

Standards: 4.1

Resources: Voc. & Gram. Transparencies: 63

Suggestions: Give other examples where the adjective has different meanings when used with **ser** or **estar:**
El niño es (está) malo. The boy is bad (sick).
Las manzanas son (están) verdes. The apples are green (unripe).

Resources: Practice Answers on Transparencies

Focus: Practicing uses of **ser** and **estar** in a cloze exercise

Suggestions: Encourage students to complete the activity without looking back at the *Gramática* for each item. Once they are finished, they can check their answers against the rules in the *Gramática* and make any necessary changes.

Common Errors: Correct usage of **ser** and **estar** is difficult for any English speaker learning Spanish. Tell students that correct usage will come with patience and practice.

Answers:
1. es   4. son   7. están
2. está   5. están   8. estamos
3. es   6. son   9. están

Resources: Audio Program: CD Cap. 2, Track 19; Resource Book: Cap. 2, Audio Script; Practice Answers on Transparencies

Focus: Listening for and using forms of **ser** and **estar**

Suggestions: Make sure students answer in complete sentences.

Answers:
1. Es argentino.
2. Es músico.
3. Está en Chicago para dar un concierto.
4. Los otros miembros del conjunto están con él.
5. El cantante es colombiano.
6. El concierto es mañana por la noche.
7. Está un poco nervioso.

Gramática · Repaso

Ser y estar

Remember that *ser* and *estar* both mean "to be." They are used in different situations and have different meanings.

Use *ser*:

- to describe permanent characteristics of objects and people
  Esa canción **es** muy original.
- to indicate origin, nationality, or profession
  Mi tía **es** escritora. **Es** de Madrid.
- to indicate when and where something takes place
  El concierto **es** el viernes. **Es** en el teatro.
- to indicate possession
  La guitarra **es** de Elisa.

Use *estar*:

- to describe temporary characteristics, emotional states, or conditions
  El teatro **está** cerrado a esta hora.
  Los actores **están** muy nerviosos.
- to indicate location
  El conjunto **está** en el escenario.
- to form the progressive tense
  El bailarín **está** interpretando a Cabral.

Some adjectives have different meanings depending on whether they are used with *ser* or with *estar*.
La bailarina **es bonita.** *The dancer is pretty. (She's a pretty person.)*
La bailarina **está** muy **bonita** hoy. *The dancer looks pretty today. (She doesn't always look this pretty.)*
El cómico **es aburrido.** *(He is boring.)* El cómico **está aburrido.** *(He is bored.)*
El cantante **es rico.** *(He is wealthy.)* El postre **está rico.** *(It tastes very good.)*

 Gramática   **Leer/Escribir**

Invitación a Caras y Caretas

El secretario del club de teatro mandó esta invitación por correo electrónico. Completa la invitación con la forma correcta de *ser* o *estar*.

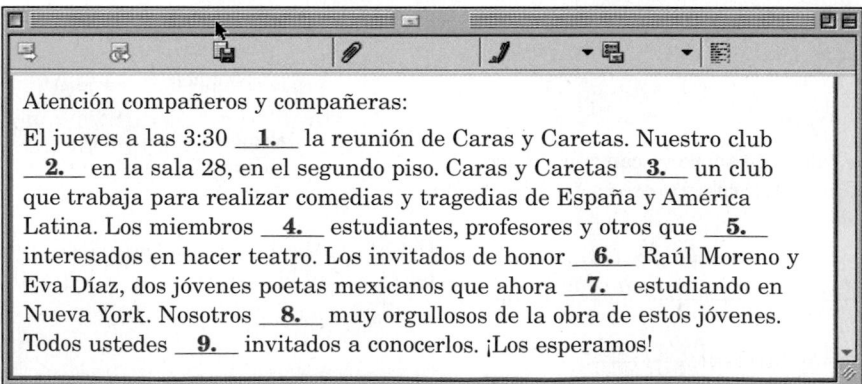

Atención compañeros y compañeras:

El jueves a las 3:30 __1.__ la reunión de Caras y Caretas. Nuestro club __2.__ en la sala 28, en el segundo piso. Caras y Caretas __3.__ un club que trabaja para realizar comedias y tragedias de España y América Latina. Los miembros __4.__ estudiantes, profesores y otros que __5.__ interesados en hacer teatro. Los invitados de honor __6.__ Raúl Moreno y Eva Díaz, dos jóvenes poetas mexicanos que ahora __7.__ estudiando en Nueva York. Nosotros __8.__ muy orgullosos de la obra de estos jóvenes. Todos ustedes __9.__ invitados a conocerlos. ¡Los esperamos!

88   ochenta y ocho
Manos a la obra 2

Universal Access

Heritage Language Learners
Have students draft an e-mail message extending an invitation to a performing arts event in their heritage country. Instruct students to identify their audience. They might be writing to a close friend or to the entire mailing list of the performing arts institution. Remind them to tailor their language accordingly.

Students with Learning Difficulties
Have students write the verb forms **es** and **está** on two separate index cards. Help them reinforce the distinction between the forms of these two verbs that both mean "to be." Provide sentences in which students must fill in the blank by holding up the appropriate card. Ask them to explain each choice.

88

Actividad 33 · Gramática · Escuchar

Entrevista en la radio

Escucha la entrevista en la radio con Carlos Galán y luego contesta las preguntas.

1. ¿De dónde es Carlos?
2. ¿Cuál es su profesión?
3. ¿Por qué está en Chicago?
4. ¿Quiénes están con Carlos?
5. ¿Quién es colombiano?
6. ¿Cuándo es el concierto?
7. ¿Cómo se siente Carlos?

Actividad 35 · Gramática · Escribir/Dibujar/Hablar

Poeta por un día

Los poemas haiku tienen tres líneas. La primera tiene 5 sílabas, la segunda tiene 7 y la tercera tiene 5. Por lo general, hablan de la naturaleza, escenas de la vida, las artes y los sentimientos que inspiran. Los sentimientos se expresan de una manera breve y sencilla.

1 Piensa en un lugar, cosa o situación que te gusta o no te gusta. Por ejemplo, un baile, una fiesta, un museo. ¿Qué sientes cuando estás allí? Mira el ejemplo e inspírate para escribir tu propio haiku. Usa el presente de *ser* o *estar* para escribir tus frases, y no olvides que necesitas 5, 7 y 5 sílabas.

2 Después de escribir tu haiku, haz un dibujo para ilustrarlo.

3 Ahora estás listo(a) para presentar tu haiku a la clase. Explica en qué te inspiraste para escribirlo y muestra la ilustración.

Actividad 34 · Gramática · Leer/Escribir/Hablar

Escena de teatro

Tú y otro(a) estudiante están hablando de una visita que hicieron al teatro. Túrnense para combinar palabras o expresiones de las dos listas y escriban frases completas con el imperfecto de *ser* o *estar*. Usen las formas correctas de los adjetivos.

Modelo

el cantante / alto y guapo
A —*¿Cómo era el cantante?*
B —*El cantante era alto y guapo.*

1. las bailarinas
2. el micrófono
3. el teatro
4. los pasos del tango
5. la melodía
6. el concierto
7. los actores
8. nosotros

a. muy difícil
b. nervioso
c. en la calle Bolívar
d. muy bonito
e. el viernes a las ocho
f. entusiasmado con el espectáculo
g. alto
h. fondo del escenario
i. argentino

En el museo las estatuas me miran. Estoy perdido.

● **Más práctica**
Practice Workbook 2-10

Go Online PHSchool.com

For: Practice with *ser* and *estar*
Visit: www.phschool.com
Web Code: jed-0207

ochenta y nueve   89
Capítulo 2

Practice and Communicate

Gramática

Verbos con distinto sentido en el pretérito y en el imperfecto

A few Spanish verbs have different meanings in the imperfect and the preterite tenses.

	IMPERFECT	PRETERITE
saber	*knew*	*found out, learned*
	¿**Sabías** que el concierto empezaba tarde?	Sí, **supe** ayer que empezaba tarde.
conocer	*knew (somebody)*	*met (somebody) for the first time*
	Pedro **conocía** muy bien a esa actriz.	Luis la **conoció** el año pasado.
querer	*wanted to*	*tried to*
	Luis **quería** comprar las entradas hoy.	Yo **quise** comprarlas, pero me enfermé.
no querer	*didn't want to*	*refused to*
	No querían ver esa obra de teatro.	**No quisieron** ver esa obra de teatro.
poder	*was able to, could*	*managed to, succeeded in*
	Ella **podía** aprender la letra de la canción.	Ella **pudo** aprender la letra de esa canción.

 Gramática **Leer/Escribir**

Una cita con Rita

1 A veces las citas no resultan como queremos. Lee estos párrafos sobre la cita que Ricardo tuvo con Rita y complétalo con el pretérito o el imperfecto de los verbos entre paréntesis.

Yo no ___1.___ *(conocer)* bien a Rita. Era sólo nuestra segunda cita. Recuerdo que la ___2.___ *(conocer)* el verano pasado en una clase de danza. Ella ___3.___ *(querer)* aprender salsa, pero no ___4.___ *(poder)* seguir bien los pasos. Yo le pregunté si ___5.___ *(saber)* los movimientos de baile. Ella me dijo que no. Entonces, yo la ayudé y al final ella ___6.___ *(poder)* aprenderlos.

Cuando salimos de la escuela de danza, Rita me dijo que ___7.___ *(querer)* comer algo. Después, me dijo que ya era tarde y que tenía una cita con otro muchacho. Me invitó a ir con ellos, pero yo no ___8.___ *(querer)* ir. Ya estaba bastante enojado. ¡Nunca más salí con ella!

2 Ahora, responde a las siguientes preguntas.

1. ¿Cuándo conoció Ricardo a Rita?
2. ¿Qué pasó cuando salieron de la escuela de danza?
3. ¿Por qué estaba enojado Ricardo?

Fondo cultural

La **salsa** tiene origen en el *son*, una mezcla de ritmos africanos y europeos que nació en Cuba. Al principio, el *son* se interpretaba con tambores y maracas. Luego se añadieron otros instrumentos como el bajo *(bass)* y la guitarra. El término *salsa* empezó a usarse en los años sesenta en Nueva York y sirve para definir una música que es mezcla del *son* cubano y otros ritmos del Caribe. La salsa es una de las danzas más populares en los Estados Unidos.

• ¿Qué nombres de cantantes o grupos de salsa conoces?

• ¿Por qué crees que la salsa tiene tanto éxito en los Estados Unidos?

Actividad 37 Gramática   Escribir/Hablar

Y tú, ¿qué dices?

1. Piensa en un momento en que quisiste hacer algo pero no pudiste. ¿Qué fue?

2. ¿Hay algo que nunca pudiste hacer bien? ¿Por qué no podías hacerlo?

3. ¿Qué poemas o canciones sabías de niño(a)? ¿Los sabías de memoria?

4. Piensa en una ocasión en que no quisiste hacer algo. ¿Qué fue?

5. ¿Conocías ya a muchos(as) de tus compañeros(as) cuando empezaste esta clase?

6. ¿Conociste a alguien famoso(a) alguna vez? ¿A quién? ¿Cómo sabías que era famoso(a)?

En voz alta

Juan Luis Guerra creció escuchando la música popular de la República Dominicana y a los Beatles en la radio. Más tarde, asistió al Conservatorio Nacional y al Berklee College of Music de Massachusetts, donde recibió la influencia del jazz. Con todas esas experiencias, Guerra comenzó a componer[1] canciones de merengue, el popular ritmo dominicano, que eran perfectas para bailar pero que tenían una música, y sobre todo una letra, mucho más rica y compleja[2] que la de los merengues tradicionales.

Escucha este fragmento de la letra de una canción de Juan Luis Guerra y luego trata de repetirla en voz alta.

_____
1 compose 2 complex

¿Recuerdas?

En español, las letras *b* y *v* se pronuncian igual. Al principio de una palabra, el sonido es similar a la *b* en *boy*. En otras posiciones, el sonido es más suave.

Amigos
de Juan Luis Guerra

Yo soy tu amigo cuando a nadie le interesas
tan sólo llámame
y enseguida tocaré a tu puerta.
Yo soy tu amigo cuando buscas y no encuentras
tan sólo llámame
y estaré a tu lado cuando quieras.
Somos el viento que despierta el alba
dos nubes blancas bajo la ventana
yo soy tu carga que no pesa nada
tú eres el río donde bebo el agua.
Tómalo todo, pide lo que quieras
haz el camino y seguiré tus huellas.

Enriching Your Teaching

Culture Note

Merengue is a rural music with roots in the Dominican Republic. Traditionally bands were composed of an accordion, a saxophone, a bass, a *tambora* drum, and a *guayano*—a metal scraper. Today however, merengue bands often achieve a big-band sound through the use of multiple saxophones, electric guitars, keyboards, and synthesizers.

Internet Search

Keywords:

Juan Luis Guerra, música merengue

Fondo cultural    *Standards:* 1.1, 1.2, 2.2, 3.1

Suggestions: Ask if any students know how to dance **la salsa** and if they would volunteer to give a demonstration. Extend this invitation to any colleagues. Some students or teachers might even be willing to give a *salsa* lesson, which would provide an excellent context for real-life use of chapter vocabulary related to dance and music.

Answers will vary.

Actividad 37   *Standards:* 1.1, 1.3

Focus: Practicing verbs whose meanings change depending on tense

Suggestions: As students hold their discussions based on the questions, have them write down any of their partner's responses that strike them as interesting. After the paired discussions, have students share with the class one interesting fact that they learned about their partner.

Answers will vary.

En voz alta

Presentation

SStandards: 1.2, 3.1, 2.2, 3.2, 5.2

Resources: Voc. & Gram. Transparencies: 16 (map); Audio Program: CD Cap. 2, Track 20

Suggestions: Show *Vocabulary & Grammar Transparency* 16 and ask a volunteer to locate **la República Dominicana.**

Before having students recite the lyrics, direct their attention to the information in the *¿Recuerdas?* Allow them a few minutes to practice with a partner. Invite students to talk about how the images in the third stanza demonstrate friendship.

Practice and Communicate

② Practice and Communicate

Actividad 38

Standards: 1.1, 1.2, 1.3, 2.2, 3.1

Resources: Practice Answers on Transparencies

Focus: Reading and answering questions about a musical theater review from Spain

Suggestions: Before students read the review, direct their attention to the *Estrategia.* Remind them that using context clues will keep them reading and prevent them from getting stuck on unfamiliar words. Using context clues develops their skills in reading Spanish faster than consulting a dictionary because they are using what they already know and making associations between words and ideas.

Have students read the review silently and answer the questions on their own. Encourage them to paraphrase information drawn directly from the review, rather than stating it verbatim. Then go through the questions with the whole class. Ask students to read their answers aloud.

Answers:
1. Se habla de una obra teatral musical. Es una buena adaptación.
2. Answers will vary.
3. Ángels Gonyalons y Josema Yuste.
4. Ella tiene una voz magnífica y hace muy bien su papel. No tiene el toque de improvisación de Meg Ryan.
5–6. Answers will vary.

Extension: When discussing students' answers for question number five, ask if anyone knows the plot of *When Harry Met Sally.* Ask any students who do to contribute to a retelling of the plot in the past tense.

Additional Resources
• Writing, Audio & Video Workbook: Cap. 2, Audio Activity 4, Track 20

Estrategia

Context clues
When you read, look for cognates (words similar to English), which will make reading easier. Then, if you do not recognize a word, look at the words around it to try and guess what it means.

Actividad 38 Leer/Escribir/Hablar................

Una reseña de teatro

Lee esta reseña de una obra musical presentada en Madrid, que fue adaptada de una película estadounidense, y luego contesta las preguntas.

Cuando Harry encontró a Sally...

TEATRO LA LATINA

Siempre asusta el hecho de ver convertida una buena película en obra teatral, pero atemoriza aún más[1] imaginarla transformada en musical. Sin embargo, se trata de una buena adaptación, con escenas escogidas y bien desarrolladas[2]. Los diálogos respetados casi literalmente con respecto a los de la película, se convierten en canciones de muy diversos estilos, sin olvidar el matiz latino que Joan Vives ha querido añadir a la adaptación.

El reparto[3] cuenta con actores como Ángels Gonyalons y Josema Yuste y más de diez valiosos actores secundarios, acompañados de los seis músicos que componen la orquesta. Ella (Sally) tiene una voz magnífica y hace muy bien su papel, aunque no tiene ese toque[4] de improvisación que caracterizaba la actuación de Meg Ryan en la película. Él (Harry), suple su carencia[5] de "voz musical" con toques de humor, pero no incluye el tono cínico que caracterizaba la actuación del Harry original. Pese a ello, sus actuaciones son impecables. Sin duda, esta comedia musical es una buena excusa para pasar un buen rato.

1 it's even more scary 2 developed 3 cast   4 touch 5 lack

1. ¿De qué tipo de espectáculo se habla en el artículo? ¿Qué dice sobre la adaptación de *Cuando Harry encontró a Sally*?

2. ¿Crees que es una buena idea convertir una película en obra teatral? ¿Por qué?

3. ¿Quiénes son los actores principales de esta obra?

4. ¿Qué elementos positivos de la actriz menciona el artículo? ¿En qué se diferencia su actuación de la actuación de Meg Ryan?

5. ¿Sabes cuál es el argumento de la obra? ¿Por qué crees que el escritor de la reseña no dice cuál es el argumento o dónde ocurre la acción?

6. ¿Crees que la persona que escribió la reseña está a favor o en contra de esta comedia musical? ¿Por qué?

Universal Access

Heritage Language Learners
Have students give a brief commentary on an adaptation or translation that they have seen or read. They might choose a book that has been made into a movie, or the Spanish-language version of an English-language film, for example. Ask them to include a brief synopsis and tell which version they enjoyed more.

Students with Learning Difficulties
Have students identify and copy key words in each of the questions following *Cuando Harry encontró a Sally.* Then have them locate these key words in the reading passage. Encourage them to use this connection to help find the answers to each question.

Actividad 39

Escribir/Hablar ....

Los críticos

1 Trabaja con otro(a) estudiante. Escojan un espectáculo que vieron, que les gustó o que no les gustó. Escriban una lista de datos del espectáculo incluyendo los siguientes:

- tipo de espectáculo (obra de teatro de la escuela, película, pieza de baile o musical, programa de televisión)
- el autor o la autora
- los personajes (cómo eran, la ropa que usaban, quiénes los representaban)
- el argumento
- dónde ocurría la acción
- la interpretación de los actores principales (cómica, aburrida)
- el orden de los sucesos
- con qué personajes se identificaron
- cómo reaccionó el público cuando terminó (lloró, se rió, aplaudió)

2 Escriban una reseña usando los datos que juntaron. Si es posible, acompañen la reseña con fotos o anuncios del espectáculo.

Modelo

La obra de teatro de Romeo y Julieta es un drama de William Shakespeare. Los personajes principales son . . . El problema es que . . . La acción tiene lugar en . . . En general, nos gustó . . . Muchas personas dijeron que la actriz se identificó bien . . . Pero otras dijeron que exageraba . . .

3 Trabajen con otra pareja y lean su reseña. Si ellos también vieron el espectáculo, ¿están de acuerdo con Uds.? Si no vieron el espectáculo, ¿qué más quieren saber? Luego hagan lo mismo con la reseña de la otra pareja.

 **Más práctica** ......

Practice Workbook
2-11, 2-12

Go Online
PHSchool.com

For: Practice with the preterite and imperfect
Visit: www.phschool.com
Web Code: jed-0209

 **Fondo cultural**

◆■◆◆■◆■◆◆■◆◆■◆◆

La zarzuela ¿Ópera . . . opereta . . . musical de Broadway? Se parece un poco a cada una de estas formas musicales, pero es una expresión de la cultura, la historia y las costumbres de España. La zarzuela nació en el siglo XVII. En el siglo XIX se construyeron los dos teatros más famosos de la zarzuela en Madrid, el Teatro de La Zarzuela (1856) y el Teatro Apolo (1873–1929), y las compañías comenzaron a visitar América Latina. Su popularidad aumentó *(increased)* en el siglo XX, cuando varias zarzuelas se llevaron al cine.

Generalmente, la zarzuela tiene partes cantadas y partes habladas. Puede ser cómica o trágica, y muchas veces el argumento es romántico.

- ¿Qué películas u obras de teatro similares a la zarzuela conoces? ¿Por qué crees que la zarzuela se hizo tan popular? Sugiere dos ideas.

Actividad 39   *Standards:* 1.1, 1.2, 1.3, 3.1
....

Focus: Combining skills to write a review of a recent performance or film

Suggestions: Point out to students that the model review contains transitions that are an important part of clear writing. Encourage them to use similar transitions when putting together the ideas they listed in step 1. Ask them to write a second draft of their review, paying attention to organization of ideas and sentence structure. Encourage them to study other examples of reviews in this chapter and use them as models for their writing.

Answers will vary.

Fondo cultural   *Standards:* 1.1, 1.2, 2.2, 3.1
■◆◆■◆■◆◆■◆◆◆

Suggestions: After students have read the information, ask comprehension questions. For example: *¿Cuáles son tres cosas que expresa la zarzuela? (Expresa la cultura, la historia y las costumbres de España.) ¿En qué siglo nació la zarzuela? (Nació en el siglo XVII.)*

Answers will vary.

Additional Resources

- Writing, Audio & Video Workbook: Cap. 2, Writing Activities 12–13
- Writing, Audio & Video Workbook: Cap. 2, Audio Activity 5, Track 21
- Resource Book: Cap. 2, Communicative Activity BLM

 Assessment

- Prueba 2-8: *Verbos con distinto sentido en el pretérito y en el imperfecto*
- Examen: Vocabulario y gramática 2

Chapter Project

Students can perform step 5 at this point. Record their presentations on cassettee or videotape for inclusion in their portfolio. (For more information, see p. 62-a.)

Enriching Your Teaching

Teacher-to-Teacher

Encourage students to keep an eye out for real-life connections to the current theme of study. The art club at your school might be planning an exhibition, or the drama club rehearsing for a new production. Perhaps an exhibition of paintings of Mexican muralists is coming to your local museum. Integrate these concrete and personal examples into language activities and exercises. Tap into students' interests and areas of expertise by inviting them to talk about their interests.

Objectives
- **Read about a famous Spanish painter**
- **Use visuals as an aid to understand the reading**
- **Relate a painter's life with his(her) work**

Puente a la cultura

Presentation

Standards: 1.2, 1.3, 2.1, 2.2, 3.1, 5.2

Resources: Fine Art Transparencies; Fine Art Transparencies Teacher's Guide

Focus: Reading to learn about the life and work of Spanish artist Francisco Goya

Suggestions:

Pre-reading: Direct students' attention to the *Estrategia*. Use the questions there and the title of the selection to help students predict what the reading is about. Ask them to write down their predictions and to return to them as they read in order to verify whether or not they were correct. As you discuss the photos on this and the next page, have volunteers read the captions aloud.

Reading: Encourage students to read through the entire passage once silently, without stopping at problem words or to ask questions. Then ask volunteers to read sections aloud. Remind students to use background knowledge, cognates, and context clues to help them understand unfamiliar words and expressions as they read.

Post-reading: Ask students to comment on the predictions they wrote down in the *Pre-reading*. Ask questions such as: *¿Tus predicciones eran correctas? ¿Tuviste que cambiar alguna predicción? ¿Cómo? ¿Leíste algo en este artículo que no esperabas? ¿Qué fue? ¿Qué más te gustaría saber sobre Francisco Goya?*

Common Errors: Point out to students the word **obra** in the first paragraph. Ask a volunteer to read aloud the sentence in which it is used. Explain that **obra** can refer to one single work, such as a painting, or to the work of an artist's entire life, as it does here.

Go Online

The online atlas will provide a more detailed map of Spain.

¡Adelante!

Puente a la cultura
El mundo de Francisco Goya

Estrategia

Using visuals
Looking at the visuals before reading a selection allows us to better understand it. What do you notice about the paintings on this page and the next one? What might your observations tell you about what you will read about the painter?

Francisco Goya nació en 1746 en España. Murió en Francia en 1828, a los 82 años de edad y sordo[1], a causa de una misteriosa enfermedad. Goya es uno de los artistas más conocidos de todos los tiempos. Su obra es extensa y muy variada. Realizó murales religiosos, retratos de la corte española, dibujos de toros, cuadros sobre la guerra, y hasta sus propias pesadillas[2] que pintó en las paredes de su casa.

Uno de sus grandes triunfos artísticos fue llegar a ser Pintor de Cámara[3], o sea el pintor oficial de los reyes. Goya pintó retratos de la familia real y de otros personajes de la corte madrileña[4]. De esta época[5] son muy conocidos los retratos que hizo de la Duquesa de Alba, según algunos, una de las mujeres más hermosas de su época. Durante 18 años, Goya trabajó para la Real Fábrica de Tapices[6] de Santa Bárbara. Allí se dedicó a dibujar bocetos[7] de escenas alegres y pintorescas, que representaban la vida cotidiana[8] en Madrid. Estos bocetos luego aparecían en tapices que adornaban las paredes de los palacios reales.

---

1 deaf 2 nightmares 3 Chamber Painter 4 Court of Madrid 5 period 6 Royal Tapestry Factory 7 sketches 8 everyday

Duquesa de Alba, (1795), Francisco Goya
194 x 130 cm. The Art Archive/Private Collection.

El quitasol, (1777), Francisco Goya
Oil on canvas, 104 x 152 cm. Museo Nacional del Prado, Madrid, Spain.

94 noventa y cuatro
¡Adelante!

Universal Access

Students with Learning Difficulties

Students may be overwhelmed by the amount of information contained in the biography of Francisco Goya. To help organize this information, have them isolate the dates included in this passage. Then have them organize the dates into a timeline, adding a short caption to each significant date.

Advanced Learners

Ask students to summarize the selection by paraphrasing each paragraph in Spanish. Suggest that they begin each paraphrase with phrases such as **El primer párrafo dice que...** or **Esta parte se trata de....**

La pintura de Goya cambió con el tiempo para mostrar los sucesos que ocurrían en su país. Los españoles lucharon[9] durante siete años contra las tropas francesas que Napoleón envió para invadir España. La obra más famosa de Goya sobre el tema de la guerra[10] contra Francia es el cuadro *El 3 de mayo de 1808.*

Al final de su vida, Goya estuvo muy enfermo. Sus obras de esta época se llaman las Pinturas Negras, ya que Goya representaba imágenes de pesadillas, como monstruos, en pinturas que eran oscuras.

Los cuadros de Goya están en los museos más importantes del mundo. Para celebrar los 250 años del nacimiento del pintor, el Museo del Prado de Madrid organizó una gran exposición en 1996. La obra de Goya es todavía muy popular hoy en día. ¿Por qué crees que es así?

El 3 de mayo de 1808, (1814), Francisco Goya
Oil on canvas, 8 ft. 9 in. x 13 ft. 4 in. Museo Nacional del Prado, Madrid. Copyright Lessing/Art Resource, NY.

9 fought **10** war

¿Comprendiste?

1. ¿Cuándo, en qué lugar y cómo se celebraron los 250 años del nacimiento de Goya?

2. ¿Por qué podemos decir que las pinturas de la página 94 son representativas de las obras de Goya cuando era Pintor de Cámara?

3. La pintura de Goya cambió según las diferentes épocas de su vida. Da dos ejemplos y explica cómo se relacionan esas pinturas con los cambios en su vida.

4. El artículo dice que Goya es uno de los artistas más conocidos de todos los tiempos. ¿Cuáles son las razones de su éxito como pintor?

Escribe tu opinión

Acabas de leer sobre los diferentes períodos de la pintura de Goya. Basado(a) en la información que leíste y las obras que ves aquí, escribe si te gustaría ver más obras de Goya, como el retrato de la *Duquesa de Alba* o *El sueño de la razón produce monstruos.*

El sueño de la razón produce monstruos, (1799), Francisco Goya
Plate 43 of 'Los Caprichos', published c. 1810 (color engraving). Bibliotheque de Nationale, Paris, France. Archives Charmet. Bridgeman Art Library, London.

Go Online
PHSchool.com

For: Internet link activity
Visit: www.phschool.com
Web Code: jed-0210

noventa y cinco **95**
Capítulo 2

Culture Note

The **Real Fábrica de Tapices de Santa Bárbara** was created in 1720 under the order of Felipe V. Goya painted for the factory from 1775 until 1800. His "cartoons" served as models for the tapestries. At times, the tapestry workers ran into difficulty transferring Goya's intricate cartoons onto fabric. In some cases, Goya had to change his original designs to suit the medium.

Enriching Your Teaching

Internet Search
Keywords:

Francisco Goya, Museo del Prado, Luis Paret y Alcázar

¿Comprendiste?
Standards: 1.2, 1.3

Resources: Fine Art Transparencies; Fine Art Transparencies Teacher's Guide; Practice Answers on Transparencies

Focus: Demonstrating reading comprehension

Suggestions: Have pairs of students answer the questions and write down their responses.

Answers:
1. Los 250 años del nacimiento de Goya se celebraron en 1996 con una gran exposición en el Museo del Prado de Madrid.
2. La pintura de la Duquesa de Alba es de un personaje de la corte madrileña. *El quitasol* es del mismo estilo realista.
3–4. Answers will vary.

Escribe tu opinión
Standards: 1.3, 3.1

Focus: Using new vocabulary and structures in a written response to a reading

Suggestions: Tell students to include one or two statements supporting their opinion.

Answers will vary.

Teaching with Art

Ask students to choose one of the paintings and not to reveal their choice to anyone. Tell them they can do one of two things:

A. Write an imaginary character sketch of one of the persons in the painting. Do not name the person, but include details about his or her life at or before the moment frozen in the painting.

B. Write a monologue that shows the thoughts going through the mind of one of the persons in the painting. Pretend to be "inside the head" of that person at the moment frozen in the painting.

Video
Presentation
Standards: 1.2

Resources: Video Program: Cap. 2

This segment introduces us to great Spanish-speaking artists representing a variety of art forms, such as Gabriel García Márquez and Diego Rivera. Dance forms such as the *tango* and *flamenco* are also highlighted. See the *Video Teacher's Guide* for additional suggestions.

¿Qué me cuentas?

Presentation

Standards: 1.1, 1.2, 2.2, 3.1, 5.2

Resources: Voc. & Fram. Transparencies: 65; Fine Art Transparencies; Fine Art Transparencies Teacher's Guide; Audio Program: CD Cap. 2, Track 23; Resource Book: Cap. 2, Audio Script; Practice Answers on Transparencies

Focus: Practicing speaking and listening comprehension within the context of two paintings

Suggestions: For step 1, use the *Audio CD* or read the descriptions aloud. Allow students to hear the descriptions twice—the first time to write their answers and the second time to check them.

In step 2, students may need some guidance in order to discuss what they think the artists wanted to express. Circulate and listen to their discussions. If necessary, help them with questions containing embedded answers: *¿Piensas que la pintura de Botero expresa la confusión o la alegría de estar en casa? ¿Y la de Dalí?*

For step 3, take a survey of the class and list on the board students' likes and dislikes with respect to the paintings.

Answers:

Step 1

1. **Dalí**	5. **Botero**
2. **Dalí**	6. **Botero**
3. **Botero**	7. **Dalí**
4. **Dalí**	8. **Botero**

Steps 2–3

Answers will vary.

Block Schedule

Ask each student to create a *naturaleza muerta* using colors, shapes, and images that reflect his or her personal style. Encourage creativity. Upon completion, give the painting to another student who will describe it.

96

¿Qué me cuentas?

Naturaleza muerta

🎧 Vas a escuchar unas descripciones sobre los dos cuadros de esta página. Escribe cada descripción e indica si pertenece al cuadro de Botero o de Dalí.

Naturaleza muerta con sopa verde, (1972), Fernando Botero
(c) Fernando Botero, courtesy, Mariborough Gallery, New York.

Naturaleza muerta, viva, (1956), Salvador Dalí
Oil on canvas. 49 1/4 x 63 inches. Collection of The Salvador Dalí Museum, St. Petersburg, Florida. Copyright 2003 Salvador Dalí Museum, Inc. (c) 2004 Artists Rights Society ARS, New York.

● Estos dos cuadros son ejemplos de naturaleza muerta. El cuadro de Botero se llama *Naturaleza muerta con sopa verde.* El de Dalí se llama *Naturaleza muerta, viva.* Piensa en los títulos de estos cuadros. ¿Por qué se llaman así? Con tus propias palabras, compara los dos cuadros, según el tema, el estilo, los colores, las imágenes y lo que quiere expresar el artista. Di cuál te gusta más y por qué. Puedes usar las frases siguientes para unir tus ideas.

Por un lado . . . *(on the one hand)*	Esto me parece más . . .	Sin embargo . . .
Por otra parte . . . *(on the other hand)*	En primer lugar . . .	En contraste . . .

● Trabaja con otro(a) estudiante para hablar sobre lo que piensan de los dos cuadros. Digan qué fue lo que más les gustó de cada cuadro y lo que menos les gustó.

96 noventa y seis
¡Adelante!

Universal Access

Heritage Language Learners

Have students add a second layer to their oral presentations. In addition to explaining why a particular heritage country artist should be voted **Artista del Milenio.** have them explain why a major competitor to this artist is not as qualified to receive the distinction.

Students with Learning Difficulties

Students may have difficulty organizing and recalling information for their oral presentations. To support them, have students provide you with a written copy of their presentation materials prior to the actual oral presentation. Use this information to provide guiding questions or cues if necessary.

Presentación oral

"Artista del Milenio"

Tarea
Imagínate que en tu clase van a seleccionar a un(a) artista como candidato(a) al premio "Artista del Milenio *(millennium)*". Puede ser un(a) pintor(a), un actor, una actriz, o un(a) cantante que te guste. Explica quién debe ser el / la candidato(a) y por qué.

① Prepárate Escoge tu artista preferido(a). Completa una tabla como ésta sobre tu candidato(a). Recuerda que puedes usar tus notas para prepararte, pero no al hacer la presentación oral.

Nombre	
Tipo de artista	
Puntos positivos	
Experiencia	
Originalidad, personalidad	
Tu recomendación	

② Practica Haz tu presentación ante el grupo. Al final, se va a hacer una votación para escoger un(a) ganador(a). Recuerda que debes:
- incluir el nombre del / de la artista, su especialidad y lo que hizo
- describir los puntos positivos del / de la candidato(a)
- decir claramente por qué debe ganar el premio
- usar el vocabulario de este capítulo

Modelo

Creo que Cabral debe ser el "Artista del Milenio". Él no fue un simple cantante, fue un símbolo de la cultura popular de su país. Su voz y su estilo de interpretar las canciones se hicieron famosos en todo el mundo.

③ Haz tu presentación Haz tu presentación ante la clase. Al final, todos los estudiantes votan para elegir al / a la "Artista del Milenio".

④ Evaluación Tu profesor(a) puede explicarte cómo va a evaluar tu presentación. Para tu profesor(a) es importante ver que:
- explicaste claramente los puntos positivos de tu candidato(a)
- el grupo entendió bien por qué escogiste a tu candidato(a)
- diste suficiente información y detalles

Estrategia
Organize information
Organize the key points you may want to talk about by listing them in a chart. This will help you give a more effective presentation.

noventa y siete   97
Capítulo 2

Presentación oral

Presentation

Standards: 1.1, 1.2, 1.3, 3.1

Resources: Voc. & Gram. Transparencies: 4

Focus: Preparing and delivering an oral presentation

Suggestions: Review the task and the four-step approach with students. Review the rubric with the class (see *Assessment* below) to explain how you will grade the performance task.

Help students decide what type of information to put in the various categories of the chart. In **Puntos positivos,** they can focus on the artistic qualities that make the artist worthy of the award. For **Experiencia,** they might list all of the artistic work they know of from that artist, such as titles of books, films, or songs. For **Originalidad, personalidad,** they can tell what they know about the artist's personal life.

Portfolio
Record students' oral presentations on audiocassette or videotape for inclusion in their portfolios.

✓ Assessment
- Assessment Program: Cap. 2, Rubrics

Give students copies of the rubric before they begin the activity. Go over the descriptions of the different levels of performance. After assessing students, help individuals understand how their performance could be improved. (See the *Teacher's Resource Book* for suggestions on using rubrics in assessment.)

Teacher-to-Teacher
Some students experience stress when asked to make oral presentations to the class. Although it is healthy and beneficial for them to confront this, allow them, at least occasionally, to record their presentations on audiocassette or videotape. This reduces stress for them and provides you with a handy tool for assessment.

Enriching Your Teaching

RUBRIC	Score 1	Score 3	Score 5
How well you provide information	You lack vital information, such as the artist's identity.	Your vital information about the artist is present.	Your information about the artist is clearly presented.
How well you support your opinion	You have little or no convincing evidence.	Your supporting evidence is present, but not developed.	Your supporting evidence is clear and convincing.
How effectively you deliver your speech	You have no eye contact with audience.	You make some eye contact. You use intonation, but not convincingly.	You make good eye contact with the audience. You have good intonation and gestures.

Presentación escrita

Presentation

Standards: 1.3, 3.1

Resources: Voc. & Gram. Transparencies: 12

Focus: Combining learned vocabulary and structures in a written presentation

Suggestions: Explain at the start the criteria you will use to evaluate students' compositions. (See step 5, *Evaluación,* in the Student Edition.)

First, direct students' attention to the *Estrategia.* Remind them that using a graphic organizer will help them prepare their evaluations. Then show *Vocabulary & Grammar Transparency* 12. Model filling in the information about an imaginary candidate. Make statements about the candidate's capabilities and ask students where the information should go in the web: *Sol Herrera es una buena escritora. Escribió dos cuentos cortos. Estos cuentos están publicados en revistas.* Once students determine that this information goes in the **Nombre, arte** and **Experiencia** sections of the web, fill it in on the transparency image. Together with students, read through the information about the imaginary candidate Vicky Lagardera in the web shown on this page. Answer any questions they may have about the graphic organizer. Then have them create on their own paper a similar, empty web and use it to prepare their evaluations of their own candidates.

Block Schedule

Encourage students to use the graphic organizer. You might have students work in small groups and share their notes. You might ask a few students to present their notes using an overhead transparency.

Presentación escrita

El mejor candidato

Objectives
• Write an evaluation about a student's audition
• Organize data into categories

Imagínate que te piden que escribas sobre un(a) artista y que digas por qué deben aceptarlo(a) en una escuela famosa. Haz un informe para explicar por qué crees que será un(a) buen(a) estudiante.

Estrategia

Categorizing
When writing a report you must include the greatest amount of information in the clearest way possible. If you organize the information into categories and write everything about one topic before going to the next one, the reader will have no trouble understanding your report.

① Antes de escribir

Para encontrar ideas, hazte preguntas como las siguientes:

• ¿Qué tipo de artista es y qué experiencia tuvo? ¿Tuvo actuaciones en público? ¿Cuándo?

• ¿Cómo es la actuación desde el punto de vista técnico? Si canta, ¿sabe la letra?, ¿sigue la música? Si baila, ¿sabe los pasos?, ¿sigue el ritmo? Si hace teatro, ¿representa bien al personaje?, ¿sabe los diálogos?

• ¿Qué aptitudes naturales tiene el(la) estudiante? Si canta, ¿tiene buena voz? Si baila, ¿tiene ritmo? Si hace teatro, ¿se identifica con el personaje?

Antes de escribir tu composición, pon en orden tus ideas para darle una estructura. Usa un organizador gráfico como éste.

Experiencia:
Aprendió los pasos de muchos bailes.
Interpretó el papel de Coppelia para el Ballet Juvenil de la escuela.

Nombre, arte:
Vicky Lagardera
danza clásica

Características técnicas:
Los movimientos siguen el ritmo.
Conoce los pasos de muchos bailes.

Características personales:
muy expresiva
con personalidad
no se desanima

Recomendación:
Admitirla.
Tiene que trabajar mucho.
Va a aprender pronto.

② Borrador

Escribe tu borrador. Escribe un informe con toda la información del organizador gráfico. Más tarde vas a tener oportunidad de revisar la organización y la ortografía de tu informe.

98 noventa y ocho
¡Adelante!

Universal Access

Heritage Language Learners
Have students identify one or two specific elements of Spanish grammar that they find challenging in their writing. Direct them to focus on these specific points while revising their written presentations.

Advanced Learners
Encourage students to interview the person they are evaluating. They can ask the person for hard facts about his or her artistic experience, such as publications or exhibits. They can also ask the artist to assess his or her own strong points. They can then translate at least some of this information to Spanish and use it in their evaluations.

Modelo

> Main topic: What is the report about?

Vicky Lagardera es un bailarina de danza clásica.

Vicky bailó desde pequeña. Estudió cinco años en la Escuela de danza Miraflores. A los once años ya bailaba en el Ballet Juvenil y . . .

> Background information: dance experience

Vicky baila con movimientos que siguen el ritmo de la música. Conoce los pasos de muchos bailes de memoria y los aprende rápidamente. A veces está nerviosa . . .

> Details: dance technique. What does the text tell about the student technique?

Tiene personalidad, es muy expresiva y . . .

> Details: personality

Debe entrar en la escuela. Tiene que trabajar mucho, pero . . .

> Conclusion: recommendation, based on the previous information.

3 Redacción/Revisión

Después de escribir el primer borrador, trabaja con otro(a) estudiante para intercambiar los trabajos y leerlos. Luego, hagan sugerencias para mejorar sus informes.

- ¿Seguiste el plan que hiciste en tu organizador gráfico? ¿Escribiste todas las ideas que querías expresar?
- ¿Están bien organizados los párrafos? ¿Comunicaste claramente la información?
- ¿Usaste los verbos y los tiempos verbales correctos?

Haz lo siguiente: Verifica si usaste correctamente los verbos en pretérito o imperfecto.

Vicky ~~bailó~~ *bailó* desde pequeña. ~~Estudiaba~~ *Estudió* cinco años en la Escuela de danza Miraflores. A los once años ya ~~bailó~~ *bailaba* en el Ballet Juvenil y . . .

4 Publicación

Antes de crear la versión final, lee de nuevo el informe y repasa los siguientes puntos:

- ¿Explica mi informe claramente lo que pienso del / de la estudiante que quiere entrar en la escuela?
- ¿Usé el vocabulario apropiado para este tema?
- ¿Debo añadir detalles importantes?

5 Evaluación

Tu profesor(a) puede explicarte cómo va a evaluar tu presentación. Probablemente para tu profesor(a) es importante ver que:

- explicaste claramente tu opinión y usaste suficientes detalles
- organizaste bien tu presentación

noventa y nueve   99
Capítulo 2

Suggestions (Cont'd):

Once students have a rough draft ready, read through the model on this page together. Help them see how information from the web on p. 98 was incorporated into this draft and to note the additional information that was added. Point out the use of past tenses and complete sentences. Encourage them to work toward similar organization, level of detail, and language use as they revise their own drafts.

Evaluation

Steps 4 and 5 overlap. Students will need evaluation by you, their peers, or self-evaluation to fine-tune and polish their drafts.

Language Arts Connection

Standards: 3.1

Remind students that in their Language Arts classes they were taught effective use of transitions in writing. As they revise their drafts in step 3, tell them to include transitions that will warn the reader that they are changing from one main idea to another. As part of the revision process, have partners comment on one another's use of transitions.

Portfolio

Keep students' final drafts in their portfolios as a writing sample.

✓ Assessment

• Assessment Program: Cap. 2, Rubrics
Give students copies of the rubric before they begin the activity. Go over the descriptions of the different levels of performance.

Teacher-to-Teacher

As students review each other's work, encourage them to begin their critiques with a positive comment or two. Remind them of how much more readily they themselves respond to positive criticism than to negative comments. Ask them to provide suggestions and additions in a constructive way.

Enriching Your Teaching

RUBRIC	Score 1	Score 3	Score 5
How well you organize information	Your vital information about the candidate is missing.	You present vital information but it's unorganized.	Your information is clearly presented and organized.
How well you support your choice	You have few or no convincing details in support of the candidate.	Your details convince us to vote for the candidate.	Your details about the candidate are organized and convincing.
Sentence structure/ grammar, spelling, mechanics	Your sentences are run-on or are fragmented with many errors.	You use sentences effectively, but with a few errors.	Your sentence structure is varied with very few errors.

Objectives
- **Read part of an autobiography**
- **Find out about the experiences of a young immigrant in New York**

Lectura

Presentation

Standards: 1.1, 1.2, 1.3, 2.1, 2.2, 3.1, 3.2, 4.1, 4.2, 5.2

Resources: Voc. & Gram. Transparencies: 16 (map)

Focus: Reading an extended passage

Suggestions:

Pre-reading: Ask a volunteer to read the title of the passage aloud. Ask students what they think is meant by the expression **Fragmento de.** If they don't know, explain that the selection is a fragment or excerpt from a longer work.

Before reading, direct students' attention to the *Estrategia* and to the *Al leer* section. Have them answer the questions and copy the graphic organizer from this page.

Consider having students read the information about the author of the autobiography in the *Fondo cultural* on p. 103 before they read the selection itself. Ask them to use what they learn from that, as well as the title of the selection and the photos, to answer the question *¿De qué tratará esta lectura?*

Lectura

Fragmento de
Cuando era puertorriqueña

Estrategia

Monitoring your reading
When you are reading a long selection, stop after each paragraph to ask yourself questions such as: What is the main idea of this paragraph? How does this idea relate to the title or the topic of the reading? This strategy will help you understand better what you are reading.

Al leer

Vas a leer un fragmento de una autobiografía. Se trata de Esmeralda Santiago, una joven puertorriqueña que emigró con su familia a Nueva York. Esmeralda da una audición en la famosa escuela secundaria Performing Arts. Mientras lees, anota en una tabla los siguientes puntos:

Qué hace y cómo se siente Esmeralda	
antes de la audición	
durante la audición	
después de la audición	

—¡Las pruebas son en menos de un mes! Tienes que aprender una escena dramática, y la vas a realizar enfrente de un jurado[1]. Si lo haces bien, y tus notas aquí son altas, puede ser que te admitan a la escuela.

El Mister Barone se encargó de prepararme para la prueba. Seleccionó un soliloquio de una obra de Sidney Howard titulada *The Silver Cord,* montada[2] por primera vez en 1926, pero la acción de la cual acontecía en una sala de estrado en Nueva York, alrededor del año 1905.

—Mister Gatti, el maestro de gramática, te dirigirá . . . Y Missis Johnson te hablará acerca de lo que te debes de poner y esas cosas.

Mi parte era la de Cristina, una joven casada confrontando a su suegra[3]. Aprendí el soliloquio fonéticamente, bajo la dirección de Mister Gatti. Mis primeras palabras eran: "You belong to a type that's very common in this country, Mrs. Phelps, a type of self-centered, self-pitying, son-devouring tigress, with unmentionable proclivities suppressed on the side."

—No tenemos tiempo de aprender lo que quiere decir cada palabra —dijo Mister Gatti—. Sólo asegúrate de que te las pronuncies todas.

Yo había soñado[4] con este momento durante varias semanas. Más que nada, quería impresionar al jurado con mi talento para que me aceptaran en Performing Arts High School y para poder salir de Brooklyn todos los días, y un día nunca volver.

Pero en cuanto me enfrenté con las tres mujeres bien cuidadas que formaban el jurado de la audición, se me olvidó el inglés que había aprendido y las lecciones que Missis Johnson me había inculcado sobre cómo portarme como una dama. En la agonía de contestar sus preguntas incomprensibles, puyaba[5] mis manos hacia aquí y hacia allá, formando palabras con mis dedos porque no me salían por la boca.

—¿Por qué no nos dejas oír tu soliloquio ahora? —preguntó la señora de los lentes colgantes.

Me paré como asustada, y mi silla cayó patas arriba como a tres pies de donde yo estaba

---

1 jury panel **2** put on stage **3** mother-in-law **4** The usage of *había* with the past participle expresses what a person *had* done. *Había soñado* = I had dreamed **5** moved, pushed

100 cien
¡Adelante!

Block Schedule

After reading the *Lectura,* ask each student to play the role of Esmeralda and do a short reading from this autobiography, perhaps one paragraph in length. Explain how it is common for authors to do "readings" of their work. Have students focus on pronunciation and personal expression, imagining how the author herself might read the selected excerpt.

Universal Access

Heritage Language Learners

After previewing the selection, have students practice and present a "dramatic reading" of this literature excerpt. Tell them to imagine that their version will be broadcast on the radio. Encourage students to assume different roles, characterizations, voices, and intonations.

Students with Learning Difficulties

As students read the excerpt aloud, model for them the appropriate intonation or expression. Have students repeat and imitate your exaggerated intonation to help support the meaning of the narrative.

parada. La fui a buscar, deseando con toda mi alma que un relámpago entrara por la ventana y me hiciera cenizas allí mismo.

—No te aflijas —dijo la señora—. Sabemos que estás nerviosa.

Cerré los ojos y respiré profundamente, caminé al centro del salón y empecé mi soliloquio.

—Llu bilón tú é tayp dats beri cómo in dis contri Missis Felps. É tayp of selfcente red self pí tí in són de baurin taygrés huid on menshonabol proclibétis on de sayd.

A pesar de las instrucciones de Mister Gatti de hablar lentamente y pronunciar bien las palabras aunque no las entendiera, recité mi monólogo de tres minutos en un minuto sin respirar ni una vez.

Las pestañas[6] falsas de la señora bajita parecían haber crecido de sorpresa. La cara serena de la señora elegante temblaba con risa controlada.

La señora alta vestida de pardo me dio una sonrisa dulce.

—Gracias, querida. ¿Puedes esperar afuera un ratito?

Resistí el deseo de hacerle reverencia. El pasillo era largo, con paneles de madera angostos pegados verticalmente entre el piso y el cielo raso.

Lámparas con bombillas grandes y redondas colgaban de cordones largos, creando charcos amarillos en el piso pulido. Unas muchachas como de mi edad estaban sentadas en sillas a la orilla del corredor, esperando su turno. Me miraron de arriba a abajo cuando salí, cerrando la puerta tras de mí. Mami se paró de su silla al fondo del corredor. Se veía tan asustada como me sentía yo.

—¿Qué te pasó?

—Na[7]—no me atrevía a hablar, porque si empezaba a contarle lo que había sucedido, empezaría a llorar enfrente de las otras personas, cuyos ojos me seguían como si

---

6 eyelashes **7** nothing

Enriching Your Teaching

Culture Note

The theme of remaining and retaining one's self in the context of a new country and culture is a popular one in contemporary U.S. literature. Esmeralda Santiago's account of a young woman from Puerto Rico growing up in New York City, feeling different, yet longing to belong, is echoed by many other works by women writers. Some notable examples include Nicholasa Mohr's *El Bronx Remembered*, and Julia Álvarez's *How the García Girls Lost Their Accents*. All of these works explore the struggle between preserving the language and culture of "home," and creating a new sense of home within U.S. language and culture.

Suggestions (Cont'd):

Reading: While reading the selection together with students, pause frequently to address comprehension issues that students may bring up. Ask your own comprehension questions to help them focus on the main idea and important details of each section. Here are some possible comprehension issues on pp. 100–101 for which you can provide some guidance:

- p. 100: Ask a volunteer to read aloud the excerpt that the author had to recite for her audition. Ask: *¿Este ejemplo de inglés es fácil o difícil?* Ask them to consider how much more difficult it would be for a person like the author, whose first language isn't English.
- p. 101, column 1: Tell students that the expression *No te aflijas* means the same as *No te preocupes.*
- p. 101, column 1: Explain that the paragraph beginning with *—Llu bilón...* is the phonetic rendition of English that the author refers to on the previous page. Read this aloud for students.
- p. 101, columns 1-2: Help students understand by pantomiming the actions in passages such as *La cara serena de la señora elegante temblaba...* and *...hacerle reverencia.*

Teacher-to-Teacher

Students may need some guidance in order to appreciate the humor in this selection. Point out humorous parts by asking questions such as *¿Piensan que el fragmento de una obra de teatro que eligieron los maestros de Esmeralda era adecuado* (adequate) *para su audición? ¿Por qué?/¿Por qué no? ¿Qué pasó cuando Esmeralda se levantó para decir su soliloquio? ¿Cómo se sintió ella? ¿Esmeralda dijo su soliloquio rápida o lentamente? ¿Cómo lo sabes?*

Suggestions (Cont'd):

Reading: Additional comprehension issues are as follows:

- p. 101, column 2: Help students through the passage about light by telling them that the key word in the passage, ***charco,*** means "puddle" or "pool."
- p. 101, column 2: Point out that ***na*** is Esmeralda's shortened, slang form of ***nada.***
- p. 102, column 1: Guide students to see the humor in Esmeralda's saying ***¡Presente! quiero decir, aquí...*** Say: *Primero, Esmeralda habla en español, pero quiere hablar en inglés. Entonces trata de corregirse* (correct herself). *¿Qué piensan que quería decir la segunda vez?* ("Here")
- p. 103: Point out the use of the participles ***jugando*** and ***chapurreando*** in participial phrases. Remind students that they reviewed this type of usage before the reading.

buscando señas de lo que les esperaba. Caminamos hasta la puerta de salida—. Tengo que esperar aquí un momentito.

—¿No te dijeron nada?

—No. Sólo que espere aquí.

Nos recostamos contra la pared. Enfrente de nosotras había una pizarra de corcho con recortes de periódico acerca de graduados de la escuela. En las orillas, alguien había escrito en letras de bloque, "P.A." y el año cuando el actor, bailarín o músico se había graduado. Cerré mis ojos y traté de imaginar un retrato de mí contra el corcho y la leyenda "P.A. '66" en la orilla.

La puerta al otro lado del pasillo se abrió, y la señora vestida de pardo sacó la cabeza.

—¿Esmeralda?

—¡Presente! quiero decir, aquí —alcé la mano.

Me esperó hasta que entré al salón. Había otra muchacha adentro, a quien me presentó como Bonnie, una estudiante en la escuela.

—¿Sabes lo que es una pantomima? —preguntó la señora. Señalé con la cabeza que sí—. Bonnie y tú son hermanas decorando el árbol de Navidad.

Bonnie se parecía mucho a Juanita Marín, a quien yo había visto por última vez cuatro años antes. Decidimos dónde poner el árbol invisible, y nos sentamos en el piso y actuamos como que estábamos sacando las decoraciones de una caja y colgándolas en las ramas.

Mi familia nunca había puesto un árbol de Navidad, pero yo me acordaba de cómo una vez yo ayudé a Papi a ponerle luces de colores alrededor de una mata de berenjenas[8] que dividía nuestra parcela de la de Doña Ana.

Empezamos por abajo, y le envolvimos el cordón eléctrico con las lucecitas rojas alrededor de la mata hasta que no nos quedaba más. Entonces Papi enchufó otro cordón eléctrico con más luces, y seguimos envolviéndolo hasta que las ramas se doblaban con el peso y la mata parecía estar prendida en llamas.

En un ratito se me olvidó dónde estaba, y que el árbol no existía, y que Bonnie no era mi hermana. Hizo como que me pasaba una decoración bien delicada y, al yo extender la mano para cogerla, hizo como que se me cayó y se rompió. Me asusté de que Mami entraría gritándonos que le habíamos roto una de sus figuras favoritas. Cuando empecé a recoger los fragmentos delicados de cristal invisible, una voz nos interrumpió y dijo:

—Gracias.

Bonnie se paró, sonrió y se fue.

La señora elegante estiró su mano para que se la estrechara.

—Notificaremos a tu escuela en unos días. Mucho gusto en conocerte.

Le estreché la mano a las tres señoras, y salí sin darles la espalda, en una neblina silenciosa, como si la pantomima me hubiera quitado la voz y el deseo de hablar.

De vuelta a casa, Mami me preguntaba qué había pasado, y yo le contestaba, "Na'. No pasó na'," avergonzada de que, después de tantas horas de práctica con Missis Johnson, Mister Barone y Mister Gatti, después del gasto de ropa y zapatos nuevos, después de que Mami

---

8 eggplant bush

Universal Access

Heritage Language Learners

Have students research and locate a Spanish-language play whose theme they find interesting. Have them design and rehearse a scene from this play. Remind them to consider characterization, costume, and movement. Encourage students to perform the scene for the class.

Advanced Learners

Invite students who enjoyed this selection to read the rest of Santiago's *Cuando era puertorriqueña.* If more than one student is interested, encourage them to form their own book club to discuss the book.

tuvo que coger el día libre sin paga para llevarme hasta Manhattan, después de todo eso, no había pasado la prueba y nunca jamás saldría de Brooklyn.

Epílogo: Un día de éstos

Diez años después de mi graduación de Performing Arts High School, volví a visitar la escuela. Estaba viviendo en Boston, una estudiante becada en la universidad Harvard. La señora alta y elegante de mi prueba se había convertido en mi mentora durante mis tres años en la escuela. Después de mi graduación, se había casado con el principal de la escuela.

—Me acuerdo del día de tu prueba —me dijo, su cara angular soñadora, sus labios jugando con una sonrisa que todavía parecía tener que controlar.

Me había olvidado de la niña flaca y trigueña[9] con el pelo enrizado, el vestido de lana y las manos inquietas. Pero ella no. Me dijo que el jurado tuvo que pedirme que esperara afuera para poderse reír, ya que les parecía tan cómico ver a aquella chica puertorriqueña de catorce años chapurreando[10] un soliloquio acerca de una suegra posesiva durante el cambio de siglo, las palabras incomprensibles porque pasaban tan rápido.

—Admiramos el valor necesario para pararte al frente de nosotras y hacer lo que hiciste.

—¿Quiere decir que me aceptaron en la escuela no porque tenía talento, sino porque era atrevida?

Nos reímos juntas.

---

9 dark haired 10 babbling

¿Comprendiste?

Con otro(a) estudiante, miren la tabla que completaron durante la lectura y revisen sus respuestas. Ahora contesten las siguientes preguntas:

1. ¿Crees que Esmeralda se preparó bien para su audición? ¿Por qué sí o por qué no?

2. ¿Cuál fue la verdadera razón por la que la aceptaron?

3. Muchos jóvenes inmigrantes se sienten atrapados *(trapped)* entre dos culturas. ¿Cómo creía Esmeralda que podía salir de esa situación?

4. Y tú, ¿tuviste alguna vez una experiencia similar a la de Esmeralda? ¿Sentiste alguna vez que no te identificabas con un grupo? Si es así, ¿cómo resolviste el problema?

5. En tu opinión, ¿cuál es el significado del título del libro? ¿Siente la autora que ahora, como estadounidense, ya no es puertorriqueña?

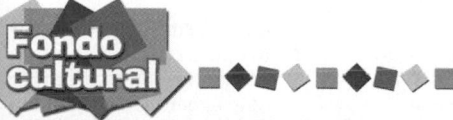

Esmeralda Santiago (1940–) nació en Puerto Rico y emigró con su familia a Nueva York. Fue a la escuela The High School for Performing Arts, de la cual salió con una beca *(scholarship)* para estudiar en Harvard. Dos de sus libros, *Cuando era puertorriqueña* y *Casi una mujer* (ambos escritos originalmente en inglés) son autobiográficos. Estos relatos describen el proceso de adaptación a otra cultura de una joven inmigrante. Aunque escribe desde el punto de vista de otra cultura, muchos de sus lectores se identifican con sus experiencias y sentimientos.

- Según tu opinión ¿cuál es una ventaja *(advantage)* de vivir entre dos culturas?

Esmeralda Santiago

ciento tres 103
Capítulo 2

Review Activities

Formas, géneros y materiales de arte/Profesiones artísticas: Have partners play **Diez preguntas.** One partner chooses a word or expression from these vocabulary categories. The other partner asks up to ten **sí/no** questions to try to determine what the word or expression is. Once the vocabulary item is determined or the asker is stumped, partners switch roles.

Para describir una obra de arte: Ask students to go back through the works of art shown in this chapter of the Student Edition or on the *Fine Arts Transparencies.* Have them take turns asking and answering questions about the works of art:

A: *¿Qué fue la fuente de inspiración para esta pintura?*

B: *Pienso que fue la alegría de estar en casa.*

En el escenario/Sobre la actuación: Ask pairs of students to make a labeled sketch or computer-generated representation of a theater with actors on stage and an audience. Have them present these to other pairs, pointing out the various parts and people of the theater. For the ***Sobre la actuación*** category, they can make comments about the actors and the audience: *Este señor se identifica con el galán.*

Otras palabras y expresiones: Students can use these words and expressions as they do the review activities for the other categories.

Sobre la música y la danza: Have pairs of students take turns giving each other TPR commands: *Toca la trompeta. Muéstrame unos pasos de tango. Canta … .*

Pretérito e imperfecto: You will need a small foam or paper cube. Write the numbers 1–4 on four of the sides. Sides 5–6 will not count. Sides 1–4 refer to the rules in the ***Pretérito e imperfecto*** chart.

Divide the class into two teams. Rotate through each team so that only one student speaks for the team at a time. However, the team "speaker" can consult with teammates for up to thirty seconds before responding.

Repaso del capítulo

Vocabulario y gramática

formas de arte

la cerámica	pottery
la escultura	sculpture
el mural	mural
la pintura	painting

géneros de arte

el autorretrato	self-portrait
la naturaleza muerta	still life
el retrato	portrait

materiales de arte

la paleta	palette
el pincel	brush

profesiones artísticas

el / la escritor(a)	writer
el / la escultor(a)	sculptor
el / la poeta	poet

para describir una obra de arte

abstracto, -a	abstract
expresar(se)	to express (oneself)
famoso, -a	famous
la figura	figure
el fondo	background
la fuente de inspiración	source of inspiration
la imagen	image
influir (i→y)	to influence
inspirar	to inspire
la obra de arte	work of art
el primer plano	foreground
representar	to represent
el sentimiento	feeling
el siglo	century
el tema	subject

en el escenario

el aplauso	applause
la entrada	ticket
el escenario	stage
el espectáculo	show
el micrófono	microphone

otras palabras y expresiones

a través de	through
mostrar(ue)	to show
parado, -a	to be standing
pararse	to stand up
parecerse (a)	to look, seem (like)
el poema	poem
realizar	to perform, to accomplish
la reseña	review
sentado, -a	to be seated
sonar (ue) (a)	to sound like
el taller	workshop
volverse (ue)	to become

sobre la música y la danza

clásico, -a	classical
el compás	rhythm
el conjunto	band
la danza	dance
la letra	lyrics
la melodía	melody
el movimiento	movement
el paso	step
el ritmo	rhythm
el tambor	drum
la trompeta	trumpet

sobre la actuación

actuar	to perform
destacar(se)	to stand out
el entusiasmo	enthusiasm
exagerar	to exaggerate
el gesto	gesture
identificarse con	to identify oneself with
la interpretación	interpretation
interpretar	to interpret

Universal Access

Students with Special Needs

Provide concrete objects or listening examples to assist visually impaired students in their review of vocabulary from the chapter. Examples might include actual art pieces, art materials, as well as audio recordings of musical or dramatic performances.

Advanced Learners

Have students use their creativity to make a video about a group of artists. Challenge them to incorporate all of the vocabulary on this page in their script. Remind them that there are many ways to do this. Some words might be seen on a sign in the background, others might occur in a letter someone reads, still others in a narration.

pretérito e imperfecto

Use the **preterite** to tell about an action that happened once and was completed. Ayer **escribí** un poema.	Use the **imperfect** to tell about habitual actions in the past. A menudo **cantábamos** juntos.	Use the **imperfect** to give background details, like time, date and weather. **Eran** las ocho y **hacía** mucho frío.	Use the **preterite** and the **imperfect** together when an action interrupts another that is taking place in the past. **Caminábamos** por el parque cuando **empezó** a llover.

estar + participio

The **past participle** is frequently used with the verb *estar*.

El teatro **está cerrado**.   El tren **está parado**.

In the following cases, the **past participle** is irregular.

hacer: **hecho**	cubrir: **cubierto**	morir: **muerto**	escribir: **escrito**
abrir: **abierto**	decir: **dicho**	poner: **puesto**	volver: **vuelto**
descubrir: **descubierto**	romper: **roto**	ver: **visto**	resolver: **resuelto**

ser y estar

Remember that *ser* and *estar* both mean **to be** in English, but have different meanings in Spanish.	Use *ser*: to describe permanent characteristics La actriz **es** bonita. to tell the date Mañana **es** miércoles. to indicate possession Los pinceles **son** de Luis.	Use *estar*: to describe temporary characteristics El escenario **está** oscuro. to indicate location **Están** sobre la mesa. to form the progressive tenses **Estoy** dibujando un retrato.	Some adjectives have different meanings depending on whether they are used with *ser* or *estar*. Los niños **están** aburridos. *(The children are bored.)* Los niños **son** aburridos. *(Children are boring.)*

verbos con significados diferentes en el pretérito y en el imperfecto

The following Spanish verbs have different meanings in the imperfect and the preterite tenses.

Yo **conocía** ese cuadro. *(I knew about that painting.)*	Él **conoció** a su maestro en Perú. *(He met his teacher in Perú.)*
No sabíamos que era tan tarde. *(We didn't know it was so late.)*	Nunca **supe** dónde estaba. *(I never found out where he/she was.)*
Ellos **querían** viajar hoy. *(They wanted to travel today.)*	Sofía **quiso ir,** pero perdió el avión. *(Sofía tried to go, but she missed the plane.)*
Antes **no podía** dibujar. *(Before, I couldn't draw.)*	Nunca **pude** dibujar. *(I was never able to draw.)*

● **Más práctica** . . . .
Practice Workbook
Organizer 2-13, 3-14

ciento cinco **105**
Capítulo 2

Enriching Your Teaching

Teacher-to-Teacher

After students review the vocabulary on the previous page, organize a "vocabulary bee." Have all students stand in a circle around the room. Give a student one item from the list. He or she has ten seconds to come up with a Spanish definition or explanation of the vocabulary or use it correctly in a sentence that clearly shows an understanding of its meaning. Students who make a mistake or run out of time sit down. The last student standing is the winner of the bee.

(Cont'd):
Team A rolls the cube and has thirty seconds to come up with a sentence that follows the rule that was rolled. If they do, they earn a point. If their sentence is incorrect or time runs out, play passes to Team B. The team with the best score out of 21 wins.

Estar + participio: Have students work in pairs. Each partner writes down five sentences about actions completed in the past tense: *Carla abrió la ventana.* They then take turns reading one sentence at a time to each other. The listener comes up with a sentence based on the one he or she hears, that uses *estar + participio: La ventana está abierta.*

Ser y estar: Play a game that is set up the same way as the one for *Pretérito e imperfecto.* For rule number 4 in the chart, allow teams double the time (one minute) to come up with two sentences that contrast two different meanings of an adjective based on its use with *ser* and *estar.* Allow them to consult the *Gramática* on p. 88.

Verbos con significados diferentes en el pretérito y en el imperfecto: Have students write their own exercises modeled after *Actividad* 36 on p. 90. Their exercises need not be in story form; a numbered list of five sentences is fine. Have them exchange quizzes, take each other's quizzes, and check and discuss answers.

Portfolio

Invite students to review the activities they completed in this chapter, including written reports, visuals, tapes of oral presentations, or other projects. Have them select one or two items that they feel best demonstrate their achievements in Spanish. Include these products in students' portfolios. Have them include this with the Chapter Checklist and Self-Assessment Worksheet.

Additional Resources

- Audio Program: CD Cap. 2, Track 24
- Resource Book: Cap. 2, Clip Art
- Assessment Program: Chapter Checklist and Self-Assessment Worksheet

Performance Tasks

Standards: 1.1, 1.2, 1.3, 3.1

Resources: Audio Program: CD Cap. 2, Track 25; Resource Book: Cap. 2, Audio Script; Practice Answers on Transparencies

1. Vocabulario

Suggestions: Encourage students to review the vocabulary from the *A primera vista* sections on pp. 68–71 and 82–85 before they complete the activity.

Answers:

1.	b	5.	b
2.	c	6.	c
3.	c	7.	c
4.	d	8.	a

2. Gramática

Suggestions: Remind students of the main points of the grammar presentations in *Capítulo 2:*

• uses of the preterite and the imperfect tenses
• constructions with **estar** + past participle
• uses of **ser** vs. **estar**
• adjectives that have different meanings when used in conjunction with the imperfect or the preterite tense

Answers:

1.	d	5.	a
2.	a	6.	a
3.	d	7.	d
4.	a	8.	c

To prepare for the test, check to see if you . . .
• know the new vocabulary and grammar
• can perform the tasks on pp. 106 and 107

Preparación para el examen

1 Vocabulario Escribe la letra de la palabra o expresión que mejor complete cada frase. Escribe tus respuestas en una hoja aparte.

1. El surrealismo fue _____ de inspiración de los pintores Miró y Dalí.
   a. el espectáculo   c. la melodía
   b. la fuente   d. la reseña

2. El actor principal _____ por su actuación y entusiasmo.
   a. se interpretó   c. se destacó
   b. se volvió   d. se inspiró

3. Si quieres bailar salsa, necesitas aprender _____ .
   a. la letra   c. los pasos
   b. los gestos   d. la actuación

4. La familia es _____ principal de muchos cuadros de Botero.
   a. el estilo   c. la forma
   b. el fondo   d. el tema

5. Picasso fue un pintor del _____ XX.
   a. estilo   c. año
   b. siglo   d. ritmo

6. Cuando termina una obra se oye _____ .
   a. un paso   c. un aplauso
   b. el micrófono   d. la paleta

7. La paleta de ese pintor _____ colores vivos como el rojo y el anaranjado.
   a. actúa   c. muestra
   b. interpreta   d. realiza

8. Los actores no dijeron nada pero se expresaron muy bien con _____ exagerados.
   a. gestos   c. escenarios
   b. poemas   d. compases

2 Gramática Escribe la letra de la palabra o expresión que mejor complete cada frase. Escribe tus respuestas en una hoja aparte.

1. La semana pasada _____ en una clase de cerámica.
   a. me inscribo   c. me inscribe
   b. me inscribía   d. me inscribí

2. No te van a oír bien porque el micrófono está _____ .
   a. roto   c. rompiendo
   b. rotas   d. romper

3. El museo estaba _____ todos los sábados.
   a. abrí   c. abiertos
   b. abriendo   d. abierto

4. Marta siempre _____ nerviosa antes de un ensayo.
   a. está   c. es
   b. están   d. era

5. Ayer, a causa de los truenos, yo no _____ dormir en toda la noche.
   a. pude   c. puedo
   b. podía   d. pudo

6. ¿Dónde _____ a tu mejor amigo?
   a. conociste   c. conocías
   b. conoces   d. conocieron

7. Nos perdimos porque no _____ bien la ciudad.
   a. conocemos   c. conocías
   b. conocimos   d. conocíamos

8. Yo _____ esta mañana que la función tuvo mucho éxito.
   a. sabía   c. supe
   b. sabe   d. saben

Universal Access

Heritage Language Learners

Have students create a brochure for their own "virtual museum." Encourage them to select artists and works from the chapter, from their own areas of interest, or from their heritage country. Remind students to tailor the language of their descriptions to the appropriate audience.

Students with Learning Difficulties

In reviewing the vocabulary and grammar of the chapter, use gestures and facial expressions to support students in their choice of the correct answer. Use TPR to support meaning of the vocabulary choices.

Preparación para el examen

Go Online
PHSchool.com

For: Test preparation
Visit: www.phschool.com
Web Code: jed-0211

En el examen vas a . . .	Éstas son las tareas de práctica que te pueden ser útiles para el examen . . .	Si necesitas repasar . . .
3 Escuchar Escuchar y comprender la descripción de un cuadro	El guía de un museo está describiendo uno de los cuadros de la galería de arte moderno. (a) ¿Qué tipo de pintura describe? (b) ¿Quién es el pintor? (c) ¿Qué se ve en primer plano? (d) ¿Qué se ve al fondo? (e) ¿Cómo son los colores?	**pp. 68–69** *A primera vista 1* **p. 73** Actividades 8–9 **p. 74** Actividad 11 **p. 75** Actividades 12, 13
4 Hablar Hablar de las actividades que tienen lugar en una escuela de arte	Un nuevo estudiante visita por primera vez tu escuela de arte. Tu tarea es mostrarle los talleres de la escuela y explicarle lo que pasa en cada clase. Incluye en tu descripción (a) las clases que ofrecen, (b) los materiales que necesitan para cada clase, (c) las actividades que hacen en cada clase, (d) las obras que los estudiantes realizan en cada clase.	**p. 68** *A primera vista 1* **p. 72** Actividad 7
5 Leer Leer y comprender las notas de un disco compacto	Lee la reseña sobre un disco compacto y di (a) ¿cuál es el tipo de música del disco compacto?, (b) ¿qué cosas le gustaron al crítico?, (c) ¿qué no le gustó?, (d) ¿qué cree que puede ser mejor? *La letra de las canciones del conjunto Sol y salsa suena a poesía. Pero creo que la interpretación puede ser mejor. El ritmo que da el tambor se destaca del de la trompeta y va bien con todo el conjunto. Me gustó mucho la melodía de la primera canción. Cuando tocan la trompeta en algunas canciones, creo que exageran. Se ve que el conjunto se inspiró mucho al tocar la música.*	**pp. 82–85** *A primera vista 2* **p. 86** Actividad 29 **p. 87** Actividad 31 **pp. 92–93** Actividades 38–39
6 Escribir Escribir una reseña sobre una obra de teatro que presentaron en tu escuela	Trabajas como reportero(a) para el periódico de la escuela y tienes que escribir una reseña sobre una obra de teatro. Incluye (a) el nombre de la obra, (b) los actores principales, (c) una breve descripción del argumento, (d) la actuación de los protagonistas.	**pp. 84–85** *A primera vista 2* **p. 89** Actividad 34 **pp. 92–93** Actividades 38–39
7 Pensar Demostrar cómo las artes pueden expresar las perspectivas y actitudes del artista	Piensa en las obras de Goya, Dalí o Botero. ¿Cómo usaron su arte para expresar sus actitudes y sus perspectivas sobre lo que pasaba en sus vidas? ¿De qué manera expresan los jóvenes de hoy sus actitudes por el arte?	**pp. 86–87** Actividades 29–31 **p. 89** Actividad 35 **pp. 94–95** *Puente a la cultura*

ciento siete   **107**
Capítulo 2

Enriching Your Teaching

Teacher-to-Teacher

Learning assessment logs are like journal entries that list and describe personal learning high and low spots for a given period of time, such as a chapter. They can take a variety of forms: a paragraph, a list, a T-chart showing pros and cons. Having your students write a learning assessment log at the end of each chapter (they can do them in Spanish) develops writing skills, helps them assess their own performance, and provides you with additional insight for assessment. Consider making learning assessment logs a regular feature of students' portfolios.

Review   2

3. Escuchar

Suggestions: Use the *Audio CD* or read from the script.

Answers:
a. un paisaje
b. Pablo Picasso
c. una casa y árboles
d. el mar Mediterráneo
e. los colores no son vivos

4. Hablar

Suggestions: Point out that this activity involves pair work. One partner should act as the new student, asking questions and making comments. The other should act as the student showing him or her around. The result is a dialogue.

Answers will vary.

5. Leer

Suggestions: Tell students to refer to pp. 68–71 and 82–85 if they have questions about vocabulary in the music review.

Answers:
a. salsa
b. el ritmo del tambor y la melodía de la primera canción
c. la trompeta en algunas canciones
d. la interpretación

6. Escribir

Suggestions: Encourage students to organize their thoughts in a list like the one on p. 93 before writing their reviews.

Answers will vary.

7. Pensar

Suggestions: Encourage students to put their thoughts down using a a T-chart. They can label the columns *Goya, Dalí, Botero* and *artistas jóvenes.*

Answers will vary.

 Assessment
• Examen del capítulo: 2
• Audio Program: CD 12, Cap. 2, Track 3
• Assessment Program: *RPH*

Alternative Assessment
• ExamView Test Bank CD-ROM
• Resource Book: Cap. 2, Situation Cards
• Resource Book: Cap. 2, Communicative Activity BLM

¿Qué haces para estar en forma?

CHAPTER OVERVIEW

¿Qué haces para estar en forma?
Vocabulary
- symptoms and remedies
- health food, nutrition, and fitness

Grammar
- affirmative and negative *tú* commands
- commands with *Ud.* and *Uds.*
- subjunctive of regular, irregular and stem-changing verbs

Cultural Perspectives:
- art of Rufino Tamayo
- medicinal plants in Latin America
- eating habits of young Spaniards
- physical education in Spain
- ancient sports in Mexico and Central America
- Spanish and Latin American teen magazines
- habits related to food and fitness, sports in Ancient American Civilizations.

Chapter Project

Buenos hábitos

Overview: Students create a poster with a complete health program that consists of three parts: 1. a healthy diet, 2. a physical exercise routine, and 3. the selection of a song in Spanish to accompany their routine. Posters should state the name of the artist and the country of origin. Students then give an oral presentation of their complete program to the class.

Materials: Poster board, markers, photos, glue, tape recorder, and a cassette or CD.

Sequence:

STEP 1. Review sections of the chapter and instructions, so students know what is expected of them. Hand out the "Chapter 3 Project Instructions and Rubric" from the *Teacher's Resource Book.*

STEP 2. Students submit a draft of the appropriate diet and matching exercises. Return the drafts with your suggestions. For vocabulary and grammar practice, ask partners to present their drafts to each other.

STEP 3. Students do a layout on poster board, leaving room for photos or drawings and descriptions.

STEP 4. Students submit completed posters.

STEP 5. Students present their posters to the class, play the accompanying song and explain why their program promotes health.

Options:
1. Students can modify and adapt their exercise programs for body building (after appropriate research).
2. Students feature only one aspect of the health program.

Assessment:
Here is a detailed rubric for assessing this project.
Chapter 3 Project: *Buenos hábitos*

RUBRIC	Score 1	Score 2	Score 3
Your evidence of planning	You have no written draft or poster layout.	Either your draft or your layout is missing.	You show evidence of corrected draft and layout.
Your use of illustrations	You have no music or song.	You are missing data about the artist.	You include music and artist's data.
Your presentation	Your presentation is weak.	Your diet and exercise program don't complement each other.	You present a coordinated program.

Bulletin Boards

Pirámide de alimentos

Ask students to cut out or draw the appropriate food groups to include in a food pyramid that they will create on the bulletin board. At the bottom of the pyramid they will have: **pan, cereales, arroz, pasta.** Above that category, they will place **frutas** on the left side and **vegetales** on the right. Above that **leche, yogur, quesos** on the left side, and **carne, pollo, pescado, huevos, guisantes** on the right side. On top of the pyramid, they will place **grasas, aceites, dulces.** This will be a visual guide of a healthy and complete diet.

Bibliography

Cruz Smith, Martin. *Aztec Herbal: The Classic Codex of 1552.* Mineola, N.Y.: Dover Publications, Inc, 2000. This sixteenth century Aztec codex was the first herbal and medical text compiled in the New World. It contains remedies for a variety of common aliments.

Del Conde, Teresa, ed. *Tamayo.* Boston, and N.Y.: Little, Brown and Company, 2000. An overview of the painter's life and analysis of his work.

Parnell, Helga. *Cooking the South American Way: Revised and Expanded to Include New Low-fat and Vegetarian Recipes.* Minneapolis: Lerner Publications, 2002. Recipes and descriptions of the land, people, and food of South America.

Sanjur, Diva. *Hispanic Foodways, Nutrition and Health.* New Jersey: Prentice Hall, 1994. A study of the links between disease and nutritional practices among the Hispanic population.

Whittington, E. Michael, ed. *The Sport of Life and Death: The Mesoamerican Ballgame.* London, England: Thames and Hudson, 2001. The world's first team sports were invented in Mexico by the Olmec, circa 1800 B.C. Played with balls made from the indigenous rubber plants, the games shared some aspects of basketball, football, and soccer and were a vital part of Mesoamerican society.

Hands-on Culture

Recipe: *Yogur de frutas helado*

This Mexican recipe provides a simple and healthy way to enjoy a nutritious dessert.

Ingredients:

2 cups of lowfat yogurt (vanilla or other flavors)

2 pears or apples

4 tablespoons of honey

4 small serving bowls

Peel and cut the fruit into small cubes. Discard the seeds.

Fill each container halfway with yogurt.

Add the fruit to each container.

Add a tablespoon of honey.

Mix the contents in each container.

Place the bowls in the refrigerator.

Game

Síntomas y remedios

Play this game in *Capítulo* 3, after students have learned vocabulary related to symptoms and remedies.

Players: Entire class

Materials: index cards, pen, a show box

Rules:

1. Students write names of symptoms on index cards and place them in a shoe box.

2. Shake the box to mix up the index cards. Then call on a volunteer to come to the front of the class. The volunteer draws an index card from the box and acts out the symptom.

3. Students take turns guessing the correct symptom. Once they guess the symptom they must provide a remedy or solution to alleviate it.
   Student 1: ¿Tienes gripe?
   Student 2: Sí.
   Student 1: Entonces debes tomar antibióticos.

4. The student that guesses the symptom and provides the correct remedy becomes the new volunteer. Play continues until every student has had a chance to ask one or two questions.

Variation: Instead of physical ailments, students will act out emotional states such as *"estoy en la luna," "me caigo de sueño,"* and so on.

Internet Search

Use the keywords to find more information.

Keywords:

gimnasia, alimentos, plantas medicinales, deportes, jugos, Día Mundial de la Salud

A ver si recuerdas

RECYCLE

Vocabulary
- Fruits and vegetables
- Descriptions
- Breakfast, lunch, and dinner

Grammar
- Direct object pronouns
- Indirect object pronouns

Chapter Overview

A primera vista 1	Manos a la obra 1	A primera vista 2	Manos a la obra 2
INPUT	**PRACTICE**	**INPUT**	**PRACTICE**

A primera vista 1 — INPUT

Objectives
- Talk about symptoms and remedies
- Give advice about health, food, and nutrition

Vocabulary
- Symptoms and remedies
- Health, food, and nutrition

Grammar
- Affirmative commands with *tú*
- Affirmative and negative commands with *Ud.* and *Uds.*

Culture
- Rufino Tamayo

Manos a la obra 1 — PRACTICE

Objectives
- Talk about symptoms and remedies
- Discuss eating habits

Vocabulary
- Practice new vocabulary

Grammar
- Affirmative commands with *tú*
- Affirmative and negative commands with *Ud.* and *Uds.*

Culture
- Healing plants in Latin America
- Eating habits of Spanish teenagers

A primera vista 2 — INPUT

Objectives
- Explain cultural perspectives about health, physical fitness, and nutrition
- Give advice

Vocabulary
- Physical fitness equipment, and exercises
- Giving advice

Grammar
- Subjunctive: regular and stem-changing verbs
- Subjunctive: irregular verbs

Culture
- World Health Day

Manos a la obra 2 — PRACTICE

Objectives
- Talk about fitness equipment
- Talk about different exercises to stay fit

Vocabulary
- Practice new vocabulary

Grammar
- Subjunctive: regular and stem-changing verbs
- Subjunctive: irregular verbs

Culture
- Physical education in Spain

¡Adelante!

APPLICATION

Objectives
- Read about an ancient team sport from Mexico and Central America
- Use different sources to understand a non-fiction article
- Summarize the information in a non-fiction article

Vocabulary
- Application

Grammar
- Application

Culture
- Magazines for teenagers
- Changing your eating habits

Repaso del capítulo

REVIEW

Objectives
- Prepare for the chapter test
- Perform the tasks on pp. 152 and 153

Vocabulary
- Review

Grammar
- Review

BEYOND THE CLASSROOM

Countries
- Mexico
- Spain

El español en el mundo del trabajo
- A bilingual counselor

Internet
- Vocabulary activities
- Grammar activities
- Internet links
- Self-tests

LEARNER SUPPORT

Strategies
- Using your prior knowledge
- Projecting your voice
- Persuasive writing
- Cause and effect

Recycling
- Prononciation of *c* after *a*, *o,* and *u*

En voz alta
- *Que te vaya bonito*

Ampliación del lenguaje
- Word families

Conexiones
- Science: teenager eating habits

Print Components

TEACHER

Teacher's Resource Book
• Chapter Table of Contents
• School-to-Home Connection
• Chapter Resource Checklist
• Input Script
• Audio Script
• Video Script
• Communicative Activities
• Situation Cards
• GramActiva Blackline Masters
• Graphic Organizers
• Answer Keys:
  Practice Workbook
  Writing, Audio & Video Workbook

Realidades para hispanohablantes
Teacher Edition

STUDENT

Practice Workbook
• Vocabulary: 3-1 – 3-4, 3-8 – 3-9
• Grammar: 3-5 – 3-7, 3-10 – 3-12
• Organizer: 3-13 – 3-14

Writing, Audio & Video Workbook
• Audio: 1–5
• Writing: 6–13
• Video: 14–17

Reading and Writing for Success
• Chapter 3, Test 30

Realidades para hispanohablantes

Transparencies

Vocabulary and Grammar Transparencies
• Vocabulary: 66–72, 76–79
• Grammar: 73–75, 80–82
• ¿Qué me cuentas?: 83

Practice Answers on Transparencies
• Cap. 3

Fine Art Transparencies
• Transparencies
• Teacher's Guide

Assessment

Assessment Program
• Pruebas:
  – Comprensión del vocabulario 1: 3-1
  – Aplicación del vocabulario 1: 3-2
  – Mandatos afirmativos con *tú*: 3-3
  – Mandatos negativos con *tú*: 3-4
  – Mandatos afirmativos y negativos con *Ud.* y *Uds.*: 3-5
  – Comprensión del vocabulario 2: 3-6
  – Aplicación del vocabulario 2: 3-7
  – El subjuntivo: Verbos regulares: 3-8
  – El subjuntivo: Verbos irregulares: 3-9
  – El subjuntivo: Verbos con cambio de raíz: 3-10
• Exámenes del capítulo
• Rubrics

Alternative Assessment
• ExamView Test Bank CD-ROM
• MindPoint Quiz Show CD-ROM
• Internet Self-test
• Situation Cards
• Communicative Activity

Assessment Program: *Realidades para hispanohablantes*

Technology

TeacherExpress™ CD-ROM
• Lesson Planner
• Teacher Resources
• Clip Art

Video Program VHS and DVD

Audio Program CDs
• A primera vista 1 y 2: Vocabulario y gramática en contexto
• Audio Activities
• ¿Qué me cuentas?
• Repaso
• Examen del capítulo: Escuchar

	Warm-up / Assess	Preview Present / Practice Communicate	Wrap-up / Homework Options
DAY 1	**Warm-up (10 min.)** • Return Examen del capítulo: Capítulo 2	**Repaso (35 min.)** • A ver si recuerdas. . .	**Wrap-up and Homework Options (5 min.)** • Practice Workbook 3-1, 3-2 • Go Online
DAY 2	**Warm-up (10 min.)** • Homework check	**Chapter Opener (10 min.)** • Objectives　• Fondo cultural **A primera vista 1 (25 min.)** • Presentation: Vocabulario y gramática en contexto • Actividades 1, 2	**Wrap-up and Homework Options (5 min.)** • Go Online • Clip Art Vocabulary
DAY 3	**Warm-up (10 min.)** • Homework check	**A primera vista 1 (35 min.)** • Presentation: La alimentación de los jóvenes • Actividades 3, 5	**Wrap-up and Homework Options (5 min.)** • Practice Workbook 3-3, 3-4　• Prueba 3-1: Vocabulary • Manos a la obra 1: Actividad 6　　recognition • Go Online
DAY 4	**Warm-up (10 min.)** • Actividad 4 • Homework check ✔**Assessment (10 min.)** • Prueba 3-1: Vocabulary recognition	**Manos a la obra 1 (25 min.)** • Actividades 7, 8, 9, 10 • Ampliación del lenguaje	**Wrap-up and Homework Options (5 min.)** • Writing Activities • Prueba 3-2: Vocabulary production
DAY 5	**Warm-up (10 min.)** • Homework check ✔**Assessment (10 min.)** • Prueba 3-2: Vocabulary production	**Manos a la obra 1 (25 min.)** • Fondo cultural　　　• Actividades 11, 12 • Presentation: Mandatos　• Writing Activity 　afirmativos con tú	**Wrap-up and Homework Options (5 min.)** • Practice Workbook 3-5 • Go Online • Prueba 3-3: Presentation: Mandatos afirmativos con tú
DAY 6	**Warm-up (10 min.)** • Homework check ✔**Assessment (10 min.)** • Prueba 3-3: Mandatos afirmativos con tú	**Manos a la obra 1 (25 min.)** • Presentation: Mandatos negativos con tú • Actividades 13, 14 • Communicative Activity	**Wrap-up and Homework Options (5 min.)** • Practice Workbook 3-6 • Go Online • Prueba 3-4: Mandatos negativos con tú
DAY 7	**Warm-up (10 min.)** • Writing Activity • Homework check ✔**Assessment (10 min.)** • Prueba 3-4: Mandatos negativos con tú	**Manos a la obra 1 (25 min.)** • Presentation: Mandatos afirmativos y negativos con Ud. y Uds. • Actividades 15, 16, 17, 20 • Writing Activity	**Wrap-up and Homework Options (5 min.)** • Practice Workbook 3-7 • Actividad 18 • Go Online • Prueba 3-5: Mandatos afirmativos y negativos con Ud. y Uds.
DAY 8	**Warm-up (10 min.)** • Actividad 19 • Homework check ✔**Assessment (10 min.)** • Prueba 3-5: Mandatos afirmitivos y negativos con Ud. y Uds.	**A primera vista 2 (25 min.)** • Presentation: Vocabulario y gramática en contexto • Actividades 21, 22, 23	**Wrap-up and Homework Options (5 min.)** • Clip Art Vocabulary • Examen: Vocabulario y gramática 1
DAY 9	**Warm-up (10 min.)** • Clip Art Vocabulary ✔**Assessment (25 min.)** • Examen: Vocabulario y gramática 1	**A primera vista 2 (10 min.)** • Presentation: ¿Qué me aconsejas?　• Presentation: Día • Actividad 24　　　　　　　　　Mundial de la Salud	**Wrap-up and Homework Options (5 min.)** • Practice Workbook 3-8, 3-9　• Prueba 3-6: Vocabulary • Go Online　　　　　　　　　recognition
DAY 10	**Warm-up (10 min.)** • Homework check • Actividades 25, 26 ✔**Assessment (10 min.)** • Prueba 3-6: Vocabulary recognition	**Manos a la obra 2 (25 min.)** • Actividades 27, 28, 29 • Fondo cultural • Audio and Video Activities	**Wrap-up and Homework Options (5 min.)** • Writing Activities • Prueba 3-7: Vocabulary production

	Warm-up / Assess	Preview Present / Practice Communicate	Wrap-up / Homework Options
DAY 11	**Warm-up (10 min.)** • Writing Activity • Homework check ✔**Assessment (10 min.)** • Prueba 3-7: Vocabulary production	**Manos a la obra 2 (25 min.)** • Presentation: El subjuntivo: Verbos regulares • Actividades 30, 31, 32 • El español en el mundo del trabajo	**Wrap-up and Homework Options (5 min.)** • Practice Workbook 3-10 • Go Online • Prueba 3-8: El subjuntivo: Verbos regulares
DAY 12	**Warm-up (10 min.)** • Actividad 33 • Homework check ✔**Assessment (10 min.)** • Prueba 3-8: El subjuntivo: Verbos regulares	**Manos a la obra 2 (25 min.)** • Presentation: El subjuntivo: Verbos irregulares • Actividades 34, 35, 37 • Presentation: El subjuntivo: Verbos con cambio de raíz • Actividad 39	**Wrap-up and Homework Options (5 min.)** • Actividad 36 • Practice Workbook 3-11, 3-12 • Go Online • Pruebas 3-9, 3-10
DAY 13	**Warm-up (10 min.)** • Actividad 38 • Homework check ✔**Assessment (15 min.)** • Pruebas 3-9, 3-10	**Manos a la obra 2 (20 min.)** • Actividad 40 • En voz alta • Communicative Activity	**Wrap-up and Homework Options (5 min.)** • Go Online • Examen: Vocabulario y gramática 2
DAY 14	**Warm-up (5 min.)** • Writing Activity ✔**Assessment (30 min.)** • Examen: Vocabulario y gramática 2	**¡Adelante! (10 min.)** • Presentación oral: Step 1	**Wrap-up and Homework Options (5 min.)** • Presentación oral: Step 2
DAY 15	**Warm-up (10 min.)** • Presentación oral: Step 2	**¡Adelante! (35 min.)** • Presentación oral: Step 3	**Wrap-up and Homework Options (5 min.)** • Un juego muy antiguo • Usa tus conocimientos • ¿Comprendiste? • Go Online
DAY 16	**Warm-up (15 min.)** • Un juego muy antiguo: ¿Comprendiste? • Homework check	**¡Adelante! (30 min.)** • ¿Qué me cuentas? 1, 2, 3 • View Video • Video Activities 1, 2, 3	**Wrap-up and Homework Options (5 min.)** • Presentación escrita: Steps 1, 2
DAY 17	**Warm-up (10 min.)** • Video Activity 4	**¡Adelante! (15 min.)** • Presentación escrita: Step 3 **Repaso (20 min.)** • Preparación para el examen: Actividades 3, 4 • MindPoint Quiz Show	**Wrap-up and Homework Options (5 min.)** • Presentación escrita: Step 4 • Fondo cultural
DAY 18	**Warm-up (10 min.)** • Homework check	**¡Adelante! (35 min.)** • Lectura • Interacción con la lectura	**Wrap-up and Homework Options (5 min.)** • Practice Workbook: Organizer 3-13, 3-14 • Go Online: Self-test
DAY 19	**Warm-up (20 min.)** • Preparación para el examen: Actividades 1, 2 • Homework check	**Repaso (25 min.)** • Preparación para el examen: Actividades 5, 6, 7 • MindPoint Quiz Show • Other review	**Wrap-up and Homework Options (5 min.)** • Examen del capítulo
DAY 20	**Warm-up (5 min.)** • Answer questions ✔**Assessment (44 min.)** • Examen del capítulo		**Wrap-up and Homework Options (1 min.)** • A ver si recuerdas: Capítulo 4 • Actividades 1-4, 6

	Warm-up / Assess	Preview Present / Practice Communicate	Wrap-up / Homework Options
DAY 1	**Warm-up (35 min.)** • Return Examen del capítulo: Capítulo 2 • A ver si recuerdas. . . • Actividad 7 • Homework check	**Chapter Opener (10 min.)** • Objectives • Fondo cultural **A primera vista 1 (30 min.)** • Presentación: Vocabulario y gramática en contexto • Actividades 1, 2 • Presentation: La alimentación de los jóvenes • Actividades 3, 4, 5 **Manos a la obra 1 (10 min.)** • Actividades 7, 8	**Wrap-up and Homework Options (5 min.)** • Practice Workbook 3-3, 3-4 • Go Online • Clip Art Vocabulary • Prueba 3-1: Vocabulary recognition
DAY 2	**Warm-up (15 min.)** • Actividad 6 • Homework check **✔Assessment (10 min.)** • Prueba 3-1: Vocabulary recognition	**Manos a la obra 1 (60 min.)** • Actividades 9, 10 • Ampliación del lenguaje • Fondo cultural • Writing or Audio Activities • Communicative Activity	**Wrap-up and Homework Options (5 min.)** • Go Online • Writing Activities • Prueba 3-2: Vocabulary production
DAY 3	**Warm-up (10 min.)** • Writing Activity • Homework check **✔Assessment (10 min.)** • Prueba 3-2: Vocabulary production	**Manos a la obra 1 (65 min.)** • Presentation: Mandatos afirmativos con *tú* • Actividades 11, 12 • Presentation: Mandatos negativos con *tú* • Actividades 13, 14 • Writing Activities	**Wrap-up and Homework Options (5 min.)** • Practice Workbook 3-5, 3-6 • Go Online • Pruebas 3-3, 3-4: Mandatos afirmativos con *tú*, mandatos negativos con *tú*
DAY 4	**Warm-up (10 min.)** • Homework check **✔Assessment (20 min.)** • Pruebas 3-3, 3-4: Mandatos afirmativos con *tú*, mandatos negativos con *tú*	**Manos a la obra 1 (35 min.)** • Presentation: Mandatos afirmativos y negativos con *Ud.* y *Uds.* • Actividades 15, 16, 17, 20 • Communicative Activity **A primera vista 2 (20 min.)** • Presentation: Vocabulario y gramática en contexto • Actividades 21, 22, 23	**Wrap-up and Homework Options (5 min.)** • Actividades 18, 19 • Practice Workbook 3-7 • Go Online • Prueba 3-5: Mandatos afirmativos y negativos con *Ud.* y *Uds.* • Examen: Vocabulario y gramática 1
DAY 5	**Warm-up (10 min.)** • Homework check **✔Assessment Options (40 min.)** • Prueba 3-5: Mandatos afirmativos y negativos con *Ud.* y *Uds.* Examen: Vocabulario y gramática 1	**A primera vista 2 (25 min.)** • Presentation: ¿Qué me aconsejas? • Actividades 24, 25, 26 **Manos a la obra 2 (10 min.)** • Actividad 29 • Fondo cultural	**Wrap-up and Homework Options (5 min.)** • Practice Workbook 3-8, 3-9 • Go Online • Prueba 3-6: Vocabulary recognition

	Warm-up / Assess	Preview Present / Practice Communicate	Wrap-up / Homework Options
DAY 6	**Warm-up (15 min.)** • Actividad 28 • Homework check ✔**Assessment (10 min.)** • Prueba 3-6: Vocabulary recognition	**Manos a la obra 2 (60 min.)** • Actividad 27 • Presentation: El subjuntivo: Verbos regulares • Actividades 30, 31, 32 • El español en el mundo del trabajo	**Wrap-up and Homework Options (5 min.)** • Practice Workbook 3-10 • Go Online • Pruebas 3-7, 3-8: Vocabulary production, El subjuntivo: Verbos regulares
DAY 7	**Warm-up (10 min.)** • Actividad 33 • Homework check ✔**Assessment (20 min.)** • Pruebas 3-7, 3-8: Vocabulary production, El subjuntivo: Verbos regulares	**Manos a la obra 2 (40 min.)** • Presentation: Subjuntivo: Verbos irregulares • Presentation: Subjuntivo: Verbos con cambio de raíz • Actividades 34, 35, 37 • Actividad 38 **¡Adelante! (15 min.)** • Presentación oral: Steps 1, 2	**Wrap-up and Homework Options (5 min.)** • Presentación oral: Step 2 • Go Online
DAY 8	**Warm-up (15 min.)** • Actividad 36 • Homework check ✔**Assessment (40 min.)** • Presentación oral: Step 3	**Manos a la obra 2 (30 min.)** • En voz alta • Actividades 39, 40 • Communicative Activity	**Wrap-up and Homework Options (5 min.)** • Practice Workbook 3-11, 3-12 • Go Online • Prueba 3-9: El Subjuntivo: Verbos irregulares • Prueba 3-10: El Subjuntivo: Verbos con cambio de raíz • Examen: Vocabulario y gramática 2
DAY 9	**Warm-up (10 min.)** • Homework check ✔**Assessment Options (30 min.)** • Prueba 3-9: El Subjuntivo: Verbos irregulares • Prueba 3-10: El Subjuntivo: Verbos con cambio de raíz • Examen: Vocabulario y gramática 2	**¡Adelante! (45 min.)** • Presentation: Un juego muy antiguo • ¿Comprendiste? • Usa tus conocimientos • ¿Qué me cuentas? 1, 2, 3 • Video • Video Activities • Presentación escrita: Step 1	**Wrap-up and Homework Options (5 min.)** • Presentación escrita: Step 2 • Go Online • Preparación para el examen: Actividades 1, 2
DAY 10	**Warm-up (20 min.)** • Presentación escrita: Step 3 • Homework check	**¡Adelante! (35 min.)** • Lectura • Interacción con la lectura • Fondo cultural **Repaso (30 min.)** • Preparación para el examen: Actividades 3, 4, 6 • MindPoint Quiz Show	**Wrap-up and Homework Options (5 min.)** • Presentación escrita: Step 4 • Practice Workbook: Organizer 3-13, 3-14 • Go Online: Self-test • Preparación para el examen: Actividades 5, 7 • Examen del capítulo
DAY 11	**Warm-up (15 min.)** • Homework check ✔**Assessment (45 min.)** • Examen del capítulo	**Theme Game (15 min.)** **A ver si recuerdas – Capítulo 4 (10 min.)** • Presentation: Vocabulario • Presentation: Gramática	**Wrap-up and Homework Options (5 min.)** • A ver si recuerdas – Capítulo 4 • Actividades 1-6 • Go Online • Practice Workbook 4-1, 4-2

A ver si recuerdas...

Vocabulario

Vocabulario

Presentation

Standards: 1.1, 1.2

Resources: Voc. & Gram. Transparencies: 66

Suggestions: Give students a few minutes to "create" a meal comprised of at least five of the foods from the lists. Then have them take turns describing and commenting on their "creations": *Es mi desayuno de sábado. Es muy sabroso. Tiene dos salchichas de cerdo, dos huevos fritos y pan tostado sin mantequilla. A veces como unas papas fritas. Para beber, hay café con leche y jugo de naranja.*

Actividad 1

Standards: 1.1, 1.3

Resources: Voc. & Gram. Transparencies: 2 (Venn diagram)

Focus: Practicing review vocabulary

Suggestions: Some students may ask for suggestions on recipes they can use for step 1. Suggest Mexican recipes with which many students will be familiar, such as **huevos rancheros, guacamole,** and **tacos.**

Answers will vary.

Actividad 2

Standards: 1.1

Focus: Practicing review vocabulary

Suggestions: Encourage students to use words from the **descripciones** category when talking about foods they like and dislike.

Answers will vary.

las frutas y las verduras

el aguacate
el ajo
la cebolla
las cerezas
el durazno
la ensalada
las fresas
los frijoles
los guisantes
las judías verdes
la lechuga
el maíz
el melón
la papa
la piña
la sandía
la sopa de verduras
el tomate
las uvas
la zanahoria

descripciones

bueno, -a / malo, -a para la salud
caliente
congelado, -a
delicioso, -a
dulce
enlatado, -a
fresco, -a
frito, -a
grasoso, -a
horrible
picante
¡Qué asco!
rico, -a
sabroso, -a

actividades

añadir
comer
cortar
probar (ue)
servir (i)

para el desayuno

el azúcar
el cereal
desayunar
el huevo
el pan con mantequilla
el pan tostado
las salchichas
el tocino
el yogur

para el almuerzo o la cena

almorzar (ue)
el arroz
el bistec
el camarón
la carne de res
cenar
la chuleta de cerdo
los dulces
los espaguetis
la galleta
el helado
los mariscos
la paella
el pastel
el pavo
el pescado
el pollo
el postre

Actividad 1 Escribir/Hablar ....

Práctica de vocabulario

❶ Haz una lista de los ingredientes que se necesitan para preparar una comida mexicana y otra lista de los ingredientes para una comida estadounidense.

❷ Con otro(a) estudiante, comparen sus listas. Trabajen juntos para preparar un menú para una comida completa.

Actividad 2 Escribir/Hablar ....

Práctica de vocabulario

Escribe una lista de tus comidas favoritas y otra de las comidas que no te gustan. Usa la lista para hablar con tu compañero(a) de las comidas que les gustan y que no les gustan y de sus hábitos alimenticios *(eating habits).* Hablen de lo que comen y por qué, cuándo y cómo lo comen.

Modelo

Me gusta el yogur. Lo como con cereal todos los días en el desayuno porque es bueno para la salud.

Universal Access

Block Schedule

Write each vocabulary word per category on individual slips of paper and place in a bag. Per category, ask a student to draw a word and act it out. Have the class guess the word being acted out.

Students with Learning Difficulties

Point to objects in the classroom and ask questions with embedded direct object pronouns. Students will restate the pronouns in their responses: Teacher: *El libro, ¿lo ves?* Student: *Sí, lo veo.* Teacher: *El reloj, ¿lo oyes?* Student: *Sí, lo oigo.*

Advanced Learners

Have students work together to create a menu for the restaurant of their dreams. Menus should include at least three different main entrées, as well as beverages and side dishes. Ask them to be creative and dream up a restaurant that they would regularly go to. They can also describe the décor.

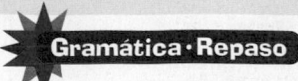

Review

Gramática · Repaso

Pronombres de complemento directo

Direct object pronouns tell who or what receives the action of the verb. They are used to replace a noun, in order not to repeat it. Remember that when the direct object is a person or group of people, you use the personal *a* before it.

—¿Probaste el pescado?   —¿Ves mucho a tus amigas?
—Sí, **lo** probé.   —Sí, **las** veo todos los días.

Here are all the direct object pronouns:

me	nos
te	os
lo / la	los / las

- Direct object pronouns generally go before the main verb. If there is a *no* before the verb, the pronoun goes between *no* and the verb.

  —Antonio comió las uvas. **Las** comió en el desayuno. Yo no **las** comí.

- If the verb is followed by an infinitive or a present participle (present progressive), the direct object pronoun may go before the main verb or be attached to the infinitive or participle.

  —¿Vas a comer el helado?   —Estoy comiéndo**lo** ahora.
  —**Lo** estoy comiendo ahora.   —No, no **lo** quiero comer. / —No, no quiero comer**lo**.

Actividad 3   Leer/Hablar

Práctica de gramática

Trabaja con otro(a) estudiante. Imaginen que él (ella) fue a un restaurante con su familia. Hablen del menú y de la comida que probaron.

Modelo

las salchichas / mi hermano
A —¿*Alguien probó las salchichas*?
B —*Sí, mi hermano* *las* *probó.*

1. los espaguetis / mi papá
2. el helado de chocolate / mi hermanita
3. la sopa de pollo / todos
4. los pasteles / nadie
5. la chuleta de cerdo / yo
6. los huevos con tocino / mi hermanita y yo
7. el yogur de durazno / mi mamá y mi papá

Actividad 4   Leer/Escribir

Práctica de gramática

Algunos estudiantes planean una cena. Lee lo que preguntan y escribe una respuesta apropiada. Usa el pronombre de complemento directo que corresponda.

Modelo

A —¿Quién va a preparar arroz?
B —*Lo va a preparar Luisa.*
o: *Luisa va a prepararlo.*

1. ¿Cómo vas a preparar las verduras?
2. ¿Quién va a comprar el pescado?
3. ¿Cuándo vamos a preparar la ensalada?
4. ¿Quién está cortando la fruta?
5. ¿Quieres preparar el postre?
6. ¿Quién está cortando las zanahorias?

ciento nueve   **109**
Capítulo 3

Enriching Your Teaching

Teacher-to-Teacher

Students tend to confuse direct and indirect object pronouns, especially when the objects are people. This *Gramática* review focuses mainly on things as direct objects. For further review of direct objects as people, ask questions such as the following and have students respond using a direct object pronoun:

¿Viste a [name of student(s)] *ayer?*

¿Conocen ustedes al (a la) señor(a) [name of teacher]*?*

¿Conoces a los (las) señores(as) [names of teachers]*?*

Gramática · Repaso

Presentation

Standards: 4.1

Resources: Voc. & Gram. Transparencies: 67

Suggestions: Cue students with sentences containing direct objects that are nouns. Have them restate each sentence, changing the direct object to a pronoun.

Actividad 3   *Standards:* 1.1

Resources: Practice Answers on Transparencies

Focus: Reviewing direct object pronouns

Suggestions: Have students switch roles, so both partners can practice asking and answering the questions.

Answers:

Student A's questions follow the pattern in the model. Student B's answers are as follows:

1. Sí, mi papá los probó.
2. Sí, mi hermanita lo probó.
3. Sí, todos la probamos (probaron).
4. No, nadie los probó.
5. Sí, yo la probé.
6. Sí, mi hermanita y yo los probamos.
7. Sí, mi mamá y mi papá lo probaron.

Actividad 4

Resources: Practice Answers on Transparencies

Focus: Reviewing direct object pronouns

Suggestions: After students complete the activity, have them take turns reading the questions and their answers aloud.

Answers will vary but should contain the following information:

1. las voy a preparar/voy a prepararlas
2. lo va a comprar/va a comprarlo
3. la vamos a preparar/vamos a prepararla
4. la está cortando/está cortándola
5. lo quiero preparar/quiero prepararlo
6. las está cortando/está cortándolas

109

Rapid Review

Play a game of **Simón dice** to review parts of the body. All students stand and listen to your (or a student leader's) commands to identify a body part: *Simón dice, "Levanta la pierna derecha."* *Simón dice, "Mueve el pie izquierdo."* Any students who fail to obey a command, or who obey a command that does not begin with the words **Simón dice,** must sit down. The last student standing wins.

Vocabulario

Presentation

Standards: 1.1

Resources: Voc. & Gram. Transparencies: 68

Suggestions: Have students choose one word or expression to pantomime from the *Vocabulario*. Have them take turns presenting their pantomimes, while others say what they are doing: *A Norberto le duele el brazo. Julia tiene frío. Miguel está tomando una pastilla.* Do your own pantomimes of words and expressions that students do not elicit.

Actividad 5

Standards: 1.1, 1.3

Focus: Practicing review vocabulary

Suggestions: Allow students to talk about real or imaginary illnesses they have had. Have them use the past tenses. They can also talk about an illness of another person, such as a family member, friend, or pet, in order to practice third-person forms.

Answers will vary.

Common Errors: Some students will consistently use possessive pronouns to identify parts of the body: *mi mano; mi estómago.* Remind them that, unlike English, Spanish usually uses the definite article with parts of the body. Model as necessary: *la mano; el estómago.*

Vocabulario

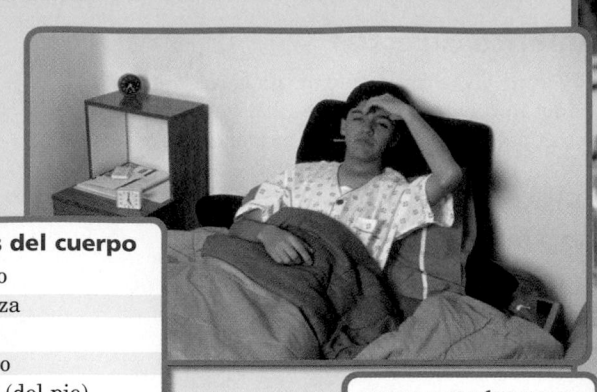

partes del cuerpo

el brazo
la cabeza
el codo
el cuello
el dedo (del pie)
la espalda
el estómago
la garganta
el hueso
la muñeca
el pie
la pierna
la rodilla
el tobillo

problemas

¡Ay!
doler (ue)
sentirse mal
tener . . .
  calor
  dolor (de)
  frío
  hambre
  sed

para mantenerse sano

caminar
correr
descansar
dormir
hacer ejercicio
levantar pesas
mover(se)
quedarse en cama

soluciones y medicinas

el enfermero, la enfermera
examinar
el médico, la médica
poner . . .
  la inyección
la radiografía
la receta
recetar . . .
  la medicina
  la pastilla
recomendar (ie)

Actividad 5 Dibujar/Escribir/Hablar..

Práctica de vocabulario

❶ Haz un dibujo sobre la última vez que estuviste enfermo(a). Luego, escribe:

- qué te pasaba
  Me sentía . . .
  Me dolía(n) (mucho / un poco) . . .

- qué te recomendó o recetó el médico
  Me recetó . . .
  Me recomendó . . .

- qué hiciste tú
  Tuve que . . .
  Debí . . .

❷ Muestra tu dibujo a dos estudiantes. Describe cómo te sentiste. Los(as) otros(as) estudiantes pueden hacerte preguntas.

¿Por cuánto tiempo . . . ?

¿También tuviste que . . . ?

110 ciento diez
A ver si recuerdas . . .

Universal Access

Heritage Language Learners

Students may use English or other alternative terms they have learned in place of some of the Spanish vocabulary: "prescription" instead of **receta;** "X-ray" (or **rayo equis**) instead of **radiografía.** Model the appropriate terms as necessary and have students repeat.

Multiple Intelligences

Musical/Rhythmic: Select a musically gifted volunteer and have him or her lead the class in a simple rap using the vocabulary for parts of the body. For example: ***El brazo, el codo y la mu-ñe-ca. La cabeza, el cuello y la es-pal-da.*** The rapper and the class should point to the parts of their bodies as they hear the words.

Gramática·Repaso

Pronombres de complemento indirecto

Indirect object pronouns indicate to whom or for whom an action is performed.

El médico **le** recetó unas pastillas a Eva.

Here are the indirect object pronouns:

me	nos
te	os
le	les

- Sometimes you can use *a + Ud. / él / ella* or a noun to clarify to whom the indirect pronouns *le* and *les* refer.

  El médico **le** dio una inyección **a ella.**
  ¿Quién **les** trajo las medicinas **a ustedes?**
  La enfermera **le** trajo la radiografía **al doctor.**

- If a verb is followed by an infinitive or a present participle (present progressive), the indirect object pronoun may go before the main verb or be attached to the infinitive or participle.

  Le tienen que hacer una radiografía a mi perro.   **Les** estoy dando las medicinas.
  Tienen que hacer**le** una radiografía a mi perro.   Estoy dánd**oles** las medicinas.

- Remember that indirect object pronouns are used with verbs like *gustar, encantar,* and *doler.*

  Me duele el brazo.   A los niños no **les** gustan las inyecciones.

 Leer/Escribir

Práctica de gramática

Unos(as) amigos(as) hablan de un accidente y de lo que les recetó el médico. Completa las oraciones con el pronombre de complemento indirecto *(me, te, le, nos, os, les)* que corresponda.

1. Yo no me puedo mover. _____ duele todo.
2. El médico va a poner_____ una inyección a José y a mí.
3. Y a Clara, ¿qué _____ recetó el doctor?
4. Ella se siente bien, a ella no _____ recetó nada.
5. Mi hermana está en cama. Yo _____ estoy dando las medicinas.
6. ¿Y a ti _____ duele el brazo?
7. No, a mí ahora empezaron a doler_____ las piernas.

 Leer/Escribir

Práctica de gramática

Completa este mensaje con los pronombres correctos.

¿Cómo estás? Hace una semana que a mi hermana Teresa y a mí **1.** duele la cabeza. A mí el médico **2.** recomendó usar anteojos. **3.** pregunté si tenía que llevarlos todo el tiempo y **4.** dijo que sí. A Teresa no **5.** dio nada.

● **Más práctica** ....
Practice Workbook 3-1, 3-2

Go Online
PHSchool.com
For: More review
Visit: www.phschool.com
Web Code: jed-0301

ciento once   **111**
Capítulo 3

Gramática·Repaso

Presentation

Resources: Voc. & Gram. Transparencies: 69

Suggestions: Have students pass around an object, such as a book. Have them use **dar** to tell about what they did, are doing, or will do: *Carlos me dio el libro. Le voy a dar el libro a María.* Change the number of recipients and guide students with questions as necessary:

¿Qué está haciendo Guillermo?
Está dándoles el libro a Gloria y a Ana.

 Standards: 1.2

Resources: Practice Answers on Transparencies

Focus: Reviewing indirect object pronouns

Suggestions: Remind students first to identify the indirect object in each item. This will help them determine which pronoun to use.

Answers:
1. Me   5. le
2. nos   6. te
3. le   7. me
4. le

 Standards: 1.2

Resources: Practice Answers on Transparencies

Focus: Reviewing indirect object pronouns

Suggestions: Ask a volunteer to read the completed message aloud, so students can check their answers.

Answers:
1. nos
2. me
3. Le
4. me
5. le

Standards for Foreign Language Learning: *Capítulo* 3

- To achieve the goals of the Standards, students will:

Communication

1.1 Interpersonal
- Talk about menus, nutrition, and the preparation and quality of foods
- Talk about physical and mental health, exercise, illnesses, and remedies
- Talk about ancient Central American ball games
- Talk about Spanish and Latin American teen magazines

1.2 Interpretive
- Read and listen to information about menus, nutrition, and the preparation and quality of foods
- Read and listen to information about physical and mental health, exercise, illnesses, and remedies
- Read about word families
- Read about the career of a bilingual student advisor
- Read about ancient Central American ball games
- Read about Spanish and Latin American teen magazines
- Read poetry by José Alfredo Jiménez

1.3 Presentational
- Write about menus, nutrition, and the preparation and quality of foods
- Write about physical and mental health, exercise, illnesses, and remedies
- Write about planning a party
- Write about ancient Central American ball games

Culture

2.1 Practices and Perspectives
- Explain the use of natural remedies in Latin America
- Explain the physical education system in Spanish schools
- Explain the practice of ball games in ancient Central America
- Explain teen reading habits in Spain and Latin America

2.2 Products and Perspectives
- Describe a Spanish nutrition study
- Discuss the poetry of José Alfredo Jiménez
- Talk about Spanish and Latin American teen magazines

Connections

3.1 Cross-curricular
- Talk about key facts about health, nutrition, remedies, and physical education
- Talk about key facts about the career of a bilingual student advisor
- Talk about key facts about the Mexican songwriter José Alfredo Jiménez
- Talk about key facts about ancient Mexico and modern Spain
- Discuss Language Arts Strategies: using prior knowledge, speech projection, persuasive writing, cause and effect

3.2 Target Culture
- Read a Spanish nutrition study report
- Read an article excerpt from a Spanish magazine
- Read song lyrics by José Alfredo Jiménez

Fondo cultural ■◆■◆◇■◆■◇■◆

Las frutas de Tamayo Rufino Tamayo (1899–1991) es un gran pintor y muralista mexicano que nació en Oaxaca, un estado conocido por sus deliciosas frutas. Cuando Tamayo era niño, su familia vendía frutas en un mercado y él aprendió mucho de ellas. Sus formas, variedad y colores lo fascinaban. Sabía cuándo tenían calidad y cuándo estaban listas para comer. Él pintó muchas frutas. Decía que su único lenguaje era la pintura porque estaba hecha de formas, como las frutas.

- ¿Qué frutas conoces que no se producen aquí y las traen de otros países? ¿Sabes de dónde las traen?

Sandías, Rufino Tamayo

Universal Access

Personalizing the Theme
Ask students to comment on perceptions about health and fitness in the United States. Ask: *¿Por qué es importante comer bien? ¿Por qué es importante hacer ejercicio? En general, ¿piensas que la gente de nuestra cultura está en buena forma física? ¿Por qué sí? ¿Por qué no?*

Students with Special Needs
Color-blind students may not be able to distinguish some of the foods in the photo. Hold up the book and point to one of the groupings of fruit. Ask volunteers to name the items.

¿Qué haces para estar en forma?

Chapter Objectives

- **Talk about symptoms and remedies**
- **Give advice about health and nutrition**
- **Express how you feel under certain circumstances**
- **Tell others what to do**
- **Understand cultural perspectives about health, physical fitness and nutrition**

Video Focus

- **Maintaining a healthy lifestyle**

Country Connection

As you learn about health, fitness and nutrition, you will make connections to these countries and places.

España

México

 Go Online
PHSchool.com
For: Online Atlas
Visit: www.phschool.com
Web Code: jee-002

ciento trece   113
Capítulo 3

Standards for Foreign Language Learning (cont'd)

Comparisons
4.1 Language
- Compare Spanish words to their English counterparts
- Compare Spanish and English commands

4.2 Culture
- Compare ancient Central American ball games to modern ones
- Compare Spanish and Latin American teen magazines and their readership to those in the United States

Communities
5.1 Beyond the School
- Link to Web sites from around the Spanish-speaking world

5.2 Lifelong Learner
- Discuss important facts about healthy lifestyles
- Discuss important facts about scientific studies
- Develop an appreciation for the art of songwriting

Chapter Opener
Presentation

Resources: Voc. & Gram. Transparencies: 14, 20 (maps)

Suggestions: Introduce students to the theme of the chapter and go over the objectives. Point out that they will learn to better communicate on the topics of health, nutrition, and feelings. Use *Vocabulary & Grammar Transparencies* 14 and 20 to locate and discuss the countries featured in the chapter.

 Fondo cultural   Standards: 1.2, 3.1

Resources: Fine Art Transparencies; Fine Art Transparencies Teacher's Guide

Suggestions: Ask: *¿Qué frutas se ven en la pintura? ¿Las comes tú?*

Answers will vary, but may include mango, guava, papaya, and kiwi.

Enriching Your Teaching

Planning for Instruction
Resources:
- Teacher Express CD-ROM or Resource Book
  - Teaching resources
  - Lesson Planner
  - Chapter Resource Checklist
  - School-to-Home Connection Letter

Culture Note
Fruits you might find in a Mexican **mercado** include **árbol de pan** (breadfruit), **guanábana** (soursop), **granadas** (pomegranates), and **granadillas** (passion fruit). But you might not have to travel as far as Mexico to find them. Mexico currently grows about 25 percent of the fruit available for purchase in the United States.

Teaching with Photos
Ask students to talk about what they see in the photo. For example: *¿Qué frutas se ven en la foto? ¿Qué piensas que dice la persona en la foto?*

Language Input

Presentation

Standards: 1.1, 1.2, 3.1

Resources: Voc. & Gram. Transparencies: 70–71; Resource Book: Cap. 3, Input Script; Audio Program: CD Cap. 3, Track 1, 3

Focus: Presenting new vocabulary and using grammar lexically in context

Suggestions: You may want to use the Input Script from the *Teacher's Resource Book* as a source of ideas for presentation of new vocabulary and comprehensible input. Meaning for most of the vocabulary in this lesson can be clarified either by pantomime or by TPR commands, and having students point to the objects named on *Vocabulary & Grammar Transparency* 71.

Actividad 1 *Standards:* 1.2

Resources: Audio Program: CD Cap. 3, Track 2; Resource Book: Cap. 3, Audio Script; Practice Answers on Transparencies

Focus: Practicing listening comprehension of new vocabulary

Suggestions: Point out to students that *Actividad* 1 focuses on the information on p. 114. Before they listen, allow students a few minutes to read over and study this page. Then play the *Audio CD* or use the script to read the activity aloud.

Answers:
1. C
2. C
3. F
4. C
5. F
6. F

Block Schedule

Have the class stand up. Call out different vocabulary words from these two pages and have students act them out. Call them out quickly and repeat words twice or three times for reinforcement. A quick pace will make the activity fun.

A primera vista 1

Vocabulario y gramática en contexto

Objectives

Read, listen to, and understand information about
• symptoms and remedies
• health, food, and nutrition

A nadie le gusta ir al médico, pero cuando estamos enfermos vamos inmediatamente a visitarlo: queremos que nos devuelva la salud en un minuto para poder seguir con nuestra vida normal. Cuando vamos al médico, a veces nos sentimos como niños que quieren la ayuda de sus papás.

Clínica de Medicina Familiar
Dr. Raúl López

Estornudo mucho. Creo que tengo una alergia.

Estoy resfriada.

Tengo fiebre de 38° (grados centígrados). Creo que tengo gripe.

Me duele el oído.

Carlitos, te duele el pecho, ¿no?, y tienes una tos muy fuerte. ¡Pobrecito!

Actividad 1 Escuchar

¿Quién está enfermo(a)?

Escribe los números del 1 al 6 en una hoja. Escucha las siguientes frases y escribe *C* (cierto) o *F* (falso).

Universal Access

Heritage Language Learners

Invite a student with outstanding pronunciation skills to take turns with you, randomly naming the vocabulary items during the presentation. This way, students will be exposed to variations in the pronunciation of the words and expressions.

Advanced Learners

Have students prepare and perform a skit set in a doctor's waiting room. Characters should include a doctor, a nurse, and at least two patients with different illnesses.

LA NUTRICIÓN

Los siguientes alimentos son nutritivos y por eso son importantes para tu alimentación.

los huevos y la leche
La leche tiene **calcio** y ayuda a tener huesos fuertes. Los huevos tienen muchas **proteínas** y **aunque** son muy buen alimento, no debes comer demasiados.

las espinacas[1]
Las espinacas **contienen** un alto **nivel** de **hierro**.

el cereal y el pan
El cereal y algunas clases de pan tienen mucha **fibra**. Los dos alimentos tienen **carbohidratos**.

las piñas y las naranjas
Tienen muchas **vitaminas**. Es bueno comer de todas las frutas con frecuencia.

los cacahuates
Tienen mucha grasa, carbohidratos y proteínas, por lo que dan **energía**, pero no debes comer muchos.

1 spinach

el jarabe

la aspirina

el antibiótico

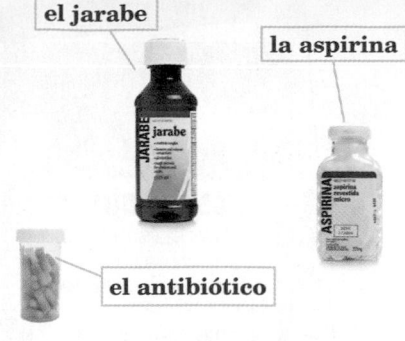

¡Ay!, doctor, me duele el estómago. Anoche comí cuatro bolsas de papas fritas y dos hamburguesas.

Tome esta medicina, pero no la tome con el estómago **vacío**. Y por favor, **evite** comer **comida basura**.

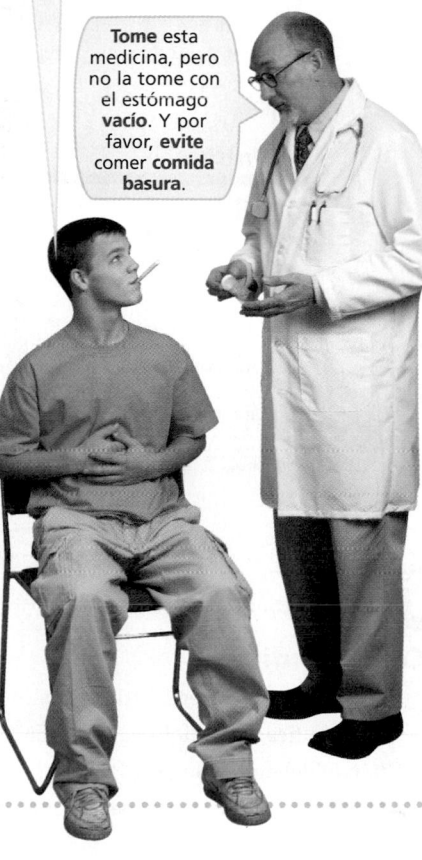

 **Escuchar** ....

La receta del doctor

Dibuja una tabla con dos columnas. En una columna, escribe *problemas de los pacientes* y en la otra, *receta del doctor.* Escucha lo que dicen el doctor López y sus pacientes y completa la tabla.

ciento quince 115
Capítulo 3

Language Input ③

Actividad 2 — *Standards:* 1.2

Resources: Audio Program: CD Cap. 3, Track 4; Resource Book: Cap. 3, Audio Script; Practice Answers on Transparencies

Focus: Practicing listening comprehension of new vocabulary

Suggestions: Use the *Audio CD* or the script. Allow students to listen more than once. Pause frequently to allow them to write the information. Then have students work in pairs to check their answers and each other's comprehension. One partner reads items from the **problemas de los pacientes** side of the chart in random order. The other responds with the appropriate **receta.**

Answers:

problemas de los pacientes
dolor de cabeza, está resfriado, no puede dormir
tos, dolor de garganta
fiebre, dolor de oído
quiere ser fuerte

receta del doctor
tomar aspirina antes de acostarse
tomar jarabe dos veces al día
tomar antibiótico
tomar vitaminas, hacer ejercicio, no comer comida basura

Extension: Have students work in pairs to come up with another idea for a patient's complaint and a doctor's prescription.

Enriching Your Teaching

Culture Note
Two grains have been Latin American staples for centuries. Quinoa (KEEN-wah) was grown by the Incas; amaranth (AH-mah-rahnth) by the Aztecs. Both are highly nutritious. Moreover, they can be grown in poor soil and arid climates. Both can now be found in many United States supermarkets.

Internet Search
Keywords:

alimentación saludable

115

Vocabulario y gramática

Presentation

Standards: 1.2, 3.1

Resources: Voc. & Gram. Transparencies: 72; Resource Book: Cap. 3, Input Script; Audio Program: CD Cap. 3, Track 5

Focus: Extending presentation of vocabulary and grammar in the context of dietary information

Suggestions:

Pre-reading: Direct students' attention to the food label and ask them to use it as a clue to predict the main idea of the information on this page.

Reading: Allow students time to read the information silently first. Then play the *Audio CD* or read the information aloud, with students reading along as they listen. Allow them to listen more than once.

Post-reading: Use gestures, explanations, and demonstrations to clarify the meaning of new vocabulary.

 **Actividad 3** *Standards:* 1.2, 1.3

Resources: Practice Answers on Transparencies

Focus: Demonstrating comprehension of the reading passage

Suggestions: Have students answer the questions in pairs, so they can share strategies for learning new words and structures as well as practice writing skills.

Answers will vary in structure but contain the following ideas:

1. Debemos leer la etiqueta para saber si debemos incluir esa comida en nuestra dieta.
2. Una dieta equilibrada es comer de todos los grupos de alimentos todos los días.
3. Debemos comer a horarios regulares y evitar muchas meriendas para tener una alimentación saludable.
4. Answers will vary.
5. Una ración tiene 160 calorías. Tiene 5 gramos de proteína.

La alimentación de los jóvenes

ARROZ CON FRIJOLES NEGROS

Datos de Nutrición
Tamaño por Ración 1/4 Taza (45g)
Raciones por Envase 5

Cantidad por Ración

Calorías 160   Cal. Grasa 0

	% Valor Diario*
Grasa Total 0 g	**0%**
Grasa Sat. 0 g	**0%**
Colesterol 0 mg	**0%**
Sodio 445 mg	**19%**
Carb. Total 34 g	**11%**
Fibra Dietética 3 g	**10%**
Azúcares 1 g	
Proteínas 5 g	

Vitamina A 0% • Vitamina C 0%
Calcio 0%   • Hierro 6%

* Los porcentajes de Valores Diarios están basados en una dieta de 2.000 calorías. Sus valores diarios pueden ser mayores o menores dependiendo de sus necesidades calóricas.

	Calorías	2.000	2.500
Grasa Total	Menos de	65g	80g
Grasa Sat.	Menos de	20g	25g
Colest.	Menos de	300mg	300mg

A veces no es tan fácil saber qué alimentos tienen mucho azúcar o demasiada grasa. Lee las etiquetas *(labels)* de la comida que compras para saber si la debes incluir en tu dieta.

¿Por qué es importante una alimentación saludable?

Una alimentación saludable es la mejor manera de:
- Tener energía todo el día y estar bien para hacer deporte y otras actividades.
- Recibir las vitaminas y el hierro que necesitas.
- Alcanzar tu estatura apropiada si no eres adulto.
- Mantener el mejor peso para tu edad y tu estatura.
- Evitar hábitos alimenticios malos.

¿Qué significa una alimentación saludable?
- Comer comidas a horarios regulares y evitar muchas meriendas.
- Mantener una dieta equilibrada, es decir, comer de todos los grupos de alimentos todos los días.
- No saltar comidas y evitar la comida basura.
- Comer cuando tienes hambre y parar cuando te sientes lleno(a).

 Actividad 3 **Escribir**

¿Comprendiste?

1. ¿Por qué debemos leer la etiqueta antes de comprar un alimento?
2. ¿Qué significa una "dieta equilibrada"?
3. ¿Cuándo debemos comer? ¿Por qué?
4. ¿Cuál de estos consejos te parece más difícil de seguir? ¿Por qué?
5. Según la información de la etiqueta, ¿cuántas calorías tiene una ración de arroz con frijoles negros? ¿Cuántos gramos de proteínas tiene una ración?

116 ciento dieciséis
A primera vista 1

Universal Access

Heritage Language Learners
Ask students to tell about foods that they eat at home that are not usually part of the local United States diet. Or, in the case of foods that have become fast food, such as the *taco,* ask them to talk about how the fast-food version differs from the version they may eat at home.

Multiple Intelligences
Naturalist: Ask students to describe fruits and vegetables only in terms of touch, smell, and taste. Ask them to imagine the taste, smell, or texture and weight of each as they describe it or hear it described. Encourage them to use the Spanish they know: *El limón no es dulce.* Provide adjectives such as *ácido* if requested.

Language Input

 Leer/Escribir . . . .

La intrusa

Escribe en una hoja de papel los números del 1 al 6. Para cada grupo de palabras, escribe la palabra o frase que no está relacionada con las otras. Luego, escribe una frase con cada una de las palabras que escribiste.

1. **a.** la dieta **b.** los hábitos alimenticios **c.** la alimentación **d.** las alergias
2. **a.** la fiebre **b.** la merienda **c.** la tos **d.** estornudar
3. **a.** lleno **b.** vacío **c.** equilibrado **d.** las proteínas
4. **a.** el peso **b.** la edad **c.** el oído **d.** la estatura
5. **a.** el calcio **b.** el pecho **c.** la cabeza **d.** el oído
6. **a.** la comida basura **b.** saludable **c.** nutritiva **d.** la dieta equilibrada

onsejos para a alimentación aludable

1. No saltes comidas. Planea tus comidas y meriendas.
• Come dos o tres meriendas al día para mantener la energía y un peso saludable.

2. Aprende maneras simples y saludables de preparar alimentos.
• Evita freír los alimentos. Es mejor hervirlos, asarlos, prepararlos al horno o cocinarlos en el microondas.
• Evita añadir mantequilla a la comida.

3. La energía que da el azúcar se gasta pronto.
• Evita tomar refrescos o bebidas que tienen mucha azúcar. Come pocos postres y dulces.

4. Presta atención a tu cuerpo y a lo que comes.
• Come despacio. Tu cuerpo necesita unos 20 minutos para sentirse lleno.
• Come comidas calientes y alimentos con mucha fibra.
• No comas comida basura. Escoge alimentos nutritivos.

5. Evita pensar en las dietas.
• Lo importante es comer de todos los alimentos sin exagerar.
• Tú eres más importante que tu peso o tu estatura. ¡Créelo!

 **Leer/Escuchar** . . . .

¿Saludable o no?

Lee este artículo. Luego escucha las frases y escribe *C* (cierto) o *F* (falso) según los "Consejos para una alimentación saludable".

grill - roast

 Más práctica . . . .

Practice Workbook 3-3, 3-4

Go Online
PHSchool.com
For: Vocabulary practice
Visit: www.phschool.com
Web Code: jed-0302

ciento diecisiete   **117**
Capítulo 3

 3

Language Input

▶ **Rapid Review**
On the board, write food categories such as *verduras, carnes,* and *frutas.* Ask pairs of students to list as many foods as they can under each category.

Actividad 4   *Standards:* 3.1

Resources: Practice Answers on Transparencies

Focus: Demonstrating comprehension of new vocabulary through categorizing

Suggestions: Ask students to explain why each odd item does not belong: *Para el número 1, las palabras de las letras a, b y c se tratan de lo que comemos, pero las alergias son problemas de la salud.*

Answers:
1. las alergias   4. el oído
2. la merienda   5. el calcio
3. las proteínas 6. la comida basura

Actividad 5   *Standards:* 1.2, 3.1

Resources: Audio Program: CD Cap. 3, Track 6; Resource Book: Cap. 3, Audio Script; Practice Answers on Transparencies

Focus: Practicing reading and listening comprehension

Suggestions: Allow students to listen to the *Audio CD* more than once.

Answers:
1. F 2. F 3. C 4. C 5. C

Additional Resources
• Resource Book: Cap. 3, Clip Art

 Assessment
• Prueba 3-1: Vocabulary recognition

Chapter Project
Give students copies of the Chapter Project outline and rubric from the *Teacher's Resource Book.* Explain the task to them, and have them perform step 1. (For more information, see p. 108-a.)

Enriching Your Teaching

Culture Note
Chili peppers are a staple not only in Mexican food. After salt, they are the world's most common form of seasoning. There are many kinds of chilis and many different tastes, some spicy enough to burn your mouth, others milder. And with twice the Vitamin C of most citrus fruits, chilis are nutritious.

Teacher-to-Teacher
The food context is an easy one in which to use manipulatives or visuals when reviewing vocabulary. Plastic imitations of many different kinds of foods are available in Teacher Stores for purchase. A more economical route is to cut pictures of foods out of magazines. Mount them on construction paper or laminate them.

Actividad 6 — Standards: 1.2

Resources: Voc. & Gram. Transparencies: 72; Practice Answers on Transparencies

Focus: Practicing new vocabulary in a cloze exercise

Suggestions: Have students briefly read the entire paragraph once for meaning before they write their answers.

Answers:
1. Tenía tos
2. Aunque
3. tenía fiebre
4. grados centígrados
5. tengo gripe
6. antibióticos

Actividad 7 — Standards: 1.1, 3.1

Resources: Practice Answers on Transparencies

Focus: Practicing new vocabulary

Suggestions: Encourage partners to ask questions and explain their answers. Remind students that everything is relative: an occasional serving of cookies and milk might be considered healthy or at least not unhealthy, but eating such foods every day is not a healthy dietary habit. Ask students to include comments about quantity and frequency as they talk about the pictures.

Answers will vary but should contain the following information:
1. Hamburguesa con papas fritas y refresco: contienen proteína y carbohidratos. No son saludables.
2. Ensalada de espinacas: contiene fibra y hierro. Es saludable.
3. Cereal con leche: contiene proteína, carbohidratos, calcio y fibra. Es nutritivo y saludable.
4. Galleta y refresco: contienen carbohidratos. No son saludables.

Manos a la obra 1

Vocabulario y gramática en uso

Objectives
- Talk about symptoms and remedies
- Discuss eating habits
- Use informal and formal commands

Actividad 6  **Leer/Escribir** B

Llegó el otoño

En el otoño los estudiantes comienzan sus clases y todo el mundo estornuda. Completa esta carta que le escribió un estudiante a su profesor con las palabras o frases del recuadro.

grados centígrados	tengo gripe
antibióticos	aunque
tenía fiebre	tenía tos

Profesor:

No puedo ir a la escuela hoy. __1.__ anoche. __2.__ tomé un jarabe que me recetó el doctor, no pude dormir. Hoy por la mañana tenía mucho frío, mi mamá me puso el termómetro debajo del brazo y me dijo que __3.__ porque tenía 39 __4.__. Ella cree que yo __5.__. En vez de recetarme __6.__, la doctora recomienda que yo descanse mucho y que beba mucha agua. ¡Siempre me pasa lo mismo en otoño! Espero regresar a clase pronto.

Tomás

Actividad 7   **Hablar**

Contiene un alto nivel de . . .

Mira las ilustraciones y explica a otro(a) estudiante lo que come cada uno de estos jóvenes y por qué es saludable o no es saludable. Usa las palabras del recuadro.

proteína	fibra	nutritivo	calcio	hierro	carbohidratos	contener

1.   2.   3.   4.

Universal Access

Multiple Intelligences
Logical/Mathematical: Bring in empty food cans and boxes. Have students review the nutrition facts information on the labels and note the amounts of *proteína, calcio, fibra, carbohidratos,* and *hierro* in each food. Ask them to make statements comparing the nutritional contents of different foods.

Students with Learning Difficulties
Review the concept of cognates and point out examples such as *alimentación* or *nutrición* on these two pages. Ask students to name other words they see that look like English words. Help students recognize a cognate like *proteína* by writing it on the board and covering the *a.*

Ampliación del lenguaje

Familias de palabras

Las familias de palabras son grupos de palabras que tienen la misma raíz *(root)*. Muchas veces podemos saber el significado *(meaning)* de una palabra si conocemos otras palabras de la misma familia. Observa la relación entre las siguientes palabras y completa las frases.

Verbos	Sustantivos	Adjetivos
alimentar	alimentación	alimenticio
equilibrar	equilibrio	equilibrada
nutrir	nutrición	nutritivo
pesar	peso	pesado

1. Para obtener una buena _____, debemos comer alimentos nutritivos.

2. Tenemos un buen hábito _____ cuando no nos alimentamos con comida basura.

Actividad 8 **Leer/Hablar/Escribir**

Preparándose para la carrera

Trabaja con otro(a) estudiante para terminar el cuento sobre este atleta. Usa por lo menos cinco palabras del recuadro.

estar resfriado	nivel	hierro	energía
carbohidratos	hábitos	aunque	evitar

Rafa era un atleta fuerte, de peso apropiado para su edad. Iba a participar en una carrera. Tenía el estómago vacío y quería comer . . .

Actividad 9 **Hablar**

¿Qué puedo hacer?

Túrnate con otro(a) compañero(a) para representar la conversación entre un(a) estudiante y su maestro(a).

Modelo

Estudiante —*Me duele la cabeza.*
Maestro(a) —*Debes tomar una aspirina.*

Estudiante

1.

2.

3.

4.

5.

Maestro(a)

Debes . . .

Tienes que . . .

Puedes tomar . . .

El médico te puede recetar . . .

ciento diecinueve **119**
Capítulo 3

Ampliación del lenguaje

Presentation

Standards: 1.2, 3.1, 4.1

Resources: Practice Answers on Transparencies

Focus: Understanding word families

Suggestions: Have groups of students use background knowledge and reference sources, such as thesauri and dictionaries, to build word families around other words: ***enfermo: enferma, enfermero(a), enfermedad, enfermería, enfermizo(a).***

Answers:
alimentación
nutritivo

 Actividad 8 *Standards:* 1.1, 1.2, 1.3

Focus: Using new vocabulary and structures to finish a story

Suggestions: As an alternative to pair work, do this activity as a round-robin. The story goes around a circle, each student adding one line that makes sense after the line before it. Have a student secretary write the story on the board as it builds.

Answers will vary.

 Actividad 9 *Standards:* 1.1

Resources: Practice Answers on Transparencies

Focus: Practicing new vocabulary and structures in a guided conversation

Suggestions: Ask partners to present one or more of their exchanges to the class.

Answers: Student B's answers will vary. Student A's statements should include the following vocabulary:

1. Me duele el codo.
2. Estornudo.
3. Tengo tos. Me duele el pecho.
4. Tengo fiebre.
5. Estoy cansado. (Estoy resfriado./Tengo gripe.)

Enriching Your Teaching

Teacher-to-Teacher

Invite students to view one or more segments of recordings of popular TV shows with a medical theme. Play your recordings without sound. Pause frequently and ask students to comment on the action, describe some of the ailments of the patients, and discuss the actions of doctors and nurses. Another alternative is to record Spanish-language versions of these shows, available in some areas, and show students all or part of an episode with sound.

3 Practice and Communicate

Rapid Review

Review various kinds of measurements. Have students refer to a metric-standard U.S. English conversion table and ask questions that help them understand the physical size and nature of measurements: *¿Cuántas libras hay en un kilo? ¿Cuántos gramos hay en una onza? ¿Cuál es más grande: una cucharada o una cucharadita?*

Actividad 10 *Standards:* 1.1, 1.2, 1.3, 3.1

Focus: Using new vocabulary and structures in a contextual discussion

Suggestions: First, have partners work together to clear up any comprehension problems they might have with the recipe. Remind students that for step 2, they should discuss a recipe that involves several ingredients rather than a single ingredient item.

Answers will vary.

Fondo cultural *Standards:* 1.1, 1.2, 2.1, 3.1

Resources: Practice Answers on Transparencies

Suggestions: Use the *Fondo cultural* information to launch a discussion about the growing popularity of natural remedies throughout the world, including the United States. Have students consult a bilingual dictionary for names of natural remedies with which they are familiar. Possibilities include ***la equinacea*** (echinacea), ***el ajo*** (garlic), and ***el hipericón (todabuena)*** (St. John's wort). Ask questions such as: *¿Para qué se usa ese remedio? ¿Cómo se toma? ¿En qué forma? ¿Cuándo se toma?*

Answers:
- **Usan la manzanilla. Usan el girasol.**
- **Answers will vary.**

Additional Resources
- Writing, Audio & Video Workbook: Cap. 3, Audio Activity 1, Track 7
- Writing, Audio & Video Workbook: Cap. 3, Writing Activity 6
- Resource Book: Cap. 3, Communicative Activity BLM

Assessment
- Prueba 3-2: Vocabulary production

Actividad 10 **Leer/Hablar/Escribir**

Una receta saludable

1 Ésta es una receta para preparar un postre nutritivo. Léela y explica a otro(a) estudiante por qué la receta es saludable. Habla de los ingredientes que tiene y de los que no tiene.

Modelo

El postre tiene avena. La avena es un cereal y tiene fibra, que es saludable.

2 Ahora, piensen en una comida que les gusta y escriban cinco ingredientes que contiene. Luego escriban tres frases que describen el valor *(value)* nutritivo de la comida.

Avena[1] con fresas

Ingredientes

3 litros de leche sabor a fresa — 1 taza llena de avena
azúcar al gusto — 1 cucharada de vainilla
1 raja de canela[2] — 10 fresas en pedazos

Preparación:

Calentar la leche a fuego bajo, junto con el azúcar y la canela, hasta que hierva. Añadir la avena y mover la mezcla hasta que se cocine. Quitarla del fuego, añadir la vainilla, y dejarla en la olla unos diez minutos. Servirla con fresas.

1 oatmeal 2 stick of cinnamon

Fondo cultural

Las plantas medicinales En América Latina, es muy común tomar remedios naturales para resolver problemas menores de salud, como la tos, la fiebre y los dolores de estómago o de cabeza. Generalmente estos remedios son plantas que usan los indígenas de la región por sus efectos saludables y curativos[1]. Muchas de estas plantas medicinales se preparan como una infusión o té para beber. Algunos ejemplos de plantas medicinales son la manzanilla[2], que se usa para los dolores de estómago, el girasol[3], para la tos y cuando estás resfriado, y la menta[4], para los dolores de cabeza y estómago. Estos remedios naturales se venden en ferias y mercados al aire libre en toda América Latina.

- ¿Qué remedios naturales usan los indígenas de América Latina para el dolor de estómago? ¿Y para la tos?
- ¿Qué remedios naturales usan en tu familia y comunidad?

1 curative 2 chamomile 3 sunflower 4 mint

Universal Access

Heritage Language Learners

Invite students to share their knowledge about folk remedies. Ask guiding questions, such as: *¿Cómo se llama el remedio? ¿Para qué se usa? Si es una planta, ¿dónde se encuentra? ¿Cómo se administra el remedio?*

Students with Learning Difficulties

Learners who have difficulty remembering the irregular ***tú*** commands may be helped by memorizing classic ***refranes,*** such as: *Dime con quien andas, y te diré quien eres. Haz bien y no mires a quien. Pon el burro delante, para que no se espante.*

Gramática · Repaso

Mandatos afirmativos con *tú*

To tell a friend or close family member to do something, use the *tú* command form. To give an affirmative command in the *tú* form, use the present indicative *Ud. / él / ella* form. This rule also applies to stem-changing verbs.

caminar → camina   comer → come   abrir → abre
jugar → juega   volver → vuelve   pedir → pide

• Some verbs have irregular *tú* commands.

decir → **di**   hacer → **haz**   ir → **ve**   mantener → **mantén**   poner → **pon**
salir → **sal**   ser → **sé**   tener → **ten**   venir → **ven**

• Attach reflexive, direct, and indirect object pronouns to the end of affirmative commands. Add an accent mark to show that the stress remains in the same place.

¡Toma esas vitaminas! **¡Tómalas** ahora mismo!
Siéntate aquí.

 **Gramática** **Leer/Escribir**

Respuestas para todo

Verónica siempre tiene una respuesta para todos los problemas. Completa lo que dice con el mandato del verbo apropiado.

1. ¿Te duelen las piernas? _____ ejercicio. *(hacer / correr)*

2. ¿Estás muy cansada? _____ un rato. *(descansar / jugar)*

3. ¿Quieres mantener tu peso? _____ la comida basura. *(comprar / evitar)*

4. ¿Tienes malos hábitos alimenticios? _____ una dieta equilibrada. *(mantener / recetar)*

5. ¿Te sientes mal? _____ al médico. *(ayudar / ir)*

6. ¿Quieres sentirte mejor? _____ bien todos los días. *(comer / pedir)*

7. ¿No tienes energía? _____ unas vitaminas en la farmacia. *(comprar / ver)*

8. ¿Estás triste? _____ con tus amigos para divertirte. *(salir / buscar)*

---

12 **Gramática**  **Leer/Hablar/Escribir**

¿Cómo se prepara?

❶ Lee la receta de la Actividad 10 y después explica a otro(a) estudiante cómo se prepara usando mandatos con *tú*.

Modelo

Primero, compra los ingredientes.

❷ Ahora, escribe cómo preparar otra receta que conoces. Usa mandatos con *tú*.

● **Más práctica**
Practice Workbook 3-5

Go Online
PHSchool.com

For: Practice with affirmative commands with *tú*
Visit: www.phschool.com
Web Code: jed-0303

ciento veintiuno   121
Capítulo 3

 **Gramática · Repaso**

Presentation

Standards: 4.1

Resources: Voc. & Gram. Transparencies: 73

Suggestions: Model giving a series of commands to a volunteer, who carries them out. Then have students work in pairs, taking turns giving each other commands and carrying them out.

 Standards: 1.2

Resources: Practice Answers on Transparencies

Focus: Practicing affirmative commands with *tú*

Suggestions: Remind students that some of the verbs in the activity have irregular command forms.

Answers:

1. Haz	5. Ve
2. Descansa	6. Come
3. Evita	7. Compra
4. Mantén	8. Sal

 Standards: 1.1, 1.2, 1.3

Focus: Practicing affirmative commands with *tú*

Suggestions: Point out to students that in step 1, they should change the infinitives they see in the recipe to affirmative commands with *tú.*

Answers will vary.

Additional Resources

• Writing, Audio & Video Workbook: Cap. 3, Writing Activity 7

 Assessment

• Prueba 3-3: *Mandatos afirmativos con* tú

Enriching Your Teaching

Teacher-to-Teacher

Have students invent and deliver "command circuits." These are a series of commands given to a partner, beginning and ending at one point. Command circuits can be written down, swapped among students, and kept on file for use in later lessons. A typical command circuit might read as follows:

Levántate. / Camina a la ventana. / Ábrela. / Ahora ciérrala. / Levanta el vaso de agua que está al lado de la planta. / Dale a la planta un poco de agua. / Pon el vaso en su lugar. / Vuelve a tu pupitre. / Siéntate.

121

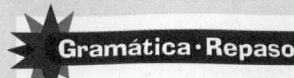

Gramática · Repaso

Mandatos negativos con *tú*

To form negative *tú* commands with regular verbs, drop the *-o* of the present tense *yo* form and add the following endings:

hablar	hablo → habl + **es**	**No hables** ahora.
comer	como → com + **as**	**No comas** tanto.
abrir	abro → abr + **as**	**No abras** la boca.

• The same rule applies to verbs whose present tense *yo* form ends in *-go*, *-zco*, *-yo*, and *-jo*.

No **salgas** si estás enferma.
No les **ofrezcas** comida basura a tus amigos.
No **escojas** comida con mucha grasa.

• The following verbs have irregular negative *tú* command forms.

dar → **no des**   ir → **no vayas**
estar → **no estés**   ser → **no seas**

• Verbs ending in *-car*, *-gar*, and *-zar* have the following spelling changes in the negative *tú* commands in order to keep the original sound.

sacar (*c → qu*)	saqu + **es**	**No saques** la basura.
llegar (*g → gu*)	llegu + **es**	**No llegues** tarde.
cruzar (*z → c*)	cruc + **es**	**No cruces** aquí.

• If you are using reflexive or object pronouns with negative commands, place them after *no*.

Estás enfermo. No **te** levantes de la cama.
No comas el pastel. No **lo** comas.

 **13** **Gramática** **Leer/Escribir**

Lo que no debes hacer

Luis sacó malas notas. Ayúdale a sacar mejores notas. Completa las frases con el mandato del verbo apropiado.

1. No _____ cuando la maestra está explicando algo. (*hablar / comer*)

2. No _____ con otro estudiante en clase. (*jugar / escribir*)

3. No _____ tarde a la clase. (*hacer / llegar*)

4. No _____ a la escuela sin hacer la tarea. (*ir / lavar*)

5. No _____ tu tarea sin leerla antes. (*entregar / comprar*)

6. No _____ tan impaciente. (*ser / tomar*)

 14 **Gramática** **Hablar**

Cuida tu salud

Tu amiga siempre está enferma. Dale siete consejos usando los verbos del recuadro. Usa mandatos afirmativos y negativos.

comer	hacer	ir	poner(se)	evitar	mantener	salir

Modelo

tomar
¡Toma tu medicina!

● **Más práctica**
Practice Workbook 3-6

Go Online
PHSchool.com
For: Practice with negative commands with *tú*
Visit: www.phschool.com
Web Code: jed-0304

Universal Access

Heritage Language Learners
Ask students to work in pairs to write sentences that demonstrate double negatives, such as **No digas nada.** Encourage them to see how many negatives they can work into a coherent sentence: **No digas nada de nada a nadie nunca.** Invite them to share their sentences with the class.

Advanced Learners
Have students choose a goal that they would like to achieve, such as keeping fit or driving safely. Ask them to create advice sheets consisting of affirmative and negative commands with **tú** that they would give to someone in order to help them achieve this goal.

Gramática · Repaso

Mandatos afirmativos y negativos con *Ud.* y *Uds.*

To give commands to people other than *tú* and to more than one person, use the *Ud.* and *Uds* commands. To form a command with *Ud.*, remove the *-s* from a negative *tú* command form. To form a command with *Uds.*, replace the *-s* of a negative *tú* command with an *-n*.

No habl**es**.	Habl**e** (Ud.).	Habl**en** (Uds.).
No traig**as** la receta.	Traig**a** (Ud.) la receta.	Traig**an** (Uds.) la receta.
No vay**as** al consultorio.	Vay**a** (Ud.) al consultorio.	Vay**an** (Uds.) al consultorio.

- To form negative *Ud.* and *Uds.* commands just add *no* before the command.

  Coma frutas, pero **no coma** muchos dulces.   **No salten** comidas.

- Attach reflexive, direct, and indirect object pronouns to the end of affirmative *Ud.* and *Uds.* commands. Add an accent mark to show that the stress remains in the same place. In negative commands, add the pronoun between *no* and the verb.

  ¡Tomen esas pastillas! **¡Tómenlas** ahora mismo!   **Lleve** la receta. Por favor, **llévela**.

  ¡Cepíllese los dientes después de comer!   **No le pidan** dulces. **Pídanle** fruta.

 15 Gramática **Escribir/Hablar**

¿Qué dicen todos?

❶ ¿Qué mandatos se oyen en diferentes lugares? Trabaja con otro(a) estudiante para escribir un mandato afirmativo y un mandato negativo con *Ud.* o *Uds.* para cada uno de los siguientes lugares.

1. en el consultorio del doctor
2. en la biblioteca
3. en el gimnasio
4. en la clase de español
5. en una fiesta
6. en la cocina
7. en una tienda de ropa

Modelo

en la sala
Apaguen el televisor.
No apaguen el televisor.

❷ Ahora, cada pareja debe leer sus mandatos a la clase, y los demás deben decir si la frase está correcta. Si está correcta la frase, y si no la tiene escrita otra pareja, gana un punto la pareja que la escribió. Gana la pareja que reúne más puntos.

ciento veintitrés   123
Capítulo 3

Enriching Your Teaching

Teacher-to-Teacher

If you had students create command circuits as suggested on p. 121, have them go through them again now with a partner. Then ask them to create new command circuits that include negative commands with *Ud.* and *Uds.* as well

as with *tú.* Volunteer yourself to follow students' command circuits with *Ud.* Have pairs of students act in unison to follow command circuits with *Uds.*

Actividad 16 *Standards:* 1.1

Focus: Practicing commands with *tú, Ud.*, and *Uds.*

Suggestions: Remind students that their commands can be negative or affirmative.

Answers will vary.

Extension: After some practice, add an element of spontaneity. After each student responds, have him or her toss a foam ball or a wadded-up sheet of paper to any other student in the group, who must say the next command.

Actividad 17 *Standards:* 1.1, 1.2, 3.1

Focus: Reading about an actual study of dietary habits conducted in Spain

Suggestions: Have students phrase their recommendations as if they were directly addressing the students in Ávila. For Advanced Learners, have students research the use and formation of *vosotros* commands to address the class accordingly, as though they were making suggestions directly to young people in Spain.

Answers will vary.

Country Connection

Presentation

Standards: 3.1

Resources: Voc. & Gram. Transparencies 20, (map)

Suggestions: Have students locate Ávila on *Vocabulary & Grammar Transparency 20* or another map of Spain. It is about 75 kilometers west-northwest of Madrid, in the autonomous region of Castilla y León. Tell students that Ávila is surrounded by a historic Romanesque wall and contains many other treasures that date back to the eleventh century. Ávila was the home of the Spanish kings until the court was moved to Madrid. A mountain range and province also bear the same name.

Actividad 16 **Gramática** **Escribir/Hablar/GramActiva**

Juego

Formen grupos de cuatro estudiantes. Cada estudiante escribe un mandato en infinitivo en un pedazo de papel y lo mete en una caja. Se turnan para sacar un papel de la caja. El(la) que saca el papel, lee el mandato. Un(a) estudiante forma un mandato con *tú*. El(la) siguiente forma el mandato con *Uds.* y el(la) último(a) añade un pronombre de complemento directo o indirecto a uno de los dos mandatos. Los mandatos pueden ser negativos o afirmativos.

Modelo

Comer manzanas verdes
No comas las manzanas verdes.
No coman las manzanas verdes.
No las comas.

Actividad 17 **Leer/Hablar**

Hábitos alimenticios de los jóvenes

Lee este artículo sobre los hábitos alimenticios de los estudiantes españoles.

Conexiones **Las ciencias**

El Centro de Salud de Ávila, en España, estudió los hábitos alimenticios de los estudiantes de 15 años. Los científicos que hicieron la encuesta piensan que es importante conocer los hábitos alimenticios que adquieren *(adopt)* los jóvenes, pues muchos los conservan toda la vida.

Desayuno	Estudiantes
Leche	96,5%
Yogur	2,6%
Jugo de frutas	20,1%
Galletas	39,8%
Cereal	26,6%
Pan	21,0%

Al final del estudio, los científicos dijeron que estaban preocupados, pues los estudiantes no estaban recibiendo en el desayuno todo el alimento que sus cuerpos necesitan para las actividades del día. Muchos científicos piensan que el desayuno es la comida más importante del día, pero el estudio de Ávila nos dice que el 38 por ciento de los estudiantes sólo toma líquidos en el desayuno.

• Observa la tabla de resultados y di a la clase qué otros alimentos deben comer los estudiantes de Ávila para tener más energía durante el día. Explica lo que tiene cada alimento (calcio, vitaminas, fibra, carbohidratos, grasa, hierro, energía) y por qué es bueno comerlo.

Universal Access

Heritage Language Learners

Have students write short descriptions of their favorite breakfast food(s) and breakfast habits. Do they eat different foods on school days and on weekends? If students have lived in a heritage country, ask them to compare and contrast the foods they ate there with those they eat now.

Multiple Intelligences

Logical/Mathematical: Have volunteers poll small groups in the class to find out what they eat for breakfast. Have them conduct their interviews in Spanish. Then have them compare their results and present their findings in a graphic organizer.

 **Gramática** ♻ **Leer/Escribir** ·

Un consejo para cada persona

¿Qué consejos les da la doctora a estos pacientes? Empareja cada frase de la columna A con un consejo de la columna B. Luego escribe un mandato con *Ud.* o *Uds.* para dar el consejo en cada caso.

Modelo
Tengo mucha sed. / tomar agua
Tome un vaso de agua.

Columna A

1. Necesitamos estar en forma.
2. No tenemos energía.
3. Tengo tos y dolor de cabeza.
4. El médico dice que necesito más calcio.
5. Creo que tengo fiebre.
6. Nos sentimos mal porque comimos mucha grasa y azúcar.

Columna B

a. ponerse el termómetro
b. tomar bastante yogur y leche
c. evitar la comida basura y los refrescos
d. tener una dieta equilibrada y no tomar muchos refrescos
e. tomar un jarabe y una aspirina
f. comprar vitaminas con hierro

 Gramática **Escribir** ·

Una gran fiesta

Imagínate que tú y seis de tus amigos(as) están planeando una fiesta en tu casa. Escribe un mensaje electrónico a tus amigos y explícales qué deben hacer. Usa los verbos del recuadro.

llegar	traer	comprar	invitar	decorar	hacer

 **Gramática** **Hablar/Escribir** ·

Guía para una vida sana

1 Vas a escribir una guía para una vida sana. Trabaja con un grupo de estudiantes. Hagan una lista de ideas sobre lo que es importante hacer y evitar para mantener la salud.

2 Escriban cinco frases para la guía usando la lista de ideas. Usen mandatos con *Ud.*

Modelo

No ponga mucha sal en la comida.

● **Más práctica** ·
Practice Workbook 3-7

3 Lean a la clase la guía que escribieron. Intercambien ideas sobre lo que recomendaron. Digan qué ideas son buenas para todas las personas, cuáles sólo sirven para los jóvenes y cuáles sólo para las personas mayores, y expliquen por qué.

PHSchool.com
For: Practice with affirmative and negative commands with *Ud.* and *Uds.*
Visit: www.phschool.com
Web Code: jed-0305

 Standards: 1.2, 3.1
· ·

Resources: Practice Answers on Transparencies

Focus: Practicing new vocabulary and command forms

Suggestions: Remind students that the subject of each sentence in the left column will help them determine to whom to address their commands.

Answers:

1. Tengan una dieta equilibrada y no tomen muchos refrescos.
2. Compren vitaminas con hierro.
3. Tome un jarabe y una aspirina.
4. Tome bastante yogur y leche.
5. Póngase el termómetro.
6. Eviten la comida basura y los refrescos.

 Standards: 1.3
· ·

Focus: Writing commands in the context of an e-mail

Suggestions: Encourage students to include some negative commands in their e-mails.

Answers will vary.

 Standards: 1.1, 1.3, 3.1
· ·

Focus: Practicing writing commands and new vocabulary in context

Suggestions: Have students work on their own to write sentences in step 2. The group will then have a greater variety of sentences in their completed health guide.

Answers will vary.

Additional Resources

• Writing, Audio & Video Workbook: Cap. 3, Audio Activity 2, Track 8
• Writing, Audio & Video Workbook: Cap. 3, Writing Activity 9

 Assessment

• Prueba 3-5: *Mandatos afirmativos y negativos con* Ud. *y* Uds.
• Examen: Vocabulario y gramática 1

Enriching Your Teaching

Culture Note

Although dietary habits in Spain have changed recently, much as they have in the United States, many people still enjoy a sweet breakfast of ***churros y chocolate.*** This is a cup of very thick hot chocolate and a small bundle of deep-fried dough sticks, whose texture resembles that of doughnuts.

Teacher-to-Teacher

Students can continue to familiarize themselves with command forms by reading a variety of authentic Spanish-language texts containing commands. Possibilities include recipes, driving manuals (available in Spanish in many towns), and Spanish-language computer software.

125

3 Language Input

Vocabulario y gramática

Presentation

Standards: 1.2, 3.1

Resources: Voc. & Gram. Transparencies: 76–77; Resource Book: Cap. 3, Input Script; Audio Program: CD Cap. 3, Track 9, 11

Focus: Presenting new vocabulary and using grammar lexically in context

Suggestions: Have students read along as you present the new vocabulary by playing the *Audio CD* or reading aloud. Use the pictures on *Vocabulary & Grammar Transparency* 76 and clarify the meaning of new vocabulary via pantomime. Check comprehension by asking questions. See the Input Scripts in the *Teacher's Resource Book* for specific questions.

Actividad 21

Standards: 1.2

Resources: Audio Program: CD Cap. 3, Track 10; Resource Book: Cap. 3, Audio Script; Practice Answers on Transparencies

Focus: Practicing listening comprehension of new vocabulary

Suggestions: Before engaging students in the listening activity, give them a few minutes to read over and study the advertisement for *Club Deportivo Las Fuentes.* Tell them to compare the information they hear to what they see in this announcement. Then play the *Audio CD* or use the script to read the activity aloud.

Answers:

1. F
2. C
3. F
4. F
5. C

Extension: After completing the activity, ask students to correct the false answers.

Block Schedule

Have students work in groups of 4 to 5 and create a brief speech by a fitness trainer giving tips for maintaining a healthy body. Use five expressions from this page and have the group act them out in front of the class.

A primera vista 2

Vocabulario y gramática en contexto

Objectives

Read, listen to, and understand information about
- physical fitness equipment
- exercises to stay fit
- giving advice

Estar en forma no es sólo tener mucho **músculo** y poca grasa en el cuerpo. Algunas personas hacen ejercicios como entrenamiento para una competencia o porque el médico les dice que lo necesitan. Pero muchos más hacen ejercicio para eliminar **el estrés** y dar a su cuerpo **fuerza** y energía. Estar en forma es también sentirse bien con uno mismo, estar saludable.

Para estar en forma

- hacer ejercicios de step
- hacer cinta
- hacer flexiones
- hacer ejercicios aeróbicos
- hacer yoga
- hacer bicicleta
- hacer abdominales

¿Se siente débil? ¿Quiere estar más fuerte?
Nunca es tarde para estar en forma

CLUB DEPORTIVO LAS FUENTES

- sala de pesas
- equipo para hacer bicicleta
- piscina
- baños sauna y jacuzzi
- clases de ejercicios aeróbicos y artes marciales
- entrenadores profesionales

Inscríbase hoy mismo y obtenga un 20% de descuento.
Tel. 555-242 677 Independencia #125

Actividad 21 Leer/Escuchar/Escribir

El Club Deportivo

Escribe en una hoja los números del 1 al 5. Escucha lo que explica esta chica a su amiga sobre el Club Deportivo Las Fuentes y escribe *C* (cierto) o *F* (falso) en cada caso.

126   ciento veintiséis
A primera vista 2

Universal Access

Heritage Language Learners

Have students list four favorite sports from their heritage country and then compare notes to see which two are the most popular. Encourage them to revise their lists during the discussion. Have them write a few lines explaining why they like or dislike one of those sports.

Advanced Learners

Ask students to work in a small group to prepare and present a TV commercial for a health club. Individuals can act as trainers or clients and do "sound bites" about the club's features and equipment and about correct and incorrect ways to do various exercises. Invite the group to record their commercial on video.

126

Para hacer ejercicio

flexionar

estirar

1 Antes de comenzar una sesión de ejercicio, es importante tener unos minutos para estirarse. Es necesario que flexiones y estires los músculos para evitar **calambres.**

2 Debemos comenzar a correr despacio, para evitar calambres. Después de un tiempo, podemos correr más rápido.

3 Es importante no hacer demasiado ejercicio sin descansar. Debemos siempre cuidar nuestro **corazón** y saber cuándo debemos parar.

4 Igualmente, al terminar el ejercicio, debe haber un tiempo para **relajarse** y **respirar** normalmente. ¡Ah, qué bien se siente uno después del entrenamiento!

 **Escuchar/Hablar** · · · · · · · · · · ·

El anuncio

Escucha el anuncio por radio de un club deportivo y busca las fotos de estas páginas que correspondan a los servicios que se anuncian. Luego, di qué ejercicios de estas páginas no están en el anuncio del club deportivo.

 **Escribir/Hablar** · · · · · · · · · · · ·

Mis favoritos

En una hoja, haz una lista de tres ejercicios que te gusta hacer que se mencionan en estas páginas y los tres servicios del club deportivo que más te gustaría usar. Comparte tu lista con otro(a) estudiante de la clase.

ciento veintisiete **127**
Capítulo 3

Language Input

3

Actividad 22 *Standards:* 1.2
· · · · · · · · · · · · · · · ·

Resources: Audio Program: CD Cap. 3, Track 12; Resource Book: Cap. 3, Audio Script; Practice Answers on Transparencies

Focus: Practicing listening comprehension of new vocabulary

Suggestions: To avoid confusion, remind students that the word *ejercicios* in the instructions refers to physical exercises, not the language activities on these pages. Use the *Audio CD* or the script. Allow students to listen more than once. Pause to monitor students, making sure they are identifying the correct illustrations.

Answers:
Photos: hacer yoga/hacer cinta/hacer bicicleta
Exercises not included: hacer flexiones/hacer abdominales/hacer ejercicios de step/hacer ejercicios aeróbicos

Actividad 23 *Standards:* 1.1
· · · · · · · · · · · · · · · ·

Resources: Voc. & Gram. Transparencies: 76–77

Focus: Listing and reading new vocabulary in the context of personal preferences

Suggestions: Encourage students to demonstrate or describe the exercises they choose in order to demonstrate comprehension of the vocabulary.

Answers will vary.

 Enriching Your Teaching

Culture Note

Baseball became popular in the Caribbean and Central America years ago. Mexico alone has over 4,000,000 amateur players. Spain can boast only a few thousand players, yet it sent a team to the Olympics in 1992—the same year that baseball became an official Olympic sport. That year, the games took place in Barcelona.

Internet Search
Keyword: educación física

127

Language Input

Vocabulario y gramática

Presentation

Standards: 1.1, 1.2, 3.1

Resources: Voc. & Gram. Transparencies: 78–79; Resource Book: Cap. 3, Input Script; Audio Program: CD Cap. 3, Track 13, 15

Focus: Extending presentation of vocabulary and grammar in context

Suggestions:

Pre-reading: Have students close their books. Show *Vocabulary & Grammar Transparency* 78. Tell students that one person in each of the pictures has a problem and ask if they can identify it.

Reading: Allow students time to read the presentation silently first, including the Web page on p. 129. Then play the *Audio CD* and have students read along as they listen. Allow them to listen more than once.

Post-reading: Check comprehension by asking questions. See the Input Script in the *Teacher's Resource Book* for specific questions.

Actividad 24

Standards: 1.2

Resources: Audio Program: CD Cap. 3, Track 14; Resource Book: Cap. 3, Audio Script; Practice Answers on Transparencies

Focus: Practicing listening comprehension of new vocabulary and structures

Suggestions: Allow students to listen to the activity once through first. Then play the *Audio CD* again, pausing after each item so students can write their answers.

Answers:
1. B   2. M   3. B   4. M   5. B   6. M

Extension: After completing the activity, ask students to replace any bad advice they heard with helpful advice.

Actividad 24 Escuchar

Escoge un buen consejo

Escribe los números del 1 al 6 en una hoja. Escucha lo que aconsejan estas personas y escribe si es un buen consejo (*B*) o un mal consejo (*M*).

Universal Access

Heritage Language Learners

Invite students who have lived in a heritage country to tell about comic strips that are popular there. Ask questions to guide them: *¿Cómo se llaman los personajes importantes? ¿Cómo son? ¿Quién lee la tira cómica típicamente? ¿Se publica en un diario o en una revista?*

Students with Learning Difficulties

Make photocopies of *Vocabulary & Grammar Transparency* 78. Have students use these to cut out the dialogue balloons. Make other copies in which the dialogue balloons have been blanked out by covering them with a piece of paper. Give students sets of dialogue balloons and dialogue-less comic strips. Have them match the dialogues to the pictures.

Address: http://www.who.int/en/

Día mundial de la salud
"Por tu salud, muévete"
7 de abril

LA ACTIVIDAD FÍSICA Y LOS JÓVENES

Según la OMS (Organización Mundial de la Salud), el ejercicio es muy importante para la salud de los jóvenes. La práctica regular del ejercicio o del deporte ayuda a los niños y a los jóvenes a **desarrollar** y mantener saludables los huesos y los músculos. También ayuda a cuidar el peso, a reducir las grasas y al buen funcionamiento del corazón.

Los juegos, los deportes y otras actividades físicas permiten a los jóvenes expresarse, tener **confianza en sí mismos** y desarrollar sentimientos de éxito. Estos efectos positivos reducen el estrés de la vida de los jóvenes de hoy.

 Actividad 25 Escribir/Hablar ·····················

¿Comprendiste?

1. ¿Por qué es buena la práctica regular de ejercicios?
2. ¿Cuáles son cuatro beneficios de hacer ejercicio?
3. ¿Cuáles son algunos efectos positivos de reducir el estrés con el ejercicio?
4. ¿Estás de acuerdo con que los juegos y deportes permiten a los jóvenes expresarse? Explica tu respuesta.

● **Más práctica** ·····················
Practice Workbook 3-8, 3-9

PHSchool.com
For: Vocabulary practice
Visit: www.phschool.com
Web Code: jed-0306

 Actividad 26 Leer/Hablar ·····················

Tu propia experiencia

Lee las frases y dile a otro(a) estudiante cuándo tienes los problemas de los que se habla aquí.

Me caigo de sueño . . .
Estoy de mal humor . . .
Me preocupo . . .
No tengo energía . . .
Estoy estresado(a) . . .
No puedo concentrarme . . .
Me quejo . . .

| Modelo |

Me siento fatal si no duermo bien.

ciento veintinueve **129**
Capítulo 3

Actividad 25 *Standards:* 1.1, 1.2, 3.1

Resources: Practice Answers on Transparencies

Focus: Demonstrating comprehension of new vocabulary

Suggestions: Have students discuss answers with a partner first. Then open the discussion up to the whole class.

Answers:
1. Es muy importante para la salud.
2. Ayuda a los niños y a los jóvenes a desarrollar y mantener saludables los huesos y los músculos. También ayuda a cuidar el peso, a reducir las grasas y al buen funcionamiento del corazón.
3. Permite a una persona expresarse, tener confianza en sí mismo y desarrollar sentimientos de éxito.
4. Answers will vary.

Actividad 26 *Standards:* 1.1

Focus: Demonstrating comprehension of new vocabulary

Suggestions: Encourage students to give realistic responses. If they don't have the problem specified, ask them to make a negative statement followed by an additional comment: *Nunca me preocupo mucho. Preocuparse mucho no resuelve ningún problema.*

Answers will vary.

Additional Resources
• Resource Book: Cap. 3, Clip Art

✓ **Assessment**
• Prueba 3-6: Vocabulary recognition

Chapter Project
Students can perform step 3 at this point. (For more information, see p. 108-a.)

 Enriching Your Teaching

Culture Note

In a Spanish custom of long ago, girls played a game called **echar los estrechos** (pick your dear one) on the last day of each year. They wrote their names on pieces of paper and put them in a bag. Then they wrote the names of boys they knew or wished they knew and put them in another bag. The girls drew pairs of papers and read aloud the names of each couple. If a pair of people named were already in a relationship, it was thought good luck. If they weren't, it was thought (or hoped!) that they would be before long.

▶ Rapid Review

Resources: Voc. & Gram. Transparencies: 70–72

Suggestions: Use *Vocabulary & Grammar Transparencies* 70–72 for a quick review of vocabulary from pp. 114–116. Ask: *¿Cuáles son unos malos hábitos alimenticios?¿Y unos buenos?* Reviewing this information will help students with step 2 of *Actividad* 27.

Standards: 1.2

Resources: Voc. & Gram. Transparencies: 80; Practice Answers on Transparencies

Focus: Demonstrating comprehension of new words and expressions

Suggestions: Show *Vocabulary & Grammar Transparency* 78 for students to use as a reference as they do step 1.

Answers:

Step 1

Some expressions are similar, and their use may vary. The following are suggestions.

1. **No tengo energía.**
2. **Estoy en la Luna.**
3. **No aguanto más.**
4. **No me puedo concentrar.**
5. **Me caigo de sueño.**
6. **Me siento fatal.**

Step 2

Answers will vary.

Extension: After completing the activity, invite pairs of students to role-play one or more of the exchanges from step 1 for the class. Encourage them to use appropriate intonation for the various expressions.

Objectives
- Talk about fitness equipment
- Talk about different exercises to stay fit
- Review the subjunctive of regular verbs
- Review the subjunctive of irregular and stem-changing verbs

Manos a la obra 2

Vocabulario y gramática en uso

Leer/Escribir

En la clase de ejercicios aeróbicos

❶ Imagina que te inscribes en una clase de ejercicios aeróbicos. Describe cómo se siente cada estudiante usando las expresiones del recuadro.

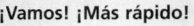

No aguanto más	No tengo energía	No me puedo concentrar
o	o	o
Me siento fatal	Me caigo de sueño	Estoy en la luna

1.

2.

3.

4.

5.

6.

❷ Escribe cinco consejos para los estudiantes de esta clase.

Modelo

Deben tomar vitaminas y desayunar mejor.

Universal Access

Students with Learning Difficulties
Before students complete *Actividad* 27, remind them that the third suggested sentence, **No me puedo concentrar** can also be stated **No puedo concentrarme.** They may have less difficulty understanding the alternative construction.

Advanced Learners
Ask students to work in a small group to prepare a brief skit set in a physical education class. One student can be the instructor leading an exercise session. The others can be students in the class, some having success and others having problems. Invite the group to present the skit to the class.

Actividad 28 Leer/Escribir

Nuestra entrenadora

Completa esta descripción de una entrenadora con las palabras apropiadas del recuadro. Usa la forma apropiada de los verbos.

consejos	exigir	confianza en sí misma
débiles	corazón	estirar y flexionar
desarrollar		

Nuestra entrenadora es una atleta que sabe mantenerse en forma y tiene mucha __1.__. Durante las prácticas, ella nos __2.__ mucho. Primero tenemos que __3.__ los músculos. Luego levantamos pesas para __4.__ más músculos en los brazos. Nuestra entrenadora siempre nos da __5.__, como "Hagan ejercicio todos los días para cuidar su __6.__". Ella no quiere que seamos __7.__.

Actividad 29 Hablar

El deportista

Éstas son las sugerencias que un(a) estudiante deportista le da a su amigo(a). Trabaja con otro(a) estudiante y escojan los mejores consejos para cada pregunta.

Modelo

estar en forma
A —¿Cómo se puede estar en forma?
B —Se debe hacer ejercicio.

Estudiante A

¿Cómo se puede . . .?
1. evitar los calambres
2. quitar el mal humor
3. cuidar el corazón
4. hacer más fuertes los músculos del estómago
5. tener brazos menos débiles

Estudiante B

Se debe . . .
Se recomienda . . .

Fondo cultural

La educación física en España es parte del programa de educación en las escuelas. Sin embargo, en los últimos años muchos estudiantes comenzaron a ir a los clubes deportivos para hacer ejercicio. ¿Por qué? Las escuelas no tienen los equipos deportivos necesarios o estos equipos son muy antiguos.

Muchos profesores de educación física están preocupados por la situación. En primer lugar, dicen ellos, los estudiantes deben tener el equipo necesario para las clases de educación física en su escuela, donde sus profesores pueden decirles qué ejercicios son mejores para su edad. En segundo lugar, muchos jóvenes tienen lesiones *(injuries)* cuando usan equipos deportivos que no conocen, sin la ayuda de un entrenador.

• ¿Qué crees que se debe hacer en las escuelas de España para mejorar esa situación? Compara su situación con la de tu escuela.

ciento treinta y uno **131**
Capítulo 3

Culture Note

About 80 percent of the people in the world rely on plants to treat illnesses. Even the other 20 percent use many prescription drugs that are plant-based. Aspirin, for example, is based on a substance found in willow bark. Plants in the rain forests of the Americas play an important part in the discovery and development of new drugs. About one half of all the plant species on earth are found there. Scientists have estimated that there may be millions of species of plants in the world, but so far, only about 250,000 have been identified. Each year, deforestation and pollution may be wiping out many species of unknown plants.

Actividad 28 Standards: 1.2

Resources: Practice Answers on Transparencies

Focus: Using new vocabulary in a cloze exercise

Suggestions: Encourage students to scan the complete paragraph before they attempt to write their answers.

Answers:
1. confianza en sí misma
2. exige
3. estirar y flexionar
4. desarrollar
5. consejos
6. corazón
7. débiles

Actividad 29 Standards: 1.1

Resources: Practice Answers on Transparencies

Focus: Practicing new vocabulary in a guided conversation

Suggestions: Have students switch roles to practice both parts of the dialogue.

Answers will vary.
Probable answers:
1. Se debe/Se recomienda estirar (flexionar).
2. … hacer yoga.
3. … hacer bicicleta.
4. … hacer abdominales.
5. … levantar pesas.

Fondo cultural Standards: 1.1, 1.2, 3.1

Suggestions: Ask: ¿Qué problema tienen muchas escuelas españolas? ¿Qué hacen los estudiantes para resolver este problema? ¿Qué pasa si un estudiante usa equipo deportivo que no conoce?

Answers will vary.

Additional Resources

• Writing, Audio & Video Workbook: Cap. 3, Audio Activity 3, Track 16
• Writing, Audio & Video Workbook: Cap. 3, Writing Activity 10
• Resource Book: Cap. 3, Communicative Activity BLM

✓ Assessment

• Prueba 3-7: Vocabulary production

131

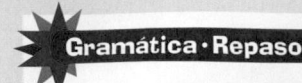

Practice and Communicate

Gramática·Repaso

Presentation

Resources: Voc. & Gram. Transparencies: 80

Suggestions: Point out that the endings used for regular verbs in the subjunctive are the same as those used for negative command forms. Refer students to pp. 122–123 for these endings.

Standards: 1.2

Resources: Practice Answers on Transparencies

Focus: Practicing forms of the present subjunctive with regular verbs

Suggestions: Ask students to pay attention to the reason for using the subjunctive in each case as they work. Then have volunteers read each sentence of the completed activity aloud, including the correct verb form.

Common Errors: Since English contains only a few vestiges of the subjunctive (such as "If I were you..."), some students have difficulty remembering to use it in Spanish. Help them by providing more examples in Spanish that require the subjunctive.

Answers:
1. comience
2. corran
3. hablen
4. hagan
5. estiremos
6. subamos

Extension: As students read through the completed activity aloud, ask them to state the reason why the subjunctive is required in each case.

Gramática·Repaso

El subjuntivo: Verbos regulares

To say that one person wants, suggests, or demands that someone else do something, use the *subjunctive mood.* A sentence that includes the subjunctive form has two parts, the main clause and the subordinate clause, connected by the word *que.*

> **Quiero que respires** lentamente. **Sugiero que bebas** agua antes de correr.
> El entrenador **exige que** los atletas **estiren** los músculos.

You can also suggest more general or impersonal ideas using expressions such as *es necesario . . . , es bueno . . . ,* and *es importante . . . ,* followed by *que* and a form of the present subjunctive.

> **Es necesario que hagas** ejercicio. **Es importante que** los jóvenes **coman** bien.

To form the subjunctive, drop the *-o* ending to the *yo* form of the present tense, and add the present subjunctive endings to the stem of the verb.

saltar

salte	saltemos
saltes	saltéis
salte	salten

conocer

conozca	conozcamos
conozcas	conozcáis
conozca	conozcan

decir

diga	digamos
digas	digáis
diga	digan

Verbs ending in *-car, -gar,* and *-zar* have a spelling change in order to keep the pronunciation consistent.

buscar (c → qu)

busque	busquemos
busques	busquéis
busque	busquen

pagar (g → gu)

pague	paguemos
pagues	paguéis
pague	paguen

cruzar (z → c)

cruce	crucemos
cruces	crucéis
cruce	crucen

 **Gramática** **Leer/Escribir**

Una clase inolvidable

¿Tuviste alguna vez una instructora de ejercicios aeróbicos que siempre estaba de mal humor? Completa la descripción con el verbo apropiado en subjuntivo.

La instructora exige que la clase __1.__ *(comenzar / cruzar)* a tiempo y que los estudiantes __2.__ *(correr / comer)* durante diez minutos antes de comenzar la sesión. Ella no permite que ellos __3.__ *(tocar / hablar)* durante la clase. A ella tampoco le gusta que __4.__ *(hacer / tener)* ruido cuando da la clase. Prefiere que nos __5.__ *(estirar / cruzar)* y que __6.__ *(apagar / subir)* escaleras para tener más energía antes de la clase.

Universal Access

Heritage Language Learners

Have students listen to conversations between family members and focus on words or phrases in the subjunctive mood. Ask them to estimate how frequently the subjunctive is used in a brief conversation. Have them write down as many of the words as they can remember. Check for spelling and structure.

Students with Learning Difficulties

Before beginning the grammar presentation on this page, remind students that they have already seen these spelling changes in other grammatical forms. On the board, write the preterite forms of *sacar, llegar,* and *empezar.* Highlight the spelling changes in the *yo* form and remind students of the spelling change rules.

Actividad 31 · Hablar

¿Qué ejercicios hago?

Imagínate que eres el(la) entrenador(a) de la escuela. Habla con otro(a) estudiante para aconsejarle algo. Usen las siguientes expresiones.

Modelo

Me duele(n) . . . / Es necesario que . . . .
A —*Me duelen las piernas cuando corro.*
B —*Es necesario que estires los músculos antes de correr.*

Estudiante A

1. ¿Qué hago para . . . ?
2. No puedo . . .
3. Estoy muy . . .
4. Quiero desarrollar . . .
5. Necesito . . .
6. Tengo . . .

Estudiante B

Te sugiero que . . .
Es importante que . . .
Para que estés más tranquilo(a), te aconsejo que . . .
Lo mejor es que practiques . . .
Es muy bueno que vayas a . . .
Para evitar los calambres quiero que . . .

El español en el mundo del trabajo

La consejera bilingüe

De niña, María Romero Thomas hablaba sólo español en su casa e inglés en la escuela. Sus padres le decían que ella no podía olvidar la cultura de sus abuelos mexicanos, pero que debía integrarse *(to integrate)* y tener éxito en la cultura estadounidense. María quiso ayudar a otros a alcanzar también esa meta y decidió estudiar para ser una consejera escolar.

La función de un(a) consejero(a) escolar es muy importante para los estudiantes y para la comunidad. Estos(as) profesionales se dedican a dar apoyo a los chicos y a guiarlos al elegir la carrera que van a seguir. También aconsejan sobre temas de salud, cómo coordinar el estudio con otras actividades como recreación, trabajo y ejercicios, en las relaciones con su familia y amigos, cómo mantener un buen estado de ánimo, y cómo desarrollar sus aptitudes en la escuela. Si ven que los chicos se sienten mal, no se pueden concentrar o están muy estresados, les recomiendan ir al médico, tener una alimentación saludable y cosas que pueden hacer para relajarse.

Al comienzo de los años ochenta, María Romero Thomas se convirtió en *(became)* la primera consejera bilingüe del Sequoia Union High School District, en California. En esos años, viajaba de una escuela a otra para implementar el primer programa bilingüe del distrito. También hablaba con los padres sobre la importancia que tenía para sus hijos recibir una buena educación.

Hoy en día, hay cientos de consejeros bilingües en los distritos escolares de los Estados Unidos que ayudan a los niños hispanohablantes a vivir entre dos culturas.

Practice and Communicate

 ③

Actividad 31

Standards: 1.1

Focus: Using the subjunctive with regular verbs in a guided conversation

Recycle: parts of the body; **poder** + infinitive

Suggestions: Allow students a few minutes on their own to prepare the problems they are going to talk about when they play the role of Student A. As they practice the dialogue together, encourage those playing the role of Student B to respond as quickly and naturally as possible with a suggestion that makes sense.

Answers will vary.

El español en el mundo del trabajo

Presentation

Standards: 1.2, 3.1, 5.1

Suggestions: Ask students, including Heritage Language Learners who may have known a bilingual advisor, to talk about their experiences with him or her. Ask: *¿Cómo ayudaba el (la) consejero(a) a los estudiantes? ¿Tenía interacción con los profesores también? ¿Y con los padres? ¿Cuáles eran algunas de sus tareas?* Then ask students: *¿Les interesa tener una carrera como consejero(a) bilingüe? ¿Por qué? ¿Por qué no?*

Teacher-to-Teacher

Prepare (or ask Advanced Learners to prepare) two sets of notecards. One set contains subordinate clauses in which the verb is in the infinitive in parentheses *...que (estudiar) mucho*. The other set is a mixture of main clauses, some that require the subjunctive in the subordinate clause and some that do not, such as **Es evidente que... or Veo que....** Students can take turns drawing one card from each pile, determining whether or not the subjunctive is needed in the subordinate clause, and if so, what its form is. Then have them read the complete complex sentence aloud: *Veo que estudias mucho.*

Enriching Your Teaching

Culture Note

For a great many Spanish-speaking people the notion of "bilingualism" has nothing to do with English. In Mexico alone, more than a hundred languages are spoken, from the **nahuatl** of the Aztecs to **amuzgo** to **zoque.** About eight percent of those who speak an indigenous language are bilingual in Spanish. Consider all of Central and South America and the Caribbean, and the number of known languages rises to almost a thousand. Indigenous languages are so important in some countries that they have been given official standing equal to Spanish. Examples include **guarani** in Paraguay and **quechua** in Peru.

Standards: 1.1

Resources: Practice Answers on Transparencies

Focus: Practicing the subjunctive with regular verbs in a guided conversation

Suggestions: Remind students that the words and expressions in the word bank are to be used to begin the main clause in Student B's sentences.

Answers: Student B's sentences will vary, but should make use of the following subjunctive forms:

saques	tomes
pongas	hagas
respires	conozcas
añadas	hagas

Focus: Practicing the subjunctive with regular verbs in the context of giving advice

Suggestions: Challenge students to be creative with their mixing and matching from the three columns, in order to make as many sentences as they can.

Answers will vary.

Students should choose from the following subjunctive verb forms, depending on the subject of each subordinate *(que)* clause:

limpies/limpie/limpiemos/limpien
llegues/llegue/lleguemos/lleguen
laves/lave/lavemos/laven
expliques/explique/expliquemos/expliquen
muestres/muestre/mostremos/muestren
te preocupes/se preocupe/nos preocupemos/se preocupen
tengas/tenga/tengamos/tengan
aprendas/aprenda/aprendamos/aprendan

Additional Resources
• Writing, Audio & Video Workbook: Cap. 3, Writing Activity 11

 Assessment
• Prueba 3-8: *El subjuntivo: Verbos regulares*

 **Gramática** **Hablar**

¿Qué le aconsejas?

Tu amigo(a) siempre se queja de sus problemas. ¿Qué le aconsejas en cada caso? Trabaja con otro(a) estudiante para darle consejos. Usa la forma correcta del subjuntivo y las expresiones del recuadro.

sugiero	recomiendo	quiero	es importante	es necesario

Modelo

Me caigo de sueño. / descansar un poco
A —*Me caigo de sueño.*
B —*Sugiero que descanses un poco.*

Estudiante A

1. Siempre estoy en la luna.
2. Quiero hacer más fuertes mi corazón y los músculos de mis piernas.
3. No tengo energía.
4. Estoy aburrido(a).
5. No aguanto más los juegos de mis amigos.
6. Siempre tengo sed.
7. Como demasiada comida basura.
8. Necesito hacer más ejercicio.

Estudiante B

sacar . . . de la biblioteca
poner . . .
respirar lentamente . . .
añadir más . . .
tomar . . .
hacer . . .
conocer . . .
hacer . . . y ejercicios . . .

¡Respuesta personal!

 Gramática **Escribir**

En el club atlético Sol y Salud

Trabajas en un club atlético y tienes que darles consejos a los miembros del club y a las personas que trabajan contigo. Combina palabras de las tres columnas para hacer frases con el subjuntivo.

Modelo

Queremos / Roberto / enseñar
Queremos que Roberto enseñe la clase de ejercicios aeróbicos.

Es importante que . . .	los entrenadores	limpiar
Sugerimos que . . .	tú	llegar a tiempo
Es mejor que . . .	David y Rita	lavar
(No) Queremos que . . .	nadie	explicar
Es necesario que . . .	ustedes	mostrar cómo
Exigimos que . . .	Julieta	no preocuparse por
	los profesores	(no) tener
	todos	aprender

● **Más práctica**
Practice Workbook 3-10

For: Practice with the subjunctive
Visit: www.phschool.com
Web Code: jed-0307

Universal Access

Students with Learning Difficulties
Ask students to search for a picture in which two or more people are interacting socially. Have them write sentences using the subjunctive that the people in the picture might be saying to one another. Ask students to cut their sentences out in the shape of dialogue balloons and paste them to the picture.

Advanced Learners
Ask students to write ten affirmative commands about eating well and keeping fit. Have them exchange sentences with a partner. Partners take turns changing the commands into suggestions, demands, or requirements that take the subjunctive: *Deja de comer comida basura./ Es mejor que dejes de comer comida basura.*

Gramática·Repaso

El subjuntivo: Verbos irregulares

The following verbs are irregular in the present subjunctive:

dar	estar	haber	ir	saber	ser
dé	esté	haya	vaya	sepa	sea
des	estés	hayas	vayas	sepas	seas
dé	esté	haya	vaya	sepa	sea
demos	estemos	hayamos	vayamos	sepamos	seamos
deis	estéis	hayáis	vayáis	sepáis	seáis
den	estén	hayan	vayan	sepan	sean

Actividad 34 · Gramática · Leer/Escribir

Cambiar los hábitos

Rocío y Manuel están estresados. Escoge el verbo correcto y completa las recomendaciones que les dio el consejero.

1. Es importante que Manuel _____ yoga dos veces por semana. *(cambiar / hacer)*

2. Les aconsejo que _____ más confianza en sí mismos. *(ser / tener)*

3. Recomiendo que los dos _____ caminatas por el campo. *(eliminar / dar)*

4. Es bueno que ustedes _____ de vacaciones al campo. *(ir / cambiar)*

5. Rocío, te recomiendo que _____ más paciente con Manuel. *(estar / ser)*

6. Por último, sugiero que cada uno _____ sus propios amigos. *(perder / tener)*

Actividad 35 · Leer/Escribir

Carta a la consejera sentimental

Completa esta correspondencia entre una joven y una consejera con las palabras apropiadas del recuadro.

decir	llegar	relajarse	hacer
estar	ser	haber	darse

Querida Ana:

Mis padres siempre me exigen demasiado. Quieren que yo siempre les __1.__ adónde voy y me exigen que __2.__ a casa antes de las 9 de la noche. Casi todos los días tenemos algún problema.
¡No aguanto más!

Frustrada en Quito

Querida Frustrada:

Primero, te aconsejo que __3.__. Es importante que __4.__ un esfuerzo para comprender lo que quieren tus padres. Ellos quieren que __5.__ segura *(safe)*. Aunque tú quieres salir con tus amigos, es necesario que __6.__ responsable. No es bueno que __7.__ problemas en tu casa, y te recomiendo que __8.__ cuenta de lo que haces. Sé paciente y trata de hablar con tus padres y las cosas van a mejorar.

Ana

Enriching Your Teaching

Teacher-to-Teacher

Invent a few scenarios in which you briefly describe an imaginary problem and ask for advice. Surprise an individual student from time to time during this chapter by taking him or her aside, presenting your "problem," and seeking his or her advice. Problem scenarios might include being tired all the time, symptoms of a minor illness such as a cold or the flu, or questions about how to create a healthy meal for your guests.

Gramática·Repaso

Presentation

Resources: Voc. & Gram. Transparencies: 81

Suggestions: Challenge students to create sentences using subjunctive verb forms that you call out.

Standards: 1.2

Resources: Practice Answers on Transparencies

Focus: Practicing forms of the present subjunctive with irregular verbs

Suggestions: Review with students the verbs in the main clause that require the subjunctive in the subordinate clause.

Answers:
1. haga
2. tengan
3. den
4. vayan
5. seas
6. tenga

Standards: 1.2

Focus: Practicing the subjunctive with irregular verbs in a cloze exercise

Suggestions: Encourage students to look for expressions such as *querer que* and *es necesario que.* Remind them that these expressions are markers for the subjunctive.

Answers:
1. diga
2. llegue
3. te relajes
4. hagas
5. estés
6. seas
7. haya
8. te des

Chapter Project

Students can perform step 4 at this point. Be sure they understand your corrections and suggestions. (For more information, see p. 108-a.)

Resources: Practice Answers on Transparencies

Focus: Practicing new vocabulary and structures via letter reading and writing

Suggestions: Encourage students to build sentences around the *sugerencias* before they organize them into a response.

Answers will vary.

Verb forms for the *sugerencias* are as follows:
cambies
estés
salgas
tengas
camines

Standards: 1.1

Resources: Practice Answers on Transparencies

Focus: Practicing new vocabulary and structures in guided conversations

Suggestions: Have groups conduct the activity in round-robin fashion. Rotate around the circle with a different student presenting the problem each time, with others eliciting possible solutions.

Answers will vary.

Students may use the following vocabulary and subjunctive forms:
1. Tengo calambres. 3. Estoy de mal humor.
2. Me caigo de sueño. 4. Estoy estresado(a).
vayas, conozcas, estés, tengas, seas, sepas

Additional Resources
• Writing, Audio & Video Workbook: Cap. 3, Writing Activity 12

Assessment
• Prueba 3-9: *El subjuntivo: Verbos irregulares*

Actividad 36 **Gramática** **Leer/Escribir**

Querida Laura . . .

Muchos jóvenes le escriben a Laura, la escritora de la columna de consejos de una revista de Madrid. Lee la carta que una joven le escribió a Laura y luego escribe la respuesta de Laura. Usa expresiones como: *te recomiendo, te sugiero, es necesario, es bueno, es importante* y la lista de sugerencias. Pon los verbos en el subjuntivo.

Querida Laura:
Me encanta la clase de yoga. Siempre me siento mejor y me relajo después de ir. Pero el problema es que no tengo tiempo. Tengo mucha tarea y también estudio piano. ¿Cómo me puedo relajar y estar tranquila si no puedo ir a yoga?

Ocupada de Burgos

Querida Ocupada de Burgos:
Si tienes tanto trabajo y no puedes ir a tu clase de yoga, te recomiendo que . . .

Sugerencias
• cambiar el horario
• estar ocupada
• salir con los(as) amigos(as)
• tener tiempo para relajarse
• caminar todos los días

Actividad 37 **Gramática** **Hablar**

Intercambio de ideas

Imagina que tú eres la persona de los dibujos. Tus compañeros(as) te van a dar sugerencias o consejos para ayudarte a resolver tus problemas. Usen los verbos del recuadro.

Modelo
A— *Estoy muy aburrido, nunca hago nada interesante.*
B— *Es importante que salgas más.*
C— *Es bueno que conozcas más gente.*

ir	conocer	estar	tener	ser	saber

1.   2.

3.    4.

● **Más práctica**
Practice Workbook 3-11

Go Online PHSchool.com
For: Practice with the subjunctive
Visit: www.phschool.com
Web Code: jed-0308

136 ciento treinta y seis
Manos a la obra 2

Universal Access

Heritage Language Learners
Advice is often given in the form of popular sayings. Cite a few examples, such as **Barriga llena, corazón contento** or **Todo lo que brilla no es oro.** Have students ask family members what their favorite saying is and write them down. Encourage them to find out if there are similar sayings in English.

Students with Special Needs
Have visually impaired students sit with a partner who can help them complete *Actividad* 37 by explaining the scene in each of the pictures.

Gramática · Repaso

El subjuntivo: Verbos con cambio de raíz

In the present subjunctive, stem-changing *-ar* and *-er* verbs have the stem change in all forms except *nosotros* and *vosotros*.

jugar (u → ue)

juegue	juguemos
juegues	juguéis
juegue	jueguen

pensar (e → ie)

piense	pensemos
pienses	penséis
piense	piensen

entender (e → ie)

entienda	entendamos
entiendas	entendáis
entienda	entiendan

• Other verbs you know that follow these patterns are:

 o → ue: contar, poder, volver, costar, probar(se), llover, doler
 e → ie: querer, sentarse, calentar, despertar(se), empezar, entender

Stem-changing *e → ie, e → i,* and *o → ue* verbs that end in *-ir* have a stem change in all forms of the subjunctive.

sentirse (e → ie)

me sienta	nos sintamos
te sientas	os sintáis
se sienta	se sientan

pedir (e → i)

pida	pidamos
pidas	pidáis
pida	pidan

dormir (o → ue)

duerma	durmamos
duermas	durmáis
duerma	duerman

• Other verbs you know that follow these patterns are:

 e → ie: divertirse, preferir
 e → i: reír, repetir, servir, vestir(se), seguir, conseguir
 o → ue: morir

Actividad 38 **Gramática** **Leer/Escribir**

¿Qué recomienda la entrenadora?

Estás en un gimnasio y la entrenadora te recomienda varias cosas. Lee lo que dice la entrenadora y escoge el verbo apropiado para completar las frases en subjuntivo.

1. Es importante que _____ mis consejos. (*sentir / seguir*)

2. Sugiero que _____ ocho horas cada noche. (*pedir / dormir*)

3. Es importante que no _____ durante las clases de ejercicio. (*sentarse / practicar*)

4. Quiero que _____ bicicleta tres veces por semana. (*repetir / hacer*)

5. También es bueno que _____ al tenis una o dos veces por semana. (*pensar / jugar*)

6. Te aconsejo que _____ con ropa cómoda. (*seguir / vestirse*)

7. Quiero que _____ durante la clase. (*concentrarse / reír*)

8. Es necesario que _____ cuántas flexiones haces. (*contar / cantar*)

ciento treinta y siete **137**
Capítulo 3

▶ **Rapid Review**
Briefly review the indicative forms of stem-changing verbs. On the board write paradigms for some of the verbs in the *Gramática* on this page. Leave some forms out of each paradigm and ask students to supply them, either by spelling them aloud or filling in the paradigm.

Gramática · Repaso

Presentation

Resources: Voc. & Gram. Transparencies: 82

Suggestions: On the board, list *...que yo ___, ...que tú ___, ...que Ud./él/ella ___, ...que nosotros(as) ___,* and *...que Uds./ellos/ellas ___.* Point to these phrases at random and call out an infinitive from the *Gramática*. Ask students to supply and spell aloud the correct subjunctive form.

Actividad 38 *Standards:* 1.2

Resources: Practice Answers on Transparencies

Focus: Practicing stem-changing subjunctive verb forms

Suggestions: Remind students to be extra careful with spelling, since that is the focus of the activity.

Answers:

1. sigas	5. juegues
2. duermas	6. te vistas
3. te sientes	7. te concentres
4. hagas	8. cuentes

Additional Resources

• Writing, Audio & Video Workbook: Cap. 3, Audio Activity 4, Track 17

Enriching Your Teaching

Teacher-to-Teacher

Supply blank index cards and have pairs of students work together to make flashcards for stem-changing verbs. They should write one verb form on each card. On the back of each card they can write the infinitive, tense, and mood. For example, "*jugar*—present subjunctive." This will help users reorganize the cards into sets when they are mixed up. Keep verb sets clipped together. Making such cards is a good exercise in itself, and they are a useful tool to be kept on hand for a great variety of practice activities.

 Gramática   Escribir/Hablar

Actividad 39

Standards: 1.1, 1.3, 3.1

Focus: Practicing new vocabulary and structures via writing and guided conversation

Suggestions: In step 1, make sure students understand from the model that the two cues should be combined to make one sentence. Remind them that the subordinate *(que)* clause of each sentence should contain a subject of their choice and a subjunctive verb form. In step 2, encourage Student B to explain in one or more sentences why he or she agrees or disagrees with the original comment.

Answers will vary.

Students should use the following expressions and subjunctive verbs:

1. Es bueno que durmamos…
2. Es mejor que perdamos…
3. Es bueno que pidamos…
4. Es bueno que volvamos…
5. Es importante que nos acostemos…
6. Es necesario que juguemos…
7. Es necesario que entendamos…
8. Es importante que sigamos…

Extension: Ask partners to report to the class on their opinions regarding a healthy lifestyle. Create a class profile by recording the information on the board.

En voz alta

Presentation

Standards: 1.2, 2.2, 3.2, 5.2

Resources: Audio Program: Cap. 3, Track 18

Suggestions: Have students read the information and the song silently. Ask comprehension questions: *¿De qué nacionalidad era José Alfredo Jiménez? ¿Por qué se conocen sus canciones? ¿De qué cosas hablan las canciones rancheras?*

Before having students read the song, direct their attention to the information in the *¿Recuerdas?* Allow them a few minutes to practice with a partner.

Decisiones

1 Con otro(a) estudiante, hagan una lista de buenos consejos para llevar una vida más saludable.

Modelo

importante / comer
Es importante que comamos verduras todos los días.

1. bueno / dormir
2. mejor / perder
3. bueno / pedir
4. bueno / volver
5. importante / acostarse
6. necesario / jugar
7. necesario / entender
8. importante / seguir

2 Léele las sugerencias que escribiste a otro(a) estudiante, quien va a decidir si está de acuerdo o no y por qué.

Modelo

A —*Es importante que comamos verduras todos los días.*
B —*Estoy de acuerdo.*
o: *No estoy de acuerdo. Es más importante que comamos comida con menos grasa.*

En voz alta

Lee una parte de la letra de una canción ranchera escrita por José Alfredo Jiménez (1923–1973), un compositor y cantante mexicano. Sus canciones se conocen por su hermosa música y por la poesía de sus letras. Cantantes internacionales como Vicki Carr, Jorge Negrete y María Dolores Pradera las han interpretado. Las canciones rancheras usan palabras sencillas y hablan del ambiente de los ranchos en México, su paisaje y sus tradiciones.

¿Recuerdas?

Cuando la letra *c* va antes de *a, o* y *u*, se pronuncia como la *c* de *cat*.

Cuando la *c* va antes de *e* o de *i*, se pronuncia como la *s* de *Sally*.

Para mantener el sonido de la *c* de *cat* antes de la *e* y la *i*, las palabras se escriben con *qu*: *busqué, aquí.*

Que te vaya bonito

de José Alfredo Jiménez

Ojalá[1] que te vaya bonito
ojalá que se acaben tus penas
que te digan que yo ya no existo
y conozcas personas más buenas
que te den lo que no pude darte
aunque yo te haya dado de todo
nunca más volveré a molestarte,
te adoré, te perdí, ya ni modo[2].

Cuántas cosas quedaron prendidas[3]
hasta dentro del fondo de mi alma[4]
cuántas luces dejaste encendidas
yo no sé cómo voy a apagarlas.

---

1 I wish, I hope **2** there's no point **3** attached **4** soul

---

Universal Access

Heritage Language Learners

Have small groups review the words in *Actividad* 39 and brainstorm other words and phrases that they know are often or always used with the subjunctive. Have the groups compare lists. Then have each group write a sentence for each of the words.

Students with Learning Difficulties

Unusual punctuation makes the song more difficult to understand. If students have difficulty, ask them to copy the lines and add the punctuation. (Add periods at the ends of lines 1, 6, and 10, a comma at the end of lines 2 and 5, and an exclamation point at the end of line 11.)

Actividad 40

Leer/Hablar • • • • • • • • • •

Cómo te beneficia el ejercicio

1 Lee este artículo que explica diferentes clases de ejercicio y los beneficios que tienen.

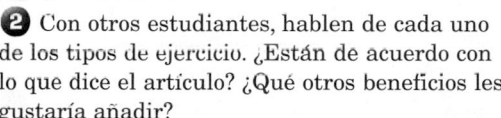

Más danza y ritmos latinos

Este tipo de danza comienza con un calentamiento de músculos. Incluye ritmos latinos y no tiene saltos.

Beneficios: Ayuda a la coordinación.

CARDIO TRAINING

Pon tu corazón en forma y, con él, todo tu organismo

Es el mejor ejercicio para estar en forma. Comienza con un calentamiento, sigue con una actividad física más intensa, como los saltos, y termina con una fase de descanso, para llevar el ritmo cardíaco a la normalidad.

Beneficios: Ayuda a la capacidad cardiovascular y todas las funciones del organismo.

STEP

Ejercicios similares al aerobic pero utilizando un escalón

Se trata de subir y bajar un escalón mientras se realizan pasos en los que se utiliza todo el cuerpo. Es como un baile. Se hace al ritmo de música disco o similar.

Beneficios: Hace más fuertes los músculos, mejora la coordinación.

2 Con otros estudiantes, hablen de cada uno de los tipos de ejercicio. ¿Están de acuerdo con lo que dice el artículo? ¿Qué otros beneficios les gustaría añadir?

3 Y a ti, ¿cuál de las clases de ejercicio te gustaría tomar? Explica tu repuesta.

4 Hagan recomendaciones a otros jóvenes. Usen formas del subjuntivo.

Modelo

Sugiero que hagas danza aeróbica si te gusta bailar. Es importante que vayas a clases de cardio training si quieres ser deportista profesional.

● **Más práctica** • • • • • • • • • • • • • • •

Practice Workbook 3-12

 Go Online
PHSchool.com

For: Practice with the subjunctive
Visit: www.phschool.com
Web Code: jed-0309

Practice and Communicate (3)

Focus: Practicing new vocabulary and structures through reading and discussion

Suggestions: Have students read the article silently twice before opening the discussion. As they discuss the article, encourage them to paraphrase parts that support the comments they make. As students complete step 4, ask: *¿Han cambiado sus opiniones o recomendaciones desde que empezamos este capítulo? ¿De qué manera?*

Answers will vary.

Additional Resources

• Writing, Audio & Video Workbook: Cap. 3, Writing Activity 13
• Writing, Audio & Video Workbook: Cap. 3, Audio Activity 5, Track 19

 ## Assessment

• Prueba 3-10: *El subjuntivo: Verbos con cambios de raíz*
• Examen: Vocabulario y gramática 2

Chapter Project

Students can perform step 5 at this point. Record their presentations on cassette or videotape for inclusion in their portfolio. (For more information, see p. 108-a.)

 Enriching Your Teaching

Culture Note

The type of song known as the *ranchera* was partly a result of a migration that occurred in the last century, when many Mexicans moved from farms to cities in search of work. Nostalgia for the way life used to be on the *rancho* bred these melancholic songs. The same nostalgia increased the popularity of *mariachi* music, as well. It is interesting to note that the term *mariachi* is thought to come from the French word "mariage" (mah-ree-AZH). This French influence is from the period of 1863–1867, when the French ruled Mexico under the emperor Maximilian. Then, as now, *mariachi* bands commonly performed at weddings.

139

Puente a la cultura

Standards: 1.1, 1.2, 2.1, 2.2, 3.1, 5.2

Focus: Reading to learn about ball games played by ancient peoples in Mexico

Suggestions:

Pre-reading: On the board, set up an **SQA** chart. This is a three-column chart with the columns labeled **Sé, Quiero saber,** and **Aprendí.** Have students duplicate the chart on their own paper. Direct their attention to the *Estrategia.* Help them access their prior knowledge on the topic by discussing the questions there. They can fill in the **Sé** column of their charts with this information. In the **Quiero saber** column, have them write at least three questions—things they would like to learn from reading **Un juego muy antiguo.**

Reading: As students read, remind them to use background knowledge, cognates, and context clues to understand unfamiliar words and expressions. Help them resolve comprehension problems by asking **sí/no** or embedded-answer questions.

Post-reading: Ask: *¿Encontraste las respuestas a todas tus preguntas en la lectura?* Have students fill in the **Aprendí** column of their **SQA** charts with any answers to the questions they wrote in the **Quiero saber** column, as well as other interesting facts they have learned from the reading.

Country Connection

Standards: 3.1

Remind students that the ancient ruins found at these places are some of Mexico's major historical and tourist attractions. Assign, or ask students to choose, one of the ancient sites and research it in an encyclopedia or on the Internet. Have them report back at least three interesting facts about the site they chose. (See *Internet Search* on p. 141 for some helpful keywords.)

Go Online

The online atlas will provide a more detailed map of Mexico.

Objectives

• **Read about an ancient team sport played by the Native Americans in Mexico and Central America**
• **Use different sources to understand a non-fiction article**
• **Summarize the information in a non-fiction article**

¡Adelante!

Puente a la cultura

Un juego muy antiguo

Estrategia

Using your prior knowledge
What do you know about competitive games in Roman and Greek times? Have you heard of the origin of games like baseball or basketball?

Remember that retrieving information you already know about the topic of your reading is always useful to help you better understand it.

Ilustración del antiguo juego olmeca de pelota

Mesoamérica va desde México hasta Panamá

La historia del juego de pelota comenzó hace unos 3,000 años alrededor del golfo de México. Los olmecas inventaron este deporte pero otros pueblos conocidos de Mesoamérica, como los mayas y los aztecas, también lo jugaban. El juego de pelota era uno de los eventos más importantes en el Nuevo Mundo.

Llamado *ullamalitzi* por los aztecas, el juego de pelota fue el primer deporte que se jugó en grupo. En la sociedad indígena, estos eventos sociales eran tanto actos religiosos como espectáculos para el público. Los pueblos indígenas creían que los dioses, la naturaleza y el ser humano no podían separarse. La vida, la astronomía y las matemáticas, la organización política y social, el arte, las guerras y hasta los deportes se relacionaban con la religión. Se cree que, para los pueblos indígenas, en el juego de pelota la competencia entre dos equipos representaba la lucha entre el Sol y otros astros[1]. Según los mayas, los dioses miraban el juego desde arriba[2]. Por eso, aunque todos podían ver el juego, solamente jugaban los nobles y los atletas entrenados por los sacerdotes[3].

Hasta hoy se han descubierto más de 600 canchas[4] de pelota en México. Todas tenían dos paredes, una en cada lado, con un anillo de piedra en el centro de cada una. Algunas eran tan grandes como una cancha de fútbol moderna. Las paredes estaban decoradas con escenas del juego.

Para jugar se necesitaba una pelota de caucho[5] que pesaba unas 8 libras[6] y era tan grande como una pelota de básquetbol.

---

1 heavenly bodies **2** above **3** priests
4 courts **5** rubber **6** pounds

Universal Access

Multiple Intelligences
Bodily/Kinesthetic: Reinforce the link between the reading and the sports context. Assign sports words by handing out papers with the words. Ask students to act out the word they received. The rest of the class calls out the appropriate sports word each time.

Advanced Learners
Encourage students to prepare more elaborate reports about the ancient site they chose in the *Country Connection*. Invite them to work together to create a bulletin board display or a graphic presentation using computer software.

La pelota no podía tocar el suelo[7] y los jugadores no podían tocarla con las manos. Usaban la cabeza, los codos, las caderas[8] y las rodillas para pasar la pelota a través de uno de los anillos.

Los atletas llevaban cascos[9] y ropa de cuero para protegerse. También llevaban uniformes especiales que se cree que formaban parte de las ceremonias religiosas anteriores al juego.

7 ground 8 hips 9 helmets

¿Comprendiste ?

1. ¿Por qué crees que los sacerdotes eran los que entrenaban a los jugadores indígenas?

2. ¿Por qué el juego de pelota tiene un significado especial? Da una explicación de origen histórico y otra de origen religioso.

3. Di dos razones por las que crees que el juego de pelota se jugaba en la sociedad indígena, y compáralas con las que la gente tiene ahora para jugar deportes.

4. ¿A qué deportes actuales se parece más el juego de pelota? ¿En qué se parecen?

Usa tus conocimientos

Imagínate que eres uno de los sacerdotes que van a entrenar a los nobles y los atletas. Piensa en una vez que te entrenaste para algo y escribe cinco ideas para explicarles cómo entrenarse, lo que es importante que hagan, cómo son las competiciones y qué deben evitar hacer.

Foto de una representación moderna de un juego de pelota

Anillo para el juego

La cancha más grande se encuentra en Chichén Itzá, México

Cerámica maya del juego de pelota

Go Online
PHSchool.com

For: Internet link activity
Visit: www.phschool.com
Web Code: jed-0310

ciento cuarenta y uno 141
Capítulo 3

¿Comprendiste?

Standards: 1.1, 1.2, 3.1, 4.2

Resources: Practice Answers on Transparencies

Focus: Demonstrating reading comprehension

Suggestions: Encourage students to support their opinions with information from the reading and their own background knowledge.

Answers:

1. Los sacerdotes eran los que entrenaban a los jugadores porque los eventos sociales eran como actos religiosos para el público.
2. El juego de pelota fue el primer deporte que se jugó en grupo. Según los mayas, los dioses miraban el juego.
3–4. Answers will vary.

Usa tus conocimientos

Standards: 1.3, 3.1

Focus: Using new vocabulary and structures in a written response to a reading

Suggestions: Have students use evidence from the reading and from the pictures on these pages to help them formulate their advice. Encourage them to use the chapter vocabulary to advise the players to train for strength and endurance and to avoid injury.

Answers will vary.

Portfolio

Invite students to organize their responses to *Usa tus conocimientos* and write them down in paragraph form. Keep the paragraphs in students' portfolios as a writing sample.

Video
Presentation

Standards: 1.2

Resources: Video Program: Cap 3

This segment features "best practices" for maintaining one's health: conscientious eating habits, adequate and varied exercise, and reasonable medical care. See the *Video Teacher's Guide* for additional suggestions.

Enriching Your Teaching

Culture Note
The ancient Mexicans discovered a way to process rubber around 1600 B.C. by harvesting latex from the rubber tree *(castilla elástica)*. They used it to make sandals and for waterproofing, among other things, but they generally considered rubber a ritual material.

Internet Search
Keywords:

Chichén Itzá, Monte Albán, Palenque, Tenochtitlán, Teotihuacán, Tikal, Tula, Veracruz

¿Qué me cuentas?

Presentation

Standards: 1.1, 1.2, 1.3

Resources: Voc. & Gram. Transparencies: 83; Audio Program: CD Cap. 3, Track 20; Resource Book: Cap. 3, Audio Script; Practice Answers on Transparencies

Focus: Practicing speaking and listening comprehension within the context of healthy lifestyles and good eating habits

Suggestions: For step 1, use the *Audio CD* or read the script aloud. Allow students to hear the descriptions twice through: the first time to write their answers and the second time to check them.

In step 2, use guiding questions as necessary in order to help students talk about important details in the pictures. Use past tenses for the discussion. For example: (picture 1) *¿En qué pensaba el chico? ¿Tenía hambre?* (picture 2) *¿El chico tenía buenos hábitos alimenticios?* (picture 3) *¿Qué comía? ¿Su comida era nutritiva o no?* (picture 4) *¿Qué decía la chica?* (picture 5) *¿De dónde crees que sacó el chico la galletita?* (picture 6) *¿Qué le pasó al chico? ¿Cuáles eran los consejos de sus compañeros?*

Students should write a sufficient amount in step 2 to be able to talk for at least a minute about each picture when they present their narration.

Answers:
Step 1
1. a 2. c 3. c 4. a 5. c 6. c

Steps 2–3
Answers will vary.

142

¿Qué me cuentas?

¿Al club o a comer?

1 🎧 Vas a escuchar un cuento acerca de tres amigos que se reúnen para hacer ejercicio. Después de cada parte vas a oír tres preguntas. Escoge la respuesta correcta.

1. **a.** al club deportivo   **b.** a un restaurante   **c.** al doctor
2. **a.** para respirar   **b.** para dormir bien   **c.** para tener músculos fuertes
3. **a.** las flexiones   **b.** los abdominales   **c.** los ejercicios aeróbicos

4. **a.** se sentía fatal   **b.** se caía de sueño   **c.** tenía hambre
5. **a.** flexiones   **b.** yoga   **c.** ir juntos al club
6. **a.** para hacer lo mismo que Manu   **b.** para estar en la luna   **c.** para relajarse, divertirse y estar de buen humor

2 Estas ilustraciones representan un cuento. Con tus propias palabras, describe lo que sucedió. Añade más información para que el cuento resulte más interesante. ¡Usa tu imaginación!

Si quieres, puedes usar las siguientes palabras o expresiones para conectar tus ideas.

luego	en primer lugar	durante
para continuar	a pesar de que *(despite the fact that)*	

1.

2.

3.

4.

5.

6.

3 Trabaja con otros dos estudiantes para narrar el cuento. Un estudiante comienza. El(la) profesor(a) avisa *(calls time)* cuando pasan dos minutos. El segundo estudiante continúa. Cuando pasan otros dos minutos, continúa el tercer estudiante. Sigan turnándose hasta completar el cuento.

Universal Access

Una vida más sana

Tarea
Imagina que tu escuela va a organizar un evento especial para que los estudiantes aprendan cómo tener una vida más sana. A ti te toca hacer una presentación. Busca algunos materiales y haz un cartel que te pueda servir para la presentación.

① Prepárate Escoge uno de los siguientes temas y prepara un cartel para organizar tu presentación.

temas	cartel
el ejercicio	deportes y tipos de ejercicio
los alimentos	alimentos nutritivos
las recetas, cómo preparar la comida	recetas saludables

② Practica Vuelve a leer la información que escribiste en el cartel. Practica varias veces tu presentación para recordar los detalles. Usa mandatos con *Uds.* o recomendaciones con el subjuntivo para explicar a tus compañeros qué deben hacer para tener una vida más sana. Recuerda:

• hablar con voz clara y mirar al público directamente
• hablar de cada uno de los temas en orden y explicar por qué es importante para la salud
• dar alguna recomendación

Modelo

Mi presentación es acerca de cómo tener una vida más sana. Voy a hablarles de qué ejercicios hacer para estar saludable. El ejercicio sirve para estar en forma. Hagan ejercicio por lo menos tres veces por semana.

③ Haz tu presentación Imagina que estás en un auditorio. Habla claro y en voz alta. Explica el tema y muestra el cartel. Al final, pregunta a los estudiantes si tienen un comentario que hacer.

④ Evaluación Tu profesor(a) puede explicarte cómo va a evaluar tu presentación. Probablemente, para tu profesor(a) es importante ver que:

• explicaste cada tema en forma clara.
• usaste un cartel apropiado para ilustrar el tema.

Estrategia
Projecting your voice
When making an oral presentation make sure you face your audience at all times. You may look at the front, middle, and back rows. Remember to speak loudly enough for all to hear, and speak clearly.

Communicate: Speaking

Presentación oral

Presentation

Standards: 1.2, 1.3, 3.1

Focus: Preparing and delivering an oral presentation

Suggestions: Review the task and the four-step approach with students. Review the rubric with the class (see *Assessment* below) to explain how you will grade the performance task. Before students begin practicing in step 2, direct their attention to the *Estrategia*. Encourage them to practice at home before a mirror or with a partner in class to develop their public speaking skills.

Portfolio
Record students' oral presentations on audiocassette or videotape for inclusion in their portfolios.

✓ Assessment
• Assessment Program: Cap. 3, Rubrics
Give students copies of the rubric before they begin the activity. Go over the descriptions of the different levels of performance. After assessing students, help individuals understand how their performance could be improved.

Teacher-to-Teacher
Provided that your school has the technology, some students may prefer to use a computer program and project their poster. Remind students that skillful use of visuals during a presentation is a valuable asset in many professions.

Enriching Your Teaching

RUBRIC	Score 1	Score 3	Score 5
How well your information is organized	Your ideas are undeveloped with incorrect or no transitions.	Some of your ideas are undeveloped. Your transitions are confusing.	Your ideas are well developed with clear transitions.
How effectively you deliver your speech	You make no eye contact with audience. You have little intonation.	You make some eye contact and use intonation.	You make good eye contact and use intonation.
How effectively you use your visuals	Your visuals don't communicate the message.	You use visuals, but not effectively.	Your visuals are very helpful and are used effectively.

143

3 Communicate: Writing

Language Arts Connection

Standards: 3.1

Help students apply the knowledge they have about writing a persuasive essay to Spanish. Have them do their planning in step 1 in small groups. Guide them with comments and questions such as the following:

1. *¿Quién es tu público? Es preferible elegir a un grupo específico, como los jóvenes de esta escuela, los atletas o los jóvenes que comen mucha comida basura. Si conoces bien a tu público, vas a saber mejor lo que tienes que decirle.*

2. *Hay que prestar atención a las palabras que usas. La condición física, por ejemplo, puede ser un tema delicado para mucha gente. Para persuadir a la gente, es muy importante que no la ofendas.*

Presentación escrita

Presentation

Standards: 1.3, 3.1

Resources: Voc. & Gram. Transparencies 4

Focus: Combining learned vocabulary and structures in a written presentation

Suggestions: Explain at the start the criteria you will use to evaluate students' compositions. (See step 5, *Evaluación,* in the Student Edition, and *Assessment* on p. 145.)

Direct students' attention to the *Estrategia*. Ask them to share additional background information they have learned in Language Arts courses about persuasive writing. Then show *Vocabulary & Grammar Transparency* 4. Have students begin a similar chart on their own paper. Guide them to add other points and to develop each point with specific details. For step 2, remind students that their persuasive essay should build through at least three arguments. They should save their strongest argument for last, rather than "bringing out the big guns" at the beginning of the article.

Presentación escrita

Por una vida más saludable

Objectives

- **Use persuasive writing to encourage people to take up a healthy practice**
- **Use the present subjunctive and commands**

Estrategia

Persuasive writing
Use persuasive writing to convince an audience about something. To write an effective persuasive composition, use words that clearly express your opinion about an issue. Always include facts and examples to support your opinions. A persuasive composition is always addressed to a specific audience. Therefore, it is important to choose words, tone and style that are directed to your audience.

Imagina que trabajas para una revista y te piden que escribas un artículo sobre cómo las personas pueden llevar una vida más saludable. Presenta razones para persuadir a las personas de que cambien sus hábitos para estar más saludables.

1 Antes de escribir

Piensa en los elementos que ayudan a llevar una vida saludable. Describe por qué son importantes y qué ocurre si no se ponen en práctica. Crea una tabla como la de abajo con la información que tienes.

Para llevar una vida saludable	Ventajas y problemas que se evitan
• mantener una dieta equilibrada	• se evitan las enfermedades • el cuerpo se mantiene sano
• mantenerse en forma	

2 Borrador

Escribe tu borrador en forma de artículo dirigido a un público específico. Usa la escritura persuasiva. Pon las ideas que anotaste en tu tabla en una composición, usando el vocabulario que aprendiste en este capítulo. Recuerda usar el subjuntivo con expresiones impersonales y los mandatos.

144 ciento cuarenta y cuatro
¡Adelante!

Universal Access

Students with Learning Difficulties

Some students may need help understanding how to use various types of graphic organizers. Show them how the table on this page works by pointing out the titles at the top and explaining the cause-and-effect relationship between the information on the left and that on the right.

Advanced Learners

Encourage students to use their skills in Spanish to incorporate into their articles even more strategies for effective persuasive writing. Have them study persuasive articles in both English and Spanish as models.

Modelo

Éstas son tres cosas necesarias para mantener una vida sana: Es necesario que mantengas una dieta equilibrada. Es importante que hagas . . . Practícalas siempre para que veas . . .

Main idea: what to do in order to stay healthy.

Persuasive writing to convince the audience.

Piensa en los alimentos que comes. Sugiero que comas frutas y verduras y alimentos con calcio y hierro. Es importante preparar los alimentos . . .

Examples to support an opinion.

Por último, . . .

Conclusion: concluding thoughts about the subject.

3 Redacción/Revisión

Después de escribir el primer borrador de tu artículo, trabaja con otro(a) estudiante para intercambiar los trabajos y leerlos. Después de leer el trabajo de tu compañero(a), sugiere cómo puede mejorar su composición y dile que haga lo mismo con la tuya. Revisen si:

- la composición se enfoca en consejos para la salud
- para persuadir al público se usan mandatos y se dan razones
- se usan expresiones impersonales para enfatizar los consejos

Haz lo siguiente: Subraya con una línea los verbos en subjuntivo, con dos líneas los mandatos, y encierra en un círculo las expresiones impersonales.

Éstas son tres cosas necesarias para mantener una vida sana: (Es necesario) que mantengas ~~mantienes~~ una dieta equilibrada. (Es importante) que hagas . . . Practícalas ~~Practícala~~ siempre para . . .

4 Publicación

Antes de hacer la versión final, lee de nuevo tu borrador y repasa los siguientes puntos:

- ¿Di suficientes razones para apoyar mis ideas?
- ¿Usé el vocabulario apropiado para convencer al público de que lea la revista donde van a publicar el artículo?

Después de revisar el borrador, escribe una copia en limpio de tu composición.

5 Evaluación

Tu profesor(a) puede explicarte cómo va a evaluar tu presentación. Probablemente, para tu profesor(a) es importante ver que:

- escribiste un artículo persuasivo, con consejos para tener una vida saludable
- incluiste razones y ejemplos para convencer al público
- usaste el vocabulario y la gramática del capítulo

ciento cuarenta y cinco **145**
Capítulo 3

Lectura

Lectura

¡Cambia tus hábitos!

Estrategia

Cause and effect
Our personality and the way we eat, sleep, or react to fear can affect our health. If we change our bad habits, we will be healthier and more productive persons. While you read this magazine article, look for other examples of cause and effect. For example, what happens if you do not eat well, you do not drink enough water, or if you do not sit correctly and comfortably?

Al leer

Nuestra vida está llena de actos que repetimos todos los días, por ejemplo, comer, dormir o estudiar. Vas a leer un artículo con recomendaciones sobre cómo cambiar tus malos hábitos para llevar una vida más saludable. Copia la tabla de la página 149. Mientras lees los artículos, llena los espacios de la gráfica con causas y efectos que encuentres en el texto.

Presta atención a los siguientes puntos:

• la importancia de tener buenos hábitos alimenticios

• la higiene personal y la salud

• cómo cuidar tu espalda aprendiendo a sentarte bien

Aliméntate bien

Meta: "Voy a desayunar todos los días."

Saltarte el desayuno no te sirve para nada. Empieza tu día con algo ligero[1], para poner a funcionar tu metabolismo. No sólo da energía sino que despierta al organismo y acelera la quema de calorías durante todo el día.

¡Lógralo!

Desayuna algo aunque sea ligero, como un jugo de naranja o una fruta, pan tostado con mermelada, cereal con leche o yogur, té o un buen vaso de leche.

Nuestros consejos:

Si tienes prisa: bebe el jugo mientras caminas a la escuela. También puedes llevar un yogur que trae una porción de cereal.

1 light

146 **ciento cuarenta y seis**
¡Adelante!

No comas comida basura

Meta: "No voy a comer tantos dulces en la escuela."

Seguro que a la hora del recreo quieres comer chocolate o una bolsa de papas fritas. Mejor escoge alimentos que echen a andar tu motor. Si comes un almuerzo nutritivo, tu rendimiento físico y mental va a ser mucho mejor y no te vas a dormir en las últimas clases.

¡Lógralo!

Lleva de tu casa zanahorias o pepinos[2]. Las palomitas de maíz[3] y las frutas deshidratadas son una buena opción en lugar de comidas fritas.

Nuestros consejos:

¡No lleves dinero! Así evitas la tentación de comprar comida basura.

---

2 cucumbers **3** popcorn

Muy limpios

Meta: "Siempre me voy a lavar las manos y los dientes."

Muchas enfermedades del estómago son producidas por las bacterias que recogemos durante el día en nuestras actividades diarias. El simple hecho de abrir la puerta para salir del baño después de lavarte las manos, ya implica una contaminación de gérmenes. Y de la boca ni hablemos, ¿quién quiere verte con el frijol entre los dientes?

¡Lógralo!

El jabón más efectivo para eliminar las bacterias en las manos es un gel que no se enjuaga[4]. Llévalo en tu mochila y úsalo cada vez que vayas al baño. En cuanto a los dientes, lávalos después de cada comida.

Nuestros consejos:

Compra un cepillo de dientes de viaje (algunos incluyen una crema de dientes pequeña) y llévalo en tu mochila junto con un hilo dental. ¿Se te olvidó lavarte los dientes o no tuviste tiempo? Usa una pastilla de menta o un chicle con clorofila para evitar el mal aliento.

---

4 rinse off

Enriching Your Teaching

③ Communicate: Reading

Suggestions (Cont'd):
Reading:

• p. 148: *Lee la parte* Más H₂O. *En la primera frase, la que empieza con "No beber …," ¿cuál es el sujeto? (No beber suficientes líquidos durante el día) ¿Qué quiere decir esta frase en inglés? (usando un participio presente: Not drinking enough water during the day)*

¿Cuál es la palabra opuesta de "hidratado"? Adivina. Busca una pista en la sección No comas comida basura en la página 147. (deshidratado)

• p. 148: *Lee la parte* ¿Una siesta? *El artículo da tres categorías de causas posibles para la falta de energía después de las clases. ¿Cuáles son? (causas fisiológicas, emocionales o relacionadas con el estilo de vida)*

• p. 148: *Lee la parte* Siéntate bien. *¿Qué parte del cuerpo tienes que pegar al asiento para sentarte bien? (toda la espalda)*

Más H₂O

Meta: "Ahora sí voy a tomar agua."

No beber suficientes líquidos durante el día puede hacer que te sientas cansado. Los refrescos te dan energía pero sólo por un momento, luego te sientes igual de cansado; los refrescos *light* tampoco ayudan, por el contrario, te quitan energía.

¡Lógralo!

Ya te lo hemos dicho mil veces: debes tomar por lo menos 8 vasos de agua al día. No sólo te mantienen hidratado, sino que ayudan al buen funcionamiento de los riñones[1].

Nuestros consejos:

¿No te gusta el agua sola? Toma jugos de fruta fresca o leche descremada durante el día.

_____

1 kidneys

¿Una siesta?

Meta: "Ya no voy a dormir cuando llegue de la escuela."

Nadie en tu casa entiende por qué cuando regresas de la escuela lo primero que haces es dormirte. Las causas pueden ser fisiológicas (como los niveles hormonales de la tiroides), emocionales (demasiado estrés), o estar relacionadas con tu estilo de vida (no dormir bien en las noches). Lo que debes hacer son unos cuantos ajustes en tu dieta diaria para combatir el cansancio.

¡Lógralo!

Si te sientes cansado, evita completamente las galletas, el pan dulce, los dulces, los refrescos y los jugos de fruta envasados, ya que contienen azúcares simples que te quitan energía; también evita la cafeína. Lo ideal es que comas proteínas con vegetales (como un pescado hervido con verduras).

Nuestros consejos:

Trata de hacer un poco de ejercicio para subir tus niveles de energía. O pon un disco compacto y ponte a bailar en tu cuarto.

Siéntate bien

Meta: "Me voy a sentar derecho en la silla."

No es nada fácil sentarte derecho por más de diez minutos, pero si sigues sentándote así, hundiéndote en[2] tu asiento de clases, tu cuerpo y sobre todo tu espalda se acostumbrarán y es probable que no se corrijan.

¡Lógralo!

Pega bien toda la espalda —baja, alta y lumbar— al asiento. Asegúrate de que tus pies estén bien apoyados en el piso y mantén las piernas juntas.

Nuestros consejos:

¿Se te hace muy difícil? Imagina que tienes un hilo que jala tu columna[3] hacia arriba para mantenerla derecha.

2 sinking yourself into 3 a string that pulls your spine

Universal Access

Heritage Language Learners
Have students discuss commands that their parents frequently give them at home. Ask volunteers to make signs of the four or five most common ones. Post these around the room in appropriate places. For example, *Siéntate bien* might be posted on the front wall.

Advanced Learners
Have students create a glossary of unfamiliar vocabulary for the article that lists items of students' choosing, along with a definition in Spanish. They can arrive at their definitions via discussion or by using a Spanish dictionary. Encourage them to paraphrase dictionary definitions and write them in their own words.

Block Schedule

Bring in magazines from different Spanish-speaking countries. Have students work with a partner and find an ad related to health. Have them explain the ad to another group. Is it an effective ad?

Interacción con la lectura

❶ Trabaja con un grupo de estudiantes para hacer una tabla de *causa y efecto*. Cada estudiante va a añadir las relaciones de causa y efecto que escribió mientras leía el artículo.

❷ Contesten las siguientes preguntas sobre el artículo y, si notan relaciones de causa y efecto que aún no incluyeron en la tabla, añádanlas.

- ¿Crees que los jóvenes en general tienen hábitos saludables? Explica tu respuesta.

- ¿Qué recomendaciones del artículo te parecen mejores o más prácticas?

- ¿Hay alguna recomendación con la que no estás de acuerdo? ¿Por qué?

- Según este artículo, ¿qué tipo de comidas y bebidas debes evitar para tener más energía? ¿Cuáles debes comer o beber?

❸ Trabaja con un grupo para hablar sobre estos temas. Hablen con la clase de lo que piensan sobre las causas y los efectos.

Causa	Efecto

Fondo cultural

Revistas para jóvenes Al igual que en los Estados Unidos, en España y América Latina hay muchas revistas para jóvenes. En ellas puedes encontrar los temas que les interesan a los chicos y las chicas de esos países, cómo se visten, qué música prefieren, y cuáles son sus sueños.

Si quieres leer más artículos relacionados con la salud, si te gustan los temas culturales y científicos o quieres mantenerte al día en deportes, música, libros o cine, existe un gran número de esas revistas que te pueden interesar. Éstas son algunas de ellas: *Ragazza* o *Junior* de España, *Tú* de México o *Pricolosa* de Argentina.

- ¿Te interesa la moda o la música de otros países?

- ¿Crees que los jóvenes de otros países tienen gustos *(taste)* similares con respecto a la moda o la música? ¿Por qué?

TECNOLOGÍA
La red
DEPORTES
ganar!
Amiga
JOVEN
tu estilo
tu salud
¡Diviértete!
¡Siéntete bien!

Interacción con la lectura

Standards: 1.1, 1.2, 1.3, 3.1

Suggestions:

Post-reading: After students revisit their **Causa/Efecto** charts and make changes or additions, have them share the information they included. Ask volunteers to read aloud or paraphrase the parts of the article that support their choices for the chart and that help them answer the *Interacción con la lectura* questions.

Answers will vary.

Fondo cultural

Standards: 1.1, 1.2, 2.2, 4.2, 5.1

Suggestions: Ask: *¿Qué revistas estadounidenses para jóvenes puedes nombrar? ¿Cuáles de estas revistas se parecen a las que ves en el* Fondo cultural? *¿Qué revistas para jóvenes lees? ¿Qué secciones de estas revistas te gustan más?* If possible, obtain some copies of the Spanish-language magazines shown and mentioned to put on display for students to peruse. Heritage language learners may have copies of Spanish-language magazines that they are willing to lend or contribute to the class.

Answers will vary.

Teacher-to-Teacher

A comparison of Spanish-language teen magazines to ones in English from the United States will provide students with valuable cultural insight. Ask students to analyze which topics are the same in the two groups of magazines. Which are noticeably different? How are the advertisements similar or different?

Enriching Your Teaching

Culture Note

The first printing press in the Americas was established in Mexico City—less than a century after Gutenberg produced his famous Bible. At the request of Juan de Zumárraga, first Bishop of Mexico, a publishing house in Sevilla set up a branch in Mexico City. The first book printed there, in 1539, was an edition of the *Breve y* *más compendiosa doctrina cristiana en lengua mexicana y castellana.* The book was part of de Zumárraga's efforts to convert the local people to Christianity. Ironically, he also destroyed many manuscripts in indigenous languages as part of his campaign.

Review Activities

Los síntomas y las medicinas: Ask students to sort the vocabulary in this section into smaller categories of their choice. Have them use a graphic organizer, such as a columnar chart or a word web to do so. Ask them to share their work, trading category names and discussing their reasons for assigning a particular item to a category.

Partes del cuerpo: Have students sketch a basic human figure and label the parts of the body. Encourage them to include labels for other parts of the body that they previously learned, or terms such as *columna (vertebral)* that they learned about in the chapter.

Actividades relacionadas con la salud/La nutrición: Have students sit in a circle. Give a foam ball to a student and say one of the words from the *actividades* or *nutrición* categories. The student has ten seconds to use the word in a sentence, then tosses the ball randomly to another student in the circle and says another word from the lists. The student catching the ball uses that word in a sentence, announces the next word, and tosses the ball again. Continue until all the words in the list have been covered at least once.

Para estar en forma/Estados de ánimo: Ask pairs of students to work together using TPR commands to demonstrate comprehension of these sections of the vocabulary: *Flexiona la rodilla derecha. Ahora estírala.*

Expresiones útiles: Students can use these words and expressions as they go over the review activities for the other categories.

Repaso del capítulo

Vocabulario y gramática

los síntomas y las medicinas

la alergia	allergy
el antibiótico	antibiotic
la aspirina	aspirin
estar resfriado, -a	to have a cold
estornudar	to sneeze
la fiebre	fever
el grado centígrado	centigrade degree
la gripe	flu
el jarabe	syrup
la tos	cough

partes del cuerpo

el corazón	heart
el músculo	muscle
el oído	ear
el pecho	chest

actividades relacionadas con la salud

aconsejar	to advise
contener	to contain
desarrollar	to develop
evitar	to avoid
exigir	to demand
incluir	to include
quejarse	to complain
saltar (una comida)	to skip (a meal)
tomar	to take, to drink

para estar en forma

abdominales	crunches
el calambre	cramp
débil	weak
ejercicios aeróbicos	aerobics
estar en forma	to be fit
estirar	to stretch
flexionar	to flex, to stretch
fuerte	strong
la fuerza	strength
hacer bicicleta	to use a stationary bike
hacer cinta	to use a treadmill
hacer flexiones	to do push-ups
relajar(se)	to relax
respirar	to breathe
yoga	yoga

la nutrición

la alimentación	nutrition, feeding
los alimentos	food
apropiado, -a	appropriate
el calcio	calcium
el carbohidrato	carbohydrate
la comida basura	junk food
la dieta	diet
la edad	age
la energía	energy
equilibrado, -a	balanced
la estatura	height
la fibra	fiber
el hábito alimenticio	eating habit
el hierro	iron
lleno, -a	full
la merienda	snack
nutritivo, -a	nutritious
el peso	weight
la proteína	protein
saludable	healthy
vacío, -a	empty
la vitamina	vitamin

expresiones útiles

aguantar	to endure, to tolerate
aunque	despite, even when
el consejo	advice
la manera	way
el nivel	level

estados de ánimo

caerse de sueño	to be exhausted, sleepy
concentrarse	to concentrate
confianza en sí mismo, -a	self-confidence
estar de buen / mal humor	to be in a good / bad mood
el estrés	stress
estresado, -a	stressed out
preocuparse	to worry
sentirse fatal	to feel awful

Universal Access

Students with Learning Difficulties

Suggest that students review the vocabulary lists in sets of three words or phrases, saying them out loud while cycling through them several times. This will also help them remember the gender of each word.

Advanced Learners

Tell students to bring in a magazine photo of a scene in a hospital or doctor's waiting room, or in a gym. Have them describe the people in the scene. Then have them write a short conversation between two or more of the people.

Mandatos afirmativos y negativos

Regular and stem-changing verbs, and verbs ending in *-car*, *-gar*, and *-zar*

	tú	Ud.	Uds.
evitar	evita, no evites	(no) evite	(no) eviten
volver	vuelve, no vuelvas	(no) vuelva	(no) vuelvan
abrir	abre, no abras	(no) abra	(no) abran
sacar	saca, no saques	(no) saque	(no) saquen
llegar	llega, no llegues	(no) llegue	(no) lleguen
cruzar	cruza, no cruces	(no) cruce	(no) crucen

Irregular verbs

	tú	Ud.	Uds.
decir	di, no digas	(no) diga	(no) digan
poner	pon, no pongas	(no) ponga	(no) pongan
ir	ve, no vayas	(no) vaya	(no) vayan
hacer	haz, no hagas	(no) haga	(no) hagan
tener	ten, no tengas	(no) tenga	(no) tengan
mantener	mantén, no mantengas	(no) mantenga	(no) mantengan
ser	sé, no seas	(no) sea	(no) sean
salir	sal, no salgas	(no) salga	(no) salgan

Placement of pronouns

Attach reflexive or object pronouns at the end of affirmative commands.
With negative commands, place them after the word *no*.

Toma esas vitaminas. ¡Tómalas ahora mismo! No las tomes.

El subjuntivo: Verbos regulares y verbos con cambios de raíz

saltar

salte	saltemos
saltes	saltéis
salte	salten

poder (o → ue)

pueda	podamos
puedas	podáis
pueda	puedan

pedir (e → i)

pida	pidamos
pidas	pidáis
pida	pidan

El subjuntivo: Verbos irregulares

dar

dé	demos
des	déis
dé	den

haber

haya	hayamos
hayas	hayáis
haya	hayan

ir

vaya	vayamos
vayas	vayáis
vaya	vayan

estar

esté	estemos
estés	estéis
esté	estén

ser

sea	seamos
seas	seáis
sea	sean

saber

sepa	sepamos
sepas	sepáis
sepa	sepan

● **Más práctica**
Practice Workbook Organizer 3-13, 3-14

Mandatos afirmativos y negativos: Have individual students write a series of commands that a partner will carry out. The commands will tell the partner how to draw something. The drawing might consist of geometric shapes or of something realistic, such as a landscape or floor plan. Then have students follow their own commands carefully, in order to create the drawing. Ask them to keep this drawing out of sight. Finally, have pairs sit back-to-back, each with pencil and paper. Students take turns reading their complete list of commands, while the partner attempts to draw based on what he or she hears. Students compare their drawings to the originals to see how well they created the commands and followed those of their partner.

El subjuntivo: Have students list at least five typical health or lifestyle complaints. Have them exchange lists with a partner and write solutions to the problems with complete sentences containing the subjunctive. As a guide for this type of sentence, write the following information on the board: Main Clause (indicative) + *que* + Subordinate Clause (subjunctive).

Alternative Assessment Options

The *El subjuntivo* activity above can be used as a way to assess students' assimilation of rules for basic formation and use of the subjunctive.

Portfolio

Invite students to review the activities they completed in this chapter, including written reports, posters or other visuals, tapes of oral presentations, and other projects. Have them select one or two items that they feel best demonstrate their achievements in Spanish. Include these products in students' portfolios. Have them include this with the Chapter Checklist and Self-Assessment Worksheet.

Additional Resources

- Audio Program: CD Cap. 3, Track 21
- Resource Book: Cap. 3, Clip Art
- Assessment Program: Chapter Checklist and Self-Assessment Worksheet

Enriching Your Teaching

Teacher-to-Teacher

Have students write the infinitives of the verbs with irregular imperative forms on slips of paper and place them in a hat or other container. Have a playing cube ready. Explain that rolling an even number means *afirmativo* and rolling an odd number means *negativo.* Students take turns rolling the cube, drawing a verb, and using it in either an affirmative or negative command.

To prepare for the test, check to see
if you . . .

• know the new vocabulary and
  grammar
• can perform the tasks on pp. 152
  and 153

Performance Tasks

Standards: 1.1, 1.2, 1.3, 2.2

Resources: Audio Program: CD Cap. 3, Track 23;
Resource Book: Cap. 3, Audio Script; Practice
Answers on Transparencies

1. Vocabulario

Suggestions: Encourage students to review
the vocabulary from the *A primera vista*
sections on pp. 114–116 and 126–129
before they complete the activity.

Answers:

1. b	5. b
2. b	6. b
3. c	7. a
4. a	8. d

2. Gramática

Suggestions: Remind students of the
main points of the grammar presentations
in *Capítulo 3*:

• affirmative commands with **tú**
• negative commands with **tú**
• affirmative and negative commands with
  Ud. and **Uds.**
• the subjunctive: regular verbs
• the subjunctive: irregular verbs
• the subjunctive: stem-changing verbs

Answers:

1. b	5. d
2. a	6. a
3. a	7. c
4. c	8. d

Preparación para el examen

❶ Vocabulario Escribe la letra de la palabra o expresión que mejor complete
cada frase. Escribe tus respuestas en una hoja aparte.

1. El médico le aconseja a Lucía que coma
   queso y tome leche todos los días porque
   contienen _____.
   a. comida basura   c. dulces
   b. calcio   d. fibra

2. Estoy enfermo(a) cuando _____.
   a. hago yoga   c. hago ejercicio
   b. tengo fiebre   d. tengo sueño

3. Te voy a recetar _____ para la tos.
   a. una gripe   c. un jarabe
   b. carbohidratos   d. una aspirina

4. Para evitar los calambres les recomiendo
   que _____.
   a. estiren los músculos c. hagan flexiones
   b. hagan abdominales d. corran rápido

5. Si _____, te aconsejo que hagas yoga.
   a. estás en la luna   c. haces cinta
   b. estás estresado   d. te caes de sueño

6. Doctor, _____ y tengo dolor de cabeza.
   a. tengo el oído   c. me duele la gripe
   b. me duele   d. estoy en forma
      el pecho

7. Tengo fiebre, cuando _____.
   a. tengo 39° centígrados c. tengo calambres
   b. evito los   d. mantengo
      antibióticos   mi dieta

8. ¡No aguanto más! significa que _____.
   a. estás muy contento(a) c. tienes energía
   b. te gusta hacer   d. estás muy
      ejercicio   estresado(a)

❷ Gramática Escribe la letra de la palabra o expresión que mejor complete
cada frase. Escribe tus respuestas en una hoja aparte.

1. Jorge, no _____ al gimnasio hoy. Está
   cerrado.
   a. vas   c. ve
   b. vayas   d. vayan

2. Sra. Díaz, por favor _____ las vitaminas
   allí.
   a. ponga   c. pongan
   b. pon   d. pones

3. El doctor me aconseja que _____ una
   dieta equilibrada.
   a. mantenga   c. mantengo
   b. mantén   d. mantener

4. ¿Estás estresado? _____ con tus amigos
   para divertirte.
   a. Salgas   c. Sal
   b. Sales   d. Salgan

5. Es importante que ustedes _____ de buen
   humor durante las clases de yoga.
   a. estemos   c. estamos
   b. están   d. estén

6. ¡Tomen las vitaminas! ¡_____ por la
   mañana!
   a. Tómenlas   c. Tómalas
   b. Tómenlo   d. Tómenlos

7. Niños, ¡_____ comida basura a la escuela!
   a. no traen   c. no traigan
   b. no traiga   d. no traes

8. Quiero que tú me _____ las reglas del club.
   a. explicas   c. explique
   b. expliquen   d. expliques

Universal Access

Students with Learning Difficulties

Tell students to look for the key word(s) in the
question and to try to visualize the action(s)
described. Encourage them to keep the visualization in mind as they look at each of the
multiple-choice answers.

Advanced Learner

Have students prepare a list of other common
illnesses and medical problems. Each student
should select one of these and create a
bilingual poster that illustrates and describes it.
If there is time, ask volunteers to talk about the
illness using the poster as a visual aid.

For: Test Preparation
Visit: www.phschool.com
Web Code: jed-0311

En el examen vas a . . .	Éstas son las tareas de práctica que te pueden ser útiles para el examen . . .	Si necesitas repasar . . .
③ Escuchar Escuchar y comprender un programa de radio sobre consejos para la salud	En este programa de radio, varias personas llaman al Dr. Salvavidas para pedirle consejos. (a) ¿Qué síntomas tiene cada uno?, (b) ¿Qué tienen que tomar?, (c) ¿Qué más les aconseja el doctor?	**pp. 114–117** *A primera vista 1* **p. 115** Actividad 2 **p. 119** Actividad 9
④ Hablar Aconsejar a otros sobre los hábitos alimenticios	La directora de la guardería infantil de tu barrio te pide que vengas a hablarles a los niños sobre lo importante que es tener buenos hábitos alimenticios. Haz cinco recomendaciones.	**p. 114–117** *A primera vista 1* **p. 116** Actividad 3 **p. 118** Actividad 7 **p. 124** Actividad 17 **p. 125** Actividades 18 y 20
 **⑤ Leer** Leer y entender un anuncio	Lucía quiere aprender a preparar alimentos nutritivos y tomar clases para tener músculos fuertes. Lee el anuncio que ella vio y dile: (a) por qué no le recomiendas las clases de ejercicio y (b) por qué debe tomar las clases para preparar alimentos. **Centro Fuente de la Salud** Si estás estresado(a) y no puedes concentrarte, tenemos clases de ejercicios para ayudarte a relajar. Aprende a tener una alimentación equilibrada. Prepara galletas nutritivas y bebidas que dan energía.	**pp. 126–129** *A primera vista 2* **p. 136** Actividad 36 **p. 139** Actividad 40
⑥ Escribir Escribir una carta para dar consejos	Tu trabajo en una revista es contestar las cartas que mandan los jóvenes. En una carta, un chico te dice que siempre se siente cansado y de mal humor. Escríbele una respuesta con por lo menos cuatro consejos.	**p. 121** Actividad 11 **p. 125** Actividad 18 **p. 129** Actividad 25 **p. 135** Actividad 35 **p. 136** Actividad 36
⑦ Pensar Pensar en los antiguos juegos de los olmecas de Mesoamérica	En tu clase puedes ganar "puntos extra" si compartes algo que aprendiste en otra clase. ¿Cómo puedes explicar el juego de pelota de los olmecas de hace 3,000 años? ¿Hoy en día hay algún juego similar? Descríbelo.	**pp. 140–141** *Puente a la cultura*

Review

3. Escuchar

Suggestions: Use the *Audio CD* or read from the script.

Answers:
a. A la señorita Juana Durante le duele el estómago después del almuerzo. El señor David Ríos tiene fiebre y tos, le duelen la garganta y el pecho.
b. La señorita Juana Durante debe cambiar sus hábitos alimenticios. El señor David Ríos debe ir al médico inmediatamente.
c. La señorita Juana Durante debe comer más frutas y verduras y menos comida basura. El señor David Ríos debe ir al médico porque necesita antibióticos.

4. Hablar

Suggestions: Remind students that they should tailor their verb forms to the situation of addressing a group of children. Have Advanced Learners use the *vosotros* forms, as if they were in Spain.

Answers will vary.

5. Leer

Suggestions: Tell students to refer to pp. 114–116 and 126–129 if they have questions about vocabulary in the review.

Answers will vary.

6. Escribir

Suggestions: Remind students that they can use either commands or sentences with the subjunctive for their advice.

Answers will vary.

7. Pensar

Suggestions: Suggest that students begin with a description of the ball game. They can then refer to this information in order to compare the ancient game to modern ones.

Answers will vary.

✓ Assessment

• Examen del capítulo: 3
• Audio Program: CD 12, Cap. 3, Track 4
• Assessment Program: *RPH*

Alternative Assessment

• ExamView Test Bank CD-ROM
• Resource Book: Cap. 3, Situation Cards
• Resource Book: Cap. 3, Communicative Activity BLM

Enriching Your Teaching

Teacher-to-Teacher

Have students create word-search puzzles that use at least ten words from the chapter vocabulary. Then have them exchange puzzles for solving by another student. Encourage students to make two copies of their puzzles and keep the clean copy on hand for photo-copying and use at a later date.

153

Capítulo 4

CHAPTER OVERVIEW

¿Cómo te llevas con los demás?
- Relationships with friends and family

Vocabulary
- personality traits and conflicts
- friends and family relationships

Grammar
- subjunctive mode with verbs of emotion
- uses of *por* and *para*
- commands with *nosotros*
- use of possesive pronouns

Cultural Perspectives
- love and friendship celebrations in the Spanish-speaking world
- depictions of family life in the art of Carmen Lomas Garza and Pablo Picasso
- love expressed through the arts in the Spanish-speaking world

Chapter Project

Anuncio ilustrado "Busco nuevos(as) amigos(as)"

Overview: Students create an illustrated ad to look for new school friends in Latin America or Spain. The ad is for the bulletin board of the school where they will be studying in summer. It should include the name of the student, his/her age, grade, phone number or email address, and photo.

Students include photos or magazine clippings with captions of two of their hobbies and two of their favorite class subjects. In a paragraph, they write why they want a new friend, two personality traits they like from a new friend, and two activities they would like to do with their new friend. Students then present their ad to the class and describe the information.

Materials: construction paper, magazines, scissors, glue and markers

Sequence: (suggestions for when to do each step are found throughout the chapter)

STEP 1. Review instructions so students know what is expected of them. Hand out the "Chapter 4 Project Instructions and Rubric" from *the Teacher's Resource Book*.

STEP 2. Students submit a draft of their ad. Return the drafts with your suggestions. For vocabulary and grammar practice, ask partners to present their drafts to each other.

STEP 3. Students do layouts on construction paper, setting space for paragraphs, photos and captions. Encourage them to try different arrangements before writing the paragraphs and gluing their photos and clippings.

STEP 4. Students submit a draft of the personal descriptions. Note your corrections and suggestions, then return drafts to students.

STEP 5. Students present their posters to the class, explaining the relationships and giving descriptions of family members.

Options:
1. Students create an ad for a newspaper instead of a bulletin board.
2. Students create an ad to look for a pen pal through a Web site.

Assessment:

Here is a detailed rubric for assessing this project:

Chapter 4 Project: *Anuncio ilustrado "Busco nuevos(as) amigos(as)"*

RUBRIC	Score 1	Score 2	Score 3
Your evidence of planning	You provide no ad layout or written draft.	You provide layout and written draft, but it is not corrected.	You show evidence of corrected draft and layout.
Your use of illustrations	You do not include photos or clippings.	You include clippings and photos but layout is unorganized.	Your ad is easy to read and photos and clippings are consistent with text.
Your presentation	You include little of the required information.	You include most of the required information.	You include all the required information.

Bulletin Boards

La amistad a través del mundo

Ask students to cut out, copy, or download photos from around the world showing manifestations of friendship among teenagers in different Spanish-speaking countries and cultures. Cluster photos into categories of countries and/or cultures so that similarities and differences are evident.

Bibliography

Jimenez, Francisco. *Breaking Through*. Houghton Mifflin Company, 2002. Having come from Mexico to California ten years ago, fourteen-year-old Francisco is still working in the fields but fighting to improve his life and complete his education.

King, Elizabeth. *Quinceañera*. Penguin Putnam Books, 1998. Focuses on describing the celebration of this rite of passage in the life of a Mexican American girl, while also presenting historical background for the occasion.

Muñoz Ryan, Pam. *Esperanza Rising*. New York: Scholastic, Inc., 2002. Based on the true-life experience of a young girl's relationship with her mother when they immigrated to California.

Soto, Gary. *Too Many Tamales*. The Putnam Publishing Group, 1996. A warm family story that combines glowing art with a well-written text to tell of a girl's dilemma.

Hands-on Culture

Art: *Mural de la amistad*

In many Latin American countries, murals are used to decorate the walls of public buildings. In schools, murals are used by students to express themselves and their feelings about events such as el *Día de la amistad*.

Materials:

butcher paper, pencils, paint brushes, paint of different colors, tape

Directions:

1. Divide students into four groups. Ask each group to brainstorm a list of ideas about the meaning of friendship. Then, each group decides the idea they are going to depict in the mural.

2. Students exchange ideas on how they are going to draw their mural. Then, they draw their mural in pencil on two large pieces of butcher paper that have been taped together.

3. Students paint their mural.

4. Display the murals on the walls of the classroom or around the school. Each group explains its mural to the class.

5. The class chooses a student from each group to organize a tour of the murals for students from other classes who might be interested.

Internet Search

Use the keywords to find more information.

Keywords:

Día de la Rosa y del Libro, Babilonia, chicanos, murales, Diego Rivera, Juana de Ibarbouru, Judith Francisca Baca, Agustín Lara, Pablo Neruda

Game

Busquemos el lado positivo

This game practices using positive and negative words to describe friendships and family relationships. Play it to review the vocabulary from *Capítulo 4*.

Players: the entire class, playing in pairs

Materials: index cards and colored pencils or markers

Rules:

1. On the board write positive and negative words and expressions from *Capítulo* 4. Write positive words such as **sincero(a)**, **comprensivo(a)**, **pedir perdón**, **perdonar**, *reaccionar, alegrarse* on the right column. On the left column, write negative words, such as **vanidoso(a)**, **conflicto**, **estar equivocado(a)**, **criticar**.

2. Ask students to write the words on their index cards, one on each card. Words from the left column should be written in blue and those from the right column should be in red.

3. Select a scorekeeper and divide the class into teams A and B. Each team A player chooses a card and thinks of a sentence that uses the negative or positive word and that can be converted to a positive or negative sentence.

4. Students go in row order, team A players alternating with players from team B. Team A player: *Una amiga que es **vanidosa** piensa sólo en ella misma*. Then, he or she says the opposite word: **considerada**. Team B player: *Es mejor ser amiga de alguien que es considerada y piensa en los demás*. This correct answer gives team B a turn.

5. Teams receive 1 point for each vocabulary word they use, as well as 1 point for each correct sentence. Each time they use a new word, the corresponding card is set aside.

6. If a team cannot make a sentence, it loses its turn. No word or sentence can be repeated. The team with the most points wins.

Variation: Players can use more than one vocabulary word in each sentence. For each additional word, they receive a point.

A ver si recuerdas
RECYCLE

Vocabulary
- Activities
- Qualities
- Time

Grammar
- Uses of reflexive verbs
- Reciprocal pronouns *nos* and *se*

Chapter Overview

A primera vista 1
INPUT

Objectives
- Describe love and friendships
- Describe personality traits
- Read surveys

Vocabulary
- Personality traits
- Love and friendships

Grammar
- Subjunctive: verbs of emotion
- *por* and *para*

Culture
- Eddie Rosado Ocasio

Manos a la obra 1
PRACTICE

Objectives
- Talk about friendships and personality traits
- Distinguish between positive and negative personal qualities
- Practice the subjunctive with verbs of emotion
- Distinguish uses of *por* and *para*

Vocabulary
- Practice new vocabulary

Grammar
- Subjunctive: verbs of emotion
- Uses of *por* and *para*

Culture
- Spanish youth
- *Día de la Rosa y del Libro* in Barcelona, Spain

A primera vista 2
INPUT

Objectives
- Talk about conflicts and how to resolve them
- Talk about friends and family relationships

Vocabulary
- Conflicts and solutions
- Friends and family relationships

Grammar
- Commands with *nosotros*
- Possessive pronouns

Culture
- Opinions of Mexican teenagers about family relationships

Manos a la obra 2
PRACTICE

Objectives
- Talk about conflicts and how to resolve them
- Commands with *nosotros*
- Use possessive pronouns

Vocabulary
- Practice new vocabulary

Grammar
- Commands with *nosotros*
- Possessive pronouns

Culture
- The soap opera in Latin America
- Carmen Lomas Garza
- Paulina Rubio

¡Adelante!
APPLICATION

Objectives
- Read about expressions of love in Latin American and Spanish arts
- Compare and contrast diverse expressions of love
- Read poems about love and friendship
- Find examples of figurative language

Vocabulary
- Application

Grammar
- Application

Culture
- Spanish and Latin American artistic contributions
- Poetry readings from Latin America and Spain

Repaso del capítulo
REVIEW

Objectives
- Prepare for the chapter test
- Perform the tasks on pp. 198 and 199

Vocabulary
- Review

Grammar
- Review

BEYOND THE CLASSROOM

Countries
- Mexico
- El Salvador
- Peru
- Chile
- Uruguay
- Spain
- United States

El español en la comunidad
- Bilingual children of Spanish-speaking families

Internet
- Vocabulary activities
- Grammar activities
- Internet links
- Self-tests

LEARNER SUPPORT

Strategies
- Using illustrations to predict outcome
- Compare and contrast
- Getting into your character
- Describing relationships

Recycling
- Possessive adjectives

- The letter *j*

Conexiones
- Math: surveys
- Social Sciences: shaking hands
- Art: Carmen Lomas Garza

En voz alta
- *Será entre tú y yo*

Ampliación del lenguaje
- Word families

Print Components

TEACHER

Teacher's Resource Book
• Chapter Table of Contents
• School-to-Home Connection
• Chapter Resource Checklist
• Input Script
• Audio Script
• Video Script
• Communicative Activities
• Situation Cards
• GramActiva Blackline Masters
• Graphic Organizers
• Answer Keys:
  Practice Workbook
  Writing, Audio & Video Workbook

Realidades para hispanohablantes
Teacher Edition

STUDENT

Practice Workbook
• Vocabulary: 4-1 – 4-4, 4-8 – 4-9
• Grammar: 4-5 – 4-7, 4-10 – 4-12
• Organizer: 4-13 – 4-14

Writing, Audio & Video Workbook
• Audio: 1–5
• Writing: 6–13
• Video: 14–17

Reading and Writing for Success
• Chapter 4, Test 31

Realidades para hispanohablantes

Transparencies

Vocabulary and Grammar Transparencies
• Vocabulary: 84–90, 93–95
• Grammar: 91–92, 96–97
• ¿Qué me cuentas?: 98

Practice Answers on Transparencies
• Cap. 4

Fine Art Transparencies
• Transparencies
• Teacher's Guide

Assessment

Assessment Program
• Pruebas:
  – Comprensión del vocabulario 1: 4-1
  – Aplicación del vocabulario 1: 4-2
  – El subjuntivo con verbos de emoción: 4-3
  – Los usos de *por* y *para*: 4-4
  – Comprensión del vocabulario 2: 4-5
  – Aplicación del vocabulario 2: 4-6
  – Mandatos con *nosotros*: 4-7
  – Pronombres posesivos: 4-8

• Exámenes del capítulo
• Rubrics

Alternative Assessment
• ExamView Test Bank CD-ROM
• MindPoint Quiz Show CD-ROM
• Internet Self-test
• Situation Cards
• Communicative Activity

Assessment Program: *Realidades para hispanohablantes*

Technology

TeacherExpress™ CD-ROM
• Lesson Planner
• Teacher Resources
• Clip Art

Video Program VHS and DVD

Audio Program CDs
• A primera vista 1 y 2: Vocabulario y gramática en contexto
• Audio Activities
• ¿Qué me cuentas?
• Repaso
• Examen del capítulo: Escuchar

Regular Schedule (50 Minutes)

For electronic lesson plans:
Teacher Express CD-ROM 💿

	Warm-up / Assess	Preview Present / Practice Communicate	Wrap-up / Homework Options
DAY 1	**Warm-up (10 min.)** • Return Examen del capítulo: Capítulo 3	**Repaso (35 min.)** • A ver si recuerdas . . . • Actividad 5	**Wrap-up and Homework Options (5 min.)** • Practice Workbook 4-1, 4-2 • Go Online
DAY 2	**Warm-up (10 min.)** • Homework check	**Chapter Opener (10 min.)** • Objectives • Fondo cultural **A primera vista 1 (25 min.)** • Presentation: Vocabulario y gramática en contexto • Actividades 1, 2	**Wrap-up and Homework Options (5 min.)** • Go Online • Clip Art Vocabulary
DAY 3	**Warm-up (10 min.)** • Homework check	**A primera vista 1 (30 min.)** • Presentation: Prueba de la amistad • Actividades 3, 4 **Manos a la obra 1 (5 min.)** • Actividad 6	**Wrap-up and Homework Options (5 min.)** • Practice Workbook 4-3, 4-4 • Go Online • Prueba 4-1: Vocabulary recognition
DAY 4	**Warm-up (10 min.)** • Homework check ✔**Assessment (10 min.)** • Prueba 4-1: Vocabulary recognition	**Manos a la obra 1 (25 min.)** • Actividades 5, 7, 8 • Ampliación del lenguaje	**Wrap-up and Homework Options (5 min.)** • Actividades 9, 10 • Writing Activities • Prueba 4-2: Vocabulary production
DAY 5	**Warm-up (10 min.)** • Fondo cultural • Homework check ✔**Assessment (10 min.)** • Prueba 4-2: Vocabulary production	**Manos a la obra 1 (25 min.)** • Presentation: El subjuntivo con verbos de emoción • Actividades 11, 13, 14, 15 • Writing Activity	**Wrap-up and Homework Options (5 min.)** • Practice Workbook 4-5 • Go Online
DAY 6	**Warm-up (10 min.)** • Actividad 12 • Homework check	**Manos a la obra 1 (35 min.)** • Actividad 16 • Communicative Activity • Presentation: Los usos de *por* y *para* • Actividad 18	**Wrap-up and Homework Options (5 min.)** • Writing Activity • Prueba 4-3: El subjuntivo con verbos de emoción
DAY 7	**Warm-up (10 min.)** • Homework check ✔**Assessment (10 min.)** • Prueba 4-3: El subjuntivo con verbos de emoción	**Manos a la obra (25 min.)** • Actividades 17, 19, 20, 21 • Communicative Activity	**Wrap-up and Homework Options (5 min.)** • Practice Workbook 4-6, 4-7 • Go Online • Prueba 4-4: Los usos de *por* y *para*
DAY 8	**Warm-up (15 min.)** • Writing Activity • Homework check ✔**Assessment (10 min.)** • Prueba 4-4: Los usos de *por* y *para*	**A primera vista 2 (20 min.)** • Presentation: Vocabulario y gramática en contexto • Actividad 22	**Wrap-up and Homework Options (5 min.)** • Clip Art Vocabulary • Examen: Vocabulario y gramática 1
DAY 9	**Warm-up (5 min.)** • Homework check ✔**Assessment (30 min.)** • Examen: Vocabulario y gramática 1	**A primera vista 2 (10 min.)** • Presentation: Hagamos las paces • Actividad 23	**Wrap-up and Homework Options (5 min.)** • Conflictos: causas y soluciones • Practice Workbook 4-8, 4-9 • Go Online • Prueba 4-5: Vocabulary recognition
DAY 10	**Warm-up (20 min.)** • Conflictos: causas y soluciones • Actividad 24 • Homework check ✔**Assessment (10 min.)** • Prueba 4-5: Vocabulary recognition	**Manos a la obra 2 (15 min.)** • Fondo cultural • Actividades 28, 29	**Wrap-up and Homework Options (5 min.)** • Actividades 26, 27 • Prueba 4-6: Vocabulary production

	Warm-up / Assess	Preview Present / Practice Communicate	Wrap-up / Homework Options
DAY 11	**Warm-up (10 min.)** • Actividad 25 • Homework check **✔Assessment (10 min.)** • Prueba 4-6: Vocabulary production	**Manos a la obra 2 (25 min.)** • Actividades 30, 32 • Actividades 33, 35 • Presentation: Mandatos • Communicative Activity con *nosotros*	**Wrap-up and Homework Options (5 min.)** • Actividad 34 • Practice Workbook 4-10 • Go Online • Prueba 4-7: Mandatos con *nosotros*
DAY 12	**Warm-up (10 min.)** • Writing Activity • Homework check **✔Assessment (10 min.)** • Prueba 4-7: Mandatos con *nosotros*	**Manos a la obra 2 (25 min.)** • Presentation: Pronombres posesivos • Actividades 36, 37, 38 • El español en la comunidad	**Wrap-up and Homework Options (5 min.)** • Practice Workbook 4-11, 4-12 • Go Online • Prueba 4-8: Pronombres posesivos
DAY 13	**Warm-up (10 min.)** • Homework check **✔Assessment (10 min.)** • Prueba 4-8: Pronombres posesivos	**Manos a la obra 2 (25 min.)** • En voz alta • Communicative Activity	**Wrap-up and Homework Options (5 min.)** • Go Online • Examen: Vocabulario y gramática 2
DAY 14	**Warm-up (8 min.)** • Writing Activity **✔Assessment (30 min.)** • Examen: Vocabulario y gramática 2	**¡Adelante! (10 min.)** • Presentación oral: Steps 1, 2	**Wrap-up and Homework Options (2 min.)** • Presentación oral: Step 2
DAY 15	**Warm-up (10 min.)** • Presentación oral: Step 2	**¡Adelante! (35 min.)** • Presentación oral: Step 3	**Wrap-up and Homework Options (5 min.)** • El amor en las artes • ¿Comprendiste? • Go Online
DAY 16	**Warm-up (15 min.)** • El amor en las artes: ¿Comprendiste? • Homework check	**¡Adelante! (30 min.)** • ¿Qué me cuentas? 1, 2, 3 • View Video • Video Activities 1, 2, 3	**Wrap-up and Homework Options (5 min.)** • Presentación escrita: Steps 1, 2
DAY 17	**Warm-up (10 min.)** • Video Activity 4	**¡Adelante! (15 min.)** • Presentación escrita: Step 3 **Repaso (20 min.)** • Preparación para el examen: Actividades 3, 4 • MindPoint Quiz Show	**Wrap Up and Homework Options (5 min.)** • Presentación escrita: Step 4
DAY 18	**Warm-up (10 min.)** • Homework check	**¡Adelante! (35 min.)** • Lectura • ¿Comprendiste? • Fondo cultural	**Wrap-up and Homework Options (5 min.)** • Practice Workbook: Organizer 4-13, 4-14 • Go Online: Self-test
DAY 19	**Warm-up (20 min.)** • Preparación para el examen: Actividades 1, 2 • Homework check	**Repaso (25 min.)** • Preparación para el examen: Actividades 5, 6, 7 • MindPoint Quiz Show • Other review	**Wrap-up and Homework Options (5 min.)** • Examen del capítulo
DAY 20	**Warm-up (5 min.)** • Answer questions **✔Assessment (44 min.)** • Examen del capítulo		**Wrap-up and Homework Options (1 min.)** • A ver si recuerdas: Capítulo 5 • Actividades 1, 2, 4, 6, 7

Block Schedule (90 Minutes)

For electronic lesson plans:
Teacher Express CD-ROM

Warm-up / Assess	Preview Present / Practice Communicate	Wrap-up / Homework Options
DAY 1		
Warm-up (35 min.) • Return Examen del capítulo: Capítulo 3 • A ver si recuerdas . . . • Actividad 5 • Homework check	**Chapter Opener (10 min.)** • Objectives • Fondo cultural **A primera vista 1 (30 min.)** • Presentation: Vocabulario y gramática en contexto • Actividades 1, 2 • Presentation: Prueba de la amistad • Actividades 3, 4 **Manos a la obra 1 (10 min.)** • Actividades 6, 7	**Wrap-up and Homework Options (5 min.)** • Practice Workbook 4-3, 4-4 • Go Online • Clip Art Vocabulary • Prueba 4-1: Vocabulary recognition
DAY 2		
Warm-up (15 min.) • Actividad 5 • Homework check ✔**Assessment (10 min.)** • Prueba 4-1: Vocabulary recognition	**Manos a la obra 1 (60 min.)** • Actividades 8, 9, 10 • Ampliación del lenguaje • Fondo cultural • Communicative Activity • Audio Activity	**Wrap-up and Homework Options (5 min.)** • Go Online • Writing Activities • Prueba 4-2: Vocabulary production
DAY 3		
Warm-up (15 min.) • Writing Activity • Homework check ✔**Assessment (10 min.)** • Prueba 4-2: Vocabulary production	**Manos a la obra 1 (60 min.)** • Presentation: El subjuntivo con verbos de emoción • Actividades 11, 12, 13, 14, 15 • Audio and Writing Activities	**Wrap-up and Homework Options (5 min.)** • Practice Workbook 4-5 • Go Online • Prueba 4-3: El subjuntivo con verbos de emoción
DAY 4		
Warm-up (10 min.) • Actividad 16 • Homework check ✔**Assessment (10 min.)** • Prueba 4-3: El subjuntivo con verbos de emoción	**Manos a la obra 1 (50 min.)** • Presentation: Los usos de *por* y *para* • Actividades 18, 19, 20, 21 • Communicative Activity **A primera vista 2 (15 min.)** • Presentation: Vocabulario y gramática en contexto • Actividad 22	**Wrap-up and Homework Options (5 min.)** • Practice Workbook 4-6, 4-7 • Go Online • Prueba 4-4: Los usos de *por* y *para* • Examen: Vocabulario y gramática 1
DAY 5		
Warm-up (15 min.) • Actividad 17 • Homework check ✔**Assessment Options (40 min.)** • Prueba 4-4: Los usos de *por* y *para* • Examen: Vocabulario y gramática 1	**A primera vista 2 (20 min.)** • Presentation: Hagamos las paces • Actividad 23 • Presentation: Conflictos: causas y soluciones • Actividad 24 **Manos a la obra 2 (10 min.)** • Actividad 25 • Fondo cultural	**Wrap-up and Homework Options (5 min.)** • Practice Workbook 4-8, 4-9 • Go Online • Prueba 4-5: Vocabulary recognition
DAY 6		
Warm-up (20 min.) • Actividades 26, 27 • Homework check ✔**Assessment (10 min.)** • Prueba 4-5: Vocabulary recognition	**Manos a la obra 2 (55 min.)** • Actividades 28, 29, 30, 32 • Presentation: Mandatos con *nosotros* • Actividades 33, 34, 35	**Wrap-up and Homework Options (5 min.)** • Practice Workbook 4-10 • Go Online • Pruebas 4-6, 4-7: Vocabulary production, Mandatos con *nosotros*

	Warm-up / Assess	Preview Present / Practice Communicate	Wrap-up / Homework Options
DAY 7	**Warm-up (15 min.)** • Actividad 31 • Homework check ✔**Assessment (20 min.)** • Pruebas 4-6, 4-7: Vocabulary production, Mandatos con *nosotros*	**Manos a la obra 2 (35 min.)** • En voz alta • Presentation: Pronombres posesivos • Actividades 36, 37, 38 • El español en la comunidad **¡Adelante! (15 min.)** • Presentación oral: Steps 1, 2	**Wrap-up and Homework Options (5 min.)** • Presentación oral: Step 2 • Go Online
DAY 8	**Warm-up (15 min.)** • Writing Activity • Homework check ✔**Assessment (40 min.)** • Presentación oral: Step 3	**Manos a la obra 2 (15 min.)** • Communicative Activity **¡Adelante! (15 min.)** • Presentation: El amor en las artes	**Wrap-up and Homework Options (5 min.)** • Practice Workbook 4-11, 4-12 • Go Online • Prueba 4-8: Pronombres posesivos • Examen: Vocabulario y gramática 2
DAY 9	**Warm-up (10 min.)** • Homework check ✔**Assessment Options (30 min.)** • Prueba 4-8: Pronombres posesivos • Examen: Vocabulario y gramática 2	**¡Adelante! (45 min.)** • El amor en las artes • ¿Comprendiste? • ¿Qué me cuentas? 1, 2, 3 • Video Activities • Presentación escrita: Step 1 • Video	**Wrap-up and Homework Options (5 min.)** • Presentación escrita: Step 2 • Go Online • Preparación para el examen: Actividades 1, 2
DAY 10	**Warm-up (20 min.)** • Presentación escrita: Step 3 • Homework check	**¡Adelante! (40 min.)** • Lectura – all pages • ¿Comprendiste? • Fondo cultural **Repaso (25 min.)** • Preparación para el examen: Actividades 3, 4, 6 • MindPoint Quiz	**Wrap-up and Homework Options (5 min.)** • Presentación escrita: Step 4 • Practice Workbook: Organizer 4-13, 4-14 • Go Online: Self-test • Preparación para el examen: Actividades 5, 7 • Examen del capítulo
DAY 11	**Warm-up (15 min.)** • Homework check ✔**Assessment (45 min.)** • Examen del capítulo	**Theme Game (15 min.)** **A ver si recuerdas – Capítulo 5 (10 min.)** • Presentation: Vocabulario • Presentation: Gramática	**Wrap-up and Homework Options (5 min.)** • A ver si recuerdas – Capítulo 5 • Actividades 1, 2, 4, 6, 7 • Go Online • Practice Workbook 5-1, 5-2

4 Review

Vocabulario

Presentation

Standards: 1.1, 1.2

Resources: Voc. & Gram. Transparencies: 84

Suggestions: Ask students to think of one person they know well. Have them tell at least two facts about the person, using vocabulary from the three categories. Tell students that vocabulary from the ***actividades*** and ***tiempo*** categories might be used in the same sentence: *Mi hermana Jane es una persona sociable. Le gusta escribir cartas a sus amigas durante sus viajes.*

Standards: 1.1, 1.3, 3.1

Resources: Voc. & Gram. Transparencies: 2

Focus: Practicing review vocabulary

Suggestions: Remind students that when making their Venn diagrams in step 1, they should fill in the overlapping parts of the diagram with qualities their friends have in common.

Common Errors: Students may forget to make an adjective agree in number and gender with the noun it modifies. Correct the error by modeling the correct form of the noun phrase and having students repeat. You can also use visual cues: hold up two fingers to elicit plural; have a flash card ready with the masculine symbol on one side and the feminine symbol on the other, and hold this up to elicit the appropriate gender.

Answers will vary.

Block Schedule

Ask each student to write a sentence of up to eight words that uses a reflexive verb in the present, past, or future tense with student(s) in the class as the subject. Put the papers in a bag. Create two teams. Alternate with individual students acting out the sentences. Allow a team up to 30 seconds to guess the sentence. Keep track of the time per sentence. The team with the lowest time wins.

154

Preparación para 4

A ver si recuerdas...

Vocabulario

actividades
charlar
divertirse
encontrarse
enviar correo electrónico
escribir cartas
jugar juegos
llevarse bien / mal
navegar en la Red
participar
pasarlo bien
pasear
quedarse en casa
reunirse
reírse
salir

cualidades

artístico, -a	inteligente
atlético, -a	nervioso, -a
bien educado, -a	reservado, -a
cortés	serio, -a
divertido, -a	simpático, -a
elegante	sociable
estudioso, -a	talentoso, -a
gracioso, -a	tranquilo, -a

tiempo
antes (de)
después (de)
hasta
los días de semana
los fines de semana
los días festivos
durante
por la mañana
por la tarde
por la noche

 **Escribir/Hablar**..

Práctica de vocabulario

1 Escoge cinco cualidades para describir a tus amigos(as). Haz una lista. Compara tu lista con la de un(a) compañero(a). Luego, hagan juntos un diagrama de Venn para ver qué cualidades comparten sus amigos(as).

2 Con tu compañero(a) hablen de las cualidades que comparten sus amigos(as) y digan por qué son importantes para ustedes.

Modelo

Nos gustan las personas divertidas porque siempre lo pasamos bien con ellas.

154 ciento cincuenta y cuatro
A ver si recuerdas . . .

Universal Access

Heritage Language Learners

Invite students with exemplary pronunciation to read the vocabulary aloud as a pronunciation model. Point out any regional differences between certain pronunciations, such as /y/ or /zh/ for *ll* in the phrase ***llevarse bien.***

Advanced Learners

Much of the review vocabulary can be applied to an animal, such as a pet, as well as a person. Ask students to use the vocabulary to write a brief paragraph about a pet or other animal they know: *Mi perro Jake es muy gracioso. Los fines de semana, vamos al parque y nos divertimos mucho jugando con su pelota.*

Gramática · Repaso

Otros usos de los verbos reflexivos

A verb is reflexive in Spanish when the subject receives the action of the verb. In English this is implied by the endings *-self* and *-selves*. In Spanish the reflexive pronouns are *me, te, se, nos, os, se*.

Ella **se** levanta.	She gets **(herself)** up.
Nosotros **nos** paramos.	We stand **(ourselves)** up.

- Many reflexive verbs in Spanish describe daily routine actions. Some verbs of this type include *despertarse* (to wake up), *ducharse* (to take a shower), *peinarse* (to comb oneself), *vestirse* (to get dressed), and *acostarse* (to go to bed).

- Other reflexive verbs describe a physical or emotional state. Verbs of this type include *divertirse* (to enjoy oneself) and *sentirse* (to feel an emotion).

- Some reflexive verbs describe a change of state and they carry the added meaning of "to get" or "to become."

Me enojé.	*I became angry (got mad).*	**Se puso** muy nervioso.	*He became very nervous.*
¿Te aburriste?	*Did you get bored?*	**Se cansan**.	*They get (become) tired.*

- Some verbs have a different meaning when used reflexively.

ir	*to go*	**irse**	*to leave*	**dormir**	*to sleep*	**dormirse**	*to fall asleep*
parecer	*to seem*	**parecerse a**	*to look like*	**quedar**	*to be located*	**quedarse**	*to stay*
quitar	*to take away*	**quitarse**	*to take off*	**volver**	*to return*	**volverse**	*to become*
perder	*to lose*	**perderse**	*to get lost*				

- Other verbs such as *darse cuenta de* (to realize), *quejarse* (to complain), and *ducharse* (to behave) are always reflexive.

- Placement of reflexive pronouns with commands and the present participle follow the same rules that apply to placement of direct and indirect object pronouns.

Actividad 2 · Escribir

Práctica de gramática

Completa este párrafo con los verbos del recuadro para describir lo que hace una familia los sábados.

quedarse	levantarse	irse
quejarse	cansarse	

Los sábados todos __1.__ temprano. Mi hermano y mi papá __2.__ con sus amigos a jugar al fútbol. Por la tarde, si hace buen tiempo, nadie quiere __3.__ en casa. Todos vamos al parque a correr. A veces, después de correr, yo __4.__ un poco pero nunca __5.__. Después de todo, lo pasamos muy bien.

Actividad 3 · Escribir

Práctica de gramática

Combina palabras de las dos listas para escribir lo que tú y tus amigos hacen los sábados.

> **Modelo**
>
> los chicos / reunirse
> *Los chicos se reúnen en la plaza.*

1. mi amigo y yo	acostarse
2. tú	divertirse
3. los chicos	aburrirse
4. yo	quedarse
5. mi amiga	irse

Gramática · Repaso

Presentation

Standards: 4.1

Resources: Voc. & Gram. Transparencies: 85

Suggestions: Show *Vocabulary & Grammar Transparency* 85. Point to the images of the various activities and have students say what is happening.

Actividad 2 *Standards:* 1.2

Resources: Practice Answers on Transparencies

Focus: Reviewing reflexive verbs

Suggestions: Remind students that the verbs in the word bank are in the infinitive form, and therefore the reflexive pronoun **se** is attached to the end. They must detach the pronoun and adapt it and the verb form to suit the subject of the sentence, if necessary (see item 3).

Answers:
1. se levantan (nos levantamos) 4. me canso
2. se van   5. me quejo
3. quedarse

Actividad 3 *Standards:* 1.3

Resources: Practice Answers on Transparencies

Focus: Reviewing reflexive verbs

Suggestions: Challenge students to compete with a partner and see who can come up with the most sentences in five minutes.

Answers will vary. Students may use the following verb forms:
1. nos acostamos/nos divertimos/nos aburrimos/nos quedamos/nos vamos
2. te acuestas/te diviertes/te aburres/te quedas/te vas
3. se acuestan/se divierten/se aburren/se quedan/se van
4. me acuesto/me divierto/me aburro/me quedo/me voy
5. se acuesta/se divierte/se aburre/se queda/se va

Enriching Your Teaching

Teacher-to-Teacher

Using video with the sound off is a good way to elicit different structures or vocabulary from students. For reflexive verbs, show a video segment from a film, a TV show, or a commercial, in which characters are going through part of a daily routine. As students watch, they say sentences about the actions, using reflexive verbs.

Vocabulario

Vocabulario

defectos
aburrido, -a
desordenado, -a
impaciente
infantil
mal educado, -a
perezoso, -a
tonto, -a

acciones
discutir
emocionarse
enojarse
gritar
importar
llorar
mentir
molestar
pelearse

reacciones
¡ay!
¡basta!
¡déjame en paz!
¡tú tampoco!
¡uf!
¡yo también!
a mí no . . .
a mí sí . . .
a mí también . . .
a mí tampoco . . .

expresiones
hablar mal (de)
llegar tarde
no pensar (en)
ponerse . . .
    furioso, -a
    nervioso, -a
quedarse
    tranquilo, -a
tener paciencia
volverse
    loco, -a

Actividad 4 · Escribir

Práctica de vocabulario

Completa las frases siguientes para describir qué cosas te molestan de tus amigos(as).

Modelo

Me pongo nervioso(a) cuando . . .
Me pongo nervioso(a) cuando mi amiga no me llama.

1. Me molesta cuando . . .
2. No me gusta nada cuando . . .
3. Me enojo cuando . . .
4. Me pongo furioso(a) cuando . . .
5. Me vuelvo loco(a) cuando . . .

Actividad 5 · Hablar

Práctica de vocabulario

Trabaja con otro(a) estudiante para leer y reaccionar a los siguientes comentarios. Usa la lista de reacciones de arriba.

Modelo

A —Me gusta cuando la profesora está contenta con mi trabajo.
B —*A mi también.*

1. ¡Vamos! ¡Levántate, perezoso!
2. ¿Me ayudas a lavar la ropa?
3. No me gustan las fresas.
4. ¡Ten cuidado! ¡Ve más despacio!
5. ¿Al cine? ¡Sí, yo quiero ir!
6. Tengo prisa. Tenemos que llegar a las tres.
7. ¿Ya estudiaste para el examen? Dicen que va a ser difícil.

156 ciento cincuenta y seis
A ver si recuerdas . . .

Gramática · Repaso

Pronombres reflexivos en acciones recíprocas

To tell what people do to or for one another use the reciprocal pronouns *nos* and *se* before the first and third person plural of certain verbs.

> Mis hermanos y yo no **nos** peleamos nunca.
> Alonso y Fernanda **se** llaman todos los días, pero **se** ven muy poco.

In the case of a verbal phrase with an infinitive or a present participle, you may place the reciprocal pronoun either before the conjugated verb or attached to the infinitive or participle. Remember to place an accent in the third to last syllable when you add the reciprocal pronoun to a present participle.

> Vamos a ver**nos** mañana.
> **Nos** vamos a ver mañana

> Rodrigo y Luisa estaban abrazándo**se** en el jardín.
> Rodrigo y Luisa **se** estaban abrazando en el jardín.

Here are some examples of reflexive verbs that are used reciprocally:

abrazarse	comprenderse	entenderse	leerse	pelearse
ayudarse	conocerse	escribirse	llamarse	saludarse
besarse	contarse	hablarse	llevarse bien / mal	verse

 Leer/Escribir

¿La pareja ideal?

Romina siempre está hablando de la relación de su hermana Analía con su novio Nicolás. Completa las siguientes frases con el verbo que corresponda, en la forma correcta. Luego, resume en una frase qué opinas tú de la relación de esta pareja.

Analía y Nicolás . . .

1. _____ *(escribirse / ayudarse)* mensajes todas las mañanas.

2. _____ *(entenderse / hablarse)* muy bien y son muy felices.

3. Nunca _____ *(besarse / pelearse)* ni tienen opiniones diferentes.

4. Siempre _____ *(comprenderse / enojarse)* y _____ *(ayudarse / conocerse)*.

5. _____ *(llamarse / leerse)* todas las noches y hablan horas por teléfono.

6. _____ *(entenderse / verse)* todos los viernes y los sábados.

7. _____ *(conocerse / contarse)* desde hace muchos años.

8. _____ *(llevarse / saludarse)* muy bien.

● **Más práctica**
Practice Workbook 4-1, 4-2

PHSchool.com

For: More review
Visit: www.phschool.com
Web Code: jed-0401

 **Gramática · Repaso**

Presentation

Resources: Voc. & Gram. Transparencies: 87

Suggestions: Ask students to create sentences using verbs from the list at the end of the *Gramática*. If a sentence contains a verb phrase, have students practice using it both ways: with the reciprocal pronoun before the conjugated verb and with the pronoun attached to the end of the infinitive or present participle.

Resources: Practice Answers on Transparencies

Focus: Reviewing reciprocal pronouns

Suggestions: Once students have written their answers, encourage them to read all the items through like a story, in order to be better able to comment on the relationship between Analía and Nicolás.

Answers:
1. Se escriben
2. Se entienden
3. se pelean
4. se comprenden/se ayudan
5. Se llaman
6. Se ven
7. Se conocen
8. Se llevan

Extension: Have students share the comments they wrote about the relationship between Analía and Nicolás. Encourage them to support their opinion with an additional comment.

Enriching Your Teaching

Teacher-to-Teacher
Even adolescents will agree that adolescence can be a very trying time of life. The vocabulary reviewed on these two pages is suitable to the complaints, discomforts, and frustrations, large and small, that many of your students go through daily. Encourage them to use, or at least think of, expressions such as *¡Uf!, ¡Basta!,* and *¡Déjame en paz!* at trying times during their day, even if the situation going on around them is in English. Such connections between genuine emotion and language use can open important portals to learning.

4 Preview

Standards for Foreign Language Learning: *Capítulo* 4

- To achieve the goals of the Standards, students will:

Communication

1.1 Interpersonal
- Talk about friendship, interpersonal relationships, personality traits, emotions, customary behavior, conflict resolution
- Talk about known artists, musicians, and poets and their work
- Talk about soap operas and poetry readings

1.2 Interpretive
- Read and listen to information about friendship, interpersonal relationships, personality traits, emotions, customary behavior, conflict resolution, family routines
- Read about known artists, musicians, and poets and their work
- Read about word families
- Read about soap operas and poetry readings
- Read about bilingual children

1.3 Presentational
- Write about friendship, interpersonal relationships, personality traits, emotions, conflict resolution, family routines
- Write about a trip and a day out
- Recite song lyrics by Paulina Rubio
- Write about the theme of love in art
- Present information orally about a student council meeting
- Write about known poets and their work

Culture

2.1 Practices and Perspectives
- Explain artistic life in Puerto Rico
- Interpret Spanish personality demographics and Mexican family dynamics
- Explain the impact of love in Spanish-speaking cultures and their art
- Explain the practice of poetry readings in Spanish

2.2 Products and Perspectives
- Talk about known artists, musicians, and poets and their work
- Talk about *telenovelas*

Connections

3.1 Cross-curricular
- Talk about psychology, conflict resolution, and interpersonal dynamics
- Talk about known artists, musicians, and poets and their work
- Work with percentages in surveys
- Describe holidays in Spain and Latin America
- Describe the history of the handshake
- Describe Spanish cities
- Discuss Language Arts strategies: compare and contrast, getting into your character, describing relationships, identifying and understanding figurative language
- Discuss conflict in fiction and drama

3.2 Target Culture
- Read a Spanish youth survey
- Read song lyrics by Paulina Rubio
- Read poetry by known poets

Fondo cultural ■◆■◇■◆■◇■◆

Madre e hijo La relación entre madre e hijo puede ser una relación muy íntima y especial. El artista español Pablo Picasso tiene una serie de cuadros de varios períodos y estilos que muestran las figuras de una madre y un hijo. En este cuadro se ve la influencia del arte africano. Las caras de las figuras se parecen a máscaras *(masks)* africanas. ¿Qué elementos usa Picasso para comunicar la relación entre estas dos personas?

- ¿Conoces otro(a) artista que muestre relaciones entre familias? Descríbelo(a).

Madre e hijo, (1907), Pablo Picasso
(c) 2003 Estate of Pablo Picasso/Artists Rights Society (ARS), New York. (c) Réunion des Musées Nationaux/Art Resource, New York.

158 ciento cincuenta y ocho

Universal Access

Personalizing the Theme
Ask students to describe the traits they think are most important in people. Ask questions such as the following: *Imagínate que estás en una fiesta donde no conoces a mucha gente. ¿Cuáles son las primeras características que notas en una persona? ¿Qué tipo de personalidad te atrae o no te atrae?*

Students with Learning Difficulties
Have students talk about the friends in the photograph using the vocabulary on p. 154. Alternatively, you can frame questions with the vocabulary to prompt discussion: *¿Crees que los chicos se divierten mucho? Sí, porque están riéndose.*

Capítulo 4

¿Cómo te llevas con los demás?

Chapter Objectives

- **Express how you relate to friends and family**
- **Explain what is needed to maintain friendships**
- **Express how you feel under certain circumstances**
- **Talk about family conflicts and how to resolve them**
- **Understand cultural perspectives on dealing with friends and family**

Video Focus

- **Characteristics of friendships and family relationships**

Country Connection

As you learn about friends and family relationships, you will make connections to these countries and places.

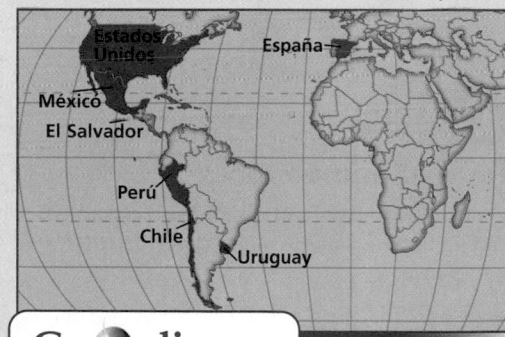

Go Online
PHSchool.com

For: Online Atlas
Visit: www.phschool.com
Web Code: jee-0002

ciento cincuenta y nueve **159**
Capítulo 4

Preview

(4)

Standards for Foreign Language Learning (cont'd)

Comparisons
4.1 Language
- Compare Spanish words to their English counterparts
- Compare English and Spanish reflexive verbs
- Compare *por* and *para* with English
- Compare *nosotros* commands with English

4.2 Culture
- Compare Spanish and U.S. teen profiles
- Compare U.S. holidays and TV shows with those in Spanish-speaking countries
- Compare works of art

Communities
5.1 Beyond the School
- Link to Web sites from around the Spanish-speaking world

5.2 Lifelong Learner
- Describe their own personalities
- Discuss techniques for conflict resolution
- Develop an appreciation for poetry

Chapter Opener
Presentation

Resources: Voc. & Gram. Transparencies: 14, 15, 19, 20, 22 (maps)

Suggestions: Introduce students to the theme of the chapter and go over the objectives. Point out that they will learn language to help them deal with their own feelings and those of others. They will also learn about how people in other cultures deal with friends and family. Use the transparencies to locate and discuss the countries featured in the chapter.

Fondo cultural *Standards:* 1.1, 1.2, 2.1, 2.2, 3.1

Resources: Fine Art Transparencies; Fine Art Transparencies Teacher's Guide

Suggestions: After students have read the information, ask: *¿Qué detalles nos muestran quién es la madre y quién es el hijo en la pintura? (La madre es más grande. Está detrás del hijo, como en muchas pinturas. El hijo tiene poco pelo, como un niño muy joven.)*

Answers will vary.

Enriching Your Teaching

Planning for Instruction
Resources:
- Teacher Express CD-ROM or Resource Book
  - Teaching resources
  - Lesson Planner
  - Chapter Resource Checklist
  - School-to-Home Connection Letter

Culture Note
The social network between family and friends is strengthened in Latin America through the tradition of **compadrazgo**. Literally translated as "copaternity," the custom is similar to that of godparents in the United States. The parents of a newborn child select a **comadre** and **compadre**. The adults agree to help the child and each other.

159

Objectives
Read, listen to, and understand information about
- love and friendship
- personality traits

Vocabulario y gramática

Presentation

Standards: 1.1, 1.2

Resources: Voc. & Gram. Transparencies: 88; Resource Book: Cap. 4, Input Script; Audio Program: CD Cap. 4, Track 1, 3

Focus: Presenting new vocabulary and using grammar lexically in context

Suggestions: You may want to use the Input Script from the *Teacher's Resource Book* as a source of ideas for presentation of new vocabulary and comprehensible input. Many meanings for the vocabulary in this lesson must be taught either via situations or by explanation. When explaining, use Spanish that students will readily understand:

Una persona egoísta sólo piensa en sí misma.

La joven de la foto es honesta, ¿verdad? Devuelve a su amigo el dinero que dejó caer.

 Standards: 1.2

Resources: Audio Program: CD Cap. 4, Track 2; Resource Book: Cap. 4, Audio Script; Practice Answers on Transparencies

Focus: Practicing listening comprehension of new vocabulary

Suggestions: Before playing the *Audio CD* or reading the script aloud, allow students to read over the selections for each item. Make sure they understand they will be drawing a conclusion about each speaker's personality.

Answers:

1. b	4. a
2. b	5. a
3. b	6. b

Block Schedule

In pairs, have students write a sentence describing each of the personality traits on p. 160. Have them work with another pair, reading the descriptions to the other students who must guess the new vocabulary word.

A primera vista 1

Vocabulario y gramática en contexto

¿Cuántas personas conoces en la escuela? ¿Cuántos amigos tienes? ¿Cómo te relacionas con ellos? Pueden ser muchas o pocas, pero no todas las personas que conoces son tus amigos. Los amigos son el mejor regalo que podemos recibir. **¡Ojalá** que tengas muchos amigos!

Un(a) buen(a) amigo(a) es . . .

Un(a) buen(a) amigo(a) no es . . .

Actividad 1 **Escuchar**

Todo el mundo dice . . .

Escucha lo que opinan algunos(as) chicos(as) sobre sus compañeros(as) y escoge la palabra que mejor describa cómo son.

1. Antonio es
   a. celoso   **b.** generoso

2. Mónica es
   a. chismosa   **b.** comprensiva

3. Francisco es
   a. honesto   **b.** cariñoso

4. Luis es
   a. vanidoso   **b.** entrometido

5. Irene es
   a. honesta   **b.** egoísta

6. Mario es
   a. generoso   **b.** egoísta

160 ciento sesenta
A primera vista 1

Universal Access

Students with Learning Difficulties
Invite students to summarize what is happening in each picture on p. 160 and to use this summary to figure out the meaning of each vocabulary word. For example: *La mujer abraza y le sonríe al niño. Creo que "cariñoso(a)" quiere decir* nice o caring.

Advanced Learners
Ask pairs of students to stretch their creativity by preparing two different pantomimes that show the meaning of each vocabulary item on this page. Have pairs present their pantomimes in random order. Those watching must guess which characteristic the partners are trying to portray.

La amistad y el amor son temas muy importantes entre los estudiantes de la escuela Las Américas en Montevideo, Uruguay. Averigua qué piensan algunos estudiantes sobre estos temas.

1 "Un amigo es alguien en quien puedes **confiar** o que sabe **guardar** bien **un secreto.** Es alguien que **se alegra** contigo en los momentos felices y **te apoya** en los momentos tristes. En pocas palabras, es alguien que se preocupa por ti."
Ricardo Rodríguez

2 "Para mí la amistad es muy importante. Mis amigos y yo **tenemos mucho en común.** Nos gusta el cine y el fútbol. Por eso lo pasamos muy bien **juntos.** También nos tenemos **confianza** para contarnos nuestros problemas. **Espero** que seamos amigos para toda la vida."
Teresa Soto

3 "Mi mejor amiga es muy **sincera.** A veces **me sorprende** cuando dice lo que realmente piensa. Pero yo sé que es muy **considerada** y que trata de no lastimar mis sentimientos con sus opiniones."
Celina Lugo

4 "Mis compañeros y yo nos llevamos bien, pero sólo dos de ellos, Julián y Mario, son mis amigos **íntimos.** Nos conocemos desde niños y sé que puedo **contar con** ellos para todo. A veces **temo** que nuestra amistad se rompa porque soy un poco chismoso. Pero mis amigos me dicen que no **desconfían** de mí. Me alegro de que me **acepten tal como soy.**"
Raúl Gutiérrez

 **Escribir/Hablar** ·

El (la) profesor(a) ideal

¿Cuáles son para ti las cinco cualidades *(qualities)* más importantes que debe tener un(a) buen(a) profesor(a)? Haz una lista e intercámbiala con tus compañeros(as).

ciento sesenta y uno **161**
Capítulo 4

 Enriching Your Teaching

Culture Note
Explain that, as in the United States, Spanish-speaking people have varying attitudes toward punctuality. Some are sticklers, and others have a more relaxed attitude. Arriving "fashionably late" to social occasions is usually considered acceptable behavior and rarely causes annoyance.

Internet Search
Keyword: | qué es un amigo |

Language Input

Vocabulario y gramática

Presentation

Standards: 1.1, 1.2

Resources: Voc. & Gram. Transparencies: 90; Resource Book: Cap. 4, Input Script; Audio Program: CD Cap. 4, Track 4

Focus: Extending presentation of vocabulary and grammar in the context of a friendship survey

Suggestions:

Pre-reading: Tell students that the survey is much like those they have probably seen in teen and fashion magazines. If possible, display another example of such a magazine survey. Clarify the meaning of *tener celos* and *cambias de opinión* using explanation or pantomime, or by setting up a situation. For *cualidades* and *amable,* point out the English cognates "qualities" and "amiable." Have students copy the answer grid to their own paper before taking the survey.

Reading: Allow students time to read the twenty questions silently. Then play the *Audio CD* or read the information aloud, with students reading along and marking their answers on their papers as they listen. In order to make the survey more interesting and enjoyable, postpone reading the *Resultados* section until students have completed the survey.

Post-reading: Have students use the completed survey as a vehicle for a discussion about friendship. Ask: ¿*Estás de acuerdo con estas cualidades para ser un buen amigo? Explica tus respuestas. ¿Crees que hay otras cualidades que deben formar parte de esta prueba?*

Chapter Project

Give students copies of the Chapter Project outline and rubric from the *Teacher's Resource Book.* Explain the task to them, and have them perform step 1. (For more information, see p. 154-a.)

Prueba de la amistad

Anímate a hacer la prueba de la amistad y averigua si tienes **cualidades** como amigo(a).

¿Sabes ser amigo(a)?

1. ¿Eres considerado(a) con los demás?
2. Cuando te peleas, ¿te quedas enojado(a) poco tiempo?
3. Si haces un error, ¿dices "lo siento"?
4. ¿Te llevas bien con muchas personas?
5. ¿Tratas de ser **amable** y de ayudar a la gente?
6. ¿Te parece tonto **tener celos** de tu mejor amigo(a)?
7. ¿Sabes escuchar a la gente?
8. ¿**Cambias de opinión** frecuentemente?
9. Si dos amigos(as) tienen un secreto, ¿tratas de guardarlo(a) y no ser entrometido(a)?
10. Si un(a) amigo(a) no sabe qué hacer, ¿tratas de darle un buen consejo?

	Sí	No
1		
2		
3		
4		
5		
6		
7		
8		
9		
10		
Total		

Resultados

Por cada sí que respondiste, cuenta dos puntos.

Entre 15 y 20 puntos: Sabes ser un(a) buen(a) amigo(a). Eres una persona muy generosa y eso hace que tus amigos(as) te quieran.

Entre 10 y 15 puntos: Tienes muchas cosas que son necesarias para ser un(a) buen(a) amigo(a), pero también algunas que no te permiten tener amistad con algunas personas. Prefieres que tus amigos(as) piensen y sean como tú. Es mejor que seas comprensivo(a) y te preocupes más por los demás.

Menos de 10 puntos: Te es difícil tener amigos(as). Eres un poco egoísta y no haces muchos esfuerzos por llevarte bien con los demás. Recuerda que la amistad es un regalo y es mejor que cambies un poco.

162 ciento sesenta y dos
A primera vista 1

Universal Access

Students with Learning Difficulties

Use the *Resultados* section of the *Prueba de la amistad* to review the subjunctive in context. Ask students to identify where the subjunctive is used. Challenge them to explain why the subjunctive is used in these cases and assist as needed.

Advanced Learners

Invite students to evaluate how well the questions in the *Prueba de la amistad* indicate whether or not a person is a good friend. Ask when a *no* answer might not necessarily indicate a poor quality in a friend. Encourage students to suggest other questions to add to the test.

Actividad 3

Leer/Hablar

Para mi mejor amiga . . .

Lee la tarjeta que Elena le mandó a Clarita y responde a las preguntas siguientes.

1. ¿Te parece que Elena y Clarita son buenas amigas? ¿Por qué?
2. Según lo que dice en la tarjeta, ¿te parece que Clarita es chismosa? ¿Por qué?
3. ¿Qué hizo Clarita que muestra su amistad por Elena?
4. ¿Qué hizo Elena que muestra su amistad por Clarita?

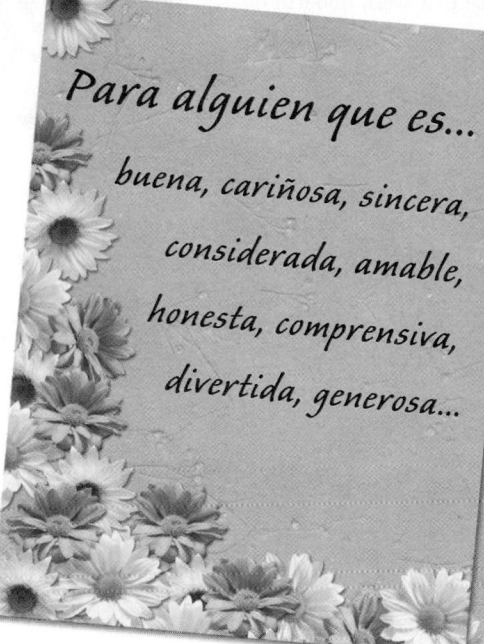

Para alguien que es...

buena, cariñosa, sincera,

considerada, amable,

honesta, comprensiva,

divertida, generosa...

...y lo más importante de todo,
¡ES MI MEJOR AMIGA!

Querida Clarita,

Gracias por tus consejos y por
guardar mi secreto. Para mí tu
amistad es muy importante y
tú siempre me apoyas cuando
tengo un problema.
¡Eres la mejor amiga
del mundo!

Besos,
Elena

Actividad 4

Escuchar/Escribir/Hablar

¿Lógico o no?

❶ En una hoja de papel escribe los números del 1 al 6. Escucha las frases y junto a cada número escribe si la frase es lógica o no. Si la frase no es lógica, corrígela.

❷ Escribe cinco frases que no sean lógicas sobre la amistad. Léeselas a tu compañero(a). Tu compañero(a) debe corregirlas para que sean lógicas.

● **Más práctica**
Practice Workbook 4-3, 4-4

PHSchool.com

For: Vocabulary practice
Visit: www.phschool.com
Web Code: jed-0402

ciento sesenta y tres **163**
Capítulo 4

Actividad 3

Standards: 1.1, 1.2

Resources: Practice Answers on Transparencies

Focus: Demonstrating reading comprehension of a friendship card and personal message

Suggestions: Read the card and have students answer the questions on their own first. Then have them discuss their work with a partner.

Answers:
1. Sí. (Reasons will vary.)
2. No. Clarita le guardó un secreto a Elena.
3. Le guardó un secreto, le dio consejos y siempre la apoya cuando tiene un problema.
4. Le mandó la tarjeta y le dijo que era su mejor amiga.

Actividad 4

Standards: 1.1, 1.2, 1.3

Resources: Audio Program: CD Cap. 4, Track 5; Resource Book: Cap. 4, Audio Script; Practice Answers on Transparencies

Focus: Practicing listening comprehension and writing

Suggestions: Tell students they will be listening to statements about personal qualities. Allow them to listen to the *Audio CD* more than once. If students have difficulty writing the illogical statements in step 2, suggest that they begin with a logical statement and change either the verb or the quality in order to make it illogical.

Answers:
1. ilógica
2. lógica
3. lógica
4. ilógica
5. ilógica
6. lógica

Additional Resources

• Resource Book: Cap. 4, Clip Art

 Assessment

• Prueba 4-1: Vocabulary recognition

Enriching Your Teaching

Teacher-to-Teacher

Invite students to use the materials of their choice, including computers, to create cards or e-cards. Their cards can be on any theme, including birthday, thank you, get well, or friendship. Encourage each student to have a friend or relative in mind as he or she makes the card, and to send it to that person. Have a few standard card envelopes on display, so students who create physical cards can design them to fit in an envelope.

Actividad 5 Standards: 1.2

Resources: Practice Answers on Transparencies

Focus: Demonstrating comprehension of new vocabulary

Recycle: subjunctive forms

Suggestions: Remind students that the items, when put together, form a letter. Tell them to scan all the items first, so that they understand the situation before attempting to complete the activity.

Answers:

1. Me preocupa
2. Es una lástima
3. Es una lástima
4. Me enoja
5. Espero
6. Es triste
7. Ojalá
8. Espero

Actividad 6 Standards: 1.1

Resources: Practice Answers on Transparencies

Focus: Practicing new vocabulary in guided conversations

Suggestions: Point out to students that the picture clues are only to elicit the various personality traits. Student B's response can be affirmative or negative. Encourage Student B to respond honestly.

Make sure students switch roles, so everyone has a chance to practice both parts of the dialogue.

Answers:

Student B's responses will vary. The following are possibilities for Student A's questions:

1. —Eres generoso(a), ¿verdad?
2. —... comprensivo(a), ...
3. —... honesto(a), ...
4. —... egoísta/vanidoso(a), ...
5. —... chismoso(a), ...

Manos a la obra 1

Vocabulario y gramática en uso

Objetives

• Communicate about friendship and personality traits
• Distinguish between positive and negative personal qualities
• Practice the subjunctive with verbs of emotion
• Distinguish uses of *por* and *para*

  Leer/Escribir

Una carta para alguien que fue mi amigo

Federico y Roberto eran amigos íntimos hasta que se pelearon. Roberto no confía en los consejos de Federico. Cree que está celoso por su relación con Teresa, que es amiga de los dos. Lee estas frases de una carta que le escribió Federico a Roberto. Escoge las palabras que completan mejor cada frase.

1. *(Me preocupa / Me alegro de)* que no me aceptes tal como soy.

2. *(Es una lástima / Me alegro de)* que desconfíes de mí.

3. *(Es una lástima / Es bueno)* que no me comprendas.

4. *(Me alegro de / Me enoja)* que siempre cambies de opinión.

5. *(Me sorprende / Espero)* que sepas que no tengo celos.

6. *(Es triste / Es bueno)* que no nos llevemos bien.

7. *(Me alegro de / Ojalá)* que no rompamos nuestra amistad.

8. *(Espero / Temo)* que todos salgamos juntos otra vez.

  Hablar

¿Cómo te relacionas con los demás?

Trabaja con otro(a) estudiante para hablar de su relación con los amigos. Usen las ilustraciones.

Modelo

A —Eres cariñoso(a), ¿verdad?
B —¡Claro que sí!, soy muy cariñoso(a).
o: No, no lo soy.
o: Pues, sí, a veces.

Estudiante A

 1.  2.  3.  4.  5.

Estudiante B

¡Respuesta personal!

Universal Access

Multiple Intelligences

Bodily/Kinesthetic: Invite students to incorporate actions or gestures into their descriptions in *Actividad 6*.

Advanced Learners

Have students write a brief sketch of a character from a popular film or TV show. Ask them not to give away the film or show the title or name the character, but to only describe his or her personality. Have students share their character sketches. Those listening can try to guess who the character is.

Actividad 7 Escribir/Hablar

Amistad y cualidades

1 Escribe un verbo o una expresión que relacionas con cada una de estas cualidades.

Modelo

amable
ayudar a los demás

1. vanidoso(a) **3.** entrometido(a) **5.** sincero(a)

2. perezoso(a) **4.** celoso(a) **6.** considerado(a)

2 Trabaja con otro(a) estudiante para hablar de las cualidades y verbos o expresiones que relacionas con la amistad.

Modelo

A —*¿Te gusta estar con personas amables?*
B —*Sí, porque siempre se preocupan por los demás.*

3 Ahora tú y tu compañero(a) deben escoger una cualidad y escribir un párrafo sobre una persona que tenga esa cualidad.

Modelo

Luisa es muy amable porque . . .

Ampliación del lenguaje

Familias de palabras

Las familias de palabras son grupos de palabras relacionadas *(related)* por tener una misma raíz. Conocer familias de palabras nos ayuda a comprender mejor el significado individual de cada palabra. Para ampliar tu vocabulario debes aprender a reconocer *(recognize)* palabras que tienen la misma raíz, por ejemplo, *celos* y *celoso*.

Lee las familias de palabras de la tabla. Piensa en palabras que conoces, que pertenecen a esas familias. Escribe en una hoja de papel las palabras que faltan para llenar los recuadros.

Luego, completa las frases utilizando la palabra correcta:

1. Carlos cuenta muchos _____, por eso todos dicen que es un _____.

Sustantivos	Adjetivos	Verbos
1. comprensión		comprender
2. alegría	alegre	
3. chisme	chismoso(a)	chismosear
4. consideración		considerar
5. sorpresa	sorprendido(a)	sorprenderse
6. reconciliación	reconciliado(a)	reconciliarse

2. Me encanta ir a las fiestas con María, pues es muy _____. Siempre me da _____ estar con ella.

3. Mi amigo se _____ mucho cuando le hicimos una fiesta _____.

Actividad 7 Standards: 1.1, 1.3

Focus: Using new vocabulary and structures in conversation and writing

Suggestions: As students share their work in step 2, encourage them to use additional verbs and expressions that pertain to each character trait. Point out that the more verbs and expressions they can think of, the more they will have to say about the person they write about in step 3.

Answers will vary.

Ampliación del lenguaje

Presentation

Standards: 1.2, 3.1, 4.1

Resources: Practice Answers on Transparencies

Focus: Understanding and using word families

Suggestions: Encourage students to copy the chart into their notebooks and make their additions there. Have them leave room, both horizontally and vertically, so they can add more word families and parts of speech at a later date.

Answers:
Chart
1. comprensivo (a)
2. alegrar
4. considerado (a)

Sentences
1. chismes/chismoso
2. alegre/alegría
3. sorprendió/sorpresa

Extension: Ask students to add a fourth column to their charts and title it **Adverbios.** Using background knowledge and dictionaries, have them work together to add adverbs to the word families on the chart. Model adding one adverb, such as **sorprendentemente.** Remind students that almost all Spanish adverbs end with the suffix **-mente.** Point out that not all word families in the chart will have an accompanying adverb.

Enriching Your Teaching

Teacher-to-Teacher

Consistent work with word families is an excellent way for students to increase their vocabularies on their own. Suggest that they devote an entire section of their notebooks to a word family chart like the one they began in the *Ampliación del lenguaje.* Each week, encourage them to spend a few minutes adding words they have learned to families that already exist on their chart or sitting with a dictionary and building new word families around words of their choice.

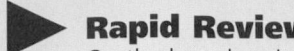

Practice and Communicate

4

On the board, write numerical sentences and have students read them aloud. For example, "26 ÷ 100 = 0.26 (26%)" reads: *Veintiséis dividido por cien son cero punto veintiséis (o veintiséis por ciento).*

Standards: 1.1, 1.2, 3.1, 3.2

Focus: Connecting new vocabulary and structures to a math context through surveys

Suggestions: For step 1, have students form questions to ask the class, such as (for the first survey): *¿Te consideras una persona sincera?* Have students answer each question clearly, restating the character trait to avoid confusion: *Sí, soy sincero(a).* Have them write their answers on blind ballots—folded slips of paper collected in a hat or other container. Ask volunteers to count the ballots for each question and tally the results on the board.

Common Errors: Without guidance, students would use the standard definite articles *el* and *la* instead of the neutral form *lo* in expressions like *ni lo uno ni lo otro.* Use this opportunity to habituate them to the sound and practice of using the neutral *lo.*

Answers will vary.

 **Leer/Hablar/Escribir** ·

Los jóvenes viéndose a sí mismos

Se hizo la siguiente encuesta a jóvenes de España, para saber qué piensan sobre las cualidades de sinceridad, solidaridad y generosidad. Lee los resultados.

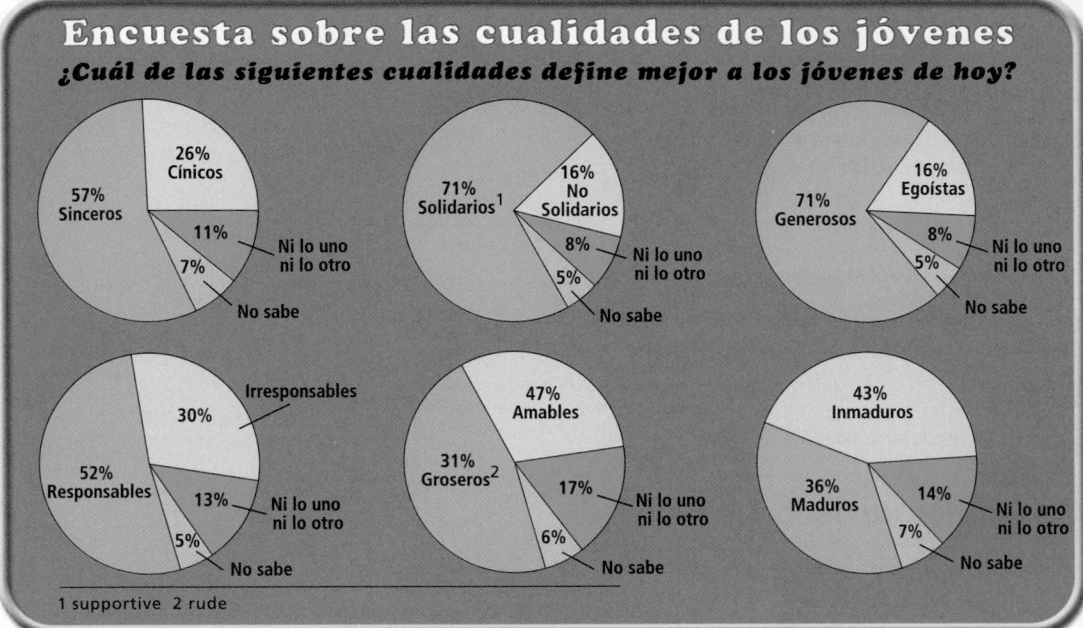

Conexiones **Las matemáticas** ——————————

Trabaja con un grupo para hacer una encuesta a tus compañeros(as) y comparar las respuestas de los jóvenes españoles con las de tu clase.

❶ Escojan un grupo de cualidades y pregúntenles a sus compañeros(as) si piensan que describen a los jóvenes de hoy.

❷ Pasen los resultados a porcentajes para poder compararlos con la encuesta española.

Recuerden que, para pasar los resultados de una encuesta a porcentajes, deben seguir los siguientes pasos:

Tomar el número de respuestas que quieren convertir y dividirlo por el número total de entrevistados. Luego, multiplicar el resultado por 100.

❸ Comenten los resultados de las encuestas. ¿Los jóvenes de España son más o menos sinceros / solidarios / generosos que los de su clase?

166 ciento sesenta y seis
Manos a la obra 1

Universal Access

Students with Learning Difficulties
Prepare students to understand and manipulate the information in the pie charts in *Actividad* 8. Explain that each piece of a pie chart represents a percentage or part of the total number of responses. The total of all the pieces adds up to 100 percent, which is represented by the complete circle.

Advanced Learners
Once groups complete their surveys, invite students to present visually the information that they have collected. They might show comparisons of percentages from each study through bar graphs or other graphic organizers.

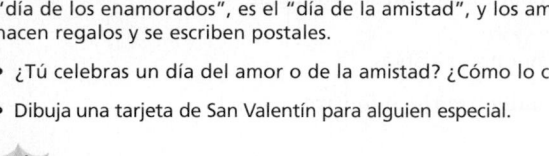

Fondo cultural

El Día de la Rosa y del Libro Muchas tradiciones de los países hispanohablantes celebran el amor y la amistad. Por ejemplo, en Cataluña, España, el 23 de abril se celebra el Día de la Rosa y del Libro. Ese día los chicos regalan a su novia una rosa roja, y las chicas regalan a su novio un libro.

En algunos países latinoamericanos el Día de San Valentín, en lugar de ser el "día de los enamorados", es el "día de la amistad", y los amigos y familiares se hacen regalos y se escriben postales.

• ¿Tú celebras un día del amor o de la amistad? ¿Cómo lo celebras?

• Dibuja una tarjeta de San Valentín para alguien especial.

Feliz Día de la Amistad

9 Escribir ··

Retrato de una amistad

Describe una relación muy importante para ti. Puede ser tu relación con un(a) amigo(a), un(a) primo(a), un familiar u otro adulto a quien quieras mucho. Describe cómo es esa amistad. Usa estos verbos como guía para escribir tu párrafo.

• conocerse
• escribirse
• contar con
• llamarse por teléfono
• enviarse mensajes electrónicos

• confiar
• apoyarse
• ayudarse
• llevarse bien
• tener en común

Modelo

Carlos y yo nos conocimos en . . . Vivíamos en el mismo barrio, pero cuando yo tenía 11 años, mi familia y yo tuvimos que irnos a . . . Ahora . . .

10 Escribir ··

Un personaje

Cuenta un hecho o describe a un personaje de un libro o película que sea un buen ejemplo de alguna de estas cualidades.

a. cariñoso(a)   **b.** chismoso(a)   **c.** comprensivo(a)   **d.** honesto(a)

Incluye:
• sus cualidades
• cómo trata a las otras personas
• ejemplos de sus acciones

Modelo

Uno de los personajes se llama Luis. Es muy amable, generoso y divertido. Sus amigos tienen mucha confianza en él.

ciento sesenta y siete   **167**
Capítulo 4

Enriching Your Teaching

Teacher-to-Teacher

In some subtle ways, functioning in a foreign language is like becoming a slightly different person. By Spanish 3, some students are becoming aware of how careful attention to the demands of Spanish causes them to think in different ways. You may find students in your class who are capable of talking in Spanish about topics they would not normally broach in English. This can be one of the greatest rewards a student earns after several years of language study. Praise and encourage students who demonstrate this.

Practice and Communicate

 Standards: 1.1, 1.2, 4.2

Resources: Voc. & Gram. Transparencies: 20 (map)

Suggestions: Have students locate *Cataluña* on *Vocabulary & Grammar Transparency* 20. Ask: *¿Qué piensas de la costumbre del Día de la Rosa y del Libro? Imagínate que vives en Barcelona, España. ¿Te gustaría recibir un libro o una rosa en este día? ¿Cómo te sentirías? ¿Qué pensarías de la persona que te lo (la) regaló?* Then invite students to talk about what they think are the differences between Valentine's Day in the United States and in Latin America.

Answers will vary.

 Standards: 1.3
·····················

Focus: Using new vocabulary and structures through writing about a relationship

Suggestions: Remind students to use the present tense to describe the relationship and past tenses to tell about its history and how it developed.

Answers will vary.

 Standards: 1.3
·····················

Focus: Using new vocabulary and structures to describe a fictional character

Suggestions: Ask students to share their descriptions and see whether or not they argree about the characters' qualities.

Answers will vary.

Additional Resources

• Writing, Audio & Video Workbook: Cap. 4, Audio Activity 1, Track 6
• Writing, Audio & Video Workbook: Cap. 4, Writing Activity 6
• Resource Book: Cap. 4, Communicative Activity BLM

✓ **Assessment**
• Prueba 4-2: Vocabulary production

167

Gramática

El subjuntivo con verbos de emoción

As you already know, we use the subjunctive after verbs indicating suggestions, desire, or demands. The subjunctive is also used after verbs and impersonal phrases indicating emotion, such as *ojalá que, temo que, tengo miedo de que, me alegro de que, me molesta que, me sorprende que, siento que, es triste que,* and *es bueno que,* among others. A sentence in the subjunctive mode has two parts, the main clause and the subordinate clause. Both clauses are connected by the word *que.*

> **Tememos que** nuestros amigos **desconfíen** de nuestras palabras.

When the sentence has only one subject, we usually use the infinitive instead of the subjunctive.

> Siento no **pasar** (yo) más tiempo con mis amigas.
> Siento que ellas no **pasen** más tiempo conmigo.

Actividad 11 **Gramática** **Escuchar/Escribir/Hablar/GramActiva**

Una amiga muy cariñosa

Alina es una amiga muy cariñosa, aunque a veces se preocupa demasiado por todos. Escribe los números del 1 al 5 en una hoja de papel. Presta atención a lo que dice Alina y escribe las frases que escuchas.

❶ Subraya con una línea los verbos en indicativo en cada frase. Subraya con dos líneas los verbos en infinitivo y encierra en un círculo los verbos en subjuntivo.

❷ Explica por qué se usó el infinitivo, el indicativo o el subjuntivo.

Actividad 12 **Gramática** **Leer/Escribir**

Una relación complicada

Soledad, una joven chilena, le escribió una carta a la consejera sentimental de una revista para jóvenes. Soledad se está llevando muy mal con su hermana y no sabe qué hacer. Completa la carta con el subjuntivo de los verbos del recuadro.

ser	desconfiar	sentirse
contarse	tener	llevar

```
Querida Consejera:
Te escribo porque mi hermana Tatiana
y yo nos estamos llevando muy mal. Me
preocupa que nuestra relación ya no
  1.  como antes. Creo que es importante
que dos hermanas   2.  sus problemas y
sus secretos. Pero ahora temo que ella
  3.  de mí. Tatiana tiene doce años.
Yo tengo quince años. A ella le
molesta que yo   4.  otros amigos de
mi edad y no le gusta que yo no la
  5.  con nosotros cada vez que salimos.
Es una lástima que ella   6.  celosa de
mis amigos. ¿Qué me aconsejas?
```

168 ciento sesenta y ocho
Manos a la obra 1

13 Gramática · **Hablar** · · · · · · · · · · · · · · · · · · ·

Díganlo de dos maneras

Trabaja con un(a) compañero(a) para hablar de las relaciones con sus amigos. Tú dices frases generales usando el infinitivo y tu compañero(a) te contesta usando el subjuntivo.

Estudiante A

1. bueno / tener mucho en común con los amigos
2. malo / tener celos de los amigos
3. importante / aceptar a los demás tal como son
4. triste / desconfiar de los amigos íntimos
5. difícil / tener buenas relaciones con los amigos

Modelo

importante / guardar secretos
me molesta / mi amigo(a) no . . .
A —*Es importante guardar secretos.*
B —*Sí, y me molesta que mi amigo(a) no guarde mis secretos.*

Estudiante B

a. siento / mi amigo(a) y yo no . . .
b. me sorprende / mi amigo(a) . . .
c. me preocupa / tú no me . . .
d. siento / mi amigo(a) . . .
e. ojalá / todos nosotros . . .

14 Gramática · **Escribir/Hablar** · · · · · · · · · · · · · · · · · · ·

Apoya a tus amigos

1 Con un(a) compañero(a) hagan una lista de ocho problemas que generalmente ocurren entre amigos o familiares.

Modelo

se pelean

2 Habla con tu compañero(a) de los problemas que incluyeron en la lista. Tu compañero(a) va a responder a cada problema con una expresión de emoción. Luego intercambien papeles.

Modelo

A —*Siempre me peleo con [nombre], él (ella) no me entiende.*
B —*Siento mucho que él (ella) no te entienda.*

ciento sesenta y nueve   **169**
Capítulo 4

Actividad 13 *Standards:* 1.1

Resources: Practice Answers on Transparencies

Focus: Using the subjunctive and infinitives with verbs of emotion in a guided conversation

Suggestions: Remind students that the determining factor for whether they use the subjunctive or an infinitive is the number of subjects in the sentence.

Answers:
1. A —Es bueno tener mucho en común con los amigos.
   B —Sí, y siento que mi amigo(a) (nombre) y yo no tengamos mucho en común.
2. A —Es malo tener …
   B —Sí, y me sorprende que mi amigo (a) (nombre) tenga …
3. A —Es importante aceptar …
   B —Sí, y me preocupa que tú no me aceptes…
4. A —Es triste desconfiar …
   B —Sí, y siento que mi amigo (a) (nombre) desconfíe …
5. A —Es difícil tener …
   B —Ojalá que todos nosotros tengamos…

Actividad 14 *Standards:* 1.1

Focus: Using the subjunctive with verbs of emotion in a guided conversation

Suggestions: Ask students to "ham it up" and present one of their exchanges to the class in the form of a vignette. Encourage them to exaggerate the emotions they are portraying.

Answers will vary.

Additional Resources
• Writing, Audio & Video Workbook: Cap. 4, Audio Activity 2, Track 8

Chapter Project
Students can perform step 2 at this point. Be sure they understand your corrections and suggestions. (For more information, see p. 154-a.)

Enriching Your Teaching

Teacher-to-Teacher
Have students fill out two strips of paper. On one they write a sentence like the ones Student A used in *Actividad* 13. On the other, they write a sentence along the lines of Student B's responses in the same activity. For example: *Es triste no confiar en los compañeros./Y temo que*

Magdalena no confíe en nadie. Mix all the sentence strips and have each student draw one. Have them circulate and say their sentences to each other until they find the person who has the sentence that corresponds to theirs.

Practice and Communicate

4

Rapid Review

Help students review negative personality traits that they will be able to use in *Actividad* 15. Have them complete the following two phrases: *No me gusta cuando un(a) amigo(a) es... Me gusta cuando un(a) amigo(a) es...* For the first sentence, pantomime and use gestures to elicit answers such as *impaciente, infantil,* or *mal educado(a).* Then have students complete the second sentence with the antonym of the word used in the first.

Actividad 15 *Standards:* 1.1, 1.3

Focus: Using the subjunctive in interviews and oral presentations

Suggestions: Ask the student pairs to prepare the chart on their own paper and to work out any comprehension problems they have with the questions in step 1, before they interview classmates.

Answers will vary.

Actividad 16 *Standards:* 1.1, 1.2, 3.1

Focus: Reading about and discussing the custom of the handshake and its origins

Suggestions: After students have read the information once, ask them to list the cognates that helped them understand the reading. They should mention words such as *personas, historiadores, estatua,* and *costumbre.*

Answers will vary.

Additional Resources

• Writing, Audio & Video Workbook: Cap. 4, Writing Activity 7

Assessment

• Prueba 4-3: *El subjuntivo con verbos de emoción*

 **Actividad 15** Gramática **Escribir/Hablar**

¿Qué te parece?

1 Trabaja con un(a) compañero(a) para entrevistar a cuatro estudiantes con las siguientes preguntas. Copien la tabla y complétenla con las respuestas de sus compañeros(as).

• ¿Cómo te gusta que sea tu mejor amigo(a)?

• ¿Qué no te gusta que haga tu mejor amigo(a)?

• ¿Qué te preocupa que opinen tus amigos(as) de ti?

• ¿Qué puede destruir una amistad?

• ¿Cuál es tu mejor cualidad como amigo(a)?

2 Luego, preparen una presentación para hacer ante la clase. Basándose en los resultados de la encuesta, expliquen qué cualidades y acciones pueden ayudar a una amistad o destruirla.

	Marisa	Rafa	Luis	Ana
¿Cómo te gusta que sea ...?	generoso(a), comprensivo(a)			
¿Qué no te gusta ...?	que no me tenga confianza			
¿Qué te preocupa ...?				
¿Qué puede destruir ...?				
¿Cuál es tu mejor ...?				

 Actividad 16 **Leer/Hablar**

Dar la mano

¿Sabes de dónde sale la costumbre de dar la mano para saludarse? Lee este artículo para enterarte.

Conexiones **Las ciencias sociales**

Nadie sabe realmente cuándo o por qué las personas comenzaron a darse la mano para saludarse. Algunos historiadores creen que todo comenzó hace 3800 años, en Babilonia. El primer día de cada año, el rey tenía que "darle la mano" a la estatua de un dios para recibir el poder *(power).*

Otros piensan que la costumbre comenzó por otra razón. Dicen que cuando dos desconocidos se encontraban en un camino o en un lugar fuera de la ciudad, se daban la mano derecha para mostrar que no tenían armas. En esos tiempos, como las mujeres no usaban armas, sólo los hombres se daban la mano.

• ¿Cómo saludas a tus amigos? ¿Y a tus familiares? ¿Les das la mano? ¿Cuándo le das la mano a alguien y cuándo lo (la) abrazas?

• ¿Conoces otros gestos o palabras de saludo? ¿Sabes cuál es su origen? Explícalo a la clase.

● **Más práctica**

Practice Workbook 4-5

For: Practice with the subjunctive
Visit: www.phschool.com
Web Code: jed-0403

Universal Access

Heritage Language Learners

Ask students to talk about how their family members use handshakes, kisses, or hugs to greet each other and friends, or to say good-bye. Encourage them to compare these practices with greeting and leave-taking customs in the United States.

Students with Learning Difficulties

Refer students to the list of uses for *por* and *para* as they complete *Actividad* 17. Encourage them to identify the point that explains each use of *por* and *para.*

Gramática · Repaso

Los usos de *por* y *para*

Both *por* and *para* are prepositions. Their usages are quite different.

Use *por* to indicate:

- length of time or distance

  Estuvieron discutiendo **por** una hora.

- place where an action takes place

  Ayer caminamos **por** el parque.

- an exchange

  Cambiamos la silla vieja **por** una nueva.

- reason or motive

  Se pelearon **por** un programa de televisión.

- substitution or action on someone's behalf

  Los padres hacen mucho **por** sus hijos.

- means of communication / transportation

  Ayer hablé con Analía **por** teléfono.

Also use *por* in certain expressions:

por ejemplo	**por lo general**
por la mañana (tarde, noche)	**por primera (segunda, tercera) vez**
por favor	**por supuesto**
por eso	

Use *para* to indicate:

- purpose (in order to)

  Salí temprano **para** ver a mis amigos.

- destination

  En unos minutos nos vamos **para** la playa.

- a point in time, deadline

  Debemos terminar el trabajo **para** el lunes.

- use, purpose

  Las tijeras sirven **para** cortar.

- opinion

  Para mí, no hay nada mejor que viajar.

  **Gramática** **Leer/Escribir**

Cosas de amigas

Dos amigas están hablando. Completa las frases con *por* o *para*, según el contexto.

A —¡Claro que sí! __1.__ supuesto que quiero ir a la fiesta. Mañana __2.__ la tarde vamos a llamar a los chicos __3.__ ver si quieren ir con nosotras.

B —¿Qué te parece si hacemos la tarea de español antes? No quiero perderme la fiesta __4.__ tener que estudiar.

A —Sí, podemos pasar __5.__ la casa de Anita __6.__ preparar la tarea todas juntas.

 Gramática **Escribir/Hablar**

Por dónde y para qué

Escribe una descripción de un viaje que hiciste y léela a un(a) compañero(a). Usa *por* y *para*. Habla de:

- tiempo
- lugar
- razón o motivo
- destino
- medio de transporte
- uso

Modelo

Viajamos a Canadá por tren. Fuimos para . . .

Presentation

Standards: 4.1

Resources: Voc. & Gram. Transparencies: 92

Suggestions: Encourage students to think of other ways to help remember some of the uses of *por* and *para.* As an example, point out that in general, when they want to say "in order to," the Spanish word they use is *para;* when they want to say "by," the word is *por.*

 Standards: 1.2

Resources: Practice Answers on Transparencies

Focus: Practicing *por* and *para* in a cloze exercise

Suggestions: Ask volunteers to supply other sample sentences for each of the usage rules for *por* and *para.*

Answers:

1. Por	4. por
2. por	5. por
3. para	6. para

 Standards: 1.3

Focus: Practicing *por* and *para* via sentence writing

Suggestions: Ask students to read their completed sentences aloud in random order. Listeners can say the rule behind each use of *por* and *para.*

Answers will vary.

 Enriching Your Teaching

Culture Note

For most Spanish speakers, a greeting includes saying hello as well as some physical gesture. Shaking hands is common. Women often kiss each other on the cheek. Men and women who are close friends or family also often hug and give a light kiss on the cheek.

Teacher-to-Teacher

In Spanish, as well as other languages, learning when to use prepositions causes the most frustration. Their correct usage is among the most difficult skills students have to master. When they make a mistake, model the correct usage and have them repeat. Eventually, they will learn to "hear" the correct usage.

Rapid Review

Review *gustar* with various combinations of subjects and indirect object pronouns. On the board write a model such as *A mí me gustan las galletitas.* Ask students to point out the subject *(las galletitas)* and the indirect object pronoun *(me).* Tell students you will use pictures to cue these two parts of the sentence. Use transparencies or pictures from books or magazines as visual cues. Display different combinations of pictures to elicit sentences such as *A ellas les gusta la película; A nosotros nos gustan los coches,* and so on.

Standards: 1.1, 1.3

Focus: Practicing *por* and *para* in sentence completions

Suggestions: Remind students to write all their sentences about the same two real or imaginary people, so that the completed activity creates a story. If they opt to write about real people they know, ask them to be considerate and sensitive to the feelings of others.

Answers will vary.

Extension: Ask students to develop their completed sentences into a comic strip about the two friends.

Standards: 1.1, 1.3, 3.1

Focus: Using the subjunctive in traded dictations and writing

Suggestions: Allow students time to figure out individually what they plan to say for step 1. This will ensure that they use varied and original ideas. As they fill out the Venn diagram in step 2, have them check to see how well their partner took down the dictation and make any necessary corrections.

Answers will vary.

Actividad 19 Gramática **Hablar/Escribir**

Por eso, para ellos . . .

Trabaja con un(a) compañero(a). Inventen una historia entre dos amigos(as) imaginarios(as) completando estas frases.

- Por lo general, ellos se divierten . . .
- La semana pasada se pelearon por . . .
- Estuvieron discutiendo por . . .
- Para [nombre] es importante . . .
- Por eso, (no) les gusta . . .
- Para llevarse bien necesitan . . .
- Por supuesto, no siempre . . .

Actividad 20   **Hablar/Escribir**

¿Tienes buenos amigos?

1 Trabaja con un(a) compañero(a). Completa las frases para decir lo que piensas de tus amigos(as), mientras tu compañero(a) las escribe. Luego, tu compañero(a) completa las frases y tú las escribes.

1. Me alegro de que . . .
2. Es una lástima que . . .
3. Me preocupa que . . .
4. Me parece importante que . . .
5. Me gusta que . . .
6. Es bueno que . . .
7. Quiero que . . .
8. Temo que . . .
9. ¡Ojalá que mis amigos(as) siempre . . . !
10. Es verdad que . . .

2 Completen el diagrama de Venn con lo que piensan.

yo   los(as) dos   mi compañero(a)

3 Escriban un breve *(short)* informe con la información de su diagrama de Venn.

Modelo

Mi compañera Marisa y yo hablamos sobre la amistad. Las dos nos alegramos de tener muchos amigos.

Universal Access

Students with Learning Difficulties

As students complete *Actividad 19*, model correct forms for completing the sentences. For example: *Por lo general, ellos se divierten jugando con su gato/nadando en el lago/jugando cartas.* Ask students to follow your model but change the content of the message.

Advanced Learners

Ask students to invent personal bios for a dating service. Their bios should use the new vocabulary and the subjunctive to provide a character sketch of an imaginary person and to explain what he or she wants and expects out of a relationship.

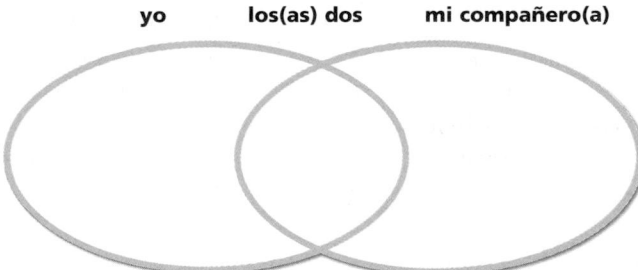

Leer/Escribir/Hablar ....

¡No me vas a creer . . . !

Muchas veces, cuando hay un problema entre amigos(as), cada persona cree que tiene la razón. Por eso, es mejor escuchar lo que tiene que decir la otra persona.

1 Lee los relatos que hacen Luis y Manuel del mismo problema y contesta las preguntas.

1. ¿Por qué crees que Luis está tan enojado?
2. ¿Te parece sincero el relato que hace Manuel?
3. ¿Qué crees que debió hacer cada uno de los cuatro personajes para evitar este problema?
4. ¿Qué deben hacer ahora para resolver el problema que tienen?

Según Manuel:

Según Luis:

Manuel era mi amigo más íntimo hasta ayer, pero me di cuenta de que es un entrometido. Ya no puedo confiar en él. Mi prima Laura me dijo que Manuel fue a pasear ayer con Clara, mi novia, y que los vio abrazándose. Lo llamé y le dije que estaba sorprendido de saber que salió con mi novia y que temo que nuestra amistad se rompa.

Me sorprende que Luis esté celoso de mí. Él sabe que somos amigos desde primer grado, que nos contamos nuestros secretos y nos apoyamos en todo. ¿Cómo puede sentir celos de mí? Clara me llamó porque quería pedirme un consejo sobre un problema que tenía. Ella es muy cariñosa y al saludarnos nos abrazamos, como siempre lo hacemos. Me preocupa que este problema pueda terminar con nuestra amistad.

2 Escribe una frase sobre cada uno de los cuatro personajes que participan en la historia, usando las palabras del recuadro.

cariñoso(a)	celoso(a)	entrometido(a)
comprensivo(a)	honesto(a)	sincero(a)

3 Imagina que eres Clara. Relata lo que sucedió desde su punto de vista.

Modelo

No me gusta que Luis esté enojado. Yo llamé a Manuel para hablar sobre un problema que tuve . . .

● **Más práctica** ....
Practice Workbook 4-6, 4-7

Go Online
PHSchool.com

For: Practice with *por* and *para*
Visit: www.phschool.com
Web Code: jed-0404

Practice and Communicate

 4

 Actividad 21   *Standards:* 1.2, 1.3
....

Focus: Using new vocabulary and structures to read, talk, and write about a situation

Suggestions: After students have read the two accounts silently in step 1, ask volunteers to read each one aloud. For step 2, point out that some of the words might be used in sentences in the indicative mood describing the people; others might be used in sentences with the subjunctive, suggesting how the people should act. Have students read their completed sentences aloud and elaborate on them orally. For step 3, have students read aloud their completed accounts by Clara. Listeners can then talk about what kind of person Clara seems to be.

Answers will vary.

Additional Resources
• Writing, Audio & Video Workbook: Cap. 4, Writing Activities 8–9
• Resource Book: Cap. 4, Communicative Activity BLM

 Assessment
• Prueba 4-4: *Los usos de* por *y* para
• Examen: Vocabulario y gramática 1

Chapter Project
Students can perform step 3 at this point. (For more information, see p. 154-a.)

Block Schedule
....

Have each students write a short note to a personal advice columnist describing a "personal problem" and asking for help. Have them sign using a fake name. Collect the questions and distribute them to different students. Each student is to write a response and then read the question and response aloud to the class. You might have the class vote on the best three "solutions."

Enriching Your Teaching

Teacher-to-Teacher
Students will learn to use prepositions more quickly if you embed the practice in a humorous context. For **por** and **para,** suggest that pairs of students prepare and present humorous dialogues in which they use the two words as often and as creatively as possible.

Vocabulario y gramática

Presentation

Standards: 1.1, 1.2, 3.1

Resources: Voc. & Gram. Transparencies: 93; Resource Book: Cap 4, Input Script; Audio Program: CD Cap. 4, Track 9

Focus: Presenting new vocabulary and using grammar lexically in context

Suggestions: Refer students to the *Estrategia.* Have them respond to the questions there by talking about the pictures and writing down their predictions about the story. Then allow students time to read the presentation silently. Have students revisit the predictions they made about the story. Ask questions such as the following: *¿Todas tus predicciones resultaron correctas? ¿Qué partes del cuento son distintas de tus predicciones?*

A primera vista 2

Vocabulario y gramática en contexto

Objectives

Read, listen to, and understand information about
- conflicts and how to resolve them
- friends and family relationships

¿Qué pasa cuando se rompe la **armonía** de una amistad por causa de **un malentendido**? Lee este cuento para ver cómo **resolvieron** sus problemas estos jóvenes.

Estrategia

Using illustrations to predict the outcome
Before reading a text, look at the illustrations. What do you think is going to happen? What details in the illustrations support your prediction? After reading, compare your prediction with what happened at the end of the story.

1 Julio y Andrés eran amigos íntimos. Tenían mucho en común, por ejemplo, a los dos les gustaba mucho el fútbol. Un día se enteraron de que la entrenadora buscaba un nuevo capitán del equipo. Los dos amigos querían ser capitán.

> Ojalá que sea yo, pero si escoge a Andrés, lo voy a apoyar en todo.

> Espero que me escoja a mí.

2 Al día siguiente, Andrés se encontró con la entrenadora y ella le preguntó si quería ser capitán o si podía recomendar a alguien. Andrés le dijo que sí, pero cuando quiso recomendar también a su amigo, la entrenadora no le **hizo caso** y lo escogió a él como capitán, sin darle **una explicación**.

174 ciento setenta y cuatro
A primera vista 2

Block Schedule

Divide students into pairs. Assign each group a scene to reenact from p. 175. You might assign each pair Scene 3, 4, or 5 so that all the scenes are covered. Have them practice and then reenact the scene in front of the class. Remind them to focus on intonation, expression, and correct pronunciation.

Universal Access

Heritage Language Learners
Remind students of strategies they can use to monitor and improve their reading comprehension. Have them pause after each section of the reading and answer *¿Qué pasó?* If they can't answer, ask them to reread the section.

Students with Learning Difficulties
Remind students that new vocabulary in the reading is identified in bold. Review the meaning of new words and phrases with them before they begin to read.

3 Cuando Julio se enteró de que Andrés era el capitán del equipo, se fue a hablar con la entrenadora.

Julio: Sra. Torres, ¿por qué escogió a Andrés?

Sra Torres: Porque me dijo que él quería ser capitán y nadie más quería serlo.

Julio: ¡Qué va! ¿Cómo **se atrevió** él a decir eso? **Está equivocada,** yo también quería ser capitán del equipo.

Sra. Torres: Entonces **pónganse de acuerdo** entre ustedes.

4 Más tarde, Julio llamó a Andrés por teléfono.

Julio: Andrés, eres un egoísta, solo **piensas en ti mismo.** ¿Por qué no le dijiste a la Sra. Torres que yo también quería ser capitán?

Andrés: No me **acuses,** yo no **tengo la culpa** de que no te escogió . . .

Julio: ¡No me hables más!

5 Unos días después, Andrés tuvo la oportunidad de darle a Julio una explicación de lo que realmente ocurrió.

Andrés: Julio, entiendo por qué estás enojado, pero yo no tengo la culpa. Cuando fui a sugerirle tu nombre, la Sra. Torres me dijo que yo era el capitán.

Julio: Tienes razón, **reconozco** que fue un malentendido. Te **pido perdón.**

Andrés: Te **perdono. Hagamos las paces,** entonces.

Julio: De acuerdo.

 Escuchar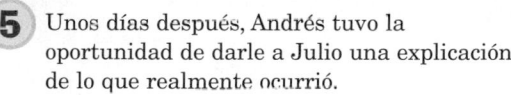

Amigos en conflicto

Escribe los números del 1 al 6 en una hoja. Vas a escuchar frases sobre el problema entre Andrés y Julio. Escribe *C* (cierto) o *F* (falso) para cada frase.

 **Language Input**

Actividad 22 *Standards:* 1.2

Resources: Voc. & Gram. Transparencies 93; Audio Program: CD Cap. 4, Track 10; Resource Book: Cap. 4, Audio Script; Practice Answers on Transparencies

Focus: Practicing listening comprehension of new vocabulary

Suggestions: Display *Vocabulary & Grammar Transparency* 93 as a reference as students complete the activity. Allow them to listen to the *Audio CD* once through first. Then play it again, pausing after each item, so they can write their answers.

Answers:

1.	F	4.	C
2.	C	5.	F
3.	F	6.	F

 Enriching Your Teaching

Culture Note

Although United States football *(el fútbol americano)* and other sports are slowly starting to gain more popularity in Latin America, soccer *(el fútbol)* continues to dominate. Besides the top-level professional *fútbol* leagues based in major cities of each country, there are also many intra-urban leagues—teams from various neighborhoods within a city. Games between neighborhood teams attract large, enthusiastic crowds. Some neighborhoods have healthy *fútbol* rivalries that go back many decades.

Vocabulario y gramática

Presentation

Standards: 1.1, 1.2, 3.1

Resources: Voc. & Gram. Transparencies: 94–95; Resource Book: Cap. 4, Input Script; Audio Program: CD Cap. 4, Tracks 11–12

Focus: Extending presentation of vocabulary and grammar in context

Suggestions:

Pre-reading: Point out that *conflictos, criticar, ignorar, reaccionar, reconciliar,* and *colaborar* are cognates. Explain that the verb *mejorar* comes from the adjective and adverb *mejor,* which students have already learned. Write on the board *mejorar = hacer mejor* and use *mejorar* in a model sentence such as *La situación se mejoró cuando hablamos del problema.*

Reading: Have students read along as you play the *Audio CD* or as you read aloud. Make sure students read the *Nota* on the next page. Use *ignorar* in model sentences like the following to demonstrate the two meanings: *Mi madre me ignora cuando grito. Mi padre no puede resolver el conflicto porque ignora los detalles.*

Post-reading: Discuss the charts and questionnaires with students and ask questions to check comprehension.

Standards: 1.3

Resources: Practice Answers on Transparencies

Focus: Demonstrating comprehension of new words and expressions

Suggestions: Encourage students to cite facts from the surveys that support their answers to the questions.

Answers:

1. Muchos conflictos ocurren cuando hay diferencias de opinión entre miembros de una familia. Answers will vary.
2. Los miembros de una familia deben pensar en los demás y colaborar para tener una buena relación.
3–5. Answers will vary.

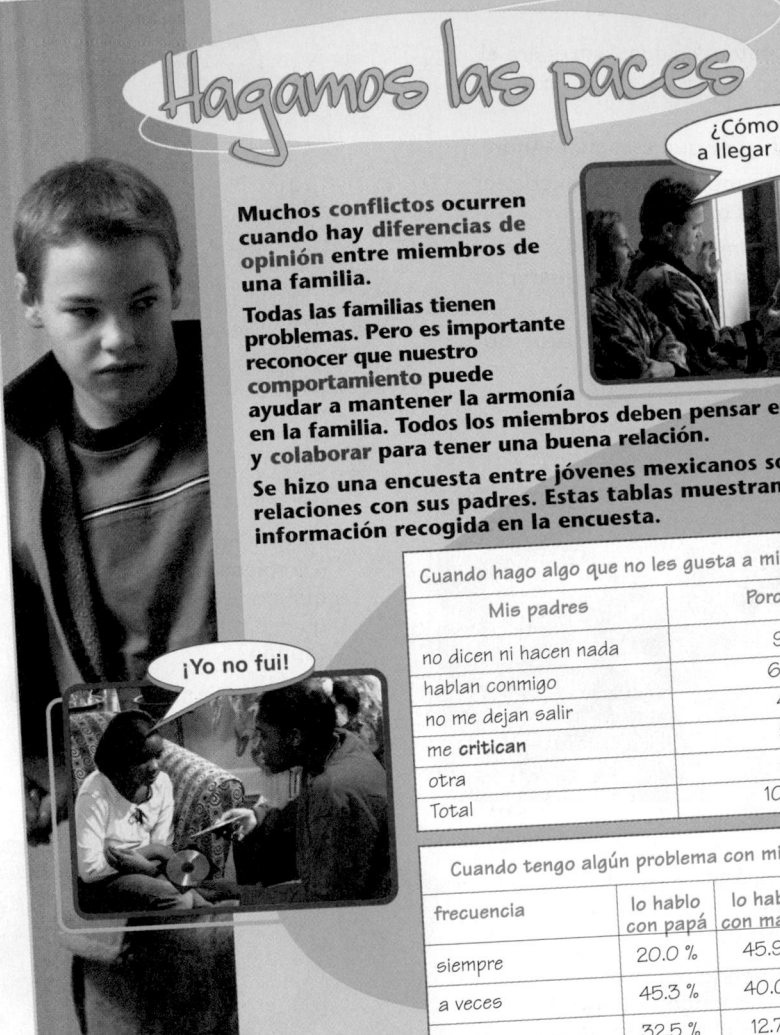

Hagamos las paces

¿Cómo **te** atreves a llegar a esta hora?

Muchos conflictos ocurren cuando hay **diferencias de opinión** entre miembros de una familia.

Todas las familias tienen problemas. Pero es importante reconocer que nuestro comportamiento puede ayudar a mantener la armonía en la familia. Todos los miembros deben pensar en los demás y colaborar para tener una buena relación.

Se hizo una encuesta entre jóvenes mexicanos sobre sus relaciones con sus padres. Estas tablas muestran la información recogida en la encuesta.

¡Yo no fui!

Cuando hago algo que no les gusta a mis padres . . .	
Mis padres	Porcentaje
no dicen ni hacen nada	9.8 %
hablan conmigo	67.7 %
no me dejan salir	4.6 %
me **critican**	9.3 %
otra	8.6 %
Total	100.0 %

Cuando tengo algún problema con mis padres . . .			
frecuencia	lo hablo con papá	lo hablo con mamá	lo hablo con los dos
siempre	20.0 %	45.9 %	16.1 %
a veces	45.3 %	40.0 %	39.7 %
nunca	32.5 %	12.7 %	36.0 %
no quiero contestar	2.2 %	1.4 %	8.2 %

Escribir/Hablar

La armonía en la familia

1. Según el artículo, ¿por qué a veces hay problemas en una familia? ¿Estás de acuerdo con esta opinión?

2. ¿Cuáles son algunas de las cosas que el artículo recomienda hacer para tener más armonía en una familia?

3. ¿Crees que por lo general las familias de esta encuesta se comunican bien o mal? ¿Por qué?

4. ¿Cómo podemos evitar conflictos?

5. Si tenemos diferencias de opinión o peleas con nuestra familia, ¿qué debemos hacer?

176 ciento setenta y seis
A primera vista 2

Universal Access

Heritage Language Learners

Draw students' attention to the title *Hagamos las paces.* Invite them to share with the class other expressions that they might use to encourage harmony within their family, such as *Ya dejemos de pelear, reconciliémonos, perdón,* or *discúlpame.*

Advanced Learners

Invite students to conduct a survey similar to the one shown on p. 176. Ask them to tally the results of their surveys and to translate these into percentages, as they did on p. 166. Have them compare the results of their class with those of the students surveyed in Spain.

Conflictos: causas y soluciones

Las preguntas de estas tablas nos pueden ayudar a saber qué hacer para mejorar nuestras relaciones con las personas que más nos quieren[1].

[1] The verb *querer* in this context means "to love" or "to like."

¿Te molesta cuando tus amigos . . .

	nunca	a veces	siempre
te **ignoran**?	❏	❏	❏
cuentan tus secretos a otros?	❏	❏	❏
no te **hacen caso**?	❏	❏	❏
tienen celos?	❏	❏	❏
no se alegran de tus éxitos?	❏	❏	❏
sólo piensan en sí mismos?	❏	❏	❏

¿Cómo reaccionas cuando tienes una pelea con un(a) amigo(a)?

	Sí	No
Gritas.	❏	❏
Dejas de hablarle.	❏	❏
Tratas de reconciliarte.	❏	❏
Lo(la) criticas.	❏	❏
Ignoras el problema.	❏	❏
Le **pides perdón**.	❏	❏

¿Cómo te reconcilias con tus padres?

	Sí	No
Hablamos del problema para resolverlo juntos.	❏	❏
Nos ponemos de acuerdo.	❏	❏
Hacemos las paces.	❏	❏
Reconocemos que estábamos equivocados.	❏	❏
Guardamos silencio hasta que pase el momento.	❏	❏

Nota
La palabra *ignorar* tiene más de un significado. Quiere decir "no prestar atención" o "no hacer caso" y, en un contexto diferente, puede significar "no saber algo".

Actividad 24

Hablar

Amistad y conflicto

Trabaja con un grupo para comparar sus respuestas a las preguntas siguientes.

1. ¿Qué nos molesta?
2. ¿Por qué nos enojamos con nuestros padres?
3. ¿Qué no nos gusta que hagan nuestros amigos?
4. ¿Qué hacemos para resolver conflictos?

● **Más práctica**
Practice Workbook 4-8, 4-9

Go Online
PHSchool.com

For: Vocabulary practice
Visit: www.phschool.com
Web Code: jed-0406

ciento setenta y siete **177**
Capítulo 4

Actividad 24
Standards: 1.1

Focus: Using new vocabulary in a guided discussion

Suggestions: Have students answer the questions individually first. Then have them meet and take turns sharing their answers. Encourage them to listen carefully to each other and to ask each other additional questions for clarification.

Answers will vary.

Additional Resources
• Resource Book: Cap. 4, Clip Art

Assessment
• Prueba 4-5: Vocabulary recognition

Chapter Project
Students can perform step 4 at this point. Be sure they understand your corrections and sugestions. (For more information, see p. 154-a.)

Enriching Your Teaching

Culture Note
As in most cultures, the family forms the most important social unit for Latin Americans. The concept of family might be considered a bit different from that in the United States. In Spain and Latin America, *familia* almost always includes not only the immediate family, but grandparents, aunts, uncles, and cousins as well. In Spanish-speaking countries, it is more common for members of three generations to live together in the same house than it is in the United States.

Standards: 1.2, 3.1

Resources: Practice Answers on Transparencies

Focus: Demonstrating comprehension of new words and expressions

Suggestions: Point out that each possible answer has two phrases that best complete the sentence.

Answers:
1. b
2. c
3. b
4. a
5. c

Extension: Have students create their own sentences in which key vocabulary words are omitted, as in *Actividad* 25. They can exchange their sentences and have classmates complete them.

Standards: 1.1, 1.2, 2.1, 2.2, 4.2

Suggestions: After students read the information, ask them to compare and contrast the concept of Latin American *telenovelas* with that of U.S. soap operas. Ask: *¿En qué se parecen una telenovela y una* soap opera? *¿En qué se diferencian? ¿Una* soap opera *dura un año o más de un año? ¿Se parecen los personajes y los argumentos?¿En qué son diferentes?*

Answers will vary.

Manos a la obra 2

Vocabulario y gramática en uso

Objectives
• Talk about conflicts and how to resolve them
• Use the *nosotros* command
• Use possessive pronouns

Leer/Escribir

Los opuestos

Completa las frases con la mejor selección de palabras opuestas *(opposite)*.

1. Es mejor vivir en _____ con nuestra familia y evitar los _____ .
   a. *pelea / comportamiento*   b. *armonía / conflictos*   c. *diferencia de opinión / paces*

2. El día que _____ estaban muy enojados, pero después _____ .
   a. *hicieron caso / ignoraron*   b. *perdonaron / acusaron*   c. *se pelearon / se reconciliaron*

3. Tú _____ , no sabes lo que dices. Alicia no quería _____ , sólo ayudarte.
   a. *haces las paces / se pelea*   b. *estás equivocado / criticarte*   c. *prestas atención / ignora*

4. Yo siempre _____ a lo que dice mi hermano y hago lo que nos pide, pero Pedro muchas veces lo _____ .
   a. *hago caso / ignora*   b. *me reconcilio / se pelea*   c. *pido perdón / acusa*

5. Amalia siempre _____ y ayuda a todo el mundo, pero su hermano es un egoísta que sólo _____ .
   a. *acusa / se reconcilia*   b. *critica / colabora*   c. *piensa en los demás / piensa en sí mismo*

Fondo cultural

La telenovela es la versión latinoamericana de la *soap opera* y generalmente la ponen entre las 8 y las 11 de la noche. El argumento es siempre una historia de amor, con personajes muy buenos o muy malos que se pelean en cada programa sin resolver sus problemas. La telenovela dura menos de un año y tiene un final emocionante, donde se resuelven los conflictos, los buenos triunfan y la muchacha y el muchacho se casan.

• ¿Qué programas similares conoces? ¿A qué horas los ponen?

• Describe un episodio de una telenovela que conoces. ¿Cuál era el conflicto? ¿Hubo un malentendido o una pelea? ¿Cómo reaccionaron los personajes? ¿Se reconciliaron al final?

Francisco y Gabriela en la telenovela mexicana "Clase 406".

Universal Access

Heritage Language Learners
Have students write a brief scene from a *telenovela* they know or one of their own invention. The script should include one of the features mentioned in the *Fondo cultural*. Encourage students to perform their scenes for the rest of the class. Remind them that *telenovelas* are usually quite dramatic. Encourage them to "ham it up!"

Advanced Learners
Ask students to prepare a general overview of a soap opera they know. Have them describe the setting, the main characters, and some long- and short-term conflicts. If students are also familiar with any *telenovelas,* have them include an overview for these programs too.

Leer/Escribir ·

Más consejos, ¡por favor!

⬤ Un chico que participó en un salón de chat escribió este mensaje. Completa el mensaje con las palabras del recuadro.

hace caso	piensa en sí mismo	¡Qué va!	colabora	peleas

Estoy colaborando con un grupo de estudiantes para hacer un informe, pero uno de mis compañeros es muy egoísta. Cuando nos debemos reunir, dice que no puede porque tiene un partido de fútbol o clases de tenis. ¡No __1.__ en nada! ¡Este chico sólo __2.__! Ya tuvimos varias __3.__ porque temo que recibamos una mala nota, pero no __4.__ y siempre que le pedimos algo él responde: " __5.__ "

⬤ Con otro(a) estudiante, da un buen consejo a la persona que escribió el mensaje.

 Leer/Escribir/Pensar ·

Lomas Garza: La gran familia chicana

La obra de Carmen Lomas Garza es como un retrato de familia de la comunidad chicana, es decir, mexicano-americana, de los Estados Unidos.

Conexiones | **El arte** —————

Carmen Lomas Garza (1948 –) es una artista chicana de Texas. Lomas Garza se inspiró en el Movimiento Chicano de los años sesenta, y desde entonces trata de representar en su obra la cultura de los chicanos. En sus cuadros, Lomas Garza ilustra las costumbres, las fiestas y la vida interesante y complicada de las personas que viven entre dos culturas, la mexicana y la estadounidense. Observa su cuadro *Cascarones (Eggshells)*, de 1989, y responde a las preguntas.

Cascarones, (1989),
Carmen Lomas Garza

Gouache painting. 15 x 20 inches.
(c) 1989 Carmen Lomas Garza. Photo
by: Wolfgang Dietze. Collection of
Gilbert Cardenas, Notra Dame, IN.

• ¿Te parece que hay armonía o conflicto en esta familia?

• ¿Por qué crees que hay una figura más grande que las otras en el cuadro? ¿Qué quiso expresar la pintora con ese detalle?

• Imagínate algo que pasa entre los miembros de esta familia. Usa las siguientes palabras para contar lo que sucede:

colaborar	hacer caso	malentendido	explicación	comportamiento

ciento setenta y nueve   179
Capítulo 4

 Standards: 1.2
· · · · · · · · · · · · · · ·

Resources: Practice Answers on Transparencies

Focus: Practicing new vocabulary in a cloze exercise

Recycle: past tenses, subjunctive

Suggestions: Explain to students that a clear understanding of the character description in the first part of the message will help them fill in the blanks in the second part. For step 2, encourage students to use expressions that take the subjunctive.

Answers:
1. colabora
2. piensa en sí mismo
3. peleas
4. hace caso
5. ¡Qué va!

Standards: 1.1, 1.2, 2.1, 2.2, 3.1
· · · · · · · · · · · · · · ·

Resources: Fine Art Transparencies; Fine Art Transparencies Teacher's Guide, Practice Answers on Transparencies

Focus: Practicing reading comprehension in a passage about an artist

Suggestions: Remind students that they can refer to *Capítulo* 2 if they need to review the fine art vocabulary used in the reading passage.

Answers will vary.

Enriching Your Teaching

Culture Note

Besides her paintings, Carmen Lomas Garza also makes prints, installations (mixed-media artworks in three dimensions, often incorporating movement), and paper and metal cutouts. Her installations tend to focus on the Day of the Dead **(el Día de los Muertos),** a Mexican feast day celebrated on November 1. Behind all of Garza's artwork lies pride in her Chicana heritage.

Actividad 28

Standards: 1.1

Resources: Practice Answers on Transparencies

Focus: Practicing new vocabulary and structures in a guided conversation

Suggestions: Remind students that the *¡Respuesta personal!* at the end of Student B's cues is an invitation for them to invent their own reactions as well as practicing those cued.

Answers will vary. Student B can use the following verb forms:

me alegro
me enojo
doy/pido una explicación
lloro
me pongo (feliz, furioso(a), contento(a))
reconozco el error/pido perdón
digo "¡Qué va!"/ "Yo no fui"

Actividad 29

Standards: 1.1, 1.2

Focus: Using new vocabulary and structures in a dramatization

Suggestions: As students are preparing the paper slips for the drawing, ask them to read all of the items and think about the dramatization they will do if they select it.

Answers will vary.

Actividad 30

Standards: 1.1

Focus: Using new vocabulary and structures in a guided conversation

Suggestions: Encourage students to supply their own personal reasons for disagreements with people they know.

Answers will vary.

 **Hablar**

¿Cómo reaccionas cuando . . . ?

Con un(a) compañero(a), habla sobre tu comportamiento en las situaciones siguientes.

Modelo

tu amigo te ignora
A —*¿Cómo reaccionas cuando tu amigo te ignora?*
B —*Generalmente le pido una explicación.*

Estudiante A  **Estudiante B**

1. tu amigo dice que estás equivocado(a)
2. tu hermano(a) te acusa de algo
3. tus padres te critican
4. tus padres te preguntan "¿por qué?"
5. alguien no te hace caso
6. alguien no quiere hacer las paces

alegrarse
enojarse
dar / pedir una explicación
llorar
ponerse (feliz, furioso, contento)
reconocer el error / pedir perdón
decir "¡Qué va!" / "Yo no fui"

¡Respuesta personal!

  Escribir/Hablar

Juego

Trabaja con un grupo y pide a cada persona que escriba una de las siguientes frases en un pedazo de papel. Luego, pónganlos todos en una caja o bolsa y tomen turnos para sacarlos. Actúa durante 20 segundos la frase que sacaste. ¡Sé dramático(a)!

1. Explícale a tu padre por qué llegaste tarde anoche.
2. Tuviste una pelea y te das cuenta de que estabas equivocado(a). ¿Qué haces?
3. Crees que tu maestro(a) está equivocado(a). ¿Qué dices / haces? Sé muy cortés.
4. Tú y tu amigo(a) se pelearon. Hay que reconciliarse. ¿Qué dices para reconciliarte?
5. Tu hermano(a) te acusa de algo que tú no hiciste. ¿Cómo reaccionas? ¿Qué dices?
6. Tu hermano(a) menor se portó mal en la tienda. ¿Qué le dices?

  Hablar

Diferencias de opinión

Trabaja con otro(a) estudiante y explícale por qué a veces peleas con estas personas. Usa las palabras del recuadro. Después, intercambien papeles.

criticar	acusar de	ignorar	atreverse
reconocer	tener la culpa	hacer	

Modelo

hermano mayor
Peleo con mi hermano mayor cuando no me deja escuchar sus discos compactos.

1. papá
2. mamá
3. hermano(a)
4. hermano(a) menor
5. mejor amigo(a)
6. primo(a)
7. compañero(a) de clase

Universal Access

Heritage Language Learners

Have students write a paragraph about one aspect of their family that they really enjoy. They might write about a relationship with a certain family member, a special family tradition, a celebration, or a memory that is important to them. Allow students to write about a close, personal friend as an option.

Advanced Learners

Ask students to interview students and teachers from other classes about their conflicts with others and how they resolve them. Have them prepare their interviews in advance by writing four or five questions they will ask. They can conduct their interviews in English and report back to the class in Spanish.

Actividad 31 · Leer/Escribir

Encuesta: ¿Para qué necesitas permiso?

Lee en la tabla la información recogida en una encuesta que se hizo entre jóvenes mexicanos con respecto a sus padres. Después, contesta las preguntas.

Actividades	Prohibido	Necesito permiso	Yo decido		No aplica	No contestó	Total
			Chicos	Chicas			
Tener novio(a)	9.3%	33.0%	35.2%	16.5%	5.2%	0.8%	**100%**
Salir con amigos	5.5%	65.1%	19.9%	7.4%	1.8%	0.3%	**100%**
Vestir como tú quieres	2.9%	10.5%	43.3%	42.0%	0.9%	0.4%	**100%**
Llegar tarde a casa	15.2%	60.1%	16.7%	5.0%	2.6%	0.4%	**100%**
Ponerte aretes	45.5%	8.0%	9.7%	6.1%	30.2%	0.5%	**100%**

1. ¿Qué actividad se prohíbe más? ¿Cuál se prohíbe menos?

2. ¿Qué información de la tabla te sorprende? ¿Por qué?

3. Mira la columna con el título "Yo decido". ¿Qué te dice esa información?

4. Un(a) chico(a) tiene prohibido llegar tarde a casa pero nunca hace caso. ¿Cómo crees que van a reaccionar los padres?

5. ¿Qué puede hacer después ese(a) chico(a) para resolver el conflicto con sus padres?

6. Si ese(a) mismo(a) chico(a) llegó tarde a casa porque no pasó el autobús, ¿crees que los padres deben enojarse? ¿Por qué?

Actividad 32 · Pensar/Escribir/Hablar

Los conflictos

1. Escribe una lista de, por lo menos, tres conflictos o malentendidos que suceden a veces en una familia. Por ejemplo: alguien no arregló su cuarto o alguien llegó muy tarde a casa.

2. ¿Quiénes son las personas que participan en cada conflicto?

3. ¿Qué pueden hacer para mejorar la situación?

4. Con otro(a) estudiante, representen el conflicto ante la clase.

5. Basado(a) en los consejos del cartel, sugiere una solución para uno de los conflictos.

PARA RESOLVER UN CONFLICTO

1. hablen para resolver el problema

2. sugieran soluciones posibles

3. sean sinceros

4. expliquen lo que pasó

ciento ochenta y uno **181**
Capítulo 4

Actividad 31
Standards: 1.2, 1.3, 2.1, 3.1, 3.2

Resources: Practice Answers on Transparencies

Focus: Practicing new vocabulary and structures via reading and discussion of a survey

Suggestions: When students have had some time to study the chart, ask additional questions: *¿Qué porcentaje de los jóvenes necesita permiso para salir con amigos? (65.1)*

Answers:
   1. Más: Ponerte aretes. Menos: vestir como tú quieres.
2–6. Answers will vary.

Actividad 32
Standards: 1.3

Focus: Practicing new vocabulary and structures through reading, writing, and dramatization

Suggestions: For item 3, ask students to think of their own ways to resolve the problems. Remind them that they do not need to have personal experience with some of the ways they mention.

Answers will vary.

Additional Resources

- Writing, Audio & Video Workbook: Cap. 4, Audio Activity 3, Track 13
- Writing, Audio & Video Workbook: Cap. 4, Writing Activity 10
- Resource Book: Cap. 4, Communicative Activity BLM

Assessment
- Prueba 4-6: Vocabulary production

Enriching Your Teaching

Culture Note

Young single adults in much of Latin America tend to live with their parents longer than their counterparts in the United States. Reasons for this vary. Sometimes they are economical; sometimes they have to do with employment; but in many cases they spring from cultural traditions that place a high value on a strong bond between the generations within a family. As in all cultures, such traditions and values are changing.

Practice and Communicate

Gramática

Presentation

Standards: 4.1

Resources: Voc. & Gram. Transparencies: 96

Suggestions: Have students write more examples using the **vamos a** + infinitive construction. Ask them to include some suggestions that use stem-changing verbs and one or more of the pronouns referred to in the *Gramática*. Have them take turns reading their suggestions aloud. Ask volunteers to convert each one to the **nosotros** command form with correct spelling and pronoun placement.

Standards: 1.2

Resources: Practice Answers on Transparencies

Focus: Practicing **nosotros** commands

Suggestions: Ask students to practice the **nosotros** commands, but remind them that the **vamos a** + infinitive construction is also an option for the items.

Answers will vary.
1. Hablemos, veamos
2. Pidámosle, prometamos
3. Ignoremos, perdonémosla
4. Démosle, terminemos
5. Atrevámonos
6. Pongámonos de acuerdo

Standards: 1.3

Resources: Practice Answers on Transparencies

Focus: Practicing new vocabulary and structures in guided conversations

Suggestions: Have groups conduct the activity in round-robin fashion.

Answers will vary. The following verb forms will be used:
compremos refrescos, lleguemos a casa, compremos las entradas, pongámonos de acuerdo, vistámonos, colaboremos, bañémonos, disfrutemos, escojamos, salgamos, comamos, lleguemos al cine

Gramática

Mandatos con *nosotros*

There are two ways to suggest that others do some activity with you *(Let's . . .)*.

You can use the construction *Vamos a* + infinitive.

> **Vamos a hacer** las paces.
> *Let's make up.*

You can also use a command with a *nosotros* form. The *nosotros* command form is the same as the *nosotros* form of the present subjunctive.

> **Resolvamos** el conflicto.
> No **reaccionemos** tan rápido.

Remember that stem-changing verbs whose infinitive ends in *-ir* have a stem change of *e → i*, or *o → u* in the *nosotros* form.

> **Pidamos** perdón por el malentendido.
> No **durmamos** al aire libre.

Verbs whose infinitive ends in *-car*, *-gar*, or *-zar* have a spelling change in the *nosotros* form of the present subjunctive, and consequently of the *nosotros* command.

> No **critiquemos** a nuestros padres.
> **Empecemos** a pensar un poco en ellos.

Direct and indirect object pronouns are attached at the end of affirmative *nosotros* commands, but precede the negative *nosotros* command form.

> **Celebremos** la amistad. **Celebrémosla.**
> **Digámosle** todo. **No le mintamos.**

When attaching reflexive or reciprocal pronouns at the end of a *nosotros* command, drop the final *-s* of the command before the pronoun.

> **¡Alegrémonos** con sus éxitos!
> **Atrevámonos** a darles nuestras opiniones.

 **Gramática** Leer/Escribir

Encontremos la solución

Miriam y Leonor se pelearon con Tamara, su hermana mayor. Completa las frases con el mandato con *nosotros* del verbo apropiado para saber qué sugieren para reconciliarse con Tamara.

1. _____ *(acusar / hablar)* con papá y _____ *(ver / ignorar)* cómo reacciona.
2. _____ *(pedirle / criticar)* perdón y _____ *(perder / prometer)* no mentir nunca más.
3. _____ *(mejorar / ignorar)* todo y _____ *(decirle / perdonarla)*.
4. _____ *(darle / reaccionar)* una explicación y _____ *(terminar / reaccionar)* la pelea.
5. _____ *(atreverse / colaborar)* a decirle que nosotras tuvimos la culpa.
6. ¡_____ *(pelear / ponerse de acuerdo)* pronto!

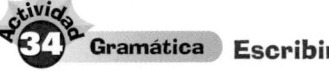 **Escribir**

Un plan para el sábado

Imagina que el sábado quieres ir al cine con tu hermano. Haz un plan de diez pasos para sugerirle lo que quieres que hagan juntos. Puedes usar las palabras del recuadro.

comprar refrescos	vestirse	escoger
llegar a casa	colaborar	salir
comprar entradas	bañarse	comer
ponerse de acuerdo	disfrutar	llegar al cine

Modelo

escoger
Primero, escojamos qué película vamos a ver.

Universal Access

Heritage Language Learners
Provide extra support to students as you discuss the letters *j* and *h* in *¿Recuerdas?* Although they rarely mispronounce Spanish words with *h*, students often make errors in spelling these words. Briefly review common errors that you see, such as misspelling **a ver** and **haber.**

Students with Special Needs
Pair advanced learners with visually impaired students in order to complete *Actividad* 35. The former can describe the actions shown in each scene. Their partners can then suggest other activities to do.

182

35 Gramática  **Hablar**

¿Y ahora qué hacemos?

Raúl y Rosalía nunca se ponen de acuerdo. Con otro(a) estudiante, hagan los papeles de Raúl y Rosalía. Uno(a) sugiere lo que aparece en el dibujo y el (la) otro(a) sugiere hacer otra cosa.

Modelo
A —*Caminemos por el parque.*
B —*Dijeron que va a llover.*
 Vayamos al cine.

1.

2.

3.

En voz alta

En 1996, la compañía discográfica EMI Latin unió en un solo disco compacto las voces de los más famosos cantantes populares de España y Latinoamérica. El objetivo del disco, *Voces unidas*, era celebrar la estrecha relación que existe entre los pueblos hispanohablantes, pues estos pueblos son como una gran familia. Escucha este fragmento de la canción "Será entre tú y yo", de la cantante mexicana Paulina Rubio. Luego trata de repetirla en voz alta.

Paulina Rubio

Será entre tú y yo
 de Paulina Rubio

**Mostremos
respeto a la adversidad
a la competencia, fidelidad¹,
fuerza espiritual unida al cuerpo,
lleguemos unidos a la final.
Juntemos los sueños que hay de ganar
y así llegarán los himnos² al cielo.
Quieres llegar, tu fuerza seré yo.
Quieres volar³ al infinito,
juntos será.**

1 loyalty 2 hymns 3 to fly

¿Recuerdas?

En español la letra *j* se pronuncia como la letra *h* en la palabra *hat* pero con un sonido más fuerte. Escucha y repite estas palabras: *juntos, juntemos.*

En español la letra *h* casi nunca suena: *hacer, himnos.*

● Más práctica
Practice Workbook 4-10

Go Online
PHSchool.com

For: Practice with *nosotros* commands
Visit: www.phschool.com
Web Code: jed-0407

ciento ochenta y tres **183**
Capítulo 4

Practice and Communicate ④

35 *Standards:* 1.1

Resources: Practice Answers on Transparencies

Focus: Practicing ***nosotros*** commands in guided conversations

Suggestions: Have students practice the exchanges with their partner. Then ask pairs of volunteers to present one of the exchanges to the class.

Answers for Student B will vary. The following are suggestions for Student A:
1. Vamos de compras.
2. Hagamos ejercicio.
3. Demos un paseo y saquemos unas fotos.

En voz alta
Presentation

Standards: 1.2, 1.3, 2.2, 3.1, 3.2, 5.2

Resources: Audio Program: CD Cap. 4, Track 14;

Suggestions: Have students read the information and the song silently. Ask comprehension questions: *¿Qué piensas del objetivo del disco* Voces unidas? *¿Por qué son los pueblos hispanohablantes como una gran familia? ¿Qué piensas de este fragmento de la canción?*

Before having students recite the song, direct their attention to the information in the *¿Recuerdas?* and have them listen to the *Audio CD.* Then allow them a few minutes to practice with a partner.

Additional Resources
• Writing, Audio & Video Workbook: Cap. 4, Writing Activity 11
• Writing, Audio & Video Workbook: Cap. 4, Audio Activity 4, Track 14

✓ **Assessment**
• Prueba 4-7: *Mandatos con* nosotros

 Enriching Your Teaching

Culture Note
The popularity of many types of Latin music continues to grow worldwide. So much so that in 2000, the first Latin Grammy Awards ceremony was held. The Latin Grammy honors artistic and technical achievements in Latin American music, awards excellence, and provides greater exposure to Latin American recording artists.

Internet Search
Keyword: | Paulina Rubio |

Gramática

Presentation

Resources: Voc. & Gram. Transparencies: 97

Suggestions: On the board, write this model: *Aquellas llaves son tuyas. Aquí tengo las mías.* Ask students to refer to other individual objects or groups of objects around the classroom and make similar pairs of sentences using possessive adjectives and pronouns.

Actividad 36

Standards: 1.2

Resources: Practice Answers on Transparencies

Focus: Practicing possessive pronouns in a cloze exercise

Suggestions: Have students first read through the entire letter for meaning. Ask them to identify the noun that is replaced by each possessive pronoun.

Answers:
1. mías
2. míos
3. mía
4. suyo
5. tuyos

Actividad 37

Standards: 1.1

Resources: Practice Answers on Transparencies

Focus: Practicing possessive pronouns

Suggestions: Have students practice third-person forms by reporting to the class on their partner's statements.

Answers will vary, but students will use the following possessive forms:

mi ropa: la tuya, la mía
mi perro: el tuyo, el mío
mi computadora: la tuya, la mía
nuestro coche: el tuyo, el nuestro
mis comidas favoritas: las tuyas, las mías
mis abuelos: los tuyos, los míos
mi hermano(a): el (la) tuyo(a), el (la) mío(a)
mi familia: la tuya, la mía
nuestros(as) amigos(as): los (las) tuyos(as), los (las) míos(as)

Gramática

Pronombres posesivos

To form the possessive pronouns, use the long form of possessive adjectives preceded by the definite article. Both the article and the possessive must agree in number and gender with the noun they replace.

> **Mis padres** son muy serios. ¿Y **los tuyos**?
> **Los míos** son bastante divertidos.

> **Tu familia** es muy pequeña. **La mía** es bastante grande.

We often omit the article between the verb *ser* and the possessive pronoun.

> Esas maletas **son nuestras**.
> Mi hermano siempre dice que toda la culpa **es mía**.

¿Recuerdas?

The long form possessive adjectives are used for clarity or emphasis.

1st, 2nd, and 3rd Person Sing.

mío(s)	mía(s)	*my, mine*
tuyo(s)	tuya(s)	*your, yours*
suyo(s)	suya(s)	*your, yours*
		his, her, hers

1st, 2nd, and 3rd Person Plural

nuestro(s)	nuestra(s)	*our, ours*
vuestro(s)	vuestra(s)	*your, yours*
suyo(s)	suya(s)	*your, yours*
		their, theirs

Actividad 36 Gramática **Leer/Escribir**

¿Cuándo vamos al cine?

Débora se enojó con Pablo porque él no pudo ir al cine con ella y le escribió una carta diciéndoselo. Entonces, Pablo le escribió una carta para reconciliarse. Completa la carta de Pablo con las formas correctas de los pronombres posesivos del recuadro. Algunas se pueden usar más de una vez.

tuyo	mío	suyo

> Querida Débora:
>
> Leí tu carta. Entiendo tus razones pero yo tengo las __1.__ para no ir al cine.
>
> Tus padres te dejan ir al cine siempre, pero los __2.__ nunca me dejan.
>
> Ayer tu mamá llamó a la __3.__ para pedirle que me dejara ir a tu casa,
>
> pero mi mamá dijo que su coche no funciona. Tu mamá dijo que podía llevarme
>
> en el __4.__, pero mi mamá no quiso. Yo quiero mucho a mis padres, pero me
>
> gustaría que fueran como los __5.__. Espero que me perdones. Creo que el
>
> sábado que viene sí me van a dejar ir contigo. ¡Nos vamos a divertir!
>
> Pablo

Universal Access

Students with Learning Difficulties

Write on the board the following sentences: *These are my books. These are mine.* Guide students to understand that *mine* is a pronoun that takes the place of *my books.* Point out that English, like Spanish, uses different words for possessive adjectives and pronouns (my/mine, your/yours, and so on.)

Advanced Learners

As students complete *Actividad 36*, ask them to tell why each form is correct. Have them say to which noun each possessive pronoun refers, identifying its number and gender. Then ask students to add two more sentences containing possessive pronouns from Pablo's letter.

 **37** **Gramática** **Hablar** ·····································

Los míos, los tuyos, los nuestros

Con otro(a) estudiante, hablen sobre los siguientes aspectos de su vida.

- mi ropa
- mi perro
- mi computadora
- nuestro coche
- mis comidas favoritas
- mis abuelos
- mi hermano(a)
- mi familia
- nuestros(as) amigos(as)

Modelo

mis padres
A —*Mis padres son serios, pero comprensivos. ¿Cómo son los tuyos?*
B —*Los míos son muy generosos, y siempre piensan en los demás.*

 **38** **Gramática** **Escribir/Hablar** ·····························

Retrato de familia

1 Piensa en una familia de una película, un libro o un programa de televisión que conoces. Imagina que eres un miembro de esa familia. Contesta las siguientes preguntas acerca de tu familia imaginaria.

1. ¿Cómo es tu familia? (cuántos son, quiénes son, cómo es cada uno)

2. ¿Quién piensa siempre en los demás y quién piensa más en sí mismo?

3. ¿Quién se pelea con los demás? ¿Quién trata de mantener la armonía?

4. ¿Cómo resuelven los conflictos?

5. ¿Qué te gusta más de tu familia?

2 Basado(a) en las respuestas a las preguntas anteriores, escribe una descripción de tu familia imaginaria.

3 Con otro(a) estudiante, hablen de las descripciones que escribieron y comparen sus familias imaginarias.

El español en la comunidad

Niños bilingües

En muchas familias latinoamericanas de Estados Unidos los niños aprenden el nuevo idioma más rápido que los adultos, y se convierten en los traductores de la familia.

A veces, esto ayuda a la armonía de la familia, pues todos colaboran para adaptarse a la nueva cultura. Pero otras veces hay conflictos, porque los padres sienten que pierden control sobre los hijos y los hijos piensan que sus padres no los entienden.

Ahora que tú sabes hablar español, puedes ser útil para tu comunidad traduciendo para los nuevos estudiantes hispanohablantes.

 Más práctica ·····························
Practice Workbook 4-11, 4-12

Go Online
PHSchool.com
For: Practice with possessive pronouns
Visit: www.phschool.com
Web Code: jed-0409

---

 38 *Standards:* 1.2, 1.3
·····························

Focus: Practicing possessive pronouns

Suggestions: Have students begin their family descriptions by identifying themselves: *Me llamo Joselito. Soy el hijo menor de la familia Cartwright....*

Answers will vary.

El español en la comunidad
Presentation
Standards: 1.2, 5.1

Suggestions: Ask students to consider what it would be like to be a parent or child in a bilingual family. If your class includes heritage language speakers, they may have a lot to offer to this discussion.

Additional Resources
- Writing, Audio & Video Workbook: Cap. 4, Writing Activities 12–13
- Writing, Audio & Video Workbook: Cap. 4, Audio Activity 5, Track 16
- Resource Book: Cap. 4, Communicative Activity BLM

 Assessment
- Prueba 4-8: *Pronombres posesivos*
- Examen: Vocabulario y gramática 2

Chapter Project
Students can perform step 5 at this point. Record their presentations on cassette or videotpae for inclusion in their portfolio. (For more information, see p. 154-a.)

Enriching Your Teaching

Culture Note
Spanish is quickly becoming an important part of many communities in the United States. According to one study, the Hispanic population has grown faster and spread out more over the past two decades than that of any immigrant group in the history of the United States. The highest rate of Hispanic population growth is occurring in smaller cities and outlying areas, places that had virtually no Hispanic population twenty years ago. Experts predict that the rapid growth of the Hispanic population will probably continue for several decades.

Puente a la cultura

Presentation

Standards: 1.1, 1.2, 1.3, 2.1, 2.2, 3.1, 3.2

Resources: Fine Art Transparencies; Fine Art Transparencies Teacher's Guide

Focus: Reading to learn about the theme of love depicted in the fine arts of Latin America and Spain

Suggestions:

Pre-reading: Refer students to the *Estrategia.* Ask them to apply their background knowledge about poetry, music, and visual arts with which they are familiar. Talk about what different kinds of love are expressed in the art they know and how it is expressed.

Reading: Encourage students to read through the entire passage once silently, without stopping at problem words or to ask questions. Remind them to use background knowledge, cognates, and context clues to help them understand unfamiliar words and expressions.

Post-reading: Ask volunteers to paraphrase the main idea and important details from the three main sections of the reading, including the introduction.

Country Connection

Presentation

Standards: 3.1

Display *Vocabulary & Grammar Transparency* 20. Point out the Spanish cities mentioned in the reading. Assign a different city to small groups. Ask them to research their city in an encyclopedia or on the Internet and report back to the class with three facts about its history, important industries, and famous sites.

Go Online

The online atlas will provide a more detailed map of Spain.

¡Adelante!

Puente a la cultura
El amor en las artes

Objectives

- Read about expressions of love in the Latin American and Spanish arts
- Compare and contrast expressions of love at different times and in diverse cultures

Estrategia

Compare and contrast
To compare, look for ways that people, events, things, or ideas are the same. To contrast, think about ways they are different. Think about their use, color, size, and shape, or other characteristics.

Madre y niño, (1926), Diego Rivera*

A través de su arte y literatura, los países de América Latina y España han expresado siempre la importancia que tiene el amor. Esta característica de la cultura del mundo hispanohablante se mantuvo a través de los siglos y sigue viva hoy.

El amor en la pintura

Quizá el sentimiento de amor más importante en la cultura latinoamericana y española es el amor a la madre. Además de poemas y estatuas, el amor a la madre ha inspirado a muchos pintores. Uno de ellos es Diego Rivera (1886–1957). Este famoso pintor y muralista disfrutaba pintando mujeres con niños, especialmente mujeres indígenas a quienes presentaba con hermosos niños, y vestidas de brillantes colores.

La pintura en murales ha sido otra forma de expresión artística del amor, el amor a la comunidad. Judith Francisca Baca es una artista de California que ha fundado programas de creación de murales. Con su arte ha ayudado a embellecer la comunidad, a hacer conocer otras culturas y a alentar[1] a miles de jóvenes a interesarse en las artes. En la creación de uno de sus murales, *The Great Wall,* participaron más de 400 jóvenes de 14 a 21 años de edad.

1 to encourage

The Great Wall of Los Angeles, (1976–1984), Judith Baca

186 ciento ochenta y seis
¡Adelante!

Universal Access

Students with Special Needs
Pair advanced learners with visually impaired students. Advanced learners can describe the Diego Rivera painting, focusing on how the painter demonstrates the love between mother and child. Advanced learners will also benefit from this analysis of the artwork.

Advanced Learners
Ask students to prepare an oral report about an important poem, song, or painting from the Spanish-speaking world that has love as a theme. This might be a work of art they have studied in earlier chapters of *Realidades.* Have them tell about the kind of love expressed and how it is expressed.

El amor en la música

La música es otra de las artes que se han usado para expresar el amor. Se escucha siempre en los grandes festivales y eventos patrióticos, en las elegantes bodas, en paseos y en funerales.

Agustín Lara (1896–1970), uno de los grandes compositores mexicanos, compuso la letra y la melodía de más de 600 canciones y sus éxitos suman cientos. La fuente de inspiración de la mayoría de sus canciones fue el amor a la mujer, ya que su vida estuvo llena de romances. Pero Agustín también fue un enamorado de España y dedicó canciones a las ciudades de Sevilla, Toledo, Navarra, Murcia, Valencia y Madrid. Su canción *Granada* ha dado la vuelta al mundo en las voces de los más famosos artistas.

El amor en la poesía

De todas las formas de expresar el amor en la literatura, quizás la más apropiada es la poesía. Un ejemplo es la obra de la gran poeta uruguaya Juana de Ibarbouru (1892–1979). Cuando Juana tenía 22 años publicó *Lenguas de diamante*, su primer libro de poesía, con el que obtuvo un éxito instantáneo. Su poesía se caracteriza por un ritmo armonioso, un amor ingenuo y transparente, sin tonos dramáticos o angustiosos[1]. Sus temas incluyen el amor, la maternidad, la belleza física y la naturaleza.

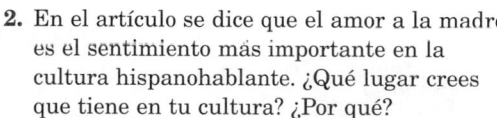

Amor

Juana de Ibarbouru

El amor es fragante como un ramo de rosas.
Amando se poseen todas las primaveras.
Eros[2] trae en su aljaba[3] las flores olorosas
De todas las umbrías[4] y todas las praderas.

1 anguished 2 god of love 3 quiver 4 shady places

¿Comprendiste?

1. Según el artículo, ¿en qué manifestaciones del arte de los países hispanohablantes se nota la importancia del amor? Da algunos ejemplos.

2. En el artículo se dice que el amor a la madre es el sentimiento más importante en la cultura hispanohablante. ¿Qué lugar crees que tiene en tu cultura? ¿Por qué?

3. Da ejemplos de otros sentimientos de amor que pueden expresarse en las artes.

4. Piensa en una expresión de amor de una canción, un poema o una pintura que conozcas. Escribe una composición para comparar tu ejemplo con el del artículo y di en qué se parecen y en qué se diferencian.

Go Online
PHSchool.com

For: Internet Link Activity
Visit: www.phschool.com
Web Code: jed-0410

Enriching Your Teaching

Culture Note

Although Mother's Day **(el Día de la Madre)** is celebrated in much of Latin America as it is in the United States, it is especially important in Mexico. There, it is celebrated on May 10, and schools are closed. During the weeks before the holiday, Mexican students spend time rehearsing elaborate performances they will put on.

Internet Search

Keywords:

Agustín Lara, Diego Rivera, Judith Francisca Baca, Juana de Ibarbouru

---

¿Comprendiste?

Standards: 1.2, 1.3, 2.1, 2.2, 3.1, 5.2

Resources: Practice Answers on Transparencies

Focus: Demonstrating reading comprehension

Suggestions: Have students read aloud or paraphrase the sections of the reading that support their answers to the first question. Use the other questions as a vehicle for discussion with the whole class.

Answers:

1. Se nota en la pintura, en la música y en la poesía. Unos ejemplos son las pinturas y los murales de Diego Rivera, las canciones de Agustín Lara y la poesía de Juana de Ibarbouru.
2–4. Answers will vary.

Teaching with Art

Help students talk about the Rivera painting by asking guiding questions: *¿Te gusta esta pintura? ¿Por qué? ¿Por qué no? ¿Qué sentimientos te inspira la pintura? ¿Qué te dice la pintura sobre el tema del amor por la madre? ¿Y del amor por el niño?*

Video
Presentation

Standards: 1.2

Resources: Video Program: Cap. 4

In this segment we become acquainted with members of the Aguilar family from Cali, Colombia, who now reside in the United States. We are shown the qualities and characteristics that allow them to be not only family members but friends. See the *Video Teacher's Guide* for additional suggestions.

Block Schedule

After the class has completed the reading, go down the rows assigning each student the number 1, 2, or 3. Each number represents a topic in the reading (1–*pintura*; 2–*música*; 3–*poesía*). Students are to write four questions about their section. Randomly create groups of 1s, 2s, and 3s. In these groups, have them ask each other their questions. This provides a fun, interactive way to review the reading.

¿Qué me cuentas?
Presentation

Standards: 1.1, 1.2, 1.3

Resources: Voc. & Gram. Transparencies: 98; Audio Program: CD Cap. 4, Track 17; Resource Book: Cap. 4, Audio Script; Practice Answers on Transparencies

Focus: Practicing speaking and listening comprehension within the context of personal relationships and conflicts

Suggestions:

For step 1, use the *Audio CD* or read the script aloud. Allow students to hear the descriptions twice through: the first time to write their answers and the second time to check them.

In step 2, ask questions such as the following to guide students in their discussion about the pictures. In order to facilitate the discussion, give names to the two characters: (picture 1) *¿Sonia y Teresa eran amigas? ¿Qué le prestó Sonia a Teresa?* (picture 2) *Teresa salió de la casa de Sonia. ¿Qué sabemos de su ropa? ¿Piensas que lleva puestos sus propios zapatos o los que le prestó Sonia?* (picture 3) *¿Qué le pasó a Teresa?* (picture 4) *¿Adónde fue Teresa después? ¿Cómo piensas que se sintió Teresa en este momento?* (picture 5) *¿Qué le dijo Teresa a Sonia?* (picture 6) *¿Piensas que Sonia era una chica comprensiva?*

Answers:
Step 1

1. b	4. a
2. a	5. a
3. b	6. b

Steps 2–3
Answers will vary.

¿Qué me cuentas?

Conflictos con y sin solución

1 🎧 Vas a escuchar lo que ocurrió entre Laura y Enrique. Después de cada descripción, vas a oír dos preguntas. Escoge la respuesta correcta para cada pregunta.

1. a. fueron a ver una película en el cine   b. fueron a dar un paseo por el barrio
2. a. tres meses   b. nueve meses
3. a. de que la cena no estaba hecha   b. de que no tenía su bolsa
4. a. Regresó al parque para ver si encontraba la bolsa.   b. Fue a la casa de Enrique para ver si él tenía la bolsa.
5. a. a Enrique con otra chica   b. a una chica con su bolsa
6. a. que lo perdonaba   b. "¡Adiós!"

2 Las ilustraciones siguientes representan un cuento. Con tus propias palabras, describe detalladamente lo que sucedió.

Puedes usar las siguientes palabras o expresiones para conectar tus ideas.

primero	más tarde	entonces	de repente	después	al final

1

2

3

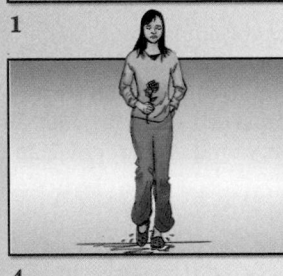
4

5

6

3 Comenta con tus compañeros(as) qué les pareció el cuento. Hablen sobre lo que les gustó más y cómo los detalles de las ilustraciones los ayudaron a saber qué sucede en el cuento. Expliquen sus respuestas.

188 ciento ochenta y ocho
¡Adelante!

Universal Access

Heritage Language Learners
Some students with a particularly strong command of spoken Spanish may be able to skip step 1 of the *Presentación oral* on the next page and offer problems and solutions orally without writing them down.

Students with Learning Difficulties
Before students begin the first part of *¿Qué me cuentas?*, review the directions, emphasizing that they will hear three descriptions and two questions after each description. Suggest that after answering questions 1 and 2, they put down their pencils and listen to the next description. The same applies after questions 3 and 4, and 5 and 6.

Una sesión del concejo estudiantil

Tarea
Los concejos estudiantiles *(student councils)* son grupos de estudiantes que ayudan a resolver problemas en la escuela. Trabaja con un grupo para representar ante la clase una sesión del concejo estudiantil.

Prepárate Al reunirse el concejo, algunos miembros deben presentar un problema y otros deben hacer sugerencias sobre cómo resolverlo. Piensen en problemas que haya en la escuela y en soluciones posibles. Anoten sus ideas en una tabla como ésta.

Problemas	Soluciones posibles
•	•
•	•

Práctica Uno(a) de ustedes explica un conflicto o problema y otro(a) sugiere una o más soluciones. Lean lo que escribieron en la tabla y asignen turnos para que todos presenten por lo menos un problema o sugieran una solución. Recuerda que deben:
- explicar claramente los conflictos
- explicar las soluciones posibles

Modelo

Miembro del concejo 1: *El problema que quiero presentar es el siguiente: Los estudiantes de los grados 10 y 11 siempre discuten en el gimnasio. Todos quieren jugar al básquetbol a la vez.*
Miembro del concejo 2: *Hablemos con el director para que tengamos recreos más largos y a horas diferentes.*
Miembro del concejo 3: *Pongámonos de acuerdo con ellos y tomemos turnos para usar el gimnasio.*

Haz tu presentación Hagan la representación ante la clase. El estudiante que presenta el problema ante el concejo puede ponerse de pie.

Evaluación Tu profesor(a) puede explicarte cómo va a evaluar tu presentación. Cada estudiante debe presentar por lo menos un conflicto o una solución. Para tu profesor(a) es importante ver que:
- describieron claramente los conflictos y sugirieron soluciones
- el público entendió la presentación

Estrategia

Getting into your character
In some cases, your oral presentation will require you to act something out. Keep in mind the character you are representing and try to act, look, and speak in the same way your character would.

For this oral presentation, remember that your character is not in front of your class, but solving a school problem at a student council meeting.

Communicate: Speaking

Presentación oral

Presentation
Standards: 1.1, 1.3, 3.1

Resources: Voc. & Gram. Transparencies: 4

Focus: Preparing and delivering an oral presentation

Suggestions: Review the task and the four-step approach with students. Review the rubric with the class (see *Assessment* below) to explain how you will grade the performance task. Before students begin practicing in step 2, direct their attention to the *Estrategia*. Encourage them to practice at home before a mirror or with a partner in class to develop their drama skills.

Portfolio
Record students' oral presentations on audiocassette or videotape for inclusion in their portfolios.

✓ **Assessment**
- Assessment Program: Cap. 4, Rubrics

Give students copies of the rubric before they begin the activity. Go over the descriptions of the different levels of performance. After assessing students, help individuals understand how their performance could be improved.

Block Schedule

You might want to set up the presentation in a way similar to a trial as seen on Court TV. Videotape each scene and encourage one of the students to "introduce" each episode.

Enriching Your Teaching

RUBRIC	Score 1	Score 3	Score 5
How well you presented a problem	You presented no problem, or your problem could not be understood.	You mentioned a problem but it wasn't clearly presented.	Your problem was clearly and completely presented.
How well you presented solutions	You offered no solutions.	You offered some solutions, but they need development.	Your solutions were clearly and completely presented.
How well you portrayed your characters	Your speakers said very little. You offered no character portrayal.	Your speakers read their lines.	Your speakers clearly portrayed realistic characters.

Presentación escrita

Presentation

Standards: 1.2, 1.3, 3.1

Resources: Voc. & Gram. Transparencies: 4

Focus: Combining learned vocabulary and structures in a written presentation

Suggestions: Begin by explaining the criteria you will use to evaluate students' compositions. (See step 5, *Evaluación*, in the Student Edition, and *Assessment* on the following page.)

Direct students' attention to the *Estrategia.* Ask them to consider how a character's actions, words, and thoughts are closely linked to what he or she is like. Ask: *Si un personaje es entrometido, ¿qué va a hacer si ve a dos personas que hablan? Si un personaje es comprensivo, ¿qué va a hacer si un amigo le pide perdón?* On their own paper, have students begin a chart like the one shown on this page. Point out that for this assignment students need to tell about an event that happened between the two characters that helps readers better see what they are like.

Language Arts Connection

Standards: 3.1

Ask students to revisit stories they have read in their Language Arts classes. Have them study scenes in which two characters interact and ask: *¿Cómo se portan los dos personajes cuando hay un conflicto? ¿Cómo nos demuestran sus cualidades? ¿Cómo influyeron las cualidades de los personajes en la resolución del conflicto?*

Block Schedule

Collect the first drafts and write sentences that show examples of errors. Distribute these to pairs of students to find and fix the errors. Do not identify which papers the errors came from. This will help them become more aware of common errors and assist them with self-editing.

Presentación escrita

Una relación

Objectives

- Write a description about a relationship
- Describe characters' relationships through their actions

Estrategia

Describing relationships
Good writers help readers deduce the relationships between characters from their actions, words, and thoughts. As you plan to write, think about what caused the conflicts or friendships between the people you will write about. How did the character's actions, thoughts, or words cause a reaction from other characters? Why?

Piensa en algún cuento que viste en un programa de televisión o una película de cine, o que leíste en un libro, sobre la amistad entre dos personas. Escribe una composición sobre los personajes del cuento. Describe cómo son, qué cosas tienen en común, en qué son diferentes y cómo es su relación.

1 Antes de escribir

Para ayudarte a recordar a los personajes de tu composición, puedes hacerte las siguientes preguntas.

- ¿Quiénes eran los personajes? ¿Qué cualidades tenían?
- ¿Qué cosas tenían en común? ¿En qué se diferenciaban?
- ¿Existía armonía entre ellos? ¿Qué problema tuvieron? ¿Cómo lo resolvieron?

Completa la tabla de abajo para prepararte para escribir tu composición. En la primera columna, apunta los nombres de los personajes. En la segunda columna haz una lista de sus cualidades. En la tercera columna, apunta las acciones de los personajes que contribuyen *(contribute)* a la armonía o al conflicto. En la cuarta columna, describe por qué los personajes hacen lo que hacen y, finalmente, en la quinta columna saca conclusiones sobre cómo las acciones y las cualidades de los personajes influyen en la relación que tienen.

Personajes	Cualidades	Acciones	¿Por qué?	Cómo influyen en la relación
Sandra	generosa, alegre, habla mucho, hace bromas	dijo que había copiado un examen	hacía muchos chistes	
Paola	callada, honesta	le dijo a Sandra que hablara con la profesora	sabía que era un malentendido	

2 Borrador

Escribe tu borrador. Para empezar, describe a los personajes. Luego cuenta qué problema tuvieron y cómo lo resolvieron. Recuerda describir claramente a los personajes y sus acciones para que el lector entienda cómo es la relación. Por último, saca conclusiones sobre la relación.

Universal Access

Heritage Language Learners

Students may sometimes confuse the letters *b* and *v* in their writing since these letters are often pronounced the same way in Spanish. As part of the revision process, have students use a dictionary to be sure that they have spelled all words with *b* and *v* correctly.

Advanced Learners

Ask students to write a short scene or part of a scene from a play in which two characters are in conflict. Students do not have to resolve the conflict in this scene. Have them share their scenes with other students, who tell what the characters are like, based on what they do, say, or think in the scene.

Modelo

Presenting the main characters: The writer describes the characters using specific words.

Sandra y Paola son amigas. Sandra es generosa y alegre. Siempre habla con todos. Paola es callada y honesta. Le preocupa que Sandra tenga problemas por hacer muchos chistes. Alguien le contó a la profesora de español que Sandra se atrevió a copiar en la prueba. Paola estaba segura de que era un chiste. Luego . . .

Main Conflict: The writer describes the characters' actions.

Conflict resolution: The writer explains the consequences of the characters' actions.

Sandra fue a hablar con la profesora para resolver el malentendido y le dio las gracias a su amiga.

Creo que estas chicas tienen una buena amistad. Lo que hizo Paola muestra que piensa en los demás, y que Sandra le hizo caso muestra que tiene confianza en su amiga.

Conclusion: The writer draws conclusions about the relationship.

3 Redacción/Revisión

Después de escribir el primer borrador de tu composición, intercambia tu trabajo con el de un(a) compañero(a) y hagan sugerencias para mejorar las composiciones. Revisen si:

- usaron palabras específicas para describir a los personajes
- hay concordancia *(agreement)* entre sustantivos, adjetivos, verbos y pronombres

Haz lo siguiente: Subraya con una línea los sustantivos, con dos líneas los adjetivos y encierra en un círculo los verbos. Asegúrate de que en cada oración haya concordancia.

Sandra es generosa y alegre. Siempre habla
con todos. Paola es callada y honesta. Le
preocupa
preocupan que Sandra tenga problemas por
hacer muchos chistes. Alguien le contó a la
profesora de español que Sandra se atrevió a
copiar en la prueba.

4 Publicación

Antes de hacer la versión final, lee tu borrador y repasa los siguientes puntos:

- ¿Describí claramente a los personajes?
- ¿Expliqué el conflicto y las acciones de los personajes?
- ¿Corresponde la conclusión a la descripción de los personajes?

Después de revisar el borrador, escribe una copia en limpio y ponle un título.

5 Evaluación

Tu profesor(a) puede explicarte cómo va a evaluar tu presentación. Probablemente, para tu profesor(a) es importante ver que:

- usaste palabras específicas para describir a los personajes
- describiste el comportamiento y los pensamientos de los personajes
- describiste las reacciones de los personajes y explicaste cómo se resolvieron los conflictos

ciento noventa y uno   191
Capítulo 4

Suggestions (Cont'd):

Once students have a rough draft ready, read through the model on this page together. Help them see how information from the chart on the previous page was incorporated into this draft and note the additional information that was added. Point out uses of the subjunctive and of *por* and *para*. Encourage them to work toward similar organization, level of detail, and language use as they revise their own drafts.

Common Errors: Students often have difficulty effectively organizing their writing. Guide them to see the organization of the model:

A. Give a general description of the characters.

B. Introduce a conflict.

C. Show how the characters acted in the conflict.

D. Show how the conflict was resolved (not all present in the model).

Tell students who are having organizational difficulties to follow these same steps in their own composition.

Evaluation

Steps 4 and 5 overlap. Students will need some evaluation by you, their peers, or some self-evaluation to fine-tune and polish their drafts.

Portfolio

Keep students' final drafts in their portfolios as a writing sample.

✓ **Assessment**

• Assessment Program: Cap. 4, Rubrics
Give students copies of the rubric before they begin the activity. Go over the descriptions of the different levels of performance.

Enriching Your Teaching

RUBRIC	Score 1	Score 3	Score 5
Your completion of task	Your lack of information or organization makes the writing unclear.	You offer descriptions, but important information is missing.	Your choice and organization of information create a convincing message.
Your description of characters	Your characters are not identified or described.	Your character descriptions need more development.	Your characters are clearly portrayed.
Sentence structure/grammar, spelling, mechanics	Your sentences are run-on or are fragmented. There are many grammar, spelling, and mechanics errors.	You use sentences consistently. Some grammar, spelling, and/or mechanics errors are present.	You use correct structure. There are few grammar, spelling, and mechanics errors.

Lectura

Presentation

Standards: 1.2, 2.1, 2.2, 3.1, 3.2, 5.2

Resources: Fine Art Transparencies; Fine Art Transparencies Teacher's Guide

Focus: Reading poems and analyzing figurative language

Suggestions:

Pre-reading: Before reading, direct students' attention to the *Al leer* section and to the *Estrategia*. Address any difficulties they may have understanding the concepts of **la metáfora** and **el símil,** and provide additional examples as necessary. Copy the graphic organizer from p. 195 and read the instructions that accompany it. Tell students that they will first work with a partner to record the examples of figurative language they find. Later, the class will compile their findings.

Reading: Have students work in pairs to read each poem using this procedure:

- Read the poem silently.
- Discuss comprehension problems, find examples of figurative language, and record these on the chart.
- Read the poem again silently.

Besides the instances of figurative language mentioned in the *¿Comprendiste?* on the next page, the following are other instances found in *Poema No. 15* that students should notice:

Metáfora

mariposa en arrullo (line 10)

Símil

Eres como la noche (line 15)

Lectura

La poesía, expresión de amor y amistad

Objectives

- **Read poems about love and friendship**
- **Find examples of figurative language**

Estrategia

Identifying and understanding figurative language
When somebody says *He ruffled his friend's feathers*, do you think that the friend is a bird? Of course not. This is a figurative language expression that means "to bother" or "to annoy". To identify figurative language, pay attention to phrases that connect two different kinds of things, for example *cheeks like roses*, or *life is a river*. Then, to figure out what the poet is trying to communicate, think what characteristics of one of the things can be used to describe the other.

Al leer

En la cultura del mundo hispanohablante la poesía es una de las formas preferidas para expresar lo que sentimos. Para crear sus poemas, los poetas usan figuras retóricas *(figures of speech)* como la metáfora y el símil.

El símil es una comparación que se hace entre dos cosas usando la palabra *como.* Por ejemplo, el poeta Pablo Neruda habla de un "silencio claro como una lámpara". Con las metáforas también se hacen comparaciones entre dos cosas, pero sin usar la palabra *como.* Por ejemplo, cuando el poeta llama a la mujer que ama "mariposa de sueño", la está comparando con una mariposa. Copia la tabla de la página 195. Mientras lees los poemas, completa los espacios en blanco de la tabla.

Presta atención a los siguientes puntos:

- cómo los poemas expresan amor o amistad
- el uso de las metáforas y los símiles
- las imágenes que usa el o la poeta

Poema No. 15
Pablo Neruda

Me gustas cuando callas[1] porque estás como ausente
y me oyes desde lejos, y mi voz no te toca.
Parece que los ojos se te hubieran volado[3] y
parece que un beso te cerrara la boca.

Como todas las cosas están llenas de mi alma[4]
emerges de las cosas, llena del alma mía.
Mariposa de sueño[5], te pareces a mi alma,
y te pareces a la palabra melancolía.

Me gustas cuando callas y estás como distante.
Y estás como quejándote, mariposa en arrullo.[6]
Y me oyes desde lejos, y mi voz no te alcanza:
déjame que me calle con el silencio tuyo.

Déjame que te hable también con tu silencio
claro como una lámpara, simple como un anillo.
Eres como la noche, callada y constelada.
Tu silencio es de estrella, tan lejano y sencillo.

Me gustas cuando callas porque estás como ausente
Distante y dolorosa como si hubieras muerto.
Una palabra entonces, una sonrisa bastan[7]. Y
estoy alegre, alegre de que no sea cierto.

---

1 you are quiet 2 absent 3 had flown 4 soul
5 dream butterfly 6 cooing 7 suffice

Universal Access

Heritage Language Learners

Have students select a Latin American artist whose works express love or friendship. They may choose a poem, a song, or a piece of visual art. Ask them to write a paragraph about how the artist expresses his or her love or friendship. Have them also mention what they like and don't like about the work.

Multiple Intelligences

Visual/Spatial: Invite students to close their eyes as you read the poems out loud. Then invite them to share the mental images that the poets' words evoked.

Homenaje a los padres chicanos

Abelardo Delgado

Con el semblante[1] callado,
con el consejo bien templado[2],
demandando siempre respeto,
con la mano ampollada[3] y el orgullo repleto,
así eres tú y nosotros te hablamos este día,
padre, papá, apá, jefito, dad, daddy . . . father,
como acostumbremos llamarte, eres el mismo.
La cultura nuestra dicta[4]
      que el cariño que te tenemos
lo demostremos poco
      y unos hasta creemos
que father's day
      es cosa de los gringos
          pero no . . .
tu sacrificio es muy sagrado
para dejarlo pasar hoy en callado.
Tu sudor[5] es agua bendita[6]
y tu palabra sabia[7],
derecha como esos surcos[8]
que con fe unos labran[9] día tras día,
nos sirve de alimento espiritual
y tu sufrir por tierras
y costumbres extrañas,
tu aguante[10], tu amparo[11], tu apoyo,
todo eso lo reconocemos y lo agradecemos
y te llamamos hoy con fuerza
          para que oigas
aun si[12] ya estás muerto,
      aun si la carga fue mucha
o la tentación bastante
      y nos abandonaste
aun si estás en la cárcel[13]
o en un hospital . . .
óyeme, padre chicano, oye también a mis
hermanos, hoy y siempre, papá, te veneramos.

---

1 face **2** tempered **3** blistered **4** dictates **5** sweat
6 holy water **7** wise **8** grooves **9** plow **10** endurance
11 protection **12** even if **13** jail

¿Comprendiste?

Trabaja con un grupo para hablar de las poesías y contestar estas preguntas:

1. ¿Qué quiere decir el poeta con "Me gusta cuando callas porque estás como ausente"?
2. ¿Qué te parece que quiere decir Neruda con "tu silencio claro como una lámpara, simple como un anillo"?
3. ¿Por qué se alegra el poeta en la última estrofa del *Poema No. 15*?
4. ¿Qué crees que quiere decir Delgado con "con la mano ampollada y el orgullo repleto"?
5. Describe las características de los padres que admira Delgado.

Enriching Your Teaching

Culture Note

Pablo Neruda (1904–1973), a Chilean poet and diplomat, won the Nobel Prize for Literature in 1971. He was politically active, holding various positions as Chilean consul to Burma, Argentina, and Mexico. In 1943, he was elected to the Chilean Senate. Much of Neruda's writing reflects political struggles, and he became known as the people's poet. Neruda is also greatly admired for his love poems. His poetry is more widely read than that of any other Latin American poet.

Suggestions (Cont'd):

Reading: Besides the instances of figurative language mentioned in the *¿Comprendiste?* on the next page, the following are other instances that students should notice:

El amor en preguntas:

Metáfora

volver a nacer (line 5)

inventar la gente (line 6)

crecer otra vez (line 9)

Point out that these are all metaphors the poet uses to describe what one must do to love and be loved. None of them are meant to be taken literally; instead they refer metaphorically to actions of the spirit.

Como tú:

Metáfora

el paisaje celeste de los días de enero (lines 3–4)

Mi sangre bulle (line 5)

Símil

la poesía es como el pan (line 9)

Teaching with Art

Standards: 3.1

Refer students to the Picasso painting on this page. Say: *Picasso era famoso por su estilo llamado cubismo. ¿Es esta obra un ejemplo de cubismo? ¿Qué mensaje te da sobre el tema del amor?*

Rimas

Gustavo Adolfo Bécquer

XXI

¿Qué es poesía? —dices mientras clavas[1]
  en mi pupila tu pupila azul—.
¿Qué es poesía? ¿Y tú me lo preguntas?
  Poesía . . . eres tú.

XXIII

Por[2] una mirada, un mundo;
por una sonrisa, un cielo,
por un beso . . . , ¡yo no sé
qué te diera[3] por un beso!

XXVIII

Los suspiros[4] son aire y van al aire.
Las lágrimas[5] son agua y van al mar.
Dime, mujer: cuando el amor se
olvida, ¿sabes tú a dónde va?

---

1 fix **2** in exchange for **3** I would give **4** sighs **5** tears

El amor en preguntas

Elizabeth Torres *15 años*

¿Qué es necesario para ser amado,
para entender la vida y saber soñar?
Tengo acaso que obtener permisos,
girar el mundo,
volver a nacer,
inventar la gente,
dar para merecer[1],
responder preguntas,
crecer[2] otra vez?

¿O se necesita estar inspirado,
abarcar[3] el mundo,
ser iluminado?

Estallar[4] el alma . . .
¡sólo para amar!

---

1 to deserve **2** to grow **3** to cover **4** to burst

194 ciento noventa y cuatro
Lectura

Como tú

Roque Dalton

Yo, como tú,
amo el amor, la vida, el dulce encanto
de las cosas, el paisaje
celeste de los días de enero.

También mi sangre bulle[1]
y río por los ojos que
han conocido el brote[2] de las lágrimas.

Creo que el mundo es bello,
que la poesía es como el pan, de todos.

Y que mis venas[3] no terminan en mí
sino en la sangre unánime
de los que luchan por la vida,
el amor,
las cosas,
el paisaje y el pan,
la poesía de todos.

---

1 boils **2** outpouring **3** veins

La salchichona, (1917), Pablo Picasso

Oil on canvas, 116 x 89cm. (c) 2004 Estate of Pablo Picasso/Artists Rights Society (ARS), New York. Musée Picasso, Barcelona, Spain. (c) Giraudon/Art Resource, NY.

Universal Access

Heritage Language Learners

Invite students with exemplary pronunciation to read aloud one stanza of each poem. After each reading, point out words that are linked together in spoken language. For example, in the first line of *Rimas,* the **e** sound in *qué* is elided with the first sound of the next word, **es.**

Advanced Learners

Ask students to read another poem by one of the poets studied and give a brief interpretation of its meaning and its use of figurative language.

Interacción con la lectura

METÁFORA	SÍMIL
_____	_____
_____	_____
_____	_____
_____	_____
_____	_____

Trabaja con la clase para completar una tabla como la de arriba y comentar lo que cada poeta quiere decir.

• Identifiquen y apunten todas las metáforas y símiles que encuentren en los poemas.

• Hablen acerca de lo que quiere trasmitir el poeta con cada uno(a).

 **Fondo cultural**

La lectura de poemas por sus propios autores es una costumbre muy popular en bibliotecas y librerías de toda España y América Latina. De igual manera, en los Estados Unidos se realiza una actividad cultural similar; en muchos centros comunitarios[1] se hacen concursos de poesía y rap, en los cuales los poetas leen sus obras ante el público. Por ejemplo, en la Ciudad de Nueva York, el *Nuyorican Poet's Cafe,* organiza concursos literarios y lecturas en español y en inglés.

• Muchas personas creen que el rap es una forma de poesía. ¿Estás de acuerdo? ¿Por qué?

• ¿Te interesa asistir a un concurso en el que los poetas de rap recitan sus poemas? ¿Por qué?

• ¿Te interesa asistir a un concurso de poesía que no sea rap? ¿Por qué?

_____

1 community centers

¿Comprendiste?

1. ¿Cuál es el tema de cada poema?

2. Según Bécquer, ¿la poesía está en las palabras de un poema? ¿Estás de acuerdo con el poeta? ¿Por qué?

3. En la "Rima XXVIII", ¿qué comparación hace el autor entre los suspiros, las lágrimas y el amor?

4. Después de leer el poema de Elizabeth Torres, ¿crees que es necesario hacer cosas extraordinarias para ser amado por las otras personas? ¿Por qué?

5. ¿Qué quiere decir Roque Dalton cuando escribe "mis venas no terminan en mí"?

6. ¿Cuál de los poemas te gustó más? ¿Por qué?

7. Forma un grupo con tres compañeros(as) para dar su opinión sobre estos temas:

• ¿Qué medios usan los jóvenes para expresar sus sentimientos? Hagan una lista.

• ¿De qué manera esas expresiones de sentimientos benefician a la comunidad?

ciento noventa y cinco **195**
Capítulo 4

Interacción con la lectura

Standards: 1.1, 1.2, 3.1

Resources: Voc. & Gram. Transparencies: 4

Suggestions:

Post-reading: Have students compile the examples of figurative language they and their partners have found into a class chart. Use this activity as a basis for further discussion of the poems.

¿Comprendiste?

Standards: 1.1, 1.2, 1.3, 3.2

Focus: Demonstrating reading comprehension and understanding of figurative language

Suggestions: For item 7, ask the small groups to divide the task in such a way that everyone participates in reporting orally.

Answers will vary.

Fondo cultural *Standards:* 1.1, 1.2, 2.1

Suggestions: After reading and discussing the information, ask interested students to work together to prepare and present a poetry reading. Students can research Spanish-language poetry at libraries and on the Internet, then present readings of the poems. Encourage them to accompany each reading with a brief interpretation of the poem's meaning.

Answers will vary.

Enriching Your Teaching

Culture Note
As students read about love in Spanish literature, explain the origins of the appellation "Don Juan." Never an actual person, Don Juan is a legendary character of Spanish folklore. The earliest-known dramatization of a Don Juan story, *El burlador de Sevilla,* was written by Tirso de Molina in 1630.

Teacher to Teacher
Help students prepare for a class poetry reading. Have them make notes for reading aloud. They can identify sounds that should elide other sounds and link words together, such as the final *s* of *suspiros* with the first *s* of *son.* Have them also note for themselves when they should not pause at the end of a line.

4 Review

Review Activities

Cualidades: Have students create a T-chart with the left column titled *Cualidades positivos* and the right titled *Cualidades negativos.* Ask them to sort the vocabulary from the **cualidades** list into these two categories and to write a brief Spanish definition for each word.

Sustantivos: Build a story using the nouns in this section of the *Vocabulario.* Have students sit in a circle. One student begins the story with a sentence that includes the word **amistad.** The student to his or her left continues by repeating that sentence and adding another that uses the word **armonía,** and so on. A variation on this is to write the words on slips of paper and place them in a hat or other container. This is passed around the circle. Students must build the story by adding a sentence that includes the word they draw from the hat.

Verbos: Have students work in pairs to invent mini-dialogues that use the verbs in the list. Each dialogue should use at least one of the verbs. Encourage them to use the verbs in different tenses, in the subjunctive, and with different subjects, in order to practice with different forms.

Expresiones: Play charades using the expressions from this list. Write the expressions on slips of paper and place them in a hat or other container. Students take turns drawing an expression and getting its meaning across to the others any way they can without speaking or writing. Use body language and strategies of traditional charades such as tugging at the ear to mean **suena como** or holding up two fingers to mean **dos palabras,** or invent your own rules.

El subjuntivo con verbos de emoción: On the board, write several subordinate *(que)* clauses, using a variety of verbs in the subjunctive. Vary the subjects of your clauses in order to use different verb forms. Precede each subordinate clause with a blank: ___ **que vayas.** ___ **que Uds. vayan a llegar tarde.** Have students supply verbs or expressions of emotion that make sense: *Te sugiero que vayas. Temo que Uds. vayan a llegar tarde.*

Repaso del capítulo

Vocabulario y gramática

cualidades

amable	kind
cariñoso, -a	loving, affectionate
celoso, -a	jealous
chismoso, -a	gossipy
comprensivo, -a	understanding
considerado, -a	considerate
egoísta	selfish
entrometido, -a	meddlesome, interfering
honesto, -a	honest
íntimo, -a	intimate
sincero, -a	sincere
vanidoso, -a	vain, conceited

sustantivos

la amistad	friendship
la armonía	harmony
el comportamiento	behaviour
la confianza	trust
el conflicto	conflict
la cualidad	quality
la explicación	explanation
el malentendido	misunderstanding
la pelea	fight
el secreto	secret

verbos

acusar	to accuse
alegrarse	to be delighted
apoyar(se)	to support, to back (each other)
atreverse	to dare
colaborar	to collaborate
confiar (i → í)	to trust
contar con	to count on
criticar	to criticize
desconfiar	to mistrust
esperar	to hope (for)
estar equivocado, -a	to be mistaken
guardar (un secreto)	to keep (a secret)
ignorar	to ignore
mejorar	to improve

pedir perdón	to ask for forgiveness
perdonar	to forgive
ponerse de acuerdo	to reach an agreement
reaccionar	to react
reconciliarse	to become friends again
reconocer (c → zc)	to admit, recognize
resolver (o → ue)	to resolve
sorprender(se)	to (be) surprised
temer	to fear

expresiones

aceptar tal como (soy)	to accept (me) the way (I am)
cambiar de opinión	to change one's mind
la diferencia de opinión	difference of opinion
hacer caso	to pay attention / to obey
hacer las paces	to make peace (with)
juntos, -as	together
ojalá	I wish, I hope
pensar en sí mismo(a)	to think of oneself
¡Qué va!	No way!
tener en común	to have in common
tener celos	to be jealous
tener la culpa	to be guilty
¡Yo no fui!	It was not me!

196 ciento noventa y seis
Repaso del capítulo

Universal Access

Students with Learning Difficulties

Whenever possible, provide students with memory clues for retaining vocabulary. For example, Say: "*Egoísta* looks like the English word 'egotistic.' Someone who is egotistic thinks a lot of him or herself and is probably selfish." Invite students to share their own memory devices.

Advanced Learners

Have students write a short letter to a friend that uses vocabulary and structures from the chapter. Letters can be one of two types: either thanking the friend for his or her positive role in resolving a problem, or reproaching the friend for an undesirable action. Have students look back through the chapter for models of similar letters, such as the ones on pp. 163 and 173.

El subjuntivo con verbos de emoción

Use the *subjunctive* following verbs indicating suggestions, desire or demands. **Te sugiero** que **vengas.** **Esperamos** que **llueva.** **Nos exigió** que **estudiemos.** **¡Ojalá** que **se diviertan!**	Use the *subjunctive* after verbs and impersonal phrases indicating emotion. **Tememos** que nuestros amigos **desconfíen** de nosotros. **Es una lástima** que no **hagan** las paces.	When the sentence has only one subject, we usually use the *infinitive* instead of the subjunctive. **Espero ir** mañana al cine. **Espero ver** esa película.

Los usos de *por* y *para*

Use *por* to indicate: length of time or distance, where an action takes place, an exchange, a reason or motive, an action on behalf of someone, a means of communication or transportation. Bailamos **por** varias horas. Busqué **por** todos los pasillos. Te cambio el café **por** un dulce. Me puse muy feliz **por** tu llegada. Fue a una marcha **por** la paz. Mandó la carta **por** avión.	Use *por* in certain expressions: **por** ejemplo **por** eso (tanto) **por** la (mañana, tarde, noche) **por** favor **por** lo general **por** primera (segunda, tercera, última) vez **por** supuesto	Use *para* to indicate: purpose, destination, a point in time, use, opinion. Estudio **para** tener un buen futuro. Salimos **para** la ciudad dentro de una hora. **Para** las ocho ya estaban allí. Ponte la chaqueta **para** no tener frío. **Para** ustedes todo es divertido.

Mandatos con *nosotros*

Regular verbs		Stem-changing verbs whose infinitive ends in –*ir*		Verbs ending in –*car*, –*gar*, and –*zar*	
olvidar	**olvidemos**	pedir	**pidamos**	criticar	**critiquemos**
pensar	**pensemos**	dormir	**durmamos**	pagar	**paguemos**
reconocer	**reconozcamos**			empezar	**empecemos**

Direct and **indirect pronouns** are attached at the end of affirmative *nosotros* commands but precede the negative *nosotros* command form. **Digámosle toda** la verdad. No **les mintamos.**	To attach **reflexive** or **reciprocal pronouns** at the end of a *nosotros* command, drop the final –*s* of the command before the pronoun. **Alegrémonos** con nuestro éxito. **Abracémonos** uno al otro.

Pronombres posesivos

To form the **possessive pronouns,** use the long form possessive adjectives preceded by the definite article. Mis padres son muy serios. ¿Y **los suyos?** Su vestido es grande. **El nuestro** es pequeño. We often omit the article between the verb *ser* and the possessive pronoun. Esas maletas **son nuestras,** pero la mochila **es suya.**

● **Más práctica** • • • • • • • • • • • • • •
Practice Workbook Organizer
4-13, 4-14

ciento noventa y siete **197**
Capítulo 4

Enriching Your Teaching

Teacher-to-Teacher
By creating their own tools for learning, students can benefit twice: once as they are creating the tool and again as they are using it. When asking students to make tools such as flashcards, for example, make sure that your instructions are clear and give several examples so students understand exactly what is needed.

Los usos de **por** *y* **para:** Have pairs write their own fill-in-the-blank quiz on the uses of **por** and **para.** Their quizzes should contain ten sentences in which one of the words is required. Tell students to include a variety of items in order to target the various rules of usage. They should make two copies, and they should also create an answer key. Then have pairs exchange their quizzes with another pair, take each other's quizzes, and check their work using the answer keys.

Mandatos con **nosotros:** Have students write three problems that need solving, such as *Mi computadora no funciona bien.* Have partners take turns reading these to each other and replying with a **nosotros** command that makes sense: *Llamemos a un técnico de computadoras.*

Pronombres posesivos: Have students create two sets of note cards. One set names individuals or groups of people, such as **María** or **los abuelos.** The other set names single or multiple nouns, such as **los problemas** or **el secreto.** Collect the cards and shuffle each set. Have students take turns drawing one card from each pile and making a sentence with a possessive pronoun: *María/los problemas: Los problemas son suyos.*

Portfolio

Invite students to review the activities they completed in this chapter, including written reports, posters or other visuals, tapes of oral presentations, or other projects. Have them select one or two items that they feel best demonstrate their achievements in Spanish. Include these products in students' portfolios. Have them include this with the Chapter Checklist and Self-Assessment Worksheet.

Additional Resources

• Audio Program: CD Cap. 4, Track 18
• Resource Book: Cap. 4, Clip Art
• Assessment Program: Chapter Checklist and Self-Assessment Worksheet

Performance Tasks

Standards: 1.1, 1.2, 1.3, 2.1

Resources: Audio Program: CD Cap. 4, Track 19; Resource Book: Cap. 4, Audio Script; Practice Answers on Transparencies

1. Vocabulario

Suggestions: Encourage students to review the vocabulary from the *A primera vista* sections on pp. 160–162 and 174–177 before they complete the activity.

Answers:

1. a   5. c
2. b   6. b
3. d   7. d
4. b   8. a

2. Gramática

Suggestions: Remind students of the main points of the grammar presentations in *Capítulo* 4:

- the subjunctive with verbs of emotion
- uses of *por* and *para*
- *nosotros* commands
- possessive pronouns

Answers:

1. c   5. a
2. a   6. d
3. b   7. b
4. b   8. a

To prepare for the test, check to see if you . . .
- know the new vocabulary and grammar
- can perform the tasks on pp. 198 and 199

Preparación para el examen

1 Vocabulario Escribe la letra de la palabra o expresión que mejor complete cada frase. Escribe tus respuestas en una hoja aparte.

1. Mis sobrinos siempre me besan y me abrazan. Son muy _____.
   a. cariñosos   c. entrometidos
   b. sinceros   d. honestos

2. Cuando dos amigos se reconcilian, _____.
   a. piensan en sí mismos   c. piensan en los demás
   b. hacen las paces   d. tienen la culpa

3. Una persona _____ no sabe guardar secretos.
   a. vanidosa   c. celosa
   b. egoísta   d. chismosa

4. Beto y Graciela son _____. Nunca mienten.
   a. armonía   c. amables
   b. sinceros   d. comprensivos

5. Cuando acusé a mi amigo de romper mi cámara, él me contestó, "_____. ¡Yo no fui!"
   a. ¡Qué lástima!   c. ¡Qué va!
   b. ¡Ojalá!   d. ¡Tienes razón!

6. Mis padres nunca me _____. Me aceptan tal como soy.
   a. hacen caso   c. temen
   b. critican   d. piden perdón

7. Mis amigos y yo tenemos _____. Nos gusta montar en monopatín y jugar videojuegos.
   a. celos   c. muchas peleas
   b. mucha confianza   d. mucho en común

8. El cariño y la confianza son dos _____ importantes en una amistad.
   a. cualidades   c. consejos
   b. conflictos   d. explicaciones

2 Gramática Escribe la letra de la palabra o expresión que complete mejor cada frase. Escribe tus respuestas en una hoja aparte.

1. Me molesta que ustedes _____ tan chismosos.
   a. son   c. sean
   b. seas   d. es

2. Ojalá que ella me _____.
   a. perdone   c. perdona
   b. perdonado   d. perdonando

3. Es triste _____ nuestra amistad.
   a. rompa   c. roto
   b. romper   d. rompo

4. Fernando y Pedro _____ todos los días.
   a. nos escribíamos   c. les escribí
   b. se escribían   d. se escribió

5. Mis hermanas y yo _____ contábamos todos los secretos.
   a. nos   c. se
   b. me   d. lo

6. Después de pelearse con su mejor amigo, Jorge le dijo: "_____ las paces".
   a. hacíamos   c. hicimos
   b. hacemos   d. hagamos

7. "¿Nos reconciliamos?", preguntó Ana. "Sí, _____," contestó Gaby.
   a. reconciliarme   c. reconciliémosnos
   b. reconciliémonos   d. reconciliamos

8. Mis padres son muy comprensivos. ¿Cómo son _____?
   a. los tuyos   c. las tuyas
   b. tuyos   d. tuyas

Universal Access

Heritage Language Learners

Remind students to take their time during both the chapter review and the actual exam. Point out that, even though they may have the necessary language skills to do well, they will have a higher chance of success if they read carefully and follow all directions.

Students with Learning Difficulties

Review test-taking strategies to prepare students for the exam. Remind them to read the directions before they begin each section. Practice using the process of elimination in items that resemble multiple-choice items on a test. Remind students that when deciding between two possible answers, first instincts are often correct.

Review 4

Go Online
PHSchool.com

For: Test preparation
Visit: www.phschool.com
Web Code: jed-0411

En el examen vas a . . .	Éstas son las tareas de práctica que te pueden ser útiles para el examen . . .	Si necesitas repasar . . .
3 Escuchar Escuchar y comprender la descripción de un buen amigo o de una buena amiga	El locutor de un canal de televisión entrevistó a varios jóvenes sobre lo que piensan de sus amigos. Escucha lo que dijo cada joven y, según lo que dijo, decide: (a) qué cualidades tiene su mejor amigo(a); (b) qué le molesta de su amigo(a); (c) qué tienen en común.	**pp. 160–163** *A primera vista 1* **pp. 164–165** Actividades 6–7 **p. 166** Actividad 8
4 Hablar Expresar opiniones y emociones sobre el comportamiento de otra persona	Estás cuidando a tu hermano menor que a veces se porta bien y a veces bastante mal. Dile a tu hermano lo que piensas y sientes acerca de su comportamiento. Usa por lo menos cinco frases. Por ejemplo, puedes decir: *Me alegro de que no tengas celos de nuestra hermanita. Es triste que no le hagas caso a mamá.*	**p. 168** *Subjuntivo con verbos de emoción* **p. 169** Actividades 13–14 **p. 170** Actividad 17 **p. 181** Actividades 31–32
5 Leer Leer y comprender un mensaje en un salón de chat	Lee este mensaje que una joven puso en un salón de chat. Decide por qué tiene tantos conflictos con sus amigos y qué debe hacer para mejorar su relación con ellos. **No entiendo por qué mis amigos están enojados conmigo. Ana dice que nunca le presto mis revistas. Lucía está enojada porque le conté a su mamá que sacó una mala nota. Luis está furioso porque llegué dos horas tarde al cine y no pudimos ver la película. En fin, ¡mi vida es un desastre! ¿Qué puedo hacer?**	**p. 161** *A primera vista 1* **p. 168** Actividad 12 **p. 173** Actividad 21 **pp. 174–176** *A primera vista 2*
6 Escribir Escribir sobre un conflicto entre amigos(as)	Escribe sobre un conflicto que ocurre entre dos amigos(as) en una película que viste o entre amigos(as) de la vida real. Explica por qué se rompe la armonía y cómo se reconcilian esas personas.	**p. 170** Actividad 15 **p. 172** Actividad 20 **p. 173** Actividad 21 **p. 179** Actividad 26 **p. 181** Actividad 32
7 Pensar Pensar en cómo se relacionan los jóvenes con sus familias	En México se hizo una serie de encuestas sobre la vida de los jóvenes y sus familias. Piensa en la información que leíste sobre este tema en el capítulo y compara las respuestas de los jóvenes mexicanos con tu propia experiencia.	**pp. 176–177** Actividades 23–24 **p. 181** Actividad 31

ciento noventa y nueve   199
Capítulo 4

---

3. Escuchar

Suggestions: Use the *Audio CD* or read from the script.

Answers:

Jorge:
a. **Su mejor amigo es muy comprensivo. Lo acepta tal como es y siempre puede contar con él.**
b. **A veces es un poco entrometido y quiere saber todo lo que hace.**
c. **A los dos les gusta jugar al béisbol.**

Cristina:
a. **Su mejor amiga es muy sincera y considerada. Siempre le da consejos y nunca la critica.**
b. **A veces es un poco vanidosa.**
c. **Las dos toman clases de danza clásica y también les gusta mucho hacer yoga.**

4. Hablar

Suggestions: Tell students to first write down five good and bad ways in which the little brother behaves. Then they can more easily come up with their comments about his behavior

Answers will vary.

5. Leer

Suggestions: Tell students to refer to pp. 160–162 and 174–177 if they have questions about vocabulary in the review.

Answers will vary, but should make use of these subjunctive forms:
prestes/no cuentes/llegues/puedas

6. Escribir

Suggestions: Remind students to be sensitive to the privacy of others if they choose to write about real-life events.

Answers will vary.

7. Pensar

Suggestions: Have students share their thoughts with each other and compare their perceptions about young people and family life in the United States.

Answers will vary.

✓ **Assessment**
• Examen del capítulo: 4
• Audio Program: CD 12, Cap. 4, Track 5
• Assessment Program: *RPH*

Alternative Assessment
• ExamView Test Bank CD-ROM
• Resource Book: Cap. 4, Situation Cards
• Resource Book: Cap. 4, Communicative Activity BLM

Enriching Your Teaching

Teacher-to-Teacher
Help students assess their own learning from this chapter. Ask them to work with a partner, reporting orally on what they learned, as though they were telling a visitor from a Spanish-speaking country about the class.

199

Trabajo y comunidad

CHAPTER OVERVIEW

Trabajo y comunidad
• jobs and volunteer work

Vocabulary
• jobs and job skills
• interviewing techniques
• volunteer work

Grammar
• present perfect
• pluperfect
• present perfect subjunctive
• demonstrative adjectives and pronouns

Cultural Perspectives
• the importance of finding a job or profession
• the art of Rufino Tamayo
• the meaning of work for young people in Latin America
• the Hispanic Heritage Awards Foundation
• work as seen through the art of Diego Rivera
• Hispanic contributions to American society

Chapter Project

Álbum de mis amigos en el futuro

Overview: Students create six pages for a scrapbook featuring photos or illustrations of their friends along with a brief description of what professions or jobs they think their friends are going to have in the future. They then give an oral presentation of their scrapbook, describing one of their friends and predicting his or her future profession or job.

Materials: construction paper, photographs of friends, drawing paper, colored pencils, markers, glue, scissors

• •

Sequence: (suggestions for when to do each step appear throughout the chapter)

STEP 1. Review instructions so students know what is expected of them. Hand out the "Chapter 5 Project Instructions and Rubric" from the *Teacher's Resource Book*.

STEP 2. Students submit a rough sketch of their scrapbook pages. Return the sketches with your suggestions. For vocabulary and grammar practice, ask pairs to present their drafts to each other.

STEP 3. Students do layouts on construction paper. Encourage them to work in pencil first and to try different arrangements before gluing photographs and writing descriptions.

STEP 4. Students submit a draft of their descriptions. Note your corrections and suggestions, then return the drafts to students.

STEP 5. Students complete and present their scrapbook to the class. They should describe one of the people in the photos or illustrations and say what profession or job they think he or she is going to have in the future.

Options:

1. Students write and create a poster with photos or descriptions about the future professions and jobs of their friends.

2. Students write a composition about the future professions and jobs of their best friends.

Assessment:

Here is a detailed rubric for assessing this project:

Chapter 5 Project: *Álbum de mis amigos en el futuro*

RUBRIC	Score 1	Score 2	Score 3
Your evidence of planning	You provide no preliminary sketch or description drafts	Your preliminary sketch and descriptions are created, but not corrected	You show evidence of corrected sketch and descriptions
Your use of illustrations	You include no photos or illustrations	You provide photos or illustrations but don't organize them	You provide well organized photos and illustrations
Your presentation	You do not include the required information	You include most of the required information	You include all of the required information

Bulletin Boards

Theme: *Trabajo y comunidad*

Ask students to cut out, copy, or download photos of people from different professions and jobs, including volunteer work. They should also include a photo of something related to each profession or job, such as a photo of a doctor along with a photo of a hospital or a patient.

Bibliography

DK Bridgman, Roger. *Technology*. London, England: Dorling Kindersley, 1999. Describes the ways technology has transformed everyday life, including jobs and careers.

Lewis, A. Barbara and Pamela Espeland. *Kid's Guide to Service Projects*. Minneapolis, MN: Free Spirit Publishing, Inc., 1995. Describes a variety of opportunities for youngsters to participate in successful community service.

Morkes, Andrew, ed. *Encyclopedia of Careers and Vocational Guidance*. Palestine, TX: Ferguson Publishing, 2002. Gives a general description and information of more than 900 careers and jobs.

Rosen, Ruth C. *The World of Work*. Sandy, UT: The Rosen Publishing Group, Incorporated, 1997. Presents information on job hunting, interviews, work objectives.

Hands-on Culture

Recipe: *Mate*

Mate is a very popular drink in Argentina. Most of the *gauchos,* Argentinian cowboys, drink mate in the afternoon while relaxing after a long day's work.

Ingredients:

1/2 oz. *mate* powder
1 cup water, hot but not boiling
pinch of sugar

Supplies:

kettle, *mate* gourd or large cup; small paper cups
bombilla (silver sipping straw with strainer at bottom) and/or paper straws

1. Put *mate* and sugar in the mate gourd (or cup) and add a cup of hot water.

2. Let the *mate* powder steep for 3-5 minutes before drinking through a bombilla or straw. Keep straws away from the grounds at bottom.

3. Tell students that the Argentines sit in a circle and pass the mate clockwise. When more water is needed, the *cebador* (server) adds hot water from the kettle.

4. Pour the *mate* into small paper cups.

Internet Search

Use the keywords to find more information.

Keywords:

Rufino Tamayo, Ignacio Rivera, Fundación de Premios de Herencia Hispana, Oscar Hijuelos, Sammy Sosa, Sociedad de Beneficencia Manuel García, servicio social, Peace Boat, Silvio Rodríguez

Game

Rueda de palabras

This memory game practices vocabulary about work and community using a spinner. Use it toward the end of *Trabajo y comunidad*, after students have practiced the vocabulary of the chapter.

Players: the entire class

Materials: spinner, pen

Rules:

1. Fill in spinner sections with the six vocabulary categories used in *Repaso del capítulo, Vocabulario y gramática*. Omit the *Acciones* and *Expresiones* categories.

2. Select a scorekeeper and divide the class into four groups. Have each group choose a writer.

3. Spin the spinner and announce the category. Groups have three minutes to write down all the Spanish words they can think of that fit the category. Words cannot be repeated from category to category.

   Spinner category: *En el trabajo*

   Team writes: *el anuncio clasificado, los beneficios, la clienta, la compañía, el gerente, el puesto, el salario, la solicitud de empleo, la computación, la recepcionista*

4. When time is up, groups take turns reading their lists one word at a time. Groups that have the same word cross it from their lists. When a category is exhausted, a tally is taken. The team with the largest number of words wins the round and spins for the next category.

5. Play until all six categories have been used.

Variation: Each team writes sentences with the words they wrote for each category. The more correct sentences they write in a given time, the more points they score.

A ver si recuerdas
RECYCLE

Vocabulary
• Work
• Community

Grammar
• Present participle
• Placement of reflexive pronouns and direct and indirect object pronouns

Chapter Overview

A primera vista 1
INPUT

Objectives
• Getting a job
• Skills and abilities needed to perform a job
• Interviewing techniques

Vocabulary
• Jobs and interviews in the workplace

Grammar
• Present perfect
• Pluperfect

Culture
• Community gardens in Latin America

Manos a la obra 1
PRACTICE

Objectives
• Talk about getting a job
• Describe skills and abilities needed to perform a job
• Review and practice the present perfect and pluperfect

Vocabulary
• Practice new vocabulary

Grammar
• Present perfect
• Pluperfect

Culture
• The meaning of work for the young people in Latin America
• The Hispanic Heritage Awards Foundation

A primera vista 2
INPUT

Objectives
• Talk about volunteer work opportunities
• Talk about how we can help our community

Vocabulary
• Volunteer work
• Community

Grammar
• Present perfect subjunctive
• Demonstrative adjectives and pronouns

Culture
• Immigrants seeking citizenship
• *Sociedad de Beneficencia Manuel García*

Manos a la obra 2
PRACTICE

Objectives
• Talk about volunteer work
• Explain how you can help your community
• Practice and review present perfect subjunctive and demonstrative adjectives and pronouns

Vocabulary
• Practice new vocabulary

Grammar
• Present perfect subjunctive
• Demonstrative adjectives and pronouns

Culture
• José Gálvez, photographer Silvio Rodríquez, singer

¡Adelante!
APPLICATION

Objectives
• Read about contributions of Spanish-speakers in society
• Comprehend the reading

Vocabulary
• Application

Grammar
• Application

Culture
• Contributions of Spanish speakers in the United States

• Story about the Maya and the meaning of death and poverty
• Community centers in Los Angeles

Repaso del capítulo
REVIEW

Objectives
• Prepare for the chapter test

• Perform the tasks on pp. 244 and 245

Vocabulary
• Review

Grammar
• Review

BEYOND THE CLASSROOM

Countries
• Mexico
• Costa Rica
• Cuba
• Spain
• United States

El español en la comunidad
• Volunteer teachers working for peace, human rights, and the environment

Internet
• Vocabulary activities
• Grammar activities
• Internet links
• Self-tests

LEARNER SUPPORT

Strategies
• Scanning
• Reading for comprehension
• Using visual aids

• Writing to persuade

Recycling
• *r* between two vowels

En voz alta
• *He andado muchos caminos*

Ampliación del lenguaje
• Nouns ending in *ero* and *era*

Conexiones
• Art: Diego Rivera

 **Print Components**

TEACHER	STUDENT

Teacher's Resource Book
• Chapter Table of Contents
• School-to-Home Connection
• Chapter Resource Checklist
• Input Script
• Audio Script
• Video Script
• Communicative Activities
• Situation Cards
• GramActiva Blackline Masters
• Graphic Organizers
• Answer Keys:
  Practice Workbook
  Writing, Audio & Video Workbook
	Practice Workbook
	• Vocabulary: 5-1 – 5-4, 5 -8 – 5-9
	• Grammar: 5-5 – 5-7, 5-10 – 5-12
	• Organizer: 5-13 – 5-14

	Writing, Audio & Video Workbook • Audio: 1–5 • Writing: 6–13 • Video: 14–17
	Reading and Writing for Success • Chapter 5, Test 32
***Realidades para hispanohablantes* Teacher Edition**	***Realidades para hispanohablantes***

Transparencies

Vocabulary and Grammar Transparencies
• Vocabulary: 99–106, 109–112
• Grammar: 107–108, 113–114
• ¿Qué me cuentas?: 115

Practice Answers on Transparencies
• Cap. 5

Fine Art Transparencies
• Transparencies
• Teacher's Guide

 **Assessment**

Assessment Program
• Pruebas:
  – Comprensión del vocabulario 1: 5-1
  – Aplicación del vocabulario 1: 5-2
  – El presente perfecto: 5-3
  – El pluscuamperfecto: 5-4
  – Comprensión del vocabulario 2: 5-5
  – Aplicación del vocabulario 2: 5-6
  – El presente perfecto del subjuntivo: 5-7
  – Los adjetivos y los pronombres posesivos: 5-8
• Exámenes del capítulo
• Rubrics

Alternative Assessment
• ExamView Test Bank CD-ROM
• MindPoint Quiz Show CD-ROM
• Internet Self-test
• Situation Cards
• Communicative Activity

Assessment Program: *Realidades para hispanohablantes*

 **Technology**

TeacherExpress™ CD-ROM
• Lesson Planner
• Teacher Resources
• Clip Art

Video Program VHS and DVD

Audio Program CDs
• A primera vista 1 y 2: Vocabulario y gramática en contexto
• Audio Activities
• ¿Qué me cuentas?
• Repaso
• Examen del capítulo: Escuchar

Capítulo 5 — Lesson Plans

Regular Schedule (50 Minutes)

For electronic lesson plans:
Teacher Express CD-ROM

	Warm-up / Assess	Preview Present / Practice Communicate		Wrap-up / Homework Options

DAY 1

Warm-up (10 min.)
• Return Examen del capítulo: Capítulo 4

Repaso (35 min.)
• A ver si recuerdas . . .
• Actividades 3, 5

Wrap-up and Homework Options (5 min.)
• Practice Workbook 5-1, 5-2
• Go Online

DAY 2

Warm-up (10 min.)
• Homework check

Chapter Opener (10 min.)
• Objectives   • Fondo cultural
A primera vista 1 (25 min.)
• Presentation: Vocabulario y gramática en contexto
• Actividades 1, 2

Wrap-up and Homework Options (5 min.)
• Go Online
• Clip Art Vocabulary

DAY 3

Warm-up (10 min.)
• Homework check

A primera vista 1 (30 min.)
• Presentation: Tú y tus habilidades;   • Actividades 3, 4, 5
  los anuncios clasificados
Manos a la obra 1 (5 min.)
• Actividad 6

Wrap-up and Homework Options (5 min.)
• Practice Workbook 5-3, 5-4
• Go Online
• Prueba 5-1: Vocabulary recognition

DAY 4

Warm-up (10 min.)
• Homework check
✔**Assessment (10 min.)**
• Prueba 5-1: Vocabulary recognition

Manos a la obra 1 (25 min.)
• Actividades 7, 8, 9, 10
• Ampliación del lenguaje

Wrap-up and Homework Options (5 min.)
• Actividad 13
• Writing Activities
• Prueba 5-2: Vocabulary production

DAY 5

Warm-up (10 min.)
• Fondo cultural
• Homework check
✔**Assessment (10 min.)**
• Prueba 5-2: Vocabulary production

Manos a la obra 1 (25 min.)
• Actividades 11, 12, 14
• Presentation: El presente perfecto

Wrap-up and Homework Options (5 min.)
• Practice Workbook 5-5
• Go Online

DAY 6

Warm-up (10 min.)
• Actividad 16
• Homework check

Manos a la obra 1 (35 min.)
• Actividades 15, 17   • Fondo cultural
• En voz alta   • Communicative Activity

Wrap-up and Homework Options (5 min.)
• Writing Activity
• Prueba 5-3: El presente perfecto

DAY 7

Warm-up (5 min.)
• Homework check
✔**Assessment (10 min.)**
• Prueba 5-3: El presente perfecto

Manos a la obra 1 (30 min.)
• Presentation: El pluscuamperfecto
• Actividades 18, 19, 20, 21
• Communicative Activity

Wrap-up and Homework Options (5 min.)
• Practice Workbook 5-6, 5-7
• Go Online
• Prueba 5-4: El pluscuamperfecto

DAY 8

Warm-up (10 min.)
• Actividad 22
• Homework check
✔**Assessment (10 min.)**
• Prueba 5-4: El pluscuamperfecto

A primera vista 2 (25 min.)
• Presentation: Vocabulario y gramática en contexto
• Actividades 23, 24

Wrap-up and Homework Options (5 min.)
• Clip Art Vocabulary
• Examen: Vocabulario y gramática 1

DAY 9

Warm-up (5 min.)
• Homework check
✔**Assessment (30 min.)**
• Examen: Vocabulario y gramática 1

A primera vista 2 (10 min.)
• Presentation: Se buscan voluntarios
• Presentation: ¿A quién van a escoger?

Wrap-up and Homework Options (5 min.)
• Actividad 25
• Practice Workbook 5-8, 5-9
• Go Online
• Prueba 5-5: Vocabulary recognition

DAY 10

Warm-up (20 min.)
• Actividades 26, 27
• Homework check
✔**Assessment (10 min.)**
• Prueba 5-5: Vocabulary recognition

Manos a la obra 2 (15 min.)
• Actividades 30, 32

Wrap-up and Homework Options (5 min.)
• Actividades 28, 29
• Prueba 5-6: Vocabulary production

	Warm-up / Assess	Preview / Practice Present / Communicate	Wrap-up / Homework Options
DAY 11	**Warm-up (10 min.)** • Homework check ✔**Assessment (10 min.)** • Prueba 5-6: Vocabulary production	**Manos a la obra 2 (25 min.)** • Actividades 31, 33 • Presentation: El presente perfecto del subjuntivo • Fondo cultural • Actividad 35	**Wrap-up and Homework Options (5 min.)** • Actividad 34 • Practice Workbook 5 -10 • Go Online • Prueba 5-7: El presente perfecto del subjuntivo
DAY 12	**Warm-up (15 min.)** • Actividad 36 • Homework check ✔**Assessment (10 min.)** • Prueba 5-7: El presente perfecto del subjuntivo	**Manos a la obra 2 (20 min.)** • Presentation: Los adjetivos y los pronombres demostrativos • Actividades 37, 39	**Wrap-up and Homework Options (5 min.)** • Practice Workbook 5-11, 5-12 • Go Online • Prueba 5-8: Los adjetivos y los pronombres demostrativos
DAY 13	**Warm-up (10 min.)** • Fondo cultural • Homework check ✔**Assessment (10 min)** • Prueba 5-8: Los adjetivos y los pronombres demostrativos	**Manos a la obra 2 (25 min.)** • Actividad 38 • Communicative Activity • El español en la comunidad	**Wrap-up and Homework Options (5 min.)** • Go Online • Examen: Vocabulario y gramática 2
DAY 14	**Warm-up (5 min.)** • Writing Activity ✔**Assessment (30 min.)** • Examen: Vocabulario y gramática 2	**¡Adelante! (10 min.)** • Presentación oral: Steps 1. 2	**Wrap-up and Homework Options (5 min.)** • Presentación oral: Step 2
DAY 15	**Warm-up (10 min.)** • Presentación oral: Step 2	**¡Adelante! (35 min.)** • Presentación oral: Step 3	**Wrap-up and Homework Options (5 min.)** • Estados Unidos . . . en español • ¿Comprendiste? • Escribe tu opinión • Go Online
DAY 16	**Warm-up (15 mln.)** • Estados Unidos . . . en español: ¿Comprendiste? • Homework check	**¡Adelante! (30 min.)** • ¿Qué me cuentas? 1, 2, 3 • View Video • Video Activities 1, 2, 3	**Wrap-up and Homework Options (5 min.)** • Presentación escrita: Steps 1, 2
DAY 17	**Warm-up (10 min.)** • Video Activity 4	**¡Adelante! (15 min.)** • Presentación escrita: Step 3 **Repaso (20 min.)** • Preparación para el examen: Actividades 3, 4 • MindPoint Quiz Show	**Wrap-up and Homework Options (5 min.)** • Presentación escrita: Step 4
DAY 18	**Warm-up (10 min.)** • Homework check	**¡Adelante! (35 min.)** • Lectura • Interacción con la lectura • Fondo cultural	**Wrap-up and Homework Options (5 min.)** • Practice Workbook: Organizer 5-13, 5-14 • Go Online: Self-test
DAY 19	**Warm-up (20 min.)** • Preparación para el examen: Actividades 1, 2 • Homework check	**Repaso (25 min.)** • Preparación para el examen: Actividades 5, 6, 7 • MindPoint Quiz Show • Other review	**Wrap-up and Homework Options (5 min.)** • Examen del capítulo
DAY 20	**Warm-up (5 min.)** • Answer questions ✔**Assessment (44 min.)** • Examen del capítulo		**Wrap-up and Homework Options (1 min.)** • A ver si recuerdas: Capítulo 6 • Actividades 4, 5, 8

Block Schedule (90 Minutes)

For electronic lesson plans:
Teacher Express CD-ROM

	Warm-up / Assess	Preview / Practice Present / Communicate	Wrap-up / Homework Options
DAY 1	**Warm-up (35 min.)** • Return Examen del capítulo: Capítulo 4 • A ver si recuerdas . . . • Actividades 3, 5 • Homework check	**Chapter Opener (10 min.)** • Objectives • Fondo cultural **A primera vista 1 (40 min.)** • Presentation: Vocabulario y gramática en contexto • Actividades 1, 2 • Presentation: Tú y tus habilidades • Actividades 3, 4 • Presentation: Los anuncios clasificados • Actividad 5	**Wrap-up and Homework Options (5 min.)** • Practice Workbook 5-3, 5-4 • Go Online • Clip Art Vocabulary • Prueba 5-1: Vocabulary recognition
DAY 2	**Warm-up (15 min.)** • Actividad 8 • Homework check ✔**Assessment (10 min.)** • Prueba 5-1: Vocabulary recognition	**Manos a la obra 1 (60 min.)** • Actividades 6, 7, 9, 10, 11, 12, 13 • Fondo cultural • Ampliación del lenguaje	**Wrap-up and Homework Options (5 min.)** • Go Online • Writing Activities • Prueba 5-2: Vocabulary production
DAY 3	**Warm-up (15 min.)** • Writing Activity • Homework check ✔**Assessment (10 min.)** • Prueba 5-2: Vocabulary production	**Manos a la obra 1 (60 min.)** • Presentation: El presente perfecto • Actividades 14, 15, 17 • En voz alta • Fondo cultural • Audio or Writing Activities	**Wrap-up and Homework Options (5 min.)** • Practice Workbook 5-5 • Go Online • Prueba 5-3: El presente perfecto
DAY 4	**Warm-up (10 min.)** • Actividad 16 • Homework check ✔**Assessment (10 min.)** • Prueba 5-3: El presente perfecto	**Manos a la obra 1 (45 min.)** • Presentation: El pluscuamperfecto • Actividades 18, 20, 21, 22 • Communicative Activity **A primera vista 2 (20 min.)** • Presentation: Vocabulario y gramática en contexto • Actividad 23, 24	**Wrap-up and Homework Options (5 min.)** • Practice Workbook 5-6, 5-7 • Go Online • Prueba 5-4: El pluscuamperfecto • Examen: Vocabulario y gramática 1
DAY 5	**Warm-up (10 min.)** • Actividad 19 • Homework check ✔**Assessment Options (40 min.)** • Prueba 5-4: El pluscuamperfecto Examen: Vocabulario y gramática 1	**A primera vista 2 (25 min.)** • Presentation: Se buscan voluntarios hispanohablantes para ayudar a inmigrantes • Actividades 25, 26 • Presentation: ¿A quién van a escoger? • Actividad 27 **Manos a la obra 2 (10 min.)** • Actividad 30	**Wrap-up and Homework Options (5 min.)** • Practice Workbook 5-8, 5-9 • Go Online • Prueba 5-5: Vocabulary recognition

	Warm-up / Assess	Preview / Practice Present / Communicate	Wrap-up / Homework Options
DAY 6	**Warm-up (20 min.)** • Actividades 28, 29 • Homework check **✔Assessment (10 min.)** • Prueba 5-5: Vocabulary recognition	**Manos a la obra 2 (55 min.)** • Actividades 31, 32, 33 • Fondo cultural • Presentation: El presente perfecto del subjuntivo • Actividades 34, 35, 36	**Wrap-up and Homework Options (5 min.)** • Practice Workbook 5-10 • Go Online • Pruebas 5-6, 5-7: Vocabulary production, el presente perfecto del subjuntivo
DAY 7	**Warm-up (15 min.)** • Writing Activity • Homework check **✔Assessment (20 min.)** • Pruebas 5-6, 5-7: Vocabulary production, el presente perfecto del subjuntivo	**Manos a la obra 2 (35 min.)** • Presentation: Los adjetivos y los pronombres demostrativos • Actividades 37, 38, 39 • El español en la comunidad • Fondo cultural **¡Adelante! (15 min.)** • Presentación oral: Steps 1, 2	**Wrap-up and Homework Options (5 min.)** • Presentación oral: Step 2 • Go Online
DAY 8	**Warm-up (15 min.)** • Writing Activity • Homework check	**¡Adelante! (40 min.)** • Presentación oral: Step 3 **Manos a la obra 2 (15 min.)** • Communicative Activity **¡Adelante! (15 min.)** • Presentation: Estados Unidos . . . en español	**Wrap-up and Homework Options (5 min.)** • Practice Workbook 5-11, 5-12 • Go Online • Prueba 5-8: Los adjetivos y los pronombres demostrativos • Examen: Vocabulario y gramática 2
DAY 9	**Warm-up (10 min.)** • Homework check	**✔Assessment Options (30 min.)** • Prueba 5-8: Los adjetivos y los pronombres demostrativos • Examen: Vocabulario y gramática 2 **¡Adelante! (45 min.)** • Estados Unidos . . . en español • ¿Comprendiste? • Escribe tu opinión • Video • Video Activities • ¿Qué me cuentas? 1, 2, 3 • Presentación escrita: Step 1	**Wrap-up and Homework Options (5 min.)** • Presentación escrita: Step 2 • Go Online • Preparación para el examen: Actividades 1, 2
DAY 10	**Warm-up (20 min.)** • Presentación escrita: Step 3 • Homework check	**¡Adelante! (40 min.)** • Lectura • Interacción con la lectura • Fondo cultural **Repaso (25 min.)** • Preparación para el examen: Actividades 3, 4, 6 • MindPoint Quiz Show	**Wrap-up and Homework Options (5 min.)** • Presentación escrita: Step 4 • Practice Workbook: Organizer 5-13, 5-14 • Go Online: Self-test • Preparación para el examen: Actividades 5, 7 • Examen del capítulo
DAY 11	**Warm-up (15 min.)** • Homework check **✔Assessment (45 min.)** • Examen del capítulo	**Theme Game (15 min.)** **A ver si recuerdas – Capítulo 6 (10 min.)** • Presentation: Vocabulario • Presentation: Gramática	**Wrap-up and Homework Options (5 min.)** • A ver si recuerdas – Capítulo 6 • Actividades 4, 5, 8 • Go Online • Practice Workbook 6-1, 6-2

Vocabulario

Presentation

Standards: 1.1, 1.2

Resources: Voc. & Gram. Transparencies: 99

Suggestions: On the board, write the following sentence: *En el (la)* lugar, *conozco a un(a)* trabajo *muy* cualidad *que* acción. Have students fill in the blanks with items from the four categories of the *Vocabulario* to create sentences that make sense: *En la* biblioteca, *conozco a una* empleada *muy* ordenada *que* usa *la* computadora.

Standards: 1.1, 1.3

Resources: Voc. & Gram. Transparencies: 4

Focus: Practicing review vocabulary

Suggestions: Use *Vocabulary & Grammar Transparency* 4 to help students create a T-chart. Encourage students to base their discussion on real-life situations as much as possible. If a job they actually have is not included in the *Vocabulario*, have them find out the Spanish term for it either in a bilingual dictionary or by asking heritage speakers. For step 3, point out that students should be commenting on the jobs their partners wrote about.

Answers will vary.

A ver si recuerdas...

Vocabulario

trabajos

el / la agente de viajes
el / la atleta
el bombero,
  la bombera
el cajero, la cajera
el camarero,
  la camarera
el científico,
  la científica
el / la dentista
el / la detective
el empleado,
  la empleada
el entrenador,
  la entrenadora
el fotógrafo
  la fotógrafa
el locutor,
  la locutora
el / la piloto
el reportero,
  la reportera
el vendedor,
  la vendedora

cualidades

animado, -a
artístico, -a
atlético, -a
bien educado, -a
cortés
interesante
obediente
ordenado, -a
paciente
trabajador, -a
tranquilo, -a

acciones

cortar el césped
cuidar niños
decorar
dibujar
hablar por teléfono
lavar el coche
lavar los platos
limpiar
pasar la aspiradora
pasear perros
sacar fotos
tocar un instrumento
usar la computadora

lugares

el banco
la biblioteca
el centro comercial
el cine
la escuela
la estación de
  servicio
la farmacia
el gimnasio
la guardería
  infantil
la librería
el museo
el restaurante
el supermercado
el teatro
la tienda

 **Hablar/Escribir** ....

Práctica de vocabulario

❶ Describe en qué trabajas ahora y qué trabajos has tenido antes.

❷ Ahora, escribe en una hoja de papel dos trabajos que te gustaría hacer y dos que no te gustaría hacer. Junto a cada trabajo, pon lo que tienes que hacer, las cualidades que se necesitan y el lugar donde se hace el trabajo.

❸ Con otro(a) estudiante, hagan y contesten preguntas sobre por qué les gustarían o no les gustarían los trabajos que escribieron.

Modelo

A —*Me gustaría ser reportero.*
B —*¿Por qué?*
A —*Un reportero escribe sobre cosas que pasan. Para ser reportero, debes saber escribir bien y sacar fotos.*

200 doscientos
    A ver si recuerdas . . .

Universal Access

Students with Special Needs

Help hearing impaired students complete step 3 of *Actividad* 1, by having them work with a partner and write out the dialogue instead of speaking it.

Advanced Learners

Have students choose one *lugar* from the *Vocabulario* and prepare a brief oral presentation telling about the different kinds of jobs encountered there, actions typically done, and one desirable quality for people to have who work there.

Gramática · Repaso

El participio presente

The present participle conveys a sense of ongoing action. To form the present participle add *-ando* to the stem of *-ar* verbs and *-iendo* to the stem of *-er* and *-ir* verbs.

trabajar	trabaj**ando**
hacer	hac**iendo**
recibir	recib**iendo**

- Verbs that have irregular third person forms in the preterite undergo the same change in the present participle.

dormir	d**u**rmiendo
pedir	p**i**diendo
decir	d**i**ciendo
reír	r**i**endo

- The verbs *ir* and *oír* and verbs ending in *-aer*, *-eer*, and *-uir* have present participles that end in *-yendo*.

ir	**yendo**
oír	**oyendo**
caer	**cayendo**
leer	**leyendo**
destruir	**destruyendo**

- The present participle is used together with a form of *estar* to form the progressive tense:

  ¡No me molestes! **Estoy leyendo.**
  Estábamos durmiendo cuando llamaste.

- Reflexive or object pronouns can be placed before the form of *estar*, or they can be attached to the end of the present participle. If they are attached to the present participle, a written accent is needed.

  Ahora **me** estoy **bañando.** / Estoy **bañándome.**
  Las está **ayudando.** / Está **ayudándolas.**

 2 Escribir

Práctica de gramática

Escribe lo que está sucediendo en la clase en este momento. Nombra a las personas que están haciendo las siguientes actividades. Usa el presente progresivo en tus frases.

leer darle observar mirar dormirse decirme

Modelo

mirar
La profesora está mirando a la clase.

 3 Hablar

Práctica de gramática

Indica quién está haciendo cada cosa en tu clase en este momento.

Modelo

escribir en su cuaderno
Laura y Miguel están escribiendo en su cuaderno.
o: *Nadie está escribiendo en su cuaderno.*

1. ayudar a otro estudiante
2. recoger los papeles del piso
3. limpiar su escritorio
4. leer el libro de español
5. poner sus cosas en la mochila

doscientos uno **201**
Capítulo 5

Enriching Your Teaching

Teacher-to-Teacher

Remind students that Spanish speakers use the present progressive in slightly different situations than do English speakers. Unless the action is happening right at the moment, Spanish speakers generally use the simple present tense. However, to emphasize that an action is taking place now, the present progressive can be used. Many English speakers tend to overuse the present progressive when speaking Spanish. Encourage students to avoid this habit and use the simple present.

Vocabulario

personas
los ancianos
la gente pobre
el niño, la niña
el paramédico,
   la paramédica
la víctima
el voluntario,
   la voluntaria

actividades
asistir a
ayudar a los demás
colaborar
conseguir
dar . . .
   ayuda
   dinero
   juguetes
   ropa
ganar dinero
hacer trabajo
   voluntario
investigar
llenar
pagar
participar
permitir
planear
recoger basura
registrar

lugares
el aeropuerto
la agencia de viajes
el club atlético
el consultorio
el laboratorio
el mercado
el quiosco
el salón de belleza

desastres
el accidente
la explosión
el huracán
el incendio
la inundación
el terremoto
la tormenta

expresiones
¿cómo se hace . . .?
ganarse la vida
no te olvides de . . .
seguir una
   carrera

 Escribir ....

Práctica de vocabulario

Haz una tabla como la de abajo. Escribe tres lugares de tu comunidad donde se pueda hacer trabajo voluntario. Al lado de cada lugar escribe qué trabajo se puede hacer y para qué o quién.

Lugar	Trabajo	Para quién / qué
el hospital	jugar	los niños enfermos

202 doscientos dos
A ver si recuerdas . . .

  Hablar ....

Práctica de vocabulario

Tu compañero(a) trabaja como voluntario(a).

❶ Pregúntale:
 • dónde trabaja
 • qué hace allí
 • a quién ayuda

❷ Tu compañero(a) te invita a trabajar con él (ella). Acepta la invitación o da una excusa.

Universal Access

Heritage Language Learners
Invite students who have lived in a heritage country to tell about volunteer work there. Encourage them to tell about the qualities needed in a person who does that kind of work.

Students with Learning Difficulties
If students have difficulty completing the chart independently, provide them with a partially completed chart and give some clues to help them finish it. For example, complete the **Lugar** column and then ask: *¿Qué trabajo se puede hacer allí?*

Gramática · Repaso

Dónde van los pronombres reflexivos y de complemento

Reflexive pronouns, as well as direct and indirect object pronouns, may be placed either before a verb or after it.

- When there are two verbs, as with a participle or an infinitive, the pronoun may come either before the first verb or after the second verb.

  Estamos divirtiéndo**nos** mucho.
  Nos estamos divirtiendo mucho.
  Voy a acostar**me** temprano.
  Me voy a acostar temprano.

- If the sentence is negative, place the pronoun between *no* and the verb.

  No **me** estoy aburriendo.
  No **las** voy a comprar.

- In affirmative commands, pronouns are attached to the end of the verb.

  Carlos, despiér**te**te.
  Chicos, láven**se** las manos.
  ¿Los niños? Cuída**los**.
  ¿El parque? Límpie**lo**.

- In negative commands, place the pronoun between *no* and the verb.

  Esa película es mala. No **la** veas.

- Notice that written accent marks must often be added when a pronoun is attached to a verb.

  Recoge la basura.   **Recógela.**
  Estoy lavando los platos. Estoy **lavándolos.**

 Leer/Escribir

Práctica de gramática

El señor Díaz es el director de un centro de ayuda y da muchos mandatos. Usa los verbos y el pronombre apropiado para completar los mandatos que les dio a sus voluntarios.

recoger limpiar servir abrir ayudar lavarse

Modelo

¿Los libros? _____ en la biblioteca.
¿Los libros? Pónganlos en la biblioteca.

1. ¿La comida? _____ al mediodía y _____ las manos antes de servirla.
2. ¿Las ventanas? No _____ ahora.
3. ¿La basura? No _____ ahora.
4. ¿Los niños? _____ con la tarea.
5. ¿El comedor? _____ después del almuerzo.

 Escribir

Práctica de gramática

Escribe cinco metas *(goals)* que quieres alcanzar *(reach)* este año. Usa los pronombres apropiados.

Modelo

No voy a quejarme. / No me voy a quejar.
Quiero ayudar a los niños. / Quiero ayudarlos.

● **Más práctica** ....
Practice Workbook 5-1, 5-2

For: More review
Visit: www.phschool.com
Web Code: jed-0501

doscientos tres **203**
Capítulo 5

Enriching Your Teaching

Teacher-to-Teacher

Assign a different everyday object to each student. Have them write as many commands as they can telling one person typical things to do and not do with the object, using a direct object pronoun each time: *la botella* – *Ábrela.*

Ciérrala. Llénala. Vacíala. Lávala. Recíclala. No la tires a la basura. For additional practice, have students repeat the commands using the **Uds.** forms.

5 **Preview**

 **Standards for Foreign Language Learning: *Capítulo* 5**

• To achieve the goals of the Standards, students will:

Communication

1.1 Interpersonal

• Talk about work, job searches, and employment types, sites, and skills
• Talk about personality traits
• Talk about community gardens
• Talk about emergencies, volunteer community organizations, and community activism
• Talk about songs with social content
• Talk about the contributions of the Spanish-speaking community in the United States

1.2 Interpretive

• Read and listen to information about work, job searches, and employment types, sites, and skills
• Read and listen to information about personality traits
• Read about community gardens
• Read and listen to information about emergencies, volunteer community organizations, and community activism
• Read about noun suffixes
• Read about known artists and poets
• Read about the contributions of the Spanish-speaking community in the United States
• Read about the Peace Boat program
• Read about songs with social content
• Read about campaigning for a public office
• Read fiction by María Luisa Góngora Pacheco

1.3 Presentational

• Write about work, job searches, and employment types, sites, and skills
• Write about what is happening right now
• Write about personality traits and personal goals
• Recite a poem by Antonio Machado
• Write about volunteer community organizations
• Write about the contributions of the Spanish-speaking community in the United States
• Present a campaign speech
• Write a cover letter for a job solicitation

Culture

2.1 Practices and Perspectives

• Explain community gardens in Latin America
• Explain teenage employment in Latin America
• Explain the contributions of the Spanish-speaking community in the United States
• Explain the Peace Boat Program
• Explain Latin American folk music
• Explain the role of indigenous Latin American writers

2.2 Products and Perspectives

• Discuss the poetry of Antonio Machado and the stories of María Luisa Góngora Pacheco
• Talk about the murals of Diego Rivera
• Talk about community organizations for Spanish-speakers in the United States

Connections

3.1 Cross-curricular

• Discuss key facts about community activities
• Discuss key facts about Latin American teenagers
• Discuss key facts about Spanish and Latin American poetry, fiction, music, and visual art

Fondo cultural ■◆◇◇■◆◇◇■◆

Jardines comunitarios En algunos pueblos de América Latina, muchas de las casas tienen pequeños jardines. A veces, dos o más casas comparten un jardín y las familias trabajan juntas para cuidarlo. Pueden sembrar *(to plant)* flores o plantas, como las toronjas *(grapefruits)* que ves en este cuadro de Rufino Tamayo (1899–1991).

• ¿Hay un jardín en tu comunidad que se comparte entre familias? ¿Qué plantas tiene?

La vendedora de toronjas, (1958), Rufino Tamayo
(c) 2004 Artists Rights Society ARS, NY. (c) Art Resource, NY.

Universal Access

Personalizing the Theme

Ask students to describe the personal rewards that come from doing volunteer work. Ask: *¿Hay cosas que uno puede aprender de los trabajos comunitarios? ¿Cuáles son? ¿Cómo te sientes cuando haces algo bueno para tu comunidad?*

Multiple Intelligences

Naturalist: Students may be aware of and interested in community gardens in their neighborhoods, but not know the names of the plants and flowers found there. Ask them to research some local plants and flowers and give a short presentation to the group about these.

Capítulo 5

Trabajo y comunidad

Chapter Objectives

- **Talk about ways of getting a job**
- **Describe skills and abilities needed to perform a job**
- **Talk about opportunities for volunteer work in your community**
- **Explain how you can help your community**
- **Understand cultural perspectives on dealing with student jobs and volunteer work**

Video Focus

- **Student volunteer work**

Country Connection

As you learn about jobs and volunteer work, you will make connections to these countries and places.

Go Online PHSchool.com

For: Online Atlas
Visit: www.phschool.com
Web Code: jee-0002

doscientos cinco **205**
Capítulo 5

Standards for Foreign Language Learning (cont'd)

- Discuss key facts about Spanish-speaking public figures
- Discuss key facts about the Peace Boat Program
- Discuss Language Arts strategies: scanning, reading for comprehension, using visual aids, writing to persuade, using context clues

3.2 Target Culture
- Read a poem excerpt by Antonio Machado
- Read a story by María Luisa Góngora Pacheco

Comparisons
4.1 Language
- Compare Spanish words to their English counterparts
- Compare the English pluperfect tense to the Spanish *pluscuamperfecto*
- Compare the Spanish present perfect subjunctive to its expression in English

4.2 Culture
- Compare Latin American community gardens to those in the United States
- Compare Latin American teenage employment to that in the United States
- Compare Latin American songs with social content to those in English
- Compare centers in the United States Spanish-speaking community to those of society in general

Communities
5.1 Beyond the School
- Discuss how to get involved in community activities and volunteer work
- Discuss job solicitation skills
- Link to Web sites from around the Spanish-speaking world

5.2 Lifelong Learner
- Develop an appreciation for poetry and fiction
- Discuss the value of community activity
- Discuss campaigning for a public office

Chapter Opener
Presentation

Resources: Voc. & Gram. Transparencies: 14, 15, 16, 20, 22 (maps)

Suggestions: Discuss the chapter theme and go over the objectives. Point out that students will improve their ability to talk and write about jobs and community work.

Enriching Your Teaching

Planning for Instruction
Resources:
- Teacher Express Pro CD-ROM or Resource Book
  - Teaching resources
  - Lesson Planner
  - Chapter Resource Checklist
  - School-to-Home Connection Letter

 **Culture Note**
In Buenos Aires, community gardens are moving from the suburbs to the city itself. Since the mid 1990s, 450,000 *huertas* or garden plots have been created within Buenos Aires. Cooperatively organized by families, schools, or community groups, these 4,000 hectares of gardens provide vegetables to city residents.

Fondo cultural *Standards:* 1.1, 1.2, 2.1, 3.1, 4.2

Resources: Fine Art Transparencies; Fine Art Transparencies Teacher's Guide

Suggestions: Ask students if they are familiar with a community garden and how it works.

Answers will vary.

Vocabulario y gramática

Presentation

Standards: 1.1, 1.2

Resources: Voc. & Gram. Transparencies: 103–104; Resource Book: Cap. 5, Input Script; Audio Program: CD Cap. 5, Track 1

Focus: Presenting new vocabulary and using grammar lexically in context

Suggestions: *El/la salvavidas* is another common form of *el/la salvavida.* Some heritage speakers may be more familiar with the former version. For visualized vocabulary such as *la salvavida, la recepcionista, la clienta,* and *el mensajero,* point to the image on *Vocabulary & Grammar Transparencies* 103–104, say the word, and have students repeat. Meaning of other vocabulary can be clarified through demonstration or explanations in Spanish. For example: *El salario es el dinero que recibe el empleado por su trabajo.*

A primera vista 1

Vocabulario y gramática en contexto

Objectives

Read, listen to, and understand information about
- getting a job
- skills and abilities needed to perform a job
- interviewing techniques

¿Has trabajado alguna vez? ¿Qué trabajo has tenido? Muchas personas **suelen** usar sus **habilidades** y sus cualidades para encontrar un trabajo que les guste, como es el caso de Miguel. A Miguel le encantan los deportes. Este verano había decidido conseguir un trabajo. Buscó en el periódico algunos trabajos que le parecieron interesantes. Sigamos a Miguel en su búsqueda.

1 Primero, **se presentó** para un trabajo en un club deportivo.

la salvavida

la recepcionista

Club Deportivo Buena Vista

2 Luego, tuvo una **entrevista** con **el gerente** del club, pero no consiguió **el puesto** porque no tenía experiencia en **computación**.

¿Sabes trabajar con programas de computadora?

206 doscientos seis
A primera vista 1

Universal Access

Students with Learning Difficulties

Help students improve their reading comprehension by discussing the boldfaced vocabulary items prior to reading each paragraph. After previewing the vocabulary, have them predict what information will be discussed in the paragraph. After reading, help them confirm and correct their predictions.

Advanced Learners

Have pairs of students prepare and present mini-dialogues. One partner plays the role of an applicant and asks a question about the job. The other plays the prospective employer and answers the question.

3 Miguel también se había entrevistado para un trabajo de **niñero**, pero era **a tiempo completo** y él buscaba un trabajo **a tiempo parcial**.

4 En el periódico había visto un trabajo de **consejero** a tiempo parcial, pero **el salario** era muy bajo.

5 Miguel **siguió solicitando** trabajo por varios días. Finalmente, después de una entrevista con el dueño, el Sr. Urbina, Miguel encontró trabajo en una tienda de equipo deportivo. A Miguel le gusta ayudar a los clientes y le encanta el horario flexible.

la clienta

el dueño

el mensajero

 Escuchar/Hablar

¿Dónde hay trabajo?

Primero, escucha las frases e indica sobre qué ilustración habla cada una. Luego, di por qué Miguel consiguió o no consiguió ese puesto.

 Escribir

Las búsquedas de Miguel

En una hoja de papel, escribe los números del 1 al 4. Lee cada una de estas frases y escribe *C* (cierto) o *F* (falso). Vuelve a escribir cada frase falsa para que sea verdadera.

1. Miguel encontró trabajo como recepcionista.
2. Miguel se entrevistó para trabajar de niñero.
3. Miguel solicitó trabajos por varios días.
4. Miguel buscaba un trabajo a tiempo completo.

Actividad 1 *Standards:* 1.2

Resources: Audio Program: CD Cap. 5, Track 2; Resource Book: Cap. 5, Audio Script; Practice Answers on Transparencies

Focus: Practicing listening comprehension of new vocabulary

Suggestions: Use the *Audio CD* or the script. Allow students to listen more than once. Remind them not to try to listen to every word, but rather for key words that will help them determine the main idea. Pause frequently to allow them to write the information.

Answers:
1. 4/El salario era muy bajo.
2. 3/El trabajo era a tiempo completo.
3. 2/No tenía experiencia en computación.
4. 5/A Miguel le gusta ayudar a los clientes y el horario es flexible.

Actividad 2 *Standards:* 1.2

Resources: Practice Answers on Transparencies

Focus: Demonstrating comprehension of new vocabulary

Suggestions: Make sure students understand that the statements pertain to the narration on pp. 206–207. Encourage them to read about Miguel again before completing the activity.

Answers:
1. F/ Miguel encontró trabajo como empleado en una tienda de equipo deportivo.
2. C
3. C
4. F/ Miguel buscaba un trabajo a tiempo parcial.

 Enriching Your Teaching

Culture Note

Point out that many Latin American and Spanish work schedules differ from those in the United States. The workday starts later, the lunch break is longer, and the day ends later. Although the total hours worked are about the same, they are more spread out. Many workers still go home to have lunch together with their families. A work day that ends later coincides with the custom in many countries of eating dinner at a later hour than in the United States, often as late as ten o'clock.

207

Vocabulario y gramática

Presentation

Standards: 1.2

Resources: Voc. & Gram. Transparencies: 105; Resource Book: Cap. 5, Input Script; Audio Program: CD Cap. 5, Tracks 3, 5

Focus: Extending presentation of vocabulary and grammar

Suggestions:

Pre-reading: Save the reading of *Los anuncios clasificados* until after students have completed *Actividades* 3 and 4.

Reading: Tell students not to fill out the *encuesta* until they have completed *Actividad* 3.

Post-reading: Use gestures, explanations, and demonstrations to clarify the meaning of the new vocabulary.

Actividad 3

Standards: 1.1, 1.2

Focus: Demonstrating comprehension of a questionnaire

Suggestions: Encourage students to answer honestly. Tell them that more than one answer is possible for each question.

Answers will vary.

Actividad 4

Standards: 1.2

Resources: Audio Program: CD Cap. 5, Track 4; Resource Book: Cap. 5, Audio Script; Practice Answers on Transparencies

Focus: Demonstrating listening comprehension of new vocabulary

Suggestions: Tell students to refer to the jobs shown on pp. 206–207.

Answers:

Sentences about each job will vary. Students should refer to the following jobs:

1. mensajero
2. salvavida
3. un puesto en el club
4. niñero
5. consejera
6. salvavida

Tú y tus habilidades

Para muchos, el mejor trabajo es aquél donde podemos usar nuestros conocimientos y habilidades. Lee la siguiente encuesta.

1 ¿Cómo eres?

- ❏ cortés
- ❏ agradable
- ❏ eficiente
- ❏ puntual
- ❏ ordenado(a)
- ❏ dedicado(a)
- ❏ flexible
- ❏ práctico(a)
- ❏ honesto(a)
- ❏ responsable
- ❏ considerado(a)
- ❏ amable
- ❏ comprensivo(a)

2 ¿Qué sabes hacer?

- ❏ cocinar
- ❏ hablar otro idioma
- ❏ usar la computadora
- ❏ reparar cosas
- ❏ nadar
- ❏ manejar un coche
- ❏ escribir bien

3 ¿Qué te gusta hacer?

- ❏ atender a la gente
- ❏ trabajar con las manos
- ❏ trabajar en equipo
- ❏ enseñar a los niños
- ❏ cuidar animales
- ❏ practicar deportes
- ❏ viajar
- ❏ leer

4 ¿Qué es más importante para ti?

- ❏ un buen salario
- ❏ un trabajo a tiempo completo
- ❏ un trabajo a tiempo parcial
- ❏ trabajar en una compañía grande
- ❏ trabajar al aire libre
- ❏ trabajar en un lugar agradable
- ❏ un horario flexible
- ❏ buenos beneficios
- ❏ vacaciones largas

 Actividad 3 · Leer/Hablar . . . .

Una encuesta

❶ Escribe tus respuestas a la encuesta en una tabla como ésta.

❷ Túrnate con otro(a) estudiante para hacer y contestar preguntas sobre la información de la encuesta. Usen sus tablas.

Modelo

A —¿Cómo eres?
B —Soy puntual y eficiente.

Soy . . .
Sé . . .
Me gusta . . .
Para mí es importante . . .

Actividad 4 · Escuchar/Escribir . . . .

Conseguir trabajo es un tremendo trabajo

Los estudiantes de la clase de Marcos no saben cuál es el mejor trabajo para ellos. Escribe en una hoja de papel los números del 1 al 6. Escucha lo que cada estudiante dice sobre sus habilidades y sus cualidades y decide cuál es el mejor trabajo para cada uno(a). Luego, describe en una frase cada trabajo que escribiste. Di de qué se trata ese trabajo y dónde se puede hacer.

Modelo

cajero
Un cajero trabaja en una tienda o en un supermercado.

208 doscientos ocho
A primera vista 1

Universal Access

Students with Learning Difficulties

For *Actividad* 4, help students with listening comprehension by playing each speaker's statement once, then pointing out key vocabulary that students should listen for before playing it a second time.

Advanced Learners

Have students create their own classified ads to advertise different job openings. Direct them to use the advertising language in *Los anuncios clasificados* as models for their own work. After checking their work for grammar and spelling, students can present their ads to the rest of the class.

∞ LOS ANUNCIOS CLASIFICADOS ∞

NIÑERO(A) CON EXPERIENCIA

Se necesita persona que tenga experiencia

Requisitos:
2 cartas de recomendación **referencias**

No recibimos solicitudes sin **la fecha nacimiento**.
Llamar al 321-4040

SECRETARIO(A)

Requisitos:

Experiencia mínima de 3 años
Conocimientos de computación
Inglés

Ofrecemos muy buenos beneficios. Interesados favor de llamar al 417-2949 o presentarse en nuestras oficinas de Hernán Cortés No. 24

CAMAREROS

Se solicitan personas con experiencia, que **cumplan** con su trabajo, para trabajar en un restaurante.

Llamar al 554-3434 y pedir una **solicitud de empleo.**

PASEAR PERROS

Se busca persona que le gusten los animales para **encargarse de** pasear a 3 perros.

Horario flexible, buen salario.

Llamar al 462-9032

ENTRENADOR(A)

Club deportivo necesita entrenador(a) para **atender** a nuevos miembros.

Venir a llenar la solicitud de empleo en nuestra oficina de calle Colón #452

REPARTIDOR(A)

Preferible con experiencia en **repartir** cosas en bicicleta. Tiempo parcial.

Enviar por fax solicitud de empleo.

Fax 771-7171

Leer/Escribir

¿Comprendes?

1. ¿Qué requisitos se solicitan generalmente en un anuncio clasificado?

2. ¿Qué cualidades se buscan generalmente en un empleado? ¿Por qué?

3. ¿Por qué es importante cumplir con el trabajo en un empleo?

4. Escoge tres de los trabajos y explica de qué se encargan las personas que hacen esos trabajos.

● **Más práctica**
Practice Workbook 5-3, 5-4

Go Online
PHSchool.com

For: Vocabulary practice
Visit: www.phschool.com
Web Code: jed-0502

doscientos nueve **209**
Capítulo 5

Standards: 1.2, 1.3

Resources: Voc. & Gram. Transparencies: 106

Focus: Demonstrating reading comprehension of classified ads

Suggestions: Before having students complete the activity, allow them to review the classified ads on p. 209.

Answers will vary. For item 1, students may mention: *una carta de recomendación, referencias, experiencia,* and so on.

Additional Resources
• Resource Book: Cap. 5, Clip Art

✓ Assessment
• Prueba 5-1: Vocabulary recognition

Teacher-to-Teacher

If possible, bring in Spanish-language newspapers. Some of your students or colleagues may be able to help you obtain them. Allow students time to pass the papers around and get an idea of their various features, including classified ads.

Chapter Project

Give students copies of the Chapter Project outline and rubric from the *Teacher's Resource Book*. Explain the task to them, and have them perform step 1. (For more information, see p. 200-a.)

Enriching Your Teaching

Culture Note
In Buenos Aires, Argentina, a common, after-school and weekend job for many young people is that of merchandise stocker. Companies hire young people to travel from store to store and stock candy, gum and other items at franchise sales displays in supermarkets and department stores. Workers usually work in teams of two.

Internet Search
Keyword: | trabajos para jóvenes |

Practice and Communicate

(5)

Actividad 6

Standards: 1.2

Resources: Audio Program: CD Cap. 5, Track 6; Resource Book: Cap. 5, Audio Script; Practice Answers on Transparencies

Focus: Practicing listening comprehension of new vocabulary

Suggestions: Before students listen to the statements, have them take a minute to look over the drawing.

Answers:
1. la Sra. Bonilla (mamá): dueña, tiene muchos clientes
2. Celia (hermana): la gerente, responsable, puntual y dedicada
3. Jorge (hermano menor): repartidor, está reparando su bicicleta
4. Laura (yo): niñera, me gusta visitar a mamá
5. Eduardo (tío): mensajero, ayuda mucho a mamá

Actividad 7

Standards: 1.2

Resources: Practice Answers on Transparencies

Focus: Practicing new vocabulary in a cloze exercise

Suggestions: Have students review the vocabulary on pp. 206–209 before completing the activity.

Answers:
1. requisitos
2. conocimientos
3. habilidades
4. una referencia
5. suelen

Actividad 8

Standards: 1.1, 1.3

Focus: Practicing new vocabulary in a paired matching activity

Suggestions: Tell students to trade with their partners only the definitions and not the answer keys they create.

Answers will vary.

Manos a la obra 1

Vocabulario y gramática en uso

Objetivos
- Talk about getting a job
- Describe the skills and abilities needed to perform a job
- Discuss interviewing techniques
- Review the present perfect tense
- Practice the pluperfect tense

Actividad 6 Escuchar/Escribir

¿Quiénes son?

La ilustración a la derecha muestra las personas que trabajan en la florería de la mamá de Laura. Escucha a Laura describir lo que hace cada persona. Identifica quién es cada persona en la ilustración. Luego, escribe dos detalles acerca de cada una.

Actividad 7 Leer/Escribir

Consejos para conseguir un trabajo

Tu amigo(a) busca trabajo. Dale consejos, usando la palabra que mejor complete la definición en la frase.

| una referencia | requisitos | habilidades | suelen | conocimientos |

1. En general, los _____ para conseguir trabajo son: ser paciente, tener habilidades para hacer el trabajo y prepararse para la entrevista.
2. Tienes _____ sobre cine, parece que has visto todas las películas. Quizás te den trabajo en una tienda de videos.
3. ¿Qué puedes hacer bien en este trabajo? ¿Tienes las _____ que se necesitan para hacerlo?
4. A veces en una entrevista te piden _____, como el nombre de una persona que te conoce.
5. Las entrevistas _____ ser formales. Debes vestirte bien.

Actividad 8 Escribir/Hablar

¿Qué quieren decir?

Escribe cinco palabras del vocabulario de las páginas 206–209 en una hoja de papel, y en otra, escribe una definición para cada una. Túrnate con otro(a) estudiante para leer las definiciones de cada uno(a) y digan de qué palabra se trata.

Universal Access

Students with Learning Difficulties
Before playing the audio selection for *Actividad 6*, help students preview some of the target language for which they will be listening. Discuss the illustration with them. Point out and briefly describe the characters, and invite students to add details.

Advanced Learners
Some students may enjoy creating informal quizzes and exercises for other students. Monitor their work carefully for spelling, grammar, and punctuation. Help them write clear and concise instructions, and teach them over time to make their activities neither too difficult nor too easy for their peers.

  **Hablar**

¿En qué te gustaría trabajar?

Imagina que solicitas un puesto de trabajo. Con otro(a) estudiante, piensen en varios trabajos a tiempo parcial, digan cuáles les gustaría hacer y por qué. Decidan qué tipo de trabajo les gustaría más conseguir.

Modelo

A —Dime, ¿qué te gustaría más, trabajar de *gerente* o de *consejero de campamento*?

B —*Me gustaría trabajar de gerente porque soy responsable.* Y a ti, ¿qué te gustaría hacer?

A —*A mí me gustaría trabajar como consejero de campamento. Me gusta mucho trabajar con niños.*

Estudiante A

1.
2.
3.
4.

Estudiante B

¡Respuesta personal!

  Hablar

¿A quién conoces?

Trabaja con otro(a) estudiante. Lean la lista de trabajos y túrnense para hacer preguntas y responderlas.

agente de viajes	reportero(a)	salvavida
gerente	camarero(a)	fotógrafo(a)
bombero(a)	locutor(a)	dentista

Modelo

A —¿A quién conoces que trabaje de *locutor*?
B —*El hermano de María es locutor.*
A —¿De qué *se encarga* él en su trabajo?

Estudiante A

1. ¿A quién conoces que trabaje de (en) . . . ?
2. ¿De qué se encarga esa persona en su trabajo?
3. ¿Qué cualidades y habilidades tiene esa persona?
4. ¿Cuándo suele trabajar?

Estudiante B

¡Respuesta personal!

 Standards: 1.1

Focus: Using new vocabulary and structures in a guided conversation

Recycle: constructions with *gustar*

Suggestions: As you go over the model with students, point out the way in which Student B politely bounces Student A's question back after answering it. Remind students that there are many ways to sustain a conversation. Encourage them to be creative and try different ways whenever they practice dialogues in which the roles are switched.

Common Errors: Some students will try to change *salvavida* to *"salvavido"* in an attempt to give it a masculine gender form. Tell them that, just as with the word *artista*, the word ends in *-a* when applied to either gender. Point out that it is a compound word made from a form of *salvar* plus *vida.*

Answers will vary.

Student A might inquire about the following jobs based on the picture clues:
1. ...de niñero(a) o de mensajero(a)?
2. ...de salvavida o de recepcionista?
3. ...de repartidor(a) o de vendedor(a)?
4. ...de camarero(a) o de cajero(a)?

 Standards: 1.1

Focus: Practicing new vocabulary and structures in a guided conversation

Suggestions: Have students take turns reading the questions aloud and answering them. Encourage them to help each other when they have difficulty answering.

Answers will vary.

Enriching Your Teaching

Teacher-to-Teacher

When students work with partners to practice dialogues and target language, end the activity by inviting pairs to present their dialogues whenever time allows. When practicing with the understanding that they will make a presentation, many students are inclined to extend their conversations and stretch their abilities. Students who find oral presentations too stressful can be assigned to the writing portion of the task.

211

Practice and Communicate

▶ Rapid Review

Review **seguir** + present participle by asking questions about their activities: *Edward, ¿sigues tocando el piano?* Have them reply in a complete sentence: *Sí, sigo tocando el piano.* Students may use the **seguir** + present participle construction in *Actividad* 11.

Standards: 1.1, 1.2, 3.1

Focus: Practicing new vocabulary and structures through reading and response

Suggestions: Refer students to the *Estrategia*. Remind them that classified ads are written for the convenience of the reader: they are categorized, and the information is presented in a similar order each time. Have them scan the ads with these things in mind.

Answers will vary.

Fondo cultural Standards: 1.1, 1.2, 2.1, 4.2

Suggestions: After students have read the information, ask: *¿Cuál es la edad oficial para poder empezar a trabajar en los Estados Unidos? En general, ¿qué creen los padres latinoamericanos que es más importante para los jóvenes: que estudien o que ganen dinero? ¿Cómo gastan los jóvenes latinoamericanos el dinero que ganan? ¿Piensan que lo gastan de la misma manera que los jóvenes de los Estados Unidos?*

Answers will vary.

Standards: 1.1, 1.3

Focus: Practicing new vocabulary and structures by writing a classified ad

Suggestions: For step 2, have students build their interviews around an ad that another group wrote.

Answers will vary.

  Leer/Escribir/Hablar

El mejor trabajo para ti

SECRETARIO(A) RECEPCIONISTA
Requisitos indispensables: Experiencia mínima de 2 años, extremadamente responsable y puntual, 2 cartas de recomendación con número telefónico, nivel intermedio de inglés y de preferencia domicilio particular cercano a nuestra zona en Distrito Federal, México.

MENSAJERO(A) / REPARTIDOR(A)
Se necesitan personas activas, excelente orientación de servicio, con iniciativa y muy responsables, para cumplir funciones de mensajero(a) y repartidor(a) motorizado(a). Se requiere la licencia de manejar correspondiente. Enviar currículum. Santiago, Chile

EMPLEADO(A) DOMÉSTICO(A)
Agencia Doña Miriam necesita urgente personas para trabajar en casas, cocinar y niñeros(as). Salarios C$1000 a C$2000. Tel 249-3736. Nicaragua

SALVAVIDAS
AQUASWIM SL necesita 25 salvavidas para trabajar la temporada de verano en la Comunidad de Madrid. Si estás interesado(a) en trabajar con nosotros, ponte en contacto llamando al tlf. 605587464. España

Estrategia
Scanning
Scanning a text such as an ad may help you to get key information.

1 Haz una lista de las habilidades y cualidades necesarias para cada trabajo mencionado en los anuncios clasificados.

2 Escoge un anuncio y escribe un mínimo de cinco preguntas para hacer una entrevista a una persona que se presenta para el puesto. Puedes preguntar datos como el horario que puede trabajar, el salario, su experiencia anterior y sus habilidades.

3 Entrevista a otro(a) estudiante para ese puesto. Luego, cambien de papeles.

Modelo
Para el puesto de secretaria:
A —*¿Trabajó usted de secretaria antes?*
B —*Sí, trabajo en una compañía desde el verano pasado.*
A —*¿Sigue trabajando allí?*
B —*Sí, pero el horario no es muy flexible.*
A —*¿Qué habilidades tiene?*
B —*Sé computación, hablo español e inglés y escribo bien en los dos idiomas.*

El trabajo y la juventud En América Latina, la edad oficial para poder empezar a trabajar suele ser 15 años. Pero socialmente no se ve bien que un joven trabaje porque los padres piensan que interfiere con la vida escolar. En todo caso, se ven jóvenes haciendo trabajos a tiempo parcial, tales como llenar bolsas para los clientes en el supermercado o servir en los restaurantes de comida rápida. Los jóvenes usan el dinero de sus salarios para salir a divertirse o comprarse cosas.

• ¿Qué piensa la gente en los Estados Unidos de los jóvenes que tienen un trabajo a tiempo parcial?

212 doscientos doce
Manos a la obra 1

Universal Access

Heritage Language Learners
Invite students who have lived in heritage countries to share their background knowledge about typical employment for young people there. Encourage them to tell about the duties, schedules, and pay rates of the various kinds of jobs.

Students with Learning Difficulties
Give each student a photocopy of one of the classified ads. Have them use a colored highlighter to shade the key words and phrases in their ad. Then have them exchange ads with a partner and analyze the partner's markings. Finally, have them scan an unmarked ad and orally share the key information.

Actividad 12 Hablar/Escribir ·········

Un anuncio clasificado

❶ Trabaja con cuatro estudiantes para escribir un anuncio clasificado. Sigan los siguientes pasos.

* Escojan un trabajo que puede hacer un estudiante y digan de qué se va a encargar.
* Determinen el horario y si el trabajo es a tiempo completo o a tiempo parcial.
* Incluyan los beneficios y el salario.
* Hagan una lista de los requisitos y de lo que el (la) candidato(a) debe llevar a la entrevista.
* Escriban el anuncio.

❷ La clase va a participar en una feria de trabajo (job fair). Cada grupo va a poner su anuncio clasificado en las paredes de la clase. Los estudiantes van a escoger un anuncio y turnarse para hacer los papeles de la persona que hace la entrevista y el (la) candidato(a).

Actividad 13 Hablar/Escribir ·········

Y tú, ¿qué dices?

1. ¿Tienes un trabajo después de las clases? ¿Qué haces? ¿Tienes un horario flexible?

2. En tu opinión, ¿cuáles son tus habilidades? Haz una lista.

3. ¿Cuáles son algunos beneficios de tener un trabajo a tiempo parcial?

4. ¿Trabajaste alguna vez como niñera(o) o salvavida? ¿Sigues haciendo ese trabajo? ¿Por qué?

5. ¿Qué tres consejos puedes dar a un(a) estudiante de tu clase que busca trabajo?

6. Escribe un párrafo en el que describas otro trabajo que hiciste y si cumpliste con lo que te pidieron. Explica qué te gustó más de ese trabajo.

Ampliación del lenguaje

Muchos sustantivos (nouns) que terminan con el sufijo *-ero, -era* se refieren a profesiones relacionadas con los sustantivos de los que se derivan.
Por ejemplo, el sustantivo *niñera(o)* nombra a la persona que cuida a niños.
Lee las palabras de la tabla siguiente y luego completa las frases.

Sustantivo	Profesión
mensaje	mensajero(a)
caja	cajero(a)
consejo	consejero(a)
carta	cartero(a)
leche	lechero(a)
niño	niñero(a)

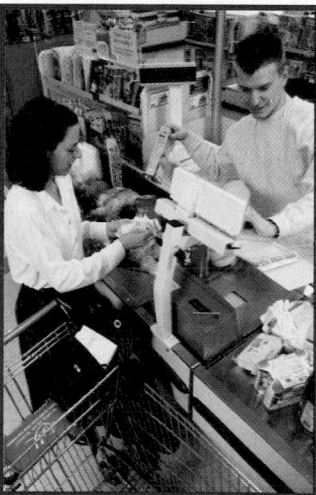

Cristina me escribió una __1.__ hace una semana. El __2.__ la dejó hoy en mi buzón.

Después de comprar la comida en el supermercado, fuimos a pagar a la __3.__ . El __4.__ tomó nuestro dinero y puso la comida en unas bolsas.

doscientos trece **213**
Capítulo 5

Actividad 13 Standards: 1.1, 1.3

Focus: Practicing new vocabulary and structures through discussion and writing

Suggestions: Have students discuss the questions orally first. This will prepare them for writing their answers. For item 1, be prepared to help students name their job in Spanish. You might have to consult a dictionary, a colleague, or another source.

Answers will vary.

Extension: Assign two or more students to be reporters of the *feria de trabajo* in *Actividad* 12. The group can videotape the various interviews and present them in the format of a news feature about the *feria*. Ask them to provide a brief introduction and a conclusion.

Ampliación del lenguaje

Presentation

Standards: 1.2, 4.1

Resources: Practice Answers on Transparencies

Focus: Understanding the noun suffixes *-ero* and *-era.*

Suggestions: For each example, ask students to use both the noun and the noun + *-ero(a)* suffix in a sentence: *Un cartero reparte cartas.*

Answers:
1. carta
2. cartero
3. caja
4. cajero

Additional Resources

* Writing, Audio & Video Workbook: Cap. 5, Audio Activity 1, Track 7
* Writing, Audio & Video Workbook: Cap. 5, Writing Activity 6
* Resource Book: Cap. 5, Communicative Activity BLM

 Assessment
* Prueba 5-2: Vocabulary production

Enriching Your Teaching

Teacher-to-Teacher

Group projects like the *feria de trabajo* in *Actividad* 12 elicit language that goes far beyond the task at hand. In order to work together, students will need to make affirmative and negative commands and to use the subjunctive in order to express necessities and preferences. Monitor them as they work and provide models of language that will help them in task-oriented communication.

Practice and Communicate

⑤

Gramática

Presentation

Standards: 4.1

Resources: Voc. & Gram. Transparencies: 107

Suggestions: Ask students to write complete, original sentences in the present perfect tense using the irregular past participles shown in the *Gramática*.

Actividad 14

Standards: 1.2

Resources: Practice Answers on Transparencies

Focus: Practicing the present perfect tense in a cloze exercise

Suggestions: Have students check their answers by reading each completed item aloud. Remind them that the initial *h-* in the forms of **haber** is always silent.

Answers:
1. ha ido
2. he respondido
3. me he puesto
4. ha dicho
5. he dado
6. ha leído

Additional Resources

• Writing, Audio & Video Workbook: Cap. 5, Audio Activity 2, Track 8

Chapter Project

Students can perform step 2 at this point. Be sure they understand your corrections and suggestions. (For more information, see p. 200-a.)

214

Gramática · Repaso

El presente perfecto

To form the present perfect tense, combine the present tense of the verb *haber* with a past participle. You generally use the Spanish present perfect in the same way you use its English equivalent.

No **he reparado** la bicicleta todavía.
I haven't repaired the bicycle yet.

¿Qué trabajos **has tenido?**
*What jobs **have you had?***

Here are the present perfect forms of *hablar.*

he hablado	hemos hablado
has hablado	habéis hablado
ha hablado	han hablado

• Recall that to form the past participle of a verb in Spanish, you add *-ado* to the stem of *-ar* verbs and *-ido* to the stem of *-er* and *-ir* verbs.

hablar → hablado   comer → comido
vivir → vivido

• Verbs that have two vowels in the infinitive form (except for *ui*) require an accent mark on the *í* in the past participle.

caer → caído   oír → oído
traer → traído   reír → reído
leer → leído   creer → creído

• Many Spanish verbs have irregular past participles. You have already learned some of these.

abrir → **abierto**   resolver → **resuelto**
decir → **dicho**   romper → **roto**
escribir → **escrito**   ser → **sido**
morir → **muerto**   ver → **visto**
poner → **puesto**

• Place negative words, object pronouns, and reflexive pronouns before the form of *haber.*

No he repartido las flores todavía.

Mi profesora **me** ha escrito una carta de recomendación.

El dueño **se** ha ido temprano a la oficina.

Actividad 14  **Leer/Escribir**

Después de la entrevista

Tamara y Juan fueron a una entrevista de trabajo. Completa la conversación que tuvieron con el presente perfecto de los verbos del recuadro.

decir	ir	dar	ponerse	leer	responder

—Juan, ¿cómo te ___**1.**___ esta manaña en la entrevista?

—Creo que no muy bien, Tamara. No ___**2.**___ a todas las preguntas.

—Yo tampoco. Además, ___**3.**___ muy nerviosa. El gerente quería gente con mucha experiencia.

—Sí, Tamara. Él me ___**4.**___ que buscaba jóvenes muy ordenados, puntuales y responsables.

—Yo le ___**5.**___ mis referencias, pero él no las ___**6.**___. Dijo que no las necesitaba.

—Bueno, a ver qué pasa . . .

214 doscientos catorce
Manos a la obra 1

Universal Access

Students with Learning Difficulties
Allow students who have difficulty reciting in front of others to record on audiocassette their recitations of the Machado poem on p. 215. You may wish to have them recite only one stanza of the poem.

Advanced Learners
Have students use the present perfect tense to tell about five things they have done that qualify them either for the job they actually have or for a job they would like to have: *Quiero ser cajera. He trabajado de cajera en la tienda de mis padres. Mi papá me ha enseñado a usar la caja...*

 **Gramática** **Escribir/Hablar/GramActiva** •••••••••••••••••

Juego

Vas a jugar con los(as) compañeros(as) de tu clase.

❶ Escribe siete preguntas para saber si tus compañeros(as) han hecho o no cosas como *trabajar en un parque de diversiones*. Para hacer tus preguntas, usa el presente perfecto de los verbos.

❷ Con otro(a) estudiante, haz y contesta las preguntas. Para conectar tus respuestas, puedes usar las siguientes palabras o expresiones.

no . . . todavía	muchas veces	varias veces	casi siempre
casi nunca	de vez en cuando	algunas veces	una vez

❸ La clase forma dos círculos concéntricos con los estudiantes cara a cara. Al oír música, los estudiantes se mueven a la derecha. Al parar la música, deben parar y hacerle una pregunta al (a la) estudiante que tienen enfrente usando el presente perfecto. Al terminar el juego, el profesor te va a hacer preguntas sobre las respuestas de tus compañeros(as).

Modelo

A —¿Has trabajado en un parque de diversiones alguna vez?
B —Sí, trabajé una vez en el verano.

En voz alta ••••••••••

El poeta español Antonio Machado (1875 – 1939) escribió poemas sencillos y hermosos que comenzaron a aparecer en España en 1901. En sus poemas, Machado parece estar hablando de sus experiencias y de las de todo el pueblo[1] español al mismo tiempo. Sus poemas hacen homenaje[2] al hombre común y su voz es a menudo la de todo el pueblo. Es por esto que todavía es el poeta de su época que más lectores ha tenido.

En *Soledades y Campos de Castilla*, Machado hace un retrato cariñoso pero crítico de la España de su época. El poema al que pertenecen estos fragmentos es un ejemplo de la manera en que Machado retrataba al hombre común. Lee los versos y trata de repetirlos en voz alta.

—————————————————————
1 people 2 pay tribute to

• ¿Crees que el autor del poema es una persona mayor o un joven? Explica por qué.

• ¿Cómo te sientes después de leer los fragmentos del poema? ¿Qué frases te hablan de cómo ve la vida el poeta?

¿Recuerdas?
Cuando la consonante *r* va entre vocales, su sonido es similar a la "dd" en la palabra inglesa *ladder*. Repite estas palabras del poema: *veredas, mares, caravanas.*

He andado muchos caminos
de Antonio Machado

He andado muchos caminos,
he abierto muchas veredas[3],
he navegado en cien mares,
y atracado[4] en cien riberas[5] . . .

Y en todas partes he visto
gentes que danzan o juegan,
cuando pueden, y laboran
sus cuatro palmos[6] de tierra.

Son buenas gentes que viven,
laboran, pasan y sueñan,
y un día como tantos,
descansan bajo la tierra.

Antonio Machado, Ignacio Rived

—————————————————————
3 trails 4 moored 5 shores 6 spans

 Standards: 1.1, 1.3
•••••••••••••••

Focus: Practicing the present perfect tense through questions and answers

Suggestions: By step 3, students should be ready to ask one of the questions they wrote or responded to in the earlier steps. Since they have had some practice, encourage them to invent new, spontaneous questions when they are in the double-circle formation.

Answers will vary.

En voz alta
Presentation

Standards: 1.2, 1.3, 2.2, 3.1, 3.2, 5.2

Resources: Audio Program: CD Cap. 5, Track 9

Suggestions: Have students read the information and the poem silently. Ask comprehension questions: *Según el texto, de todos los poetas españoles de la época de Machado, ¿quién ha tenido el mayor número de lectores? ¿A qué obra pertenecen los fragmentos del texto?*

Before having students recite the poem, direct their attention to the information in the *¿Recuerdas?* Have students repeat your models of words with the intervocalic *r* sound, such as the names of jobs they studied in the *Ampliación del lenguaje* on p. 213: *mensajera, cajero, consejero, cartero, lechero,* and *niñera.* Then allow them a few minutes to practice reciting the poem excerpt with a partner.

Answers will vary.

Enriching Your Teaching

Culture Note
Antonio Machado belongs to the Generation of 1898, a group of Spanish writers whose work is marked by reflections on personal and national identity. In Machado's lifetime, Spain underwent enormous political upheaval—revolution, loss of its remaining colonial empire, and a civil war that drove Machado to die in exile.

Teacher-to-Teacher
Many students take pleasure in the practice and perfection of the sounds of a new language. Encourage them by setting up a regularly scheduled recital period. Aside from pronunciation practice, regular recitals or readings of poetry, song lyrics, or fiction excerpts strengthen students' reading skills.

Block Schedule
•••••••••••••••••

After completing *En voz alta,* have students write their own version of the first stanza of the poem. Model it after the Machado poem using the present perfect tense as he did. Have students read their poems aloud in small groups.

215

Actividad 16 Standards: 1.2, 1.3

Focus: Practicing the present perfect tense through reading and writing about jobs and job qualifications

Suggestions: Remind students that in real life a paragraph like the one they are writing has the value of creating a favorable first impression.

Answers will vary.

Actividad 17 Standards: 1.2, 1.3

Focus: Practicing the present perfect tense in guided conversations

Suggestions: For step 3, remind students that most Spanish speakers would address each other with **Ud.** rather than **tú** during an interview.

Answers will vary.

Fondo cultural Standards: 1.1, 1.2

Resource: Practice Answers on Transparencies

Suggestions: After students have read the information, ask them to name other prominent people of Spanish or Latin American heritage in the United States. Have them tell what each person does or has done.

Answers will vary.

Additional Resources

• Writing, Audio & Video Workbook: Cap. 5, Writing Activity 7

Assessment
• Prueba 5-3: *El presente perfecto*

Actividad 16 Gramática **Leer/Escribir**

¿Cómo te describes a ti mismo?

Imagina que estás buscando trabajo y lees en el periódico este anuncio clasificado. Para contestar al anuncio, escribe un breve párrafo sobre tus cualidades y las cosas que has hecho hasta ahora. Si no te interesa este trabajo, escoge uno de los trabajos que se anuncian en la página 209.

> Se busca joven responsable y cortés para trabajar en un campamento de verano. Debe gustarle la naturaleza y los niños.
> Enviar breve párrafo describiendo sus cualidades y lo que ha hecho en materia de trabajo y estudio.

Modelo

Mi nombre es Enrique y he trabajado con niños desde que tengo 12 años. Siempre he sido responsable, puntual y he cumplido con mi trabajo.

Actividad 17 Gramática **Escribir/Hablar**

Preparación para una entrevista

① Haz una lista de cinco cosas que has hecho para prepararte para una entrevista.

Modelo

He leído los anuncios clasificados.

② Piensa en un trabajo específico y escribe cinco preguntas que puedan hacerte en la entrevista.

③ Ensaya la entrevista con otro(a) estudiante.

La Fundación de Premios de Herencia Hispana (*Hispanic Heritage Awards Foundation*) es una organización establecida para promover una mayor comprensión de las contribuciones que han hecho los hispanoamericanos a los Estados Unidos. Cada año, la Fundación premia a hispanoamericanos prominentes, entre ellos, científicos, artistas y atletas. Los ganadores suelen ser profesionales y líderes que se han destacado en su campo profesional. Una de las ganadoras del Premio fue Ellen Ochoa, una astronauta de NASA. Otros ganadores anteriores incluyen Oscar Hijuelos (literatura) y Sammy Sosa (deportes).

• ¿Qué otros premios conoces que reconozcan a personas que se han destacado en sus profesiones?

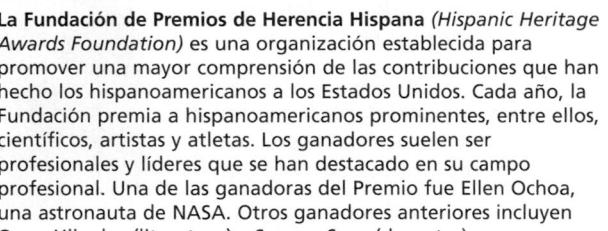
Dra. Ellen Ochoa

● **Más práctica**
Practice Workbook 5-5

For: Practice with the present perfect
Visit: www.phschool.com
Web Code: jed-0503

Universal Access

Heritage Language Learners
Have students pretend they are announcers presenting a Hispanic Heritage Award to an accomplished member of the Hispanic American community in the United States. Encourage them to use target language from the chapter. Provide feedback on errors they may make.

Students with Learning Difficulties
Have students work with a partner to complete steps 1 and 2 of *Actividad* 17. Allow partners to prepare one set of questions that can be used twice.

Gramática

El pluscuamperfecto

You use the pluperfect tense to describe an action in the past that occurred *before* another action in the past. To form the pluperfect tense, combine the imperfect tense of the verb *haber* with a past participle. You generally use the Spanish pluperfect in the same way you use its English equivalent.

Cuando llegué a la oficina, el gerente ya **había leído** mis cartas de recomendación.

*When I arrived in the office, the manager **had** already **read** my letters of recommendation.*

Después de la entrevista, yo estaba muy nerviosa porque la dueña de la compañía me **había pedido** referencias.

*After the interview, I was feeling nervous because the owner of the company **had asked** me for references.*

Here are the pluperfect forms of *hablar*:

había hablado	habíamos hablado
habías hablado	habíais hablado
había hablado	habían hablado

 18 Gramática Leer/Escribir

En la agencia de empleos

Jorge y Agustín fueron a una agencia de empleos a pedir trabajo. Completa las siguientes frases con los verbos del recuadro en la forma correcta del pluscuamperfecto.

encargarse	tener	escribir	llenar
pedir	atender	cumplir	solicitar

1. Antes de ir a la agencia, Jorge y Agustín _____ varias solicitudes de empleo.

2. Antes de llenar las solicitudes, Agustín ya _____ una lista de sus habilidades.

3. El año pasado, durante varios meses, Jorge _____ de cuidar niños.

4. Estaban sorprendidos porque la recepcionista los _____ muy rápido.

5. Poco después de entrar a la oficina, el gerente les _____ cartas de recomendación y les _____ referencias.

6. En un momento durante la entrevista, les preguntó qué salario ellos _____ en sus otros trabajos.

7. Cuando terminó la entrevista, la recepcionista ya _____ con su trabajo.

Gramática · Repaso

Presentation

Standards: 4.1

Resources: Voc. & Gram. Transparencies: 108

Suggestions: Tell students you will say two events that happened in the past. Ask them to combine your two sentences into one using the pluperfect tense.

Teacher: *Primero, entré en la cocina. Después, sonó el teléfono.*

Student: *Había entrado en la cocina cuando sonó el teléfono.*

18 *Standards:* 1.2

Resources: Practice Answers on Transparencies

Focus: Practicing the pluperfect tense in a cloze exercise

Suggestions: Remind students to look over the exercise carefully first in order to decide how best to use the answers in the word bank.

Common Errors: Some students will try to make the past participle agree in number with the subject: **habían idos.** Remind them that the verb **haber** is the only part of the verb phrase that must agree in number with the subject: **habían ido.**

Answers:
1. habían llenado
2. había escrito
3. se había encargado
4. había atendido
5. había solicitado/había pedido
6. habían tenido
7. había cumplido

Extension: For extra practice, have students rewrite the subordinate clauses of the sentences using the preterite tense. For example: *Jorge y Agustín llenaron varias solicitudes de empleo.*

Enriching Your Teaching

Teacher-to-Teacher

Set up a situation, such as a family going to bed at night. Use an adverbial clause such as **antes de acostarse....** Ask students to tell one thing that each member of the family had done before retiring. Then have them write sentences using the pluperfect: *Antes de acostarse, papá había apagado las luces.*

217

5 Practice and Communicate

Actividad 19

Standards: 1.2

Resources: Practice Answers on Transparencies

Focus: Practicing formation of the pluperfect tense

Suggestions: Point out that for this activity, students already know the tense they need to use each time. All they need to focus on is choosing the correct verb and forming the pluperfect tense correctly. Ask volunteers to take turns reading the completed story aloud, so students have a chance to concentrate on meaning.

Answers:
1. había buscado
2. había conseguido
3. había preparado
4. había estado
5. se había presentado
6. se había levantado
7. había andado
8. había querido

Actividad 20

Standards: 1.1, 1.3

Focus: Practicing the pluperfect tense through writing

Suggestions: Invite students to use this activity as an opportunity to get to know someone better. Suggest that they learn something about a parent or other family member by using him or her as the subject of their paragraph in step 2.

Answers will vary.

 **Actividad 19** **Gramática** **Leer/Escribir** ....

Trabajos en bicicleta

Ayer Andrés empezó a trabajar. Lee lo que le sucedió y completa el relato con el pluscuamperfecto del verbo apropiado.

Andrés __1.__ (buscar / creer) trabajo por mucho tiempo. Finalmente __2.__ (destruir / conseguir) un trabajo como mensajero en bicicleta, en la compañía donde trabajaba su amigo Luis. Ayer era su primer día. Él __3.__ (preparar / comer) sus cosas desde el día anterior para no llegar tarde. Esa mañana, Luis lo __4.__ (oír / estar) esperando en la parada del autobús para irse juntos a trabajar. Como Andrés no llegaba, Luis lo llamó a la casa. Andrés nunca antes __5.__ (presentarse / entrar) tarde a una cita. La mamá le dijo que Andrés __6.__ (levantarse / acostarse) hacía diez minutos y se estaba duchando. Luis se fue entonces solo en autobús. Cuando llegó a la compañía, Andrés ya estaba allí. Él __7.__ (correr / andar) en bicicleta hasta allí. Más tarde, Andrés le explicó que __8.__ (caer / querer) dar una buena impresión el primer día.

 Actividad 20 **Gramática** **Escribir/Hablar** ....

Una persona que trabaja

❶ Piensa en una persona que conozcas bien y que tenga un trabajo. Haz una línea de tiempo como la de abajo para indicar qué había hecho esa persona antes de conseguir este trabajo. Responde a las siguientes preguntas como ayuda.

- ¿De qué trabaja esa persona ahora?
- ¿Qué trabajo o responsabilidades tenía el año pasado?
- ¿De qué otras responsabilidades se había encargado antes?

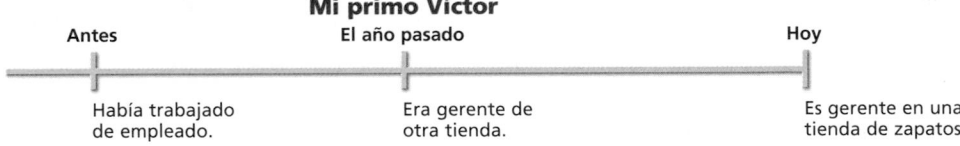

Mi primo Víctor

Antes	El año pasado	Hoy
Había trabajado de empleado.	Era gerente de otra tienda.	Es gerente en una tienda de zapatos.

❷ Escribe un párrafo describiendo a esta persona y sus experiencias en el mundo del trabajo.

❸ Intercambia papeles con otro(a) estudiante. Háganse preguntas sobre las experiencias de la persona que han descrito.

218 **doscientos dieciocho**
Manos a la obra 1

Universal Access

Students with Special Needs
Ask an advanced learner to describe the Rivera painting on p. 219 in detailed language for visually impaired students.

Advanced Learners
Ask students to interview their parents or other adults about things they had already done by the time they were the student's age. Then have students report back to the class in Spanish. For example: *Antes de tener dieciséis años, mi mamá había viajado en avión.*

 **21 Gramática** **Hablar** ....

Mi trabajo el año pasado

Habla con otro(a) estudiante y dile tres cosas que hiciste durante el año pasado. Luego, dile si habías hecho lo mismo antes del año pasado.

Modelo

A —*El año pasado ganamos el campeonato de fútbol.*

B —*¿Habían ganado el campeonato antes?*

 22 Leer/Escribir ....

El trabajo en el arte

El tema del trabajo siempre estuvo presente en la obra de Diego Rivera, el gran pintor de México.

Conexiones | El arte ———————

En los años 1920, el tema principal de la pintura de Diego Rivera fue los campesinos mexicanos. Sin embargo, en los Estados Unidos Rivera pintó obras en las que el trabajador estadounidense era el tema central. Ya en 1930, Rivera había pintado obras importantes en San Francisco y era un artista conocido en los Estados Unidos.

Henry Ford, el dueño de la compañía Ford, y su hijo Edsel, pidieron a Rivera que pintara un mural en el Detroit Institute of Arts. Rivera comenzó a pintarlo en 1932. Había escogido a los trabajadores de Ford como tema de su obra.

Desde 1930, las ideas políticas que Rivera expresaba en sus obras habían causado muchas críticas. Cuando terminó su obra del Detroit Institute en 1933, muchos la criticaron por esa razón. Pero gracias al apoyo de Edsel Ford, el mural sigue hoy en su lugar.

- Mira el detalle *(detail)* del mural que aparece en esta página. ¿Qué crees que nos quiere decir el artista?

- ¿Conoces otro artista al que han criticado por las ideas políticas que expresa en sus obras? ¿Qué piensas tú sobre su obra?

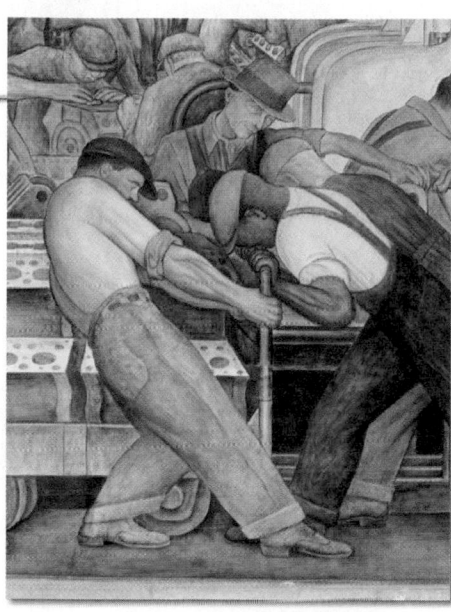

Detalle del mural del Detroit Institute of Arts

Detroit Industry, (1933), Diego Rivera. (c) Banco de México Diego Rivera & Frida Kahlo Museums Trust. Av. Cinco de Mayo No. 2, Col. Centro, Del. Cuauhtemoc 06059, México, D.F. Reproduction authorized by the *Instituto Nacional de Bellas Artes y Literatura*. The Detroit Institute of Arts, USA/Bridgeman Art Library.

 **Más práctica** ....
Practice Workbook 5-6, 5-7

Go Online
PHSchool.com
For: Practice with the pluperfect
Visit: www.phschool.com
Web Code: jed-0504

doscientos diecinueve **219**
Capítulo 5

Vocabulario y gramática

Presentation

Standards: 1.1, 1.2, 5.1

Resources: Voc. & Gram. Transparencies: 109–110; Resource Book: Cap. 5, Input Script; Audio Program: CD Cap. 5, Tracks 10, 12

Focus: Presenting new vocabulary and using grammar lexically in context

Suggestions: Have students read along as you present the new vocabulary by playing the *Audio CD* or reading the text aloud. Use the pictures on *Vocabulary & Grammar Transparencies* 109–110 and questions with embedded answers to elicit the vocabulary from students: *¿Este hombre está en el centro de la comunidad o en el comedor de beneficencia?* Check for comprehension by asking other questions. See the Input Scripts in the *Teacher's Resource Book* for specific questions.

Standards: 1.2

Resources: Audio Program: CD Cap. 5, Track 11; Resource Book: Cap. 5, Audio Script; Practice Answers on Transparencies

Focus: Practicing listening comprehension of new vocabulary

Suggestions: Ask students to tell about what they see happening in the photos on this page and what they think typically happens in each place. Guide them with questions as necessary: *¿Quién come en el comedor de beneficencia?*

Answers:

1. el comedor de beneficencia
2. el centro recreativo
3. el centro de la comunidad
4. el hogar de ancianos
5. el centro de rehabilitación

A primera vista 2

Vocabulario y gramática en contexto

Objectives

Read, listen to, and understand information about
- volunteer work opportunities in our community
- how you can help your community

¿Has trabajado como voluntario? Ojalá lo hayas hecho, si no, nunca es tarde para ayudar a otros. Hay organizaciones en tu comunidad que buscan **proteger** y **beneficiar** a otras personas. Aquí tienes algunos lugares donde puedes colaborar como voluntario y ayudar.

el centro de rehabilitación

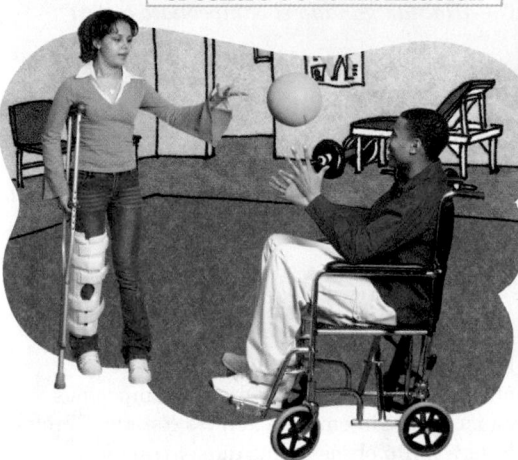

el hogar de ancianos

el centro recreativo

el comedor de beneficencia

el centro de la comunidad

Escuchar/Escribir

Dónde buscar ayuda

Escribe los números del 1 al 5 en una hoja. Escucha la descripción de estos lugares y escribe el nombre del lugar.

220 doscientos veinte
A primera vista 2

Universal Access

Heritage Language Learners

Have students create original announcements to post on the *Boletín de la Comunidad.* Encourage them to consider volunteer opportunities in their community and in places they have visited. Provide feedback on errors in Spanish and then invite them to share their work with the class.

Advanced Learners

Ask small groups of students to obtain leaflets or flyers from community organizations, preferably in Spanish. Have students scan the papers for words and pictures that relate to the new vocabulary, cut them out, and create a collage.

Boletín de la Comunidad
marzo-abril

Queremos dar las gracias a todos los que han colaborado como voluntarios este mes. Esperamos que ésta haya sido una buena experiencia. Éstas son algunas de las actividades que organizamos:

¡Ayuda ahora!

1 Jóvenes de la escuela La Libertad participaron en **la marcha** para **juntar fondos** (obtener dinero) para las víctimas de los huracanes del mes pasado.

2 Los jóvenes de la escuela Simón Bolívar participaron en **una manifestación** en contra de la contaminación del medio ambiente. Luego sembraron árboles para apoyar la causa.

donar

3 La organización Hermanos solicita suéteres y abrigos para la gente sin hogar que no tiene un lugar donde vivir.

Se Aceptan **DONACIONES**

Sembrar un árbol

¿Quieren ayudar a conseguir abrigos? A mí **me es imposible,** tengo que estudiar.

A mí **me encantaría,** me gusta ayudar a los demás.

Me interesaría . . . ¿Qué tengo que hacer?

Escribir

¿Vas a ser voluntario?

En el boletín se habla de diferentes proyectos de trabajo voluntario. Imagínate que te invitan a participar en ellos este sábado. Completa la tabla con las actividades del boletín según tu disponibilidad (*availability*) e interés.

Me es imposible . . .	Me encantaría . . .	Me interesaría . . .

doscientos veintiuno **221**
Capítulo 5

Actividad 24   *Standards:* 1.2, 1.3

Focus: Writing new vocabulary

Suggestions: Explain to students that there are a variety of ways to talk about the different projects. They should study the presentation text on this page to decide on the phrasing they will use in their chart.

Answers will vary.

Extension: Have students talk about the information on their charts and add a sentence elaborating on each entry: *Me es imposible participar en la manifestación. Tengo que ayudar a mi padre.*

Enriching Your Teaching

Teacher-to-Teacher
Take advantage of the community-oriented context of this part of the chapter to get students out and learning about organizations in their own community. Encourage them to visit places where volunteer work is done, to ask pertinent questions, and to bring in any available literature. Tell them to look for brochures and other print material in Spanish.

Vocabulario y gramática

Presentation

Standards: 1.1, 1.2, 3.1, 5.1

Resources: Voc. & Gram. Transparencies: 111–112; Resource Book: Cap. 5, Input Script; Audio Program: CD Cap. 5, Tracks 13, 15

Focus: Extending presentation of vocabulary and grammar in context

Suggestions:

Pre-reading: Present the readings on this and the next page one at a time, along with their respective activities.

Reading: Allow students time to read each presentation silently first before they listen to the *Audio CD.*

Post-reading: Check comprehension by asking questions.

 Actividad 25   *Standards:* 1.2, 1.3

Resources: Practice Answers on Transparencies

Focus: Writing answers to demonstrate comprehension of a reading

Suggestions: Have students share and discuss their answers.

Answers:
1. Pueden ayudarlos a llenar los formularios y a estudiar para el examen de ciudadanía.
2–4. Answers will vary.

 Actividad 26   *Standards:* 1.2

Resources: Audio Program: CD Cap. 5, Track 14; Resource Book: Cap. 5, Audio Script; Practice Answers on Transparencies

Focus: Practicing listening comprehension of new vocabulary and structures

Suggestions: Before students hear the conversation, have them read items 1–4 and the choices offered in parentheses. In this way they will be better prepared for the task and know what to listen for.

Answers:
1. solicitar la ciudadanía
2. llenar los formularios
3. la historia del país
4. es imposible

Se buscan voluntarios hispanohablantes para ayudar a inmigrantes

★★★★★★★★★★★★★★★★★★★★

¿No sabes qué hacer con tu tiempo libre? Ayuda a un inmigrante a hacerse **ciudadano.**

Buscamos voluntarios para dar clases a inmigrantes. El objetivo de las clases es educar a los inmigrantes para conseguir la ciudadanía.

¿Qué hacen los voluntarios en las clases?

Un abogado[1] explica **las leyes de inmigración** y luego, los voluntarios ayudan a las personas a **llenar los formularios** y a estudiar para el examen de ciudadanía.

Para más información, visítanos en Roosevelt Ave. y 84th St., Queens, NY

1 lawyer

 Actividad 24   Escribir/Hablar

¿Comprendiste?

1. ¿Qué pueden hacer los voluntarios para beneficiar a los inmigrantes?

2. ¿Te interesaría ayudar a los inmigrantes? ¿Qué conocimientos crees que se necesitan para ayudarlos a obtener la ciudadanía?

3. ¿Por qué es importante que los inmigrantes comprendan las leyes antes de obtener la ciudadanía?

4. ¿Crees que todos debemos ayudar y educar a las personas que lo necesitan? ¿Por qué?

222 doscientos vientidós
A primera vista 2

 Actividad 26   Escuchar

Ayuda a inmigrantes

Escucha la conversación de unos jóvenes voluntarios. Luego, completa cada frase según lo que dijeron los jóvenes.

1. Un abogado explicó cómo (*llenar los formularios / solicitar la ciudadanía*).

2. Los voluntarios ayudaron a (*hacer el examen / llenar los formularios*).

3. Paola tuvo que estudiar (*las leyes de inmigración / la historia del país*).

4. A Luis le (*es imposible / encantaría*) ayudar en las clases para inmigrantes.

Universal Access

Heritage Language Learners

Ask students to research the United States citizenship test on the Internet. Then have them prepare a mini-lesson in which they act as volunteer teachers for Spanish-speaking immigrants and the rest of the class acts as the immigrants.

Students with Learning Difficulties

Have students list the main ideas from the paragraphs about the candidates on this page. This will help them focus on key language for the *Actividad* 27. Allow them to refer to their lists as they complete the activity.

¿A quién van a escoger?

La Sociedad de Beneficencia Manuel García

La Sociedad es una organización que tiene un hogar de ancianos y un hospital para niños. Cada cuatro años se hace una **campaña** para elegir (elect) un presidente. Lee sobre los candidatos de este año y sus causas, es decir, lo que piensan que es más importante.

Soy María Luna de Soto. Estoy **a favor de** proteger **los derechos** de todos los niños, por eso quiero que haya más programas de **servicio social**. Debemos **garantizar** los fondos para comprar medicinas para nuestros ciudadanos más jóvenes, los niños, y buscar voluntarios que ayuden a las personas que lo necesitan. Es **injusto** que sólo algunas personas reciban cuidado y ayuda.

Soy Mauricio Gutiérrez. Pienso que ser presidente de la Sociedad de Beneficencia es una gran **responsabilidad**. Estoy a favor de comprar equipo médico y garantizar así una mejor atención a la salud de nuestros pacientes. También quiero **construir** un centro recreativo junto al hogar de ancianos. Me parece **justo** que los ancianos tengan un lugar donde descansar y recibir todo el cuidado que ellos necesitan.

 Escuchar ·

¿Quién está a favor de esto?

En una hoja, escribe los números del 1 al 6. Después de leer sobre los dos candidatos, escucha estas frases y escribe *Mauricio* o *María* según quién haya expresado esa idea.

● **Más práctica** · · · · · · · · · · · · · ·
Practice Workbook 5-8, 5-9

PHSchool.com
For: Vocabulary practice
Visit: www.phschool.com
Web Code: jed-0506

doscientos veintitrés 223
Capítulo 5

 Standards: 1.2
27
· ·

Resources: Audio Program: CD Cap. 5, Track 16; Resource Book: Cap. 5, Audio Script; Practice Answers on Transparencies

Focus: Practicing listening comprehension of new vocabulary and structures

Suggestions: Prepare students for the listening activity by asking comprehension questions about the main points of each candidate's statements.

Answers:
1. María
2. Mauricio
3. María
4. Mauricio
5. María
6. María

Additional Resources
• Resource Book: Cap. 5, Clip Art

✓ Assessment
• Prueba 5-5: Vocabulary recognition

Chapter Project
Students can perform step 4 at this point. Be sure they understand your corrections and suggestions. (For more information, see p. 200-a.)

Enriching Your Teaching

Culture Note
Many volunteer organizations protect the rights and aid in the welfare of children throughout Latin America and Spain. Some of them are worldwide organizations, while others are based in individual countries. Some examples are the Homeless Children's Network, Amnesty International, and Doctors Without Borders.

Teacher-to-Teacher
Invite volunteers to perform dramatic readings of the paragraphs about María Luna de Soto and Mauricio Gutiérrez. After they read their speeches, invite the class to ask questions about their positions on issues mentioned in the paragraph. Readers can improvise their answers.

Practice and Communicate

5

Actividad 28

Standards: 1.2

Resources: Practice Answers on Transparencies

Focus: Practicing new vocabulary in a cloze exercise

Recycle: preterite tense, imperfect tense

Suggestions: Encourage students to read the entire paragraph before filling in the blanks. When they have finished, have students read the paragraph again and make sure they understand Rocío's description of her efforts.

Answers:

1. responsabilidad
2. ciudadana
3. campaña
4. servicio social
5. dona
6. juntar fondos
7. sociedad
8. comedores de beneficencia
9. donen
10. construir
11. gente sin hogar

Actividad 29

Standards: 1.2, 1.3, 3.1

Resources: Practice Answers on Transparencies

Focus: Demonstrating comprehension of new vocabulary through reading and responding to questions

Recycle: *nosotros* forms of *-ar* verbs

Suggestions: After students have read the announcement, ask them to discuss whether they think the ad is successful in its objective.

Answers:

1. La responsabilidad de los ciudadanos es la de votar.
2. El objetivo principal es juntar fondos para la campaña para votar.
3. Beneficia a los ancianos para que entiendan sus derechos y ayuda a los inmigrantes a solicitar la ciudadanía.
4. Answers will vary.

Manos a la obra 2

Vocabulario y gramática en uso

Objetivos

- Talk about volunteer work opportunities in your community
- Explain how you can help your community
- Practice the present perfect subjunctive
- Review demonstrative adjectives and pronouns

Actividad 28

 Leer/Escribir

Ayudar es fácil

Completa la entrevista con la estudiante Rocío Hernández sobre su campaña.

servicio social	campaña	ciudadana
dona	responsabilidad	juntar fondos

Cuando supe que 24,000 personas en el mundo mueren de hambre cada día y que el 75% son niños, pensé que era mi __1.__, como __2.__ del mundo, ayudar a eliminar el hambre. Decidí crear una __3.__ de __4.__ en mi escuela con el nombre de "Ayudachicos". Allí buscamos diferentes maneras de ayudar. Por ejemplo, encontramos un sitio en la Red que se llama "Hunger Site". Cada vez que haces un clic, se __5.__ comida a los ciudadanos de un país pobre. También hicimos una marcha para __6.__ que luego enviamos a UNICEF.

comedores de beneficencia	gente sin hogar	construir
donen	sociedad	

Además, escribimos a varias compañías de comida enlatada¹ para que donen parte de sus productos a la __7.__ de Aldeas Infantiles SOS. En nuestro pueblo, pedimos donaciones de comida y las llevamos a los __8.__. Ahora, vamos a solicitar a arquitectos y a compañías de construcción que __9.__ materiales y proyectos de construcción a "Hábitat para la humanidad", que se encarga de __10.__ casas para la __11.__.

1 canned food

Actividad 29

  Leer/Escribir

Jóvenes ciudadanos

Lee este anuncio de una organización que beneficia a la comunidad y responde a las preguntas.

1. Según el anuncio, ¿cuál es la responsabilidad de los ciudadanos?
2. Observa el título *(title)* de este proyecto. ¿Cuál es el objetivo principal de esta organización?
3. ¿A qué dos grupos beneficia esta organización? ¿Cómo los ayuda?
4. ¿Te interesaría participar en este proyecto? ¿Estás a favor o en contra de su causa? ¿Por qué?

¡CAMPAÑA PARA VOTAR!

¿Quiere cumplir con su responsabilidad como ciudadano?

- Educamos a los ancianos a entender sus derechos
- Ayudamos a los inmigrantes a solicitar la ciudadanía
- Juntamos fondos para la campaña

Reuniones cada jueves a las 5:00 PM
931 E. Market St. Salinas, CA 93905

Proyecto ¡Vote!
Beneficiamos la sociedad

224 doscientos veinticuatro
Manos a la obra 2

Universal Access

Students with Learning Difficulties

To help students complete *Actividad* 28, encourage them to read each sentence and fill in the blank with a word or phrase that they think would make sense. Then have them search the choices for a word or phrase that is similar to their own idea.

Advanced Learners

Have students contact a community organization that employs Spanish speakers as staff or volunteers. Ask students to arrange for someone from the organization to speak to the class about volunteer work and areas in which Spanish-speaking volunteers are needed.

Actividad 30

Hablar

El servicio social

Habla con un(a) compañero(a) sobre el servicio social.

Modelo

A —¿Te interesaría hacer servicio social en
una escuela primaria?

B —Sí, me encantaría porque me gusta
encargarme de los niños.

o: No, me es imposible porque _tengo miedo de
hablar frente a un grupo._

Estudiante A

1.
2.
3.
4.
5.
6.

Estudiante B

Me encantaría
Me interesaría
No me gustaría
Me es imposible
¡Respuesta personal!

Actividad 31

Pensar/Escribir/Hablar/Dibujar

Compañeros voluntarios . . .

1 Haz una lista de cinco acciones que benefician a la sociedad, tales como
donar ropa a la gente sin hogar.

2 En grupos de cuatro estudiantes, hablen de las acciones que todos
escribieron. ¿Cuáles creen que son las cinco más importantes? ¿Por qué?

Modelo

A —Es importante donar ropa a la gente sin hogar.
B —Estoy de acuerdo, pero para mí es más importante
que los niños tengan comida.

3 En grupo, escriban las acciones en orden de importancia (1 = lo más
importante; 5 = lo menos importante). Escojan las tres acciones que a
ustedes les parecen más importantes y hagan un cartel para animar a
otros(as) jóvenes a hacer trabajo voluntario.

doscientos veinticinco **225**
Capítulo 5

Practice and Communicate

5

Actividad 30

Standards: 1.1

Resources: Practice Answers on Transparencies

Focus: Using new vocabulary in guided conversations

Suggestions: Have partners practice all the dialogues, switching roles. Then ask them to choose one dialogue to present to the class.

Answers will vary. Student A will use the following vocabulary:

1. un hogar de ancianos
2. un centro de rehabilitación
3. un centro de la comunidad
4. un centro recreativo
5. un comedor de beneficencia
6. un jardín comunitario

Actividad 31

Standards: 1.1, 1.3

Focus: Practicing new vocabulary via discussion and writing an announcement

Suggestions: Remind students that expressions such as **es importante que** take the subjunctive. Point out that their announcement in step 3 should include either subjunctive expressions, infinitive expressions, or imperatives.

Answers will vary.

Enriching Your Teaching

Teacher-to-Teacher

If your school has a charitable organization or a club that contributes to such efforts, ask your students to create a Spanish-language poster for it. Obtain permission to place several of these on the school grounds. The posters will help the organization, and your students will benefit from the experience.

225

Standards: 1.2

Actividad 32

Resources: Audio Program: CD Cap. 5, Track 17; Resource Book: Cap. 5, Audio Script; Practice Answers on Transparencies

Focus: Practicing listening comprehension of new vocabulary

Suggestions: First, allow students to listen to the *Audio CD* and read the sentences. Then play the *Audio CD* again, pausing after each item, so they can write their answers.

Answers:
1. la compañía "El Salvador"
2. un millón de bolívares
3. es nuestra responsabilidad
4. los ancianos de esta ciudad
5. siente la responsabilidad de ayudar a todos los ciudadanos

Standards: 1.1, 1.2

Actividad 33

Focus: Practicing new vocabulary and structures by responding to discussion questions

Suggestions: Remind students that when talking about opinions and values, the subjunctive is often required.

Answers will vary.

Standards: 1.1, 1.2, 2.1, 3.1, 5.1

Fondo cultural

Suggestions: Ask students to research José Gálvez and his work on the Internet and hold a follow-up discussion in which they tell about their findings.

Answers will vary.

Additional Resources
- Writing, Audio & Video Workbook: Cap. 5, Audio Activity 3, Track 18
- Writing, Audio & Video Workbook: Cap. 5, Writing Activity 10
- Resource Book: Cap. 5, Communicative Activity BLM

✓ Assessment
- Prueba 5-6: Vocabulary production

Actividad 32 **Escuchar/Escribir** • • • • • • • • • • • • • • • • • • •

Un reportaje especial

Imagina que estás en Caracas, Venezuela y que escuchas este reportaje en la radio. Completa las frases siguientes con la información del reportaje. Luego, usa esta información para hacer un resumen.

1. Sepúlveda es dueño de _____.
2. Donó _____.
3. La campaña se llama "Educar _____".
4. La escuela va a beneficiar a _____.
5. Sepúlveda decide ayudar porque _____.

Actividad 33 **Escribir/Hablar** •

Y tú, ¿qué dices?

1. ¿Qué servicios sociales hay en la comunidad donde vives? ¿A quién(es) beneficia(n)? En tu opinión, ¿cuál es el más importante? ¿Por qué?
2. ¿En cuál de estos servicios sociales participas o has participado? Si no has participado en ninguno, ¿en cuál te gustaría participar?
3. Piensa en tus habilidades o conocimientos. ¿Cómo los puedes usar para mejorar tu comunidad?
4. Imagina que vas a crear una organización de servicio social. ¿Qué organización puede beneficiar más a tu comunidad? ¿Por qué?

Fondo cultural ■◆■■◆■■◆■■◆■■◆■■◆■◆■◆■

José Gálvez, fotógrafo En todos los tiempos, los artistas han utilizado el arte como una forma de protesta social. Hoy en día puedes ver arte de artistas chicanos que expresan posiciones a favor de algo o en su contra.

José Gálvez creció en Tucson, Arizona. Era fotógrafo para los periódicos *The Arizona Daily Star* y *The Los Angeles Times*. Siempre tenía su cámara y siempre estaba preparado para capturar la experiencia de la comunidad hispanohablante. En 1984 ganó el Premio Pulitzer por una serie de fotos sobre la experiencia mexicano-americana en Los Ángeles. Aunque ha visto muchos cambios en su vida, dice que una cosa que no cambia en la comunidad mexicano-americana es "el respeto por la familia y la herencia mexicana". Dice, "ésta es mi cultura y estoy muy orgulloso de ella."

- Compara la protesta social de los artistas con la de las personas que participan en una marcha o una manifestación. ¿En qué se parecen y en qué son diferentes?
- Habla con otros(as) estudiantes sobre personas que han logrado cambios con protestas sociales.

José Gálvez

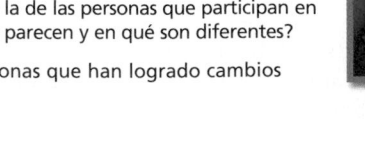

Universal Access

Heritage Language Learners
Students may be familiar with additional expressions of emotion that require the present perfect subjunctive. Invite them to share other expressions that are not listed in *Capítulo* 4 by using them in sentences.

Multiple Intelligences
Musical/Rhythmic: Help students obtain first-hand knowledge about Latin American musicians whose work has a social message. Have them listen to a song of your choice by the contemporary Mexican band Los Tigres del Norte and discuss the message of the song.

Gramática

El presente perfecto del subjuntivo

The present perfect subjunctive refers to actions or situations that may have occurred before the action in the main verb.

Me alegro de que **hayas trabajado** de voluntario.
*I'm glad that you **have worked** as a volunteer.*

Estoy orgullosa de que Julián **haya trabajado** en el centro de rehabilitación.
*I am proud that Julian **has worked** in the rehabilitation center.*

Ojalá que ellos **hayan juntado** mucho dinero.
*I hope that they **have collected** a lot of money.*

Siento que no **hayan participado** en la campaña.
*I'm sorry that you **haven't participated** in the campaign.*

To form the present perfect subjunctive, we use the present subjunctive of the verb *haber* with a past participle. Here are the present perfect subjunctive forms of *trabajar*.

haya trabajado	hayamos trabajado
hayas trabajado	hayáis trabajado
haya trabajado	hayan trabajado

• The present perfect subjunctive uses the same regular and irregular past participles as the other perfect tenses you have learned. To review irregular past participles see pages 214–217.

34 **Gramática** **Leer/Escribir**

La bienvenida al comedor

1 Santiago es el presidente de un comedor de beneficencia. Cada año, da las gracias a las personas que trabajaron allí como voluntarios. Completa lo que dice con el presente perfecto del subjuntivo del verbo apropiado.

| juntar | escribir | decidir | tener | colaborar | organizar | enviar |

Queridos voluntarios:

Me alegro de que ustedes __1.__ trabajar como voluntarios en el comedor. Creo que es justo que los ancianos y la gente sin hogar __2.__ esta oportunidad de recibir alimentos todos los días. Es muy bueno que un voluntario __3.__ fondos para comprar alimentos y espero que yo __4.__ para hacer más fácil su trabajo. Ojalá que cuando termine este año, nosotros __5.__ mejor la forma de servir la comida. Estoy contento de que ustedes __6.__ sus comentarios y los __7.__ a la dirección electrónica que les di. Muchas gracias a todos.

2 Escribe dos frases más que Santiago puede decirles a los voluntarios. Usa el presente perfecto del subjuntivo.

doscientos veintisiete **227**
Capítulo 5

Practice and Communicate

 Rapid Review

Before presenting the present perfect subjunctive, have students create sentences using expressions of emotion and the present subjunctive. Examples of expressions of emotion can be found in *Capítulo 4* on p. 168.

Gramática

Presentation

Standards: 4.1

Resources: Voc. & Gram. Transparencies: 113

Suggestions: Have students use vocabulary from pp. 220–221 in sentences with **Ojalá** and the present perfect subjunctive: *Ojalá que muchos hayan participado en la manifestación.*

 34 *Standards:* 1.2

Resources: Practice Answers on Transparencies

Focus: Using the present perfect subjunctive in a cloze exercise and in written statements

Suggestions: Have students read over the entire thank-you message before completing the activity. Ask them to point out the verbs of emotion that require the subjunctive.

Answers:

Step 1
1. hayan decidido
2. hayan tenido
3. haya juntado
4. haya colaborado
5. hayamos organizado
6. hayan escrito
7. hayan enviado

Step 2
Answers will vary.

Enriching Your Teaching

Teacher-to-Teacher

Have students devote a section of their notebook to the subjunctive. This ready reference can include rules and examples on the formation of the various tenses in the subjunctive mood, as well as situations and expressions that require its use.

Practice and Communicate

5

Actividad 35

Standards: 1.1

Focus: Practicing the present perfect subjunctive in a guided conversation

Suggestions: In step 1, remind students that in most Spanish-speaking countries, people in this situation would address each other using *Ud.* Have them use the *Ud.* forms for their conversations.

Answers will vary.

Actividad 36

Standards: 1.1, 1.3

Focus: Practicing the present perfect subjunctive in writing and in a guided group discussion

Suggestions: Encourage students to be honest when creating their lists in step 1. This will contribute to a realistic assessment of the group during the discussion in step 2.

Answers will vary.

Additional Resources

• Writing, Audio & Video Workbook: Cap. 5, Writing Activity 11

 Assessment

• Prueba 5-7: *El presente perfecto del subjuntivo*

Block Schedule

Actividad 36: Have students work in groups of 4 or 5. On strips of paper, have one student write out the four expressions in *Actividad* 36. Place them face down in one pile. Then have each student write out on three separate strips of paper any subject and any infinitive: *David/trabajar.* Place in a second pile, face down. One student is to select a strip from each pile and create a sentence, receiving a point if the sentence is correct and makes sense. Place strips at the bottom of each pile and continue to play. The winner is the student with the most points.

228

 **Actividad 35** Gramática Escribir/Hablar

¿Qué hacen cada día?

❶ Imagina que eres voluntario(a) de un centro de rehabilitación. Escribe cinco preguntas que puedes hacerle al (a la) director(a) del centro para saber lo que ha pasado y lo que debes hacer.

❷ Trabaja con otro(a) estudiante. Hagan los papeles del (de la) director(a) y el (la) voluntario(a). El (la) director(a) explica lo que no se ha hecho todavía y por qué es importante que se haga.

> **Modelo**
> A —*¿Los pacientes han hecho sus ejercicios de rehabilitación?*
> B —*No sé. Espero que ya los hayan hecho. Es importante que hagan sus ejercicios todos los días.*

 **Actividad 36** Gramática Escribir/Hablar

Ayudando a otros

❶ Haz una lista de trabajos que hayas hecho para ayudar a otros.

> **Modelo**
> *He atendido a ancianos.*
> *He cocinado para mis catorce primos.*

❷ Trabaja con un grupo de estudiantes. Comenten lo que han hecho y escriban una lista de todos los trabajos. Observen la lista y piensen en algunos trabajos que no hayan hecho y que pueden ayudar a la comunidad. Usen las expresiones siguientes para comentar sobre lo que han hecho y lo que no han hecho.

| estoy orgulloso(a) de . . . | me alegro de . . . |
| es una lástima que . . . | me sorprende que . . . |

> **Modelo**
> *Me alegro de que varios estudiantes hayan donado ropa a la gente sin hogar. Me sorprende que nadie haya trabajado como voluntario en un hogar de ancianos.*

● **Más práctica**
Practice Workbook 5-10

For: Practice with the present perfect subjunctive
Visit: www.phschool.com
Web Code: jed-0507

228 doscientos veintiocho
Manos a la obra 2

Universal Access

Advanced Learners

Ask students to think of a scene in which something has gone wrong. For example: *Un coche está parado en la calle y le está saliendo humo del motor.* Other students tell what has happened using verbs of emotion and the present perfect subjunctive: *Es una lástima que se haya descompuesto el coche.*

Multiple Intelligences

Visual/Spatial: Ask students to create visuals to help them remember demonstrative pronouns and adjectives. Tell them to include either a caption or speech bubble that shows which word they are illustrating.

Gramática · Repaso

Los adjetivos y los pronombres demostrativos

Remember that you use demonstrative adjectives to point out people or things that are nearby and farther away. A demonstrative adjective always comes before the noun and agrees with it in gender and number.

Me gusta mucho trabajar en **este** centro recreativo.
*I really like to work at **this** recreation center.*

¿Quién donó **esa** comida?
*Who donated **that** food?*

Voy a ayudar a **aquellos** pacientes.
*I'm going to help **those** patients.*

Demonstrative adjectives can also be used as pronouns to replace nouns. To distinguish them from demonstrative adjectives, they have a written accent.

Me es imposible trabajar para **este** candidato, pero me encantaría trabajar para **ése**.
*It's impossible for me to work for **this** candidate, but I would love to work for **that one**.*

¿Ves **esas** bolsas? Por favor, recoge **ésa**, pero no recojas **aquélla**.
*Do you see **those** bags? Please pick up **that one**, but don't pick up **that one over there**.*

To refer to an idea, or something that has not been identified, use the demonstrative pronouns *esto*, *eso*, or *aquello*. None of them has an accent mark.

Esto es injusto.	***This** is unfair.*
Me encantaría **eso**.	*I would love **that**.*
¿Qué es **aquello**?	*What is **that (over there)**?*

• Here are all the demonstrative adjectives and pronouns.

	Close to you		Closer to the person you are talking to		Far from both of you	
Adjectives	este	estos	ese	esos	aquel	aquellos
	esta	estas	esa	esas	aquella	aquellas
Pronouns	éste	éstos	ése	ésos	aquél	aquéllos
	ésta	éstas	ésa	ésas	aquélla	aquéllas

Éste es un perro marrón.

Ése es un perro blanco.

Aquél es un perro negro.

Gramática

Presentation

Standards: 4.1

Resources: Voc. & Gram. Transparencies: 114

Suggestions: Have students talk in pairs about classroom objects using demonstrative adjectives and pronouns. Then ask students to make cards for the chapter vocabulary. Two or three cards are needed for each vocabulary item. Place the cards around the room. Students can stand in one position and create a series of sentences that use the vocabulary along with demonstrative adjectives and pronouns: *Trabajo en este centro recreativo. Ese centro recreativo es donde trabaja mi hermano. Me gustaría saber quién trabaja en aquel centro recreativo.*

Additional Resources

• Writing, Audio & Video Workbook: Cap. 5, Audio Activity 4, Track 19

Enriching Your Teaching

Teacher-to-Teacher

Write the demonstrative adjectives on note cards. Have students take turns drawing a card and using the demonstrative adjective in a sentence. Sentences should refer to an object whose relative distance makes it clear that the student understands the adjective. Students can also use the demonstrative adjective in a comparison in order to make the meaning clear: *Me gusta más esta obra de arte que aquélla al lado de la puerta.*

229

Practice and Communicate

Actividad 37 *Standards:* 1.2

Resources: Practice Answers on Transparencies

Focus: Practicing demonstrative adjectives and pronouns

Suggestions: Tell students that they must carefully consider accent marks and gender and number agreement as they complete this activity.

Answers:
1. Esta/ Aquélla
2. Éstos/este
3. aquello
4. Aquel/ ése
5. Aquéllas
6. este
7. Éstas
8. esto
9. esas/Ésta
10. Éste

El español en la comunidad

Presentation

Standards: 1.2, 5.1

Suggestions: Once students have read the information, ask comprehension questions. For example: *¿Por qué se ofrecen clases de español a bordo del* Peace Boat? *(Se ofrecen clases de español porque muchos de los participantes no hablan español, pero el barco visita muchos países hispanohablantes.) ¿Cuál es el objetivo principal del* Peace Boat? *(El objetivo es ayudar a grupos que promueven los derechos humanos, la paz y la protección del medio ambiente.)*

Chapter Project

Students can perform step 5 at this point. Record their presentations on cassette or videotape for inclusion in their portfolio. (For more information, see p. 200-a.)

Actividad 37 **Gramática** Leer/Escribir

¿Éste o aquél?

Margarita es voluntaria en el centro de la comunidad. El supervisor del centro le dice lo que tiene que hacer. Completa las siguientes frases con el adjetivo demostrativo o el pronombre demostrativo correcto.

1. *(Esta / Ésta)* lista no es la de los nuevos ciudadanos. *(Aquella / Aquélla)* es la lista.
2. *(Estos / Éstos)* son los fondos que juntó el centro *(este / estos)* mes.
3. Todo *(aquel / aquello)* beneficia al centro que organiza la marcha.
4. *(Aquel / Aquél)* escritorio no es el tuyo, *(esa / ése)* es el tuyo.
5. *(Aquéllas / Esas)* son las donaciones de alimentos que trajo la gente.
6. Debes leer *(esto / este)* artículo sobre el medio ambiente.
7. *(Esas / Éstas)* son las plantas que deben sembrarse en el parque.
8. Tenemos que publicar en nuestro informe *(esto / esos)* que dice el artículo sobre los servicios sociales.
9. No tienes que leer todas *(ésas / esas)* páginas. *(Esta / Ésta)* es la más importante.
10. *(Éste / este)* es el informe que tienes que leer.

El español en la comunidad

Profesores voluntarios por la paz, los derechos humanos y el medio ambiente

Peace Boat es una organización no gubernamental (ONG) que tiene como objetivo ayudar a grupos que promueven *(promote)* los derechos humanos, la paz y la protección del medio ambiente en distintos países. Para alcanzar su objetivo, *Peace Boat* organiza viajes en un barco alrededor del mundo para visitar países donde se pueda dar ayuda.

Como muchos de los países que el barco visita son hispanohablantes, y muchos de los participantes no hablan español, en el barco se ofrecen clases de español todos los días durante el viaje. Todos los profesores de español de *Peace Boat* son voluntarios. La organización paga solamente el boleto, la comida y las medicinas para los profesores. Todos los pasajeros pueden asistir a las clases, que se ofrecen en un "curso intensivo" para las personas que tienen bastante tiempo para estudiar. Y pueden participar en "clases libres" los pasajeros que no tienen tiempo para estudiar todos los días pero quieren disfrutar y aprender un poquito de español. Es una hermosa manera *(way)* de enseñar español, promover la paz y los derechos humanos y ayudar a proteger el medio ambiente, todo a la misma vez.

Universal Access

Students with Learning Difficulties

Help students understand demonstrative adjectives and pronouns by making spatial relationships clear. On three cards, write, for example, **esta, esa,** and **aquella.** Place each card beside three similar objects, such as chairs, that are arranged at three different distances from the student. Ask the student to remain in place, point, and say or repeat sentences such as *Esta es una silla. Esa también es una silla. Aquella silla está lejos.*

 **38** Gramática · Hablar ··········

Ésta, ésa, aquélla

Imagina que te estás preparando para participar en una manifestación. Habla con un(a) compañero(a) sobre los preparativos (*preparations*). Usa los pronombres demostrativos apropiados.

Estudiante A

1. carteles
2. banderas
3. anuncios
4. tambores
5. libros
6. camisetas de la manifestación

Estudiante B

en el piso
en el armario
de color azul
sobre la mesa
allí
al lado de la puerta

Modelo

artículo / en la página 2 del periódico
A —*¿Cuál es el artículo que habla sobre la manifestación?*
B —*Éste, el que está en la página 2 del periódico.*

 **39** Gramática · Escribir/Hablar ··········

A sugerir soluciones

1 La clase va a dividirse en dos grupos. Un grupo cree que el trabajo voluntario debe ser obligatorio para la graduación; el otro piensa que no. Cada grupo trata de convencer al otro. Hablen sobre:

• tipos de trabajo
• cuándo deben hacer el trabajo (después de clases, fines de semana, en vacaciones)
• si debe ser parte del currículum o no
• los beneficios que puede tener para el futuro

2 Formen grupos y preparen la representación de una marcha o una manifestación. Escojan la causa y decidan:

• a favor o en contra de qué o de quiénes protestan
• qué exigen o qué resultados esperan
• qué pasará si no consiguen lo que quieren

3 Uno o dos estudiantes pueden representar a reporteros de televisión y entrevistar a los que protestan.

Silvio Rodríguez es el cantante más importante del "Movimiento de la Nueva Trova", un movimiento musical que apareció en Cuba en los años 60 y tuvo gran influencia en América Latina. Aunque ha escrito canciones de amor, frecuentemente en sus letras habla de los problemas de la sociedad, de lo que cree que es justo o injusto, de las causas que apoya.

• ¿Qué cantante conoces que hable en sus canciones de la sociedad o del medio ambiente?

• ¿Crees que es bueno que los cantantes hablen de problemas sociales en sus canciones? ¿Por qué?

Silvio Rodríguez

 **Más práctica** ··········

Practice Workbook 5-11, 5-12

Go Online
PHSchool.com

For: Practice with demonstrative adjectives and pronouns
Visit: www.phschool.com
Web Code: jed-0509

doscientos treinta y uno **231**
Capítulo 5

Puente a la cultura

Standards: 1.2, 3.1

Focus: Reading to learn about the contributions of the Spanish-speaking population of the United States

Suggestions:

Pre-reading: Refer students to the *Estrategia.* Remind them to use their knowledge of cognates, word families, and context clues to keep reading through difficult parts of passages.

Reading: Help students resolve comprehension problems by asking **sí/no** or embedded-answer questions: *¿César Chávez organizó a los trabajadores del campo o a los trabajadores en las fábricas? (a los trabajadores del campo) ¿Linda G. Alvarado es la Tesorera de los Estados Unidos? (No. La Tesorera es Rosario Marin.)*

Post-reading: On the board, begin a concept web with the words **contribuciones de los hispanohablantes** in the center. Use the web as a vehicle to discuss the article. Record in it students' responses about the people mentioned in the article, as well as other information they may supply from their background knowledge about the topic.

Standards: 3.1

Resources: Voc. & Gram. Transparencies 16 (map)

Remind students that Nydia Velázquez is Puerto Rican. Ask a volunteer to locate Puerto Rico on *Vocabulary & Grammar Transparency* 16. Remind students that the island is the only United States territory where **Cristóbal Colón** actually set foot. He landed there on his second voyage to the Americas in 1493. Puerto Rico is a commonwealth associated with the United States. Large numbers of Puerto Ricans have made permanent homes in Florida, New York City, and elsewhere on the mainland.

¡Adelante!

Puente a la cultura
Los Estados Unidos . . . en español

Estrategia

Reading for comprehension
Read without stopping at unknown words. Then go back, decide if the words are important, and see if you can guess the meaning. If you do not understand the meaning, then look at the footnotes or a dictionary.

César Chávez

Desde el origen de nuestro país, los hispanohablantes han hecho importantes contribuciones. Ya en 1776, el capitán Jorge Ferragat había venido desde España para luchar por la independencia. Hoy día los hispanohablantes son una importante parte de la población[1] y sus contribuciones se pueden observar en todas las áreas de la sociedad.

La población[1]

Según datos del censo del año 2000, la población hispanohablante representa el 13 por ciento del total de la población y es el grupo minoritario más grande de los Estados Unidos. Durante los años noventa, este grupo tuvo un gran crecimiento. Según la Oficina del Censo, el número de estadounidenses que hablan español en el hogar aumentó[2] más del 50 por ciento en la década de los noventa. Hoy, uno de cada diez estadounidenses habla español. Como hay casi 27 millones de hispanohablantes, el español tiene cada vez más fuerza e influye en muchos campos del país. Por eso podemos decir que el español es ahora parte importante de la cultura de los Estados Unidos.

La política

En 1993 murió César Chávez, un mexicano americano de familia pobre que fue activista laboral. Chávez organizó y dirigió a los braceros o trabajadores mexicanos migrantes de California para obtener mejores condiciones de trabajo. Creó la Farm Workers Association, de donde luego se formó el fuerte sindicato United Farm Workers of America. Chávez creía en el derecho a ser parte del "sueño americano" y mantener la cultura mexicana al mismo tiempo. En su época, éste era un concepto muy nuevo.

Nydia Velázquez es la primera hispanohablante elegida[3] al Consejo de la Ciudad de Nueva York y la primera puertorriqueña que llegó a ser miembro del Congreso de los Estados Unidos. Además de ella, hay 21 miembros hispanohablantes en el Congreso, y su número e influencia están aumentando.

1 population **2** grew **3** elected

Nydia Velázquez

232 doscientos treinta y dos
¡Adelante!

Students with Learning Difficulties
Some students may be intimidated by long reading passages. Provide a jigsawing option for small groups in which each student reads one section of the passage and reports key information to the rest of the group.

Advanced Learners
Ask students to choose one of the people mentioned in the article or another Spanish speaker for further research. Have them present brief oral reports about their choice. Students can also make posters with photos that can be placed in the classroom or around the school.

Rosario Marin, una inmigrante que vino de México, es la Tesorera de los Estados Unidos y la hispanohablante de más alto nivel que sirve en la administración del presidente George W. Bush.

Los negocios[4]

De las 1,000 compañías que la revista *Fortune* considera las más importantes de los Estados Unidos, trece tienen directores(as) hispanohablantes. Algunas de ellas son: ALCOA, BankBoston, CHS Electronics, Kellog Co., WalMart y Office Depot.

Además, de cada cinco hispanohablantes en los consejos de administración de esas compañías, una es mujer. Linda G. Alvarado, por ejemplo, además de ser directora general de su propia compañía, Alvarado Construction, es también presidenta de los consejos de administración de otras cinco compañías.

Linda G. Alvarado

Las ciencias

Los hispanohablantes se han destacado[5] también como científicos. Por ejemplo, el Dr. Luis W. Álvarez recibió el Premio Nobel de Física por sus estudios sobre partículas elementales[6] y el Dr. Severo Ochoa ganó el Premio Nobel de Medicina por sus estudios sobre el ADN y el ARN[7].

Dr. Severo Ochoa

---

4 business **5** have stood out **6** elementary particles **7** DNA and RNA

¿Comprendiste?

1. ¿Puede decirse que la población hispanohablante es una minoría importante en Estados Unidos? ¿Por qué? ¿Qué ha pasado con esta población desde los años noventa?

2. ¿En qué campos trabajan y hacen importantes contribuciones los hispanohablantes de Estados Unidos?

3. ¿Los hispanohablantes participan en la política de Estados Unidos? Da un ejemplo.

Escribe tu opinión

Después de leer el artículo, piensa cómo puede servirle aprender español a una persona que no lo habla. Escribe un párrafo en el que expliques cómo el español puede ayudar a esa persona a encontrar un trabajo.

Rosario Marin

Go Online
PHSchool.com
For: Internet Link Activity
Visit: www.phschool.com
Web Code: jed-0510

doscientos treinta y tres **233**
Capítulo 5

Presentation

Standards: 1.1, 1.2, 1.3

Resources: Voc. & Gram. Transparencies 115; Audio Program: CD Cap. 5, Track 21; Resource Book: Cap. 5, Audio Script; Practice Answers on Transparencies

Focus: Practicing speaking and listening comprehension within the context of jobs and volunteer work

Suggestions:

For step 1, use the *Audio CD* or read the script aloud. Allow students to hear the descriptions twice through: the first time to write their answers and the second time to check them.

For step 2, guide students to using the present perfect subjunctive. One way they can do this is by having the young man apologize in picture 5 for having stayed up too late the night before in picture 2. Have students tell the story in the past, since this will facilitate using the present perfect subjunctive and the pluperfect tense.

Answers:

Step 1

1. **a**
2. **a**
3. **b**
4. **a**
5. **b**

Steps 2–3
Answers will vary.

¿Qué me cuentas?

En busca de empleo

1 🎧 Vas a escuchar una narración en tres partes. Después de cada parte, vas a oír una o dos preguntas. Escoge la respuesta que corresponda a cada pregunta.

1. **a.** comedor de beneficencia   **b.** hogar de niños   **c.** centro recreativo
2. **a.** llevarlas a la entrevista   **b.** pedirlas a los ancianos   **c.** leerlas
3. **a.** si tenía responsabilidad   **b.** si le gustaba ser voluntario   **c.** si sabía cocinar
4. **a.** de horario flexible   **b.** sólo a tiempo parcial   **c.** fácil
5. **a.** si donan fondos   **b.** cuál es el salario   **c.** ¡Felicitaciones!

2 Las ilustraciones que aparecen a continuación representan un cuento. Con tus propias palabras, describe detalladamente lo que sucedió. Añade más información para que el cuento sea más interesante. ¡Usa tu imaginación!

Si quieres, puedes usar las siguientes palabras o expresiones para conectar tus ideas.

| en cuanto *(as soon as)* | mientras | a pesar de que *(in spite of)* | cuando |
| para empezar | al mismo tiempo *(at the same time)* | | durante |

1

2

3

4

5

6

3 Trabaja con un grupo de estudiantes. Hablen de los problemas que tuvo el estudiante del cuento anterior. Hagan sugerencias de lo que puede hacer para que la siguiente entrevista sea mejor.

234 doscientos treinta y cuatro
¡Adelante!

Block Schedule

Step 2: In partners, have one student retell the story looking at the pictures. The other student has to act out what he or she hears, without looking at the book. Then switch roles and encourage the second student to change a few details when retelling the picture sequence!

Universal Access

Heritage Language Learners
After students have told a story about the pictures, invite them to improvise a short skit based on their story. Allow them some time to practice. Provide feedback on errors they may make in Spanish, and then have them perform their skits for the class.

Students with Learning Difficulties
Students who find it difficult to create their own speech will benefit from working with an advanced learner first. Together they can complete the chart in step 1 before splitting off to write their speeches individually. Alternatively, allow students to keep track of their classmates' speeches by recording each speaker's main points in a similar chart.

Presentación oral

La elección de la clase

Tarea

Imagina que decides presentarte como candidato(a) a presidente(a) de la clase. Prepara un discurso para convencer a los estudiantes de que eres el (la) mejor porque has ayudado a los demás y eres responsable. Acompaña tu presentación con un cartel.

1 Prepárate Para hacer tu discurso, es necesario que pongas tus ideas en orden. Anota en una tabla como la siguiente las razones por las que piensas que eres el (la) mejor candidato(a) para el trabajo.

Cualidades y habilidades	Éxitos importantes	Trabajos realizados	Problemas de la clase	Ideas para resolverlos

2 Practica Vuelve a leer la información y organízala para preparar tu discurso. Explica tus cualidades y lo que has hecho, los problemas de la clase y tus soluciones. Usa tus notas para practicar, pero no al hablar ante la clase. Recuerda:

- expresar tus ideas en forma convincente *(a convincing way)*
- hablar con voz clara

Modelo

Soy la mejor candidata para presidenta de la clase. Siempre me han preocupado los problemas de mis compañeros. Siempre he ayudado a todos. Tengo muchas ideas para mejorar . . .

3 Haz tu presentación Piensa que tus compañeros(as) de clase son los que van a votar a favor del (de la) mejor candidato(a). Usa un cartel u otra ayuda gráfica para apoyar tu presentación.

4 Evaluación Tu profesor(a) puede explicarte cómo va a evaluar tu presentación. Probablemente, para tu profesor(a) es importante ver que:

- explicaste con ejemplos por qué eres el (la) mejor candidato(a)
- tu público entendió el mensaje de tu discurso

Estrategia

Using visual aids
If you create visual aids such as graphs and charts to support the topic of your speech, they will strengthen your argument while adding visual appeal.

doscientos treinta y cinco **235**
Capítulo 5

Communicate: Speaking

Presentación oral

Presentation

Standards: 1.2, 1.3, 3.1

Resources: Voc. & Gram. Transparencies 4

Focus: Preparing and delivering an oral presentation

Suggestions: Review the task and the four-step approach with students. Before students begin, direct their attention to the *Estrategia*. Encourage them to design their visual aid to be simple, clear, and large enough to be seen by everyone in their audience. Help them organize their information by using *Vocabulary & Grammar Transparency* 4 as a model. You must add a fifth column to the chart.

Portfolio

Record students' oral presentations on audiocassette or videotape for inclusion in their portfolios.

✓ Assessment

• Assessment Program: Cap. 5, Rubrics

Give students copies of the rubric before they begin the activity. Go over the descriptions of the different levels of performance. After assessing students, help individuals understand how their performance could be improved.

Enriching Your Teaching

RUBRIC	Score 1	Score 3	Score 5
How well your information is organized	Your ideas are undeveloped with incorrect or no transitions.	You leave some ideas undeveloped, with some confusing details.	Your ideas are well developed with clear, consistent transitions.
How convincing you are	Your supporting evidence is weak. Your speech is read.	Some of your evidence is convincing. You make some eye contact with audience.	All your evidence is convincing. You have good eye contact and use of gestures.
How effectively you use your visuals	You hardly use visuals, or they don't communicate the message.	You use visuals sometimes, but they're not always effective.	Your visuals are very helpful and are used effectively.

235

Presentación escrita

Standards: 1.2, 1.3, 3.1, 5.1

Resources: Voc. & Gram. Transparencies:12

Focus: Combining learned vocabulary and structures in a written presentation

Suggestions: Begin by explaining the criteria you will use to evaluate students' compositions. (See step 5, *Evaluación*, in the Student Edition, and *Assessment* on the following page.)

Direct students' attention to the *Estrategia*. Ask them to share additional background information they have learned in Language Arts courses about persuasive writing. Remind them that they also developed some effective persuasion strategies in the *Presentación oral* on the previous page. Use *Vocabulary & Grammar Transparency* 12 to model the organization of the persuasive letter. Adapt the transparency for your purposes by writing your main idea in the center box and using the four outer boxes for the four parts of the letter.

Language Arts Connection

Standards: 3.1

Remind students that in today's busy world, the most important qualities for messages such as the letter they are writing are clarity and brevity. Have them consult reference sources from their Language Arts classes for models of a persuasive cover letter. They can use and adapt information from those models for this assignment.

Presentación escrita

La carta para solicitar empleo

Objectives
- To write a cover letter to express interest in a job
- To include a description of the student's qualities and work experience in the letter

Estrategia

Writing to persuade
When you write to persuade, you want to convince someone else to do or think the way you do. In this case, you are offering to be the best candidate for an opening. When you write to persuade you should do the following:
- Think about the needs of the person you are writing to.
- Think of the reasons why you might be the best candidate.
- Organize the reasons and let the person you are writing to know you are the solution.
- Invite your reader to take action.

Imagina que quieres pedir trabajo en un centro recreativo. Vas a enviar una carta en la que expliques tus cualidades, tu experiencia y las razones por las que te gustaría trabajar allí. Escribe una carta para solicitar empleo.

1 Antes de escribir

Piensa en los datos que quieres incluir en la carta. Crea una gráfica, como la siguiente, con la información que debes poner en cada parte de la carta. Imagina el nombre de la organización y del gerente al que le escribes la carta.

CARTA PARA SOLICITAR EMPLEO PARA:
Centro Recreativo Avellaneda
Gerente: Sr. Jorge Ríos

SALUDO/INTRODUCCIÓN
Razones por las que le escribo:
- He leído el anuncio y me interesa el trabajo.
- Me gusta ayudar.
- Me gusta trabajar con niños.

DESARROLLO
Cualidades/Experiencia:
- ordenado, puntual, responsable
- He trabajado como consejero en un campamento de verano.
- Antes había juntado fondos para . . .

CONCLUSIÓN
- Tengo las cualidades y la experiencia que se necesitan para hacer bien el trabajo.
- Voy a llamarlo la semana que viene.

DESPEDIDA
- Atentamente

2 Borrador

Escribe tu borrador. Recuerda que la carta es para el gerente del centro recreativo en el que quieres trabajar. Escribe tus ideas siguiendo el orden de la gráfica. Recuerda usar la gramática y el vocabulario de este capítulo.

Universal Access

Students with Special Needs
Allow students with fine motor skill difficulties to dictate their ideas to another student. The second student also benefits from this arrangement, since he or she is exposed to new ideas.

Advanced Learners
Have pairs of students create a humorous skit about a person who lacks the qualities they described in their letters interviewing for a job. Ask them to act out their "How Not to Get a Job" skits for the class.

Modelo

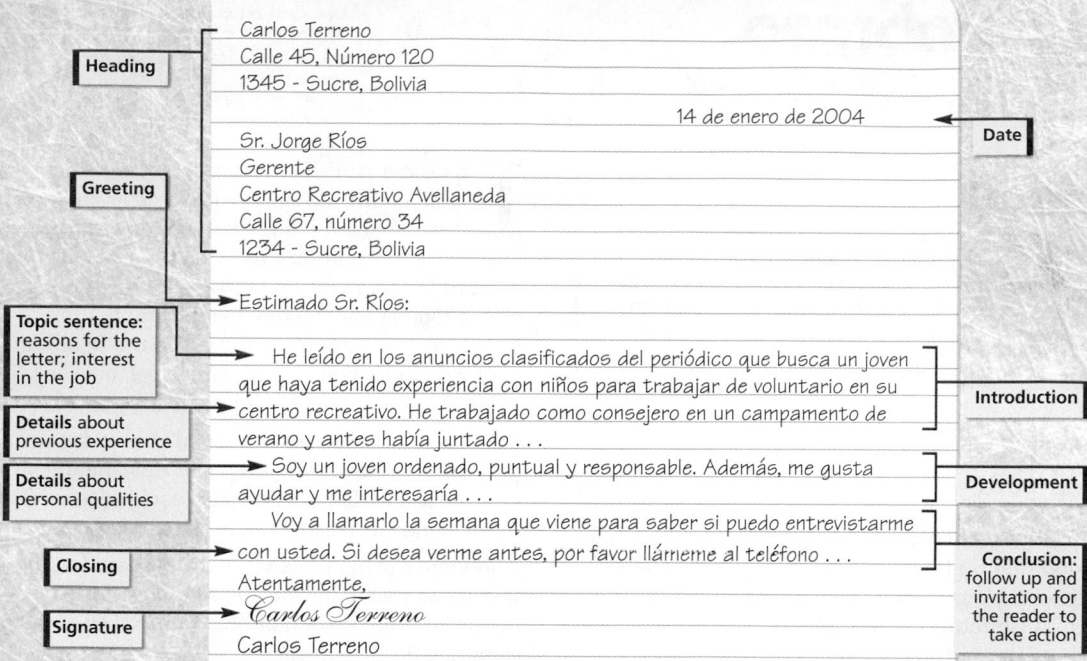

Heading

Carlos Terreno
Calle 45, Número 120
1345 - Sucre, Bolivia

14 de enero de 2004 — **Date**

Greeting

Sr. Jorge Ríos
Gerente
Centro Recreativo Avellaneda
Calle 67, número 34
1234 - Sucre, Bolivia

Estimado Sr. Ríos:

Topic sentence: reasons for the letter; interest in the job

He leído en los anuncios clasificados del periódico que busca un joven que haya tenido experiencia con niños para trabajar de voluntario en su centro recreativo. He trabajado como consejero en un campamento de verano y antes había juntado . . . — **Introduction**

Details about previous experience

Details about personal qualities

Soy un joven ordenado, puntual y responsable. Además, me gusta ayudar y me interesaría . . . — **Development**

Voy a llamarlo la semana que viene para saber si puedo entrevistarme con usted. Si desea verme antes, por favor llámeme al teléfono . . . — **Conclusion:** follow up and invitation for the reader to take action

Closing

Atentamente,

Signature

Carlos Terreno
Carlos Terreno

3 Redacción/Revisión

Después de escribir el primer borrador de tu carta, trabaja con otro(a) estudiante para intercambiar los trabajos y leerlos. Digan qué aspectos de las cartas son más efectivos.

Haz lo siguiente: Subraya con una línea los verbos en presente perfecto, con dos los verbos en pluscuamperfecto, y encierra en un círculo los verbos en presente perfecto del subjuntivo. Corrige los errores de verbos, ortografía y concordancia.

He leído en los anuncios clasificados del periódico que busca un joven que (haya tenido) experiencia con niños para trabajar como voluntario en su centro recreativo. He trabajé como consejero en un campamento de verano y antes habíamos juntado . . .

4 Publicación

Antes de escribir la versión final, lee de nuevo tu carta y repasa los siguientes puntos:

- ¿Sigue mi carta el formato de una carta para solicitar empleo?
- ¿Puse detalles sobre mis cualidades y mi experiencia de trabajo?

Después de revisar el borrador, escribe una copia en limpio de tu carta.

5 Evaluación

Tu profesor(a) puede explicarte cómo va a evaluar tu presentación. Probablemente, para tu profesor(a) es importante ver que:

- seguiste el formato de una carta para solicitar empleo
- usaste detalles para demostrar que eres el (la) mejor candidato(a)

doscientos treinta y siete   237
Capítulo 5

Suggestions (Cont'd):

In step 2, students should concentrate on how to develop the ideas in the chart from step 1 and include them in the appropriate sequence in a letter. Explain that the three parts of their chart called *Introducción, Desarrollo,* and *Conclusión* should each become a paragraph in their letter.

For step 3, encourage students to focus on sentence structure, transitions, use of the pluperfect tense and the present perfect subjunctive, and use of demonstrative adjectives and pronouns. In this step, they should also include and arrange the *Saludo, Despedida,* date, and necessary addresses in their letter. Have them follow the suggestions shown.

Evaluation

Steps 4 and 5 overlap. Students will need evaluation by you, their peers, or self-evaluation to fine-tune and polish their drafts.

Portfolio

Keep students' final drafts in their portfolios as a writing sample.

✓ **Assessment**

- Assessment Program: Cap. 5, Rubrics

Give students copies of the rubric before they begin the activity. Go over the descriptions of the different levels of performance.

Enriching Your Teaching

RUBRIC	Score 1	Score 3	Score 5
Completion of task	Important parts of your letter are missing.	Minor parts of your letter are missing or incorrect.	All your information is included and effectively organized.
Ability to persuade	Your lack of information or organization makes the message unclear.	Your message is present, but sometimes unconvincing.	Your choice and organization of information create a clear, convincing message.
Sentence structure/grammar, spelling, mechanics	Your sentences are run on or are fragmented with many errors.	You use sentences consistently, but they contain some errors.	Your sentence structure is correct and varied with very few errors.

Lectura

Presentation

Standards: 1.2, 2.1, 2.2, 3.1, 3.2

Resources: Voc. & Gram. Transparencies: 4

Focus: Reading an extended passage

Suggestions:

Pre-reading: Before reading, direct students' attention to the *Al leer* section. Have them copy the graphic organizer from p. 241 and make sure they understand how they will use it. Address any comprehension problems they may have with the three points at the end of *Al leer,* and remind them to focus on these points as they read. Also refer them to the *Estrategia.* In order to answer the question there, ask them to watch for the words **poblado, ramas,** and **deshacerse** as they read.

Country Connection

Presentation

Standards: 3.1

Resources: Voc. & Gram. Transparencies 14 (map)

After reading the *Al leer* section, refer students to *Vocabulary & Grammar Transparency* 14. Ask a volunteer to point out the Yucatán peninsula. Remind them that this part of Mexico was the home of the great civilization of the ancient Mayas, whose descendents still live there. Ask students to name famous sites with Mayan ruins, such as Chichén Itzá and Tulum in Mexico or Tikal in Guatemala.

Lectura

La Pobreza

Objectives

- **Read about a Mayan folktale**
- **Use context clues to find meaning of unfamiliar words**
- **Understand the meaning of the story**

Estrategia

Using context clues

If you don't recognize a word in a selection, use other words in the sentence or paragraph to guess its meaning. Which context clues may help you to guess the meaning of words such as *poblado, ramas,* and *deshacerse*?

Al leer

Muchas personas se dedican a tratar de cambiar algo que no les parece bueno o justo. Quieren tener un efecto en la vida de los demás. María Luisa Góngora Pacheco se ha dedicado a conservar la tradición de los pueblos mayas de Yucatán, sus narraciones orales, su teatro popular, su artesanía y su cocina. Vas a leer un cuento escrito por ella.

En este cuento, *La Pobreza*, la autora trata de mostrarnos lo que piensan los mayas sobre la muerte y la pobreza a través de sus propias narraciones orales, que transmiten de padres a hijos.

Antes de leer el cuento, copia la tabla de la página 241. Llena la segunda columna mientras lees y presta atención a los siguientes puntos:

- cómo describe la autora a la Muerte
- la descripción del personaje de la Pobreza
- cómo ve la gente del pueblo a los dos personajes

238 doscientos treinta y ocho
Lectura

El señor Aurelio Zumárraga cuenta que hubo una vez cierta viejita cuyo nombre era Pobreza y que vivía en las afueras de la población. En la puerta de su casa había sembrado una mata de huaya[1] y ésta le daba frutos todo el año. Lo que le molestaba a la viejita es que a aquel que veía el fruto le daban ganas de[2] comérselo y sin pedirle permiso se subía a la mata y se anolaba[3] las huayas.

Un día, cuando la viejita llegó al centro del poblado, vio que un viejito pedía limosna, pedía aunque sea le dieran algo para comer en vez de unas monedas, pero nadie lo tomaba en cuenta.

A la viejita le dio pena verlo en ese estado tan lastimoso y se lo llevó a su casa para darle de almorzar. Cuando el hombrecito terminó de comer, le dijo a la viejita:

—Ahora que ya comí lo que me diste, pídeme lo que quieras, que yo puedo concedértelo[4].

---

1 guava bush 2 felt like 3 ate 4 grant it

Universal Access

Heritage Language Learners

Have students ask family members about folk tales from their heritage country, and invite them to share these tales with the class. Some family members might even enjoy visiting the class and sharing these folk tales themselves.

Students with Learning Difficulties

Stop periodically and help students summarize what they have read so far. By breaking up the selection into smaller chunks, you provide students with a better chance for successful reading comprehension.

—Buen hombre —dijo la viejita—, lo único que quiero es que le digas a la huaya que no deje bajar al que se suba a sus ramas, hasta que yo se lo mande.

—¡Que se cumpla lo que pides! —contestó el viejito y se fue satisfecho.

La viejita se quedó muy complacida al ver que se cumplía lo prometido por el viejito.

Pasaron muchos años, y un día llegó con la viejita el señor de la Muerte quien le ordenó:

—Ya es tiempo de que vengas conmigo vieja Pobreza, por eso te vine a buscar.

Ella pensó rápidamente la forma de deshacerse de la Muerte y le dijo: —Me voy contigo, pero primero quiero que bajes unas huayas para que yo anole.

—Bien, en seguida lo haré —contestó la Muerte. Se dirigieron al árbol y ya debajo, la viejita le dijo a la Muerte:

—Sube hasta allá en lo más alto, ahí se encuentran las más grandes y hermosas huayas, de ésas quiero.

La Muerte, muy segura de sí misma, trepó a la mata, pero no pudo bajarse.

La Pobreza al ver lo que sucedía, se metió a su casa y se desajenó³ de todo.

Así pasaron muchos años y la Muerte no llegaba a nadie, aunque se enfermara la persona. Los doctores veían con asombro que la viejita Pobreza no moría aun buscando alguna manera para hacerlo.

Un día, uno de los doctores fue a casa de la viejita y lo primero que vio fue la mata llena de frutos, dándole tantas ganas de comer algunos se subió y no pudo bajar. En las ramas encontró al señor de la Muerte y le preguntó:

---

3 washed her hands of

Enriching Your Teaching

Culture Note
María Luisa Góngora Pacheco is one of the most important writers of Mayan culture. She has conducted many activities related to preserving the language, medicines, and traditions of her people. One of her current interests is to develop a Web site in order to preserve samples of the Mayan language and provide information about Mayan traditions for future generations to enjoy. Thanks to her work, Mayan folklore and traditions are enjoying renewed popularity not only in Mexico but internationally.

Suggestions (Cont'd):

Reading: Allow students time to read the entire selection on their own silently. You might assign this task for homework. This will allow you to capitalize on class time to read it again together with students. When reading together, pause frequently to address comprehension issues that students may bring up and to allow them to fill in their **_Claves del contexto_** charts from p. 241. The following questions and possible thought processes refer to the three words mentioned in the _Estrategia_. Encourage students to use similar reasoning as they complete the rest of the chart.

• p. 238: _¿Qué claves del contexto usaste para comprender la palabra_ **poblado?** _(Sé que es un lugar porque la viejita llegó allí. Tiene un centro. Se parece a las palabras_ **pueblo** _y_ **población**. _Es probablemente un sinónimo de_ **pueblo**._)_

• p. 239: _¿Qué claves del contexto usaste para comprender la palabra_ **ramas?** _(Son una parte de una planta que da frutas. La gente sube a las ramas. Sé que muchos árboles dan frutas y que la gente las sube para recoger las frutas. Entonces_ **ramas** _probablemente quiere decir "branches.")_

• p. 239: _¿Qué claves del contexto usaste para comprender la palabra_ **deshacerse?** _(A nadie le gusta que le venga el señor de la Muerte. Cuando viene, la viejita piensa rápidamente la forma de_ **deshacerse** _de él. Después, engaña a (tricks) al señor de la Muerte que se queda en el árbol. Creo que es así que la viejita se_ **deshizo** _de él. También la palabra tiene el prefijo_ **des-** _y sé que este prefijo quiere decir algo negativo._ **Deshacerse** _debe significar algo como "have nothing to do with" o "get rid of.")_

Teacher-to-Teacher
A successful strategy for teaching reading skills is articulating your thoughts in words, as if you were thinking aloud in order to answer a question. In Spanish, this process not only guides students in how to implement a reading strategy; it provides excellent listening practice.

Suggestions (Cont'd):

Reading: The following questions can be used to help students comprehend the portion of the reading on this page:

¿Piensas que la Muerte habla rápidamente o lentamente? ¿Qué te da esa impresión? (Parece que habla rápidamente. No habla con frases, sino con muchas ideas a la vez, separadas por comas.)

¿Habla formalmente o informalmente con el doctor? ¿Cómo lo sabes? (Le dice "tú." Usa palabras informales.)

¿A quién se refiere el pronombre del complemento indirecto "les" en la frase "Bajen, —les decían"? (a los que están en el árbol)

Según el señor de la Muerte, ¿por qué no puede llevarse a la Pobreza con él al final del cuento? (Tiene demasiado trabajo.)

Post-reading: As students discuss the story and complete the activities in *Interacción con la lectura* on the next page, remind them that the two main characters are meant to represent more than just two inhabitants in a village. Their names, *la Pobreza* and *la Muerte,* are what make the folk tale timeless and larger than life.

—¿Qué haces aquí?, todos te andan buscando, pues ya quieren morirse y tú no llegas para llevártelos.

—Mira, lo que pasó fue que esa mentecata[4] de viejita de la casa, me fregó[5], pues vine a buscarla y la muy taimada[6] me dijo que se iría conmigo, pero que antes le bajara unas cuantas huayas. Al subir no pude bajarme y aquí me tienes, y todo aquel que se sube, se queda y hasta tú te quedarás —contestó la Muerte.

—Entonces, a eso se debe que no mueran las personas —dijo el doctor. —Lo que debemos hacer es bajar —y empezó a gritar: —¡Vengan aquí, vengan aquí, la Muerte está en mi poder, vengan a verla!

Fue tanto lo que gritó y tan fuerte, que la gente de la población se reunió debajo del árbol.

—Bajen —les decían.

—No podemos, todo el que se sube, se queda aquí —contestó el doctor.

Entonces la gente acordó cortar el árbol para que bajaran el doctor y la Muerte. Al momento que lo iban a comenzar a cortar, se asomó la viejita Pobreza.

—¿Qué pretenden hacer, si quieren bajar a los que están en la mata de huaya, por qué no me lo dicen?

—Discúlpenos[7], —dijeron los allí reunidos. La vieja Pobreza se volvió hacia el árbol y le dijo:

—¡Deja que todos bajen!

Cuando todos bajaron, el señor de la Muerte le dijo:

—Vieja Pobreza, por dejarme bajar del árbol, ahora tengo mucho trabajo y no te puedo llevar, otro día será.

Se fue el señor de la Muerte y la Pobreza se quedó en la tierra. Por eso hasta ahora la tenemos con nosotros.

4 silly, stupid **5** ruined my plans **6** sly, crafty **7** excuse us

Block Schedule

After the class has read the story, create "story experts." Divide the story in four sections and give students numbers 1, 2, 3, or 4. This "expert" is to create five questions about his or her section of the story. Create groups of four students, each with a different "expert." Have them direct their questions to other members of the group.

Universal Access

Multiple Intelligences
Interpersonal/Social: Invite students to discuss ways they can use their interpersonal skills to better the community by working with people of their own age. In small groups, they can brainstorm community needs and possible solutions that they and groups from other schools can help bring about.

Advanced Learners
Students who enjoyed reading this folk tale might wish to use the Internet to find out more about María Luisa Góngora Pacheco and her work preserving the traditions of the Mayas.

Interacción con la lectura

1 Completa la tabla con claves del contexto.

CLAVES DEL CONTEXTO		
palabra desconocida	palabras clave	significado
limosna		
lastimoso		
rama		
satisfecho		
complacida		
deshacerse		
trepó		
acordó		
se asomó		

2 Trabaja con un grupo de estudiantes. Completen sus tablas. Usen las palabras clave que escribieron para decir cuál creen que es el significado de las palabras desconocidas. Escriban el significado de cada palabra en la columna vacía.

3 Comenta con tu grupo lo que escribieron en sus tablas y contesta las preguntas.

- ¿Qué hizo la Pobreza para deshacerse del señor de la Muerte cuando vino a buscarla?
- ¿Cuál era más importante para la vieja Pobreza, la mata de huaya o la Muerte? ¿Por qué?
- ¿Qué significa cuando la autora dice que el señor de la Muerte no se llevó a la Pobreza aunque era vieja?
- Da algunas características del personaje de la Muerte en este cuento. ¿La autora lo presenta como un personaje trágico y serio o no?

4 ¿Conoces otros cuentos o mitos que traten de la Muerte? Escribe un párrafo que diga cómo hablan de ella.

Fondo cultural

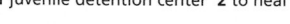

Vuelta de hoja La vida de Luis Rodríguez iba por un camino peligroso. A los 7 años, ya era un ladrón. No pasaba de los 13 años, cuando estuvo en un centro de detención juvenil[1] y a los 15, dejó la escuela. Pero a los 18 años "comencé a darle vuelta a mi vida", recuerda Rodríguez. Con ayuda, empezó a trabajar. "Pero a lo largo de todo, leí todo lo que pude. Los libros salvaron mi vida", dice Rodríguez.

Hace más de un año, Rodríguez abrió al noreste de Los Ángeles el Café Cultural Tía Chucha, para los jóvenes hispanohablantes y sus familias. Allí tienen charlas de historia y libros, presentaciones musicales y exhibiciones de películas. Rodríguez quiere ayudar a otros jóvenes a desarrollar sus habilidades y a curarse[2] ellos mismos, tal como él se curó. Él es un escritor y activista mexicano-americano que nació en El Paso, Texas. Su padre, Alfonso, un director de escuela en México, fue quien fomentó su amor por los libros.

- ¿Conoces algún centro de la comunidad en tu barrio que te haya ayudado a ti o a algún(a) joven que conoces? ¿Cómo se llama el centro y cómo los(as) ayudó?
- ¿Por qué crees que el café de Rodríguez puede gustarle a los(as) jóvenes? ¿Qué otras cosas crees que puede añadir al café?

Luis Rodríguez en el Café Cultural Tía Chucha

---

1 juvenile detention center **2** to heal

doscientos cuarenta y uno **241**
Capítulo 5

Interacción con la lectura

Standards: 1.1, 1.3, 3.1

Resources: Practice Answers on Transparencies

Suggestions: After students share the thought processes they followed to complete the *Claves del contexto* chart, encourage them to go back and read over sections of the story, now that they have a better understanding of the vocabulary.

Answers:

Steps 1, 2, 4
Answers will vary.

Step 3
La Pobreza le dijo al señor de la Muerte que se subiera a la mata de huaya.
Answers will vary for the remaining bulleted questions.

Fondo cultural

Standards: 1.1, 1.2, 5.1, 5.2

Suggestions: After students have read the information silently, ask comprehension questions. For example: *Da unos ejemplos del "camino peligroso" por donde iba Luis Rodríguez durante la primera parte de su vida. (Era ladrón y miembro de una pandilla. Estuvo en un centro de detención juvenil. Se dedicó a la violencia y a las drogas.) ¿Qué ocurre típicamente en el Café Cultural Tía Chucha? (charlas, presentaciones musicales y exhibiciones de películas)*

Answers will vary.

Teacher-to-Teacher

Help students personalize the information about Luis Rodríguez. Use it as a vehicle for discussion about social issues that affect them and your community.

Enriching Your Teaching

Culture Note

In addition to being a successful and important community leader, Luis Rodríguez is a renowned writer. He has published memoirs, fiction, nonfiction, children's literature, and poetry. His work has also won numerous awards, including a Poetry Center Book Award, a Parent's Choice Award, and the Carl Sandberg award. Rodríguez named his café after his aunt, who was an inspiration to him, just as he has now become for other young people.

En el trabajo/Los trabajos/Para la entrevista: Have students prepare their own Spanish definition for each vocabulary item in these categories. Then have teams of two students play against each other in a game of "Password." One student on a team gives his or her partner a definition. The partner must name the vocabulary item defined to earn a point. If he or she cannot, the other team gets a chance at the same definition. The team that correctly matches the greatest number of definitions and vocabulary items wins.

Cualidades y características: Have students work in pairs. One student describes a personality trait of someone he or she knows: *Tengo una hermana que nunca llega tarde.* The partner responds by restating the information using an appropriate adjective: *Así es, tienes una hermana muy puntual.*

Actividades/Acciones: Have students write their own cloze exercises for the items in this category. Explain that, to make a cloze exercise, they use the word or expression correctly in a sentence, then delete the word or expression and replace it with a blank. Ask them to make an answer key to accompany their exercise. Students might enjoy creating their exercises using computer word-processing software. Have partners trade exercises, complete them, and check their work together.

La comunidad: Have students work in pairs and play "Hangman" using the words and expressions in this category.

Expresiones: Students can use these words and expressions as they do the review activities for the other categories.

Repaso del capítulo

Vocabulario y gramática

en el trabajo

el anuncio clasificado	classified ad
los beneficios	benefits
el / la cliente(a)	client
la compañía	firm / company
el / la dueño(a)	owner
la fecha de nacimiento	date of birth
el / la gerente	manager
el puesto	position
el salario (o el sueldo)	salary
la solicitud de empleo	job application

los trabajos

la computación	computer science
el / la consejero(a)	counselor
el / la mensajero(a)	messenger
el / la niñero(a)	babysitter
el / la repartidor(a)	delivery person
el / la recepcionista	receptionist
el / la salvavida	lifeguard

cualidades y características

agradable	pleasant
dedicado, -a	dedicated
flexible	flexible
injusto, -a	unfair
justo, -a	fair
puntual	punctual
la responsabilidad	responsibility
responsable	responsible

para la entrevista

los conocimientos	knowledge
la entrevista	interview
la habilidad	skill
la referencia	reference
el requisito	requirement

el trabajo

a tiempo completo	full time
a tiempo parcial	part time

actividades

atender	to help, to assist
construir (i→y)	to build
cumplir con	to carry out, to perform
donar	to donate
encargarse (de)(g→gu)	to be in charge of
juntar fondos	to fundraise
presentarse	to apply for a job
reparar	to repair
repartir	to deliver
seguir (+ gerund)	to keep on (doing)
sembrar (ie)	to plant
soler (ue)	to usually do something
solicitar	to request

la comunidad

la campaña	campaign
el centro de la comunidad	community center
el centro de rehabilitación	rehabilitation center
el centro recreativo	recreation center
la ciudadanía	citizenship
el / la ciudadano(a)	citizen
el comedor de beneficencia	soup kitchen
los derechos	rights
la gente sin hogar	homeless people
el hogar de ancianos	home for the elderly
la ley	law
la manifestación	demonstration
la marcha	march
el medio ambiente	environment
el servicio social	social service
la sociedad	society

acciones

beneficiar	to benefit
educar	to educate
garantizar	to guarantee
organizar	to organize
proteger	to protect

expresiones

a favor de	in favor of
en contra (de)	against
me es imposible	It is impossible for me . . .
me encantaría	I would love to. . .
me interesaría	I would be interested . . .

Universal Access

Students with Learning Difficulties

Have students write down words or phrases they are having difficulty remembering. Place these in a hat. Then invite a volunteer to choose two words from the hat and work with a more advanced learner to come up with a sentence using the two words. Students can share their sentences with the class.

Advanced Learners

Invite students to create and trade crossword puzzles using the chapter vocabulary. Tell them they can be creative with their clues, but they must be accurate. You may wish to provide or have students use computer software to make the crossword puzzles.

El presente perfecto

To form the **present perfect tense**, combine the present tense of the verb *haber* with a past participle.

he hablado	hemos hablado
has hablado	habéis hablado
ha hablado	han hablado

To form the past participle of a verb, add *-ado* to the stem of *-ar* verbs and *-ido* to the stem of *-er* and *-ir* verbs.

hablar → hablado   comer → comido   vivir → vivido

Some verbs that have a double vowel in the infinitive (except for *ui*) require an accent mark on the *i* in the past participle.

caer → caído   oír → oído

Many Spanish verbs have irregular past participles:

abrir	→	**abierto**	morir	→	**muerto**	romper →	**roto**
decir	→	**dicho**	poner	→	**puesto**	ser →	**sido**
escribir	→	**escrito**	resolver	→	**resuelto**	ver →	**visto**

When using the present perfect tense, place negative words, object pronouns and reflexive pronouns before the form of *haber*.

No he repartido las flores.
Mi profesora **me** ha escrito un poema.
El dueño **se** ha ido temprano a la oficina.

El pluscuamperfecto

To form the **pluperfect,** combine the imperfect tense of the verb *haber* with a past participle.

había hablado	habíamos hablado
habías hablado	habíais hablado
había hablado	habían hablado

El presente perfecto del subjuntivo

To form the **present perfect subjunctive,** use the present subjunctive of the verb *haber* with a past participle.

haya trabajado	hayamos trabajado
hayas trabajado	hayáis trabajado
haya trabajado	hayan trabajado

Los adjetivos y los pronombres demostrativos

	Close to you		Closer to the person you are talking to		Far from both of you	
Adjectives	este	estos	ese	esos	aquel	aquellos
	esta	estas	esa	esas	aquella	aquellas
Pronouns	éste	éstos	ése	ésos	aquél	aquéllos
	ésta	éstas	ésa	ésas	aquélla	aquéllas

To refer to an idea, or something that has not been identified, we use the demonstrative pronouns *esto, eso,* or *aquello.*

⬤ **Más práctica** . . . .
Practice Workbook Organizer 5-13, 5-14

Enriching Your Teaching

Teacher-to-Teacher
Building on activities within the same context, as in the first three activity suggestions on this Teacher's Edition page, is an excellent way to clarify the meaning of verb tenses and moods and show how they interrelate.

El presente perfecto: Have students write five sentences in the present perfect tense about the actions of five different people they know or people in the news during the past week. Tell students not to name the people in their sentences, and encourage them to vary the subject each time. Have them share their sentences with other students, who must identify who the subject is: *Hemos ganado el partido de básquetbol contra Wilford Heights. (los miembros del equipo de básquetbol de nuestra escuela)*

El pluscuamperfecto: Students can use the sentences they wrote in the previous activity. This time, listeners add a fact about what had happened previously: *Hemos ganado el partido de básquetbol contra Wilford Heights. Antes no habíamos ganado ni un solo partido.*

El presente perfecto del subjuntivo: Have students continue using the same contexts from the previous two activities. This time, they use *Ojalá que* and the present perfect subjunctive to make an additional statement: *Hemos ganado el partido de básquetbol contra Wilford Heights. Antes no habíamos ganado ni un solo partido. Ojalá que nuestro equipo se haya entrenado mejor y no haya sido sólo suerte.*

Los adjetivos y los pronombres demostrativos: Have partners choose three objects to refer to. Pairs take turns giving demonstrations using the demonstrative adjectives and pronouns. They place the objects around the room, stand at opposite ends, and make sentences: *Estas llaves (las que están aquí cerca de mí) son mías. Ésas (las que están cerca de ti)...*

Portfolio

Invite students to review the activities they completed in this chapter, including written reports, posters or other visuals, tapes of oral presentations, and other projects. Have them select one or two items that they feel best demonstrate their achievements in Spanish. Include these products in students' portfolios. Have them include this with the Chapter Checklist and Self-Assessment Worksheet.

Additional Resources

• Audio Program: CD Cap. 5, Track 22
• Resource Book: Cap. 5, Clip Art
• Assessment Program: Chapter Checklist and Self-Assessment Worksheet

243

Performance Tasks

Standards: 1.1, 1.2, 1.3

Resources: Audio Program: CD Cap. 5, Track 23; Resource Book: Cap. 5, Audio Script; Practice Answers on Transparencies

1. Vocabulario

Suggestions: Encourage students to review the vocabulary from the *A primera vista* sections on pp. 206–209 and 220–223 before they complete the activity.

Answers:

1. b	5. c
2. a	6. a
3. d	7. d
4. b	8. a

2. Gramática

Suggestions: Remind students of the main points of the grammar presentations in *Capítulo* 5:
• the present perfect tense
• the pluperfect tense
• the present perfect subjunctive
• demonstrative adjectives and pronouns

Answers:

1. b	5. c
2. c	6. b
3. a	7. d
4. a	8. a

Preparación para el examen

To prepare for the test, check to see if you . . .
• know the new vocabulary and grammar
• can perform the tasks on pp. 244 and 245

① Vocabulario Escribe la letra de la palabra o expresión que mejor complete cada frase. Escribe tus respuestas en una hoja aparte.

1. Cuando llenas una solicitud de empleo te piden tu _____.
   a. derecho
   b. fecha de nacimiento
   c. requisito
   d. entrevista

2. Vamos a participar en una _____ para proteger a la gente sin hogar.
   a. campaña
   b. ciudadanía
   c. rehabilitación
   d. responsabilidad

3. No quiero trabajar todos los días. Necesito un puesto a tiempo _____.
   a. puntual
   b. completo
   c. clasificado
   d. parcial

4. Una recepcionista debe _____ bien a los clientes.
   a. reparar
   b. atender
   c. repartir
   d. conseguir

5. ¿Quieres ayudarnos a _____ árboles en el jardín de la comunidad?
   a. educar
   b. beneficiar
   c. sembrar
   d. solicitar

6. Me gustaría trabajar de _____ en una piscina.
   a. salvavida
   b. mensajero
   c. vendedor
   d. repartidor

7. Las leyes de nuestro país _____ educar a todos los niños.
   a. benefician
   b. solicitan
   c. rescatan
   d. garantizan

8. Muchos jóvenes voluntarios _____ casas para la gente sin hogar.
   a. construyen
   b. destruyen
   c. limpian
   d. protegen

② Gramática Escribe la letra de la palabra o expresión que mejor complete cada frase. Escribe tus respuestas en una hoja aparte.

1. Antes de trabajar en el hogar de ancianos, Pilar_____ en un centro recreativo.
   a. ha trabajado
   b. había trabajado
   c. está trabajando
   d. trabaja

2. Me interesaría este puesto, pero prefiero más _____.
   a. aquella
   b. aquellos
   c. aquél
   d. aquellas

3. Espero que mi profesora me _____ una buena carta de referencia.
   a. haya escrito
   b. había escrito
   c. ha escrito
   d. está escribiendo

4. No sé dónde está el gerente. No lo _____ en varias horas.
   a. he visto
   b. había visto
   c. veía
   d. haya visto

5. Quiero que te encargues de _____ solicitudes de empleo.
   a. estos
   b. esto
   c. estas
   d. este

6. Espero que ustedes _____ suficientes fondos para el hogar de ancianos.
   a. han juntado
   b. hayan juntado
   c. habían juntado
   d. juntan

7. "¿Cuántas bicicletas ya _____ este año?", le preguntó a Julio el dueño del taller.
   a. estás reparando
   b. reparabas
   c. hayas reparado
   d. has reparado

8. Cuando llegué al comedor de beneficencia, los voluntarios ya _____ la mesa.
   a. habían puesto
   b. han puesto
   c. van a poner
   d. hayan puesto

Universal Access

Heritage Language Learners

Ask students to write down changes that have occurred in their Spanish due to what they have learned in *Capítulo* 5. These might include corrections of grammar or spelling errors, improvements in vocabulary or pronunciation, or elimination of Anglicisms. Have them keep a running list of such changes in their portfolios.

Students with Learning Difficulties

Before asking students to complete each activity on p. 245, review with them the chapter material that pertains to the activity. If students still have difficulty, encourage them to review together in study groups.

Go Online
PHSchool.com
For: Test preparation
Visit: www.phschool.com
Web Code: jed-0511

En el examen vas a . . .	Éstas son las tareas de práctica que te pueden ser útiles para el examen . . .	Si necesitas repasar . . .
❸ **Escuchar** Escuchar a varios estudiantes en entrevistas de trabajo e identificar los empleos que están solicitando	Escucha lo que dicen estos estudiantes en sus entrevistas de trabajo. Presta atención a lo que dicen y di a qué empleo se presentaron Verónica, Ariel, José y Patricia.	**pp. 206–209** *A primera vista 1* **p. 211** Actividad 9 **p. 212** Actividad 11 **p. 213** Actividad 12
❹ **Hablar** En una feria de trabajo, hablar de tu experiencia y hacer preguntas sobre los empleos	Imagina que vas a una feria de trabajo. Di lo que le dirías a un consejero acerca de tus conocimientos y habilidades, en qué te interesaría trabajar y en qué has trabajado antes. También haz preguntas sobre el empleo, por ejemplo: el horario, el sueldo y los beneficios.	**p. 211** Actividad 9 **p. 212** Actividad 11 **p. 212** Actividad 12 **p. 215** Actividad 15 **p. 216** Actividad 17
❺ **Leer** Leer y comprender un anuncio clasificado	Lee este anuncio. ¿Qué tipo de empleo se ofrece? ¿Es un trabajo a tiempo completo o a tiempo parcial? ¿Qué conocimientos o habilidades se necesitan? **Recepcionista.** Se necesita joven bilingüe, puntual y responsable para atender el teléfono y otros trabajos de oficina. Otros requisitos: saber trabajar con computadoras y tener buenas referencias. Lunes a viernes de 8 a.m. a 5 p.m. Buenos beneficios y salario. Presentarse en nuestras oficinas de la Avenida Bolívar # 534.	**p. 209** *A primera vista 1* **p. 212** Actividad 11 **p. 216** Actividad 16
❻ **Escribir** Escribir una carta para solicitar empleo	Imagina que vas a solicitar empleo. Piensa qué tipo de trabajo es, y escribe una carta para solicitar empleo. En tu carta di (a) por qué te interesa el trabajo, (b) qué cualidades personales tienes por las que serías el (la) mejor para ese puesto y (c) qué experiencia de trabajo tienes.	**p. 213** Actividad 13 **p. 226** Actividad 33 **pp. 236–237** *Presentación escrita*
❼ **Pensar** Pensar en las contribuciones de los hispanohablantes a los Estados Unidos	¿Cuál es el impacto de algunos hispanohablantes en la cultura de los Estados Unidos? También piensa en cómo les influimos a ellos en sus países, como en la política, los negocios, las artes, las ciencias y el deporte.	**p. 226** *Fondo cultural* **pp. 232–233** *Puente a la cultura*

Review

3. Escuchar

Suggestions: Use the *Audio CD* or read from the script.

Answers:
Verónica: empleada en una tienda de animales
Ariel: voluntario en un hogar de ancianos
José: salvavida
Patricia: recepcionista

4. Hablar

Suggestions: Remind students that in this situation they would most likely address the people to whom they are speaking with *Ud.*

Answers will vary.

5. Leer

Suggestions: Tell students to refer to pp. 206–209 and 220–223 if they have questions about vocabulary in the review.

Answers:
Recepcionista.
Es un trabajo a tiempo completo.
Se necesita ser bilingüe, puntual y responsable. Hay que saber trabajar con computadoras y tener buenas referencias.

6. Escribir

Suggestions: Tell students to use their own cover letters in their portfolios as a model.

Answers will vary.

7. Pensar

Suggestions: Ask students if their perceptions of the Spanish-speaking population have changed in any way because of what they have learned.

Answers will vary.

✓ **Assessment**
• Examen del capítulo: 5
• Audio Program: CD 12, Cap. 5, Track 6
• Assessment Program: *RPH*

Alternative Assessment
• ExamView Test Bank CD-ROM
• Resource Book: Cap. 5, Situation Cards
• Resource Book: Cap. 5, Communicative Activity BLM

Enriching Your Teaching

Teacher-to-Teacher

Ask pairs of students to read the want ads section of the newspaper and find a job opening requiring knowledge of Spanish. Then have them create a skit in which one student plays the role of the employer and the other student is the job applicant.

245

¿Qué nos traerá el futuro?

CHAPTER OVERVIEW

Capítulo **6**

¿Qué nos traerá el futuro?
• Careers, professions, and technology

Vocabulary
• careers and professions
• plans for the future
• impact of science and technology

Grammar
• future
• future of probability
• future perfect
• uses of direct and indirect object pronouns

Cultural Perspectives
• Chilean surrealist painter Roberto Matta
• living arrangements of young people in Spain
• internships in Washington, D.C. for young Spanish speakers
• the international baccalaureate program
• Spanish and Latin American architects

Chapter Project

La evolución de los inventos

Overview: Students create a Web page featuring items that have evolved throughout time and will continue to change in the future. Students should show when each item was invented, what it looked like then, what it looks like now, and what it is going to look like in the future. They should insert a brief description of the changes in the history of each product. Students then present their Web page to the class, describing all the information featured on the page.

Materials: poster board, magazines, colored pencils, markers, glue, scissors, bilingual dictionary

Sequence: (suggestions for when to do each step appear throughout the chapter)

STEP 1. Review instructions so students know what is expected of them. Hand out the "Chapter 6 Project Instructions and Rubric" from the *Teacher's Resource Book*.

STEP 2. Students submit a rough draft of their Web page. Return the drafts with your suggestions. For vocabulary and grammar practice, ask students to work in pairs and present their drafts to each other.

STEP 3. Students create layouts on poster board. Encourage students to work in pencil first and to try different arrangements before gluing photographs and writing descriptions. Encourage students to use as much of the vocabulary from *Capítulo* 6 as possible in the descriptions. Also, encourage them to use a bilingual dictionary for any words they would like to use, but do not yet know.

STEP 4. Students submit a draft of their descriptions. Note your corrections and suggestions, then return the drafts to students.

STEP 5. Students complete and present their Web page to the class. They describe all the information featured on the page.

Options:
1. Students create a poster for their school instead of a Web page.
2. Students write an article for the school newspaper about the inventions.

Assessment:
Here is a detailed rubric for assessing this project:

Chapter 6 Project: *La evolución de los inventos*

RUBRIC	Score 1	Score 3	Score 5
Your evidence of planning	You provide no written draft or page layout.	Your draft was written and layout created, but not corrected.	You show evidence of corrected draft and layout.
Your use of illustrations	You include photos or visuals.	Your photos or visuals were included, but the layout was unorganized.	Your Web page was easy to read, complete, and accurate.
Your presentation	You include little of the required information.	You include most of the required information.	You include all of the required information.

Bulletin Boards

Theme: *¿Qué nos traerá el futuro?*

Ask students to cut out, copy, or download photos or pictures of projects or things for the future, and people whose careers are related to the future. Cluster photos or pictures according to these themes. Add brief captions to the photos or pictures explaining what the project or item for the future is about.

Bibliography

DK Bridgman, Roger. *Technology.* Dorling Kindersley, 1999. Describes the ways technology has transformed everyday life, including jobs and careers.

Newcomb, Rexford. *Spanish-Colonial Architecture in the United States.* Mineola, N.Y.: Dover Publishers, 1990. Spanish architecture throughout the United States.

Rubie, Peter, and Luis Reyes. *Los Hispanos en Hollywood: Celebrando 100 Años en el Cine y la Televisión.* New York: Random House Español, 2002. Contributions of Spanish speakers in television and movies.

DK Wilson, Anthony. *Visual Timelines of Transportation.* New York: Dorling Kindersley, 2002. Charts of development of all forms of transportation.

Yenne, Bill, and Morton Grosser. *100 Inventions that Shaped World History.* San Francisco: Bluewood Books, 1993. Describes and illustrates technological inventions that changed the world.

Hands-on Culture

Recipe: *Gallo pinto*

The national dish of Costa Rica is *gallo pinto*, which stands for "refried beans". The *gallo pinto* is served at breakfast, lunch, or dinner, with fried eggs, sour cream, and hot *tortillas*.

Ingredients:

1 cup white rice
1-3/4 cups water
1 tablespoon olive oil
1 medium onion, diced
1/2 red bell pepper, seeded and diced
1 jalapeño pepper, seeded and minced
2 cloves garlic, minced
1 handful chopped cilantro leaves
16 ounces canned black beans, drained
Salt to taste
1 teaspoon Tabasco sauce
2 tablespoons Worcestershire sauce

Supplies:

- frying pan
- 2 qt. saucepan
- serving dish

1. Wash the rice in cold water, drain, and put it in a pot with the water and a pinch of salt. Bring the rice to a boil, stir, cover, and lower the heat to a simmer. Cook the rice until the water is absorbed, about 20 minutes. Let the rice stand for 10 minutes, then fluff it with a fork.
2. Heat the olive oil in a skillet over medium-high heat. Add the onions and peppers and sauté, stirring for 5 minutes. Stir in the garlic and sauté for another 2 minutes. Add the cilantro and sauté for 1 minute more.
3. Spoon the rice and beans into the skillet, mix well, and heat everything through. Season the dish to taste with salt and a combination of Worcestershire sauce and Tabasco sauce.

Internet Search

Use the keywords to find more information.

Keywords:

Roberto Matta, Congressional Hispanic Caucus Institute, Gustavo Adolfo Bécquer, futurólogo, robots, genética, Bachillerato Internacional, diario digital

Game

Cosas del futuro

This game practices grammar and vocabulary about the future. Use it toward the end of *Manos a la obra 2*, after students have practiced the chapter vocabulary.

Players: the entire class

Materials: paper, pencils, markers, pen

Rules:

1. Divide the class into small groups.
2. Have each group think of an invention for the future, such as a special machine that does homework for students.
3. Ask them to make a drawing of the invention and to write down a clue about its function. The clue could be one word or a phrase.
4. Call one group to come to the front of the class. The group shows their drawing to the class. Meanwhile you write the drawing's clue on the board so everybody can read it.
5. The rest of the students take turns asking the members of the group *sí/no* questions in an attempt to determine what the object is for.

Student 1: ¿Es una máquina?
Group: Sí.
Student 2: ¿Se usa en la escuela?
Group: No.
Student 3: ¿Es para los estudiantes?
Group: Sí.
Student 4: ¿Reemplaza a una máquina que existe en la actualidad?
Group: No.
Student 5: ¿Es una máquina que te hace las tareas?
Group: ¡Sí!

6. When a student correctly guesses what the object is, his or her group gets one point and is the next one to come to the front of the class and show their drawing. Play continues in this manner until every group has had the chance of showing their drawings and answering questions. The group with more points wins the game.

Variation: Instead of drawing the objects, students can write clues in the form of sentences so students guess what the object is.

Capítulo 6 Overview

A ver si recuerdas — RECYCLE	Vocabulary	Grammar
	• Careers and jobs • Technology and environment	• *saber* vs. *conocer* • Impersonal *se*

Chapter Overview

A primera vista 1 INPUT	Manos a la obra 1 PRACTICE	A primera vista 2 INPUT	Manos a la obra 2 PRACTICE
Objectives • Talk about careers and professions • Talk about future relationships	**Objectives** • Discuss different professions • Talk about plans for the future	**Objectives** • Talk about changes in technology • Explain the impact of science and technology in our lives	**Objectives** • Discuss technology changes • Talk about the impact of technology in our lives
Vocabulary • Careers and professions • Plans for the future	**Vocabulary** • Practice and use new vocabulary	**Vocabulary** • Advances in technology • Careers in the future	**Vocabulary** • Practice and use new vocabulary
Grammar • Future • Future of probability	**Grammar** • Future • Future of probability	**Grammar** • Future perfect tense • Uses of the direct and indirect pronouns	**Grammar** • Future perfect tense • Uses of the direct and indirect pronouns
Culture • Surrealism in art	**Culture** • Spanish young people still living with their parents • Hispanic youth working in Washington, D.C.	**Culture** • Technology of the future	**Culture** • International high school • Life in the future

¡Adelante! — APPLICATION

Objectives		Vocabulary	Culture
• Read about the architecture of the future • Write a comparison about the past and the present	• Describe change in today's world	• Application **Grammar** • Application	• Architecture of the future • Fiction by Ángel Balzarino • Virtual School of the University of Puerto Rico

Repaso del capítulo — REVIEW

Objectives		Vocabulary	Grammar
• Know the new vocabulary and grammar	• Perform the tasks on pages 290 and 291	• Review	• Review

BEYOND THE CLASSROOM

Countries	El español en la comunidad	Internet
• Mexico • Argentina • Puerto Rico • Spain • Chile • United States	• Digital newspapers	• Vocabulary activities • Grammar activities • Internet links • Self-tests

LEARNER SUPPORT

Strategies		Recycling	Ampliación del lenguaje
• Circumlocution • Look at illustrations • Mapping your speech using main idea and details	• Compare and contrast • Coping with unknown words	• Combining letters when speaking • Verbs with irregular participles **En voz alta** • *Rima LIII*	• Professions **Conexiones** • Social Studies: television in Mexico

Print Components

TEACHER

Teacher's Resource Book
• Chapter Table of Contents
• School-to-Home Connection
• Chapter Resource Checklist
• Input Script
• Audio Script
• Video Script
• Communicative Activities
• Situation Cards
• GramActiva Blackline Masters
• Graphic Organizers
• Answer Keys:
  Practice Workbook
  Writing, Audio & Video Workbook

***Realidades para hispanohablantes*
Teacher Edition**

STUDENT

Practice Workbook
• Vocabulary: 6-1 – 6-4, 6-8 – 6-9
• Grammar: 6-5 – 6-7, 6-10 – 6-12
• Organizer: 6-13 – 6-14

Writing, Audio & Video Workbook
• Audio: 1–5
• Writing: 6–13
• Video: 14–17

Reading and Writing for Success
• Chapter 6, Test 33

Realidades para hispanohablantes

Transparencies

Vocabulary and Grammar Transparencies
• Vocabulary: 116–123, 126–129
• Grammar: 124–125, 130–131
• ¿Qué me cuentas?: 132

Practice Answers on Transparencies
• Cap. 6

Fine Art Transparencies
• Transparencies
• Teacher's Guide

Assessment

Assessment Program
• Pruebas:
  – Comprensión del vocabulario 1: 6-1
  – Aplicación del vocabulario 1: 6-2
  – El futuro: 6-3
  – El futuro de probabilidad: 6-4
  – Comprensión del vocabulario 2: 6-5
  – Aplicación del vocabulario 2: 6-6
  – El futuro perfecto: 6-7
  – Uso de los complementos directos e indirectos: 6-8

• Exámenes del capítulo

• Rubrics

Alternative Assessment
• ExamView Test Bank CD-ROM
• MindPoint Quiz Show CD-ROM
• Internet Self-test
• Situation Cards
• Communicative Activity

Assessment Program: *Realidades para hispanohablantes*

Technology

TeacherExpress™ CD-ROM
• Lesson Planner
• Teacher Resources
• Clip Art

Video Program VHS and DVD

Audio Program CDs
• A primera vista 1 y 2: Vocabulario y gramática en contexto
• Audio Activities
• ¿Qué me cuentas?
• Repaso
• Examen del capítulo: Escuchar

Regular Schedule (50 Minutes)

For electronic lesson plans:
Teacher Express CD-ROM

	Warm-up / Assess	Preview Present / Practice Communicate		Wrap-up / Homework Options

DAY 1

Warm-up (10 min.)
• Return Examen del capítulo: Capítulo 5

Repaso (35 min.)
• A ver si recuerdas
• Actividades 1, 2, 3, 6, 7

Wrap-up and Homework Options (5 min.)
• Practice Workbook 6-1, 6-2
• Go Online

DAY 2

Warm-up (10 min.)
• Homework check

Chapter Opener (10 min.)
• Objectives   • Fondo cultural

A primera vista 1 (25 min.)
• Presentation: Vocabulario y gramática en contexto
• Actividad 1

Wrap-up and Homework Options (5 min.)
• Go Online
• Clip Art Vocabulary

DAY 3

Warm-up (10 min.)
• Homework check

A primera vista 1 (30 min.)
• Presentation: Los estudiantes y su futuro • Actividades 2, 3

Manos a la obra 1 (5 min.)
• Actividades 4, 5

Wrap-up and Homework Options (5 min.)
• Practice Workbook 6-3, 6-4
• Manos a la obra 1: Actividad 6
• Go Online   • Prueba 6-1: Vocabulary recognition

DAY 4

Warm-up (10 min.)
• Homework check
✔**Assessment (10 min.)**
• Prueba 6-1: Vocabulary recognition

Manos a la obra 1 (25 min.)
• Actividades 7, 8, 9
• Fondo cultural
• Ampliación del lenguaje

Wrap-up and Homework Options (5 min.)
• Actividad 10
• Writing Activities
• Prueba 6-2: Vocabulary production

DAY 5

Warm-up (15 min.)
• Homework check • Audio Activity
• Communicative Activity
✔**Assessment (10 min.)**
• Prueba 6-2: Vocabulary production

Manos a la obra 1 (20 min.)
• Presentation: El futuro
• Actividades 11, 12, 13
• Writing Activity

Wrap-up and Homework Options (5 min.)
• Practice Workbook 6-5
• Go Online

DAY 6

Warm-up (10 min.)
• Homework check

Manos a la obra 1 (35 min.)
• Actividades 14, 15
• Fondo cultural
• Presentation:El futuro de probabilidad
• Actividades 16, 17

Wrap-up and Homework Options (5 min.)
• Practice Workbook 6-6, 6-7
• Go online
• Prueba 6-3: El futuro

DAY 7

Warm-up (10 min.)
• Homework check
✔**Assessment (10 min.)**
• Prueba 6-3: El futuro

Manos a la obra 1 (25 min.)
• Actividades 18, 19
• Communicative Activity
• En voz alta

Wrap-up and Homework Options (5 min.)
• Writing Activity
• Prueba 6-4: El futuro de probabilidad

DAY 8

Warm-up (10 min.)
• Homework check
✔**Assessment (10 min.)**
• Prueba 6-4: El futuro de probabilidad

A primera vista 2 (25 min.)
• Presentation: Vocabulario y gramática en contexto
• Actividades 20, 21

Wrap-up and Homework Options (5 min.)
• Clip Art Vocabulary
• Examen: Vocabulario y gramática 1

DAY 9

Warm-up (5 min.)
• Homework check
✔**Assessment (30 min.)**
• Examen: Vocabulario y gramática 1

A primera vista 2 (10 min.)
• Presentation: Tres campos que tienen futuro
• Actividad 22

Wrap-up and Homework Options (5 min.)
• Actividad 23
• Practice Workbook 6-8, 6-9
• Go Online
• Prueba 6-5: Vocabulary recognition

DAY 10

Warm-up (20 min.)
• Homework check
✔**Assessment (10 min.)**
• Prueba 6-5: Vocabulary recognition

Manos a la obra 2 (15 min.)
• Actividades 24, 25, 26
• Fondo cultural

Wrap-up and Homework Options (5 min.)
• Actividades 27, 28

	Warm-up / Assess	Preview Present / Practice Communicate	Wrap-up / Homework Options
DAY 11	**Warm-up (15 min.)** • Homework check	**A primera vista 2 (15 min.)** • Actividad 29 • Communicative Activity • Writing Activity **Manos a la obra 2 (15 min.)** • Presentation: El futuro perfecto • Actividades 30, 32	**Wrap-up and Homework Options (5 min.)** • Practice Workbook 6-10 • Go Online • Prueba 6-6: Vocabulary production

DAY 12	**Warm-up (10 min.)**
	• Homework check
	✔**Assessment (10 min.)**
	• Prueba 6-6: Vocabulary production
		Manos a la obra 2 (25 min.)
		• Actividad 31 • Writing Activity
		• Presentation: Uso de los • Actividades 33, 34
		  complementos directos • El español en la comunidad
		  e indirectos
			Wrap-up and Homework Options (5 min.)
			• Practice Workbook 6-11, 6-12
			• Go Online
			• Prueba 6-7: El futuro de probabilidad

DAY 13	**Warm-up (10 min.)** • Homework check ✔**Assessment (10 min.)** • Prueba 6-7	**Manos a la obra 2 (25 min.)** • Actividades 35, 36, 37 • Audio Activity • Writing Activity	**Wrap-up and Homework Options (5 min.)** • Writing Activity • Prueba 6-8: Uso de los complementos directos e indirectos
DAY 14	**Warm-up (10 min.)** • Communicative Activity ✔**Assessment (10 min.)** • Prueba 6-8	**¡Adelante! (25 min.)** • Puente a la cultura: La • El futuro de la comunidad arquitectura del futuro • Presentación oral: Step 1 • ¿Comprendiste?	**Wrap-up and Homework Options (5 min.)** • Examen: Vocabulario y gramática 2
DAY 15	**Warm-up (5 min.)** • Answer questions ✔**Assessment (25 min.)** • Examen: Vocabulario y gramática 2	**¡Adelante! (15 min.)** • Presentación oral: Step 2	**Wrap-up and Homework Options (5 min.)** • Presentación oral: Step 3 • Go Online
DAY 16	**Warm-up (5 min.)** • Homework check	**¡Adelante! (40 min.)** • Presentación oral: Step 3 (half class) • ¿Qué me cuentas? 1, 2, 3	**Wrap-up and Homework Options (5 min.)** • Presentación escrita: Steps 1, 2
DAY 17	**Warm-up (10 min.)** • Homework check	**¡Adelante! (35 min.)** • Presentación oral: Step 3 (half class) • View Video • Video Activities 1, 2, 3 • Presentación escrita: Step 3	**Wrap-up and Homework Options (5 min.)** • Presentación escrita: Step 4 • Preparación para el examen: 1, 2
DAY 18	**Warm-up (10 min.)** • Homework check	**Repaso (10 min.)** • Preparación para el examen: Actividades 3, 4 **¡Adelante! (25 min.)** • Lectura • ¿Comprendiste? • Fondo cultural	**Wrap-up and Homework Options (5 min.)** • ¿Comprendiste? • Practice Workbook: Organizer 6-13, 6-14 • Go Online: Self-test
DAY 19	**Warm-up (15 min.)** • Homework check	**Repaso (30 min.)** • Preparación para el examen: Actividades 5, 6, 7 • MindPoint Quiz Show • Other review	**Wrap-up and Homework Options (5 min.)** • Examen del capítulo
DAY 20	**Warm-up (5 min.)** • Answer questions ✔**Assessment (44 min.)** • Examen del capítulo		**Wrap-up and Homework Options (1 min.)** • A ver si recuerdas: Capítulo 7

	Warm-up / Assess	Preview Present / Practice Communicate	Wrap-up / Homework Options
DAY 1	**Warm-up (35 min.)** • Return Examen del capítulo: Capítulo 6 • A ver si recuerdas • Homework check	**Chapter Opener (10 min.)** • Objectives • Fondo cultural **A primera vista 1 (30 min.)** • Presentation: Vocabulario y gramática en contexto • Actividad 1 • Presentation: Los estudiantes hablan del futuro • Actividades 2, 3 **Manos a la obra 1 (10 min.)** • Actividades 4, 5, 6	**Wrap-up and Homework Options (5 min.)** • Practice Workbook 6-3, 6-4 • Go Online • Clip Art Vocabulary • Prueba 6-1: Vocabulary recognition
DAY 2	**Warm-up (20 min.)** • Homework check • Actividades 7, 8, 9 ✔**Assessment (10 min.)** • Prueba 6-1: Vocabulary recognition	**Manos a la obra 1 (55 min.)** • Actividad 10 • Ampliación del lenguaje • Audio Activity • Writing Activity • Communicative Activity	**Wrap-up and Homework Options (5 min.)** • Prueba 6-2: Vocabulary production
DAY 3	**Warm-up (5 min.)** • Homework check ✔**Assessment (10 min.)** • Prueba 6-2: Vocabulary production	**Manos a la obra 1 (70 min.)** • Presentation: El futuro • Actividades 11, 12, 13, 14, 15 • Fondo cultural • Writing Activity	**Wrap-up and Homework Options (5 min.)** • Actividad 15: Step 3 • Practice Workbook 6-5 • Go Online • Prueba 6-3: El futuro
DAY 4	**Warm-up (10 min.)** • Homework check ✔**Assessment (10 min.)** • Prueba 6-3: El futuro	**Manos a la obra 1 (50 min.)** • Presentation: El futuro de probabilidad • Actividades 16, 17, 18, 19 • En voz alta • Writing Activity • Communicative Activity **A primera vista 2 (15 min.)** • Presentation: Vocabulario y gramática en contexto • Actividades 20, 21	**Wrap-up and Homework Options (5 min.)** • Practice Workbook 6-6, 6-7 • Go Online • Prueba 6-4: El futuro de probabilidad • Examen: Vocabulario y gramática 1
DAY 5	**Warm-up (10 min.)** • Homework check ✔**Assessment Options (40 min.)** • Prueba 6-4: El futuro de probabilidad • Examen: Vocabulario y gramática 1	**A primera vista 2 (20 min.)** • Presentation: Tres campos que tienen futuro • Actividades 22, 23 **Manos a la obra 2 (15 min.)** • Actividades 25, 26	**Wrap-up and Homework Options (5 min.)** • Practice Workbook 6-8, 6-9 • Actividades 27, 28 • Clip Art • Go Online • Prueba 6-5: Vocabulary recognition
DAY 6	**Warm-up (35 min.)** • Homework check • Actividades 26, 29 • Audio Activity • Writing Activity • Communicative Activity ✔**Assessment (10 min.)** • Prueba 6-5: Vocabulary recognition	**Manos a la obra 2 (40 min.)** • Presentation: El futuro perfecto • Actividades 30, 31, 32 • Writing Activities	**Wrap-up and Homework Options (5 min.)** • Practice Workbook 6-10 • Go Online • Pruebas 6-6, 6-7: Vocabulary production, El futuro perfecto

	Warm-up / Assess	Preview Present / Practice Communicate	Wrap-up / Homework Options
DAY 7	**Warm-up (10 min.)** • Homework check ✔**Assessment (20 min.)** • Pruebas 6-6, 6-7: Vocabulary production, El futuro perfecto	**Manos a la obra 2 (40 min.)** • Presentation: El uso de los complementos directos e indirectos • Actividades 33, 34, 35, 36, 37 • Audio Activity • Writing Activity • El español en la comunidad **¡Adelante! (15 min.)** • Presentación oral: Steps 1, 2	**Wrap-up and Homework Options (5 min.)** • Practice Workbook 6-11, 6-12 • Go Online • Prueba 6-8: El uso de los complementos directos e indirectos • Presentación oral: Step 2 • Go Online
DAY 8	**Warm-up (15 min.)** • Homework check • Communicative Activity ✔**Assessment (10 min.)** • Prueba 6-8: El uso de los complementos directos e indirectos	**¡Adelante! (35 min.)** • Presentación oral: Step 3 **¡Adelante! (25 min.)** • Presentation: La arquitectura del futuro • ¿Comprendiste? • El futuro de tu comunidad	**Wrap-up and Homework Options (5 min.)** • ¿Comprendiste? • El futuro de tu comunidad • Examen: Vocabulario y gramática 2
DAY 9	**Warm-up (5 min.)** • Homework check ✔**Assessment Options (30 min.)** • Examen: Vocabulario y gramática 2	**¡Adelante! (50 min.)** • ¿Qué me cuentas? 1, 2, 3 • Video • Video Activities • Presentación escrita: Step 1	**Wrap-up and Homework Options (5 min.)** • Presentación escrita: Step 2 • Go Online • Preparación para el examen: Actividades 1, 2
DAY 10	**Warm-up (20 min.)** • Homework check • Presentación escrita: Step 3	**¡Adelante! (35 min.)** • Lectura • ¿Comprendiste? • Fondo cultural **Repaso (30 min.)** • Preparación para el examen: Actividades 3, 4, 6 • MindPoint Quiz Show	**Wrap-up and Homework Options (5 min.)** • Presentación escrita: Step 4 • Practice Workbook: Organizer 6-13, 6-14 • Go Online: Self-test • Preparación para el examen: Actividades 5, 7 • Examen del capítulo
DAY 11	**Warm-up (15 min.)** • Homework check ✔**Assessment (45 min.)** • Examen del capítulo	**Theme Game (15 min.)** **A ver si recuerdas – Capítulo 7 (10 min.)** • Presentation: Vocabulario • Presentation: Gramática	**Wrap-up and Homework Options (5 min.)** • A ver si recuerdas – Capítulo 7 • Actividades 1-6 • Practice Workbook 7-1, 7-2 • Go Online

A ver si recuerdas...

Vocabulario

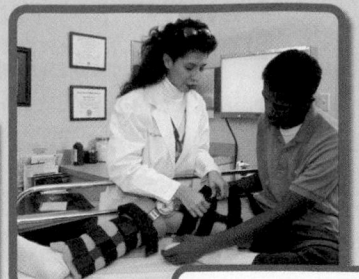

Vocabulario

Presentation

Standards: 1.1, 1.2

Resources: Voc. & Gram. Transparencies: 116

Suggestions: Have students copy the names of the five categories onto their own paper. Show *Vocabulary & Grammar Transparency* 116. With books closed, have students work in pairs and list as many words as they can remember in each category.

Standards: 1.1

Resources: Practice Answers on Transparencies

Focus: Practicing review vocabulary

Suggestions: Encourage students to use vocabulary and structures from previous chapters in step 2. For example, they might use the present perfect tense when referring to the experiences needed for a particular profession: *Si alguien ha trabajado mucho con los animales, puede estudiar para ser veterinario(a).*

Common Errors: Some students may use a feminine article when they refer to a male *artista, policía,* or *dentista.* Remind them that although these nouns end in *-a,* they apply to either gender. Students should use them with masculine articles when talking about males: *Conozco a un artista que se llama Guillermo.*

Answers:
Step 1
1. e   4. b
2. d   5. c
3. a
Step 2
Answers will vary.

el mundo del espectáculo
el actor, la actriz
el bailarín, la bailarina
el/la cantante
el crítico, la crítica

trabajos en la comunidad
el agricultor, la agricultora
el bombero, la bombera
el cajero, la cajera
el cartero, la cartera
el/la dependiente
el empleado, la empleada
el/la gerente
el mecánico, la mecánica
el paramédico, la paramédica
el/la policía
el político, la política
el secretario, la secretaria

los estudios
la graduación
la universidad

el mundo de las ciencias y la tecnología
el/la dentista
el enfermero, la enfermera
el médico, la médica
el técnico, la técnica
el veterinario, la veterinaria

el mundo de las artes
el/la artista
el escritor, la escritora
el escultor, la escultora
el pintor, la pintora

 Hablar ....

Práctica de vocabulario

1 Trabaja con otro(a) estudiante para emparejar cada actividad o área de trabajo con una profesión.

1. actuar, el teatro   **a.** policía
2. los animales, las ciencias naturales **b.** escritor(a)
3. cuidar y proteger a la gente   **c.** abogado(a)
4. los libros, escribir   **d.** veterinario(a)
5. las leyes, las ciencias sociales   **e.** actor, actriz

2 Con tu compañero(a), habla de qué cualidades o estudios se necesitan para trabajar en las profesiones de las listas en el *Vocabulario.*

Modelo

investigar / científico(a)
Si te gusta investigar, puedes ser científico.

246   doscientos cuarenta y seis
A ver si recuerdas . . .

Block Schedule

Extend *Actividad* 1 by asking students to write clues or associations for ten additional jobs. Have them read the list to a partner who will try to guess the job being described.

Universal Access

Multiple Intelligences
Bodily/Kinesthetic: Have students play a game of charades in which they physically act out the movements associated with different professions. After the professions have been identified, have all students review by performing the actions while repeating the vocabulary.

Advanced Learners
Have students choose one profession from the *Vocabulario* and prepare a brief oral presentation telling what a person in that profession does, where he or she works, and what skills and studies he or she needs.

Gramática · Repaso

Saber vs conocer

Both *saber* and *conocer* mean "to know."

You use *saber* to talk about knowing facts or information.

Nadie **sabe** la fecha del examen.   ¿**Saben** Uds. quién es ese actor?

Saber followed by an infinitive means "to know how to do something."

Por supuesto, yo **sé usar** la computadora.   No, mi hermanito no **sabe manejar**.

Conocer means "to know" in the sense of being acquainted or familiar with a person, place, or thing.

Conocemos al Dr. Fernández y a toda su familia.   ¿**Conocen** Uds. el jardín zoológico de Mérida?

In the preterite, *conocer* means "to meet someone for the first time."

Conocí a dos críticos que trabajan para el periódico.   ¿Los **conociste** en la conferencia de ayer?

Actividad 2 · Hablar

Práctica de gramática

¿Qué es necesario saber hacer en cada profesión? Con tu compañero(a) escoge cuatro profesiones de la lista en la pág. 246. Túrnate con tu compañero(a) para decir qué se debe saber hacer en cada una.

Modelo

periodista
Un periodista debe saber escribir bien.

Actividad 3 · Hablar

Práctica de gramática

Túrnate con tu compañero(a) para hacer y contestar preguntas usando *saber* y *conocer*.

Modelo

el número de teléfono de (nombre) . . .
A —¿Sabes el número de teléfono de Alex?
B —Sí, lo sé, es 555-1719. / No, no lo sé.

- la fecha de hoy
- la respuesta
- al profesor (nombre)
- la Ciudad de México
- alguna canción en español
- montar en bicicleta
- alguna mujer de negocios
- a qué hora abre el museo

Actividad 4 · Leer/Escribir

Práctica de gramática

Dos amigos hablan en una fiesta. Completa la conversación con el verbo *saber* o *conocer* según corresponda.

A —¿ __1.__ quién es esa señora?

B —Es la doctora Rubio. Yo __2.__ a sus hijos. Los __3.__ el año pasado.

A —¿De veras? ¿Dónde los __4.__ ?

B —En la universidad. Ellos __5.__ a mi amiga Elena.

A —¿Elena Peña? Yo también la __6.__ .

Gramática · Repaso

Presentation

Standards: 4.1

Resources: Voc. & Gram. Transparencies: 117

Suggestions: Call out words or phrases and have students associate them with the correct verb.

Teacher: *la dirección*
Student: *saber*

Actividad 2

Standards: 1.1

Focus: Reviewing *saber* + infinitive

Suggestions: Encourage students to say more than one thing a person needs to know how to do for each profession.

Answers will vary.

Actividad 3

Standards: 1.1

Resources: Practice Answers on Transparencies

Focus: Reviewing *saber* vs. *conocer*

Suggestions: Remind students that Student A's question tells Student B which verb to use.

Answers:

saber	saber
saber	saber
conocer	conocer
conocer	saber

Actividad 4

Standards: 1.2

Resources: Practice Answers on Transparencies

Focus: Reviewing *saber* vs. *conocer*

Suggestions: Remind students to make each verb agree in person and number with the subject, and to watch for correct use of tense.

Answers:

1. Sabes	4. conociste
2. conozco	5. conocen
3. conocí	6. conozco

247

Vocabulario

Presentation

Standards: 1.1, 1.2

Resources: Voc. & Gram. Transparencies: 118

Suggestions: Ask students to create sentences that use items from at least two of the categories in the *Vocabulario*. For example: *Me gusta mi computadora portátil porque la puedo llevar conmigo y trabajar en casa o en la escuela.*

Standards: 1.1, 1.3

Focus: Practicing review vocabulary

Suggestions: As students share their sentences, encourage them to elaborate on each other's comments.

Answers will vary.

Extension: Ask students to say what changes they have made in their personal lives due to the changes in their community: *He tenido que cambiar mi rutina de la mañana. Hoy día es necesario que salga más temprano.*

Standards: 1.1

Focus: Practicing review vocabulary

Suggestions: Point out to students that *había* remains singular, even if they are referring to plural objects: *... no había videocaseteras.*

Answers will vary.

Vocabulario

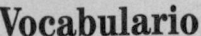

la tecnología
la computadora
la computadora portátil
el correo electrónico
el disco compacto
el disquete
la página web
la Red
el salón de chat
el televisor
el video
la videocasetera

la ciudad
el apartamento
el barrio
la calle
la casa
la comunidad
el edificio de
  apartamentos
la gente
el tráfico

el medio ambiente
el agua
el aire
los animales
limpio, -a
la naturaleza
puro, -a
sucio, -a

acciones
beneficiar
cambiar
construir
crear
darse cuenta de
eliminar
mejorar
obtener
preocuparse
proteger
realizar
tener lugar

para comparar
ahora
antes
desafortunadamente
hace . . . que
hasta
más . . . (que)
mejor
menos . . . (que)
peor
pero

  Escribir/Hablar . . . .

Práctica de vocabulario

Haz una lista de cuatro cosas que hayan cambiado en tu barrio o comunidad en los últimos años. Luego escribe frases comparando cómo son las cosas ahora y cómo eran antes. Usa las palabras de la lista. Comparte tus frases con un(a) compañero(a).

Modelo

tráfico
El tráfico en mi comunidad es ahora peor que antes porque hay más gente que vive en el barrio.

  Hablar . . . .

Práctica de vocabulario

Túrnate con un(a) compañero(a) para decir qué había o no había en los períodos de tiempo indicados. Usen las palabras o expresiones de las listas.

Modelo

Hace 50 años . . .
Hace 50 años había televisión pero no había videocaseteras.

1. Hace 40 años . . .   4. Hace 10 años . . .
2. En 1975 . . .   5. En 1930 . . .
3. El año pasado . . .   6. Hace 20 años . . .

Universal Access

Heritage Language Learners

Ask students who have lived in a heritage country to discuss changes that have taken place there as well as in their current community. Have them predict future changes.

Students with Learning Difficulties

Help students organize their sentence ideas for *Actividad 5*. On a piece of paper, have them label two columns *antes* and *ahora.* Ask them to write a simple sentence in each column. Then guide them to connect the two ideas into a complex sentence.

Gramática · Repaso

El *se* impersonal

In English you often use *they, you, one,* or *people* in an impersonal or an indefinite sense meaning "people in general." In Spanish you use *se* + the *Ud. /él /ella* or the *Uds. /ellos /ellas* form of the verb.

> **Se** habla español.   **Se** venden computadoras baratas.

• Note that you don't know who performs the action. The word that follows the verb determines whether the verb is singular or plural.

> **Se creó** una página web.   **Se crearon** páginas web.

• When the word following the conjugated verb is an infinitive, the verb form is singular.

> **Se necesita construir** un nuevo edificio.

Actividad 7 — Hablar

Práctica de gramática

Trabaja con otro(a) estudiante para hacer la pregunta *¿Dónde . . . ?* y contestarla. Luego inventen y contesten tres preguntas más con *¿Dónde?*

Modelo

escribir reseñas
A —*¿Dónde se escriben reseñas?*
B —*En el periódico se escriben reseñas.*

1. ver mucha gente tomando el sol
2. no permitir sacar fotos
3. vender ropa barata
4. poder esquiar
5. comer muy bien
6. ¡Respuesta personal!

Actividad 8 — Escribir

Práctica de gramática

Trabajas en la sección de anuncios clasificados de un periódico. En una hoja aparte escribe títulos para anuncios usando los siguientes verbos y las palabras de abajo. Recuerda que si la palabra que va después del verbo es plural el verbo debe ir en plural.

| vender | reparar | alquilar |
| necesitar | buscar | comprar |

1. un coche
2. computadoras
3. apartamento nuevo
4. personas con experiencia
5. bicicletas usadas
6. joven cortés
7. casas viejas
8. videos y discos compactos

● **Más práctica**
Practice Workbook 6-1, 6-2

Go Online
PHSchool.com
For: More review
Visit: phschool.com
Web Code: jed-0601

doscientos cuarenta y nueve **249**
Capítulo 6

Gramática · Repaso

Presentation

Standards: 4.1

Resources: Voc. & Gram. Transparencies: 119

Suggestions: Explain that in most cases the *se* construction in the *Gramática* can also be compared to the English passive voice. Provide examples of the English passive voice, such as "Spanish is spoken here." *(Se habla español aquí.)*

Actividad 7

Standards: 1.1

Resources: Practice Answers on Transparencies

Focus: Reviewing impersonal constructions

Common Errors: Students may treat the word *gente* as plural. Remind them that *gente* is always singular and takes singular forms of verbs, adjectives, and articles: *La gente está tomando el sol.*

Suggestions: Encourage students to use vocabulary from the previous page in their sentences.

Answers:
Student B's answers will vary. Student A's questions will use the following verb forms:

1. se ve   4. se puede
2. no se permite   5. se come
3. se vende   6. Answers will vary.

Actividad 8

Standards: 1.3

Resources: Practice Answers on Transparencies

Focus: Reviewing impersonal constructions

Suggestions: Remind students that, as in English, Spanish ad titles often omit smaller function words, such as articles.

Answers will vary. The following are likely results:

1. Se vende coche
2. Se reparan computadoras
3. Se alquila apartamento nuevo
4. Se buscan personas con experiencia
5. Se compran bicicletas usadas
6. Se necesita joven cortés
7. Se reparan casas viejas
8. Se venden videos y discos compactos

Standards for Foreign Language Learning: *Capítulo* 6

• To achieve the goals of the Standards, students will:

Communication

1.1 Interpersonal
• Talk about careers and professions and necessary qualities for them
• Talk about virtual and physical communities
• Talk about past, present, and future changes
• Talk about lifestyles of Spanish youth
• Talk about educational organizations

1.2 Interpretive
• Read and listen to information about careers and professions and necessary qualities for them
• Read about virtual and physical communities
• Read and listen to information about past, present, and future changes
• Read about lifestyles of Spanish youth
• Read about educational organizations
• Read about word families in the world of professions
• Read poetry by Gustavo Adolfo Bécquer and fiction by Ángel Balzarino
• Read about online Spanish-language newspapers
• Read about speech preparation and compare and contrast essays

1.3 Presentational
• Write and present information orally about careers and professions and necessary qualities for them
• Write and present information orally about past, present, and future changes
• Recite poetry by Gustavo Adolfo Bécquer

Culture

2.1 Practices and Perspectives
• Explain the lifestyles of Spanish youth
• Explain the work of educational organizations
• Explain the readership of online Spanish-language newspapers
• Explain the changing roles of Mexican television
• Explain the perspectives of Spanish-speaking architects

2.2 Products and Perspectives
• Discuss the poetry of Gustavo Adolfo Bécquer and the fiction of Ángel Balzarino
• Discuss the products of Spanish-speaking architects

Connections

3.1 Cross-curricular
• Discuss key facts about Spanish youth
• Discuss key facts about educational organizations
• Discuss key facts about the poetry of Gustavo Adolfo Bécquer and the fiction of Ángel Balzarino
• Discuss key facts about employment demographics and futurology
• Discuss key facts about Spanish speakers' use of the Internet and television
• Discuss key facts about architecture
• Use Language Arts Strategies: circumlocution, compare and contrast, mapping your speech using main idea and details, coping with unknown words

3.2 Target Culture
• Read a university workshop announcement
• Read poetry by Gustavo Adolfo Bécquer and fiction by Ángel Balzarino

 **Fondo cultural** ■◆◾◇■◆◇◻◆

Matta y el surrealismo

El surrealismo fue un movimiento literario y artístico muy importante de la primera mitad *(half)* del siglo XX. Entre sus artistas principales se destaca el pintor chileno Roberto Matta (1911–2002). Matta vivió la mayor parte de su vida en Europa y Estados Unidos, y sus influencias más importantes fueron Dalí y Picasso. Sus obras se caracterizan por el uso de figuras abstractas, el espacio, la transparencia, el movimiento, la energía y los colores brillantes *(bright)*. Este cuadro es un ejemplo de la pintura surrealista.

• ¿Cómo crees que se diferencia el realismo del surrealismo en la pintura?

L'Etang de No, (1958), Roberto Matta

(c) 2003 Artists Rights Society ARS, New York. Musée National d'Art Moderne, Centre Georges Pompidou. Giraudon/Art Resource, New York.

250 doscientos cincuenta

Universal Access

Personalizing the Theme

Ask students to talk about their current plans for life after high school. Ask guiding questions, such as: *¿Vas a asistir a una universidad? ¿Sabes a cuál? ¿Has pensado en qué vas a estudiar? ¿A qué profesión o trabajo quieres dedicarte? ¿Qué te gustaría hacer después de graduarte?*

Heritage Language Learners

Students may already know the future tense but be more comfortable expressing future actions by using *ir* + *a* + infinitive. Have them write a short paragraph about their future plans, and ask them to focus on using future tense verb forms.

¿Qué nos traerá el futuro?

Chapter Objectives

- **Talk about careers and professions**
- **Talk about plans for the future**
- **Explain the impact of science and technology on our lives**
- **Understand cultural perspectives on jobs and technology**

Video Focus

- **The effects of technology on society**

Country Connection

As you learn about careers and technology, you will make connections to these countries and places.

Estados Unidos
España
Puerto Rico
México
Chile
Argentina

Go Online
PHSchool.com

For: Online Atlas
Visit: phschool.com
Web Code: jee-0002

doscientos cincuenta y uno **251**
Capítulo 6

 **Standards for Foreign Language Learning (cont'd)**

Comparisons

4.1 Language

- Compare the Spanish impersonal *se* to the English passive voice
- Compare Spanish and English future and future perfect tenses
- Compare Spanish words to their English counterparts

4.2 Culture

- Compare the lifestyles of young people from Spain and the United States
- Compare the roles of television in Mexico and in the United States
- Compare distance education in Puerto Rico and in the United States

Communities

5.1 Beyond the School

- Link to Web sites from around the Spanish-speaking world
- Describe strategies for obtaining employment and keeping up with employment trends
- Discuss distance education and attending universities abroad

5.2 Lifelong Learner

- Discuss important facts about going to college
- Prepare for the future
- Develop an appreciation for poetry and fiction

Chapter Opener

Presentation

Resources: Voc. & Gram. Transparencies: 14, 16, 18, 20, 22 (maps)

Suggestions: Introduce students to the theme of the chapter and go over the objectives. Point out that they will improve their ability to talk and write about the future and their own development within professions and skills. Use the transparencies to locate and discuss the countries featured in the chapter.

 Fondo cultural   *Standards:* 1.1, 1.2, 2.2, 3.1

Resources: Fine Art Transparencies; Fine Art Transparencies Teacher's Guide

Suggestions: After students have read the information, ask comprehension questions. For example: *¿Qué artistas tuvieron una gran influencia sobre la obra de Matta?* (Dalí y Picasso)

Answers will vary.

Planning for Instruction
Resources:
- Teacher Express CD-ROM or Resource Book
  - Teaching resources
  - Lesson Planner
  - Chapter Resource Checklist
  - School-to-Home Connection Letter

Culture Note
Completed in 1963, the Arecibo Radio Telescope is the largest single-dish telescope in the world. Measuring approximately 305 meters across, the telescope is located in a valley in Puerto Rico. One of the telescope's major accomplishments was the first discovery of planets outside our solar system.

Vocabulario y gramática

Presentation

Standards: 1.1, 1.2, 5.1

Resources: Voc. & Gram. Transparencies: 120–121; Resource Book: Cap. 6, Input Script; Audio Program: CD Cap. 6, Track 1

Focus: Presenting new vocabulary and using grammar lexically in context

Suggestions: Show *Vocabulary and Grammar Transparencies* 120–121. Say the names of visualized vocabulary items, have students repeat, and ask volunteers to point to the appropriate image on the transparency. For non-visualized vocabulary such as ***diseñar, cuidadoso(a),*** and ***eficiente,*** give an explanation and ask students to identify the vocabulary item explained: *Una persona que hace su trabajo con mucho cuidado es una persona … (cuidadosa).*

A primera vista 1

Vocabulario y gramática en contexto

Objectives

Read, listen to, and understand information about
• professions
• future relationships

¿Qué planes tienes para el futuro? **Te graduarás** de la escuela secundaria y, ¿qué harás después? En poco tiempo **tomarás decisiones** muy importantes.

Será bueno que hables con un(a) consejero(a), con tus padres o con otras personas sobre este tema. Ellos te pueden ayudar a ver qué profesiones se relacionan con tus intereses y habilidades.

el programa

el científico

3 Te gustan las computadoras. Te gusta resolver problemas y buscar soluciones porque eres **emprendedor.**

2 Te interesan **las finanzas** y el dinero. Los hombres y mujeres de negocios confían en ti porque eres honesto e inteligente.

1 Te gusta hacer investigaciones científicas en el laboratorio. Eres ordenado y **cuidadoso.** Te importan mucho los detalles.

el banquero

la mujer de negocios

el hombre de negocios

Block Schedule

Have students work in pairs to draw two illustrations similar to the photos on these pages to represent two additional jobs. Have one pair of students exchange drawings with another group. Each group will write a description for the illustrations using the descriptions on these two pages as models. Have the pairs then read their descriptions to each other.

Universal Access

Students with Learning Difficulties

Using note cards, have students write words associated with each profession. Tell them not to write the names of the professions. Shuffle the cards and read them aloud. Have students identify the profession associated with each word they hear. Remind them that some words might pertain to more than one profession.

Advanced Learners

Ask students to talk about a person they know whose profession is one of those in the *Vocabulario*. Have them tell the person's profession, some of the activities he or she does, and at least one quality necessary for that type of work.

el redactor

el diseñador

4 Te es fácil escribir y eres cuidadoso. **Además de** escribir, eres **capaz** de leer el trabajo de otros escritores y hacer correcciones.

la jueza

la abogada

el abogado

5 Te interesa la moda y eres capaz de **diseñar** ropa nueva y original. Tienes mucho talento artístico.

el cocinero

7 Te gusta mucho cocinar, eres **eficiente** y algo artístico.

6 Te encanta leer sobre la ley. Eres una persona justa y te importan los derechos de los ciudadanos.

Actividad 1

Escuchar/Escribir/Hablar ··

¿Con quién debo hablar?

1 En una hoja, escribe los números del 1 al 7. Después, escucha lo que necesitan las personas y escribe con qué profesional necesitan hablar.

2 Escribe dos cualidades que se necesitan para cada una de las profesiones que escribiste. Compara tu lista con la de otro(a) estudiante.

doscientos cincuenta y tres **253**
Capítulo 6

Language Input ⑥

Actividad 1 *Standards:* 1.2
·······················

Resources: Voc. & Gram. Transparencies: 120–121; Audio Program: CD Cap. 6, Track 2; Resource Book: Cap. 6, Audio Script; Practice Answers on Transparencies

Focus: Practicing listening comprehension of new vocabulary

Suggestions: Remind students to listen for key words that will help them determine the answers. Use the *Audio CD* or read the script. Allow students to listen more than once.

Answers:

Step 1
1. el (la) abogado(a)
2. el (la) banquero(a)
3. el (la) redactor(a)
4. el (la) diseñador(a)
5. el (la) programador(a)
6. el (la) científico(a)
7. el (la) cocinero(a)

Step 2
Answers will vary.

Enriching Your Teaching

Culture Note

One of the world's most renowned fashion designers, Oscar de la Renta, is a Spanish speaker. He was born in Santo Domingo, Dominican Republic. As a young man, he left home to study painting in Madrid. There, he started his career in design by drawing for fashion houses. De la Renta worked with accomplished designers in Paris before establishing himself at Elizabeth Arden in New York City. In 1965, de la Renta started his own company, known for fashions, accessories, and fragrances.

Vocabulario y gramática

Presentation

Standards: 1.2

Resources: Voc. & Gram. Transparencies: 122–123; Resource Book: Cap. 6, Input Script; Audio Program: CD Cap. 6, Track 3

Focus: Extending presentation of vocabulary and grammar

Suggestions:

Pre-reading: Have students look at the photos and predict the content of each interview.

Reading: Allow students time to read the interviews silently first. Then play the *Audio CD* or read the interviews aloud, with students reading along as they listen. Allow them to listen more than once. Another option after silent reading is to have volunteers take turns reading each interview aloud, playing the roles of the two speakers.

Post-reading: To clarify the meaning of new vocabulary, provide synonyms and alternative meanings and ask students to tell which vocabulary item you are talking about: *¿Qué expresión quiere decir "vamos a vivir en otra casa"?* **(nos mudaremos)**

Los estudiantes hablan de su futuro

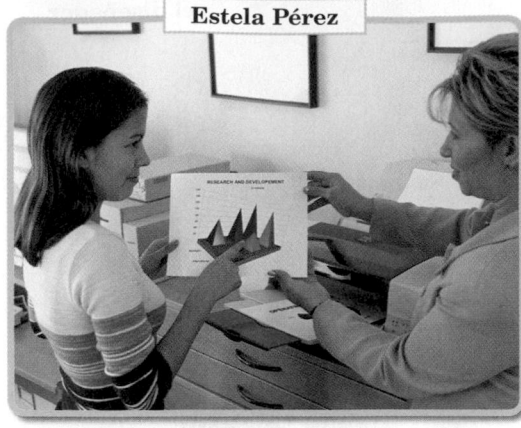
Estela Pérez

Manolo Sánchez

1 —¿Seguirás estudiando después de terminar la escuela secundaria?

—¡Sí, por supuesto! Para mí lo más importante es tener una buena educación. Soy **ambiciosa**, quiero ganar un buen salario, **así que** estudiaré finanzas. Buscaré trabajo y poco a poco **lograré** conseguir un puesto como directora o **jefa** de una oficina.

—Tu hermana quiere **seguir una carrera** similar, ¿no?

—Sí, ella quiere ser **contadora**. Es muy buena con los números. ¡Ya se encarga del dinero de la familia!

2 —¿Qué harás en cinco años?

—Me gustan los coches, así que **me dedicaré** a la mecánica. Quisiera ser dueño de un taller mecánico. Así no tendré otro jefe y **haré lo que me dé la gana**.

—¿Crees que te quedarás en casa con tus padres?

—Eso depende. Si estoy **casado**, mi esposa y yo **nos mudaremos** a una casa. Si estoy **soltero**, es posible que me quede con mis padres.

Ana María Sosa López

3 —¿Qué harás después de graduarte? Sabemos que eres bilingüe y que has hecho traducciones aquí en la escuela. ¿Serás **traductora**?

—Sí, me gusta **traducir** pero lo que más me interesa es viajar. **Por lo tanto** quiero **desempeñar un cargo** de traductora en **una empresa** que tenga oficinas en varios países.

—¿Te gustará vivir en otro país?

—Sí, porque realizaré mi sueño *(dream)* de viajar y conocer el mundo.

254 doscientos cincuenta y cuatro
A primera vista 1

Universal Access

Heritage Language Learners
Ask students if any of them have considered a career that would utilize their language skills. Some examples might include translator, court interpreter, teacher, international business person, or diplomat. Ask them to share the stories of people they know who utilize two or more languages on the job.

Students with Learning Difficulties
After students have read the interviews, ask them to identify just the questions by pointing to them in the text. Then ask students to provide personal responses to the questions.

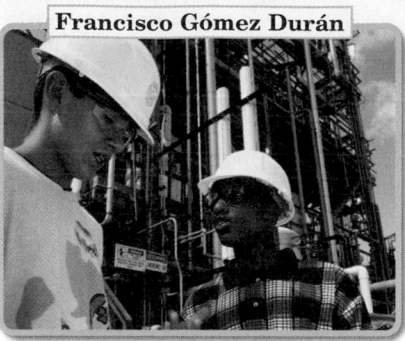

Francisco Gómez Durán

Belinda Domínguez

4 —El consejero te dijo que eres **maduro** y estudioso . . . y sé que te gustan las matemáticas. **¿Te harás** banquero?

—No. Siempre me han fascinado los castillos históricos y también los edificios modernos. Algún día quiero ser **arquitecto** o **ingeniero.**

—¿De veras? ¿A qué universidad irás el año **próximo**?

—No lo sé todavía. Tengo que investigar para **averiguar** qué universidades ofrecen esas carreras y qué requisitos piden.

5 —¿Qué crees que harás al terminar la escuela?

—Buscaré empleo. Necesito trabajar un poco y **ahorrar** antes de estudiar.

—¿Para qué estudiarás?

—Estudiaré para ser **peluquera** en un salón de belleza.

 **Leer/Escribir** · · · · · · · · · · · · · · ·

Lo que quieren ser

Escribe la palabra o las palabras que sean necesarias para completar las siguientes frases según lo que dijeron los estudiantes.

1. Estela es ＿＿ y quiere ser ＿＿. Estudiará ＿＿.
2. Manolo se dedicará a la ＿＿. Quiere ser el ＿＿ de un taller mecánico.
3. Ana es ＿＿. Quiere desempeñar un cargo de ＿＿. Su sueño es ＿＿.
4. Francisco es ＿＿ y ＿＿. Dice que será ＿＿ o ＿＿.
5. Belinda buscará ＿＿. Después estudiará para ser ＿＿.

 Escuchar · · · · · · · · · · · · · · ·

Planes para el futuro

En una hoja escribe los números del 1 al 5. Después, escucha lo que dicen las personas y escribe si es lógico o ilógico. Corrige las oraciones ilógicas.

● **Más práctica** ·

Practice Workbook 6-3, 6-4

For: Vocabulary practice
Visit: phschool.com
Web Code: jed-0602

doscientos cincuenta y cinco **255**
Capítulo 6

Language Input **6**

 2 *Standards:* 1.2

Resources: Practice Answers on Transparencies

Focus: Writing to demonstrate reading comprehension of new vocabulary

Suggestions: Point out that the sentences in the activity are about the students interviewed. Students can find the answers to each item by referring to the appropriate interview.

Answers:
1. ambiciosa/jefa (directora)/finanzas
2. mecánica/dueño
3. bilingüe/traductora/viajar y conocer el mundo
4. maduro/estudioso/arquitecto/ingeniero
5. empleo/peluquera

 3 *Standards:* 1.2

Resources: Voc. & Gram. Transparencies: 122–123; Audio Program: CD Cap. 6, Track 4; Resource Book: Cap. 6, Audio Script; Practice Answers on Transparencies

Focus: Demonstrating listening comprehension of new vocabulary

Suggestions: Point out that there may be more than one way for students to correct the illogical sentences.

Answers:
1. ilógico. Por eso voy a ser mecánico.
2. ilógico. Quiero estar soltera./Por eso me casaré.
3. lógico
4. lógico
5. ilógico. Así que me dedicaré a la medicina.

Additional Resources

• Resource Book: Cap. 6, Clip Art

 Assessment

• Prueba 6-1: Vocabulary recognition

Chapter Project

Give students copies of the Chapter Project outline and rubric from the *Teacher's Resource Book.* Explain the task to them, and have them perform step 1. (For more information, see p. 246-a.)

Enriching Your Teaching

Culture Note

Traditionally, a workday in Spain or Mexico contained a two-to-three-hour midday break for lunch and *siesta.* Today, multinational corporations are influencing this daily routine. Many firms have adopted a so-called *horario americano,* which resembles the nine-to-five schedule of the United States.

Teacher-to-Teacher

Invite colleagues, friends, or other professionals whom you know that use Spanish in their careers to come talk to your class. You may wish to have such speakers come in from time to time as a recurring "career day" event.

255

6 Practice and Communicate

 Actividad 4 *Standards:* 1.1, 1.2

Resources: Audio Program: CD Cap. 6, Track 5; Resource Book: Cap. 6, Audio Script; Practice Answers on Transparencies

Focus: Practicing listening comprehension of new vocabulary

Suggestions: Remind students that some of the ads they will hear are missing definite and indefinite articles. Have them listen to the *Audio CD* more than once.

Answers:
1. jefe; persona madura, con experiencia
2. peluquero; capaz de trabajar rápido; amable y sociable
3. redactor; con experiencia, emprendedor y responsable, capaz de trabajar en equipo
4. cocinero; eficiente y creativo

Actividad 5 *Standards:* 1.2

Resources: Practice Answers on Transparencies

Focus: Practicing new vocabulary in a cloze exercise

Suggestions: Have students review the vocabulary on pp. 252–255 before completing the activity.

Answers:
1. próximo
2. Además de
3. por lo tanto
4. casado
5. soltero

Actividad 6 *Standards:* 1.1, 1.3, 3.1

Focus: Practicing new vocabulary in a paired matching activity

Recycle: adjectives describing personality

Suggestions: Refer students to the *Estrategia*. Remind them that you often use circumlocution when introducing new vocabulary to the class.

Answers will vary.

Manos a la obra 1

Vocabulario y gramática en uso

Objectives
- To discuss different professions
- To talk about plans for the future
- To practice the future tense
- To practice the future of probability

 **Actividad 4** **Escuchar/Escribir/Hablar**

Las cualidades necesarias

En una hoja, escribe los números del 1 al 4. Escucha los anuncios clasificados y escribe la profesión y la cualidad o las cualidades que se necesitan para cada trabajo. Compara tu lista con la de otro(a) estudiante.

 Actividad 5 **Leer**

Los 17 años

A los 17 años, los jóvenes también tienen nuevas responsabilidades y problemas. Completa lo que dicen estos dos amigos sobre esta edad.

por lo tanto	casado(a)	soltero(a)	además de	próximo

—¿Sabes a qué universidad vas a asistir el año __1.__, Roberto?

—No lo sé todavía, Luisa. __2.__ la Universidad San Ignacio, he escrito a cuatro universidades. Todas están lejos de aquí, __3.__ sé que voy a tener que mudarme.

—Me dicen que en San Ignacio te ayudan a alquilar apartamento si estás __4.__ porque reconocen que es más difícil para dos personas.

—Pues a mí no me importa eso. Voy a estar __5.__ hasta cumplir los 30 años.

—¡Yo también!

   Actividad 6 **Escribir/Hablar**

¿Cómo se dice?

❶ Imagina que te olvidaste de estas palabras. Escribe frases que quieran decir lo mismo.

> **Modelo**
> responsable
> *persona que es capaz de tomar decisiones y desempeñar un cargo*

1. amable
2. emprendedor
3. ambicioso
4. honesto
5. capaz
6. maduro
7. cuidadoso
8. puntual

❷ Con otro(a) estudiante, decidan qué características deben tener los siguientes profesionales: ingeniero(a), contador(a), hombre / mujer de negocios, mecánico(a), peluquero(a).

256 doscientos cincuenta y seis
Manos a la obra 1

Estrategia

Circumlocution
When you can't remember or don't know a word, you can use circumlocution to describe or exemplify it without naming it (e.g., *the thing you open a door with* for *doorknob*).

Universal Access

Heritage Language Learners
In addition to definitions, have students brainstorm synonyms for the adjectives in *Actividad* 6. For example: *amable/simpático(a); capaz/talentoso(a).* Invite students to share their synonyms with the class.

Advanced Learners
Ask students to write their own classified ad. In it, they should name the position they are trying to fill and briefly describe the qualities of an ideal candidate.

Actividad 7 Hablar

¿Qué quieres ser?

Con un(a) compañero(a) hablen sobre los trabajos que les gustaría o no tener algún día.

Modelo

A —*¿Te gustaría ser banquero?*
B —*Sí, porque me fascinan los números y soy muy cuidadoso.*
o: *¿Yo? ¡Qué va! No me interesan nada los números.*

Estudiante A

1. 2. 3. 4. 5 6

Estudiante B

organizado(a)
eficiente
responsable
creativo(a)
capaz
amable
ambicioso(a)
emprendedor(a)

¡Respuesta personal!

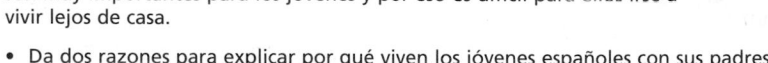

Fondo cultural

En casa de mamá Según un estudio del Instituto de la Juventud de España, el 77% de los jóvenes españoles menores de 30 años vive con sus padres. ¿Por qué vivirán tantos jóvenes españoles en casa de sus padres? El estudio dice que hay varias razones importantes. En España es bastante difícil para los jóvenes conseguir un empleo que les permita ganar el dinero necesario para vivir solos. Además, no es fácil conseguir una casa o un apartamento barato para mudarse.

Otras personas dicen que el problema es que los jóvenes no quieren tener responsabilidades y por eso prefieren vivir con sus padres. También hay personas que piensan que en la cultura española la familia y los padres son muy importantes para los jóvenes y por eso es difícil para ellos irse a vivir lejos de casa.

- Da dos razones para explicar por qué viven los jóvenes españoles con sus padres.
- ¿Crees que en los Estados Unidos la mayoría de los jóvenes menores de 30 años vive con sus padres? ¿Por qué?
- Compara la situación de los jóvenes españoles y los estadounidenses. ¿Qué tienen en común? ¿Cuál es la diferencia más importante que ves entre ellos?

Actividad 7 *Standards:* 1.1

Resources: Practice Answers on Transparencies

Focus: Using new vocabulary and structures in guided dialogues

Suggestions: Encourage students to switch roles and to read each dialogue more than once. Student B's response should be different each time.

Answers will vary. Students will use the following vocabulary:

1. **juez**
2. **científico(a)**
3. **diseñador(a)**
4. **programador(a)**
5. **redactor(a)**
6. **contador(a)**

Fondo cultural *Standards:* 1.1, 1.2, 2.1, 3.1, 4.2

Suggestions: After students have read the information, ask: *¿Qué piensas de esta información? ¿A ti te gustaría vivir con tus padres tanto tiempo? ¿Cuáles son los beneficios posibles de este estilo de vida? ¿Cuáles son los puntos negativos?*

Answers:
Una razón es porque es difícil encontrar un empleo que les permita ganar el dinero necesario para vivir solos. Otra es que no es fácil conseguir una casa o un apartamento barato.
Other answers will vary.

Enriching Your Teaching

Culture Note

Children in Spain attend elementary school from ages 6 to 12 and secondary school from ages 12 to 16. After secondary school, students may either go on to one to two years of vocational study or complete the ***bachillerato,*** a two-year course that prepares them for university study.

Teacher-to-Teacher

When students do pair work, such as in *Actividad* 7, encourage them to work with a different partner each time, and avoid the habit of the same partners working together day after day. Working with new partners is a good strategy for keeping students on task.

Actividad 8

Standards: 1.1, 1.2, 3.2

Resources: Practice Answers on Transparencies

Focus: Practicing new vocabulary and structures through reading and response

Suggestions: Assist students as needed with the meaning of any unknown vocabulary.

Answers: Some answers may vary. The following are likely results:
1. **Creación e introducción a la poesía argentina**
2. **Redacción asertiva**
3. **Expresión teatral**
4. **Negociación y debate**
5. **Comunicación persuasiva / Negociación y debate**
6. **Creación e introducción a la poesía argentina**
7. **Comunicación persuasiva**
8. **Danza contemporánea**

▶ **Rapid Review**

Item 3 in step 2 of *Actividad* 9 asks students to make recommendations for which they will need to use the subjunctive. Prepare them for this by asking them to make up sentences with *Es necesario que...* and the subjunctive.

Actividad 9

Standards: 1.1, 1.2

Focus: Practicing new vocabulary and structures through discussion

Suggestions: Ask groups to appoint a spokesperson to report the results of their discussion to the class.

Answers will vary.

Actividad 8 **Leer/Hablar** ....

Talleres de verano

Mira el anuncio sobre los talleres de verano. ¿A qué taller(es) van a asistir las personas que quieran seguir las siguientes carreras? Trabaja con un grupo de tres estudiantes para decidir. Expliquen sus respuestas.

1. escritor(a)
2. redactor(a)
3. actor / actriz
4. abogado(a)
5. hombre / mujer de negocios
6. poeta
7. político(a)
8. bailarín / bailarina

Actividad 9 **Leer/Hablar** ....

Hablar sobre el trabajo

1 La búsqueda de trabajo es un tema sobre el que todo el mundo tiene diferentes opiniones. Lee la siguiente encuesta *(survey)* que se hizo a un grupo de jóvenes sobre de qué depende encontrar un trabajo.

¿De qué depende encontrar un buen trabajo? ¿Y en segundo lugar?		
	Primer lugar (%)	Segundo lugar (%)
De estar bien preparado	50	27
De tener buenas recomendaciones	28	30
De la buena suerte	16	23
De saber hablar bien	3	11
De ser guapo(a)	2	7
No sé	1	2

2 Trabaja con un grupo de estudiantes para hablar de la encuesta y responder a las siguientes preguntas.

1. ¿Están de acuerdo con los resultados de la encuesta? ¿Por qué? Traten de dar ejemplos de algunas personas que conocen.
2. ¿Pueden añadir alguna otra razón a la lista?
3. Si todas estas razones son ciertas, ¿qué recomendaciones pueden darle a una persona que quiera seguir una carrera o comenzar una nueva profesión?

UNIVERSIDAD RODRIGO CABEZAS

DEPARTAMENTO DE ACTIVIDADES CULTURALES

FACULTAD DE HUMANIDADES

TALLERES DE VERANO

6 de diciembre al 12 de febrero

CREACIÓN E INTRODUCCIÓN A LA POESÍA ARGENTINA
Profesor: Fabián Díaz, poeta, doctor en Literatura Argentina

DANZA CONTEMPORÁNEA
Profesor: Lucía Suárez, bailarina y coreógrafa

EXPRESIÓN TEATRAL
Profesor: Javier Jiménez, actor y director

NEGOCIACIÓN Y DEBATE
Profesor: Oliverio Rojas, periodista, licenciado en Comunicación Social

REDACCIÓN ASERTIVA
Profesora: Sarah Vázquez, periodista

COMUNICACIÓN PERSUASIVA
Profesor: Ramón Santiago, actor y dramaturgo

Inscripciones e Informaciones hasta el 2 de diciembre en San Martín 301

Universal Access

Multiple Intelligences
Logical/Mathematical: Have groups of students conduct their own polls on the topic of what it takes to find a good job. Have them record their data and present it in the form of a chart. Invite different groups to compare their results.

Students with Learning Difficulties
Distribute props or pictures associated with the professions listed in *Ampliación del lenguaje*. Ask students to say three simple sentences to accompany their props: *Yo soy cocinero(a). Yo cocino. Aquí está la cocina.* Redistribute props among male and female students, so they can practice both masculine and feminine endings.

Actividad 10 — Escribir/Hablar

Y tú, ¿qué dices?

1. ¿A qué se dedican tus padres? ¿Vas a seguir la misma carrera? ¿Por qué?
2. ¿Cuál es el sueño que quieres realizar? ¿Qué quieres lograr en el futuro?
3. ¿Te gustaría mudarte a otra ciudad, otro estado u otro país? ¿Por qué?
4. Imagina que no necesitas ahorrar dinero. ¿A qué te gustaría dedicarte después de graduarte de la universidad?
5. ¿Qué carreras no te gustaría seguir? ¿Por qué?
6. ¿Qué te gustaría hacer con tu tiempo libre?
7. ¿Cuáles son las mayores responsabilidades que tienes a tu edad? ¿Y los problemas? ¿Qué quieres cambiar o lograr en el futuro?

Ampliación del lenguaje

Profesiones

En español hay varios sufijos que indican profesión. Muchas palabras que terminan con los sufijos *-or / -ora, -ero / -era, -ario / -aria* nombran profesiones que tienen relación con los verbos o sustantivos de los que derivan.

Verbo	Sustantivo	Profesión
vender	venta	vendedor(a)
traducir	traducción	traductor(a)
escribir	escrito	escritor(a)
programar	programa	programador(a)
redactar	redacción	redactor(a)
dirigir	dirección	director(a)
diseñar	diseño	diseñador(a)
	barco	barquero(a)
	carta	cartero(a)
cocinar	cocina	cocinero(a)
	banco	banquero(a)

Lee las palabras de la tabla y escribe ocho frases en las que uses las profesiones y los verbos o sustantivos relacionados.

Modelo

vender / vendedor(a)
Un vendedor trabaja tratando de vender cosas a otras personas.

carta / cartero(a)
Mi tío es cartero. Entrega cartas en las casas y apartamentos de nuestra ciudad.

Actividad 10

Standards: 1.1, 1.3

Focus: Practicing new vocabulary and structures

Suggestions: This activity is ideal as a homework assignment. Encourage students to take the questions seriously and sit in a quiet place to answer them, giving them careful thought. Then invite them to share their answers with the class during a subsequent session.

Answers will vary.

Ampliación del lenguaje

Presentation

Standards: 1.2, 1.3, 3.1, 4.1

Focus: Understanding suffixes in nouns that name professions

Suggestions: Ask students to use more than one variation of the word in the same sentence. Encourage them to make it clear from their sentences that they understand the meaning of each word.

Answers will vary.

Additional Resources

- Writing, Audio & Video Workbook: Cap. 6, Audio Activity 1, Track 6
- Writing, Audio & Video Workbook: Cap. 6, Writing Activity 6
- Resource Book: Cap. 6, Communicative Activity BLM

 Assessment
- Prueba 6-2: Vocabulary production

Enriching Your Teaching

Teacher-to-Teacher

Regularly refer to and isolate word parts such as prefixes and suffixes, and ask students to do the same. Such attention to meaningful chunks of words is an excellent way for language learners to expand their vocabularies. Once students know that suffixes like those shown in the *Ampliación del lenguaje* indicate professions, they can experiment with them on their own to build new words. Parallels can often be drawn between Spanish and English word parts. For example, the suffixes shown in the *Ampliación del lenguaje* can be compared to English *-er*, as in "teacher" or "baker."

259

Practice and Communicate

Presentation

Resources: Voc. & Gram. Transparencies: 124

Suggestions: Ask students to take turns telling about their plans for next summer, using the future tense. If necessary, cue them with questions that elicit verbs of various kinds, including those with the irregular stems shown in the *Gramática*.

Actividad 11

Standards: 1.2

Resources: Practice Answers on Transparencies

Focus: Practicing the future tense in a cloze exercise

Suggestions: Remind students to first look over the entire paragraph about Lorena in order to get an idea of its meaning.

Answers:

1. haré	7. podré
2. iré	8. regresaré
3. realizaré	9. llamará
4. Estudiaré	10. diseñaré
5. pasaré	11. tendré
6. visitaré	12. disfrutarán

Extension: Conduct a question-and-answer session with students, using the completed activity as a base.

Teacher: *¿Qué decidió Lorena hoy?*

Student: *Decidió lo que hará el año*

Block Schedule

Have students work in pairs to practice the different irregular forms of the future. Have one student select an infinitive and then provide different subject pronouns. The partner has to quickly provide the correct verb conjugation. Switch roles with each verb.

Gramática·Repaso

El futuro

You can express the future in Spanish in three ways: by using *ir + a + infinitive*, the present tense, or the future tense. In the future tense, all verbs have the same endings. For most verbs, attach the endings to the infinitive.

Here are the future tense forms of the regular verbs *pasar, comer,* and *pedir*:

pasaré	comeré	pediré
pasarás	comerás	pedirás
pasará	comerá	pedirá
pasaremos	comeremos	pediremos
pasaréis	comeréis	pediréis
pasarán	comerán	pedirán

Some verbs have irregular stems in the future tense. Note that their future endings (*-é, -ás, -á, -emos, -éis, -án*) are the same as those of regular verbs.

haber	→	habr-
poder	→	podr-
querer	→	querr-
saber	→	sabr-
poner	→	pondr-
salir	→	saldr-
tener	→	tendr-
venir	→	vendr-
decir	→	dir-
hacer	→	har-

-é
-ás
-á
-emos
-éis
-án

¿Cómo será el planeta en 100 años?

Actividad 11 **Gramática** **Leer**

Los sueños

Lorena escribe en su diario sobre sus experiencias y sueños para el futuro. Completa este fragmento de su diario con el futuro de los verbos del recuadro.

poder	estudiar	hacer	visitar
pasar	realizar	ir	

disfrutar	regresar	tener	llamar
diseñar			

Hoy, después de regresar del parque, decidí lo que __1.__ el año próximo. Yo __2.__ a una universidad famosa y allí __3.__ mi sueño. __4.__ arquitectura. Después de estudiar, __5.__ unos años en Japón y __6.__ los parques más famosos. Así __7.__ aprender mucho.

Finalmente, __8.__ a este país para crear mi propia empresa. Se __9.__ "Parques y jardines de oriente" y yo __10.__ los jardines. Estoy segura de que __11.__ mucho éxito y muchas personas __12.__ de mis jardines y parques.

Universal Access

Heritage Language Learners

Have students with exemplary pronunciation model the pronunciation of future verb forms. Ask them to be especially aware of the written accent on the last syllable on all but the ***nosotros*** forms, and have all students repeat.

Advanced Learners

Ask students to talk about habits they or someone they know used to have but now no longer engage in. For the old habit they use the imperfect tense, and for the change they use the future tense: *Antes solía charlar mucho en la cafetería. No charlaré más allí porque no tengo tiempo.*

  **Gramática** **Hablar**

En el futuro

¿Sabes lo que quieres hacer en el futuro? Pregúntale a otro(a) estudiante sobre sus planes. Después, intercambien papeles.

Estudiante A

1. seguir una carrera después de graduarse
2. dedicarse a hacer trabajo de voluntario
3. averiguar información sobre la carrera de ingeniería
4. ir a ver a un consejero
5. hacer lo que le dé la gana
6. tener un trabajo y ahorrar mucho dinero
7. estudiar finanzas en unos años
8. tomar decisiones importantes para una empresa

Modelo

mudarse a otra ciudad para estudiar
A —*¿Te mudarás a otra ciudad para estudiar en la universidad?*
B —*No, iré a la universidad de mi ciudad.*

Estudiante B

¡Respuesta personal!

 Gramática **Leer/Escribir**

¿Qué hará . . . ?

Piensa en personas de tu escuela, familia, comunidad o programa de televisión favorito que correspondan a estas descripciones. ¿Qué harán en el futuro? Usa el futuro de los verbos del recuadro para escribir frases sobre lo que hará cada persona.

hacerse . . .	estudiar para ser . . .	trabajar como / en . . .
tener . . .	lograr ser . . .	mudarse a . . .
dedicarse a . . .	ser . . .	

Modelo

Pinta cuadros muy bonitos.
Santiago será un pintor famoso.

1. Le encanta arreglarles el pelo a sus amigas.
2. Le gusta planear y construir caminos y puentes.
3. Le gustan los animales.
4. Es cuidadoso(a) y escribe muy bien.
5. Le gustan las matemáticas.
6. Me fascina traducir textos.
7. Tiene mucho talento artístico.
8. Le interesan los negocios y las finanzas.

SERVICIOS MUNDIALES, S.A.

Isabela Ruiz
Contadora

Calle Flores, no.85
Caracas, Venezuela

Tel: 224-6560
Fax: 224-6586

Enriching Your Teaching

Teacher-to-Teacher

Young people are as interested in making New Year's resolutions as many adults. You can take advantage of this custom at any time of the year. An enjoyable way to help them practice using the future tense is to ask them to make a short list of resolutions for the coming week or month. At the end of the time period, check back with students to see whether they kept their resolutions, giving them an opportunity to review the past tenses.

 Actividad 12 *Standards:* 1.1

Resources: Practice Answers on Transparencies

Focus: Practicing the future tense in guided dialogues

Suggestions: Point out to students that in the future tense, reflexive and object pronouns are placed in the same position in relation to the verb as they are in other tenses of conjugated verb forms.

Answers: Student B's responses will vary. Student A's questions will use the following verb forms:

1. **Seguirás**
2. **Te dedicarás**
3. **Averiguarás**
4. **Irás**
5. **Harás**
6. **Tendrás**
7. **Estudiarás**
8. **Tomarás**

Actividad 13 *Standards:* 1.2, 1.3

Resources: Practice Answers on Transparencies

Focus: Practicing the future tense by responding to questions

Suggestions: Tell students to demonstrate their comprehension of new vocabulary by making a logical connection between each cue and the future plans of their chosen person. Remind them that some of their sentences can be negative.

Answers will vary. Third-person, singular future forms of the verbs in the word bank are as follows:

se hará	logrará
tendrá	será
se dedicará	trabajará
estudiará	se mudará

Chapter Project

Students can perform step 2 at this point. Be sure they understand your corrections and suggestions. (For more information, see p. 246-a.)

Standards: 1.1

Resources: Practice Answers on Transparencies

Focus: Practicing the future tense

Suggestions: Ask Student B to think of real people and to provide an additional detail or two, as the model does.

Answers: Students A and B will use the following verb forms respectively:

1. **se escribirán/nos escribiremos**
2. **asistirán/asistiremos**
3. **tendrán/tendremos**
4. **sabrán/sabremos**
5. **saldrán/saldremos**
6. **recordarán/recordaremos**
7. **se dedicarán/nos dedicaremos**

Standards: 1.1, 1.3

Focus: Practicing the future tense

Suggestions: Tell students to use *nosotros* forms in the left column of the chart in step 2. The right column will most likely contain a negative statement about one partner and an affirmative one about the other.

Answers: Students will use the following verb forms for step 1:

me quedaré/me mudaré	viajaré
asistiré/encontraré	me casaré/seguiré
seguiré	tendré

Steps 2–3

Answers will vary.

Standards: 1.1, 1.2, 3.1

Suggestions: After students have read the information, ask: *¿Te gustaría trabajar en un programa como éste? ¿Trabajarás para el gobierno en el futuro?*

Answers will vary.

Additional Resources

• Writing, Audio & Video Workbook: Cap. 6, Writing Activity 7

Assessment
• Prueba 6-3: *El futuro*

262

  **Hablar** ....

Después de . . .

Con un(a) compañero(a), hablen de cómo serán sus relaciones en el futuro usando las frases de abajo. Pueden hablar de sus relaciones con los amigos, la familia, o las personas de la escuela o de la comunidad.

Modelo

verse cada semana

A —*En diez años, ¿tus amigos y tú se verán cada semana?*
B —*No, no nos veremos cada semana pero quizás cada mes.*

1. escribirse por correo electrónico
2. asistir a la misma universidad
3. tener mucho en común
4. saber dónde viven sus amigos de la escuela
5. salir juntos los fines de semana
6. recordar todo lo que pasó en la escuela secundaria
7. dedicarse a diferentes intereses

 **Fondo cultural** ◼◆◼◆◆◆◼◆◼◆◼◆◼◆

Jóvenes hispanohablantes trabajando en Washington El *Congressional Hispanic Caucus Institute,* CHCI, selecciona todos los años a unos 30 jóvenes para participar en su programa de pasantías[1] de verano. Los seleccionados pasan parte del verano en Washington, D.C., disfrutando de las ventajas de poder observar al gobierno en acción. "CHCI se siente orgulloso de ofrecerle a los mejores representantes de la comunidad hispanohablante la oportunidad de crecer como líderes y miembros de dicha comunidad", dijo la presidenta del instituto, Ingrid M. Durán.

• ¿Por qué es importante para los estudiantes participar en un programa de pasantías?

_____

1 internships

 **Más práctica** ....
Practice Workbook 6-5

 **Escribir/Hablar**

¿Cómo será tu vida en el futuro?

❶ Escribe sobre tu futuro. Incluye la siguiente información:

• quedarse en la misma ciudad o mudarse
• asistir a la universidad o encontrar trabajo
• seguir una carrera
• viajar y adónde
• casarse o seguir soltero(a)
• tener hijos y cuántos

❷ Ahora, compara tus respuestas con las de un(a) compañero(a). Completen una tabla como la siguiente con las semejanzas y las diferencias.

SEMEJANZAS	DIFERENCIAS

❸ Usa la tabla para escribir un párrafo acerca de tu futuro y el futuro de tu compañero(a).

Go Online
PHSchool.com

For: Practice with the future
Visit: phschool.com
Web Code: jed-0603

Universal Access

Heritage Language Learners

In preparation for the *Gramática* on p. 263, ask students to prepare a short skit portraying a situation in which there is some element of doubt. Instruct them to use the future tense to express this uncertainty at least once in the dialogue. A possible theme might be *¿Dónde estará mi tarea para mañana?*

Students with Learning Difficulties

Before students begin *Actividad* 14, allow them time to make notes on the future forms of the verbs presented. Point out that they will be using the *Uds.* and *nosotros* forms. Give students similar time and guidance for *Actividad* 15.

Gramática

El futuro de probabilidad

In Spanish, you use the future tense to express uncertainty or probability in the present.

¿Qué hora será?
I wonder what time it is.

Serán las seis.
It's probably six o'clock.

Estarán debajo de tu cama.
They must be under your bed.

The English equivalents in these cases are
I wonder, it's probably, it must be, and so on.

¿Dónde estarán mis zapatos?
Where can my shoes *be?*

Presentation

Standards: 4.1

Resources: Voc. & Gram. Transparencies: 125

Suggestions: Have students talk about the picture using the future tense to express uncertainty: *¿Quién será la persona que está a la derecha? Será…*

---

16 Gramática · Leer/Escribir

Probablemente . . .

En una fiesta, conoces a las siguientes personas y comienzas a imaginarte qué cosas tendrán o qué harán en sus trabajos. Lee las siguientes frases. Escribe una segunda frase relacionada con la primera. Usa la forma correcta de los verbos del recuadro en el futuro para indicar probabilidad.

Modelo
Marcela es escritora.
Tendrá muchos libros.

tener	saber	vender	comprar	trabajar
estudiar	dedicarse	ser	aprender	seguir

1. El Sr. Paz es abogado.
2. Carmen es una mujer de negocios.
3. Andrés quiere ser traductor.
4. La Sra. Dávila es peluquera.
5. Héctor espera ser ingeniero.

6. Los hermanos González son agricultores.
7. Roberto quiere ser diseñador.
8. Margarita quiere ser científica.
9. El Sr. Pérez es juez.
10. Jaime y Elena quieren ser cocineros.

Standards: 1.3

Resources: Practice Answers on Transparencies

Focus: Practicing the future tense to express probability or uncertainty

Suggestions: To avoid confusion, remind students that the meaning of the word *conoces* in the first line of the instructions is "to meet someone" rather than "to know someone."

Answers will vary. Students will choose from the following verb forms, depending on the subject of their sentence:
tendrá/tendrán
estudiará/estudiarán
sabrá/sabrán
se dedicará/se dedicarán
venderá/venderán
será/serán
comprará/comprarán
aprenderá/aprenderán
trabajará/trabajarán
seguirá/seguirán

Extension: Once students have completed the activity, challenge them to add another logical sentence about each person. They can use a verb from the word bank or another verb of their choice in the future tense.

---

doscientos sesenta y tres 263
Capítulo 6

Enriching Your Teaching

Teacher-to-Teacher

Making a connection between a grammar point and something in students' everyday lives leads to meaningful language practice and helps students solidify their understanding of the grammar point. Remind students that we frequently make predictions as we look forward to elections, sports events, or award ceremonies.

Choose an upcoming school event, such as a sports match, and ask students to write their predictions about it. Take a survey to see how many of them predict each possible outcome. After the event, ask students to state whether their predictions were correct.

Additional Resources

• Writing, Audio & Video Workbook: Cap. 6, Audio Activity 2, Track 7

En voz alta

Presentation

Standards: 1.2, 1.3, 2.2, 3.1, 3.2, 5.2

Resources: Audio Program: Cap. 6, Track 8

Suggestions: Have students read the information and the poem silently. Help them understand the complicated syntax. For example, point out that **volverán** in the first line is only part of a verb phrase. Ask: *¿Cuáles son las demás palabras que completen esta frase? (a colgar)* Remind them that for effect, poets like Bécquer often invert the positions of subjects and verbs.

Before having students recite the poem, direct their attention to the information in the *¿Recuerdas?* Then allow them a few minutes to practice reciting the poem excerpt with a partner.

Common Errors: When working with pronunciation in the *¿Recuerdas?*, students may interrupt the elision of the vowel sounds with a glottal stop (a stoppage of air at the back of the throat). Model pronouncing the word groups without interruption and have students repeat.

Standards: 1.1, 1.3

Resources: Practice Answers on Transparencies

Focus: Practicing the future tense

Suggestions: Tell students that their predictions must be at least one complete sentence in length. They need not make all their predictions about the same person or persons.

Answers will vary. The following are third-person singular and plural forms of the verbs in the word bank:

será/serán
logrará/lograrán
trabajará/trabajarán
estará/estarán
se dedicará/se dedicarán
tendrá/tendrán
realizará/realizarán
hará/harán
se mudará/se mudarán
ahorrará/ahorrarán
desempeñará/desempeñarán
podrá/podrán

En voz alta

El poeta español Gustavo Adolfo Bécquer nació en Sevilla en 1836. Era hijo de un pintor famoso que murió cuando Bécquer tenía sólo 5 años. Desde joven, Bécquer comenzó a escribir poesía. A los 22 años conoció a Julia Espín, la mujer que inspiró la mayoría de sus famosas *Rimas*. El poeta murió en 1870, a los 34 años de edad.

Bécquer fue quizás el último de los poetas románticos. Sus *Rimas* fueron durante mucho tiempo los poemas de amor más famosos en el mundo hispanohablante.

Lee este fragmento de la *Rima LIII* y luego trata de repetirlo en voz alta.

Rima LIII
de Gustavo Adolfo Bécquer

**Volverán las oscuras golondrinas[1]
en tu balcón sus nidos[2] a colgar[3],
y otra vez con el ala[4] a sus cristales
jugando llamarán.**

**Pero aquellas que el vuelo refrenaban[5]
tu hermosura y mi dicha[6] a contemplar,
aquellas que aprendieron nuestros nombres...
Ésas... ¡no volverán!**

---

1 swallows **2** nests **3** hang **4** wing **5** slowed down **6** happiness

¿Recuerdas?

Al hablar en voz alta muchas veces se combinan la última vocal de una palabra con la primera vocal de la siguiente en una sola sílaba. Por ejemplo: *que aprendieron; que el.*

 **Gramática** **Escribir/Hablar**

¿Dónde estarán en diez años?

1 Haz predicciones sobre tus amigos, profesores, artistas o políticos famosos. Completa la tabla usando por lo menos seis verbos de la lista en futuro.

ser	trabajar	dedicarse	realizar	mudarse	desempeñar
lograr	estar	tener	hacer	ahorrar	poder

¿Cuándo?	Predicción
El próximo año	(Nombre) tendrá...
En cinco años	
En diez años	
En veinte años	

2 Ahora, habla con un(a) compañero(a) sobre las predicciones que hizo cada uno. Escojan una de ellas, digan si están de acuerdo o no, y vuelvan a contarla añadiendo más detalles. Usen su imaginación y añadan todos los detalles que puedan.

Modelo

en diez años / mujer presidenta

A —*En diez años, una mujer será presidenta de los Estados Unidos.*
B —*Sí, primero será abogada y trabajará para la gente de su estado. Será muy popular.*

264 **doscientos sesenta y cuatro**
Manos a la obra 1

Universal Access

Students with Special Needs
Help hearing impaired students appreciate the rhythm and style of *Rima LIII* by Gustavo Adolfo Bécquer. After the class has read the poem aloud, ask students to compose a series of rhythmic gestures to accompany the text. Invite everyone to participate in the movements.

Advanced Learners
Ask students to imagine that they will be attending their ten-year high school reunion. Have them use the future tense in as many sentences as they can to describe their classmates as they might appear ten years from now. Monitor for appropriate language usage.

Actividad 18 · Gramática · Escribir

¿Qué lograrás?

¿Qué harás en las siguientes situaciones? Completa las frases de una manera original usando el futuro.

Modelo

Si ahorro mucho dinero . . .
Si ahorro mucho dinero podré viajar a Guinea Ecuatorial.

1. Si consigo el empleo de mis sueños . . .
2. Si conozco a un(a) chico(a) que me gusta mucho . . .
3. Si encuentro un millón de dólares en la calle . . .
4. Si logro entrar en la universidad . . .
5. Si me ofrecen estudiar en el extranjero . . .
6. Si mis padres se mudan a otro estado . . .
7. Si logro tener mi propia empresa . . .
8. Si me piden trabajar como voluntario(a) . . .

> **Nota**
> Cuando una frase comienza con *si* + presente indicativo, generalmente es seguida de una frase que usa el futuro.

Actividad 19 · Gramática · Leer/Hablar

Los trabajos del futuro

❶ ¿Qué profesiones serán importantes para el año 2030? Lee el artículo y haz una lista con un(a) compañero(a).

❷ Expliquen de qué hablan las predicciones del artículo. Busquen ejemplos que apoyen estas opiniones.

❸ Escojan dos profesiones y hablen de por qué son o serán importantes. Pueden ser profesiones de ahora o del futuro.

⬤ Más práctica

Practice Workbook 6-6, 6-7

For: Practice with the future of probability
Visit: phschool.com
Web Code: jed-0604

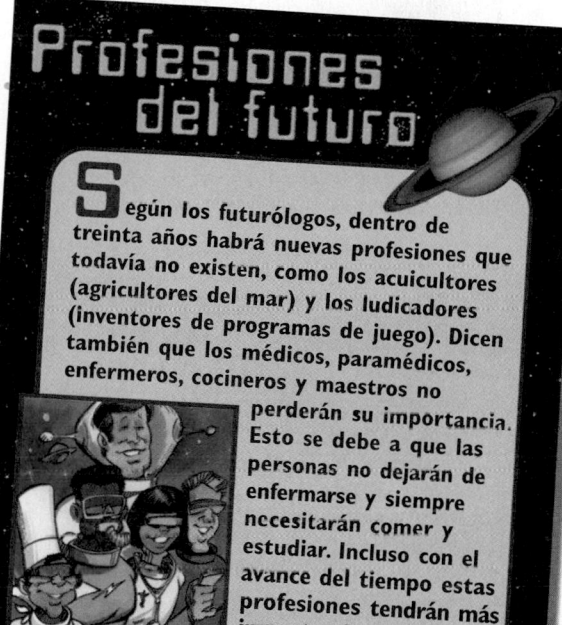

Profesiones del futuro

Según los futurólogos, dentro de treinta años habrá nuevas profesiones que todavía no existen, como los acuicultores (agricultores del mar) y los ludicadores (inventores de programas de juego). Dicen también que los médicos, paramédicos, enfermeros, cocineros y maestros no perderán su importancia. Esto se debe a que las personas no dejarán de enfermarse y siempre necesitarán comer y estudiar. Incluso con el avance del tiempo estas profesiones tendrán más importancia que ahora.

doscientos sesenta y cinco **265**
Capítulo 6

Practice and Communicate

Actividad 18 · *Standards:* 1.3

Focus: Practicing the future tense

Suggestions: Once students have prepared their answers, encourage them to share them. They can invite others' responses with questions such as **Y tú, ¿qué harás si...?**

Answers will vary.

Actividad 19 · *Standards:* 1.1, 1.2

Resources: Practice Answers on Transparencies

Focus: Practicing new vocabulary and structures through reading and discussion about future professions

Suggestions: Before students read the information, have them predict what they think will be important jobs or professions in the future.

Answers:
Step 1
acuicultores, ludicadores, médicos, paramédicos, enfermeros, cocineros y maestros

Steps 2–3
Answers will vary.

Additional Resources

• Writing, Audio & Video Workbook: Cap. 6, Writing Activities 8–9
• Resource Book: Cap. 6, Communicative Activity BLM

✓ **Assessment**
• Prueba 6-4: *El futuro de probabilidad*
• Examen: Vocabulario y gramática 1

Chapter Project

Students can perform step 3 at this point. (For more information, see p. 246-a.)

Enriching Your Teaching

Culture Note

In addition to writing poetry, Gustavo Adolfo Bécquer composed music, wrote **zarzuelas,** and painted. He was influenced by **coplas,** two-to-three-line poems, usually sung, that were a popular poetic style of the time. Bécquer composed 76 **rimas** in all. Although

Bécquer is considered one of the major figures of Spanish romanticism, he published only one book within his lifetime, a volume entitled **Los Templos de España,** which he also illustrated.

Internet Search

Keyword: profesiones del futuro

Vocabulario y gramática

Presentation

Standards: 1.1, 1.2, 5.1

Resources: Voc. & Gram. Transparencies: 126–127; Resource Book: Cap. 6, Input Script; Audio Program: CD Cap. 6, Track 9

Focus: Presenting new vocabulary and using grammar lexically in context

Suggestions: Ask students to look at the seven numbered photos on these pages. Have a volunteer read the titles at the top of the photos. Ask: *¿Esta información se trata de avances tecnológicos o avances artísticos? (tecnológicos)* Play the *Audio CD* or read the text and have students follow along. Point out cognates that will aid in comprehension, such as *inventos, máquinas, satélite, reducir,* and *energía,* among others. Use circumlocution to explain the meaning of other vocabulary: *¿Qué palabra significa el lugar donde se producen cosas como coches? (fábrica)*

Block Schedule

Have students work in pairs to write out definitions of five of the words on these two pages. This will practice the skill of circumlocution. Have them work with another pair of students. Each pair will read aloud the definitions. The other pair has to guess the word being described.

266

A primera vista 2
Vocabulario y gramática en contexto

Objectives

Read, listen to, and understand information about
- changes in technology
- the impact of technology on our lives

¿Ya estamos viviendo en el futuro? Hace unos años se hablaba de la llegada del siglo XXI. El siglo XXI ya llegó, y con éste muchos **avances** de la tecnología que cambiarán nuestras vidas.

1 Avances científicos y **tecnológicos**

Muchos trabajos peligrosos son hechos ahora por **máquinas** o robots. Se **predice** que en el futuro menos gente trabajará en **las fábricas**. Habrá más tiempo de **ocio**, o sea que la gente tendrá más tiempo para divertirse o para viajar.

2 Nuevos **inventos**

Inventos como la televisión digital y los discos digitales ofrecen imágenes más claras y mejor sonido. En muchas casas, los discos digitales están **reemplazando** a las videocaseteras.

3 Realidad virtual

La tecnología llamada realidad virtual permite vivir una experiencia a través de computadoras **como si fuera** real. Esta nueva tecnología ya se usa para entrenar a los pilotos.

Si queremos un futuro mejor, debemos prepararnos desde ahora. ¿Qué podemos hacer?

Hay que **tener en cuenta** la importancia del medio ambiente.

De hoy en adela[...] debemos dedicarr[...] proteger el agu[...]

Universal Access

Students with Learning Difficulties

Encourage students to use the photographs on these two pages to help predict the main idea of each paragraph. Ask embedded-answer questions to help them understand the passages: *¿Quién hará muchos trabajos peligrosos en el futuro, la gente o las máquinas?*

Advanced Learners

Have students brainstorm and "invent" a technological advancement that might be possible 100 years from now. Individuals or small groups should describe in detail their prediction and include a drawing that can be shown to the class.

4 Medios de comunicación

Gracias a **aparatos** como el teléfono celular podemos **comunicarnos** desde muchos lugares. Desde que **se inventó** la televisión **vía satélite**, podemos ver imágenes y **enterarnos** inmediatamente de lo que pasa en todo el mundo.

5 Vivienda

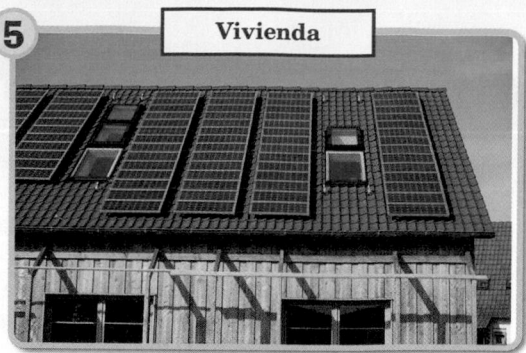

El uso de otras **fuentes de energía**, como la energía solar, permitirá calentar **las viviendas** sin **contaminar** el medio ambiente y, además, será mucho más barato.

6 Transporte

Algunas compañías han presentado los primeros coches eléctricos que ayudarán a **reducir** la contaminación del aire.

7 Medicina

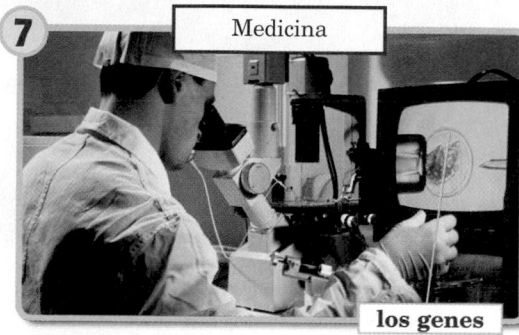

los genes

Cada año, los científicos **descubren** más cosas fascinantes sobre el cuidado de la salud. Avances en **la genética** harán posible **curar** muchas de **las enfermedades**, como el cáncer. Algunas enfermedades **desaparecerán** gracias a los nuevos medicamentos, que **prolongarán** la vida de muchas personas.

20 Escuchar/Escribir

Radio Futura

En una hoja de papel escribe los números del 1 al 6. Vas a escuchar lo que se dice en un programa de radio sobre avances científicos que van a ayudar a resolver muchos problemas en el mundo. Escucha cada frase y escribe si es lógica o ilógica. Si la frase no es lógica, corríjela.

21 Escribir

Avances de la tecnología

Escribe dos ejemplos de avances que se han logrado en cada una de las siguientes categorías.

- tecnología
- medicina
- medios de comunicación
- vivienda

Language Input (6)

20 *Standards:* 1.2

Resources: Audio Program: CD Cap. 6, Track 10; Resource Book: Cap. 6, Audio Script; Practice Answers on Transparencies

Focus: Practicing listening comprehension of new vocabulary

Suggestions: Remind students that they are only commenting on whether or not each statement is logical. Whether they agree or not with the future possibilities has no bearing on their answers.

Answers:
1. lógica
2. ilógica
3. lógica
4. ilógica
5. lógica
6. lógica

21 *Standards:* 1.3

Resources: Practice Answers on Transparencies

Focus: Practicing writing of new vocabulary

Suggestions: Invite students to answer with complete sentences if they choose, but to paraphrase the information, rather than stating it verbatim from the *Vocabulario* presentation.

Answers will vary but should contain the following basic information:
- menos trabajadores en las fábricas; más tiempo de ocio
- avances en la genética; algunas enfermedades desaparecerán; la vida de muchas personas se prolongará
- nos comunicaremos desde muchos lugares; nos enteraremos inmediatamente de lo que pasa
- nuevas fuentes de energía no contaminarán el medio ambiente; será más barata

Enriching Your Teaching

Culture Note

In 1950, with its population growing rapidly, Mexico City began work on a modern transportation system. The first line of the Mexico City Metro was opened in 1969. Today the system is still expanding and modernizing to meet the needs of the future. Plans are currently in place to introduce light rail lines into the suburbs.

Teacher-to-Teacher

Young people enjoy talking about the future, and many will have a lot to say in discussions. Encourage them to stretch their skills in Spanish and experiment with ways of articulating their ideas about the future.

Language Input

Vocabulario y gramática

Presentation

Standards: 1.1, 1.2, 3.1, 5.1

Resources: Voc. & Gram. Transparencies: 128–129; Resource Book: Cap. 6, Input Script; Audio Program: CD Cap. 6, Tracks 11–12

Focus: Extending presentation of vocabulary and grammar in context

Suggestions:

Pre-reading: Have students look at the photos and talk about what they see. Ask a volunteer to read the title and the photo captions. Give explanations or ask questions that help clarify the meaning of new vocabulary. For example, point to photo number 1 and say: *Una empresa es una organización que emplea gente. ¿Puedes nombrar algunas empresas de nuestra comunidad?*

Reading: Allow students time to read the information on this and the next page silently first. Then play the *Audio CD* and have students read along as they listen. Allow them to listen more than once.

Post-reading: Check comprehension by asking questions, including those found in *Actividad* 23.

TRES CAMPOS QUE TIENEN FUTURO

Según estudios de los últimos años, para el año 2050 habrá desaparecido la mayoría de los trabajos que ahora existen. Aunque habrá demanda de médicos, abogados y economistas, éstos son los campos con más futuro:

Servicios a empresas

Las empresas en general tendrán menos empleados, pero necesitarán de los servicios de profesionales como vendedores, secretarios y diseñadores gráficos.

Con el uso de las computadoras y de la Red, la informática es la profesión del futuro. Por todo el mundo, los ingenieros de sistemas y programadores se dedican al desarrollo de nuevos y mejores programas de computación.

Informática

Habrá mucho trabajo en hoteles y empresas turísticas. Se necesitarán cocineros, agentes de viaje, camareros y administradores.

Industria de la hospitalidad

268 doscientos sesenta y ocho
A primera vista 2

Universal Access

Heritage Language Learners

Ask students if they have ever had occasion to interpret for someone. Ask them to discuss the circumstances that called for an interpreter, as well as comment on the experience. Was it exciting to serve as a bridge between two languages? Was it challenging?

Students with Special Needs

Provide visually impaired students with a partner who can verbally describe the photographs under *Tres campos que tienen futuro.* Instruct the partners to focus on details associated with the profession being discussed.

Traducciones

✓ **Traducciones bilingües: inglés-español, español-inglés**

✓ **Especializados en documentos legales, informes de mercadeo, libros científicos**

✓ **Servicio rápido y eficiente**

✓ **Traductores certificados**

AGENCIA TRADUCE

Calle 49, número 456
San José, Costa Rica
Tel: 555-5555

La demanda de traductores aumentará porque habrá más comercio entre los diferentes países.

Las personas que trabajan en el campo de mercadeo desarrollan estrategias para vender los productos.

UNA DELICIOSA BEBIDA

Actividad 22 **Escuchar** • • • • • • • • • • • •

Campos de trabajo

Escribe los números del 1 al 5 en una hoja de papel. Escucha la descripción de cada trabajo y escribe a qué campo se refiere.

● **Más práctica** • • • • • • • • • • • •
  Practice Workbook 6-8, 6-9

Go Online
PHSchool.com

For: Vocabulary practice
Visit: www.phschool.com
Web Code: jed-0606

Actividad 23 **Escribir/Hablar** • • • • • • • • • •

¿Comprendiste?

1. ¿Qué empleados(as) se necesitarán para ofrecer servicios a empresas?

2. Según lo que leíste, ¿cuál es la profesión del futuro? ¿Por qué?

3. ¿Por qué se necesitarán más traductores en el futuro?

4. ¿Por qué crees que habrá más demanda de empleados en la industria de la hospitalidad?

5. ¿Puedes describir una estrategia de mercadeo que se usa para vender un producto que conoces?

doscientos sesenta y nueve 269
Capítulo 6

Enriching Your Teaching

Culture Note

Some students involved in the ***Bachillerato Internacional*** go on to special programs of study for careers in interpretation and translation. Students involved in these programs study the difference between *simultaneous* interpretation, listening and speaking at the same time, and *consecutive* interpretation, waiting for pauses every two to three sentences. They also master *phrase* interpretation, which is word-for-word translation, and *summary* interpretation, providing the main idea of what a speaker has said. Students often develop an expertise in a particular field, such as court interpretation or medical translation.

Manos a la obra 2

Vocabulario y gramática en uso

Actividad 24 **Leer**

¿Nos ayudarán los robots?

Muchas personas creen que el uso del robot cambiará mucho nuestra vida en el futuro. Completa cada frase con la palabra correcta.

1. En el futuro, ¿nos darán los robots más tiempo para dedicarlo al_____y al descanso?

   a. uso   **b.** ocio   **c.** avance

2. La _____ de las fábricas ya tienen o pronto tendrán robots para hacer gran parte del trabajo allí.

   a. máquina   **b.** tecnología   **c.** mayoría

3. La _____ para vender los robots al público será a través de la Red.

   a. estrategia   **b.** informática   **c.** vía satélite

4. Veremos robots en muchas _____ también. Los usarán en casas y apartamentos para los trabajos diarios.

   a. demandas   **b.** viviendas   **c.** enfermedades

5. Muchas personas que predicen el futuro creen que el robot será uno de los _____ tecnológicos más importantes del siglo.

   a. avances   **b.** genes   **c.** campos

Actividad 25 **Leer**

Una vida diferente

¿Qué piensas acerca de las computadoras? Completa el párrafo con las palabras o expresiones del recuadro.

el uso	reemplazar	predecir	la realidad virtual	los inventos
como si fuera	los avances	el campo	tener en cuenta	

Es imposible __1.__ el futuro, pero no hay duda de que __2.__ de la tecnología va a aumentar. Cada día, los ingenieros de sistemas escriben programas que cambian nuestra vida. Claro, las computadoras nunca van a __3.__ a las personas, pero __4.__ como __5.__, muestran cómo una computadora puede funcionar __6.__ una persona. Pero con todos __7.__ en __8.__ de la informática, es importante __9.__ que las computadoras nunca serán personas.

Actividad 26 — Leer/Escribir/Hablar

Las profesiones del mañana

❶ En otro papel, escribe los números del 1 al 8. Escribe la información apropiada para cada espacio en blanco de la tabla.

❷ Con otro(a) estudiante hablen de cuál o cuáles de esos trabajos les gustaría hacer y por qué.

❸ Habla con tu compañero(a) sobre la importancia de estas profesiones ahora y en el futuro.

Industria	Profesión	Servicio / Producto
transporte	científico	1.
medios de comunicación	2.	teléfono celular
finanzas	3.	cajero automático
4.	5.	programa de computación
medicina	6.	7.
8.	mujer de negocios	estrategias para vender productos

Actividad 27 — Escribir/Hablar

Y tú, ¿qué dices?

Imagina que vas a vivir solo(a) durante ocho semanas en un observatorio, en medio del desierto. Haz una lista de los aparatos, la tecnología o los inventos que te gustaría tener allí.

1. ¿Cuáles te parecen más importantes? ¿Cuáles crees que usarás más frecuentemente?

2. ¿Cuáles de esos aparatos o inventos crees que desaparecerán en el futuro? ¿Por qué?

3. ¿Cuáles crees que serán los mejores avances que verás en el futuro?

4. ¿Qué cosas piensas que habrá en el futuro que no te gustarán? ¿Qué crees que se puede hacer para evitarlas?

Bachillerato Internacional El Bachillerato Internacional es un programa de estudios común para las escuelas preparatorias de América Latina y otros países. Actualmente[1], más de 1,400 colegios[2] en 114 países forman parte del programa. Tiene una gran ventaja[3] para los estudiantes que cambian de país con frecuencia ya que pueden ir, sin problemas, de un colegio de Bachillerato Internacional a otro.

Los programas se enseñan en el idioma del país. Por ejemplo, un estudiante de Francia que estudia en España tiene el mismo currículum que el de su país, pero lo aprende en español. El programa empezó en 1968 y es reconocido por universidades de todo el mundo. Busca la excelencia académica, desarrolla el pensamiento crítico y ayuda a la comprensión intercultural entre los jóvenes de todos los países.

1 Currently 2 high schools 3 advantage

• ¿Has oído hablar del Bachillerato Internacional? ¿Conoces alguna escuela que ofrece este programa?

• ¿Qué opinas de un programa de estudios que es igual en todo el mundo? ¿Es buena idea? ¿Por qué? ¿Por qué no?

Practice and Communicate

 Actividad 26 — Standards: 1.1

Resources: Voc. & Gram. Transparencies: 8

Focus: Practicing new vocabulary via note-taking and discussion

Suggestions: Show *Vocabulary and Grammar Transparency* 4 as a reference while students fill in the chart for step 1.

Answers will vary.

 Actividad 27 — Standards: 1.3

Focus: Writing answers to demonstrate comprehension of new vocabulary and structures

Suggestions: Point out that questions 1 and 2 deal with the desert observatory situation. Questions 3 and 4 require more open-ended, personal responses.

Answers will vary.

 Fondo cultural — Standards: 1.1, 1.2, 3.1, 5.1, 5.2

Suggestions: After students read the information, ask comprehension questions such as the following: *¿Qué tipo de escuela forma parte del Bachillerato Internacional? ¿Cómo beneficia el programa a los jóvenes?*

Common Errors: Some students will assume that **actualmente** means the same as the English "actually." Remind them that this is a false cognate and means "currently."

Answers will vary.

Chapter Project

Students can perform step 4 at this point. Be sure they understand your corrections and suggestions. (For more information, see p. 246-a.)

Enriching Your Teaching

Teacher-to-Teacher

Play "Concentration." Prepare twenty notecards. On ten of them, write the name of an area of employment or a profession. On the other ten, write a word or expression that is clearly associated with each area. Example: *el (la) abogado(a)/la ley.* Write the numbers 1–20 in random order on the back of the cards. Tape them to the board in numerical order in a grid. Divide students into two teams. A player from Team A chooses two cards, which are turned over and read aloud. If they match, they are removed from the grid. Team A scores a point and goes again. If the cards don't match, they are returned to their positions and it is Team B's turn.

Standards: 1.1, 1.2

Resources: Practice Answers on Transparencies

Focus: Practicing new vocabulary in a cloze exercise

Suggestions: Refer students to p. 260 for forms of the future tense.

Answers:
Step 1

1. reemplazarán	6. Nos enteraremos
2. curarán	7. Desaparecerán
3. Nos comunicaremos	8. Inventarán
4. prolongarán	9. aumentarán
5. reducirán	10. descubrirán

Step 2
Answers will vary.

Standards: 1.1, 1.2, 3.1

Focus: Demonstrating comprehension of new vocabulary and structures through reading and response

Suggestions: For step 1, students can read the article in pairs. Ask them to help each other with any comprehension problems they may have.

Answers will vary.

Additional Resources

- Writing, Audio & Video Workbook: Cap. 6, Audio Activity 3, Track 14
- Writing, Audio & Video Workbook: Cap. 6, Writing Activity 10
- Resource Book: Cap. 6, Communicative Activity BLM

Assessment

- Prueba 6-6: Vocabulary production

 **Leer/Hablar** ....

Predicciones

1 Averigua qué piensan tus compañeros(as) sobre cómo será la vida en 50 años. Completa las siguientes preguntas con el futuro del verbo correcto.

aumentar	comunicarse	curar	desaparecer	descubrir
enterarse	inventar	prolongar	reducir	reemplazar

1. ¿Los robots _____ a los empleados de las fábricas?

2. En el campo de la medicina, ¿_____ a las personas que sufren de cáncer?

3. ¿_____ nosotros con extraterrestres?

4. ¿Nuevas medicinas _____ la vida hasta los cien años?

5. ¿Nuevos métodos tecnológicos _____ la contaminación del aire?

6. ¿_____ nosotros de las causas del cáncer?

7. ¿_____ las enfermedades, como el resfriado común?

8. ¿_____ los ingenieros nuevos aparatos que harán más fáciles los quehaceres diarios?

9. ¿Los autobuses eléctricos _____ el ahorro de gasolina?

10. ¿Los científicos _____ nuevas fuentes de energía en el medio ambiente?

2 Con otro(a) estudiante preparen respuestas para tres de las preguntas y expliquen por qué dieron esas respuestas.

  Leer/Hablar ....

Los futurólogos predicen . . .

1 Lee estos fragmentos de un artículo sobre la vida en el año 2050.

▶▶▶▶▶ LA VIDA EN EL 2050

Los futurólogos no son psíquicos, son científicos que basan sus predicciones en el estado de la ciencia y la sociedad del presente. Predicen que en el 2050 los aparatos de la casa podrán encenderse con un solo control remoto. La realidad virtual nos permitirá visitar lugares o amigos en el otro lado del mundo, en segundos. La prensa escrita desaparecerá por completo y también los libros y revistas. Leeremos todo en pequeños aparatos digitales. En cuanto al mundo del trabajo, dicen los futurólogos que se trabajará sólo 20 horas por semana y mucha gente trabajará desde su casa, gracias a la computadora y a la Red.

2 Trabaja con otro(a) estudiante para decir cómo será más fácil la vida y cómo podremos hacer más rápidamente las cosas, según el artículo.

3 Expliquen por qué son positivos o negativos los cambios que se mencionan en el artículo.

Universal Access

Heritage Language Learners

Have students exchange papers and edit each other's work for *Actividad* 30. Direct them to focus on the correct placement of accent marks, as well as the correct spelling of past participles. Allow students to discuss their editorial changes with their partners.

Students with Learning Difficulties

Help students divide *Actividad* 28 into several steps. First, have them read over each sentence for meaning. Second, have them identify the subject of the sentence. Third, have them choose the appropriate verb from the word bank. Finally, have them write the correct future verb form in the blank.

Gramática

El futuro perfecto

Use the future perfect tense to express what will have happened by a certain time. To form the future perfect, use the future of the verb *haber* with the past participle of the verb.

Here are all the future perfect tense forms of *inventar*:

habré inventado	habremos inventado
habrás inventado	habréis inventado
habrá inventado	habrán inventado

Para el año 2050 los científicos **habrán descubierto** otras fuentes de energía.
*By 2050, scientists **will have discovered** other energy sources.*

• The future perfect tense is often used with *dentro de* + time.

Dentro de cinco años, **habremos aprendido** mucho sobre la genética.
*In five years, we **will have learned** a lot about genetics.*

• You also use the future perfect tense to speculate about something that may have happened in the past.
—Laura no me llamó. ¿Qué le **habrá pasado**?
—**Se habrá enterado** de que no ibas.

—*Laura didn't call me. What **could have happened** to her?*
—***Perhaps she found out** you were not coming.*

¿Recuerdas?

Varios verbos tienen participios irregulares, como *escribir, escrito* y *volver, vuelto.* Los participios pasados de los verbos *descubrir* y *resolver* también son irregulares: *descubierto, resuelto.*

Actividad 30 **Gramática** Leer

¿Qué habremos logrado para el año . . .?

Imagina que hablas con otros(as) estudiantes sobre lo que habrán logrado dentro de varios años. Completa las siguientes predicciones con el futuro perfecto del verbo correcto.

1. En unos diez años, la mejor estudiante de geología de mi clase _____ (*descubrir / desaparecer*) nuevos materiales de la Luna.

2. Dentro de veinte años, nuestra amiga escritora _____ (*conseguir / permitir*) el Premio Nobel de literatura.

3. Para las próximas Olimpiadas, mi patinadora favorita _____ (*inventar / reemplazar*) a la campeona mundial.

4. Si sigo estudiando, dentro de dos años _____ (*aumentar / eliminar*) mi vocabulario de español.

5. Dentro de 20 años, probablemente todos nosotros _____ (*prolongar / mudarse*) de casa alguna vez.

6. Dicen mis padres que como trabajamos mucho y somos dedicados, dentro de 15 años _____ (*alcanzar / diseñar*) nuestras metas.

doscientos setenta y tres **273**
Capítulo 6

Rapid Review

Before presenting the future forms of **haber** in the *Gramática* on this page, review with students the present tense and imperfect forms. Have students use these forms in sentences in the present perfect and past perfect tenses.

Gramática

Presentation

Standards: 4.1

Resources: Voc. & Gram. Transparencies: 130

Suggestions: Refer students to the *¿Recuerdas?* Have them list other irregular past participles that they can remember. Point out that all the perfect tenses they have learned so far use the auxiliary verb **haber.** Explain that this verb's conjugated forms are most often used in perfect tenses.

 Actividad 30 *Standards:* 1.2

Resources: Practice Answers on Transparencies

Focus: Using the future perfect tense in a word-choice exercise

Suggestions: Tell students to complete the exercise in steps. First, choose the verb that makes sense. Second, convert the verb to its past participle form. Third, add the appropriate future tense form of *haber* before the participle.

Answers:
1. habrá descubierto
2. habrá conseguido
3. habrá reemplazado
4. habré aumentado
5. nos habremos mudado
6. habremos alcanzado

Enriching Your Teaching

Culture Note

According to The Second World Assembly on Aging, which met in Madrid in 2001, there will be two billion people over the age of 60 in the world in the year 2050, and for the first time, the number of people over 60 will outnumber those under 14. Ask students to discuss the implications of this trend.

Teacher-to-Teacher

Ask students to write three sentences using the future perfect tense to tell what they will have done one week from now, one month from now, and one year from now.

Additional Resources

• Writing, Audio & Video Workbook: Cap. 6, Audio Activity 4, Track 15

6 Practice and Communicate

Standards: 1.1, 1.3

Focus: Practicing the future perfect tense through discussion about a fact table

Suggestions: As part of their discussion, ask students to compute the year in which the use of each invention became widespread.

Answers will vary.

Standards: 1.1

Focus: Practicing the future perfect tense through discussion in context

Suggestions: As students discuss their predictions, encourage them to choose a secretary for the group who notes down students' comments by category.

Answers will vary.

Extension: After students' discussions, have them report to the class on what other members of their group said. This will elicit third-person forms of the future perfect tense.

Additional Resources

• Writing, Audio & Video Workbook: Cap. 6, Writing Activity 11

✓ **Assessment**
• Prueba 6-7: *El futuro perfecto*

 Gramática Leer/Hablar

Más y más rápido

Muchas veces, pasan años antes de que la gente empiece a usar los inventos. Lee la tabla siguiente. Con otro(a) estudiante, piensa por qué unos inventos habrán tardado mucho *(taken a long time)* en usarse mientras que otros inventos habrán tardado poco. Escojan cuatro inventos y preparen explicaciones.

Modelo

electricidad / 46 años

A —*¿Por qué habrán pasado 46 años entre el invento de la electricidad y su uso masivo?*

B —*Habrá pasado mucho tiempo porque . . .*

MÁS Y MÁS RÁPIDO		
Invento	Fecha	Años para su uso masivo *(widespread)*
Electricidad	1873	46
Teléfono	1876	35
Coche	1886	55
Radio	1906	22
Televisión	1926	26
Microondas	1953	30
Minicomputadora	1975	16
Teléfono celular	1983	13
La Red	1991	7

Coche antiguo

 Gramática Hablar

Predicciones para el año 2030

En grupos de cuatro, hagan predicciones para el año 2030. ¿Qué habrá pasado en el mundo? ¿Qué pasará? Piensen en sus metas, su escuela, su comunidad, sus viajes de vacaciones, los deportes, la moda y los alimentos.

Modelo

Para el año 2030, habré terminado una carrera y estaré trabajando como abogada.

● **Más práctica**
Practice Workbook 6-10

Go Online
PHSchool.com

For: Practice with the future perfect
Visit: www.phschool.com
Web Code: jed-0607

Universal Access

Students with Learning Difficulties

Guide students to focus on the first sentence or clause of each item in *Actividad* 33. Instruct them to copy the noun that will become an object pronoun in the second part of the item. Then have them convert each noun to the appropriate object pronoun, insert it in the second part of the sentence, and read the entire item aloud.

Advanced Learners

Ask students to use the Internet to investigate other technological advances like those in *Actividad* 31. They might research the creation and widespread use of audio CDs, DVDs, or fax machines. Have them prepare brief reports telling when the device was invented and about what year its use became widespread.

Gramática

Uso de los complementos directos e indirectos

You already know the direct object pronouns *(me, te, lo, la, nos, os, los, las)* and the indirect object pronouns *(me, te, le, nos, os, les)* in Spanish.

When you use a direct and an indirect object pronoun together, place the indirect object pronoun before the direct object pronoun.

—Si necesitas un teléfono celular, yo **te lo** doy. ¿Quién **te** prestará la computadora?

—Octavio **me la** prestará.

When the indirect object pronoun *le* or *les* comes before the direct object pronoun *lo, la, los,* or *las,* change *le* or *les* to *se.* In these cases, you often add the prepositional phrase *a Ud., a él, a ella,* etc. or *a* + a noun or a person's name for clarification.

—¿A quién **le** comunicarán la noticia del descubrimiento?

—**Se la** comunicaremos **a Carlos**.

—José y Adela quieren leer los libros sobre el nuevo invento. ¿Puedes **prestárselos**?

When you attach two object pronouns to an infinitive, a command, or a present participle, you must add an accent mark to preserve the original stress.

—Quiero ver las fotos que van a usar para el mercadeo. **Dámelas,** por favor.

—No puedo **dártelas** hoy, espera hasta mañana.

 33 Gramática Leer

Sobre el futuro

Carla y Laura quieren estar preparados para el futuro. Completa lo que dicen con los complementos apropiados.

1. Laura quiere que le preste mi libro sobre genética pero no *(se lo / me lo)* _____ voy a prestar.

2. ¿Viste el programa vía satélite sobre la importancia del español en el mundo? *(Se lo / Te lo)* _____ recomiendo.

3. No recibimos la información sobre los nuevos aparatos eléctricos. El gerente de la empresa dice que *(nos la / se la)* _____ enviará la próxima semana.

4. Sé que ustedes comprarán una televisión digital. *(Me la / Se la)* _____ pediré prestada.

5. Quiero leer el artículo sobre informática. ¿*(Me lo / Te lo)* _____ das?

6. Nos explicaron la tarea sobre las nuevas fuentes de energía que habrá en el 2020, pero no *(te la / nos la)* _____ explicaron muy bien.

7. Me compré un programa de realidad virtual. *(Se lo / Te lo)* _____ mostraré cuando vengas a casa.

doscientos setenta y cinco **275**
Capítulo 6

 Gramática

Presentation

Resources: Voc. & Gram. Transparencies: 131

Suggestions: On the board or a transparency, cue students with sentences of various types that contain both a direct and an indirect object as nouns. Ask students to restate the sentences, changing the objects to pronouns.

 33 *Standards:* 1.2

Resources: Practice Answers on Transparencies

Focus: Practicing combinations of direct and indirect object pronouns

Suggestions: Remind students to use the *se* form of the third-person indirect object pronoun. Point out that Spanish never has the pronoun combinations *le lo, le la, le los,* or *le las.*

Answers:

1. se lo	5. Me lo
2. Te lo	6. nos la
3. nos la	7. Te lo
4. Se la	

Enriching Your Teaching

Teacher-to-Teacher

Using one word per sheet of paper, write a sentence such as *Juan da el libro a María.* Write the direct and indirect object pronouns, including *se,* on separate sheets. Distribute the words to students. Say the sentence in English: "Juan gives the book to María." Students who have the words go to the front of the class and stand in the correct order. Then say, "Juan gives it to María." The student holding *lo* comes up, the student with *el libro* sits down, and those standing must form the sentence: *Juan lo da a María.* Continue in this way, saying "Juan gives the book to her," and "Juan gives it to her." Prepare several sentences in this manner.

275

El español en la comunidad

Presentation

Standards: 1.2, 5.1

Suggestions: Once students have read the information, ask comprehension questions. For example: *¿Cuál es la idea principal de esta lectura? ¿Cómo ayudan los diarios digitales a los hispanohablantes en los Estados Unidos?*

Standards: 1.1

Focus: Practicing combinations of direct and indirect object pronouns

Suggestions: Encourage students to practice alternative placements of object pronouns: *Voy a dársela a Marta./Se la voy a dar a Marta.*

Answers will vary.

▶ Rapid Review

Prepare students for *Actividad 35* by briefly reviewing vocabulary associated with volunteer work and community centers. This can be found in the *A primera vista* 2 section of *Capítulo* 5.

Standards: 1.1

Focus: Practicing combinations of direct and indirect object pronouns

Suggestions: As students have their group discussions, ask them to be ready to report to the rest of the class on their donation strategy.

Answers will vary.

El español en la comunidad

Diarios digitales

Las personas hispanohablantes de los Estados Unidos siempre han querido enterarse de las noticias de sus países. Es lógico, allí tienen sus raíces y parte de su familia. Hasta hace unos años, la única fuente de información en español que tenían eran algunos periódicos y canales de televisión en español de los Estados Unidos.

Ahora, gracias a los diarios digitales que hay en la Red, los hispanohablantes pueden leer periódicos de sus países todos los días.

La Red también les ofrece a los estudiantes de español la oportunidad de practicar el idioma y aprender sobre los países hispanohablantes. Pueden saber, por ejemplo, no sólo las noticias importantes de Quito, sino también qué restaurante está de moda, qué película es más popular o qué obra de teatro están poniendo. La Red ha hecho del mundo un lugar verdaderamente pequeño.

 **Gramática** **Hablar**

¿Qué les darás?

❶ Imagina que vas a mudarte a un apartamento muy pequeño. Haz una lista de las cosas que no vas a necesitar y que les puedes regalar a tus amigos.

❷ Intercambia tu lista con la de un(a) compañero(a). Tu compañero(a) te va a preguntar a quién le darás cada una de tus cosas.

Modelo

la televisión

A —*¿A quién le vas a dar la televisión?*

B —*Voy a dársela a Marta.*

276 doscientos setenta y seis
Manos a la obra 2

 Gramática **Hablar**

¿Qué les podemos ofrecer?

❶ Tú y tus amigos van a donar cosas a las siguientes personas que las necesitan. Para cada persona, escribe una cosa que le puedes ofrecer.

- un inmigrante que acaba de llegar
- una mujer sin hogar
- una persona de un hogar de ancianos
- un niño de un centro de rehabilitación

Modelo

un paciente de un centro de rehabilitación
unas revistas o una novela

❷ Trabaja con otro(a) estudiante. Hablen de las cosas que pueden ofrecer, cuándo las donarán y cómo las entregarán.

Modelo

A —*¿Qué le podemos ofrecer a un paciente de un centro de rehabilitación?*

B —*Le podemos ofrecer unos refrescos.*

A —*¡Buena idea! ¿Cuándo podemos llevárselos?*

B —*Se los podemos llevar este fin de semana.*

Universal Access

Heritage Language Learners

Ask students who have lived in a heritage country to discuss the role of television there. What are some of the most popular programs? Who are some of the most popular actors or personalities? Ask them to express their opinion on the influence of television. Do they find it positive or negative?

Students with Learning Difficulties

After students have chosen their topics for *Actividad 36*, instruct them to reread sections of the chapter pertaining to that topic. Help them find these sections and suggest that they write down vocabulary and phrases that might be useful to their presentations.

Actividad 36 — Hablar/Escribir/Escuchar

Las cosas que traerá el futuro

❶ Trabaja en un grupo de tres o cuatro estudiantes. Escojan uno de los temas de la lista y hagan predicciones sobre ese tema. Luego, preparen una pequeña presentación para la clase. Mientras escuchan las presentaciones de los demás grupos, tomen notas.

- la vivienda
- la tecnología
- las carreras
- los medios de comunicación
- el ocio
- los alimentos

❷ Con tu compañero(a), usen sus notas para hablar sobre lo que dijeron los demás grupos. Escriban algunas frases que digan si las predicciones de los(as) demás estudiantes son lógicas o ilógicas y por qué.

 Standards: 1.1, 1.3

Focus: Using new vocabulary and structures in an oral presentation

Suggestions: As students do their planning in step 1, have them brainstorm a list of details associated with their chosen topic. They can use this list to help them develop their oral presentation.

Answers will vary.

Actividad 37 — Leer/Escribir

Cómo la televisión hizo historia

Pocos avances tecnológicos han tenido una influencia tan grande como la televisión. En México, la televisión ha sido un agente de cambio que ha jugado papeles muy diferentes en distintos momentos históricos.

Conexiones | Las ciencias sociales

La primera transmisión de televisión en México fue el 16 de mayo de 1935, y tuvo lugar en la sede[1] del partido político que gobernó[2] ese país por más de 70 años. Los líderes del partido pensaban que con la televisión en sus manos podían decidir qué ideas, noticias y opiniones iba a recibir el pueblo. Por mucho tiempo, la televisión fue un instrumento de los líderes del país.

1. ¿Por qué se puede decir que la televisión ha tenido una gran influencia en la historia de México?

2. ¿Qué papel juega la televisión en la política de tu país?

1 headquarters 2 ruled

● **Más práctica**
Practice Workbook 6-11, 6-12

Go Online
PHSchool.com

For: Practice with direct and indirect object pronouns
Visit: www.phschool.com
Web Code: jed-0608

 Standards: 1.2, 3.1, 4.2

Focus: Using new vocabulary and structures to read and respond

Suggestions: Have students read the information silently once. Then ask volunteers to read it aloud in sections. Before students answer the questions, address any reading comprehension issues they may have.

Answers:
1. La televisión fue un instrumento de los líderes políticos. Pensaban que con la televisión podían decidir lo que iba a recibir el pueblo.
2. Answers will vary.

Additional Resources
- Writing, Audio & Video Workbook: Cap. 6, Writing Activities 12–13
- Writing, Audio & Video Workbook: Cap. 6, Audio Activity 5, Track 16
- Resource Book: Cap. 6, Communicative Activity BLM

 Assessment
- Prueba 6-8: *Uso de los complementos directos e indirectos*
- Examen: Vocabulario y gramática 2

Chapter Project
Students can perform step 5 at this point. Record their presentations on cassette or videotape for inclusion in their portfolios. (For more information, see p. 474-a.)

 ### Enriching Your Teaching

Culture Note

Statistics show that there are approximately 200 million televisions in homes throughout North and South America. Sixty percent of these are in North America and 40 percent in South America. This gap is quickly shrinking, however. In fact, 85 percent of households in Latin America own a television set. At first, this number seems to contradict the aforementioned percentages, but this is because many households in the United States have two or more television sets. Mexico alone has 17 million sets.

277

Puente a la cultura

Presentation

Standards: 1.1, 1.2, 2.2, 3.1

Focus: Reading to learn about the designs of well-known Spanish-speaking architects

Suggestions:

Pre-reading: Refer students to the *Estrategia* and have them answer the questions there. Then, based on the title of the selection, pictures, and captions, ask: *Después de leer este artículo, ¿qué tipo de comparación piensas que podremos hacer? (Podremos comparar ejemplos de la arquitectura del futuro; Podremos comparar la arquitectura del futuro con la de hoy día.)*

Reading: Encourage students to read through the entire passage once silently, without stopping at problem words or to ask questions. Then, for the second time through, ask volunteers to read sections aloud. Remind students to use background knowledge, cognates, and context clues to help them understand unfamiliar words and expressions as they read.

Post-reading: Ask students to work in small groups to complete a graphic organizer, such as a chart or a concept web, that shows the reading's main ideas and important supporting details.

Country Connection

Presentation

Standards: 3.1

Resources: Voc. & Gram. Transparency: 14

Remind students that Luis Barragán is from Mexico. Tell them that Monterrey, Mexico's third-largest city, is not only the country's leading industrial center, but also home to seven universities.

Go Online

The online atlas will provide more detailed maps of Argentina, Mexico, and Spain.

¡Adelante!

Puente a la cultura
La arquitectura del futuro

Objectives

- Read about the architecture of the future and the Latin American architects that are shaping it
- Compare and contrast different modern buildings
- Make predictions about the architecture of the future

Estrategia

Look at Illustrations

Pictures, photographs, and other graphics are often used to emphasize a written message.

You can anticipate what the content of a text will be by examining the illustrations.

The article on this page is about architecture. Look at the photos on these pages and think about the style of the buildings. What might the article be about?

¿Te has preguntado alguna vez cómo serán los edificios del futuro? La mayoría de los arquitectos están de acuerdo en que serán más eficientes, mejores y más inteligentes pero, ¿qué quiere decir eso?

Seguramente, los edificios del futuro usarán menos ladrillo[1] y piedra, pues tendrán materiales como el titanio y las fibras de carbón y grafito[2], siguiendo el ejemplo de los aviones y coches. Cada vez habrá más edificios "inteligentes", en otras palabras, edificios en los que una computadora central controla todos los aparatos y servicios para aprovechar[3] mejor la energía eléctrica, la calefacción y el aire acondicionado en el interior.

El argentino César Pelli es uno de los arquitectos que diseñan los edificios del futuro. Una de sus obras más importantes son las Torres Petronas, en Kuala Lumpur, Malasia, consideradas los edificios más altos del mundo. Estas torres, con su planta en forma de estrella y construidas de cristal, acero[4] y concreto, tienen un diseño que es a la vez futurista e influenciado por la arquitectura islámica.

---

1 brick **2** titanium, and carbon and graphite fibers **3** to utilize **4** steel

Faro del Comercio

Hotel Camino Real

Torres Petronas

278   doscientos setenta y ocho
¡Adelante!

Universal Access

Students with Learning Difficulties
Before they read *La arquitectura del futuro,* have students create a chart with the following headings: *nombre del arquitecto, edificio, ciudad, diseño.* After an initial read, have them re-read to find the information necessary to complete the chart.

Advanced Learners
As a group project, have students design and then talk about a futuristic building of their own creation. They should illustrate or discuss how the building will be used, what its appearance will be, and so on.

Otro edificio futurista es el Faro del Comercio, en Monterrey, México, diseñado por el arquitecto mexicano Luis Barragán. La arquitectura de Barragán reúne en un mismo diseño líneas simples y modernas con el uso de colores, texturas y materiales que recuerdan la cultura popular mexicana y los colores de la naturaleza.

Ricardo Legorreta, otro reconocido arquitecto mexicano, ha diseñado el Hotel Camino Real en Cancún, México. La arquitectura de Legorreta se caracteriza por ambientes con diseños geométricos, una armoniosa combinación de espacio y color y un uso funcional y decorativo de la luz.

Un edificio que impresiona por su estilo futurístico es el Milwaukee Art Museum, diseñado por el arquitecto español Santiago Calatrava. Este museo se destaca por su forma única que combina elementos de arte y arquitectura.

Vistas del interior y del exterior del Milwaukee Art Museum

¿Comprendiste?

1. ¿Qué materiales se usarán para construir los edificios del futuro? ¿Por qué crees que se usarán esos materiales?

2. ¿Qué influencias se pueden ver en las Torres Petronas y en el Faro del Comercio? ¿Conoces algún edificio similar? Explica las razones para diseñarlo así.

3. Compara uno de los edificios futuristas de estas páginas con algún edificio moderno que te guste. ¿En qué se parecen? ¿En que se diferencian?

El futuro de tu comunidad

Usa la información del texto y las fotos para hacer predicciones sobre los edificios del futuro de tu comunidad. ¿Cómo será la escuela?, ¿la biblioteca?, ¿el hospital? Escribe un párrafo sobre alguno de esos edificios.

Go Online
PHSchool.com
For: Internet Link Activity
Visit: www.phschool.com
Web Code: jed-0610

doscientos setenta y nueve **279**
Capítulo 6

¿Comprendiste?

Standards: 1.2, 1.3

Resources: Practice Answers on Transparencies

Focus: Demonstrating reading comprehension

Suggestions: Tell students that questions 1 and 2 are fact-based, and the answers to them can be found in the reading. Questions 3 and 4 are more open-ended. Encourage them to talk about their personal tastes and values while answering question 3.

Answers:
1. Se usarán titanio y fibras de carbón y grafito. Seguirán el ejemplo de los aviones y coches.
2. Se pueden ver las influencias futuristas. Answers will vary.
3–4. Answers will vary.

El futuro de tu comunidad

Standards: 1.3

Focus: Combining learned structures in a written response to a reading

Suggestions: Encourage students to use chapter vocabulary and structures, such as the future perfect tense, in their paragraphs. Remind them that other technological advances, such as those in electronics, will have an effect on the buildings of the future.

Answers will vary.

Portfolio

Keep students' paragraphs from *El futuro de tu comunidad* in their portfolios as a writing sample.

Video
Presentation

Standards: 1.2

Resources: Video Program: Cap. 6

In this segment we meet a young Venezuelan professor, Antonio Cortez, who tells us how he combines his professional interests of photography and technology through his work with his students at the New England School of Photography. See the *Video Teacher's Guide* for additional suggestions.

Enriching Your Teaching

Culture Note
César Pelli has also designed many performing arts centers in the United States. The Aronoff Center in Cincinnati features the use of brick and stone, traditional building materials for the area. Pelli's design for the Performing Arts Center of Greater Miami reflects the city's tropical climate and multicultural ambience.

Internet Search
Keywords:

César Pelli, Luis Barragán, Ricardo Legorreta, Santiago Calatrava + arquitecto

279

¿Qué me cuentas?

Presentation

Standards: 1.1, 1.2, 1.3

Resources: Voc. & Gram. Transparencies: 132; Audio Program: CD Cap. 6, Track 17; Resource Book: Cap. 6, Audio Script; Practice Answers on Transparencies

Focus: Practicing speaking and listening comprehension

Suggestions:

For step 1, use the *Audio CD* or read the script aloud. Allow students to hear the descriptions twice through: the first time to write their answers and the second time to check them.

For step 2, guide students to use the future perfect, as well as the future tense. Encourage them to talk about the accomplishments each child will have achieved as an adult. Encourage them to use their imaginations and humor.

Answers:

Step 1
1. b   2. c   3. a   4. c   5. b   6. b

Steps 2–3
Answers will vary.

¿Qué me cuentas?

Cuando sea mayor

1 🎧 Vas a escuchar una serie de descripciones. Después de cada descripción, vas a oír dos preguntas. Escoge la respuesta correcta para cada pregunta.

1. **a.** avances tecnológicos   **b.** programas de dibujos animados   **c.** productos de mercadeo

2. **a.** insectos   **b.** medios de comunicación   **c.** cómo curar enfermedades

3. **a.** el mercadeo   **b.** las comunicaciones   **c.** la medicina

4. **a.** una gerente   **b.** una cocinera   **c.** una arquitecta

5. **a.** un disco digital   **b.** una calculadora   **c.** un teléfono celular

6. **a.** una contadora   **b.** una actriz cómica   **c.** una abogada

2 Observa las siguientes ilustraciones. Imagina a los niños dentro de 20 años. Con tus propias palabras, predice lo que estarán haciendo entonces. Describe con detalles tus predicciones para que resulten más interesantes. ¡Usa tu imaginación!

Si quieres, puedes usar las siguientes palabras o expresiones para conectar tus ideas.

para entonces	cuando	dentro de	así que
por eso	por lo tanto	porque	después de

1

2

3

4

5

6

3 Trabaja con tres compañeros(as) para comparar sus predicciones. Decidan cuál fue la más lógica, la más creativa y la más cómica.

280   doscientos ochenta
¡Adelante!

Block Schedule

Ask each students to write five statements about the picture sequence that are false. Place the students in pairs. Have them read the sentences to each other with the other student correcting each of the false statements.

Universal Access

Multiple Intelligences
Visual/Spatial: After students have made their predictions based on the illustrations in step 2, ask them to select their favorite example. Have students create their own pictures to illustrate how they envision the character in the future.

Students with Learning Difficulties
Help students organize information for their oral presentations. Model how to turn each question in the chart into an informative sentence. *¿Quiénes darán las clases? Los estudiantes darán las clases.*

Mi escuela del futuro

Tarea
Imagina que dentro de 10 años regresas a tu escuela y que serás el(la) nuevo(a) director(a). ¿Qué cambios harás para adaptar la escuela a los avances tecnológicos que habrá entonces? Tienes que preparar un discurso para decir lo que harás.

1 **Prepárate** Responde a las preguntas sobre los cambios que harás en tu escuela. Usa una tabla como ésta para escribir tus respuestas.

¿Quiénes darán las clases y cómo las darán?	
¿Qué materias enseñarán?	
¿Qué cambios harás en el edificio?	
¿Cómo harán sus tareas los estudiantes?	
¿Cómo se comunicarán los estudiantes dentro y fuera de la escuela?	

2 **Practica** Vuelve a leer la información que anotaste en la tabla. Puedes usar tus notas para practicar, pero no al hablar ante la clase. Recuerda:
- explicar con detalles lo que harás y por qué
- mirar directamente al público al hablar
- usar los tiempos futuros y el vocabulario del capítulo

Modelo
Los estudiantes podrán estudiar desde sus casas. Por las tardes, un robot ayudará a todos los estudiantes con sus tareas. Cada estudiante tendrá una computadora muy avanzada, que será casi humana . . .

3 **Haz tu presentación** Imagina que las personas que escuchan no saben cómo será tu escuela en el futuro. Descríbeles con detalles las cosas que harás para adaptar tu escuela a los avances del futuro.

4 **Evaluación** Tu profesor(a) puede explicarte cómo va a evaluar tu presentación. Probablemente, para tu profesor(a) es importante ver que:
- investigaste y te preparaste bien para hacer la presentación
- diste suficientes detalles e información a tu público

Estrategia
Mapping your speech using main idea and details
To organize a speech you can *map* it in advance. Think of your presentation as an organized way to communicate your ideas. You should start with an opening statement of the main idea. Then, use the items in the chart you wrote as subtopics. As you speak, introduce each subtopic one at a time, and elaborate on it by adding details. End your presentation with a closing statement that reinforces the main idea or your opinion about it.

Presentación oral
Presentation
Standards: 1.2, 1.3, 3.1

Resources: Voc. & Gram. Transparencies: 4

Focus: Preparing and delivering an oral presentation

Suggestions: Review the task and the four-step approach with students. Review the rubric with the class (see *Assessment* below) to explain how you will grade the performance task. Before students begin, direct their attention to the *Estrategia*. Point out that the chart shown in step 1 is one way of mapping a speech. Help them organize their information by using *Vocabulary & Grammar Transparency* 4 as a model. Show students how to set up their own charts by copying the questions into the left column of the transparency. Leave plenty of space between questions and tell students to use that space to write their answers in the right column of their own charts. The answers they write will be the details they use to support each main idea in their speech.

Portfolio
Record students' oral presentations on audiocassette or videotape for inclusion in their portfolios.

✓ **Assessment**
• Assessment Program: Cap. 6, Rubrics
Give students copies of the rubric before they begin the activity. Go over the descriptions of the different levels of performance. After assessing students, help individuals understand how their performance could be improved.

Enriching Your Teaching

RUBRIC	Score 1	Score 3	Score 5
How well your information is organized	Your ideas are undeveloped or not addressed at all.	You tend to skip around from idea to idea.	Your ideas are presented in a logical, planned order.
How well you support your main ideas	Your supporting evidence is absent.	Some of your supporting evidence is weak.	All your main ideas are supported with interesting details.
How effectively you deliver your speech	You read your speech. You have no eye contact with the audience and little or no intonation.	You make some eye contact. You use intonation, but not convincingly.	You have good eye contact with the audience. Your intonation helps get the message across.

Standards: 1.2, 1.3, 3.1

Resources: Voc. & Gram. Transparencies: 2

Focus: Combining learned vocabulary and structures in a written presentation

Suggestions: Begin by explaining the criteria you will use to evaluate students' compositions. (See step 5, *Evaluación*, in the Student Edition, and *Assessment* on the following page.)

Direct students' attention to the *Estrategia*. Ask them to share additional background information they have learned in Language Arts courses about comparing and contrasting. Use *Vocabulary & Grammar Transparency* 2 to model brainstorming and recording ideas for a comparison and contrast essay.

Language Arts Connection

Standards: 3.1

Point out to students that there are two ways they can organize their compare and contrast essay. They can tell all about one period of time first, then compare it to the other in another paragraph. Or they can go back and forth between one period of time and the other, showing how they are alike or different in various ways. Remind them that this latter alternative will require them to use more transitions in their writing.

Presentación escrita

El futuro según el presente

Objectives
- **Write a comparison about the past and the present**
- **Organize similarities and differences using a Venn diagram**

Estrategia

Compare and contrast
When you are writing, if you want to compare issues, use signal words to mark their similarities and their differences . . . You can say, for instance, *"En el pasado había muchas enfermedades, pero hoy, con los avances en la medicina, podemos curarlas"* or *"Antes, los viajes tardaban mucho tiempo, pero ahora tardan sólo unas horas."* Other expressions are: *"Antes . . . pero ahora . . .", "en el pasado, ambos . . . y hoy . . .", "ni entonces ni ahora . . . ."*

Signal words and phrases give you clues about the structure of the passage.

Para nosotros, el futuro es siempre incierto *(uncertain)*. Tenemos una idea de lo que sucederá y cómo será la vida en unos años, pero no podemos estar completamente seguros de ello. Podemos hacer predicciones. Para la gente que vivió en tiempos pasados el futuro también fue incierto. Escoge un período del pasado y compáralo con el presente. Escribe un ensayo *(essay)* con tus comparaciones, teniendo en cuenta la pregunta: "¿El futuro será siempre mejor que el presente?".

1 Antes de escribir

Usa un diagrama como éste para anotar las semejanzas y las diferencias *(similarities and differences)* entre el período del pasado que escogiste y el presente.

Siglo XIX   **Presente**

- mucha gente no iba a la escuela
- había muchas enfermedades
- no había medios de comunicación muy avanzados

- curiosidad por el futuro
- importancia de la familia

- importancia de la educación
- avances en los descubrimientos para curar enfermedades
- comunicaciones muy avanzadas

2 Borrador

Escribe tu borrador en forma de ensayo. Comienza con la pregunta de la introducción y presenta las épocas *(time periods)* que vas a describir. Explica las diferencias y semejanzas entre los dos períodos, según lo que escribiste en el diagrama de Venn. Usa expresiones como *pero* y *sin embargo* para comparar y contrastar.

Universal Access

Heritage Language Learners
Students may have difficulty correctly placing commas in complex sentences. Have students trade drafts of their essay with a partner and read the drafts aloud. Remind students that in many cases, when they sense a pause in the text, a comma should be inserted.

Advanced Learners
Ask students to imagine they have taken a trip back in time to a point of their choice. Have them explain to a person of that period how one or more aspects of everyday life will have changed. Challenge them to focus on something they take for granted that didn't exist during their chosen period of the past.

Modelo

> Muchas veces nos preguntamos si el futuro será mejor que el presente. Esa pregunta no la podemos responder ahora, porque no sabemos lo que pasará. ← **Introduction** to present the topic
>
> Por ejemplo, si comparamos el siglo XIX con el presente, encontraremos que éstos son dos momentos de la historia muy diferentes. La gente del siglo XIX no sabía lo que iba a ocurrir en el futuro; pero nosotros tampoco lo sabemos. En el siglo XIX no había . . . ← **Details** of the past
>
> **Comparison** of the past and the present →
>
> El mundo siempre tiene problemas diferentes; sin embargo, siempre habrá un futuro. Esto es lo que hace que . . . ← **Conclusion** on how the past and the present are similar

Suggestions (Cont'd):

In step 2, students should decide on the organization of their essays. Will they make a side-by-side comparison, or will they describe one time period all at once and then compare and contrast the other in a separate paragraph? Explain that the organization strategy they choose depends on how much they have to say about each time period. If they are comparing several details, suggest that they use the latter strategy, focusing on one period at a time, in separate paragraphs.

For step 3, encourage students to focus on sentence structure, transitions, and use of past, present, and future tenses. Have them follow the suggestions shown.

Evaluation

Steps 4 and 5 overlap. Students will need evaluation by you, their peers, or self-evaluation to fine-tune and polish their drafts.

3 Redacción/Revisión

Después de escribir el primer borrador de tu ensayo, intercambia tu trabajo con el de otro(a) estudiante. Léanlos y hagan sugerencias sobre cómo mejorarlos. Decidan qué aspectos de los ensayos son más o menos efectivos. Fíjense en cómo el escritor del modelo incluyó detalles en su ensayo. Hagan sugerencias sobre cómo mejorar los ensayos.

Haz lo siguiente: Subraya con una línea los verbos en presente y con dos los verbos en futuro.

- ¿Hay concordancia entre los verbos y el sujeto?
- ¿El presente y el futuro están empleados correctamente?

> nos preguntamos
> Muchas veces ~~preguntamos~~ si el futuro ~~es~~ será
> el presente
> mejor que ~~presente.~~ No ~~sabemos~~ lo que
> pasarán
> ~~pasará~~ en 50 años. Ignoramos lo que se habrá
> descubierto entonces. Esa pregunta no la
> podemos
> ~~podremos~~ responder ahora, ya que . . .

4 Publicación

Antes de escribir la versión final, lee de nuevo tu borrador y repasa los siguientes puntos:

- ¿Sigue mi ensayo un orden lógico?
- ¿Comparé claramente los dos períodos?
- ¿Añadí detalles a mis descripciones?
- ¿La conclusión es resultado de lo que dice el ensayo?

Después de revisar el borrador, escribe una copia en limpio de tu ensayo.

5 Evaluación

Tu profesor(a) puede explicarte cómo va a evaluar tu presentación. Probablemente, para tu profesor(a) es importante ver que:

- tus frases tienen sentido y expresan una idea completa
- usaste correctamente la estrategia de comparar y contrastar
- usaste el vocabulario y la gramática que aprendiste en este capítulo

Portfolio

Keep students' final drafts in their portfolios as a writing sample.

✓ **Assessment**
• Assessment Program: Cap. 6, Rubrics

Give students copies of the rubric before they begin the activity. Go over the descriptions of the different levels of performance.

doscientos ochenta y tres   283
Capítulo 6

Enriching Your Teaching

RUBRIC	Score 1	Score 3	Score 5
Completion of task	Your main idea is unclear, not stated, or not developed.	Your main idea is stated, but development is weak.	Your main idea is clearly stated and developed.
Development of comparison and contrast	Your essay does not present two time periods for comparison and contrast.	You presented two time periods, but few details are compared or contrasted.	You compared and contrasted time periods clearly with good use of supporting details.
Sentence structure/ grammar, spelling, mechanics	Your sentences run on or are fragmented with many grammar, spelling, mechanics errors.	You used sentences consistently. You have some grammar, spelling, and/or mechanics errors.	Your sentence structure is correct and varied with few grammar, spelling, mechanics errors.

Lectura

Presentation

Standards: 1.2, 1.3, 2.2, 3.1, 3.2, 5.2

Resources: Voc. & Gram. Transparencies: 3

Focus: Reading an extended passage

Suggestions:

Pre-reading: Before reading, direct students' attention to the *Al leer* section. Have them copy the graphic organizer from p. 287 and make sure they understand how they will use it. Also refer students to the *Estrategia*. Remind them that, besides using context clues as suggested, they know other strategies to help them understand difficult words and passages: they can use their knowledge of cognates and word families.

Reading: When reading together with students, pause frequently to address comprehension issues they may have and to allow them to fill in their *Elementos del cuento* charts from p. 287. Here are some possible comprehension issues on this page for which you can provide some guidance:

• After students have read the first part of the story, ask: *¿Cuántos personajes están presentes al principio del cuento? ¿Cómo se llaman? ¿Qué relación existe entre ellos? ¿Son miembros de la misma familia? ¿Son amigas? ¿Trabajan juntas? ¿De qué gran cambio están hablando? (Son tres: Rosa, Betty y Carmen; trabajan juntas; hablan del cambio de puesto de Rosa.)*

• *En esta escena, ¿cómo tratan de ayudar Betty y Carmen a Rosa? (Tratan de animarla, de hacerle sentirse mejor.)*

• *Mira las dos primeras preguntas en la sección Al leer. ¿Cómo las puedes contestar ahora?*

Lectura

Rosa

Estrategia

Coping with unknown words

When you encounter a word you don't know, try to infer its meaning from the context of the sentence. If you can't guess the meaning, skip the word and continue reading. If the word is essential and the reading doesn't help you understand it, look it up in the dictionary.

Al leer

Vas a leer un cuento de Ángel Balzarino, escritor argentino nacido en 1943. Al leer el cuento verás que el autor no nos explica dónde ocurre la acción, ni nos dice claramente quiénes son o qué hacen los personajes. De esta manera, el autor añade un elemento de suspenso. Lee el cuento una primera vez para tener una idea general de lo que pasa. Luego, copia la tabla que aparece al final de la lectura. Mientras lees por segunda vez, completa la tabla. Presta atención a los siguientes puntos:

• quiénes son los personajes

• las emociones de los personajes al principio del cuento

• la importancia de trabajar y la satisfacción de un trabajo bien realizado

• el final sorprendente *(surprising)*

Objectives

• **Read a short story**
• **Understand change in today's world**
• **Understand unknown words by inferring their meaning through context**

—¡Hoy es el día! —el tono de Rosa expresó cierta zozobra[1], la sensación de una derrota[2] ineludible—. ¿Por qué habrán decidido eso?

—Nadie lo sabe, querida —respondió Betty.

—Así es. Son órdenes[3] superiores —Carmen pareció resignada[4] ante esa realidad—. Simplemente debemos obedecer.

Aunque la explicación resultaba clara y sencilla, no logró convencer a Rosa. Ya nada la consolaría[5]. Ahora sólo deseaba sublevarse[6], expresar abiertamente la indignación que sentía desde hacía una semana, cuando le comunicaron la orden increíble de sacarla de allí.

—¡No quiero separarme de ustedes! —ahora su voz tuvo el carácter de un ruego angustioso[7]—. ¡No puedo aceptarlo!

—Nosotras tampoco lo deseamos, Rosa.

—Posiblemente te lleven a un sitio más importante —dijo Carmen dulcemente, tratando de animarla—. Tus antecedentes son extraordinarios. Sin duda los han tenido en cuenta para esa resolución.

—Por supuesto —confirmó Betty—. ¿Adónde te gustaría trabajar ahora?

Se produjo un largo silencio; embargada[8] por la duda, Rosa demoró[9] una respuesta concreta, como si aún no hubiera contemplado esa posibilidad.

—No lo sé. No tengo ambiciones. Me gusta estar aquí.

—Pero ya estuviste mucho tiempo, ¿no te parece?

1 uneasiness, anxiety **2** defeat **3** orders **4** resigned
5 would comfort **6** to revolt **7** anguished plea
8 overwhelmed **9** delayed

Universal Access

Heritage Language Learners

After students have read the selection for comprehension, assign them the roles of the different characters in the story and have them prepare a dramatic reading. Encourage them to focus on pronunciation and expression.

Students with Learning Difficulties

Some students may have difficulty keeping track of the characters in the story. On a piece of paper, have them copy the names **Rosa, Betty,** and **Carmen.** After reading each paragraph, have them stop and record a key phrase related to the character who has just spoken or been described.

—Tal vez sí. ¡Cuarenta y tres años! —la pesadumbre[10] de Rosa se transformó de pronto en una ráfaga de orgullo[11]—. Fui la primera que empezó a trabajar en el Control de Datos Generales. Siempre me encargaron las tareas más complicadas. Nunca tuve un problema, nadie me ha hecho una corrección.

—Lo sabemos, Rosa.

—¡Una trayectoria realmente admirable!

—Por eso querrán trasladarte. Necesitarán tus servicios en otra parte. Quizá te lleven al Centro Nacional de Comunicaciones.

Las palabras de Betty reflejaron un vibrante entusiasmo, casi tuvieron una mágica sonoridad[12]. Trabajar en ese lugar constituía un hermoso privilegio. A pesar de ser un anhelo[13] común, todas comprendían que eran remotas las posibilidades de realizarlo, como si debieran recorrer un camino lleno de escollos[14]. Preferían, tal vez para evitar una desilusión, descartar la esperanza[15] de ser escogidas.

---

10 sorrow **11** burst of pride **12** harmony **13** yearning
14 stumbling blocks **15** to leave aside any hope

—A cualquiera le gustaría estar allí —dijo Rosa sin énfasis—. Pero creo que ya soy demasiado vieja.

—Precisamente por eso te habrán escogido —dijo Betty con fervor—. Para trabajar allí se necesita tener mucha experiencia.

—Las cosas están cambiando, Rosa —confirmó Carmen—. Todo se presenta bajo un aspecto nuevo, casi sorprendente. Es un proceso de reestructuración. Ellos parecen decididos a dar a cada cosa el lugar que le corresponde. Sin duda comprendieron que era hora de darte una merecida recompensa[16].

—Quizá tengan razón —dijo Rosa modestamente—. Cuarenta y tres años de eficiente labor tienen un gran significado. Aunque nunca me interesó recibir un premio. Simplemente me dediqué a trabajar de la mejor manera.

—Siempre serás un ejemplo para nosotras, Rosa.

—Nadie será capaz de reemplazarte. Estamos seguras.

—Sin embargo, desearía saber a quién pondrán en mi lugar.

---

16 deserved reward

doscientos ochenta y cinco **285**
Capítulo 6

Suggestions (Cont'd):

Reading: Here are some possible comprehension issues on this page for which you can provide some guidance:

• *Uno de los personajes usa una palabra que se parece a la palabra* trajectory *en inglés. Un sinónimo de la palabra en español es "carrera." ¿Qué palabra es? (trayectoria)*

• *Según dicen los personajes, ¿qué es más prestigioso* (prestigious): *trabajar en el Control de Datos Generales o trabajar en el Centro Nacional de Comunicaciones? ¿Qué partes del texto te ayudan a contestar esta pregunta? (en el Centro Nacional de Comunicaciones; "un hermoso privilegio"; "A cualquiera le gustaría estar allí.")*

• *¿Qué cualidades tiene Rosa como trabajadora? (es eficiente y dedicada)*

• *Ahora, ¿cómo contestas la tercera pregunta en Al leer? (Los personajes piensan que trabajar bien da mucha satisfacción, tiene importancia y merece un premio.)*

Teacher-to-Teacher

When discussing a reading together, ask questions that require students to refer to the text in order to answer them. This causes them to approach the text with a purpose, which is an important reading strategy.

Enriching Your Teaching

Culture Note

Ángel Balzarino was born in 1943 in Villa Trinidad, Argentina. The recipient of many awards and honors, Balzarino has dedicated his writing to the art and craft of the short story. He is the author of many collections of short stories, including ***Las otras manos*** and ***La visita del general.*** In addition, many of his works appear in anthologies or other collected editions. Given the theme of the story ***Rosa,*** it is interesting to note that many of Balzarino's short stories are currently available to read on the Internet.

Las palabras de Rosa quedaron de repente superadas[17] por el ruido de unos pasos cada vez más cercanos; entonces, algo sobresaltadas[18] por esa señal que parecía anunciar una grave amenaza[19], las tres se quedaron a la expectativa.

—¡Allí vienen!

—Sí —Rosa no se preocupó en disimular su consternación—. ¡Ha llegado el momento!

Carmen y Betty se vieron contagiadas[20] por ese estado de ánimo; después, con forzada exaltación, sólo pudieron decir a modo de despedida:

—¡Mucha suerte en tu nuevo trabajo, Rosa!

La puerta se abrió de repente y cuatro hombres jóvenes, de cuerpos esbeltos y vigorosos, entraron en el lugar donde se amontonaban[21] diversas máquinas y pantallas a las que las luces incandescentes les daban un aspecto limpio, reluciente, casi de implacable frialdad[22].

—¿Cuál es? —preguntó uno de ellos.

El Suplente pasó lentamente la vista a su alrededor, en una especie de reconocimiento, hasta que extendió una mano.

—Aquélla. Se la conoce con el nombre de Rosa.

Los tres hombres se acercaron con pasos firmes y decididos hacia la computadora más grande, cuyo material parecía algo deteriorado por el uso y los años.

—¿La llevamos al lugar de costumbre?

—Sí, a la Cámara[23] de Aniquilación.

—Está bien.

Mientras los hombres llevaban la vieja y pesada computadora, el Suplente fue a ocupar su puesto. Entonces no pudo evitar una franca sonrisa de seguridad, de absoluto triunfo al comprender que ya estaba a punto de finalizar la Era de las Máquinas.

---

17 overcome **18** alarmed **19** serious threat **20** infected
21 piled up **22** coldness

23 Chamber

Interacción con la lectura

1 Llena la tabla con información del cuento.

ELEMENTOS DEL CUENTO

nombre del personaje principal	
dos palabras que describen al personaje	
una frase que dice cuál es el problema	
una frase que dice cuál es el final	

2 Trabaja con un grupo de estudiantes para comentar lo que escribieron en sus tablas.

- ¿Cuál es el problema que se presenta en el cuento? ¿Quién habrá decidido sacar a Rosa de la oficina?

- Carmen dice que quizás lleven a Rosa a un lugar más importante. ¿Lo habrá hecho porque lo cree o para animar a Rosa?

- ¿Cómo apoyan a Rosa sus compañeras? ¿Te parece que así debe ser?

- ¿Cuál será el futuro de Rosa? ¿Por qué habrá dicho que no tiene ambiciones?

- ¿Qué te parece el final del cuento? ¿Te parece optimista o pesimista? Explica por qué.

3 Trabaja con tu grupo para buscar palabras de la lectura que no conocían o no recordaban. Hablen sobre cómo lograron determinar o recordar el significado de esas palabras para entender mejor la lectura.

4 Y tú, ¿qué piensas? ¿Somos en realidad "arquitectos de nuestro propio futuro"? ¿O crees que otras personas deciden todo por nosotros?

 **Fondo cultural**

El Proyecto de la Escuela Virtual de la Universidad de Puerto Rico sigue buscando maestros para un entrenamiento que transformará las clases que se dan a los estudiantes de una futura escuela virtual del Departamento de Educación.

Los interesados deben tener habilidades para el trabajo con computadoras, y tener cuentas (accounts) privadas de acceso a la Red. Se les darán materiales y un poco de dinero a los escogidos. El proyecto durará dos años.

- ¿Crees que en el futuro toda la educación será a distancia?

- ¿Cuáles serán las ventajas (advantages) de estos cursos? ¿Cuáles serán las desventajas?

- ¿Has pensado alguna vez en tomar clases a distancia? ¿Conoces alguna universidad o escuela que las ofrezca?

Instituto de Educación a Distancia, Universidad de Puerto Rico

doscientos ochenta y siete 287
Capítulo 6

Culture Note

Today it is not only possible to study using the Internet, it is also possible to study abroad "virtually." Distance-learning programs, some of them in Spanish, allow students to take courses at colleges and universities throughout the world. Interactive online programs provide language and culture activities in real time. International chat rooms create a place to meet and practice language skills with friends from around the world. Many popular cultural and tourist destinations are also available for exploration via their own Web sites.

287

Review Activities

Profesiones y oficios/Sustantivos asociados con el futuro: Have students prepare cards or slips of paper for each vocabulary item in these categories. Divide students into groups and assign each group a section of the vocabulary items. Place the cards or slips from each category into two separate containers. Have students take turns drawing an item from each pile. If there is an obvious connection between the two items drawn, the student makes that connection in a sentence that uses both items. If there is not, the student tells about a connection that might exist in the future. For example: ***el (la) peluquero(a)/el aparato*** – *Una peluquera usa varios aparatos eléctricos en su trabajo.* ***el (la) peluquero(a)/el gen*** – *El peluquero del futuro cambiará los genes de sus clientes para que tengan el pelo perfecto.*

Cualidades/Campos y carreras del futuro: Have students use these items in sentences that make it clear they understand their meanings.

Verbos: Have students work in pairs. Partners take turns using a verb in a sentence that either makes sense or doesn't. If the sentence makes sense, the other partner says so and goes to the next verb. If the sentence does not make sense, the partner must explain why it doesn't or correct it so that it does.

Otras palabras y expresiones: Students can use these words and expressions as they go over the review activities for the other categories.

Repaso del capítulo

Vocabulario y gramática

profesiones y oficios

el / la abogado(a)	lawyer
el / la arquitecto(a)	architect
el / la banquero(a)	banker
el / la científico(a)	scientist
el / la cocinero(a)	cook
el / la contador(a)	accountant
el / la diseñador(a)	designer
la empresa	business
las finanzas	finance
el hombre de negocios, la mujer de negocios	businessman, businesswoman
el / la ingeniero(a)	engineer
el / la jefe(a)	boss
el / la juez(a)	judge
el / la peluquero(a)	hairstylist
el / la programador(a)	programmer
el / la redactor(a)	editor
el / la traductor(a)	translator

cualidades

ambicioso, -a	ambitious
capaz	able
cuidadoso, -a	careful
eficiente	efficient
emprendedor, -a	enterprising
maduro, -a	mature

verbos

ahorrar	to save
aumentar	to increase
averiguar	to find out
comunicarse	to communicate
contaminar	to pollute
curar	to cure
dedicarse a	to dedicate oneself to
desaparecer	to disappear
descubrir	to discover
desempeñar un cargo	to hold a position
diseñar	to design
enterarse	to find out
graduarse (u → ú)	to graduate
hacerse	to become
inventar	to invent
lograr	to achieve, to manage (to)
mudarse	to move to
predecir	to predict
prolongar	to prolong, to extend

reducir (zc)	to reduce
reemplazar	to replace
seguir una carrera	to pursue a career
tomar decisiones	to make decisions
traducir	to translate

sustantivos asociados con el futuro

el aparato	gadget
el avance	advance
el desarrollo	development
la enfermedad	illness
la fábrica	factory
la fuente de energía	energy source
el gen, *pl.* los genes	gene
la genética	genetics
el invento	invention
la máquina	machine
la mayoría	the majority
los medios de comunicación	media
el ocio	free time
la realidad virtual	virtual reality
tecnológico, -a	technological
el uso	use
vía satélite	via satellite
la vivienda	housing

otras palabras y expresiones

así que	therefore
además de	in addition to
casado, -a	married
como si fuera	as though it were
de hoy en adelante	from now on
haré lo que me dé la gana	I'll do as I please
por lo tanto	therefore
próximo, -a	next
soltero, -a	single
tener en cuenta	to take into account

campos y carreras del futuro

el campo	field
la demanda	demand
la estrategia	strategy
la hospitalidad	hospitality
la industria	industry
la informática	information technology
el mercadeo	marketing
el producto	product
el servicio	service

Universal Access

Students with Learning Difficulties

To help students reinforce vocabulary comprehension, have them create their own flashcards. On one side of the card, have them write a vocabulary word. On the other side, they can draw a picture or write a Spanish synonym or other clue.

Advanced Learners

Invite students to create a video about a profession of the future. This could be a future version of a profession that exists today or one that is yet unheard of. Have one or more students dramatize the profession while a narrator explains it.

el futuro

To express the future in Spanish, you can use *ir + a + infinitive*, the present tense, or the future. For most verbs, attach the endings (*-é, -ás, -á, -emos, -éis, -án*) to the infinitive.

pasar *to pass*

pasaré	pasaremos
pasarás	pasaréis
pasará	pasarán

comer *to eat*

comeré	comeremos
comerás	comeréis
comerá	comerán

pedir *to ask*

pediré	pediremos
pedirás	pediréis
pedirá	pedirán

Other verbs have irregular stems in the future but have the same endings as the regular verbs.

haber	habr-
hacer	har-
saber	sabr-
tener	tendr-
poder	podr-
decir	dir-
salir	saldr-
querer	querr-
poner	pondr-
venir	vendr-

el futuro de probabilidad

In Spanish the future tense can express uncertainty or probability in the present.

¿Qué hora **será**? *(I wonder what time it is.)*

el futuro perfecto

Use the future perfect tense to express what will have happened by a certain time. To form the future perfect, use the future of the verb *haber* with the past participle of the verb.

pasar *to pass*

ha**bré** pasado	ha**bremos** pasado
ha**brás** pasado	ha**bréis** pasado
ha**brá** pasado	ha**brán** pasado

el uso de los complementos directos e indirectos

The indirect object pronoun goes before the direct object pronoun.

Te los traduciré. (los libros)

In the third person, the indirect objects *le / les* become *se* before the indirect objects *lo / la, los / las*. You can add the prepositional phrase *a Ud., a él, a ella*, etc., or *a* + a noun / name for clarification.

Se los traduciré a ella.

When the object pronouns are attached to an infinitive, a command, or a present participle, you must add an accent mark to keep the stress: *traducírmelos, tradúcemelos, traduciéndomelos.*

● **Más práctica** ....
Practice Workbook Organizer 6-13, 6-14

Teacher-to-Teacher
Using imperative forms and pronouns are some of the most difficult skills your students have to learn, and yet they are a common part of everyday speech. Provide students with plenty of accurate models and give them every opportunity possible to practice using these structures.

El futuro: Ask students to pretend they are a wizard from 300 years ago who is very good at making accurate predictions about what life will be like in the twenty-first century. Have them tell about life today: *Cada casa tendrá una caja mágica que da visiones de las cosas que pasan en otras partes del mundo. En vez de leer libros, la gente mirará las imágenes en esta caja mágica.*

El futuro de probabilidad: Have students work in pairs, sitting back to back. One partner performs a simple action that the other can't see. Actions might include writing, holding up a number of fingers, or putting on a hat. The other partner tries to guess the action using the future tense: *¿Escribirás algo? ¿No tendrás unos dedos en el aire? ¿Llevarás puesto tu sombrero?*

El futuro perfecto: Have students make predictions about things that will have happened by the year 2110: *Habremos colonizado otros planetas. Gracias a la genética, todas las enfermedades habrán desaparecido.*

El uso de los complementos directos e indirectos: Have students work in groups of three. Individually, they think of two sentences describing actions that they can perform in the group. Each action should involve a direct object and refer to one or both of the other students as the indirect object. For example: *Les digo un secreto a Uds. dos* or *Le doy mi cuaderno a Mark.* Have them take turns saying their sentences. The other two protest and turn the sentence into a negative command using pronouns: *¡No, no nos lo digas! ¡No, no se lo des!*

Portfolio

Invite students to review the activities they completed in this chapter, including written reports, posters or other visuals, tapes of oral presentations, and other projects. Have them select one or two items that they feel best demonstrate their achievements in Spanish. Include these products in students' portfolios. Have them include this with the Chapter Checklist and Self-Assessment Worksheet.

Additional Resources

• Audio Program: CD Cap. 6, Track 18
• Resource Book: Cap. 6, Clip Art
• Assessment Program: Chapter Checklist and Self-Assessment Worksheet

Performance Tasks

Standards: 1.1, 1.2, 1.3, 4.2

Resources: Audio Program: CD Cap. 6, Track 19; Resource Book: Cap. 6, Audio Script; Practice Answers on Transparencies

1. Vocabulario

Suggestions: Encourage students to review the vocabulary from the *A primera vista* sections on pp. 252–255 and 266–269 before they complete the activity.

Answers:

1. b	5. c
2. b	6. c
3. a	7. a
4. a	8. b

2. Gramática

Suggestions: Remind students of the main points of the grammar presentations in *Capítulo* 6:

• the future tense
• the future tense used for probability
• the future perfect tense
• use of direct and indirect object pronouns together

Answers:

1. b	5. a
2. b	6. a
3. c	7. a
4. d	8. d

To prepare for the test, check to see if you . . .

• **know the new vocabulary and grammar**
• **can perform the tasks on pp. 290 and 291**

Preparación para el examen

1 **Vocabulario** Escribe la letra de la palabra o expresión que mejor complete cada frase. Escribe tus respuestas en una hoja aparte.

1. Tengo que _____ qué cursos ofrecen en la universidad.
   a. desarrollar   c. inventar
   b. averiguar   d. prolongar

2. Después de terminar sus estudios, mi hermano piensa _____ a otro estado.
   a. dedicarse   c. enterarse
   b. mudarse   d. comunicarse

3. Cuando una persona sabe hacer algo bien, se dice que es _____.
   a. capaz   c. madura
   b. entrometida   d. sincera

4. Gracias a _____ como el teléfono celular podemos comunicarnos desde muchos lugares.
   a. aparatos   c. campos
   b. transportes   d. servicios

5. Los avances en la genética harán posible curar _____.
   a. la contaminación   c. las enfermedades
   b. las viviendas   d. el ocio

6. La _____ te permite vivir una experiencia como si fuera real.
   a. vivienda   c. realidad virtual
   b. genética   d. informática

7. A Jorge le gusta resolver problemas y tomar decisiones sin ayuda. Es muy _____.
   a. emprendedor   c. honesto
   b. cuidadoso   d. puntual

8. Creo que _____ me voy a dedicar a la medicina.
   a. así que   c. tener en cuenta
   b. de hoy en adelante d. como si fuera

2 **Gramática** Escribe la letra de la palabra o expresión que mejor complete cada frase. Escribe tus respuestas en una hoja aparte.

1. El año próximo _____ mi sueño de viajar por todo el mundo.
   a. realicé   c. realizo
   b. realizaré   d. estoy realizando

2. Andrés quiere ser traductor. El año que viene _____ en las Naciones Unidas.
   a. trabaja   c. está trabajando
   b. trabajará   d. trabajaba

3. No tengo reloj. ¿Qué hora _____?
   a. estará   c. será
   b. saldrá   d. era

4. Si necesitas un texto de genética, yo _____ prestaré.
   a. te la   c. se lo
   b. te los   d. te lo

5. ¿Vio usted el programa sobre los inventos del siglo XX? _____ prestaré.
   a. Se lo   c. Me lo
   b. Se la   d. Te la

6. Quiero ver las fotos que sacaste ayer. _____ por favor.
   a. Dámelas   c. Déle
   b. Dáselas   d. Déselas

7. Dentro de 20 años, ya _____ otras fuentes de energía.
   a. habrán descubierto c. descubrieron
   b. han descubierto   d. están descubriendo

8. Para el año 2020, muchos aparatos que ahora se usan ya _____.
   a. han desaparecido   c. están desapareciendo
   b. desaparecen   d. habrán desaparecido

Universal Access

Heritage Language Learners

Ask students to draft their own set of multiple-choice review questions based on the vocabulary and grammar points of the chapter. Have them trade questions with a partner. Students should not only choose the correct answer, but also proofread their partner's questions for errors.

Students with Special Needs

Give hearing impaired students a transcribed or illustrated version of the conversation in the listening section of the exam. Have students work in pairs and track the appropriate text as the dialogue is played.

Review   6

Go Online
PHSchool.com

For: Test preparation
Visit: www.phschool.com
Web Code: jed-0611

En el examen vas a . . .	Éstas son las tareas de práctica que te pueden ser útiles para el examen . . .	Si necesitas repasar . . .
❸ **Escuchar** Escuchar y comprender una conversación entre dos jóvenes	Félix y Carmen hablan sobre sus planes para el futuro. Escucha su conversación y di (a) qué intereses y habilidades tiene cada uno; (b) cuáles son sus planes para después de graduarse de la escuela secundaria; (c) cuáles son sus sueños para su carrera.	**pp. 252–255** *A primera vista 1* **p. 253** Actividad 1 **p. 255** Actividades 2–3 **p. 261** Actividad 12
❹ **Hablar** Hablar sobre lo que quieres hacer en el futuro	Imagina que te entrevistas con una consejera que te ayudará a decidir qué carrera debes estudiar y a qué universidad debes ir. Explícale cuáles son tus intereses y cualidades, qué trabajo te gustaría tener, qué sueños quieres realizar, qué quieres lograr, en fin, explícale qué quieres hacer con tu vida.	**p. 258** Actividad 9 **p. 259** Actividad 10 **p. 261** Actividad 12 **p. 262** Actividad 15
❺ **Leer** Leer y comprender las predicciones de un futurólogo	Lee este fragmento del artículo de un futurólogo. ¿Esta persona cree que el futuro será mejor o peor que el presente? ¿Por qué? *En el futuro viviremos en paz, pues en unos años habrá nuevos inventos y aparatos que permitirán una mejor comunicación entre las personas. Además, gracias a ciencias nuevas como la informática y la genética, en 50 ó 60 años no habrá hambre ni enfermedades. Todos vivirán 100 años y trabajarán mucho menos que nosotros.*	**pp. 266–269** *A primera vista 2* **p. 270** Actividad 25 **p. 272** Actividades 28, 29 **p. 277** Actividad 36
❻ **Escribir** Escribir sobre los avances que habrá en el futuro	Escribe sobre los principales avances y problemas que crees que habrá en los 50 años que vienen. Di dos cosas que crees que habrán ocurrido. ¿Cómo cambiará la vida de la gente? ¿Cuáles serán los problemas más difíciles que tendrán que resolver?	**p. 265** Actividad 19 **p. 267** Actividad 21 **p. 269** Actividad 23 **p. 271** Actividad 27 **p. 273** Actividad 30 **p. 274** Actividades 31–32
❼ **Pensar** Pensar en la actitud de algunos jóvenes españoles que prefieren vivir con sus padres al terminar de estudiar	Piensa por qué te gustará o no te gustará vivir con tus padres cuando termines tus estudios. Compara tus razones con las de algunos jóvenes españoles.	**p. 257** *Fondo cultural*

doscientos noventa y uno **291**
Capítulo 6

Enriching Your Teaching

Teacher-to-Teacher

Ask students to interview a parent or other family member about his or her job or profession. Will the work they do exist 50 years from now? Will it be more or less important? Why? Have students report on the interview to the class in Spanish.

---

3. Escuchar

Suggestions: Use the *Audio CD* or read from the script.

Answers:
a. **Intereses y habilidades:**
   Félix: finanzas, banquero; eficiente, emprendedor
   Carmen: le gustan los libros, es bilingüe
b. **Carmen y Félix piensan seguir estudiando para ser traductora y banquero.**
c. **Sus sueños:**
   Félix: ganar mucho dinero y hacer lo que le dé la gana. Quiere ser banquero.
   Carmen: Quiere ser traductora. Quiere viajar al extranjero y aprender más sobre los países del mundo.

4. Hablar

Suggestions: Point out that this activity requires students to use a variety of tenses. They might use the present tense to talk about their personal qualities and the future tenses and subjunctive mood to tell about their plans for the future.

Answers will vary.

5. Leer

Suggestions: Tell students to refer to pp. 252–255 and 266–269 if they have questions about vocabulary in the review.

Answers:
Esta persona cree que el futuro será mejor que el presente.
Answers will vary.

6. Escribir

Suggestions: After students have completed their writing, ask them how their perceptions of the future have changed since they began *Capítulo* 6.

Answers will vary.

7. Pensar

Suggestions: Encourage students to write down their thoughts in a T-chart with the two columns entitled *A favor de* and *En contra de.*

✓ **Assessment**
- Examen del capítulo: 6
- Audio Program: CD 13, Cap. 6, Track 9
- Assessment Program: *RPH*

Alternative Assessment
- ExamView Test Bank CD-ROM
- Resource Book: Cap. 6, Situation Cards
- Resource Book: Cap. 6, Communicative Activity BLM

291

¿Mito o realidad?

CHAPTER OVERVIEW

¿Mito o realidad?

Vocabulary
- archeological discoveries and mysteries
- description of objects
- myths and legends

Grammar
- present and present perfect subjunctive after expressions of doubt, uncertainty, or disbelief
- uses of *pero* and *sino*
- subjunctive in adjective clauses

Cultural Perspectives
- prehispanic civilizations as viewed in the art of Diego Rivera
- two wonders of Peru: the Inca Trail and Machu Picchu
- Aztec myths and legends
- contributions of the Mayan and Aztec civilizations
- mysteries of pre-Columbian civilizations

Chapter Project

Cartel de arte indígena

Overview: Students create an illustrated poster to show a piece of indigenous art. They research art of an indigenous group they know from the United States or Latin America and choose one or more images to create an interesting visual composition. Posters should include a message or two and a title. Students then present their poster to the class and describe what the art means, the indigenous group it belongs to, and why they chose those images.

Materials: pencil, crayons, paint of different colors, poster board, and construction paper

Sequence: (suggestions for when to do each step are found throughout the chapter)

STEP 1. Review instructions so students know what is expected of them. Hand out the "Chapter 7 Project Instructions and Rubric" from the *Teacher's Resource Book*.

STEP 2. Students submit a sketch of their poster. Return the sketches with your suggestions.

STEP 3. Students do layouts on construction paper, setting space for the messages. Encourage them to try different arrangements before drawing their images.

STEP 4. Students submit a draft of the messages and a paragraph for the presentation. Note your corrections and suggestions, then return drafts to students.

STEP 5. Students make a brief presentation of their posters to the class.

Options:

1. Students create computer art using a painting or drawing software.

2. Students make a brief presentation of the indigenous group they chose.

Assessment:

Here is a detailed rubric for assessing this project:

Chapter 7 Project: *Cartel de arte indígena*

RUBRIC	Score 1	Score 3	Score 5
Your evidence of planning	You provide no poster layout or written draft.	You provide a layout and written draft, but they are not corrected.	You show evidence of corrected draft and layout.
Your use of illustrations	You include no art images, or they are not indigenous art.	You include images, but layout is not well organized.	Your poster is carefully done and images are consistent with text.
Your presentation	You include little of the required information.	You include most of the required information.	You include all of the required information.

Chapter Support

Bulletin Boards

Theme: *Las culturas indígenas latinoamericanas*

Ask students to cut out, copy, or download images of the Aztecs, Mayas, or other indigenous groups in Latin America. Images can include examples of clothing, folk art, crafts, and food. Cluster photos around the name of each group that is chosen.

Bibliography

DK Baquedano, Elizabeth. *Aztec, Inca and Maya*. New York: DK Publishing, Inc., 2000. Chronicles the history, beliefs, and everyday lives of the ancient Aztec, Inca, and Maya peoples.

Brown, Barbara. *Weekend with Diego Rivera*. New York: Rizzoli International, 1994. In this beautiful and informative book, Rivera talks in the first person and tells the reader of his life, love of Mexico, and his desire to create art for the people.

Kalman, Bobbie and David Schimpky. *Peru: The Land*. New York: Crabtree Publishing, 1994. Contemporary examination of Peru, its peoples, and its cultures.

Temko, Florence. *Traditional Crafts from Mexico and Central America*. Minneapolis: Lerner Publications, 1996.

Wood, Marion. *Growing up in Aztec Times*. Memphis: Troll Communications L.L.C., 1993. Describes the daily life of the Aztecs, discussing life in the city, life in the country, education, food and drink, and other aspects.

Hands-on Culture

Music: *Songs from Spain and Latin America*

The fusion of old and new music styles has revived many traditional beats and sounds, especially flamenco, salsa, Mexican boleros, and more.

Directions:

1. Type out names of Hispanic musical artists and distribute copies to students. Some artists to look for are: Gypsy Kings and Carlos Villalobos (flamenco), Gloria Estefan (salsa), Tito Puente, Tish Hinojosa (salsa, boleros, cumbia), and Inti Illimani (Andean).

2. Divide students into four groups. If possible, assign one or two students with strong artistic skills to each group.

2. Ask students to do research about their artist on the Internet and, if possible, record some music clips or obtain a cassette or CD.

3. Each group types out a fact sheet about their artist with information from the research and makes copies to distribute to the class. They can download the artist's photo and include it in the fact sheet.

4. Each group chooses a leader, who makes a presentation of their artist to the class.

5. The leader reads the fact sheet and plays some music by the artist to the class.

Internet Search

Use the keywords to find more information.

Keywords:

Machu Picchu, Diego Rivera, Atlántida, música latinoamericana, música española, leyendas indígenas, aztecas, mayas, olmecas, Palenque, Cuzco, Tiahuanaco, Incas, Nazca, Miguel de Cervantes

Game

Encuentra dónde estamos

Play this game to review the information about archaeological sites from *Capítulo 7*.

Players: the whole class, playing in teams

Materials: slips of paper, a large world map, markers, pins or masking tape

Preparation: Prepare ahead. Draw with different color markers in the map the outlines of Mexico, Peru, Bolivia, Guatemala, and Isla de Pascua. On slips of paper, write the names of different ancient cities and indigenous groups described in *Capítulo 7*, such as *ruinas de Palenque, los aztecas, los mayas, ruinas de Cobá y Tulúm, ciudad de Teotihuacán, cabezas de los olmecas, Chichen Itzá, Líneas de Nazca, estatuas moai, indígenas quichés, ciudad de Machu Picchu, ciudad de Tiahuanaco*. Place the slips of paper in a bag.

Rules:

1. Students should prepare ahead for the game. Ask them to review *Capítulo 7*, paying special attention to the location of the archaeological sites and the indigenous groups described there.

2. Divide the class into teams.

3. Have members of the teams take turns drawing a slip of paper from the bag.

4. If the student can tape the note in the correct place on the map, the team receives 5 points.

5. If he or she can also give cultural, historical, architectural, or other information about that place or indigenous group, the team receives an additional 5 points.

6. The team with the most points when the bag is empty wins.

Variation: Names of indigenous groups from the United States can also be written on the slips of paper. In this case, the outline of the United States should be included.

A ver si recuerdas
RECYCLE

Vocabulary
- Architecture and materials
- Nature, animals, and places

Grammar
- Negative constructions
- Adjectives used as nouns

Chapter Overview

A primera vista 1
INPUT

Objectives
- Describe what archaeologists do
- Talk about archaeological mysteries of other civilizations
- Give your opinion about mysterious events

Vocabulary
- Description of objects
- Archaeological discoveries

Grammar
- Present subjunctive and present perfect subjunctive with expressions of doubt

Culture
- Diego Rivera

Manos a la obra 1
PRACTICE

Objectives
- Talk about archaeological mysteries
- Talk about ancient civilizations

Vocabulary
- Practice and use new vocabulary

Grammar
- Present subjunctive and present perfect subjunctive with expressions of doubt

Culture
- Atlantis: mystery or historical fact?
- Inca trail to Machu Picchu

A primera vista 2
INPUT

Objectives
- Read about myths and legends from the Spanish-speaking world
- Talk about the contributions of the Mayan and Aztec civilizations

Vocabulary
- Myths and legends
- Ancient civilizations

Grammar
- Uses of *pero* and *sino*
- Subjunctive with adjective clauses

Culture
- Mayan and Aztec cultures

Manos a la obra 2
PRACTICE

Objectives
- Communicate about myths and legends
- Explore the contributions of ancient civilizations

Vocabulary
- Practice and use new vocabulary

Grammar
- Uses of *pero* and *sino*
- Subjunctive with adjective clauses

Culture
- Aztec calendar
- A Quiché legend

¡Adelante!
APPLICATION

Objectives
- Read about mysteries of past civilizations in Latin America
- Write a legend about something in the past
- Use different sources to investigate mysteries of the past
- Read a piece of fiction

Vocabulary
- Application

Grammar
- Application

Culture
- Fragment of *Don Quijote de la Mancha*
- Miguel de Cervantes Saavedra

Repaso del capítulo
REVIEW

Objectives
- Know the new vocabulary and grammar
- Perform the tasks on pages 336 and 337

Vocabulary
- Review

Grammar
- Review

BEYOND THE CLASSROOM

Countries
- Mexico
- Colombia
- Peru
- Chile
- Guatemala
- Honduras
- Spain

El español en el mundo del trabajo
- Antigua, Guatemala

Internet
- Vocabulary activities
- Grammar activities
- Internet links
- Self-tests

LEARNER SUPPORT

Strategies
- Cooperative learning
- Using illustrations
- Maintaining your focus
- Combining sentences
- Characters and actions

Recycling
- Pronunciation of dipthong *ue*
- Pronouns *vosotros* and *vosotras*

En voz alta
- *Sueño cuarto (la luz)*

Ampliación del lenguaje
- Word families

Conexiones
- History: Machu Picchu

Print Components

TEACHER

Teacher's Resource Book
• Chapter Table of Contents
• School-to-Home Connection
• Chapter Resource Checklist
• Input Script
• Audio Script
• Video Script
• Communicative Activities
• Situation Cards
• GramActiva Blackline Masters
• Graphic Organizers
• Answer Keys:
  Practice Workbook
  Writing, Audio, & Video Workbook

Realidades para hispanohablantes
Teacher Edition

STUDENT

Practice Workbook
• Vocabulary: 7-1 – 7-4, 7-8 – 7-9
• Grammar: 7-5 – 7-7, 7-10 – 7-12
• Organizer: 7-13 – 7-14

Writing, Audio & Video Workbook
• Audio: 1–5
• Writing: 6–13
• Video: 14–17

Reading and Writing for Success
• Chapter 7, Test 34

Realidades para hispanohablantes

Transparencies

Vocabulary and Grammar Transparencies
• Vocabulary: 133–140, 142–145
• Grammar: 141, 146–147
• ¿Qué me cuentas?: 148

Practice Answers on Transparencies
• Cap. 7

Fine Art Transparencies
• Transparencies
• Teacher's Guide

Assessment

Assessment Program
• Pruebas:
  – Comprensión del vocabulario 1: 7-1
  – Aplicación del vocabulario 1: 7-2
  – El presente y el presente perfecto del subjuntivo con expresiones de duda: 7-3
  – Comprensión del vocabulario 2: 7-4
  – Aplicación del vocabulario 2: 7-5
  – *Pero y sino:* 7-6
  – El subjuntivo en cláusulas adjetivas: 7-7
• Exámenes del capítulo
• Rubrics

Alternative Assessment
• ExamView Test Bank CD-ROM
• MindPoint Quiz Show CD-ROM
• Internet Self-test
• Situation Cards
• Communicative Activity

Assessment Program: *Realidades para hispanohablantes*

Technology

TeacherExpress™ CD-ROM
• Lesson Planner
• Teacher Resources
• Clip Art

Video Program VHS and DVD

Audio Program CDs
• A primera vista 1 y 2: Vocabulario y gramática en contexto
• Audio Activities
• ¿Qué me cuentas?
• Repaso
• Examen del capítulo: Escuchar

Regular Schedule (50 Minutes)

For electronic lesson plans:
Teacher Express CD-ROM

	Warm-up / Assess	Preview Present / Practice Communicate	Wrap-up / Homework Options
DAY 1	**Warm-up (10 min.)** • Return Examen del capítulo: Capítulo 6	**Repaso (35 min.)** • A ver si recuerdas Actividades 1, 2, 4, 5, 7	**Wrap-up and Homework Options (5 min.)** • Practice Workbook 7-1, 7-2 • Go Online
DAY 2	**Warm-up (10 min.)** • Homework check	**Chapter Opener (10 min.)** • Objectives • Fondo cultural **A primera vista 1 (25 min.)** • Presentation: Vocabulario y gramática en contexto • Actividades 1, 2	**Wrap-up and Homework Options (5 min.)** • Go Online • Clip Art Vocabulary
DAY 3	**Warm-up (10 min.)** • Homework check	**A primera vista 1 (20 min.)** • Presentation: Misterios arqueológicos • Actividad 3 **Manos a la obra 1 (15 min.)** • Actividades 4, 5	**Wrap-up and Homework Options (5 min.)** • Practice Workbook 7-3, 7-4 • Manos a la obra 1: Actividad 8 • Go Online • Prueba 7-1: Vocabulary recognition
DAY 4	**Warm-up (10 min.)** • Homework check ✔**Assessment (10 min.)** • Prueba 7-1: Vocabulary recognition	**Manos a la obra 1 (25 min.)** • Actividades 6, 7, 9, 10 • Audio Activity • Ampliación del lenguaje	**Wrap-up and Homework Options (5 min.)** • Writing Activities • Prueba 7-2: Vocabulary production
DAY 5	**Warm-up (15 min.)** • Homework check • Communicative Activity ✔**Assessment (10 min.)** • Prueba 7-2: Vocabulary production	**Manos a la obra 1 (20 min.)** • Presentation: Subjuntivo con expresiones de duda • Actividad 11, 12, 13	**Wrap-up and Homework Options (5 min.)** • Practice Workbook 7-5, 7-6, 7-7 • Go Online
DAY 6	**Warm-up (10 min.)** • Homework check	**Manos a la obra 1 (35 min.)** • Actividades 14, 15, 16 • Fondo cultural	**Wrap-up and Homework Options (5 min.)** • Actividad 19
DAY 7	**Warm-up (10 min.)** • Homework check	**Manos a la obra 1 (35 min.)** • Actividad 17, 18, 19 • Writing Activity • Communicative Activity • En voz alta	**Wrap-up and Homework Options (5 min.)** • Writing Activity Prueba 7-3: Subjuntivo con expresiones de duda
DAY 8	**Warm-up (10 min.)** • Homework check ✔**Assessment (10 min.)** • Prueba 7-3	**A primera vista 2 (25 min.)** • Presentation: Vocabulario y gramática en contexto • Actividades 20, 21	**Wrap-up and Homework Options (5 min.)** • Clip Art Vocabulary • Examen: Vocabulario y gramática 1
DAY 9	**Warm-up (5 min.)** • Homework check ✔**Assessment (30 min.)** • Examen: Vocabulario y gramática 1	**A primera vista 2 (10 min.)** • Presentation: Los mayas y los aztecas • Actividades 22	**Wrap-up and Homework Options (5 min.)** • Practice Workbook 7-8, 7-9 • Go Online • Prueba 7-4: Vocabulary recognition
DAY 10	**Warm-up (20 min.)** • Homework check ✔**Assessment (10 min.)** • Prueba 7-4: Vocabulary recognition	**Manos a la obra 2 (15 min.)** • Actividades 23, 24, 25	**Wrap-up and Homework Options (5 min.)** • Actividades 26, 27

	Warm-up / Assess	Preview Present / Practice Communicate	Wrap-up / Homework Options
DAY 11	**Warm-up (15 min.)** • Homework check	**A primera vista 2 (15 min.)** • En voz alta • Audio • Writing Activity • Communicative Activity **Manos a la obra 2 (15 min.)** • Presentation: *Pero* y *sino* • Actividades 28, 29	**Wrap-up and Homework Options (5 min.)** • Practice Workbook 7-10 • Go Online • Prueba 7-5: Vocabulary production
DAY 12	**Warm-up (10 min.)** • Homework check ✔**Assessment (10 min.)** • Prueba 7-5: Vocabulary production	**Manos a la obra 2 (25 min.)** • Writing Activity 11 • Presentation: El subjuntivo en cláusulas adjetivas • Actividades 30, 31, 32	**Wrap-up and Homework Options (5 min.)** • Practice Workbook 7-11, 7-12 • Go Online • Prueba 7-6: *Pero* y *sino*
DAY 13	**Warm-up (10 min.)** • Homework check ✔**Assessment (10 min.)** • Prueba 7-6: *Pero* y *sino*	**Manos a la obra 2 (25 min.)** • Actividades 33, 34, 35 • El español en el mundo del trabajo	**Wrap-up and Homework Options (5 min.)** • Writing Activity • Prueba 7-7: El subjuntivo en cláusulas adjetivas
DAY 14	**Warm-up (10 min.)** • Communicative Activity • Audio Activity ✔**Assessment (10 min.)** • Prueba 7-7: El subjuntivo en cláusulas adjetivas	**¡Adelante! (25 min.)** • Puente a la cultura • ¿Comprendiste? • Investiga • Presentación oral: Step 1	**Wrap-up and Homework Options (5 min.)** • Examen: Vocabulario y gramática 2
DAY 15	**Warm-up (10 min.)** • Answer questions ✔**Assessment (20 min.)** • Examen: Vocabulario y gramática 2	**¡Adelante! (15 min.)** • Presentación oral: Step 2	**Wrap-up and Homework Options (5 min.)** • Presentación oral: Step 3 • Go Online
DAY 16	**Warm-up (15 min.)** • Homework check	**¡Adelante! (30 min.)** • Presentación oral: Step 3 • ¿Qué me cuentas? 1, 2, 3	**Wrap-up and Homework Options (5 min.)** • Presentación escrita: Steps 1, 2
DAY 17	**Warm-up (10 min.)** • Homework check	**¡Adelante! (35 min.)** • Presentación oral: Step 3 • View Video • Video Activities 1, 2, 3 • Presentación escrita: Step 3	**Wrap-up and Homework Options (5 min.)** • Presentación escrita: Step 4 • Preparación para el examen: 1, 2
DAY 18	**Warm-up (10 min.)** • Homework check	**¡Adelante! (25 min.)** • Lectura • Interacción • Fondo cultural **Repaso (10 min.)** • Preparación para el examen: Actividades 3, 4	**Wrap-up and Homework Options (5 min.)** • ¿Comprendiste? • Practice Workbook: Organizer 7-13, 7-14 • Go Online: Self-test
DAY 19	**Warm-up (15 min.)** • Homework check	**Repaso (30 min.)** • Preparación para el examen: Actividades 5, 6, 7 • MindPoint Quiz Show • Other review	**Wrap-up and Homework Options (5 min.)** • Examen del capítulo
DAY 20	**Warm-up (5 min.)** • Answer questions	✔**Assessment (44 min.)** • Examen del capítulo	**Wrap-up and Homework Options (1 min.)** • A ver si recuerdas: Capítulo 8

Capítulo 7 — Lesson Plans

Block Schedule (90 Minutes)

For electronic lesson plans:
Teacher Express CD-ROM

	Warm-up / Assess	Preview Present / Practice Communicate	Wrap-up / Homework Options
DAY 1	**Warm-up (35 min.)** • Return Examen del capítulo: Capítulo 6 • A ver si recuerdas • Homework check	**Chapter Opener (10 min.)** • Objectives • Fondo cultural **A primera vista 1 (30 min.)** • Presentation: Vocabulario y gramática en contexto • Actividades 1, 2 • Presentation: Misterios arqueológicos • Actividad 3 **Manos a la obra 1 (10 min.)** • Actividades 4, 5	**Wrap-up and Homework Options (5 min.)** • Practice Workbook 7-3, 7-4 • Go Online • Clip Art Vocabulary • Prueba 7-1: Vocabulary recognition
DAY 2	**Warm-up (15 min.)** • Homework check • Actividades 6, 7 ✔**Assessment (15 min.)** • Prueba 7-1: Vocabulary recognition	**Manos a la obra 1 (55 min.)** • Actividades 8, 9, 10 • Ampliación del lenguaje • Audio Activity • Writing Activity • Communicative Activity	**Wrap-up and Homework Options (5 min.)** • Prueba 7-2: Vocabulary production
DAY 3	**Warm-up (5 min.)** • Homework check ✔**Assessment (10 min.)** • Prueba 7-2: Vocabulary production	**Manos a la obra 1 (70 min.)** • Presentation: Subjuntivo con duda • Actividades 11, 12, 13, 14, 15, 16 • Fondo cultural	**Wrap-up and Homework Options (5 min.)** • Fondo cultural • Actividad 19 • Practice Workbook 7-5, 7-6, 7-7 • Go Online
DAY 4	**Warm-up (10 min.)** • Homework check	**Manos a la obra 1 (50 min.)** • Actividades 17, 18 • Writing Activity • Communicative Activity **A primera vista 2 (25 min.)** • Presentation: Vocabulario y gramática en contexto • Actividades 20, 21	**Wrap-up and Homework Options (5 min.)** • Prueba 7-3: El subjuntivo con duda • Examen: Vocabulario y gramática 1
DAY 5	**Warm-up (10 min.)** • Homework check ✔**Assessment Options (40 min.)** • Prueba 7-3: El subjuntivo con duda • Examen: Vocabulario y gramática	**A primera vista 2 (20 min.)** • Presentation: Los mayas y los aztecas • Actividad 22 **Manos a la obra 2 (15 min.)** • Actividades 23, 24, 25	**Wrap-up and Homework Options (5 min.)** • Practice Workbook 7-8, 7-9 • Actividades 26, 27 • Clip Art • Go Online • Prueba 7-4: Vocabulary recognition

	Warm-up / Assess	Preview Present / Practice Communicate	Wrap-up / Homework Options
DAY 6	**Warm-up (35 min.)** • Homework check • En voz alta • Audio Activity • Writing Activity ✔**Assessment (10 min.)** • Prueba 7-4 Vocabulary recognition	**Manos a la obra 2 (40 min.)** • Presentation: *Pero* y *sino* • Actividades 28, 29 • Writing Activity 11	**Wrap-up and Homework Options (5 min.)** • Practice Workbook 7-10 • Go Online • Pruebas 7-5, 7-6: Vocabulary production, *pero* y *sino*
DAY 7	**Warm-up (10 min.)** • Homework check • Communicative Activity ✔**Assessment (20 min.)** • Pruebas 7-6, 7-7: Vocabulary production, *pero* y *sino*	**Manos a la obra 2 (40 min.)** • Presentation: Subjuntivo en cláusulas adjetivas • Actividades 30, 31, 32, 33, 34, 35 • El español en el mundo del trabajo **¡Adelante! (15 min.)** • Presentación oral: Steps 1, 2	**Wrap-up and Homework Options (5 min.)** • Practice Workbook 7-11, 7-12 • Writing Activity 12-13 • Go Online • Prueba 7-7 • Presentación oral: Step 2 • Go Online
DAY 8	**Warm-up (25 min.)** • Homework check • Communicative Activity ✔**Assessment (20 min.)** • Prueba 7-7	**¡Adelante! (40 min.)** • Presentación oral: Step 3 • Presentation: Misterios del pasado • ¿Comprendiste?	**Wrap-up and Homework Options (5 min.)** • ¿Comprendiste? • Investiga • Examen: Vocabulario y gramática 2
DAY 9	**Warm-up (10 min.)** • Homework check ✔**Assessment Options (25 min.)** • Examen: Vocabulario y gramática 2	**¡Adelante! (50 min.)** • Video • Video Activities • ¿Qué me cuentas? 1, 2, 3 • Presentación escrita: Step 1	**Wrap-up and Homework Options (5 min.)** • Presentación escrita: Step 2 • Go Online • Preparación para el examen: Actividades 1, 2
DAY 10	**Warm-up (20 min.)** • Homework check • Presentación escrita: Step 3	**¡Adelante! (35 min.)** • Lectura • Interacción • ¿Comprendiste? • Fondo cultural **Repaso (30 min.)** • Preparación para el examen: Actividades 3, 4, 6 • MindPoint Quiz Show	**Wrap-up and Homework Options (5 min.)** • Presentación escrita: Step 4 • Practice Workbook: Organizer 7-13, 7-14 • Go Online: Self-test • Preparación para el examen: Actividades 5, 7 • Examen del capítulo
DAY 11	**Warm-up (15 min.)** • Homework check ✔**Assessment (45 min.)** • Examen del capítulo	**Theme Game (15 min.)** **A ver si recuerdas – Capítulo 8 (10 min.)** • Presentation: Vocabulario • Presentation: Gramática	**Wrap-up and Homework Options (5 min.)** • A ver si recuerdas – Capítulo 8 • Actividades 1-6 • Practice Workbook 8-1, 8-2 • Go Online

7 Review

Vocabulario

Presentation

Standards: 1.1, 1.2

Resources: Voc. & Gram. Transparencies: 133

Suggestions: Challenge students to create sentences that use vocabulary from as many categories as possible. For example: *Dentro de un palacio en el bosque, descubrimos una hermosa escultura de piedra.* This can be set up as a game. Students earn a point for every *Vocabulario* item used in a sentence that makes sense. Sentences in which items from all five categories are successfully used earn double, or ten, points. Sentences that don't make sense or are faultily constructed earn no points. The student who earns the most points wins.

Actividad 1

Standards: 1.1

Focus: Practicing review vocabulary

Suggestions: In step 1, encourage students to use the impersonal *se* when telling about what can be found in the various places. Provide a model such as *En la selva tropical de Honduras se pueden encontrar monumentos antiguos.*

Answers will vary.

Block Schedule

Group composition: Divide the class into groups of five. Each student is to begin a paragraph with a sentence that includes one of the negative expressions. Each student passes the paper with the first sentence to the student to his or her left. That student adds a sentence with a negative to the story. Pass to the left, again. Each student in turn adds a sentence to the story. When the paragraph returns to the first writer, have the group read each paragraph aloud to each other and determine the best "story." Have the group read the "best story" aloud for the class.

292

Preparación para 7

A ver si recuerdas...

Vocabulario

materiales
el oro
la piedra
el plástico
la plata
el vidrio

descripciones
antiguo, -a
enorme
hermoso, -a
histórico, -a
impresionante
increíble
moderno, -a

acciones
buscar
dejar
descubrir
encontrar
explicar
impresionar
investigar
olvidar
perder
representar

construcciones
el castillo
el edificio
la escalera
la escultura
la figura
la fuente
el monumento
el palacio
la plaza
el templo

lugares
el bosque
el desierto
el mar
las montañas
el océano
el río
la selva tropical
el valle

Actividad 1  **Escribir/Hablar** ....

Práctica de vocabulario

❶ Haz una lista de:
- dos lugares que visitaste o te gustaría visitar
- dos construcciones que puedes encontrar en esos lugares
- tres palabras que describan cada lugar

❷ Intercambia tu lista con un(a) compañero(a). Hablen sobre por qué escogieron esos lugares, cómo son y qué se encuentra allí.

292 doscientos noventa y dos
A ver si recuerdas . . .

Universal Access

Heritage Language Learners

Have students who have lived in a heritage country create a travel brochure for that country. They may choose a place they know there or research another place. Encourage them to use words from the *Vocabulario* in order to create a vivid picture of the place.

Advanced Learners

Have students prepare an oral description of a famous monument. Ask them to give as many details as they can about the monument without naming it. Have them give their descriptions to the class who can guess which monument is being described. They can also tell which descriptive details helped them identify the monument.

Gramática · Repaso

Las construcciones negativas

Here are some affirmative and negative words that you already know. Remember that they are antonyms.

AFFIRMATIVE	
alguien	*someone*
algo	*something*
alguno, alguna *(pron.)*	*some*
algún, alguna *(adj.)*	*some*
algunos, algunas *(pron., adj.)*	*some*
siempre	*always*
también	*also*

NEGATIVE	
nadie	*no one*
nada	*nothing*
ninguno, ninguna *(pron.)*	*none, not any*
ningún, ninguna *(adj.)*	*no, not any*
ningunos, ningunas *(pron., adj.)*	*none, not any*
nunca	*never*
tampoco	*neither, either*

- *Alguno, alguna, algunos, algunas,* and *ninguno, ninguna* have the same number and gender as the noun they modify.

- When *alguno* and *ninguno* come before a masculine singular noun, they become *algún* and *ningún*.

- To make a sentence negative in Spanish, put *no* in front of the conjugated verb.

  No pudieron encontrar **nada**.

- If a sentence begins with a negative word, like *nunca* or *nadie,* you don't need to use the word *no* in front of the verb.

  Nunca investigaron bien el interior del templo.

Actividad 2 · Hablar

Práctica de gramática

Tu hermano vuelve a casa después de un viaje y quiere saber qué pasó mientras él no estaba. Túrnate con tu compañero(a) para contestar sus preguntas. Todas las respuestas son negativas.

Modelo

A —¿Me llamó alguien por teléfono?
B —*No, nadie te llamó.*

1. ¿Alguien preguntó por mí?
2. ¿Pasó algo interesante?
3. ¿Vino algún amigo a verme?
4. Y Susana, ¿vino a verme?
5. ¿Llegó alguna carta para mí?

Actividad 3 · Leer

Práctica de gramática

Laura le escribe a Isabel. Escoge la expresión adecuada para completar su mensaje electrónico.

```
¡Hola Isabel!

¡Qué pena! No tengo __1.__ (algo /
nada) para contarte. He estado muy
ocupada estudiando y no ha pasado
__2.__ (nada / nadie) interesante. No
he visto a __3.__ (alguien / nadie).
No he ido a __4.__ (nada / ninguna)
parte. No he visto __5.__ (ningún /
ninguno) programa de televisión ni
visto __6.__ (nada / ninguna)
película. ¡Estoy muy aburrida!
Saludos, Laura
```

doscientos noventa y tres 293
Capítulo 7

Teacher-to-Teacher

You can review vocabulary or structures that operate in pairs using the round-robin approach. Students need not form a circle; the process can also run up and down rows. To review the words in the *Gramática* on this page, for example, have the first student in a row say one of the words to the second student. The second student gives the opposite and says another word to the third student, and so on:

A: *Nadie.*
B: *Alguien. Siempre.*
C: *Nunca. Tampoco.*
D: *También…*

Gramática · Repaso

Presentation

Standards: 4.1

Resources: Voc. & Gram. Transparencies: 134

Suggestions: Have pairs of students practice the words in the *Gramática* by asking negative questions and giving affirmative answers:

A: —*¿No ves a nadie en la plaza?*
B: —*Sí, veo a alguien.*

Actividad 2   *Standards:* 1.1

Resources: Practice Answers on Transparencies

Focus: Practicing negative constructions

Suggestions: Tell Student B to listen carefully for the affirmative word in the question in order to build the answer around its negative form.

Answers:

Wording of Sudent B's answers may vary. The following are likely results:

1. No, nadie preguntó por ti.
2. No, no pasó nada interesante.
3. No, ningún amigo vino a verte.
4. No, Susana tampoco vino a verte.
5. No, no llegó ninguna carta (ninguna carta llegó) para ti.

Actividad 3   *Standards:* 1.2

Resources: Practice Answers on Transparencies

Focus: Practicing negative constructions

Suggestions: Have students briefly review the *Gramática* before completing the activity and focus on which words are used for people, places, times, count nouns, and mass (collective) nouns.

Answers:

1. nada	4. ninguna
2. nada	5. ningún
3. nadie	6. ninguna

Vocabulario

fenómenos naturales
el granizo
el huracán
el incendio
la inundación
la lluvia
la nieve
el relámpago
el terremoto
la tormenta
el trueno

las estaciones
el invierno
el otoño
la primavera
el verano

para dar tu opinión
creo . . .
es / no es cierto que . . .
lo bueno / lo malo es que . . .
me parece que . . .
pienso que . . .

animales
la cebra
el elefante
el gato
el hipopótamo
la hormiga
el jaguar
el mono
la mosca
el mosquito
el oso
el pájaro
los peces
el perro
el tigre

sucesos
matar
morirse
nacer
ocurrir
pasar
suceder
tener lugar

Actividad 4 **Hablar/Escribir** . . . .

Práctica de vocabulario

Escoge dos animales de la lista. Luego, con un(a) compañero(a), copien en una hoja una tabla como la que sigue. Escriban en la tabla los nombres de los animales que han escogido y las características de cada animal.

Animal favorito
Lugar donde vive
Fenómeno natural que lo afecta
Tu opinión sobre el animal

Actividad 5 **Hablar/Escribir** . . . .

Práctica de vocabulario

Trabaja con otro(a) estudiante para emparejar cada descripción con el fenómeno de la naturaleza que corresponde. Luego escoge dos de esos fenómenos que hayan ocurrido recientemente y escribe una frase diciendo cuándo y dónde sucedió cada uno.

1. lluvia, truenos y relámpagos
2. luz muy viva producida en una tormenta
3. movimiento de tierra
4. ruido fuerte que se oye en una tormenta
5. viento muy fuerte y violento

a. trueno
b. tormenta
c. huracán
d. relámpago
e. terremoto

294 doscientos noventa y cuatro
A ver si recuerdas . . .

Gramática·Repaso

Los adjetivos usados como sustantivos

When you talk about two similar things in Spanish you can avoid repeating the noun by using the adjective as a noun.

> ¿Qué prefieres, los edificios antiguos o **los modernos**?
> ¿Quieres un gato blanco o **uno gris**?

- Note that in both cases the noun is dropped in the second part of the sentence, and the definite *(el, la, los, las)* or indefinite article *(un, una, unos, unas)* comes before the adjective.

- The adjective agrees in gender and number just as if the noun were still there; also the indefinite article *un* becomes *uno* when it is not followed by the noun.

> No me gustan los edificios antiguos ni **los modernos**.
> No quiero un gato blanco ni **uno gris**.

- The same applies to a prepositional phrase beginning with *a, de,* or *para.*

> ¿Prefieres las esculturas de la derecha o **las de la izquierda**?
> ¿El informe es para esta semana o **para la próxima**?

A masculine singular adjective can be made into a noun by placing *lo* before it.

> **Lo bueno** del verano es que tenemos vacaciones.

---

 6 Leer

Práctica de gramática

Dos amigos visitan el zoológico. Completa su conversación con *el, la, los, las* o *lo* según corresponda.

A —¿Vamos a la sección de los pájaros o a __1.__ de los reptiles?

B —A mí me gusta más __2.__ de los reptiles.

A — ¡Mira ese cocodrilo! ¿No es impresionante?

B — ¿Cuál, __3.__ más grande?

A — No, __4.__ pequeño. ¡Mira sus dientes! Para mí, __5.__ más interesante son los dientes. Y, ¿para ti?

B —A mí, __6.__ que más me interesa es no acercarme demasiado. ¡Me dan mucho miedo!

● **Más práctica**
Practice Workbook 7-1, 7-2

 7 Hablar

Práctica de gramática

Una mamá le ofrece cosas a un niño, pero él quiere algo diferente. Con un(a) compañero(a) hagan los papeles de la mamá y del niño.

Modelo

querer / helado de chocolate / (vainilla)
A —¿Quieres un helado de chocolate?
B —¡No, quiero uno de vainilla!

1. comprar / el globo rojo / (azul)
2. conseguir / un perrito pequeño / (grande)
3. comer / los dulces de fresa / (de limón)
4. ponerse / los pantalones largos / (cortos)

For: More review
Visit: www.phschool.com
Web Code: jed-0701

doscientos noventa y cinco **295**
Capítulo 7

Enriching Your Teaching

Teacher-to-Teacher

Ask pairs of students to compare and contrast two pictures of similar items, such as food items or animals. Point out to them that, in order not to repeat nouns unnecessarily, they must determine a way to identify each picture.

Sometimes this might be an adjective that describes the pictured item, and sometimes it might be simply the relative positions of the pictures themselves: *la rana de la izquierda* vs. *la de la derecha.*

Gramática·Repaso

Presentation

Resources: Voc. & Gram. Transparencies: 136

Suggestions: Have students write one sentence in which they talk about two similar things. Ask them to take turns reading their sentences and have volunteers adapt the second part so that an adjective is used as a noun.

 6 *Standards:* 1.2

Resources: Practice Answers on Transparencies

Focus: Reviewing the use of adjectives as nouns

Suggestions: Remind students to pay attention to the gender and number of the noun they are referring to. Point out that sometimes they must refer to the previous sentence in order to do this.

Answers:

1. la
2. la
3. el
4. el
5. lo
6. lo

 7 *Standards:* 1.1

Resources: Practice Answers on Transparencies

Focus: Reviewing the use of adjectives as nouns

Suggestions: Encourage Student B to use exaggerated intonation for the child's role. Have pairs of students take turns performing one of the dialogues for the class.

Answers will vary. The following are likely results:

1. A—¿Compras el globo rojo?
   B—¡No, compro el azul!
2. A—¿Consigues un perrito pequeño?
   B—¡No, consigo uno grande!
3. A—¿Comes los dulces de fresa?
   B—¡No, como los de limón!
4. A—¿Te pones los pantalones largos?
   B—¡No, me pongo los cortos!

295

(7) Preview

Standards for Foreign Language Learning: *Capítulo 7*

• To achieve the goals of the Standards, students will:

Communication

1.1 Interpersonal
• Talk about tourist sites, animals, and natural phenomena
• Talk about muralist Diego Rivera
• Talk about archaeology and mysteries past and present
• Talk about shapes and measurements
• Talk about the 1938 "War of the Worlds" scare
• Talk about family and community
• Talk about pre-Columbian indigenous civilizations in America
• Talk about classified ads
• Talk about Miguel Cervantes and Don Quijote de la Mancha

1.2 Interpretive
• Read about tourist sites, animals, and natural phenomena
• Read about muralist Diego Rivera
• Read and listen to information about archaeology and mysteries past and present
• Read about shapes and measurements
• Read about word families
• Read about the 1938 "War of the Worlds" scare
• Read and listen to information about pre-Columbian indigenous civilizations in America
• Read about Feliciano Sánchez Chan and his poetry
• Read about speech preparation and writing a legend
• Read about Miguel Cervantes and Don Quijote de la Mancha

1.3 Presentational
• Write and present information orally about tourist sites, animals, and natural phenomena
• Write and present information orally about archaeology and mysteries past and present
• Write and present information orally about shapes and measurements
• Write and present information orally about a panic like the 1938 "War of the Worlds" scare
• Write about family and community
• Recite poetry by Feliciano Sánchez Chan
• Write about pre-Columbian indigenous civilizations in America
• Write classified ads
• Write legends
• Write and present information orally about Miguel Cervantes and Don Quijote de la Mancha

Culture

2.1 Practices and Perspectives
• Describe the perspectives of muralist Diego Rivera
• Describe some practices and perspectives of pre-Columbian indigenous civilizations in America
• Interpret the perspectives of indigenous Latin American writers
• Interpret the work of the Academia de Español de Guatemala
• Interpret the perspectives of Miguel Cervantes

2.2 Products and Perspectives
• Describe the work of muralist Diego Rivera
• Describe the creations and contributions of ancient civilizations
• Discuss the fiction of Miguel Cervantes

Connections

3.1 Cross-curricular
• Discuss key facts about muralist Diego Rivera

Fondo cultural ■◆■◇■◇◆◇■◆

Diego Rivera, el gran pintor mexicano, basó su obra en temas políticos y sociales. Siempre tuvo un gran interés por la historia de su país, y muchas de sus pinturas representan elementos históricos. Estos elementos son una forma de honrar y preservar la herencia *(heritage)* cultural de las antiguas civilizaciones prehispánicas. En este caso, se puede apreciar un detalle del fresco *La civilización Totonaca*, que muestra a los jefes de los poztecas con las pirámides al fondo.

• ¿Qué construcciones indígenas conoces en los Estados Unidos? ¿Dónde están?

Detalle de *La civilización Totonaca*, (1950), Diego Rivera

(c) Banco de México Diego Rivera & Frida Kahlo Museums Trust. Av. Cinco de Mayo No. 2, Col. Centro, Del. Cuauhtemoc 06059, Mexico, D.F. Reproduction authorized by the *Instituto Nacional de Bellas Artes y Literatura*. CORBIS, Inc.

296   doscientos noventa y seis

Universal Access

Personalizing the Theme
Ask students to share their background knowledge about indigenous Latin American peoples. Ask guiding questions such as: *¿Cuáles son unos nombres de pueblos indios de América Latina? ¿En qué países de hoy vivían antes los mayas? ¿Y los incas?*

Heritage Language Learners
Have students share with the class legends from their heritage cultures. They may have heard the stories growing up. If not, suggest that they ask family members about them. Point out legends that are popular in more than one country and compare different versions of the same legend.

Capítulo 7

¿Mito o realidad?

Chapter Objectives

- **Describe what archaeologists do**
- **Identify and describe some extraordinary phenomena**
- **Give your opinion about mysterious events**
- **Talk about the contributions of the Maya and Aztec civilizations**
- **Compare some myths and legends from the Spanish-speaking world with those of the United States**

Video Focus

- **Famous archaeological sites in the Spanish-speaking world**

Country Connection

As you learn about cultures and mysteries of the Spanish-speaking world, you will make connections to these countries and places.

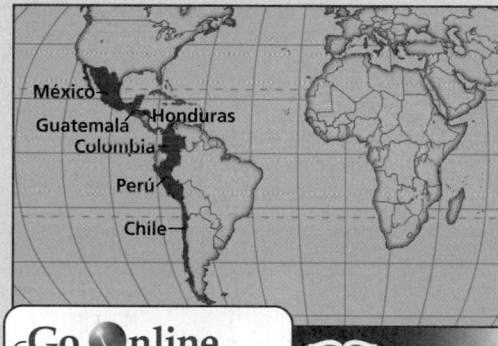

México
Guatemala Honduras
Colombia
Perú
Chile

For: Online Atlas
Visit: www.phschool.com
Web Code: jee-0002

doscientos noventa y siete **297**
Capítulo 7

Preview

Standards for Foreign Language Learning (cont'd)

- Discuss key facts about ancient civilizations
- Discuss key facts about the 1938 "War of the Worlds" scare
- Discuss key facts about Mayan writer Feliciano Sánchez Chan
- Discuss key facts about Antigua, Guatemala
- Discuss key facts about myths and legends
- Discuss key facts about Miguel Cervantes and his times
- Use language arts strategies: using illustrations, maintaining your focus, combining sentences, characters and actions

3.2 Target Culture
- Read poetry by Feliciano Sánchez Chan
- Read fiction by Miguel Cervantes

Comparisons
4.1 Language
- Compare pero and sino to English "but" and "but rather"
- Compare Spanish words to their English counterparts

4.2 Culture
- Compare ancient myths with modern scientific explanations

Communities
5.1 Beyond the School
- Link to Web sites from around the Spanish-speaking world

5.2 Lifelong Learner
- Develop an appreciation for fine art
- Develop an appreciation for poetry and literature

Chapter Opener

Presentation

Resources: Voc. & Gram. Transparencies: 14, 15, 19 (maps)

Suggestions: Introduce students to the theme of the chapter and go over the objectives. Point out that they will improve their ability to talk and write about extraordinary events and about the Aztec and Mayan civilizations. Use *Vocabulary & Grammar Transparencies* 12, 13, 15, 16, and 17 to locate and discuss the countries featured in the chapter.

Fondo cultural *Standards:* 1.1, 1.2, 2.1, 2.2, 3.1, 5.2
■◆■◆■◆■◆■◆■◆■◆■◆

Resources: Fine Art Transparencies; Fine Art Transparencies Teacher's Guide

Suggestions: After students read the information, ask comprehension questions. For example: *¿En qué basó Diego Rivera su obra? (La basó en temas políticos y sociales.) ¿Qué trató de preservar en su obra? (Trató de preservar la herencia cultural de las antiguas civilizaciones prehispánicas.)*

Answers will vary.

Enriching Your Teaching

Planning for Instruction
Resources:
- Teacher Express CD-ROM or Resource Book
  - Teaching resources
  - Lesson Planner
  - Chapter Resource Checklist
  - School-to-Home Connection Letter

Culture Note
Also known as the Pyramid of Kukulkán, El Castillo of Chichén Itzá rises 75 feet into the air. This ancient Mayan structure, built on the site of a previous pyramid, is astrologically aligned. There are 354 stairs and a platform on each side; these 365 steps represent the days in the year.

297

Vocabulario y gramática

Presentation

Standards: 1.1, 1.2, 3.1

Resources: Voc. & Gram. Transparencies: 137–138; Resource Book: *Cap. 7, Input Script;* Audio Program: CD Cap. 7, Track 1

Focus: Presenting new vocabulary and using grammar lexically in context

Suggestions: You may want to use the Input Script from the *Teacher's Resource Book* as a source of ideas for presentation of new vocabulary and comprehensible input. Meaning for vocabulary such as *calcular, medir, excavar, pesar,* and *trazar* can be clarified by pantomime. Visualized vocabulary, such as the various forms and measurements, can be taught using TPR commands. Name an object and then have the class repeat the name while a volunteer points to its image on *Vocabulary & Grammar Transparency* 137 or 138.

A primera vista 1

Vocabulario y gramática en contexto

Objectives

Read, listen to, and understand information about
- what archaeologists do
- archaeological mysteries of other civilizations

1 ❝ ¡Hola! Soy Sabrina. El mes pasado, mis compañeros y yo fuimos a visitar **las ruinas** de **una civilización** que vivió hace muchos siglos. Las civilizaciones antiguas son **pueblos** que **existieron** hace muchos años. ¡Fue muy interesante! ❞

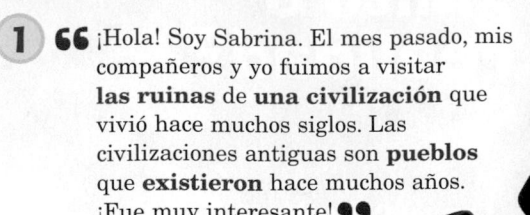

2 ❝ Entre las ruinas se destacaba **el observatorio.** Allí se estudiaban los movimientos de la **Luna** y el Sol y se calculaba el tiempo. ❞

3 ❝ También vimos un monumento de piedra enorme y calculamos que **pesaba** varias **toneladas.** Es imposible saber qué **función** tenía. ❞

¿Pesará más de 3 toneladas? — calcular

4 ❝ Las paredes de los templos y **las pirámides** tenían **diseños geométricos** muy bonitos. ❞

el triángulo   el rectángulo

el diámetro

el círculo

el óvalo

298 doscientos noventa y ocho
A primera vista 1

Universal Access

Advanced Learners

First have students draw a simple design using one or two geometric shapes or lines. Ask them not to show their drawings to anyone. Then have partners sit back-to-back with pencils and pads, looking at their own drawings. Have them take turns using affirmative and negative commands to tell their partner, step by step, how to reproduce their drawing. When finished, have them compare the two drawings and discuss the reasons for any differences between them.

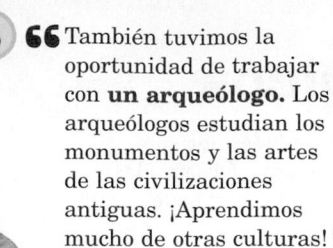

5 “También tuvimos la oportunidad de trabajar con **un arqueólogo.** Los arqueólogos estudian los monumentos y las artes de las civilizaciones antiguas. ¡Aprendimos mucho de otras culturas!”

6 “Aprendimos a excavar para buscar cosas del pasado.”

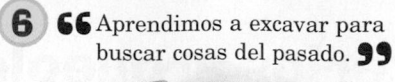

excavar

el ancho   **el centímetro**

7 “**Medimos** algunas piedras y **estructuras** como las que se usaron para construir monumentos.”

el largo   **el alto**

8 “Pesamos cosas de cerámica.”

9 “También trazamos una línea en la tierra para medir **la distancia** entre dos piedras.”

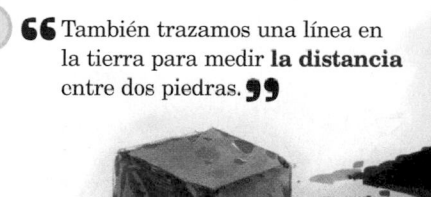

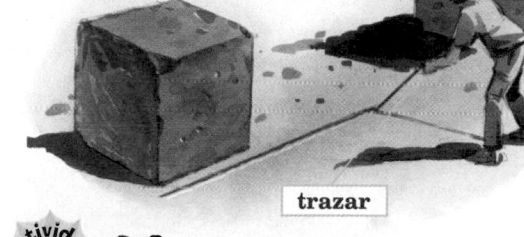

trazar

 Actividad 1   Escuchar · · · · · · · · · · · · · · ·

¿Qué hicieron Sabrina y sus compañeros?

En una hoja escribe los números del 1 al 6. Escucha las frases. Escribe *C* si la frase es cierta o *F* si la frase es falsa.

Actividad 2   Hablar · · · · · · · · · · · · · · ·

Trabajo de arqueólogos

Imagina que trabajaste con un(a) arqueólogo(a). Dile a un(a) compañero(a) lo que hiciste en tu trabajo. Puedes ayudarte usando las ilustraciones de esta página. Por ejemplo: *Excavamos para buscar cosas del pasado.*

doscientos noventa y nueve 299
Capítulo 7

Actividad 1   *Standards:* 1.2

Resources: Voc. & Gram. Transparencies: 137–138; Audio Program: CD Cap. 7, Track 2; Resource Book: Cap. 7, Audio Script; Practice Answers on Transparencies

Focus: Practicing listening comprehension of new vocabulary

Suggestions: Before students listen, point out that the statements they will hear are related directly to the story about Sabrina and her friends on this and the previous page. Use the *Audio CD* or read the text. Allow students to listen more than once.

Answers:

1. F	4. C
2. F	5. F
3. C	6. C

Extension: Ask students to correct the false statements. Have them do so by changing information, rather than making the false statement negative.

Actividad 2   *Standards:* 1.1

Focus: Practicing new vocabulary in a guided conversation

Suggestions: As students talk together, encourage them to use gestures that show that they understand the meaning of the vocabulary items.

Answers will vary.

Enriching Your Teaching

Culture Note

The largest pyramid in the world by volume is located in Cholula, Mexico, two hours southeast of Mexico City. This colossal structure was only discovered in 1910 during the construction of a nearby building. Grassy vegetation had grown and covered the pyramid, making it look like a huge hill. A church was even built on it. Archaeologists have dug about five miles of tunnels inside the pyramid to study its history. The pyramid consists of several layers of construction that were built over ten centuries. Cholula was conquered by various tribes, including the Olmecs, the Toltecs, and the Aztecs, each building a larger pyramid around the existing one.

Misterios arqueológicos

Muchas civilizaciones antiguas construyeron grandes ciudades que son **un misterio**. No se sabe por qué y para qué se construyeron. Observa las fotos que enviaron los estudiantes de diferentes países explicando qué lugares o cosas **misteriosas** hay en sus países.

Analía, de Ciudad de México

Éste es el dibujo que se encontró en la piedra que **cubría** la tumba del misterioso señor Pakal, en la ciudad de Palenque. El hombre del dibujo parece estar sentado en **una nave espacial**. Algunas personas creen que esto es **una evidencia** de la presencia de extraterrestres en los tiempos de los mayas. ¿Es **probable**, no?

José, de Cuzco, Perú

Éstas son las ruinas de la misteriosa ciudad inca de Machu Picchu. Es posible que los incas hayan construido esta ciudad para protegerse de las invasiones o que haya sido un centro comercial. También es un misterio cómo unieron las piedras de sus muros[1] **ya que** no usaron argamasa[2]. No se sabe si van a **resolver** este misterio.

1 walls 2 mortar

300 trescientos
A primera vista 1

Universal Access

Heritage Language Learners
As students use the new vocabulary, remind them to be careful with spellings of cognates, such as **pirámide.** Also remind them of differences in capitalization rules between English and Spanish: *The Incas* versus **los incas.**

Students with Special Needs
Have partners describe the images in each photo so that visually impaired students can better understand the context of each caption. For example, for the fourth photo: *Vemos a una chica que toca una piedra perfectamente redonda. El diámetro de la piedra debe ser de tres pies, más o menos.*

María, de La Paz, Bolivia

es envío esta foto de la ciudad de Tiahuanaco, a La Paz. Esta ciudad es un enigma ya que está ena de monumentos construidos con enormes iedras. Los arqueólogos no **dudan** que estas iedras son de un lugar que está a 80 ilómetros de Tiahuanaco. Lo que resulta **nexplicable** es cómo llevaron las piedras de un lugar a otro si no tenían animales para transportarlas.

Roberto, de San José, Costa Rica

*En Costa Rica sucedió **un fenómeno muy extraño**: un día se encontraron piedras perfectamente **redondas** en la costa del Pacífico. Es **improbable** que descubramos de dónde vienen.*

Actividad 3 Escuchar

¿Cuál es el lugar?

Escucha las descripciones y escoge la cultura o ciudad que corresponda.

1. a. Canadá   b. Costa Rica   c. Cuzco
2. a. Palenque   b. Honduras   c. Tiahuanaco
3. a. Inca   b. Pakal   c. Machu Picchu
4. a. Machu Picchu b. Palenque   c. Tiahuanaco
5. a. Palenque   b. Cuzco   c. Machu Picchu

 Más práctica

Practice Workbook 7-3, 7-4

Go Online
PHSchool.com

For: Vocabulary practice
Visit: www.phschool.com
Web Code: jed-0702

trescientos uno   **301**
Capítulo 7

Actividad 3

Standards: 1.2

Resources: Voc. & Gram. Transparencies: 139–140; Audio Program: CD Cap. 7, Track 4; Resource Book: Cap. 7, Audio Script; Practice Answers on Transparencies

Focus: Practicing listening comprehension of new vocabulary

Suggestions: Allow students to listen to the *Audio CD* more than once. Remind them to listen for key words that will guide them toward a correct answer, rather than trying to understand every word.

Answers:

1. b	4. b
2. c	5. c
3. b	

Extension: Have students tell as much as they can about the other places listed in numbers 1–5. For example: *Cuzco es una ciudad en Perú. Está cerca de las ruinas de Machu Picchu.*

Additional Resources

• Resource Book: Cap. 7, Clip Art

✓ Assessment

• Prueba 7-1: Vocabulary recognition

Teacher-to-Teacher

Many students are intrigued by the mysteries associated with Latin American ruins. Encourage students, including heritage language learners, to share their background knowledge about these places. Suggest that they talk to their social studies teachers about them and report back with information.

Chapter Project

Give students copies of the Chapter Project outline and rubric from the *Teacher's Resource Book*. Explain the task to them, and have them perform step 1. (For more information, see p. 292-a.)

Enriching Your Teaching

Culture Note

Thousands of these spherical stones, ranging from a few inches in diameter to eight feet around, have been discovered in Costa Rica. Even the largest of the spheres are so perfect in shape that modern tests show no imperfections. This degree of precision would have required great mathematical ability as well as an advanced knowledge of stoneworking. In addition, many of the spheres are made of granite, quarries of which are up to thirty miles away from where the largest stones were found. How did anyone move such large pieces of granite through the dense bush of the region? So far, no written record has been found.

Actividad 4

Standards: 1.2, 3.1

Resources: Practice Answers on Transparencies

Focus: Practicing new vocabulary

Suggestions: Remind students that the items are presented as analogies. A single colon means "is to" and a double colon means "as."

Answers:
1. línea
2. medir
3. óvalo
4. astrónomo
5. centímetro
6. triángulo
7. arqueóloga

Actividad 5

Standards: 1.2

Resources: Practice Answers on Transparencies

Focus: Practicing new vocabulary through reading, listing, and discussion

Suggestions: Remind students that reading through the entire announcement first will help them place their answers correctly.

Answers:
1. misterios
2. existen
3. que
4. cubría
5. se excavaron
6. extraños
7. redondas
8. arqueólogos
9. probable

Steps 2–3
Answers will vary.

Manos a la obra 1

Vocabulario y gramática en uso

Objectives
- Talk about archaeological mysteries
- Talk about ancient civilizations
- Use the present and the present perfect subjunctive after expressions of doubt, uncertainty or disbelief

Actividad 4 Leer/Escribir/Pensar

A recordar palabras

Completa cada analogía con una palabra correcta del recuadro. Sigue el modelo.

triángulo	astrónomo	medir	centímetro
arqueóloga	línea	óvalo	

Modelo

cierta : verdad :: inexplicable : *improbable*

1. cortar : papel :: trazar : _____

2. kilo : pesar :: centímetro : _____

3. reloj : círculo :: huevo : _____

4. laboratorio : científico :: observatorio : _____

5. el peso : tonelada :: el largo : _____

6. puerta : rectángulo :: pared de una pirámide : _____

7. enseñar : maestra :: excavar : _____

Actividad 5 Leer/Escribir

¡A viajar!

❶ Imagina que quieres irte de viaje con tu familia. Completa este anuncio de un viaje arqueológico usando las palabras del recuadro.

redondas	arqueólogos	ya que
se excavaron	probable	extraños
misterios	cubría	existen

❷ ¿Qué otro misterio arqueológico te gustaría visitar? ¿Por qué?

❸ Haz una lista de tres cosas interesantes que puedes ver en un viaje como éste.

Viaje Arqueológico

Los __1__ de los mayas

¿Sabías que…

…todavía __2__ muchas estructuras antiguas __3__ estaban construidas de piedra?

…la tierra __4__ muchos monumentos importantes hasta que __5__?

…hay sitios misteriosos y __6__ con piedras perfectamente __7__?

Explora las ruinas del Yucatán y de Centroamérica con un equipo de __8__ en la selva tropical. Visita Cobá, uno de los sitios más antiguos de los mayas. Ven a Tulum y disfruta de las aguas azules del Caribe.

¡Es muy __9__ que te diviertas!

Viajes Paraíso
Calle 55, esquina Lago
Ciudad de México, México

Universal Access

Students with Learning Difficulties

For *Actividad* 4, explain that to solve an analogy, students must find a word that completes the second pair. The first two words are always related; the second two must be related in the same way. Help students identify the relationship in order to solve the second analogy in each item.

Advanced Learners

Ask students to create more word analogies similar to the ones in *Actividad* 4. Have them refer to previous chapters for vocabulary sets.

Actividad 6 **Hablar** ....

Preguntas de arqueólogos

Un buen arqueólogo se hace muchas preguntas. Trabaja con una(a) compañero(a) para hablar de las fotos y los dibujos de los lugares en las páginas 298 a 301. Sigue el modelo.

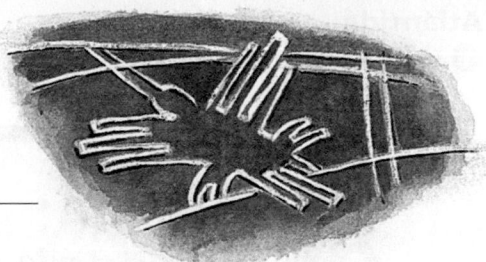

líneas de Nazca

Modelo

líneas de Nazca / ¿quiénes trazaron?

A —¿Quiénes trazaron las líneas de Nazca?

B —Los extraterrestres las trazaron, según algunas personas.

Estudiante A

1. observatorio / ¿qué calculaban?
2. paredes de los templos / ¿qué tipo de dibujos muestran?
3. el monumento / ¿cuánto pesa?
4. las paredes de la pirámide / ¿qué forma tienen?
5. la evidencia de la presencia de extraterrestres en la región maya / ¿cuál puede ser?
6. las ruinas de Machu Picchu / ¿cuál era el misterio?
7. las piedras misteriosas que se encontraron en Costa Rica / ¿cómo eran?

Estudiante B

triángulo
más de 3 toneladas
cómo unieron las piedras de las paredes
perfectamente redondas
una nave espacial dibujada en una piedra que cubría una tumba
los extraterrestres, según algunas personas
diseños geométricos
el tiempo y el movimiento del Sol y de la Luna

Actividad 7 **Hablar** ....

Juego

Tú y tus compañeros(as) van a jugar al juego de las veinte preguntas. Cada estudiante piensa en un objeto sin decir lo que es y sus compañeros tienen que hacerle preguntas que sólo pueden ser contestadas con *sí* o *no*.

❶ Cada estudiante escribe una descripción de un objeto de la sala de clases. Pueden usar las palabras del recuadro.

Es un objeto redondo. Tiene números . . .

está hecho(a) de	pesa	mide	el ancho	el alto	el largo
óvalo	círculo	triángulo	rectángulo	redondo	sirve para

❷ Los estudiantes hacen preguntas para identificar el objeto. El (La) estudiante que identifica el objeto gana dos puntos.

Modelo

¿Tiene el objeto más de 20 centímetros de largo?
¿Tiene forma redonda?

Nota

Para expresar en español el largo, ancho o alto de un objeto, puedes usar estas mismas palabras precedidas por la preposición **de**.

El monumento mide tres metros **de alto** y dos metros **de ancho**.

trescientos tres **303**
Capítulo 7

Practice and Communicate

 7

Actividad 6 *Standards:* 1.1

Resources: Practice Answers on Transparencies

Focus: Using new vocabulary and structures in guided dialogues

Suggestions: Point out to students that there will be more than one way to ask and answer the questions. Encourage them to use their language skills to create the most clear and efficient questions and answers possible.

Answers:

Questions and answers will vary. The following are suggestions:

1. A —¿Qué calculaban en el observatorio?
   B —Calculaban el tiempo y el movimiento del Sol y de la Luna.
2. A —¿Qué tipo de dibujos muestran en las paredes de los templos?
   B —Muestran diseños geométricos.
3. A —¿Cuánto pesa el monumento?
   B —Pesa más de 3 toneladas.
4. A —¿Qué forma tienen las paredes de la pirámide?
   B —Tienen la forma de un triángulo.
5. A —¿Cuál puede ser la evidencia de la presencia de los extraterrestres en la región maya?
   B —Una nave espacial dibujada en una piedra que cubría una tumba puede ser esa evidencia.
6. A —¿Cuál era el misterio de las ruinas de Machu Picchu?
   B —El misterio era cómo unieron las piedras de las paredes.
7. A —¿Cómo eran las piedras misteriosas que se encontraron en Costa Rica?
   B —Eran perfectamente redondas.

Actividad 7 *Standards:* 1.1

Focus: Using new vocabulary to ask for and provide descriptions of objects

Suggestions: As students describe and ask about the objects, encourage them to include as much new shape and measurement vocabulary as they can.

Answers will vary.

Enriching Your Teaching

Teacher-to-Teacher
The game "Twenty Questions" is a tried-and-true language-teaching strategy. It is easily adaptable to all sorts of vocabulary and grammar teaching targets. Any variation that you can think of for the game (such as

Actividad 7 on this page) will provide students with excellent real-life language practice. The game requires students to engage in question formation and a true exchange of information within any context you decide to apply.

303

Rapid Review

Remind students of the spelling changes in the preterite forms of verbs like *creer* and *leer.* On the board, begin a preterite conjugation of one or more of these verbs, supplying some of the preterite forms. Have volunteers finish the conjugation, including third-person, plural preterite forms like *creyeron* and *leyeron.*

Actividad 8

Standards: 1.1, 1.2, 1.3, 3.1

Resources: Practice Answers on Transparencies

Focus: Practicing new vocabulary and structures through reading and response

Suggestions: First, have students read the article on their own and write their answers to the questions in step 2. Have them share these answers when they meet in groups for step 3. Doing so will help them address together any reading comprehension problems they may have.

Answers:

Wording of answers may vary. The following are likely results:

1. **Trata del misterio de la Atlántida.**
2. **Atlántida es el nombre de una antigua civilización que se hundió rápidamente en el mar. Muchas personas creen que la historia de Atlántida es verdad. Otras no la creen.**
3. **Creta fue completamente cubierta por una ola gigantesca.**
4. **Los dos lugares fueron destruidos por el mar. La destrucción de los dos lugares ocurrió en la misma época.**
5. **Answers will vary.**

 **Actividad 8** **Leer/Escribir/Hablar** ....

Atlántida

❶ Lee el siguiente artículo sobre el misterio de la Atlántida.

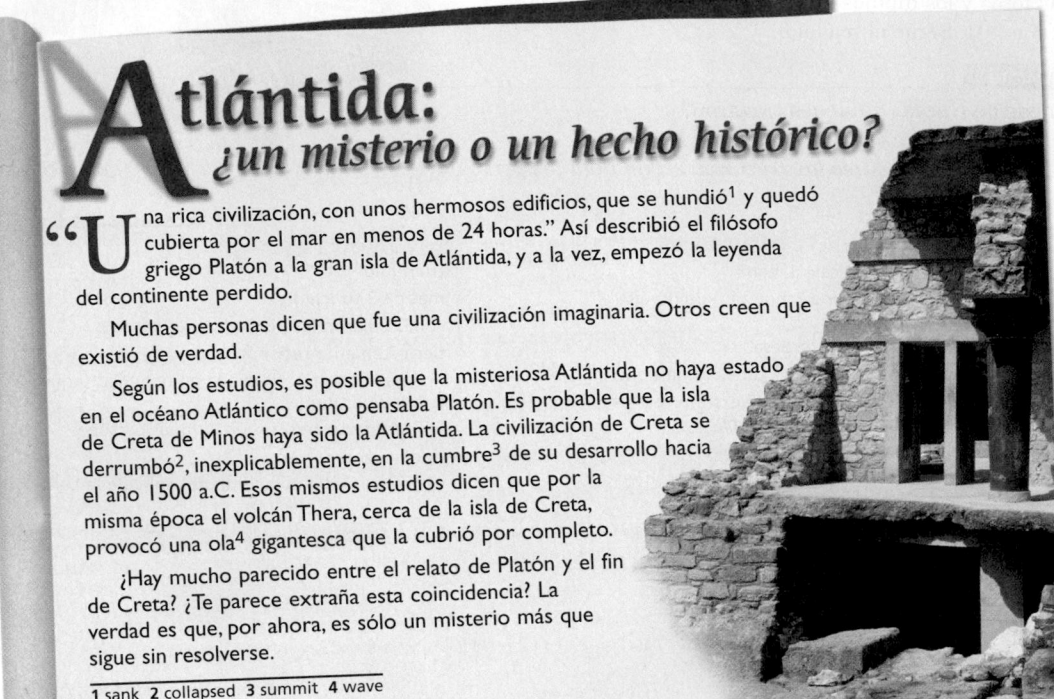

Atlántida: ¿un misterio o un hecho histórico?

"Una rica civilización, con unos hermosos edificios, que se hundió[1] y quedó cubierta por el mar en menos de 24 horas." Así describió el filósofo griego Platón a la gran isla de Atlántida, y a la vez, empezó la leyenda del continente perdido.

Muchas personas dicen que fue una civilización imaginaria. Otros creen que existió de verdad.

Según los estudios, es posible que la misteriosa Atlántida no haya estado en el océano Atlántico como pensaba Platón. Es probable que la isla de Creta de Minos haya sido la Atlántida. La civilización de Creta se derrumbó[2], inexplicablemente, en la cumbre[3] de su desarrollo hacia el año 1500 a.C. Esos mismos estudios dicen que por la misma época el volcán Thera, cerca de la isla de Creta, provocó una ola[4] gigantesca que la cubrió por completo.

¿Hay mucho parecido entre el relato de Platón y el fin de Creta? ¿Te parece extraña esta coincidencia? La verdad es que, por ahora, es sólo un misterio más que sigue sin resolverse.

1 sank **2** collapsed **3** summit **4** wave

❷ Ahora responde a las preguntas sobre lo que dice el artículo.

1. ¿De qué trata el artículo?
2. ¿Qué es la Atlántida y qué creen las personas acerca de la Atlántida?
3. ¿Qué sucedió con Creta?
4. ¿En qué se relacionan Creta y la Atlántida?
5. ¿Habías visto o leído antes algo sobre la Atlántida, en películas, documentales, dibujos animados, libros o artículos? ¿Qué explicación se daba allí? ¿Era parecida a la de este artículo?

❸ En grupo, comenten lo que dice la leyenda. ¿Cuántos creen que es cierta? ¿Creen que hay suficiente evidencia de que la Atlántida realmente existió?

Universal Access

Students with Learning Difficulties

Point out to students that *a.C.* means *antes de Cristo.* Draw a timeline on the board. Label the points *1500 a.C., el año 1 (nacimiento de Jesucristo),* and *20xx* (the current year). Use this visual to demonstrate adding 1,500 years + 2,0(xx) years to determine how many years ago the civilization of Crete was destroyed.

Multiple Intelligences

Logical/Mathematical: As the class completes *Actividad* 10, challenge students to convert answers to the metric system. Remind them that the metric system is used throughout Latin America, Spain, and many other countries. Provide them with the following information: 2.2 pounds = 1 kilogram; 3.3 feet = 1 meter; 1.6 miles = 1 km.

Hablar/Escribir · · · · · · · · · · · · ·

Compara los misterios

1 Trabaja con un(a) compañero(a). Hagan una lista de los misterios que han estudiado hasta ahora en el capítulo. Añadan otros misterios que conozcan.

2 Escojan dos misterios y compárenlos. ¿En qué se parecen? ¿En qué se diferencian? Pueden usar un diagrama de Venn como el siguiente para compararlos.

3 Usando el diagrama de Venn, escriban frases para comparar los misterios.

Machu Picchu   **Atlántida**

ciudad inca   isla

Ampliación del lenguaje

Familia de palabras

Muchas veces podemos averiguar el significado de una palabra si conocemos otras palabras de la misma familia. Observa la relación entre las siguientes palabras. Luego completa las frases.

1. La piedra es muy _____. _____ 20 kilos.
2. Nadie puede _____ ese fenómeno. Es _____.

verbo	sustantivo	adjetivo
calcular	la calculadora	
cubrir		cubierto(a)
diseñar	el diseño	
dudar	la duda	dudoso(a)
	la evidencia	evidente
explicar	la explicación	inexplicable
	el fenómeno	fenomenal
funcionar	la función	
medir	la medida	
	el misterio	misterioso(a)
pesar	el peso	pesado(a)

 Escribir/Hablar · · · · · · · · · · · · ·

Y tú, ¿qué dices?

1. ¿Cuánto crees que pesa tu pupitre? ¿Y el escritorio del (de la) profesor(a)? ¿Y un árbol?

2. ¿Qué objeto o edificio en los Estados Unidos tiene el alto de una pirámide? ¿Qué río crees que es el más largo del mundo?

3. ¿Cuál es mayor, el diámetro de la Luna o el de la Tierra? ¿Y qué distancia crees que es mayor, la de la Tierra al Sol o la de la Tierra a la Luna?

4. Busca formas geométricas en la clase. ¿Qué cosas tienen forma de rectángulo, triángulo, círculo u óvalo?

trescientos cinco **305**
Capítulo 7

Practice and Communicate

 7

 Standards: 1.1, 1.3, 3.1
9
· · · · · · · · · · · · · · · · ·

Focus: Practicing new vocabulary and structures via discussion and note-taking

Suggestions: If students can't name other mysteries in step 1, suggest well-known ones such as *las predicciones de Nostradamus* or *el Yeti.*

Answers will vary.

10 *Standards:* 1.1, 1.3
· · · · · · · · · · · · · · · · ·

Focus: Practicing new vocabulary and structures

Suggestions: As students talk about their answers, they will be making comparisons. Model comparative and superlative structures as necessary.

Answers will vary.

Ampliación del lenguaje

Presentation

Standards: 1.2, 3.1

Resources: Practice Answers on Transparencies

Focus: Understanding word families

Suggestions: Ask pairs of students to build word families around other verbs such as *expresar* or *impresionar.*

Answers:
pesada; pesa
explicar; inexplicable

Additional Resources

• Writing, Audio & Video Workbook: Cap. 7, Audio Activity 1, Track 5
• Writing, Audio & Video Workbook: Cap. 7, Writing Activity 6
• Resource Book: Cap. 7, Communicative Activity BLM

 Assessment
• Prueba 7-2: Vocabulary production

Enriching Your Teaching

Teacher-to-Teacher

A good way to draw students into a discussion is to use "faulty" questions. A "faulty" question is one that doesn't supply all the information necessary for it to be clearly answered. For example, a question such as *¿Cuánto pesa un perro?* might elicit further

comments, questions, and comparisons such as: *Bueno, ¿qué clase de perro es? Un labrador pesará más que un chihuahua. Es necesario saber la edad del perro también. ¿Come bien el perro? ¿Es un perro delgado o gordo?*

Gramática

Presentation

Standards: 4.1

Resources: Voc & Gram. Transparencies: 141

Suggestions: Ask students to use the expressions in the *Gramática* in sentences with the subjunctive or the indicative, as appropriate. Encourage them to make comments about the mysteries already discussed in the chapter or about current events. If necessary, ask guiding questions such as: *¿Piensas que los extraterrestres estaban presentes durante la civilización maya?*

11

Standards: 1.2

Resources: Practice Answers on Transparencies

Focus: Practicing the subjunctive with expressions of doubt

Suggestions: Remind students that these are complex sentences with more than one set of subject and verb. Tell them to carefully determine the subject of the subordinate clause before writing each answer, since their verb form must agree in person and number with that subject.

Answers:
1. excaven
2. pueda
3. pesen
4. calculen
5. pese/pesa
6. son

Additional Resources

• Writing, Audio & Video Workbook: Cap. 7, Audio Activity 2, Track 6

Gramática

El presente y el presente perfecto del subjuntivo con expresiones de duda

To express doubt, uncertainty, or disbelief about actions in the present, you use the present subjunctive. To express doubt, uncertainty, or disbelief about actions in the past, you use the present perfect subjunctive. Recall that the present perfect subjunctive is formed with the present subjunctive of *haber* and a past participle.

doubt, uncertainty		subjunctive
Dudo que . . . **Es posible** que . . . **Es dudoso** que . . .	**+**	**existan** los extraterrestres *extraterrestrials **exist, do exist, will exist***

disbelief		
No creo que . . . **Es imposible** que . . .	**+**	**hayan existido** los extraterrestres *extraterrestrials **existed, have existed***

Expressions of belief, knowledge or certainty are usually followed by the indicative.

Creo que . . . **Estoy segura** que . . . **Es evidente** que . . . **Es verdad** que . . . **Sabemos** que . . . **No dudo** que . . .	**+**	ésas **son** ruinas mayas

11 **Gramática** **Leer**

Lo dudo

Jorge está leyendo una revista de arqueología. Completa lo que piensa con el presente del indicativo o el presente del subjuntivo del verbo apropiado.

1. Dudo que los arqueólogos _____ en lugares donde no exista evidencia de otras civilizaciones. *(excavar)*

2. Es improbable que una persona sin experiencia artística _____ trazar los diseños incas. *(poder)*

3. Es posible que las ruinas de los palacios _____ muchas toneladas. *(pesar)*

4. No creo que los científicos _____ el diámetro de una estructura sin ver antes la evidencia. *(calcular)*

5. Es imposible que el antiguo observatorio _____ más que un edificio moderno. Creo que el observatorio _____ menos que un edificio moderno. *(pesar)*

6. Estoy seguro de que los científicos _____ capaces de resolver muchos misterios. *(ser)*

306 trescientos seis
Manos a la obra 1

Universal Access

Students with Learning Difficulties
Point out that these sentences have two clauses, each with its own subject and verb that must agree. Provide models of different subjects with ***haber*** to form the present perfect subjunctive: *Es imposible que él haya creído esta leyenda. No creo que tú hayas visto un extraterrestre. Es dudoso que haya aterrizado una nave espacial.*

Advanced Learners
Have students write three false statements about real-life events: *Shirley sacó una mala nota en el examen de inglés.* Have them exchange sentences with a partner and take turns commenting on each statement using the present perfect subjunctive: *Dudo que haya sacado una mala nota porque estaba muy bien preparada.*

Actividad 12 Gramática — Leer/Hablar

¿Qué opinas?

Trabaja con un(a) compañero(a) para dar su opinión sobre la información y las teorías que acaban de leer. Usen frases de las dos columnas.

Modelo

Los extraterrestres vivían en la ciudad de Palenque.
Dudo que los extraterrestres hayan vivido en la ciudad de Palenque.

columna A

Los seres humanos han transportado las piedras de Tihuanaco.

Los incas construyeron Machu Picchu para protegerse de las invasiones.

El señor Pakal está sentado en una nave espacial.

Las piedras que se encontraron en Costa Rica son perfectamente redondas.

Atlántida fue en realidad la isla de Creta de Minos.

columna B

Dudo que . . .

Creo que . . .

Estoy seguro(a) de que . . .

Es imposible que . . .

Es probable / improbable que . . .

Actividad 13 — Leer/Hablar/Escribir

Noticias increíbles

Lee este artículo sobre algo que sucedió en 1938.

1 Contesta las preguntas.

1. ¿De qué se trataba el programa de radio?
2. ¿Qué causó el pánico?
3. ¿Cree el señor en la calle que existen los extraterrestres?
4. ¿Qué cree la señorita?

2 Trabaja con un grupo para pensar en un evento o un fenómeno que pueda causar pánico al público hoy día. Escriban entre todos un guión *(script)* de un programa sobre el evento o fenómeno.

3 "Transmitan" su programa a la clase.

---

31 de octubre, 1938

¡Pánico por supuesta invasión de marcianos!

Programa de radio causó gran revuelo[1]

Orson Welles adaptó y transmitió por radio ayer La guerra de los mundos *de H.G. Wells, de manera tan realista que la gente creyó que estaba escuchando las noticias de una invasión extraterrestre. Aquí les damos la opinión del público en las calles cuando todo se aclaró.*

Periodista: ¡Señor, señor! ¿Qué cree usted que ha sucedido? ¿Es posible que nos invadan los marcianos?

Señor en la calle: Quizás todos hayamos pensado que era verdad. Pero no creo que una invasión así sea posible.

Periodista: ¿Y usted, señorita?

Chica en la calle: Yo me asusté, pero en realidad, dudo que existan los marcianos.

[1] commotion

trescientos siete **307**
Capítulo 7

Practice and Communicate

 Actividad 12   *Standards:* 1.1

Resources: Practice Answers on Transparencies

Focus: Practicing the subjunctive with expressions of doubt

Suggestions: Make sure partners switch roles in order to practice both halves of the dialogues. Encourage Student B to answer truthfully when expressing either doubt or certainty.

Answers will vary. The following are the possible combinations of expressions and verb forms:

doubt, uncertainty, disbelief
> **Dudo que; Es imposible que; Es probable/ improbable que/hayan transportado; hayan construido; esté sentado; sean; haya sido**

certainty
> **Creo que; Estoy seguro(a) de que/han transportado (transportaron); construyeron; está sentado; son; fue**

 Actividad 13   *Standards:* 1.1, 1.2, 1.3, 3.1

Resources: Practice Answers on Transparencies

Focus: Practicing the subjunctive through reading and response

Suggestions: Remind students that when answering questions 3 and 4 in step 1, they must use third-person verb forms. Encourage them to record their transmission for step 3 on audiocassette or videotape.

Answers: Wording of answers may vary. The following are likely results:
- **Se trataba de una invasión de marcianos.**
- **El público creyó que la invasión era verdadera.**
- **Sí, el señor cree que existen los extraterrestres.**
- **La señorita duda que existan los extraterrestres.**

Chapter Project

Students can perform step 2 at this point. Be sure they understand your corrections and suggestions. (For more information, see p. 292-a.)

Enriching Your Teaching

Teacher-to-Teacher

When students work on group projects, such as the creation of the transmission in *Actividad* 13, monitor them to make sure that everyone is contributing to the best of his or her ability. Whenever possible, allow them to organize themselves according to their skills. It will sometimes be necessary, however, to assign specific tasks to specific students. Those with stronger language skills might be given more of the writing task, for example, while those who are struggling might contribute to the more technical and hands-on parts of the task.

307

Practice and Communicate

7

14 *Standards:* 1.1

Resources: Practice Answers on Transparencies

Focus: Practicing the present perfect subjunctive with expressions of doubt

Suggestions: Tell students that Student A may interpret the art in more than one way in order to form the question. Student B should listen carefully and respond using a direct object pronoun that refers to the direct object that Student A used.

Answers:

Direct objects may vary. Direct object pronouns shown in Student B's answers replace the direct objects shown in Student A's questions.

1. A —¿Marcia ya excavó las ruinas?
   B —No, no creo que las haya excavado.
2. A —¿Tú ya pesaste las piedras?
   B —No, no creo que las haya pesado.
3. A —¿Carlos y Raúl ya trazaron las formas geométricas?
   B —No, no creo que las hayan trazado.
4. A —¿Usted ya calculó el diámetro del círculo?
   B —No, no creo que lo haya calculado.
5. A —¿Mateo ya estudió el monumento?
   B —No, no creo que lo haya estudiado.
6. A —¿Teresa y Emilio ya buscaron el templo?
   B —No, no creo que lo hayan buscado.

Block Schedule

After completing *Actividad* 15, divide students into groups of four. Have one student write out each of the expressions on a strip of paper. Place these face down in one pile. Then have students write on a a strip of paper a subject/verb combination: *El arqueólogo/encontrar* and place it in a second pile. One student selects a strip from each pile and creates a sentence combining both elements. The student receives one point if the sentence is correct and logical. Return the strips to the bottom of each pile. Continue play until each student gets three chances to create a sentence. The winner is the student with the most points.

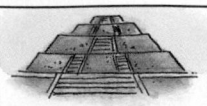

14 **Gramática** **Hablar** . . . .

Los arqueólogos

Imagina que estás trabajando en una excavación arqueológica. Algunos de tus compañeros se olvidaron de hacer sus tareas, y tú quieres confirmar que se han hecho. Observa los dibujos, y con un(a) compañero(a) hagan y contesten preguntas según el modelo.

Modelo

Pedro / medir
A —¿Pedro ya midió la pirámide?
B —No, no creo que la haya medido.

1. Marcia / excavar

2. tú / pesar

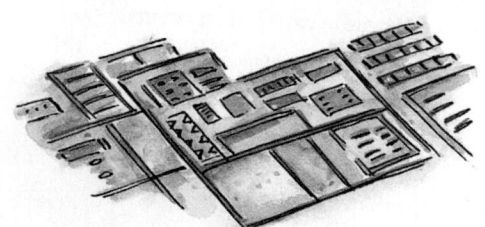

3. Carlos y Raúl / trazar

4. usted / calcular

5. Mateo / estudiar

6. Teresa y Emilio / buscar

308 trescientos ocho
Manos a la obra 1

Universal Access

Students with Learning Difficulties

Make sure students understand the scenario of *Actividad* 16. Then have them read the questions in part 2 to set a purpose for listening. Play the interview once for students to get the gist. Have them revisit the questions and answer any that they can. Play the interview two more times so they can listen for any answers they missed.

Students with Special Needs

In order to complete *Actividad* 14, students with visually impaired partners will need to describe the object illustrated for each sentence. For example: *El dibujo es de un pueblo muy antiguo. Parece que lo están excavando.*

 **Escribir/Hablar** ············

Y tú, ¿qué crees?

Escribe tres frases acerca de tu escuela, familia, comunidad o país, y léeselas a otro(a) estudiante. Tu compañero(a) debe responder usando las expresiones del recuadro.

(no) es cierto que	(no) dudar que	(no) creer que
es (im)probable que	es (im)posible que	(no) estar seguro(a) de que

Modelo

A —*Creo que nuestro equipo de béisbol puede ganar el campeonato este año.*
B —*Estoy seguro de que nuestro equipo puede ganar el campeonato.*
o: *Dudo que nuestro equipo pueda ganar este año porque Tomás Álvarez era el mejor jugador y acaba de romperse la muñeca.*

 Gramática **Escuchar/Hablar/Escribir** ·····················

La civilización misteriosa

❶ Un famoso arqueólogo ha descubierto las ruinas de una antigua ciudad de una misteriosa civilización. Escucha la entrevista que le hace una periodista al arqueólogo. Observa el dibujo mientras escuchas la entrevista.

❷ Ahora, contesta las siguientes preguntas según la entrevista.

1. ¿Por qué no cree el Dr. Romero que haya existido esta civilización hace millones de años?
2. ¿El Dr. Romero cree que se puede calcular la edad de las ruinas?
3. ¿Qué formas geométricas se han usado en los diseños de los edificios?
4. Según el Dr. Romero, ¿quiénes fueron los habitantes de esta civilización?

❸ Escribe un párrafo sobre cómo te imaginas tú que haya sido esta misteriosa civilización.

 Standards: 1.1, 1.3
············

Focus: Practicing the present perfect subjunctive with expressions of doubt

Suggestions: Suggest that students write some sentences about things they are sure about and some about things they are unsure about. This way, expressions of both doubt and certainty can be used meaningfully in the speaking part of the activity.

Answers will vary.

 Standards: 1.2, 1.3
············

Resources: Audio Program: CD Cap. 7, Track 7; Resource Book: Cap. 7, Audio Script; Practice Answers on Transparencies

Focus: Practicing listening comprehension and writing of the subjunctive with expressions of doubt

Suggestions: Play the *Audio CD* or read from the script. Then allow students two minutes to look over the comprehension questions. Allow them to listen again before they write their answers to the questions.

Answers:
1. Es imposible que la ciudad se haya conservado tan bien por tantos años.
2. Sí, está seguro de que se puede calcular.
3. Se han usado círculos, óvalos y triángulos.
4. Dice que es posible que hayan sido extraterrestres, pero todavía esto no se puede saber.

Enriching Your Teaching

Teacher-to-Teacher

Students intrigued by the mysteries mentioned in this chapter might wish to create their own "mystery." Encourage them to do so and suggest different formats. Some might write a story or a scene that takes place within a lost civilization. Others might prepare and record a news flash about the discovery of a mysterious object or structure.

Actividad 17 Standards: 1.1, 1.2

Focus: Practicing the subjunctive with expressions of doubt

Suggestions: Tell students to respond to the questions in step 1 as though the excursion happened in the past. They should also practice the past tenses in step 3 when telling about their discoveries.

Answers will vary.

Fondo cultural Standards: 1.1, 1.2, 3.1, 5.2

Resources: Voc. & Gram. Transparencies 17 (map); Practice Answers on Transparencies

Suggestions: After students read the information, show *Vocabulary and Grammar Transparency* 17. Ask a volunteer to use the transparency to show the extent of the **Camino Inca** in relation to all of South America. Then ask comprehension questions such as: *¿Por qué recorren hoy en día muchos turistas el Camino Inca?*

Answers:
- Los incas construyeron tantos caminos para poder comunicarse con todas las ciudades de su imperio inmenso.
- Other answers will vary.

Chapter Project

Students can perform step 3 at this point. (For more information, see p. 292-a.)

 **Actividad 17 Gramática** **Hablar/Dibujar/GramActiva**

La misteriosa civilización

1 Imagina que eres un(a) arqueólogo(a) y te envían a trabajar a un lugar misterioso. En grupos pequeños, imaginen cómo fue su viaje. Respondan a las siguientes preguntas. Recuerden que van a inventar una civilización y que deben ser creativos al responder a las preguntas.

1. ¿Adónde fueron? *(desierto, montaña, bosque, mar, playa, etc.)* ¿En qué país estaba ese lugar?
2. ¿Encontraron ruinas? ¿Cómo eran?
3. ¿Qué objetos encontraron? ¿Qué forma tenían esos objetos?
4. ¿Qué estructuras encontraron? ¿Qué creen que representan?
5. ¿Cómo se imaginan que era la civilización? ¿Creen que la crearon extraterrestres?

2 Ahora, dibujen lo que sucedió en el viaje. Pueden ilustrar las respuestas a las preguntas anteriores.

3 Cada grupo debe contar su viaje a la clase mientras muestran los dibujos que hicieron. Los estudiantes deben responderles usando diferentes expresiones del recuadro de gramática de la página 306.

Modelo
Es imposible que las personas de esa civilización hayan sido extraterrestres porque los extraterrestres nunca dejan evidencia.

 **Fondo cultural**

El Camino Inca Antes de la llegada de los españoles, el imperio[1] inca iba desde lo que es hoy el norte de Chile hasta Colombia. Para poder comunicarse con todas las ciudades de este imperio tan inmenso, los incas construyeron más de 15,000 millas de caminos. El Camino Real, también llamado Camino Inca, va desde Colombia hasta Chile y tiene 3,250 millas de largo. (Es más largo que el camino más largo construido por los romanos, que iba desde Jerusalén hasta Escocia.) El camino pasa a través de montañas, selvas y desiertos, y llega a muchas de las antiguas ciudades del imperio.

Hoy en día, muchos turistas recorren[2] el Camino Inca para visitar las ruinas de ciudades como Machu Picchu y también para ver los impresionantes paisajes de la geografía de América del Sur.

[1] empire [2] travel (along)

Camino Inca a Machu Picchu

- ¿Por qué construyeron los incas tantos caminos? ¿Qué nos dice esto acerca de la civilización inca?
- ¿Te gustaría recorrer como turista el Camino Inca? ¿Por qué?
- ¿Qué sistema de caminos o carreteras conoces que se parezca al que construyeron los incas? ¿Para qué se construyó?

Universal Access

Students with Learning Difficulties
Provide questions for the last three bulleted items in *Actividad* 18 to guide students in looking for information. For the first of the questions, ask: *¿Qué dice la leyenda? ¿Hay diferentes versiones?* For the second, ask: *¿Qué parte de la leyenda está basada en la verdad? ¿Qué es todavía un misterio?* For the third, ask: *¿Qué crees tú?*

Advanced Learners
Have students read more about the Incan civilization in encyclopedias or on the Internet. Ask them to report two facts about the Incas not mentioned in the *Fondo cultural*.

Actividad 18
Leer/Escribir/Hablar

¿Cómo se explica?

¿Te has preguntado alguna vez sobre los misterios? En grupos de tres o cuatro estudiantes van a investigar y presentar ante la clase algunos misterios inexplicables del mundo.

1 Investiguen uno de los misterios que estudiaron en este capítulo u otros fenómenos inexplicables, como el monstruo de Loch Ness o el triángulo de las Bermudas. Deben:

- investigar en periódicos, revistas, libros o en la Red, cuándo, dónde y qué sucedió
- describir los cuentos populares y leyendas que haya sobre ese misterio
- incluir las explicaciones científicas
- dar la opinión que ustedes tienen sobre ese misterio

2 Luego, hagan una presentación a la clase. Incluyan todo lo que encontraron y sus opiniones. Pueden usar fotos o ilustraciones sacadas de periódicos, revistas o la Red.

Para decir más

el fantasma	*ghost*
el OVNI	*UFO*
la casa encantada	*haunted house*
el poltergeist	*poltergeist*
el amuleto	*amulet*

Actividad 19

Leer/Escribir

Machu Picchu

En 1911, el norteamericano Hiram Bingham descubrió unas ruinas en las montañas del Perú. Cuando se excavaron las estructuras cubiertas por la selva, se descubrió una ciudad maravillosa.

Conexiones La historia

Ubicado[1] a 2,400 metros sobre el nivel del mar, Machu Picchu es uno de los lugares más impresionantes del planeta. Esta ciudad de los incas, de casi un kilómetro de extensión, tenía aproximadamente 1,000 habitantes durante el siglo XV. Su diseño es extraordinario, y sus muros[2], acueductos y observatorios fueron perfectamente construidos sin usar ni cemento ni pegamento[3].

Machu Picchu es considerado uno de los monumentos arquitectónicos y arqueológicos más importantes del mundo, pero la historia y función de Machu Picchu siguen siendo un misterio. Algunos creen que era una fortaleza; otros creen que era un monasterio.

_____
1 located **2** walls **3** glue

- ¿Por qué es un fenómeno arquitectónico Machu Picchu?
- ¿Qué se cree que era la función de Machu Picchu?
- Si los incas vivían en el siglo XV, ¿por qué crees que no se descubrieron las ruinas hasta 1911?

Más práctica
Practice Workbook 7-5, 7-6, 7-7

Go Online
PHSchool.com

For: Practice with the subjunctive with expressions of doubt
Visit: www.phschool.com
Web Code: jed-0703

Actividad 18
Standards: 1.2, 1.3, 3.1

Focus: Using learned vocabulary and structures to research and report

Suggestions: Encourage students to do the initial research on their own. They can then work together to compile their notes, work them into a report, and decide which visuals to use and how to most effectively use them.

Answers will vary.

Actividad 19
Standards: 1.1, 1.2, 2.1, 3.1, 5.2

Resources: Practice Answers on Transparencies

Focus: Practicing new vocabulary and structures through reading and discussion

Suggestions: Once students have read the information silently, ask comprehension questions before moving on to the discussion questions. For example: *¿Qué palabra en la primera frase es un sinónimo de "encontrado"? (Ubicado) Esta palabra nombra una estructura que se parece a un puente para el agua. ¿Qué palabra es? (el acueducto)*

Answers:
- Es un fenómeno arquitectónico porque sus muros, acueductos y observatorios fueron perfectamente construidos sin cemento ni pegamento.
- Algunos creen que era una fortaleza; otros creen que era un monasterio.
- Answers will vary.

Additional Resources
- Writing, Audio & Video Workbook: Cap. 7, Writing Activities 7–9
- Resource Book: Cap. 7, Communicative Activity BLM

Assessment
- Prueba 7-3: *El presente y el presente perfecto del subjuntivo con expresiones de duda*
- Examen: Vocabulario y gramática 1

311

A primera vista 2

Vocabulario y gramática en contexto

Read, listen to, and understand information about
- myths and legends
- contributions from ancient civilizations

¿Cómo se explican los misterios del mundo?

En el mundo de hoy, los científicos desarrollan **teorías** para explicar **cualquier** fenómeno natural. En tiempos antiguos, la gente contaba cuentos para explicar los misterios del **universo** y los fenómenos de la naturaleza. Con el tiempo estos relatos se desarrollaron en **leyendas**, cuentos exagerados basados en personajes o temas históricos. También se crearon **mitos** para explicar los fenómenos de la naturaleza. Los mitos y las leyendas llegaron a formar parte de la cultura de los pueblos.

Uno de estos pueblos, los aztecas, tenía **creencias** muy interesantes para explicar fenómenos naturales como las inundaciones, el fuego y **el origen** del día y de la noche. Es importante comprender que los aztecas tenían muchos **dioses**: un dios del conocimiento y la civilización llamado Quetzalcóatl, un dios de la lluvia, una diosa del agua y una diosa del maíz. Los dioses eran una parte fundamental de la cultura azteca.

312 **trescientos doce**
A primera vista 2

Universal Access

Students with Learning Difficulties
Before students begin to read, draw their attention to the boldface words in the text. Remind them that these are all vocabulary words that are listed at the end of the chapter. Encourage students to refer to the chapter vocabulary list as they read, if necessary.

Advanced Learners
On note cards or slips of paper, write several terms, such as ***Quetzalcóatl, el mito de la luna,*** and ***la creación del sol.*** Once students have read the selection, have them close their books. Place the cards or slips in a container and have students take turns drawing one at a time and explaining it in their own words.

Así es cómo los aztecas explicaban el origen del día y de la noche . . .

"Todos los dioses querían ser el centro del universo, y por eso compitieron varias veces para **convertirse** en el sol. Durante estos **intentos**, destruyeron a **los habitantes** de **la Tierra** con inundaciones y fuego. El último intento tuvo lugar en Teotihuacán, la ciudad **sagrada** de los dioses. Allí, uno de los dioses saltó al fuego y se convirtió en el sol. Pero el sol no se movía. Entonces, los demás dioses **se arrojaron** al fuego y el sol pudo moverse por el cielo."

Con estos actos, según los aztecas, también se crearon la luna y las estrellas, **o sea que** nacieron el día y la noche.

Así es cómo los aztecas explicaban por qué la luna tiene sombras . . .

"Cuando el sol **apareció**, también apareció la luna. Los dioses se enojaron porque la luna **brillaba** tanto como el sol. Así que le arrojaron **un conejo** a la luna para cubrir su luz."

Según los aztecas, esto explica por qué alguna gente puede ver la imagen de un conejo en la luna.

 20 Escuchar . . . .

¿Cómo se explica?

Escribe en una hoja los números del 1 al 6. Escucha las frases. Escribe *C* (cierto) o *F* (falso) para cada frase.

 **21** Leer . . . .

¿Cómo se creó el sol según los aztecas?

Según el relato azteca del origen del mundo, ¿en qué orden sucedieron los siguientes sucesos? Numéralos del 1 al 5.

- Como el sol no se movía, los otros dioses se arrojaron al fuego.
- Uno de los dioses saltó al fuego y salió el sol.
- Los dioses destruyeron a los habitantes de la Tierra.
- Los dioses se reunieron en el sitio sagrado de Teotihuacán.
- Se crearon la luna, el día, la noche y las estrellas.

 20   *Standards:* 1.2, 2.1, 2.2, 3.1

Resources: Audio Program: CD Cap. 7, Track 9; Resource Book: Cap. 7, Audio Script; Practice Answers on Transparencies

Focus: Practicing listening comprehension of new vocabulary

Suggestions: Before engaging students in the listening activity, give them a few minutes to read the information on these two pages silently and address any comprehension problems they may still have. Then play the *Audio CD* or read from the script. Allow students to listen more than once.

Answers:

1. C	4. F
2. F	5. C
3. C	6. F

Extension: Have students correct the answers they marked *falso.* Have them do so by first making the original statement negative, then stating the correct fact: *En los mitos no se explicaban el arte y la cultura de la civilización. Explicaban los fenómenos naturales.*

 21   *Standards:* 1.2, 2.2, 3.1

Resources: Practice Answers on Transparencies

Focus: Practicing reading comprehension and writing of new vocabulary

Suggestions: If students have difficulty ordering the events, model for them how to scan the text on these two pages in order to reference each event.

Answers:

4
3
1
2
5

Enriching Your Teaching

Teacher-to-Teacher

Some students may be curious about the notion of the rabbit in the moon. Invite them to share their background knowledge about moon lore, such as the man in the moon or the moon being made of green cheese. Encourage students to use a visual to show the position of the rabbit in the moon, and to look for it during the next full moon.

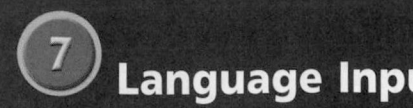

Vocabulario y gramática

Presentation

Standards: 1.1, 1.2, 3.1, 5.2

Resources: Voc. & Gram. Transparencies: 144–145; Resource Book: Cap. 7, Input Script; Audio Program: CD Cap. 7, Track 10

Focus: Extending presentation of vocabulary and grammar in context

Suggestions:

Pre-reading: Ask a volunteer to read aloud the main title. Say: *El título principal nos dice que esta lectura se trata de los mitos de dos culturas. ¿Cuáles son las dos culturas que van a compararse? (los mayas y los aztecas)* Point out new vocabulary items that are cognates: *astrónomos, planetas, eclipses,* and *símbolos.*

Reading: Allow students time to read the information on this page and the next silently first. Then play the *Audio CD* or read the text and have students read along as they listen. Allow them to listen more than once. Demonstrate the meaning of *al igual que* by saying *Al igual que inglés, Uds. también hablan español.* Ask students what verb they think the noun *escritura* comes from *(escribir).*

Post-reading: Check comprehension by asking questions. See the Input Script in the *Teacher's Resource Book* for specific questions.

Los mayas y los aztecas

Los mayas y los aztecas eran dos pueblos que existían en México y Centroamérica cuando llegaron los españoles en el siglo XV. Las dos culturas **contribuyeron** mucho a la civilización mundial de hoy.

Algunos símbolos de la escritura azteca

La escritura y los números

Hoy día, es común que las lenguas *(languages)* del mundo se hablen y se escriban. Pero no ha sido siempre así. Los mayas desarrollaron un sistema de **escritura** que expresaba la lengua que hablaban. Este sistema tenía cerca de 800 **símbolos.** La lengua de los mayas se habla todavía en partes de México y Centroamérica.

La escritura de los aztecas mezclaba dibujos y símbolos. Por ejemplo, el número cinco era el dibujo de una mano, porque la mano tiene cinco dedos.

"El Castillo," un templo maya sobre una pirámide en Chichén Itzá en México

Los templos

Templo azteca

Los mayas y los aztecas tenían pirámides como parte de su cultura. Como los dioses eran muy importantes, las dos civilizaciones construyeron sus templos sobre las pirámides.

Universal Access

Heritage Language Learners

Have students use the Internet to learn more about one of the topics presented in the reading. Invite them to present their findings orally to the class.

Students with Learning Difficulties

Read the introductory paragraph. Then draw students' attention to *Actividad* 22 and the chart that they will fill out after they read. Have students look at the headings in the reading and help them decide in which section they will probably find each piece of information.

Los números y el calendario

Los mayas fueron grandes matemáticos. Descubrieron el concepto del cero, un concepto fundamental en las matemáticas que usamos hoy día. Los aztecas, **al igual que** los mayas, eran grandes **astrónomos.** Los mayas observaron los movimientos del Sol desde que salía por la mañana hasta que **se ponía** por la noche. No sólo estudiaron el Sol, **sino también** las estrellas, **los planetas** y la Luna.

Observatorio "El Caracol (snail)" en la ciudad maya de Chichén Itzá

Calendario azteca, también llamado, "Piedra del Sol"

Los mayas y los aztecas tenían dos calendarios distintos. Uno, el sagrado, estaba basado en los dioses y la religión. El otro era como el que usamos nosotros, basado en el año solar de 365 días. Los mayas no sabían cómo ocurrían **los eclipses,** pero creían que cuando el Sol estaba oscuro era porque los dioses estaban enojados.

Escribir
22

¿Con qué contribuyeron?

Después de leer la información de estas páginas, completa el cuadro sobre lo que contribuyeron los mayas y los aztecas.

● **Más práctica**
Practice Workbook, 7-8, 7-9

	Mayas	Aztecas
Astronomía		
Calendario		
Escritura		
Números		
Templos		

Go Online
PHSchool.com

For: Vocabulary practice
Visit: www.phschool.com
Web Code: jed-0706

---

22 *Standards:* 1.2

Resources: Practice Answers on Transparencies

Focus: Practicing writing of new vocabulary and structures

Suggestions: Some students may prefer to complete the chart on their own, while others will prefer to work in pairs. Suggest that students paraphrase their answers, instead of copying word for word from the reading.

Answers:

Mayas
Estudiaron los movimientos de las estrellas, los planetas, el Sol y la Luna.
Crearon dos calendarios, uno de los cuales es muy parecido al nuestro.
Desarrollaron un sistema con cerca de 800 símbolos.
Usaron el cero por primera vez.
Construyeron sus templos sobre las pirámides.

Aztecas
Eran grandes astrónomos.
Tenían dos calendarios, uno solar y otro de los dioses.
Su escritura mezclaba dibujos y símbolos.
Representaban sus números con dibujos.
Construyeron sus templos sobre las pirámides.

Additional Resources
• Resource Book: Cap. 7, Clip Art

✓ **Assessment**
• Prueba 7-4: Vocabulary recognition

Enriching Your Teaching

Culture Note

The Temple of Kukulkán (plumed serpent god) is the most important structure at Chichén Itzá. The pyramid preserves information about the Mayan calendar. Each of its four sides has 91 steps, which, with the common platform at the top, add up to 365, the number of days in a year. On each side the stairs separate nine terraces into 18 parts, representing the 18 months of the Mayan calendar. Twice a year the pyramid's alignment provides a unique display. Each equinox, the sun hits the steps and creates a shadow that resembles a snake's body slithering down the pyramid; Kukulkán's head rests at the base of the stairs, completing the illusion.

315

Resources: Practice Answers on Transparencies

Focus: Demonstrating comprehension of new vocabulary

Suggestions: At first glance, students may think there is more than one correct answer for some the items. Encourage them to scan the entire activity first and to use the process of elimination to determine which one answer is best for each item.

Answers:

1. leyendas
2. astrónomo
3. dioses
4. eclipse
5. conejo
6. símbolos

Resources: Practice Answers on Transparencies

Focus: Practicing new vocabulary in a word-choice exercise

Suggestions: Encourage students to scan the complete paragraph before they attempt to write their answers.

Answers:

1. se movían
2. planeta
3. dios
4. símbolos
5. creencia
6. habitantes

Manos a la obra 2

Vocabulario y gramática en uso

Actividad 23 Leer ·

Un poco de todo . . .

Completa las siguientes frases con las palabras del recuadro.

conejo	dioses	leyendas	eclipse	astrónomo	símbolos

1. Los aztecas crearon _____ para explicar el origen del universo.
2. El _____ estudia los planetas y las estrellas desde el observatorio.
3. Las civilizaciones antiguas creían en muchos _____.
4. Durante un _____, la Luna cubre el Sol y la Tierra se queda a oscuras.
5. En la Luna se puede observar la imagen de un _____.
6. La escritura maya tiene una gran cantidad de _____.

Actividad 24 Leer ·

El calendario azteca

Completa este párrafo con la palabra correcta que describe el calendario azteca.

El calendario azteca fue uno de los objetos más importantes de esa cultura. No sólo mostraba los días, sino que mostraba cómo __1.__ *(se movían / se convertían)* el Sol, la Luna y el __2.__ *(estrella / planeta)* Venus. El calendario es una piedra muy grande en forma de círculo y pesa 20 toneladas. En su centro está la cara de Tonatiuh, el __3.__ *(conejo / dios)* del sol que, rodeada[1] por otros __4.__ *(símbolos / mitos)*, representa el universo. Los aztecas tenían la __5.__ *(creencia / línea)* de que para mantener el orden del sistema del universo debían hacer ciertas ceremonias. Por ejemplo, los antiguos __6.__ *(sistemas / habitantes)* de la Ciudad de México ponían el calendario en posición horizontal como si fuera un espejo del cielo.

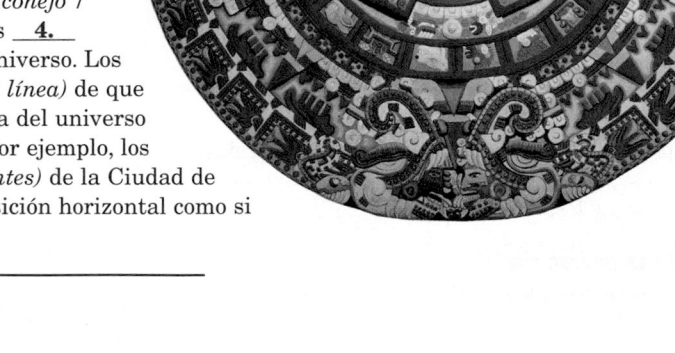

---

1 surrounded

Actividad 25 — Hablar

Según la leyenda . . .

Trabaja con tu compañero(a) para hablar sobre lo que están aprendiendo de las civilizaciones antiguas. Sigue el modelo.

Estudiante A

Según una leyenda/un mito/una creencia . . .

1. los dioses hacían muchos intentos para convertirse en el sol
2. unos extraterrestres trazaron las líneas de Nazca
3. los dioses se enojaron porque la luna brillaba tanto como el sol
4. los eclipses ocurrían cuando los dioses estaban enojados
5. los extraterrestres existían en los tiempos de los mayas
6. Atlántida fue una gran civilización en el Mediterráneo
7. Machu Picchu fue un centro comercial importante

Modelo

A —*Según una leyenda mexicana, dos volcanes eran antes unos novios, ¿no?*

B —*Sí, se casaron contra los deseos de sus padres.*

Estudiante B

la erupción de un volcán causó su destrucción

los científicos no están seguros del origen de estas ruinas

las trazaron para saber dónde aterrizar (land) sus naves espaciales

mientras, los habitantes de la Tierra fueron destruidos con inundaciones y fuego

le arrojaron un conejo para hacer sombra y cubrir su luz

cubrían la luz del sol con la luna

un dibujo que se encontró en Palenque representa una nave espacial

En voz alta

En México, muchos escritores contemporáneos de ascendencia maya están escribiendo en el idioma nativo de sus antepasados[1]. Lo hacen para mantener vivos su idioma y su cultura y para conservar los cuentos y las creencias que antes se trasmitían sólo por tradición oral.

Feliciano Sánchez Chan nació en el pequeño poblado de Xaya, Tekax, Yucatán, en 1960. Sus obras "Retazos[2] de vida" y "X-Marcela" han sido premiadas en concursos de literatura de la lengua maya.

Escucha el poema de Sánchez Chan y trata de repetirlo en voz alta.

• Nombra tres elementos naturales que se mencionan en el poema. ¿Crees que es importante la naturaleza en la cultura del poeta? ¿Por qué?

---

1 ancestors 2 snippets

Sueño cuarto (la luz)

de Feliciano Sánchez Chan

**Soy el trueno que ha venido
con su luz
de eternas profundidades
para alumbrar[3] el camino blanco
por donde transitan tus hijos, Madre.**

. . .

**El señor fuego es mi hermano mayor.
Hoy he venido
con mis cuatro hermanas:
la lluvia del oriente[4],
la lluvia del poniente[5],
la lluvia del norte
y la lluvia del sur.**

. . .

¿Recuerdas?

In Spanish the diphthong *ue* is pronounced "we" as in "wet." Read and pronounce: *trueno, fuego.*

---

3 to light 4 east 5 west

 Actividad 25 *Standards:* 1.1, 1.2

Resources: Practice Answers on Transparencies

Focus: Practicing new vocabulary and structures via note-taking and discussion

Suggestions: Explain that Student B must read to determine the correct cue and adapt it for his or her response.

Answers will vary. The following answers show the relationship between the comments of both partners:

1. A —Según una leyenda azteca, los dioses hacían muchos intentos para convertirse en el sol.
   B —Sí, y mientras, los habitantes de la Tierra fueron destruidos con inundaciones y fuego.
2. A —Según poca/mucha gente, unos extraterrestres trazaron….
   B —Sí, las trazaron para saber….
3. A —Según un mito azteca, los dioses se enojaron….
   B —Sí, por eso le arrojaron un conejo….
4. A —Según los mayas, los eclipses ocurrían cuando….
   B —Sí, pero nosotros sabemos que cubrían….
5. A —Según mucha gente, los extraterrestres existían….
   B —Sí, porque un dibujo….
6. A —Según poca/mucha gente, Atlántida fue una gran civilización….
   B —Sí, pero la erupción de un volcán….
7. A —Según algunos arqueólogos, Machu Picchu fue….
   B —Sí, pero los científicos no están….

En voz alta

Presentation

Standards: 1.2, 1.3, 2.1, 2.2, 3.1, 3.2, 5.2

Resources: Audio Program: Cap. 7, Track 11; Practice Answers on Transparencies

Suggestions: Have students practice reciting with a partner first, then ask volunteers to recite the poem fragment for the class.

Answers:

• el trueno, la luz, la lluvia; Remainder of answer will vary.

Chapter Project

Students can perform step 4 at this point. Be sure they understand your corrections and suggestions. (For more information, see p. 292-a.)

Actividad 26

Standards: 1.3, 3.1

Focus: Practicing writing new vocabulary

Suggestions: Remind students that they are to use their imaginations. Their explanations might resemble those in Mayan or Aztec legends, but they should invent their own.

Common Errors: Students will sometimes confuse *por qué* and *porque.* Remind them that the first is a question and the second an answer. Point out that they can use the accent mark in *por qué* as a reminder, since they know that accent marks appear in question words.

Answers will vary.

Actividad 27

Standards: 1.2, 1.3, 2.1, 2.2, 3.1, 3.2, 5.2

Resources: Practice Answers on Transparencies

Focus: Demonstrating comprehension of new vocabulary and structures through reading and response

Suggestions: Have students read through the legend once on their own, then a second time with a partner. During the second reading, partners can help each other with difficult words or sentences.

Answers:
1. Quetzal era el hijo del cacique de una tribu quiché. Chiruma era el hermano del cacique (el tío de Quetzal).
2. Chiruma le robó la pluma de colibrí que lo protegía.
3. La pluma de colibrí es un símbolo de la buena suerte.
4. Quetzal se convirtió en un hermoso pájaro.

Additional Resources

- Writing, Audio & Video Workbook: Cap. 7, Audio Activity 3, Track 12
- Writing, Audio & Video Workbook: Cap. 7, Writing Activity 10
- Resource Book: Cap. 7, Communicative Activity BLM

Assessment

- Prueba 7-5: Vocabulary production

Actividad 26 Escribir

Mitos y leyendas

En los mitos y las leyendas la gente inventa razones para explicar ciertas cosas. Usa tu imaginación para escribir una frase sobre seis de los siguientes fenómenos de la naturaleza. Explica por qué . . .

Modelo

. . . hay truenos
Hay truenos porque los dioses están tocando los tambores.

1. . . . cae lluvia
2. . . . hace viento
3. . . . se pone el sol
4. . . . ocurre un eclipse
5. . . . aparecen sombras
6. . . . brillan las estrellas
7. . . . salta un conejo
8. . . . el agua se convierte en hielo

Actividad 27 Leer/Escribir

Una leyenda quiché

Lee esta leyenda de los indígenas quichés de Guatemala sobre el pájaro quetzal, símbolo de la libertad y nombre de su moneda.

Quetzal nunca muere

Quetzal era el hijo del cacique[1] de una tribu[2] quiché[3]. Todos los habitantes lo admiraban y sabían que un día Quetzal se iba a convertir en el jefe de la tribu. Pero Chiruma, el hermano del cacique, estaba celoso de Quetzal.

Cuando Quetzal fue mayor, el adivino[4] le dijo: "No morirás nunca, Quetzal. Vivirás eternamente." Durante una lucha contra otra tribu, Chiruma se dio cuenta de que las flechas[5] que le arrojaban a Quetzal nunca lo herían[6]. Entonces Chiruma pensó que debía tener un amuleto. Esa noche, cuando Quetzal dormía, Chiruma entró en su cuarto y descubrió al lado de Quetzal una pluma de colibrí[7]. Recordó que el colibrí era un símbolo de la buena suerte[8] y robó la pluma.

Cuando murió el cacique, los ancianos escogieron a Quetzal para ser el nuevo jefe. Un día Quetzal caminaba por el bosque cuando de repente apareció un colibrí. El colibrí le dijo a Quetzal: "Soy tu protector y vengo a decirte que alguien quiere matarte".

De pronto oyó un silbido[9] y una flecha penetró en su pecho. Quetzal cayó sobre la hierba[10] verde y murió. Pero los dioses, que habían predicho una vida eterna, lo convirtieron en un hermoso pájaro. Su cuerpo tomó el color del césped, su pecho conservó el color de la sangre y el sol puso en su larga cola[11] muchos colores.

---

1 chief 2 tribe 3 indigenous people of Guatemala 4 fortune-teller 5 arrows 6 wounded 7 hummingbird's feather 8 luck 9 whistling sound 10 grass 11 tail

¿Comprendiste?

1. ¿Quién es Quetzal? ¿Quién es Chiruma?
2. ¿Qué hizo Chiruma para vengarse *(get revenge)* cuando no lo escogieron para ser el cacique de la tribu?
3. ¿Qué representa el símbolo de la pluma de colibrí?
4. ¿En qué se convirtió Quetzal?

318 trescientos dieciocho
Manos a la obra 2

Universal Access

Heritage Language Learners
Encourage students to read Spanish-language materials recreationally for at least five to ten minutes per day. Allow them to read a book, magazine, or a newspaper of their choice. As students learn to enjoy reading recreationally in Spanish, they will improve their academic reading skills as well.

Multiple Intelligences
Verbal/Linguistic: Challenge students to pronounce the names of the Aztec gods in the Nahuatl language. When the letters *tl* occur together, they are pronounced as a single consonant, but not as a separate syllable (there is no vowel sound). Have students produce the sound by saying "nightly" without the final /i/ sound.

Gramática

Pero y sino

The word *pero* is usually the equivalent of the English conjunction *but*. However, there is another word in Spanish, *sino*, that also means *but*. *Sino* is used after a negative, in order to offer the idea of an alternative: not this, *but rather* that.

No voy a beber jugo de frutas **sino** agua.

• You can also use *sino* with *no sólo. . . sino también. . . (not only . . . but also)*

Apareció **no sólo** el sol **sino también** la luna.

• You use *sino que* instead of *sino* when there is a conjugated verb in the second part of the sentence.

No vendí mis libros **sino que** los regalé.

 Gramática **Leer**

¿Qué dice el artículo?

Imagina que estás leyendo diferentes noticias y artículos. Decide si la palabra que completa cada frase es *pero* o *sino*.

1. Hizo varios intentos por convertirse en astrónomo _____ no lo consiguió.
2. No construirán un nuevo observatorio _____ que repararán el viejo.
3. No sólo se ven sombras en la luna _____ también figuras oscuras.
4. Creía que el lugar era sagrado _____ ahora no estoy seguro.
5. Según la creencia, no fue un solo dios _____ todos.
6. Tenían no sólo información _____ también evidencia importante.

 Gramática  **Leer/Hablar**

Dioses de los aztecas

Lee la lista de los dioses de los aztecas. Trabaja con otro(a) compañero(a) para hacer frases sobre los dioses usando *sino* y *pero*.

Modelo

Quetzalcóatl no sólo era el dios del conocimiento sino también de la civilización. Era el dios de la civilización pero no el dios del fuego.

Los DIOSES importantes de los AZTECAS

Coatlicue– La primera diosa: creó la Luna y las estrellas

Huitzilopochtli– Dios de la guerra y el Sol

Quetzalcóatl– Dios del conocimiento y la civilización

Mictantecuhtle– Dios de los muertos

Ehecatl– Dios del viento

Tláloc– Dios de la lluvia

Xiuhtecuhtle– Dios del fuego

● **Más práctica**
Practice Workbook 7-10

Go Online
PHSchool.com

For: Practice with *pero* and *sino*
Visit: www.phschool.com
Web Code: jed-0707

 Gramática

Presentation

Standards: 4.1

Resources: Voc. & Gram. Transparencies: 146

Suggestions: Provide students with pairs of cues and ask them to make sentences like the models shown in the *Gramática*. Tell them to make their sentences using past tenses. For example **ver la película en el cine/verla en casa**: *No vi la película en el cine, sino que la vi en casa.*

 Standards: 1.2

Resources: Practice Answers on Transparencies

Focus: Using *pero* and *sino* in a word-choice exercise

Suggestions: Remind students that *no sólo* in the first part of a sentence is a hint telling them that they must use *sino también* in the second part.

Answers:

1. pero   4. pero
2. sino   5. sino
3. sino   6. sino

 Standards: 1.2, 2.2, 3.1

Focus: Using *pero* and *sino* in written sentences

Suggestions: Invite pairs of students to share their sentences with others. Encourage them to turn the sharing into a conversation by asking each other questions about the gods:

A —¿Tláloc era el dios del sol?

B —Tláloc no era el dios del sol, sino de la lluvia.

Answers will vary.

Additional Resources

• Writing, Audio & Video Workbook: Cap. 7, Writing Activity 11

 Assessment

• Prueba 7-6: *Pero y sino*

Enriching Your Teaching

Teacher-to-Teacher

When talking about ancient Latin American civilizations, many unusual words appear, such as the names of the gods mentioned in *Actividad* 29. Point out that, since these names come from ancient languages, the spellings that we see are inventions by Spanish speakers who used the Spanish alphabet. Help students apply the Spanish phonics skills they have developed. Ask them to sound out the words syllable by syllable using Spanish sounds.

Practice and Communicate

Gramática

Presentation

Resources: Voc. & Gram. Transparencies: 147

Suggestions: By now, students have seen enough uses for the subjunctive to be able to begin to make subtle associations regarding its meaning. Ask them to give English equivalents for the Spanish models in the *Gramática*. Point out that the subjunctive mood often has the connotation of hypothesis, which can be translated by the English auxiliary verb "might." For this reason, *Busco un libro que tenga un artículo sobre los mayas* can be translated to "I'm looking for a book that might have an article about the Maya."

30 Standards: 1.2

Resources: Practice Answers on Transparencies

Focus: Practicing the subjunctive in adjective clauses

Suggestions: Remind students that the subjunctive is used when referring to something that only hypothetically exists. This is true when we refer to things we haven't found or aren't sure of yet. Once we begin talking about something or someone we definitely know of, we use the indicative.

Answers:

1. sea
2. hace
3. tiene
4. sepa
5. pueda
6. guste
7. sirva

Additional Resources

- Writing, Audio & Video Workbook: Cap. 7, Audio Activity 4, Track 13

Gramática

El subjuntivo en cláusulas adjetivas

Sometimes you use an entire clause to describe a noun. This is called an adjective clause.

- When you have a specific person or thing in mind, you use the indicative.

  Este libro tiene un artículo **que habla** sobre los mayas.

- If you don't have a specific person or thing in mind, or if you are not sure the person exists, you use the subjunctive. Sometimes *cualquier(a)* is used in these expressions.

  Busco un libro **que tenga** un artículo sobre los mayas.
  Escoge **cualquier** cosa **que te guste**.

- You also use the subjunctive in an adjective clause when it describes a negative word such as *nadie, nada,* or *ninguno(a)*.

  No hay **nadie que conozca** los símbolos aztecas.

To refer to something or someone unknown in the past, you can use the present perfect subjunctive.

  Busco una joven **que haya estudiado** arqueología.
  No hay nadie **que haya visto** un extraterrestre.

30 Gramática Leer

El proyecto sobre culturas antiguas

Un grupo de estudiantes va a hacer un proyecto para representar algunos aspectos artísticos de las culturas antiguas. Están tratando de decidir a quiénes y qué necesitan para hacer su proyecto. Completa las siguientes frases con el presente del subjuntivo o del indicativo.

—Necesitamos encontrar a un estudiante que __1.__ *(ser)* muy artístico para hacer dibujos de los dioses.

—Pues, yo conozco a una chica que siempre __2.__ *(hacer)* dibujos muy bonitos en su cuaderno durante mi clase de inglés.

—Fernando compró un libro que __3.__ *(tener)* unos diseños de la Pirámide del sol. Podemos hacer un modelo de ella. ¿Conocemos a alguien que __4.__ *(saber)* hacer construcciones de cerámica?

—No puedo pensar en ningún estudiante que __5.__ *(poder)* hacer un modelo de la pirámide.

—El calendario azteca es fascinante. Podemos dibujarlo y pintarlo usando cualquier sistema de colores que nos __6.__ *(gustar)*.

—Buena idea. Vamos a buscar un dibujo o una foto que nos __7.__ *(servir)* de modelo.

320 **trescientos veinte**
Manos a la obra 2

Universal Access

Students with Learning Difficulties

Review how to form the present subjunctive and give examples: 1) form the first person singular in the present tense: *hablo, vengo;* 2) take away **o**: *habl-, veng-;* 3) add "opposite" endings (**-e** for **-ar** verbs and **a** for **-er** and **-ir** verbs): *hable, venga;* 4) make verbs agree with subjects: *que yo hable, que ella venga.*

Advanced Learners

Have students write three sentences that set up a situation in which there is a need. Have them trade sentences with a partner, who then makes a suggestion: A —*Tengo que hacer una investigación sobre el calendario azteca, pero no sé cómo empezar.* B —*Necesitas encontrar un sitio en el Internet que pueda ayudarte.*

Actividad 31 Gramática Leer/Escribir

Investigación sobre las culturas antiguas

Imagina que tienes que investigar acerca de las culturas antiguas. Usa tu imaginación y completa las frases usando la forma correcta del verbo. Añade detalles a cada frase.

Modelo

Busco una biblioteca que (estar). . .
Busco una biblioteca que esté cerca de mi casa.

1. Necesito un libro que (explicar). . .
2. Yo sé de un libro que (hablar). . .
3. No hay nadie que (conocer). . .
4. No hay nada que (decir). . .
5. Escogeré cualquier artículo que (gustar). . .
6. Quiero encontrar una página Web que (tener). . .
7. Mi amigo tiene varios artículos que (aparecer). . .
8. Tengo que hablar con las personas que (contribuir). . .

Actividad 32 Gramática  Hablar

¿A quién conoces que sepa . . . ?

Trabaja con otro(a) estudiante para identificar a personas de tu escuela o comunidad que hayan hecho o sepan hacer diferentes cosas.

Modelo

A —*¿Hay alguien en nuestra escuela que sepa hablar tres idiomas?*
B —*Sí, el padre de Berta sabe hablar español, italiano e inglés.*
o: —*No sé. No conozco a nadie que sepa hablar tres idiomas.*

Estudiante A

1. tener un coche deportivo
2. conocer a una persona famosa
3. haber ganado un campeonato de deportes
4. ser actor / actriz de cine
5. haber vivido en un país extranjero por más de un año
6. contribuir su tiempo como voluntario(a)

Estudiante B

¡Respuesta personal!

trescientos veintiuno **321**
Capítulo 7

Practice and Communicate ⑦

Actividad 31 Standards: 1.2, 1.3

Resources: Practice Answers on Transparencies

Focus: Practicing the subjunctive in adjective clauses

Suggestions: Remind students to stay within the context of the research project that is set up in the instructions. All of their completed sentences should make sense within that context.

Answers:
Wording of sentences will vary. Students will use the following verb forms:

1. explique
2. habla
3. conozca
4. diga
5. guste
6. tenga
7. aparecen
8. contribuyen

Actividad 32 Standards: 1.1

Resources: Practice Answers on Transparencies

Focus: Practicing the subjunctive in adjective clauses

Suggestions: Point out that since Student A is asking if a certain kind of person exists, that person is only hypothetical, and so the subjunctive must be used in the question. If Student B doesn't know of anyone, then such a person remains hypothetical and the subjunctive continues to be used.

Answers:
Students will choose from among the following verb forms. Student A will always use the subjunctive in the question. Student B will use the indicative if he or she knows of a particular person, and the subjunctive if not.

1. tenga/tiene
2. conozca/conoce
3. haya ganado/ha ganado
4. sea/es
5. haya vivido/ha vivido (vivió)
6. contribuya/contribuye

Enriching Your Teaching

Teacher-to-Teacher

Students tend to have difficulty understanding the subjunctive since it has all but disappeared in English. Point out that it did once exist in English, however. Give them the example "If I were you…." Since the situation is hypothetical, we don't use the indicative "am." Instead, "were" acts as a vestige of the old English subjunctive. British English retains a few other vestiges of the subjunctive. When referring to something that may or may not happen (again, a hypothetical situation), British people often use "should" to indicate the subjunctive mood: "I think it should be quite nice if you phoned me sometime."

321

Rapid Review
Briefly review with students vocabulary associated with jobs and job qualifications. This can be found in the *A ver si recuerdas* and *A primera vista* sections of *Capítulos* 5 and 6.

Actividad 33 *Standards:* 1.1, 1.3

Focus: Practicing the subjunctive in adjective clauses

Suggestions: Remind students to use the subjunctive in an adjective clause that modifies someone or something that they are searching for. If an adjective clause modifies something that is already known about, such as a course or a facility at a school, they must use the indicative.

Answers will vary.

El español en el mundo del trabajo

Presentation

Standards: 1.2, 5.1

Suggestions: Once students have read the information, ask comprehension questions. For example: *¿Para qué profesiones dan cursos en español?* **(diferentes profesiones, incluyendo guías de turismo)** *En tus propias palabras, describe un paseo típico que da un profesor para guías de turismo.*

 **Gramática** **Escribir/Hablar** · · · · · · · · · · ·

Tu anuncio clasificado

1 Imagina que decides aprender otro idioma o cambiar de trabajo. Escribe un anuncio clasificado para el periódico solicitando un(a) maestro(a) o una escuela de idiomas o pidiendo trabajo.

Modelo

Busco una escuela de idiomas que dé clases de chino.

2 Ahora, trabaja con otro(a) estudiante para intercambiar los anuncios que hicieron. Cada uno(a) debe responder al anuncio con un mensaje breve.

Modelo

A — *Busco una escuela de idiomas que dé clases de chino.*
B — *Yo conozco una escuela que da clases de chino.*

El español en el mundo del trabajo

Antigua, en Guatemala, es una de las ciudades más bellas de América Latina. Está llena de bellos edificios y plazas coloniales. También hay muchas ruinas de edificios antiguos destruidos por los terremotos que ocurren en la región.

En esta ciudad se encuentra la Academia de Español de Guatemala. Allí se dan cursos de español especialmente diseñados para diferentes profesiones.

La escuela tiene un curso muy interesante para guías de turismo. Muchas veces, los estudiantes de este curso salen a pasear por la ciudad mientras el profesor les enseña todas las palabras que deben saber para describir los edificios y las ruinas. Estos estudiantes aprenden a usar el español para hacer un trabajo útil e interesante.

Una calle de Antigua

Universal Access

Heritage Language Learners
Encourage students to take on the role of editor in *Actividad* 35. As group members suggest potential phrases and sentences, heritage learners can offer more commonly used alternatives.

Students with Learning Difficulties
Remind students that in *Actividad* 33 they are composing an ad for a person or thing that they want to find. They can't be sure that the person or thing exists. So, as explained in the *Gramática* on p. 320, they need to put the verb in the subordinate clause in the subjunctive.

Actividad 34 **Escribir/Hablar** ....

Juego

❶ En grupos, piensen en algún programa de televisión, libro o película que trate sobre extraterrestres o fenómenos inexplicables. Completen una tabla como la siguiente sobre el programa, el libro o la película.

Nombre del programa, libro o película	
Argumento general	
Ejemplos de fenómenos inexplicables	
Personajes	
¿Dónde ocurre?	
¿Cuándo ocurre?	
¿Cuál es el final?	

El monstruo de Loch Ness

❷ Ahora, jueguen a adivinar qué programa de televisión, libro o película escogió cada grupo. Por turnos, cada grupo pasa al frente de la clase y relata de qué trata el programa, el libro o la película que escogió sin dar el título. Pero, para hacer el juego más divertido, tienen que cambiar uno de los elementos que pusieron en sus tablas. Por ejemplo, pueden cambiar el nombre de los personajes principales o el lugar donde ocurre la historia. Gana el grupo que haya adivinado más programas, libros o películas.

  Actividad 35 **Hablar/Escribir** ....

¿Recuerdas la leyenda?

Trabaja con un grupo para escribir con tus propias palabras una leyenda conocida.

❶ Escojan una leyenda que conozcan.

❷ Hagan una tabla con lo siguiente y complétenla con los datos de la leyenda que escogieron.

- el tema
- la situación
- los personajes
- el lugar y la época
- el conflicto
- cómo se resuelve el conflicto

❸ Escriban la leyenda. No se olviden de escribir el título.

❹ Pueden ilustrar la leyenda e incluir música.

Estrategia
Cooperative learning
You might assign roles to each member of the group. These roles might include:

- secretary
- editor
- illustrator
- story-teller / presenter

● **Más práctica** ....
Practice Workbook 7-11, 7-12

Go Online
PHSchool.com

For: Practice with the subjunctive with adjective clauses
Visit: phschool.com
Web Code: jed-0709

trescientos veintitrés **323**
Capítulo 7

 Enriching Your Teaching

Culture Note
When assigning *Actividad* 35, tell students an ancient Aztec legend called **La Llorona.** It is still told throughout Mexico and Guatemala today in several versions. Generally, the story is of a beautiful young woman who married a handsome man. They had two children, but eventually the man tired of the woman. The man continued to pay attention to his children but ignored his wife. The woman, crazed with jealousy, killed her children. Struck with remorse, she wandered the town at night, weeping and searching for her lost children. Parents warn their children that if they are out at night, the woman might mistake them for her own and take them away.

¡Adelante!

Puente a la cultura
Misterios del pasado

Estrategia

Using illustrations
You can preview what you are about to read by looking at the illustrations or photos that accompany the text. You can also look at the illustrations to locate details while reading. Before starting to read, look at the photos on these pages and make a prediction about what the text is about. After you finish reading, check if your prediction was right.

Cuando los europeos llegaron a América a partir de 1492, se encontraron con muchos pueblos indígenas. Hoy día no hay nadie que pueda explicar la desaparición de la cultura de algunos de estos pueblos.

La Isla de Pascua

En el medio del océano Pacífico se encuentra la Isla de Pascua, de unos 167 metros cuadrados. Allí se encuentran los moai, unas estatuas enormes de piedra que representan enormes cabezas con orejas largas y torsos pequeños. Se encuentran en toda la isla y miran hacia el cielo como esperando a algo o alguien. Pero la pregunta es ¿cómo las construyeron y las movieron los habitantes indígenas a la isla? Se sabe que no conocían ni el metal ni la rueda. Cuando se les pregunta a los habitantes de hoy cómo llegaron las estatuas al lugar, ellos responden: —¡A pie!

Muchos esperan que aparezca la verdad acerca de estas estatuas. Hay quienes dicen que las estatuas representan a los primeros habitantes de la isla, que creen que eran polinesios. Otros dicen que representan a los dioses y muchos creen que eran extraterrestres. Quizás algún día descubramos el misterio de esta pequeña isla.

Los moai en la Isla de Pascua

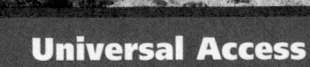

Universal Access

Heritage Language Learners

Invite students with exemplary pronunciation to read short sections aloud as a model of fluency and pronunciation.

Advanced Learners

Ask students to research one of the mysteries they read about in the *Puente a la cultura*. Have them present brief oral reports to the class about their chosen mystery.

Los olmecas

Más de 1,500 años antes de los mayas y 25 siglos antes de los aztecas existieron los olmecas, la primera gran civilización de Mesoamérica. Entre sus ruinas se descubrieron unas cabezas de piedra gigantes que no sólo miden entre dos o tres metros de alto sino que pesan entre 11 y 24 toneladas. Pero en esa zona de México no existen piedras tan grandes. Se supone que[1] los olmecas tuvieron que mover esas piedras más de 129 kilómetros. ¿Cómo lo hicieron? Es un misterio.

Cabeza olmeca

Las líneas de Nazca

En 1927, un arqueólogo que recorría[2] el sur de Perú observó unas largas líneas de muchas formas a los lados de la carretera. Observó las líneas desde una meseta, las dibujó en un papel y descubrió que un dibujo tenía la forma de un pájaro volando. Más tarde se encontraron en las Pampas de Nazca, al sur de Perú, más de 30 dibujos que representan animales y figuras geométricas y humanas. Lo interesante de estos dibujos es que las formas solamente pueden verse desde el aire. ¿Para qué servían las líneas? ¿Cómo se hicieron?

1 supposedly 2 travelled

¿Comprendiste?

1. ¿Qué son los moai? ¿Qué representan?
2. ¿Qué se descubrió entre las ruinas de los olmecas? ¿Por qué es un misterio?
3. ¿Qué descubrió un arqueólogo que recorría el sur de Perú?
4. ¿Qué representan los dibujos que forman las líneas de Nazca?
5. ¿Por qué es un misterio las líneas de Nazca?

Investiga

Busca en la biblioteca o en la Internet información sobre algún otro misterio del pasado, como el hombre de Palenque o la Atlántida. Escribe un pequeño párrafo que describa el misterio y tu opinión sobre el tema.

Líneas de Nazca

Go Online
PHSchool.com

For: Internet link activity
Visit: phschool.com
Web Code: jed-0710

trescientos veinticinco   325
Capítulo 7

¿Qué me cuentas?

Presentation

Standards: 1.1, 1.2, 1.3, 2.2, 3.1

Resources: Voc. & Gram. Transparencies 148;
Audio Program: CD Cap. 7, Track 15; Resource
Book: Cap. 7, Audio Script; Practice Answers on
Transparencies

Focus: Practicing speaking and listening
comprehension

Suggestions:

For step 1, use the *Audio CD* or read the
script aloud. Allow students to hear the
descriptions twice through: the first time
to write their answers and the second time
to check them.

In step 2, use guiding questions as
necessary in order to help students talk
about important details in the pictures. For
example: (picture 1) *¿Qué hacían los
muchachos?* (picture 2) *¿Qué vieron de
repente?* (picture 3) *¿Los muchachos se
escondieron o no?* (picture 4) *¿Quién
salió?* (picture 5) *¿Qué hicieron los
extraterrestres? ¿Quién los ayudaron?*
(picture 6) *¿Se puede explicar lo que hizo
la nave espacial cuando salió?*

Answers:
Step1
1. b   2. b   3. a   4. b   5. a   6. b

Steps 2–3
Answers will vary.

¿Qué me cuentas?

Ver para creer

1 🎧 Escucha las siguientes descripciones. Después de cada descripción, vas a oír
dos preguntas. Escoge la mejor respuesta para cada pregunta.

1. **a.** del descubrimiento de América
   b. de su último trabajo arqueológico en América Central

2. **a.** conocer a un grupo de arqueólogos
   b. las ruinas de un antiguo palacio olmeca

3. **a.** diseños geométricos y símbolos de soles y dioses
   b. dibujos de animales

4. **a.** Leyeron las notas que dejaron los olmecas.
   b. Midieron las piedras y calcularon su peso.

5. **a.** un hombre misterioso que apareció y les contó acerca de una leyenda
   b. que nadie sabía que esa estructura existiera

6. **a.** porque la leyenda decía que ese lugar no existía
   b. porque existía una leyenda y la creencia de que allí vivían extraterrestres

2 Las ilustraciones a continuación representan un cuento. Con tus propias
palabras, describe detalladamente lo que sucedió. Puedes usar las siguientes
palabras o expresiones para conectar tus ideas.

finalmente	después	entonces
mientras	más tarde	de repente

1

2

3

4

5

6

3 Trabaja con un grupo de estudiantes. Comparen los detalles de los
cuentos que escucharon. ¿Qué fue lo más interesante? ¿Qué fue lo más
extraño? ¿Y lo más misterioso?

**326   trescientos veintiséis
      ¡Adelante!**

Block Schedule

After completing *Ver para creer*, Step 2, ask
students to draw a 4- to 6-panel story
about extraterrestrials on Earth. Encourage
creativity! Then place students in groups of
four and have them talk about each
student's picture sequence. Have students
alternate telling about the story with each
student contributing one sentence at a time.

Universal Access

Heritage Language Learners
Have students periodically watch Spanish-
language television programs or videos so that
they also, along with their classmates, can
benefit from exposure to different accents and
language use.

Students with Learning Difficulties
Read the directions to the first task with students.
Emphasize that they will: 1) hear a description;
2) hear two questions; 3) choose *a* or *b* to
answer each question. Also before listening, have
students read each pair of possible answers to
help them focus on their listening task. Remind
them to listen for one of the two choices.

Tu descubrimiento científico

Tarea
Imagínate que eres un(a) científico(a), que creaste una teoría para explicar un fenómeno extraño y tienes que convencer *(convince)* a la clase de que tu explicación tiene sentido.

Prepárate Completa un organizador gráfico como éste sobre tu descubrimiento. Escribe en el rectángulo de la izquierda el nombre y una descripción del fenómeno inexplicable, y en los de la derecha, tus explicaciones de lo que sucedió. Puedes inventar el fenómeno y las teorías para tratar de explicarlo.

Fenómeno inexplicable: _____

Practica Vuelve a leer la información del organizador. Practica tu presentación para recordar los detalles. Puedes usar tus notas para practicar, pero no al hablar ante la clase. Recuerda:
- explicar claramente de qué fenómeno inexplicable estás hablando
- dar razones convincentes *(convincing)* que traten de explicarlo
- mirar directamente al público al hablar

Modelo
No hay nadie que haya descubierto qué les sucedió a los habitantes de la Atlántida. Yo creo que unos extraterrestres aparecieron en la Atlántida y se convirtieron en sus habitantes. Dudo que el clima les haya gustado, por eso se mudaron a un pueblo de Alaska.

Haz tu presentación Haz la presentación de forma convincente para que tus compañeros de clase entiendan el fenómeno y cómo se resuelve según tu teoría. Puedes acompañar tu presentación con un dibujo o un organizador gráfico sobre el fenómeno.

Evaluación Tu profesor(a) puede explicarte cómo va a evaluar tu presentación. Probablemente, para él (ella) es importante ver que:
- te preparaste bien para hacer tu presentación
- diste suficiente información a la clase
- usaste el vocabulario del capítulo

Estrategia
Maintaining your focus
It is important that when you are doing your speech you maintain your focus. Your focus is the message you want to communicate to your audience. Concentrate on the topic of your message and make sure that it is clearly understood by your audience. Avoid adding information not directly related to the topic that might interfere with the purpose of your speech.

Presentación oral
Presentation
Standards: 1.2, 1.3, 3.1

Resources: Voc. & Gram. Transparencies 12

Focus: Preparing and delivering an oral presentation

Suggestions: Review the task and the four-step approach with students. Review the rubric with the class (see *Assessment* below) to explain how you will grade the performance task. Before students begin, direct their attention to the *Estrategia*. Point out that the key to maintaining their focus in a speech or in writing is to organize their ideas first. This is what they should do in step 1. Show *Vocabulary and Grammar Transparency* 12 and have students create a similar chart on their own paper, leaving out the rectangle farthest to the right. Model how to fill in a sample mysterious phenomenon and at least one explanation it. Encourage students to use their imaginations to create their own explanations which, although they may be invented, should be plausible.

Portfolio
Record students' oral presentations on audiocassette or videotape for inclusion in their portfolios.

✓ Assessment
- Assessment Program: Cap. 7, Rubrics

Give students copies of the rubric before they begin the activity. Go over the descriptions of the different levels of performance. After assessing students, help individuals understand how their performance could be improved.

Enriching Your Teaching

RUBRIC	Score 1	Score 3	Score 5
How well you maintain your focus	Your theory is undeveloped. You miss important ideas.	You present a theory, but your ideas are disorganized.	Your theory is presented in a logical, organized way.
How convincing you are	Your supporting explanations are weak.	Your supporting explanations are somewhat convincing.	You use convincing explanations.
How effectively you deliver your speech	You read your speech and make no eye contact with your audience.	You make some eye contact and you use some intonation.	Your eye contact is good. Your intonation helps get the message across.

327

Presentación escrita

Presentation

Standards: 1.2, 1.3, 3.1

Resources: Voc. & Gram. Transparencies: 4

Focus: Combining learned vocabulary and structures in a written presentation

Suggestions: Begin by explaining the criteria you will use to evaluate students' compositions. (See step 5, *Evaluación,* in the Student Edition, and *Assessment* on the following page.)

Direct students' attention to the *Estrategia.* Point out that in *Capítulo* 7, they have learned how to use the present perfect subjunctive and **sino,** as well as the subjunctive in adjective clauses. All three of these are valuable tools they can use to combine sentences more effectively. Then show *Vocabulary & Grammar Transparency* 4. Fill in the left side of the chart on the transparency and model for students how to add one or two pieces of information to the right side when they create their own charts.

Language Arts Connection

Standards: 3.1

Remind students that the subjunctive usually occurs in complex sentences. Point out that the sentences in which they learned to use **sino** in this chapter are compound sentences. Ask them to use their knowledge from their Language Arts courses to talk about the differences between compound and complex sentences.

Presentación escrita

Tu leyenda

Objectives
- Write a legend about something or someone from the past
- Combine sentences in order to add interest to the story
- Add details in order to improve the story

Estrategia

Combining sentences
The paragraphs in your story may lose their impact if you use only short, choppy sentences. One way to improve the flow of your paragraphs is to combine sentences with conjunctions like *y, o,* or *pero.* For example, *"Todos los habitantes del pueblo conocen la leyenda pero ninguno habla de ella"* is more interesting than *"Todos los habitantes del pueblo conocen la leyenda. Ninguno habla de ella."* Likewise, *"El hombre no tenía ni familia ni amigos"* sounds better than *"El hombre no tenía familia. El hombre no tenía amigos."*

Ahora es tu turno de inventar una leyenda. Usa tu imaginación y escribe una leyenda acerca de algún personaje o lugar imaginario. Puedes también escribir acerca de alguna leyenda ya conocida pero añadiéndole detalles propios.

1 Antes de escribir

Responde a las preguntas como ayuda para encontrar ideas para tu leyenda.

- ¿En dónde ocurre la historia?
- ¿Quién o quiénes son los protagonistas de tu historia?
- ¿Cuál es el misterio o fenómeno inexplicable principal? ¿Qué sucede?
- ¿El misterio o fenómeno inexplicable se resuelve o tiene un final abierto?
- ¿Qué título tiene la leyenda?

Recuerda que una leyenda tiene la estructura de un cuento, es decir, una introducción, un desarrollo y un final. Completa una tabla como ésta para ordenar tus ideas sobre la leyenda que vas a escribir.

Título de la leyenda	La leyenda del extraterrestre del valle
Introducción	Un hombre estaba dando un paseo por el valle cuando de repente apareció un extraterreste . . .
Desarrollo	Se hicieron amigos y el hombre decidió acompañar al extraterrestre a su planeta . . .
Final	Nunca más se supo del hombre . . .

2 Borrador

Escribe tu borrador utilizando la información de la tabla. Recuerda que al escribir una leyenda debes añadir todos los detalles que sean posibles y combinar las oraciones para que los párrafos sean más interesantes. La leyenda debe ser misteriosa e interesante. No te olvides de usar el vocabulario y la gramática que aprendiste en este capítulo.

328 trescientos veintiocho
¡Adelante!

Universal Access

Heritage Language Learners
Before students write final drafts of their legends, have them proofread for correct use of accent marks. Review frequently misspelled words that have homonyms, such as **como/cómo, que/qué, se/sé.**

Advanced Learners
Invite students to have a discussion in Spanish about other ways to create more varied and interesting sentences. Encourage them to talk about other types of subordinate clauses by helping them with vocabulary such as **cláusula adverbial** and **cláusula sustantiva.**

Modelo

> Según cuenta la leyenda, un hombre estaba dando un paseo por el valle del pueblo cuando de repente apareció una figura muy extraña. Tenía una cabeza redonda sin pelo y sus ojos eran muy grandes y ovalados. "Dudo que existan extraterrestres", pensó el hombre en ese momento, "pero ahora no estoy tan seguro"...
>
> El desconocido se le acercó y le dijo: "Es verdad, soy un extraterrestre, pero no tenga miedo. Yo sólo busco un hombre que quiera ser mi amigo." El hombre le respondió que no tenía amigos pero que podía hacer una excepción. Después de hablar por muchas horas, el extraterrestre le ofreció llevarlo a conocer su planeta. Como el hombre no tenía ni familia ni amigos, aceptó la invitación. Entonces...
>
> Nunca más se supo del hombre...

Topic sentence: Sets the story.

Description of a character: What did the stranger look like?

Development: What happened after the two characters met.

Conclusion: Explains the mystery or leaves it to the reader's imagination.

---

3 Redacción/Revisión

Después de escribir el primer borrador de la leyenda, trabaja con otro(a) estudiante para intercambiar los trabajos y leerlos. Decidan qué aspectos son más efectivos. Fíjense en cómo el(la) escritor(a) del modelo incluyó detalles en su composición. Cada uno puede sugerir qué cambios hacer para mejorar las leyendas.

Haz lo siguiente: Verifica si usaste correctamente las formas del indicativo y del subjuntivo.

> El desconocido se le acercó y le dijo : "Es verdad, ~~sea~~ soy un extraterrestre, pero no ~~tienes~~ tenga miedo. Yo sólo busco un hombre que ~~quiere~~ quiera ser mi amigo."

4 Publicación

Antes de hacer la versión final, lee de nuevo tu borrador y repasa lo siguiente:

- ¿La leyenda tiene un orden lógico?
- ¿Es interesante la introducción?
- ¿Incluí suficientes detalles que den un ambiente *(feeling)* a la historia?
- ¿Es misterioso el final de la leyenda?

Después de revisar el borrador, escribe tu composición en limpio.

5 Evaluación

Tu profesor(a) puede explicarte cómo va a evaluar tu presentación. Probablemente, para tu profesor(a) es importante ver que:

- las oraciones tienen sentido y expresan ideas completas
- la leyenda sigue un orden lógico
- incluiste detalles en la leyenda
- usaste correctamente la gramática y el vocabulario del capítulo

---

Suggestions (Cont'd):

Once students have a rough draft ready, read through the model on this page together. Help them see how information from the chart on the previous page was incorporated into this draft and to note the additional information that was added. Point out the use of the subjunctive in an adjective clause in the first paragraph: *Yo sólo busco un hombre **que quiera ser mi amigo.*** Encourage them to work toward similar organization, level of detail, and language use as they create their own drafts.

For step 3, encourage students to experiment with various ways of combining sentences. Have them follow the suggestions shown.

Evaluation

Steps 4 and 5 overlap. Students will need evaluation by you, their peers, or self-evaluation to fine-tune and polish their drafts.

Portfolio

Keep students' final drafts in their portfolios as a writing sample.

✓ **Assessment**

- Assessment Program: Cap. 7, Rubrics

Give students copies of the rubric before they begin the activity. Go over the descriptions of the different levels of performance. After assessing students, help individuals understand how their performance could be improved.

Enriching Your Teaching

RUBRIC	Score 1	Score 3	Score 5
Completion of task	Your writing cannot be defined as a legend.	You present an idea for a legend, but you miss important elements.	Your writing is an interesting legend, containing all necessary elements.
Use of varied sentence structure	Your sentences are all the same length.	You combine some sentences but miss some opportunities.	Your sentences are varied, interesting, and effective.
Grammar, spelling, mechanics	Your grammar, spelling, and mechanics errors make for difficult reading.	You make some grammar, spelling, and/or mechanics errors.	You make very few grammar, spelling, or mechanics errors.

Lectura

Presentation

Standards: 1.2, 2.2, 3.1, 3.2, 5.2

Resources: Voc. & Gram. Transparencies: 4

Focus: Reading an extended passage

Suggestions:

Pre-reading: Before reading, direct students' attention to the *Al leer section.* Have them begin a T-chart similar to the one on p. 333 and make sure they understand how they will use it. Also refer them to the *Estrategia.* Point out that their T-charts will help them keep track of the characters and their actions.

Reading: When reading together with students, pause frequently to address comprehension issues they may have and to allow them to fill in their charts for *Interacción con la lectura.* Here is an example: Point out that in Spanish, the noun to which a possessive adjective refers is not always immediately obvious. We have to use background knowledge and context clues in order to know. In the first paragraph, we know that **su escudero** means "his, her, or their squire." Since we learned earlier who Sancho Panza is, we can deduce that **su** refers to Don Quijote and not the guards or their prisoners.

Country Connection

Presentation

Standards: 3.1

Resources: Voc. & Gram. Transparencies 20 (map)

What was known as La Mancha in Cervantes' day is currently the **región autónoma** called Castilla-La Mancha. Display *Vocabulary & Grammar Transparency* 20 and point out the region on the map. It is a large area in the central part of the country, east and southeast of Madrid. Before the **regiones autónomas** were created, Spain was divided into smaller provinces named after important cities. Castilla-La Mancha is comprised of five of these older provinces called Guadalajara, Cuenca, Albacete, Ciudad Real, and Toledo.

Go Online

The online atlas will provide a more detailed map of Spain.

330

Lectura

Fragmento de
Don Quijote de la Mancha
Capítulo XXII

Objectives

- Read a piece of fiction
- Understand the reasoning of a character who lives his own fantasy

Estrategia

Characters and actions
Read the passage once through to understand the events of the story. When you have read through once, think about the characters in the story. What are they like? Then, re-read the story and write down the events.

Al leer

El personaje más famoso de la literatura española es Don Quijote de la Mancha, el protagonista de la novela del mismo nombre que escribió Miguel de Cervantes. La historia cuenta que el Quijote leyó tantos libros sobre caballeros andantes *(knights),* que un día perdió el juicio *(lost his mind)* y decidió ser uno de ellos. En la época en que él vive (el siglo XVII) ya no hay caballeros andantes, pero en su imaginación, el Quijote ve a las sirvientas *(maids)* como princesas, las posadas *(inns)* como castillos y los molinos *(windmills)* como gigantes contra los que tiene que pelear. El conflicto entre la fantasía del Quijote y la realidad produce situaciones cómicas que hacen reír.

El fragmento que vas a leer es una adaptación del Capítulo XXII, en el que Don Quijote y su escudero *(squire)* y amigo Sancho Panza se encuentran con unos prisioneros.

Copia la tabla de la página 333. Complétala mientras lees. Ésta te ayudará a contestar las preguntas que aparecen al final.

on Quijote vio que por el camino venían doce hombres atados[1] con una gran cadena[2] de hierro por el cuello, y todos con esposas[3] en las manos. Venían con ellos dos hombres a caballo y dos a pie. Su escudero Sancho Panza dijo:

—Ésta es una cadena de prisioneros, gente forzada[4] por el rey, que va a las galeras[5].

—¿Cómo gente forzada? —preguntó Don Quijote—. ¿Es posible que el rey haga fuerza a alguien?

—No digo eso —respondió Sancho—, son personas que, por sus crímenes, van condenadas a servir al rey en las galeras por fuerza.

1 tied **2** chain **3** handcuffs **4** forced **5** galleys

330 trescientos treinta
Lectura

Universal Access

Multiple Intelligences

Bodily/Kinesthetic: Invite students to interpret the excerpt from *Don Quijote* by performing it as a skit for the class. They may use the excerpt as a script, adding inflection and gestures, or they may keep the general idea but improvise the lines. Have students work together to plan and perform their skit.

Students with Learning Difficulties

Have students read through the chart and comprehension questions on p. 333 before they begin to read the excerpt. They can use the questions to set a purpose for reading and to maintain a focus.

—Entonces —contestó Don Quijote— esta gente, aunque los llevan, van de por fuerza, y no porque ellos quieren.

—Así es —dijo Sancho.

—Pues —dijo su amo—, aquí puedo hacer mi tarea: deshacer fuerzas y ayudar a los miserables.

Don Quijote se acercó y le preguntó al primero que por qué crímenes iba a las galeras. Él le respondió que por enamorado.

—¿Por eso no más? —replicó Don Quijote—. Pues, si por enamorados echan a galeras, yo estaría en ellas desde hace tiempo.

—No son los amores como los que usted piensa —dijo el prisionero—; que los míos fueron que quise tanto a una cesta llena de ropa blanca, que la abracé conmigo tan fuertemente que, a no quitármela la justicia por fuerza, aún la tendría.

—Éste, señor, va por músico y cantor, le dijeron.

—Pues, ¿cómo —repitió Don Quijote—, por músicos y cantores van también a galeras?

Pero uno de los guardas le explicó:

—Señor caballero, cantar es confesar en el tormento[6].

Luego al tercero que le preguntó Don Quijote, éste le dijo:

—Yo voy por cinco años porque me faltaron diez monedas de oro.

—Yo daré veinte de muy buena gana[7] —dijo Don Quijote— por libraros[8] de las galeras.

—Eso me parece —respondió el prisionero— como quien tiene dineros en mitad del mar y se está muriendo de hambre, sin tener adónde comprar lo que necesita. Si hubiera tenido el dinero necesario para cambiar la opinión del juez, hoy estaría paseando por la plaza de Toledo y no camino a las galeras.

Al final venía un hombre con más cadenas que los demás.

—¿Cuál es su crimen? —preguntó Don Quijote.

—Va por diez años por ladrón —replicó el guarda—. Este hombre tiene solo más crímenes que todos los otros juntos. Es el famoso Ginés de Pasamonte.

—Para servir a Dios y al rey, otra vez he estado cuatro años, —respondió Ginés—; y no me pesa mucho ir a ellas, porque allí tendré lugar de acabar de escribir mi libro.

Dijo entonces Don Quijote:

—De todo lo que me habéis dicho, he sacado en limpio que, aunque os han castigado[9] por vuestros crímenes, las penas que vais a padecer[10] no os dan mucho gusto, y que vais a ellas muy de mala gana y muy contra vuestra voluntad. Me parece duro caso hacer esclavos[11] a los que Dios y la naturaleza hizo libres. Estos pobres no han cometido nada contra vosotros, guardias. Pido que los dejéis libres pero si no lo hacen, por fuerza haré que lo hagáis.

---

6 torture 7 willingly 8 *libraros* means *librarlos*; the ending *-os* is the pronoun corresponding to *vosotros* 9 punished 10 to suffer
11 slaves

Enriching Your Teaching

Culture Note

Don Quijote de la Mancha is the most well-known work of literature in the Spanish language. It has been translated into more than 60 languages. Cervantes' novel is a comic satire, intended to poke fun at the popular chivalric romances of the time. The novel is entertaining, but it also carries a message. The author criticizes the greed, pride, and violence of society at the time. Don Quijote's insanity also demonstrates a form of wisdom. He sees humble people as noble, while the rich and members of the clergy are targets of his wrath.

Suggestions (Cont'd):

Reading: Here are some possible comprehension issues on this page for which you can provide some guidance:

• Refer students to the *¿Recuerdas?* Remind them that verb forms that look unfamiliar to them as they read might be **vosotros** forms.

• If students have difficulty understanding the paragraph that begins **—De gente bien educada...,** explain that Don Quijote sometimes uses archaic syntax when he speaks. Restate the first sentence using modern syntax: *La gente bien educada está siempre agradecida por los beneficios que recibe.*

• Ask students to work together to tell in their own words the sequence of events beginning the moment Don Quijote decides to free the prisoners.

Post-reading: Ask students to talk about the humor in the Cervantes excerpt. Guide them to talk about the situational irony of the character of Don Quijote, totally dedicated to his mission, a mission that has no place in the world in which he lives and which turns him into a clown, no matter how seriously he takes himself. Ask students to draw analogies to such a situation in the present day. For example, Don Quijote might be compared to a man who decides to dress like a cowboy hero and sets out to roam the streets of a modern city on a quest to help the downtrodden.

Block Schedule

After the class has read the excerpt from *Don Quijote,* create "story experts." Divide the story in four sections and give students numbers 1, 2, 3, or 4. This "expert" is to create five questions about his or her section of the story. Create groups of four students, each with a different "expert." Have them ask their questions to other members of the group.

¿Recuerdas?

En el español antiguo, se utilizaban los pronombres personales *vosotros* y *vosotras,* y las formas verbales correspondientes. En la actualidad, estas formas casi no se usan en los países de habla hispana con excepción de España.

Pero los guardias no hicieron caso y le dijeron:

— No ande buscando tres pies al gato[12].

—¡Vos sois el gato, y el ratón, y el bellaco! —respondió Don Quijote furioso y atacó[13] a los guardias. Sancho ayudó a dar la libertad a los prisioneros. Muy sorprendidos y asustados, los guardas se escaparon.

Don Quijote llamó entonces a los prisioneros y así les dijo:

—De gente bien educada es agradecer[14] los beneficios que reciben. Les pido que vayan a la ciudad del Toboso, y allí os presentéis ante la señora Dulcinea del Toboso y le digáis que su caballero, el de la Triste Figura, ha tenido esta famosa aventura.

Respondió por todos Ginés de Pasamonte, y dijo:

—Lo que vuestra merced[15] nos manda, señor y libertador nuestro, es imposible de toda imposibilidad cumplirlo. Lo que podemos hacer es rezar[16] por usted.

—¡No! —dijo Don Quijote furioso.

Pasamonte, que ya se había dado cuenta que Don Quijote no era muy cuerdo[17], empezó con los demás prisioneros a arrojarle piedras a Don Quijote, le quitaron la ropa a Sancho y huyeron[18]. Solos quedaron Sancho y Don Quijote; Don Quijote, muy triste de verse tan malparado[19] por los mismos a quien tanto bien había hecho.

---

12 looking for a problem where there is none **13** attacked **14** to thank **15** archaic usage for *Usted* **16** to pray **17** sane **18** fled **19** left in such a sorry state

332 trescientos treinta y dos
¡Adelante!

Universal Access

Students with Learning Difficulties

After students read the *¿Recuerdas?,* write on the board verbs from the text in the **vosotros** form. Demonstrate pronunciation of these words by comparing them to words that are familiar to students. For example, the vowels in the last syllables of **presentéis** and **vais** sound much like those in **seis** and **país.**

Advanced Learners

Invite students to read another excerpt from *Don Quijote de la Mancha,* such as his famous battle with the windmill giant, and tell about it in their own words.

Interacción con la lectura

❶ Completa una tabla como la siguiente a medida que lees.

Preguntas	Respuestas
1. ¿Cuál es la situación?	
2. ¿Qué piensa Don Quijote que ocurre?	
3. ¿Qué sucede en realidad?	
4. ¿Qué hace Don Quijote?	
5. ¿Qué resultados tiene su acción?	

❷ Trabaja con otro(a) compañero(a) para comparar la información de las tablas de cada uno(a). Añadan cualquier otro detalle interesante que recuerden.

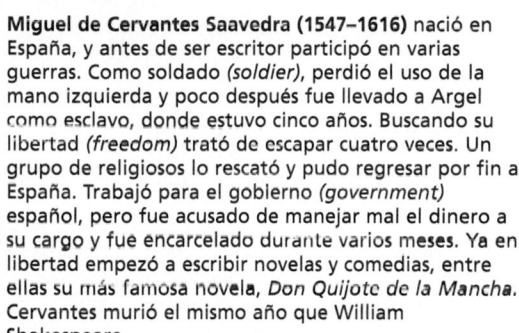

Fondo cultural ■◆●■◆●■◆●■◆● ■◆●◆◆●■◆● ■◆●◆■◆●

Miguel de Cervantes Saavedra (1547–1616) nació en España, y antes de ser escritor participó en varias guerras. Como soldado (*soldier*), perdió el uso de la mano izquierda y poco después fue llevado a Argel como esclavo, donde estuvo cinco años. Buscando su libertad (*freedom*) trató de escapar cuatro veces. Un grupo de religiosos lo rescató y pudo regresar por fin a España. Trabajó para el gobierno (*government*) español, pero fue acusado de manejar mal el dinero a su cargo y fue encarcelado durante varios meses. Ya en libertad empezó a escribir novelas y comedias, entre ellas su más famosa novela, *Don Quijote de la Mancha*. Cervantes murió el mismo año que William Shakespeare.

• Da un ejemplo de un conflicto entre la fantasía y la realidad que hayas leído en algún libro. Explica cómo presenta el autor este conflicto y qué crees que quiere decir.

¿Comprendiste?

1. ¿Qué cree Don Quijote que es su misión en la vida?

2. Don Quijote escucha las historias de los prisioneros. ¿Cómo reacciona Don Quijote después de escucharlas? ¿Considera que el castigo (*punishment*) de los prisioneros es justo?

3. ¿Por qué quiere Don Quijote que los prisioneros ya libres vayan a ver a la señora Dulcinea? ¿Qué nos dice de su personalidad?

4. Don Quijote ve las cosas de manera diferente que los demás personajes. ¿Crees que él piensa que dice la verdad? ¿Crees que él ve las cosas como son? ¿Crees que Sancho ve las cosas como son?

5. Piensa en algún ejemplo de la vida real en el que dos personas vean una misma cosa de diferente forma. ¿Por qué crees que puede ser eso? Di qué pueden hacer para ponerse de acuerdo.

6. En tu opinión, ¿qué quiere expresar el autor al escribir acerca de Don Quijote?

Miguel de Cervantes Saavedra

trescientos treinta y tres 333
Capítulo 7

Interacción con la lectura

Standards: 1.1, 1.2

Suggestions: After students finish and discuss their charts, encourage them to go back and read the excerpt again, now that they have a better understanding of Don Quijote's character and of Cervantes's use of language.

Answers will vary.

¿Comprendiste?

Standards: 1.3

Resources: Practice Answers on Transparencies

Suggestions: Have students write the answers to the questions on their own first, then use them as a basis for class discussion.

Answers:
1. Don Quijote piensa que su misión es deshacer fuerzas y ayudar a los miserables.
2. Don Quijote reacciona con sorpresa y enojo. Piensa que los castigos son injustos.
3. Don Quijote quiere que los prisioneros vayan a decirle a Dulcinea el bien que ha hecho. Answers will vary.
4–6. Answers will vary.

Fondo cultural *Standards:* 1.1, 1.2, 2.2, 3.1
■◆●■◆●■◆●■◆●■◆●

Suggestions: After students have read the information silently, ask comprehension questions. For example: *¿Cuál fue la situación de Cervantes en Argel?* (Fue llevado allí como esclavo.) *¿Por qué fue encarcelado Cervantes en España durante varios meses?* (Lo acusaron de haber manejado mal el dinero a su cargo.) *¿En qué año murió William Shakespeare?* (1616)

Answers will vary.

Enriching Your Teaching

Culture Note

Miguel de Cervantes Saavedra was shot in his left hand at the battle of Lepanto. He lost the use of this hand and was subsequently nicknamed **el manco** (the maimed) **de Lepanto.** He was proud of both his participation in the battle and his nickname. This nickname is still commonly associated with the author today.

Review Activities

Descubrimientos/Mitos y leyendas/Para hablar de los fenómenos inexplicables:
Have students number the items in these three categories. Ask them to write these numbers on slips of paper and put them into a hat or other container. Have students take turns drawing four numbers each, writing their numbers down, and then returning the slips to the hat or other container for the next person. Challenge students to write a sentence which uses the four words whose numbers they have drawn. Have them pass the hat more than once. Invite them to share their sentences.

Para describir objetos/Para indicar duda:
Have students sketch the ruins of an imaginary ancient civilization and use as many words in this category as they can to label their sketch. Ask them to assume the role of archaeologists and show their sketch to their classmates, describing the ruins and telling what functions the various structures and monuments supposedly served.

El universo: Ask students to create a "size-line" on which they arrange the items in this category in a line from largest to smallest. They should show each item on the "size-line" using a simple sketch or symbol accompanied by a label.

Verbos: Ask students to invent a false definition for each of the verbs. Have them work in pairs and take turns defining the verbs. Students decide each time whether their definition will be the correct one or their invented false one. If the definition is correct, the partner says *Tienes razón.* If it is false, the partner says, for example: *No, trazar no significa "llenar," sino "dibujar."*

Otras palabras/Expresiones: Students can use these words and expressions as they go over the review activities for the other categories.

Repaso del capítulo

Vocabulario y gramática

descubrimientos

el / la arqueólogo(a)	archaeologist
la civilización	civilization
la escritura	writing
la pirámide	pyramid
las ruinas	ruins
sagrado, -a	sacred
el símbolo	symbol

mitos y leyendas

la creencia	belief
el / la dios(a)	god, goddess
la leyenda	legend
el mito	myth
la nave espacial	spaceship
el origen	origin

para hablar de los fenómenos inexplicables

la estructura	structure
la evidencia	proof, evidence
extraño, -a	strange
el fenómeno	phenomenon
la función	function
la imagen	image
inexplicable	inexplicable
el misterio	mystery
misterioso, -a	mysterious
la teoría	theory

para describir objetos

el alto	height
el ancho	width
el centímetro	centimeter
el círculo	circle
el diámetro	diameter
el diseño	design
la distancia	distance
geométrico, -a	geometric(al)
el largo	length
el óvalo	oval
el rectángulo	rectangle
redondo, -a	round
la tonelada	ton
el triángulo	triangle

otras palabras

el conejo	rabbit
cualquier, -a	any
el intento	attempt

para indicar duda

improbable	unlikely
probable	likely

el universo

el / la astrónomo(a)	astronomer
el eclipse	eclipse
el / la habitante	inhabitant
la Luna	moon
el observatorio	observatory
el planeta	planet
el pueblo	people
la sombra	shadow
la Tierra	Earth
el universo	universe

expresiones

al igual que	as, like
o sea que	in other words
sino	but
ya que	because, due to

verbos

aparecer (zc)	to appear
arrojar(se)	to throw (oneself)
brillar	to shine
calcular	to calculate, to compute
convertirse (en)	to turn (into), to become
contribuir (u→y)	to contribute
cubrir	to cover
dudar	to doubt
excavar	to excavate
existir	to exist
medir (e→i)	to measure
pesar	to weigh
ponerse (el sol)	to set (sun)
resolver (o→ue)	to solve
trazar	to trace, to draw

Universal Access

Multiple Intelligences

Verbal/Linguistic: Remind students that many words in English come from Latin, with stops in Spanish and French along the way. Have students help their classmates by pointing out meaningful similarities between parts of Spanish and English words, such as "spaceship" and *(nave) espacial,* or "brilliant" and ***brillar.***

Advanced Learners

Have students use their creativity to make an audio or video recording about a group of archaeologists at the moment they discover an important find. Challenge them to use as much as they can of the chapter vocabulary in their script.

El presente y el presente perfecto del subjuntivo con expresiones de duda

Use the present subjunctive after expressions of doubt, uncertainty, or disbelief.

Dudo que **haya** una nave espacial en el pueblo.

To express doubt, uncertainty, or disbelief about actions in the past, Spanish uses the present perfect subjunctive mode.

Es probable que los arqueólogos **hayan encontrado** nuevas evidencias.

Expressions starting with *creo, no dudo, estoy seguro(a)* are usually followed by the indicative since they do not express doubt, disbelief or uncertainty.

Estoy seguro de que aquellas piedras **pertenecen** a los mayas.

Pero y sino

The word **pero** is usually the equivalent of the English conjunction *but*. The word **sino** also means *but*. *Sino* is used when the idea being conveyed is *not this*, *but rather* that.

No voy a comer carne **sino** vegetales.

You can also use *sino* with *no sólo . . . sino también . . .*

Vino **no sólo** María **sino también** Ana.

You use *sino que* when there is a conjugated verb in the second part of the sentence.

No salí a pasear **sino que** me quedé en casa.

El subjuntivo en cláusulas adjetivas

You can use an entire clause to describe a noun. This is an adjective clause. When you have a specific person or thing in mind, you use the indicative.

Busco a la arqueóloga **que trabaja** con ruinas aztecas.

If you don't have a specific person or thing in mind, or if you are not sure the person exists, you use the subjunctive. To refer to something or someone in the past, you use the present perfect subjunctive.

Necesito un artículo **que hable** sobre las pirámides.
Busco un joven **que haya estudiado** español.

You also use the subjunctive in an adjective clause when it describes a negative word such as *nadie, nada,* or *ninguno(a)*.

No hay **nadie que tenga** tiempo libre.

You use the subjunctive in an adjective clause when it doesn't describe a specific person or thing, using words such as *cualquier* or *cualquiera*.

Escoge **cualquier** cosa **que quieras**.

● **Más práctica** . . . .
Practice Workbook Organizer 7-13, 7-14

El presente y el presente perfecto del subjuntivo con expresiones de duda: Ask students to think about the mysteries described in *Capítulo 7* as well as other mysteries and unanswered questions about our world or the universe in general. Have each student write on a slip of paper a statement of opinion about one mystery. Ask them to write their statement as though it were a fact, avoiding expressions of doubt. For example: *Los extraterrestres tenían una presencia en la civilización maya.* Mix the slips of paper. Have students take turns drawing one and giving their own opinion about the mystery, using an expression of certainty or uncertainty: *Es improbable que los extraterrestres hayan tenido una presencia en la civilización maya.*

Pero y sino: Ask students to comment on unexplained phenomena using ***sino, sino que,*** or ***sino también.*** For example: *Los extraterrestres no sólo tenían una influencia en la civilización maya sino también en otras civilizaciones.*

El subjuntivo en cláusulas adjetivas: Ask students to pretend they are employment counselors. Have them write two sentences. In the first, they tell what type of position needs to be filled: *Se busca secretaria.* In the second, they tell about a desirable quality or skill needed for the job: *La secretaria tiene que ser organizada.* Have them trade pairs of sentences with a partner, who combines them into a single sentence with an adjective clause: *Se busca una secretaria que sea organizada.*

Portfolio

Invite students to review the activities they completed in this chapter, including written reports, posters or other visuals, tapes of oral presentations, and other projects. Have them select one or two items that they feel best demonstrate their achievements in Spanish. Include these products in students' portfolios. Have them include this with the Chapter Checklist and Self-Assessment Worksheet.

Additional Resources

- Audio Program: CD Cap. 7, Track 16
- Resource Book: Cap. 7, Clip Art
- Assessment Program: Chapter Checklist and Self-Assessment Worksheet

Enriching Your Teaching

Teacher-to-Teacher

Make clear to students the value of using study groups to prepare for exams and other assessment activities. Encourage them to conduct all the activities of the group in Spanish. Besides sharing their knowledge about the vocabulary or grammatical structures under review, students in a study group must also use vital, everyday language necessary for the performance of group activities: taking turns, giving and following commands, offering suggestions and opinions, and so on.

Performance Tasks

Standards: 1.1, 1.2, 1.3, 2.1, 2.2, 3.1

Resources: Audio Program: CD Cap. 7, Track 17; Resource Book: Cap. 7, Audio Script; Practice Answers on Transparencies

1. Vocabulario

Suggestions: Encourage students to review the vocabulary from the *A primera vista* sections on pp. 298–301 and 312–315 before they complete the activity.

Answers:

1. b	5. a
2. d	6. d
3. a	7. d
4. c	8. b

2. Gramática

Suggestions: Remind students of the main points of the grammar presentations in *Capítulo 7*:

• the present and present perfect subjunctive used with expressions of doubt

• the use of **pero** and **sino**

• the subjunctive in adjective clauses

Answers:

1. d	5. d
2. b	6. d
3. c	7. a
4. b	8. c

3. Escuchar

Suggestions: Use the *Audio CD* or read from the script.

Answers:

a. Estudió la civilización de los olmecas.
b. Excavó una roca con símbolos muy antiguos.
c. No son símbolos sino letras en un idioma muy extraño.
d. El locutor cree que los mitos muchas veces son realidad.

To prepare for the test, check to see if you . . .
• know the new vocabulary and grammar
• can perform the tasks on pp. 336 and 337

Preparación para el examen

1 Vocabulario Escribe la letra de la palabra o expresión que mejor complete cada frase. Escribe tus respuestas en una hoja aparte.

1. Un huevo tiene forma de _____ .
   a. triángulo
   c. pirámide
   b. óvalo
   d. rectángulo

2. El arqueólogo midió _____ de la roca.
   a. el mito y el origen
   c. el fenómeno y
   b. el planeta y   el misterio
      el observatorio
   d. el ancho y el largo

3. Cada civilización tenía sus teorías sobre el _____ del mundo.
   a. origen
   c. universo
   b. pueblo
   d. habitante

4. Los astrónomos mayas observaban _____ y los eclipses.
   a. las ruinas
   c. los planetas
   b. el símbolo
   d. el círculo

5. A un fenómeno extraño e inexplicable lo llamamos _____ .
   a. misterio
   c. evidencia
   b. geométrico
   d. estructura

6. El arqueólogo _____ el diámetro del calendario azteca.
   a. cubrió
   c. pesó
   b. dudó
   d. midió

7. A las seis de la tarde se _____ el sol.
   a. excavó
   c. calculó
   b. resolvió
   d. puso

8. Los astrónomos _____ en la reunión con información sobre los planetas.
   a. brillaron
   c. se arrojaron
   b. contribuyeron
   d. existían

2 Gramática Escribe la letra de la palabra o expresión que mejor complete cada frase. Escribe tus respuestas en una hoja aparte.

1. Dudo que _____ naves espaciales en el imperio maya.
   a. existió
   c. existen
   b. existirán
   d. hayan existido

2. Algunos creen que es probable que los extraterrestres _____ las líneas de Nazca.
   a. trazaron
   c. trazan
   b. hayan trazado
   d. tracen

3. La arqueóloga está segura de que esta pirámide _____ a la civilización azteca.
   a. pertenecerá
   c. pertenece
   b. haya pertenecido
   d. pertenecerían

4. No conozco ningún arqueólogo que _____ el nombre de todos los dioses aztecas.
   a. sabe
   c. sabían
   b. sepa
   d. supo

5. Necesitan un científico que _____ la edad del templo.
   a. calcula
   c. calculo
   b. calculen
   d. calcule

6. Es improbable que los aztecas _____ a la luna.
   a. han viajado
   c. hayas viajado
   b. viajan
   d. hayan viajado

7. No conozco a nadie que _____ para buscar ruinas de la cultura azteca.
   a. haya excavado
   c. han excavado
   b. excava
   d. hayan excavado

8. El sol no desapareció _____ que se puso.
   a. también
   c. sino
   b. pero
   d. sólo

Universal Access

Heritage Language Learners

Have students review their past exams, portfolios, and pieces of writing on which you have given them feedback. Have them identify errors that they consistently make, including errors with accent marks and spelling. Guide them to make notes that will help them to not repeat these errors as they complete the writing portion of the exam

Students with Learning Difficulties

Guide students to use the process of elimination by first determining which answers they are sure are incorrect and ignoring them. Help them begin by eliminating answers that do not agree in tense, person, or number with the rest of the sentence.

Go Online
PHSchool.com

For: Test Preparation
Visit: www.phschool.com
Web Code: jed-0711

En el examen vas a . . .	Éstas son las tareas de práctica que te pueden ser útiles para el examen . . .	Si necesitas repasar . . .
3 Escuchar Escuchar y comprender una entrevista con un arqueólogo que acaba de regresar de una excavación	Escucha una entrevista entre un locutor de una estación de radio y la famusa arqueóloga Dr. Cruz, y responde a las siguientes preguntas: (a) ¿Qué civilización estudió? (b) ¿Qué excavó? (c) ¿Cómo explicó lo que encontró? (d) ¿El locutor cree que es un mito o la realidad?	**pp. 298–301** *A primera vista 1* **p. 299** Actividades 1–2 **p. 301** Actividad 3 **p. 305** Actividad 9 **p. 309** Actividad 16
4 Hablar Hablar sobre un misterio o fenómeno inexplicable del pasado o del presente	Piensa en un misterio o fenómeno inexplicable que te interese. Descríbelo y sugiere una explicación lógica de por qué existe o se produce dicho misterio o fenómeno.	**p. 305** Actividad 9 **p. 308** Actividad 14 **p. 309** Actividad 16 **p. 310** Actividad 17
5 Leer Leer y comprender una leyenda	Lee este relato azteca. Según el relato, ¿cuál es la explicación para el principio de la lluvia? (a) A los dioses les gustaba el templo que los aztecas construyeron. (b) Para que lloviera, siete hombres cantaban cuatro canciones. (c) La luna aparcció por 28 días. *Cuenta el relato que los antiguos aztecas construyerom un templo a los dioses del fuego y de la lluvia en una montaña. Y siete hombres se reunían cuando llegaba el tiempo de sembrar la tierra, llamaban al dios de la lluvia y cantaban cuatro canciones, porque cuatro por siete es 28, y veintiocho días tiene el mes de la luna. Poco después, comenzaba a llover.*	**p. 304** Actividad 8 **p. 311** Actividad 19 **pp. 312–315** *A primera vista 2* **p. 312** Actividad 21 **p. 318** Actividad 27 **pp. 324–325** *Puente a la cultura*
6 Escribir Escribir sobre un misterio arqueológico	Escoge una de las ruinas misteriosas de las que se han hablado en este capítulo y escribe un párrafo sobre lo que piensas de ella. ¿Cuál crees que fue el origen y la función de esa construcción? ¿Está relacionada con algún mito o leyenda de esa civilización? ¿Crees que algún día se descubrirán sus misterios?	**p. 304** Actividad 8 **p. 305** Actividad 9 **p. 309** Actividad 16 **p. 311** Actividad 18 **p. 318** Actividad 27 **pp. 324–325** *Puente a la cultura*
7 Pensar Pensar en un mito y buscar una explicación posible	Piensa en alguna leyenda o mito que has estudiado en este capítulo. Busca una razón posible para explicar el origen de este mito y la función que tenía.	See *Actividades* referenced in #6 Escribir p. 337.

trescientos treinta y siete **337**
Capítulo 7

---

4. Hablar

Suggestions: Encourage students to use an expression of doubt or of certainty when giving their explanation for the phenomenon.

Answers will vary.

5. Leer

Suggestions: Tell students to refer to pp. 298–301 and 312–315 if they have questions about vocabulary in the review.

Answers:
b

6. Escribir

Suggestions: Encourage students to use subordinate clauses in their paragraphs in order to make their sentences varied and interesting.

Answers will vary.

7. Pensar

Suggestions: Ask students how their personal opinions regarding unexplained phenomena have changed, if at all, due to what they have learned in *Capítulo* 7. Ask them also to summarize the new information they have learned from the chapter.

Answers will vary.

✓ **Assessment**
• Examen del capítulo: 7
• Audio Program: CD 13, Cap. 7, Track 10
• Assessment Program: *RPH*

Alternative Assessment
• ExamView Test Bank CD-ROM
• Resource Book: Cap. 7, Situation Cards
• Resource Book: Cap. 7, Communicative Activity BLM

Enriching Your Teaching

Teacher-to-Teacher

Invite students to create their own four-page brochure that summarizes the important points learned in the chapter. The first page might be a table of contents for the chapter. Other pages might include captioned sketches, drawings, or photos that organize chapter information.

Capítulo 8

Encuentro entre culturas

CHAPTER OVERVIEW

8 Encuentro entre culturas
• Interactions between different cultures

Vocabulary
• fusion of cultures in Spain
• fusion of cultures in the Americas

Grammar
• conditional
• imperfect subjunctive

Cultural Perspectives
• the fusion of different cultures evidenced in the architecture and culture and lifestyles of Spain
• Buenos Aires, a city where cultures, religions and traditions mix
• the Paraguayan harp and its European origin
• Texmex food, a mixture of two cultures
• the missions of California

Chapter Project

Carteles del encuentro entre culturas

Overview: Students create a poster about the arrival of the Spaniards or other explorers in the Americas. They can focus on one of the many topics presented on pages 356-358. The poster must feature labeled photos or illustrations related to the topic they have selected. Students then give an oral presentation of their poster, describing briefly the culture they are showing and what happened during that period in history.

Materials: construction paper, photographs or pictures from magazines or downloaded from the Web, drawing paper, colored pencils, markers, glue, scissors

• •

Sequence: (suggestions for when to do each step appear throughout the chapter)

STEP 1. Review instructions so students know what is expected of them. Hand out the "Chapter 8 Project Instructions and Rubric" from the *Teacher's Resource Book*.

STEP 2. Students choose their topic and submit a rough sketch of their poster. Return the sketches with your suggestions. For vocabulary and grammar practice, ask students to work in pairs and present their drafts to each other.

STEP 3. Students do layouts on construction paper. Encourage students to work in pencil first and to try different arrangements before gluing photographs or illustrations and writing descriptions.

STEP 4. Students submit a draft of their descriptions. Note your corrections and suggestions, then return the drafts to students.

STEP 5. Students complete and present their posters to the class. They should describe one of the images in the photos or illustrations and give a brief summary of what is shown in the whole poster.

Options:

1. Instead of a poster, students design a Web page with similar information.
2. Students design a timeline beginning with the arrival of the Spaniards in Mexico up to and including the establishment of colonies.

Assessment:

Here is a detailed rubric for assessing this project:

Chapter 8 Project: *Carteles del encuentro entre culturas*

RUBRIC	Score 1	Score 3	Score 5
Your evidence of planning	You provide no preliminary proposal or descriptions.	Your preliminary proposal and descriptions are not revised.	You show evidence of corrected proposal and descriptions.
Your use of illustrations	Your photos or illustrations are incorrectly labeled.	Your photos or illustrations are disorganized.	Your photos or illustrations are organized. Your presentation is easy to read.
Your presentation	You do not include the required information.	You include most of the required information.	You include all of the required information.

Bulletin Boards

Theme: *Mezcla de culturas en España*

Ask students to cut out, copy or download pictures showing evidence of the exchange between diferent cultures in Spain from the Roman conquest, through the Arab occupation, to the reconquering of Granada. They can include pictures of diferent architectural structures, musical instruments, samples of writings, mathematical symbols, food, and other examples of how Spain assimilated elements from different cultures. The pictures and illustrations should be labeled and organized on the bulletin board.

Bibliography

De Virien, Claire. *Alhambra: A Moorish Paradise*. August 1999. A photographic essay about the Alhambra and its wonderful architecture.

MacDonald, Fiona. *Step into the Aztec and Maya Worlds*. New York: Lorenz Books, 1998. History and culture of the Aztec and Mayan civilizations.

Newcomb, Rexford. *Spanish-colonial Architecture in the United States*. Mineola, N.Y.: Dover Publishers, 1990. Spanish architectural traditions and Spanish architecture thoughout the United States.

Stevens, Kathryn. *Argentina*. Countries — Faces and Places Series. Chanhasse, Minn.: Childs World, 2001. Information about Argentina, its people, and its culture.

Hands-on Culture

Craft: *Azulejo de maravilla*

Arab architects, artists, and craftmen were responsible for creating some of the most wonderful pieces of architecture in Spain. Students will imagine they are creating beautifully decorated *azulejos* (tiles) to be used in the construction of the Alhambra corridors and fountains.

Materials: Internet access or books and magazines about Moorish architecture in Spain (optional), tracing or drawing paper, carbon paper, 2 square or octagonal cardboard or plastic tiles per student, white or beige enamel, paint brushes, permanent markers in a variety of colors and tips

Directions:

1. Students cover each of their tiles with one or two layers of enamel and let it dry overnight.
2. Students either research in the Internet, books, or magazines for examples of Arab designs like the ones used in the tiles of the Alhambra and copy them on tracing paper, or make their own designs on drawing paper.
3. Once the enamel on the tiles dries out, students transfer their designs to the painted surface of each tile by placing a piece of carbon paper on the tile and the design on top of it and tracing with a pointed pencil.
4. Students use permanent markers in their choice of colors to decorate the tiles with the designs just transferred.

Internet Search

Use the keywords to find more information.

Keywords:

Moros en España, judíos + sinagoga + España, Buenos Aires + cosmopolita, Hernán Cortés, Moctezuma, imperio azteca

Game

Dominó de palabras

This domino game practices vocabulary about cultural exchange during the Spanish conquest of the Americas and the Middle Ages in Spain. Use it after students have practiced the vocabulary of the chapter.

Players: the entire class

Materials: index cards, at least five per student, pens or markers

Rules:

1. Distribute five or more index cards to each student. Ask students to draw a vertical line on each card, dividing it in two halves.

2. Ask students to select any words they like from the chapter vocabulary and write them on the cards, one word per half. They can mix and match words on the cards any way they like.

3. Collect the finished "domino" pieces, shuffle them, and redistribute them evenly to the students.

4. Play! Students form a big circle and start playing domino with the cards. The criteria for matching domino halves will be that matching words should fall within the same category or be directly related to each other. This way, *conquista*, could be paired with either *árabes, Cortés, aztecas, reconquistar,* or *soldados;* but *árabes* and *Cortés* could not be paired to each other. *La Giralda, azulejos, maravilla,* and *arco,* can all be paired with each other and with *arquitectura.*

5. Students take turns setting one of their domino pieces on the table, and arranging them in creative domino designs. If a student cannot match any of his or her pieces to the free ends of the domino, he or she skips the round and keeps the pieces. The objective is to be the first to set all the pieces on the table.

Variation: Instead of playing traditional domino, in which only one piece can be attached to each free end, students can attach up to three matching words to each word, thus making a multi-lineal design.

Capítulo 8 Overview

A ver si recuerdas
RECYCLE

Vocabulary
- Conquest and empires
- Fusion of different cultures

Grammar
- Interrogative words
- Verbs with changes in the preterite

Chapter Overview

A primera vista 1
INPUT

Objectives
- Interaction between cultures
- Fusion of different cultures in Spain before 1492

Vocabulary
- Ethnic groups
- Conquest and occupation
- Architecture and culture

Grammar
- Conditional

Culture
- Sevilla, Toledo, and Barcelona

Manos a la obra 1
PRACTICE

Objectives
- Describe how different cultures interact
- Talk about the fusion of different cultures in Spain before 1492

Vocabulary
- Practice and use new vocabulary

Grammar
- Conditional

Culture
- Moorish and Christian architecture in Spain
- The Paraguayan harp

A primera vista 2
INPUT

Objectives
- Talk about cultural interaction
- Talk about the fusion of different cultures in the Americas

Vocabulary
- Conquest, trade, and missions
- Ancestors and cultural heritage

Grammar
- Imperfect subjunctive
- Imperfect subjunctive with *si*

Culture
- Aztecs and Hernán Cortés
- Spanish colonialism

Manos a la obra 2
PRACTICE

Objectives
- Describe how different cultures intreract
- Talk about the fusion of different cultures in the Americas

Vocabulary
- Practice and use new vocabulary

Grammar
- Imperfect subjunctive
- Imperfect subjunctive with *si*

Culture
- Empires
- Texmex food
- Luis Palés Matos and the Black Poetry Movement in the Caribbean
- Bilingual professionals in Texas

¡Adelante!
APPLICATION

Objectives
- Read about Spanish missions in California
- Distinguish between fact and opinion

Vocabulary
- Application

Grammar
- Application

Culture
- Catholic missions in California and the role of Junípero Serra
- Fiction by Elías Miguel Muñoz
- Aztec heritage

Repaso del capítulo
REVIEW

Objectives
- Prepare for the chapter test
- Perform the tasks on pages 382 and 383

Vocabulary
- Review

Grammar
- Review

BEYOND THE CLASSROOM

Countries
- Argentina
- Cuba
- Mexico
- Paraguay
- Spain
- United States

El español en el mundo del trabajo
- Bilingual professionals working at Houston's Health and Science Museum

Internet
- Vocabulary activities
- Grammar activities
- Internet links
- Self-tests

LEARNER SUPPORT

Strategies
- Fact and opinion
- Speaker's purpose
- Chronological ordering

Recycling
- Skipping words and guessing
- The verb *haber* in the preterite
- The preterite of verbs

En voz alta
- *Calabó y bambú*

Ampliación del lenguaje
- Words of Arab origin

Conexiones
- Music: Arab contributions to the music in Spain

Print Components

TEACHER

Teacher's Resource Book
- Chapter Table of Contents
- School-to-Home Connection
- Chapter Resource Checklist
- Input Script
- Audio Script
- Video Script
- Communicative Activities
- Situation Cards
- GramActiva Blackline Masters
- Graphic Organizers
- Answer Keys:
  Practice Workbook
  Writing, Audio & Video Workbook

Realidades para hispanohablantes
Teacher Edition

STUDENT

Practice Workbook
- Vocabulary: 8-1 – 8-4, 8-8 – 8-9
- Grammar: 8-5 – 8-7, 8-10 – 8-12
- Organizer: 8-13 – 8-14

Writing, Audio & Video Workbook
- Audio: 1–5
- Writing: 6–13
- Video: 14–17

Reading and Writing for Success
- Chapter 8, Test 35

Realidades para hispanohablantes

Transparencies

Vocabulary and Grammar Transparencies
- Vocabulary: 149–156, 158–161
- Grammar: 157, 162–163
- ¿Qué me cuentas?: 164

Practice Answers on Transparencies
- Cap. 8

Fine Art Transparencies
- Transparencies
- Teacher's Guide

Assessment

Assessment Program
- Pruebas:
  – Comprensión del vocabulario 1: 8-1
  – Aplicación del vocabulario 1: 8-2
  – El condicional: 8-3
  – Comprensión del vocabulario 2: 8-4
  – Aplicación del vocabulario 2: 8-5
  – El imperfecto del subjuntivo: 8-6
  – El imperfecto del subjuntivo con *si*: 8-7
- Exámenes del capítulo
- Rubrics

Alternative Assessment
- ExamView Test Bank CD-ROM
- MindPoint Quiz Show CD-ROM
- Internet Self-test
- Situation Cards
- Communicative Activity

Assessment Program: *Realidades para hispanohablantes*

Technology

TeacherExpress™ CD-ROM
- Lesson Planner
- Teacher Resources
- Clip Art

Video Program VHS and DVD

Audio Program CDs
- A primera vista 1 y 2: Vocabulario y gramática en contexto
- Audio Activities
- ¿Qué me cuentas?
- Repaso
- Examen del capítulo: Escuchar

Capítulo 8 — Lesson Plans

Regular Schedule (50 Minutes)

For electronic lesson plans:
Teacher Express CD-ROM

	Warm-up / Assess	Preview Present / Practice Communicate	Wrap-up / Homework Options
DAY 1	**Warm-up (10 min.)** • Return Examen del capítulo: Capítulo 7	**Repaso (35 min.)** • A ver si recuerdas • Actividad 7	**Wrap-up and Homework Options (5 min.)** • Practice Workbook 8-1, 8-2 • Go Online
DAY 2	**Warm-up (10 min.)** • Homework check	**Chapter Opener (10 min.)** • Objectives • Fondo cultural **A primera vista 1 (25 min.)** • Presentation: Vocabulario y gramática en contexto • Actividad 1	**Wrap-up and Homework Options (5 min.)** • Go Online • Clip Art Vocabulary
DAY 3	**Warm-up (10 min.)** • Homework check	**A primera vista 1 (35 min.)** • Presentation: España: Una gran mezcla de culturas • Actividades 2, 3, 4	**Wrap-up and Homework Options (5 min.)** • Practice Workbook 8-3, 8-4 • Go Online • Manos a la obra 1: Actividad 6 • Prueba 8-1: Vocabulary recognition
DAY 4	**Warm-up (10 min.)** • Homework check ✔**Assessment (10 min.)** • Prueba 8-1: Vocabulary recognition	**Manos a la obra 1 (25 min.)** • Actividades 5, 7, 8, 9, 10 • Ampliación del lenguaje	**Wrap-up and Homework Options (5 min.)** • Writing Activities • Prueba 8-2: Vocabulary production
DAY 5	**Warm-up (10 min.)** • Homework check ✔**Assessment (10 min.)** • Prueba 8-2: Vocabulary production	**Manos a la obra 1 (25 min.)** • Presentation: El condicional • Actividades 12, 13, 14 • Writing Activity	**Wrap-up and Homework Options (5 min.)** • Practice Workbook 8-5 • Go Online
DAY 6	**Warm-up (10 min.)** • Actividad 11 • Homework check	**Manos a la obra 1 (35 min.)** • Actividades 15, 16 • Audio or Writing Activity	**Wrap-up and Homework Options (5 min.)** • Practice Workbook 8-6, 8-7 • Writing Activity • Prueba 8-3: El condicional
DAY 7	**Warm-up (10 min.)** • Fondo cultural • Homework check ✔**Assessment (10 min.)** • Prueba 8-3: El condicional	**Manos a la obra 1 (10 min.)** • Communicative Activity **A primera vista 2 (15 min.)** • Presentation: Vocabulario y gramática en contexto • Actividad 17	**Wrap-up and Homework Options (5 min.)** • Go Online • Examen: Vocabulario y gramática 1
DAY 8	**Warm-up (15 min.)** • Writing Activity • Homework check ✔**Assessment (30 min.)** • Examen: Vocabulario y gramática 1		**Wrap-up and Homework Options (5 min.)** • Clip Art Vocabulary
DAY 9	**Warm-up (5 min.)** • Homework check	**A primera vista 2 (25 min.)** • Presentation: La fusión y la herencia • Actividades 18, 19 • Audio and Writing Activities **Manos a la obra 2 (15 min.)** • Actividades 21, 22	**Wrap-up and Homework Options (5 min.)** • Practice Workbook 8-8, 8-9 • Go Online • Prueba 8-4: Vocabulary recognition
DAY 10	**Warm-up (15 min.)** • Actividad 20 • Homework check ✔**Assessment (10 min.)** • Prueba 8-4: Vocabulary recognition	**Manos a la obra 2 (20 min.)** • Actividades 23, 24, 25	**Wrap-up and Homework Options (5 min.)** • Fondo cultural • Prueba 8-5: Vocabulary production

	Warm-up / Assess	Preview Present / Practice Communicate	Wrap-up / Homework Options
DAY 11	**Warm-up (10 min.)** • Writing Activity • Homework check ✔**Assessment (10 min.)** • Prueba 8-5	**Manos a la obra 2 (25 min.)** • Presentation: El imperfecto del subjuntivo • En voz alta • Actividades 26, 27, 29 • Communicative Activity	**Wrap-up and Homework Options (5 min.)** • Actividad 28 • Prueba 8-6: El imperfecto • Practice Workbook 8-10 del subjuntivo • Go Online
DAY 12	**Warm-up (10 min.)** • Actividad 30 • Homework check ✔**Assessment (10 min.)** • Prueba 8-6: El imperfecto del subjuntivo	**Manos a la obra 2 (25 min.)** • El español en el mundo del trabajo • Presentation: El imperfecto del subjuntivo con *si* • Actividades 33, 34, 35	**Wrap-up and Homework Options (5 min.)** • Practice Workbook 8-11, 8-12 • Go Online • Prueba 8-7: El imperfecto del subjuntivo con *si*
DAY 13	**Warm-up (20 min.)** • Actividad 31, 32 • Homework check ✔**Assessment (10 min)** • Prueba 8-7: El imperfecto del subjuntivo con *si*	**Manos a la obra 2 (15 min.)** • Communicative Activity	**Wrap-up and Homework Options (5 min.)** • Go Online • Examen: Vocabulario y gramática 2
DAY 14	**Warm-up (10 min.)** • Writing Activity ✔**Assessment (25 min.)** • Examen: Vocabulario y gramática 2	**¡Adelante! (10 min.)** • Presentación oral: Steps 1, 2	**Wrap-up and Homework Options (5 min.)** • Presentación oral: Step 2
DAY 15	**Warm-up (10 min.)** • Presentación oral: Step 2	**¡Adelante! (35 min.)** • Presentación oral: Step 3	**Wrap-up and Homework Options (5 min.)** • Las misiones de California • Go Online • ¿Comprendiste?
DAY 16	**Warm-up (15 min.)** • Las misiones de California: ¿Comprendiste? • Homework check	**¡Adelante! (30 min.)** • ¿Qué me cuentas? 1, 2, 3 • Video Activities 1, 2, 3 • View Video	**Wrap-up and Homework Options (5 min.)** • Presentación escrita: Steps 1, 2
DAY 17	**Warm-up (10 min.)** • Video Activity 4	**¡Adelante! (15 min.)** **Repaso (20 min.)** • Presentación escrita: Step 3 • Preparación para el examen: Actividades 3, 4 • MindPoint Quiz Show	**Wrap-up and Homework Options (5 min.)** • Presentación escrita: Step 4
DAY 18	**Warm-up and Bellringer (10 min.)** • Homework check	**¡Adelante! (35 min.)** • Lectura • Fondo cultural • Interacción con la lectura	**Wrap-up and Homework Options (5 min.)** • Practice Workbook: Organizer 8-13, 8-14 • Go Online: Self-test
DAY 19	**Warm-up (20 min.)** • Preparación para el examen: Actividades 1, 2 • Homework check	**Repaso (25 min.)** • Preparación para el examen: Actividades 5, 6, 7 • MindPoint Quiz Show • Other review	**Wrap-up and Homework Options (5 min.)** • Examen del capítulo
DAY 20	**Warm-up (5 min.)** • Answer questions ✔**Assessment (44 min.)** • Examen del capítulo		**Wrap-up and Homework Options (1 min.)** • A ver si recuerdas: Capítulo 9

Warm-up / Assess	Preview Present / Practice Communicate	Wrap-up / Homework Options
DAY 1 **Warm-up (25 min.)** • Return Examen del capítulo: Capítulo 7 • A ver si recuerdas • Actividad 7 • Homework check	**Chapter Opener (10 min.)** • Objectives • Fondo cultural **A primera vista 1 (40 min.)** • Presentation: Vocabulario y gramática en contexto • Actividad 1 • Presentation: España: Una gran mezcla de culturas • Actividades 2, 3, 4 **Manos a la obra 1 (10 min.)** • Actividad 7	**Wrap-up and Homework Options (5 min.)** • Practice Workbook 8-3, 8-4 • Go Online • Clip Art Vocabulary • Prueba 8-1: Vocabulary recognition
DAY 2 **Warm-up (15 min.)** • Actividad 5 • Homework check **✔Assessment (10 min.)** • Prueba 8-1: Vocabulary recognition	**Manos a la obra 1 (60 min.)** • Actividades 6, 8, 9, 10 • Ampliación del lenguaje • Communicative Activity	**Wrap-up and Homework Options (5 min.)** • Go Online • Writing Activities • Prueba 8-2: Vocabulary production
DAY 3 **Warm-up (15 min.)** • Writing Activity • Homework check **✔Assessment (10 min.)** • Prueba 8-2: Vocabulary production	**Manos a la obra 1 (60 min.)** • Presentation: El condicional • Actividades 11, 12, 13, 14, 15, 16 • Fondo cultural • Audio and Writing Activities	**Wrap-up and Homework Options (5 min.)** • Practice Workbook 8-5, 8-6, 8-7 • Go Online • Prueba 8-3: El condicional
DAY 4 **Warm-up (15 min.)** • Writing Activity • Homework check **✔Assessment (10 min.)** • Prueba 8-3: El condicional	**Manos a la obra 1 (20 min.)** • Communicative Activity **A primera vista 2 (40 min.)** • Presentation: Vocabulario y gramática en contexto • Actividad 17 • Presentation: La fusión y la herencia • Actividades 18, 19	**Wrap-up and Homework Options (5 min.)** • Practice Workbook 8-8, 8-9 • Go Online • Examen: Vocabulario y gramática 1
DAY 5 **Warm-up (10 min.)** • Actividad 19 • Homework check **✔Assessment Options (30 min.)** • Examen: Vocabulario y gramática 1	**A primera vista 2 (20 min.)** • Audio or Writing Activities **Manos a la obra 2 (25 min.)** • Actividades 21, 22, 23 • En voz alta	**Wrap-up and Homework Options (5 min.)** • Actividades 20, 24 • Go Online • Prueba 8-4: Vocabulary recognition

	Warm-up / Assess	Preview Present / Practice Communicate	Wrap-up / Homework Options
DAY 6	**Warm-up (20 min.)** • Actividad 25 • Homework check ✔**Assessment (10 min.)** • Prueba 8-4: Vocabulary recognition	**Manos a la obra 2 (55 min.)** • Fondo cultural • Presentation: El imperfecto del subjuntivo • Actividades 26, 27, 29, 30 • El español en el mundo del trabajo • Writing Activities	**Wrap-up and Homework Options (5 min.)** • Practice Workbook 8-10 • Go Online • Pruebas 8-5, 8-6: Vocabulary production, el imperfecto del subjuntivo
DAY 7	**Warm-up (10 min.)** • Actividad 28 • Homework check ✔**Assessment (20 min.)** • Pruebas 8-5, 8-6: Vocabulary production, el imperfecto del subjuntivo	**Manos a la obra 2 (40 min.)** • Presentation: El imperfecto del subjuntivo con *si* • Actividades 31, 32, 33, 34, 35 **¡Adelante! (15 min.)** • Presentación oral: Steps 1, 2	**Wrap-up and Homework Options (5 min.)** • Presentación oral: Step 2 • Go Online
DAY 8	**Warm-up (15 min.)** • Writing Activity • Homework check ✔**Assessment (40 min.)** • Presentación oral: Step 3	**Manos a la obra 2 (15 min.)** • Communicative Activity **¡Adelante! (15 min.)** • Presentation: Las misiones de California	**Wrap-up and Homework Options (5 min.)** • Practice Workbook 8-11, 8-12 • Go Online • Prueba 8-7: El imperfecto del subjuntivo con *si* • Examen: Vocabulario y gramática 2
DAY 9	**Warm-up (10 min.)** • Homework check ✔**Assessment Options (30 min.)** • Prueba 8-7: El imperfecto del subjuntivo con *si* • Examen: Vocabulario y gramática 2	**¡Adelante! (45 min.)** • Las misiones de California • ¿Comprendiste? • ¿Qué me cuentas? 1, 2, 3 • Video • Video Activities • Presentación escrita: Step 1	**Wrap-up and Homework Options (5 min.)** • Presentación escrita: Step 2 • Go Online • Preparación para el examen: Actividades 1, 2
DAY 10	**Warm-up (20 min.)** • Presentación escrita: Step 3 • Homework check	**¡Adelante! (35 min.)** • Lectura • Interacción con la lectura • Fondo cultural **Repaso (30 min.)** • Preparación para el examen: Actividades 3, 4, 6 • MindPoint Quiz Show	**Wrap-up and Homework Options (5 min.)** • Presentación escrita: Step 4 • Practice Workbook: Organizer 8-13, 8-14 • Go Online: Self-test • Preparación para el examen: Actividades 5, 7 • Examen del capítulo
DAY 11	**Warm-up (15 min.)** • Homework check ✔**Assessment (45 min.)** • Examen del capítulo	**Theme Game (15 min.)** **A ver si recuerdas – Capítulo 9 (10 min.)** • Presentation: Vocabulario • Presentation: Gramática	**Wrap-up and Homework Options (5 min.)** • A ver si recuerdas – Capítulo 9 • Actividades 1, 2, 3, 6, 8 • Go Online • Practice Workbook 9-1, 9-2

Vocabulario

Presentation

Standards: 1.1

Resources: Voc. & Gram. Transparencies: 149

Suggestions: Ask students to make a map of an imaginary neighborhood. Their map should include labels calling out several of the *construcciones* shown in the *Vocabulario*. Ask them to include some of the terms from the *para describir* and *en la ciudad* categories as well. Have students exchange maps with a partner and ask and answer questions about each other's maps:

A —*¿Cómo voy de la vieja sinagoga al nuevo museo?*

B —*Sal de la sinagoga y sigue por la Avenida Martín. Dobla a la derecha en la Calle del Museo. Camina dos cuadras y verás el museo.*

Actividad 1

Standards: 1.1

Focus: Practicing review vocabulary

Suggestions: Encourage students to invent Spanish names for places and buildings that are known by English names. Their Spanish names should be translations that are direct enough so that their partner can recognize them. If this proves too difficult, allow them to use the English name.

Answers will vary.

Block Schedule

Twenty Questions: Divide the class into groups of four or five to play Twenty Questions. Each student will assume the identify of a person, living or dead. The group asks up to twenty questions to determine the identity of the mystery person.

A ver si recuerdas...

Vocabulario

construcciones
el edificio histórico
la fuente
la iglesia
la mezquita
el monumento
el museo
el palacio
la plaza
el puente
la sinagoga
el teatro

para indicar el lugar
a la derecha
a la izquierda
al lado de
cerca de
debajo de
delante de
detrás de
entre
lejos de

para indicar el tiempo
¿Cuánto tiempo hace que . . . ?
desde
la fecha
hace . . . dos, tres, cuatro años
hace mucho / poco tiempo
recientemente

para describir
antiguo, -a
enorme
grande
horrible
moderno, -a
nuevo, -a
pequeño, -a
viejo, -a

en la ciudad
la avenida
la calle
la cuadra
la esquina

Actividad 1 Escribir/Hablar ....

Práctica de vocabulario

● Haz una lista con tres lugares o edificios famosos de tu pueblo, de tu ciudad o de tu estado, por ejemplo: un monumento, una calle, un teatro o una plaza. En una tabla como la siguiente, escribe dónde quedan esos lugares o edificios, cómo son y cuándo los visitaste. Usa las palabras de la lista de vocabulario. NO escribas el nombre de la construcción.

¿Qué es?	¿Dónde queda?	¿Cómo es?	¿Cuándo lo visitaste?
1. [lugar o edificio]			
2. [lugar o edificio]			

● Hazle preguntas a otro(a) estudiante sobre los lugares de su lista. Pregúntale sobre la información que escribió y trata de identificar los lugares.

Modelo

A —*¿Cuándo visitaste el lugar?*
B —*Lo visité hace un año.*

338 trescientos treinta y ocho
A ver si recuerdas . . .

Universal Access

Heritage Language Learners

Ask students to share the names and types of buildings prevalent in, or specific to, their heritage country. Have them use specific vocabulary to describe some of the noteworthy structures found in their heritage country.

Advanced Learners

Have students write step-by-step directions in order to travel from one place in your community to another. Their directions should be clear and detailed enough so that a person following them would arrive at the destination. Have them read their directions to each other. Ask listeners to identify the destination.

Gramática·Repaso

Las palabras interrogativas

Remember that you use interrogative words to ask questions. In Spanish, all interrogative words have a written accent mark.

The interrogative words *¿cómo?, ¿cuándo?, ¿dónde?, ¿adónde?, ¿qué?, ¿para qué?, ¿por qué?* are invariable—they do not change in gender or number.

¿Cuándo vas al museo?   **¿Por qué** vamos a la plaza?

The interrogative words *¿cuál? / ¿cuáles?*, and *¿quién? / ¿quiénes?* have both singular and plural forms, but do not change in gender.

¿Cuáles son tus amigos?   **¿Quién** es tu mejor amiga?

The interrogative words *¿cuánto? / ¿cuántos? / ¿cuánta? / ¿cuántas?* agree both in number (singular / plural) and gender (masculine / feminine) with the noun they modify.

¿Cuánto dinero?   **¿Cuántas** horas?

In Spanish, prepositions always precede interrogative words.

¿Para qué hiciste eso?   **¿Con quién** fuiste tú?

Just as in direct questions, interrogative words have a written accent when they are used in indirect questions.

Quiero saber **quiénes** van a la fiesta.   Me preguntó **cuál** era mi mochila.

 Leer

Práctica de gramática

Dos amigas quieren ir al museo. Completa el diálogo con las palabras interrogativas que correspondan.

A —¿ __1.__ vamos al museo, en autobús o a pie?

B —Depende . . . ¿tú sabes a __2.__ cuadras de aquí está el museo?

A —Creo que a unas veinte . . . ¿ __3.__ no vamos en autobús?

B —Sí, mejor. Estoy cansada. ¿Sabes __4.__ está la parada del autobús?

A —Aquí, pero . . . mira, aquí paran cuatro autobuses. ¿ __5.__ tomamos? ¿A __6.__ le preguntamos?

 Escribir/Hablar

Práctica de gramática

Tú y tu compañero(a) trabajan para una organización de turismo. Deben entrevistar a los turistas que visitan un centro cultural, un teatro o un museo. Escriban diez preguntas para hacerles a los turistas. Lean sus preguntas a la clase. Pueden representar la entrevista con otros(as) compañeros(as).

Modelo

¿De dónde es usted?
¿Por qué ha venido a . . . ?

Enriching Your Teaching

Teacher-to-Teacher

Challenge students to write sentences that contain many different types of information. For example: *La plaza vieja está a una distancia de tres cuadras de la plaza nueva. Jorge llegó allí a las seis con su hermana Gloria.* Have them trade sentences with a partner, who writes as many questions as possible about it. Here are some possible questions based on the sample sentences: *¿A qué distancia está la plaza vieja de la plaza nueva? ¿A cuántas cuadras está la plaza vieja de la plaza nueva? ¿Quién llegó a la plaza vieja? ¿Con quién llegó Jorge? ¿A qué hora llegaron Jorge y su hermana?*

Gramática·Repaso

Presentation

Resources: Voc. & Gram. Transparencies: 150

Suggestions: Have students fold a sheet of paper in half to create a flashcard. On one side of the card, have them write a large accent mark. Tell them to leave the other side blank. Say sentences that contain the words reviewed in the *Gramática.* Some of your models should use the words to form questions, and others should use them in subordinate clauses in which no accent is required: *Cuando llegamos al museo, tú no estabas.* Have students flash the accent side their cards if they hear an interrogative word that requires an accent, and the blank side if a similar word they hear requires no accent

---

 Standards: 1.2

Resources: Practice Answers on Transparencies

Focus: Reviewing interrogative words

Suggestions: Have students scan the entire dialogue for meaning before they begin writing their answers.

Answers:
1. Cómo	4. dónde
2. cuántas	5. Cuál
3. Por qué	6. quién

Extension: Ask pairs of students to practice and present the dialogue for the class.

 Standards: 1.3

Focus: Reviewing interrogative words

Suggestions: Encourage students to ask questions that a tour agency might really ask in order to improve business.

Answers will vary.

8 Review

Vocabulario

Presentation

Standards: 1.1

Resources: Voc. & Gram. Transparencies: 151

Suggestions: Ask students to write sentences using each of the verbs in the *reacciones* and *acciones* categories. In each of their sentences, challenge them to use items from at least one of the other categories as well.

Standards: 1.1, 1.2, 1.3

Actividad 4

Resources: Practice Answers on Transparencies

Focus: Practicing review vocabulary

Suggestions: Once students have matched the items and written their definitions, ask them to identify prefixes and suffixes such as *des-* and *-ía* and explain how they are used.

Answers will vary.

1. c   4. a
2. d   5. b
3. e

Standards: 1.1, 3.1

Actividad 5

Focus: Practicing review vocabulary

Suggestions: As students discuss their word webs, ask them to explain how the solution to the conflict determines how we perceive its causes and reactions. Point out that when a conflict is not yet resolved, there is still confusion as to what its causes are and who is reacting to whom.

Answers will vary.

Vocabulario

el arte
la artesanía
la creación
la joya
la melodía
el oro
la plata

el comercio
cambiar
comprar
el mercado
pagar
el producto
regatear
vender

reacciones
asustarse
enojarse
estar asustado, -a
estar enojado, -a
ponerse enojado, -a
temer
tener miedo de

acciones
atreverse
capturar
destruir
escaparse
luchar
matar
morirse
refugiarse
salvar

las relaciones
colaborar
comunicarse
el conflicto
desconfiar
llevarse bien / mal
la pelea
pelearse
ponerse de acuerdo
reaccionar
relacionarse

 **Actividad 4** Leer/Escribir/Hablar ....

Práctica de vocabulario

Empareja cada definición con la palabra correspondiente. Luego, usa las definiciones como modelos y escribe tus propias definiciones de cuatro palabras o expresiones de las listas. Lee tus definiciones a un(a) compañero(a) para ver si puede identificar las palabras apropiadas.

1. arte u obra con una marca personal
2. evitar un peligro
3. no confiar
4. lugar donde la gente compra y vende productos
5. discutir el precio de algo

a. mercado
b. regatear
c. artesanía
d. salvarse
e. desconfiar

 **Actividad 5** Escribir/Hablar ....

Práctica de vocabulario

Piensa en un conflicto que hayas tenido en casa o en la escuela. Haz una red de palabras como la que sigue y complétala. Usa las palabras del vocabulario. Compara tu red con las de otros(as) compañeros(as). Hablen sobre las causas de los conflictos y sus soluciones.

PARTICIPANTES — CONFLICTO — REACCIÓN
CAUSA — SOLUCIÓN

---

340 trescientos cuarenta
A ver si recuerdas . . .

Universal Access

Multiple Intelligences

Interpersonal/Social: Have students choose 8 to 10 words from the *Vocabulario* on pp. 338 and 340. Have them role-play a "walk around the city." Instruct students to meet their "neighbors" and chat about people, places, and reactions. Direct them to use each one of their chosen words before they can "stroll back home."

Students with Learning Difficulties

Students may have difficulty memorizing past forms of irregular verbs, especially verbs with irregular stems. Have students create their own reference cards for each of these verbs. On each card, students should list present, preterite, and imperfect forms. Encourage students to write clearly for quick reference.

340

Gramática · Repaso

Verbos con cambios en el pretérito

Verbs like *oír*, *leer*, and *creer* change the *i* to *y* in the *Ud./él/ella* and *Uds./ellos/ellas* forms: *leí, leíste, leyó, leímos, leísteis, leyeron.*

Stem-changing *-ir* verbs like *dormir, morir* (o → ue), *sentir, preferir* (e → ie), and *pedir, repetir* (e → i) have changes in the *Ud./él/ella* and the *Uds./ellos/ellas* form of the preterite.

> dormir: durmió, durmieron
> sentir: sintió, sintieron

Some verbs, such as *decir, traer,* and *traducir* have irregular stems in the preterite but they share the same endings:

> decir: dije, dijiste, dijo, dijimos, dijisteis, dijeron
> traer: traje, trajiste, trajo, trajimos, trajisteis, trajeron
> traducir: traduje, tradujiste, tradujo, tradujimos, tradujisteis, tradujeron

The following verbs also have irregular stems in the preterite and share the following endings: *-e, -iste, -o, -imos, isteis, -ieron.*

tener	estar	saber	poner	andar	poder	venir	hacer
tuv-	estuv-	sup-	pud-	anduv-	pud-	vin-	hic-

¿Recuerdas?

El verbo *haber* en el pretérito se conjuga *hubo.* Se usa para indicar que algo sucedió en el pasado en un momento específico en el tiempo, no algo que sucedía siempre.

Anoche *hubo* luna llena.

 Leer

Práctica de gramática

Escribe la forma correcta del pretérito para completar este informe sobre un día en la vida de dos estudiantes.

Ayer, ellos **1.** (tener) muchas actividades. Primero, **2.** (andar) un rato por el parque. Después, sus amigos **3.** (venir) a la casa de visita. Luego, **4.** (estar) en la biblioteca e **5.** (hacer) varias tareas para sus clases. **6.** (leer) un cuento para la clase de inglés y **7.** (traducir) algunas frases del español al inglés. Al salir, **8.** (querer) llamar a Pablo e Isabel pero no **9.** (poder) porque su teléfono no funcionaba. **10.** (ir) a un café y **11.** (pedir) unos pasteles con café. ¡Una manera perfecta de descansar después de un día tan ocupado!

  Hablar

Práctica de gramática

Entrevista a tu compañero(a) sobre la última película que fueron a ver sus amigos(as). Túrnense para hacer preguntas y contestarlas. Usen los siguientes verbos: *ir, estar, andar, dormir, preferir, comenzar, terminar.*

Modelo

ir
¿Qué película fueron a ver?

● **Más práctica**
Practice Workbook 8-1, 8-2

For: More review
Visit: www.phschool.com
Web Code: jed-0801

trescientos cuarenta y uno **341**
Capítulo 8

Gramática · Repaso

Presentation

Resources: Voc. & Gram. Transparencies: 152

Suggestions: Have students use three different verbs from the *Gramática* in sentences with third-person singular or plural subjects. Ask volunteers to write their sentences on the board and point out the spellings of the irregular verb forms.

 Standards: 1.2

Resources: Practice Answers on Transparencies

Focus: Reviewing irregular preterite verb forms

Common Errors: Students may forget to use irregular preterite verb stems when speaking or writing. Model the correct forms as necessary.

Suggestions: Remind students to pay particular attention to spelling, since that is the focus of the activity.

Answers:
1. tuvieron
2. anduvieron
3. vinieron
4. estuvieron
5. hicieron
6. Leyeron
7. tradujeron
8. quisieron
9. pudieron
10. Fueron
11. pidieron

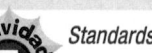 *Standards:* 1.1

Focus: Reviewing irregular preterite verb forms

Suggestions: Remind students that they are asking about a film their friends saw and should use the ***Uds.*** verb forms. Point out they should practice careful pronunciation, since many of the irregular verb forms contain spelling changes.

Answers will vary but should include the following verb forms:

fueron, estuvieron, anduvieron, durmieron, prefirieron, comenzaron, terminaron

---

Teacher-to-Teacher

Ask students to talk about the histories of their family or the family of someone they know. Give them a few minutes to prepare what they plan to say. Encourage them to use verbs with irregular preterite forms: *Mis abuelos vinieron de Italia en 1930. Dejaron todo que tenían en Italia y trajeron muy poco con ellos. Sabían que algún día iban a tener una casa, pero no pudieron comprar una por mucho tiempo porque....*

8 Preview

 Standards for Foreign Language Learning: *Capítulo 8*

- To achieve the goals of the Standards, students will:

Communication

1.1 Interpersonal
- Talk about city sights and their relative positions
- Talk about childhood and conflict resolution
- Talk about travel and favorite films
- Talk about Spanish painter Joaquín Sorolla y Bastida
- Talk about cultural and social interaction and fusion
- Talk about Spanish history, including colonial expansion
- Talk about Quechua music

1.2 Interpretive
- Read about city sights and their relative positions
- Read about conflict resolution
- Read about travel and daily activities
- Read about Spanish painter Joaquín Sorolla y Bastida
- Read and listen to information about cultural and social interaction and fusion
- Read about word families
- Read and listen to information about Spanish history, including colonial expansion
- Read about Quechua music
- Read poetry by Luis Palés Matos and fiction by Elías Miguel Muñoz
- Read about Houston's Museo de Salud y Ciencia
- Read about speech and composition preparation

1.3 Presentational
- Present information orally about travel and city sights
- Write about conflict resolution
- Write and present information orally about cultural and social interaction and fusion
- Write and present information orally about Spanish history, including colonial expansion
- Present information orally about childhood
- Recite poetry by Luis Palés Matos

Culture

2.1 Practices and Perspectives
- Interpret cultural and social interaction and fusion
- Interpret cultural influences in Spanish history, including colonial expansion
- Interpret cultural perspectives in Quechua music and the poetry of Luis Palés Matos

2.2 Products and Perspectives
- Describe the art of Joaquín Sorolla y Bastida, the poetry of Luis Palés Matos, and the fiction of Elías Miguel Muñoz
- Discuss cultural and social interaction and fusion
- Discuss Quechua music
- Discuss Spanish history, including colonial expansion

Connections

3.1 Cross-curricular
- Discuss key facts about visual fine art, poetry, fiction, music, and cuisine
- Discuss key facts about history, social studies, and architecture
- Discuss key facts about Houston's Museo de Salud y Ciencia
- Use Language Arts strategies: fact and opinion, speaker's purpose, chronological ordering, skipping and guessing

3.2 Target Culture
- Read poetry by Luis Palés Matos and fiction by Elías Miguel Muñoz

Fondo cultural

Juaquín Sorolla y Bastida (1863–1923) fue un pintor español. Su obra refleja una gran habilidad para capturar los efectos de la luz. En este cuadro de Granada, Sorolla captura la majestad de la Alhambra y de la Sierra Nevada usando el contraste entre la luz y la sombra.

- ¿Conoces otros pintores que sean famosos por su uso de la luz? ¿Quiénes son?

Granada, (1920), Joaquín Sorolla y Bastida
Museo Sorolla, Madrid, Spain/Bridgeman Art Library.

Universal Access

Personalizing the Theme
Ask students to share their background knowledge about the different cultures that have always defined the United States. Ask guiding questions, such as: *¿De qué país vinieron los primeros exploradores de las Américas? Después de los viajes de Cristóbal Colón, ¿de qué otros países europeos vinieron muchas personas?*

Heritage Language Learners
Ask students to share a brief description of the history of Spanish-speaking people in their heritage country. If they are unsure of the historic details, ask them to speak about the history of their own families. Where did their ancestors live or come from?

Capítulo 8

Encuentro entre culturas

Chapter Objectives

- **Describe how different cultures interact**
- **Talk about the fusion of cultures in Spain before 1492**
- **Talk about fusion of different cultures in the Americas after the Europeans arrived**
- **Understand cultural perspectives of different ethnic groups in the United States**

Video Focus

- **Cultural diversity in the Spanish-speaking world**

Country Connection

As you learn about different cultures in Spain and the Americas, you will make connections to these countries and places.

For: Online Atlas
Visit: www.phschool.com
Web Code: jee-0002

trescientos cuarenta y tres 343
Capítulo 8

Preview

Standards for Foreign Language Learning (cont'd)

Comparisons

4.1 Language
- Compare the Spanish to the English conditional
- Compare Spanish use of the imperfect subjunctive with English if/then sentences
- Compare Spanish words to their English counterparts

4.2 Culture
- Compare cultural fusion in the Spanish-speaking world with that in the United States
- Compare Tex-Mex and Latin American food with traditional fare in the United States
- Compare indigenous influence in Latin America with that in the United States

Communities

5.1 Beyond the School
- Link to Web sites from around the Spanish-speaking world

5.2 Lifelong Learner
- Develop an appreciation for poetry, fiction, and music

Chapter Opener

Presentation

Resources: Voc. & Gram. Transparencies: 14, 18, 20, 22 (maps);

Suggestions: Introduce students to the theme of the chapter and go over the objectives. Point out that they will improve their ability to communicate on the topic of the migrations and intermixing of cultures over the centuries. Use the transparencies to locate and discuss the countries featured in the chapter.

Fondo cultural *Standards:* 1.1, 1.2, 2.2, 3.1

Resources: Fine Art Transparencies; Fine Art Transparencies Teacher's Guide

Suggestions: After students read the information, ask comprehension questions. For example: *¿Qué habilidad se refleja en la obra de Sorolla? (Se refleja la habilidad para capturar los efectos de la luz.) ¿Qué combinación de elementos se ve en la pintura? (Se ve una combinación de la arquitectura, el agua y la luz.)*

Answers will vary.

Enriching Your Teaching

Planning for Instruction
Resources:
- Teacher Express CD-ROM or Resource Book
  - Teaching resources
  - Lesson Planner
  - Chapter Resource Checklist
  - School-to-Home Connection Letter

Culture Note
Mexico's cultural heritage includes influences of indigenous peoples, such as the Mayan, Aztec, and Huichol, as well as the Spanish. However, other ethnic groups have also played a role in the country's history. In the early twentieth century, many Chinese immigrated to Mexico to work on building the country's irrigation systems.

343

Presentation

Standards: 1.1, 1.2, 2.2, 3.1, 5.1

Resources: Voc. & Gram. Transparencies: 153–154; Resource Book: Cap. 8, Input Script; Audio Program: CD Cap. 8, Track 1

Focus: Presenting new vocabulary and using grammar lexically in context

Suggestions: Show *Vocabulary and Grammar Transparencies* 153 and 154. Say the names of visualized vocabulary items, have students repeat, and ask volunteers to point to the appropriate image on the transparency. For non-visualized vocabulary such as **asimilaron, maravilla,** and **anteriormente,** use explanation, circum-locution, synonyms, antonyms, or gestures along with exaggerated intonation to clarify meaning: ***Anteriormente** significa **antes.** El Gran Cañón es **una maravilla** natural. La Alhambra en Granada es **una maravilla** de la arquitectura.* Ask students to point out cognates such as **influencia** and **invadieron** and challenge them to invent Spanish definitions for the words.

A primera vista 1

Vocabulario y gramática en contexto

66 Mis compañeros y yo fuimos de viaje a España. Visitamos las ciudades de Córdoba, Granada y Sevilla, y aprendimos mucho sobre la historia. Es interesante que hayan vivido allí **judíos, musulmanes** y **cristianos. La influencia** de cada cultura se puede ver en la **arquitectura** de los edificios y otras construcciones. ¡La mezcla de culturas es fascinante! 99

el acueducto

el arco

Acueducto de Segovia

Invasión árabe

La Mezquita de Córdoba

Siglo III a.C. - V d.C.[1]	711	785
El imperio romano **dominaba** la península. **Los romanos** trajeron a España **la unidad** política, vías (calles), acueductos y puentes, y la religión cristiana.	**Los árabes** vinieron de África, **invadieron** España y **conquistaron** gran parte de la península. La **ocuparon** por casi 800 años.	Los árabes trajeron la religión musulmana a España. Durante **la conquista**, se construyeron impresionantes mezquitas, como la de Córdoba.

---

1 *a.C. (antes de Cristo)* and *d.C. (después de Cristo)* are equivalent to B.C. and A.D. in English.

344 trescientos cuarenta y cuatro
A primera vista 1

Block Schedule

School Year Timeline: Divide the class into groups of three. Have them construct a timeline for the school year placing six significant events on it. Have them provide a brief description as to what happened on each date. Use the timeline on pp. 344–345 as a model.

Universal Access

Students with Learning Difficulties
Ask students to identify the main idea in each paragraph below the timeline on pp. 344 and 345. Have them copy this main idea onto a card. Direct students to mix the cards, and then put the events back into chronological order.

Advanced Learners
Have students draw on their learning from social studies classes and tell what other countries besides Spain were influenced by the Roman Empire.

Language Input

Actividad 1 Escuchar

Estilos y culturas

Escucha lo que dicen los jóvenes y señala la fotografía que corresponda al lugar del que hablan.

la torre

La Giralda

Sinagoga de Córdoba

Patio de los Leones

Los reyes católicos

Ferdinand and Isabella, Eugene Deveria (1808-1865). Art Resource, NY.

1248	1315	1377	1492
Cuando los cristianos **reconquistaron** Sevilla, construyeron la Catedral de Sevilla donde **anteriormente** había una mezquita musulmana. La **única** parte de la construcción original que existe todavía es la torre, que se llama la Giralda.	Se construyó la sinagoga de Córdoba, en donde se observa cómo los judíos **asimilaron** el arte árabe y lo combinaron con sus propias decoraciones.	Los cristianos continuaron la Reconquista. Granada fue la última ciudad que ocuparon los árabes. Al final de esta **época**, se construyó el Patio de los Leones en la Alhambra, en Granada, que es **una maravilla**.	Los cristianos **expulsaron** a los árabes de España. Isabel de Castilla y Fernando de Aragón, "los reyes católicos," **gobernaron** España. Cristóbal Colón llegó a América.

trescientos cuarenta y cinco   345
Capítulo 8

Actividad 1

Standards: 1.2

Resources: Voc. & Gram. Transparencies: 153–154; Audio Program: CD Cap. 8, Track 2; Resource Book: Cap. 8, Audio Script; Practice Answers on Transparencies

Focus: Practicing listening comprehension of new vocabulary

Suggestions: Before playing the *Audio CD* or reading aloud the text, allow students to read over the information on pp. 344–345. Remind them to use familiar key words to help them comprehend what they hear. Allow them to listen more than once.

Answers:
1. el acueducto
2. La Giralda
3. el Patio de los Leones Granada
4. la sinagoga de Córdoba
5. el acueducto
6. los reyes católicos
7. el mapa de España

Enriching Your Teaching

Culture Note

The history of the **Mezquita de Córdoba** is a reflection of the history of Spain. The **Mezquita** was first built by Abd al-Rahman I in 785 A.D. The mosque was built on the site of the Visigoth Christian Church of St. Vincent, which had replaced a Roman pagan temple. In the sixteenth century, when Christians reconquered Córdoba, the mosque was converted to a cathedral. The cathedral's tower was constructed directly over the Islamic Minaret.

Internet Search

Keyword: mihrab + Cordoba

Language Input

Vocabulario y gramática

Presentation

Standards: 1.1, 1.2, 2.1, 2.2, 3.1

Resources: Voc. & Gram. Transparencies: 155–156; Resource Book: Cap. 8, Input Script; Audio Program: CD Cap. 8, Tracks 3–4

Focus: Extending presentation of vocabulary and grammar

Suggestions:

Pre-reading: Ask a volunteer to read aloud the main title of the selection, ***Una gran mezcla de culturas.*** To help students understand the reading, say: *Mira las dos páginas. Estos artículos se tratan de tres ciudades españolas. ¿Cuáles son?*

Reading: Allow students time to read the selections silently first. Then play the *Audio CD* or read the text, with students reading along as they listen. Allow them to listen more than once. Another option is to have students listen and read along first, then have volunteers take turns reading the articles aloud in chunks.

Post-reading: Check comprehension by asking questions. See the Input Scripts in the *Teacher's Resource Book* for specific questions.

Standards: 1.3

Focus: Writing to demonstrate reading comprehension of new vocabulary

Suggestions: Invite students who have appropriate background knowledge to write about places other than those mentioned in the articles.

Answers will vary.

El Alcázar Real

balcón

rejas

España

Una gran mezcla de culturas

Sevilla

En la provincia de Andalucía y su capital, Sevilla, los romanos y los árabes, entre otros grupos, **dejaron su huella** en la arquitectura. También lo dejaron en la gente y en **el idioma**, al que se asimilaron numerosas palabras árabes. En Sevilla, el Alcázar Real es **una construcción** de estilo mudéjar, una mezcla de la influencia cristiana y del islam. Tiene arcos con **maravillosas** decoraciones de **azulejos**. En el barrio de Triana, muchas de las casas tienen balcones adornados con hermosas rejas de hierro. El viejo barrio de Santa Cruz fue un barrio judío.

 Escribir . . . .

Un viaje por España

Imagina que tú y tus compañeros van a viajar a España. Escribe tres lugares que te gustaría conocer. Explica por qué te gustaría conocerlos.

346 **trescientos cuarenta y seis**
A primera vista 1

Universal Access

Students with Learning Difficulties
Provide students with a graphic organizer to help support understanding of the passages on pp. 346 and 347. Have students create three columns on a piece of paper: ***ciudad, culturas, ejemplo de la mezcla de culturas.*** Then have them reread the selection to fill in the chart.

Students with Special Needs
Help visually impaired students experience the architecture of the cities portrayed in the photographs on pp. 346 and 347. Assist them in tracing shapes and structures, such as the arches in Sevilla or the tower in Toledo.

Un ejemplo de cómo **se integran** las culturas en la época moderna es la ciudad de Barcelona, capital de Cataluña. Por estar cerca de Francia **la población** de Cataluña tiene varias formas de expresión de influencia francesa. Una es el idioma catalán, que ha tomado muchas palabras del francés.

Toledo

Señales en catalán y español

La ciudad de Toledo es ejemplo de la colaboración entre diferentes **grupos étnicos**. En 1085, el rey Alfonso VI reunió en Toledo a los más importantes científicos y filósofos árabes, judíos y cristianos de la época. En este período se **fundó** la famosa Escuela de Traductores de Toledo. En ella se traducían al latín los libros que tenían gran demanda en Europa. Más tarde, en el siglo XIII, la ciudad fue centro cultural de España y de toda Europa.

La otra es la comida, con platos como la butifarra, similar al "saucisson[1]" francés.

[1] cold sausage

Actividad 3 Hablar

Las culturas de una ciudad

Conversa con un(a) compañero(a) sobre las diferentes culturas que se ven hoy o que se veían en el pasado en las ciudades de estas páginas.

Modelo

En Toledo había muchas culturas y grupos étnicos que se integraron.

● **Más práctica**
Practice Workbook 8-3, 8-4

Actividad 4 Escribir

Construcciones famosas

Haz una tabla con tres columnas. Escribe una lista de seis construcciones sobre las que has leído. Di dónde están, cuándo se construyeron y si las construyeron los árabes, los judíos o los cristianos.

Go Online
PHSchool.com
For: Vocabulary practice
Visit: www.phschool.com
Web Code: jed-0802

trescientos cuarenta y siete **347**
Capítulo 8

Focus: Demonstrating reading comprehension via discussion

Suggestions: Encourage students to paraphrase information about the three cities, rather than reciting parts of the text verbatim. Point out that other places they discuss do not have to be in Spain. Students can discuss any place in which there is a variety of cultures.

Answers will vary.

Resources: Practice Answers on Transparencies

Focus: Demonstrating reading comprehension via note-taking

Suggestions: On the board, create a three-column chart. Label the columns *la construcción, el lugar,* and *la cultura.*

Answers will vary. Students should choose from among the following structures for their lists:

**las vías, los puentes, los acueductos
la mezquita de Córdoba
la Giralda de Sevilla
la sinagoga de Córdoba
la Alhambra de Granada
los balcones de Sevilla
la Escuela de Traductores de Toledo**

Additional Resources

• Resource Book: Cap. 8, Clip Art

 Assessment

• Prueba 8-1: Vocabulary recognition

Chapter Project

Give students copies of the Chapter Project outline and rubric from the *Teacher's Resource Book*. Explain the task to them, and have them perform step 1. (For more information, see p. 338-a.)

Enriching Your Teaching

Teacher-to-Teacher

Whenever students record information—while reading, during class discussions, when preparing for tests—encourage them to organize thoughts and information graphically. Help them become familiar with the various types of graphic organizers by regularly modeling their use and working with a variety of them in your teaching.

Rapid Review

Briefly review rules for accent marks with students. On the board write words that require accent marks, but don't include them as you write. Ask students to say which letter in the word has an accent mark over it.

Standards: 1.2, 3.1

Resources: Practice Answers on Transparencies

Focus: Demonstrating comprehension of new vocabulary

Suggestions: Tell students to complete the activity in three steps: 1. briefly read the word bank and the paragraph, 2. write the answers, 3. read the completed paragraph again.

Answers:

1. unidad	6. judíos
2. ocuparon	7. maravillas
3. musulmanes	8. reconquistó
4. población	9. única
5. étnicos	10. se integraron

Actividad 6 *Standards:* 1.3, 2.2

Focus: Practicing new vocabulary via writing

Suggestions: Remind students to present their descriptions of the photo in a logical way. Suggest that they start with the foreground, continue with the background, and save their impressions for last.

Answers will vary.

Manos a la obra 1

Vocabulario y gramática en uso

Objectives
- Describe how different cultures interact
- Talk about the fusion of different cultures in Spain before 1492
- Practice the conditional tense

  Leer/Hablar ....

¡Bienvenido a Toledo!

Completa la siguiente información con las palabras del recuadro. Después, habla con otro(a) compañero(a) y pregúntale si le gustaría visitar Toledo y por qué.

ocuparon	musulmanes	reconquistó	población	étnicos
judíos	maravillas	única	se integraron	unidad

Durante siglos, la ciudad de Toledo ha mantenido su __1.__ mientras recibía la influencia de muchas culturas y religiones. Los romanos entraron en la ciudad en 193 a.C. y la __2.__. Siglos después, los __3.__ que vinieron desde el sur de España y desde África conquistaron Toledo. Durante la Edad Media (*Middle Ages*), que se extendió aproximadamente desde el año 476 al 1492, Toledo fue un centro intelectual y artístico, con una gran __4.__ formada por varios grupos __5.__, como musulmanes, __6.__ y cristianos. El palacio musulmán, llamado El Alcázar, fue construido en 1531 y es una de las verdaderas __7.__ de la ciudad. Más adelante, durante la Reconquista, el rey Alfonso XIII __8.__ la ciudad en 1085 y volvieron a gobernar los reyes cristianos. Toledo no es la __9.__ ciudad de España donde __10.__ muchas culturas y religiones, pero es uno de los mejores ejemplos.

 Escribir ....

Un patio andaluz

Observa la foto de un patio en España. Luego, escribe una descripción de lo que ves y tus impresiones. Incluye las palabras siguientes.

azulejos	rejas	influencia
balcón	arquitectura	arco
construcción	maravilloso(a)	musulmán

Patio de Andalucía, España

Universal Access

Students with Learning Difficulties

Before students complete *Actividad* 5, have them separate the word choices into the following categories: people, things, descriptions, and actions. As students read through the paragraph, assist them in choosing the correct word by asking what type of word is missing.

Advanced Learners

Ask students to write their own fill-in-the-blank vocabulary exercises. These can either be in paragraph form or presented as separate sentences. Have students number each blank and make an answer sheet. Have them exchange their work with a partner, complete each other's exercises, and check their answers together.

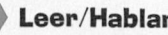

Leer/Hablar ···

Una breve historia de España

Para entender bien las culturas de hoy, es importante que conozcas la historia de otros países. Lee la línea cronológica de esta página. Con otro(a) estudiante, habla de la historia de España. Trata de usar todos los verbos siguientes.

invadir	ocupar	asimilarse	llegar	contribuir
reconquistar	gobernar	expulsar	integrarse	dominar

Modelo

A —¿Qué pasó en el año 1085?
B —Los cristianos reconquistaron Toledo.

218 a.C.
Romanos: Conquista de España, construcción de puentes y acueductos

711
Llegada de los musulmanes de África; contribuciones en las matemáticas, las ciencias, el papel, los números que usamos hoy; integración de muchos grupos étnicos en España

1085
Cristianos: reconquista de Toledo

1236
Musulmanes: gobiernan desde La Alhambra de Granada

1492
Reyes Católicos: reconquista y ocupación de Granada; expulsión del último rey musulmán, Boabdil; expulsión de los judíos de España

Ampliación del lenguaje

Palabras árabes

Durante los ochocientos años que los árabes estuvieron en España, muchas palabras del árabe pasaron a formar parte del español. Muchas de ellas entraron también en otros idiomas de Europa, incluyendo el inglés. Lee las palabras de la tabla y escoge las que mejor completan las frases.

Palabras de origen árabe	
alcázar	¡hola!
algodón	jarabe
alfombra	limón
barrio	mezquita
baño	naranja
café	¡ojalá!
chisme	taza
guitarra	

1. En el _____ donde vivo hay una _____ adonde van los musulmanes.

2. El músico estaba tocando su _____ , pero cuando me vio me saludó diciendo " _____ ".

3. En mi casa tenemos una _____ en el piso que está hecha de _____ .

4. Todas las mañanas, mi mamá bebe una _____ de _____ y un jugo de _____ .

trescientos cuarenta y nueve **349**
Capítulo 8

Practice and Communicate

Focus: Practicing new vocabulary and structures through reading and response

Suggestions: First, have students silently read the article and answer questions 1–2 on their own. Invite them to share their answers to these questions in their small groups before they complete the chart for item 3.

Answers:
1. Answers to the first part will vary, but might include: los italianos, ingleses, judíos, rusos, árabes y bolivianos.
2. Es bueno porque hace que una ciudad sea multicultural y cosmopolita.
3. Answers will vary.

Actividad 8   Leer/Escribir/Hablar ....

Mi Buenos Aires querido

¿Has oído alguna vez hablar de la ciudad de Buenos Aires y su origen?
Lee el siguiente artículo sobre Buenos Aires y contesta las preguntas.

Conexiones | **Las ciencias sociales** _____

Buenos Aires

Desde que se fundó Buenos Aires en 1536, allí se han mezclado distintas culturas, religiones y tradiciones. Aunque el idioma oficial de Argentina es el español, en la ciudad hay barrios en los que el idioma que más se habla es el italiano, el inglés, el yiddish, el ruso o el árabe y donde se pueden ver mezquitas, sinagogas e iglesias. Anteriormente, la mayoría de los inmigrantes que llegaban a Buenos Aires venían de Europa, pero en los últimos tiempos la mayoría ha llegado de otros países latinoamericanos, sobre todo de Bolivia.

Esta inmigración de diferentes grupos étnicos ha hecho de Buenos Aires una ciudad multicultural y cosmopolita. En algunos casos los inmigrantes se han asimilado a la manera de vivir del lugar. Por ejemplo, aunque muchos hablan sus propios idiomas, la mayoría habla también español.

También puedes encontrar que en un mismo barrio se practican las religiones judía, cristiana y musulmana, y se comen platos que vienen de muchos lugares, como la pasta de Italia o los guisos (stews) de España.

Buenos Aires no es la única ciudad de América del Sur con esta mezcla maravillosa de culturas pero es una de las más conocidas por su variedad.

1. ¿Cuáles son algunos de los inmigrantes y grupos étnicos que se establecieron en Buenos Aires?

2. ¿Por qué es bueno que muchas personas de diferentes culturas vivan en una misma ciudad?

3. Trabaja con tres estudiantes. Copien esta tabla, complétenla y comparen su ciudad o comunidad con la ciudad de Buenos Aires.

	Buenos Aires	Mi ciudad / comunidad
¿Dónde está?		
¿Cuál es el idioma oficial?		
¿Qué religiones se practican?		
¿Hay muchos inmigrantes?		
¿De dónde son?		

Universal Access

Heritage Language Learners
After students have completed the table on p. 350 with reference to Buenos Aires and their own communities, ask them to answer the same questions with reference to their heritage country in general. What are some of the aspects of its culture?

Students with Learning Difficulties
Help students identify key words or phrases in each of the questions on p. 350. Instruct them to locate these words or phrases in the passage. Then have them reread around the key word or phrase to find the answer.

Actividad 9 · Leer/Escribir

La cultura en la arquitectura

Puedes aprender sobre otras culturas al observar su arte y su arquitectura. Mira el anuncio y contesta las preguntas.

1. ¿Sobre qué es la exposición (exhibit)?

2. ¿De dónde son los arquitectos? ¿Son todos de la misma cultura étnica?

3. ¿Crees que las construcciones que se presentan en la exposición van a ser similares? ¿Por qué? ¿Por qué no?

4. Imagina que puedes dejar una huella en tu comunidad. ¿Qué contribución te gustaría hacer? Haz un folleto como éste que la represente.

Museo Regional del Sur y Museo Histórico Arqueológico presentan

HUELLAS DE IDENTIDAD:
ASIMILACIÓN CULTURAL EN LA ARQUITECTURA CHILENA

23 de enero–12 de mayo

▸ 5 arquitectos de la época moderna
▸ diversas influencias étnicas
▸ construcciones únicas

Avenida de la Cruz, no. 32
Valparaíso

Actividad 10 · Escribir/Hablar

Y tú, ¿qué dices?

1. ¿Qué cultura(s) representas tú? ¿De dónde eran tus abuelos y bisabuelos (great-grandparents)? ¿Qué idioma(s) hablaban? ¿Lo(s) siguen hablando? ¿Por qué?

2. ¿Qué culturas han contribuido a la cultura de los Estados Unidos? ¿Qué huellas han dejado?

3. ¿Alguna vez has tenido que integrarte a una nueva cultura o grupo? ¿Cuándo? ¿Cómo te sentiste? ¿Qué diferencias notaste entre tu manera de ser y la de ellos?

4. Imagina que hay un nuevo estudiante de otro país en tu clase. Di al menos cinco cosas que puedes hacer para ayudarle a integrarse.

Actividad 9 · Standards: 1.2

Resources: Practice Answers on Transparencies

Focus: Practicing new vocabulary

Suggestions: After students have read and discussed the ad, have them work in small groups to create their own ad for item 4.

Answers:
1. Es sobre la asimilación cultural en la arquitectura chilena.
2. Son de Chile. No.
3.–4. Answers will vary.

Actividad 10 · Standards: 1.1, 1.3, 4.2, 5.2

Focus: Practicing new vocabulary and structures by responding to questions

Suggestions: Many heritage language learners will have particularly insightful responses to question 4. Invite them to share these with the class.

Answers will vary.

Additional Resources

• Writing, Audio & Video Workbook: Cap. 8, Audio Activity 1, Track 5
• Writing, Audio & Video Workbook: Cap. 8, Writing Activity 6
• Resource Book: Cap. 8, Communicative Activity BLM

 Assessment
• Prueba 8-2: Vocabulary production

Enriching Your Teaching

Teacher-to-Teacher
Take this opportunity to initiate a thoughtful and sensitive discussion with students on the topic of ethnic and cultural differences. Discuss how these differences can enrich our lives. Help students understand that ethnic stereotypes are inaccurate generalizations based on fear or a lack of knowledge.

Gramática

El condicional

You use the conditional in Spanish to express what a person would do or what a situation would be like.

Me **gustaría** leer un libro sobre el budismo.   Yo le **pediría** ese libro a Tomás.

- As with the future tense, you form the conditional by adding the endings to the infinitive. The conditional endings are the same for all verbs. Here are the conditional forms of *hablar, ser,* and *ir*.

hablar		ser		ir	
hablaría	hablaríamos	sería	seríamos	iría	iríamos
hablarías	hablaríais	serías	seríais	irías	iríais
hablaría	hablarían	sería	serían	iría	irían

- All verbs that are irregular in the future tense have the same irregular stems in the conditional.

decir	dir-	poder	podr-	saber	sabr-	tener	tendr-
haber	habr-	poner	pondr-	salir	saldr-	querer	querr-
hacer	har-	componer	compondr-	venir	vendr-	contener	contendr-

Actividad 11   Gramática Leer

La Ruta Quetzal

El año pasado tu amiga participó en la Ruta Quetzal, un viaje que muchos jóvenes hacen por España y América Latina. Tú quieres hacer el viaje el año próximo, y ella te cuenta cómo sería. Completa el párrafo con el condicional del verbo apropiado.

¿Te interesa participar en la Ruta Quetzal? Esta experiencia __1.__ (tener / ser) fantástica para ti. El viaje __2.__ (ocupar / comenzar) en España. Para decidir quiénes __3.__ (ir / poder), tú y los otros estudiantes __4.__ (contribuir / salir) ideas sobre los lugares que se __5.__ (fundar / poder) visitar. Al terminar la experiencia, Uds. __6.__ (saber / fundar) mucho más sobre la integración de la cultura española con la americana y __7.__ (poner / poder) apreciar más las dos culturas. Cuando yo fui, mis padres me dijeron que me __8.__ (ayudar / preferir) a juntar dinero. ¿Te __9.__ (saber / dar) dinero tus padres? ¡No importa! Tienes que ir.

Universal Access

Heritage Language Learners

Ask students to model speech in the conditional tense. Ask them to speculate on what their life would be like if they were living in a different country. They might focus on their heritage country or another country with which they are familiar.

Advanced Learners

Have students write a paragraph telling what their daily routine would be if they lived in a place very unlike where they are. If you live in a city, have them tell what their routines would be if they lived in the countryside, or vice versa.

 **12** **Gramática** **Hablar** ....

¡Ganamos!

Tu familia participa en un concurso para ganar una casa que se construiría según el estilo musulmán. Como a tu mamá le encanta este tipo de arquitectura, ella se imagina cómo sería. Habla con otro(a) estudiante para describir su nueva casa. Usen elementos de cada columna.

Modelo

Mi mamá tendría una ventana con un balcón.

Yo	tener	balcón
Nosotros	poner	rejas
Mis hermanos	construir	azulejos
Mi hermano(a)	gustar	flores
Mi mamá (o papá)	querer	fuente
Mis padres	pedir	arcos
¡Respuesta personal!	hacer	torre
	preferir	patio
	¡Respuesta personal!	jardín
		¡Respuesta personal!

 13 **Gramática** **Hablar** ....

No sabía que en . . .

Piensa en una ciudad que visitaste y en las cosas que encontraste que no te habías imaginado. Escoge entre las cuatro columnas para decir tus frases a un(a) compañero(a).

Modelo

No me había dado cuenta de que vería grupos étnicos tan diferentes.

no podía creer que	haber	cosas tan . . .	divertido
no sabía que	encontrar	grupos étnicos tan . . .	interesante
no me di cuenta de que	ver	construcciones tan . . .	alto
nunca pensé que	comer	la influencia de . . .	impresionante
¡Respuesta personal!	escuchar	música tan . . .	diferente
	visitar	comida tan . . .	similar
	hacer	puntos de interés tan . . .	maravilloso
	¡Respuesta personal!	personas tan . . .	único
		¡Respuesta personal!	¡Respuesta personal!

 Actividad 12 *Standards:* 1.1

Resources: Practice Answers on Transparencies

Focus: Practicing the conditional tense in a guided conversation

Suggestions: Point out to students that for the **respuesta personal,** they should use a verb of their own choosing that is different from the rest of those in the chart.

Answers will vary. Students will choose from among the following verb forms:
**tendría/tendríamos/tendrían
pondría/pondríamos/pondrían
construiría/construiríamos/construirían
gustaría/gustarían
querría/querríamos/querrían
pediría/pediríamos/pedirían
haría/haríamos/harían
preferiría/preferiríamos/preferirían**

 Actividad 13 *Standards:* 1.1

Resources: Practice Answers on Transparencies

Focus: Practicing the conditional tense in a guided conversation

Suggestions: Remind students to make the adjectives in the fourth column agree in number and gender with the nouns they modify.

Answers will vary. Students will use the following verb forms:

habría	escucharía
encontraría	visitaría
vería	haría
comería	

Chapter Project

Students can perform step 2 at this point. Be sure they understand your corrections and suggestions. (For more information, see p. 338-a.)

<hr>

Enriching Your Teaching

Teacher-to-Teacher

Invite students to use the conditional tense to write a description of the school of their dreams. Ask guiding questions as necessary. For example: *¿Cómo serían las aulas? ¿Qué cursos* *habría? ¿Cómo serían los profesores? ¿Qué harías durante un día típico? ¿De qué consistirían los almuerzos?* Invite students to share and discuss their completed descriptions.

Actividad 14 *Standards:* 1.1

Resources: Practice Answers on Transparencies

Focus: Practicing the conditional tense via guided dialogues

Suggestions: Ask students to complete the *Actividad* twice, switching roles. Student B's answers should be different each time.

Answers will vary. Students will use the following verb forms:

1. Vivirían   4. Tendría
2. podría   5. encontraría
3. Sería   6. debería

Actividad 15 *Standards:* 1.1, 1.3

Focus: Practicing the conditional tense

Suggestions: If students have difficulty thinking of questions, ask them to consider things they like to do, list them, and use the list as a source of ideas for questions.

Answers will vary.

 **Actividad 14** **Gramática** **Hablar**

Conoce nuestra comunidad

Imagina que un(a) estudiante de otro país te hace preguntas para informarse sobre tu comunidad. Trabaja con otro(a) estudiante para hacer los papeles de estudiante y estudiante extranjero(a). Usen el condicional.

Modelo

¿Qué *(tener)* que ponerme para ir a la escuela?
A —¿Qué *tendría* que ponerme para ir a la escuela?
B —*Podrías llevar jeans y una camiseta.*

Estudiante A

1. ¿*(Vivir)* muchos o pocos grupos étnicos en tu comunidad?
2. ¿A qué lugares *(poder)* ir para ver la vida típica de los jóvenes en tu comunidad?
3. ¿*(Ser)* fácil o difícil asimilarme en tu escuela?
4. ¿*(Tener)* que hablar inglés todo el tiempo?
5. ¿Qué religiones diferentes *(encontrar)*?
6. ¿Qué más *(deber)* hacer para integrarme a la nueva cultura?

Estudiante B

¡Respuesta personal!

 **Actividad 15** **Gramática** **Pensar/Escribir/Hablar**

En tu comunidad

❶ Imagina que acabas de mudarte a otro estado y quieres aprender más sobre tu nueva comunidad. Haz una lista de preguntas que le harías a un(a) jóven que vive en esa comunidad.

Modelo

¿Adónde podría ir para encontrar jóvenes de mi edad?
¿Cuál es el equipo de deportes más popular?
¿Cuál es el restaurante más popular entre los jóvenes?

❷ Trabaja con un grupo para escoger un mínimo de seis preguntas. Contesten las preguntas y usen las respuestas para escribir un breve párrafo en el cual describen su comunidad.

Modelo

Si quieres conocer a jóvenes de tu edad, podrías ir al café La Paz por la tarde porque allí van muchos chicos después de la escuela.

354 trescientos cincuenta y cuatro
Manos a la obra 1

Universal Access

Heritage Language Learners

Ask students to comment on the musical traditions of their heritage country. Phrase questions so that they may be answered using the conditional tense. You might ask what kinds of instruments one would see, what kinds of sounds one would hear, or what kinds of locations one could visit to listen to music.

Multiple Intelligences

Musical/Rhythmic: Ask students who play a musical instrument to bring their instruments to share with the group. Ask them to research and discuss the history of their instruments, and the cultures in which they are prevalent. Have students play a short selection.

Actividad 16

Leer/Hablar ·

La música llegó por España

Durante la conquista árabe, España se convirtió en la puerta por donde entraban a Europa las nuevas ideas y descubrimientos.

laúd

Conexiones **La música**

Durante la época que los árabes ocuparon España, Europa recibió muchos instrumentos y conceptos musicales de ese pueblo.

Los árabes fundaron escuelas de música en España. Instrumentos musicales como la guitarra, el órgano y el laúd *(lute)* no se conocían en Europa hasta que los árabes los llevaron a España. Pero quizás la contribución más importante fue el concepto de armonía, que cambió la historia de la música europea.

• ¿Por qué crees que se dice que España era la puerta por donde entraban las nuevas ideas a Europa?

• ¿Cuáles fueron las contribuciones árabes a la música europea?

Fondo cultural ■◆■◆■◆■◆■◆■◆■◆

El arpa paraguaya nació cuando se asimilaron dos culturas, la española y la indígena guaraní del territorio que sería Paraguay. El arpa es originaria de Egipto y es uno de los instrumentos más antiguos que se conocen. Los exploradores españoles que viajaron por el Río de la Plata en 1526 fueron acompañados de un hombre que tocaba el arpa. Los guaraníes, que amaban la música, adoptaron el arpa, la cambiaron a su manera y la hicieron parte de su vida diaria. El resultado fue maravilloso: un instrumento ligero hecho de madera *(wood)* americana, y frecuentemente, con cuerdas *(strings)* de colores diferentes.

Los guaraníes enseñan a sus niños a tocar con una técnica propia que pasa de padres a hijos. La música que ha resultado de este instrumento, que llegó con los españoles y que ha sido integrado en la cultura indígena, es muy especial y bella.

• ¿Qué contribuyó España a la música paraguaya? ¿Cómo la han asimilado los guaraníes a su cultura?

• ¿Puedes nombrar un instrumento u otra expresión artística en los Estados Unidos que haya tenido su origen en otra cultura?

● **Más práctica** · · · · · · · · · · · · · · ·
Practice Workbook 8-5, 8-6, 8-7

Go Online
PHSchool.com
For: Practice with the conditional
Visit: www.phschool.com
Web Code: jed-0803

Actividad 16

Standards: 1.1, 1.2, 2.1, 3.1
· · · · · · · · · · · · · · · · ·

Resources: Practice Answers on Transparencies

Focus: Practicing new vocabulary and structures via reading and response

Suggestions: Have students read the information on their own first, then discuss the questions with a partner. Invite partners to share their responses to the questions with the rest of the class.

Answers:
• **Se dice esto porque España era el país que recibió la mayor cantidad de las influencias importantes del mundo árabe.**
• **Los árabes contribuyeron con instrumentos musicales como la guitarra, el órgano y el laúd. La contribución más importante fue el concepto de armonía.**

Fondo cultural

Standards: 1.1, 1.2, 2.1, 2.2, 3.1, 5.2
■◆■◆■◆■◆■◆■◆■◆■◆

Suggestions: After students have read the information, ask comprehension questions. For example: *¿Puedes nombrar a un pueblo indígena que vive en Paraguay? (los guaraníes) ¿Qué pasó en 1526? (Los españoles viajaron por el Río de la Plata)*

Answers:
• **España contribuyó con la idea del arpa, un elemento importante de la música paraguaya. Los guaraníes han cambiado los materiales que se usan para construir el arpa. También han adaptado la técnica de tocar ese instrumento.**
• **Answers will vary.**

Additional Resources
• Writing, Audio & Video Workbook: Cap. 8, Writing Activities 7–9

✓ **Assessment**
• Prueba 8-3: *El condicional*
• Examen: Vocabulario y gramática 1

Enriching Your Teaching

Culture Note
The harp is thought to have originally developed as a musical evolution of a hunter's bow. Variations of the instrument can be found throughout the world. They include the Adunga, a nine-string arched harp from Uganda, the Celtic or Irish Harp, the Chinese Konghou, the Burmese Saung-Gauk, and of course, the Paraguayan Harp. The Veracruz Harp is common throughout Mexico and Latin America. It first came from Spain around the 1500s.

Internet Search
Keyword: música guaraní

Vocabulario y gramática

Presentation

Standards: 1.1, 1.2, 2.1, 2.2, 3.1

Resources: Voc. & Gram. Transparencies: 158–159; Resource Book: Cap. 8, Input Script; Audio Program: CD Cap. 8, Track 7

Focus: Presenting new vocabulary and using grammar lexically in context

Suggestions: Ask volunteers to read the main title and the captions on these pages. Invite students to talk about what they see in the pictures. Have students point out cognates such as *europeos, colonia,* and *adoptaran* from among the new vocabulary. Play the *Audio CD* or read the text and have students follow along. Check comprehension by asking questions. See the Input Script in the *Teacher's Resource Book* for specific questions.

Block Schedule

Have each student write six *Cierto/Falso* statements from the information on pp. 356–367. Have them work in pairs and read statements to each other. The partner states whether the statement is *cierto* or *falso* and then corrects the information that is false.

A primera vista 2

Vocabulario y gramática en contexto

Objectives

Read, listen to, and understand information about
• interaction between cultures
• fusion of different cultures in the Americas after the arrival of the Europeans

Con la llegada de los españoles y otros exploradores **europeos** a las Américas al final del siglo XV, se produjo **un encuentro** que iba a cambiar para siempre la vida en los dos hemisferios.

La llegada: los aztecas y Hernán Cortés

1 En el siglo XIII, llegó a la región central de México un grupo de **indígenas** llamados aztecas. Estos indígenas, más tarde llamados *mexicas,* **establecieron** entre dos lagos la ciudad de Tenochtitlán, la cual llegó a ser la capital de su **imperio**. En esta **tierra** creció el imperio azteca que dominó el centro y el sur de México a finales del siglo XV. El imperio azteca estaba basado en la agricultura, el comercio, la religión y **la guerra.**

Tenochtitlán era una ciudad con una gran población y **una riqueza** increíble.

2 En 1519, el español Hernán Cortés llegó a la costa de México cerca de Veracruz. Desde allí salió para Tenochtitlán con un grupo de **soldados** montados a caballo y con **armas** de fuego. Los aztecas **se rebelaron** contra los españoles, con quienes **se enfrentaron** y **lucharon** en numerosas **batallas.** En 1521, Hernán Cortés logró conquistar al **poderoso** imperio azteca y a su emperador, Moctezuma. Así se creó el gobierno español en las Américas, llamado *virreinato*. Éste duró hasta 1821, año en que México ganó su independencia de España.

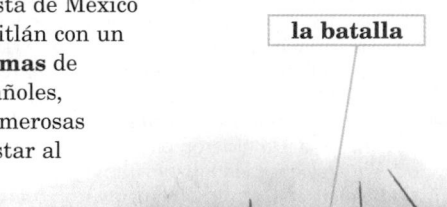

la batalla

Los aztecas describían a los españoles como seres[1] con dos cabezas, una de hombre y otra de animal, y cuatro patas.[2]

_____

1 beings **2** legs

Universal Access

Students with Learning Difficulties
Students may have difficulty with comprehension of the text on pp. 356 and 357. To help organize the information presented, have students find the dates mentioned in sections 1 and 2 of the reading. Then have them create a timeline with a simple caption for each year or century mentioned.

Advanced Learners
Ask students to write paraphrases for each of the four sections on these pages on separate sheets of paper. Collect and mix all the paraphrases. Have students arrange them into sets of four in chronological order and discuss similarities and differences among the different paraphrased versions.

El intercambio

3 **Al llegar** los españoles, se estableció **una colonia** con **el poder** de España, que se llamó Nueva España. Después de poco tiempo, empezó **un intercambio** de mercancías entre Europa y las Américas. Los españoles se llevaron café, chocolate y maíz, hasta entonces **desconocidos** en Europa, y trajeron a Nueva España caballos, pollo y arroz.

las mercancías

la misión

el misionero

4 Los españoles cambiaron muchos aspectos de la vida de los indígenas. Ellos querían que los indígenas **adoptaran** su religión, su **lengua** y su cultura. Muchos religiosos de varias órdenes, como los Dominicanos y los Franciscanos, llegaron a la colonia. Esos misioneros construyeron misiones para enseñarles a los indígenas su religión. Los españoles también trajeron su arquitectura, su comida y sus tradiciones. Con la poca **semejanza** entre la cultura española y la indígena, el encuentro entre los dos mundos cambió para siempre la historia de las Américas.

 17 Escuchar ·····································

Diferentes opiniones

Escribe los números del 1 al 6 en una hoja. Escucha cada frase sobre la historia del encuentro entre los aztecas y los españoles y escribe *C* si es cierta o *F* si es falsa.

 *Standards:* 1.2
17 ·····················

Resources: Audio Program: CD Cap. 8, Track 8; Resource Book: Cap. 8, Audio Script; Practice Answers on Transparencies

Focus: Practicing listening comprehension of new vocabulary

Suggestions: Before students listen, allow them a few minutes to silently read over the information on these two pages. Play the *Audio CD* or read from the script. Allow students to listen more than once.

Answers:
1. F	4. C
2. F	5. F
3. C	6. C

Chapter Project

Students can perform step 3 at this point. (For more information, see p. 338-a.)

Enriching Your Teaching

Teacher-to-Teacher

Use visuals on these pages to elicit as much language as possible from students. They can describe what they see, practice various tenses to say what happened, is happening, or will happen in a picture, or offer opinions or value statements based on their interpretation of a picture.

Internet Search

Keyword: Hernán Cortés

Language Input

Vocabulario y gramática

Presentation

Standards: 1.1, 1.2, 2.1, 2.2, 3.1

Resources: Voc. & Gram. Transparencies: 160–161; Resource Book: Cap. 8, Input Script; Audio Program: CD Cap. 8, Tracks 9–10

Focus: Extending presentation of vocabulary and grammar in context

Suggestions:

Pre-reading: Point out cognates such as *descendencia, africana,* and *resultado* that will help students better understand the text as they read. Remind students that the information here is an extension of the historical treatment on pp. 356–357.

Reading: Allow students time to read the information on this and the next page silently first. Then play the *Audio CD* and have students read along as they listen. Allow them to listen more than once.

Post-reading: Check comprehension by asking questions. For example: *¿La celebración del Día de los Muertos es una fusión de elementos de qué religiones? ¿La herencia de Sandra es una fusión de qué tres culturas?*

---

18 *Standards:* 1.2

Resources: Practice Answers on Transparencies

Focus: Practicing reading comprehension of new vocabulary and structures

Suggestions: Encourage students to review the material presented on pp. 356–359 before completing the activity.

Answers:
1. Se veía la influencia de las tradiciones indígenas, europeas y africanas.
2. Se combinan los elementos de la religión católica y la indígena.
3. Porque la comida combina los productos nativos con los de Europa y Asia.
4. Porque sus antepasados son de las tres culturas principales: indígena, española y africana.

La fusión

Durante la época colonial (1521–1821) se mezclaron diferentes **razas**, religiones y costumbres. No sólo había gente de **descendencia** europea, sino también indígena y **africana**. Como **resultado** de esta **mezcla**, hay una gran **variedad** de tradiciones y culturas en América.

1 Los indígenas influyeron en las prácticas religiosas cristianas que trajeron los españoles. En la celebración del Día de los Muertos, que tiene lugar el dos de noviembre para recordar a los familiares que han muerto, se combinan elementos de las religiones católicas e indígenas.

Celebración del Día de los Muertos

2 Una de las cosas en que se vio la influencia española fue la comida. Durante la época colonial, la alimentación de los indígenas cambió debido a los productos traídos por los españoles. Es en esta época que aparecen muchos de los platos mexicanos de hoy día. Por ejemplo, el mole poblano, una salsa típica de la cocina mexicana, fue creado por las monjas[1] de una misión utilizando productos mexicanos, asiáticos y europeos.

El mole poblano

---

1 nuns

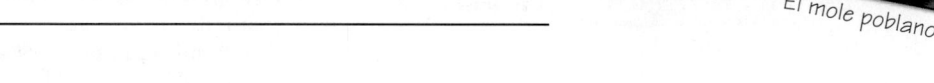
18 **Escribir** ....

Contesta las preguntas con la información de las páginas 358–359.

1. En la fusión que tenía lugar durante la época colonial, ¿se veía la influencia de qué tres tradiciones?

2. ¿La celebración del Día de los Muertos representa la combinación de elementos de qué religiones?

3. ¿Por qué dicen que la comida representa una fusión?

4. ¿Por qué representa la herencia de Sandra lo más noble de la historia de las Américas?

Universal Access

Heritage Language Learners
Ask students to talk about traditional or typical foods in their heritage country. Ask them to discuss the history of these foods in the culture or in their own families. How did the recipes, ingredients, and traditions begin?

Students with Learning Difficulties
Students may have difficulty with the concept of analogies in *Actividad* 19. Provide students with visual clues to help establish the relationship between the first two words in the analogy. For example, for the first item, *europeo: Europa,* draw a person and a simple map.

La herencia

Esta mezcla de culturas sigue presente hoy en día.

❝ Me llamo Sandra y vivo en los Estados Unidos. Mi herencia **se compone de** elementos de varias culturas diferentes. **Los antepasados** de mi familia representan lo más noble de la historia de las Américas: los indígenas americanos que vivían aquí desde hace mucho tiempo, los españoles que llegaron a la costa de México en el siglo XVI, y los africanos con sus tradiciones tan ricas. Estoy muy orgullosa de que mi herencia sea de estas tres culturas. Uno de mis **retos** es aprender sobre las contribuciones de estas culturas a mi país. ❞

Actividad 19 · Leer/Escribir ·······································

Las analogías

Escoge la mejor palabra para completar cada analogía.

africano	europeo	poderoso
luchar	desconocido	lengua

1. europeo: Europa; _____ : África
2. igual : diferente; _____ : débil
3. indígena: azteca; _____ : español
4. escribir : lápiz; _____ : arma
5. justo : injusto; _____ : familiar
6. volver : regresar; _____ : idioma

● **Más práctica** ·····························
Practice Workbook 8-8, 8-9

Go Online
PHSchool.com

For: Vocabulary practice
Visit: www.phschool.com
Web Code: jed-0806

Actividad 19 · *Standards:* 1.2, 3.1
·······························

Resources: Practice Answers on Transparencies

Focus: Writing answers to demonstrate comprehension

Suggestions: Remind students that the items are presented as analogies. A single colon means "is to" and a double colon means "as."

Answers:
1. africano
2. poderoso
3. europeo
4. luchar
5. desconocido
6. lengua

Extension: After students complete the activity, ask them to point out words that are synonyms, such as *idioma* and *lengua,* and antonyms, such as *familiar* and *desconocido.*

Additional Resources
• Resource Book: Cap. 8, Clip Art

✓ **Assessment**
• Prueba 8-4: Vocabulary recognition

Enriching Your Teaching

Culture Note

The Aztecs and the Incas first cultivated the tomato as a crop around 700 A.D. The fruit was brought to Europe by explorers in the sixteenth century. The cuisines of France, Italy, and Spain quickly utilized the new ingredient. The French called it "the apple of love," and the Germans called it "the apple of paradise." As the tomato traveled north, however, its mystery increased. The British actually believed that the tomato was poisonous, a myth that traveled to the American colonies, and was believed by many until the nineteenth century.

Standards: 1.1, 1.3, 3.1

Focus: Demonstrating comprehension of new vocabulary

Suggestions: Remind students that a valid definition of a word does not reuse the word or any other form of the word as part of the definition. Encourage them to consider which part of speech each word is before attempting to define it.

Answers will vary.

Rapid Review
Students will hear a combination of the imperfect and preterite tenses in *Actividad* 21. Briefly review the uses of the two tenses. Make statements that use both the imperfect and the preterite tenses. Have students tell why each tense was used.

Standards: 1.2, 3.1

Resources: Fine Art Transparencies; Fine Art Transparencies Teacher's Guide; Audio Program: CD Cap. 8, Track 11; Resource Book: Cap. 8, Audio Script; Practice Answers on Transparencies

Focus: Practicing listening comprehension of new vocabulary and structures

Suggestions: Point out to students that the description they will hear is a running narrative rather than several independent sentences. Show the *Fine Art Transparency* as you play the *Audio CD* or read from the script. Allow students to listen more than once.

Answers:
1. F; Cortés entró a Tenochtitlán después de que Moctezuma envió a sus mensajeros para invitarlo a entrar en la ciudad.
2. C
3. F; Cortés conoció a Moctezuma en Tenochtitlán.
4. C
5. F; Moctezuma le regaló riquezas importantes a Cortés.

Manos a la obra 2
Vocabulario y gramática en uso

 **Escribir** ·············

¿Qué significa esta palabra?
Trabaja con otro(a) estudiante para escribir definiciones de las palabras siguientes.

Modelo
poderoso
Una persona que es poderosa tiene mucha influencia.

1. la semejanza
2. el imperio
3. la riqueza
4. la batalla
5. el encuentro
6. el resultado
7. la mezcla
8. la mercancía
9. la misión
10. el reto

 Escuchar/Escribir ··········

Cortés llega a Tenochtitlán
Escucha una descripción de la entrada de Cortés a Tenochtitlán. Después, lee cada frase y escribe si es cierta (*C*) o falsa (*F*). Si la frase es falsa, vuelve a escribirla para que diga algo cierto.

1. Cortés entró a Tenochtitlán después de una batalla contra los mensajeros de Moctezuma.
2. Los conquistadores no siguieron el camino a Tenochtitlán que les sugirieron los aztecas.
3. Cortés nunca llegó a conocer al líder del imperio azteca.
4. Moctezuma y Cortés se encontraron en un palacio muy grande.
5. Moctezuma le dio armas a Cortés como regalos.

Primera entrada de Cortés y sus soldados en Tenochtitlán

Universal Access

Heritage Language Learners
As students write their definitions for the vocabulary words in *Actividad* 20, ask them to also brainstorm a synonym for each word. Then have students discuss the subtle differences in meaning between the original word and its close relation.

Advanced Learners
Have students compare and contrast the two pictures of the encounter between Cortés and Moctezuma that accompany *Actividades* 21 and 22. Encourage them to paraphrase information they heard in *Actividad* 21 in order to talk about the events depicted.

Hablar ....

A describir el cuadro

Mira este cuadro que representa el encuentro entre Cortés y los representantes de Moctezuma. Describe lo que ves a un(a) compañero(a).

Modelo

Los soldados de Cortés tenían caballos.

Cortés ofrece un banquete a los enviados de Moctezuma

 Leer/Escribir/Hablar ....

¿Imperio del siglo XXI?

¿Sabes qué es un imperio? Lee este párrafo para aprender qué es un imperio y cuáles son sus ventajas y desventajas.

Conexiones | **Las ciencias sociales** ————

Un imperio es un grupo importante de territorios que dependen de un mismo gobierno. Los territorios que dependen del gobierno central se llaman colonias. Los ciudadanos de las colonias disfrutan por lo general de los mismos derechos y beneficios que los ciudadanos del país del gobierno central. Sin embargo, esto no ha sido siempre así. Como consecuencia, las colonias se han ido separando del gobierno central, creando sus propios gobiernos.

• ¿Cuáles son las características de un imperio? Trabaja con otro(a) estudiante para hacer una lista usando las palabras del recuadro.

componerse	poder	reto	variedad
riqueza	poderoso	luchar	establecer
invadir	batalla	soldado	intercambio

 Standards: 1.1, 1.3
....

Resources: Fine Art Transparencies; Fine Art Transparencies Teacher's Guide

Focus: Practicing new vocabulary

Suggestions: Show the *Fine Art Transparency* as students describe the picture.

Answers will vary.

Standards: 1.2, 1.3, 3.1
....

Focus: Practicing new vocabulary and structures via reading and response

Suggestions: Ask students to share their background knowledge about colonies and colonial situations past and present. Challenge their critical thinking skills by asking: *Si los ciudadanos de las colonias disfrutan de los mismos derechos que los ciudadanos del gobierno central, ¿por qué siempre terminan votando o luchando por su libertad?*

Answers will vary.

Chapter Project

Students can perform step 4 at this point. Be sure they understand your corrections and suggestions. (For more information, see p. 338-a.)

Enriching Your Teaching

Culture Note

On September 15, 1821, five Latin American countries gained independence from Spain. They included Costa Rica, El Salvador, Guatemala, Honduras, and Nicaragua. September 15th is the national holiday of independence in each of these countries. For this reason, we now celebrate Hispanic Heritage Month from September 15th to October 15th. Mexico achieved its independence a few years earlier, but one day later, on September 16, 1810.

361

Standards: 1.2, 2.1, 2.2, 3.1, 3.2
Actividad 24

Resources: Practice Answers on Transparencies

Focus: Practicing new vocabulary and structures via reading and response

Suggestions: As students read the information silently, ask them to note down words or phrases at spots in which they have comprehension problems. Address these problem spots and have students read the material again before answering the questions.

Answers:

1. Su herencia está formada de tres culturas: la africana, la indígena y la española.
2. Sus antepasados son de África, la República Dominicana y España.
3. La cultura dominicana ha influido más en su vida.
4. Aprende sobre su cultura dominicana cuando visita la República Dominicana. También aprende mucho porque la cultura dominicana ha influido mucho en la Ciudad de Nueva York, donde vive.
5. Ella se siente orgullosa de su herencia.
6. Answers will vary.

Fondo cultural Standards: 1.1, 1.2, 2.1, 2.2, 3.1, 4.2

■◆◈◆■◆◈■◆◈■◆◈■◆

Suggestions: Before students read the information, ask them to share their background knowledge about Tex-Mex food. Then help them increase their knowledge by asking questions that have answers they will discover as they read. For example: *No sólo dos sino tres culturas han influido en la comida texmex. ¿Cuáles son?*

Answers will vary.

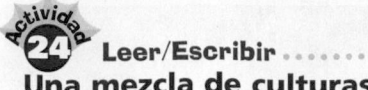
Actividad 24 **Leer/Escribir**

Una mezcla de culturas

Lee la lectura y contesta las preguntas.

Mi herencia africana

Mi nombre es Noemí y nací en la ciudad de Santo Domingo, en la República Dominicana. Soy resultado de una mezcla de razas y culturas. De mi padre recibí mi herencia africana. Los antepasados de mi madre eran españoles e indígenas. De niña, la cultura dominicana tuvo más influencia en mi vida. Ahora vivo en los Estados Unidos y me encanta ir a la República Dominicana, donde hay mucha riqueza cultural y donde lo paso muy bien con mi familia y mis amigos. Sin embargo, cuando estoy en la República Dominicana quiero volver a los Estados Unidos, porque también me identifico con este país.

Vivo en Nueva York, una ciudad donde se encuentran y se mezclan muchas culturas: la cultura dominicana, la estadounidense y la africana, entre otras. Para mí, en Nueva York es fácil aprender sobre mi herencia cultural. Voy a una iglesia dominicana, escucho cantantes dominicanos y españoles en la radio y voy a festivales de música y presentaciones de arte africano. Las culturas que forman mi herencia han influido mucho en la vida de toda la ciudad. Me siento orgullosa de mi herencia.

1. ¿De cuántas culturas está formada la herencia de Noemí? Di cuáles son.
2. ¿De dónde son los antepasados de la autora?
3. ¿Cuál es la cultura que más ha influido en la vida de la autora?
4. ¿Cómo aprende sobre su cultura dominicana?
5. ¿Cómo se siente ella de su herencia?
6. ¿Hay una variedad de culturas en tu comunidad? Descríbelas.

Fondo cultural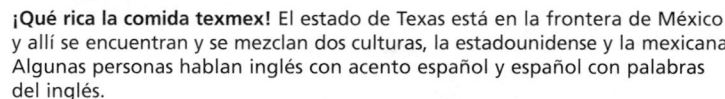

¡Qué rica la comida texmex! El estado de Texas está en la frontera de México y allí se encuentran y se mezclan dos culturas, la estadounidense y la mexicana. Algunas personas hablan inglés con acento español y español con palabras del inglés.

La comida texmex es otro resultado de ese encuentro. Es una mezcla de la cocina mexicana y la texana, con influencia de la cocina cajún del Sur de los Estados Unidos. El arroz, los frijoles, el chile y las tortillas de maíz se mezclan con las cebollas texanas y los mariscos del Golfo, para lograr un resultado exquisito.

La comida texmex ya no se encuentra sólo en Texas; en todas las ciudades grandes de los Estados Unidos hay restaurantes de estilo texmex. La próxima vez que veas uno de ellos, no dejes de entrar.

• ¿Has ido a algún restaurante texmex o de comida latinoamericana? Compara la comida que había allí con la que comes generalmente en casa.

362 trescientos sesenta y dos
Manos a la obra 2

Universal Access

Heritage Language Learners
Have students share their own personal versions of **Una mezcla de culturas** in *Actividad* 24. Ask them to reread the passage, substituting their own information about their heritage country and culture. For example, *Mi nombre es ___ y nací en la ciudad ___, en ___.*

Multiple Intelligences
Musical/Rhythmic: Divide students into small groups. Have each group rehearse a choral reading of **Calabó y bambú.** Instruct students to create their own rhythmic gestures and percussion accompaniment using hand claps, finger snaps, and knee slaps.

En voz alta

En los años 20 aparece en varios países del Caribe el movimiento de poesía negra. Los poetas de este movimiento tratan de reflejar el ritmo de la música africana con las palabras y expresiones de los caribeños descendientes de africanos.

El puertorriqueño Luis Palés Matos (1898–1959) es uno de los poetas más importantes de este movimiento. Nació en Guayama, Puerto Rico. Sus padres eran poetas. Comenzó a escribir poesía desde muy joven, pero su primer poema con tema africano fue *Pueblo negro*, que publicó en 1926. Él llegó a ser un poeta reconocido en el Caribe y también en América del Sur. Escucha este fragmento y trata de repetirlo en voz alta.

- Según el poeta, ¿dónde vibra el alma africana?
- ¿Qué nos dice este poema sobre la cultura del Caribe?

Calabó y bambú
(fragmento)
Luis Palés Matos
(1898–1959)

Calabó y bambú.
Bambú y calabó.
Es el sol de hierro que arde[1] en Tombuctú[2].
Es la danza negra de Fernando Poo[3].
El alma africana que vibrando[4] está
en el ritmo gordo[5] del mariyandá.
Calabó y bambú.
Bambú y calabó.
El Gran Cocoroco dice: tu-cu-tú.
La Gran Cocoroca dice: to-co-tó.

---

1 burns 2 African city 3 African island 4 vibrating 5 fat

Hablar

¿De dónde venimos?

Trabaja con otro(a) estudiante para contestar las preguntas.

1. ¿Cómo se muestran las diferentes herencias culturales en tu comunidad? ¿Y en los Estados Unidos?
2. Habla de algunas celebraciones que tengan raíces *(roots)* culturales.
3. ¿Cómo se ve la influencia de diferentes herencias en la lengua que hablamos? ¿Puedes pensar en algún ejemplo?
4. ¿Hay influencia indígena en el lugar donde vives? ¿En qué cosas la ves?

trescientos sesenta y tres   363
Capítulo 8

En voz alta

Presentation

Standards: 1.2, 1.3, 2.1, 2.2, 3.1, 3.2, 5.2

Resources: Audio Program: Cap. 8, Track 12

Suggestions: As students are preparing to read the poem aloud, ask them to read fragments they feel best reflect *el ritmo de la música africana.*

Answers:
- Vibra en el ritmo gordo del mariyandá.
- Answers will vary.

 Standards: 1.1, 1.3, 4.2

Focus: Using new vocabulary and structures in a discussion

Suggestions: For question 3, encourage students to consider the influences Arabic has had on Spanish as well as those that Spanish has had on English. Ask them to give examples of each type of influence.

Answers will vary.

Additional Resources

- Writing, Audio & Video Workbook: Cap. 8, Audio Activity 3, Track 13
- Writing, Audio & Video Workbook: Cap. 8, Writing Activity 10
- Resource Book: Cap. 8, Communicative Activity BLM

✓ **Assessment**
- Prueba 8-5: Vocabulary production

Enriching Your Teaching

Culture Note

Not only were Luis Palés Matos' parents poets, his brothers, Vicente and Gustavo were also writers. Matos self-published his first collection of poems **Azaleas** (1915). His second manuscript was heavily influenced by his grief after the death of his wife. Entitled **El palacio en sombras,** this manuscript was never published.

Teacher-to-Teacher

During discussions about cultural influences, play background music that showcases these cultures. Most public libraries have recordings of music from Africa, the Caribbean, and many parts of Latin America. Background music may stimulate the discussion and arouse students' curiosity about its cultural roots.

Practice and Communicate

8

Gramática

Presentation

Resources: Voc. & Gram. Transparencies: 162

Suggestions: As you explain the points in the *Gramática,* point out to students the difference between the use of the *presente perfecto del subjuntivo,* which they learned in *Capítulo* 7, and the current lesson, the *imperfecto del subjuntivo.* We use the former when the main clause is in the present tense and expresses doubt or uncertainty about a situation in the past. We use the *imperfecto del subjuntivo* when the main clause is in one of the past tenses.

Actividad 26

Standards: 1.2, 3.1

Resources: Practice Answers on Transparencies

Focus: Practicing the imperfect subjunctive

Suggestions: As students complete the activity, ask them to focus on the clauses that make up each sentence. Remind them that in all cases, the main clause (containing an expression of emotion, doubt, or uncertainty) is in a past tense, thus requiring the imperfect subjunctive in the subordinate clause.

Answers:

1. fuera
2. tuvieran
3. fuera
4. hubiera
5. pudiera
6. supieran

Block Schedule

Play the Cube Game with three cubes. In groups of two, give students three cubes. Cube 1: write six infinitives including some irregular verbs from p. 364. Cube 2: six expressions that use the subjunctive. Cube 3: subject pronouns. Have students roll the cubes and provide a sentence combining information on the three cubes: *Mi padre quería que yo estudiara.*

364

Gramática

El imperfecto del subjuntivo

You know that you use the subjunctive to persuade someone else to do something, to express emotions about situations, and to express doubt and uncertainty. If the main verb is in the present tense, use the present subjunctive. If the main verb is in the preterite or imperfect, use the imperfect subjunctive.

> Los indígenas **dudan** que los europeos **aprendan** su lengua.
> Los indígenas **dudaban** que los europeos **aprendieran** su lengua.

> El profesor **sugiere** que **aprendamos** los nombres de las colonias.
> El profesor **sugirió** que **aprendiéramos** los nombres de las colonias.

• To form the imperfect subjunctive, take the *Uds./ellos/ellas* form of the preterite and replace the ending *-ron* with the imperfect subjunctive endings. Here are the forms of the imperfect subjunctive for *cantar, aprender,* and *vivir:*

cantar		aprender		vivir	
cantara	cantáramos	aprendiera	aprendiéramos	viviera	viviéramos
cantaras	cantarais	aprendieras	aprendierais	vivieras	vivierais
cantara	cantaran	aprendiera	aprendieran	viviera	vivieran

• Note that the *nosotros* form has a written accent.

Irregular verbs, stem-changing verbs, and spelling-changing verbs follow the same rule for forming the imperfect subjunctive.

ir: fueron → fue-	El rey les dijo que **fueran** al Nuevo Mundo.
haber: hubieron → hubie-	Dudaba que **hubiera** semejanzas.
pedir: pidieron → pidie-	No era necesario que **pidieran** tantas armas.
construir: construyeron → construye-	Los europeos querían que los habitantes **construyeran** una iglesia.

Actividad 26 **Gramática** **Leer**

Historia de la conquista

Bernal Díaz del Castillo (1492–1581) escribió un libro sobre la conquista de México. Completa las frases con el imperfecto del subjuntivo del verbo apropiado.

1. Era impresionante que la capital de los aztecas *(ser / ver)* tan enorme.
2. Era increíble que los edificios de la ciudad *(tener / traer)* torres tan altas.
3. Dudábamos que lo que veíamos *(ser / decir)* verdad.
4. Nos gustó mucho que *(saber / haber)* tantos árboles en los jardines.
5. No podíamos creer que la gente *(creer / poder)* navegar por la ciudad.
6. Nos parecía interesante que los indígenas *(saber / decir)* cultivar el maíz en un lago.

364 trescientos sesenta y cuatro
Manos a la obra 2

Universal Access

Students with Learning Difficulties

Students may have difficulty grasping the distinction between the present subjunctive and past subjunctive. Before they attempt *Actividad* 26, provide them with additional examples. Provide a sentence utilizing the subjunctive in the present, discuss its meaning, and then transform that sentence using a past tense and the imperfect subjunctive.

Advanced Learners

Ask students to revisit *Actividad* 11 on p. 306 in *Capítulo* 7. Challenge them to change the verbs in each item's main clause to the imperfect or preterite tense, and make the resulting change to the imperfect subjunctive in the subordinate clause.

Actividad 27 Gramática Leer

Durante la conquista . . .

Imagina que estuviste presente cuando Cortés llegó a México. Tu trabajo era relatar lo que veías. Completa las siguientes oraciones con el imperfecto del subjuntivo del verbo apropiado.

ser	rebelarse	comprender
establecer	adoptar	

1. Era imposible que los aztecas _____ la lengua de los españoles.

2. Los españoles esperaban que los indígenas _____ sus costumbres inmediatamente.

3. Los reyes querían que las colonias _____ un intercambio de mercancías.

4. Según los aztecas era posible que los españoles _____ enviados por sus antepasados.

5. Los españoles temían que los indígenas _____ contra ellos.

 Actividad 28 Gramática Escribir

Nuestra herencia

Para la familia de Carlos es muy importante mantener su herencia. Completa las frases de Carlos de una manera original, usando el imperfecto del subjuntivo de los verbos del recuadro.

hablar	aprender	comer
adoptar	venir	ir
haber	sentirse	abandonar

Modelo

Papá quería que todos nosotros . . . (hablar)
Papá quería que todos nosotros habláramos la lengua de nuestros antepasados.

1. Mis padres preferían que mis hermanos y yo . . .

2. Mi mamá exigía que todos . . .

3. Mis padres no querían que yo . . .

4. Todos estábamos orgullosos que nuestros antepasados . . .

5. Mi hermana tenía miedo que nuestro hermano . . .

6. A mis abuelos no les gustaba que los jóvenes de la familia . . .

7. Nadie creía que . . .

8. Era importante que todos nosotros . . .

El español en el mundo del trabajo

Salud y ciencia . . . en español

La ciudad de Houston, en Texas, es la quinta de los Estados Unidos con mayor número de hispanohablantes. Sin embargo, al abrir sus puertas en marzo de 1996, el Museo de Salud y Ciencia de Houston sólo tenía un trabajador bilingüe.

Hoy la situación es muy diferente. El museo tiene profesionales bilingües que ofrecen visitas guiadas en español. También hay videos educativos del museo con subtítulos en español. Además, se publica una guía en español y el servicio telefónico de atención al público tiene menús bilingües.

trescientos sesenta y cinco **365**
Capítulo 8

 Actividad 27 *Standards:* 1.2, 3.1

Resources: Practice Answers on Transparencies

Focus: Practicing the imperfect subjunctive

Suggestions: Remind students to form the imperfect subjunctive beginning with the correct stem for regular verbs: the third-person plural stem from the preterite tense.

Answers:
1. comprendieran
2. adoptaran
3. establecieran
4. fueran
5. se rebelaran

Actividad 28 *Standards:* 1.3

Focus: Practicing the imperfect subjunctive

Suggestions: Point out to students that number 7 provides no subject for the subordinate clause. They must choose their own subject and make the imperfect subjunctive form of the verb agree with it.

Answers will vary.

El español en el mundo del trabajo

Presentation

Standards: 1.2, 5.1

Suggestions: Once students have read the information, ask comprehension questions. For example: *¿Cuántas ciudades estadounidenses tienen un mayor número de hispanohablantes que Houston? (cuatro) ¿Quiénes ofrecen visitas guiadas en el Museo de Salud y Ciencia de Houston? (los profesionales bilingües)*

Enriching Your Teaching

Culture Note
The 2000 Census shows that the Spanish-speaking population in the United States is increasing quickly and dramatically. Since 1990, the Hispanic population in the United States has risen by 58 percent.

Teacher-to-Teacher
Invite students to practice the imperfect subjunctive in a discussion about their first year of high school. They can use sentences similar to those in *Actividad 28*, changing the subjects to ones such as **Los profesores, Los demás estudiantes,** or **Mis amigos.**

Actividad 29  Gramática  Hablar

¿Qué querían que hicieras?

Piensa en las cosas que esperaban tus familiares u otras personas que hicieras de pequeño(a). Trabaja con otro(a) estudiante para hablar sobre lo que querían esas personas que hiciera cada uno(a) de pequeño(a). Añadan detalles a sus frases.

Modelo

los maestros / querer / compartir

A —*¿Qué querían los maestros de la escuela primaria?*

B —*Los maestros querían que compartiéramos los materiales con nuestros compañeros.*

Estudiante A

los maestros	querer
mi mamá	esperar
mi papá	pedir
mis padres / abuelos	decir
mi(s) hermano(s)	prohibir
mi(s) hermana(s)	aconsejar
el(la) director(a) de la escuela	sugerir
mi entrenador(a)	exigir
¡Respuesta personal!	

Estudiante B

respetar
adoptar
salir
llevarse bien
ir
dormir
jugar
despertarse
¡Respuesta personal!

Actividad 30 Gramática Leer/Hablar

¿Qué pasó?

Piensa en un momento importante de tu niñez. Según lo que recuerdas, completa las siguientes frases.

1. Yo esperaba que . . .
2. Yo quería que . . .
3. [Nombre de un(a) amigo(a) o un pariente] quería que . . .
4. Era importante que . . .
5. (No) me sorprendió que . . .
6. Me gustó que . . .
7. Me molestó que . . .
8. Me pareció interesante que . . .

● **Más práctica**
Practice Workbook 8-10

For: Practice with the imperfect subjunctive
Visit: www.phschool.com
Web Code: jed-0807

Universal Access

 **Gramática**

El imperfecto del subjuntivo con *si*

Use the imperfect subjunctive after *si* when a situation is unlikely, impossible, or not true.

> **Si tuviera** tiempo, aprendería más sobre las misiones.
> *If I had time, I'd learn more about the missions.*

> **Si viviéramos** en México, adoptaríamos las costumbres del país.
> *If we lived in Mexico, we'd adopt the customs of the country.*

> Ese imperio sería más poderoso **si tuviera** oro.
> *That empire would be more powerful if it had gold.*

- Notice that you use the imperfect subjunctive form after *si*, and the conditional in the main clause.

After *como si* ("as if") you always use the the imperfect subjunctive regardless of the tense of the first verb in the sentence. Notice that the other verb can be in either the present or the past tense.

> Él se vestía **como si fuera** un rey.
> *He dressed as if he were a king.*

> Hablan **como si supieran** la lengua desde niños.
> *They speak as if they knew the language since childhood.*

 Gramática   Leer

A pensar . . .

Imagina que has ido a ver un espectáculo de bailes tradicionales de diferentes países de América Latina. Completa el texto con el imperfecto del subjuntivo del verbo apropiado.

Si las personas que crearon los bailes __1.__ *(enfrentarse / vivir)* ahora, les gustaría mucho ver a los bailarines interpretarlos. Ellos bailaban como si __2.__ *(estar / establecer)* en una gran fiesta. Las joyas que llevaban brillaban como si __3.__ *(ser / ir)* de oro. Si los antepasados los __4.__ *(ver / adoptar)* bailar, se emocionarían mucho. Si yo __5.__ *(poder / querer)*, aprendería más sobre las tradiciones y herencias de los países de América Latina. Me gustaría estudiar sobre los países que no __6.__ *(salir / tener)* muchas semejanzas con el mío.

trescientos sesenta y siete **367**
Capítulo 8

 Gramática

Presentation

Standards: 4.1

Resources: Voc. & Gram. Transparencies: 163

Suggestions: Say clauses in which the verb is in the conditional: *...todos iríamos para ver el partido; ...aprenderías muy rápidamente el español.* Ask volunteers to supply subordinate *(si)* clauses that make sense. Point out the cause-and-effect relationship between the clauses in this type of complex sentence.

Actividad 31   *Standards:* 1.2

Resources: Practice Answers on Transparencies

Focus: Practicing the imperfect subjunctive with *si*

Suggestions: Have students complete the activity in pairs and discuss their reasoning behind each answer.

Answers:
1. vivieran   4. vieran
2. estuvieran   5. pudiera
3. fueran   6. tuvieran

Additional Resources
- Writing, Audio & Video Workbook: Cap. 8, Audio Activity 4, Track 14

Enriching Your Teaching

Teacher-to-Teacher

Have students imagine a situation in which everything goes wrong on what should be a dream vacation. The flight is late; the weather turns out to be terrible; the hotel is less than adequate; the food is horrific; and so on. Ask them to work with a partner and come up with as many sentences as they can, saying what they would do if things were different: *Si los servicios del hotel no fueran tan malos, podríamos pasarlo bien adentro. Si el mesero no me hablara tan antipáticamente, le daría una buena propina.*

Practice and Communicate

Actividad 32

Standards: 1.3

Resources: Practice Answers on Transparencies

Focus: Practicing the imperfect subjunctive with *si*

Suggestions: If students have difficulty, help them by telling them that they should use the expression *como si* in all the items.

Answers:
1. Antes de la obra el director les habló a los jóvenes como si supieran lo que estaban haciendo.
2. Las armas de los actores brillaron como si fueran de oro.
3. Los jóvenes lucharon como si participaran en una batalla.
4. El actor principal actuó como si fuera un rey de verdad.
5. El jóven que hizo el papel de misionero actuó como si sintiera compasión.
6. La actriz principal actuó como si estuviera enamorada del rey.
7. El público aplaudió como si hubiera visto una obra de teatro de Broadway.

Actividad 33

Standards: 1.1, 1.3

Focus: Practicing the imperfect subjunctive with *si*

Suggestions: If students need ideas, suggest that they talk about things such as governments, education, the economy, employment, and cultural interaction.

Answers will vary.

 **Gramática** Escribir

Como si . . .

En la escuela Gabriela Mistral los estudiantes están participando en una obra musical sobre la conquista de México. Describe lo que pasó usando expresiones de las dos columnas y el imperfecto del subjuntivo.

Modelo

Los estudiantes actuaron . . . / ser actores profesionales
Los estudiantes actuaron como si fueran actores profesionales.

Columna A	Columna B
1. Antes de la obra el director les habló a los jóvenes . . .	estar enamorada del rey
2. Las armas de los actores brillaron . . .	sentir compasión
3. Los jóvenes lucharon . . .	haber visto una obra de teatro de Broadway
4. El actor principal actuó . . .	ser un rey de verdad
5. El jóven que hizo el papel de misionero actuó . . .	ser de oro
6. La actriz principal actuó . . .	saber lo que estaban haciendo
7. El público aplaudió . . .	participar en una batalla

 **Gramática** Hablar/Escribir

Nuestra sociedad

En grupo hablen sobre las características y los problemas de la sociedad actual. Escriban ocho frases usando el imperfecto del subjuntivo con *si*.

Modelo

Si los jóvenes y los adultos trataran de comprenderse mejor, no habría tantos conflictos sobre la música en nuestras casas.

Universal Access

Advanced Learners

Have students work in pairs to create two sets of cards. On one set they write only subordinate clauses with *si.* On the other they write corresponding main clauses that make sense with the *si* clauses. Have partners mix the cards in each set and exchange them with another pair of students. Students then match the sentence halves of the cards they have received. Some sentence halves may have more than one match. Have students discuss these instances with those who wrote the cards.

Actividad 34 Gramática Leer/Hablar

Si pudiera . . .

❶ Lee el siguiente anuncio de una agencia de viajes y completa las frases.

Modelo

Si nada me parara . . .
Si nada me parara, invitaría a mi mejor amigo(a) a un viaje a la Antártida.

❷ Ahora, trabaja con otro(a) estudiante para comparar lo que escribieron.

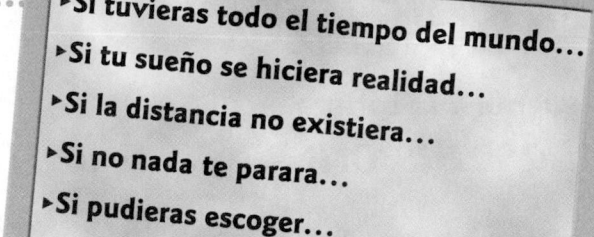

▸Si tuvieras todo el tiempo del mundo...
▸Si tu sueño se hiciera realidad...
▸Si la distancia no existiera...
▸Si no nada te parara...
▸Si pudieras escoger...

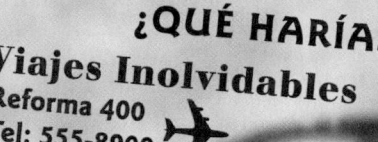

¿QUÉ HARÍAS?

Viajes Inolvidables
Reforma 400
Tel: 555-8900

Actividad 35 Hablar/Escribir

Encuentros

❶ En grupo, van a describir un encuentro de dos culturas del pasado. Pueden tomar ideas de este capítulo o de la clase de estudios sociales. Describan lo siguiente:

• ¿Qué culturas se encontraron?
• ¿Cuándo y dónde fue el encuentro?
• ¿Cómo fue el encuentro?
• ¿Exigía un grupo que el otro hiciera algo?
• ¿Cambió un grupo más que el otro?
• ¿Cuál fue el resultado del encuentro?

❷ Comparen el encuentro sobre el que escribieron con una situación del presente. Analicen qué cosas tienen en común.

● **Más práctica**
Practice Workbook 8-11, 8-12

Go Online
PHSchool.com

For: Practice with the imperfect subjunctive after *si*
Visit: www.phschool.com
Web Code: jed-0808

trescientos sesenta y nueve **369**
Capítulo 8

 8

Actividad 34

Standards: 1.1, 1.2, 1.3

Focus: Practicing the imperfect subjunctive

Suggestions: Point out to students that they should complete all the sentences about themselves, using *yo* as the subject.

Common Errors: Students may mistakenly drop *-ar, -ir,* or *-er* infinitive endings when forming the conditional. Remind them that conditional endings are added to the complete infinitive forms of regular verbs.

Answers will vary.

Extension: After students complete step 2, ask them to use third-person forms to report on their partner's responses: *Si no le parara nada, mi compañero(a)....*

Actividad 35

Standards: 1.1

Focus: Practicing the imperfect subjunctive

Suggestions: Encourage students to discuss current world events as they decide on and develop their present-day situation for step 2.

Answers will vary.

Additional Resources

• Writing, Audio & Video Workbook: Cap. 8, Writing Activities 12–13
• Writing, Audio & Video Workbook: Cap. 8, Audio Activity 5, Track 15
• Resource Book: Cap. 8, Communicative Activity BLM

✓ Assessment

• Prueba 8-7: *El imperfecto del subjuntivo con* si
• Examen: Vocabulario y gramática 2

Chapter Project

Students can perform step 5 at this point. Record their presentations on cassette or videotape for inclusion in their portfolios. (For more information, see p. 338-a.)

Enriching Your Teaching

Teacher-to-Teacher

Help students develop their critical thinking skills. Invite them to research current or recent events for information that will add to class discussions about encounters between different cultures. Besides obtaining information from encyclopedias, newspapers, magazines, personal interviews, and the Internet, they might use information they learned from discussions in their Social Studies courses. Encourage them to synthesize information they glean from a variety of sources, both English and Spanish, in order to verify their facts and develop objective opinions.

Puente a la cultura

Presentation

Standards: 1.1,1.2, 2.1, 2.2, 3.1, 5.1, 5.2

Resources: Voc. & Gram. Transparencies 4

Focus: Reading to learn about the Spanish missions in California

Suggestions:

Pre-reading: Refer students to the *Estrategia.* Show *Vocabulary and Grammar Transparency* 4 and model setting up a T-chart with the two columns labeled *los hechos* and *las opiniones.* Have students set up a similar chart on their own paper and use it to record facts and opinions as they read the selection.

Reading: As students read, remind them to use background knowledge, cognates, and context clues to understand unfamiliar words and expressions. Help them resolve comprehension problems by asking *sí/no* or embedded-answer questions.

Post-reading: After students have read the selection, allow them to complete their *los hechos/las opiniones* charts and share the information they recorded there. Use the information from the *las opiniones* column as a springboard to discussion about the cultural encounter between the Spanish colonizers and the indigenous peoples of California.

Country Connection

Presentation

Standards: 3.1

Resources: Voc. & Gram. Transparencies 22 (map)

Use *Vocabulary and Grammar Transparency* 22 and the map on p. 371 to show the relative location of the *Camino Real.* Explain to students that some of the California missions developed into modern-day cities, the names of which still retain at least part of the name of the original missions. The largest of these are Los Angeles and San Francisco. Smaller cities include Santa Barbara and San Luis Obispo. Other missions, such as San Antonio de Padua, never grew into cities, and today they remain isolated in rural areas.

Objectives

- **Read about Spanish missions in California and learn about their role in California's history**
- **Distinguish between fact and opinion**

¡Adelante!

Puente a la cultura
Las misiones de California

Estrategia

Fact and opinion
As a critical reader, you must distinguish between the facts and opinions of your source to judge the information's reliability. As you read, try to determine if any of the information presented is the opinion of the author, or whether it is based on facts.

Estatua del Fray *(Brother)* Junípero Serra

Misión de San Diego de Alcalá, la más antigua de las misiones

Durante el siglo XVIII, los españoles colonizaron el territorio de California. En 1767, el gobierno español y la Iglesia Católica les dieron la tarea a los padres franciscanos de construir misiones y encargarse de ellas.

Las misiones fueron creadas no sólo para enseñar la religión cristiana a los indígenas sino también para enseñarles tareas que pudieran realizar en la nueva sociedad española. Asimismo[1] tenían la función de recibir y alimentar a las personas que viajaban a través del territorio desconocido de California.

Las misiones incluían una iglesia, cuartos para los sacerdotes, depósitos, casas para mujeres solteras, barracas para los soldados, comedores y talleres. Los indígenas casados vivían en una villa cerca de la misión.

---

1 likewise

Universal Access

Students with Learning Difficulties
Provide students with a concept web to help support their comprehension of *Las misiones de California.* Use the question words *¿Qué? ¿Quién? ¿Cuándo? ¿Dónde?* and *¿Por qué?* as the components of the web. After students have read the passage, have them supply information relevant to each of the question words.

Advanced Learners
Invite students to search the Internet for more information about one or more of the missions along the *Camino Real.* Ask them to present the information they find in a brief report to the class. Encourage them to show downloaded photos and share a few facts that are specific to each mission.

Fray Junípero Serra fue escogido por los españoles para fundar las misiones. Serra fundó nueve misiones en California. Las mismas se encuentran en el Camino Real, una ruta que va desde San Diego hasta la Bahía de San Francisco. Muchas personas recorren hoy el Camino Real para visitar las misiones y aprender sobre su historia.

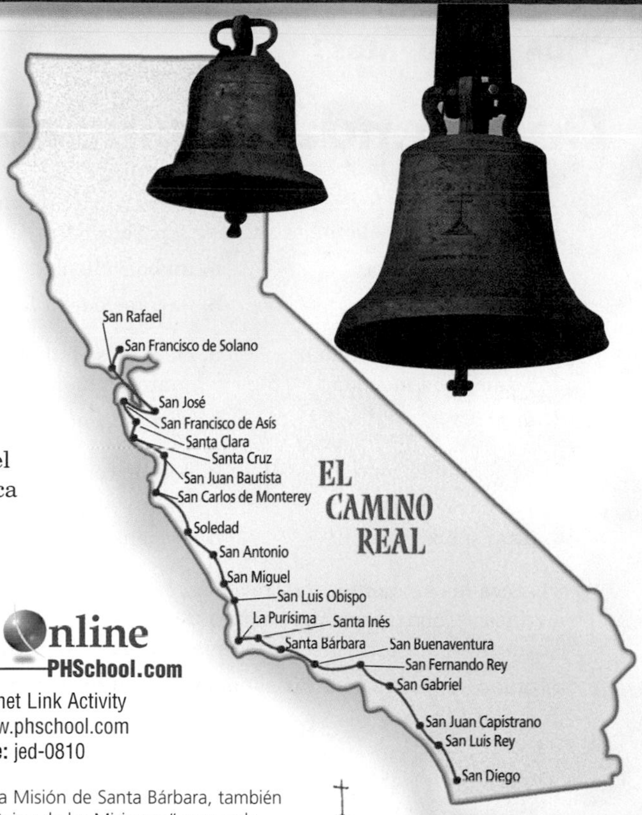

EL CAMINO REAL
San Rafael
San Francisco de Solano
San José
San Francisco de Asís
Santa Clara
Santa Cruz
San Juan Bautista
San Carlos de Monterey
Soledad
San Antonio
San Miguel
San Luis Obispo
La Purísima
Santa Inés
Santa Bárbara
San Buenaventura
San Fernando Rey
San Gabriel
San Juan Capistrano
San Luis Rey
San Diego

¿Comprendiste?

1. ¿Para qué fueron creadas las misiones?
2. ¿Qué hizo Fray Junípero Serra?
3. ¿Conoces otros edificios que representen el encuentro entre distintas culturas? Explica tu respuesta.

Go Online PHSchool.com

For: Internet Link Activity
Visit: www.phschool.com
Web Code: jed-0810

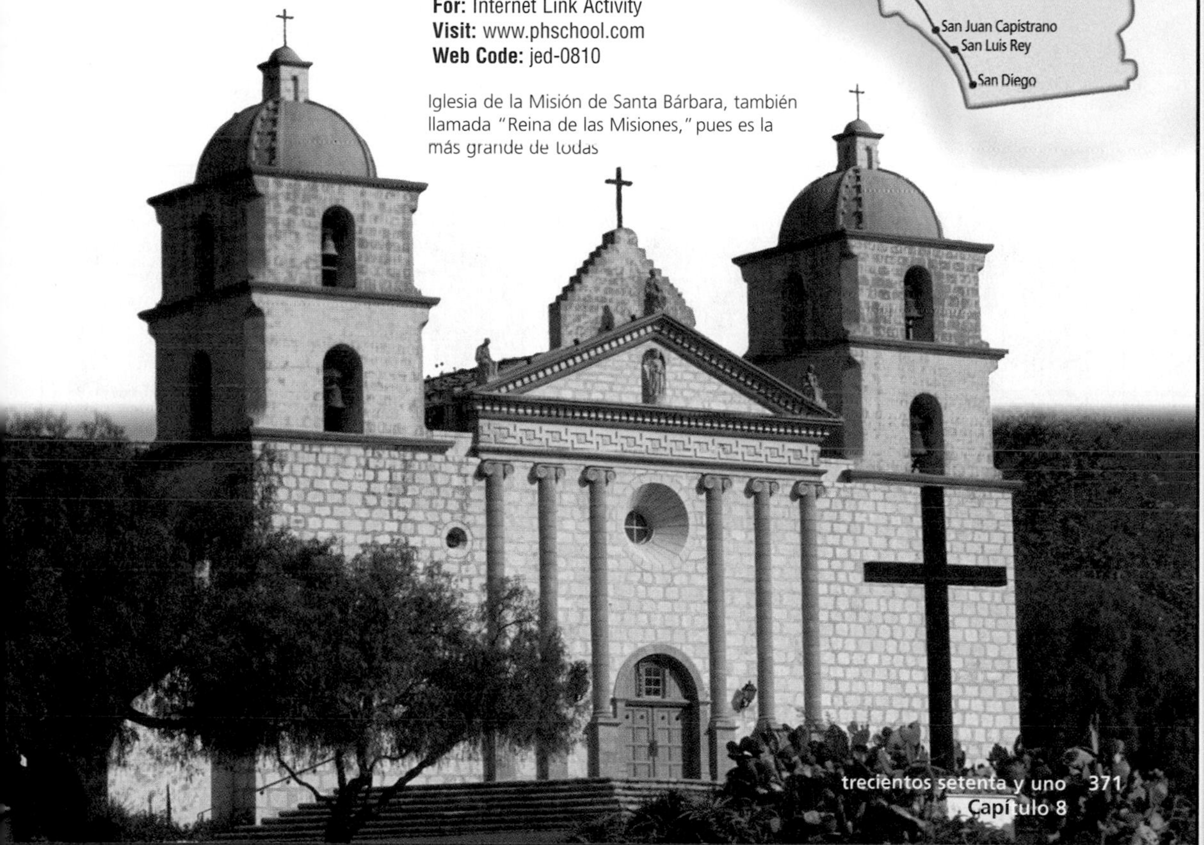

Iglesia de la Misión de Santa Bárbara, también llamada "Reina de las Misiones," pues es la más grande de todas

Culture

8

¿Comprendiste?

Standards: 1.2, 1.3

Resources: Practice Answers on Transparencies

Focus: Demonstrating reading comprehension

Suggestions: Have students first write answers to the questions on their own. Then ask them to share their answers in a class discussion.

Answers:

1. **Fueron creadas para enseñar la religión cristiana a los indígenas y también para enseñarles tareas que pudieron realizar en la nueva sociedad española.**
2. **Fundó nueve misiones en California.**
3. **Answers will vary.**

Go Online

The online atlas will provide a more detailed map of California.

Video Presentation

Standards: 1.2

Resources: Video Program, Cap. 8

Throughout the Spanish-speaking world, people of diverse cultural backgrounds come together, forming communities that combine many cultures. This segment offers several examples of this sharing of cultures as seen in word development architecture, and foods. See the *Video Teacher's Guide* for additional suggestions.

Enriching Your Teaching

Culture Note

Early Spanish influence in California is still very visible and strongly felt today. Most of the early missions are still intact. Many have been completely restored and are open to visitors as museums and as functioning Catholic churches. The Spanish names of towns, streets, and geographical features fill any map of California, although the pronunciation of many of them, such as Los Angeles, has been anglicized.

Internet Search

Keyword: Padre Junípero Serra

Standards: 1.1, 1.2, 1.3

Resources: Voc. & Gram. Transparencies: 164; Audio Program: CD Cap. 8, Track 16; Resource Book: Cap. 8, Audio Script; Practice Answers on Transparencies

Focus: Practicing speaking and listening comprehension

Suggestions:

For step 1, use the *Audio CD* or read the script aloud. Allow students to hear the descriptions twice through: the first time to write their answers and the second time to check them.

For step 2, encourage students to use the imperfect subjunctive at least once as they talk about the pictures. Suggest to them that one way they can do this is by stating an opinion or making a value judgment about the scene in the first picture: ***Parecía imposible que....***

Answers:

Step 1
1. b 2. a 3. c 4. b 5. c 6. c

Steps 2–3
Answers will vary.

¿Qué me cuentas?

De leyendas y ciudades

1 Escucha la leyenda. Después de cada párrafo vas a oír dos preguntas. Escoge la mejor respuesta para cada pregunta.

1. **a.** una mercancía
   b. un bolso lleno de oro
   c. un azulejo

2. **a.** devolvérselo a su dueño
   b. llevárselo a su familia
   c. comprar muchas cosas

3. **a.** en el bolso no había ninguna moneda
   b. en el bolso había cuarenta monedas
   c. faltaban dos monedas en el bolso

4. **a.** al rey
   b. al representante del rey
   c. a sus amigos

5. **a.** porque le contó su historia
   b. porque compró pocas cosas con el oro
   c. porque devolvió el bolso

6. **a.** al señor español
   b. al mensajero
   c. al señor azteca

2 Observa las siguientes ilustraciones. Las dos muestran un lugar de una ciudad en épocas distintas. Con tus propias palabras, compara las dos ilustraciones. Añade datos históricos y culturales para que tu comparación sea más interesante. ¡Usa tu imaginación!

Si quieres, puedes usar las siguientes palabras o expresiones para conectar tus ideas.

al principio	antes de	porque
anteriormente	también	así
sin embargo	para ilustrar	durante

1

2

3 Trabaja con otro(a) compañero(a) para hablar sobre las ilustraciones. Túrnense para describir las características de cada ilustración. Al terminar, den a la clase su opinión sobre lo que creen que ocurrió en cada época.

372 trescientos setenta y dos
¡Adelante!

Heritage Language Learners

After each oral presentation, ask students to play the part of tourists in the city. Encourage them to ask follow-up questions of the tour guide, and to discuss how this city compares to other cities with which they are familiar, perhaps in their heritage country.

Students with Learning Difficulties

Encourage students to organize and record the information for their oral presentations on index cards. Remind them not to read from their cards, but to refer to their notes during the course of the presentation.

Una visita a . . .

Tarea
Imagínate que eres guía turístico(a) en una ciudad multicultural. Tienes que planear una visita a los lugares más importantes de la ciudad.

1 Prepárate Escoge la ciudad en la que te gustaría organizar una visita. Completa una tabla como la siguiente sobre las características de la ciudad y sus habitantes.

nombre de la ciudad	
herencia cultural	
religiones	
restaurantes típicos	
edificios históricos	

Puedes dibujar un plano de la ciudad y marcar con una flecha *(arrow)* los lugares sobre los que hablarás.

2 Practica Vuelve a leer la información que anotaste en la tabla. Practica varias veces tu presentación para recordar todos los detalles. Puedes usar tus notas para practicar, pero no al hablar ante la clase. Recuerda:

- describir con detalles la parte de la ciudad de la que hablas
- añadir detalles sobre cómo se relacionan entre sí los diferentes grupos culturales de la ciudad
- mirar directamente al público
- usar el vocabulario y la gramática del capítulo

Modelo
Hoy visitaremos el centro de la ciudad de San Cristóbal de las Casas. La ciudad tiene herencia cultural española e indígena. La religión de sus habitantes es la cristiana, por eso tiene muchas iglesias . . .

3 Haz tu presentación Imagina que tus compañeros de clase son los turistas. Explícales cómo es la ciudad, como si estuvieran allí.

4 Evaluación Tu profesor(a) puede explicarte cómo va a evaluar tu presentación. Probablemente, para él (ella) es importante ver que:

- te preparaste bien para hacer tu presentación
- diste suficiente información sobre la ciudad
- tu presentación se entendió bien

Estrategia
Speaker's purpose
Before giving an oral presentation, you must think what the purpose of your speech is. Do you want to inform, persuade, or entertain your audience?

In this case, your purpose will be to inform. You need your audience—the tourists—to be both interested in the tour and informed. Use interesting facts about the city and present them in an engaging way.

trescientos setenta y tres **373**
Capítulo 8

Presentación oral
Presentation
Standards: 1.2, 1.3, 3.1

Resources: Voc. & Gram. Transparencies 4

Focus: Preparing and delivering an oral presentation

Suggestions: Review the task and the four-step approach with students. Review the rubric with the class (see *Assessment* below) to explain how you will grade the performance task. Before students begin, direct their attention to the *Estrategia*. Then ask a volunteer to read the *Modelo* in step 2. Ask students if they think the speaker's purpose is evident in this sample speech introduction. Tell them that they should not only clarify their purpose in their own minds but make it clear to their audience as well by stating it at the beginning of their speech.

Portfolio
Record students' oral presentations on audiocassette or videotape for inclusion in their portfolios.

✓ Assessment
- Assessment Program: Cap. 8, Rubrics

Give students copies of the rubric before they begin the activity. Go over the descriptions of the different levels of performance. After assessing students, help individuals understand how their performance could be improved.

Enriching Your Teaching

RUBRIC	Score 1	Score 3	Score 5
How clearly you state your purpose	Your purpose is not stated or evident.	You hint at a purpose but don't clearly state it.	You clearly state your purpose at the beginning.
How well you organize and present information	You give very little information.	You lack important information. You do not organize your information.	Your information is complete, interesting, and well-organized.
How effectively you deliver your speech	Your speech is read. You make no eye contact with the audience.	You make some eye contact with the audience.	You make good eye contact with the audience.

8

Communicate: Writing

Language Arts Connection

Standards: 3.1

Have students consult models of narratives they have encountered in their Social Studies courses, including narratives they themselves may have created. Ask them to focus on how chronological order was used in those narratives and the transitions that were used to connect ideas. Have them incorporate successful organizational strategies from these models into their narrative compositions.

Presentación escrita

Presentation

Standards: 1.2, 1.3, 3.1

Resources: Voc. & Gram. Transparencies 4

Focus: Combining learned vocabulary and structures in a written presentation

Suggestions: Begin by explaining the criteria you will use to evaluate students' compositions. (See step 5, *Evaluación,* in the Student Edition, and *Assessment* on the following page.)

Direct students' attention to the *Estrategia.* Ask them to share additional background information they have learned in Language Arts courses about chronological order. Use *Vocabulary & Grammar Transparency* 4 to model brainstorming and recording ideas for a personal experience narrative. Have students create a similar chart on their own paper, adding a fifth column.

Presentación escrita

Mi experiencia con otras culturas

Objectives
- **Narrate a personal experience**
- **Order facts chronologically**
- **Add details to make the story more interesting**

Estrategia

Chronological ordering
Putting events in chronological order means listing them in the order they occurred. This usually means starting with the first event and continuing to the last. You can also use reverse chronological order if it's more appropriate for the story you are telling. Remember to use signal words that indicate chronological order, like *primero, luego, después, segundo, finalmente, por último.*

¿Cómo sería ir a vivir a otro país? ¿Te mudaste de país en algún momento de tu vida? ¿Tus padres nacieron en otro país? ¿Conservan en tu familia tradiciones de sus antepasados? ¿Conoces a alguna persona que haya nacido en otro país y esté viviendo aquí? Escribe un episodio *(episode)* autobiográfico sobre alguna de estas cosas. Escribe desde el punto de vista de tu experiencia propia, o bien inventa una historia. Puedes relatar cómo te sentiste cuando llegaste al país, qué cosas encontraste, qué piensas de la integración con otras culturas o qué tradiciones conserva tu familia.

1 Antes de escribir

Piensa en ideas para tu episodio autobiográfico. A medida que pienses en posibles temas, hazte las siguientes preguntas:

- ¿Con qué claridad recuerdo o me imagino la experiencia?
- ¿Estoy listo(a) para compartir la experiencia con otros?
- ¿Qué aprendí o aprendería de la experiencia?

Para ordenar tus ideas para el episodio autobiográfico, completa una tabla como la que aparece a continuación.

Personajes	Lo que sucedió	Época	Lugar	Pensamientos/Sentimientos
yo, mamá, papá, abuela	mudarnos a Estados Unidos	cinco años atrás	Nueva York	• triste por dejar a mis amigos • nervioso por ir a un país desconocido

2 Borrador

Escribe tu borrador de un episodio autobiográfico. Escribe tus ideas en orden lógico, así tu relato va a ser más interesante y más fácil de leer. Añade todos los detalles que sean necesarios. Recuerda usar el vocabulario y la gramática de este capítulo.

Universal Access

Heritage Language Learners
Ask willing students to serve as interviewees for other students. Encourage them to share their own experiences or those of family members. Have the interviewers show their questions to you first, and remind all participants to conduct these personal interviews with respect and consideration.

Advanced Learners
Invite students to write a short story or dramatic scene. Their story or scene should convey the emotional impact that arises from an encounter between two cultures. Encourage students to limit the number of characters in their story or scene to two or three.

Modelo

Topic sentence and introductory paragraph: What is the composition about?

Hace cinco años que vivo con mi familia en los Estados Unidos. Antes vivíamos en México, en la ciudad de Aguascalientes. Tenía muchos amigos allí. Cuando mi papá me dio la noticia de que íbamos a mudarnos a los Estados Unidos, mis amigos no querían que los dejara. Yo les pedí que fueran a . . .

Recuerdo que cuando llegamos a Nueva York me sentía feliz. Nuestro apartamento estaba . . .

Details: The writer expresses his or her feelings in the autobiographic composition.

Signal words: The writer uses words that indicate the chronological order of events.

Al principio no sentí mucho la diferencia, pues todas las personas del barrio hablaban español. Era increíble que hasta en los almacenes y los restaurantes yo encontrara personas que hablaban el mismo idioma que yo . . .

Finalmente, me dí cuenta de que debía aprender inglés porque . . .

Conclusion: The writer uses a signal word that indicates chronological order.

3 Redacción/Revisión

Después de escribir el primer borrador, trabaja con otro(a) estudiante para intercambiar los trabajos y leerlos. Luego, hagan sugerencias para mejorar sus composiciones.

Haz lo siguiente: Subraya con una línea los verbos en pretérito o en imperfecto y con dos líneas los verbos en imperfecto del subjuntivo.

• ¿Siguieron el plan de la tabla que hicieron?

• ¿Organizaron la información en orden cronológico?

• ¿Están empleados correctamente el pretérito, el imperfecto y el imperfecto del subjuntivo?

Cuando mi papá me <u>dio</u> la noticia de que <u>íbamos</u> a mudarnos a los Estados Unidos, mis amigos no <u>querían</u> que los <u>deje</u> _{dejara}. Yo les <u>pediré</u> _{pedí} que <u>fueran</u> a . . .

4 Publicación

Antes de crear la versión final, lee de nuevo tu borrador y repasa los siguientes puntos:

• ¿Incluí detalles para expresar mis sentimientos?

• ¿Estoy relatando un episodio interesante?

• ¿Refleja la integración con otras culturas?

Después de revisar el borrador, escribe en limpio tu composición.

5 Evaluación

Tu profesor(a) puede explicarte cómo va a evaluar tu presentación. Probablemente, para tu profesor(a) es importante ver que:

• las frases tienen sentido y expresan una idea completa

• la composición tiene un orden lógico

• usaste correctamente el vocabulario y la gramática del capítulo

---

Suggestions (Cont'd):

Once students have a rough draft ready, read through the model on this page together. Help them see how information from the chart on p. 374 was incorporated into this draft and to note transitions that were used. Ask them to identify uses of the imperfect subjunctive. Encourage them to work toward a similar level of organization, detail, and language use, even if they have chosen a different chronological order for their own personal experience narratives.

For step 3, encourage students to focus on sentence structure, transitions, and use of the imperfect subjunctive. Have them follow the suggestions shown.

Evaluation

Steps 4 and 5 overlap. Students will need evaluation by you, their peers, or self-evaluation to fine-tune and polish their drafts.

Portfolio

Keep students' final drafts in their portfolios as a writing sample.

✓ Assessment

• Assessment Program: Cap. 8, Rubrics

Give students copies of the rubric before they begin the activity. Go over the descriptions of the different levels of performance. After assessing students, help individuals understand how their performance could be improved.

Enriching Your Teaching

RUBRIC	Score 1	Score 3	Score 5
Completion of task	Your main idea is not stated or unclear. There is little or no development of it.	Your main idea is hinted at, but your development of it is weak.	Your main idea is clear and interestingly developed.
Use of chronological order and transitions	You present too few events and use no transitions.	Some of your events are out of order or lacking helpful transitions.	You sequence events and use effective transitions.
Sentence structure/ grammar, spelling, mechanics	Sentences run on or are fragmented. You make many grammar, spelling, mechanics errors.	You use sentences consistently. You make some grammar, spelling, mechanics errors.	Your sentence structure is correct and varied. You make few grammar, spelling, mechanics errors.

Lectura

Presentation

Standards: 1.2, 2.1, 2.2, 3.1, 3.2, 5.2

Resources: Voc. & Gram. Transparencies: 4

Focus: Reading an extended passage

Suggestions:

Pre-reading: Before reading, direct students' attention to the *Al leer* section. Have them copy the graphic organizer from p. 379 and make sure they understand how they will use it. If necessary, use *Vocabulary and Grammar Transparency* 4 to model setting up a similar chart, leaving one of the columns empty. Explain that **Antes** refers to the point at which the story begins or before, and **Ahora** refers to the end of the story. Point out the relationship between the five questions in *Al leer* and the information in the left column of the chart. Also refer them to the *Estrategia.* Remind them to follow the suggestions there and to read the selection the first time without stopping.

Reading: Allow students time to read the entire selection on their own silently. You might assign this task for homework. This will allow you to capitalize on class time to read it again together with students. When reading together, pause frequently to address comprehension issues they may have and to allow them to fill in their **Cambios en la narración** charts from p. 379. Here are some possible comprehension issues on this page for which you can provide some guidance:

• Explain that the first, italicized paragraph is a summary. It is important to understand this summary of who the characters Daniel and Chalchi are in order to follow the rest of the story.

• *¿En qué tiempo está la narración del cuento, en el presente o en el pasado? (el presente)*

• *¿Daniel se da cuenta de qué cambios en su situación mientras se despierta? (Su ropa y su cama han cambiado.)*

• *¿A quién se parece la mujer que está llamando a Daniel? (Se parece a su novia Chalchi.)*

• *¿Qué nombre es una forma corta de Chalchiunenetl? (Chalchi)*

Lectura

El último sol
fragmento adaptado

Objectives

• **Read and understand a story based on historical facts**

• **Acquire vocabulary as you read**

Estrategia

Skipping and guessing
When reading for pleasure, you may try to skip unfamiliar words. If the word is truly essential to the meaning of the passage, try to guess the word's meaning. If you guess correctly, the text will make sense!

Al leer ·····

¿Alguna vez has sentido que nadie te entiende? Vas a leer un cuento de Elías Miguel Muñoz, un destacado novelista y cuentista cubano que reside en los Estados Unidos. Al leer este cuento te verás transportado(a) a otro mundo, el mundo del México antiguo, Tenochtitlán. Lee el cuento una primera vez sin pararte. No te preocupes por las palabras que no conozcas. Trata de adivinarlas. Cuando leas el cuento por segunda vez, mira los significados para ver si las entendiste. Mientras lees, presta atención a los siguientes puntos para que puedas llenar la tabla que aparece al final de la lectura:

• quiénes son los personajes

• dónde ocurre la acción, cómo cambia

• cómo cambia la relación de los personajes

• cómo reacciona el narrador

• cómo se siente el narrador al final de la lectura

---

*D*ANIEL, *el protagonista de* El último sol *es un joven que estudia en la Ciudad de México. A Daniel le encanta compartir pasajes de la historia de México con su novia Chalchi. Un día Daniel se queda dormido y sueña con la Piedra del Sol, el calendario azteca que había visto en el Museo de Antropología. Cuando se despierta, Daniel se encuentra en un mundo diferente . . .*

"¡Tozani!" Escucho una voz de mujer que viene de lejos. "¡Tozani!" Trato de despertar, pero me pesan los párpados[1]. Siento mucho frío. "¡Tozani!" La voz se hace más fuerte. Abro por fin los ojos y veo mi cuerpo, casi desnudo. Sólo llevo un taparrabo[2] y estoy acostado en una cama que no es la mía; es un petate[3]. Busco a la dueña de la voz y por fin la veo, parada frente a mí.

—Despierta ya —me dice ella.

Habla un idioma extraño que yo, de una manera también muy extraña, puedo comprender. Sus palabras llegan a mí como filtradas por el aire frío de este cuarto.

—Despierta —repite—. Es hora de ir al lago.

La observo. Es una muchacha joven, hermosa. Tiene el cabello atado atrás, con dos trenzas[4] sobre la frente. Lleva un vestido largo, blanco; en la cintura, un amplio cincho[5] bordado. Sus ojos son de un verde intenso. Se parece tanto a Chalchi que la llamo por ese nombre, Chalchiunenetl, y ella responde . . .

—Sí. Has dormido mucho, Tozani.

—¿Tozani? Yo no me llamo Tozani —le digo, confundido. Y ella me mira sonriendo.

—Levántate ya, esposo.

---

1 eyelids **2** loincloth **3** bedroll **4** braids **5** belt

---

Universal Access

Students with Learning Difficulties

Students may be confused by the main character's own confusion in **El último sol.** To help clarify the plot, assign small groups of students different sections of the excerpt. Have each group choose a narrator and the necessary characters. Give students the opportunity to quickly rehearse and present their dramatic interpretation of events.

Students with Special Needs

Provide visually impaired students with partners to describe the illustrations on pp. 377 and 378. Instruct these partners to provide details regarding the setting, calendar, and dress shown. How do these images differ from what Daniel must have been used to?

¡Me ha llamado *esposo*! Miro a mi alrededor y descubro que no estoy en casa de mis padres. Este lugar es mucho más grande; las paredes son blancas y a lo largo de cada una hay tiestos[6] enormes con flores de varios tipos y colores. Los muebles son escasos pero hermosos, de madera densa: un pequeño armario, una mesa baja y dos sillas. Hay una armonía total en este sitio. La puerta que da a la calle está inundada de luz.

¿Dónde estoy?

• • • • • • • • • • • • • • • •

Trato de ordenar mis pensamientos. Debo estar soñando. Cierro los ojos. Me golpeo la cara para despertar, ¡una, dos, tres veces! Y escucho la voz asustada de Chalchi; sus manos sujetan las mías.

—¡Tozani! —exclama—. ¡¿Qué haces?! ¿Por qué te golpeas?

No puedo contestarle. Algo en la garganta me impide hablar.

—Estabas soñando, esposo —me dice ella, mientras me acaricia.

—¿Soñando? —le pregunto, incrédulo.

—Sí. Pero ya, por fin, empiezas a despertar.

Me muevo. Respiro. Tengo los ojos muy abiertos. Sí. Estoy despierto.

—Cuando regreses del lago, comeremos —me dice Chalchi. Y se va a otro cuarto.

El lago. ¿Qué tendré que hacer en el lago? Me acuesto otra vez en el petate incómodo. ¿Cómo explicar todo esto?

6 flowerpots

trescientos setenta y siete 377
Capítulo 8

Suggestions (Cont'd):

Reading: Here are some possible comprehension issues on this page for which you can provide some guidance:

• *En el primer párrafo, hay una palabra que significa lo mismo que harmony en inglés. Adivina qué palabra es.* (armonía)

• *¿Cuáles son los muebles que Daniel ve?* (un armario, una mesa y dos sillas) *¿Estos son muchos o pocos muebles?* (pocos) *Entonces, ¿qué quiere decir la palabra "escasos": "muchos" o "pocos"?* (pocos)

• *¿Por qué no puede hablar Daniel?* (Algo en su garganta le impide.) *¿Qué palabra en inglés significa lo mismo que "impide"?* (impede)

Teacher-to-Teacher

When having students read selections aloud, try assigning roles to volunteers. In this story, you could choose one or more narrators, who rotate reading paragraphs of the narration. Two other volunteers can assume the roles of Daniel-Tozani and Chalchiunenetl.

Enriching Your Teaching

Culture Note
Built in the center of Lake Texcoco, the Aztec city of Tenochtitlán was one of the biggest metropolitan areas of its era. With causeways linking the city to the mainland, the city featured a number of engineering advances. Aqueducts, sewers, and irrigation systems were all part of the city's design. Although the area was marshy, the agricultural skills of the Aztecs prevailed. They created "floating gardens," bundles of sticks and earth that supported crops. The city sustained a population of approximately 200,000 to 300,000 people until 1521 and the arrival of Cortés.

Suggestions (Cont'd):

Reading: Here are some possible comprehension issues on this page for which you can provide some guidance:

• *¿Cuál es la fecha, exactamente, en el calendario moderno? (el 29 de junio de 1519)*

• *Moctezuma quiere que Daniel-Tozani sea responsable de una misión importante. ¿Qué verbo usa Chalchi que significa "hacer responsable"? (encomendar)*

• *¿Qué expresión usa Chalchi para decir que los seres blancos son altos? (son grandes de estatura)*

Post-reading: Have students complete their **Cambios en la narración** charts, referring to the story as necessary. Ask volunteers to read aloud or paraphrase parts of the story that support their choices for the chart.

Block Schedule

Expert Groups: After the class has read the story, give each student the number 1, 2, or 3. The story is divided into three sections. Indicate to the students which section they are to focus on. Each student is to write eight questions about their section. Then divide the class into groups of three, with a Number 1, 2, and 3 in each group. Have each student read his or her questions starting with the 1s. If a student needs assistance with a particular section, he or she can "ask the expert."

—¡Chalchi! —la llamo, y ella aparece ante mí.

—Estoy amasando *tlaxcalli*[7], preparando tu *atolli*[8]. ¿Por qué no te has ido al lago?

—¡Porque no sé para qué tengo que ir al lago!

—¿Estás soñando otra vez, querido mío? —ella me dice, sonriendo—. Tienes que ir al lago para bañarte, claro. Luego te vestirás de guerra para asistir al Templo Mayor. No olvides que el Reverendo Padre quiere verte.

—¿El Reverendo Padre?

—Sí. El señor emperador, Moctezuma.

—¡¿Quién?!

—Pobre de ti. Ese sueño de anoche te obsesiona.

—¿En qué año estamos, Chalchi?

—Acatl. El año 1-Caña[9], el día de 2-Casas.

Trato de recordar el calendario azteca. Un escalofrío[10] me invade el cuerpo cuando por fin descifro el significado de aquella fecha. *Acatl*, equivalente al año 1519 del calendario cristiano. El día 2-Casas, o sea, el 29, probablemente del mes de junio. Un mes antes de la entrada de Hernán Cortés en Tenochtitlán.

• • • • • • • • • • • • • • • •

—Chalchi, ¿por qué quiere verme Moctezuma?

Ella me mira como diciéndome, "despierta ya, querido esposo". Exasperada y sin comprender mi pregunta, me explica:

—El reverendo señor Moctezuma, *Huey-Tlatoani* de los aztecas, quiere encomendarte una misión muy importante . . .

—¿Qué misión es?

—¿Tampoco lo recuerdas? ¡Ese sueño de anoche te ha convertido en otro hombre, Tozani!

—Mi misión tiene que ver con los "dioses blancos", ¿verdad?

—Sí. En la última reunión del consejo gobernante, nuestro emperador decidió enviar una comisión para recibir a los seres blancos, para llevarles regalos y guiarlos hasta nuestra ciudad. El consejo te escogió a ti para encabezar la comisión.

---

[7] corn tortillas [8] corn gruel [9] 1-Reed, represents a month in the Aztec calendar [10] chill

—Esos seres no son dioses, Chalchi.

—¿Cómo lo sabes?

—Lo sé. Simplemente lo sé.

Chalchi se queda pensativa unos minutos. Luego me dice, agitada:

—Los mensajeros de Moctezuma que han visto a esos seres, cuentan que son grandes de estatura, que tienen la cara cubierta de cabello. Y algunos de ellos tienen cuatro patas enormes y dos cabezas, una de animal y otra de hombre . . .

—Son los españoles, Chalchi —le digo, sabiendo que no me entenderá. Repito: —Son los soldados de Cortés.

—Los soldados . . . ¿de quién?

—De Cortés, un hombre que viene a destruirnos.

—¡No! Moctezuma dice que son dioses. Dice que nuestro creador, Quetzalcóatl, ha regresado para recuperar su reino.

—¡Está loco el emperador!

Universal Access

Heritage Language Learners
Ask students to choose an interesting and/or important historical event from their heritage country. Have students briefly discuss what it would be like to return to that event. Who would they wish to be? How might their perspective on the event be different given their present-day knowledge?

Advanced Learners
Have students choose one word or expression from the story that they consider new or difficult and write it on a slip of paper. Mix the slips and have students take turns drawing one. Ask them to use background knowledge or reference materials to write a definition or explanation of the item they drew.

Interacción con la lectura

1 Llena la tabla con la información del cuento.

CAMBIOS EN LA NARRACIÓN		
	Antes	Ahora
Nombre de los dos personajes principales		
Cuándo ocurre la acción		
Lugar donde ocurre la acción		
Cuál es la relación entre los personajes		
Cómo se siente el personaje		

2 Trabaja con un grupo de estudiantes para comentar lo que escribieron en sus tablas y contestar las siguientes preguntas.

- ¿Qué le ha ocurrido a Daniel? ¿Cómo lo sabes?
- ¿Cómo es la nueva vida de Daniel?
- ¿Por qué es importante la fecha? ¿Quiénes son esos seres con dos cabezas y cuatro patas?
- ¿Qué tarea le ha encargado el emperador a Daniel?
- ¿Qué sabe Daniel que nadie más sabe?
- ¿Daniel puede cambiar lo que ocurrirá?

3 Trabaja con tu grupo para describir a los personajes en el mundo azteca: ¿Cómo se vestían? ¿Qué comían? Usa el vocabulario de la lectura.

4 Conocemos el final de la historia: Hernán Cortés conquistó el imperio Azteca. ¿Qué crees que hizo Daniel? ¿Trató de prevenir *(warn)* a los demás? ¿Trató de parar a los españoles? Comenta tus ideas con tus compañeros.

La herencia azteca Aunque el mundo de los aztecas desapareció con la llegada de Hernán Cortés en 1519, en México todavía se siente la herencia azteca en el lenguaje y las costumbres. En México todavía usan petates para acostarse en el campo y los niños toman atole en la merienda y los adultos en las celebraciones. Además, en todo el mundo se usan las palabras *tomate, chocolate, chile, coyote.* Las otras lenguas americanas de Norteamérica, el Caribe y Sudamérica también han contribuido con palabras que se usan hoy en todo el mundo: *caimán, canoa, caribú, cóndor, gaucho, huracán, iglú, iguana, jaguar, maíz, mocasín, papaya, poncho, puma.* Generalmente, estas palabras se refieren a objetos que se desconocían en Europa antes del descubrimiento de América.

- ¿Conoces más palabras como éstas?
- ¿Qué tipos de palabras pasan de una lengua a otra? ¿Por qué?
- ¿Tú usas palabras nuevas o distintas a las que usan los demás? ¿De dónde vienen? ¿Por qué las usas?

trescientos setenta y nueve **379**
Capítulo 8

Interacción con la lectura

Standards: 1.1, 1.2, 3.1

Resources: Practice Answers on Transparencies

Suggestions: Explain that the last piece of information in the chart in step 1, **Cómo se siente el personaje,** refers to Daniel-Tozani.

Answers:

Step 1
Daniel/Tozani; Chalchi/Chalchiunenetl
hoy en día/en el año 1519
Ciudad de México/Tenochtitlán
novios/esposos
Answers for how Daniel-Tozani feels will vary.

Step 2
- **Daniel se ha despertado en otro mundo. En la introducción es un joven de la Ciudad de México de hoy en día. De repente se encuentra en el mundo precolonial de los aztecas.**
- **Su vida es muy distinta a la vida de hoy en día.**
- **Es una fecha importante porque es un mes antes de la llegada de los europeos. Son soldados españoles montados a caballo.**
- **El emperador ha encargado a Daniel con la tarea de recibir a los europeos.**
- **Daniel sabe que los seres blancos no son dioses sino los españoles.**
- **Answers will vary.**

Steps 3–4
Answers will vary.

Fondo cultural *Standards:* 1.1, 1.2, 2.1, 2.2, 3.1

Suggestions: After students have read the information silently, ask them to work in pairs or small groups and develop lists of other words borrowed from indigenous American languages and used in either English or Spanish. Remind them of the many place names in the United States that come from indigenous languages. Encourage them to find out what some of these names mean in their original languages.

Answers will vary.

Enriching Your Teaching

Culture Note
Today maize is the third most planted field crop in the world (first and second being wheat and rice). Maize is actually a domesticated grass first cultivated and developed by the Aztecs. A chief staple of their diet, maize also played an important religious role. Of the Aztecs' many gods, *Xilonen* was the god of the "young maize ear." The name maize, however, is not an indigenous word. It's thought to have evolved from Columbus' entourage encountering Tahino people, and their *mahis,* which means "source of life." *Mahis* developed into the word *maíz.*

Review Activities

Para hablar de construcciones: Ask students to work in pairs to quiz each other. Have them take turns sketching and identifying the various items.

Para hablar del descubrimiento de América: Have students work in groups to create a summary of the discovery and early contact in the Americas. Their summary should include all of the words in the category. Invite them to present their summaries orally. Have the class discuss differences and similarities between the various summaries they hear.

Para hablar del encuentro de culturas: Ask students to prepare brief oral reports about a cultural encounter of their choice, past or present. Encourage each student to base the report on his or her own cultural heritage. Their reports should include as many of the words in the category as possible. Ask students to be prepared to field questions from the audience after their report.

Verbos: Have students choose any five of the verbs and use them in the imperfect subjunctive in complex sentences. Then have students share their sentences.

Otras expresiones y palabras: Students can use these words and expressions as they go over the review activities for the other categories.

Repaso del capítulo

Vocabulario y gramática

para hablar de construcciones

el acueducto	aqueduct
el arco	arch
la arquitectura	architecture
el azulejo	tile
el balcón, *pl.* los balcones	balcony
la construcción	construction
la reja	railing, grille
la torre	tower

para hablar de la llegada a las Américas

anteriormente	before
el arma, *pl.* las armas	weapon
la batalla	battle
la colonia	colony
la conquista	conquest
el imperio	empire
el / la indígena	native
la maravilla	marvel, wonder
la misión	mission
el / la misionero(a)	missionary
la población	population
el poder	power
poderoso, -a	powerful
el reto	challenge
la riqueza	wealth
el / la soldado	soldier
la tierra	land

para hablar del encuentro de culturas

africano, -a	African
el antepasado	ancestor
el / la árabe	Arab
cristiano, -a	Christian
la descendencia	descent, ancestry
desconocido, -a	unknown
el encuentro	meeting
la época	time, era
europeo, -a	European

la guerra	war
el grupo étnico	ethnic group
la herencia	heritage
el idioma	language
la influencia	influence
el intercambio	exchange
el / la judío(a)	Jewish
la lengua	language
la mercancía	merchandise
la mezcla	mix
el musulmán, la musulmana	Muslim
el / la romano(a)	Roman
la raza	race
el resultado	result, outcome
la semejanza	similarity
la unidad	unity
la variedad	variety

verbos

adoptar	to adopt
asimilar(se)	to assimilate
componerse de	to be formed by
conquistar	to conquer
dejar huellas	to leave marks, traces
dominar	to dominate
enfrentarse	to face, to confront
establecer (zc)	to establish
expulsar	to expel
fundar(se)	to found
gobernar (ie)	to rule, to govern
integrarse	to integrate
invadir	to invade
luchar	to fight
ocupar	to occupy
rebelarse	to rebel, to revolt
reconquistar	to reconquer

otras expresiones y palabras

al llegar	upon arriving
maravilloso, -a	wonderful
único, -a	only

Universal Access

Students with Learning Difficulties

Divide students into pairs. Instruct them to use the vocabulary on p. 380 as a guide. One partner should choose a word and read it aloud. The other partner should review the chapter to locate a picture of, or reference to that word. Have students use the information they have found to formulate a sentence using the word.

Advanced Learners

Have students assume the role of a politician, either local, national, or international. Ask them to prepare and deliver a brief message in which they suggest one or more ways to improve relations between two cultures. Tell them that their message can be created as though it were part of a longer speech.

el condicional

Use the conditional to express what you would do or what a situation would be like.

hablar

hablaría	hablaríamos
hablarías	hablaríais
hablaría	hablarían

ser

sería	seríamos
serías	seríais
sería	serían

ir

iría	iríamos
irías	iríais
iría	irían

Verbs that are irregular in the future tense have the same irregular stems in the conditional.

tener

tendría	tendríamos
tendrías	tendríais
tendría	tendrían

future and conditional stems of other irregular verbs:

decir	**dir-**	poder	**podr-**	saber	**sabr-**
haber	**habr-**	poner	**pondr-**	salir	**saldr-**
hacer	**har-**	querer	**querr-**	venir	**vendr-**

el imperfecto del subjuntivo

Use the subjunctive to say what one person asks, hopes, tells, insists, or requires someone else to do. If the main verb is in the preterite or imperfect tense, use the imperfect subjunctive.

cantar

cantara	cant**áramos**
cantaras	cantar**ais**
cantara	cantar**an**

aprender

aprendi**era**	aprendi**éramos**
aprendi**eras**	aprendi**erais**
aprendi**era**	aprendi**eran**

vivir

vivi**era**	vivi**éramos**
vivi**eras**	vivi**erais**
vivi**era**	vivi**eran**

el imperfecto del subjuntivo con *si*

Use the imperfect subjunctive after *si* when a situation is unlikely, impossible, or not true. Use the conditional in the main clause.

Si hablaras más, **tendrías** muchos amigos.
Si Marcos **no fuera** tan travieso, lo llevaría de paseo.

After *como si* you always use the imperfect subjunctive.

Ella se sentía **como si estuviera** en un lugar desconocido.

● **Más práctica** ....
Practice Workbook Organizer 8-13, 8-14

El condicional: Tell students that Mateo is a very popular boy. Everyone always needs to talk to him or has something to do with him. Ask students to think of at least two questions concerning Mateo that they might ask a friend, such as: ¿*Hablarás con Mateo hoy?* The friend responds using the conditional, saying that he or she would do that thing, but Mateo is not to be found: *Le hablaría, pero no lo encuentro.* Another example might be: ¿*Harás tu tarea con Mateo hoy? La haria con él, pero no lo encuentro.* Have partners take turns asking and answering each other's questions.

El imperfecto del subjuntivo: Ask students to think of five wishes they have always had. On the board write the sentence starter **Siempre he querido que....** Have students use the sentence starter five times to write their wishes: *Siempre he querido que el año escolar no fuera tan largo.*

El imperfecto del subjuntivo con si: Challenge students to write comparisons using complex sentences with **como si:** *Entró en el cuarto como si fuera una reina.* Encourage them to make their comparisons humorous: *Estaba tan alegre como si fuera una tortuga con patines.*

Portfolio

Invite students to review the activities they completed in this chapter, including written reports, posters or other visuals, tapes of oral presentations, and other projects. Have them select one or two items that they feel best demonstrate their achievements in Spanish. Include these products in students' portfolios. Have them include this with the Chapter Checklist and Self-Assessment Worksheet.

Additional Resources

• Audio Program: CD Cap. 8, Track 17
• Resource Book: Cap. 8, Clip Art
• Assessment Program: Chapter Checklist and Self-Assessment Worksheet

Enriching Your Teaching

Teacher-to-Teacher
Have students create a practice test covering the vocabulary and grammar structures. Encourage them to use multiple choice, true/false, or short answer questions. Have them exchange tests with a partner or compile the questions and answer them in a game show format.

Performance Tasks

Standards: 1.1, 1.2, 1.3, 3.1

Resources: Audio Program: CD Cap. 8, Track 18; Resource Book: Cap. 8, Audio Script; Practice Answers on Transparencies

1. Vocabulario

Suggestions: Encourage students to review the vocabulary from the *A primera vista* sections on pp. 344–347 and 356–359 before they complete the activity.

Answers:

1. b	5. d
2. c	6. d
3. b	7. b
4. c	8. c

2. Gramática

Suggestions: Remind students of the main points of the grammar presentations in *Capítulo 8:*

• the conditional
• the imperfect subjunctive
• the imperfect subjunctive with *si*

Answers:

1. c	5. a
2. b	6. b
3. c	7. a
4. a	8. d

3. Escuchar

Suggestions: Use the *Audio CD* or read from the script.

Answers: Wording of answers will vary. The following are likely results:

a. Es famoso por su maravillosa artesanía. Dice que la arquitectura es un resultado de la influencia española durante la colonia.
b. Le impresiona más la variedad de las mercancías. El mercado le recuerda de lo que describió Hernán Cortés en sus Cartas de relación.
c. Encuentra hamacas, joyas de plata y cerámica y también canoas.
d. Lo compara con un mercado de hace siglos.

To prepare for the test, check to see if you . . .

• **know the new vocabulary and grammar**
• **can perform the tasks on pp. 382 and 383**

Preparación para el examen

❶ Vocabulario Escribe la letra de la palabra o expresión que mejor complete cada frase. Escribe tus respuestas en una hoja aparte.

1. Un ejemplo de un _____ fue el pueblo romano, porque tuvo tanto poder que pudo decidir el futuro de otros pueblos.
   a. misionero   c. arte
   b. imperio   d. arma

2. Empezó un intercambio de _____ entre Europa y las Américas.
   a. riquezas   c. mercancías
   b. banderas   d. libertad

3. Cuando un país invade a otro país y se queda allí por muchos años, decimos que lo _____.
   a. expulsa   c. lucha
   b. ocupa   d. permite

4. Como resultado de la mezcla de españoles, indígenas y africanos hay una gran _____ de culturas en América.
   a. batalla   c. variedad
   b. reja   d. mercancía

5. La Mezquita de Córdoba es un ejemplo de la arquitectura árabe porque tiene muchos _____, igual que la Alhambra, en Granada.
   a. caballos   c. budistas
   b. retos   d. arcos

6. Los misioneros tenían opiniones diferentes sobre _____ de los españoles en la vida de los indígenas.
   a. la semejanza   c. la arquitectura
   b. el azulejo   d. la influencia

7. España era un imperio _____ en la época de la conquista de América.
   a. único   c. débil
   b. poderoso   d. africano

8. Cuando los cristianos reconquistaron Sevilla, muchos árabes se habían _____ con los españoles.
   a. rebelado   c. asimilado
   b. reconquistado   d. expulsado

❷ Gramática Escribe la letra de la palabra o expresión que mejor complete cada frase. Escribe tus respuestas en una hoja aparte.

1. Yo _____ con Luisa por teléfono todos los días si tuviera tiempo, pero estoy muy ocupada.
   a. hablo   c. hablaría
   b. he hablado   d. hablaba

2. Nosotros _____ al balcón, pero hace mucho frío y está lloviendo.
   a. saldremos   c. salíamos
   b. saldríamos   d. saldrían

3. El arquitecto le dijo al dueño de la casa que _____ el azulejo de color amarillo porque era mejor.
   a. compré   c. comprara
   b. compró   d. compras

4. El rey de España lo miró como si _____ que estaba mintiendo.
   a. creyera   c. creía
   b. crea   d. creerá

5. La madre le dijo al niño que _____ a la escuela después de comprar la comida.
   a. vendría   c. vinieron
   b. vienen   d. viene

6. Si _____ todas tus riquezas, te regalaría mis caballos, le dijo el español al indígena.
   a. me das   c. me diste
   b. me dieras   d. me dieron

7. Aprenderíamos otros idiomas, como el chino, si _____ la oportunidad de estudiarlos en la escuela.
   a. tuviéramos   c. tuvieran
   b. tuvimos   d. tuvieras

8. Los misioneros querían que los indígenas _____ su religión.
   a. adoptáramos   c. adoptamos
   b. adoptaron   d. adoptaran

Universal Access

Heritage Language Learners

Ask students to identify a writing skill that they would like to improve. Examples might include spelling, punctuation, or organization. Have students create a draft of an essay based on the topic on p. 383. Then, have them revise their drafts, focusing on the skill they are trying to improve.

Students with Learning Difficulties

Direct students to focus on the verb(s) in each example of the *Gramática* review. Help them establish the time frame of each sentence. Then, instruct students to choose the verb form that corresponds to both the time frame and meaning of the sentence.

Go Online
PHSchool.com

For: Test preparation
Visit: www.phschool.com
Web Code: jed-0811

En el examen vas a . . .	Éstas son las tareas de práctica que te pueden ser útiles para el examen . . .	Si necesitas repasar . . .
3 **Escuchar** Escuchar y comprender la descripción de una visita a un pueblo indígena	La visitante describe su visita a un pueblo. (a) ¿Por qué es famoso ese pueblo? ¿Qué dice de la arquitectura? (b) ¿Qué le impresiona más? ¿Qué le recuerda el mercado? (c) ¿Qué otras cosas encuentra allí? (d) ¿Con qué compara al pueblo?	pp. 344–347 *A primera vista 1* p. 347 Actividad 4 p. 350 Actividad 8 p. 354 Actividad 15 p. 379 *Interacción con la lectura*
4 **Hablar** Presentar una visita guiada para conocer una ciudad	Escoge una ciudad que te guste. Imagina que le hablas de esta ciudad a un recién llegado. Menciona (a) los edificios históricos, (b) las culturas y religiones, (c) una breve historia de la ciudad y (d) lugares donde los jóvenes se divierten.	p. 350 Actividad 8 p. 354 Actividad 15 p. 373 *Presentación oral*
5 **Leer** Leer y comprender un cuento	Lee este párrafo sobre las aventuras de un indígena azteca y di (a) ¿En qué ciudad crees que se despierta Maco? ¿En qué época sería? (b) ¿Qué lengua habla la gente? (c) ¿Crees que es un sueño o es la realidad? *Un día, Maco, un joven indígena azteca, cerró sus ojos y cuando los abrió se vio en medio de una ciudad muy diferente a la que vivía. La gente era alta con los cabellos claros. Llevaban ropas largas y zapatos. Hablaban una lengua familiar, parecida a la de las personas que habían llegado a su tierra hacía poco tiempo. La gente lo miraba, pero nadie se paraba a hablarle...*	pp. 376–379 *Lectura*
6 **Escribir** Escribir una reseña sobre la herencia	Escribe una reseña sobre qué cosas pueden hacer las familias para mantener su herencia cultural y las tradiciones de sus antepasados. Sugiere qué pueden hacer para mantener el idioma, las comidas y otras tradiciones familiares.	p. 351 Actividad 9 p. 351 Actividad 10 pp. 374–375 *Presentación escrita*
7 **Pensar** Pensar en ejemplos de intercambio cultural en el mundo de hoy y decir si son positivos o no	Da un ejemplo de un intercambio entre culturas en el mundo de hoy en día. Di por qué crees que ese intercambio es positivo o crea conflictos. ¿Crees que ayuda a que las personas se integren o no?	p. 350 Actividad 8 p. 362 Actividad 24 pp. 370–371 *Puente a la cultura*

trescientos ochenta y tres **383**
Capítulo 8

Review

4. Hablar

Suggestions: Encourage students to combine ideas into complex sentences as they describe their city.

Answers will vary.

5. Leer

Suggestions: Tell students to refer to pp. 344–347 and 356–359 if they have questions about vocabulary in the review.

Answers:
a. Cities named should be major Spanish cities. Es la época moderna.
b. La gente habla español.
c. Answers will vary between *sueño* and *realidad*.

6. Escribir

Suggestions: Encourage students to work in pairs or groups to gather ideas for their *reseñas*.

Answers will vary.

7. Pensar

Suggestions: Ask students to consider how their thoughts about cultural fusion have changed, based on what they have learned in *Capítulo* 8.

Answers will vary.

✓ **Assessment**
• Examen del capítulo: 8
• Audio Program: CD 13, Cap. 8, Track 11
• Assessment Program: *RPH*

Alternative Assessment
• ExamView Test Bank CD-ROM
• Resource Book: Cap. 8, Situation Cards
• Resource Book: Cap. 8, Communicative Activity BLM

Enriching Your Teaching

Teacher-to-Teacher
Have students choose a Spanish or Latin American city, research it, and write a proposal outlining why it should become a sister community of your own. Ask them to focus on how similarities and differences between the two communities might help to create a healthy cultural exchange.

Capítulo 9

Cuidemos nuestro planeta

CHAPTER OVERVIEW

Cuidemos nuestro planeta
• local and global environmental concerns

Vocabulary
• environmental issues
• endangered species

Grammar
• conjunctions used with the subjunctive and the indicative
• relative pronouns *que, quien, lo que*

Cultural Perspectives
• traffic restrictions in Chile
• ecotourism in Costa Rica
• protection of Magellanic penguins
• endangered species of the Galapagos Islands
• life cycle of the Monarch butterfly

Chapter Project

Visita un parque nacional

Overview: Students create a brochure for a national park in Central or South America featuring the flora and fauna of the area, as well as conservation programs sponsored by the park. They should include illustrations of some species found in the area accompanied by a brief description of each. Illustrations could be obtained from magazines, travel brochures or downloaded from the Web. Students then give an oral presentation of their brochure describing the park and trying to convince their listeners to support the conservation program sponsored by the park.

Materials: construction paper, magazines, travel brochures, scissors, glue, colored pencils and markers

Sequence: (suggestions for when to do each step appear throughout the chapters)

STEP 1. Review instructions so students know what is expected of them. Hand out the "Chapter 9 Project Instructions and Rubric" from the *Teacher's Resource Book*.

STEP 2. Students submit a rough sketch of their brochure. Return the sketches with your suggestions. For vocabulary and grammar practice, ask students to work in pairs and present their sketches to each other.

STEP 3. Students create layouts on construction paper. Encourage students to work in pencil first and to try different arrangements before drawing pictures or gluing magazine clippings and writing the contents of the brochure.

STEP 4. Students submit a draft of their brochure. Note your corrections and suggestions, then return the drafts to students.

STEP 5. Students complete and present their brochure to the class, trying to convince their fellow students to support the conservation program sponsored by the park.

Options:
1. Students create a poster for the national park instead of a brochure.
2. Students write an article for the school newspaper about a national park.

Assessment:
Here is a detailed rubric for assessing this project:
Chapter 9 Project: *Visita un parque nacional*

RUBRIC	Score 1	Score 3	Score 5
Your evidence of planning	You provide no written draft or page layout.	Your draft and layout are provided, but not corrected.	You show evidence of corrected draft and layout.
Your use of illustrations	You include no photos or visuals.	You include photos or visuals, but your layout is disorganized.	Your brochure is easy to read, complete, and accurate.
Your presentation	You include little of the required information.	You include some of the required information. You attempted to convince.	You include all of the required information. You convinced us to support the program.

Chapter Support

Bulletin Boards

Theme: *Animales en peligro de extinción*

Ask students to cut out, copy, or download photos or pictures of animals in danger of extinction. Place photos around a world map with leader lines from animals to their respective habitats. Add brief captions to the photos or pictures explaining why these animals are in danger of extinction.

Bibliography

Bowden, Rob. *Waste, Recycling and Reuse*. Texas: Raintree Publishers, 2002. Looks at the impact human development is having on the planet and how this could affect our future.

DK Burnie, David. *Animal*. New York: Dorling Kindersley, 2001. Illustrates, describes, and explains the incredible range of creatures that make up the animal kingdom.

Chapman, Matthew, and Rob Bowden. *Air Pollution*. Texas: Raintree Publishers, 2002. Explores the debates surrounding air pollution, discussing its causes and prevention.

Fridell, Ron. *Global Warming*. New York: Scholastic Library Publishing, 2002. Describes different theories on the causes and solutions of global warming.

Morris, Scott Edward. *The Endangered World*. Pennsylvania: Chelsea House Publishers, 1993. Eighteen spreads of maps highlight the damage pollution has done to our world.

Hands-on Culture

Art: *Un móvil de mariposas*

Mobiles of butterflies are a popular decoration in homes throughout the Spanish-speaking world.

Materials: construction paper, pencil, scissors, hole punch, pipe cleaners, thread, large upholstery needle, 3 twigs (about 1 ft long each), markers or crayons, glitter glue or glitter (optional)

1. Fold a piece of construction paper in half and cut along the fold. (This will make 2 butterflies). You will need to make 4 or more butterflies for the mobile.

2. Fold one of these pieces of paper in half. Draw half of a butterfly along the fold line.

3. Fold a small piece of black or brown paper in half. Draw the body and head of a butterfly on it. Make it the same length as your butterfly. Cut them out. Glue a body on each side of your butterfly.

4. Using a hole punch, make two holes in the butterfly's head. Cut a pipe cleaner in half. Thread it through the holes in the butterfly's head as antennae.

5. Decorate both sides of your butterfly using crayons, markers, glitter, or glitter glue.

6. Using a needle, pull a short length of knotted thread through the balancing point of the butterfly (near its middle). Tie the other end of the thread to the end of a twig.

7. On the other end of the twig, attach another butterfly in the same way.

8. Tie a thread to the middle of this twig and attach it to the end of another twig. Attach a butterfly to the end of this twig.

9. Using a short length of thread, attach what you've made to the end of another twig. Attach a butterfly to the other end of this twig.

10. Tie a longer length of thread to the top twig. If you want the twigs to remain horizontal, tie the thread where the mobile will balance.

Game

En las noticias

Play this game to review the material from *Capítulo 9*.

Players: the whole class

Materials: index cards, pen

Rules:

1. On index cards, write vocabulary words, expressions and verbs from *Capítulo 9*. Place the cards in a box.

2. Have a student draw an index card from the box. Ask him / her to begin a story for a news article for the newspaper, using the word on the card in a sentence. Write the student's sentence on the board. Ask the class to make any necessary corrections.

3. Call on another volunteer to pick up a card and to continue the story, doing the same thing. Write the second volunteer's sentence on the board, and have the class make any necessary corrections. Continue in this manner until the class feels the story has reached a logical conclusion. If every student has not had the chance to contribute to the story, begin a second story.
   Student 1: (drew **capa de ozono**) *El problema del agujero en la capa de ozono es cada vez más grave.*
   Student 2: (drew **disminuir**) *Si no disminuimos el uso de aerosoles, podrían producirse más agujeros en la capa de ozono.*
   Student 3: (drew **amenaza**) *Este problema es una amenaza para la vida del planeta.*

Variation: Play the game at the end of *Capítulo 9*, writing only verbs on the index cards. Have students tell the story using conjunctions.

Internet Search

Use the keywords to find more information.

Keywords:

Puerto Rico: Programa Industria y Comercio Pro-Reciclaje (ICPRO), reciclar, población del mundo, lluvia ácida, derrames de petróleo, animales en peligro de extinción, Punta Arenas, Parque Nacional de Guanacaste, pingüinos magallánicos, Pablo Neruda, Santuario Ballenero del Atlántico Sur, rescatista, islas Galápagos, mariposa monarca

A ver si recuerdas
RECYCLE

Vocabulary
- Recycling and community
- Places and natural phenomena

Grammar
- Verbs like *gustar*
- Uses of the definite article

Chapter Overview

A primera vista 1	Manos a la obra 1	A primera vista 2	Manos a la obra 2
INPUT	**PRACTICE**	**INPUT**	**PRACTICE**
Objectives • Talk about environmental concerns in the community • What we can do to protect the environment	**Objectives** • Talk about environmental issues • Discuss what we can do to protect the environment	**Objectives** • Talk about environmental issues and endangered species • Talk about measures to protect endangered species	**Objectives** • Discuss environmental issues • Talk about animals in danger of extinction
Vocabulary • Pollution • Environment	**Vocabulary** • Practice and use new vocabulary	**Vocabulary** • Natural resources • Animals	**Vocabulary** • Practice and use new vocabulary
Grammar • Conjunctions used with the subjunctive and the indicative tenses • Relative pronouns *que, quien,* and *lo que*	**Grammar** • Conjunctions used with the subjunctive and the indicative tenses • Relative pronouns *que, quien,* and *lo que*	**Grammar** • Conjunctions used with the subjunctive and the indicative tenses	**Grammar** • Conjunctions used with the subjunctive and the indicative tenses
Culture • Diego Rivera • Puerto Rico	**Culture** • Restrictions on driving cars • Acid rain	**Culture** • Punta Arenas, Chile • National Park of Guanacaste, Costa Rica	**Culture** • Magellanic penguins • Tropical forests of Costa Rica • International rescuers

¡Adelante!
APPLICATION

Objectives
- Read about the history of the Galapagos Islands
- Write a petition letter to an oil company
- Read an article about the Monarch butterfly

Vocabulary
- Application

Grammar
- Application

Culture
- Galapagos Islands
- Monarch butterfly

Repaso del capítulo
REVIEW

Objectives
- Know the new vocabulary and grammar
- Perform the tasks on pages 428 and 429

Vocabulary
- Review

Grammar
- Review

BEYOND THE CLASSROOM

Countries
- Mexico
- Ecuador
- Puerto Rico
- Costa Rica
- Chile
- United States

El español en el mundo del trabajo
- International rescuers in South America

Internet
- Vocabulary activities
- Grammar activities
- Internet links
- Self-tests

LEARNER SUPPORT

Strategies
- Using topic sentences to orient you
- Finding good details
- Good conclusions
- Context clues

Recycling
- Syllabication

En voz alta
- *Versos sencillos*

Ampliación del lenguaje
- Word families

Conexiones
- Science: acid rain

Print Components

TEACHER

Teacher's Resource Book
- Chapter Table of Contents
- School-to-Home Connection
- Chapter Resource Checklist
- Input Script
- Audio Script
- Video Script
- Communicative Activities
- Situation Cards
- GramActiva Blackline Masters
- Graphic Organizers
- Answer Keys:
  Practice Workbook
  Writing, Audio & Video Workbook

Realidades para hispanohablantes
Teacher Edition

STUDENT

Practice Workbook
- Vocabulary: 9-1 – 9-4, 9-8 – 9-9
- Grammar: 9-5 – 9-7, 9-10 – 9-12
- Organizer: 9-13 – 9-14

Writing, Audio and Video Workbook
- Audio: 1–5
- Writing: 6–13
- Video: 14–17

Reading and Writing for Success
- Chapter 9, Test 36

Realidades para hispanohablantes

Transparencies

Vocabulary and Grammar Transparencies
- Vocabulary: 165–172, 175–178
- Grammar: 173–174, 179
- ¿Qué me cuentas?: 180

Practice Answers on Transparencies
- Cap. 9

Fine Art Transparencies
- Transparencies
- Teacher's Guide

Assessment

Assessment Program
- Pruebas:
  – Comprensión del vocabulario 1: 9-1
  – Aplicación del vocabulario 1: 9-2
  – Conjunciones que se usan con el subjuntivo y el indicativo: 9-3
  – Los pronombres relativos *que, quien* y *lo que*: 9-4
  – Comprensión del vocabulario 2: 9-5
  – Aplicación del vocabulario 2: 9-6
  – Conjunciones que se usan con el subjuntivo y el indicativo: 9-7
- Exámenes del capítulo
- Rubrics

Alternative Assessment
- ExamView Test Bank CD-ROM
- MindPoint Quiz Show CD-ROM
- Internet Self-test
- Situation Cards
- Communicative Activity

Assessment Program: *Realidades para hispanohablantes*

Technology

TeacherExpress™ CD-ROM
- Lesson Planner
- Teacher Resources
- Clip Art

Video Program VHS and DVD

Audio Program CDs
- A primera vista 1 y 2: Vocabulario y gramática en contexto
- Audio Activities
- ¿Qué me cuentas?
- Repaso
- Examen del capítulo: Escuchar

	Warm-up / Assess	Preview Present / Practice Communicate	Wrap-up / Homework Options
DAY 1	**Warm-up (10 min.)** • Return Examen del capítulo: Capítulo 8	**Repaso (35 min.)** • A ver si recuerdas • Actividades 1–8	**Wrap-up and Homework Options (5 min.)** • Practice Workbook 9-1, 9-2 • Go Online
DAY 2	**Warm-up (10 min.)** • Homework check	**Chapter Opener (10 min.)** • Objectives • Fondo cultural **A primera vista 1 (25 min.)** • Presentation: Vocabulario y gramática en contexto • Actividades 1, 2	**Wrap-up and Homework Options (5 min.)** • Go Online • Clip Art Vocabulary
DAY 3	**Warm-up (10 min.)** • Homework check	**A primera vista 1 (35 min.)** • Presentation: ¿Cómo cuidas tu planeta?; Puerto Rico: cómo conservar bella la isla • Actividad 3	**Wrap-up and Homework Options (5 min.)** • Practice Workbook 9-3, 9-4 • Go Online • Manos a la obra 1: Actividad 4 • Prueba 9-1: Vocabulary recognition
DAY 4	**Warm-up (10 min.)** • Homework check ✔**Assessment (10 min.)** • Prueba 9-1: Vocabulary recognition	**Manos a la obra 1 (25 min.)** • Actividades 6, 7, 8, 9	**Wrap-up and Homework Options (5 min.)** • Actividades 5, 10 • Writing Activities • Prueba 9-2: Vocabulary production
DAY 5	**Warm-up (10 min.)** • Homework check ✔**Assessment (10 min.)** • Prueba 9-2: Vocabulary production	**Manos a la obra 1 (25 min.)** • Fondo cultural • Presentation: Conjunciones que se usan con el subjuntivo y el indicativo 1 • Actividades 11, 12; Ampliación del lenguaje	**Wrap-up and Homework Options (5 min.)** • Practice Workbook 9-5 • Go Online
DAY 6	**Warm-up (10 min.)** • Actividad 13 • Homework check	**Manos a la obra 1 (35 min.)** • Actividades 14, 15, 16 • Communicative Activity • Presentation: Los pronombres relativos *que, quien* y *lo que* • Actividad 18	**Wrap-up and Homework Options (5 min.)** • Writing Activity • Prueba 9-3: Conjunciones que se usan con el subjuntivo y el indicativo 1
DAY 7	**Warm-up (10 min.)** • Actividad 17 • Homework check ✔**Assessment (10 min.)** • Prueba 9-3	**Manos a la obra 1 (25 min.)** • Actividad 19 • Communicative Activity	**Wrap-up and Homework Options (5 min.)** • Practice Workbook 9-6, 9-7 • Go Online • Prueba 9-4: Los pronombres relativos *que, quien* y *lo que*
DAY 8	**Warm-up (15 min.)** • Writing Activity • Homework check ✔**Assessment (10 min.)** • Prueba 9-4	**A primera vista 2 (20 min.)** • Presentation: Vocabulario y gramática en contexto • Actividades 20, 21	**Wrap-up and Homework Options (5 min.)** • Clip Art Vocabulary • Examen: Vocabulario y gramática 1
DAY 9	**Warm-up (5 min.)** • Homework check ✔**Assessment (30 min.)** • Examen: Vocabulario y gramática 1	**A primera vista 2 (10 min.)** • Presentation: Punta Arenas • Presentation: El Parque Nacional de Guanacaste	**Wrap-up and Homework Options (5 min.)** • Actividad 22 • Practice Workbook 9-8, 9-9 • Go Online • Prueba 9-5: Vocabulary recognition
DAY 10	**Warm-up (10 min.)** • Actividad 23 • Homework check ✔**Assessment (10 min.)** • Prueba 9-5: Vocabulary recognition	**Manos a la obra 2 (25 min.)** • Actividades 26, 27 • Fondo cultural	**Wrap-up and Homework Options (5 min.)** • Actividades 24, 25 • Prueba 9-6: Vocabulary production

	Warm-up / Assess	Preview Present / Practice Communicate	Wrap-up / Homework Options
DAY 11	**Warm-up (10 min.)** • Writing Activity • Homework check ✔**Assessment (10 min.)** • Prueba 9-6: Vocabulary production	**Manos a la obra 2 (25 min.)** • Actividades 28, 29 • Communicative Activity	**Wrap-up and Homework Options (5 min.)** • Actividad 30 • Writing Activity
DAY 12	**Warm-up (10 min.)** • Homework check	**Manos a la obra 2 (35 min.)** • Presentation: Conjunciones que se usan con el subjuntivo y el indicativo 2 • Actividades 31, 32, 34 • En voz alta	**Wrap-up and Homework Options (5 min.)** • Actividad 33 • Practice Workbook 9-11, 9-12 • Go Online • Prueba 9-7: Conjunciones con el subjuntivo y el indicativo 2
DAY 13	**Warm-up (10 min.)** • Homework check ✔**Assessment (10 min.)** • Prueba 9-7	**Manos a la obra 2 (25 min.)** • Actividades 35, 36 • El español en el mundo del trabajo • Communicative Activity	**Wrap-up and Homework Options (5 min.)** • Go Online • Examen: Vocabulario y gramática 2
DAY 14	**Warm-up (8 min.)** • Writing Activity ✔**Assessment (30 min.)** • Examen: Vocabulario y gramática 2	**¡Adelante! (10 min.)** • Presentación oral: Steps 1, 2	**Wrap-up and Homework Options (2 min.)** • Presentación oral: Step 2
DAY 15	**Warm-up (10 min.)** • Presentación oral: Step 2	**¡Adelante! (35 min.)** • Presentación oral: Step 3	**Wrap-up and Homework Options (5 min.)** • Galápagos: el encuentro con la naturaleza • ¿Comprendiste? • Go Online
DAY 16	**Warm-up (15 min.)** • Galápagos: el encuentro con la naturaleza: ¿Comprendiste? • Homework check	**¡Adelante! (30 min.)** • ¿Qué me cuentas? 1, 2, 3 • View Video • Video Activities 1, 2, 3	**Wrap-up and Homework Options (5 min.)** • Presentación escrita: Steps 1, 2
DAY 17	**Warm-up (10 min.)** • Video Activity 4	**¡Adelante! (15 min.)** • Presentación escrita: Step 3 **Repaso (20 min.)** • Preparación para el examen: Actividades 3, 4 • MindPoint Quiz Show	**Wrap-up and Homework Options (5 min.)** • Presentación escrita: Step 4
DAY 18	**Warm-up and Bellringer (10 min.)** • Homework check	**¡Adelante! (35 min.)** • Lectura • Interacción con la lectura • Fondo cultural	**Wrap-up and Homework Options (5 min.)** • Practice Workbook: Organizer 9-13, 9-14 • Go Online: Self-test
DAY 19	**Warm-up (20 min.)** • Preparación para el examen: Actividades 1, 2 • Homework check	**Repaso (25 min.)** • Preparación para el examen: Actividades 5, 6, 7 • MindPoint Quiz Show • Other review	**Wrap-up and Homework Options (5 min.)** • Examen del capítulo
DAY 20	**Warm-up (5 min.)** • Answer questions ✔**Assessment (44 min.)** • Examen del capítulo		**Wrap-up and Homework Options (1 min.)** • A ver si recuerdas: Capítulo 10

Block Schedule (90 Minutes)

For electronic lesson plans:
Teacher Express CD-ROM 💿

	Warm-up / Assess	Preview Present / Practice Communicate	Wrap-up / Homework Options
DAY 1	**Warm-up (35 min.)** • Return Examen del capítulo: 8 • A ver si recuerdas • Actividades 4, 5, 7 • Homework check	**Chapter Opener (10 min.)** • Objectives • Fondo cultural **A primera vista 1 (30 min.)** • Presentation: Vocabulario y gramática en contexto • Actividades 1, 2 • Presentation: ¿Cómo cuidas tu planeta?; Puerto Rico: cómo conservar bella la isla • Actividad 3 **Manos a la obra 1 (10 min.)** • Actividades 7, 8	**Wrap-up and Homework Options (5 min.)** • Practice Workbook 9-3, 9-4 • Go Online • Clip Art Vocabulary • Prueba 9-1: Vocabulary recognition
DAY 2	**Warm-up (15 min.)** • Actividad 4 • Homework check ✔**Assessment (10 min.)** • Prueba 9-1: Vocabulary recognition	**Manos a la obra 1 (60 min.)** • Actividades 5, 6, 9, 10 • Communicative Activity	**Wrap-up and Homework Options (5 min.)** • Go Online • Writing Activities • Prueba 9-2: Vocabulary production
DAY 3	**Warm-up (10 min.)** • Writing Activity • Homework check ✔**Assessment (15 min.)** • Prueba 9-2: Vocabulary production	**Manos a la obra 1 (60 min.)** • Presentation: Conjunciones con el subjuntivo y el indicativo 1 • Actividades 11, 12, 13, 14, 15 • Ampliación del lenguaje • Audio and Writing Activities	**Wrap-up and Homework Options (5 min.)** • Practice Workbook 9-5 • Go Online • Prueba 9-3: Conjunciones con el subjuntivo y el indicativo 1
DAY 4	**Warm-up (10 min.)** • Actividad 16 • Homework check ✔**Assessment (10 min.)** • Prueba 9-3: Conjunciones con el subjuntivo y el indicativo 1	**Manos a la obra 1 (50 min.)** • Presentation: Los pronombres relativos *que, quien* y *lo que* • Actividades 17, 18, 19 • Communicative Activity **A primera vista 2 (15 min.)** • Presentation: Vocabulario y gramática en contexto • Actividades 20, 21	**Wrap-up and Homework Options (5 min.)** • Practice Workbook 9-6, 9-7 • Go Online • Prueba 9-4: Los pronombres relativos *que, quien* y *lo que* • Examen: Vocabulario y gramática 1
DAY 5	**Warm-up (10 min.)** • Writing Activity • Homework check ✔**Assessment Options (40 min.)** • Prueba 9-4: Los pronombres relativos *que, quien* y *lo que* • Examen: Vocabulario y gramática 1	**A primera vista 2 (20 min.)** • Presentation: Punta Arenas: miedo al sol • Actividad 22 • Presentation: El Parque Nacional de Guanacaste • Actividad 23 **Manos a la obra 2 (15 min.)** • Actividades 26, 27 • Fondo cultural	**Wrap-up and Homework Options (5 min.)** • Practice Workbook 9-8, 9-9 • Go Online • Prueba 9-5: Vocabulary recognition

	Warm-up / Assess	Preview Present / Practice Communicate	Wrap-up / Homework Options
DAY 6	**Warm-up (20 min.)** • Actividades 24, 25 • Homework check ✔**Assessment (10 min.)** • Prueba 9-5: Vocabulary recognition	**Manos a la obra 2 (55 min.)** • Actividades 28, 29, 30 • Actividades 31, 32, 33 • Presentation: Conjunciones con • En voz alta el subjuntivo y el indicativo 2 • Writing Activities	**Wrap-up and Homework Options (5 min.)** • Practice Workbook 9-10 • Go Online • Prueba 9-6: Vocabulary production
DAY 7	**Warm-up (10 min.)** • Homework check ✔**Assessment (10 min.)** • Prueba 9-6: Vocabulary production	**Manos a la obra 2 (45 min.)** • Actividades 34, 35, 36 • El español en el mundo del trabajo • Communicative Activity **¡Adelante! (20 min.)** • Presentación oral: Steps 1, 2	**Wrap-up and Homework Options (5 min.)** • Presentación oral: Step 2 • Go Online
DAY 8	**Warm-up (15 min.)** • Writing Activity • Homework check ✔**Assessment (40 min.)** • Presentación oral: Step 3	**¡Adelante! (30 min.)** • Presentation: Galápagos: el encuentro con la naturaleza • ¿Comprendiste?	**Wrap-up and Homework Options (5 min.)** • Practice Workbook 9-11, 9-12 • Go Online • Prueba 9-7: Conjunciones con el subjuntivo y el indicativo 2 • Examen: Vocabulario y gramática 2
DAY 9	**Warm-up (10 min.)** • Homework check ✔**Assessment Options (40 min.)** • Prueba 9-7: Conjunciones con el subjuntivo y el indicativo 2 • Examen: Vocabulario y gramática 2	**¡Adelante! (35 min.)** • ¿Qué me cuentas? 1, 2, 3 • Presentación escrita: Step 1 • Video • Video Activities	**Wrap-up and Homework Options (5 min.)** • Presentación escrita: Step 2 • Go Online • Preparación para el examen: Actividades 1, 2
DAY 10	**Warm-up (20 min.)** • Presentación escrita: Step 3 • Homework check	**¡Adelante! (35 min.)** • Lectura • Interacción con la lectura • Fondo cultural **Repaso (30 min.)** • Preparación para el examen: Actividades 3, 4, 6 • MindPoint Quiz Show	**Wrap-up and Homework Options (5 min.)** • Presentación escrita: Step 4 • Practice Workbook: Organizer 9-13, 9-14 • Go Online: Self-test • Preparación para el examen: Actividades 5, 7 • Examen del capítulo
DAY 11	**Warm-up (15 min.)** • Homework check ✔**Assessment (45 min.)** • Examen del capítulo	**Theme Game (15 min.)** **A ver si recuerdas – Capítulo 10 (10 min.)** • Presentation: Vocabulario • Presentation: Gramática	**Wrap-up and Homework Options (5 min.)** • A ver si recuerdas – Capítulo 10 • Go Online • Practice Workbook 10-1, 10-2

Vocabulario

Presentation

Standards: 1.1, 1.2

Resources: Voc. & Gram. Transparencies: 165

Suggestions: Number the categories of the *Vocabulario* from 1 to 6, proceeding from left to right on the page: *la basura* is number 1, *la comunidad* is number 2, and so on. Have students roll a numbered cube three times and write down the numbers that they roll. These pertain to the categories of the *Vocabulario*. Ask them to write a sentence using one word from each of the three categories they rolled. Have them roll and write as often as possible in an amount of time that you set.

Actividad 1

Standards: 1.1

Focus: Practicing review vocabulary

Suggestions: Allow students to convert some of the sentences they wrote for the *Presentation* above to questions for this *Actividad*.

Answers will vary.

Extension: Have students report to the class about what is important to their partner. Remind them to use third-person verb forms and indirect object pronouns.

Actividad 2

Focus: Practicing review vocabulary

Suggestions: Remind students that antonyms sometimes work well to define words. Have them use the sentence starter *Es el contrario de...* when using an antonym to define a word.

Answers will vary.

A ver si recuerdas...

Vocabulario

la basura
- la campaña
- el centro de reciclaje
- la contaminación
- el medio ambiente
- reciclar
- recoger
- separar

la comunidad
- la avenida
- el barrio
- la calle
- la carretera
- la gente
- el lago
- el parque
- la plaza
- el pueblo
- el río
- los vecinos

para reciclar
- la botella
- el cartón
- la lata
- el plástico
- el vidrio

opiniones
- me encanta(n)
- me gusta(n)
- me importa(n)
- me interesa(n)
- me molesta(n)
- me parece(n)
- me preocupa(n)

el tráfico
- la ambulancia
- el camión
- el coche
- el peatón
- la sirena
- la zona escolar
- la zona de construcción

actividades
- adoptar
- arrojar
- beneficiar
- colaborar
- contar con
- establecer
- evitar
- mejorar
- obligar
- prevenir
- reducir

 **Actividad 1** Escribir/Hablar ....

Práctica de vocabulario

¿Te importa el medio ambiente? Escribe cinco preguntas que le puedes hacer a un(a) compañero(a) para saber si le importa a él / ella. Luego, trabaja con tu compañero(a) para hacer preguntas y contestarlas.

Modelo

A —*¿Te importa reciclar el vidrio?*
B —*Sí, me importa mucho. Mi familia y yo siempre reciclamos.*

 Actividad 2 Escribir/Hablar ....

Práctica de vocabulario

Trabaja con otro(a) estudiante para escribir definiciones de las palabras siguientes. Lean sus definiciones a otros estudiantes para ver si pueden identificar las palabras correctas.

1. tráfico
2. carretera
3. arrojar
4. botella
5. peatones
6. evitar
7. sirena
8. vecinos

Universal Access

Multiple Intelligences
Visual/Spatial: Have students create a map of a fictional community that is environmentally conscious. Instruct them to include the items listed in *la comunidad, el tráfico,* and *para reciclar.* Have students label the areas and objects shown on their maps using the vocabulary.

Advanced Learners
Have students list five *Vocabulario* items from any of the categories except *opiniones* and exchange lists with a partner. Partners have three minutes to create a drawing that includes all of the items in the list, complete with labels. Then have partners talk about their drawings.

Gramática·Repaso

Verbos como *gustar*

You know that *gustar* is used to talk about likes and dislikes. When you use *gustar*, the subject of the sentence is what is liked or disliked. You use the singular form *gusta* when what is liked is a singular noun or an action (an infinitive). You use the plural form *gustan* when what is liked is a plural noun.

Nos **gusta** este barrio.   Le **gusta** trabajar para la comunidad.
Me **gustan** las calles de este barrio.

Use the indirect object pronoun to indicate to whom something is pleasing.

Me gustaría participar en la campaña de reciclaje.

Other Spanish verbs that often follow the same pattern as *gustar* are:

doler *to ache, to be painful*	importar *to matter*	parecer *to seem*
encantar *to love*	interesar *to interest*	preocupar *to worry*
faltar *to lack, to be missing*	molestar *to bother*	quedar (bien / mal) *to fit*

• The personal *a* plus a pronoun or a person's name can be used for emphasis, or to make clear to whom you are referring.

A nosotros nos preocupa la contaminación del aire.
¿Le interesaron **a Sergio** los libros?

---

 3 Leer

Práctica de gramática

Un grupo de vecinos escribe una carta al periódico. Escoge las expresiones adecuadas para completarla.

Estimado Sr. Director:
Le escribimos porque __1.__ *(preocupar / interesar)* la interrupción del tráfico en la calle Ramos. Aunque a todos nosotros __2.__ *(importar / interesar)* que se construya un nuevo centro médico, la construcción __3.__ *(importar / molestar)* diariamente. A mí no __4.__ *(importar / molestar)* sólo el problema del tráfico, __5.__ *(preocupar / interesar)* también la basura que se está acumulando en el lugar. Favor de mejorar la situación.
Atentamente,
Los vecinos de la calle Ramos

  4 Hablar

Práctica de gramática

Tu compañero(a) describe a sus amigos y a su familia usando las palabras siguientes. Responde a lo que dice tu compañero(a) con ejemplos de tu propia experiencia.

Modelo
A mi hermano(a) y a mí *(molestar)* ...
A —*A nosotros(as) nos molesta el frío.*
B —*A mis hermanos(as) no les molesta nada el frío.*

1. A mí *(molestar)*
2. A mi compañero(a) *(interesar)*
3. A mis amigos(as) *(preocupar)*
4. A mi madre (padre) no *(gustar)*
5. A mí *(faltar)*
6. A mi mejor amigo(a) *(encantar)*

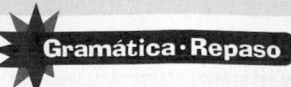

Gramática·Repaso

Presentation

Standards: 4.1

Resources: Voc. & Gram. Transparencies: 166

Suggestions: Ask students to write three questions they can ask a partner, using three of the verb phrases from the *Gramática*. Have partners take turns asking and answering questions. Then have them report to the class on their partner's answers.

 3 *Standards:* 1.2

Resources: Practice Answers on Transparencies

Focus: Practicing verbs like *gustar*

Suggestions: Point out the use of the expressions *Estimado* and *Atentamente* in the salutation and closing of the letter. Remind students that these are good expressions to use in more formal letters.

Answers:
1. nos preocupa
2. nos importa
3. nos molesta
4. me molesta
5. me preocupa

 4 *Standards:* 1.1

Resources: Practice Answers on Transparencies

Focus: Practicing verbs like *gustar*

Suggestions: Encourage students to listen to each other and to be inventive with their responses. Explain that using the cues to create a natural, flowing conversation is preferable to a rigid, A-B-A-B exchange.

Answers will vary. Students will use the following verb forms and indirect object pronouns:
1. me molesta(n)
2. le interesa(n)
3. les preocupa(n)
4. le gusta(n)
5. me falta(n)
6. le encanta(n)

Enriching Your Teaching

Teacher-to-Teacher

Fill your classroom with posters, advertisements, displays, photos, signs, and anything you can find that corresponds to the environmental theme. Provide students with a center containing articles, suggested Web sites, magazines, and books to browse on the topic.

A classroom environment that is linguistically rich and full of information will enhance learning and provide students with interesting facts and details they can use to contribute to class discussions.

Vocabulario

Presentation

Standards: 1.1, 1.2

Resources: Voc. & Gram. Transparencies: 167

Suggestions: Have students sit in a circle. Give one student a foam ball and have him or her give a definition of a vocabulary item from one of the lists. That student tosses the ball to another and names a term from a different *Vocabulario* category. Whoever catches the ball gives a brief definition of that term and tosses the ball to another student, and so on.

Actividad 5

Standards: 1.1

Focus: Practicing review vocabulary

Common Errors: Even with regular review, students may make verbs like *gustar* agree with the indirect object rather than the subject. Remind them that **gustar** means "to please" rather than "to like," and provide models as necessary.

Suggestions: Encourage students to consider all five senses when talking about why they are or are not partial to the various places.

Answers will vary.

Actividad 6

Standards: 1.2

Resources: Practice Answers on Transparencies

Focus: Practicing review vocabulary

Suggestions: Remind students that, since the items are headlines, their structure is different from that of complete sentences.

Answers:
1. Incendio; árboles
2. mosquitos; insectos
3. inundaciones; lluvias
4. océano; peces

Vocabulario

lugares
el bosque
el campo
el desierto
el fondo del mar
las montañas
el océano
el parque nacional
la selva tropical
la sierra
los valles

fenómenos naturales
la explosión
el huracán
el incendio
la inundación
la lluvia
la nieve
el relámpago
el terremoto
la tormenta
el trueno

acciones
capturar
cuidar
eliminar
matar
permitir
prohibir
proteger
rescatar
salvar

animales
el caballo
la cebra
el conejo
el elefante
el gato
el hipopótamo
la hormiga
los insectos
el jaguar
el mono
la mosca
el mosquito
el oso
el pájaro
los peces
el perro
el tigre

Actividad 5 **Hablar/Escribir**

Práctica de vocabulario

Decide con tu compañero(a) qué lugares de la lista les interesan más y cuáles les interesan menos y por qué. Hagan una tabla como la siguiente y compartan los resultados con la clase.

Nos gustan más . . .	Porque . . .	Nos gustan menos . . .	Porque . . .
1. las montañas		1. el desierto	
2. el océano		2. las sierras	

Actividad 6 **Leer**

Práctica de vocabulario

Lee con un(a) compañero(a) los siguientes titulares y anuncios de periódicos y luego complétenlos con estas palabras o expresiones.

insectos	óceano	mosquitos
árboles	incendio	inundaciones
peces	lluvias	

1. ¡_____ en el bosque! Se quemaron miles de _____.

2. Si quiere que los _____ se mantengan lejos, use el repelente de _____.

3. Grandes _____ en Zamora a causa de las _____ recientes.

4. Una exploración del _____ descubre nuevas especies de _____.

386 trescientos ochenta y seis
A ver si recuerdas . . .

Universal Access

Heritage Language Learners
Ask students to model additional examples of cases in which the definite article is used in Spanish, but not in English. Then, have students create a short "fill in the blank" exercise for their peers.

Students with Learning Difficulties
Help students reinforce the vocabulary presented on p. 386. Encourage them to create small picture clues for words that are unfamiliar. Ask students to share their picture clues with the group, and have other students guess the word indicated.

Gramática · Repaso

Usos del artículo definido

In general, the definite article *(el, la, los, las)* is used in Spanish the same way it is in English. In the following cases, however, it is used in Spanish but not in English.

When people are referred to by name and an accompanying title, preceding the title (but not when people are addressed directly using a title):

La profesora Estévez enseña ciencias.   Buenas tardes, **doctor Zabala**.

Before the name of a street, avenue, park, or other proper names:

Los vecinos de **la calle Ramos** se quejaron.

Before any noun representing an entire species, institution, or general concept:

El perro es el mejor amigo del hombre.   **La educación** es muy importante.

With certain time expressions:

Llegó a **las siete** de la tarde. *(hours)*   Me encanta **la primavera**. *(seasons)*
Van a reunirse **el lunes** próximo. *(days)*   Salió de su país a **los diez años**. *(age)*

When it is an inseparable part of the name of a country, such as *El Salvador* and of some cities, such as *El Cairo, La Habana, El Havre, La Haya, La Paz.*

The words *al* and *del* result from contracting the prepositions *a* and *de* with the article *el*, but there is no contraction when *El* is part of a proper name.

Vamos **al** parque. Venimos **del** bosque.   Vamos a **El Paso**. Venimos de **El Paso**.

7 **Hablar**

Práctica de gramática

Con un(a) compañero(a) escriban sustantivos (con su correspondiente artículo definido) que sirvan para completar las frases siguientes.

Modelo

_____ es bueno para la salud.
El aire puro / El ejercicio / El jugo de naranja es bueno para la salud.

1. _____ Romero nos recibirá a las cuatro.

2. _____ es / no es un país de Asia.

3. _____ son / no son muy caros.

4. Generalmente _____ por la tarde practicamos en el club.

8 **Leer** ....

Práctica de gramática

Completa los diálogos con artículos definidos o con las contracciones *al* o *del*. Si el artículo no es necesario, deja el espacio en blanco.

1. —Lo siento, ya son _____ siete y debo irme.
   —Claro, Carmen, nos vemos _____ miércoles. Recuerda que es _____ reunión.

2. — ¡Mira! Aquí llega _____ doctora López.
   —¿Cómo está, _____ doctora López?

● **Más práctica** ....
Practice Workbook 9-1, 9-2

Go Online
PHSchool.com
For: More review
Visit: www.phschool.com
Web Code: jed-0901

trescientos ochenta y siete **387**
Capítulo 9

Gramática · Repaso

Presentation

Standards: 4.1

Resources: Voc. & Gram. Transparencies: 168

Suggestions: Have students write five sentences or parts of sentences in which they incorrectly use a definite article. Collect their papers and shuffle and redistribute them. Have them correct the errors and discuss their reasoning behind the corrections.

 Standards: 1.1

Resources: Practice Answers on Transparencies

Focus: Reviewing the use of definite articles

Suggestions: Ask students which rule from the *Gramática* applies to each use of the definite article.

Answers will vary. Students may use articles and nouns such as the following:
1. **El ingeniero/La doctora/La señorita**
2. **El Salvador/La República Dominicana/Los Estados Unidos**
3. **Los coches/Los zapatos/Los discos compactos**
4. **los fines de semana/los sábados/los domingos**

 Standards: 1.2

Resources: Practice Answers on Transparencies

Focus: Reviewing the use of definite articles

Suggestions: Remind students to read through each item first before attempting to write their answer.

Answers:
1. las; el; la
2. la; leave blank

Enriching Your Teaching

Teacher-to-Teacher

Applying the correct gender to nouns is one of the more difficult skills that English-speaking learners of Spanish must master. Students frequently succumb to misconceptions along the way, such as the one that says all nouns ending in *-a* are feminine and all those ending in *-o* are masculine. (*La mano* and *el problema* are two of many possible examples to use to remind them that this is not true.) Encourage students to invent their own mnemonic devices for remembering genders. One way is to associate the noun with an oft-heard, tell-tale modifier: ***Buenos Aires, Santa Fe, sangre fría.***

Standards for Foreign Language Learning: *Capítulo* 9

• To achieve the goals of the Standards, students will:

Communication

1.1 Interpersonal
• Talk about interests, neighborhoods, regions, and weather
• Talk about Diego Rivera, José Martí, and their work
• Talk about environmental issues and endangered species
• Talk about post-high-school plans
• Talk about the Galápagos Islands and monarch butterflies
• Talk about a festival in Michoacán, Mexico

1.2 Interpretive
• Read about interests, neighborhoods, regions, and weather
• Read about Diego Rivera, José Martí, and their work
• Read and listen to information about environmental issues and endangered species
• Read about word families
• Read about the Galápagos Islands, monarch butterflies, and magellanic penguins
• Read about *turrones*
• Read about Latin American rescue teams
• Read about a festival in Michoacán, Mexico
• Read about speech preparation and persuasive letters

1.3 Presentational
• Write and present information orally about environmental issues and endangered species
• Write and present information orally about the Galápagos Islands and monarch butterflies

Culture

2.1 Practices and Perspectives
• Interpret Latin American perspectives and practices regarding the environment and endangered species
• Describe Latin American rescue operations
• Describe Ecuador's policies regarding the Galápagos Islands
• Describe Mexican events spurred by monarch butterfly migration

2.2 Products and Perspectives
• Discuss Diego Rivera, José Martí, and their work
• Describe a Puerto Rican recycling program
• Describe Ecuadorian national parks

Connections

3.1 Cross-curricular
• Discuss key facts about Diego Rivera, José Martí, and their work
• Discuss key facts about ecological science, biology, and demographics
• Discuss key geographical facts about Puerto Rico, Chile, Mexico, Costa Rica, and Ecuador
• Discuss key facts about emergency organizations
• Use Language Arts Strategies: using topic sentences, finding good details, good conclusions, context clues

3.2 Target Culture
• Read poetry by José Martí

Fondo cultural ■◆■◇▽■◆◇▽◆■◇

Diego Rivera (1886–1957) En 1921, el pintor Diego RIvera conoció a José Vasconcelos, que estaba a cargo del Ministerio de Educación de México. Una de las ideas de Vasconcelos era crear murales en edificios públicos para educar al pueblo. En 1922, Vasconcelos le encomendó (*commissioned*) a Rivera su primer mural. Este mural se llamó *Creación*. En este mural Rivera combina elementos de la tradición indígena, como se ve en el dibujo del jaguar, con elementos religiosos e intelectuales basados en el arte clásico europeo.

•¿Qué otras cosas asocias con la tradición indígena mexicana?

Creación, (1922–1923), Diego Rivera
(c) Banco de México Diego Rivera & Frida Kahlo Museums Trust. Av. Cinco de Mayo No. 2, Col. Centro, Del. Cuauhtemoc 06059, México, D.F. Reproduction authorized by the *Instituto Nacional de Bellas Artes y Literatura*. Art Resource, NY.

Universal Access

Personalizing the Theme
Ask students to share their background knowledge about environmental concerns. Ask guiding questions such as: *¿Hay problemas hoy en día con el agua del mundo y con el aire que respiramos? ¿Dónde hay contaminación?*

Heritage Language Learners
Ask students who have lived in a heritage country to share their knowledge and experience with environmental issues in that country. What have been the major problems or breakthroughs? What are the predictions for the future?

Capítulo
9

Cuidemos nuestro planeta

Chapter Objectives

- **Talk about environmental concerns in the community**
- **Discuss how to solve local and global environmental problems**
- **Express attitudes and opinions about the environment**
- **Understand cultural perspectives on dealing with conservation and the environment**

Video Focus

- **Protecting our natural environment**

Country Connection

As you learn about the environment, you will make connections to these countries and places.

Puerto Rico
Costa Rica
Chile
Argentina

Go Online PHSchool.com
For: Online Atlas
Visit: www.phschool.com
Web Code: jee-0002

trescientos ochenta y nueve   389
Capítulo 9

Standards for Foreign Language Learning (cont'd)

Comparisons
4.1 Language
- Compare use of Spanish verbs like **gustar** to that of their English counterparts
- Compare Spanish and English relative pronouns and conjunctions
- Compare Spanish words to their English counterparts

4.2 Culture
- Compare Latin American environmental and recycling problems and programs to those in the United States
- Compare nature-based festivals in Mexico and the United States

Communities
5.1 Beyond the School
- Link to Web sites from around the Spanish-speaking world
- Describe urban vehicle restriction laws

5.2 Lifelong Learner
- Develop an appreciation for poetry and the visual arts
- Discuss ecological trends and possibilities for community involvement

Chapter Opener
Presentation

Resources: Voc. & Gram. Transparencies: 14, 15, 16, 17, 18 (maps)

Suggestions: Introduce students to the theme of the chapter and go over the objectives. Point out that they will improve their ability to talk and write about environmental concerns. Use *Vocabulary & Grammar Transparencies* 14, 15, 16, 17, and 18 to locate and discuss the countries featured in the chapter.

Fondo cultural *Standards:* 1.1, 1.2, 2.2, 3.1, 4.1, 5.2

Resources: Fine Art Transparencies; Fine Art Transparencies Teacher's Guide

Suggestions: After students read the information, ask comprehension questions. For example: *¿Cuál era la idea de José Vasconcelos? (Su idea era crear unos murales para educar al pueblo.)*

Answers will vary.

Enriching Your Teaching

Planning for Instruction
Resources:
- Teacher Express CD-ROM or Resource Book
  - Teaching resources
  - Lesson Planner
  - Chapter Resource Checklist
  - School-to-Home Connection Letter

Culture Note
South America's Amazon Basin is the largest rainforest area in the world. Rainforests currently cover 6 percent of the globe's surface. They originally covered 14 percent. The Amazon rainforest alone provides 20 percent of the Earth's oxygen supply.

Vocabulario y gramática

Presentation

Standards: 1.1, 1.2, 3.1

Resources: Voc. & Gram. Transparencies: 169–170; Resource Book: Cap. 9, Input Script; Audio Program: CD Cap. 9, Track 1

Focus: Presenting new vocabulary and using grammar lexically in context

Suggestions: You may want to use the Input Script from the *Teacher's Resource Book* as a source of ideas for presentation of new vocabulary and comprehensible input. While presenting the vocabulary, capitalize on cognates, such as *contaminadas, petróleo,* and *conservar.* Since most of the vocabulary is not visualized, encourage students to use context clues to help themselves understand the meanings of new words and expressions.

A primera vista 1

Vocabulario y gramática en contexto

Objectives

Read, listen to, and understand information about

• environmental issues
• what we can do to protect the environment

La contaminación del aire, de los ríos y de los mares es un problema gigante. En estas páginas el Dr. Biente contesta algunas preguntas sobre este problema y sobre lo que podemos hacer para ayudar a resolverlo.

1 66 La contaminación es uno de los problemas más **graves** del mundo. Hasta que tomemos **medidas** apropiadas para reducirla, este hermoso planeta estará en peligro. 99

los desperdicios

la fábrica

el veneno

2 —Dr. Biente, en mi barrio hay una fábrica de **pesticidas** y otros productos **químicos** que arroja los desperdicios al río. ¿Cree que es peligroso?

—¡Claro! **Debido a** estas prácticas peligrosas, los peces del río pueden morir en las aguas **contaminadas**. No debemos **echar** desperdicios en los ríos.

3 —Dr. Biente, ¿qué haremos cuando no haya **recursos naturales** tan importantes como **el petróleo**? ¿Cómo podremos usar los coches?

—En el futuro no podremos **depender del** petróleo para producir energía; algún día **se agotará**. Tenemos que **fomentar** el uso de fuentes de energía más eficientes **tan pronto como** sea posible. Creo que en el futuro todos los coches serán eléctricos, pues son **económicos** y limpios.

390 trescientos noventa
A primera vista 1

Universal Access

Advanced Learners

Have students research a picture or bring in an object that represents one kind of threat to the environment. Ask them to use the picture or object as the basis for a short oral presentation about one kind of pollution. They can tell why they chose that particular picture or object, what kind of environmental problem it represents, their feelings about the seriousness of the problem, and then offer one or more possible solutions to the problem.

4 —La población está **creciendo** y cada día hay más gente en el planeta. ¿Cómo vamos a evitar que haya una **escasez**, o sea, una falta de recursos naturales?

—Es cierto que nos **amenaza** el peligro de la escasez. Por eso todos los seres humanos tenemos que tomar medidas para **conservar** los recursos que tenemos.

5 —¿Y **el gobierno** no puede hacer nada para proteger el medio ambiente?

—El gobierno **está a cargo de** hacer leyes para proteger el ambiente y **castigar** con multas a quienes no las obedezcan. Pero recuerden, no podemos esperar hasta que el gobierno haga algo, nosotros tenemos que cuidar el ambiente cada día.

 Escuchar ·······································

Cómo cuidar el medio ambiente

Escribe los números del 1 al 6 en una hoja. Escucha lo que dice cada persona y di si es cierto *(C)* o falso *(F)*.

 Leer ···

Los consejos del Dr. Biente

Completa estos consejos con la palabra apropiada.

1. Los *(desperdicios / gobiernos)* no se deben echar en los ríos.

2. Debemos *(agotar / fomentar)* nuevas fuentes de energía.

3. Los gobiernos deben *(tomar medidas contra / depender de)* la contaminación.

4. En el futuro debemos construir menos *(recursos naturales / fábricas)* en las ciudades.

5. El gobierno debe *(estar a cargo de / castigar a)* las personas que echan desperdicios a los ríos.

6. Todos debemos colaborar para *(contaminar / proteger)* el medio ambiente.

Actividad 1   *Standards:* 1.2

Resources: Audio Program: CD Cap. 9, Track 2; Resource Book: Cap. 9, Audio Script; Practice Answers on Transparencies

Focus: Practicing listening comprehension of new vocabulary

Suggestions: Before students listen, give them a few minutes to review the information on these two pages. Use the *Audio CD* or read the text. Allow students to listen more than once.

Answers:

1. F	4. C
2. C	5. F
3. C	6. F

Extension: Ask students to correct the false statements. Have them do so by changing information, rather than making the false statement negative. For example: *Los pesticidas no limpian, sino contaminan las aguas de los ríos.*

Actividad 2   *Standards:* 1.2

Resources: Practice Answers on Transparencies

Focus: Practicing new vocabulary in a word-choice exercise

Suggestions: After students have written their answers, challenge them to explain why the answer they chose makes sense and the other does not. If they cannot do this at this point, allow them to wait until later in the chapter, since the focus here is on vocabulary recognition.

Answers:

1. desperdicios
2. fomentar
3. tomar medidas contra
4. fábricas
5. castigar a
6. proteger

 Enriching Your Teaching

Culture Note

As urbanization and development increase, motor vehicles are quickly becoming the main source of air pollution in Latin America. Air pollution can lead to such health problems as coughing, bronchitis, and lung cancer. The air in Mexico City, for example, was ranked the most contaminated by the World Health Organization. Other Mexican cities, such as Guadalajara and Ciudad Juárez are also affected by emissions from vehicles and assembly plants. Some efforts to curtail air pollution include a focus on alternative fuels, public transportation, and non-motorized transportation, such as bicycles.

Vocabulario y gramática

Presentation

Standards: 1.1, 1.2, 3.1, 4.2

Resources: Voc. & Gram. Transparencies: 171–172; Resource Book: Cap. 9, Input Script; Audio Program: CD Cap. 9, Tracks 3–4

Focus: Extending presentation of vocabulary and grammar

Suggestions:

Pre-reading: Point out that all of the information on this page is a survey, and that the next page contains a separate article. Have students copy the answer grid to their own paper before taking the survey.

Reading: Have students read the survey questionnaire first and then present the new vocabulary to them. Ask them to cover the ***Resultados*** part of the survey with a piece of paper, so they are not tempted to read ahead, which may affect their answers. Cover the ***Resultados*** portion on *Vocabulary and Grammar Transparency* 171 as well. After all the new vocabulary has been presented, ask them to complete the survey on their own and read the ***Resultados*** part silently. For the article on the next page, play the *Audio CD* or read aloud from the text as students follow along. Allow them to listen more than once.

Post-reading: Use *Vocabulary and Grammar Transparency* 171 to compile students' information from the survey. Use tallies or a percentage to show the class results for each question.

Block Schedule

After students complete the survey on p. 392, total the responses of the entire class. Discuss how the entire class ranks. Is the class surprised by the results? Why?

¿Cómo cuidas tu planeta?

Contesta las preguntas para ver si estás haciendo todo lo que puedes por la protección del medio ambiente.

1. ¿**Colocas los recipientes** plásticos y de vidrio en el depósito de reciclaje?
2. ¿Evitas poner **las pilas** (baterías) viejas con el resto de la basura?
3. ¿Apagas el televisor cuando no lo estás viendo?
4. ¿Cierras la llave *(faucet)* del agua cuando te lavas los dientes?
5. ¿Apagas las luces antes de salir de una habitación para ahorrar **electricidad**?
6. Cuando vas a acampar, ¿evitas dejar basura en el campo?
7. ¿Usas papel reciclado? ¿Tratas de no **desperdiciar** papel?
8. ¿Tratas de usar el transporte público?
9. ¿Sabes lo **suficiente** sobre los problemas de contaminación de tu comunidad? ¿Tratas de conservar el medio ambiente?
10. ¿Tratas de **limitar** el uso de productos que contaminen el medio ambiente?

	Sí	No
1		
2		
3		
4		
5		
6		
7		
8		
9		
10		
Total		

Resultados

Por cada sí que respondiste, cuenta dos puntos.

Entre 15 y 20 puntos: **Eres una persona preocupada por el medio ambiente. Sabes lo que puedes hacer para reducir la contaminación ambiental y lo haces cuando puedes.**

Entre 10 y 14 puntos: **Te preocupas por el medio ambiente y no haces nada que sepas que lo puede dañar pero no tienes toda la información necesaria.**

Menos de 10 puntos: **Como no tienes mucha información, haces cosas que podrían aumentar la contaminación en vez de reducirla. Debes buscar más información sobre este tema en cuanto puedas.**

Universal Access

Heritage Language Learners

Ask students to briefly debate the issues presented in each of the survey questions. Are there reasons one might not turn off a light or use recycled paper? Perhaps there are security or cost concerns. Encourage students to consider possible arguments and discuss them fully.

Students with Learning Difficulties

Assign each of the survey questions on p. 392 to a pair or small group of students. Direct students to act out their question to make its meaning clear. Encourage them to provide two versions of the action. For example, have them act out turning off the faucet, and *not* turning off the faucet.

Puerto Rico: *cómo conservar bella la isla*

Como todos sabemos, Puerto Rico es famoso por sus bellos paisajes y sus playas de aguas azules y calientes. Sin embargo, para cuidar esa belleza el gobierno y los habitantes de la isla han tenido que buscar desde hace años nuevas maneras de **deshacerse** de la basura.

Con este objetivo, un grupo de hombres y mujeres de negocios decidió unirse en 1993 para formar el programa Industria y Comercio Pro-Reciclaje (ICPRO). Esta organización se dedica a **promover** programas educativos sobre el ahorro y reciclaje de recursos

en escuelas y comunidades alrededor de la isla.

El ICPRO también ha organizado un concurso de artes plásticas llamado "Basurarte" para los jóvenes de escuela secundaria y la universidad. Los jóvenes artistas tratan de hacer obras de arte con materiales recogidos en la basura. Con sus obras de arte, los jóvenes quieren educar a la gente sobre la importancia del reciclaje y el cuidado del medio ambiente.

 3 Escribir

¿Comprendiste?

1. ¿Qué han tenido que hacer desde hace años los habitantes y el gobierno de Puerto Rico? ¿Por qué?

2. ¿Qué es ICPRO y a qué se dedica? ¿En tu comunidad hay programas educativos que informen a la gente sobre los beneficios del reciclaje?

3. ¿Qué tipo de concurso organizó el programa ICPRO?

4. ¿Quiénes participaron en ese concurso y para qué lo hicieron?

Más práctica
Practice Workbook 9-3, 9-4

For: Vocabulary practice
Visit: phschool.com
Web Code: jed-0902

Enriching Your Teaching

Culture Note

In addition to the **Basurarte** contest, ICPRO organizes other events to promote recycling and reuse of resources. The **Recyclaton** is a one-day event where people bring their recyclable items to a central location. In return, they receive small prizes and incentives, as well as information about recycling. ICPRO also

organizes pro-recycling clubs. Decreasing the amount of landfill garbage is especially crucial in an island environment, such as Puerto Rico. It is estimated that Puerto Rico produces 8,500 tons of solid waste per day, and that approximately 18 percent of that is recycled.

Language Input

 Rapid Review
Both the article on this page and *Actividad* 3 require students to use the present perfect tense. Briefly review this tense and ask students what they have done, eaten, heard, and seen today.

Actividad 3 *Standards:* 1.2, 1.3, 3.1

Resources: Practice Answers on Transparencies

Focus: Practicing reading comprehension of new vocabulary

Common Errors: Some students may pronounce the **sh** in **deshacerse** as the English *sh* consonant blend. Model correct pronunciation. Remind students that the prefix **des-** is pronounced with a final, hard **s,** and that **h** is always silent in Spanish.

Suggestions: Encourage students to answer the questions in their own words, rather than reading their answers from the article.

Answers:
1. Han tenido que buscar nuevas maneras de deshacerse de la basura porque quieren conservar la belleza de su isla.
2. ICPRO es el programa Industria y Comercio Pro-Reciclaje. Se dedica a promover programas educativos sobre el ahorro y reciclaje de recursos en escuelas y comunidades en Puerto Rico. Remainder of answer will vary.
3. Organizó un programa de artes plásticas.
4. Los jóvenes de la escuela secundaria y la universidad participaron porque querían educar a la gente sobre la importancia del reciclaje y el cuidado del medio ambiente.

Additional Resources
• Resource Book: Cap. 9, Clip Art

 Assessment
• Prueba 9-1: Vocabulary recognition

Chapter Project
Give students copies of the Chapter Project outline and rubric from the *Teacher's Resource Book*. Explain the task to them, and have them perform step 1. (For more information, see p. 384-a.)

393

Practice and Communicate

Actividad 4

Standards: 1.2, 3.1

Resources: Practice Answers on Transparencies

Focus: Practicing new vocabulary

Suggestions: Remind students that in each item, both possible answers are the correct part of speech, but only one makes sense in the sentence. They must choose their answer based solely on meaning.

Answers:
1. castiga
2. en vez de/la pila
3. contaminado/grave
4. coloca
5. energía
6. escasez/conservar

Extension: After students complete the activity, ask volunteers to summarize what they have learned about some environmental problems and solutions in a few countries.

Actividad 5

Standards: 1.1, 1.2, 1.3, 3.1

Resources: Practice Answers on Transparencies

Focus: Practicing new vocabulary through reading and response

Recycle: *por* and *para,* imperatives

Suggestions: Encourage students to read the entire poster before answering any questions. Have them work with a partner to resolve comprehension problems.

Answers:

Step 1
1. No usar más bolsas de las que se necesitan, comprar productos en recipientes grandes, evitar los productos desechables.
2. Reciclar es devolver a las fábricas todos los materiales que se pueden volver a usar.
3. El objetivo es reducir, reutilizar y reciclar la basura y educar a la gente sobre el reciclaje.

Step 2
Answers will vary.

Manos a la obra 1

Vocabulario y gramática en uso

Objectives
- Talk about environmental issues
- Discuss what we can do to protect the environment
- Practice the subjunctive after conjunctions
- Practice the relative pronouns *que, quien, lo que*

Actividad 4 Leer

Problemas y soluciones del medio ambiente

Lee las siguientes frases que describen problemas del medio ambiente y las soluciones. Escoge la palabra que mejor complete cada frase.

1. En la capital de Chile, se *(castiga / desperdicia)* con una multa a las personas que echan basura en la calle.

2. En España, reciclan los teléfonos celulares *(en vez de / a cargo de)* echarlos a la basura, pero primero se separa *(el veneno / la pila)* del teléfono.

3. En la Ciudad de México, el aire *(contaminado / económico)* es un problema tan *(químico / grave)* que se prohíbe el uso del coche ciertos días de la semana.

4. En Perú, para reciclar, se *(agota / coloca)* el vidrio y el papel en un recipiente especial.

5. Argentina tiene mucho gas natural, que sirve para producir *(desperdicios / energía)*.

6. Debido a la *(escasez / medida)* en la Ciudad de México, hay que *(promover / conservar)* el agua.

  Actividad 5 Leer/Escribir

Un cartel ecológico

1 Lee el cartel y responde a las preguntas.

1. ¿Qué consejos da el cartel para reducir la basura?

2. Según el cartel, ¿qué es reciclar?

3. ¿Cuál es el objetivo de este cartel?

2 Piensa en las tres "R"s de las que habla el cartel. Escribe otros dos consejos sobre cosas específicas que la gente pueda hacer para reducir, reciclar y reutilizar. Piensa en tu propia experiencia y en cosas que se hayan hecho en tu comunidad.

394 trescientos noventa y cuatro
Manos a la obra 1

REDUCIR
- No use más bolsas de las que necesita.
- Compre productos en recipientes grandes.
- Evite los productos desechables[1].

RECICLAR
- Reciclar es devolver a las fábricas todos los materiales que se pueden volver a usar, como el cartón y el vidrio.

REUTILIZAR
- Dé a cada producto todo el uso posible antes de considerarlo basura.
- Es importante ser consumidores responsables y pedir a las empresas que vendan productos que se puedan reutilizar.

1 disposable

Universal Access

Heritage Language Learners
The level of recycling activity and awareness varies greatly depending on country and community. Ask students who have lived in a heritage country to comment on recycling in that country. Were the programs and awareness more or less developed than in their current communities?

Advanced Learners
Invite students to work in a small group to create a Spanish-language poster about environmental programs in your community. If the technology is available in your school, have them generate the poster using computer software. Then they can obtain permission to create multiple copies and post them.

6 Leer/Escribir

Las cosas que contaminan

En cada grupo de palabras busca algo que contamina el medio ambiente. Después, escribe frases que describan cómo esas cosas contaminan el medio ambiente. Además, sugiere una solución al problema.

Modelo

el petróleo
El petróleo que se usa en los coches contamina mucho.
Tenemos que inventar coches que no usen petróleo.

1. **a.** el reciclaje   **b.** las medidas   **c.** los productos químicos
2. **a.** el recipiente   **b.** el gobierno   **c.** los pesticidas
3. **a.** el veneno   **b.** la protección   **c.** la electricidad
4. **a.** las verduras   **b.** la energía   **c.** la pila
5. **a.** la población   **b.** los desperdicios   **c.** los derechos
6. **a.** la basura   **b.** lo suficiente   **c.** el ambiente

  7 Hablar

En el futuro

Muchos jóvenes se preocupan por el futuro, pues no saben cómo se resolverán los problemas de contaminación y la escasez de recursos naturales que tenemos hoy. Habla sobre este tema con otro(a) estudiante.

fomentar

Modelo

A —*En el futuro, ¿crees que se fomentará el uso del transporte público?*

B —*Sí, porque es mucho más económico.*

Estudiante A

1. dañar
2. fomentar
3. limitar
4. agotarse
5. **¡Respuesta personal!**

Estudiante B

económico(a)
grave
medida
escasez
¡Respuesta personal!

 Standards: 1.3

Resources: Practice Answers on Transparencies

Focus: Practicing new vocabulary

Suggestions: After students make their selections, have them check their work with a partner before writing sentences for the second part of the activity.

Answers: Choices for the first part are as follows. Sentences for the second part will vary:

1. c   4. c
2. c   5. b
3. a   6. a

 Standards: 1.1

Resources: Practice Answers on Transparencies

Focus: Practicing new vocabulary and structures in guided dialogues

Suggestions: As you go over the model with students, point out the use of **porque** as a transition in Student B's response. Encourage students to be creative with their language and vary the way in which they respond to each other's comments.

Answers will vary. Student A will use the following vocabulary and future forms of verbs:

1. **las fábricas/dañarán**
2. **la energía solar/fomentará**
3. **los pesticidas/se limitarán**
4. **el agua/se agotará**

Enriching Your Teaching

Culture Note

Extended Producer Responsibility is the concept that a manufacturer's responsibility for the environmental effects of its product does not end when the product is sold. Rather, producers retain a role in the recycling, reuse, or disposal of the product and/or its packaging. In 2000, Peru became the first Latin American country to institute a packaging take-back law. Started in response to a landfill crisis in Germany in 1991, take-back programs require producers to accept responsibility for the waste management of their packaging, even after the product has been sold to and used by the consumer.

Actividad 8

Standards: 1.1, 1.2, 1.3

Resources: Voc. & Gram. Transparencies: 4

Focus: Practicing new vocabulary and structures

Recycle: impersonal *se,* pronoun placement

Suggestions: Have students copy the chart to their own paper. Use *Vocabulary and Grammar Transparency* 4 to model adding one other problem to the chart. Leave the right column empty on the transparency.

Answers will vary.

Actividad 9

Standards: 1.1, 1.3

Focus: Practicing new vocabulary and structures through writing and discussion

Suggestions: Students may wish to consult each other or a bilingual dictionary for pertinent vocabulary to add to the discussion.

Answers will vary.

Fondo cultural

Standards: 1.1, 1.2, 2.1, 3.1, 4.2

Suggestions: After students have read the information, ask comprehension questions. For example: *¿Por qué han establecido la "restricción vehicular" en Santiago? (La han establecido porque el aire está muy contaminado.) Si vives en Santiago y el número de patente de tu coche termina con el 2, ¿irías en coche a la escuela el jueves? (No. La restricción está en efecto.)*

Answers will vary.

  **Escribir/Hablar** . . . .

Para proteger el futuro

❶ Piensa en los problemas del medio ambiente y lo que se puede hacer para protegerlo. Copia la tabla y complétala con, por lo menos, cuatro problemas.

el problema	lo que se puede hacer	quiénes están a cargo (todos los ciudadanos, el gobierno, las industrias, etc.)
contaminación del océano	no echar basura	los ciudadanos
los desperdicios industriales		

❷ Cuando hayas completado tu tabla, trabaja con otro(a) estudiante. Hablen de las medidas que indicaron en sus tablas y expliquen quiénes deben estar a cargo de tomar esas medidas.

Modelo

proteger el océano

A —*¿Qué medidas se pueden tomar para proteger el océano de la contaminación?*

B —*No debemos echar basura ni desperdicios al océano.*

A —*¿Quiénes están a cargo de protegerlo?*

B —*Todos los ciudadanos podemos proteger el océano al no echar basura.*

❸ Ahora, hagan una presentación para explicar a la clase los problemas y las soluciones de los que han hablado.

 Escribir/Hablar . . . .

Y tú, ¿qué dices?

1. ¿Qué problemas ambientales existen en tu comunidad?

2. ¿Qué medidas toman tú, tu familia y tu comunidad para proteger el medio ambiente? ¿Qué pueden hacer que no estén haciendo ya?

3. Nombra al menos una cosa que quieras . . .
   a. no desperdiciar   c. limitar
   b. promover   d. conservar

4. ¿De qué fuentes de energía depende más tu comunidad? ¿Qué otras fuentes de energía eficientes y económicas están tratando de fomentar?

 **Fondo cultural** ◼◼

Restricción de vehículos
El aire en la ciudad de Santiago de Chile está muy contaminado. El problema es tan grave, que el gobierno ha tenido que establecer la "restricción vehicular". Eso quiere decir que algunos días de la semana no puedes usar tu coche en la ciudad. El día depende del último número de la patente *(license plate)* del coche. Por ejemplo: si miras la tabla del periódico *El Mercurio,* verás que los coches que tienen una patente que termina con los números 5 ó 6, no pueden usarse los lunes.

Día	Terminación de patente
Lunes	5 y 6
Martes	7 y 8
Miércoles	9 y 0
Jueves	1 y 2
Viernes	3 y 4

- ¿Hay algún tipo de restricción vehicular en tu comunidad? Descríbela, y explica qué le pasa a la persona que no la obedezca.

396 trescientos noventa y seis
Manos a la obra 1

Universal Access

Heritage Language Learners
Ask students who have lived in a heritage country to discuss the issues of vehicular traffic and water availability in those countries. Are there specific problems or programs in place? If these issues are not at the forefront, are there other, more pressing environmental concerns?

Students with Learning Difficulties
Encourage students to plan out their responses for *Actividad* 9. Before they write their answers, have them record possible ideas in list form. Then, help them use elements of the question and their lists to formulate a complete response.

Actividad 10 Leer/Escribir

La población crece

❶ Lee la tabla y contesta las preguntas.

1. Según la tabla, ¿en qué siglo creció más la población?

2. ¿Qué problemas crees que ha causado este gran aumento en la población?

❷ Ahora, lee el artículo siguiente y contesta las preguntas.

EVOLUCIÓN DE LA POBLACIÓN DEL MUNDO EN LOS ÚLTIMOS 2,000 AÑOS
(en millones de habitantes)

El número de habitantes de la Tierra se ha multiplicado por diez en los últimos tres siglos.

Año 0	100	500	1000	1500	1600	1700	1800	1900	1960	1976	1987	1999	2000
170	180	190	265	425	545	680	980	1,645	3,000	4,000	5,000	6,000	6,228

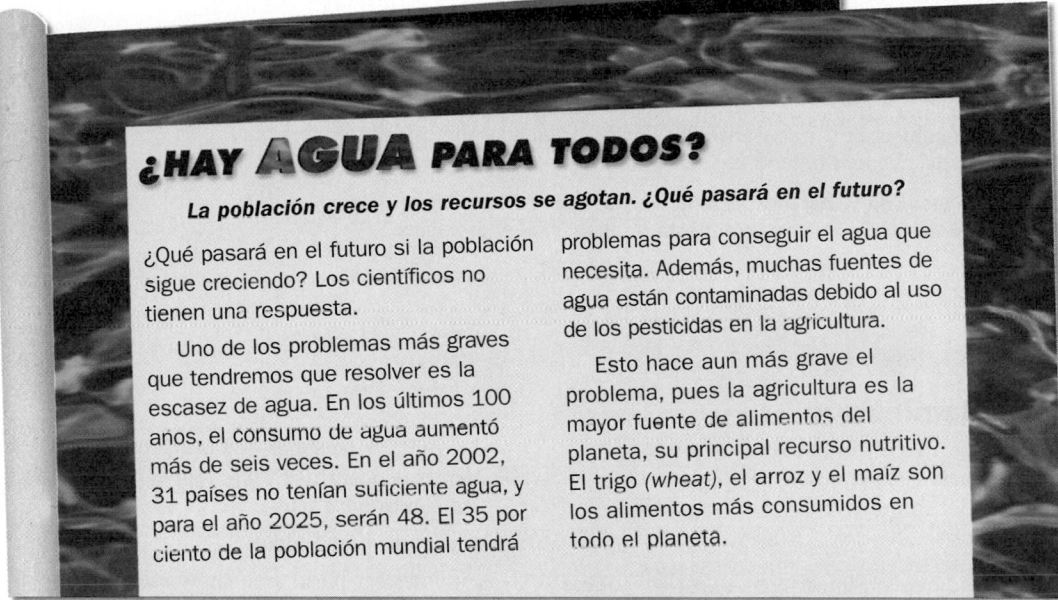

¿HAY AGUA PARA TODOS?

La población crece y los recursos se agotan. ¿Qué pasará en el futuro?

¿Qué pasará en el futuro si la población sigue creciendo? Los científicos no tienen una respuesta.

Uno de los problemas más graves que tendremos que resolver es la escasez de agua. En los últimos 100 años, el consumo de agua aumentó más de seis veces. En el año 2002, 31 países no tenían suficiente agua, y para el año 2025, serán 48. El 35 por ciento de la población mundial tendrá problemas para conseguir el agua que necesita. Además, muchas fuentes de agua están contaminadas debido al uso de los pesticidas en la agricultura.

Esto hace aun más grave el problema, pues la agricultura es la mayor fuente de alimentos del planeta, su principal recurso nutritivo. El trigo (*wheat*), el arroz y el maíz son los alimentos más consumidos en todo el planeta.

¿Comprendiste?

1. ¿Cuál será uno de los problemas más graves si la población sigue creciendo?

2. ¿Cuáles son los alimentos más consumidos en todo el planeta?

3. En tu opinión, ¿quién debe tomar medidas para resolver estos problemas: los gobiernos de cada comunidad, los gobiernos de cada país, las Naciones Unidas o los ciudadanos?

 Enriching Your Teaching

Culture Note

Because of its geography, Santiago suffers from greater air pollution even compared to cities with similar vehicle emissions levels. Located between two mountain ranges, the Andes and the Cordillera de la Costa, the air pollution tends to remain over the city.

Teacher-to-Teacher

Challenge students' math skills by asking them to use information from the chart in *Actividad 10* to extrapolate the rate of growth to several points over the next 100 years. Have them discuss their reasoning in Spanish.

 Actividad 10 *Standards:* 1.2, 1.3, 3.1

Resources: Practice Answers on Transparencies

Focus: Practicing new vocabulary and structures via reading and response

Suggestions: In addition to answering the questions in step 1, encourage students to comment on the rate of population growth over the years.

Answers:

Step 1
1. La población creció más en el siglo XX.
2. Answers will vary.

Step 2
1. Uno de los problemas más graves será la escasez de agua.
2. Los alimentos más consumidos en el planeta son el trigo, el arroz y el maíz.
3. Answers will vary.

Additional Resources

• Writing, Audio & Video Workbook: Cap. 9, Audio Activity 1, Track 5
• Writing, Audio & Video Workbook: Cap. 9, Writing Activity 6
• Resource Book: Cap. 9, Communicative Activity BLM

 Assessment

• Prueba 9-2: Vocabulary production

Block Schedule

Inside-Outside Circles. Have students go through the information on pp. 390–397. Have each student create a question and write it on a sheet of paper. Have students count off as 1 or 2. All number 1s form the outside circle. All number 2s form the inside circle, facing out. Each student should be paired. Have each student ask their questions and then the outside circle moves two people to the left. Each partner asks the questions again. Rotate until the class rotates back to the original partner.

397

▶ Rapid Review

Briefly review with students the formation and use of the subjunctive before beginning the next *Gramática* presentation and series of *Actividades*.

 **Gramática**

Presentation

Standards: 4.1

Resources: Voc. & Gram. Transparencies: 173

Suggestions: In random order, call out the conjunctions shown in the *Gramática* and ask volunteers to use them in sentences. Make sure students understand that the two rules given after the word bank apply to all the conjunctions shown in the word bank, not just to those shown in sample sentences.

 Standards: 1.2

Resources: Practice Answers on Transparencies

Focus: Practicing the subjunctive and the indicative with time-related conjunctions

Suggestions: Have students read the entire dialogue for meaning before they write their answers.

Answers:
1. tome
2. eche
3. se agoten
4. estén
5. sepan

Chapter Project

Students can perform step 2 at this point. Be sure they understand your corrections and suggestions. (For more information, see p. 384-a.)

✦ **Gramática**

Conjunciones que se usan con el subjuntivo y el indicativo

Certain conjunctions related to time are followed by either the indicative or the subjunctive.

después (de) que *after*	**mientras** *while, as long as*	**cuando** *when*
en cuanto *as soon as*	**tan pronto como** *as soon as*	**hasta que** *until*

You use the subjunctive after these conjunctions when the action that follows has not yet taken place.

> Van a seguir contaminando **hasta que** el gobierno los castigue.
> Habrá menos contaminación **cuando haya** menos fábricas.

You use the indicative after these conjunctions when the action that follows has already taken place or if it occurs regularly.

> Siempre apagamos las luces en cuanto **salimos** del cuarto.
> La empresa cerró tan pronto como **se puso** grave el problema.

• The conjunction *antes de que* is always followed by the subjunctive.

> Siempre se agotan los boletos **antes de que yo compre** el mío.

• If the subject of the sentence does not change, use the infinitive after *antes de*, *después de* and *hasta*:

> **Después de visitar** (nosotros) la fábrica, debemos escribir el informe.
> Marisa no piensa descansar **hasta resolver** (ella) el problema.

 Gramática **Leer**

La contaminación

Dos estudiantes están hablando sobre la contaminación. Completa el diálogo con el presente del subjuntivo del verbo apropiado del recuadro.

estar	echar	tomar	saber	agotarse

—La contaminación es un problema muy grave. Va a seguir aumentando hasta que el gobierno __1.__ medidas serias.

—Sí, seguro. Mientras la gente __2.__ desperdicios en lugares públicos, no vamos a resolver el problema.

—La gente debe saber que tan pronto como los recursos naturales __3.__, no vamos a tener lo suficiente para poder vivir.

—¡Debemos hacer algo!

—Sí. Podemos hacer una campaña en la escuela. Mientras los estudiantes __4.__ en recreo, pueden informarse sobre cómo conservar los recursos naturales.

—Después de que nuestros compañeros __5.__ más sobre el tema, todos van a querer colaborar.

Universal Access

Students with Learning Difficulties

Lead students through *Actividad* 11 step by step. First, ask them to select the correct verb for the sentence based on meaning. Then, have them create the present subjunctive form of that verb. Last, ask them to explain why the subjunctive is necessary given the conjunction used and the time frame of the sentence.

Advanced Learners

Ask students to write two ways in which people commonly hurt the environment or waste resources. Have them read their sentences to a partner, who responds using a time-related conjunction: A —*Mucha gente no conserva el agua cuando se ducha.* B —*Verdad. Conservaremos el agua tan pronto como desaparezca.*

Ampliación del lenguaje

Familias de palabras

Las familias de palabras son grupos de palabras relacionadas por tener una misma raíz. Lee las familias de palabras de la tabla. Piensa en palabras que conoces que pertenezcan a esas familias. Escribe en una hoja de papel las palabras que faltan para llenar los recuadros.

Sustantivos	Adjetivos	Verbos
1. desperdicios	desperdiciado(a)	
2. contaminación		contaminar
3.	protegido(a)	proteger
4. amenaza	amenazante	
5. agotamiento	agotado(a)	
6. economía		economizar

Ampliación del lenguaje

Presentation

Standards: 1.2

Resources: Practice Answers on Transparencies

Focus: Understanding word families

Suggestions: Ask pairs of students to build word families around other words such as **conservar** or **fábrica**.

Answers:

1. desperdiciar
2. contaminado(a)
3. protección
4. amenazar
5. agotar
6. económico(a)

  **12** **Gramática** **Hablar**

¿Cuándo?

Tu compañero(a) quiere saber cuándo se van a reconocer las amenazas del futuro. Responde a sus preguntas usando las conjunciones *antes de que, cuando, tan pronto como, después de que, mientras, hasta que, en cuanto.*

Modelo

el gobierno *(tomar)* medidas para fomentar la protección de la Tierra / reducir los recursos naturales
A —¿Cuándo va a tomar medidas el gobierno para fomentar la protección de la Tierra?
B —Cuando se reduzcan los recursos naturales.

Estudiante A

1. las fábricas *(deshacerse)* de los desperdicios sin contaminar
2. voluntarios *(fomentar)* el cuidado de la comunidad
3. *(promoverse)* leyes para proteger los recursos naturales
4. los ciudadanos *(colocar)* los objetos reciclables en lugares apropiados
5. las compañías que producen coches *(limitar)* el uso de petróleo

Estudiante B

castigarlas el gobierno
poder organizarse y recibir fondos
agotarse los recursos naturales
ser fácil y económico hacerlo
dejar de comprar coches ineficientes
tener más influencia los ciudadanos que las empresas
reconocer que el problema es grave

 12

Standards: 1.1

Resources: Practice Answers on Transparencies

Focus: Practicing the subjunctive and the indicative with time-related conjunctions

Suggestions: Point out that Student B has a choice of more responses than there are questions. Students should choose responses that reflect their opinions and make sense.

Answers will vary. The following are some likely results.

1. A —¿Cuándo van a deshacerse las fábricas de los desperdicios sin contaminar?
   B —Tan pronto como el gobierno las castigue.
2. A —¿Cuándo fomentarán los voluntarios el cuidado de la comunidad?
   B —En cuanto se pueden organizar y recibir fondos.
3. A —¿Cuándo se promoverán leyes para proteger los recursos naturales?
   B —No hasta que tengan más influencia los ciudadanos que las empresas.
4. A —¿Cuándo colocarán los ciudadanos los objetos reciclables en lugares apropiados?
   B —En cuanto sea fácil y económico hacerlo.
5. A —¿Cuándo van a limitar las compañías que producen coches el uso de petróleo?
   B —Después de que se agoten los recursos naturales.

trescientos noventa y nueve 399
Capítulo 9

Enriching Your Teaching

Teacher-to-Teacher

Have students prepare interviews which they can conduct with local business people, merchants, farmers, or community leaders who speak Spanish. Tell students that the purpose of their interviews should be to find out more about what people in your community are doing to protect the environment and conserve natural resources. Ask students to prepare a draft of several questions, then convene in a group to exchange ideas and correct any grammar errors their questions may have. Ask students to conduct their interviews and report back to the class with the results.

Additional Resources

• Writing, Audio & Video Workbook: Cap. 9, Audio Activity 2, Track 6

Actividad 13 — Leer/Escribir

¡No a la contaminación!

Lee el siguiente folleto *(brochure)* sobre una fábrica de tu comunidad y responde a las preguntas que aparecen a continuación.

Marcha en contra de la CONTAMINACIÓN

¿Sabías que la fábrica de pesticidas no respeta el medio ambiente? Contamina el agua del río con los desperdicios y también contamina el aire. Aunque el gobierno ha promovido leyes para la protección de la comunidad, esta fábrica continúa deshaciéndose de su basura en nuestras aguas y en nuestro aire.

Mientras fábricas como ésta no respeten las medidas de protección, van a dañar cada vez más a nuestro planeta. ¡Debemos exigir que la fábrica coloque sus desperdicios en lugares apropiados antes de que sea demasiado tarde! Juntos, podemos fomentar un cambio. ¡Toma medidas para proteger al planeta! ¡Deja de comprar los pesticidas! ¡Exige que la fábrica use recipientes apropiados para sus productos químicos!

Para mostrar tu apoyo, puedes participar en la marcha frente a la fábrica, o puedes firmar una petición en contra de la persona que está a cargo.

La protección de la comunidad depende de ti.

1. ¿Cómo contamina el medio ambiente la fábrica de pesticidas?
2. ¿Existen leyes para proteger a la comunidad? ¿Las obedece la fábrica?
3. ¿Qué medidas pueden tomar los ciudadanos? Nombra dos medidas.
4. ¿Cómo pueden apoyar la causa los ciudadanos?
5. ¿Puedes pensar en otras maneras de apoyar la causa de la que se habla en el folleto?

Actividad 14 — Gramática  Escribir/Hablar

Problemas y soluciones

1 Con otro(a) estudiante, escribe cinco frases que identifiquen amenazas en tu comunidad respecto al medio ambiente y soluciones posibles, usando las conjunciones *antes de que, cuando, tan pronto como, después de que, mientras, hasta que.*

Modelo

Los ciudadanos no ahorran electricidad. Hasta que los ciudadanos hagamos un esfuerzo por ahorrar electricidad tendremos problemas.

2 Cada pareja va a compartir sus ideas con la clase. Para cada problema que se menciona, la clase va a sugerir soluciones.

Universal Access

Heritage Language Learners
Ask students to model the use of the time-related conjunctions in *Actividad* 15. After they have written their responses, have them go back and circle each verb that follows a conjunction. Ask students to confirm and explain why each verb requires the indicative or the subjunctive. Also, have students confirm the spelling of these verb forms.

Students with Learning Difficulties
Encourage students to circle a key word in each of the questions following the brochure in *Actividad* 13. Instruct students to search for these key words in the text to help locate the information required to answer each question.

400

 **Gramática** **Escribir/Hablar** ....

En cuanto podamos . . .

❶ Trabaja con otro(a) estudiante. Imaginen que se reunieron para hablar sobre lo que harán después de graduarse de la escuela. Hagan una lista de cosas que pueden hacer.

Modelo

- ir a la universidad
- buscar un trabajo
- viajar

❷ Escojan una idea de su lista y hablen de los pasos necesarios para realizarla, usando las siguientes conjunciones.

después de que	tan pronto como	después de	mientras
cuando	hasta que	en cuanto	

Modelo

ir a la universidad
A —*En cuanto me gradúe iré a la universidad.*
B —*Me quedaré con mis padres hasta que empiecen las clases.*

 Leer/Hablar ....

La lluvia ácida

Lee el siguiente artículo sobre la lluvia ácida y contesta las preguntas que aparecen a continuación.

Conexiones **Las ciencias** _____

En más de una docena de países europeos está ocurriendo una corrosión acelerada en los edificios y monumentos históricos. Así, por ejemplo, el Partenón ha sufrido más el efecto de la erosión en los últimos 30 años que durante los 2,400 años anteriores, y en España las pinturas del museo del Prado se han estado deteriorando a causa de la contaminación.

Todo ello es debido a las emisiones de dióxido de azufre *(sulfur)* y óxidos de nitrógeno, que se convierten en ácidos fuertes y atacan tanto a edificios antiguos como nuevos. Los más afectados son los objetos y estructuras de materiales fácilmente degradables, como la piedra caliza *(limestone)* y la arenisca *(sandstone)*.

- ¿Qué otros ejemplos de corrosión por lluvia ácida conoces?
- ¿Hay corrosión por lluvia ácida en tu comunidad? Descríbela.

● **Más práctica** ....
Practice Workbook 9-5

For: Practice with conjuctions
Visit: www.phschool.com
Web Code: jed-0903

cuatrocientos uno 401
Capítulo 9

Practice and Communicate   9

 Standards: 1.1
....

Focus: Practicing the subjunctive and the indicative with time-related conjunctions

Suggestions: Point out that the future activities in the model are suggestions only. Encourage students to talk about their actual plans after high school.

Answers will vary.

 Standards: 1.1, 1.2, 3.1
....

Focus: Practicing new vocabulary and structures via reading and response

Suggestions: Have students read the information silently. Help them address any comprehension problems they may have. Ask them to share background knowledge they may have about the major causes of acid rain.

Answers will vary.

Additional Resources

- Writing, Audio & Video Workbook: Cap. 9, Writing Activity 7

 Assessment

- Prueba 9-3: *Conjunciones que se usan con el subjuntivo y el indicativo*

 Enriching Your Teaching

Culture Note

Many of the earth's ancient treasures are threatened by acid rain. In the Mexico City basin, acid rain is eroding the ancient ruins of the Aztecs at Tenochtitlán. In the Yucatán Peninsula, it is accelerating the erosion of the Mayan ruins. In Peru, it is attacking the Nazca Lines. Projects and studies around the world are dedicated to solving the problem of acid rain, but many of them lack funds.

Internet Search

Keywords:

lluvia ácida + (nombre de lugar)

401

Gramática

Presentation

Standards: 4.1

Resources: Voc. & Gram. Transparencies: 174

Suggestions: Say two short sentences referring to the same thing or person: *La señora Martínez es profesora. Hablé con la señora Martínez ayer.* Ask students to combine the two sentences using a relative pronoun from the *Gramática: La señora Martínez es la profesora con quien hablé ayer.*

Actividad 17 *Standards:* 1.2

Resources: Practice Answers on Transparencies

Focus: Practicing the relative pronouns *que, quien,* and *lo que*

Suggestions: Suggest that students follow three steps to complete the activity. First, read and understand the sentence. Second, locate the noun that will be replaced by the relative pronoun. Third, choose the correct relative pronoun.

Common Errors: Some students will follow English grammatical logic and use *quien* to refer to people, even when the pronoun doesn't follow a preposition: *Melina es una persona quien conozco.* Remind them that in Spanish, *que* is used to refer to both things and people unless a preposition precedes the relative pronoun: *Melina es una persona que conozco.*

Answers:

1. que
2. Lo que
3. quien
4. que
5. que
6. quienes

Actividad 18 *Standards:* 1.1

Focus: Practicing the relative pronouns *que, quien,* and *lo que*

Suggestions: Point out to students that they are creating complex sentences. The relative pronoun serves as the subject of the subordinate clause they are adding. They must supply the verb phrase for that subordinate clause.

Answers will vary.

Gramática

Los pronombres relativos *que, quien* y *lo que*

You use relative pronouns to combine two sentences or to give clarifying information. The most common relative pronoun in Spanish is *que*. It can mean "that," "which," "who," or "whom," and it may refer either to persons or to things.

> Ésta es la fábrica **que** visité ayer.
> La fábrica, **que** hace productos químicos, fomenta la protección del medio ambiente.
> El Sr. Ríos es el profesor **que** nos llevó a la fábrica.

After a preposition, use *que* to refer to things and *quien(es)* to refer to people.

> No encuentro el papel **en que** escribí tu dirección.
> El problema **del que** te hablé ocurrió en otro barrio.
> La señora **a quien** te presenté trabaja en una fábrica de recipientes.

- Use the relative phrase *lo que* to refer to a situation, concept, action, or object not yet identified.

> No recuerdo **lo que** me dijo.
> **Lo que** más me gusta es estar a cargo del proyecto.

Actividad 17 **Leer**

El medio ambiente

Muchas de las noticias del periódico hablan sobre el medio ambiente. Completa las frases con los pronombres relativos *que, quien(es)* o *lo que*.

1. El gobierno anunció las medidas _____ limitan el uso de pesticidas.

2. _____ más amenaza a la población es la escasez de recursos.

3. La persona de _____ habla el artículo tira los desperdicios en el río.

4. Las medidas _____ fueron tomadas por el gobierno no resuelven los problemas más graves.

5. El petróleo _____ se echa en el océano produce contaminación.

6. Las personas a _____ ayudó el gobierno viven ahora en una zona sin contaminación.

Actividad 18 **Hablar**

Lo que a mí me parece es . . .

Completa las frases siguientes con tus opiniones personales.

1. Lo que más me molesta de la contaminación es . . .

2. El gobierno es la organización que . . .

3. Nuestros padres son las personas con quienes . . .

4. (Nombres) son las personas que . . .

5. No estoy de acuerdo con lo que . . .

Universal Access

Advanced Learners

On the board, write questions that ask for identifying information that students can supply: *¿Quién es el señor Harler? ¿Qué es la lluvia ácida?* Then answer the questions with complex sentences containing relative pronouns: *El señor Harler es el profesor que enseña matemáticas. La lluvia ácida es un problema que destruye los monumentos antiguos.* Have students write three similar questions and exchange them with a partner, who answers them using complex sentences with relative pronouns.

El petróleo

1 En grupo, lean el siguiente artículo sobre el petróleo en el mar.

Petróleo en el mar

En nuestra sociedad, el petróleo y sus derivados son imprescindibles[1] como fuente de energía y para la fabricación[2] de productos químicos, alimentos, medicinas, etc.

Por otro lado, alrededor del 0.1% al 0.2% de la producción mundial de petróleo termina en el mar. Esto produce la contaminación de las aguas y daña el ecosistema marino. Aves[3] y mamíferos mueren constantemente a causa del petróleo en sus cuerpos.

¿Cómo llega el petróleo al mar? El petróleo debe ser transportado muchas millas por el mar hasta llegar al lugar donde se va a usar. En el camino se producen a veces accidentes que pueden ser muy graves. Pero, la mayor parte del petróleo que termina en el mar procede de la tierra, de desperdicios de las casas, automóviles, combustible, fábricas, etc.

En la actualidad[4] se usan productos de limpieza especiales para limpiar el petróleo, pero evitar la contaminación es la única solución verdaderamente aceptable.

1 Indispensable, essential 2 manufacture
3 Birds 4 currently, today

2 Decidan cuáles son las ideas más importantes del artículo. Escríbanlas en una lista y añadan detalles.

Modelo
Necesitamos el petróleo como fuente de energía.

3 Usen las ideas que anotaron para pensar en una propuesta sobre cómo resolver el problema del petróleo en el mar y en cómo se puede evitar la contaminación de las aguas. Pueden usar la Internet o la biblioteca para investigar sobre el tema.

Modelo
Cuando se transporta el petróleo por mar,
se deben usar barcos que sean más modernos.

4 Presenten sus ideas a la clase.

● **Más práctica** · · · · · · · · · · · · ·
Practice Workbook 9-6, 9-7

For: Practice with relative pronouns
Visit: www.phschool.com
Web Code: jed-0905

cuatrocientos tres 403
Capítulo 9

 Enriching Your Teaching

Culture Note

Oil was first discovered in Venezuela in 1921. In 1960, the country became a founding member of OPEC. In 1976, the oil industry was nationalized. Currently, as the world's fifth-largest producer, oil is undoubtedly the lifeblood of the Venezuelan economy. The oil industry accounts for about 80 percent of Venezuela's export earnings. The barrels of crude oil produced each day account for approximately 5 percent of world production. In the late 1990s, roughly 50 percent of this was exported to the United States, 10 percent of the total national supply.

 Actividad 19 *Standards:* 1.1, 1.2, 1.3, 3.1
· · · · · · · · · · · · · · · · · · · ·

Focus: Practicing new vocabulary and structures via reading and response

Suggestions: For steps 2–3, encourage students to use a graphic organizer, such as a three-column chart, to record the main ideas and important details of the article. They can write their proposed solutions in the third column.

Answers will vary.

Additional Resources
- Writing, Audio & Video Workbook: Cap. 9, Writing Activities 8–9
- Resource Book: Cap. 9, Communicative Activity BLM

 Assessment
- Prueba 9-4: *Los pronombres relativos que, quien y lo que*
- Examen: Vocabulario y gramática 1

Chapter Project
Students can perform step 3 at this point. (For more information, see p. 384-a.)

403

Presentation

Standards: 1.1, 1.2, 3.1

Resources: Voc. & Gram. Transparencies: 175; Resource Book: Cap. 9, Input Script; Audio Program: CD Cap. 9, Track 7

Focus: Presenting new vocabulary and using grammar lexically in context

Suggestions: Have students look over the four numbered reading sections on these pages. Ask questions to help them achieve a general idea of what they will read. For example: *¿Piensas que esta lectura se trata más de la literatura o de las ciencias?* **(las ciencias)** Ask students to describe what they see in the photos. Encourage them to use background knowledge from their science and other courses in this discussion. Use *sí/no* or embedded answer questions to elicit new vocabulary from students. For example, looking at the diagram for section 1, ask: *¿Se atrapa el calor del sol en la tierra o en la atmósfera?* **(en la atmósfera)** Looking at the diagram for section 3, ask: *¿Los problemas del medio ambiente ponen a los animales en peligro de extinción?* **(Sí.)** Then have students read along as you present the new vocabulary by playing the *Audio CD* or reading the text aloud. Check for comprehension by asking other questions. See the Input Scripts in the *Teacher's Resource Book* for specific questions.

A primera vista 2

Vocabulario y gramática en contexto

Objectives

Read, listen to, and understand information about
- environmental issues and endangered species
- measures to protect the environment and endangered species

¿Has escuchado decir alguna vez que **el clima** de la Antártida es muy frío o que en el Caribe hace mucho calor? Cada región del planeta tiene su propio clima. La flora y la fauna de cada región, es decir las plantas y los animales que viven en ella, están adaptados a su clima.

1 La actividad de los seres humanos puede cambiar el clima de una región o de todo el planeta. Por ejemplo, el CO_2 que **producen** los automóviles y las plantas generadoras de energía **atrapa** el calor del sol en **la atmósfera**. Este fenómeno, llamado **efecto invernadero**, ha hecho que las temperaturas de muchas regiones aumenten.

la piel

la foca

2 Los seres humanos también pueden causar cambios en las condiciones de vida de un lugar. Cuando se **produce un derrame de petróleo**, muchos peces y otros animales marinos de la región pueden morir. **La limpieza** de estos derrames y **el rescate** de los animales de esa región cuesta mucho trabajo y dinero.

el ave

la pluma

404 **cuatrocientos cuatro**
A primera vista 2

Universal Access

Students with Learning Difficulties
Before students write their definitions for *Actividad* 21, instruct them to locate each word in the reading. Model for students how to use context clues in the reading to come up with a definition for each word.

Advanced Learners
Have students create a large greenhouse effect diagram like the one in section 1 of the reading. Ask them to include labels in their diagram. Have them use the diagram as a visual aid for a brief oral presentation about **el efecto invernadero.**

3 Los cambios en el clima, además de **la caza** y **la pesca excesivas** han puesto muchos animales **salvajes** en **peligro de extinción**. La escasez de alimentos y **la falta** de agua son dos resultados principales de la expansión de las ciudades y de otras actividades humanas. **La selva tropical** es un lugar que ha sido **explotado** sin control. Se han cortado tantos árboles que el número de **especies** que viven allí ha **disminuido**. **La preservación** de todas las especies es nuestra responsabilidad y podemos hacer cambios **con tal que** hagamos un esfuerzo.

Animales en peligro de extinción

el águila calva

la ballena

4 Los científicos dicen que **el recalentamiento global**, es decir, el aumento de las temperaturas en todo el planeta, puede **derretir** la nieve y **el hielo** de los polos y las montañas. Muchas ciudades quedarán bajo el agua **a menos que detengamos** el recalentamiento global.

 Escuchar/Escribir

¿Será cierto?

Escribe los números del 1 al 6 en una hoja. Escucha cada frase y escribe C *(cierta)* o F *(falsa)*. En el caso de las falsas, vuelve a escribir la frase para que sea cierta.

  Escribir/Hablar

Definiciones

Trabaja con otro(a) estudiante para escribir definiciones de estas palabras y expresiones. Luego, escriban frases usando tres de las palabras y expresiones.

1. el efecto invernadero
2. la caza
3. derretir
4. el rescate
5. disminuir

cuatrocientos cinco **405**
Capítulo 9

 Standards: 1.2

Actividad 20

Resources: Voc. & Gram. Transparencies: 176; Audio Program: CD Cap. 9, Track 8; Resource Book: Cap. 9, Audio Script; Practice Answers on Transparencies

Focus: Practicing listening comprehension of new vocabulary

Suggestions: Display *Vocabulary & Grammar Transparency* 176 as a reference as students complete the activity. Allow them to listen to the *Audio CD* once through first. Then play it again, pausing after each item, so they can write their answers.

Answers:
1. C
2. F Si no detenemos el recalentamiento global, muchas ciudades se quedarán bajo el agua.
3. F Muchas especies están en peligro de extinción a causa de los cambios en el clima.
4. C
5. C

Standards: 1.1, 1.3

Actividad 21

Resources: Practice Answers on Transparencies

Focus: Demonstrating comprehension of new vocabulary

Suggestions: Allow students to use phrases and sentence fragments to define the words and expressions in the first part of the activity. This way they can focus on meaning.

Answers: Sentences and wording of definitions will vary. Definitions should contain the following basic information:
1. el calor del sol que queda atrapado en la atmósfera
2. el acto de seguir a los animales para matarlos
3. calentar el hielo para hacerlo líquido
4. liberación del peligro
5. hacer menos

Enriching Your Teaching

Teacher-to-Teacher

Many of your students are already well versed in the area of pollution and other environmental problems. Throughout *Capítulo 9*, encourage them to draw on this information and use their Spanish skills and reference materials such as bilingual dictionaries to synthesize it for discussions and writing in Spanish.

Internet Search

Keyword: efecto invernadero

Vocabulario y gramática

Presentation

Standards: 1.1, 1.2, 3.1

Resources: Voc. & Gram. Transparencies: 177–178; Resource Book: Cap. 9, Input Script; Audio Program: CD Cap. 9, Tracks 9–10

Focus: Extending presentation of vocabulary and grammar in context

Suggestions:

Pre-reading: Before reading, point out that *ozono, aerosoles,* and *afecta* are cognates. Show how removing the initial *a-* from the verb *amenazar* makes it closely resemble the English verb "menace," and explain that the meaning is the same. Have volunteers read aloud the titles on this and the next page to help students focus on the main ideas of the two readings.

Reading: Allow students time to read the information on this and the next page silently first. Then play the *Audio CD* or read the text and have students read along as they listen. Allow them to listen more than once.

Post-reading: Check comprehension by asking questions, including those in *Actividad* 22. See the Input Script in the *Teacher's Resource Book* for other questions.

Standards: 1.2, 1.3, 3.1

Resources: Practice Answers on Transparencies

Focus: Writing answers to demonstrate reading comprehension

Suggestions: Have students answer the questions on their own. Then invite them to share their responses.

Answers:
1. La capa de ozono es importante porque nos protege de los rayos ultravioleta del sol. Si no la cuidamos, afectará nuestra vida diaria.
2. Punta Arenas está en Chile. Está en la región con el agujero más grande de la capa de ozono.
3. Los habitantes pueden llevar ropa que protege todo el cuerpo, ponerse anteojos de sol y loción protectora para el sol.
4–5. Answers will vary.

Punta Arenas: miedo al sol

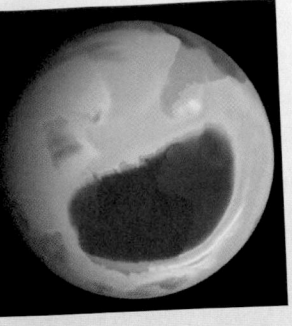

¿Has oído hablar de **la capa de ozono**? El ozono es un gas que forma una capa en la atmósfera que nos protege de los rayos ultravioleta del sol. A veces esta capa contiene **agujeros** a causa del uso excesivo de productos que usamos todos los días, como **los aerosoles**. Es importante **tomar conciencia** de este problema, ya que **afecta** nuestra vida diaria.

Punta Arenas, en Chile, es una de las ciudades más cercanas al polo Sur. Y es en esa región donde está el agujero más grande de la capa de ozono.

Desde hace años, los habitantes de Punta Arenas viven bajo **la amenaza** de los rayos ultravioleta y ajustan *(adjust)* sus vidas a los niveles de ozono de la atmósfera. Si las noticias del tiempo indican que los niveles de ozono son muy altos, se recomienda llevar ropa que proteja todo el cuerpo, ponerse anteojos de sol y loción protectora para el sol.

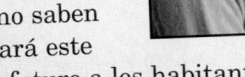

Los científicos no saben aún cómo afectará este fenómeno en el futuro a los habitantes de esta ciudad.

 Leer/Escribir..

La amenaza del sol

1. ¿Por qué es importante la capa de ozono? ¿Qué pasará si no la cuidamos?

2. ¿Dónde está Punta Arenas? ¿Qué problema hay allí?

3. ¿Qué pueden hacer los habitantes de Punta Arenas para protegerse de los rayos ultravioleta?

4. ¿Cómo crees que se sentirán los habitantes de esa ciudad viviendo bajo esta amenaza todos los días?

5. ¿Qué podemos hacer para que la gente tome conciencia de la importancia que tiene cuidar nuestro medio ambiente?

Universal Access

Heritage Language Learners
Students may not be familiar with specific scientific vocabulary. Have them read through the passages on pp. 406 and 407 to find terms with which they are not familiar. Then, have them create a simple scientific glossary with explanations of each of these terms.

Students with Special Needs
Help students with visual impairments experience the images of *El Parque Nacional de Guanacaste.* Locate a recording that features some of the sounds one would hear at a Costa Rican nature preserve. These might include the sounds of the weather, birds, and animals.

El Parque Nacional de Guanacaste

En los últimos años se ha hecho muy popular el ecoturismo. Los turistas ecológicos no sólo quieren visitar lugares hermosos, sino que desean aprender sobre la fauna y la flora de la región, las características del terreno *(terrain)* y su clima. Este tipo de turista desea ayudar a cuidar y preservar la naturaleza.

1 Uno de los países que promueve el ecoturismo es Costa Rica. El Parque Nacional de Guanacaste, en la región del Pacífico Norte, por ejemplo, es un refugio para muchos animales y plantas, pero también uno de los lugares favoritos de los ecoturistas. En los años 80, se creó un Programa de Ecoturismo para que los visitantes pudieran disfrutar de los hermosos paisajes mientras participan en los programas educativos.

2 Guanacaste es una **reserva natural** para muchos animales y plantas, pues en sus **tierras** hay varios tipos de bosques. Según los científicos, este parque tiene 3,000 tipos de plantas, 300 especies de aves y mamíferos, como el armadillo, el puma y el mono de cara blanca, y 5,000 especies de mariposas.

  Escribir/Hablar

Actividad 23

Cuando vaya a Guanacaste . . .

Haz una lista de los esfuerzos que hacen en un parque nacional de Costa Rica por proteger el medio ambiente. Habla con otro(a) estudiante sobre lo que hacen.

● **Más práctica**
Practice Workbook 9-8, 9-9

For: Vocabulary practice
Visit: www.phschool.com
Web Code: jed-0906

cuatrocientos siete **407**
Capítulo 9

 Enriching Your Teaching

Culture Note
Although Costa Rica faces the same development concerns as many other countries, including a growing population and high deforestation, the small Central American country has taken a leadership role in the development of ecotourism. With only .03 percent of the world's total land mass, Costa Rica is home to 6 percent of the globe's biodiversity. Currently, national parks and reserves constitute approximately 25 percent of the country's area. Hundreds of thousands of ecotourists visit each year to view, study, and appreciate Costa Rica's natural resources, and these numbers are projected to grow. By 2006, it is estimated that over 1.5 million tourists will visit Costa Rica.

407

Objectives
- Discuss environmental issues
- Talk about animals in danger of extinction
- Use the subjunctive after conjunctions

Manos a la obra 2

Vocabulario y gramática en uso

 **Leer/Escribir** . . . .

Definiciones ambientales

Indica a qué palabra se refiere cada definición. Luego, escribe un párrafo en el que usas por lo menos tres de las palabras.

1. mamífero (*mammal*) enorme que vive en el agua
2. animal con piel que vive en el mar y en la tierra
3. acción de limpiar
4. cubre el cuerpo del ave
5. hacer o causar algo
6. parar
7. agua sólida
8. ave que representa un símbolo de los Estados Unidos

a. el águila calva
b. el hielo
c. detener
d. producir
e. la ballena
f. la pluma
g. la foca
h. la limpieza

 Leer . . . .

El efecto invernadero

Completa esta conversación entre Tomás y Ana con las palabras del recuadro.

una amenaza	el recalentamiento global	la capa de ozono	los aerosoles
el clima	efecto invernadero	la atmósfera	

Tomás: —Hace mucho calor, ¿verdad?

Ana:　—Sí, mucho. Tal vez es a causa del __1.__.

Tomás: —¿Qué es eso?

Ana:　—Es la producción de gases que atrapan el calor del sol en __2.__. Cuando estos gases aumentan, hay cambios graves en __3.__ del mundo. Hace más calor o llueve más.

Tomás: —Pero __4.__ protege la Tierra de los rayos del sol, ¿verdad?

Ana:　—Sí, pero __5.__ y otros productos químicos son __6.__ para la capa de ozono. Ya han creado un agujero en la capa de ozono sobre la Antártida. Un resultado es __7.__ en todas partes del mundo. El sol es tan fuerte en Australia, por ejemplo, que los estudiantes tienen que llevar sombreros especiales para protegerse la cabeza y el cuello.

Universal Access

Students with Learning Difficulties

Have students label the words in *Actividad* 24 with one of the following codes: **an (animal), c (cosa),** or **ac (acción).** Then ask students to determine whether each definition applies to an animal, a thing, or an action. Have them choose the correct word from the smaller group of choices.

Advanced Learners

Have pairs or small groups of students use vocabulary from *Actividades* 24 and 25 to write and present their own conversations. Encourage them to create situations in which the vocabulary would arise naturally, such as a conversation between ecotourists and a park ranger, or between a museum guide and museum goers.

Actividad 26

Escribir/Hablar ....

Peligros

1 Escribe una lista de cinco cosas que pueden afectar la vida y la salud de los animales y de los seres humanos. Puedes usar las palabras del recuadro.

escasez	contaminado(a)	derrame de petróleo	caza excesiva	explotar
derretir	capa de ozono	especie	falta	amenaza

2 Luego, intercambia tu lista con la de otro(a) estudiante, piensa en qué se puede hacer para solucionar los problemas y habla de tus soluciones con tu compañero(a).

Modelo

la pesca excesiva

A —*La pesca excesiva es una amenaza a la población de peces.*
B —*Podemos establecer leyes en contra de la pesca excesiva.*

Actividad 27

  Leer/Pensar/Hablar ....

Un rescate problemático

Imagina que hay un derrame de petróleo y tienes que llevar a la otra orilla *(bank)* del río a una anaconda, un cocodrilo y un ave. En el barco hay lugar sólo para ti y uno de ellos. Como no puedes dejarlos juntos en ninguna orilla porque la anaconda se comería al cocodrilo o el cocodrilo se comería al ave, ¿cómo podrías rescatar a todos sin problemas? Con un(a) compañero(a), piensen en las soluciones posibles.

Fondo cultural

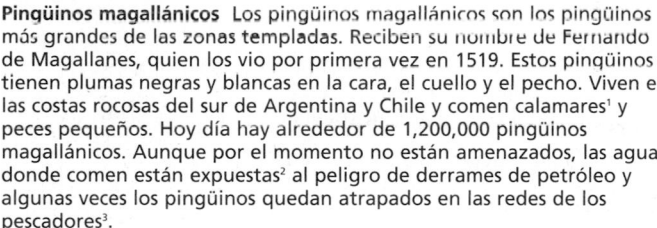

Pingüinos magallánicos Los pingüinos magallánicos son los pingüinos más grandes de las zonas templadas. Reciben su nombre de Fernando de Magallanes, quien los vio por primera vez en 1519. Estos pingüinos tienen plumas negras y blancas en la cara, el cuello y el pecho. Viven en las costas rocosas del sur de Argentina y Chile y comen calamares[1] y peces pequeños. Hoy día hay alrededor de 1,200,000 pingüinos magallánicos. Aunque por el momento no están amenazados, las aguas donde comen están expuestas[2] al peligro de derrames de petróleo y algunas veces los pingüinos quedan atrapados en las redes de los pescadores[3].

• ¿Dónde viven los pingüinos magallánicos? ¿Qué comen?
• ¿Qué peligros hay en las aguas donde viven los pingüinos?

1 squid **2** exposed **3** fishermen's nets

cuatrocientos nueve **409**
Capítulo 9

Practice and Communicate

 9

 Actividad 26 — *Standards:* 1.1, 3.1

Focus: Practicing new vocabulary and structures via note-taking and discussion

Suggestions: Remind students that the vocabulary in the word bank is there to give them ideas. Encourage them to use the word bank, but to go beyond it as well, and use other pertinent vocabulary they may already know.

Answers will vary.

 Actividad 27 — *Standards:* 1.1, 1.2, 3.1

Focus: Practicing new vocabulary and structures through problem-solving

Suggestions: Suggest strategies in which students take two animals across, leave one, and return with the other to pick up the third.

Answers will vary.

 Fondo cultural — *Standards:* 1.1, 1.2, 3.1

Suggestions: After students have read and discussed the information, ask: *¿Qué sabes de los otros animales que viven en la tierra o en el mar en la parte sur de América del Sur? ¿Cómo se llaman? ¿Qué información interesante puedes decir sobre ellos?*

Answers:
• Viven en las costas rocosas del sur de Argentina y Chile. Comen calamares y peces pequeños.
• Las aguas están expuestas al peligro de derrames de petróleo y los pingüinos pueden quedar atrapados en las redes de los pescadores.

Enriching Your Teaching

Culture Note
Magellanic penguins are not the only things in the Southern Atlantic to receive the name of Fernando de Magallanes. The Strait of Magellan is the name of the body of water that separates the island of Tierra del Fuego from the tip of South America. Today, ecotours and cruises are available in and around the "land of fire."

Teacher-to-Teacher
Problem-solving activities like *Actividad* 27 are an excellent way to get groups of students speaking in Spanish. Many books are available containing such activities. Although the problems you find will most likely be in English, they can readily be converted and solved in Spanish.

Rapid Review

Before students complete *Actividad* 28, briefly review the uses of *por* and *para*. The *Gramática* presentation for these is in *Capítulo* 4 on p. 171.

Actividad 28 Standards: 1.1, 1.2, 1.3, 3.1, 5.2

Resources: Practice Answers on Transparencies

Focus: Practicing new vocabulary and structures via reading and response

Suggestions: For the slogans or announcements in step 3, encourage students to make their message more effective by using poetic devices such as rhyme or alliteration.

Answers:

Step 2

1. Se cortan los árboles para hacer cosas de madera y tener tierras libres para que coman las vacas.
2. El gobierno trata de fomentar más interés por la ecología.
3. Nelly recomienda educar a la gente para que no contamine la atmósfera.

Step 3

Answers will vary.

Extension: After students have completed the activity, ask pairs of volunteers to perform a dramatic reading of the interview with Nelly Anderson.

Actividad 28 Leer/Hablar/Escribir

Las selvas tropicales de Costa Rica

❶ Lee la siguiente entrevista de Nelly Anderson, una estudiante de Costa Rica que se dedica a la preservación de la flora y la fauna de su país.

Entrevista con Nelly Anderson

¿Por qué te interesa la ecología?
Porque Costa Rica tiene muchas especies de plantas y animales salvajes.

¿Cuáles son los problemas que afectan a las selvas tropicales y la naturaleza en el mundo?
Muchos países han explotado las selvas sin control. Se cortan los árboles para hacer cosas de madera[1] y tener tierras libres para que coman las vacas[2]. Ahora hay una escasez de recursos naturales.

¿Quién debe ejercer[3] este control?
El gobierno y todos los habitantes de países como Costa Rica. Además, los agricultores no deben cortar tantos árboles y deben respetar la naturaleza.

¿Qué hace el gobierno de Costa Rica ante este problema?
El gobierno ayuda al Instituto Costarricense de Turismo. Los turistas vienen a Costa Rica por su flora y fauna. Por lo tanto, el gobierno trata de fomentar más interés por la ecología.

¿Qué se puede hacer para que los niños y los adultos tomen conciencia del medio ambiente?
Pienso que la gente no tiene suficiente información. Por eso usan productos como aerosoles y pesticidas, que contaminan la atmósfera. Hay que educarlos.

1 wood   2 cows   3 exercise

❷ Contesta las preguntas sobre la entrevista.

1. ¿Por qué se cortan muchos árboles?
2. ¿Qué hace el gobierno de Costa Rica para apoyar la causa de Nelly?
3. ¿Qué recomienda Nelly para que la gente tome conciencia del problema?

❸ Trabaja con un(a) compañero(a) para crear un slogan o un anuncio que ayude a la gente a tomar conciencia de la importancia de no destruir las selvas tropicales.

410 cuatrocientos diez
Manos a la obra 2

Universal Access

Heritage Language Learners

Ask students who have lived in a heritage country if they would volunteer to be interviewed. As the topic, ask them to identify a natural resource or geographic area of the heritage country. Have other students model their questions on those posed to Nelly Anderson in *Actividad* 28.

Multiple Intelligences

Visual/Spatial: Once students have chosen the theme that concerns them the most in *Actividad* 30, have them create a public awareness poster or pamphlet. How could they use art and design to inform the public and improve the situation?

Actividad 29 — Hablar/Escribir

Para el futuro

❶ En grupos de tres o cuatro estudiantes escojan uno de estos temas. Hagan una lista de todas las palabras o expresiones relacionadas con ese tema.

- los derrames de petróleo
- se disminuyen los árboles en las selvas tropicales
- los animales que están en peligro de extinción
- el agujero en la capa de ozono
- el recalentamiento global
- la falta de preservación de la flora del planeta

❷ Luego diseñen un cartel para que la gente de su comunidad tome conciencia del problema que han escogido. Indiquen qué cosas hace la gente diariamente que producen el problema y lo que se puede hacer para mejorar la situación.

Cada vez que usas un vaso de plástico cuando puedes usar un vaso de vidrio, creas basura que no es necesaria.

Actividad 30 —  Leer/Escribir/Hablar

Y tú, ¿qué dices?

1. ¿Puedes nombrar animales en el mundo que estén en peligro de extinción? Usa un diccionario para buscar los nombres en español. ¿Por qué es importante salvar a los animales que están en peligro de extinción?

2. ¿Cómo han cambiado la Tierra las personas? Escribe una lista de cuatro o cinco cosas que han hecho.

3. ¿Qué te preocupa más? Pon en orden la lista de temas, de lo más a lo menos serio, en tu opinión. Después explica por qué te preocupa el tema que escogiste como el más serio.

   a. el recalentamiento global
   b. la amenaza de una guerra nuclear
   c. la destrucción de las selvas tropicales
   d. la caza excesiva de los animales
   e. la falta o escasez de recursos naturales
   f. la contaminación de las aguas
   g. el derretimiento de los glaciares
   h. las nuevas enfermedades
   i. la violencia en la sociedad

4. ¿De qué se preocupan tus compañeros(as)? Haz una encuesta en tu clase para conocer la opinión de los demás estudiantes. Comparte los resultados con el resto de la clase.

Practice and Communicate (9)

Actividad 29

Standards: 1.1, 1.2, 1.3

Focus: Using new vocabulary and structures in the creation of a poster

Suggestions: Allow students to use and expand upon their slogans or ads from *Actividad* 28 in the posters they create here.

Answers will vary.

Actividad 30

Standards: 1.1, 1.2, 3.1

Focus: Practicing new vocabulary and structures

Recycle: present perfect tense

Suggestions: Have groups compile the information that they wrote in item 2. Encourage them to use some of this information, as well as the prioritizing they did in item 3, when they conduct their interviews in item 4.

Answers will vary.

Additional Resources

- Writing, Audio & Video Workbook: Cap. 9, Audio Activity 3, Track 11
- Writing, Audio & Video Workbook: Cap. 9, Writing Activity 10
- Resource Book: Cap. 9, Communicative Activity BLM

✓ **Assessment**
- Prueba 9-6: Vocabulary production

 Enriching Your Teaching

Culture Note

In 1998, together with the Costa Rican National Accreditation Commission, the Costa Rican Tourism Institute developed a "Certification for Sustainable Tourism." Tourism companies, from guides to hotels, apply to be rated on a system of sustainability levels from 0 to 5; 0 being unsustainable and 5 being the most sustainable. Companies are rated according to their management of natural, cultural, and social resources. The ratings help tourists choose companies that work to sustain the country's natural and cultural resources. They also prevent companies from using labels such as "eco" or "green" without following through on those efforts.

Block Schedule

Total the individual class results for *Actividad* 30, item 3. Determine the top three environmental concerns. Ask students to write whether they agree or disagree with the top choices. Have each student present their opinion to the class.

411

Gramática
Presentation

Standards: 4.1

Resources: Voc. & Gram. Transparencies: 179

Suggestions: Point out to students that here, just as in past *Gramática* presentations concerned with the subjunctive, the key to understanding its use is the concept of hypothetical actions or situations. If a situation has not yet occurred, or is only being considered as a possibility, the subjunctive is used.

Actividad 31

Standards: 1.2

Resources: Practice Answers on Transparencies

Focus: Practicing the subjunctive and the indicative with conjunctions

Suggestions: Ask students to complete the activity on their own. Then have them share their answers and discuss their reasons for choosing the subjunctive or the indicative.

Answers:
1. sepamos
2. se molesten
3. disminuya
4. haya
5. desaparezcan

Actividad 32

Standards: 1.2, 1.3

Focus: Practicing the subjunctive with conjunctions

Suggestions: Encourage students to refer back to the rules in the *Gramática* as often as necessary in order to complete the activity.

Answers will vary. Students will use subjunctive verb forms in the subordinate clauses.

Gramática

Más conjunciones que se usan con el subjuntivo y el indicativo

The following conjunctions are usually followed by the subjunctive to express the purpose or intention of an action:

a menos que *unless*
sin que *without*
con tal (de) que *provided (that)*

para que *so that*
aunque *although, even though*

Te doy este libro **para que** tengas más información sobre la capa de ozono.

If the subject of the sentence does not change, use the infinitive after *para* and *sin*.

No puedes saber el final **sin ver** la película.

With the conjunction *aunque*, use the subjunctive to express uncertainty. Use the indicative when there is no uncertainty. Compare the following:

Aunque llueve vamos a la reserva natural.
Although it is raining, we're going to the nature preserve.

Aunque llueva, vamos a la reserva natural.
Although it may rain, we're going to the nature preserve.

Actividad 31 **Gramática** **Leer/Escribir**

En el zoológico

Completa las frases sobre el zoológico con el subjuntivo del verbo apropiado.

1. Nos han dado información para que (nosotros) *(producir / saber)* más.
2. El guardia del zoológico limpia el lugar de las focas sin que (ellas) *(molestarse / derretirse)*.
3. Un cartel dice que la ballena azul desaparecerá a menos que su caza *(disminuir / aumentar)*.
4. Aunque *(explotar / haber)* contaminación el río parece limpio.
5. Se construyen reservas para que los animales salvajes no *(desaparecer / afectar)*.

Actividad 32 **Gramática** **Leer/Hablar**

El rescate

Imagina que se produjo un derrame de petróleo y estás organizando la limpieza y el rescate de animales. Completa las frases de una manera lógica.

1. Nosotros vamos a trabajar hasta tarde con tal de que Uds. . . .
2. No pueden tocarles la piel a las focas a menos que . . .
3. Leonardo y María, Uds. deben limpiar el área sin . . .
4. Vayan a hablar con la gente del barco que lleva petróleo aunque ellos . . .
5. Escribe un informe sobre el rescate para que la gente . . .

412 cuatrocientos doce
Manos a la obra 2

Universal Access

Advanced Learners

On separate slips of paper, have students write three subordinate clauses beginning with conjunctions taught in the *Gramática* on this page. If they use **aunque,** allow them to use either the infinitive or the subjunctive in the clause. Collect the strips, mix them, and place them in a container. Have students meet in a circle, take turns drawing one subordinate clause at a time, and completing a complex sentence by inventing a suitable independent clause.

Actividad 33 Gramática Leer/Escribir

¡Delicioso!

Una empresa que crea anuncios para revistas necesita tu ayuda. Completa los anuncios usando la conjunción apropiada de la página 412. Usa como modelo el anuncio sobre el turrón, un alimento dulce en forma de tableta típico de España.

1. El chocolate . . . cómelo _____ te sientas más dulce.

2. ¡No manejes este coche _____ todos lleven su cinturón de seguridad (seat belts)!

3. El único teléfono celular que funciona _____ estés bajo tierra.

4. El reloj que sigue funcionando durante un año _____ cambies la pila.

5. ¡Salgan de casa! Vengan de viaje con nosotros . . . ¡_____ tengan niñero!

En voz alta

José Martí (1853–1895) fue una de las grandes figuras históricas y literarias de América. Además de escribir poesía, artículos periodísticos y muchísimos ensayos, Martí dedicó su vida a la lucha por la libertad de Cuba. Fue uno de los fundadores del modernismo, un estilo literario que se caracteriza por su interés en la belleza y el estilo. La poesía de Martí es directa y clara. *Versos sencillos,* del cual las siguientes estrofas representan una pequeña parte, refleja la visión que tenia del mundo. Escucha las estrofas y luego contesta las preguntas.

• Según el poema, ¿cómo es el poeta?

• ¿Cómo el poeta le da importancia a la naturaleza en el poema?

De versos sencillos, 1891
José Martí

Yo soy un hombre sincero
de donde crece la palma,
y antes de morirme, quiero
echar mis versos del alma.[1]

Yo vengo de todas partes,
y hacia todas partes voy:
arte soy entre las artes,
en los montes,[2] monte soy.

---

1 Soul 2 forests

¿Recuerdas?

Generalmente se divide una palabra en sílabas después de una vocal o entre las consonantes. Cada línea de estas estrofas de *Versos sencillos* tiene ocho sílabas. Escribe el poema en una hoja de papel y divide las palabras en sílabas.

Actividad 33

Standards: 1.2

Resources: Practice Answers on Transparencies

Focus: Practicing the subjunctive with conjunctions

Suggestions: Students will enjoy sharing their responses for these items. After they complete the activity, invite them to do so in round-robin fashion.

Answers:
1. para que
2. a menos que / sin que
3. aunque
4. sin que
5. Answers will vary.

En voz alta

Presentation

Standards: 1.1, 1.2, 2.2, 3.1, 3.2, 5.2

Resources: Audio Program: Cap. 9, Track 13

Suggestions: After students read the poem, encourage them to write a few lines of poetry to describe themselves and their relationship with nature.

Answers:
• Es un hombre sincero que quiere escribir poesía.
• Dice que, en los montes, el poeta es monte también; por lo tanto, el poeta es parte de la naturaleza.

Additional Resources

• Writing, Audio & Video Workbook: Cap. 9, Audio Activity 4, Track 12

Enriching Your Teaching

Culture Note

Turrón, translated as "nougat," is a Spanish sweet with Arabic origins. The traditional recipe calls for almonds, honey, and eggs. These ingredients can be combined to form *alicante,* a hard nougat with whole almonds, or *jijona,* a soft nougat with crushed almonds. *Turrones* are traditionally eaten at Christmas time, especially after Christmas dinner with coffee. Today, many varieties of the traditional candy are available, including nougats made with peanuts, hazelnuts, coconut, or covered in chocolate.

Actividad 34

Standards: 1.1

Focus: Practicing the subjunctive with conjunctions

Suggestions: Remind students that the model shows just one possible way to use the cues. Encourage Student A to begin the questions in other ways besides **¿Qué va a suceder....** If necessary, suggest other possibilities, such as: **¿Estaremos capaces de parar...?** or **¿Qué se puede hacer con respecto a...?**

Answers will vary. Student B will use the subjunctive after the conjunction.

Actividad 35

Standards: 1.1, 1.2

Focus: Practicing the subjunctive and the indicative with conjunctions

Suggestions: Point out to students that not all of the subordinate clauses they write must begin with **tú.** It is a given in items 2 and 6, but in the other items they can use different subjects.

Answers will vary. Students will use the subjunctive in the subordinate clauses, with the possible exception of number 5 after **aunque.**

Chapter Project

Students can perform step 5 at this point. Record their presentations on cassette or videotape for inclusion in their portfolios. (For more information, see p. 384-a.)

Actividad 34 **Gramática** **Hablar**

Cómo cuidar el planeta

Imagina que vas a una conferencia sobre cómo cuidar el planeta en que vivimos. En ella se habla sobre diferentes temas ambientales. Trabaja con un(a) compañero(a) para hacer preguntas y respuestas sobre los temas de la conferencia.

Modelo

el recalentamiento global / a menos que
A —¿Qué va a suceder con el recalentamiento global?
B —A menos que los gobiernos no tomen conciencia del problema, el recalentamiento global aumentará cada año.

¡Cuidemos el planeta!

Conferencia sobre el medio ambiente

• Oportunidades para hacer trabajo voluntario
• Ideas para tu comunidad
• Nuevos productos para proteger el planeta

sábado 3 de mayo

Proyecto Limpieza

Estudiante A

1. la caza excesiva
2. la destrucción de árboles en la selva tropical
3. la capa de ozono
4. las reservas naturales del planeta
5. la contaminación de los ríos
6. la extinción de algunos animales
7. los derrames de petróleo

Estudiante B

a menos que
para que
sin que
con tal (de) que
aunque
sin

Actividad 35 **Gramática** **Leer/Hablar**

Ecoturismo en Chile

Imagina que vas a hacer ecoturismo a Chile con un(a) amigo(a). Como él (ella) todavía no ha llegado, le cuentas tus planes por teléfono. Completa las frases de una manera apropiada.

1. Visitaremos varias reservas naturales a menos que . . .

2. No saldré hasta que tú . . .

3. Iremos a una conferencia sobre la capa de ozono con tal que . . .

4. Sacaremos fotos de las especies del lugar para que . . .

5. Nos quedaremos en un pueblo cerca del océano aunque . . .

6. No haré nada sin que tú . . .

7. Planearemos nuestras excursiones en cuanto . . .

414 cuatrocientos catorce
Manos a la obra 2

Universal Access

Students with Learning Difficulties

Before students read **Victoria parcial para las ballenas** on p. 415, ask them to preview the questions. Have them record a "shorthand" for the main idea of each question. For example: **1) ¿religioso o natural? 2) ¿Qué dos votaciones?** Remind students to consider these notes as they read the passage.

Advanced Learners

Have students create an adapted version of *Actividad* 35. In their version, ask them to include information about an actual ecotourism spot in Latin America. They can research this information on the Internet.

Actividad 36 Gramática Leer/Escribir

Las ballenas en peligro

1 Lee la noticia del periódico acerca de la reunión anual de la Comisión Ballenera Internacional.

2 Ahora, responde a las preguntas.

1. En el artículo se habla de un santuario. En este contexto, ¿un santuario es un lugar religioso o un refugio natural?

2. ¿Qué dos votaciones se realizaron en la reunión de la Comisión Ballenera Internacional?

3. ¿Crees que ha sido un hecho positivo que Japón no haya obtenido votos suficientes en la votación?

4. ¿Qué se lograría con la creación del santuario de las ballenas?

5. ¿Has ido alguna vez a un lugar donde se pueda observar a las ballenas? Descríbelo.

Victoria parcial para las ballenas

Con una derrota (defeat) para la ambición de Japón de volver a practicar la caza comercial de ballenas, finalizó la reunión anual de la Comisión Ballenera Internacional. El gobierno de Japón no pudo obtener votos suficientes para que se le permitiera continuar con la caza de ballenas.

En tanto, el proyecto presentado por los gobiernos de Argentina y Brasil de crear un Santuario Ballenero del Atlántico Sur no obtuvo el 75% de los votos necesarios en la votación para ser aprobado.

Desde hace más de tres años las organizaciones ecológicas trabajan para lograr la creación de un santuario en el Atlántico Sur que ofrecería la protección que las ballenas necesitan y beneficiaría a las actividades científicas, educativas y turísticas en la región.

El español en el mundo del trabajo

Rescatista internacional en Sudamérica

En los países de habla hispana existen brigadas de rescate que ayudan a las víctimas de tragedias como, por ejemplo, la ocurrida en el terremoto del 13 de enero de 2001 en San Vicente, El Salvador. Para desempeñar (perform) este trabajo se necesita entrenamiento, equipo y conocimiento del idioma para comunicarse y coordinarse con los demás rescatistas (rescuers). No importa cual sea la especialidad del rescatista: primeros auxilios, excavación, demolición o control de incendios, hablar español le permite al rescatista trabajar en equipo con las otras organizaciones nacionales. Hoy día, existen numerosos grupos, tanto oficiales como no oficiales, que desempeñan esta labor tan importante.

• ¿Conoces a algún grupo de rescatistas?

• ¿Te gustaría trabajar como rescatista?

● **Más práctica**
Practice Workbook 9-10, 9-11, 9-12

Go Online PHSchool.com

For: Practice with the subjunctive after conjuctions
Visit: www.phschool.com
Web Code: jed-0908

cuatrocientos quince **415**
Capítulo 9

 9

Practice and Communicate

Actividad 36
Standards: 1.1, 1.2, 3.1

Focus: Practicing new vocabulary and structures via reading and response

Suggestions: Have students note down their ideas for responses to the questions on their own. Tell them their notes do not have to be in the form of complete sentences. Have them use these notes as they discuss the questions with a partner or in a group.

Answers:
1. En este contexto un santuario es un refugio natural.
2. Se votó para que no se permitiera a Japón continuar con la caza de ballenas y sobre un proyecto para crear un santuario ballenero.
3–5. Answers will vary.

El español en el mundo del trabajo
Presentation

Standards: 1.1, 1.2, 3.1, 5.2

Suggestions: Once students have read the information, ask comprehension questions. For example: *¿Cuáles son unas especialidades de los rescatistas? (Son primeros auxilios, excavación, demolición y control de incendios.)*

Answers will vary.

Additional Resources
• Writing, Audio & Video Workbook: Cap. 9, Audio Activity 5, Track 14
• Writing, Audio & Video Workbook: Cap. 9, Writing Activities 11–13
• Resource Book: Cap. 9, Communicative Activity BLM

 Assessment
• Prueba 9-7: *Conjunciones que se usan con el subjuntivo y el indicativo*
• Examen: Vocabulario y gramática 2

Enriching Your Teaching

Culture Note

In 1998, Brazil and Argentina proposed a South Atlantic whale sanctuary, stretching from the equator to Antarctica, and from the eastern coast of South America to the western coast of Africa. But the idea of whale sanctuaries is not new. In 1979, the IWC instituted a sanctuary in the Indian Ocean, and in 1994 the whales around Antarctica came under protection. Although there has been an international moratorium on commercial whaling since 1986, some countries still find loopholes that allow them to hunt these great mammals. Before whaling, there were 100,000 humpbacks in the waters of the Southern Hemisphere. Today, there are estimated to be only 10,000.

Puente a la cultura

Presentation

Standards: 1.2, 3.1

Focus: Reading to learn about the Galápagos Islands

Suggestions:

Pre-reading: Refer students to the *Estrategia* and have them read the topic sentences from the selection in order to better understand the information. Ask them to share background knowledge they may have about the function of topic sentences from their Language Arts courses.

Reading: Help students resolve comprehension problems by asking *sí/no* or embedded-answer questions: *En el siglo XVI, ¿los barcos españoles fueron atacados por los piratas ingleses o por los piratas peruanos? (por los piratas ingleses) ¿El exceso de tortugas es uno de los problemas que enfrenta las islas Galápagos? (No, pero un problema es el exceso de la población humana.)*

Post-reading: Ask volunteers to tell in their own words about the important details that support the topic sentence in each paragraph of the selection.

Country Connection

Presentation

Standards: 3.1

Resources: Voc. & Gram. Transparencies: 17 (map)

Ecuador's official name for the Galápagos Islands is the ***Archipiélago de Colón.*** Before the historical events presented on these pages, it is thought that people from the northern part of the Incan Empire, the Chimu, were present here. The islands were "discovered" by Europeans in 1535, when the Bishop of Panama's ship was blown off course on its way to Peru. The archipelago consists of eight major islands, thirteen smaller ones, and forty islets. Besides the turtles mentioned in the reading selection, the islands are famous for their iguanas, of which there are two types: the sea iguana and the land iguana (pictured on p. 417).

¡Adelante!

Puente a la cultura

Galápagos: el encuentro con la naturaleza

Objectives

- Read about the history of the Galapagos islands
- Learn about the endangered species of the Galapagos
- Use topic sentences for reading comprehension

Estrategia

Using topic sentences to orient you
In this text, you will read about the history of a particular place. As you read, notice how the topic sentence of each paragraph helps orient you. Each topic sentence contains a date, and the paragraph then discusses a particular period in history. As you read, think about what other information the topic sentence provides to set the scene for the rest of the paragraph.

Las islas Galápagos son un archipiélago de más de cincuenta islas que se encuentran en el Océano Pacífico a 800 kilómetros de la costa del Ecuador. Estas islas, que forman una provincia del Ecuador, son de origen volcánico y se ubican[1] directamente en la línea ecuatorial. Las islas son famosas por sus tortugas gigantes, que pueden vivir más de 100 años.

A finales del siglo XVI los piratas ingleses se establecieron en el archipiélago para atacar los barcos españoles que traían riquezas del Perú. Los piratas descubrieron que la carne de las tortugas gigantes era una excelente fuente de alimentos. Además, las tortugas podían vivir en los barcos, sin comida ni agua, por muchos meses.

A finales del siglo XVIII llegaron los balleneros. Pronto comenzaron a cazar las tortugas con la misma velocidad con que cazaban las ballenas. Se cree que mataron alrededor de 200,000 tortugas.

En 1835, un joven inglés de 22 años llamado Charles Darwin llegó a las islas en el barco *H.M.S. Beagle* y pasó cinco semanas estudiando su fauna. Las ideas centrales de su libro fundamental, *El origen de las especies*, nacieron a partir de su viaje en el *Beagle*. La teoría propone[2] que las tortugas son las especies más fuertes que sobreviven[3] a través del tiempo.

1 they are located 2 proposes 3 survive

416 cuatrocientos dieciséis
¡Adelante!

Universal Access

Students with Learning Difficulties
Assign each paragraph of the reading to a small group of students. Direct each group to create a picture based on the main idea of their paragraph. Then, have students arrange their pictures by date to create a pictorial timeline of the reading's main ideas.

Advanced Learners
Ask students to research a Galápagos animal on the Internet. Have them present brief oral reports in which they present a few interesting facts about their chosen animal.

En 1935 el gobierno ecuatoriano decidió establecer una reserva natural de flora y fauna en las islas. En esa época, 3 de las 14 especies de tortugas habían desaparecido junto con algunos mamíferos y aves del lugar. En 1959 se creó la Fundación Charles Darwin para las islas Galápagos. Su trabajo de investigación y protección de los animales logró salvar varias especies que estaban por desaparecer.

El turismo organizado comenzó en 1970, pero se han implementado estrictas reglas para el cuidado de la fauna del lugar. Hoy en día las islas enfrentan muchos problemas, como el exceso de población y la falta de recursos del gobierno ecuatoriano para proteger su flora y fauna. Pero muchos colaboran para preservar este lugar único . . . y sus tortugas gigantes.

¿Comprendiste?

1. Usando las frases que empiezan cada párrafo, dibuja una línea de tiempo identificando los períodos de tiempo en la historia de las islas Galápagos de los que habla el artículo.

2. ¿A qué país pertenecen las islas Galápagos? ¿Dónde se encuentran?

3. ¿Por qué se establecieron en Galápagos los piratas ingleses?

4. ¿Qué logró la Fundación Charles Darwin para las islas Galápagos?

5. ¿Qué problemas enfrentan hoy en día las islas?

Go Online
PHSchool.com

For: Internet link activity
Visit: www.phschool.com
Web Code: jed-0910

Galápagos Islands
ECUADOR

cuatrocientos diecisiete   417
Capítulo 9

¿Comprendiste?

Standards: 1.2, 1.3

Resources: Practice Answers on Transparencies

Focus: Demonstrating reading comprehension

Suggestions: Have students write their responses to the questions on their own. For item 1, ask them to write a brief identifying detail at each point on their time line.

Answers:
1. Siglo XVI, piratas ingleses descubren las tortugas gigantes; siglo XVIII, llegada de los balleneros; 1835, llegada de Charles Darwin; 1935, creación de la reserva natural; 1959, Fundación Charles Darwin para las islas Galápagos; 1970, comienzo del turismo organizado
2. Las islas Galápagos forman una provincia del Ecuador. Se ubican directamente en la línea ecuatorial en el Océano Pacífico, a 800 kilómetros de la costa del Ecuador.
3. Los piratas ingleses se establecieron en Galápagos porque querían atacar los barcos españoles que traían riquezas del Perú.
4. La Fundación Charles Darwin logró salvar varias especies que estaban por desaparecer.
5. Hoy en día las islas enfrentan muchos problemas, como el exceso de población y la falta de recursos del gobierno ecuatoriano para proteger su flora y fauna.

Portfolio

Keep students' responses to the *¿Comprendiste?* questions in their portfolios as a writing sample.

Go Online

The online atlas will provide a more detailed map of Ecuador and the Archipiélago de Colón.

Video
Presentation

Standards: 1.2

Resources: Video Program, Cap. 9

In this segment we explore the importance of establishing a balance between the world's economic needs and the desire to protect the natural environment in Latin America. Nature reserves in San Ramón, Costa Rica and the Galapagos Islands are highlighted. See the *Video Teacher's Guide* for additional suggestions.

Enriching Your Teaching

Culture Note
The Galápagos Islands are part of Ecuador's national park system. The human population lives in roughly five percent of the islands' area that is not a park. One of the main challenges facing the wildlife of the islands today is the introduction by humans of animals such as pigs and goats, which destroy natural habitats, and rats, which prey on the young of wild animals.

Internet Search
Keyword: Archipiélago de Colón

417

¿Qué me cuentas?

Presentation

Standards: 1.1, 1.2, 1.3

Resources: Voc. & Gram. Transparencies: 180; Audio Program: CD Cap. 9, Track 15; Resource Book: Cap. 9, Audio Script; Practice Answers on Transparencies

Focus: Practicing speaking and listening comprehension

Suggestions:

For step 1, use the *Audio CD* or read the script aloud. Allow students to hear the descriptions twice through: the first time to write their answers and the second time to check them.

For step 2, have students review the rules on pp. 398 and 412 for use of the subjunctive or the indicative after conjunctions, before they complete the task.

Answers:

Step1
1. b   2. a   3. a   4. b   5. b   6. a

Steps 2–3
Answers will vary.

¿Qué me cuentas?

Unas vacaciones inolvidables

1 🎧 Escucha estas descripciones. Después de cada párrafo vas a oír dos preguntas. Escoge la mejor respuesta para cada una.

1. a. Se quemó en una fogata en una excursión de cámping.
   b. Se quemó en el sol.

2. a. Le explicó que en esa zona existía un agujero en la capa de ozono.
   b. Le explicó que en esa zona existía el efecto invernadero.

3. a. Le aconsejó que se cubriera el cuerpo si iba a la playa.
   b. Le aconsejó que se quedara en el mar si iba a la playa.

4. a. Catalina fue a la playa con sus amigas y llevó crema protectora.
   b. Catalina pasó unos días sin ir a la playa.

5. a. Empezó a pensar que la crema protectora para el sol era muy buena.
   b. Empezó a pensar en el medio ambiente.

6. a. Decidió proteger más el medio ambiente.
   b. Decidió usar más recursos naturales en su comunidad.

2 Estas ilustraciones representan un cuento. Con tus propias palabras, describe detalladamente lo que sucedió. Recuerda que no puedes usar tus notas mientras cuentas el cuento. Añade información para que el cuento resulte más interesante. ¡Usa tu imaginación!
Puedes usar las siguientes palabras o expresiones para conectar tus ideas.

antes de que	tan pronto como	cuando	en cuanto
hasta que	después (de) que	mientras	aunque

1

2

3

4

5

3 Trabaja con un grupo de seis estudiantes. Cada miembro del grupo describe uno de los dibujos. Uno de los miembros toma notas de las descripciones. Al terminar, lee sus notas y comenta con sus compañeros los detalles del cuento.

418 cuatrocientos dieciocho
¡Adelante!

Campaña para limpiar la comunidad

Tarea
Imagínate que vas a organizar una campaña para limpiar tu comunidad. Tienes que convencer a tus compañeros de que es necesario mantener limpia la ciudad para evitar la contaminación. Haz un discurso persuasivo para presentar tus ideas.

1 Prepárate
Completa una red de palabras como la siguiente con las razones de por qué es importante mantener limpia la comunidad.

¿Por qué hay que mantener limpia la comunidad?

2 Practica
Vuelve a leer la información de la tabla. Practica tu presentación para recordar los detalles. Puedes usar tus notas para practicar, pero no al hablar ante la clase. Recuerda:

- explicar cada razón en forma clara
- presentar un plan a tus compañeros de lo que deben hacer
- mirar al público y hablar con voz clara y persuasiva
- usar el vocabulario que aprendiste en el capítulo

Modelo
Existen muchas razones para que mantengamos limpia nuestra comunidad. Es importante que sepamos que la contaminación se puede evitar. Cada uno de nosotros puede contribuir con la tarea.

3 Haz tu presentación
Imagina que tus compañeros de clase son los que van a ayudar a limpiar la comunidad. Explícales por qué es importante mantener limpia la comunidad.

4 Evaluación
Tu profesor(a) puede explicarte cómo va a evaluar tu presentación. Probablemente, para el (ella) es importante ver que:

- tu presentación fue convincente
- diste suficientes razones y soluciones
- tu conclusión resumió las ideas principales del discurso

Estrategia

Finding good details
When giving a speech, you need to include appropriate details in order to make sense when talking about your topic. Interesting details add color and life to what you talk about and give it more substance. A good way to choose the right details to include is to ask these questions: *Who? What? Where? Why? When? How?*

cuatrocientos diecinueve 419
Capítulo 9

Presentación oral

Presentation

Standards: 1.1, 1.2, 1.3, 3.1, 5.1

Resources: Voc. & Gram. Transparencies 5

Focus: Preparing and delivering an oral presentation

Suggestions: Review the task and the four-step approach with students. Review the rubric with the class (see *Assessment* below) to explain how you will grade the performance task. Before students begin, direct their attention to the *Estrategia*. Remind students of how the inclusion of details made for interesting reading in the *Puente a la cultura* section on pp. 416–417. Show *Vocabulary and Grammar Transparency* 5 and have students create a similar word web on their own paper. Model how to include in the web some details related to the topic that would make for an interesting and persuasive speech. These might be details about a litter problem or a clean-up program at your own school.

Portfolio

Record students' oral presentations on audiocassette or videotape for inclusion in their portfolios.

✓ Assessment

• Assessment Program: Cap. 9, Rubrics

Give students copies of the rubric before they begin the activity. Go over the descriptions of the different levels of performance. After assessing students, help individuals understand how their performance could be improved.

Enriching Your Teaching

RUBRIC	Score 1	Score 3	Score 5
How well you organize information	The information you present is not well organized.	Your information is somewhat organized but hard to follow.	Your information is well organized and easy to follow.
How well you use details	You do not include details that make your speech interesting.	Your details are too few; some do not belong with your main idea.	Your details are interesting and support your main idea.
How effectively you deliver your speech	You read your speech and make no eye contact with your audience.	You make some eye contact, and you use some intonation.	Your eye contact is good. Your intonation helps you persuade.

Block Schedule

You might videotape the presentations and have each student watch his or her presentation at a later time. Have each student evaluate the presentation from the perspective of being effective:
Good eye contact, clear speaking voice, convincing tone of voice.

Communicate: Writing

9

Presentación escrita

Presentation

Standards: 1.3, 3.1

Resources: Voc. & Gram. Transparencies 4

Focus: Combining learned vocabulary and structures in a written presentation

Suggestions: Begin by explaining the criteria you will use to evaluate students' compositions. (See step 5, *Evaluación*, in the Student Edition, and *Assessment* on the following page.)

Direct students' attention to the *Estrategia*. Remind them that an effective conclusion of a composition or letter almost always restates the main idea in other words. For this assignment, it should also help persuade. Then show *Vocabulary & Grammar Transparency* 4. Model filling in information like that shown in the chart on this page, and have students follow along on their own paper. Have them continue adding ideas to their charts that will help them develop their own compositions. Encourage them to do some outside research in order to find additional facts and interesting details that will improve their compositions.

Language Arts Connection

Standards: 3.1

Encourage students to draw on background knowledge they have from their Language Arts courses about introductions and conclusions in formal speaking and writing. Remind them that introductions and conclusions act as signposts to prepare the reader for the information presented and to summarize the information so it is easier to remember.

Presentación escrita

Cuidemos nuestros océanos

Objectives

- Write a petition letter to an oil company
- Give reasons and details to explain why the petition is being made
- Summarize ideas in a conclusion

Estrategia

Good conclusions
It's always a good idea to end what you write with a good conclusion that draws your main ideas together. For example, your conclusion can review ideas you introduced earlier and give a few sentences that tie them together. Your conclusion can also summarize your main idea in other words, or it can close with an interesting comment that leaves your reader wanting to know more about your topic.

Imagínate que trabajas como voluntario(a) en una asociación de defensa de la preservación de los océanos. Tienes que escribir una carta a una empresa petrolera para que tome conciencia de los problemas que producen los derrames de petróleo en las aguas del planeta y qué cosas se pueden hacer para evitarlos. Puedes concentrarte en los problemas que producen en su flora y fauna y las consecuencias que esto tiene para las personas.

Antes de escribir

Completa una tabla como la siguiente para reunir datos sobre los problemas que producen los derrames de petróleo en las aguas de los océanos.

Problemas que causan los derrames	Cómo se pueden evitar
• destrucción de las plantas	• tener cuidado
• contaminación del alimento de los peces	• tomar conciencia de los peligros
•	•
•	•
•	•

2 Borrador

Escribe tu borrador de la carta. Explica cómo afectan los derrames de petróleo a las aguas de los océanos y qué se puede hacer para evitarlos. Añade todos los detalles que sean necesarios. Recuerda usar el vocabulario y la gramática de este capítulo.

420 cuatrocientos veinte
¡Adelante!

Universal Access

Heritage Language Learners

Students may have difficulty organizing their writing into formal, cohesive paragraphs. Have students write the topic sentence of each paragraph they plan to include at the top of an index card. Then have them add supporting details below. Remind them that each card will constitute one paragraph.

Advanced Learners

Encourage students to experiment with more than one attempt at a concluding paragraph for their letters. They might simply summarize the ideas presented in the body of the composition, restate the introduction in other words, or ask a question or two that will keep their readers thinking about the implications of what they have said.

Modelo

Estimado Sr. López:

Mi nombre es Enrique Lomas y trabajo como voluntario en una asociación de defensa de la preservación de los océanos. Le escribo esta carta para que ustedes tomen conciencia de lo importante que es la preservación de las aguas de nuestro planeta y de la flora y la fauna que viven en ellas.

Topic sentence: set the purpose of the letter.

Details: add information about the topic.

Es importante que se eviten los derrames de petróleo en los océanos antes de que sea demasiado tarde. Los derrames de petróleo destruyen y contaminan los animales y las plantas que viven en los océanos. Esto afecta también a las personas . . .

Mi intención con esta carta es comunicarles que mientras la vida en los océanos no sea respetada no vamos a poder...

Conclusion: ties everything together.

3 Redacción/Revisión

Después de escribir el primer borrador, trabaja con otro(a) compañero(a) para intercambiar los trabajos y leerlos. Decidan qué aspectos son más efectivos. Luego, hagan sugerencias para mejorar sus composiciones. Fíjense si:

- ¿Se usó correctamente el subjuntivo o el indicativo después de las conjunciones?
- ¿Hay concordancia *(agreement)* entre los sujetos y los verbos?
- ¿Existen errores de ortografía?

En caso de algún error, corríjanlo.

4 Publicación

Antes de hacer la versión final, lee de nuevo tu borrador y repasa los siguientes puntos:

- ¿Muestra la carta mi punto de vista respecto al tema?
- ¿Incluí detalles para expresar lo que pienso?
- ¿Refleja la importancia de comprender el problema?
- ¿Presenta una conclusión interesante?

Después de revisar el borrador, escribe una copia en limpio de tu composición.

Le escribo esta carta para que ustedes
~~toman~~ tomen conciencia de lo importante
que ~~son~~ es la ~~preservasión~~ preservación de las aguas de
nuestro planeta y de la flora y la fauna que
viven en ellas.

5 Evaluación

Tu profesor(a) puede explicarte cómo va a evaluar tu presentación. Probablemente, para tu profesor(a) es importante ver que:

- usaste suficientes detalles para hacer tu punto más interesante
- las frases tienen sentido y expresan una idea completa
- la carta muestra claramente tu opinión sobre el tema
- tu conclusión resume las ideas principales de la carta

cuatrocientos veintiuno   421
Capítulo 9

Suggestions (Cont'd):

In step 2, students should concentrate on how to develop and organize their ideas from the chart from step 1 into an effective sequence. This is also the step in which they should focus on an effective conclusion for their persuasive letter. Encourage them to work toward organization, level of detail, and language use similar to that shown in the model.

For step 3, encourage students to experiment with various ways of combining sentences. Remind them that this often entails use of the subjunctive. Have them follow the revision suggestions shown.

Evaluation

Steps 4 and 5 overlap. Students will need evaluation by you, their peers, or self-evaluation to fine-tune and polish their drafts.

Portfolio

Keep students' final drafts in their portfolios as a writing sample.

✓ **Assessment**

• Assessment Program: Cap. 9, Rubrics

Give students copies of the rubric before they begin the activity. Go over the descriptions of the different levels of performance. After assessing students, help individuals understand how their performance could be improved.

Enriching Your Teaching

RUBRIC	Score 1	Score 3	Score 5
Completion of task	Important parts of your letter are missing.	Parts of your letter are missing or disorganized.	You include and organize all the parts needed for a persuasive letter.
Effective Conclusion	Your letter lacks an effective conclusion.	Your letter has a conclusion, but it is not effective.	Your include an effective conclusion that helps persuade your readers.
Grammar, spelling, mechanics	You make many errors in grammar, spelling, and punctuation.	You make some errors in grammar, spelling, and punctuation.	You make very few errors in grammar, spelling, and punctuation.

Lectura

Presentation

Standards: 1.2, 3.1

Resources: Voc. & Gram. Transparencies: 4

Focus: Reading an extended passage

Suggestions:

Pre-reading: Before reading, direct students' attention to the *Estrategia* and *Al leer* sections. Have them begin a T-chart similar to the one on p. 425 and make sure they understand how they will use it. Point out that their T-charts will help them keep track of important details related to the points listed in *Al leer*. Have a volunteer read the subtitles of the passage aloud, so that the class can get an idea of how the information about monarch butterflies will be presented.

Reading: Allow students time to read the selection on their own silently. Consider assigning this task for homework. This will allow you to capitalize on class time to read it again together with students. When reading together, pause frequently to address comprehension issues they may have and to allow them to fill in their *Mariposa monarca* charts from p. 425. Ask comprehension questions to help them focus on the main idea and important details in sections of the reading. Suggestions for these begin on the next page.

Country Connection
Presentation

Standards: 3.1

Resources: Voc. & Gram. Transparencies 14 (map)

The state of Michoacán lies to the west of the state of México, (where Ciudad de México is located). Since it extends from the center of Mexico to the Pacific coast, Michoacán has a variety of climactic zones and terrains. It is primarily an agricultural and livestock-raising zone, specializing in lemons, corn, cotton, sugar cane, beef cattle and pigs. The capital of Michoacán is Morelia, a city with a population of nearly one million.

Go Online
The online atlas will provide a more detailed map of Mexico.

Lectura

La mariposa monarca

Estrategia

Context clues
It is impossible to know the meaning of every word you read, but by developing your guessing ability, you will be able to understand enough to guess at the total meaning of a sentence, paragraph, or essay. Sometimes you can discover the meaning of a word from other words, punctuation, or sentences in the paragraph. These clues are often called context clues.

Al leer

Vas a leer un artículo sobre la mariposa monarca. Como ocurre casi siempre en los textos de no ficción, encontrarás palabras relacionadas con el tema de las mariposas que quizás no conozcas. Recuerda que debes tratar de determinar su significado a partir del contexto antes de consultar el diccionario o pedir ayuda a otra persona. Antes de leer, copia la tabla que aparece al final de la lectura. Mientras lees, complétala para que puedas contestar las preguntas sobre la lectura. Presta atención a los siguientes puntos:

- la migración de la mariposa monarca
- características que diferencian a esta mariposa de las demás
- los problemas que amenazan a la mariposa monarca

Objectives

- **Read an article**
- **Understand the uniqueness of the Monarch butterfly**
- **Use context clues to figure out the meaning of a word**

Tres cuartas partes de los animales que viven en la tierra son insectos. De todos los insectos, quizás el más hermoso sea la mariposa monarca. Este insecto, además de ser increíblemente bello, es un importante agente polinizador[1] y un factor de equilibrio ecológico.

Las mariposas, en general, viven alrededor de 24 días; sin embargo, la mariposa monarca llega a vivir 9 meses, es decir, 12 veces más que las otras especies de mariposas. Además, es muy resistente a las condiciones del clima.

[1] pollen carrier

Universal Access

Heritage Language Learners
Ask students to read **La mariposa monarca** aloud. Have them model pronunciation, and encourage them to follow the rules of punctuation in their reading. They should briefly pause at each comma, and pause a bit longer at each period.

Students with Learning Difficulties
Students may have difficulty organizing the wealth of information provided in the non-fiction passage. Have them create their own concept webs around the theme of **la mariposa monarca.** As they encounter interesting facts in the reading, instruct them to record the information on their webs.

Llegada a México

Cada año, millones de mariposas monarca vuelan desde Canadá, lugar de donde provienen[2], hasta México. Llegan a fines de octubre a la zona entre Michoacán y el Estado de México y a mediados[3] de abril comienzan el viaje de regreso al norte. Es un viaje de más de 4,000 kilómetros.

En el camino, las mariposas se alimentan de asclepias[4], unas plantas que contienen una sustancia que es venenosa para otras especies. Esta sustancia le da a la mariposa un sabor y un olor desagradables, y esto le sirve de protección contra otros animales. La mariposa monarca también ayuda a la asclepia, pues es su agente de polinización.

Las condiciones de las montañas michoacanas son ideales para las mariposas: hay mucho oxígeno, están protegidas del viento y la temperatura es casi siempre agradable. Por otra parte, gracias a que los millones de mariposas que llegan a esta zona son agentes de polinización, hay una gran variedad de plantas en esta región.

Hibernación

Durante mucho tiempo se pensó que la mariposa monarca pasaba el invierno en zonas tropicales; pero nadie sabía adónde iban. Fue un misterio hasta 1975, en que después de décadas de investigación se encontró su lugar de hibernación. Para sorpresa de muchos, estaba en una zona donde las temperaturas normales están cerca de cero grados centígrados, en una región boscosa[5] entre valles y montañas. Esta región tiene una altitud promedio[6] de 3,300 metros sobre el nivel del mar, y se encuentra en la majestuosa Sierra Madre de México, entre Michoacán y el Estado de México.

Como la mariposa es un insecto de sangre fría, puede ajustar[7] la temperatura de su cuerpo al medio ambiente, lo que le permite conservar una gran cantidad de energía y grasa para su largo viaje de regreso.

Migración

Las mariposas monarca deben migrar en invierno porque el clima de Canadá es extremadamente frío durante esa estación. Para asegurar su sobrevivencia[8], las mariposas comienzan a desplazarse[9] al sur a medida que se acerca el invierno. Al llegar a las zonas de hibernación entre los estados de México y Michoacán, las mariposas buscan los lugares con la mejor temperatura para hibernar.

2 come from 3 in the middle of 4 milkweed

5 wooded 6 average 7 to adjust 8 survival 9 travel

La ruta de *las mariposas* monarca

CANADÁ
ESTADOS UNIDOS
MÉXICO

cuatrocientos veintitrés   423
Capítulo 9

Enriching Your Teaching

Teacher to Teacher

Monarch butterflies are present in many parts of the United States during one part of the year or another. Invite students to talk about personal sightings of monarch butterflies or other experiences they have had with insects. At what time of the year are they seen in your area?

If milkweed grows nearby, ask volunteers to bring in samples and tell where they found them. Interested students may wish to create a ***Centro de mariposas monarca*** in which they display photos and other information about the presence of monarch butterflies in your area.

El número de mariposas que llega a los diferentes refugios del Estado de México y Michoacán está entre los 100 y los 140 millones, de acuerdo con las condiciones de su hábitat de verano en Canadá y los Estados Unidos.

Sobrevivir[10] el invierno es una tarea difícil para las monarcas. También es importante el papel que juegan los depredadores[11], aves y pequeños mamíferos, ya que de las mariposas muertas el 50% muestra mutilaciones y señales de ataque. La mortalidad natural en invierno se acerca al 35% aunque cambia de acuerdo a las condiciones del clima.

Refugios

Los refugios son lugares donde se reúnen las monarcas para pasar el invierno y reproducirse; se trata de bosques localizados en las laderas de las montañas y que están resguardados[12] del aire polar y de los cambios del clima. Los refugios se localizan entre los 2,700 y 3,200 metros de altitud sobre el nivel del mar, dependiendo de las condiciones del clima de cada año.

Peligros

El 20 de mayo de 2001 hubo un incendio en la zona entre el Estado de México y Michoacán en donde se reproduce la mariposa monarca. A pesar de los esfuerzos, se quemaron más de 500 hectáreas de la reserva natural. Se cree que el fuego fue causado por un grupo de turistas que hicieron una fogata y no la apagaron totalmente cuando se fueron del lugar. Afortunadamente las mariposas no sufrieron daños, pues habían emigrado a Canadá desde marzo.

En febrero de 2003 el diario *The New York Times* informó que una tormenta de invierno en la zona de hibernación había causado la muerte de miles de mariposas durante el año anterior. Sin embargo, los científicos habían podido comprobar[13] que un año después la población de mariposas parecía haber recuperado[14] su nivel de años anteriores.

Las mariposas monarca son insectos bellos, útiles y resistentes. Debemos hacer todo lo posible para proteger los increíbles habitantes que comparten este planeta con nosotros.

10 to survive 11 predators 12 protected

13 to prove 14 recovered

Universal Access

Students with Learning Difficulties

Model for students how to transform each question into the base for their answer. For example: *¿Cuáles son los principales problemas que enfrentan las mariposas monarca? Los principales problemas que enfrentan las mariposas monarca son...*

Advanced Learners

Invite students to research and prepare brief reports on another kind of butterfly common to your area. Encourage them to make comparisons between the butterfly they research and the monarch.

Interacción con la lectura

1 Trabaja con un grupo de estudiantes para comentar lo que escribieron en sus tablas.

Mariposa monarca	
¿Dónde vive?	
¿Cuánto tiempo vive?	
¿De qué se alimenta?	
Otras características importantes	
¿Qué peligros la amenazan?	

- ¿En qué se diferencia la mariposa monarca de las demás mariposas?

- ¿Conoces otros animales que migran para pasar el invierno en otras zonas? ¿En qué se diferencian esos animales de las mariposas monarca?

- ¿Por qué podemos decir que las mariposas monarca no son solamente hermosas sino también muy útiles?

- ¿Cuáles son los principales problemas que enfrentan las mariposas monarca? ¿Qué podemos hacer para protegerlas?

2 Trabaja con tu grupo para buscar palabras de la lectura que no conocían. Hablen sobre cómo lograron determinar el significado de esas palabras para entender la lectura.

3 Y tú, ¿qué piensas? ¿Crees que las mariposas monarca son animales extraordinarios o no? ¿Qué otro animal conoces que te parece extraordinario? Habla de ese animal a tu grupo.

Fondo cultural

Festival Cultural de la Mariposa Monarca Desde hace 10 años, en los pueblos de Michoacán cercanos a los lugares donde hibernan las mariposas monarca, se celebra el Festival Cultural de la Mariposa Monarca. El Festival tiene como objetivo promover las artes de esos pueblos y el ecoturismo en la región oriental del estado de Michoacán.

La fiesta incluye música, danza, pintura y artesanías. La sede central del festival es Angangueo, ciudad que se hizo famosa desde que en 1976 se descubrió cerca de allí el primer santuario de las mariposas monarca. Durante los 16 días de festival, los artesanos trabajan en las plazas de los pueblos y venden sus obras a los visitantes.

- ¿Conoces algún festival que celebre la flora o fauna de tu región? Si es así, descríbelo.

cuatrocientos veinticinco **425**
Capítulo 9

Interacción con la lectura

Standards: 1.1, 1.2, 1.3, 3.1

Suggestions: As students work together in step 2, ask them to use their combined knowledge and context clues to resolve comprehension problems. Encourage them to use dictionaries as a last resort.

Answers:

Step 1
- **La mariposa monarca se diferencia de las demás mariposas porque vive 12 veces más que las otras especies. Además es muy resistente a las condiciones del clima.**
- **Answers will vary.**
- **Las mariposas monarca no son solamente hermosas sino también muy útiles porque son un importante agente polinizador y un factor de equilibrio ecológico.**
- **Los principales problemas que enfrentan son el clima, los depredadores y los incendios. The remainder of this answer will vary.**

Steps 2–3
Answers will vary.

Fondo cultural
Standards: 1.1, 1.2, 2.1, 3.1, 4.2

Suggestions: After students have read the information and answered the question, invite them to draft a letter to festival organizers in Mexico, telling them about a festival in your area that celebrates some plant or animal. In their letter, they should compare and contrast features of the *Festival Cultural de la Mariposa Monarca* and your local festival.

Answers will vary.

Enriching Your Teaching

Culture Note
One of the greatest threats to the monarch butterfly is to its natural environment. The forests in Michoacán offer a unique ecosystem. Hanging from fir trees, the monarchs achieve the perfect temperature for their winter hibernation. Unfortunately, this forest ecosystem only constitutes 2 percent of the total forest area in Mexico. In addition, there are people who depend on the logging and development of these areas for economic reasons. In 1986, the Reserva de la Biosfera Mariposa Monarca created two zones within the butterfly's habitat. In the "nuclear zone," no logging is allowed; in the "buffer zone," only limited logging is permitted.

Review Activities

Sobre la contaminación/Sobre el medio ambiente: Have students prepare their own Spanish definition for each vocabulary item in these categories. Then have teams of two students play against each other in a game of "Password." One student on a team gives his or her partner a definition. The partner must name the vocabulary item defined to earn a point. If he or she cannot, the other team gets a chance at the same definition. The team that correctly matches the greatest number of definitions and vocabulary items wins.

Sobre los recursos naturales: On their own, have students write three other words or expressions that are clearly associated with each item in this category. For example, for ***la protección,*** a student might write ***un santuario ballenero, una ley,*** and ***una reserva natural.*** Have students conduct the next part of the activity in round-robin fashion. One student says a word that he or she has written. The next student says which ***recursos naturales*** word it is associated with and explains the association.

Animales/Sobre los animales: Have students create their own fill-in-the-blanks exercises for these words. Tell them to create answer keys as well. Have them exchange exercises with a partner, complete each other's exercise, and check their answers together.

Otras palabras y expresiones: Students can use these words and expressions as they go over the review activities for the other categories and in the grammar review activities on the next page.

Verbos: Ask students to perform actions that they think portray the meanings of the verbs. Those watching must guess which verb is being acted out. Some verbs, such as ***derretir*** and ***castigar*** will be easy and fun to act out. Others like ***fomentar*** and ***promover*** present more of a challenge.

Repaso del capítulo

Vocabulario y gramática

sobre la contaminación

el aerosol	aerosol
la contaminación	pollution
contaminado, -a	polluted
el derrame de petróleo	oil spill
el desperdicio	waste
la fábrica	factory
el pesticida	pesticide
el petróleo	oil
la pila	battery
químico, -a	chemical
el recipiente	container
el veneno	poison

sobre los recursos naturales

económico, -a	economical
la protección	protection
el recurso natural	natural resource
suficiente	enough

verbos

afectar	to affect
agotar(se)	to exhaust, to run out
amenazar	to threaten
atrapar	to catch, to trap
castigar	to punish
colocar	to put, place
conservar	to preserve
crecer	to grow
dañar	to damage
depender de	to depend on
derretir	to melt
deshacerse de	to get rid of
desperdiciar	to waste
detener	to stop
disminuir	to decrease, to diminish
echar	to throw (away)
explotar	to exploit, to overwork
fomentar	to encourage
limitar	to limit
producir	to produce
promover (ue)l	to promote

sobre los animales

la caza	hunting
(en) peligro de extinción	(in) danger of extinction, endangered
la piel	skin
la pluma	feather
salvaje	wild

otras palabras y expresiones

el agujero	hole
la amenaza	threat
a menos que	unless
con tal que	provided that, as long as
debido a	due to
la electricidad	electricity
en cuanto	as soon as
la escasez	shortage
estar a cargo de	to be in charge of
excesivo, -a	excessive
la falta	lack
el gobierno	government
grave	serious
la limpieza	cleaning
tan pronto como	as soon as
tomar conciencia de	to become aware of
tomar medidas	to take steps (to)

sobre el medio ambiente

a atmósfera	atmosphere
la capa de ozono	ozone layer
el clima	weather
el efecto invernadero	greenhouse effect
el hielo	ice
la preservación	conservation
el recalentamiento global	global warming
el rescate	rescue
la reserva natural	nature preserve
la selva tropical	tropical forest
la tierra	land

animales

el ave	bird
el águila calva, *pl.* las águilas calvas	bald eagle
la ballena	whale
la especie	species
la foca	seal

Universal Access

Heritage Language Learners

Have students provide examples of sentences utilizing each of the conjunctions reviewed on p. 427. Ask them to explain why they used the indicative or the subjunctive following each conjunction. Then have them write down their examples focusing on the spelling of the appropriate verb forms.

Advanced Learners

Invite students to create and exchange word-search puzzles using the chapter vocabulary. Remind them that the words hidden in their grids of letters can be written vertically, horizontally, or diagonally. Remind them to blend in the Spanish letters ***ñ*** and ***ll*** throughout their word-search grids.

Conjunciones que se usan con el subjuntivo y el indicativo

Certain conjunctions related to time are followed by either the indicative or the subjunctive.

en cuanto	tan pronto como	cuando
mientras	hasta que	después (de) que

You use the subjunctive after these conjunctions when the action that follows has not yet taken place. You use the indicative with these conjunctions when the action that follows has already taken place or if it occurs regularly.

Van a producir petróleo **hasta que** se agote.
En cuanto salgo del cuarto, siempre apago las luces.

• The conjunction *antes de que* is always followed by the subjunctive.

Pon el helado en el refrigerador **antes de que** se derrita.

• If the subject of a sentence does not change, use the infinitive after *antes de, después de, hasta.*

Después de salir del trabajo, voy a visitar a mi amigo Juan.

Más conjunciones que se usan con el subjuntivo y el indicativo

The following conjunctions are usually followed by the subjunctive to express the purpose or intention of an action:

a menos que	para que	sin que	con tal (de) que	aunque

No haré la limpieza de la casa **a menos que** me ayudes.

• If the subject of the sentence does not change, use the infinitive after *para* and *sin*.

Debemos dejar de usar aerosoles **para** detener la destrucción de la capa de ozono.

• With the conjunction *aunque*, use the subjunctive to express uncertainty. Use the indicative when there is no uncertainty.

Aunque produzcan más petróleo no podrán depender de este recurso por mucho tiempo.
No quiero ver ese programa sobre las ballenas **aunque** todos dicen que es muy bueno.

Los pronombres relativos *que, quien* y *lo que*

You use relative pronouns to combine two sentences or to give clarifying information. The most common relative pronoun in Spanish is *que*. It can mean "that," "which," "who," or "whom," and it may refer either to persons or to things.

El artículo **que** salió en el periódico habla sobre la contaminación.

After a preposition, use *que* to refer to things and *quien(es)* to refer to people.

El problema **del que** te hablé es muy grave.   La persona **de quien** te hablé se llama Adriana.

Use the relative phrase *lo que* to refer to a situation, concept, action, or object not yet identified.

Te cuento **lo que** me explicó el científico.

● **Más práctica** . . . .
Practice Workbook Organizer 9-13, 9-14

cuatrocientos veintisiete 427
Capítulo 9

Conjunciones que se usan con el subjuntivo y el indicativo: In this activity, students can review the conjunctions from both the first and second grammar explanations on this page. On their own, have students use each of the eleven conjunctions in a written sentence. Tell them to use the subjunctive or indicative incorrectly in about half of their sentences and to randomly mix these incorrect sentences in with the rest. Then have students trade papers. Ask them to mark the correct sentences they see with a **C,** and to correct any errors they see in the use of the subjunctive versus the indicative. Have them read the corrected sentences aloud to their partners and explain the corrections they made.

Los pronombres relativos que, quien *y* lo que**:** Have students use the pronouns to create definitions of the chapter vocabulary on the previous page. For example: *Una selva tropical es un bosque cerca del ecuador que recibe una gran cantidad de lluvia. Los senadores son unas personas a quienes podemos escribir sobre la protección del medio ambiente. Crecer es lo que hacen las plantas en la primavera.*

Alternative Assessment Options
The activity above under ***Los pronombres relativos*** que, quien *y* lo que can be used as a way to assess students' assimilation of the rules for use of the subjunctive vs. the indicative, as well as their understanding of chapter vocabulary.

Portfolio

Invite students to review the activities they completed in this chapter, including written reports, posters or other visuals, tapes of oral presentations, and other projects. Have them select one or two items that they feel best demonstrate their achievements in Spanish. Include these products in students' portfolios. Have them include this with the Chapter Checklist and Self-Assessment Worksheet.

Additional Resources
• Audio Program: CD Cap. 9, Track 16
• Resource Book: Cap. 9, Clip Art
• Assessment Program: Chapter Checklist and Self-Assessment Worksheet

---

Enriching Your Teaching

Teacher-to-Teacher
Play "Concentration." Prepare twenty note cards. On ten, write an indicative form of one of the verbs from the list on p. 426. On the other ten, write a the corresponding subjunctive form. A sample pair might be *coloca/coloque.* Number the cards randomly 1–20 on the reverse side. Tape them to the board in numerical order in a grid.

Divide students into two teams. A player from Team A chooses two cards, which are turned over and read aloud. If they match, they are removed from the grid. Team A scores a point and goes again. If the cards don't match, they are returned to their positions and it is Team B's turn.

427

Performance Tasks

Standards: 1.1, 1.2, 1.3, 3.1

Resources: Audio Program: CD Cap. 9, Track 17; Resource Book: Cap. 9, Audio Script; Practice Answers on Transparencies

1. Vocabulario

Suggestions: Encourage students to review the vocabulary from the *A primera vista* sections on pp. 390–393 and 404–407 before they complete the activity.

Answers:

1. b   5. b
2. c   6. d
3. b   7. a
4. a   8. b

2. Gramática

Suggestions: Remind students of the main points of the grammar presentations in *Capítulo* 9:

• conjunctions that use the subjunctive and the indicative

• the relative pronouns *que, quien* and *lo que*

Answers:

1. a   5. d
2. a   6. a
3. d   7. c
4. a   8. b

3. Escuchar

Suggestions: Use the *Audio CD* or read from the script.

Answers:

a. **El problema de la contaminación de los ríos.**

b. **Que el gobierno tome las medidas apropiadas para castigar las fábricas que continúan echando desperdicios al agua.**

Chapter Review

To prepare for the test, check to see if you . . .
• know the new vocabulary and grammar
• can perform the tasks on pp. 428 and 429

❶ Vocabulario Escribe la letra de la palabra o expresión que mejor complete cada frase. Escribe tus respuestas en una hoja aparte.

1. Muchos animales salvajes están en peligro de _____ a causa de la caza.
   a. preservación   c. población
   b. extinción   d. amenaza

2. El uso excesivo de _____ puede destruir la capa de ozono.
   a. venenos   c. aerosoles
   b. derrames   d. recipientes

3. Es muy peligroso cuando las fábricas arrojan _____ al río.
   a. peces   c. recursos
   b. desperdicios   d. medidas

4. ¿Qué haremos cuando se acaben los recursos naturales como _____?
   a. el petróleo   c. el terreno
   b. la energía   d. el clima

5. El número de ballenas ha disminuido a causa de _____ de petróleo.
   a. la contaminación c. la piel
   b. los derrames   d. la electricidad

6. Hay que buscar nuevas maneras de _____ de la basura.
   a. depender   c. promover
   b. castigar   d. deshacerse

7. El _____ es un fenómeno que ocurre cuando las temperaturas suben.
   a. efecto invernadero c. producto químico
   b. derrame de petróleo d. medio ambiente

8. Muchos se dedican a la caza de las focas para usar sus _____.
   a. alimentos   c. plumas
   b. pieles   d. dientes

❷ Gramática Escribe la letra de la palabra o expresión que mejor complete cada frase. Escribe tus respuestas en una hoja aparte.

1. No van a parar de tirar desperdicios hasta que los _____.
   a. castiguen   c. castigaran
   b. castigaron   d. castigan

2. Mientras la gente no _____ conciencia de los problemas de la contaminación, no podrán disminuirla.
   a. tome   c. haya tomado
   b. tomará   d. toma

3. Después de _____ los ríos, tendremos que tomar medidas para reducir el número de fábricas.
   a. limpiemos   c. limpiaremos
   b. limpiamos   d. limpiar

4. Mientras no _____ leyes más justas no voy a contribuir a su campaña.
   a. promuevan   c. promoviendo
   b. promueven   d. promovieron

5. Allí está el refugio de vida silvestre _____ visitamos el año pasado.
   a. quien   c. lo que
   b. del que   d. que

6. _____ más le molesta a la gente es el recalentamiento global.
   a. Lo que   c. Que
   b. El que   d. En que

7. La señora _____ te hablé trabaja en una reserva natural.
   a. a quien   c. de quien
   b. del que   d. que

8. Siempre _____ las luces en cuanto salimos de casa.
   a. apaguemos   c. apagaron
   b. apagamos   d. apaguen

Universal Access

Heritage Language Learners

Encourage students to review the standard format for a business or professional letter on p. 421. Discuss how a letter to the editor of a newspaper or to an environmental group would differ in form and content from a casual letter to a friend or family member.

Students with Learning Difficulties

Have students identify and copy the conjunction used in each sentence of the *Gramática* review. Have them refer to the chart on p. 427 to review the rules for each conjunction. Then direct them to apply the appropriate rule to select the correct choice.

For: Test preparation
Visit: www.phschool.com
Web Code: jed-0911

En el examen vas a . . .	Éstas son las tareas de práctica que te pueden ser útiles para el examen . . .	Si necesitas repasar . . .

3 Escuchar Escuchar y comprender unas descripciones sobre la contaminación del medio ambiente

Escucha a una persona que llama al locutor de un programa popular en la radio. Quiere expresar sus opiniones sobre los problemas y las soluciones del medio ambiente. Identifica a) el problema que menciona y b) la solución que sugiere.

pp. 390-393
A primera vista 1
p. 396 Actividades 8–9

4 Hablar Hacer unas sugerencias sobre cómo proteger el medio ambiente de la comunidad

Trabajas para un centro comunitario y te piden que hables con un grupo de jóvenes sobre cómo proteger el medio ambiente en sus vidas personales. Diles qué hacer en a) casa, b) la escuela y c) la comunidad.

p. 394 Actividad 5
p. 396 Actividades 8–9
p. 400 Actividad 13
p. 419 *Presentación oral*

5 Leer Leer y comprender declaraciones sobre los problemas del medio ambiente

Lee este artículo sobre un reciente derrame de petróleo y di a) ¿dónde tuvo lugar el derrame?, b) ¿por qué ha sido un desastre para el turismo?, c) ¿qué medidas deberían tomarse para prevenir estos accidentes?

El derrame de petróleo cerca de la costa de Galicia, en España, ha causado grandes problemas para el turismo y el trabajo en la región. El gobierno ha gastado millones de euros en la limpieza de las playas y el rescate de la fauna marina. Miles de peces y otras especies marinas han desaparecido. A menos que no haya leyes más estrictas para prevenir desastres de este tipo, la vida marina y el turismo seguirán amenazados.

pp. 404–407
A primera vista 2
p. 410 Actividad 28
p. 415 Actividad 36

6 Escribir Escribir una carta al periódico sobre los problemas del medio ambiente

Eres miembro de un grupo que se encarga de la protección del ambiente y tienes que escribir una carta a los jóvenes de tu zona para que tomen conciencia de lo que pueden hacer para proteger la comunidad. Describe por lo menos dos problemas y explica las consecuencias si no se toman las medidas necesarias. Al final, diles qué pueden hacer ellos para ayudar.

p. 394 Actividad 5
p. 396 Actividad 9
p. 400 Actividad 14
p. 411 Actividad 29
pp. 420–421
Presentación escrita

7 Pensar Pensar en los problemas ecológicos globales

Piensa en uno de los problemas y su solución mencionados en el capítulo. Descríbelo y piensa si en los Estados Unidos existe o no ese problema y cómo lo resolverías tú.

pp. 390–393; 404–407
p. 397 Actividad 10
p. 403 Actividad 19

cuatrocientos veintinueve   429
Capítulo 9

---

4. Hablar

Suggestions: Encourage students to use in their answer at least one of the conjunctions studied in this chapter that take either the subjunctive or the indicative.

Answers will vary.

5. Leer

Suggestions: Tell students to refer to pp. 390–393 and 404–407 if they have questions about vocabulary in the review.

Answers:

a. El derrame tuvo lugar cerca de la costa de Galicia, en España.
b. Ha causado grandes problemas para el turismo porque ha ensuciado las playas.
c. Debe haber leyes más estrictas para prevenir desastres de este tipo.

6. Escribir

Suggestions: Remind students of what they learned about effective conclusions in this chapter's *Presentación escrita*. Have them apply that learning to their writing here.

Answers will vary.

7. Pensar

Suggestions: Encourage students to review current events on the Internet or in your local newspaper in light of what they have learned about the environment in *Capítulo* 9.

Answers will vary.

✓ Assessment

• Examen del capítulo: 9
• Audio Program: CD 13, Cap. 9, Track 12
• Assessment Program: *RPH*

Alternative Assessment

• ExamView Test Bank CD-ROM
• Resource Book: Cap. 9, Situation Cards
• Resource Book: Cap. 9, Communicative Activity BLM

Enriching Your Teaching

Teacher-to-Teacher

Encourage students to enhance their skills in Spanish by regularly listening to Spanish-language news broadcasts. *Telemundo* is the largest televised Spanish-language news entity in the United States, with daily programs on many network stations throughout the country. Those of your students who have cable television will be able to find other Spanish-language news programs as well. Tuning in regularly to such programs will not only improve their listening comprehension, but also inform them and broaden their perspectives on environmental issues and other current concerns and events.

Capítulo 10

¿Cuáles son tus derechos y deberes?

CHAPTER OVERVIEW

¿Cuáles son tus derechos y deberes?
• Rights and responsibilities

Vocabulary
• rights and responsibilities at home and in school
• rights in society guaranteed by the Constitution

Grammar
• passive voice
• present perfect subjunctive and imperfect subjunctive
• pluperfect subjunctive
• conditional perfect

Cultural Perspectives
• find out what young people think about their rights and world problems
• interpret cultural perspectives on rights and responsibilities
• heroes of the Latin American independence movement

Chapter Project

Web pages for *Club los Ruidosos*

Overview: Students work in teams of four to create illustrated pages for a Web site of fans and members of a music-sharing club. The home page should include an introduction and an index to three pages.

Materials: construction paper, crayons and markers and, if computers are not available, poster boards, magazines, glue, scissors

Sequence: (suggestions for when to do each step appear throughout the chapter)

STEP 1. Review instructions so students know what is expected of them. Hand out the "Chapter 10 Project Instructions and Rubric" from the *Teacher's Resource Book*.

STEP 2. Students submit sketches of their Web pages. Return the sketches with your suggestions.

STEP 3. Students do layouts of Web pages on construction paper. Encourage them to try different arrangements before drawing pictures or gluing photos from magazines.

STEP 4. Students submit a draft of the texts for each page. Note your corrections and suggestions, then return drafts to students.

STEP 5. Students complete and present their Web pages to the class, reading and / or describing all the information featured in the pages.

Option:
Students create Web pages for a club of book fans.

Assessment:
Here is a detailed rubric for assessing this project:
Chapter 10 Project: *Web pages for Club los Ruidosos*

RUBRIC	Score 1	Score 3	Score 5
Your evidence of planning	You provide no layout or written draft.	Your layout and written draft are provided, but not corrected.	You show evidence of corrected draft and layout.
Your use of illustrations	You include no images and little of the required information.	You include images, but your layout is disorganized.	Your Web pages are carefully done and images are consistent with text.
Your presentation	You include little of the required information.	You include most of the required information.	You include all the required information.

Bulletin Boards

Theme: *Derechos y deberes*

Have students work in pairs to brainstorm about their rights and duties at home, at school, and with their friends, and then collect magazine clippings to illustrate them. The class then arranges the information on the bulletin board under *Derechos* and *Deberes*.

Bibliography

Altman, Linda Jacobs. *Human Rights: Issues for a New Millennium.* Springfield, NJ: Enslow Publishers, Inc., 2002.

Goodnough, David. *Simón Bolívar: South American Liberator.* Springfield, NJ: Enslow Publishers, 1998.

Hudson, David L. *Bill of Rights: The First Ten Amendments of the Constitution.* Springfield, NJ: Enslow Publishers, 1998. Traces the history of the writing of the first ten amendments to the Constitution.

Tingay, Graham I., and Antony Marks. *The Romans.* Illustrated World History Series. Tulsa, Ok: EDC Publications, 1991. Describes the Roman empire.

Waldron, Ann. *Francisco Goya.* New York: Harry N. Abrams, Inc., 1992. A biography of the Spanish painter, a forerunner of the impressionist movement.

Hands-on Culture

Recipe: *Queso fundido*

This is an authentic recipe to help you celebrate Mexican Independence Day. This delicious fondue takes only about 20 minutes to make. It serves six and can be served on *tortillas* or scooped up with chips.

Ingredients:

> 1 lb. Mexican *queso Cacique* or any other *queso blanco* (light white cheese), cut into small chunks
>
> 3 to 4 cloves garlic, minced
>
> juice of 4 limes, or 1/4 cup lime juice
>
> 6 to 8 drops of Tabasco, or other hot pepper sauce

Directions:

1. Slowly melt cheese in a medium saucepan over slow heat. Stir continuously with a wooden spoon.
2. When almost melted, add the garlic, lime, and Tabasco, and heat through.
3. Serve immediately with *tortillas* or chips.

Internet Search

Use the keywords to find more information.

Keywords:

> derechos de los niños, constitución de los Estados Unidos, Naciones Unidas

Game

Derechos contra obligaciones

Play this game to review the objectives and the vocabulary from *Capítulo 10.*

Players: the entire class

Materials: pens, paper, a stop watch

Rules:

1. Divide the class into two teams: *los derechos* and *las obligaciones. Los derechos* team generates a list of rights that parents, children, and teachers have. *Las obligaciones* group generates a list of responsibilities for those same categories.

2. Teams have ten minutes to generate their lists.

3. When time is up, toss a coin to determine which team begins the game.

4. The team member who plays first tells a *derecho/obligación* from the list. For example, a *derechos* player says: *Un niño tiene derecho a jugar todos los días.*

5. The member of the opposite team should tell an obligation the same child should have. For example, *Un niño debe cumplir con sus deberes de la escuela todos los días.*

6. Play continues until a team is stumped and cannot think of a reply.

7. No repeated sentences are allowed.

Variation: Apply the game to rights of animals, communities, or countries.

A ver si recuerdas

RECYCLE

Vocabulary
- Rights and obligations
- People and organizations

Grammar
- Preterite vs. imperfect

- Conflicts
- Solutions

- Verbs with different meanings in the imperfect and the preterite tenses

---

Chapter Overview

A primera vista 1	Manos a la obra 1	A primera vista 2	Manos a la obra 2
INPUT	**PRACTICE**	**INPUT**	**PRACTICE**
Objectives • Talk about rights and responsibilites at home and in school • Talk about parents' rights	**Objectives** • Discuss rights and responsibilities that people have	**Objectives** • Read about individual rights in society and the role of government • Listen to what young people think about world problems and their solutions	**Objectives** • Talk about rights guaranteed by the Constitution • Discuss how these rights apply to individuals in society
Vocabulary • Children's rights and responsibilites • Parents' rights and responsibilites	**Vocabulary** • Practice and use new vocabulary	**Vocabulary** • Individual rights in society • Role of the government	**Vocabulary** • Practice and use new vocabulary
Grammar • Passive voice • Present perfect subjunctive and imperfect subjunctive	**Grammar** • Passive voice • Present perfect subjunctive and imperfect subjunctive	**Grammar** • Pluperfect subjunctive • Conditional perfect	**Grammar** • Pluperfect subjunctive • Conditional perfect
Culture • Francisco Goya	**Culture** • *Consulta infantil y juvenil 2000*	**Culture** • Teenagers and world problems	**Culture** • José Vasconcelos, politician and educator • Juan Lovera, painter

---

¡Adelante!

APPLICATION

Objectives
- Read about heroes of the Latin American independence movement
- Write an editorial essay in a newspaper

- Read an autobiographical account and understand the author's reason for writing the selection

Vocabulary
- Application

Grammar
- Application

Culture
- Fragment of *Si me permiten hablar* by Domitila Barrios Chungara

---

Repaso del capítulo

REVIEW

Objectives
- Prepare for the chapter test

- Perform the tasks on pages 474 and 475

Vocabulary
- Review

Grammar
- Review

BEYOND THE CLASSROOM

Countries
- Mexico
- Cuba
- Peru
- Venezuela
- Bolivia
- United States
- Spain

El español en la comunidad
- Use of the media by candidates who speak Spanish

Internet
- Vocabulary activities
- Grammar activities
- Internet links
- Self-tests

LEARNER SUPPORT

Strategies
- Creating a timeline
- Think, plan, then speak
- Snappy introductions

- Investigate the author's reasons

Recycling
- Pronunciation of dipthong *ue*
- Pronouns *vosotros* and *vosotras*

En voz alta
- *Subjuntivo*

Ampliación del lenguaje
- Suffix -*miento*

Conexiones
- The Arts: Juan Lovera

Print Components

TEACHER

Teacher's Resource Book
- Chapter Table of Contents
- School-to-Home Connection
- Chapter Resource Checklist
- Input Script
- Audio Script
- Video Script
- Communicative Activities
- Situation Cards
- GramActiva Blackline Masters
- Graphic Organizers
- Answer Keys:
  Practice Workbook
  Writing, Audio & Video Workbook

Realidades para hispanohablantes
Teacher Edition

STUDENT

Practice Workbook
- Vocabulary: 10-1 – 10-4, 10-8 – 10-9
- Grammar: 10-5 – 10-7, 10-10 – 10-12
- Organizer: 10-13 – 10-14

Writing, Audio & Video Workbook
- Audio: 1–5
- Writing: 6–13
- Video: 14–17

Reading and Writing for Success
- Chapter 10, Test 37

Realidades para hispanohablantes

Transparencies

Vocabulary and Grammar Transparencies
- Vocabulary: 181–188, 191–194
- Grammar: 189–190, 195–196
- ¿Qué me cuentas?: 197

Practice Answers on Transparencies
- Cap. 10

Fine Art Transparencies
- Transparencies
- Teacher's Guide

Assessment

Assessment Program
- Pruebas:
  – Comprensión del vocabulario 1: 10-1
  – Aplicación del vocabulario 1: 10-2
  – La voz pasiva: *ser* + participio pasado: 10-3
  – El presente y el imperfecto del subjuntivo: 10-4
  – Comprensión del vocabulario 2: 10-5
  – Aplicación del vocabulario 2: 10-6
  – El pluscuamperfecto del subjuntivo: 10-7
  – El condicional perfecto: 10-8
- Exámenes del capítulo
- Rubrics

Alternative Assessment
- ExamView Test Bank CD-ROM
- MindPoint Quiz Show CD-ROM
- Internet Self-test
- Situation Cards
- Communicative Activity

Assessment Program: *Realidades para hispanohablantes*

Technology

TeacherExpress™ CD-ROM
- Lesson Planner
- Teacher Resources
- Clip Art

Video Program VHS and DVD

Audio Program CDs
- A primera vista 1 y 2: Vocabulario y gramática en contexto
- Audio Activities
- ¿Qué me cuentas?
- Repaso
- Examen del capítulo: Escuchar

Regular Schedule (50 Minutes)

For electronic lesson plans:
Teacher Express CD-ROM

	Warm-up / Assess	Preview Present / Practice Communicate	Wrap-up / Homework Options
DAY 1	**Warm-up (10 min.)** • Return Examen del capítulo: Capítulo 9 • Homework check	**Repaso (35 min.)** • A ver si recuerdas Actividades 1–8	**Wrap-up and Homework Options (5 min.)** • Practice Workbook 10-1, 10-2 • Go Online
DAY 2	**Warm-up (10 min.)** • Homework check	**Chapter Opener (10 min.)** • Objectives • Fondo cultural **A primera vista 1 (25 min.)** • Presentation: Vocabulario y gramática en contexto • Actividades 1, 2	**Wrap-up and Homework Options (5 min.)** • Go Online • Clip Art Vocabulary
DAY 3	**Warm-up (10 min.)** • Homework check	**A primera vista 1 (35 min.)** • Presentation: Derechos • Actividades 3, 4 **Manos a la obra 1** • Actividades 5, 6	**Wrap-up and Homework Options (5 min.)** • Practice Workbook 10-3, 10-4 • Actividad 4 • Go Online • Prueba 10-1: Vocabulary recognition
DAY 4	**Warm-up (10 min.)** • Homework check • Audio Activity **✔Assessment (10 min.)** • Prueba 10-1: Vocabulary recognition	**Manos a la obra 1 (25 min.)** • Actividades 7, 8, 9, 10 • Fondo cultural	**Wrap-up and Homework Options (5 min.)** • Actividad 11 • Writing Activities • Prueba 10-2: Vocabulary production
DAY 5	**Warm-up (15 min.)** • Homework check • Communicative Activity **✔Assessment (10 min.)** • Prueba 10-2: Vocabulary production	**Manos a la obra 1 (20 min.)** • Presentation: La voz pasiva • Actividades 12, 13 • Writing Activity	**Wrap-up and Homework Options (5 min.)** • Practice Workbook 10-5 • Go Online
DAY 6	**Warm-up (10 min.)** • Homework check	**Manos a la obra 1 (35 min.)** • Presentation: El presente y el imperfecto del subjunctivo • Actividades 14, 15, 16, 17	**Wrap-up and Homework Options (5 min.)** • Practice Workbook 10-6, 10-7 • Go Online • Prueba 10-3: La voz pasiva
DAY 7	**Warm-up (10 min.)** • Homework check **✔Assessment (10 min.)** • Prueba 10-3: La voz pasiva	**Manos a la obra 1 (25 min.)** • Writing Activity • Communicative Activity • En voz alta	**Wrap-up and Homework Options (5 min.)** • Writing Activity • Prueba 10-4: El presente y el imperfecto del subjuntivo
DAY 8	**Warm-up (10 min.)** • Homework check **✔Assessment (10 min.)** • Prueba 10-4	**A primera vista 2 (25 min.)** • Presentation: Vocabulario y gramática en contexto • Actividades 18, 19	**Wrap-up and Homework Options (5 min.)** • Clip Art Vocabulary • Examen: Vocabulario y gramática 1
DAY 9	**Warm-up (5 min.)** • Homework check **✔Assessment (30 min.)** • Examen: Vocabulario y gramática 1	**A primera vista 2 (10 min.)** • Presentation: Jóvenes por el desarrollo y la paz • Actividades 20, 21	**Wrap-up and Homework Options (5 min.)** • Actividad 22 • Practice Workbook 10-8, 10-9 • Go Online • Prueba 10-5: Vocabulary recognition
DAY 10	**Warm-up (20 min.)** • Homework check **✔Assessment (10 min.)** • Prueba 10-5: Vocabulary recognition	**Manos a la obra 2 (15 min.)** • Actividades 23, 24, 25 • Fondo cultural	**Wrap-up and Homework Options (5 min.)** • Actividades 29, 30

Warm-up / Assess	Preview Present / Practice Communicate		Wrap-up / Homework Options
DAY 11 **Warm-up (10 min.)** • Homework check	**A primera vista 2 (20 min.)** • Actividades 26, 27, 28 • Audio Activity • Writing Activity	**Manos a la obra 2 (15 min.)** • Presentation: El pluscuamperfecto del subjunctivo • Actividades 31, 32	**Wrap-up and Homework Options (5 min.)** • Practice Workbook 10-10 • Go Online • Prueba 10-6: Vocabulary production
DAY 12 **Warm-up (10 min.)** • Homework check • Communicative Activity ✔**Assessment (10 min.)** • Prueba 10-6: Vocabulary production	**Manos a la obra 2 (25 min.)** • Actividades 33, 34 • Writing Activity • Presentation: El condicional perfecto • Actividades 35, 36		**Wrap-up and Homework Options (5 min.)** • Practice Workbook 10-11, 10-12 • Go Online • Prueba 10-7: El pluscuamperfecto del subjuntivo
DAY 13 **Warm-up (10 min.)** • Homework check ✔**Assessment (10 min.)** • Prueba 10-7	**Manos a la obra 2 (25 min.)** • Actividades 37–40 • Audio Activity • Writing Activity		**Wrap-up and Homework Options (5 min.)** • Prueba 10-8: El condicional perfecto
DAY 14 **Warm-up (10 min.)** • Communicative Activity ✔**Assessment (10 min.)** • Prueba 10-8	**¡Adelante! (25 min.)** • Puente a la cultura: Héroes de América Latina • ¿Comprendiste? • Cronología • Presentación oral: Step 1		**Wrap-up and Homework Options (2 min.)** • Examen: Vocabulario y gramática 2
DAY 15 **Warm-up (5 min.)** • Answer questions ✔**Assessment (25 min.)** • Examen: Vocabulario y gramática 2	**¡Adelante! (15 min.)** • Presentación oral: Step 2		**Wrap-up and Homework Options (5 min.)** • Presentación oral: Step 3 • Go Online
DAY 16 **Warm-up (5 min.)** • Homework check	**¡Adelante! (40 min.)** • Presentación oral: Step 3 (half class) • ¿Qué me cuentas? 1, 2, 3		**Wrap-up and Homework Options (5 min.)** • Presentación escrita: Steps 1, 2
DAY 17 **Warm-up (10 min.)** • Homework check	**¡Adelante! (35 min.)** • Presentación oral: Step 3 (half class) • View Video • Video Activities 1, 2, 3 • Presentación escrita: Step 3		**Wrap-up and Homework Options (5 min.)** • Presentación escrita: Step 4 • Preparación para el examen: 1, 2
DAY 18 **Warm-up (10 min.)** • Homework check	**Repaso (10 min.)** • Preparación para el examen: Actividades 3, 4	**¡Adelante! (25 min.)** • Lectura • Interacción • ¿Comprendiste? • Fondo cultural	**Wrap-up and Homework Options (5 min.)** • ¿Comprendiste? • Practice Workbook: Organizer 7-13, 7-14 • Go Online: Self-test
DAY 19 **Warm-up (15 min.)** • Homework check	**Repaso (30 min.)** • Preparación para el examen: Actividades 5, 6, 7 • MindPoint Quiz Show • Other review		**Wrap-up and Homework Options (5 min.)** • Examen del capítulo
DAY 20 **Warm-up (5 min.)** • Answer questions ✔**Assessment (45 min.)** • Examen del capítulo			

	Warm-up / Assess	Preview Present / Practice Communicate	Wrap-up / Homework Options
DAY 1	**Warm-up (35 min.)** • Return Examen del capítulo: Capítulo 9 • A ver si recuerdas • Homework check	**Chapter Opener (10 min.)** • Objectives • Fondo cultural **A primera vista 1 (30 min.)** • Presentation: Vocabulario y gramática en contexto • Actividades 1, 2 • Presentation: Derechos . . ., El gobierno . . . • Actividades 3, 4 **Manos a la obra 1 (10 min.)** • Actividades 5, 6, 7	**Wrap-up and Homework Options (5 min.)** • Practice Workbook 10-3, 10-4 • Go Online • Clip Art Vocabulary • Prueba 10-1: Vocabulary recognition
DAY 2	**Warm-up (15 min.)** • Homework check • Actividades 8, 9 ✔**Assessment (10 min.)** • Prueba 10-1: Vocabulary recognition	**Manos a la obra 1 (60 min.)** • Actividades 10, 11 • Fondo cultural • Ampliación del lenguaje • Audio Activity • Writing Activity • Communicative Activity	**Wrap-up and Homework Options (5 min.)** • Prueba 10-2: Vocabulary production
DAY 3	**Warm-up (5 min.)** • Homework check ✔**Assessment (10 min.)** • Prueba 10-2: Vocabulary production	**Manos a la obra 1 (70 min.)** • Presentation: La voz pasiva • Actividades 12, 13 • Presentation: El presente y el imperfecto del subjuntivo • Actividades 14, 15 • Writing Activity	**Wrap-up and Homework Options (5 min.)** • Practice Workbook 10-5 • Go Online • Prueba 10-3: La voz pasiva
DAY 4	**Warm-up (10 min.)** • Homework check ✔**Assessment (10 min.)** • Prueba 10-3: La voz pasiva	**Manos a la obra 1 (50 min.)** • Actividades 16, 17 • En voz alta • Writing Activity • Communicative Activity **A primera vista 2 (15 min.)** • Presentation: Vocabulario y gramática en contexto • Actividades 18, 19	**Wrap-up and Homework Options (5 min.)** • Practice Workbook 10-6, 10-7 • Go Online • Prueba 10-4: El presente y el imperfecto del subjuntivo • Examen: Vocabulario y gramática 1
DAY 5	**Warm-up (10 min.)** • Homework check ✔**Assessment Options (40 min.)** • Prueba 10-4: El presente y el imperfecto del subjuntivo Examen: Vocabulario y gramática 1	**A primera vista 2 (20 min.)** • Presentation: Jóvenes por el desarrollo y la paz • Actividades 20, 21, 22 **Manos a la obra (15 min.)** • Actividades 23, 24	**Wrap-up and Homework Options (5 min.)** • Practice Workbook 10-8, 10-9 • Actividad 25 • Clip Art • Go Online • Prueba 10-5: Vocabulary recognition

	Warm-up / Assess	Preview Present / Practice Communicate	Wrap-up / Homework Options
DAY 6	**Warm-up (35 min.)** • Homework check • Fondo cultural • Actividades 26, 27, 28 • Audio Activity • Writing Activity • Communicative Activity **✔Assessment (10 min.)** • Prueba 10-5: Vocabulary recognition	**Manos a la obra (40 min.)** • Presentation: El pluscuamperfecto del subjuntivo • Actividades 31, 32, 33, 34 • El español en la comunidad	**Wrap-up and Homework Options (5 min.)** • Actividades 29, 30 • Practice Workbook 10-10 • Go Online • Pruebas 10-6, 10-7: Vocabulary production, El pluscuamperfecto del subjuntivo
DAY 7	**Warm-up (10 min.)** • Homework check **✔Assessment (20 min.)** • Pruebas 10-6, 10-7: Vocabulary production, El pluscuamperfecto del subjuntivo	**Manos a la obra 2 (40 min.)** • Presentation: El condicional perfecto • Actividades 35, 36, 37, 38, 39, 40 • Audio Activity • Writing Activity **¡Adelante! (15 min.)** • Presentación oral: Steps 1, 2	**Wrap-up and Homework Options (5 min.)** • Practice Workbook 10-11, 10-12 • Go Online • Prueba 10-8: El condicional perfecto • Presentación oral: Step 2 • Go Online
DAY 8	**Warm-up (15 min.)** • Homework check • Communicative Activity **✔Assessment (20 min.)** • Prueba 10-8: El condicional perfecto	**¡Adelante! (35 min.)** • Presentación oral: Step 3 **¡Adelante! (15 min.)** • Presentation: Héroes de América Latina • ¿Comprendiste?	**Wrap-up and Homework Options (5 min.)** • ¿Comprendiste? • Cronología • Examen: Vocabulario y gramática 2
DAY 9	**Warm-up (10 min.)** • Homework check **✔Assessment Options (30 min.)** • Examen: Vocabulario y gramática 2	**¡Adelante! (45 min.)** • ¿Qué me cuentas? 1, 2, 3 • Presentación escrita: Step 1 • Video • Video Activities	**Wrap-up and Homework Options (5 min.)** • Presentación escrita: Step 2 • Go Online • Preparación para el examen: Actividades 1, 2
DAY 10	**Warm-up (20 min.)** • Homework check • Presentación escrita: Step 3	**¡Adelante! (35 min.)** • Lectura • Interacción • ¿Comprendiste? • Fondo cultural **Repaso (30 min.)** • Preparación para el examen: Actividades 3, 4, 6 • MindPoint Quiz Show	**Wrap-up and Homework Options (5 min.)** • Presentación escrita: Step 4 • Practice Workbook: Organizer 10-13, 10-14 • Go Online: Self-test • Preparación para el examen: Actividades 5, 7 • Examen del capítulo
DAY 11	**Warm-up (20 min.)** • Homework check **✔Assessment (45 min.)** • Examen del capítulo	**Theme Game (25 min.)**	

Review ⑩

Vocabulario

Presentation

Standards: 1.1, 1.2

Resources: Voc. & Gram. Transparencies: 181

Suggestions: Have students copy the names of the five categories to their own paper. Show *Vocabulary & Grammar Transparency* 181. With books closed, have students work in pairs and list as many words and expressions as they can remember in each category.

Actividad 1 *Standards:* 1.1, 1.2, 1.3

Resources: Practice Answers on Transparencies

Focus: Practicing review vocabulary

Suggestions: Remind students to consider parts of speech when completing the matching activity. Explain that a definition beginning with a verb is most likely matched with a verb; one that begins with a noun is mostly likely matched with a noun.

Answers:

1. f	5. a
2. d	6. b
3. e	7. g
4. c	

Actividad 2 *Standards:* 1.1, 1.3

Focus: Practicing review vocabulary

Suggestions: Point out to students that when listing permitted or prohibited activities, they can use either the impersonal *se* or *estar* + past participle: *se prohíbe/está prohibido.*

Answers will vary.

Block Schedule

Have students write five questions, each using a different vocabulary word from the organizer. Have them ask a partner the questions.

430

A ver si recuerdas...

Vocabulario

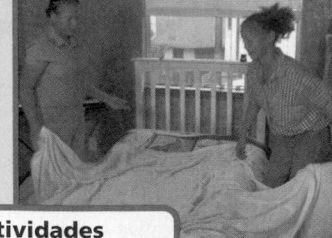

la sociedad
- la comunidad
- la costumbre
- los / las demás
- la escuela
- la familia
- el hermano, la hermana
- los padres
- la sociedad
- el vecino, la vecina

condiciones
- la edad
- injusto, -a
- justo, -a
- libre
- mayor
- menor

derechos y obligaciones
- el derecho
- la injusticia
- la ley
- las medidas
- la obligación
- las reglas
- la responsabilidad
- la seguridad
- las tareas

actividades
- alcanzar
- beneficiar
- conseguir
- cumplir (con)
- disfrutar (de)
- encargarse (de)
- luchar
- obtener
- proteger

expresiones
- a favor
- de niño
- de pequeño
- en contra
- (me) parece justo / injusto
- se permite
- se prohibe

Actividad 1 **Hablar/Escribir..............**

Práctica de vocabulario

Trabaja con otro(a) estudiante para emparejar cada definición con la palabra correspondiente. Luego, escoge 4 palabras y escribe un cuento.

1. cuidar a alguien de cualquier tipo de peligro
2. lo contrario de justo
3. las personas que viven en el mismo barrio
4. lo contrario de prohibir
5. hacer lo que se debe
6. la regla establecida por una autoridad
7. tomar la responsabilidad de hacer algo

    a. cumplir
    b. la ley
    c. permitir
    d. injusto
    e. los vecinos
    f. proteger
    g. encargarse

430 cuatrocientos treinta
A ver si recuerdas . . .

Actividad 2  **Escribir/Hablar..............**

Práctica de vocabulario

Haz una lista de tres actividades que se prohíban y tres actividades que se permitan en tu casa o en tu escuela. Compara la lista con la de un(a) compañero(a). Escriban una frase entre los (las) dos para expresar su opinión. Compartan su oración con la clase.

Modelo

En la escuela se prohibe hablar mientras la profesora habla.
Nos parece justo para mantener el orden en la clase.

Universal Access

Heritage Language Learners

After the class writes their accounts of experiences in *Actividad 4*, have them exchange papers. Ask students with strong grammar skills to identify errors they see in their partners' work without correcting them. Then have the writers revise their work based on this feedback.

Advanced Learners

Challenge students to create sentences that use vocabulary from as many categories as possible. For example: *En mi familia, los niños mayores disfrutan de más derechos que los niños menores.*

Gramática · Repaso

Pretérito vs. imperfecto

Remember that when speaking in Spanish about the past, you can use either the preterite or the imperfect, depending on the sentence and the meaning you want to convey. Compare:

El sábado pasado me **permitieron** llegar tarde a casa.
De niño nunca me **permitían** llegar tarde.

Use the preterite:

• to tell about past actions that happened and are complete.

Las mujeres **protestaron** para obtener los mismos derechos.

• to give a sequence of actions in the past.

Llegamos al restaurante, **nos sentamos** y **comimos**.

Use the imperfect:

• to tell about habitual actions in the past.

Ellas no **tenían** los mismos derechos que los hombres.

• to give background details such as time, location, weather, mood, age, and physical and mental descriptions.

Era tarde, **hacía** frío, **estábamos** cansados y **teníamos** hambre.

• when two or more actions are taking place simultaneously in the past.

Mientras nosotros **comíamos**, mis hermanos **se peleaban**.

Use the preterite and the imperfect together when an action (preterite) interrupts another that is taking place in the past (imperfect).

Estábamos comiendo cuando **llegó** mi hermano.

 3 Leer

Práctica de gramática

Esteban se asustó ayer por la noche al volver a su casa. Para saber qué le pasó, completa estas frases con el tiempo verbal correcto.

Ayer __1.__ (eran / fueron) las once de la noche cuando Esteban __2.__ (regresó / regresaba) a su casa. __3.__ (Estaba / Estuvo) muy oscuro y no se __4.__ (vio / veía) nada. De repente __5.__ (se escuchó / se escuchaba) un extraño ruido en la noche. Esteban __6.__ (salió / salía) corriendo y __7.__ (se escondió / se escondía) detrás de un árbol. ¿ __8.__ (Fue / Era) un fantasma quien __9.__ (se acercó / se acercaba)? ¡No! __10.__ (Fue / Era) un gato que __11.__ (tuvo / tenía) hambre y __12.__ (buscó / buscaba) algo para comer.

  4 Escribir/Hablar

Práctica de gramática

Con un(a) compañero(a) escribe un relato sobre algo que les haya sucedido, usando el pretérito y el imperfecto. Primero, escojan algo en lo que los (las) dos participaron. Luego, formen frases sobre:

• la causa de lo que sucedió
• la hora de llegada y una descripción del ambiente
• qué hacía la gente
• algo que pasó

Compartan su relato con otros(as) compañeros(as).

Modelo

Era el cumpleaños de [nombre] y él (ella) hacía una fiesta.

Presentation

Resources: Voc. & Gram. Transparencies: 182

Suggestions: Have students write three sentences using past tenses. Encourage them to use more than one verb in each sentence. Have them take turns reading their sentences aloud and explaining their reason for using the preterite tense or the imperfect tense in each case.

 3 Standards: 1.2

Resources: Practice Answers on Transparencies

Focus: Practicing the preterite tense vs. the imperfect tense

Suggestions: Have students number the rules in the Gramática from 1 to 6. As they complete Actividad 3, have them write the rule number that applies beside each sentence.

Answers:

1. eran
2. regresó
3. Estaba
4. veía
5. se escuchó
6. salió
7. se escondió
8. Era
9. se acercó
10. Era
11. tenía
12. buscaba

 4 Standards: 1.1, 1.3

Focus: Practicing the preterite tense vs. the imperfect tense

Suggestions: Before students begin writing, encourage them to decide which tense they think should be used with each of the four cues that are given. Point out that the verbs in the clues provide some guidance on which tenses they should use.

Answers will vary.

Enriching Your Teaching

Teacher-to-Teacher

Correct use of the imperfect tense vs. the preterite tense is a difficult skill for language learners to master. Remind them that mastery comes through patience and practice. Whenever students are engaged in oral communication, correct errors that they may make by modeling the correct usage and having them repeat. Better yet, create a cue card with *imperfecto* written on one side and *pretérito* on the other. Flash the appropriate side of this card when you hear an error, and have the student self-correct.

Review

Vocabulario

Presentation

Standards: 1.1, 1.2

Resources: Voc. & Gram. Transparencies: 183

Suggestions: Ask students to create sentences that use items from at least three of the categories in the *Vocabulario*. For example: *El juez resolvió el problema entre los dos ciudadanos.*

Actividad 5 *Standards:* 1.2

Resources: Practice Answers on Transparencies

Focus: Practicing review vocabulary

Suggestions: Have students read the sentences first and make tentative decisions about how they will use the words in the word bank. Remind them to complete the items about which they are the most certain first.

Answers:
1. manifestación
2. habitantes; gobierno
3. víctimas; juez
4. campaña; población
5. beneficios

Actividad 6 *Standards:* 1.1, 3.1

Focus: Practicing review vocabulary

Suggestions: As students discuss their conflicts in step 2, remind them to use the preterite and the imperfect tenses appropriately.

Answers will vary.

Vocabulario

expresiones
decir la verdad
tener la culpa
tener razón

personas y organizaciones
la campaña
el ciudadano, la ciudadana
la gente
el gobierno
el / la habitante
la manifestación
la organización
la población
la reunión
el sistema

profesiones
el abogado, la abogada
el juez, la jueza
el / la policía

soluciones
los beneficios
la confianza
confiar
garantizar
obedecer
perdonar
resolver
reunirse
solicitar

conflictos
acusar
arrestar
capturar
el conflicto
desconfiar
limitar
mentir
molestar
la pelea
pelearse
el problema
quejarse
rebelarse
temer
la víctima

Actividad 5 Leer ....

Práctica de vocabulario

Estos titulares y anuncios aparecieron recientemente en los periódicos. Léelos y luego complétalos con las palabras o expresiones que siguen.

campaña	gobierno	beneficios
juez	habitantes	víctimas
manifestación	población	

1. ¡Arrestaron a quince personas en la _____ de ayer!
2. El conflicto entre los _____ del valle causa problemas al _____.
3. Las _____ del accidente aparecen ante *(before)* el _____.
4. La _____ de limpieza de la plaza Tribunales cuenta con el apoyo de la _____ de ese lugar.
5. Los ciudadanos quieren garantizar _____ para los ancianos.

Actividad 6 Escribir/Hablar ....

Práctica de vocabulario

❶ Piensa en un conflicto que haya sucedido en tu familia, escuela o comunidad recientemente. Luego, copia esta tabla en una hoja y complétala.

¿Quiénes participaron?	¿Qué hicieron?	¿Por qué?	¿Tenían o no razón?
_____	_____	_____	_____

❷ Usando la información que escribiste en la tabla, cuéntale a otro(a) estudiante la historia del conflicto.

432 cuatrocientos treinta y dos
A ver si recuerdas . . .

Universal Access

Students with Learning Difficulties
Students may have difficulty establishing the contexts in *Actividades* 7 and 8. Give them the opportunity to act out the events described in both activities. This will help them grasp each situation, which will in turn help them choose correct answers.

Advanced Learners
Ask students to model using the vocabulary in context. Give them time to think about the words, then ask them to create a fictional story about a courtroom scene that uses as many of the words as possible.

Gramática·Repaso

Verbos con distinto sentido en el pretérito y en el imperfecto

A few Spanish verbs have different meanings in the imperfect and the preterite tenses.

	IMPERFECT	PRETERITE
saber	*knew* ¿**Sabías** que Ángel Suárez había ganado las elecciones?	*found out, learned* Sí, lo **supe** esta mañana por el periódico.
conocer	*knew (somebody)* Mi padre lo **conocía** cuando era pequeño.	*met (somebody) for the first time* Ellos se **conocieron** en la escuela.
(no) querer	*wanted to* Mi hermana **quería** ir a la manifestación.	*tried to* Yo también **quise** hacerlo pero no pude.
	didn't want to No **querían** decirle la verdad a su familia.	*refused to* No **quisieron** decirle la verdad a su familia.
poder	*was able to, could* Ella **podía** encontrar la solución en un minuto.	*managed to, succeeded in* Ella **pudo** encontrar la solución en un minuto.

 7 Leer ....

Práctica de gramática

Dos amigos hablan sobre sus actividades. Completa esta conversación con el pretérito o el imperfecto del verbo apropiado.

conocer	poder	querer	saber

A — ¿Pudiste estudiar el sábado por la tarde?

B — No, no __1.__. Pablo y Agustín estuvieron en casa toda la tarde.

A — ¡Ah! Pablo es el chico que yo __2.__ el verano pasado, ¿no?

B — No, tú no lo __3.__.

A — Bueno, yo __4.__ conocerlo, pero no __5.__ conocerlo en persona. Lo __6.__ por teléfono.

B — ¿Tú hablaste por teléfono con él? ¡Yo nunca lo __7.__! A mí él nunca me dijo nada.

● **Más práctica** ....
Practice Workbook 10-1, 10-2

8 Leer ....

Práctica de gramática

Escoge el verbo que corresponda para completar lo que escribió Teresa anoche en su diario.

Querido diario:
Hoy __1.__ (conocí / conocía) a un chico guapísimo. Julia y yo __2.__ (quisimos / queríamos) ir al cine, pero no __3.__ (pudimos / podíamos). No había más entradas para la película que __4.__ (quisimos / queríamos) ver. Al salir nos encontramos con el chico guapísimo. Yo no lo __5.__ (conocí / conocía), pero Julia me contó que ella lo __6.__ (conoció / conocía) en una fiesta. Él __7.__ (quiso / quería) ir a tomar algo pero Julia no __8.__ (quiso / quería).

Go Online
PHSchool.com
For: More review
Visit: www.phschool.com
Web Code: jed-01001

cuatrocientos treinta y tres **433**
Capítulo 10

Gramática·Repaso

Presentation

Standards: 4.1

Resources: Voc. & Gram. Transparencies: 184

Suggestions: Have students write question-and-answer dialogues practicing the verbs in the preterite tense: —*¿Jorge escribió su composición? —Quiso escribirla pero dice que era demasiado difícil.*

 7 *Standards:* 1.2
....

Resources: Practice Answers on Transparencies

Focus: Reviewing verbs with different meanings in the preterite and imperfect tenses

Common Errors: Some students may spell preterite forms of **querer** with **-c-** instead of **-s-** in the middle. On the board, model as necessary the correct spellings of the forms of this irregular verb.

Suggestions: Remind students that the items in the activity are part of a dialogue. They need to keep track of the meaning of what has already been said in order to better know which verb form to use.

Answers:

1. **pude**	5. **pude**
2. **conocí**	6. **conocí**
3. **conociste**	7. **sabía**
4. **quería**	

 8 *Standards:* 1.2
....

Resources: Practice Answers on Transparencies

Focus: Reviewing verbs with different meanings in the preterite and imperfect tenses

Suggestions: Remind students to read the entire diary entry before attempting to write their answers.

Answers:

1. **conocí**	5. **conocía**
2. **queríamos**	6. **conoció**
3. **pudimos**	7. **quería**
4. **queríamos**	8. **quiso**

Enriching Your Teaching

Teacher-to-Teacher

A great way to get students on-task at the beginning of the class is to put a short written exercise on an overhead transparency. Stand at the door as students enter and hand them copies of the accompanying activity to complete (or instruct them to write answers on their own paper) and have them begin immediately. These should be short activities that students can complete in two to three minutes. Use this time to take attendance or collect homework. Word-choice activities of your own creation, similar to *Actividad 8*, work very well for this type of beginning-of-the-class activity. Limit the content of such activities to review.

Standards for Foreign Language Learning: *Capítulo* 10

• To achieve the goals of the Standards, students will:

Communication

1.1 Interpersonal
• Talk about problems, rights, responsibilities, and the role of government
• Talk about Francisco Goya, Hilario Barrero, Juan Lovera, and their work
• Talk about Peruvian schools and a Mexican referendum
• Talk about famous people who fought for justice
• Talk about heroes of Latin American independence

1.2 Interpretive
• Read and listen to information about problems, rights, responsibilities, and the role of government
• Read about Francisco Goya, Hilario Barrero, Juan Lovera, and their work
• Listen to information about Peruvian schools
• Read about a Mexican referendum
• Read about the suffix *-miento*
• Read about famous people who fought for justice
• Read about Spanish-language electoral campaigns in the United States
• Read about heroes of Latin American independence
• Read about Bolivian Domitila Barrios Chungara's struggle for justice

1.3 Presentational
• Write and present information orally about problems, rights, responsibilities, and the role of government
• Recite poetry by Hilario Barrero
• Write a news report
• Write and present information orally about famous people who fought for justice
• Write about heroes of Latin American independence
• Write about Bolivian Domitila Barrios Chungara's struggle for justice

Culture

2.1 Practices and Perspectives
• Interpret the cultural perspectives of important artists
• Interpret student rights and responsibilities in Spain and Peru
• Interpret the vision of Mexican politician and educator José Vasconcelos
• Interpret the perspectives of heroes of Latin American independence

2.2 Products and Perspectives
• Discuss the work of Francisco Goya, Hilario Barrero, Juan Lovera
• Discuss Latin American independence movements
• Discuss a book by Bolivian writer Domitila Barrios Chungara

Connections

3.1 Cross-curricular
• Discuss key facts about art, poetry, literature, and important artists
• Discuss key social and geographical facts about many Latin American countries and Spain
• Discuss key facts about civics studies and social studies
• Use Language Arts Strategies: creating a time line; think, plan, then speak; snappy introductions; investigate the author's reasons

Fondo cultural ■◆◆◇■◆◇■◇■◆

Escenas de la vida

La obra de Francisco Goya (1746–1828) cubrió un período de más de 60 años. En su juventud, cuando pintó este cuadro, Goya aceptó felizmente el mundo tal como era.

Años más tarde, Goya comenzó a sentirse desilusionado con la gente y la sociedad. Como resultado, pintó escenas que criticaban la política de la época. Su selección de temas es evidencia de que creía en el derecho del artista de pintar el mundo tal como lo veía.

•¿Crees que un artista debe tener el derecho de pintar lo que le dé la gana? ¿Por qué? ¿Por qué no?

El baile a orillas del Manzanares, (1777), Francisco de Goya y Lucientes
(c) 2003 SCALA/Art Resource, New York.

Universal Access

Personalizing the Theme
Ask students to share their background knowledge about rights and responsibilities at home, at school, and in society. Ask: *¿Cuáles son algunas de tus responsabilidades como estudiante en esta escuela? ¿Cuáles son unos de los derechos que garantiza la Constitución de los Estados Unidos?*

Multiple Intelligences
Interpersonal/Social: In small groups, ask students to imagine that they were charged with starting a new country. Have them discuss their country's form of government, rules and laws, and rights of citizens.

Capítulo 10

¿Cuáles son tus derechos y deberes?

Chapter Objectives

- Talk about rights and responsibilities at home and in school
- Discuss rights in society guaranteed by the Constitution
- Talk about the role of government
- Learn what young people think about the world problems they face and the solutions they propose
- Understand cultural perspectives on rights and responsibilities

Video Focus

- Human rights education

Country Connection

As you learn about rights and responsibilities in the Spanish-speaking world, you will make connections to these countries and places.

Go Online
PHSchool.com

For: Online Atlas
Visit: www.phschool.com
Web Code: jee-0002

cuatrocientos treinta y cinco **435**
Capítulo 10

Preview

Standards for Foreign Language Learning (cont'd)

3.2 Target Culture
- Read a pamphlet from Spain
- Read a transcript of an interview with a Peruvian student
- Read poetry by Hilario Barrero
- Read literature by Domitila Barrios Chungara

Comparisons
4.1 Language
- Compare the passive voice in Spanish and English
- Compare the use of Spanish **como si** with that of the English "as if"
- Compare the Spanish conditional perfect with that of English
- Compare Spanish words with their English counterparts

4.2 Culture
- Compare student rights and responsibilities in Spain and Mexico with those in the United States
- Compare Venezuelan historical art with that of the United States
- Compare Latin American independence movements with that of the United States
- Compare a Bolivian civil rights movement with those in the United States

Communities
5.1 Beyond the School
- Link to Web sites from around the Spanish-speaking world

5.2 Lifelong Learner
- Develop an appreciation for visual art, poetry, and literature
- Discuss the individual's place in society

Chapter Opener
Presentation

Resources: Voc. & Gram. Transparencies: 14, 16, 18, 20 (maps)

Suggestions: Introduce students to the theme of the chapter and go over the objectives. Point out that they will improve their ability to talk and write about individual rights and responsibilities. Use the map transparencies to locate and discuss the countries featured in the chapter.

Enriching Your Teaching

Planning for Instruction
Resources:
- Teacher Express CD-ROM or Resource Book
  - Teaching resources
  - Lesson Planner
  - Chapter Resource Checklist
  - School-to-Home Connection Letter

Culture Note
In a UNICEF-sponsored series of youth opinion polls conducted from 1999-2001, Latin Americans from ages 9 to 18 said they were most concerned with access to education, violence in their communities, and social justice.

Fondo cultural | *Standards:* 1.1, 1.2, 2.1, 2.2, 3.1
■◆■◆■◆■◆■◆■◆■◆■◆■◆■◆

Resources: Fine Art Transparencies; Fine Art Transparencies Teacher's Guide

Suggestions: After students read the information, ask: *¿Cómo comenzó a sentirse Goya durante la segunda parte de su vida? (Se desilusionó con la gente y la sociedad.)*

Answers will vary.

Vocabulario y gramática

Presentation

Standards: 1.1, 1.2

Resources: Voc. & Gram. Transparencies: 185–186; Resource Book: Cap. 10, Input Script; Audio Program: CD Cap. 10, Track 1

Focus: Presenting new vocabulary and using grammar lexically in context

Suggestions: You may want to use the Input Script from the *Teacher's Resource Book* as a source of ideas for presentation of new vocabulary and comprehensible input. While presenting the vocabulary, point out cognates, such as *adolescentes, injusticia, libertad, respeto* and *tolerancia.* Since most of the vocabulary is not visualized, encourage students to use context clues to help themselves understand the meanings of new words and expressions.

Block Schedule

Divide the class into two sections. Have students from one half work in groups of three and create three additional *derechos de los adolescentes.* Have the other half work in threes and write three additional *derechos de los padres.* Ask each group to present their statements to the groups. Write different *derechos* on the board and have the class vote on the best three.

A primera vista 1

Vocabulario y gramática en contexto

Los adolescentes sienten a veces que tienen tantos **deberes** o responsabilidades como los adultos, pero menos derechos que los niños. ¿Crees que los problemas de Laura son comunes entre los adolescentes de hoy?

Laura: ¿Puedo ir a la fiesta el sábado?

Madre: El sábado vamos a ver a tu abuela.

Laura: ¡Es una **injusticia**! Tengo 16 años y no tengo **libertad** para decidir qué voy a hacer el sábado. . .

Ustedes dicen que quieren mi **felicidad**, pero no sé hasta qué punto es justo que me **traten** como a una niña, **de ese modo** no soy feliz.

Padre: Laura, claro que queremos que seas feliz y que sientas nuestro **apoyo**. Para nosotros también es difícil saber cómo tratar a una chica de 16 años.

Laura: Pero, ¿por qué tienen que **obligarme** a ir a casa de la abuela un sábado por la noche?

Creo que tengo una idea para resolver este **asunto.**

Derechos de los Adolescentes

▶ Iré siempre donde yo quiera ir.

▶ Podré usar la ropa que yo quiera.

▶ Nadie podrá prohibirme que me pinte el pelo de cualquier color.

▶ Hablaré por teléfono con mis amigas todo el tiempo que sea necesario.

▶ Nadie me prohibirá navegar en la Red.

▶ Nadie entrará en mi cuarto sin permiso.

Universal Access

Advanced Learners

Ask students to work in a small group to compare and contrast the rights and responsibilities they and their classmates have at home. They can begin by telling about their own rights and responsibilities in round-robin fashion, and then commenting on similarities and differences among them. Encourage them to compile information on the group in a T-chart with the two headings *nuestros derechos en casa* and *nuestras responsabilidades en casa.* Invite the group to share their findings with the rest of the class.

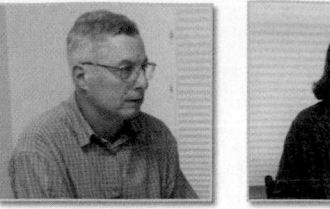

Padre: Ana, nosotros nunca hemos **maltratado** a Laura. . . **ambos** queremos su felicidad. ¿Por qué está tan enojada con nosotros?

Madre: Pedro, si tú tuvieras 16 años, ¿no te sentirías como ella?

Padre: Quizás. Pero creo que debe tratarnos con **respeto** y **tolerancia**. ¿O es que los padres no tenemos derechos?

Derechos de los padres

1. Nos dirás siempre adónde vas.

2. Si te vas a cambiar el color del pelo, pedirás permiso.

3. Estableceremos un horario para hablar por teléfono.

4. Estableceremos un horario para usar la Red.

5. Mantendrás tu cuarto ordenado y limpio.

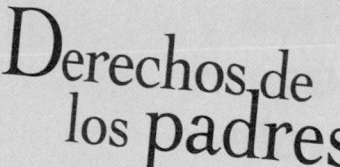

Laura: Papá, creo que mi lista de derechos es muy **adecuada**, ¿verdad?

Padre: Pues yo también hice una lista, pero de los derechos de los padres. ¿Qué te parece?

 **Escuchar**

Los derechos de cada uno

Escribe los números del 1 al 5 en una hoja de papel. Escucha cada frase y escribe *C* (cierta) o *F* (falsa).

 Hablar

Lo mejor de las listas

Piensa si estás de acuerdo con las listas que escribieron Laura y su papá. De ambas listas, escoge cuatro frases con las que estés de acuerdo y di por qué estás de acuerdo. Habla con otro(a) estudiante sobre tus opiniones.

cuatrocientos treinta y siete **437**
Capítulo 10

Language Input

Actividad 1 *Standards:* 1.2

Resources: Voc. & Gram. Transparencies: 185–186; Audio Program: CD Cap. 10, Track 2; Resource Book: Cap. 10, Audio Script; Practice Answers on Transparencies

Focus: Practicing listening comprehension of new vocabulary

Suggestions: Remind students to listen for key words that will help them determine the answers. Use the *Audio CD* or read the script. Allow students to listen more than once.

Answers:
1. C   4. C
2. F   5. C
3. C

Actividad 2 *Standards:* 1.1

Resources: Voc. & Gram. Transparencies: 185–186

Focus: Practicing new vocabulary in a guided conversation

Suggestions: Use the instructions to clarify the meaning of **ambos(as).** Point to both lists on *Vocabulary and Grammar Transparencies* 185–186 and say: *Voy a seleccionar de ambas listas. Esto quiere decir que voy a usar las dos listas y seleccionar un número total de cuatro frases.*

Answers will vary.

Enriching Your Teaching

Culture Note

Many families in Spanish-speaking countries still take the time to discuss daily events, make plans, and resolve conflicts in a conversation around the table after dinner. There is even a name for this custom of after-dinner conversation: *la sobremesa.* Depending on the household, dessert and coffee may remain on the table during *la sobremesa,* or other foods, such as fruit or cheeses, may be served. On special days, when guests are invited to the house, *la sobremesa* may last for hours. *Una sobremesa* after a Sunday lunch, for example, may last right into dinnertime!

437

Vocabulario y gramática

Presentation

Standards: 1.1, 1.2, 2.1, 2.2, 3.1, 3.2

Resources: Voc. & Gram. Transparencies 187–188; Resource Book: Cap. 10, Input Script; Audio Program: CD Cap. 10, Tracks 3–4

Focus: Extending presentation of vocabulary and grammar

Suggestions:

Pre-reading: Explain to students that the readings on these two pages are separate and will be read and discussed individually. Before beginning, write on the board *responsabilidades = deberes* and say: *Estas dos palabras son sinónimos. En estas lecturas se usan "deberes."*

Reading: After students read the brochure on this page, have them complete *Actividad 3* before they go on to read the article on p. 439 and complete *Actividad 4.*

Post-reading: After an initial reading of each of the selections, clarify the meaning of new vocabulary as necessry. Point out cognates such as *satisfactoria* and *abusos.* Ask a volunteer to read aloud the definition for *estado* that is included in the article on p. 439. **(todas las instituciones del gobierno).** Use circumlocution, synonyms, antonyms, and demonstrations to teach the meanings of other non-visualized words and expressions.

Standards: 1.2, 1.3, 3.1, 4.2

Focus: Practicing new vocabulary via note-taking and discussion

Suggestions: Encourage students to add to their discussion other pertinent student rights and responsibilities that the Spanish brochure does not address.

Answers will vary.

Derechos y deberes en la escuela

En todas las escuelas, los estudiantes tienen ciertos derechos y deberes. Sin embargo, no en todos los países, ni en todas las escuelas, son iguales. Por ejemplo, en tu escuela, ¿hay un **código de vestimenta** o todo el mundo puede llevar la ropa que más le guste? Y **en cuanto a los armarios** de los estudiantes, ¿los maestros tienen derecho a registrarlos?

Para resolver estas preguntas de manera **satisfactoria**, el gobierno en España estableció una ley de los derechos y deberes de los estudiantes.

 **Hablar/Escribir** · · · · · · · · ·

Los derechos en tu escuela

Con otro(a) estudiante, comenta los derechos y deberes de los estudiantes españoles. Hablen de los derechos y deberes que tienen ustedes en su escuela y escríbanlos en una hoja de papel. Luego, compárenlos con los de los estudiantes en España.

Los estudiantes tienen el deber de:

- cumplir y respetar los horarios para el desarrollo de las actividades de la escuela
- respetar **la autoridad** de los maestros
- respetar el derecho al estudio de sus compañeros
- respetar la libertad de expresión y **pensamiento** de sus compañeros
- no **discriminar** a ningún o ninguna estudiante por **motivos** personales o sociales
- cuidar y utilizar correctamente las escuelas; ayudarlas a **funcionar** bien
- participar en la vida y funcionamiento de las escuelas

Los estudiantes tienen derecho a:

- recibir una **enseñanza** gratuita
- no ser **discriminados** por causas personales o sociales
- **votar** a sus representantes en el Consejo Escolar
- **gozar de** libertad de expresión y pensamiento
- reunirse y utilizar las escuelas para actividades educativas

438 cuatrocientos treinta y ocho
A primera vista 1

Universal Access

Advanced Learners

Invite students to convert their notes from *Actividad 3* into an "official" ***Panfleto de los deberes y derechos de los estudiantes*** for your school. They can use the Spanish brochure as a model. If they have computer software available to them, encourage them to design the pamphlet for reproduction and posting in the classroom or, with permission, in other parts of the school. Interested students may want to bring the contents of their pamphlet before your school's student council for consideration.

El gobierno y los derechos de la niñez

El estado, o sea todas las instituciones del gobierno, son responsables de **aplicar** las leyes que protegen a la niñez. Los gobiernos deben:

1. Garantizar que los niños y adolescentesvivan en **paz**.

2. Garantizar que los niños no **estén sujetos** a **maltratos** ni **abusos** por parte de las personas que se encargan de ellos.

3. Dar ayuda a los niños que **sufren** de mucha **pobreza**.

4. Prohibir que se discrimine por **razones** de raza, nacionalidad o sexo.

5. Reconocer **la igualdad** de derechos ante la ley.

 Escribir

La felicidad de los más jóvenes

1. Según el documento, ¿qué derechos debe garantizar el gobierno para los niños?

2. Indica dos cosas que, según el documento, el gobierno debe prohibir.

3. ¿Qué quiere decir "reconocer la igualdad de todas las personas ante la ley"? ¿Por qué es importante?

● **Más práctica**
Practice Workbook 10-3, 10-4

PHSchool.com
For: Vocabulary practice
Visit: www.phschool.com
Web Code: jed-1002

Actividad 4   *Standards:* 1.2, 1.3, 3.1

Resources: Practice Answers on Transparencies

Focus: Practicing reading comprehension of new vocabulary

Suggestions: Encourage students to paraphrase information from the article in order to answer the questions.

Answers:

1. El gobierno debe garantizar que los niños y adolescentes vivan en paz y que no estén sujetos a maltratos ni abusos por parte de las personas que los cuidan.

2. El gobierno dcbc prohibir que se discrimine por razones de raza, nacionalidad o sexo. También debe prohibir los maltratos y abusos de los niños y adolescentes.

3. Answers will vary.

Additional Resources

• Resource Book: Cap. 10, Clip Art

 Assessment

• Prueba 10-1: Vocabulary recognition

Chapter Project

Give students copies of the Chapter Project outline and rubric from the *Teacher's Resource Book*. Explain the task to them, and have them perform step 1. (For more information, see p. 430-a.)

 Enriching Your Teaching

Culture Note

Many schools and organizations in Spanish-speaking countries post information about student rights and responsibilities on the Internet. Examples of such rights and responsibilities include: "that students' freedom of choice as well as their religious, moral, and ideological convictions be respected" and "that students respect the right of their classmates to study."

Internet Search

Keywords:

derechos y deberes en la escuela

439

Manos a la obra 1
Vocabulario y gramática en uso

Actividad 5 Leer/Escribir

Lo positivo y lo negativo

En una hoja de papel, copia esta tabla. Lee las palabras y escríbelas en la columna apropiada. Luego, escribe frases con tres de las palabras.

lo positivo	lo negativo

la libertad   el respeto   la felicidad   el abuso
el deber   discriminar   la tolerancia   el apoyo
maltratar   sufrir   el maltrato   gratuito(a)
la paz   la injusticia la igualdad   adecuado(a)

Actividad 6 Leer/Escuchar/Escribir

Entrevista con una peruana

❶ Lee esta entrevista con Viviana Gallegos, una adolescente del Perú.

Una entrevista con

Viviana Gallegos...

¿Qué nacionalidad tienes?
Soy peruana.

¿Es gratuita la enseñanza en Perú?
Hay colegios privados y colegios del estado. Los colegios del estado son gratuitos.

¿Hay un código de vestimenta en las escuelas?
Sí, tenemos que usar uniformes. Cada escuela tiene su uniforme. Unos uniformes son más bonitos que otros.

¿Hay servicios médicos adecuados para todos los ciudadanos?
Sí, se llaman postas médicas. Son centros médicos pequeños. Ofrecen consultas con médicos y dan vacunas (*vaccines*). Ambos servicios son gratuitos.

❷ Ahora, escucha las preguntas y contéstalas en clase.

Universal Access

Heritage Language Learners
Ask students who have lived in a heritage country if they would let others interview them on the topic of schools and the educational system in the heritage country. Interviewers can base their questions on the interview with Viviana Gallegos in *Actividad* 6.

Students with Learning Difficulties
Help students grasp the abstract concepts listed in *Actividad 8*. Provide them with photographs or icons that represent each of the issues described. For example, a photograph of people protesting might represent *la libertad de expresión y pensamiento.*

Actividad 7

Leer/Escribir/Hablar · · · · · · · · · · · ·

Los derechos en nuestra escuela

Túrnate con un(a) compañero(a) para indicar si estás de acuerdo o no con las frases siguientes sobre tu escuela, y explícale por qué. Tu compañero(a) va a tomar apuntes sobre lo que dices, y luego ambos van a compartir sus ideas con la clase.

1. No es necesario seguir un código de vestimenta en esta escuela.

2. Los adolescentes deben tratar a los maestros con más respeto y, de ese modo, respetar su autoridad.

3. En nuestras clases, los chicos tienen más libertad que las chicas.

4. La enseñanza en esta escuela es adecuada para prepararme para lo que voy a hacer en el futuro.

5. Todos los estudiantes tienen derecho a gozar de libertad de expresión.

6. Los profesores deben tener la autoridad y el deber de registrar los armarios.

7. Todos los estudiantes deben estar sujetos a las mismas reglas.

Actividad 8

 Escribir/Hablar ·

En nuestro país

1 Piensa en los siguientes temas sociales. En tu opinión, ¿cuál es el más importante? ¿Y el menos importante? Ponlos en orden de importancia.

1. la libertad de expresión y pensamiento
2. la igualdad entre los hombres y las mujeres
3. cómo tratar a los animales
4. los servicios médicos
5. el apoyo a los niños
6. la pobreza
7. las reglas para manejar
8. los deberes del estado

2 Dile tu opinión a un(a) compañero(a) sobre los temas mencionados en la parte anterior. Usa las palabras del recuadro.

adecuado(a)	satisfactorio(a)	injusticia	en cuanto a
abuso	respeto	gratuito(a)	ambos(as)

Modelo

la alimentación
A —*La alimentación en nuestro país es satisfactoria.*
B —*Pues yo no estoy de acuerdo. La gente come demasiada comida basura y . . .*

 Actividad 7 *Standards:* 1.1, 1.2, 1.3
· · · · · · · · · · · · · · · · ·

Focus: Using new vocabulary in a contextualized discussion

Suggestions: Remind students that when they report on their pair work, they will change verb forms frequently in order to tell about what their partner said.

Answers will vary.

 Actividad 8 *Standards:* 1.1, 1.2
· · · · · · · · · · · · · · · · ·

Focus: Using new vocabulary in a contextualized discussion

Recycle: conjunctions that take the subjunctive or the indicative

Suggestions: For step 1, tell students to copy each item entirely for writing practice, rather than using numbers to order the items.

Answers will vary.

Enriching Your Teaching

Teacher-to-Teacher

Invite students who have cameras to create photo essays about student rights and responsibilities in your school. They can take pictures of their friends studying, participating in extracurricular activities, having lunch in the cafeteria, taking breaks, making visits to their lockers, interacting with faculty and administration, and so on. Have them assemble the photos in a visual display, complete with a title, a brief statement about the purpose of the display, and a caption for each photo, explaining how it represents a student right or responsibility.

Actividad 9 *Standards:* 1.1, 1.3, 3.1

Resources: Voc. & Gram. Transparencies 4

Focus: Practicing new vocabulary via note-taking and discussion

Suggestions: This activity can be conducted with the whole class. Use *Vocabulary and Grammar Transparency* 4 to begin the chart, and have students follow along on their own paper. Use guiding questions to elicit from students the information to record on the chart. Record it there yourself or have a volunteer do so as the class follows along.

Answers will vary.

Actividad 10 *Standards:* 1.1

Focus: Practicing new vocabulary through discussion

Suggestions: Encourage students to use background knowledge they have gained in their Language Arts or Social Studies classes to answer the questions.

Answers will vary.

Ampliación del lenguaje

Presentation

Standards: 1.2, 3.1

Resources: Practice Answers on Transparencies

Focus: Understanding the suffix **-miento**

Suggestions: After students complete the chart, encourage them to experiment using **-miento** to form other nouns from verbs. They can use a dictionary to check their work.

Answers:

Chart

3. pensamiento
4. mejoramiento
5. conocimiento
6. comportamiento
7. descubrimiento
8. movimiento

Sentences
1. descubrimiento; descubrir
2. mejorar; mejoramiento

Actividad 9 **Hablar/Escribir**

Derechos y responsabilidades

❶ Ser adolescente quiere decir tener muchos derechos pero también responsabilidades. En grupo, completen una tabla como la siguiente con los derechos y responsabilidades que tienen los adolescentes.

❷ ¿Cómo se comparan los derechos y responsabilidades de los adolescentes con los de los adultos? Usen sus tablas para responder.

Derechos	Responsabilidades
1.	1.
2.	2.
3.	3.

Actividad 10 **Escribir/Hablar**

Y tú, ¿qué dices?

1. ¿Por qué crees que hay códigos de vestimenta en muchas escuelas? ¿Crees que es buena idea tener un código de vestimenta? ¿Por qué?

2. Describe el asunto de tu comunidad que sea más importante para ti. ¿Cómo se debe resolver ese asunto?

3. En tu opinión, ¿por qué la gente discrimina? ¿Tiene motivos personales? Explica.

4. ¿Hasta qué punto piensas que en nuestra sociedad hay igualdad?

Ampliación del lenguaje

El sufijo *–miento*

Un sustantivo que termina en el sufijo *–miento* tiene como base un verbo. Para formar sustantivos, a los verbos en infinitivo que terminan en *-ar*, quítales la *r* y añádeles el sufijo *-miento (tratar → tratamiento*), y a los que terminan en *-er* y en *-ir* quítales la terminación y agrégales una *i* antes del sufijo *(vencer → vencimiento)*. Los sustantivos con *-miento* son masculinos. Copia la tabla y escribe los sustantivos. Luego, completa las frases.

verbo	sustantivo
1. funcionar	funcionamiento
2. nacer	nacimiento
3. pensar	
4. mejorar	
5. conocer	
6. comportar	
7. descubrir	
8. mover	

1. El ____ de la electricidad hizo que la vida de mucha gente fuera más fácil. Pero ____ la electricidad tomó mucho tiempo.

2. Muchos científicos trabajan juntos para ____ el medio ambiente. El ____ del medio ambiente es importante.

Universal Access

Heritage Language Learners

Ask students who have lived in a heritage country to comment on the issue of equality in that country. Do they feel equality exists? If not, along which lines do inequalities appear? Invite all students to compare these descriptions to the situation in their present community.

Students with Learning Difficulties

Before students speak about their opinions in *Actividad* 10, give them the opportunity to brainstorm and plan their responses. Suggest that students write down a few notes on each of the topics.

Actividad 11

Escribir/Dibujar

Una tarjeta especial

Vas a entrar en un concurso para hacer tarjetas que digan algo sobre los derechos y las responsabilidades de la gente. Dibuja una tarjeta y añádele un deseo o derecho. Usa el vocabulario de este capítulo.

Modelo

Es importante que todos los ciudadanos voten en las elecciones del estado.

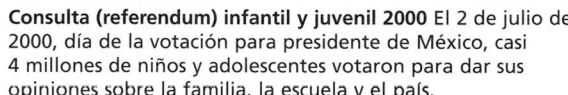

Consulta (referendum) infantil y juvenil 2000 El 2 de julio de 2000, día de la votación para presidente de México, casi 4 millones de niños y adolescentes votaron para dar sus opiniones sobre la familia, la escuela y el país.

Mira las gráficas para comparar lo que piensan los niños y los adolescentes sobre el respeto en las escuelas y lee la tabla de abajo que muestra opiniones de los adolescentes.

• ¿Son ustedes respetados en la escuela?

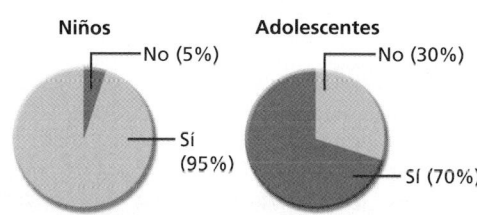

Niños
No (5%)
Sí (95%)

Adolescentes
No (30%)
Sí (70%)

Adolescentes	Sí	No
¿Son tomados en cuenta en su familia?	95%	5%
¿Son tomados en cuenta en la comunidad?	83%	17%
¿Son tomados en cuenta en el país?	61%	39%
¿Participan en las decisiones del país?	32%	68%
¿Hay igualdad entre hombres y mujeres en el país?	37%	63%

• ¿Por qué crees que la opinión de los niños y de los adolescentes sobre la escuela es diferente?

• Compara lo que dicen los adolescentes mexicanos sobre el respeto en las escuelas con lo que piensan tus compañeros(as). ¿Crees que ellos opinan lo mismo? ¿Por qué?

Practice and Communicate

  10

Actividad 11

Standards: 1.3

Focus: Practicing new vocabulary

Suggestions: Encourage students to research greeting card stores or the Internet to find creative ideas for their cards.

Answers will vary.

Fondo cultural

Standards: 1.1, 1.2, 2.1, 3.1, 4.2

Suggestions: After students have read the information, ask: *¿Quiénes votaron en la consulta? (niños y adolescentes) Según las gráficas, ¿hay más o menos adolescentes que niños que piensan que son respetados en la escuela? (menos) ¿Cuánto menos? (casi el 25 por ciento menos)*

Answers will vary.

Additional Resources
• Writing, Audio & Video Workbook: Cap. 10, Audio Activity 1, Track 6
• Writing, Audio & Video Workbook: Cap. 10, Writing Activity 6
• Resource Book: Cap. 10, Communicative Activity BLM

 Assessment
• Prueba 10-2: Vocabulary production

Enriching Your Teaching

Teacher-to-Teacher

The *Consulta infantil y juvenil 2000* was considered a success by its organizers and by the Mexican press. To conduct the referendum, more than 15,000 polling places were set up throughout the country, and the turnout was considerable. More children under twelve voted than adolescents. Youngsters were presented with ballots that differed according to their age group. There was a ballot for 6–9-year-olds, one for 10–13-year-olds, and one for 14–17-year-olds. All ballots contained *sí/no* questions that varied according to the age groups, as well as one open-ended question that read: *Yo quiero que en México nunca más haya....*

Gramática

Presentation

Standards: 4.1

Resources: Voc & Gram. Transparencies: 189

Suggestions: Ask questions about what students do to elicit the passive voice: —*¿Por quién fue cerrada la puerta? —La puerta fue cerrada por (nombre de estudiante).*

12 *Standards:* 1.2, 1.3

Resources: Audio Program: CD Cap. 10, Track 8; Resource Book: Cap. 10, Audio Script; Practice Answers on Transparencies

Focus: Practicing the passive voice

Suggestions: Pause the *Audio CD* after each item, so students can write their answers.

Answers:
1. un perro; fue maltratado; su dueño
2. varios jóvenes; fueron discriminados; no se sabe
3. los dueños de una fábrica; fueron acusados de abuso; no se sabe
4. dos adolescentes; fueron obligados a devolver un televisor robado; no se sabe
5. la víctima; fue apoyada; los abogados
6. un hombre; fue criticado; otros ciudadanos
7. los criminales; fueron perdonados; el juez

13 *Standards:* 1.1

Resources: Practice Answers on Transparencies

Focus: Practicing the passive voice

Suggestions: Have students switch roles, so everyone has a chance to practice.

Answers: Passive subjects will vary. The following are possible results.
1. —¿Quién curó a los niños?
—Fueron curados por….
2. —¿Quién respetó la igualdad?
—La igualdad fue respetada por….
3. —¿Quién aplicó las leyes?
—Las leyes fueron aplicadas por….
4. —¿Quién leyó el discurso?
—El discurso fue leído por….

Additional Resources

• Writing, Audio & Video Workbook: Cap. 10, Audio Activity 2, Track 7

Gramática

La voz pasiva: *ser* + participio pasado

In a sentence, the subject usually performs the action. This is called active voice. Sometimes, the subject does not "do" the action but rather has the action "done to it" or receives the action. This is called passive voice.

> Santiago **estableció** las reglas del club.
> Las reglas del club **fueron establecidas** por Santiago.

In Spanish, like in English, you form the passive voice by using *ser* + past participle. Since the past participle is an adjective, it agrees in number and gender with the subject.

> Las reglas **son aplicadas** por el estado.

• If you mention "who" or "what" performs the action, you use *por* to mean "by".

• You often use the impersonal *se* when the subject is unknown.

> **Se necesita** una persona para trabajar en el centro comunitario.

12 **Gramática** **Escuchar/Escribir/Hablar**

Las noticias del día

Imagina que enciendes la radio y escuchas las noticias del día. Para cada frase que escuches, llena una tabla como ésta. Después, usa tus notas para contar de nuevo las noticias.

¿Quién(es) fue(ron) afectado(s)?	¿Qué le(s) pasó?	¿Por quién(es)?
un niño	*fue asustado*	*un oso*
1.		

Modelo

Un niño fue asustado por un oso que había escapado del zoológico.

13 **Gramática** **Hablar**

¿Quién lo hizo?

Con un(a) compañero(a), comenta por quién o quiénes fueron hechas estas cosas. Sigue el modelo.

Modelo

escribir / artículo
A —*¿Quién escribió el artículo sobre la adolescencia?*
B —*El artículo fue escrito por un reportero.*

Estudiante A
1. curar / niños
2. respetar / igualdad
3. leyes / aplicar
4. leer / discurso
5. entrevistar / adolescentes
6. (nombre) / escoger
7. promover / paz
8. evitar / injusticias

Estudiante B
autoridades
gobierno
estudiantes
maestro (a)
médico (a)
reportero (a)
juez

● **Más práctica**
Practice Workbook 10-3, 10-4

For: Practice with the passive voice
Visit: www.phschool.com
Web Code: jed-1007

Universal Access

Students with Learning Difficulties

Before students make their choices in *Actividad 14*, first have them identify the verb in the main clause of each sentence. Second, ask them to determine the tense based on that verb. Third, have them choose the correct answer based on that tense.

Advanced Learners

Have students prepare brief news reports about current events. Tell them to use at least one sentence in the passive voice for each report.

Practice and Communicate

 (cont'd)

5. —¿Quién entrevistó a los adolescentes?
   —Los adolescentes fueron entrevistados por….
6. —¿Quién escogió…?
   —…fue escogido por…
7. —¿Quién promovió la paz?
   —La paz fue promovida por….
8. —¿Quién evitó las injusticias?
   —Las injusticias fueron evitadas por….

 Gramática

El presente y el imperfecto del subjuntivo

Use the present or the present perfect subjunctive when the verb in the main clause is in the:

Present	**Espero** que **hayan votado**.
Command form	**Dile** que **vote** mañana en las elecciones.
Present perfect	No **hemos establecido** ninguna regla que **sea** injusta.
Future	El sistema **funcionará** mejor cuando **se cambien** las leyes.

Use the imperfect subjunctive when the verb in the main clause is in the:

Preterite	Mi mamá me **pidió** que **tratara** con más respeto a mi hermano.
Imperfect	Mis padres **querían** que mi hermano y yo **nos lleváramos** bien.
Pluperfect	El profesor nos **había exigido** que ambos **tuviéramos** más tolerancia.
Conditional	Al jefe le **gustaría** que los empleados **llegaran** a tiempo.

 Rapid Review
Before completing the next *Gramática* presentation and accompanying series of activities, briefly review with students the formation of the imperfect subjunctive.

 Gramática

Presentation

Focus: Voc. & Gram. Transparencies: 190

Suggestions: Have students invent sentences to demonstrate their understanding of each of the rules for use of the present subjunctive, present perfect subjunctive, and imperfect subjunctive.

Actividad 14 **Gramática** **Leer**

Responsabilidades como estudiante

Imagina que hablas con un adulto acerca de las responsabilidades que tenía cuando iba a la escuela. Completa el párrafo con el tiempo correcto del subjuntivo de los verbos.

Cuando era joven, el director de la escuela quería que los estudiantes __1.__ *(sigan / siguieran)* un código de vestimenta. A mí no me gustaba que __2.__ *(tenga / tuviera)* que usar ropa especial para ir a clases. Yo quería que nosotros __3.__ *(gocemos / gozáramos)* de la libertad de vestirnos de cualquier manera, como ahora. ¡Tú tienes suerte! Los maestros no pueden prohibir que __4.__ *(lleves / llevaras)* pantalones rotos ni zapatos viejos. Siempre me ha sorprendido que ahora los maestros no __5.__ *(obliguen / obligaran)* a los estudiantes a sentarse cuando empieza la clase. Es curioso que tampoco les __6.__ *(pidan / pidieran)* la tarea todos los días. En mis clases era común que todas las semanas nos __7.__ *(den / dieran)* un examen, y de ese modo, hacían que __8.__ siempre *(estudiáramos / estudiemos)*. También querían que los estudiantes __9.__ *(hagamos / hiciéramos)* proyectos especiales después de la escuela. Pero hoy es diferente. Este sistema de enseñanza menos formal funciona bien, a menos que los jóvenes __10.__ *(se rebelen / se rebelaran)*. Ojalá no __11.__ *(pase / pasara)* eso. Sería triste que los estudiantes __12.__ *(sufran / sufrieran)* por una falta de organización en la escuela.

 Actividad 14 *Standards:* 1.2

Resources: Practice Answers on Transparencies

Focus: Using various tenses in the subjunctive

Suggestions: Remind students to focus on the verb in the main clause of each sentence in order to determine which tense to use in the subordinate clause.

Answers

1. siguieran	7. dieran
2. tuviera	8. estudiáramos
3. gozáramos	9. hiciéramos
4. lleves	10. se rebelen
5. obliguen	11. pase
6. pidan	12. sufrieran

Enriching Your Teaching

Teacher-to-Teacher

Have students interview a family member from an earlier generation, such as a parent, grandparent, aunt or uncle, about similarities and differences between family dynamics when they were adolescents and now. What where their rights and responsibilities when they were young? How were those the same or different from the rights and responsibilities of adolescents today? Ask students to report on the family member's comments. In order to practice using various tenses in the subjunctive, include that person's value judgments or opinions: *Los padres de mi abuelo siempre exigían que él hiciera….*

Additional Resources
• Writing, Audio & Video Workbook: Cap. 10, Writing Activity 7

 Assessment
• Prueba 10-3: *La voz pasiva: ser + participio pasado*

445

10 Practice and Communicate

Standards: 1.1

Focus: Using various tenses in the subjunctive

Suggestions: Tell students to use one of the words or expressions from Column B in the sentence about the past as well as in the one about the present.

Answers will vary.

Standards: 1.1, 1.3

Focus: Using various tenses in the subjunctive

Suggestions: Suggest that students begin their preparation in step 1 by writing a key word or two about something interesting they would like to ask their interview subject. Then they can determine which verbs they will use and begin to construct the necessary questions for their interview.

Answers will vary.

Block Schedule

Cube Game with *Actividad* 15: Divide the class into groups of three. Give each group two game cubes or two small six-sided boxes. Have students write on each side of one cube a word from Column A. Then have them write one verb from Column B on each side of the other box. Have each student roll the cubes and create a sentence combining the words that show face-up on the cubes.

446

 **Gramática** **Hablar**

Los primeros años . . .

¿Cómo fueron tus primeros años de escuela? Con un(a) compañero(a), comparen las responsabilidades que tenían en sus primeros años de escuela con las que tienen ahora. Usen palabras de las dos columnas.

Modelo

Antes, la maestra prefería que yo hiciera la tarea con mis padres. Ahora, mis profesores quieren que haga la tarea solo(a).

Columna A	Columna B
mis padres	exigir
mis maestros(as)	dudar
mis profesores(as)	aconsejar
mis amigos(as)	ser común que
mi entrenador(a)	querer
mis hermanos(as)	sugerir
mis compañeros(as) de clase	preferir
	recomendar
	ser importante que

 **Gramática** **Escribir/Hablar**

Una biografía

Imagina que tienes que escribir una biografía de un(a) compañero(a).

1 Escribe cinco preguntas que le puedes hacer a tu compañero(a) sobre su niñez y sobre cómo es diferente hoy por las experiencias que ha tenido.

Modelo

A —¿De qué tenías miedo cuando eras niño(a)?
B —Tenía miedo de que mis padres me castigaran.
A —Y ahora, ¿de qué tienes miedo?
B —Ahora tengo miedo de que las clases de la universidad sean más difíciles.

2 Haz las preguntas a tu compañero(a) y toma apuntes mientras las contesta. Luego, intercambien papeles.

3 Usa tus notas para escribir una biografía breve.

446 cuatrocientos cuarenta y seis
Manos a la obra 1

Universal Access

Heritage Language Learners
Before partners complete *Actividad* 16, ask students who have lived in a heritage country to serve as models. Ask questions that highlight the differences between childhood in the heritage country and childhood in the United States.

Multiple Intelligences
Musical Rhythmic: In small groups, have students rehearse choral readings of Hilario Barrero's ***Subjuntivo.*** Discuss how punctuation, word choice, and line breaks impact the rhythm of the poem. Have students compare and contrast the different interpretations they hear.

 **Hablar/Escribir**

Los adolescentes en el mundo de hoy

Tu clase va a escribir un informe sobre los adolescentes de hoy.

1 Para juntar información, trabajen en grupos de cuatro estudiantes y completen las siguientes frases con tres diferentes respuestas.

- Nos importa que . . .
- Nos sorprende que . . .
- Queremos que . . .
- Nos alegramos de que . . .
- Es una lástima que . . .
- Nos molesta que . . .

2 Compartan sus respuestas con los otros grupos. Escojan las respuestas que más se repitieron y digan en qué orden de importancia las colocarían.

3 Ahora, imaginen que pueden hablar con las autoridades del gobierno para informarles cómo se sienten ustedes como adolescentes. Deben presentarles una propuesta *(proposal)* sobre cuáles son los temas más importantes para los adolescentes. Escríbanlos en forma de frase, dando buenas razones de por qué son importantes.

Modelo

Nos parece injusto que no podamos votar hasta los 18 años. Tenemos . . .

En voz alta

Escucha el poema que escribió Hilario Barrero (Toledo, 1948–), un escritor, traductor y poeta español que vive en Nueva York y también da clases en una universidad. Trata de repetir el poema en voz alta. Luego, contesta las preguntas.

- ¿Por qué dice el poeta que el maestro les roba su tiempo a los estudiantes?
- ¿Crees que los estudiantes están interesados en lo que les quiere enseñar el profesor? Repite alguna de las frases del poema para dar un ejemplo.
- ¿Te parece que para el autor es fácil o difícil enseñar a los estudiantes? ¿Por qué?

Subjuntivo
de Hilario Barrero

Y tener que explicar de nuevo el subjuntivo,
. . . cuando lo que desean es (. . .)
y olvidarse del viejo profesor que les roba
su tiempo inútilmente.
Mientras copian los signos del lenguaje,
emotion, doubt, volition, fear, joy . . .,
y usando el subjuntivo de mi lengua de humo[1]
mi deseo es que tengan un amor como el nuestro,
pero sé que no escuchan la frase
que les pongo para ilustrar su duda
ansiosos como están de usar el indicativo.
(. . .)

_____
1 smoke

● Más práctica . . . .
Practice Workbook 10-6, 10-7

Go Online
PHSchool.com
For: : Practice with present subjunctive and imperfect subjunctive
Visit: www.phschool.com
Web Code: jed-1005

Enriching Your Teaching

Culture Note
Hilario Barrero's poetry has won awards and been published in numerous anthologies and literary magazines. Besides writing poetry and teaching Spanish, Barrero has translated to Spanish the poetry of Robert Frost, Jane Kenyon, and Donald Hall, among others.

Internet Search
Keyword: | Hilario Barrero |

 Actividad 17   *Standards:* 1.1, 1.3

Focus: Using various tenses in the subjunctive

Suggestions: For step 1, point out that the verbs in all the cues are in the present tense. Ask: *¿En qué tiempo estarán los verbos que escriben Uds? (en el presente o el presente perfecto del subjuntivo)*

Answers will vary.

En voz alta
Presentation
Standards: 1.1, 1.2, 1.3, 2.1, 2.2, 3.1, 3.2, 5.2
Resources: Audio Program: Cap. 10, Track 9

Suggestions: Before students read the poem, prepare them by saying: *Este poema se trata de los pensamientos de un profesor de español.* When students recite the poem, encourage them to use expression appropriate to the professor's thoughts.

Answers will vary.

Additional Resources
- Writing, Audio & Video Workbook: Cap. 10, Writing Activities 8–9
- Resource Book: Cap. 10, Communicative Activity BLM

 Assessment
- Prueba 10-4: *El presente y el imperfecto del subjuntivo*
- Examen: Vocabulario y gramática 1

Chapter Project
Students can perform step 2 at this point. Be sure they understand your corrections and suggestions. (For more information, see p. 430-a.)

Language Input

Presentation

Standards: 1.1, 1.2, 3.1

Resources: Voc. & Gram. Transparencies: 191–192; Resource Book: Cap. 10, Input Script; Audio Program: CD Cap. 10, Track 10

Focus: Presenting new vocabulary and using grammar lexically in context

Suggestions: Have students read along as you present the new vocabulary by playing the *Audio CD* or reading the text aloud. Use the pictures on *Vocabulary & Grammar Transparencies* 191–192 and questions with embedded answers to elicit the vocabulary from students: *¿La igualdad es esencial para que tengamos justicia o injusticia? (justicia) ¿Lo contrario de inocente es acusado o culpable? (culpable)* Check for comprehension by asking other questions. See the Input Scripts in the *Teacher's Resource Book* for specific questions.

A primera vista 2

Vocabulario y gramática en contexto

Read, listen to, and understand information about
- **individual rights in society**
- **role of government**

¿Te preguntaste alguna vez de dónde vienen tus derechos? **La garantía** de decir lo que piensas, de reunirte con otros, y de sentirte tranquilo(a) forman parte de la Constitución de los Estados Unidos. Son parte de las diez primeras enmiendas[1] que se añadieron a la Constitución en 1791 para garantizar la libertad de expresión y otros derechos **fundamentales**.

1 amendments

"La libertad de expresión es la base de una sociedad **democrática**. Debemos proteger la libertad de **prensa, de modo que** todos tengamos acceso a los diferentes **puntos de vista** que se expresan en los medios de comunicación."

La igualdad es esencial si queremos tener una sociedad **libre** y con **justicia** para todos. Hay que **asegurar** que todas las personas, en todo el mundo, **lleguen a** gozar de los mismos derechos.

448 cuatrocientos cuarenta y ocho
A primera vista 2

Universal Access

Students with Learning Difficulties

Before students read or listen to the text on pp. 448–449, ask them to preview the passages to look for cognates. Some examples might include *garantía, fundamentales, justicia,* or *democrática.* Discuss how these words can help students decipher meaning from the text.

Advanced Learners

Have students search newspapers, magazines, and the Internet for pictures of such things as the Bill of Rights, trials, juries, defendants, and judges. Have them work together in a group to assemble these visuals into a display, complete with captions and labels, about individual rights and the role of government.

"Debido a que todos gozamos de derechos, la policía no puede **detener** a una persona sin acusarla de un crimen específico. Tampoco puede registrar la casa del acusado sin un documento que indique que es **sospechoso** de haber **violado** la ley."

"La Declaración garantiza los derechos del acusado a tener **un juicio** rápido y público, a ser **juzgado** por **un jurado** imparcial del estado y a no recibir **castigos** crueles."

el acusado

El acusado es **inocente** hasta que se muestre, con testigos y pruebas, que es **culpable**."

la testigo

Actividad 18 · Escuchar/Escribir

Los derechos del pueblo

Escribe los números del 1 al 6 en una hoja de papel. Escucha lo que dicen estos jóvenes y en cada caso escribe *C* (cierto) o *F* (falso). Vuelve a escribir las frases falsas, de manera que sean ciertas.

Actividad 19 · Escribir

Tus derechos

Escribe una lista de los tres derechos que te parecen más importantes para que una sociedad sea democrática. Puedes usar los que aparecen en estas páginas u otros que conozcas.

cuatrocientos cuarenta y nueve   **449**
Capítulo 10

Actividad 18 *Standards:* 1.2

Resources: Audio Program: CD Cap. 10, Track 11; Resource Book: Cap. 10, Audio Script; Practice Answers on Transparencies

Focus: Practicing listening comprehension of new vocabulary

Suggestions: Allow students to silently review the material on these two pages before they complete the listening activity. Use the *Audio CD* or read from the script. Allow students to listen more than once.

Answers:
1. C
2. F La libertad de prensa es necesaria para tener acceso a los puntos de vista de los medios de comunicación.
3. F Es necesario asegurar que haya igualdad en la sociedad.
4. C
5. F Las personas son inocentes hasta que se muestre que son culpables.
6. C

Actividad 19 *Standards:* 1.3

Focus: Writing new vocabulary in a list

Suggestions: Point out to students that they need not use the word *derecho* in each item in their list. Have them study the material on these two pages as a model for how to express various rights.

Answers will vary.

Enriching Your Teaching

Teacher-to-Teacher

The constitutions of Spain and Latin American countries are readily available on the Internet. Have students choose, or assign them, a constitution to study. They can compare its structure and contents to the United States Constitution, find out which rights it guarantees, analyze verb tenses used in the text, and so on.

Internet Search

Keywords:

constitución + (adjetivo de nacionalidad)

Vocabulario y gramática

Presentation

Standards: 1.1, 1.2

Resources: Voc. & Gram. Transparencies: 193–194; Resource Book: Cap. 10, Input Script; Audio Program: CD Cap. 10, Tracks 12–13

Focus: Extending presentation of vocabulary and grammar in context

Suggestions:

Pre-reading: Present the readings on this and the next page one at a time, along with their respective activities.

Reading: Allow students time to read each presentation silently first before they listen to the *Audio CD.*

Post-reading: Check comprehension by asking questions. See the *Teacher's Resource Book* for specific questions.

Standards: 1.3

Focus: Writing new vocabulary in a list

Suggestions: Encourage students to think of other problems they consider important and list them as well as the problems they see on this page.

Answers will vary.

Block Schedule

Have students work in pairs and rank the problems listed on p. 450 from most to least serious. Have each group report back on their top four and summarize the results of each group to create a class summary.

Jóvenes por el desarrollo y la paz

Los jóvenes tienen gran fuerza en el mundo de hoy. El desarrollo de los países depende, entre otras cosas, de la participación de los jóvenes. Hay organizaciones internacionales, como la Red de Jóvenes y Estudiantes, que reúnen grupos de jóvenes de todo el mundo. Allí **intercambian** sus ideas y hacen **propuestas** sobre los diferentes **modos** de resolver sus propios problemas y los de otros jóvenes.

A medida que participan en estas reuniones, los jóvenes aprenden a respetar la diferencia de opiniones de otros grupos. Juntos **proponen** soluciones a sus problemas y a los problemas del mundo.

Éstos son algunos problemas que enfrentan los jóvenes:

- **las desigualdades** sociales, económicas y políticas
- **el desempleo**
- la discriminación por sexo
- los jóvenes sin hogar
- los conflictos **mundiales**
- la contaminación ambiental
- las enfermedades, el hambre y la mala nutrición
- los problemas en la familia
- **la falta de** oportunidades de educación y entrenamiento

Escribir

Problemas de los jóvenes

Haz una lista de los problemas que tienen los jóvenes de hoy. Empieza con los que creas que son más importantes y termina con los menos importantes.

450 cuatrocientos cincuenta
A primera vista 2

Universal Access

Heritage Language Learners

Ask students who have lived in a heritage country to share their views on the biggest problems facing the youth in that country. Are the issues similar to or different from those faced by young people in the United States?

Students with Learning Difficulties

Ask students to provide each other with brief definitions or explanations of each of the issues listed on p. 450. For example: *¿Qué es el desempleo? ¿Cuáles son algunos ejemplos de problemas en la familia?*

Qué proponen los jóvenes?

Lydia, de San Luis Obispo, California. Ella quiere ser representante **ante** la Organización de las Naciones Unidas. ▶

66 **En lugar de** pensar sólo en nosotros mismos, somos responsables de hablar por los jóvenes del mundo que llevan una vida difícil. Ellos también tienen derecho a lograr sus **aspiraciones. 99**

◀ Mark, de Atlanta, Georgia. Mark dice que trabajará en el gobierno.

66 **El fin** de la democracia es que tengamos más libertad para expresar sin miedo lo que **opinamos.** La libertad de expresión es **un valor** democrático fundamental. **99**

Yamiko y Alicia, de Providence, Rhode Island. Ellas quieren ser consejeras de estudiantes. ▶

66 Si la gente se reúne con fines **pacíficos** e intercambia opiniones cuando no está de acuerdo, puede encontrar soluciones a muchos problemas. Así, habrá menos guerras y también menos problemas en las escuelas. **99**

 Escuchar ·

Hagamos algo

Escucha las frases. Después de oír cada frase, di quién de los estudiantes de esta página crees que dijo cada cosa.

 **Escribir** · · · · · · · · · · · · · · · · · · ·

Y tú, ¿qué propones?

Imagina que te invitan a representar a los jóvenes de tu país, o de otro país que conozcas, en alguna organización internacional. Escribe cinco problemas y cinco propuestas que harías para mejorar las condiciones de los jóvenes de ese país.

● **Más práctica** · · · · · · · · · · · · · ·
Practice Workbook 10-8, 10-9

For: Vocabulary practice
Visit: www.phschool.com
Web Code: jed-1006

cuatrocientos cincuenta y uno **451**
Capítulo 10

Language Input

Actividad 21 *Standards:* 1.2
· · · · · · · · · · · · · · · ·

Resources: Audio Program: CD Cap. 10, Track 14; Resource Book: Cap. 10, Audio Script; Practice Answers on Transparencies

Focus: Practicing listening comprehension of new vocabulary

Suggestions: Remind students that the comments they will hear are by the four people shown on this page.

Answers:
1 Lydia
2 Mark
3. Yamiko y Alicia
4. Mark
5. Lydia

Actividad 22 *Standards:* 1.3
· · · · · · · · · · · · · · · ·

Focus: Practicing new vocabulary through writing in context

Suggestions: Once students have written their five problems and solutions, invite them to share them in a class discussion.

Answers will vary.

Additional Resources
• Resource Book: Cap. 10, Clip Art

✓ **Assessment**
• Prueba 10-5: Vocabulary recognition

Chapter Project
Students can perform step 3 at this point. (For more information, see p. 430-a.)

 Enriching Your Teaching

Culture Note

La Red de Jóvenes y Estudiantes, mentioned on p. 450, belongs to the Mexican section of Amnesty International, and some of its campaigns are operated through that organization. Their mission is to encourage youth involvement in the promotion and defense of human rights. Each year, Amnesty International unites the energy and ideas of young Mexicans of *la Red* with other young people all over the world in a unified action. They call attention to one place in the world in which human rights are in jeopardy and put pressure on authorities and organizations in that place to respect human rights.

Practice and Communicate

Actividad 23 Standards 1.2

....

Resources: Practice Answers on Transparencies

Focus: Demonstrating comprehension of new vocabulary

Suggestions: Make sure students are given adequate writing practice by having them write the entire answer and not just the corresponding letter.

Answers:

1. c
2. b
3. a
4. c
5. a
6. b
7. c (a)

Actividad 24 Standards 1.2, 1.3

....

Resources: Practice Answers on Transparencies

Focus: Demonstrating comprehension of new vocabulary

Suggestions: After students have completed the activity, have them share their work, reading each item as a complete sentence.

Answers:

1. dar a cada persona lo que es de esa persona
2. cuando todos participan en el gobierno de un país
3. cuando la policía le quita la libertad a una persona porque cree que es sospechosa
4. las da el estado cuando asegura derechos para todos sus ciudadanos
5. las cosas que los ciudadanos pueden hacer o exigir de acuerdo con la ley
6. no respetar una ley

Manos a la obra 2
Vocabulario y gramática en uso

Objectives
- Talk about the rights guaranteed by the Constitution
- Discuss how these rights apply to individuals in society
- Practice the pluperfect subjunctive
- Practice the conditional perfect

Actividad 23 Leer ....

En la sala de justicia

¿Quién dijo cada frase en la sala de justicia?

1. Hay que prometer decir la verdad, sólo la verdad.

   a. el inocente   **b.** el juicio   **c.** el juez

2. Desde donde yo estaba, pude ver muy bien lo que hizo el criminal.

   a. el sospechoso   **b.** el testigo   **c.** la acusada

3. Lo siento, señor juez, pero esa mujer no ha dicho la verdad. Yo no lo hice.

   a. el acusado   **b.** el jurado   **c.** la víctima

4. No hay suficiente información. ¡El acusado es inocente!

   a. la justicia   **b.** la policía   **c.** la abogada

5. Sí, soy inocente. ¡Tienen que creerme!

   a. el acusado   **b.** el juicio   **c.** el castigo

6. Hemos decidido quién es culpable.

   a. el inocente   **b.** el jurado   **c.** la acusada

7. El jurado deberá juzgar al acusado con justicia.

   a. el juez   **b.** los valores   **c.** la prensa

Actividad 24 Leer/Escribir ....

¿Qué quieren decir?

Para poder defender nuestros derechos, es importante saber lo que quieren decir las palabras de la Declaración de derechos. Empareja cada palabra con su significado. Luego, escribe dos frases usando cuatro palabras de la primera columna.

1. la justicia   dar a cada persona lo que es de esa persona

2. democrático(a)   no respetar una ley

3. detener   las cosas que los ciudadanos pueden hacer o exigir de acuerdo con la ley

4. las garantías   cuando todos participan en el gobierno de un país

5. los derechos   cuando la policía le quita la libertad a una persona porque cree que es sospechosa

6. violar   las da el estado cuando asegura derechos para todos sus ciudadanos

452 cuatrocientos cincuenta y dos
Manos a la obra 2

Universal Access

Students with Learning Difficulties
Assign students the roles outlined in *Actividad* 23, and provide each character with a label card. Ask them to stand at the front of the class, holding their label card. Read the quotes from the activity and ask students to call out the character who would say those words.

Advanced Learners
Have students write sentences containing the unused words from *Actividad* 23. Ask them to read their sentences to each other and listen to make sure the words are used correctly.

Escribir/Hablar . . . .

¿Que dicen los titulares?

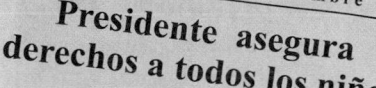

☀ El Sol

Santiago, 23 de septiembre

Presidente asegura derechos a todos los niños.

❶ Usa elementos de cada columna para escribir titulares *(headlines)*.

1. la Organización de las Naciones Unidas	detener	puntos de vista con fines pacíficos
2. la policía	votar	competencia mundial de atletismo
3. el Congreso	asegurar	garantías y derechos de los ciudadanos
4. el juez	proponer	el castigo del culpable
5. la declaración	reunirse	los valores democráticos
6. el presidente del club atlético	defender	los sospechosos
7. el grupo para la defensa de los niños	intercambiar	el derecho a la educación y la alimentación

❷ Imagina que eres reportero(a). Trabaja con otro(a) estudiante para escribir tres frases sobre uno de los titulares.

Fondo cultural ■◆■◆■■◆■◆◆■◆■◆◆■◆

Políticos y educadores ¿Sabías que muchos líderes políticos en los países hispanohablantes fueron educadores o maestros? Un político famoso, el mexicano José Vasconcelos (1882–1959), también fue educador, además de filósofo, abogado, historiador y escritor. Después de luchar en la Revolución Mexicana, fue rector de la Universidad Nacional y creó la Secretaría de Educación Pública. La dividió en cuatro departamentos: el de Escuelas, para desarrollar la enseñanza técnica y científica; el de Bibliotecas, para promover la lectura en todo el país; el de Bellas Artes, para desarrollar la cultura artística; y el de Enseñanza indígena para enseñar a los indígenas a leer ya que no tenían acceso a la educación. En su época, miles de campesinos y obreros aprendieron a leer y a escribir y se dio el más importante avance de la educación en México. Los estudiantes lo llamaron "Maestro de las juventudes de América".

Vasconcelos, además, creó la orquesta sinfónica de México y promovió la pintura mural y la obra de los grandes muralistas Diego Rivera y José Clemente Orozco.

José Vasconcelos

• ¿Por qué es importante que los políticos sean maestros?

cuatrocientos cincuenta y tres 453
Capítulo 10

Actividad 25 *Standards:* 1.1, 4.1
. . . .

Focus: Practicing new vocabulary via guided writing

Suggestions: Remind students that the structure of a *titular* is different from that of a complete sentence. Point out the model *titular* at the top of the page, and ask them to use it as a model.

Answers will vary.

Fondo cultural *Standards:* 1.1, 1.2, 3.1

 ■◆■◆■◆■◆■■◆◆■■◆◆■◆

Suggestions: After students have read and discussed the information, ask comprehension questions. For example: *¿Cuáles eran las profesiones de José Vasconcelos? (político, educador, filósofo, abogado, historiador, escritor) ¿Cuáles eran los cuatro departamentos de la Secretaría de Educación Pública que él creó? (los departamentos de Escuelas, Bibliotecas, Bellas Artes y Enseñanza indígena)*

Answers will vary.

 Enriching Your Teaching

Culture Note

José Vasconcelos considered it one of his most important missions as a leader to reach out to the indigenous peoples of Mexico through education. As part of this mission, he started the "muralist movement," which helped launch the artistic careers of Diego Rivera, José Clemente Orozco, and Alfaro Siqueiros.

Teacher-to-Teacher

Invite students to prepare brief reports in Spanish on a politician of their choice who is or was also an educator. United States politicians who fit this profile include S. I. Hayakawa, Horace Mann, Al Gore, Barbara Jordan, and Booker T. Washington.

Standards: 1.2

Resources: Audio Program: CD Cap. 10, Track 15; Resource Book: Cap. 10, Audio Script; Practice Answers on Transparencies

Focus: Practicing listening comprehension of new vocabulary

Suggestions: Before students listen, tell them that they will hear five separate, short news reports. Encourage them to write their responses in their own words.

Answers: Wording of answers will vary. The following contain the main ideas:
1. está acusado de tratar de robar un banco.
2. pidiendo una solución al problema del tráfico.
3. fueron a varios países para hablar de los derechos y los valores democráticos.
4. de la tienda Alegría.
5. castigará a quien viole la ley contra el ruido.

Standards: 1.1

Focus: Practice new vocabulary in discussions around themes

Recycle: subjunctive with verbs of emotion or doubt

Suggestions: Have students take turns being the one to launch each interchange.

Answers will vary.

Standards: 1.1, 1.3

Focus: Practice new vocabulary via an oral news report

Recycle: preterite and imperfect tenses

Suggestions: Encourage students to present their report as though it were part of a real news program. The narrator should introduce the witness.

Answers will vary.

454

 Escuchar/Escribir

Escucha la radio

A veces parece que las noticias siempre son malas. Escucha la radio y completa las frases para hacer un resumen de las noticias.
1. En Santa Ana, un grupo de personas . . .
2. En Ciudad Luna, hubo una manifestación . . .
3. Representantes de la organización mundial Los Amigos . . .
4. Desaparecieron 200 cajas de juguetes . . .
5. El alcalde Marino dijo que . . .

   **Leer/Hablar**

¿Qué opinas? o "la libertad de opinión"

Trabaja con otro(a) estudiante. Usa tu derecho a la libertad de opinión y di si estás de acuerdo o no con las siguientes frases. Usa expresiones como: *creo que, me parece que, me preocupa que, dudo que.*

Modelo

(no) proteger los derechos fundamentales
A —*Debemos proteger los derechos fundamentales.*
B —*Creo que debemos proteger los derechos fundamentales para no perderlos.*

1. (no) detener a los sospechosos
2. los testigos de un crimen (no) ayudar a la víctima
3. (no) ser culpables los padres de jóvenes desobedientes
4. (no) apoyar la participación de jóvenes en manifestaciones pacíficas
5. (no) luchar contra la falta de justicia en otros países
6. (no) construir más carreteras
7. (no) controlar lo que pueden hacer los jóvenes
8. (no) proponer soluciones pacíficas

  **Hablar/Escribir**

El noticiero

Con un(a) compañero(a), escribe un breve reportaje sobre "el misterio de la desaparición de una bicicleta" para el programa de noticias. Describe lo que pasó e incluye un comentario de un testigo. Pueden usar las palabras del recuadro. Presenten su reportaje a otra pareja. Uno(a) es reportero(a) del noticiero y otro(a) es testigo.

el / la testigo	culpable	en lugar de	sospechoso(a)
inocente	detener	el punto de vista	opinar

Universal Access

Students with Learning Difficulties

For *Actividad* 28, help students first note down ideas for events involved in the theft of a bicycle. Have them use a flow chart or other graphic organizer for this purpose. Ask what would happen: first the discovery that the bicycle is missing, then asking family members or neighbors, and so on. Guide them to use the vocabulary in the word bank.

Students with Special Needs

You may need to provide impaired students with a copy of the script in order for them to complete listening activities like *Actividad* 26.

Actividad 29 · Leer/Hablar

Momentos históricos

En todas las épocas hay artistas que representan momentos históricos de la vida de sus países y de sus héroes. Uno de esos momentos es cuando se firman *(sign)* documentos fundamentales, como las declaraciones de independencia y las constituciones. Lee sobre un pintor de la historia de Venezuela y contesta las preguntas.

Conexiones | Las artes

Juan Lovera (1776–1841) es un pintor que inició el género de pintura histórica en Venezuela. En su obra, *El 5 de julio de 1811*, retrata a más de cien personajes y deja testimonio de un suceso de gran importancia para Venezuela, la firma de la declaración de independencia de España. La pintura muestra con detalles y de manera fiel a los hechos la ropa y la posición de los criollos *(native born)* de esa época. Además de los dibujos de cada uno de los personajes principales, tiene escritos sus nombres. Esta obra muestra la misión de las artes para preservar la historia.

• ¿Por qué piensas que las pinturas eran más importantes testimonios históricos antes que ahora?

• ¿Recuerdas alguna pintura que muestre un momento de la historia de los Estados Unidos?

El 5 de Julio de 1811, Juan Lovera, (Venezuelan)

Actividad 30 · Hablar/Escribir

Y tú, ¿qué respondes?

❶ Imagina que estás en tu clase de Educación cívica. Discute y contesta estas preguntas con un(a) compañero(a):

1. En tu opinión, ¿qué debe garantizar el gobierno a los ciudadanos?

2. ¿Qué debe garantizar el(la) director(a) de tu escuela a los(as) estudiantes?

3. ¿Conoces países donde no respetan el punto de vista de la gente? ¿Puedes mencionar algunos de esos países?

4. ¿El desempleo existe en todos los países del mundo? ¿Cómo crees que afecta a las familias que sufren debido al desempleo?

5. ¿Qué organizaciones mundiales conoces que tengan fines pacíficos? Descríbelas.

6. ¿Conoces países que aseguran una educación gratuita para los ciudadanos?

❷ Escribe un párrafo sobre lo que significa para ti la democracia de los Estados Unidos.

Actividad 29
Standards: 1.1, 1.2, 2.2, 3.1, 4.2

Focus: Practicing new vocabulary via reading and response

Suggestions: Have students read the information about Juan Lovera in pairs and help each other with any comprehension problems they may have.

Answers will vary.

Actividad 30
Standards: 1.1, 1.3

Focus: Practicing new vocabulary

Recycle: subjunctive, country names

Suggestions: For step 2, encourage students to consider and comment on their partner's opinions as well as their own.

Answers will vary.

Additional Resources

• Writing, Audio & Video Workbook: Cap. 10, Audio Activity 3, Track 16

• Writing, Audio & Video Workbook: Cap. 10, Writing Activity 10

• Resource Book: Cap. 10, Communicative Activity BLM

✓ Assessment

• Prueba 10-6: Vocabulary production

Block Schedule

After completing *Actividad* 30 #2, have each student write on the board one statement from his or her paragraph. Use these ideas as a brainstorm. Have each student take these ideas and write a new paragraph. Select the top two paragraphs and send them to a local Spanish newspaper to be published or submit them to the school literary magazine.

Enriching Your Teaching

Culture Note

Juan Lovera is Venezuela's most outstanding artist of the school known as *arte republicana,* which portrayed historical events. He eventually became known as *El pintor de los Próceres.* His paintings on a grand scale like *El 5 de julio de 1811* are known for their composition and perspective. For a time Lovera worked as an art instructor with the musician Lino Gallardo and other known Venezuelan artists of the day in an art institute that they themselves founded.

Gramática

Presentation

Standards: 4.1

Resources: Voc. & Gram. Transparencies: 195

Suggestions: On the board, write sentence frames consisting of a verb in the preterite, the imperfect, or the past perfect tense, followed by *que,* followed by an infinitive. The three parts should be able to work together as building blocks for a complex sentence. Here are some examples:

dudó + que + terminar

quería + que + invitar

habíamos pedido + que + servir

Challenge students to put the parts together to make complex sentences using the pluperfect subjunctive. Tell them they can use whatever subject they wish in the subordinate clause. The above frames might result in sentences like the following:

Papá dudó que Benito hubiera terminado el maratón antes de la puesta del sol.

Yo quería que tú me hubieras invitado.

Habíamos pedido que Ud. nos hubiera servido antes.

Actividad 31

Standards: 1.2

Resources: Practice Answers on Transparencies

Focus: Practicing the pluperfect subjunctive

Suggestions: In addition to forming the pluperfect subjunctive for the correct verb, encourage students to think about the time relationships in the sentences.

Answers:

1. hubiera detenido
2. hubieran destruido
3. hubiera castigado
4. hubieran sido
5. hubiera garantizado
6. hubiera opinado
7. hubiera robado
8. hubiera sabido

Gramática

El pluscuamperfecto del subjuntivo

You use the pluperfect subjunctive to describe actions in the past, when one action takes place before the other. In such cases, the action that takes place before is in the pluperfect subjunctive, and the action that takes place after is in the preterite, the imperfect or the pluperfect of the indicative.

> Carlos **se sorprendió** que su amigo **hubiera comprado** todos los materiales.
> **Esperaba** que **hubieran ido** a la fiesta con los niños.
> Yo **había querido** que mis hermanos **hubieran venido** a la casa de la abuela.

You form the pluperfect subjunctive using the past subjunctive of *haber* + the past participle of the verb.

hubiera salido	hubiéramos salido
hubieras salido	hubierais salido
hubiera salido	hubieran salido

- You also use the pluperfect subjunctive when the verb in the main clause is in the conditional.

> ¿**Sería** posible que Teresa **hubiera terminado** el informe?

- Note that since the expression *como si* (as if) always refers to something that is contrary to the truth, or unreal, it must always be followed by the subjunctive, either the imperfect subjunctive or the pluperfect subjunctive.

> Estaba tan cansada **como si hubiera corrido** todo el día.
> Sergio descansa **como si no tuviera** nada que hacer.

31 **Gramática** **Leer**

Las noticias del día

Imagina que estás leyendo el periódico. Completa las siguientes frases con la forma correcta del verbo en el pluscuamperfecto del subjuntivo.

1. Fue una sorpresa que el gobierno _____ (detener / proponer) a tantas personas en el aeropuerto.

2. Los ciudadanos se enojaron porque los aerosoles _____ (opinar / destruir) tanto el medio ambiente.

3. Los estudiantes dudaban que la policía _____ (castigar / asegurar) al presidente de la universidad.

4. Los testigos esperaban que las noticias _____ (estar / ser) más positivas.

5. Los ciudadanos de ese país esperaban que el gobierno _____ (garantizar / juzgar) la libertad de prensa y de expresión.

6. Me sorprendía que el juez _____ (opinar / violar) de esa manera.

7. ¿Sería verdad que el actor _____ (juzgar / robar) el coche de su novia?

8. El testigo desapareció como si _____ (saber / violar) algo acerca del acusado.

456 **cuatrocientos cincuenta y seis**
Manos a la obra 2

Universal Access

Advanced Learners

On separate slips of paper, have students write three subordinate clauses beginning with conjunctions taught in the *Gramática* on this page. If they use **aunque,** allow them to use either the indicative or the subjunctive in the clause. Collect the strips, mix them, and place them in a container. Have students meet in a circle, take turns drawing one subordinate clause at a time, and completing a complex sentence by inventing a suitable main clause.

 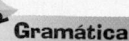

Actividad 32 Gramática · Hablar

En tu comunidad

Imagina que te encuentras con un(a) amigo(a) y conversan sobre las cosas que sucedieron en tu barrio. Trabaja con un(a) compañero(a). Tu compañero(a) te dice lo que pasó en el barrio y tú le respondes cómo te hizo sentir, usando un verbo de emoción y el pluscuamperfecto del subjuntivo.

Modelo

Roberto / celebrar su cumpleaños
A —*Roberto celebró su cumpleaños.*
B —*Me alegré mucho que hubiera celebrado su cumpleaños.*

Estudiante A

1. la abuela de Pedro / enfermarse
2. los hijos de Ana / cambiarse de escuela
3. la familia Ortiz / irse de viaje
4. el dueño del supermercado / acusar al vecino
5. los padres de Luisa / comprarse una casa

Estudiante B

Me alegré . . .
Fue una lástima . . .
Me sorprendió . . .
Me enojó . . .
Fue maravilloso . . .

El español en la comunidad

El español y las campanas electorales

Cada día más, en las campañas electorales en los Estados Unidos los candidatos dedican tiempo a comunicarse en español con la comunidad hispanohablante. Además de que ya hay boletas para votar traducidas al español, en las elecciones para presidente del 2000, por ejemplo, los candidatos usaron las estaciones de radio y televisión en español para trasmitir sus mensajes, y fueron entrevistados en programas de la televisión en español. Pero esta idea no es nueva, el presidente John F. Kennedy fue el primero que grabó mensajes en español durante su campaña, en 1960.

Como la población de hispanohablantes está creciendo en los Estados Unidos, se espera que durante las campañas presidenciales próximas, los candidatos usarán aún más el español para convencer *(convince)* a los hispanohablantes de votar por ellos. Es probable que entonces quienes puedan hablar los dos idiomas, ¡tendrán más posibilidades de ganar!

Actividad 32 *Standards:* 1.1

Resources: Practice Answers on Transparencies

Focus: Practicing the pluperfect subjunctive

Suggestions: Make sure both partners have a chance to assume the role of Student B.

Answers: Student B's choices of verbs of emotion will vary. The following are likely results:

1. —La abuela de Pedro se enfermó.
   —Fue una lástima que ella se hubiera enfermado.
2. —Los hijos de Ana se cambiaron de escuela.
   —Me sorprendió que ellos se hubieran cambiado de escuela.
3. —La familia Ortiz se fue de viaje.
   —Fue maravilloso que ellos se hubieran ido de viaje.
4. —El dueño del supermercado acusó al vecino.
   —Me enojó que él lo hubiera acusado.
5. —Los padres de Luisa se compraron una casa.
   —Fue maravilloso que ellos se hubieran comprado una casa.

El español en la comunidad
Presentation

Standards: 1.2, 3.1, 5.1

Suggestions: Once students have read the information, ask comprehension questions. For example: *¿De qué manera se comunican los candidatos con la comunidad? (Hay boletas para votar traducidas al español. Usan la radio y la televisión para transmitir sus mensajes. Se entrevistan en programas de la televisión en español.)*

Answers will vary.

Chapter Project

Students can perform step 4 at this point. Be sure they understand your corrections and suggestions. (For more information, see p. 430-a.)

Enriching Your Teaching

Culture Note

Business leaders and politicians from the Spanish-speaking community in the United States have made great progress in broadcasting their messages in the past thirty years. Besides many Spanish-language media tools, such as radio stations and TV channels at their disposal throughout the country, there is also Hispanic Heritage Month. It runs from September 15 to October 15 of each year and celebrates contributions to United States society from anyone in the Spanish-speaking community. It was originally approved by Congress as National Hispanic Heritage Week in 1968, and was expanded to an entire month in 1988.

Actividad 33 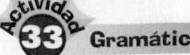 **Gramática** **Escribir** ....

El culpable

Imagina que eres un(a) detective que investigó un robo en una tienda. Entrevistaste a diferentes personas y su comportamiento fue muy sospechoso. Usa la expresión *como si* y el pluscuamperfecto del subjuntivo para explicar cómo actuaron.

Modelo

el chofer *(reaccionar)* / estar enojado con la dueña
El chofer reaccionó como si hubiera estado enojado con la dueña.

1. el vecino *(actuar)* / no importarle nada
2. el contador *(responder)* / estar loco
3. la vendedora *(mirar)* / esconder algo
4. la dueña *(hablar)* / enojarse con la vendedora
5. el cliente *(reírse)* / asustarse con las preguntas

Actividad 34  **Gramática** **Hablar/Escribir** ....

Por una sociedad mejor

1 En grupo, investiguen sobre la vida de una persona famosa que luchó o que lucha por una sociedad más justa. Pueden buscar información en la biblioteca o en la Red. La persona puede ser:

• un(a) presidente(a)
• un(a) escritor(a)
• un(a) pintor(a)
• un(a) héroe(a)
• un(a) científico(a)

2 Preparen un cuestionario sobre la vida de la persona que escogieron, por ejemplo, dónde nació, cómo fue su niñez, a qué se dedicaba, cuáles eran o son sus razones para luchar por una sociedad mejor, qué logró hacer. Escriban en una hoja de papel aparte las respuestas a las preguntas del cuestionario.

Modelo

¿Cómo reaccionó el país cuando se murió Lincoln?
El país se sorprendió de que el presidente Lincoln hubiera muerto.

3 Intercámbiense los cuestionarios entre los grupos para responderlos. Luego, devuélvanlos al grupo que los hizo para que revise las respuestas.

4 Corrijan las respuestas y compartan su información sobre la persona famosa con el resto de la clase.

● **Más práctica** ....
Practice Workbook 10-10

For: Practice with the pluperfect subjunctive
Visit: www.phschool.com
Web Code: jed-1007

Universal Access

Heritage Language Learners

For *Actividad* 34, encourage students who have lived in a heritage country to suggest famous persons from that country for their group to investigate. They can provide valuable cultural insight on the famous person's achievements.

Advanced Learners

Have students use the pluperfect subjunctive to tell about three outstanding events in their lives and their reactions—or the reactions of others—to those events. Provide an example, such as: *Mis padres no pudieron creer que yo hubiera ganado el concurso de poesía.*

Gramática

El condicional perfecto

You use the conditional perfect to express what would or should have happened at some point in the past.

Y tú, ¿qué **habrías dicho** en esa situación?
*And you, what **would you have done** in that situation?*

Yo le **habría dado** un buen consejo.
*I **would have given** him(her) good advice.*

You form the conditional perfect using the conditional of *haber* + the past participle of the verb.

habría trabajado	habríamos trabajado
habrías trabajado	habríais trabajado
habría trabajado	habrían trabajado

- The conditional is used with *si* clauses to say what might have been if things had been different. In these sentences you use the past perfect subjunctive and the conditional perfect together.

Si **hubiera sabido** que estabas interesada, te **habría invitado** a la reunión.
*If **I had known** you were interested, I **would have invited** you to the meeting.*

Si no **hubieran venido** a este país, no los **habrías conocido**.
*If they **hadn't come** to this country, you **would not have met** them.*

Actividad 35 · Gramática · Leer

Lo habrían hecho pero, . . .

Muchas personas quieren resolver problemas, pero no siempre pueden. Completa las frases con el condicional perfecto del verbo apropiado.

1. Yo *(participar / detener)* en la reunión, pero no pude porque estaba enferma.

2. Los profesores *(obligar / asegurar)* el respeto a los derechos de los estudiantes si hubieran ido a la manifestación.

3. Si las personas no hubieran actuado de una manera tan sospechosa, la policía no los *(detener / intercambiar)*.

4. Si yo fuera el profesor, *(decir / proponer)* otro código de vestimenta.

5. Si ellos no hubieran tenido problemas, no *(aceptar / sufrir)* nuestra ayuda.

6. Si hubiera tenido problemas como tú, yo *(buscar / asegurar)* el apoyo de mis padres.

7. Creo que con un buen traductor, la confusión entre los dos países *(proponerse / resolverse)*.

cuatrocientos cincuenta y nueve **459**
Capítulo 10

Practice and Communicate · 10

Gramática

Presentation

Standards: 4.1

Resources: Voc. & Gram. Transparencies: 196

Suggestions: To help students become familiar with using the past perfect subjunctive and the conditional perfect together, write on the board English sentences like the examples in the second part of the *Gramática* and have students translate them to Spanish.

Actividad 35

Standards: 1.2

Resources: Practice Answers on Transparencies

Focus: Practicing the conditional perfect

Common Errors: Some students will confuse verb forms of **haber** when working with the past perfect subjunctive and the conditional perfect. Write the forms of **haber** for the former tense on the left side of the board and those for the latter tense on the right side, and allow students to refer to them as they complete the activities.

Suggestions: Once students have written the answers on their own, invite them to take turns reading the completed sentences aloud.

Answers:
1. habría participado
2. habrían asegurado
3. habría detenido
4. habría propuesto
5. habrían aceptado
6. habría buscado
7. se habría resuelto

Additional Resources
- Writing, Audio & Video Workbook: Cap. 10, Audio Activity 4, Track 17

Enriching Your Teaching

Teacher-to-Teacher

If you use a predictable system for calling on volunteers, such as going up and down rows, some students will determine which item they are going to be held responsible for and "drop out" of the activity until it is their turn. When conducting activities together with the whole class, as suggested for *Actividad 34*, it is preferable to randomize the way in which you choose volunteers to complete items. This keeps everyone on task since students don't know whom you might call on next.

Practice and Communicate

10

Actividad 36

Standards: 1.3

Resources: Practice Answers on Transparencies

Focus: Practicing the pluperfect subjunctive and conditional perfect

Suggestions: Encourage students to use humor in some of their responses.

Answers will vary. Students will use *habría* in all main clauses, since they are talking about themselves. Pluperfect subjunctive forms for the subordinate *(si)* clauses follow:

1. hubiera estado
2. hubiera perdido
3. hubiera llegado
4. hubiera ganado
5. hubiera sido
6. hubiera empezado
7. hubiera encontrado
8. hubiera tenido
9. hubiera visto
10. hubiera tenido

Actividad 37

Standards: 1.1

Resources: Practice Answers on Transparencies

Focus: Practicing the pluperfect subjunctive and conditional perfect

Recycle: past participle formation, reflexive verbs

Suggestions: Encourage students to answer honestly and completely in order to practice useful, real-world vocabulary.

Answers will vary. Students will use the following pluperfect subjunctive forms:

1. hubieras ido
2. hubieras perdido
3. hubiera ocurrido
4. te hubieran invitado
5. te hubiera detenido
6. hubiera desaparecido
7. te hubieras enterado
8. te hubieran ignorado

Actividad 38

Standards: 1.1, 1.3

Focus: Practicing the conditional perfect

Suggestions: For step 2, encourage students to talk about their partners as well as themselves in order to practice different verb forms.

Answers will vary.

Actividad 36   **Gramática**   **Escribir** ....

¿Qué habrías hecho?

Imagina que te sucedieran las siguientes cosas. Escribe frases sobre lo que habrías hecho si hubieras estado en estas situaciones.

> **Modelo**
> ser testigo
> *Si hubiera sido testigo en un juicio, me habría olvidado de todo lo que sabía.*

1. estar acusado
2. perder (una cosa)
3. llegar tarde
4. ganar un premio
5. ser sospechoso(a)
6. empezar a trabajar
7. encontrar (una cosa)
8. tener derecho a (algo)
9. ver un extraterrestre
10. tener conocimiento de (una cosa)

 **Actividad 37**   **Gramática**   **Hablar** ....

¿Qué habría hecho yo?

Habla con un(a) compañero(a) de lo que habrías hecho si hubieran pasado las siguientes cosas. Usen la información para hacer la pregunta *¿Qué habrías hecho si . . .?* y contéstenla.

> **Modelo**
> mudarse nuevos vecinos a tu barrio
> **A** —*¿Qué habrías hecho si se hubieran mudado nuevos vecinos a tu barrio?*
> **B** —*Yo habría ido a conocerlos.*

1. (no) ir de vacaciones
2. perder mucho dinero
3. ocurrir un accidente en la calle
4. invitarte a ir a una fiesta
5. detenerte la policía
6. desaparecer tu coche
7. enterarte de un crimen
8. ignorarte tus amigos

 **Actividad 38**   **Gramática**   **Hablar/Escribir** ....

Cómo me habría gustado

❶ ¿Qué habrías hecho para mejorar la vida de los jóvenes de tu país y del mundo en el siglo XX? Trabaja con otro(a) estudiante para hacer una lista. Habla de los siguientes temas:

- la escuela
- la comunidad
- los países pobres
- el gobierno

> **Modelo**
> *Yo habría quitado el código de vestimenta para dar más libertad a los estudiantes.*

❷ Ahora, cada pareja debe presentar sus ideas a la clase. La clase debe hacer comentarios y preguntas sobre las ideas.

460   cuatrocientos sesenta
Manos a la obra 2

Universal Access

Students with Learning Difficulties

Use English and basic physical demonstrations to point out to students the cause-and-effect nature of situations that require the conditional perfect. For example, drop a piece of chalk and say, "The chalk broke. Why? Because I dropped it. If I hadn't dropped the chalk, it wouldn't have broken."

Advanced Learners

Invite students to talk about how things would have turned out differently if certain events had or had not happened in the past. Encourage them to mention world as well as local events: *Si no hubieran inventado el Internet, yo no me habría comunicado tanto con mi tía en España.*

39 Gramática Escribir/Hablar ··········

En otro país

❶ Imagina cómo habría sido tu vida si hubieras nacido en otro país. Piensa en un país que te interese. Investiga cómo vive la gente en ese lugar. Escribe un párrafo describiendo cómo habría sido tu vida en ese país.

Modelo

Si yo hubiera nacido en España, habría hablado español. Me habría gustado la comida con pescado y mariscos, así como . . .

❷ Trabaja con otro(a) estudiante. Lean los párrafos que escribieron y digan por qué eligieron ese lugar. Añadan detalles de ese país, como el clima, los lugares que pueden visitar, la comida, el idioma y la música.

Madrid, España

40 Gramática Leer/Escribir/Hablar ····················

Por los derechos de los animales

❶ Lee el siguiente folleto que se repartió en una manifestación en España a favor de los derechos de los animales.

❷ Responde a las siguientes preguntas sobre el folleto.

1. Según el folleto, ¿cuál es la situación de los perros en España? ¿Cómo ayudan los suizos?

2. ¿Cuál habría sido tu reacción si hubieras recibido este folleto?

3. ¿Qué opinas sobre los derechos de los animales? ¿Piensas que todos los animales deben gozar de los mismos derechos? ¿Por qué?

❸ En grupo, comparen sus respuestas a las preguntas anteriores. Piensen qué otras cosas se podrían hacer para proteger a los animales. Hagan un folleto para proponer sus ideas y explicar por qué la gente debe cuidar a los animales.

● **Más práctica** ·············
Practice Workbook 10-11, 10-12

> **Situación de los perros en España**
>
> Estoy obligado a escribir esto, después de toda la información que he recibido sobre el maltrato que dan a muchos animales en España. Ahora vivo en Zurich (Suiza), y me sorprende que la gente de este país tenga que solucionar nuestros problemas. Cada semana, llegan perros de España que son salvados de su sacrificio o rescatados de alguna otra situación difícil.
>
> Por favor, firmen esta petición de apoyo.
>
> *Amante de los animales*

 Go Online
PHSchool.com
For: Practice with the conditional perfect
Visit: www.phschool.com
Web Code: jed-1009

Focus: Practicing the conditional perfect

Suggestions: In step 2, encourage students to make suggestions to their partner on what else he or she might have done: *Habrías visitado la ciudad de...; Habrías ido a un concierto de....*

Answers will vary.

Focus: Practicing new vocabulary and structures via reading and response

Suggestions: Display students' leaflets from step 3 around the classroom.

Answers will vary.

Additional Resources

• Writing, Audio & Video Workbook: Cap. 10, Writing Activities 12–13

• Writing, Audio & Video Workbook: Cap. 10, Audio Activity 5, Track 18

• Resource Book: Cap. 10, Communicative Activity BLM

 Assessment

• Prueba 10-8: *El condicional perfecto*
• Examen: Vocabulario y gramática 2

Chapter Project

Students can perform step 5 at this point. Record their presentations on cassette or videotape for inclusion in their portfolios. (For more information, see p. 430-a.)

Enriching Your Teaching

Culture Note

Attitudes towards animals vary greatly throughout the world, but in the past few decades, the notion of animal rights has been receiving wider and wider popularity. Animal rights groups are springing up around the world, addressing issues ranging from the treatment of cats and dogs to the protection of whales. Many of these are in Spanish-speaking countries. Some include **Alternativa de la Liberación Animal** in Spain, **Ánima** and **Asociación para la Defensa de los Derechos del Animal** in Argentina, and Mexico's **Conservación de Mamíferos Marinos de México.** All of these groups have signed the UDAR, or Universal Declaration of Animal Rights.

Puente a la cultura

Presentation

Standards: 1.1, 1.2, 2.1, 2.2, 3.1,4.1

Focus: Reading to learn about heroes of Latin American independence

Suggestions:

Pre-reading: Refer students to the *Estrategia*. Then, based on a brief survey of the selection's main title, subtitles, pictures, and captions, ask: *Si vamos a crear una línea cronológica para esta lectura, ¿de qué se tratará: la historia social y política en América Latina o el desarrollo de las artes en América Latina? (la historia social y política en América Latina)*

Reading: Encourage students to read through the entire passage once silently, without stopping at problem words or to ask questions. Then, for the second time through, ask volunteers to read sections aloud. Remind students to use background knowledge, cognates, and context clues to help them understand unfamiliar words and expressions as they read.

Post-reading: Ask students to paraphrase the main accomplishments of each of the three heroes mentioned in the reading.

Country Connection
Presentation

Standards: 3.1

Resources: Voc. & Gram. Transparencies: 17 (maps)
Venezuela's large size and latitudinal location result in a variety of topographies and climates. The country has four main climactic zones, all of which fall under the main category of "tropical." These include rain forest (a large part of the Amazon) in the south, savannah in the center and northwest, semi-arid tropical regions along the coasts, and highlands. The different areas—some of them huge—as well as the difficulty of overland travel, have given rise to many different indigenous cultures throughout the country. These, along with strong Spanish and African influences, are what create Venezuela's incredibly rich blend of dialects, foods, music, and folklore.

Go Online

The online atlas will provide a more detailed map of Venezuela.

¡Adelante!

Puente a la cultura
Héroes de América Latina

Objectives

- Read about heroes of the Latin American independence movement
- Compare and contrast the independence movements of the U.S. and of Spanish-speaking countries
- Create a timeline to organize and compare historical data

Simón Bolívar

Estrategia

Creating a timeline
Graphic aids are always useful to show data in a visual way. *Timelines* are graphic aids used to organize data in chronological order. Use them when you have historical information to organize and compare.

Durante la época colonial, España dominaba un territorio desde California hasta el Cabo de Hornos, al extremo sur de Sudamérica. Este territorio tenía aproximadamente 17 millones de habitantes y estaba dividido en cuatro virreinatos, o unidades políticas. Los representantes de la Corona[1] española controlaban no sólo la política en las colonias sino también los impuestos[2], el comercio, y así la vida de los habitantes.

Los habitantes de las colonias en América criticaban a España por su gran poder, pero en 1808, la monarquía española tuvo una crisis. Al sentir que la monarquía estaba débil, los criollos, o hijos de españoles nacidos en América, se rebelaron contra la Corona, iniciando así un movimiento de independencia en las colonias. Este movimiento resultó en la independencia de los países de América Latina.

Aquí hablamos de tres de los héroes de este movimiento. Aunque la historia de cada uno es my diferente, sus sueños de crear naciones independientes en América son muy similares.

Simón Bolívar: El Libertador de América

Simón Bolívar (1783–1830) nació en Caracas, Venezuela. Su sueño era liberar a las colonias españolas y unirlas en una gran patria[3]. Casi lo logró en 1819 cuando, después de muchos éxitos militares, creó la República de la Gran Colombia y fue su presidente. La Gran Colombia incluía los territorios que hoy forman Colombia, Venezuela, Panamá y Ecuador. Para 1826, Bolívar ya era también jefe supremo del Perú y presidente de Bolivia. Pero Bolívar murió sin realizar su sueño. Nunca pudo unir las repúblicas hispanoamericanas ya que había divisiones entre ellas. Bolivia se independizó en 1829 y Venezuela se separó de Colombia.

---

1 (Spanish) crown **2** taxes **3** homeland

Universal Access

Students with Learning Difficulties
Help students focus on the theme of national heroes by asking them to talk briefly about heroes they know of from United States history. Connect this to the reading by saying: *En América Latina también hay héroes. Ellos lucharon por la independencia de sus países. Esta lectura se trata de ellos.*

Advanced Learners
Ask students to do further research on one of the figures from the selection, or on another of their choice from Latin American history, such as José de San Martín.

José Martí: El apóstol de la independencia cubana

Además de gran poeta e intelectual, José Martí (1853–1895) es el héroe nacional y el apóstol de la independencia de Cuba. Desde los dieciséis años, ya participaba en la vida política y estuvo en prisión por haber escrito en publicaciones contra las autoridades coloniales españolas. Lo deportaron a España y de allí, fue a Nueva York, donde escribió la mayoría de sus obras. Luego, fundó el Partido Revolucionario Cubano en 1892. Regresó a Cuba cuando comenzó la guerra por la independencia en 1895 y murió en una batalla.

Miguel Hidalgo: El precursor de la independencia de México

Miguel Hidalgo se destaca en la historia de México como uno de los precursores de la independencia de ese país. Muchos lo criticaron porque era miembro del clero y tenía ideas revolucionarias. En 1810, durante un sermón, llamó al pueblo a luchar. Miles de indígenas que habían sufrido largos años de maltrato y explotación, decidieron seguirlo junto con los criollos. Miguel Hidalgo y su representante, el general Allende, organizaron el movimiento que llevó a la independencia en 1821.

¿Comprendiste?

1. ¿En qué siglo se iniciaron los movimientos de independencia de las naciones hispanohablantes de América y cuáles fueron sus causas?

2. ¿Qué tienen en común los héroes del artículo? Da dos ejemplos.

3. Menciona dos héroes de otros países y di quiénes eran y qué hicieron.

4. Compara el movimiento de independencia de los Estados Unidos con el de las naciones hispanohablantes. Di sus semejanzas y diferencias.

Cronología de la independencia latinoamericana

Copia la línea cronológica y complétala con la información del texto que leíste.

1808	1810	1819	1821	1826	1829	1895
____	Movimiento de independencia de México	____	____	____	Independencia de Bolivia	____

José Martí

Miguel Hidalgo

Go Online
PHSchool.com

For: Internet Link Activity
Visit: www.phschool.com
Web Code: jed-1010

Enriching Your Teaching

Culture Note
José Martí was unwelcome in many countries because of his political outspokenness. Once he moved to New York City, he spent most of his time there until the year of his death. He had a variety of jobs, including editor, journalist, and foreign correspondent for several magazines. He even worked as a Spanish teacher at New York's Central High School. The popular song *Guantanamera* is based on Martí's poetry.

Internet Search
Keywords:

> independencia + (nombre de país)

¿Comprendiste?

Standards: 1.1, 1.2, 1.3, 2.1, 2.2, 3.1, 4.2

Resources: Practice Answers on Transparencies

Focus: Demonstrating reading comprehension

Suggestions: Before discussing, have students first write answers to the questions on their own.

Answers:
1. En el siglo XIX; La monarquía española estaba débil.
2. La causa de Bolívar era unir a las colonias en una gran patria. La de Martí era la independencia de Cuba. Hidalgo luchaba contra la esclavitud y por los derechos de los indígenas.
3. Answers will vary.

Cronología de la independencia latinoamericana

Standards: 1.2, 3.1

Resources: Practice Answers on Transparencies

Focus: Demonstrating reading comprehension

Suggestions: Have students complete their time lines together in pairs or small groups.

Answers will vary, but should include the following information:

1808: Rebelión de los criollos latinoamericanos
1819: Creación de la República de la Gran Colombia por Bolívar
1821: Organización del movimiento independentista mexicano
1826: Bolívar: jefe supremo en Perú, presidente en Bolivia
1895: Se muere José Martí

Portfolio
Keep students' responses to the *¿Comprendiste?* questions and their time lines in their portfolios as writing samples.

Video

Presentation

Standards: 1.2

Resources: Video Program: Cap. 10
In this segment we learn of the Latino political organization OÍSTE, located in Massachusetts. See the *Video Teacher's Guide* for additional suggestions.

¿Qué me cuentas?

Presentation

Standards: 1.1, 1.2, 1.3

Resources: Voc. & Gram. Transparencies 197; Audio Program: CD Cap. 10, Track 19; Resource Book: Cap. 10, Audio Script; Practice Answers on Transparencies

Focus: Practicing speaking and listening comprehension

Suggestions:

For step 1, use the *Audio CD* or read the script aloud. Allow students to hear the descriptions twice through: the first time to write their answers and the second time to check them.

For step 2, suggest that students give names to the characters, at least the two main ones, in order to make the story-telling task easier. Challenge them to come up with ways to use tenses such as the present perfect subjunctive and the conditional perfect.

Answers:

Step1

1. b   **2.** a   **3.** b   **4.** a   **5.** c   **6.** c

Steps 2–3

Answers will vary.

Justicia para todos

1 Escucha el siguiente diálogo entre Sergio y su padre. Después de cada sección del diálogo vas a oír tres preguntas. Escoge la mejor respuesta para cada pregunta.

1. a. a una propuesta   **b.** a un juicio   **c.** a un castigo

2. a. un jurado, un juez y testigos   **b.** una secretaria y dos policías   **c.** un representante del estado

3. a. un libro   **b.** un video   **c.** una obra de teatro

4. a. gozarían de igualdad ante la ley   **b.** todos serían culpables   **c.** no podría haber testigos

5. a. el juez   **b.** el abogado   **c.** el estado

6. a. es interesante   **b.** es entretenido   **c.** es muy necesario

2 Las ilustraciones a continuación representan un cuento. Con tus propias palabras, describe detalladamente lo que sucedió. Recuerda que no puedes usar tus notas mientras cuentas el cuento. Añade información para que el cuento resulte más interesante y ponle un título. ¡Usa tu imaginación!

Puedes usar las siguientes palabras o expresiones para conectar tus ideas.

primero	antes de	después	finalmente
por eso	porque	cuando	entonces

1

2

3

4

5

6

3 Trabaja con un grupo de estudiantes. Cada miembro del grupo cuenta su cuento. ¿Qué conclusiones sacan sobre las reglas de los miembros de una familia a partir de los cuentos?

464   cuatrocientos sesenta y cuatro
    ¡Adelante!

Universal Access

Students with Learning Difficulties

For the *Presentación* oral, allow students the option of describing rules and regulations your school already has.

Students with Special Needs

Record on audiocassette oral descriptions of the pictures in step 2 of *¿Qué me cuentas?* for visually impaired students. They can then perform the task on their own, including for homework.

Los derechos de los estudiantes

Tarea
Imagina que el director de la escuela ha decidido que los estudiantes propongan qué reglas y derechos les gustaría tener en su escuela. Prepara un discurso para presentar las reglas y los derechos que tú propondrías.

Estrategia

Think, plan, then speak
Before proposing a list of rules, think about what you're going to include. Make a plan and use a table or graphic to organize your thoughts. Then, speak using the information that you have gathered.

1 Prepárate Completa una tabla como la siguiente con las reglas y los derechos que quieres proponer.

Reglas de la escuela	Derechos de los estudiantes

2 Practica Vuelve a leer la información que anotaste en la tabla. Practica varias veces tu discurso para recordar las reglas y los derechos que vas a proponer. Presenta razones por las que crees que estos derechos y reglas son beneficiosos. Usa tus notas para practicar, pero no al hablar ante la clase. Recuerda:

- explicar cada regla y derecho en forma clara y persuasiva
- presentar las razones por las que estos derechos y reglas serían beneficiosos
- mirar directamente al público y hablar con voz clara

Modelo

Los estudiantes deberíamos tener derecho a vacaciones más largas. Si hubiéramos tenido antes más tiempo para relajarnos, habríamos aprendido más y mejor. También la escuela debería tener derecho a exigir que . . .

3 Haz tu presentación Imagina que tus compañeros son los que van a analizar las reglas y los derechos que propongas. Debes convencerlos de que tu propuesta beneficiará tanto a los estudiantes como a los profesores.

4 Evaluación Tu profesor(a) puede explicarte cómo va a evaluar tu presentación. Probablemente, para tu profesor(a) es importante ver que:

- tu discurso fue convincente y se entendió bien
- diste suficientes razones de por qué los derechos y las reglas que propones son beneficiosos para todos.

Communicate: Speaking

10

Presentación oral

Presentation

Standards: 1.2, 1.3, 3.1

Resources: Voc. & Gram. Transparencies: 4

Focus: Preparing and delivering an oral presentation

Suggestions: Review the task and the four-step approach with students. Review the rubric with the class (see *Assessment* below) to explain how you will grade the performance task. Before students begin, direct their attention to the *Estrategia.* Show *Vocabulary and Grammar Transparency* 4 and have students create a similar word chart on their own paper. Model how to include in the chart an idea or two for proposed student rules and rights. Encourage them to use other graphic organizers as well, such as concept webs, that they may find beneficial in developing their speeches. Remind them that they will submit and be evaluated on their use of one or more organizers.

Portfolio

Record students' oral presentations on audiocassette or videotape for inclusion in their portfolios.

✓ Assessment

- Assessment Program: Cap. 10, Rubrics

Give students copies of the rubric before they begin the activity. Go over the descriptions of the different levels of performance. After assessing students, help individuals understand how their performance could be improved.

Enriching Your Teaching

RUBRIC	Score 1	Score 3	Score 5
How well you use organizers	Your speech notes include no organizers.	You use one or more organizers, but they contain little useful information.	You use organizer(s) effectively to plan your speech.
How convincing you are	You miss important arguments. Your arguments are weak.	You present some convincing arguments.	You present convincing arguments.
How effectively you deliver your speech	You read your speech and make no eye contact with your audience.	You make some eye contact, and you use some intonation.	Your eye contact is good. Your intonation helps get your message across.

Presentación escrita

Presentation

Standards: 1.2, 1.3, 3.1

Resources: Voc. & Gram. Transparencies 4

Focus: Combining learned vocabulary and structures in a written presentation

Suggestions: Begin by explaining the criteria you will use to evaluate students' compositions. (See step 5, *Evaluación,* in the Student Edition, and *Assessment* on the following page.)

Direct students' attention to the *Estrategia.* Suggest than another idea for a snappy introduction for this particular essay might be to include an interesting comment from one of the people interviewed. Such a comment should catch readers' attention and give an idea of what the subject of the essay will be. Then show *Vocabulary & Grammar Transparency* 4. Model filling in part of a column with information like that shown in the chart on this page. Have students begin a similar columnar chart on their own paper. Tell them to use one column for the responses of each person that they interview, and to interview at least two people.

Language Arts Connection

Standards: 3.1

Encourage students to draw on background knowledge they have from their Language Arts courses about introductions used in writing. Remind them that an effective introduction provides readers with a context for what is to follow—a kind of mental "shelf" on which to place the information they will read. Without an effective introduction, an essay is bound to quickly lose readers' attention.

Presentación escrita

¿Cuáles son sus derechos?

Objectives

- Write an editorial essay to be published in a newspaper
- Present other people's opinions about a subject

Estrategia

Snappy introductions
An interesting introduction will get your reader involved in your essay immediately. One good way to begin is to ask a question to pique his or her curiosity. Another way to hook your reader is to start with an interesting fact or incident related to your story.

Imagínate que eres reportero(a) y tienes que hacer un ensayo editorial sobre lo que saben los ciudadanos de los Estados Unidos acerca de los derechos y las garantías que tienen según la Constitución. Puedes entrevistar *(interview)* a personas de diferentes edades y usar sus respuestas para escribir tu ensayo.

1 Antes de escribir

Usa las siguientes preguntas para entrevistar a las personas sobre lo que saben acerca de sus derechos y garantías como ciudadanos(as) de los Estados Unidos. Escribe sus respuestas en una tabla como la siguiente.

1. ¿Es ciudadano(a) de los Estados Unidos?
2. ¿A qué se dedica?
3. ¿Sabe qué derechos y garantías tiene como ciudadano(a) de los Estados Unidos?
4. ¿Cómo usa usted sus libertades?
5. ¿Cómo compara su situación en este país con respecto a otros países?

Entrevista a: Ingrid Ramírez	**Entrevista a:** Jorge Ríos
1. ciudadana de los Estados Unidos	1. ciudadano de los Estados Unidos
2. maestra en Nueva York	2. mecánico en Miami
3. derecho a la libertad de expresión, libertad de prensa, libertad de religión	3. derecho a la libertad de decir lo que uno quiere
4. "Trabajo, me expreso y viajo libremente; tengo la religión que quiero."	4. "Puedo tener una vida cómoda, trabajar y viajar."
5. muy buena situación con respecto a otros países	5. mejor situación que en otros países

1 Borrador

Escribe tu borrador del ensayo. Presenta las opiniones de las personas entrevistadas sobre lo que saben de los derechos y las garantías que tienen como ciudadanos(as). Añade todos los detalles que sean necesarios. Recuerda usar el vocabulario y la gramática de este capítulo.

466 cuatrocientos sesenta y seis
¡Adelante!

Universal Access

Students with Learning Difficulties

Suggest that students interview their Social Studies teachers for the *Presentación escrita*. If possible, meet with the teachers beforehand and tell them what type of research students are doing, so that they can provide guidance to students during the interviews.

Advanced Learners

Have students prepare and present orally their own Spanish paraphrases of the ten amendments to the United States Constitution in the Bill of Rights.

Modelo

> **Snappy introduction** uses a question to get the readers' attention.

Nuestra Constitución determina los derechos y las garantías que tienen los ciudadanos de este país. Pero, ¿sabe realmente la gente de qué tratan esos derechos y garantías? La mayoría de nosotros vivimos sin preguntarnos qué habría sido de nuestra vida si no se hubieran creado los derechos de los ciudadanos . . .

> **Examples** of how people think about the topic.

Por ejemplo Ingrid, una maestra de Nueva York, dice que goza de sus libertades ya que trabaja, se expresa y viaja libremente . . .

> **Conclusion** ties everything together.

Al igual que Ingrid, muchas personas que hubieran vivido en este país en las últimas décadas, habrían . . .

3 Redacción/Revisión

Después de escribir el primer borrador, trabaja con otro(a) compañero(a) para intercambiar los trabajos y leerlos. Decidan qué aspectos son más interesantes. Luego, hagan sugerencias para mejorar sus composiciones y corregir los errores.

- ¿Se usó correctamente el pluscuamperfecto del subjuntivo y el condicional perfecto?
- ¿Existen errores de ortografía?

> mayoría
> La ~~mayorías~~ de nosotros vivimos sin
> habría
> preguntarnos qué ~~habrían~~ sido de nuestra
> hubieran
> vida si no se ~~hubiera~~ creado los derechos
> de los ciudadanos . . .

4 Publicación

Antes de hacer la versión final, lee de nuevo tu borrador y repasa los siguientes puntos.

- ¿Presenta el ensayo una idea clara sobre el tema?
- ¿Incluí opiniones de otras personas para explicar el tema?
- ¿Muestra el ensayo la importancia del tema?
- ¿Presenta una conclusión interesante?

Después de revisar el borrador, escribe una copia en limpio de tu composición.

5 Evaluación

Tu profesor(a) puede explicarte cómo va a evaluar tu ensayo. Probablemente, para tu profesor(a) es importante ver que:

- explicaste tu punto de vista sobre el tema
- presentaste detalles para explicar el tema
- las frases tienen sentido (make sense) y expresan una idea completa
- usaste correctamente el vocabulario y la gramática

Suggestions (Cont'd):

For step 1, encourage students to interview at least one Spanish-speaking person, if possible. Help them agree upon effective English translations of the five interview questions to use when interviewing people in English. Remind them that they must convert the information gained in English interviews to Spanish.

In step 2, students should concentrate on developing the information they obtained in their interviews into a rough draft. This is also the step in which they should focus on an effective introduction for their essay. Encourage them to work toward organization, level of detail, and language use similar to that shown in the model.

For step 3, encourage students to experiment with various ways of combining sentences. Suggest that they use the pluperfect subjunctive and the conditional perfect at least once by mentioning how some aspect of United States society would have developed differently without the rights guaranteed by the Constitution and the Bill of Rights.

Evaluation

Steps 4 and 5 overlap. Students will need evaluation by you, their peers, or self-evaluation to fine tune and polish their drafts.

Portfolio

Keep students' final drafts in their portfolios as a writing sample.

✓ Assessment

- Assessment Program: Cap. 10, Rubrics

Give students copies of the rubric before they begin the activity. Go over the descriptions of the different levels of performance. After assessing students, help individuals understand how their performance could be improved.

Enriching Your Teaching

RUBRIC	Score 1	Score 3	Score 5
Completion of task	Important parts of your essay are missing.	Information in your essay is disorganized and hard to follow.	You include and organize all the parts needed for an effective essay.
Effective introduction	Your essay lacks an introduction.	You attempt an introduction, but it is not effective.	Your introduction is effective, attracting and orientating readers.
Grammar, spelling, mechanics	You make many errors in grammar, spelling, and punctuation.	You make some errors in grammar, spelling, and punctuation.	You make very few errors in grammar, spelling, and punctuation.

Lectura

Presentation

Standards: 1.2, 2.1, 3.1, 3.2, 5.2

Resources: Voc. & Gram. Transparencies: 4

Focus: Reading an extended passage

Suggestions:

Pre-reading: Before reading, direct students' attention to the *Estrategia* and *Al leer* sections. Have them copy the T-chart on p. 471 to their own paper and make sure they understand how they will use it. Explain that, since this reading is based on an oral account, the language used is more informal than in other readings. Point out as examples of this the use of **Bueno** at the outset of the reading and the frequent use of informal and creative diminutives, such as **otrita** and **cajoncito** in the first paragraph. Ask students to pay attention to other examples of informal language as they read.

Reading: When reading together with students, pause frequently to address comprehension issues they may have and to allow them to fill in their charts from p. 471. Here are some suggestions for providing comprehension guidance on this page:

• Ask: *¿En qué año empieza la historia? (1954)*

• Ask: *En tus propias palabras, describe qué verías si la joven Domitila y sus hermanas te pasaran en la calle delante de la escuela.*

Country Connection

Presentation

Standards: 3.1

Resources: Voc. & Gram. Transparencies 17 (map)

After students have read the *Al leer* section, show *Vocabulary and Grammar Transparency* 17 and ask a volunteer to point out Bolivia. Explain to students that historically mining was the most important attraction that the country held for Europeans. At the end of the sixteenth century, for example, the city of Potosí was the largest urban center in South America, due to its surrounding silver mines. Those mines are now depleted.

Go Online

The online atlas will provide a more detailed map of Bolivia.

468

Si me permiten hablar . . .
(Fragmento)

Estrategia

Investigate the author's reasons
Authors must decide which materials are most appropriate for describing the events they want to include in the narration of their experiences. The setting, the selection of special memories and how they affected his or her life, the use of particular details to describe feelings and personal opinions and the inclusion of anecdotes to liven up the narration, all these elements will give you clues to the author's reasons for writing.

Al leer

Este fragmento de *Si me permiten hablar . . .* es parte de una historia oral basada en las experiencias de Domitila Barrios Chungara en las minas de cobre *(copper mines)* de Bolivia. En este fragmento, Domitila cuenta cómo tenía que luchar para quedarse en la escuela y continuar su educación. Su testimonio revela a una joven cuyo coraje y determinación lograron vencer los obstáculos y prejuicios que formaban parte de la vida diaria de las mujeres en los pueblos mineros. Mientras lees este relato, presta atención a los siguientes puntos y luego completa la tabla que aparece en la página 471 con la siguiente información:

• el ambiente de pobreza en el hogar de la protagonista

• los errores que cometió y cómo logró superarlos

• los obstáculos que tuvo que enfrentar

• la actitud del padre de Domitila

Bueno, en el 54 me fue difícil regresar a la escuela después de las vacaciones, porque nosotros teníamos una vivienda que consistía en una pieza pequeñita donde no teníamos patio y no teníamos dónde ni con quiénes dejar a las wawas[1]. Entonces consultamos al director de la escuela y él dio permiso para llevar a mis hermanitas conmigo. El estudio se hacía por las tardes y por las mañanas. Yo tenía que combinar todo: casa y escuela. Entonces yo llevaba a la más chiquita cargada y a la otra agarrada de la mano y Marina llevaba las mamaderas[2] y las mantillas[3] y mi hermana la otrita llevaba los cuadernos. Y así todas nos íbamos a la escuela. En un rincón teníamos un cajoncito donde dejábamos a la más chiquita mientras seguíamos estudiando. Salía de la escuela, tenía que cargarme la niñita, nos íbamos a la casa y tenía yo que cocinar, lavar, planchar, atender a las wawas. Me parecía muy difícil todo eso. ¡Yo deseaba tanto jugar! Y tantas otras cosas deseaba, como cualquier niña.

Dos años después, ya la profesora no me dejó llevar a mis hermanitas porque ya metían bulla[4]. Mi padre no podía pagar a una sirvienta, pues no le alcanzaba su sueldo ni para la comida y la ropa de nosotras. En la casa, por ejemplo, yo andaba siempre descalza, usando los zapatos solamente para ir a la escuela.

---

1 small children 2 baby bottles 3 swaddling clothes 4 made noise

Universal Access

Heritage Language Learners

When the class reads the Bolivian slang term **wawas,** ask students to mention other slang terms for children that they may know. They may wish to comment on other elements of Domitila Chungara's informal style, as well.

Students with Learning Difficulties

Write a paragraph-by-paragraph paraphrase of the reading selection for students, using language suitable to their level. Consider jigsawing this task and assigning paragraphs or sections to interested Advanced Learners.

Bueno, como la profesora no me había dado aquella orden, entonces yo empecé a irme sola a la escuela. Echaba llave a la casa y tenían que quedarse las wawas en la calle, porque la vivienda era oscura, no tenía ventana y les daba mucho terror cuando se la cerraba. Era como una cárcel[5], solamente con una puerta. Y no había dónde dejar a las chicas, porque en ese entonces vivíamos en un barrio de solteros, donde no había familias, puros hombres vivían allí.

Entonces mi padre me dijo que dejara la escuela, porque ya sabía leer y leyendo podía aprender otras cosas. Pero yo no acepté y me puse fuerte[6] y seguí yendo a la escuela.

Mi padre gestionó[7] en la empresa minera de Pulacayo para que le diera una vivienda con patiecito, porque era muy difícil vivir donde estábamos. Y el gerente, a quien mi papá le arreglaba sus trajes, ordenó que le diera una vivienda más grande con un cuarto, una cocina y un corredorcito donde se podía dejar a las chicas.

Sufríamos hambre a veces y no nos satisfacían los alimentos porque era poco lo que podía comprar mi papá. Ha sido duro vivir con

privaciones y toda clase de problemas cuando pequeñas. Pero eso desarrolló algo en nosotras: una gran sensibilidad, un gran deseo de ayudar a toda la gente. Nuestros juegos de niños siempre tenían algo relacionado con lo que vivíamos y con lo que deseábamos vivir. Además, en el transcurso de nuestra infancia habíamos visto eso: mi madre y mi padre, a pesar de que teníamos tan poco, siempre estaban ayudando a algunas familias de Pulacayo. Entonces, cuando veíamos pobres por la calle mendigando[8], yo y mis hermanas nos poníamos a soñar. Y soñábamos que un día íbamos a ser grandes, que íbamos a tener tierras, que íbamos a sembrar y que a aquellos pobres les íbamos a dar de comer.

Y bueno, así era nuestra vida. Yo tenía entonces 13 años. Mi padre siempre insistía en que no debía seguir en la escuela. Pero yo le iba rogando[9], rogando y seguía yendo. Claro, siempre me faltaba material escolar[10]. Entonces, algunos maestros me comprendían, otros no.

5 jail 6 got stubborn 7 negotiated 8 begging
9 pleading 10 school supplies

cuatrocientos sesenta y nueve 469
Capítulo 10

Suggestions (Cont'd):

Reading: Here are some suggestions for providing comprehension guidance on this page:

• After reading the first paragraph ask: *¿Qué expresión significa que Domitila cerraba la puerta de la casa con llave? (Echaba llave a la casa.)*

• After reading the third paragraph, say: *Recuerda que el padre de Domitila era sastre* (tailor)*. ¿Cómo le ayudó a su padre influir al gerente de la mina? (El padre podía influir al gerente porque le arreglaba sus trajes.)*

• After reading the fourth paragraph, ask: *¿Qué expresión significa "durante nuestra infancia"? (en el transcurso de nuestra infancia)*

Enriching Your Teaching

Culture Note

Bolivia offers many attractions for tourists. There is the capital La Paz, with all its record-breaking statistics, including world's highest large city, world's highest capital, and world's highest major airport. Even higher in the Andes is **el lago Titicaca,** the highest lake in the world and one of the earliest centers of human population in South America. One of the reasons for this is because its waters cause local temperatures to be more moderate, allowing for cultivation of wheat and maize at much higher altitudes than usual. But Bolivia isn't all mountainous. It also contains part of the Amazon rainforest, an area called Beni, which is about the size of the United Kingdom.

Suggestions (Cont'd):

Reading: Here are some suggestions for providing comprehension guidance on this page:

• After reading the second paragraph, write on the board in English:

A. "In the sixth grade I had a great teacher who knew how to understand me."

B. "In the sixth grade I had a great teacher who learned how to understand me."

Then ask: *¿Cuál es la mejor traducción de la primera frase de este párrafo, A o B? ¿Por qué? (B. El pretérito de* saber *quiere decir* "learned.")

• After reading the first column, ask: *¿Qué significa la expresión "a la salida": "en la puerta del aula» o «después de la clase"? (después de la clase)*

• After reading the second column, ask: *¿Creían los vecinos de Domitila en educar a las niñas? (No. Creían que no se debe eseñar a leer a las mujeres.)*

• *¿Tenía Domitila un hermano? ¿Qué parte del texto te lo dice? (No tenía hermano. "cinco mujeres, ningún varón")*

Post-reading: When students finish reading, ask: *¿Qué inferencia podemos hacer al fin de la historia? ¿Qué decidió hacer el maestro de Domitila? (Parece que decidió darle a Domitila el material escolar que necesitaba.)* Then ask them to go back and identify other examples of informal language they can find in the reading.

El problema es que habíamos hecho un trato[11] mi papá y yo. Él me había explicado que no tenía dinero, que no me podía comprar material, que no podía dar nada para la escuela. Y de ahí que me arreglaba como podía. Y por eso tenía yo problemas.

En el sexto curso tuve como profesor a un gran maestro que me supo comprender. Era un profesor bastante estricto, y los primeros días que no llevé el material completo, me castigó severamente. Tuve que irme a la casa, llorando. Pero al día siguiente, volví. Y de la ventana miraba lo que estaban haciendo los chicos.

En uno de esos momentos, el profesor me llamó.

—Seguramente no ha traído su material —me dijo. Yo no podía contestar y me puse a llorar.

—Entre. Ya pase, tome su asiento. Y a la salida se ha de quedar usted.

A la salida me quedé y entonces él me dijo:

—Mira, yo quiero ser tu amigo, pero necesito que me digas qué pasa con vos[12]. ¿Es cierto que no tienes tu mamá?

—Sí, profesor.

—¿Cuándo se murió?

—Cuando estaba todavía en el primer curso.

—Y tu padre, ¿dónde trabaja?

—En la policía minera, es sastre[13].

—Bueno, ¿qué es lo que pasa? Mira, yo quiero ayudarte, pero tienes que ser sincera. ¿Qué es lo que pasa?

Yo no quería hablar, porque pensé que iba a llamar a mi padre como algunos profesores lo hacían cuando estaban enojados. Pero el profesor me hizo otras preguntas y entonces le conté todo. También le dije que podía hacer mis tareas, pero que no tenía mis cuadernos, porque éramos bien pobres y mi papá no podía comprar y que, años atrás, ya mi papá me había querido sacar de la escuela porque no podía hacer ese gasto más. Y que con mucho sacrificio y esfuerzo había yo podido llegar hasta el sexto curso. Pero no era que mi papá no quisiera, sino porque no podía, porque, incluso, a pesar de toda la creencia que había en Pulacayo de que a la mujer no se le debía enseñar a leer, mi papá siempre quiso que supiéramos por lo menos eso.

Sí, mi papá siempre se preocupó por nuestra formación[14]. Cuando murió mi mamá, la gente nos miraba y decía: "Ay, pobrecitas, cinco mujeres, ningún varón . . . ¿Para qué sirven? . . . Mejor si se mueren". Pero mi papá muy orgulloso decía: "No, déjenme a mis hijas, ellas van a vivir". Y cuando la gente trataba de acomplejarnos[15] porque éramos mujeres y no servíamos para gran cosa, él nos decía que todas las mujeres tienen los mismos derechos que los hombres. Y decía que nosotras podíamos hacer las hazañas[16] que hacen los hombres. Nos crió siempre con esas ideas. Sí, fue una disciplina muy especial. Y todo eso fue muy positivo para nuestro futuro. Y de ahí que nunca nos consideramos mujeres inútiles.

El profesor comprendía todo esto, porque yo le contaba. E hicimos un trato de que yo le iba a pedir todo el material que necesitaba. Y así pude terminar mi último año escolar.

---

11 deal **12** with you **13** tailor **14** education **15** make us feel bad **16** feats

Universal Access

Heritage Language Learners
Ask students who have lived in heritage countries to share what they know about student-teacher relations in schools there.

Advanced Learners
Invite students to compare Domitila Barrios Chungara's account with readings from past *Capítulos.* Can they find a similar theme of overcoming obstacles in the other readings? What are the obstacles? How are they overcome?

Interacción con la lectura

1 Completa la tabla siguiente para investigar por qué Domitila Barrios de Chungara escribió este relato autobiográfico.

Razones de Domitila	Ejemplos
describir las condiciones en que ella y su familia vivían	vivienda pobre, pasar hambre
analizar sus errores para prevenirlos en el futuro	
explicar su actitud frente a los obstáculos que tenía que enfrentar	
explicar el comportamiento de sus maestros	
explicar el comportamiento de su padre	

2 Trabaja con otro(a) compañero(a) para analizar la información de las tablas de cada uno(a). Comenten cuáles son las razones principales que llevaron a Domitila Barrios de Chungara a escribir este relato autobiográfico.

¿Comprendiste?

1. ¿Por qué dice Domitila que le fue difícil regresar a la escuela después de las vacaciones de 1954? ¿Qué tenía que hacer ella después de la clase?

2. Según Domitila, ¿qué aspecto positivo surgió de las privaciones que ella y su familia tuvieron que pasar?

3. ¿Cuál era la actitud del pueblo de Pulacayo hacia las mujeres?

4. ¿Qué piensas de la actitud del padre hacia los derechos de las mujeres?

5. ¿Piensas que Domitila logró superar los obstáculos que tuvo que enfrentar? Explica tu respuesta.

 **Fondo cultural**

Domitila Barrios Chungara (1937–) nació en Pulacayo, un pueblo minero de Bolivia. Años después recogió sus memorias de este pueblo en su obra *Si me permiten hablar . . .* Desde muy pequeña, Domitila estaba consciente del sufrimiento de su pueblo, en particular, la falta de educación, de empleo, de vivienda y de comida. Su ambición era mejorar las condiciones de vida de los campesinos y mineros de Bolivia. En 1952 se casó con un minero y empezó a participar en el Comité de Amas de Casa *(Homemakers)* del Distrito Minero Siglo XXI, y después, fue nombrada su Secretaria General. Su participación en las protestas contra las injusticias del gobierno causó que la encarcelaran *(jailed)*. Después tuvo que exiliarse *(go into exile)* en Europa. A pesar de estas terribles experiencias, Domitila sigue su campaña por los derechos de los pobres, los niños y las mujeres.

Domitila Barrios Chungara

• ¿Has participado alguna vez en un movimiento u organización que se dedica a luchar por los derechos de la gente? ¿Qué motivo tuviste para hacerlo? Si no lo has hecho, ¿te gustaría participar en el futuro?

Interacción con la lectura

Standards: 1.1, 1.2, 1.3

Suggestions: Have students work together to complete their charts in step 1. Encourage them to help each other paraphrase the pertinent parts of the text.

Answers will vary.

¿Comprendiste?

Standards: 1.1, 1.2, 1.3

Resources: Practice Answers on Transparencies

Suggestions: Have students first write the answers to the questions on their own. Then invite them to share their answers as a basis for discussion of the reading.

Answers:
1. Fue difícil porque tenía que llevar a sus hermanitas a la escuela. Después de la clase, tenía que cargar a sus hermanitas a la casa, cocinar, lavar, planchar y atender a las niñas.
2. Ella desarrolló una sensibilidad y un deseo de ayudar a los demás.
3. Ellos no creían en la educación de las mujeres.
4–5. Answers will vary.

Fondo cultural  *Standards:* 1.1, 1.2, 3.1

Suggestions: After students have read the information, ask: *¿Cuál fue el resultado de las protestas de Domitila Barrios Chungara contra las injusticias del gobierno? (La encarcelaron y tuvo que exiliarse en Europa.)*

Answers will vary.

Enriching Your Teaching

Teacher-to-Teacher
Invite interested students to research and report more about Domitila Barrios Chungara. Encourage them to read her book, the full title of which is *Si me permiten hablar: testimonio de una mujer en las minas de Bolivia*. It has also been tranlated to English and given the title *Let Me Speak* (Monthly Review Press, Boulder, 1978.)

Review Activities

Sobre tus derechos y responsabilidades/Sobre los derechos de los ciudadanos/Sobre los derechos de todas las personas: On strips of paper, have students write a phrase or sentence using each word in these three categories. You can divide this task among small groups. Students' phrases or sentences should connote either a right or a responsibility. For example: ***que los niños no sufran*** or ***Gozamos de una prensa libre.*** Collect all strips and place them in a container. Have students sit in a circle. They take turns drawing one slip at a time, reading it aloud, and stating whether the phrase or sentence connotes a ***derecho*** or a ***responsabilidad.***

En el hogar: Have students work in pairs and play *hangman* using the words and expressions in this category.

En la escuela: Play charades using the words and expressions in this category. Write them on slips of paper and place them in a container. Students take turns drawing an expression and getting its meaning across to the others any way they can without speaking or writing. Use body language and strategies of traditional charades such as tugging at the ear to mean ***suena como*** or holding up two fingers to mean ***dos palabras***—or invent your own rules.

Otros adjetivos y expresiones: Students can use these words and expressions as they go over the review activities for the other categories and in the grammar review activities on the next page.

Repaso del capítulo

Vocabulario y gramática

sobre tus derechos y responsabilidades

aplicar (las leyes)	to apply (the law)
discriminado, -a	discriminated
discriminar	to discriminate
funcionar	to function
gozar (de)	to enjoy
maltratar	to mistreat
obligar	to force
sufrir	to suffer
tratar	to treat
votar	to vote

en el hogar

el abuso	abuse
el / la adolescente	adolescent
el apoyo	support
la libertad	liberty
la niñez	childhood
la pobreza	poverty

en la escuela

el armario	locker
la autoridad	authority
el código de vestimenta	dress code
el deber	duty
la enseñanza	teaching
la igualdad	equality
el maltrato	mistreatment
el motivo	cause
el pensamiento	thought
la razón	reason
el respeto	respect

otros adjetivos y expresiones

adecuado, -a	adequate
ambos	both
de ese modo	in that way
en cuanto a	with respect to, as for
estar sujeto(a) a	to be subject to
satisfactorio, -a	satisfactory

sobre los derechos de los ciudadanos

el / la acusado(a)	accused, defendant
asegurar	to assure
el castigo	punishment
la desigualdad	inequality
el desempleo	unemployment
detener	to detain
el estado	the state
la felicidad	happiness
fundamental	fundamental, vital
la injusticia	injustice
el juicio	judgement
el jurado	jury
la justicia	justice
juzgar	to judge
la paz	peace
la prensa	the press
la propuesta	proposal
sospechoso, -a	suspicious
el / la testigo	witness
la tolerancia	tolerance
violar	to violate

sobre los derechos de todas las personas

la aspiración	aspiration
el fin	purpose
la garantía	guarantee
la igualdad	equality
intercambiar	to exchange
libre	free
mundial	worldwide
opinar	to think
pacífico, -a	peaceful
proponer	to propose, to suggest
el punto de vista	point of view
el valor	value

otros adjetivos y expresiones

a medida que	as
ante	before
culpable	guilty
democrático, -a	democratic
de modo que	so, so that
el modo	the way
en lugar de	instead of
la falta de	lack of
inocente	innocent
llegar a	to reach, to get to

472 cuatrocientos setenta y dos
Repaso del capítulo

Students with Learning Difficulties

For additional vocabulary practice, have students make vocabulary flashcards for the vocabulary words. Tell them to write the word on one side of the card, and on the other to include a photo, sketch, synonym, antonym, or whatever other clue helps them remember the word. Have pairs of students quiz each other using their cards.

Advanced Learners

Invite students to create and trade crossword puzzles using the chapter vocabulary. Tell them they can be creative with their clues, but they must be accurate. You may wish to provide or have students use computer software to make the crossword puzzles.

La voz pasiva: *ser* + *participio pasado*

Form the passive voice by using *ser* + past participle. The past participle is an adjective, so it agrees in number and gender with the subject. However, use the impersonal *se* when the subject is unknown.

Las reglas **son aplicadas** por el estado.   Se **necesita** una persona para trabajar con nosotros.

El presente y el imperfecto del subjuntivo

Use the present subjunctive when the verb in the main clause is in the present, present perfect, command or future tense.

Dile que **vote** mañana en las elecciones.   Armando cantará cuando **se lo pidan**.
No hemos dicho que ella **sea** nuestra amiga.

Use the imperfect subjunctive when the verb in the main clause is in the preterite, imperfect, pluperfect or conditional.

Mi maestra me pidió que **bailara**.   El adolescente había tratado que **nos conociéramos**.
El presidente quería que todos **votaran**.   Le gustaría a mamá que **llegáramos** a tiempo.

pluscuamperfecto del subjuntivo

Use the pluperfect subjunctive when the verb of the main clause is in the preterite, the imperfect or the pluperfect of the indicative.

Esperaba que **hubieran ido** a la fiesta con los niños.
Carlos no pensó que Juan **hubiera intercambiado** su pluma.
Había querido que la prensa **hubiera dicho** la verdad.

To form the pluperfect subjunctive use the past subjunctive of *haber* + the past participle of the verb.

hubiera	salido	hubiera	salido	hubierais	salido
hubieras	salido	hubiéramos	salido	hubieran	salido

Also use the pluperfect subjunctive when the verb in the main clause is in the conditional.

¿**Sería** posible que él **hubiera terminado** la tarea?

After the expression *como si* (as if), use either the imperfect subjunctive or the pluperfect subjunctive.

Estaba tan alegre **como si hubiera dormido**.   El niño descansa **como si no tuviera** nada que hacer.

El condicional perfecto

Form the conditional perfect using the conditional of *haber* + the past participle of the verb.

habría	trabajado	habría	trabajado	habríais	trabajado
habrías	trabajado	habríamos	trabajado	habrían	trabajado

In sentences with *si* clauses, use the past perfect subjunctive and the conditional perfect together.

Si **hubieras ido** a la fiesta, te **habrías divertido**.   Si **hubieran venido** aquí, no **habrían estudiado**.

● **Más práctica** ·
Practice Workbook Organizer 10-13, 10-14

La voz pasiva: **ser** + *participio pasado:*
Ask students to write five sentences that contain a transitive verb and a direct object. Have them exchange sentences with a partner, who converts them to the passive voice: *Tina leyó un libro sobre los derechos de la gente./Un libro sobre los derechos de la gente fue leído por Tina.*

El presente y el imperfecto del subjuntivo: Ask students to write two opinions they have about rights and responsibilities. Encourage them to begin each opinion with an expression that requires the subjunctive and to sign their opinions. For example: *Es importante que el gobierno asegure la protección de los niños—Pedro.* Have them place these in a "time capsule." Pretend that 100 years have passed and the class is opening the time capsule. Students read the opinions, converting them to the past tense: *Pedro dijo que era importante que el gobierno asegurara la protección de los niños.*

El pluscuamperfecto del subjuntivo: Have students write humorous expressions using **como si** and the pluperfect subjunctive: *La muchacha bailó como si hubiera tenido alitas en los tobillos.*

El condicional perfecto: Have students write five things to tell a partner that he or she should have done. For example: *Deberías haber ido a la fiesta.* Ask them to take turns reading their statements to a partner, who asks *¿Por qué?* The first student then responds with a suitable sentence using the conditional perfect: *Habrías bailado mucho.*

Portfolio

Invite students to review the activities they completed in this chapter, including written reports, posters or other visuals, tapes of oral presentations, and other projects. Have them select one or two items that they feel best demonstrate their achievements in Spanish. Include these products in students' portfolios. Have them include this with the Chapter Checklist and Self-Assessment Worksheet.

Additional Resources

• Audio Program: CD Cap. 10, Track 20
• Resource Book: Cap. 10, Clip Art
• Assessment Program: Chapter Checklist and Self-Assessment Worksheet

---

Enriching Your Teaching

Teacher-to-Teacher

As students read more and more in Spanish, help them improve their skills in dictionary use by offering this suggestion. Tell them that each time they look up a word in their own dictionary, they should place a small dot beside the entry. If they look up a word and find a dot already there, they know this is the second time they have looked up the word. If they see two dots beside a word, they know it is one that they need frequently, and they should take steps to internalize it.

Performance Tasks

Standards: 1.1, 1.2, 1.3, 3.1

Resources: Audio Program: CD Cap. 10, Track 21; Resource Book: Cap. 10, Audio Script; Practice Answers on Transparencies

1. Vocabulario

Suggestions: Encourage students to review the vocabulary from the *A primera vista* sections on pp. 436–439 and 448–451 before they complete the activity.

Answers:

1. c	5. a
2. d	6. a
3. c	7. c
4. b	8. b

2. Gramática

Suggestions: Remind students of the main points of the grammar presentations in *Capítulo* 10:

- the passive voice
- the present and imperfect subjunctive
- the pluperfect subjunctive
- the conditional perfect

Answers:

1. d	5. a
2. c	6. d
3. c	7. c
4. a	8. d

3. Escuchar

Suggestions: Use the *Audio CD* or read from the script.

Answers:

a. un deber
b. podrán votar
c. serán castigados
d. Answers will vary.

To prepare for the test, check to see if you . . .
- know the new vocabulary and grammar
- can perform the tasks on pp. 474 and 475

Preparación para el examen

① Vocabulary Escribe la letra de la palabra o expresión que mejor complete cada frase. Escribe tus respuestas en una hoja aparte.

1. El _____ de las opiniones de los demás ayuda a que la gente viva de manera pacífica.
   a. valor   c. respeto
   b. código de vestimenta d. maltrato

2. Antes, era muy difícil recibir las noticias _____ si vivías en un pueblo pequeño.
   a. inocentes   c. enseñanzas
   b. propuestas   d. mundiales

3. La justicia y la paz son _____ que tienen los países de todo el mundo.
   a. democráticas   c. aspiraciones
   b. injusticias   d. castigos

4. A medida que le hacían preguntas, el sospechoso de _____ la ley se asustaba más.
   a. intercambiar   c. opinar
   b. violar   d. proponer

5. En los libros que usan los abogados encontrarás frecuentemente las palabras juicio, _____ y juzgar.
   a. jurado   c. desempleo
   b. armario   d. felicidad

6. Cuando pasan de _____ , muchos adolescentes creen que pueden hacer todo sin avisar a sus padres.
   a. la niñez   c. la injusticia
   b. la pobreza   d. la libertad

7. La policía tiene _____ de detener a las personas cuando existe un motivo.
   a. la igualdad   c. el deber
   b. la tolerancia d. el pensamiento

8. _____ guardar para sus estudios el dinero que ganó con el premio, lo gastó en divertirse.
   a. A pesar de   c. Ante
   b. En lugar de   d. Debido a

② Gramática Escribe la letra de la palabra o expresión que mejor complete cada frase. Escribe tus respuestas en una hoja aparte.

1. Luis no esperaba que su jefe lo _____ a quedarse trabajando toda la noche.
   a. obligará   c. habrá obligado
   b. habían obligado d. hubiera obligado

2. Las leyes que prohiben maltratar a los animales _____ en muchas ciudades.
   a. aplicarán   c. están aplicadas
   b. son aplicados d. son aplicadas

3. Si _____ una educación adecuada, todos los jóvenes se habrían graduado.
   a. tienen   c. hubieran tenido
   b. tenían   d. han tenido

4. La acusada hablaba sobre el asunto como si _____ la autoridad para acusar a otros durante su propio juicio.
   a. hubiera gozado de   c. habría gozado de
   b. han gozado de   d. ha gozado de

5. Dile al candidato que te _____ que va a luchar contra la desigualdad.
   a. asegure   c. asegura
   b. asegurará   d. ha asegurado

6. Si _____ sujeto a todos los problemas que sufrió ese adolescente, tu punto de vista sería muy distinto.
   a. estabas   c. hubiste estado
   b. estás   d. hubieras estado

7. Ambos estudiantes le pidieron al profesor que _____ de convencer a toda la clase para que votaran por su candidata.
   a. tratará   c. tratara
   b. hubiera tratado d. trataría

8. Su amigo le _____ el apoyo que necesitaba si él no lo hubiera tratado así.
   a. sería dado   c. había dado
   b. habrá dado   d. habría dado

Universal Access

Students with Learning Difficulties

Refer students to their portfolios. Have them look at chapter exams from past chapters. Lay three or four exams side-by-side and point out the similarities in structure between them. Remind students that knowing how a test is laid out helps them know what to expect next and reduces stress.

Advanced Learners

Provide students with additional vocabulary practice by asking them to use the incorrect answers from performance task 1 in sentences.

For: Test preparation
Visit: www.phschool.com
Web Code: jed-1011

En el examen vas a . . .	Éstas son las tareas que te pueden ser útiles para el examen . . .	Si necesitas repasar . . .
❸ **Escuchar** Escuchar y comprender la descripción de las reglas de un club deportivo	Responde a las preguntas sobre las reglas del Club Deportivo Veloz. (a) ¿Respetar el código de vestimenta es un derecho o un deber de los miembros? (b) ¿Qué significa que los miembros tendrán derecho de opinar? (c) ¿Qué les pasa a los que no obedecen las reglas? (d) ¿Crees que hay igualdad entre los derechos y los deberes de los miembros? Di por qué.	**pp. 436–439** *A primera vista 1* **p. 437** Actividad 2 **p. 442** Actividad 9 **p. 465** *Presentación oral*
❹ **Hablar** Hacer una presentación para explicar por qué los animales también tienen derechos	Haz una presentación a los jóvenes del barrio sobre lo que deben hacer para cuidar a los animales. Incluye (a) una explicación de los problemas que sufren los animales, (b) qué derechos deberían tener, (c) lo que pueden hacer los jóvenes para protegerlos.	**p. 438** Actividad 3 **p. 461** Actividad 40 **p. 465** *Presentación oral*
❺ **Leer** Leer y comprender un párrafo de un ensayo editorial	Lee un párrafo de un ensayo editorial sobre el mar y Chile. (a) ¿Qué solución propone el autor para desarrollar al país? (b) ¿Quién es el libertador de Chile? (c) ¿De qué depende Chile? *Ante lo que he dicho antes, propongo que hagamos una campaña para que Chile vuelva a mirar hacia el mar como solución para desarrollar al país. Para terminar, debemos recordar a nuestro libertador, Don Bernardo O'Higgins, quien dijo que el pueblo de Chile, "desde siempre y para siempre, depende del mar".*	**pp. 448–451** *A primera vista 2* **p. 455** Actividad 29 **pp. 468–471** *Lectura*
❻ **Escribir** Escribir un cuestionario sobre cómo hacer uso de un parque	En un parque sembraron césped y flores y construyeron un camino para bicicletas, pero la gente no está de acuerdo en cómo usarlos. Escribe un cuestionario para preguntarles cómo habrían usado el parque si hubiera sido de ellos. Incluye (a) el horario, (b) las obligaciones y los derechos, (c) lo que debe garantizar la ciudad.	**p. 438** Actividad 3 **p. 442** Actividad 9 **p. 447** Actividad 17 **p. 460** Actividades 36–38 **pp. 436–437** *A primera vista 1*
❼ **Pensar** Decir de qué derechos deberían gozar los niños	Piensa en lo que leíste sobre Domitila Barrios de Bolivia y di tres derechos que deberían tener todos los niños del mundo.	**p. 439** *A primera vista 1* **p. 439** Actividad 4 **pp. 468–471** *Lectura*

cuatrocientos setenta y cinco **475**
Capítulo 10

4. Hablar

Suggestions: Encourage students to use sentences in which they say what will happen to the animals if they are not cared for and protected.

Answers will vary.

5. Leer

Suggestions: Tell students to refer to pp. 436–439 and 448–451 if they have questions about vocabulary in the review

Answers:
a. Propone una campaña para que el país use el mar.
b. Don Bernardo O'Higgins
c. Chile depende del mar.

6. Escribir

Suggestions: Remind students of what they learned about effective introductions in this chapter's *Presentación escrita*. Have them apply that learning to their writing here.

Answers will vary.

7. Pensar

Suggestions: Encourage students to review the reading on pp. 468–470 before they make their recommendations.

Answers will vary.

✓ **Assessment**
• Examen del capítulo: 10
• Audio Program: CD 13, Cap. 10, Track 13
• Assessment Program: *RPH*

Alternative Assessment
• ExamView Test Bank CD-ROM
• Resource Book: Cap. 10, Situation Cards
• Resource Book: Cap. 10, Communicative Activity BLM

Enriching Your Teaching

Teacher-to-Teacher
Help students prioritize what they need to study. One way to do this is by having them use colored sticky notes to identify important areas of the text. One color can be used to label helpful activities. With another color, students can point out items that they only need to review briefly. They should use a third color for high-priority items that they have not yet mastered. Have them monitor their progress by removing the colored sticky notes as they master the skills.

Vocabulario adicional

El equipo para ir de cámping

el abrelatas can opener

la balsa raft

el bote inflable inflatable boat

la cantimplora canteen

la caña de pescar fishing rod

el casco helmet

el chaleco salvavidas lifesaving jacket

los fósforos matches

la leña firewood

el remo paddle

Para indicar cuando sucede algo

el amanecer dawn

el atardecer dusk

el mediodía noon

la puesta del sol sunset

la salida del sol sunrise

Expresiones para los deportes

empatar to tie (a game)

la cancha (sports) field

el podio podium

Los materiales

la acuarela watercolor

el barro clay

el caballete easel

el lienzo canvas

el óleo oleo (paint)

la témpera gouache

Las expresiones de teatro

la escenografía stage scenography

---

la iluminación lighting

la ovación ovation

poner en escena (una obra) to stage (a play)

el telón curtain

la utilería stage scenery

el vestuario costumes

Los instrumentos musicales

el arpa harp

el contrabajo double bass

la flauta flute

el instrumento de cuerda string instrument

el instrumento de percusión percussion instrument

el instrumento de viento wind instrument

el violoncelo cello

La literatura

la autobiografía autobiography

la biografía biography

el ensayo essay

la estrofa stanza

la ficción fiction

la prosa prose

la rima rhyme

Las expresiones para la salud

el análisis clínico laboratory test

el / la especialista specialist

el estetoscopio stetoscope

el medicamento medicine

los minerales minerals

la presión arterial blood presure

los primeros auxilios first aid

la respiración breathing

el síntoma symptom

el termómetro thermometer

Las máquinas de ejercicio

la caminadora treadmill

la máquina de remar rowing machine

la máquina de subir escaleras stair master

las pesas libres free weights

Los condimentos

la mayonesa mayonnaise

la mostaza mustard

la salsa de tomate ketchup

Otro tipo de comidas

los fideos noodles

Los estados de ánimo

ansioso, -a anxious

abrumado, -a overwhelmed

agotado, -a exhausted

rendido, -a worn out

Las relaciones con los demás

agradecer to thank

chismear to gossip

disculpar to excuse

insultar to insult

opinar to give / to have an opinion

querer (a alguien) to love (someone)

soportar to tolerate

Expresiones para empleo y trabajo voluntario

comunitario, -a community related

la destreza skill

los estudios (cursados) studies (completed)

el patrón / la patrona boss

los recursos humanos human
  resources

el / la supervisor(a) supervisor

sin fines de lucro non profit

Otras profesiones

el / la aprendiz apprentice

el / la camarógrafo(a) cameraman,
  camerawoman

el / la cirujano(a) surgeon

el /la intérprete interpreter

el / la jardinero(a) gardener

el / la modista(a) dressmaker,
  designer

cl /la oculista eye doctor

Las ciencias

la astronomía astronomy

la física physics

la química chemistry

La tecnología

la energía nuclear nuclear energy

el facsímil fax

la fotocopiadora copier

inalámbrico, -a wireless

el microscopio electrónico
  electronic microscope

el rayo / la luz láser laser beam /
  light

el telescopio telescope

La arqueología

abandonar to abandon

el / la antropólogo(a)
  anthropologist

avanzado, -a advanced

los datos data, information

la desaparición disappearance

descifrar to decipher

desenterrar to unearth

la evolución evolution

el / la geólogo(a) geologist

el jeroglífico hieroglyph

la prueba proof

el significado meaning

surgir to arise

Para hablar del universo

la constelación constellation

la galaxia galaxy

intergaláctico, -a intergalactic

el sistema solar solar system

Otras formas geométricas

el cuadrado square

la circunferencia circumference

el cubo cube

la esfera sphere

la rueda wheel

La arquitectura

la capilla chapel

la cúpula dome

el muro wall

la muralla (de la ciudad) wall (of
  a city)

Expresiones para la historia de América

la armadura armor

las armas de fuego fire weapons,
  fire-arms

el arribo arrival

cabalgar to ride a horse

la carabela caravel

el escudo shield

la lanza spear

la nave (a vela) sail ship

la pólvora gunpowder

unificar to unify

el yelmo helmet

Expresiones sobre el cuidado del planeta

la atmósfera atmosphere

la biosfera biosphere

descomponer(se) to decompose

los desechos industriales
  industrial waste

el /la ecólogo(a) ecologist

la erosión erosion

la radioctividad radioactivity

radiactivo,-a radiactive

la superpoblación overpopulation

la sustancia substance

la tala de bosques felling of forests

Las leyes y los derechos

apelar to appeal

el congreso congress

la Declaración de Derechos Bill
  of Rights

la democracia democracy

los derechos civiles civil rights

los derechos humanos human
  rights

encarcelar to put in jail

las enmiendas ammendments

el himno nacional national anthem

la monarquía monarchy

la patria mother country

el patriotismo patriotism

el senado senate

Resumen de gramática

Grammar Terms

Adjectives describe nouns: *a **red** car.*

Adverbs usually describe verbs: *He read it **quickly**.* Adverbs can also describe adjectives or other adverbs: ***very** tall, **quite** well.*

Articles are words in Spanish that can tell you whether a noun is masculine, feminine, singular, or plural. In English, the articles are ***the, a,*** and ***an.***

Commands are verb forms that tell people to do something: ***Work!***

Comparatives compare people or things.

Conditional tense is used to express what a person would do or what a situation would be like: *I **would like** to write a book.*

Conjugations are verb forms that add endings to the stem in order to tell who the subject is and what tense is being used: *escrib**o**, escrib**iste.***

Conjunctions join words or groups of words. The most common ones are ***and, but,*** and ***or.***

Direct objects are nouns or pronouns that receive the action of a verb: *I read the **book**. I read **it**.*

Future tense is used to talk about actions in the future: *Tomorrow **we will begin** working.*

Gender in Spanish tells you whether a noun, pronoun, or article is masculine or feminine.

Imperfect tense is used to talk about actions that happened repeatedly in the past; to describe people, places, and situations in the past; to talk about a past action or situation where no beginning or end is specified; and to describe an ongoing action in the past.

Imperfect progressive tense is used to describe something that was taking place over a period of time in the past: *He **was skiing** when he broke his leg.*

Indicative mood refers present, past of futures actions or states based on reality. *It **snowed** all night. It's **snowing** right now. **Will it snow** tomorrow?*

Indirect objects are nouns or pronouns that tell you to whom / what or for whom / what something is done: *I gave **him** the book.*

Infinitives are the basic forms of verbs. In English, infinitives have the word "to" in front of them: ***to walk.***

Interrogatives are words that ask questions: ***What** is it? **Who** is he?*

Nouns name people, places, or things: ***students, Mexico City, books.***

Number tells you if a noun, pronoun, article, or verb is singular or plural.

Past participles are verb forms that are used with forms of *haber* to form compound tenses. *He **escrito** una carta.* When a participle is used with *estar*, it functions as an adjective. *La mesa **está puesta**.*

Prepositions show relationship between their objects and another word in the sentence: *He is **in** the classroom.*

Present tense is used to talk about actions that always take place, or that are happening now: *I always **take** the bus; I **study** Spanish.*

Present perfect tense is used to say what a person had done: *We **have seen** the new movie.*

Present progressive tense is used to emphasize that an action is happening *right now: I **am doing** my homework; he **is finishing** dinner.*

Preterite tense is used to talk about actions that were completed in the past: *I **took** the train yesterday.*

Pronouns are words that take the place of nouns: ***She** is my friend.*

Reflexive verbs are used to say that people do something to or for themselves: *I **wash my** hair.* Reflexive verbs often describe a change in emotional or physical state, and express the idea that someone "gets" or "becomes": *They **became** angry.*

Subjects are the nouns or pronouns that perform the action in a sentence: ***John** sings.*

Subjunctive mood is used to say that one person influences the actions of another: *I **recommend that you study** more.* It is also used after verbs and expressions of doubt or uncertainty: ***It's possible that there's** enough food.*

Verbs show action or link the subject with a word or words in the predicate (what the subject does or is): *Ana **writes**; Ana **is** my sister.*

Nouns, Number, and Gender

Nouns refer to people, animals, places, things, and ideas. Nouns are singular or plural. In Spanish, nouns have gender, which means that they are either masculine or feminine.

Singular Nouns	
Masculine	**Feminine**
libro	carpeta
pupitre	casa
profesor	noche
lápiz	ciudad

Plural Nouns	
Masculine	**Feminine**
libros	carpetas
pupitres	casas
profesores	noches
lápices	ciudades

Definite Articles

El, la, los, and *las* are definite articles and are the equivalent of "the" in English. *El* is used with masculine singular nouns; *los* with masculine plural nouns. *La* is used with feminine singular nouns; *las* with feminine plural nouns. When you use the words *a* or *de* before *el*, you form the contractions *al* and *del: Voy **al** centro; Es el libro **del** profesor.*

Masculine	
Singular	**Plural**
el libro	los libros
el pupitre	los pupitres
el profesor	los profesores
el lápiz	los lápices

Feminine	
Singular	**Plural**
la carpeta	las carpetas
la casa	las casas
la noche	las noches
la ciudad	las ciudades

Indefinite Articles

Un and *una* are indefinite articles and are the equivalent of "a" and "an" in English. *Un* is used with singular masculine nouns; *una* is used with singular feminine nouns. The plural indefinite articles are *unos* and *unas.*

Masculine	
Singular	**Plural**
un libro	unos libros
un baile	unos bailes

Feminine	
Singular	**Plural**
una revista	unas revistas
una mochila	unas mochilas

Pronouns

Subject pronouns tell who is doing the action. They replace nouns or names in a sentence. Subject pronouns are often used for emphasis or clarification: *Gregorio escucha música. **Él** escucha música.*

A *direct object* tells who or what receives the action of the verb. To avoid repeating a direct object noun, you can replace it with a *direct object pronoun*. Direct object pronouns have the same gender and number as the nouns they replace: *¿Cuándo compraste **el libro**? **Lo** compré ayer.*

An *indirect object* tells to whom or for whom an action is performed. *Indirect object pronouns* are used to replace an indirect object noun: ***Les** doy dinero. (I give money to them.)* Because *le* and *les* have more than one meaning, you can make the meaning clear, or show emphasis, by adding *a* + the corresponding name, noun, or pronoun: ***Les** doy el dinero a **ellos.***

When two object pronouns are used together, the indirect object pronoun comes before the direct object pronoun: *Si necesitas este libro, **te lo** doy.*

The direct object pronoun *le* or *les* becomes *se* before the direct object pronoun *lo, la, los,* or *las. María quiere escuchar esta canción. **Se la** voy a cantar.*

A *reflexive pronoun* is used to show that someone does an action to or for themselves. Each reflexive pronoun corresponds to a different subject and always agrees with the subject pronoun. *Todos los días **me ducho** y **me arreglo** el pelo.*

The personal a

When the direct object is a person, a group of people, or a pet, use the word *a* before the object. This is called the "personal a": *Visité **a** mi abuela. Busco **a** mi perro, Capitán.*

Subject Pronouns		Direct Object Pronouns		Indirect Object Pronouns		Reflexive Pronouns		Objects of Prepositions	
Singular	**Plural**	**Singular**	**Plural**	**Singular**	**Plural**	**Singular**	**Plural**	**Singular**	**Plural**
yo	nosotros, nosotras	me	nos	me	nos	me	nos	(para) mí, conmigo	nosotros, nosotras
tú	vosotros, vosotras	te	os	te	os	te	os	(para) ti, contigo	vosotros, vosotras
usted (Ud.)	ustedes (Uds.)	lo, la	los, las	le	les	se	se	Ud.	Uds.
él, ella	ellos, ellas							él, ella	ellos, ellas

Adjectives

Words that describe people and things are called adjectives. In Spanish, most adjectives have both masculine and feminine forms, as well as singular and plural forms. Adjectives must agree with the noun they describe in both gender and number. When an adjective describes a group including both masculine and feminine nouns, use the masculine plural form.

Masculine	
Singular	**Plural**
alto	altos
inteligente	inteligentes
trabajador	trabajadores
fácil	fáciles

Feminine	
Singular	**Plural**
alta	altas
inteligente	inteligentes
trabajadora	trabajadoras
fácil	fáciles

Shortened Forms of Adjectives

When placed before masculine singular nouns, some adjectives change into a shortened form.

bueno	→	buen chico
malo	→	mal día
prime	→	primer trabajo
tercero	→	tercer plato
grande	→	gran señor

One adjective, **grande,** changes to a shortened form before any singular noun: *una **gran** señora, un **gran** libro.*

Possessive Adjectives and Pronouns

Possessive adjectives are used to tell what belongs to someone or to show relationships. Like other adjectives, possessive adjectives agree in number with the nouns that follow them.

Only *nuestro* and *vuestro* have different masculine and feminine endings. *Su* and *sus* can have many different meanings: *his, her, its, your,* or *their.*

The long forms of possessive adjectives are used for emphasis and come *after* the noun. They may also be used without a noun: *¿Esta chaqueta es **tuya?** Sí, es **mía.***

Singular	**Plural**
mi	mis
tu	tus
su	sus
nuestro, -a	nuestros, -as
vuestro, -a	vuestros, -as
su	sus

Singular	**Plural**
mío/mía	míos/mías
tuyo/tuya	tuyos/tuyas
suyo/suya	suyos/suyas
nuestro/nuestra	nuestros/nuestras
vuestro/vuestra	vuestros/vuestras
suyo/suya	suyos/suyas

Possessive pronouns use the long form possessive adjectives preceded by the definite article. *Tu cuarto es grande. **El mío** es pequeño.*

Demonstrative Adjectives and Pronouns

Demonstrative adjectives are used to point out people or things that are nearby and farther away. A demonstrative adjective agrees in gender and number with the noun that follows it.

Use *este, esta, estos, estas* ("this" / "these") before nouns that name people or things that are close to you. Use *ese, esa, esos, esas* ("that" / "those") before nouns that name people or things that are at some distance from you.

	Close to you		Closer to the person you are talking to		Far from both of you	
Adjectives	este	estos	ese	esos	aquel	aquellos
	esta	estas	esa	esas	aquella	aquellas
Pronouns	éste	éstos	ése	ésos	aquél	aquéllos
	éstas	ésta	ésa	ésas	aquélla	aquéllas

Use *aquel, aquella, aquellos,* or *aquellas* ("that one [those] over there") before nouns that name people or things that are far from both you and the person you are speaking to.

Demonstrative adjectives can be used as pronouns to replace nouns. To distinguish them from demonstrative adjectives they have a written accent.

Interrogative Words

You use interrogative words to ask questions. When you ask a question with an interrogative word, you put the verb before the subject. All interrogative words have a written accent mark.

¿Adónde?	¿Cuándo?	¿Dónde?
¿Cómo?	¿Cuánto, -a?	¿Por qué?
¿Con quién?	¿Cuántos, -as?	¿Qué?
¿Cuál?	¿De dónde?	¿Quién?

Comparatives and Superlatives

Comparatives Use *más . . . que* or *menos . . . que* to compare people or things: *más interesante que . . . , menos alta que . . .*

When talking about number, use *de* instead of *que: Tengo más de cien monedas en mi colección.*

To compare people or things that are equal, use *tan . . . como: tan popular como . . . Tanto / tanta . . . como* is used to say "as much as" and *tantos / tantas . . . como* is used to say "as many as": *tanto dinero como . . . tantas amigas*

como . . . Tanto and *tanta* match the number and gender of the noun to which they refer.

Superlatives Use this pattern to express the idea of "most" or "least."

el
la   + *noun* + más / menos + *adjective*
los
las

Es la chica más seria de la clase.
Son los perritos más pequeños.

Several adjectives are irregular when used with comparisons and superlatives.

older	mayor
younger	menor
better	mejor
worse	peor

Affirmative and Negative Words

To make a sentence negative in Spanish, *no* usually goes in front of the verb or expression. To show that you do not like either of two choices, use *ni . . . ni.*

Alguno, alguna, algunos, algunas and *ninguno, ninguna* match the number and gender of the noun to which they refer. *Ningunos* and *ningunas* are rarely used. When *alguno* and *ninguno* come before a masculine singular noun, they change to *algún* and *ningún.*

Affirmative	Negative
algo	nada
alguien	nadie
algún	ningún
alguno, -a, -os, -as	ninguno, -a, -os, -as
siempre	nunca
también	tampoco

Adverbs

To form an adverb in Spanish, *-mente* is added to the feminine singular form of an adjective. This *-mente* ending is equivalent to the "-ly" ending in English. If the adjective has a written accent, such as *rápida, fácil,* and *práctica,* the accent appears in the same place in the adverb form.

general	→	generalmente
especial	→	especialmente
fácil	→	fácilmente
feliz	→	felizmente
rápida	→	rápidamente
práctica	→	prácticamente

Past Participles

Past participles are used with forms of the verb *haber* to form compound tenses. **Había escrito** *un poema muy hermoso.* They can also be used as adjectives: *El espejo estaba* **roto**.
To form a past participle, add *-ado* to the root of *-ar* verbs and *-ido* to the root of *-er* and *-ir* verbs.

Some past participles are irregular.

| decorar | decorado | conocer | conocido | preferir | preferido |

abrir: abierto	morir: muerto
cubrir: cubierto	poner: puesto
decir: dicho	resolver: resuelto
descubrir:	romper: roto
descubierto	ver: visto
escribir: escrito	volver: vuelto
hacer: hecho	

Por and *para*

Both *por* and *para* are prepositions. Their usages are quite different.

Use *por* to indicate:	
length of time or distance	Caminamos **por** dos horas.
where an action is done	El perro corría **por** la playa.
an exchange	Le doy diez pesos **por** ese dibujo.
an action on behalf of someone or something	Vamos a la marcha **por** la paz.
a means of communication or transportation	Lo vimos **por** televisión.

Use *por* in certain expressions:
por ejemplo
por eso (tanto)
por la (mañana, tarde, noche)
por favor
por lo general
por primera (segunda, tercera, última) vez
por supuesto

Use *para* to indicate:	
purpose	Como frutas **para** tener vitaminas.
destination	Hace una hora salieron **para** la playa.
a point in time	**Para** mañana ya tendrás lo que encargaste.
use	¿Dónde hay una cuchara **para** sopa?
opinion	**Para** los niños el helado es muy rico.

Pero and *sino*

The word *pero* is usually the equivalent of the English conjunction *but*. The word *sino*, also means *but*.

Sino is used after a negative, to convey the idea of an alternative: "not this, but rather that."

No compré pastel *sino* helado.

Yo can also use *sino* with *no sólo . . . sino también.*

Me regaló *no sólo* dulces *sino* también flores.

You use *sino que* when there is a conjugated verb in the second part of the sentence.

No fuimos a la ciudad *sino que* salimos a navegar.

Relative Pronouns *que, quien,* and *lo que*

You use relative pronouns to combine two sentences or to give clarifying information. The most common relative pronoun in Spanish is *que*. It can mean *that, which, who,* or *whom,* and it may refer either to persons or to things.

*El artículo **que** salió en el periódico habla sobre la contaminación.*

After a preposition, use *que* to refer to things and *quien(es)* to refer to people.

El problema **del que** te hablé es muy grave.
La persona **de quien** te hablé se llama Adriana.

Use the relative phrase *lo que* to refer to a situation, concept, action, or object not yet identified.

Te cuento **lo que** me explicó el científico.

Conjuntions used with the subjunctive and the indicative

Certain conjunctions related to time are followed by either the indicative or the subjunctive:

antes de que	**tan pronto como**	**cuando**	**en cuanto**
después (de) que	**hasta que**	**mientras**	

You use the subjunctive after these conjunctions when the action that follows has not yet taken place. You use the indicative with these conjunction when the action that follows has already taken place or if it occurs regularly.

Van a producir petróleo **hasta que** se agote.
En cuanto salgo del cuarto, siempre apago las luces.

The conjunction *antes de que* is always followed by the subjunctive.

Pon el helado en el refrigerador **antes de que** se derrita.

If the subject of a sentence does not change, use the infinitive after *antes de, después de* and *hasta*.

Después de la escuela, voy a visitar a mi amigo Juan.

The following conjunctions are usually followed by the subjunctive to express the purpose or intention of an action:

a menos que	**para que**	**sin que**
a fin de que	**aunque**	**con tal (de) que**

No haré la limpieza de la casa **a menos que** me ayudes.

If the subject of the sentence does not change, use the infinitive after *para* and *sin*.

Debemos dejar de usar aerosoles **para** detener la destrucción de la capa de ozono.

With the conjunction *aunque*, use the subjunctive to express uncertainty. Use the indicative when there is no uncertainty.

Aunque produzcan más petróleo no podrán depender de este recurso por mucho tiempo.
No quiero ver ese programa sobre las ballenas **aunque** todos dicen que es muy bueno.

Verbos

Regular Verbs

Here are the conjugations for regular -ar, -er, and -ir verbs in the indicative (present, preterite, imperfect, future and conditional) and the present and imperfect subjunctive.

Infinitive Present Participle Past Participle	Present		Preterite		Imperfect	
estudiar	estudio	estudiamos	estudié	estudiamos	estudiaba	estudiábamos
estudiando	estudias	estudiáis	estudiaste	estudiásteis	estudiabas	estudiábais
estudiado	estudia	estudian	estudió	estudiaron	estudiaba	estudiaban
correr	corro	corremos	corrí	corrimos	corría	corríamos
corriendo	corres	corréis	corriste	corristeis	corrías	corríais
corrido	corres	corren	corrió	corrieron	corría	corrían
vivir	vivo	vivimos	viví	vivimos	vivía	vivíamos
viviendo	vives	vivís	viviste	vivisteis	vivías	vivíais
vivido	vive	viven	vivió	vivieron	vivía	vivían

Present Progressive and Imperfect Progressive

Progressive tenses are formed with a form of *estar* and the present participle

Present progressive	Present participle	Imperfect progressive	Present participle
estoy		estaba	
estás		estabas	
está	estudiando	estaba	estudiando
estamos	corriendo	estábamos	corriendo
estáis	viviendo	estabais	viviendo
están		estaban	

Reflexive Verbs

Infinitive and Present Participle	Present	Preterite	Subjunctive
lavarse	me lavo	me lavé	me lave
lavándose	te lavas	te lavaste	te laves
	se lava	se lavó	se lave
	nos lavamos	nos lavamos	nos lavemos
	os laváis	os lavasteis	os lavéis
	se lavan	se lavaron	se laven

Regular Verbs (continued)

Future		Conditional		Present Subjunctive		Imperfect Subjunctive	
estudiaré	estudiaremos	estudiaría	estudiaríamos	estudie	estudiemos	estudiara	estudiáramos
estudiarás	estudiaréis	estudiarías	estudiaríais	estudies	estudiéis	estudiaras	estudiárais
estudiará	estudiarán	estudiaría	estudiaría	estudie	estudien	estudiara	estudiaran
correré	correremos	correría	correríamos	corra	corramos	corriera	corriéramos
correrás	correréis	correrías	correríais	corras	corráis	corrieras	corriérais
correrá	correrán	correría	correrían	corra	corran	corriera	corrieran
viviré	viviremos	viviría	viviríamos	viva	vivamos	viviera	viviéramos
vivirás	viviréis	vivirías	viviríais	vivas	viváis	vivieras	viviérais
vivirá	vivirán	viviría	vivirían	viva	vivan	viviera	viviéran

Perfect Tenses

Perfect tenses are formed with an auxiliary verb *(haber)* and a past participle.

Present Perfect		Pluperfect		Future Perfect		Present Perfect Subjunctive		Past Perfect Subjunctive		Conditional Perfect	
he		había		habré		haya		hubiera		habría	
has	estudiado	habías	estudiado	habrás	estudiado	hayas	estudiado	hubieras	estudiado	habrías	estudiado
ha	corrido	había	corrido	habrá	corrido	haya	corrido	hubiera	corrido	habría	corrido
hemos	vivido	habíamos	vivido	habremos	vivido	hayamos	vivido	hubiéramos	vivido	habríamos	vivido
habéis		habíais		habréis		hayáis		hubierais		habriais	
han		habían		habrán		hayan		hubieran		habrían	

Stem-changing Verbs

Here is a list of the stem-changing verbs. Only conjugations with changes are shown.

Infinitive in -ar

Infinitive	Present Indicative		Present Subjunctive	
pensar (e→ie)	pienso	pensamos	piense	pensemos
	piensas	pensáis	pienses	penséis
	piensa	piensan	piense	piensen
Verbs like **pensar:** calentar, comenzar, despertar(se), recomendar, tropezar				
contar (o→ue)	cuento	contamos	cuente	contemos
	cuentas	contáis	cuentes	contéis
	cuenta	cuentan	cuente	cuenten
Verbs like **contar:** acostar(se), almorzar, costar, encontrar(se), probar(se), recordar				
jugar (u→ue)	juego	jugamos	juegue	juguemos
	juegas	jugáis	juegues	juguéis
	juega	juegan	juegue	jueguen

Infinitive in -er

	Present Indicative		Present Subjunctive	
entender (e→ie)	entiendo	entendemos	entienda	entendamos
	entiendes	entendéis	entiendas	entendáis
	entiende	entienden	entienda	entiendan
Verbs like **entender:** encender, perder				
devolver (o→ue)	devuelvo	devolvemos	devuelva	devolvamos
past participle:	devuelves	devolvéis	devuelvas	devolváis
devuelto	devuelve	devuelven	devuelva	devuelvan
Verbs like **devolver:** mover(se), resolver, torcer(se), volver (past participle: **vuelto**)				

Stem-changing Verbs (continued)

Infinitive in -ir

	Indicative				Subjunctive	
	Present		**Preterite**		**Present**	
pedir (e→i) (e→i)	pido	pedimos	pedí	pedimos	pida	pidamos
present participle: pidiendo	pides	pedís	pediste	pedisteis	pidas	pidáis
	pide	piden	pidió	pidieron	pida	pidan
Verbs like pedir: conseguir, despedir(se), repetir, seguir, vestir(se)						
preferir (e→ie) (e→i)	prefiero	preferimos	preferí	preferimos	prefiera	prefiramos
present participle:	prefieres	preferís	preferiste	preferisteis	prefieras	prefiráis
prefiriendo	prefiere	prefieren	prefirió	prefirieron	prefiera	prefieran
Verbs like preferir: divertir(se), hervir, mentir, sugerir,						
dormir (o→ue) (o→u)	duermo	dormimos	dormí	dormimos	duerma	durmamos
present participle:	duermes	dormís	dormiste	dormisteis	duermas	durmáis
durmiendo	duerme	duermen	durmió	durmieron	duerma	duerman
Verbs like **dormir**: morir(se) (past participle: **muerto**)						

Spelling-changing Verbs

These verbs have spelling changes in the present, preterite, and/or the subjunctive tenses. The spelling changes are indicated in boldface.

Infinitive Present Participle Past Participle	Present		Preterite		Subjunctive	
almorzar (z→c) almorzando almorzado	See regular *-ar* verbs		**almorcé** almorzaste almorzó	almorzamos almorzasteis almorzaron	**almuerce** **almuerces** **almuerce**	**almorcemos** **almorcéis** **almuercen**
buscar (c→qu) buscando buscado	See regular *-ar* verbs		**busqué** buscaste buscó	buscamos buscasteis buscaron	**busque** **busques** **busque**	**busquemos** **busquéis** **busquen**
comunicarse (c→qu) comunicándose	See reflexive verbs		See reflexive verbs and **buscar**		See reflexive verbs and **buscar**	
conocer (c→zc) conociendo conocido	**conozco** conoces conoce	conocemos conocéis conocen	See regular *-er* verbs		conozca conozcas conozca	conozcamos conozcáis conozcan
creer (i→y) creyendo creído	See regular *-er* verbs		creí creíste creyó	creímos creísteis creyeron	See regular *-er* verbs	
empezar (z→c) empezando empezado	See stem-changing verbs		empecé empezaste empezó	empezamos empezasteis empezaron	See stem-changing verbs	
enviar (i→í) enviando enviado	**envío** **envías** **envía**	enviamos enviáis **envían**	See regular *-ar* verbs		envíe envíes envíe	enviemos enviéis envíen
escoger escogiendo escogido	**escojo** escoges escoge	escogemos escogéis escogen	See regular *-er* verbs		escoja escojas escoja	escojamos escojáis escojan
esquiar (i→í) esquiando esquiado	See **enviar**		See regular *-ar* verbs		See **enviar**	
jugar (g→gu) jugando jugado	See stem-changing verbs		**jugué** jugaste jugó	jugamos jugasteis jugaron	See stem-changing verbs	
leer (i→y) leyendo leído	See regular *-er* verbs		See **creer**		See **creer**	
obedecer (c→zc) obedeciendo obedecido	See **conocer**		See regular *-er* verbs		See **conocer**	

Spelling-changing Verbs (continued)

Infinitive Present Participle Past Participle	Present		Preterite	Subjunctive	
ofrecer (c→zc) ofreciendo ofrecido	See **conocer**		See regular -*er* verbs	See **conocer**	
pagar (g→gu) pagando pagado	See regular -*ar* verbs		See **jugar**	**pague** **pagues** **pague**	**paguemos** **paguéis** **paguen**
parecer (c→zc) pareciendo parecido	See **conocer**		See regular -*er* verbs	See **conocer**	
practicar (c→qu) practicando practicado	See regular -*ar* verbs		See **buscar**	See **buscar**	
recoger (g→j) recogiendo recogido	**recojo** **recoges** **recoge**	**recogemos** **recogéis** **recogen**	See regular -*er* verbs	See **escoger**	
sacar (c→qu) sacando sacado	See regular -*ar* verbs		See **buscar**	See **buscar**	
tocar (c→qu) tocando tocado	See regular -*ar* verbs		See **buscar**	See **buscar**	

Irregular Verbs

These verbs have irregular patterns.

	1		2		3		4	
Infinitive Present Participle Past Participle	**Present**			**Preterite**		**Imperfect**		
dar	doy	damos	di	dimos	daba	dábamos
dando	das	dais	diste	disteis	dabas	dabais
dado	da	dan	dio	dieron	daba	daban
decir	digo	decimos	dije	dijimos	decía	decíamos
diciendo	dices	decís	dijiste	dijisteis	decías	decíais
dicho	dice	dicen	dijo	dijeron	decía	decían
estar	estoy	estamos	estuve	estuvimos	estaba	estábamos
estando	estás	estáis	estuviste	estuvisteis	estabas	estabais
estado	está	están	estuvo	estuvieron	estaba	estaban
haber	he	hemos	hube	hubimos	había	habíamos
habiendo	has	habéis	hubiste	hubisteis	habías	habíais
habido	ha	han	hubo	hubieron	había	habían
hacer	hago	hacemos	hice	hicimos	hacía	hacíamos
haciendo	haces	hacéis	hiciste	hicisteis	hacías	hacíais
hecho	hace	hacen	hizo	hicieron	hacía	hacían
ir	voy	vamos	fui	fuimos	iba	íbamos
yendo	vas	vais	fuiste	fuisteis	ibas	ibais
ido	va	van	fue	fueron	iba	iban
oír	oigo	oímos	oí	oímos	oía	oíamos
oyendo	oyes	oís	oíste	oísteis	oías	oíais
oído	oye	oyen	oyó	oyeron	oía	oían
poder	puedo	podemos	pude	pudimos	podía	podíamos
pudiendo	puedes	podéis	pudiste	pudisteis	podías	podíais
podido	puede	pueden	pudo	pudieron	podía	podían
poner	pongo	ponemos	puse	pusimos	ponía	poníamos
poniendo	pones	ponéis	pusiste	pusisteis	ponías	poníais
puesto	pone	ponen	puso	pusieron	ponía	ponían

Irregular Verbs (continued)

	5		6		7		8
Future		**Conditional**		**Present Subjunctive**		**Imperfect Subjunctive**	
daré	daremos	daría	daríamos	dé	demos	diera	diéramos
darás	dareis	darías	daríais	des	deis	dieras	dierais
dará	darán	daría	darían	dé	den	diera	dieran
diré	diremos	diría	diríamos	diga	digamos	dijera	dijéramos
dirás	diréis	dirías	diríais	digas	digáis	dijeras	dijerais
dirá	dirán	diría	dirían	diga	digan	dijera	dijeran
estaré	estaremos	estaría	estaríamos	esté	estemos	estuviera	estuviéramos
estarás	estaréis	estarías	estaríais	estés	estéis	estuviera	estuvierais
estará	estarán	estaría	estarían	esté	estén	estuvieras	estuvieran
habré	habremos	habría	habríamos	haya	hayamos	hubiera	hubiéramos
habrás	habréis	habrías	habríais	hayas	hayáis	hubieras	hubierais
habrá	habrán	habría	habrían	haya	hayan	hubiera	hubieran
haré	haremos	haría	haríamos	haga	hagamos	hiciera	hiciéramos
harás	haréis	harías	haríais	hagas	hagáis	hicieras	hicierais
hará	harán	haría	harían	haga	hagan	hiciera	hicieran
iré	iremos	iría	iríamos	vaya	vayamos	fuera	fuéramos
irás	iréis	irías	iríais	vayas	vayáis	fuera	fuerais
irá	irán	iría	irían	vaya	vayan	fuera	fueran
oiré	oiremos	oiría	oiríamos	oiga	oigamos	oyera	oyéramos
oirás	oiréis	oirías	olríals	oigas	oigáis	oyeras	oyerais
oirá	oirán	oiría	oirían	oiga	oigan	oyera	oyeran
podré	podremos	podría	podríamos	pueda	podamos	pudiera	pudiéramos
podrás	podréis	podrías	podríais	puedas	podáis	pudieras	pudierais
podrá	podrán	podría	podrían	pueda	puedan	pudiera	pudieran
pondré	pondremos	pondría	pondríamos	ponga	pongamos	pusiera	pusiéramos
pondrás	pondréis	pondrías	pondríais	pongas	pongáis	pusieras	pusierais
pondrá	pondrán	pondría	pondrían	ponga	pongan	pusiera	pusieran

Irregular Verbs (continued)

	1		2		3		4
	Infinitive Present Participle Past Participle		Present		Preterite		Imperfect
querer	quiero	queremos	quise	quisimos	quería	queríamos
queriendo	quieres	queréis	quisiste	quisisteis	querías	queríais
querido	quiere	quieren	quiso	quisieron	quería	querían
saber	sé	sabemos	supe	supimos	sabía	sabíamos
sabiendo	sabes	sabéis	supiste	supisteis	sabías	sabíais
sabido	sabe	saben	supo	supieron	sabía	sabían
salir	salgo	salimos	salí	salimos	salía	salíamos
saliendo	sales	salís	saliste	salisteis	salías	salíais
salido	sale	salen	salió	salieron	salía	salían
ser	soy	somos	fui	fuimos	era	éramos
siendo	eres	sois	fuiste	fuisteis	eras	erais
sido	es	son	fue	fueron	era	eran
tener	tengo	tenemos	tuve	tuvimos	tenía	teníamos
teniendo	tienes	tenéis	tuviste	tuvisteis	tenías	teníais
tenido	tiene	tienen	tuvo	tuvieron	tenía	tenían
traer	traigo	traemos	traje	trajimos	traía	traíamos
trayendo	traes	traéis	trajiste	trajisteis	traías	traíais
traído	trae	traen	trajo	trajeron	traía	traían
venir	vengo	venimos	vine	vinimos	venía	veníamos
viniendo	vienes	venís	viniste	vinisteis	venías	veníais
venido	viene	vienen	vino	vinieron	venía	venían
ver	veo	vemos	vi	vimos	veía	veíamos
viendo	ves	veis	viste	visteis	veías	veíais
visto	ve	ven	vio	vieron	veía	veían

Irregular Verbs (continued)

	5		6		7		8
Future		**Conditional**		**Present Subjunctive**		**Imperfect Subjunctive**	
querré	querremos	querría	querríamos	quiera	queramos	quisiera	quisiéramos
querrás	querréis	querrías	querríais	quieras	queráis	quisieras	quisierais
querrá	querrán	querría	querrían	quiera	quieran	quisiera	quisieran
sabré	sabremos	sabría	sabríamos	sepa	sepamos	supiera	supiéramos
sabrás	sabréis	sabrías	sabríais	sepas	sepáis	supieras	supierais
sabrá	sabrán	sabría	sabrían	sepa	sepan	supiera	supieran
saldré	saldremos	saldría	saldríamos	salga	salgamos	saliera	saliéramos
saldrás	saldréis	saldrías	saldríais	salgas	salgáis	salieras	salierais
saldrá	saldrán	saldría	saldrían	salga	salgan	saliera	salieran
seré	seremos	sería	seríamos	sea	seamos	fuera	fuéramos
serás	seréis	serías	seríais	seas	seáis	fueras	fuerais
será	serán	sería	serían	sea	sean	fuera	fueran
tendré	tendremos	tendría	tendríamos	tenga	tengamos	tuviera	tuviéramos
tendrás	tendréis	tendrías	tendríais	tengas	tengáis	tuvieras	tuvierais
tendrá	tendrán	tendría	tendrían	tenga	tengan	tuviera	tuvieran
traeré	traeremos	traería	traeríamos	traiga	traigamos	trajera	trajéramos
traerás	traeréis	traerías	traeríais	traigas	traigáis	trajeras	trajerais
traerá	traerán	traería	traerían	traiga	traigan	trajera	trajeran
vendré	vendremos	vendría	vendríamos	venga	vengamos	viniera	viniéramos
vendrás	vendréis	vendrías	vendríais	vengas	vengáis	vinieras	vinierais
vendrá	vendrán	vendría	vendrían	venga	vengan	viniera	vinieran
veré	veremos	vería	veríamos	vea	veamos	viera	viéramos
verás	veréis	verías	veríais	veas	veáis	vieras	vierais
verá	verán	vería	verían	vea	vean	viera	vieran

Affirmative and negative commands

To form an affirmative *tú* command, use the present-tense indicative *Ud.* / *él* / *ella* form. This rule also applies to stem-changing verbs. Some verbs have an irregular affirmative *tú* command.

To form a command with *Ud.*, remove the *-s* from a negative *tú* command form. To form a command with *Uds.*, replace the *-s* of a negative *tú* command with an *-n*.

Regular and stem-changing verbs, and verbs ending in *-car*, *-gar* and *-zar*

Infinitive	Tú	Negative tú	Usted	Ustedes
estudiar	estudia	no estudies	(no) estudie	(no) estudien
volver	vuelve	no vuelvas	(no) vuelva	(no) vuelvan
abrir	abre	no abras	(no) abra	(no) abran
sacar	saca	no saques	(no) saque	(no) saquen
llegar	llega	no llegues	(no) llegue	(no) lleguen
cruzar	cruza	no cruces	(no) cruce	(no) crucen

Irregular verbs

Infinitive	Tú	Negative tú	Usted	Ustedes
decir	di	no digas	(no) diga	(no) digan
hacer	haz	no hagas	(no) haga	(no) hagan
ir	ve	no vayas	(no) vaya	(no) vayan
mantener	mantén	no mantengas	(no) mantenga	(no) mantengan
poner	pon	no pongas	(no) ponga	(no) pongan
salir	sal	no salgas	(no) salga	(no) salgan
ser	sé	no seas	(no) sea	(no) sean
tener	ten	no tengas	(no) tenga	(no) tengan
venir	ven	no vengas	(no) venga	(no) vengan

Placement of pronouns with commands

Attach reflexive or object pronous at the end of affirmative commands. With negative commands, place them after the word *no*.

Toma esas vitaminas.
¡Tómalas ahora mismo!
No las tomes.

Expresiones útiles para conversar

Making an apology

Perdóname. Forgive me.

Lo siento mucho. I'm very sorry.

Fue un malentendido. It was a misunderstanding.

Hagamos las paces. Let's make up.

Reconciliémonos. Let's reconcile.

Te pido perdón. I'm asking for your forgiveness.

Estoy equivocado, -a. I'm wrong.

Pongámonos de acuerdo. Let's come to an agreement.

Yo tengo la culpa. It's my fault.

Talking about friendship

Tenemos mucho en común. We have a lot in common.

Te acepto tal como eres. I accept you just the way you are.

Tengo celos. I'm jealous.

No me hace caso. He / She doesn't pay any attention to me.

Sólo piensa en sí mismo, -a. He / She only thinks about himself / herself.

Confío en ti. I trust you.

Cuento contigo. I count on you.

Sé guardar un secreto. I can keep a secret.

Resolvamos este conflicto. Let's resolve this conflict.

Tenemos una diferencia de opinión. We disagree.

Me identifico contigo. I identify with you.

De hoy en adelante . . . From now on . . .

Ten en cuenta . . . Keep in mind . . .

Tengo derecho a . . . I have a right to . . .

Expressing disagreement

Qué va. No way.

Yo no fui. I didn't do it.

No es cierto que . . . It's not true that . . .

No es verdad que . . . It's not true that . . .

No estoy de acuerdo. I disagree.

Me parece que no tienes razón. I think you're wrong.

Expressing interest

Me es posible. I can.

Me gustaría . . . I'd like to . . .

Me encantaría . . . I'd love to . . .

Expressing certainty or possibility

Es cierto que . . . It's true that . . .

Estoy seguro, -a que . . . I'm sure that . . .

Es probable que . . . It's probable that . . .

Puede ser que . . . It's possible that . . .

Es posible que . . . It's possible that . . .

Es evidente que . . . It's clear that . . .

Quizás . . . Perhaps . . .

Expressing doubt or uncertainty

Dudo que . . . I doubt that . . .

No creo que . . . I don't think that . . .

No estoy seguro, -a que . . . I'm not sure that . . .

Es imposible que . . . It's impossible that . . .

Talking about how you feel physically

Me siento fatal. I feel awful.

Me caigo de sueño. I'm exhausted.

Estoy resfriado, -a. I have a cold.

Tengo tos. I have a cough.

Estornudo mucho. I'm sneezing a lot.

Tengo gripe. I have the flu.

Tengo fiebre. I have a fever.

Tengo alergia a . . . I'm allergic to . . .

Talking about how you feel emotionally

Estoy en la luna. I'm spaced-out.

No puedo concentrarme. I can't concentrate.

No aguanto más. I can't take it anymore.

Estoy de buen humor. I'm in a good mood.

Estoy de mal humor. I'm in a bad mood.

Estoy estresado, -a. I'm stressed-out.

Me preocupo por . . . I'm worried about . . .

Me emociono mucho. I'm very emotional.

Estoy orgulloso, -a de . . . I'm proud of . . .

Estoy animado, -a. I'm excited.

Tengo confianza en mí mismo, -a. I have confidence in myself.

Me vuelvo loco, -a. I'm going crazy.

He cambiado de opinión. I've changed my mind.

Me doy cuenta de que . . . I realize that . . .

Me vuelvo . . . I'm getting . . .

Haré lo que me dé la gana. I'll do whatever I want.

Talking about personal goals

Alcancé mi meta. I achieved my goal.

Hice un esfuerzo. I made an effort.

Salí campeón. I won (I was the winner).

¡Felicitaciones! Congratulations!

Eres mi fuente de inspiración. You're my inspiration.

Describing things or people

Se parece a . . . It / He / She looks like . . .

Suena a . . . It / He / She sounds like . . . .

Está basado, -a en . . . It's based on . . .

Se destaca. It / He / She stands out.

Está a cargo de . . . He / She is in charge of . . .

Vocabulario español-inglés

The *Vocabulario español-inglés* contains all active vocabulary from the text, including vocabulary presented in the grammar sections.

A dash (—) represents the main entry word. For example, **pasar la —** after **la aspiradora** means **pasar la aspiradora.**

The number following each entry indicates the chapter in which the word or expression is presented. A Roman numeral (I) indicates that the word was presented in REALIDADES 1. A Roman numeral (II) indicates that the word was presented in REALIDADES 2.

The following abbreviations are used in this list: *adj.* (adjective), *dir. obj.* (direct object), *f.* (feminine), *fam.* (familiar), *ind. obj.* (indirect object), *inf.* (infinitive), *m.* (masculine), *pl.* (plural), *prep.* (preposition), *pron.* (pronoun), *sing.* (singular).

A . . . .

a to (*prep.*) (I)
   — ... le gusta(n) he / she likes (I)
   — ... le encanta(n) he / she loves (I)
   — casa (to) home (I)
   — causa de because of (II)
   — favor de in favor of (5-2)
   — la derecha (de) to the right (of) (I)
   — la izquierda (de) to the left (of) (I)
   — la parrilla on the grill (II)

   — la una de la tarde at one (o'clock) in the afternoon (I)
   — las ocho de la mañana at eight (o'clock) in the morning (I)
   — las ocho de la noche at eight (o'clock) in the evening, at night (I)
   — mano by hand (II)
   — medida que as (10-2)
   — menos que unless (9-2)
   — menudo often (I)
   — pesar de despite (10-2)
   — mí también. I do (like to) too. (I)
   — mí tampoco. I don't (like to) either. (I)
   ¿— qué hora? (At) what time? (I)
   — tiempo on time (II)
   — tiempo completo full time (5-1)
   — tiempo parcial part time (5-1)
   — través de through (2-1)
   — veces sometimes (I)
   — ver. Let's see. (I)
al *(a + el),* **a la** to the (I)
al amanecer at dawn (1-1)
al anochecer at dusk (1-1)
al horno baked (II)
al igual que as (7-2)
al lado de next to (II)
al llegar upon arriving (8-2)
al principio at the beginning (1-2)
abdominales crunches (3-2)
abierto, -a open (II)
el **abogado, la abogada** lawyer (II, 6-1)
abordar to board (II)
abrazar(se) to hug (II)
el **abrigo** coat (I)
abril April (I)

abrir to open (I)
abstracto, -a abstract (2-1)
el **abuelo, la abuela** grandfather, grandmother (I)
los **abuelos** grandparents (I)
aburrido, -a boring (I)
aburrir to bore (I)
aburrirse to get bored (II)
me aburre(n) it bores me (they bore me) (I)
el **abuso** abuse (10-1)
acabar de + *inf.* to have just... (I)
el **accidente** accident (II)
el **aceite** cooking oil (II)
aceptar to accept
   — tal como (soy) to accept (me) the way (I am) (4-1)
acercarse a to approach (1-1)
acompañar to accompany (II)
aconsejar to advise (3-2)
acostarse (o → ue) to go to bed (II)
las **actividades extracurriculares** extracurricular activities (II)
el **actor** actor (I)
la **actriz,** *pl.* **las actrices** actress (I)
la **actuación** acting (II)
actuar to perform (2-2)
el **acueducto** aqueduct (8-1)
acuerdo:
   Estoy de —. I agree. (I)
   No estoy de —. I don't agree. (I)
el **acusado, la acusada** accused (10-2)
acusar to accuse (4-2)
adecuado, -a adequate (10-1)
además de in addition to, besides (II, 6-1)
¡Adiós! Good-bye! (I)
la **adolescencia** adolescence (10-1)

el / la adolescente adolescent (10-1)

¿Adónde? (To) where? (I)

adoptar to adopt (8-2)

la aduana customs (II)

el aduanero, la aduanera customs officer (II)

el aeropuerto airport (II)

el aerosol aerosol (9-2)

afectar to affect (9-2)

afeitarse to shave (II)

el aficionado, la aficionada fan (II)

afortunadamente fortunately (II)

africano, -a African (8-2)

la agencia de viajes travel agency (II)

el / la agente de viajes travel agent (II)

agitado, -a agitated (II)

agosto August (I)

agotar(se) to exhaust, to run out (9-1)

agradable pleasant (5-1)

el agricultor, la agricultora farmer (II)

el agua *f.* water (I)

el — de colonia cologne (II)

el aguacate avocado (II)

aguantar to endure, to tolerate (3-2)

el águila calva, *pl.* **las águilas calvas** bald eagle (9-2)

el agujero hole (9-2)

ahora now (I)

ahorrar to save (II, 6-1)

el aire acondicionado air conditioner (II)

el ajedrez chess (II)

el ajo garlic (II)

al *(a + el),* **a la** to the (I)

— aire libre outdoors (II)

— amanecer at dawn (1-1)

— anochecer at dusk (1-1)

— final at the end (II)

— horno baked (II)

— igual que as (7-2)

— lado de next to (I)

— llegar upon arriving (8-2)

— principio at the beginning (1-2)

alcanzar to reach (1-2)

alegrarse to be delighted (4-1)

alegre happy (II)

la alergia allergy (3-1)

la alfombra rug (I)

algo something (I)

¿— más? Anything else? (I)

el algodón cotton (II)

alguien someone, anyone (II)

algún, alguno, -a some (II)

— día some day (II)

algunos, as any (II)

la alimentación nutrition, feeding (3-1)

los alimentos food (3-1)

allí there (I)

una vez — once there (1-1)

el almacén, *pl.* **los almacenes** department store (I)

almorzar (o → ue) to have lunch (II)

el almuerzo lunch (I)

en el — for lunch (I)

alquilar to rent (II)

alrededor de around (II)

alto, -a tall (I); high (II)

el alto height (7-1)

amable kind, nice (4-1)

el amanecer dawn (1-1)

al — at dawn (1-1)

amarillo, -a yellow (I)

ambicioso, -a ambitious (6-1)

ambos both (10-1)

la ambulancia ambulance (II)

la amenaza threat (9-2)

amenazar to threaten (9-1)

la amistad friendship (4-1)

el amor love (II)

añadir to add (II)

anaranjado, -a orange (I)

ancho, -a wide (II)

el ancho width (7-1)

el anciano, la anciana older man, older woman (I)

los ancianos older people (I)

andar to walk, to move (1-1)

el anillo ring (I)

animado, -a excited (1-2)

el animador, la animadora cheerleader (II)

el animal animal (I)

el aniversario anniversary (II)

anoche last night (I)

los anteojos de sol sunglasses (I)

el antepasado, la antepasada ancestor (8-2)

antes de before (I, II)

antiguo, -a old, antique (II)

el año year (I)

el — pasado last year (I)

¿Cuántos —s tiene(n)...? How old is / are...? (I)

Tiene(n)...—s. He / She is / They are...(years old). (I)

el anochecer dusk (1-1)

al — at dusk (1-1)

ante before (10-2)

anteriormente before (8-1)

el antibiótico antibiotic (3-1)

antiguo, -a old / antique (II)

anunciar to announce (II)

el anuncio announcement (II)

el — clasificado classified ad (5-1)

apagar to put out *(fire)* (II); to turn off (II)

el aparato gadget (6-2)

aparecer (zc) to appear (7-2)

el **apartamento** apartment (I)

aplaudir to applaud (II)

el **aplauso** applause (2-2)

aplicar (las leyes) to apply (the law) (10-1)

apoyar(se) to support, to back (each other) (4-1)

el **apoyo** support (10-1)

aprender (a) to learn (I)

— **de memoria** to memorize (II)

apretado, -a tight (II)

apropiado, -a appropriate (3-1)

aproximadamente approximately (II)

aquel, aquella that one (over there) (II)

aquellos, aquellas those (over there) (II)

aquí here (I)

el / la **árabe** Arab (8-1)

el **árbol** tree (I)

el **arco** arch (8-1)

los **aretes** earrings (I)

el **argumento** plot (II)

el **arma,** *pl.* **las armas** weapon (8-2)

el **armario** closet, locker (I, II, 10-1)

la **armonía** harmony (4-2)

el **arqueólogo, la arqueóloga** archaeologist (7-1)

el **arquitecto, la arquitecta** architect (II, 6-1)

la **arquitectura** architecture (8-1)

arreglar (el cuarto) to straighten up (the room) (I)

arreglarse (el pelo) to fix (one's hair) (II)

arrestar to arrest (II)

arrojar (se) to throw (7-2)

el **arroz** rice (I)

el **arte:**

la **clase de** — art class (I)

la **obra de** — work of art (2-1)

las **artes** the arts (II)

las — **marciales** martial arts (II)

la **artesanía** handicrafts (II)

el **artículo** article (II)

el **artista, la artista** artist (II)

artístico, -a artistic (I)

asado, -a grilled (II)

asar to grill (II)

el **ascensor** elevator (II)

asco:

¡Qué —**!** How awful! (I)

asegurar to assure (10-2)

así this way (1-1)

— **que** therefore (6-1)

el **asiento** seat (II)

asimilar(se) to assimilate (8-1)

asistir a to attend (II)

la **aspiración** aspiration (10-2)

la **aspirina** aspirin (3-1)

el **astrónomo, la astrónoma** astronomer (7-2)

el **asunto** matter (10-1)

asustado, -a frightened (II)

asustar to scare (1-1)

atender to help, to assist (5-1)

atento, -a attentive (II)

el / la **atleta** athlete (II)

la **atmósfera** atmosphere (9-2)

la **atracción,** *pl.* **las atracciones** attraction (I)

atrapar to catch, trap (9-2)

atreverse to dare (4-2)

atrevido, -a daring (I)

la **audición,** *pl.* **las audiciones** audition (II)

el **auditorio** auditorium (II)

aumentar to increase (6-2)

aunque despite, even when (3-1)

el **autobús,** *pl.* **los autobuses** bus (I)

la **autoridad** authority (10-1)

el **autorretrato** self-portrait (2-1)

el / la **auxiliar de vuelo** flight attendant (II)

el **avance** advance (6-2)

el **ave** bird (9-2)

la **avenida** avenue (II)

averiguar to find out (6-1)

el **avión** airplane (I)

¡Ay! ¡Qué pena! Oh! What a shame / pity! (I)

ayer yesterday (I)

la **ayuda** help (II)

ayudar to help (I)

el **azúcar** sugar (I)

azul blue (I)

el **azulejo** tile (8-1)

bailar to dance (I)

el **bailarín, la bailarina** dancer (II)

el **baile** dance (I)

bajar to go down (II)

bajar (información) to download (I)

bajo, -a short *(stature)* (I); low (II)

el **balcón**, *pl.* **los balcones** balcony (8-1)

la **ballena** whale (9-2)

el **banco** bank (II)

la **banda** (musical) band (II)

la **bandera** flag (I)

el **banquero, la banquera** banker (6-1)

bañarse to take a bath (II)

el **baño** bathroom (I)

el **traje de —** swimsuit (I)

barato, -a inexpensive, cheap (I)

el **barco** boat, ship (I)

el **barrio** neighborhood (I)

¡Basta! Enough! (II)

el **básquetbol:**

jugar al — to play basketball (I)

bastante enough, rather (I)

la **batalla** battle (8-2)

batir to beat (II)

el **bebé, la bebé** baby (II)

beber to drink (I)

las **bebidas** drinks (I)

béisbol:

jugar al — to play baseball (I)

bello, -a beautiful (II)

beneficiar to benefit (5-2)

los **beneficios** benefits (II, 5-1)

besar(se) to kiss (II)

la **biblioteca** library (I)

bien well (I)

— educado, -a well-behaved (II)

pasarlo — to have a good time (1-1)

bienvenido, -a welcome (II)

bilingüe bilingual (II)

los **binoculares** binoculars (1-1)

el **bistec** beefsteak (I)

blanco, -a white (I)

los **bloques** blocks (II)

la **blusa** blouse (I)

la **boca** mouth (I)

la **boda** wedding (II)

el **boleto** ticket (I)

el **bolígrafo** pen (I)

los **bolos:**

jugar a los — to bowl (II)

la **bolsa** bag, sack (I)

el **bolso** purse (I)

el **bombero, la bombera** firefighter (II)

bonito, -a pretty (I)

el **bosque** wood, forest (II, 1-1)

las **botas** boots (I)

el **bote:**

pasear en — to go boating (I)

el **— de vela** sailboat (II)

la **botella** bottle (I)

el **brazo** arm (I)

brillar to shine (7-2)

la **brújula** compass (1-1)

bucear to scuba dive, to snorkel (I)

bueno (buen), -a good (I)

Buenas noches. Good evening. (I)

Buenas tardes. Good afternoon. (I)

Buenos días. Good morning. (I)

buscar to look for, to search (for) (I)

la **búsqueda** search (II)

hacer una — to do a search (II)

el **buzón**, *pl.* **los buzones** mailbox (II)

el **caballo:**

montar a — to ride horseback (I)

la **cabeza** head (I)

cada día every day (I)

la **cadena** chain (I)

caer granizo to hail (1-1)

caerse to fall (II)

— de sueño to be exhausted, sleepy (3-2)

(yo) me caigo I fall (II)

(tú) te caes you fall (II)

el **café** coffee, café (I)

la **caja** box (I); cash register (II)

el **cajero, la cajera** cashier (II)

el **— automático** ATM (II)

el **calambre** cramp (3-2)

los **calcetines** socks (I)

el **calcio** calcium (3-1)

la **calculadora** calculator (I)

calcular to calculate, to compute (7-1)

el **caldo** broth (II)

la **calefacción** heat (II)

calentar (e → ie) to heat (II)

caliente hot (II)

la **calle** street, road (I)

calor:

Hace —. It's hot. (I)

tener — to be warm (I)

la **cama** bed (I)

hacer la — to make the bed (I)

la **cámara** camera (I)

la — digital digital camera (I)

el **camarero, la camarera** waiter, waitress (I)

el **camarón**, *pl.* **los camarones** shrimp (II)

cambiar to change, to exchange (II)

   — de opinión to change one's mind (4-1)

caminar to walk (I)

la **caminata** walk (II)

   dar una — take a walk (II)

el **camión,** *pl.* **los camiones** truck (II)

la **camisa** shirt (I)

la **camiseta** T-shirt (I)

el **campamento** camp (I)

la **campaña** campaign (5-2)

el **campeón, la campeona,** *pl.*

los **campeones** champion (II)

el **campeonato** championship (II)

el **campo** countryside, field (I, 6-2)

el **canal** (TV) channel (I)

la **canción,** *pl.* **las canciones** song (I, II)

   canoso: pelo — gray hair (I)

   cansado, -a tired (I)

el / la **cantante** singer (II)

   cantar to sing (I)

la **capa de ozono** ozone layer (9-2)

   capaz able (6-1)

   capturar to capture (II)

la **cara** face (II)

   cara a cara face-to-face (I)

   caramba good gracious (II)

el **carbohidrato** carbohydrate (3-1)

   cariñoso, -a loving, affectionate (4-1)

la **carne** meat (I)

   la — de res steak (II)

el **carnet de identidad** I.D. card (II)

   caro, -a expensive (I)

la **carpeta** folder (I)

   la — de argollas three-ring binder (I)

la **carrera** race (II, 1-2); career (II)

la **carretera** highway (II)

la **carta** letter (I, II)

   echar una — to mail a letter (II)

el **cartel** poster (I)

la **cartera** wallet (I)

el **cartero, la cartera** mail carrirer (II)

el **cartón** cardboard (I)

la **casa** home, house (I)

   a — (to) home (I)

   en — at home (I)

   — de cambio money exchange (II)

   casado, -a married (6-1)

   casarse (con) to get married (II)

   casi almost (I, II)

   castaño:

   pelo — brown (chestnut) hair (I)

   castigar to punish (9-1)

el **castigo** punishment (10-2)

el **castillo** castle (II)

la **catedral** cathedral (II)

   catorce fourteen (I)

la **causa** cause (II)

la **caza** hunting (9-2)

la **cebolla** onion (I)

   celebrar to celebrate (I)

   celoso, -a jealous (4-1)

   tener celos to be jealous (4-1)

la **cena** dinner (I)

el **centímetro** centimeter (7-1)

el **centro** center, downtown (I, II)

   el — comercial mall (I)

   el — de la comunidad community center (5-2)

   el — de reciclaje recycling center (I)

   el — de rehabilitación rehabilitation center (5-2)

   el — recreativo recreation center (5-2)

   cepillarse (los dientes) to brush (one's teeth) (II)

el **cepillo** brush (II)

   el — de dientes toothbrush (II)

la **cerámica** pottery (2-1)

   cerca (de) close (to), near (I)

el **cerdo** pork (II)

   la chuleta de — pork chop (II)

el **cereal** cereal (I)

la **ceremonia** ceremony (1-2)

la **cereza** cherry (II)

   cero zero (I)

   cerrado, -a closed (II)

   cerrar to close (II)

el **certificado** certificate, diploma (1-2)

la **cesta** basket (II)

el **champú** shampoo (II)

la **chaqueta** jacket (I)

   charlar to chat (II)

el **cheque:**

   cobrar un — to cash a check (II)

   el — de viajero traveler's check (II)

   el — personal personal check (II)

la **chica** girl (I)

el **chico** boy (I)

   chismoso, -a gossipy (4-1)

   chocar con to crash into, to collide with (II)

la **chuleta de cerdo** pork chop (II)

el **cielo** sky (II)

   cien one hundred (I)

las **ciencias:**

   la clase de — naturales science class (I)

la clase de — sociales social studies class (I)

el científico, la científica scientist (II, 6-1)

(es) cierto (it is) certain (II)

cinco five (I)

el círculo circle (7-1)

cincuenta fifty (I)

el cine movie theater (I)

la cinta adhesiva transparent tape (II)

el cinturón, *pl.* **los cinturones** belt (II)

la cita date (II)

la ciudad city (I)

la ciudadanía citizenship (5-2)

el ciudadano, la ciudadana citizen (5-2)

la civilización civilization (7-1)

claro, -a light *(color)* (II)

la clase class (I)

la sala de clases classroom (I)

    ¿Qué — de...? What kind of...? (I)

clásico, -a classical (2-2)

el cliente, la clienta client (5-1)

el clima weather (9-2)

el club, *pl.* **los clubes** club (II)

    el — atlético athletic club (II)

cobrar un cheque to cash a check (II)

el coche car (I)

la cocina kitchen (I)

cocinar to cook (I)

el cocinero, la cocinera cook (6-1)

el código de vestimenta dress code (10-1)

el codo elbow (II)

    colaborar to collaborate (4-2)

la colección, *pl.* **las colecciones** collection (II)

coleccionar to collect (II)

el colegio secondary school, high

school (II)

la colina hill (II)

el collar necklace (I)

la colonia colony (8-2)

el color, *pl.* **los colores** (I)

    ¿De qué — ...? What color...? (I)

colocar to put (9-1)

la comedia comedy (I)

el comedor dining room (I)

el — de beneficencia soup kitchen (5-2)

el comentario commentary (II)

comenzar (e → ie) to start (II)

comer to eat (I)

cómico, -a funny, comical (I)

la comida food, meal (I)

    la — basura junk food (3-1)

como likc, as (I)

    — si fuera as though it were (6-2)

¿Cómo?:

    ¿— eres? What are you like? (I)

    ¿— es? What is he / she like? (I)

    ¿— está Ud.? How are you? *formal* (I)

    ¿— estás? How are you? *fam.* (I)

    ¿— lo pasaste? How was it (for you)? (I)

    ¿— se dice...? How do you say...? (I)

    ¿— se escribe...? How is...spelled? (I)

    ¿— se hace...? How do you make...? (II)

    ¿— se llama? What's his / her name? (I)

    ¿— se va...? How do you go to...? (II)

    ¿— te llamas? What is your name? (I)

    ¿— te queda(n)? How does it (do they) fit (you)? (I)

¡Cómo no! Of course! (II)

la cómoda dresser (I)

cómodo, -a comfortable (II)

la compañía firm, company (5-1)

compartir to share (I)

el compás rhythm (2-2)

la competencia competition (II)

competir (e → i) to compete (II)

complicado, -a complicated (I, II)

componerse de to be formed by (8-2)

el comportamiento behavior (4-2)

la composición, *pl.*

las composiciones composition (I)

comprar to buy (I)

    comprar recuerdos to buy souvenirs (I)

comprender to understand (I)

comprensivo, -a understanding (4-1)

la computación computer science (5-1)

la computadora computer (I)

    la — portátil laptop computer (I)

    usar la — to use the computer (I)

comunicarse to communicate (I, 6-2)

(tú) te comunicas you communicate (I)

(yo) me comunico I communicate (I)

la comunidad community (I)

con with (I)

    — destino a going to (II)

    — mis / tus amigos with my / your friends (I)

    — tal que provided that (9-2)

    ¿— qué se sirve? What do you serve it with? (II)

¿— quién? With whom? (I)

concentrarse to concentrate (3-2)

el **concierto** concert (I)

el **concurso** contest (II)

el **— de belleza** beauty contest (II)

el **conductor, la conductora** driver (II)

el **conejo** rabbit (7-2)

confianza trust (4-1)

— en sí mismo, -a self-confidence (3-2)

confiar (i → í) to trust (4-1)

el **conflicto** conflict (4-2)

congelado, -a frozen (II)

el **conjunto** band (2-2)

conmigo with me (I)

conocen you know (II)

conocer to know, to be acquainted with (I, II)

los **conocimientos** knowledge (5-1)

la **conquista** conquest (8-1)

conquistar to conquer (8-1)

conseguir (e → i) to obtain (II)

el **consejero, la consejera** counselor (5-1)

el **consejo** advice (3-2)

consentido, -a spoiled (II)

conservar to conserve (II, 9-1)

considerado, -a considerate (4-1)

la **construcción** construction (8-1)

construir (i → y) to build (5-2)

el **consultorio** doctor's /dentist's office (II)

el **contador, la contadora** accountant (II, 6-1)

la **contaminación** pollution (II, 9-1)

contaminado, -a polluted (II, 9-1)

contaminar to pollute (6-2)

contar (chistes) (o → ue) to tell (jokes) (II)

— con to count on (4-1)

contener to contain (3-1)

contento, -a happy (I)

contestar to answer (II)

contigo with you (I)

contra against (II, 1-2)

en — (de) against (5-2)

contribuir (u → y) to contribute (7-2)

convertirse (en) to turn (into), to become (7-2)

el **corazón** heart (3-2)

la **corbata** tie (I)

el **coro** chorus, choir (II)

el **correo** post office (II)

el **correo electrónico** e-mail (I)

escribir por — to write e-mail (I)

correr to run (I)

cortar to cut (I, II)

— el césped to mow the lawn (I)

— se to cut oneself (II)

— se el pelo to cut one's hair (II)

cortés, *pl.* **corteses** polite (II)

las **cortinas** curtains (I)

corto, -a short *(length)* (I)

los pantalones —s shorts (I)

la **cosa** thing (I)

costar (o → ue) to cost (I)

¿Cuánto cuesta(n)...? How much does (do)…cost? (I)

la **costumbre** custom (II)

crear to create (I)

— una página Web to create a Web page (II)

recer to grow (9-1)

la **creencia** belief (7-2)

creer:

Creo que... I think… (I)

Creo que no. I don't think so. (I)

Creo que sí. I think so. (I)

el **crimen** crime (II)

el / la **criminal** criminal (II)

cristiano, -a Christian (8-1)

criticar to criticize (4-2)

el **crítico, la crítica** critic (II)

el **cruce de calles** intersection (II)

cruzar to cross (II)

el **cuaderno** notebook (I)

la **cuadra** block (II)

el **cuadro** painting (I)

¿Cuál? Which? What? (I)

¿— es la fecha? What is the date? (I)

la **cualidad** quality (4-1)

cualquier, -a any (7-2)

¿Cuándo? When? (I)

¿Cuánto?:

¿— cuesta(n)...? How much does (do)...cost? (I)

¿— tiempo hace que...? How long...? (II)

¿Cuántos, -as? How many? (I)

¿—s años tiene(n)...? How old is / are...? (I)

cuanto:

en — a with respect to (10-1)

en — as soon as (9-1)

cuarenta forty (I)

cuarto, -a fourth (I)

y — quarter past *(in telling time)* (I)

el **cuarto** room (I)

cuatro four (I)

cuatrocientos, -as four hundred (I)

cubrir to cover (7-1)

la **cuchara** spoon (I)

la **cucharada** tablespoon(ful) (II)

el **cuchillo** knife (I)

el **cuello** neck (II)

la cuenta bill (I)

   tener en — to take into account (6-2)

la cuerda rope (II)

el cuero leather (II)

cuidadoso, -a careful (6-1)

cuidar a to take care of (II)

culpable guilty (10-2)

el cumpleaños birthday (I)

   ¡Feliz —! Happy birthday! (I)

cumplir años to have a birthday (II)

cumplir con to carry out, to perform (5-1)

el cupón de regalo, *pl.* **los cupones de regalo** gift certificate (II)

curar to cure (6-2)

el curso:

   tomar un curso to take a course (I)

D . . . .

la danza dance (2-2)

dañar to damage (9-1)

dar to give (I)

   — + *movie or TV program* to show (I)

   — de comer al perro to feed the dog (I)

   — puntadas to stitch *(surgically)* (II)

   — un discurso to give a speech (II)

   — un paseo to take a walk, to stroll (1-1)

   — una caminata to take a walk (II)

   dar(se) la mano to shake hands (II)

   darse cuenta de to realize (1-2)

de of, from (I)

   — acuerdo. OK. Agreed. (II)

   — algodón cotton (II)

   — cuero leather (II)

   ¿— dónde eres? Where are you from? (I)

   — ida y vuelta round trip (II)

   — la mañana / la tarde / la noche in the morning / afternoon / evening (I)

   — lana wool (II)

   — negocios business (II)

   — niño as a child (II)

   — oro gold (II)

   — pequeño as a child (II)

   — plata silver (II)

   — plato principal as a main dish (I)

   — postre for dessert (I)

   — prisa in a hurry (II)

   ¿— qué color...? What color...? (I)

   ¿— qué está hecho, -a? What is it made of? (II)

   — repente suddenly (II)

   — seda silk (II)

   — sólo un color solid-colored (II)

   — tela sintética synthetic fabric (II)

   ¿— veras? Really? (I)

   — vez en cuando once in a while (II)

debajo de underneath (I)

deber should, must (I)

el deber duty (10-1)

debido a due to (10-2)

débil weak (3-2)

decidir to decide (I)

décimo, -a tenth (I)

decir to say, to tell (I)

   — la verdad to tell the truth (II)

   ¿Cómo se dice...? How do you say...? (I)

dime tell me (I)

   ¡No me digas! You don't say! (I)

   ¿Qué quiere —...? What does...mean? (I)

   Quiere — ... It means... (I)

   Se dice... You say... (I)

las decoraciones decorations (I)

decorar to decorate (I)

dedicado, -a dedicated (5-1)

dedicarse a to be involved in (6-1)

el dedo finger (I)

Déjame en paz. Leave me alone. (II)

dejar to leave, to let (II)

   — de to stop (doing something) (1-1)

   — huellas to leave footprints (8-1)

   no dejes don't leave, don't let (II)

503

delante de in front of (I)

delicioso, -a delicious (I)

la **demanda** demand (6-2)

los **demás, las demás** others (I)

demasiado too (I)

democrático, -a democratic (10-2)

el / la **dentista** dentist (II)

dentro de inside (II)

depende it depends (II)

depender de to depend on (9-1)

el **dependiente, la dependienta** salesperson (I)

deportista athletic, sports-minded (I)

derecha:

a la — (de) to the right (of) (I)

derecho straight (II)

el **derecho** *(study of)* law (II)

los **derechos** rights (5-2)

el **derrame de petróleo** oil spill (9-2)

derretir to melt (9-2)

desafortunadamente unfortunately (1-2)

desanimado, -a discouraged (1-2)

desaparecer to disappear (6-2)

desarrollar to develop (3-2)

el **desarrollo** development (6-2)

el **desayuno** breakfast (I)

en el — for breakfast (I)

descansar to rest, to relax (I)

la **descendencia** offspring, descendants (8-2)

desconfiar to mistrust (4-1)

desconocido, -a unknown (8-2)

descubrir to discover (6-2)

los **descuentos:**

la tienda de — discount store (I)

desde from, since (II)

desear to wish (I)

¿Qué desean (Uds.)? What would you like? *formal* (I)

desempeñar un cargo to hold a position (6-1)

el **desempleo** unemployment (10-2)

el **desfile** parade (II)

deshacerse de to get rid of (9-1)

el **desierto** desert (II, 1-1)

la **desigualdad** inequity (10-2)

desobediente disobedient (II)

el **desodorante** deodorant (II)

desordenado, -a messy (I)

despacio slowly (II)

el **despacho** office (home) (I)

despedirse (e → i) de to say good-bye (II)

el **despertador** alarm clock (I)

desperdiciar to waste (9-1)

el **desperdicio** waste (9-1)

despertarse (e → ie) to wake up (II)

después (de) afterwards, after (I)

destacar(se) to stand out (2-2)

la **destrucción** destruction (II)

destruir (i → y) to destroy (II)

el / la **detective** detective (II)

detener to detain (10-2), to stop (9-2)

detrás de behind (I)

devolver (o → ue) (un libro) to return (a book) (II)

el **día** day (I)

Buenos —s. Good morning. (I)

cada — every day (I)

el — festivo holiday (II)

¿Qué — es hoy? What day is today? (I)

todos los —s every day (I)

el **diámetro** diameter (7-1)

la **diapositiva** slide (I)

dibujar to draw (I)

el **diccionario** dictionary (I)

diciembre December (I)

diecinueve nineteen (I)

dieciocho eighteen (I)

dieciséis sixteen (I)

diecisiete seventeen (I)

los **dientes** teeth (II)

cepillarse — to brush one's teeth (II)

el cepillo de — toothbrush (II)

la **dieta** diet (3-1)

diez ten (I)

la **diferencia de opinión** difference of opinion (4-2)

difícil difficult (I)

digital:

la cámara — digital camera (I)

dime tell me (I)

el **dinero** money (I)

— en efectivo cash (II)

el **dinosaurio** dinosaur (II)

el **dios, la diosa** god, goddess (7-2)

la **dirección,** *pl.* **las direcciones** direction (II)

la — electrónica e-mail address (I)

directo, -a direct (II)

el **director, la directora** (school) principal (II)

el **disco compacto** compact disc (I)

grabar un — to burn a CD (I)

discriminar to discriminate (10-1)

el **discurso** speech (II)

discutir to discuss (II)

el **diseñador, la diseñadora** designer (II, 6-1)

diseñar to design (6-1)

el **diseño** design (7-1)

disfrutar de to enjoy (II)

disminuir to decrease, to diminish (9-2)

el **disquete** diskette (I)

la **distancia** distance (7-1)

divertido, -a amusing, fun (I)

divertirse (e → ie) to have fun (II)

doblar to turn (II)

doce twelve (I)

el **documento** document (I)

doler (o → ue) to hurt (I, II)

el **dolor** pain (II)

dominar to dominate (8-1)

domingo Sunday (I)

donar to donate (5-2)

dónde:

    ¿—? Where? (I)

    ¿De — eres? Where are you from? (I)

dormido, -a asleep (II)

dormir (o → ue) to sleep (I)

    —se to fall asleep (II)

    el saco de — sleeping bag (1-1)

el **dormitorio** bedroom (I)

dos two (I)

los / las **dos** both (I)

doscientos, -as two hundred (I)

el **drama** drama (I)

la **ducha** shower (II)

ducharse to take a shower (II)

dudar to doubt (II, 7-1)

el **dueño, la dueña** owner (II, 5-1)

dulce sweet (II)

los **dulces** candy (I)

durante during (I)

durar to last (I, II)

el **durazno** peach (II)

duro, -a hard (1-2)

E..

echar to throw, to throw away (9-1)

    — una carta to mail a letter (II)

el **eclipse** eclipse (7-2)

ecológico, -a ecological (II)

económico, -a economical (II, 9-1)

la **edad** age (3-1)

el **edificio de apartamentos** apartament building (II)

la **educación física:**

    la clase de — physical education class (I)

educar to educate (5-2)

efecto:

    el — invernadero greenhouse effect (9-2)

los **efectos especiales** special effects (II, 6-1)

eficiente efficient (II)

egoísta selfish (4-1)

el **ejercicio:**

    hacer — to exercise (1)

ejercicios aeróbicos aerobics (3-2)

el *m. sing.* the (I)

él he (I)

la **electricidad** electricity (II, 9-1)

los **electrodomésticos:**

    la tienda de — household-appliance store (I)

electrónico, -a:

    la dirección — e-mail address (I)

elegante elegant (II)

eliminar to eliminate (II, 1-2)

ella she (I)

ellas *f.* they (I)

ellos *m.* they (I)

emocionado, -a excited, emotional (II)

emocionante touching (I)

emocionarse to be moved (1-2)

el **empate** tie (II)

empezar (e → ie) to begin, to start (I, II)

el **empleado, la empleada** employee (II)

emprendedor, -a enterprising (6-1)

la **empresa** business (6-1)

en in, on (I)

    — + *vehicle* by, in, on (I)

    — casa at home (I)

    — contra (de) against (5-2)

    — cuanto as soon as (9-1)

    — cuanto a with respect to (10-1)

    — la...hora in the...hour (class period) (I)

    — la Red online (I)

    — lugar de instead of (10-2)

    — medio de in the middle of (II)

    — punto exactly (II)

    ¿— qué puedo servirle? How can I help you? (I)

    — realidad really (II)

    — seguida right away (II)

    — vez de instead of (10-1)

enamorado, -a de in love with (II)

enamorarse (de) to fall in love (with) (II)

encantado, -a delighted (I)

encantar to please very much, to love (I)

    a él / ella le encanta(n) he / she loves (I)

    me encantaría I would love to... (5-2)

    me / te encanta(n)... I / you love... (I)

encargarse (de) (g → gu) to be in charge of (5-1)

encender (e → ie) to turn on, to light (II)

encima de on top of (I)

encontrar (o → ue) to find (II)

el **encuentro** meeting (8-2)

la **energía** energy (II, 3-1)

   la fuente de — energy source (6-2)

enero January (I)

la **enfermedad** illness (6-2)

el **enfermero, la enfermera** nurse (II)

enfermo, -a sick (I)

enfrentarse to face, to confront (8-2)

enlatado, -a canned (II)

enojado, -a angry (II)

enojarse to get angry (II)

enorme enormous (II)

la **ensalada** salad (I)

   la — de frutas fruit salad (I)

ensayar to rehearse (II)

el **ensayo** rehearsal (II)

la **enseñanza** teaching (10-1)

enseñar to teach (I)

entender (e → ie) to understand (II)

enterarse to find out (6-2)

entonces then (I)

la **entrada** entrance (II), ticket (2-2)

entrar to enter (I)

entre among, between (II)

la **entrega de premios** awards ceremony (1-2)

entregar to turn in (II)

   — la tarea a tiempo to turn in homework on time (II)

el **entrenador, la entrenadora** coach, trainer (II)

el **entrenamiento** training (1-2)

entrenarse to train (1-2)

la **entrevista** interview (II, 5-1)

entrevistar to interview (II)

entrometido, -a meddlesome (4-1)

el **entusiasmo** enthusiasm (2-2)

enviar to send (I, II)

la **época** period, time (8-1)

equilibrado -a balanced (3-1)

el **equipaje** luggage (II)

   facturar el — to check luggage (II)

el **equipo** team (II)

   el — de sonido sound (stereo) system (I)

   el — deportivo sports equipment (II)

¿Eres...? Are you...? (I)

es is; (he / she / it) is (I)

   — cierto it's true (II)

   — el *(number)* **de** *(month)* it is the... of... *(in telling the date)* (I)

   — el primero de *(month).* It is the first of... (I)

   — la una. It is one o'clock. (I)

   — necesario. It's necessary. (I)

   — un(a)... It's a... (I)

la **escala** stopover (II)

escalar to climb (a rock or mountain) (1-1)

la **escalera** stairs, stairway (I), ladder (II)

escaparse to escape (II)

la **escasez** shortage (9-1)

la **escena** scene (II)

el **escenario** stage (2-2)

escoger to choose (II)

esconder(se) to hide (oneself) (II)

escribir:

   ¿Cómo se escribe...? How is...spelled? (I)

   — cuentos to write stories (I)

   — por correo electrónico to write e-mail (I)

   — un informe sobre... to write a report about...

   Se escribe... It's spelled... (I)

el **escritor, la escritora** writer (II, 2-2)

el **escritorio** desk (I)

la **escritura** writing (7-2)

escuchar música to listen to music (I)

la **escuela primaria** primary school (I)

la **escuela técnica** technical school (II)

el **escultor, la escultora** sculptor (2-1)

la **escultura** sculpture (2-1)

ese, esa that (I, II)

   de — modo in that way (10-1)

eso:

   por — that's why, therefore (I)

esos, esas those (I, II)

el **espacio** outer space (II)

los **espaguetis** spaghetti (I)

la **espalda** back (II)

el **español:**

   la clase de — Spanish class (I)

especial special (II)

especialmente especially (I)

la **especie** species (9-2)

el **espectáculo** show (2-2)

el **espejo** mirror (I)

esperar to hope (for) (4-1), to wait (II)

la **esposa** wife (I)

el **esposo** husband (I)

el **esquí acuático** waterskiing (II)

esquiar to ski (I)

la **esquina** corner (II)

Está hecho, -a de... It is made of... (II)

establecer (zc) to establish (8-2)

la **estación,** *pl.* **las estaciones** season (I)

    la **— de servicio** service station (II)

el **estadio** stadium (I)

el **estado** state (10-1)

el **estante** shelf, bookshelf (I)

estar to be (I)¿

    Cómo está Ud.? How are you? *formal* (I)

    ¿Cómo estás? How are you? *fam.* (I)

    — + *present participle* to be + *present participle* (I)

    — a cargo de to be in charge of (9-1)

    — basado, -a en to be based on (II)

    — de buen / mal humor to be in a good / bad mood (3-2)

    — de moda to be in fashion (II)

    — en línea to be online (I)

    — enamorado, -a de to be in love with (II)

    — equivocado, -a to be mistaken (4-2)

    — orgulloso / orgullosa de to be proud of (1-2)

    — resfriado, -a to have a cold (3-1)

    — seguro, -a to be sure (II)

    — sujeto a to be subject to (10-1)

    Estoy de acuerdo. I agree. (I)

    No estoy de acuerdo. I don't agree. (I)

la **estatua** statue (II)

la **estatura** height (3-1)

este, esta this (I, II)

esta noche this evening (I)

esta tarde this afternoon (I)

este fin de semana this weekend (I)

el **estilo** style (II)

estirar to stretch (3-2)

el **estómago** stomach (I)

estornudar to sneeze (3-1)

estos, estas these (I, II)

    ¿Qué es esto? What is this? (I)

Estoy de acuerdo. I agree. (I)

la **estrategia** strategy (6-2)

estrecho, -a narrow (II)

la **estrella (del cine)** (movie) star (II)

el **estrés** stress (3-2)

estresado, -a stressed out (3-2)

la **estructura** structure (7-1)

el / la **estudiante** student (I)

estudiar to study (I)

estudioso, -a studious (I)

la **estufa** stove (II)

estupendo, -a stupendous, wonderful (II)

europeo, -a European (8-2)

la **evidencia** proof, evidence (7-1)

el **evento especial** special event (II)

evitar to avoid (3-1)

exagerado, -a outrageous (II)

exagerar to exaggerate (2-2)

excavar excavate (7-1)

excesivo, -a excessive (9-2)

exigir to demand (3-2)

existir to exist (7-1)

el **éxito** success (II)

    tener — to be successful (II)

examinar to examine, to check (II)

la **excursión,** *pl.* **las excursiones** excursion, short trip (II)

la **experiencia** experience (I)

la **explicación** explanation (4-2)

explicar to explain (II)

la **explosión,** *pl.* **las explosiones** explosion (II)

explotar to exploit, to overwork (9-2)

expresar(se) to express (oneself) (2-1)

expulsar to expel (8-1)

extracurricular extracurricular (II)

extinción:

    (en) peligro de — (in) danger of extinction (9-2)

extranjero, -a foreign (II)

extraño, -a strange (7-1)

el / la **extraterrestre** alien (II)

F . . . .

la **fábrica** factory (6-2)

fácil easy (I)

facturar (el equipaje) to check (luggage) (II)

la **falda** skirt (I)

la **falta** lack (9-2)

    la — de lack of (10-2)

faltar to be missing (I)

famoso, -a famous (II, 2-1)

fantástico, -a fantastic (I)

la **farmacia** pharmacy (II)

fascinante fascinating (I)

fascinar to fascinate (II)

favorito, -a favorite (I)

febrero February (I)

la **fecha:**

    ¿Cuál es la —? What is the date? (I)

    la — de nacimiento date of birth (5-1)

la **felicidad** happiness (10-1)

¡Felicidades! Congratulations! (II)

¡Felicitaciones! Congratulations! (1-2)

felicitar to congratulate (II)

¡Feliz cumpleaños! Happy birthday! (I)

fenomenal phenomenal (II)

el **fenómeno** phenomenon (7-1)

feo, -a ugly (I)

la **fibra** fiber (3-1)

la **fiebre** fever (3-1)

la **fiesta** party (I)

    la — de sorpresa surprise party (II)

la **figura** figure (2-1)

el **fin,** *pl.* **los fines** purpose (10-2)

el **fin de semana:**

    este — this weekend (I)

los **fines de semana** on weekends (I)

las **finanzas** finance (6-1)

flexible flexible (5-1)

flexionar to flex, to stretch (3-2)

flojo, -a loose (II)

la **flor,** *pl.* **las flores** flower (I)

la **foca** seal (9-2)

la **fogata** bonfire (II)

fomentar to encourage (9-1)

el **fondo** background (2-1)

el **fósforo** match (II)

la **foto** photo (I)

la **fotografía** photography (II)

el **fotógrafo, la fotógrafa** photographer (II)

el **fracaso** failure (II)

frecuentemente frequently (II)

el **fregadero** sink (II)

freír (e → í) to fry (II)

las **fresas** strawberries (I)

fresco, -a fresh (II)

los **frijoles** beans (II)

el **frío:**

    Hace —. It's cold. (I)

    tener — to be cold (I)

frito, -a fried (II)

fue it was (I)

    — un desastre. It was a disaster. (I)

el **fuego** fire (II)

los **fuegos artificiales** fireworks (II)

la **fuente** fountain (II); source (II)

    la — de energía energy source (6-2)

    la — de inspiración source of inspiration (2-1)

fuera (de) outside (II)

fuerte strong (3-1)

la **fuerza** strength (3-2)

la **función** function (7-1)

funcionar to function, to work (II, 10-1)

fundamental fundamental (10-2)

fundar to found (8-1)

furioso, -a furious (II)

el **fútbol:**

    jugar al — to play soccer (I)

el **fútbol americano:**

    jugar al — to play football (I)

el **futuro** future (II)

G

el **galán** leading man (II)

la **galleta** cookie (I)

ganar to win (I); to earn *(money)* (II)

— **se la vida** to make a living (II)

la **ganga** bargain (II)

el **garaje** garage (I)

la **garantía** guarantee (10-2)

garantizar to guarantee (5-2)

la **gasolina** gasoline (II)

gastar to spend (II)

el **gato** cat (I)

el **gel** gel (II)

el **gen** *pl.* **los genes** gene, genes (6-2)

generalmente generally (I)

generoso, -a generous (II)

la **genética** genetics (6-2)

¡Genial! Great! (I)

la gente people (I)

la — **sin hogar** homeless people (5-2)

geométrico, -a geometric(al) (7-1)

el / la **gerente** manager (II, 5-1)

el **gesto** gesture (2-2)

la **gimnasia** gymnastics (II)

el **gimnasio** gym (I)

el **globo** balloon (I)

gobernar (ie) to rule, to govern (8-1)

el **gobierno** government (9-1)

el **gol** goal *(in sports)* (II)

meter un — to score a goal (II)

el **golf:**

jugar al — to play golf (I)

la **gorra** cap (I)

gozar (de) to enjoy (10-1)

grabar to record (II)

— **un disco compacto** to burn a CD (I)

gracias thank you (I)

gracioso, -a funny (I)

el **grado centígrado** centigrade degree (3-1)

la **graduación,** *pl.*

las **graduaciones** graduation (II)

graduarse (u → ú) to graduate (II, 6-1)

los **gráficos** computer graphics (I)

grande large (I)

el **granizo** hail (1-1)

caer — to hail (1-1)

la **grapadora** stapler (II)

grasoso, -a greasy (II)

gratuito, -a free (10-1)

grave serious (II, 9-1)

la **gripe** flu (3-1)

gris gray (I)

gritar to scream (II)

el **grupo étnico** ethnic group (8-1)

los **guantes** gloves (I)

guapo, -a good-looking (I)

guardar (un secreto) to keep (a secret) (4-1)

la **guardería infantil** day-care center (II)

la **guerra** war (II, 8-2)

el / la **guía** guide (II)

la **guía** guidebook (II)

los **guisantes** peas (I)

gustar:

a él / ella le gusta(n) he / she likes (I)

(A mí) me gusta... I like to... (I)

(A mí) me gusta más... I like to...better (I prefer to...) (I)

(A mí) me gusta mucho... I like to...a lot (I)

(A mí) no me gusta... I don't like to... (I)

(A mí) no me gusta nada... I don't like to...at all. (I)

Le gusta... He / She likes... (I)

Me gusta... I like... (I)

Me gustaría... I would like... (I)

Me gustó. I liked it. (I)

No le gusta... He / She doesn't like... (I)

¿Qué te gusta hacer? What do you like to do? (I)

¿Qué te gusta hacer más? What do you like better (prefer) to do? (I)

Te gusta... You like... (I)

¿Te gusta...? Do you like to...? (I)

¿Te gustaría? Would you like? (I)

¿Te gustó? Did you like it? (I)

H..

haber to have
(as an auxiliary verb) (II)
había there was / there were (II)
la **habilidad** skill (5-1)
la **habitación,** *pl.* **las
habitaciones** room (II)
la — **doble** double occupancy
(II)
la — **individual** single
occupancy (II)
el / la **habitante** inhabitant (7-2)
el **hábito alimenticio** eating
habit (3-1)
hablar to talk (I)
— **por teléfono** to talk on
the phone (I)
habrá there will be (II)
hacer to do (I)
hace + *time expression* ago (I)
Hace + *time* **+ que...** It has
been... (II)
Hace calor. It's hot. (I)
Hace frío. It's cold. (I)
Hace sol. It's sunny. (I)
— **bicicleta** to use a
stationary bike (3-2)
— **caso** to pay attention, to
obey (4-2)
— **cinta** to use a treadmill
(3-2)
— **ejercicio** to exercise (I)
— **el papel de** to play the
role of (II)
— **escala** to stop over (II)
— **flexiones** to do push ups
(3-2)
— **gimnasia** to do gymnastics
(II)
— **la cama** to make the bed (I)
— **la maleta** to pack the
suitcase (II)

— **las paces** to make peace
with (4-2)
— **ruido** to make noise (II)
— **un esfuerzo** to make an
effort (1-2)
— **un picnic** to have a picnic
(II)
— **un proyecto** to do a
project (II)
— **un viaje** to take a trip (II)
— **un video** to videotape (I)
— **una búsqueda** to do a
search (II)
— **una gira** to take a tour (II)
— **una parrillada** to have a
barbecue (II)
— **una pregunta** to ask a
question (II)
haz *(command)* do, make (I)
¿Qué hiciste? What did you
do? (I)
¿Qué tiempo hace? What is
the weather like? (I)
(tú) haces you do (I)
(yo) hago I do (I)
hacerse to become (6-1)
hacia toward (1-1)
hambre:
Tengo —. I'm hungry. (I)
la **hamburguesa** hamburger (I)
haré lo que me dé la gana I'll
do as I please (6-1)
la **harina** flour (II)
has visto you have seen (II)
hasta until (II); as far as, up to
(II)
— **luego.** See you later. (I)
— **mañana.** See you
tomorrow. (I)
hay there is, there are (I)
— **que** one must (I)
haya *(subjunctive)* there is,
there are (II)

he visto I have seen (II)
el **helado** ice cream (I)
la **herencia** heritage (8-2)
herido, -a injured (II)
el **herido, la herida** injured
person (II)
el **hermano, la hermana** brother,
sister (I)
el **hermanastro, la hermanastra**
stepbrother, stepsister (I)
los **hermanos** brothers, brother(s)
and sister(s) (I)
hermoso, -a beautiful (1-1)
el **héroe** hero (II)
la **heroína** heroine (II)
hervir (e → ie) (e → i) to boil
(II)
el **hielo** ice (9-2)
el **hierro** iron (3-1)
el **hijo, la hija** son, daughter (I)
los **hijos** children, sons (I)
histórico, -a historical (II)
el **hockey** hockey (II)
hogar:
el — **de ancianos** home for
the elderly (5-2)
la **gente sin —** homeless
people (5-2)
la **hoja de papel** sheet of paper (I)
¡Hola! Hello! (I)
el **hombre** man (I)
el — **de negocios**
businessman (II, 6-1)
el **hombro** shoulder (II)
honesto, -a honest (4-1)
la **hora:**
en la... — in the...hour (class
period) (I)
¿A qué —? (At) what time? (I)
el **horario** schedule (I)
la **hormiga** ant (II)
el **horno** oven (II)
al — baked (II)

horrible horrible (I)

el **horror:**
    la película de — horror movie (I)

el **hospital** hospital (I)

la **hospitalidad** hospitality (6-2)

el **hotel** hotel (I)

hoy today (I)
    de — en adelante from now on (6-2)
    hubo there was (II)

el **hueso** bone (II)

los **huevos** eggs (I)

el **humo** smoke (II)

el **huracán,** *pl.* **los huracanes** hurricane (II)

I ....

ida y vuelta round-trip (II)

identificarse con to identify oneself with (2-2)

el **idioma** language (II)

la **iglesia** church (I)

ignorar to ignore (4-2)

la **igualdad** equality (10-1)

igualmente likewise (I)

la **imagen** image (2-1)

impaciente impatient (I)

el **imperio** empire (8-2)

importante important (I)

impresionante impressive (I)

impresionar to impress (1-1)

improbable unlikely (7-1)

el **incendio** fire (II)

incluir to include (3-1)

increíble incredible (I)

el / la **indígena** native (8-2)

la **industria** industry (6-2)

inexplicable inexplicable (7-1)

infantil childish (I)

la **influencia** influence (8-1)

influir (i → y) to influence (2-1)

la **información** information (I)

la **informática** information technology (6-2)

el **informe** report (I, II)

el **ingeniero, la ingeniera** engineer (II, 6-1)

el **inglés:**
    la clase de — English class (I)

el **ingrediente** ingredient (II)

inhumano, -a inhuman (10-1)

la **injusticia** injustice (10-1)

injusto, -a unfair (5-2)

inmediatamente immediately (II)

inocente innocent (10-2)

inolvidable unforgettable (I)

inscribirse to register (1-2)

la **inscripción** registration (1-2)

insistir en to insist (II)

la **inspección,** *pl.* **las inspecciones de seguridad** security checkpoint (II)

inspirar to inspire (2-1)

integrarse to integrate (8-1)

inteligente intelligent (I)

el **intento** attempt (7-2)

intercambiar to exchange (10-2)

el **intercambio** exchange (8-2)

el **interés** interest (II)

interesante interesting (I)

interesar to interest (I)

me **interesa(n)** it interests me (they interest me) (I)

me **interesaría** I would be interested… (5-2)

la **interpretación** interpretation (2-2)

interpretar to interpret (2-2)

íntimo, -a intimate (4-1)

la **inundación,** *pl.* **las inundaciones** flood (II)

invadir to invade (8-1)

inventar to invent (6-2)

el **invento** invention (6-2)

investigar to investigate (II)

el **invierno** winter (I)

la **inyección,** *pl.* **las inyecciones** injection, shot (II)

ir to go (I)
    — a + *inf.* to be going to + *verb* (I)
    — a la escuela to go to school (I)
    — a pie to go on foot (II)
    — de cámping to go camping (I)
    — de compras to go shopping (I)
    — de pesca to go fishing (I)
    — de vacaciones to go on vacation (I)

¡Qué va! No way! (4-2)
¡Vamos! Let's go! (I)
el **itinerario** itinerary (II)
la **izquierda:**
   a la — (de) to the left (of) (I)

J . . . .
el **jabón** soap (II)
el **jarabe** syrup (3-1)
el **jardín** garden, yard (I)
los **jeans** jeans (I)
el **jefe, la jefa** boss (6-1)
joven *adj.* young (I)
el / la **joven** young man, young
   woman (I)
los **jóvenes** young people (II)
las **joyas (de oro, de plata)**
   (gold, silver) jewelry (II)
la **joyería** jewelry store (I)
las **judías verdes** green beans (I)
el **judío, la judía** Jew(ish) (8-1)
jueves Thursday (I)
el **juez, la jueza,** *pl.* **los jueces**
   judge (II, 6-1)
el **jugador, la jugadora** player (II)
jugar (a) (u → ue) to play
   (games, sports) (I)
   — a los bolos to bowl (II)
   — al básquetbol to play
      basketball (I)
   — al béisbol to play baseball
      (I)
   — al fútbol to play soccer (I)
   — al fútbol americano to
      play football (I)
   — al golf to play golf (I)
   — al tenis to play tennis (I)
   — al vóleibol to play
      volleyball (I)
   — videojuegos to play video
      games (I)
el **jugo:**
   el — de manzana apple juice
   (I)
   el — de naranja orange juice
   (I)
el **juguete** toy (I)

el **juicio** trial (10-2)
julio July (I)
junio June (I)
juntar fondos to fundraise (5-2)
juntarse to join (II)
juntos -as together (4-1)
el **jurado** jury (10-2)
la **justicia** justice (10-2)
justo, -a fair (5-2)
juzgar to judge (10-2)

la the *f. sing.* (I); it, her *f. dir. obj. pron.* (I)

los labios lips (II)

el laboratorio laboratory (I, II)

el lado:

    al — de next to (I)

el ladrón, la ladrona, *pl.* **los ladrones** thief (II)

el lago lake (I)

la lámpara lamp (I)

la lana wool (II)

el lápiz, *pl.* **los lápices** pencil (I)

largo, -a long (I)

el largo length (7-1)

las the *f. pl.*; them *f. dir. obj. pron.* (I)

    — dos, los dos both (I)

lastimarse to hurt oneself (II)

lástima:

    ¡Qué —! What a shame! (II)

la lata can (I)

lavar to wash (I)

    — el coche to wash the car (I)

    — la ropa to wash the clothes (I)

    — los platos to wash the dishes (I)

    — se la cara to wash one's face (II)

le (to / for) him, her, *(formal)* you *sing. ind. obj. pron.* (I)

    — gusta... He / She likes... (I)

    — traigo... I will bring you... (I)

    No — gusta... He / She doesn't like... (I)

la lección, *pl.* **las lecciones de piano** piano lesson (class) (I)

la leche milk (I)

la lechuga lettuce (I)

el lector DVD DVD player (I)

leer revistas to read magazines (I)

lejos (de) far (from) (I)

la lengua language (8-2)

lentamente slowly (II)

la leña firewood (II)

les (to / for) them, *(formal);* you *pl. ind. obj. pron.* (I)

la letra lyrics (2-2)

el letrero sign (II)

levantar pesas to lift weights (I)

levantarse to get up (II)

la ley law, rule (II, 5-2)

la leyenda legend (7-2)

la libertad liberty (10-1)

libre free (10-2)

la librería bookstore (I)

el libro book (I)

la liga league (II)

limitar to limit (9-1)

la limonada lemonade (I)

limpiar el baño to clean the bathroom (I)

la limpieza cleaning (9-2)

limpio, -a clean (I)

la línea:

    estar en — to be online (I, II)

    la — aérea airline (II)

la linterna flashlight (1-1)

la liquidación, *pl.* **las liquidaciones** sale (II)

listo, -a ready (II)

llamar:

    — por teléfono to call on the phone (II)

    ¿Cómo se llama? What's his / her name? (I)

    ¿Cómo te llamas? What is your name? (I)

    Me llamo... My name is... (I)

la llave key (II)

el llavero key chain (I)

la llegada arrival (II)

llegar. to arrive

al — upon arriving (8-2)

    — a to reach, to get to (10-2)

    — tarde to arrive late (II)

llenar (el tanque) to fill (the tank) (II)

lleno, -a full (3-1)

llevar to wear (I); to take to carry, to bring (I)

llevarse bien / mal to get along well / badly (II)

llorar to cry (II)

llover (o → ue) to rain (II)

Llueve. It's raining. (I)

la lluvia rain (II)

lo que what (II)

lo it, him *m. dir. obj. pron.* (I)

    — siento. I'm sorry. (I)

el locutor, la locutora announcer (II)

lograr to achieve (6-1)

los the *m. pl.* (I); them *m. dir. obj. pron* (I)

    — dos, las dos both (I)

    — fines de semana on weekends (I)

    — lunes, los martes... on Mondays, on Tuesdays... (I)

luchar to fight (II, 8-2)

luego then (II)

el lugar place (I)

    en — de instead of (10-2)

    tener — to take place (1-2)

la Luna the Moon (II)

lunes Monday (I)

los lunes on Mondays (I)

la luz, *pl.* **las luces** light (I)

M ·

la **madrastra** stepmother (I)

la **madre (mamá)** mother (I)

maduro, -a mature (6-1)

el **maíz** corn (II)

mal bad, badly (I)

  pasarlo — to have a bad time (1-1)

el **malentendido** misunderstanding (4-2)

la **maleta** suitcase (II)

malo, -a bad (I)

maltratar to mistreat (10-1)

el **maltrato** mistreatment (10-1)

manejar to drive (II)

la **manera** way, manner (II, 3-1)

la **manifestación** demonstration (5-2)

la **mano** hand (I)

  darse la — to shake hands (II)

mantener:

  para — la salud to maintain one's health (I)

la **mantequilla** butter (I)

la **manzana** apple (I)

  el jugo de — apple juice (I)

mañana tomorrow (I)

la **mañana:**

  a las ocho de la — at eight (o'clock) in the morning (I)

  de la — in the morning (I)

el **maquillaje** make-up (II)

la **máquina** machine (6-2)

el **mar** sea (I)

la **maravilla** marvel, wonder (8-1)

maravilloso, -a wonderful (8-1)

la **marca** brand (II)

la **marcha** march (5-2)

los **mariscos** shellfish (II)

marrón brown (I)

martes Tuesday (I)

  los martes on Tuesdays (I)

marzo March (I)

más:

  ¿Qué —? What else? (I)

  — ...que more...than (I)

  — de more than (I)

  — o menos more or less (I)

matar to kill (II)

las **matemáticas:**

  la clase de — mathematics class (I)

los **materiales** supplies, materials (II)

mayo May (I)

la **mayonesa** mayonnaise (II)

mayor, *pl.* **mayores** *adj.* older (I)

los **mayores** grown-ups (II)

la **mayoría** the majority (6-2)

me (to / for) me *ind. obj. pron.* (I)

  — aburre(n) it / they bore(s) me (I)

  — encantaría I would love to... (5-2)

  — es imposible It is imposible for me ... (5-2)

  — estás poniendo nervioso, -a. You are making me nervous. (II)

  — falta(n)... I need... (I)

  — gustaría I would like (I)

  — gustó. I liked it. (I)

  — interesa(n) it / they interest(s) me (I)

  — interesaría I would be interested… (5-2)

  — llamo... My name is... (I)

  — importa(n) it matters (it's important) they matter to me (II)

  — parece que it seems to me (II)

  — queda(n) bien / mal. It / They fit(s) me well / poorly. (I)

  — quedo en casa. I stay at home. (I)

  ¿— trae...? Will you bring me...? *formal* (I)

el **mecánico, la mecánica** mechanic (II)

la **medalla** medal (1-2)

media, -o half (I)

  y — thirty, half past (I)

mediano, -a medium (II)

la **medicina** medicine (II)

el **médico, la médica** doctor (II)

el **medio ambiente** environment (II, 5-2)

los **medios de comunicación** media (6-2)

medir (e → i) to measure (7-1)

mejor:

  el / la —, los / las —es the best (I)

  —(es) que better than (I)

mejorar to improve (II, 4-2)

la **melodía** melody (2-2)

el **melón,** *pl.* **los melones** melon (II)

menor younger (I)

menos:

  a — que unless (9-2)

  más o — more or less (I)

  — ...que less / fewer...than (I)

  — de less / fewer than (I)

el **mensajero, la mensajera** messenger (5-1)

mentir (e → ie) to lie (II)

el **menú** menu (I)

menudo:

  a — often (I)

el **mercadeo** marketing (6-2)

el **mercado** market (II)

la **mercancía** merchandise (8-2)

la **merienda** snack (3-1)

el **mes** month (I)

la **mesa** table (I)

    poner la — to set the table (I)

la **mesita** night table (I)

la **meta** goal (1-2)

    meter:

        meter un gol to score a goal (II)

el **metro** subway (II)

la **mezcla** mixing (8-2)

    mezclar to mix (II)

la **mezquita** mosque (I)

    mi, mis my (I)

    mí:

        a — también I do (like to) too (I)

        a — tampoco I don't (like to) either (I)

        para — in my opinion, for me (I)

el **micrófono** microphone (2-2)

el **microondas** microwave (II)

el **miedo: tener — (de)** to be scared (of), to be afraid (of) (I)

el **miembro** member (II)

    ser miembro to be a member (II)

    mientras (que) while (II)

    miércoles Wednesday (I)

    mil thousand (I)

    militar *(adj.)* military (II)

    un millón de / millones de a million / millions of (II)

    mío, -a, -os, -as mine (II)

    mirar to look (at) (I)

la **misión** mission (8-2)

el **misionero, la misionera** missionary (8-2)

    mismo, -a same (I)

        pensar en sí — to think of one's self (4-2)

el **misterio** mystery (7-1)

    misterioso, -a mysterious (7-1)

el **mito** myth (7-2)

la **mochila** bookbag, backpack (I)

los **modales** manners (II)

el **modo** the way (10-2)

    de ese — in that way (10-1)

    de — que so, so that (10-2)

    mojado, -a wet (II)

    molestar to bother (II)

el **momento:**

    un — a moment (I)

la **moneda** coin (II)

el **mono** monkey (I)

las **montañas** mountains (I)

    montar:

        — a caballo to ride horseback (I)

        — en bicicleta to ride a bicycle (I)

        — en monopatín to skateboard (I)

el **monumento** monument (I)

    morado, -a purple (I)

    morirse to die (II)

la **mosca** fly (II)

la **mostaza** mustard (II)

    mostrar (ue) to show (2-1)

el **motivo** cause (10-1)

la **moto acuática** jetski (II)

    moverse (o → ue) to move (II)

el **movimiento** movement (2-1)

    mucho, -a a lot (I)

        — gusto pleased to meet you (I)

    muchos, -as many (I)

    mudarse to move to (6-1)

los **muebles** furniture (II)

    muerto, -a dead (II)

        la naturaleza muerta still life (2-1)

la **mujer** woman (I)

    la — de negocios businesswoman (II, 6-1)

las **muletas** crutches (II)

la **multa** ticket (II)

    mundial worldwide (10-2)

el **mundo** world (II)

la **muñeca** doll (II); wrist (II)

el **muñeco** action figure (II)

el **mural** mural (2-1)

el **músculo** muscle (II)

el **museo** museum (I)

el **músico, la música** musician (II)

el **musulmán, la musulmana** Muslim (8-1)

    muy very (I)

        — bien very well (I)

N

nacer to be born (II)
nada nothing (I)
  (A mí) no me gusta — ... I don't like to...at all. (I)
nadar to swim (I)
nadie no one, nobody (II)
la **naranja:**
  el jugo de — orange juice (I)
la **nariz,** *pl.* **las narices** nose (I)
la **natación** swimming (II)
la **naturaleza** nature (II, 1-1)
  la — muerta still life (2-1)
la **nave espacial** spaceship (7-1)
navegar to sail, to navigate (II)
  — en la Red to surf the Web (I, II)
necesario:
  Es —. It's necessary. (I)
necesitar:
  necesitas you need (I)
  necesito I need (I)
los **negocios** business (II)
  el hombre de — businessman (II, 6-1)
  la mujer de — businesswoman (II, 6-1)
negro:
  el pelo negro black hair (I)
nervioso, -a nervous (II)
nevar (e → ie) to snow (II)
Nieva. It's snowing. (I)
ni...ni neither...nor, not...or (I)
ningún, ninguno,-a no, none (II)
el **niñero, la niñera** babysitter (5-1)
la **niñez** childhood (10-1)
el **niño, la niña** young boy, young girl (I)
los **niños** children (I)
el **nivel** level (3-1)

No comas. Don't eat. (II)
No dejes Don't leave, don't let (II)
No escribas. Don't write. (II)
No estoy de acuerdo. I don't agree. (I)
No hables. Don't speak. (II)
¡No me digas! You don't say! (I)
no...todavía not yet (II)
la **noche:**
  a las ocho de la — at eight (o'clock) in the evening, at night (I)
  Buenas —s. Good evening. (I)
  de la — in the evening, at night (I)
  esta — this evening (I)
nos (to / for) us *ind. obj. pron.* (I)
  ¡— vemos! See you later! (I)
nosotros, -as we (I)
la **nota** grade, mark (in school) (II)
  sacar una buena — to get a good grade (II)
el **noticiero** newscast (II)
novecientos, -as nine hundred (I)
noveno, -a ninth (I)
noventa ninety (I)
noviembre November (I)
el **novio, la novia** boyfriend, girlfriend (I)
la **nube** cloud (II)
nuestro, -a, -os, -as our (I)
nueve nine (I)
nuevo, -a new (I)
el **número** shoe size (II)
nunca never (I)
nutritivo, -a nutritious (3-1)

O

o or (I)
  — sea que in other words (7-2)
obedecer to obey (II)
obediente obedient (II)
obligar to force (10-1)
la **obra:**
  la — de arte work of art (2-1)
  la — de teatro play (I)
observar to observe (II)
el **observatorio** observatory (7-1)
obtener to obtain, to get (1-2)
ochenta eighty (I)
ocho eight (I)
ochocientos, -as eight hundred (I)
el **ocio** free time (6-2)
octavo, -a eighth (I)
octubre October (I)
ocupado, -a busy (I)
ocupar to occupy (8-1)
ocurrir to occur (II)
ofender to offend (II)
la **oficina** office (II)
ofrecer to offer (II)
el **oído** ear (3-1)
oír to hear (II)
ojalá I wish (4-1)
el **ojo** eye (I)
la **olla** pot (II)
el **olor** odor (II)
olvidarse de to forget about (II)
  no te olvides de don't forget about (II)
once eleven (I)
opinar to think (10-2)
la **oportunidad** opportunity (II)
ordenado, -a neat (I)
organizar to organize (5-2)
el **origen** origin (7-2)
el **oro** gold (II)

la **orquesta** orchestra (II)

os (to / for) you *pl. fam. ind. obj. pron.* (I)

oscuro, -a dark (II)

el **oso de peluche** teddy bear (II)

el **otoño** fall, autumn (I)

otro, -a other, another (I)

otra vez again (I)

el **óvalo** oval (7-1)

¡Oye! Hey! (I)

ozono:

la **capa de —** ozone layer (9-2)

P . . . .

la **paciencia** pacience (II)

tener — to be patient (II)

paciente *adj.* patient (I)

pacífico, -a peaceful (10-2)

el **padrastro** stepfather (I)

el **padre (papá)** father (I)

los **padres** parents (I)

pagar (por) to pay (for) (I)

la **página Web** Web page (I)

el **país** country (I)

el **paisaje** landscape (1-1)

el **pájaro** bird (I)

la **palabra** word (II)

el **palacio** palace (II)

la **paleta** palette (2-1)

el **palo de golf** golf club (II)

el **pan** bread (I)

el **— tostado** toast (I)

la **pantalla** (computer) screen (I)

los **pantalones** pants (I)

los **— cortos** shorts (I)

las **papas** potatoes (I)

las **— fritas** French fries (I)

el **papel** role (II)

el **— picado** cut-paper decorations (I)

hacer el — de to play the role of (II)

la **papelera** wastepaper basket (I)

para for (I)

— + *inf.* in order to (I)

— la salud for one's health (I)

— mantener la salud to maintain one's health (I)

— mí in my opinion, for me (I)

¿ — qué sirve? What's it (used) for? (I)

— ti in your opinion, for you (I)

parado, -a to be standing (2-1)

el **paramédico, la paramédica** paramedic (II)

parar to stop (II)

pararse to stand up (2-2)

parecer:

me parece que it seems to me (II)

¿Qué te parece? What do you think? / How does it seem to you? (II)

parecerse a to look, to seem (like) (2-2)

la **pared** wall (I)

los **parientes** relatives (II)

el **parque** park (I)

el **— de diversiones** amusement park (I)

el **— nacional** national park (I)

la **parrilla** grill (II)

el / la **participante** participant (1-2)

participar (en) to participate (in) (II)

el **partido** game, match (I)

el **pasajero, la pasajera** passenger (II)

el **pasaporte** passport (II)

pasar to pass, to go (II)

¿Cómo lo pasaste? How was it (for you)? (I)

— la aspiradora to vacuum (I)

— tiempo con amigos to spend time with friends (I)

¿Qué pasa? What's happening? (I)

¿Qué te pasó? What happened to you? (I, II)

pasarlo bien / mal to have a good time / bad time (1-1)

el **pasatiempo** pastime (II)

pasear en bote to go boating (I)

el **pasillo** aisle (II)

el **paso** step (2-2)

la **pasta dental** toothpaste (II)
pastel *adj.* pastel (colors) (II)
el **pastel** cake (I)
los **pasteles** pastries (I)
las **pastillas** pills (II)
patinar to skate (I)
los **patines** skates (II)
el **patio de recreo** playground (II)
el **pavo** turkey (II)
la **paz** peace (II, 10-1)
    hacer las paces to make
    peace with (4-2)
el **peatón,** *pl.* **los peatones**
    pedestrian (II)
el **pecho** chest (3-1)
el **pedazo** piece, slice (II)
pedir (e → i) to order, to ask
    for (I)
    — ayuda to ask for help (II)
    — prestado, -a (a) to borrow
    (from) (II)
    — perdón to ask for
    forgiveness (4-2)
el **peine** comb (II)
pelar to peel (II)
la **pelea** fight (4-2)
    pelearse to fight (II)
la **película** film, movie (I)
    la — de acción action film
    (II)
    la — de ciencia ficción
    science fiction movie (I)
    la — de horror horror movie
    (I)
    la — policíaca crime movie,
    mystery (I)
    la — romántica romantic
    movie (I)
    ver una — to see a movie (I)
peligro:
    (en) peligro de extinción in
    danger of extinction,
    endangered (II, 9-2)

peligroso, -a dangerous (II)
pelirrojo, -a red-haired (I)
el **pelo** hair (I, II)
    el — canoso gray hair (I)
    el — castaño brown
    (chestnut) hair (I)
    el — negro black hair (I)
    el — rubio blond hair (I)
la **pelota** ball (II)
el **peluquero, la peluquera**
    hairstylist (6-1)
el **pensamiento** thought (10-1)
pensar (e → ie) to plan, to
    think (I)
    — en sí mismo(a) to think of
    one's self (4-2)
peor:
    el / la —, los / las —es the
    worst (I)
    —(es) que worse than (I)
pequeño, -a small (I)
perder (e → ie) to lose (II)
    — el equilibrio to lose one's
    balance (1-1)
perderse to get lost (1-1)
Perdón. Excuse me. (I)
perdonar to forgive (4-2)
perezoso, -a lazy (I)
el **perfume** perfume (I)
el **periódico** newspaper (I)
el **permiso de manejar** driver's
    license (II)
permitir to permit, to allow (II)
pero but (I)
el **perrito caliente** hot dog (I)
el **perro** dog (I)
la **persona** person (I)
el **personaje principal** main
    character (II)
pesar to weigh (7-1)
    a — de despite (10-2)
pesas:
    levantar — to lift weights (I)

el **pescado** fish *(as a food)* (I)
el **peso** weight (3-1)
el **pesticida** pesticide (9-1)
el **petróleo** oil (9-1)
    el derrame de — oil spill
    (9-2)
el **pez,** *pl.* **los peces** fish (II)
    picante spicy (II)
    picar to chop (II)
el **picnic** picnic (II)
el **pie** foot (I)
la **piedra** rock (II)
la **piel** skin (9-2)
la **pierna** leg (I)
la **pila** battery (9-1)
el / la **piloto** pilot (II)
la **pimienta** pepper (I)
el **pincel** brush (2-1)
    pintarse (las uñas) to paint, to
    polish (one's nails) (II)
el **pintor, la pintora** painter (II)
la **pintura** painting (2-1)
la **piña** pineapple (II)
la **piñata** piñata (I)
la **pirámide** pyramid (7-1)
la **piscina** swimming pool (I)
el **piso** story, floor (I)
    primer — second floor (I)
    segundo — third floor (I)
la **pizza** pizza (I)
    planear to plan (II)
el **planeta** planet (7-2)
la **planta** plant (II)
la **planta baja** ground floor (I)
el **plástico** plastic (I)
la **plata** silver (II)
el **plátano** banana (I)
el **plato** plate, dish (I)
    de — principal as a main
    dish (I)
    el — principal main dish (I)
la **playa** beach (I)
la **plaza** plaza (II)

la pluma feather (9-2)

la población population (8-1)

pobre poor (I)

pobrecito, -a poor thing (II)

la pobreza poverty (10-1)

poco:

   un — (de) a little (I)

poder to be able to (I)

(tú) puedes you can (I)

(yo) puedo I can (I)

el poder power (8-2)

poderoso, -a powerful (8-2)

el poema poem (2-2)

el / la poeta poet (2-2)

el / la policía police officer (II)

policíaca:

   la película — crime movie, mystery (I)

la política politics (II)

el político, la política politician (II)

el pollo chicken (I)

poner to put, to place (I)

pon *(command)* put, place (I)

   — la mesa to set the table (I)

   — una multa to give a ticket (II)

   — se to apply, to put on *(clothing, make up, etc.)* (II); to become (II)

(tú) pones you put (I)

(yo) pongo I put (I)

ponerse:

   — de acuerdo to reach an agreement (4-2)

   — el sol to set (the sun) (7-2)

por for (how long) (II); by, around, along, through (II)

   — ejemplo for example (II)

   — eso that's why, therefore (I)

   — lo general in general (II)

   — lo tanto therefore (6-1)

   ¿— qué? Why? (I)

— supuesto of course (I)

—...vez for the...time (II)

porque because (I)

portarse bien / mal to behave well / badly (II)

la posesión, *pl.* **las posesiones** possession (I)

el postre dessert (I)

   de — for dessert (I)

la práctica practice (II)

practicar deportes to play sports (I)

práctico, -a practical (I)

el precio price (I, II)

predecir to predict (6-2)

preferir (e [set arrow] ie) to prefer (I)

   (tú) prefieres you prefer (I)

   (yo) prefiero I prefer (I)

la pregunta question (II)

   hacer una — to ask a question (II)

el premio prize (II)

la prensa the press (10-2)

preocuparse worry (3-2)

preparar to prepare (I)

   —se to get ready (II)

la presentación, *pl.* **las presentaciones** presentation (I)

el presentador, la presentadora presenter (II)

presentarse to apply for a job (5-1)

la preservación conservation (9-2)

prestar atención to pay attention (II)

la primavera spring (I)

primer (primero), -a first (I)

   — piso second floor (I)

   el — plano foreground (2-1)

el primo, la prima cousin (I)

los primos cousins (I)

prisa hurry (II)

   tener — to be in a hurry (II)

probable likely (7-1)

probar (o → ue) to taste, to try (II)

probarse (o → ue) to try on (II)

el problema problem (I)

producir to produce (9-2)

el producto product (6-2)

la profesión, *pl.* **las profesiones** profession (II)

el profesor, la profesora teacher (I)

el programa program, show (I)

   el — de concursos game show (I)

   el — de dibujos animados cartoon (I)

   el — de entrevistas interview program (I)

   el — de estudios course of studies (II)

   el — de la vida real reality program (I)

   el — de noticias news program (I)

   el — deportivo sports program (I)

   el — educativo educational program (I)

   el — musical musical program (I)

el programador, la programadora programmer (6-1)

prohibir:

   se prohíbe it is forbidden (II)

prolongar to prolong, to extend (6-2)

promover (ue) to promote (9-1)

pronto soon (II)

   tan — como as soon as (9-1)

la **propina** tip (II)

propio, -a own (I)

proponer to propose, to suggest (10-2)

la **propuesta** proposal (10-2)

la **protección** protection (9-1)

proteger to protect (II, 5-2)

la **proteína** protein (3-1)

próximo, -a next (6-1)

el **proyecto** project (II)

   el **— de construcción** construction project (I)

el **público** audience (II)

el **pueblo** people (7-1), town (II)

puedes:

   (tú) — you can (I)

puedo:

   (yo) — I can (I)

el **puente** bridge (II)

la **puerta** door (I)

   la — de embarque departure gate (II)

pues well *(to indicate pause)* (I)

el **puesto** position (5-1), food stand (II)

la **pulsera** bracelet (I)

el **reloj —** watch (I)

las **puntadas** stitches (II)

   dar — to stitch *(surgically)* (II)

el **punto de vista** point of view (10-2)

puntual punctual (II, 5-1)

el **pupitre** desk (I)

puro, -a pure (II)

Q ●

que who, that (I)

qué:

   ¿Para — sirve? What's it (used) for? (I)

   ¡— + *adj.!* How...! (I)

   ¡— asco! How awful! (I)

   ¡— buena idea! What a good / nice idea! (I)

   ¿— clase de...? What kind of... ? (I)

   ¿— desean (Uds.)? What would you like? *formal* (I)

   ¿— día es hoy? What day is today? (I)

   ¿— es esto? What is this? (I)

   ¿— hiciste? What did you do? (I)

   ¿— hora es? What time is it? (I)

   ¡— lástima! What a shame! (II)

   ¿— más? What else? (I)

   ¿— pasa? What's happening? (I)

   ¡— pena! What a shame / pity! (I)

   ¿— quiere decir... ? What does...mean? (I)

   ¿— tal? How are you? (I)

   ¿— tal es...? How is (it)...? (II)

   ¿— te gusta hacer? What do you like to do? (I)

   ¿— te gusta hacer más? What do you like better (prefer) to do? (I)

   ¿— te parece? What do you think? / How does it seem to you? (I, II)

   ¿— te pasó? What happened to you? (I, II)

   ¿— tiempo hace? What's the weather like? (I)

   ¡— va! No way! (4-2)

quedar to fit, to be located (I, II)

quedarse to stay (II)

el **quehacer (de la casa)** (household) chore (I)

quejarse to complain (3-2)

quemar(se) to burn (oneself), to burn up (II)

querer (e → ie) to want (I)

   ¿Qué quiere decir...? What does...mean? (I)

   Quiere decir... It means... (I)

   quisiera I would like (I)

   (tú) quieres you want (I)

   (yo) quiero I want (I)

¿Quién? Who? (I)

químico, -a chemical (9-1)

quince fifteen (I)

quinientos. -as five hundred (I)

quinto, -a fifth (I)

el **quiosco** newsstand (II)

quisiera I would like (I)

quitar to take away, to remove (II)

   — el polvo to dust (I)

quizás maybe (I)

R •

la **radiografía** X-ray (II)

rápidamente quickly (I, II)

la **raqueta de tenis** tennis racket (II)

un rato a while (1-1)

el **ratón,** *pl.* **los ratones** (computer) mouse (I)

la **raza** race (8-2)

razón reason (10-1)

   tener — to be correct (I)

reaccionar to react (4-2)

la **realidad virtual** virtual reality (6-2)

realista realistic (I)

realizar to perform, to accomplish (2-2)

rebelarse to rebel, revolt (8-2)

el **recalentamiento global** global warming (9-2)

la **recepción** reception desk (II)

el / la **recepcionista** receptionist (5-1)

la **receta** prescription (II); recipe (II)

recetar to prescribe (II)

recibir to receive (I)

reciclar to recycle (I)

recientemente recently (II)

el **recipiente** container (9-1)

recoger to collect, to gather (I)

recomendar (e →ie) to recommend (II)

reconciliarse to become friends again (4-2)

reconocer (c → zc) to accept (4-2)

reconquistar to reconquer (8-1)

recordar (o → ue) to remember (II)

el **rectángulo** rectangle (7-1)

los **recuerdos** souvenirs (I)

   comprar — to buy souvenirs (I)

el **recurso natural** natural resource (9-1)

la **Red:**

   en la — online (I)

   navegar en la — to surf the Web (I)

el **redactor, la redactora** editor (6-1)

redondo,-a round (7-1)

reducir (zc) to reduce (II, 6-2)

reemplazar to replace (6-2)

la **referencia** reference (5-1)

el **refresco** soft drink (I)

el **refrigerador** refrigerator (II)

refugiarse to take shelter (1-1)

el **refugio** refuge, shelter (1-1)

regalar to give (II)

el **regalo** gift, present (I)

regatear to bargain (II)

registrar to inspect, to search *(luggage)* (II)

la **regla** rule (II)

regresar to return (I)

regular okay, so-so (I)

la **reina** queen (II)

reírse (e → í) to laugh (II)

la **reja** grate (8-1)

relajar(se) to relax (3-2)

el **relámpago** lightning (1-1)

el **reloj** clock (I)

   el — pulsera watch (I)

reparar to repair (5-1)

el **repartidor, la repartidora** delivery person (5-1)

repartir to deliver (5-1)

el **repelente de insectos** insect repellent (1-1)

repetir (e → i) to repeat (II)

el **reportero, la reportera** reporter (II)

el / la **representante** representative (1-2)

representar to represent (2-1)

el **requisito** requirement (5-1)

la **res** cattle (II)

rescatar to rescue (II)

el **rescate** rescue (9-2)

la **reseña** review (2-2)

la **reserva natural** nature preserve (9-2)

la **reservación,** *pl.* **las reservaciones** reservation (II)

reservado, -a reserved, shy (I)

resolver (o → ue) to resolve (4-2, 7-2), to solve (II)

respetar to respect (II)

el **respeto** respect (10-1)

respirar to breathe (3-2)

la **responsabilidad** responsibility (5-2)

responsable responsible (5-1)

el **restaurante** restaurant (I)

el **resultado** result, outcome (8-2)

resultar to result, to turn out (II)

el **reto** challenge (8-2)

el **retraso** delay (II)

el **retrato** portrait (2-1)

la **reunión,** *pl.* **las reuniones** meeting, gathering (II)

reunirse (u → ú) to meet (II)

el **rey** king (II)

rico, -a rich, tasty (I)

el **río** river (I)

la **riqueza** wealth (8-2)

el **ritmo** rhythm (2-2)

robar to rob, to steal (II)

la **roca** rock (1-1)

la **rodilla** knee (II)

rojo, -a red (I)

el **romano, la romana** Roman (8-1)

romántico, -a:

   la película — romantic movie (I)

romper to break (I)

—se to break, to tear (II)

la **ropa:**

la **tienda de —** clothing store (I)

rosado, -a pink (I)

roto, -a broken (II)

rubio, -a blond (I)

el **ruido** noise (II)

las **ruinas** ruins (II, 7-1)

S ·

sábado Saturday (I)

saber to know (how) (I, II)

(tú) sabes you know (how to) (I)

(yo) sé I know (how to) (I)

el **sabor** taste (II)

sabroso, -a tasty, flavorful (I)

el **sacapuntas,** *pl.* los **sacapuntas** pencil sharpener (I)

sacar:

— fotos to take photos (I)

— la basura to take out the trash (I)

— un libro to take out, to check out a book (II)

— una buena nota to get a good grade (II)

el **saco de dormir** sleeping bag (1-1)

sagrado, -a sacred (7-2)

la **sal** salt (I)

la **sala** living room (I)

la **— de clases** classroom (I)

la **— de emergencia** emergency room (II)

el **salario** (*o* el **sueldo**) salary (II, 5-1)

la **salchicha** sausage (I)

la **salida** exit (II); departure (II)

salir to leave, to go out (I)

— campeón, campeona to become the champion (1-2)

el **salón de belleza,** *pl.* los **salones de belleza** beauty salon (II)

los **salones de chat** chat rooms (II)

la **salsa** salsa, sauce (II)

la **— de tomate** ketchup (II)

saltar:

— a la cuerda to jump rope (II)

— una comida to skip a meal (3-1)

la **salud:**

para la — for one's health (I)

para mantener la — to maintain one's health (I)

saludable healthy (3-1)

saludar(se) to greet (II)

salvaje wild (9-2)

salvar to save (II)

el / la **salvavida** lifeguard (5-1)

la **sandía** watermelon (II)

el **sándwich de jamón y queso** ham and cheese sandwich (I)

la **sangre** blood (II)

la **sartén** frying pan (II)

satélite:

vía satélite via satellite (6-2)

satisfactorio, -a satisfactory (10-1)

se abre opens (II)

se cierra closes (II)

se me olvidó I forgot (II)

se murieron they died (II)

se prohíbe... it's forbidden... (II)

se puede you can (II)

sé:

(yo) — I know (how to) (I)

el **secador** blow dryer (II)

secarse to dry (II)

seco, -a dry (II)

el **secretario, la secretaria** secretary (II)

el **secreto** secret (4-1)

sed:

Tengo —. I'm thirsty. (I)

la **seda** silk (II)

seguir (e → i) to follow, to continue (II)

— (+ gerund) to keep on (doing) (5-1)

— una carrera to pursue a career (II, 6-1)

según according to (I)

— mi familia according to my family (I)

segundo, -a second (I)

— **piso** third floor (I)

seguro, -a sure (II)

seis six (I)

seiscientos, -as six hundred (I)

el **sello** stamp (II)

la **selva tropical** tropical rainforest (II, 9-2)

el **semáforo** stoplight (II)

la **semana** week (I)

este fin de — this weekend (I)

la — pasada last week (I)

los fines de — on weekends (I)

sembrar (ie) to plant (5-2)

la **semejanza** similarity (8-2)

el **sendero** trail (II)

sentado, -a to be seated (2-1)

el **sentimiento** feeling (2-1)

sentirse (e → ie) to feel (II)

— **fatal** to feel awful (3-2)

la **señal** sign (II)

la — de parada stop sign (II)

señor (Sr.) sir, Mr. (I)

señora (Sra.) madam, Mrs. (I)

señorita (Srta.) miss, Miss (I)

separar to separate (I)

septiembre September (I)

séptimo, -a seventh (I)

ser to be (I)

¿Eres...? Are you...? (I)

es he / she is (I)

fue it was (I)

no soy I am not (I)

— **miembro** to be a member (II)

soy I am (I)

ser:

será it, he, she will be (II)

serio, -a serious (I)

el **servicio** service (6-2)

el — social social service (5-2)

la **servilleta** napkin (I)

servir (e → i) to serve, to be useful (I)

¿En qué puedo —le? How can I help you? (I)

¿Para qué sirve? What's it (used) for? (I)

sirve para it is used for (I)

sesenta sixty (I)

setecientos, -as seven hundred (I)

setenta seventy (I)

sexto, -a sixth (I)

si if, whether (I)

sí yes (I)

siempre always (I)

siento:

Lo —. I'm sorry. (I)

la **sierra** sierra, mountain range (1-1)

siete seven (I)

el **siglo** century (2-1)

siguiente next, following (II)

la **silla** chair (I)

la — de ruedas wheelchair (II)

el **símbolo** symbol (7-2)

simpático, -a nice, friendly (I)

sin without (I)

— **duda** without a doubt (II)

— **embargo** however (1-2)

la **sinagoga** synagogue (I)

sincero, -a sincere (4-1)

sino but (7-2)

el **sitio Web** Web site (I)

sobre about (I)

sociable sociable (I)

la **sociedad** society (5-2)

¡Socorro! Help! (II)

el **software** software (I)

el **sol:**

Hace —. It's sunny. (I)

los anteojos de — sunglasses (I)

tomar el — to sunbathe (I)

solar solar (II)

el / la **soldado** soldier (8-2)

soler (ue) to usually do something (5-1)

solicitar to request (5-1)

la **solicitud de empleo** job application (5-1)

sólo only (I)

solo, -a alone (I)

soltero, -a single (6-1)

la **sombra** shadow (7-2)

Son las... It is... *(in telling time)* (I)

sonar (ue) (a) to sound like (2-2)

sonreír (e → í) to smile (II)

la **sopa de verduras** vegetable soup (I)

sorprenderse to be surprised (4-1)

la **sorpresa** surprise (II)

sospechoso, -a suspicious (10-2)

el **sótano** basement (I)

soy I am (I)

su, sus his, her, your *formal,* their (I)

subir to go up (II)

suceder to occur (1-1)

sucio, -a dirty (I)

la **sudadera** sweatshirt (I)

el **suelo** ground, floor (II)

sueño:

tener — to be sleepy (I)

el **suéter** sweater (I)

suficiente enough (9-1)

sufrir to suffer (10-1)

sugerir (e → ie) to suggest (II)

el **supermercado** supermarket (II)

supuesto:

por — of course (I)

el **surf de vela** windsurf (II)

T . . . .

tal:

   ¿Qué — ? How are you? (I)

tal vez maybe, perhaps (II)

talentoso, -a talented (I)

la **talla** size (II)

el **taller** workshop (2-1)

también also, too (I)

   a mí — I do (like to) too (I)

el **tambor** drum (2-2)

tampoco:

   a mí — I don't (like to) either (I)

tan so (II)

   — +*adj.*** so + ***adj.*** (II)

   — + ***adj.* + como** as + ***adj.*** + as (II)

   — pronto como as soon as (9-1)

el **tanque** tank (II)

el **tanteo** score (II)

tanto so much (I)

   por lo — therefore (6-1)

tantos, -as + ***noun*** + **como** as much / many + ***noun*** + as

tarde late, afternoon (I)

   a la una de la — at one (o'clock) in the afternoon (I)

   Buenas —s. Good afternoon. (I)

   de la — in the afternoon (I)

   esta — this afternoon (I)

   llegar — to arrive late (II)

la **tarea** homework (I)

la **tarjeta** card (I, II)

   la — de crédito credit card (II)

   la — de embarque boarding pass (II)

   la — postal postcard (II)

la **taza** cup (I)

te (to / for) you *sing. ind. obj. pron.* (I)

¿— gusta...? Do you like to...? (I)

¿— gustaría? Would you like? (I)

¿— gustó? Did you like it? (I)

— importa(n) it matters (it's important), they matter to you (II)

— ves (bien) you look (good) (II)

el **té** tea (I)

   el — helado iced tea (I)

el **teatro** theater (I)

   la obra de — play (2-1)

el **teclado** (computer) keyboard (I)

el **técnico, la técnica** technician (II)

la **tecnología** technology / computers (I)

   la clase de — technology / computer class (I)

tecnológico, -a technological (6-2)

la **tela sintética** synthetic fabric (II)

la **telenovela** soap opera (I)

el **televisor** television set (I)

el **tema** subject (2-1)

temer to fear (4-1)

el **templo** temple, Protestant church (I)

temprano early (I)

el **tenedor** fork (I)

tener to have (I)

   ¿Cuántos años tiene(n)...? How old is / are...? (I)

   — calor to be warm (I)

   — celos to be jealous (4-1)

   — cuidado to be careful (II)

   — en común to have in common (4-1)

   — en cuenta to take into account (6-2)

   — éxito to succeed, to be successful (II)

   — frío to be cold (I)

   — la culpa to be guilty (4-2)

   — lugar to take place (1-2)

   — miedo (de) to be scared (of), to be afraid (of) (I)

   — paciencia to be patient (II)

   — prisa to be in a hurry (II)

   — razón to be correct (I)

   — sueño to be sleepy (I)

Tengo hambre. I'm hungry. (I)

Tengo que... I have to... (I)

Tengo sed. I'm thirsty. (I)

Tiene(n)...años. He / She is / They are...(years old). (I)

el **tenis:**

   jugar al — to play tennis (I)

la **teoría** theory (7-2)

tercer (tercero), -a third (I)

terminar to finish, to end (I)

el **terremoto** earthquake (II)

el / la **testigo** witness (10-2)

ti you *fam. after prep.*

   ¿Y a —? And you? (I)

   para — in your opinion, for you (I)

el **tiempo:**

   a — on time (II)

   a — completo full time (5-1)

   a — parcial part time (5-1)

   el — libre free time (I)

   pasar — con amigos to spend time with friends (I)

   ¿Qué — hace? What's the weather like? (I)

la **tienda** store (I)

   la — de acampar tent (1-1)

   la — de descuentos discount store (I)

   la — de electrodomésticos household-appliance store (I)

la — de ropa clothing store (I)

Tiene(n)...años. He / She is / They are...(years old). (I)

la Tierra Earth (II, 7-2), **la tierra** land (8-2)

las tijeras scissors (II)

tímido, -a timid (II)

típico, -a typical (II)

el tío, la tía uncle, aunt (I)

los tíos uncles, aunt(s) and uncle(s) (I)

tirar to spill, to throw away (II)

no tires don't spill, don't throw away (II)

la toalla towel (II)

el tobillo ankle (II)

tocar la guitarra to play the guitar (I)

el tocino bacon (I)

todavía still (II)

todo el mundo everyone (II)

todos, -as all (I)

— los días every day (I)

la tolerancia tolerance (10-1)

tomar to take, to drink (3-1)

— conciencia de to become aware of (9-2)

— decisiones to make decisions (6-1)

— el sol to sunbathe (I)

— lecciones to take lessons (II)

— un curso to take a course (I)

los tomates tomatoes (I)

la tonelada ton (7-1)

tonto, -a silly, stupid (I)

torcerse (o → ue) to twist, to sprain (II)

la tormenta storm (II)

la torre tower (8-1)

la tortuga turtle (II)

la tos cough (3-1)

trabajador, -ora hardworking (I)

trabajar to work (I)

el trabajo work, job (I)

el — voluntario volunteer work (I)

traducir to translate (6-1)

el traductor, la traductora translator (6-1)

traer:

Le traigo... I will bring you... (I)

¿Me trae...? Will you bring me...? *formal* (I)

el tráfico traffic (II)

el traje suit (I)

el — de baño swimsuit (I)

tranquilo, -a calm (II)

tratar to treat (10-1)

— de to try to (II)

tratarse de to be about (II)

travieso, -a naughty, mischievous (II)

trazar to trace, to draw (7-1)

trece thirteen (I)

treinta thirty (I)

treinta y uno thirty-one (I)

tremendo, -a tremendous (I)

el tren train (I)

el — eléctrico electric train (II)

tres three (I)

trescientos, -as three hundred (I)

el triángulo triangle (7-1)

el triciclo tricycle (II)

triste sad (I)

el trofeo trophy (1-2)

la trompeta trumpet (2-2)

tropezar (e → ie) (con) to trip (over) (II)

el trueno thunder (1-1)

tu, tus your (I)

tú you *fam.* (I)

el / la turista tourist (II)

tuyo, -a, -os, -as yours (II)

U

Ud. (usted) you *formal sing.* (I)
Uds. (ustedes) you *formal pl.*
(I)
¡Uf! ugh!, yuck! (I)
último, -a the last / final (II)
un, una a, an (I)
— poco (de) a little (I)
la **una:**
    a la — at one o'clock (I)
único, -a only (8-1)
la **universidad** university (II)
uno one (I)
unos, -as some (I)
las **uñas** nails (II)
la **unidad** unity (8-1)
el **universo** universe (7-2)
usado, -a used (I)
usar la computadora to use
the computer (I)
el **uso** use (6-2)
usted (Ud.) you *formal sing.* (I)
ustedes (Uds.) you *formal pl.*
(I)
las **uvas** grapes (I)

V

las **vacaciones:**
    ir de — to go on vacation (I)
vacío, -a empty (3-1)
valiente brave (II)
el **valle** valley (II, 1-1)
el **valor** value (10-2)
¡Vamos! Let's go! (I)
vanidoso, -a vain, conceited
(4-1)
la **variedad** variety (8-2)
varios, -as various, several (II)
el **vaso** glass (I)
el **vecino, la vecina** neighbor (II)
veinte twenty (I)
veintiuno (veintiún)
twenty-one (I)
la **vela** sail (II)
vencer to beat (1-2)
la **venda** bandage (II)
el **vendedor, la vendedora**
vendor (II)
vender to sell (I)
el **veneno** poison (9-1)
venir to come (I)
la **ventana** window (I)
la **ventanilla** (airplane) window (II)
ver to see (I)
    a — ... Let's see... (I)
    ¡Nos vemos! See you later! (I)
    — la tele to watch television
    (I)
    — una película to see a
    movie (I)
el **verano** summer (I)
veras:
    ¿De —? Really? (I)
la **verdad** truth (II)
¿Verdad? Really? (I)
verde green (I)
el **vestido** dress (I)
vestirse (e → i) to get dressed
(II)

el **veterinario, la veterinaria**
veterinarian (II)
la **vez,** *pl.* **las veces:**
    a veces sometimes (I)
    en — de instead of (10-1)
    otra — again (I)
    una — allí once there (1-1)
vía satélite via satellite (6-2)
viajar to travel (I)
el **viaje** trip (I)
la **víctima** victim (II)
la **vida** life (II)
el **video** videocassette (I)
la **videocasetera** VCR (I)
los **videojuegos:**
    jugar — to play video games
    (I)
el **vidrio** glass (I)
viejo, -a old (I)
viernes Friday (I)
el **vinagre** vinegar (II)
violar to violate (10-2)
la **violencia** violence (II)
violento, -a violent (I)
visitar to visit (I)
    — salones de chat to visit
    chat rooms (I, II)
la **vitamina** vitamin (3-1)
la **vivienda** housing (6-2)
vivir to live (I)
vivo, -a bright *(color)* (II);
living, alive (II)
el **vóleibol:**
    jugar al — to play volleyball (I)
volver (o → ue) to return (II)
    —se loco, -a to go crazy (II)
volverse (ue) to become (2-1)
votar to vote (10-1)
la **voz,** *pl.* **las voces** voice (II)
el **voluntario, la voluntaria**
volunteer (I)
vosotros, -as you *fam. pl.* (I)
el **vuelo** flight (II)
vuestro, -a, -os, -as your (I)

Vocabulario inglés-español

The *English-Spanish Vocabulary* contains all active vocabulary from the text, including vocabulary presented in the grammar sections.

A dash (—) represents the main entry word. For example, **to play —** after **baseball** means **to play baseball.**

The number following each entry indicates the chapter in which the word or expression is presented. A Roman numeral (I) indicates that the word was presented in REALIDADES 1. A roman numeral II indicates the word was presented in REALIDADES 2.

The following abbreviations are used in this list: *adj.* (adjective), *dir. obj.* (direct object), *f.* (feminine), *fam.* (familiar), *ind. obj.* (indirect object), *inf.* (infinitive), *m.* (masculine), *pl.* (plural), *prep.* (preposition), *pron.* (pronoun), *sing.* (singular).

A ·

a, an un, una (I)
a little un poco (de) (I)
a lot mucho, -a (I)
a while un rato (1-1)
able capaz (6-1)
able:
to **be — to** poder (o → ue) (I)
about sobre (I)
abstract abstracto, -a (2-1)
abuse el abuso (10-1)
to **accept** reconocer (c → z) (4-2)
—(me) the way (I am)
aceptar tal como soy (4-1)
accident el accidente (II)
to **accompany** acompañar (II)
to **accomplish** realizar (2-2)

according to según (I)
— my family según mi familia (I)
accountant el contador, la contadora (II, 6-1)
to **accuse** acusar (4-2)
accused el acusado, la acusada (10-2)
to **achieve** lograr (6-1)
acquainted:
to be — with conocer (I, II)
acting la actuación (II)
action figure el muñeco (II)
actor el actor (I)
actress la actriz, *pl.* las actrices (I)
to **add** añadir (II)
address:
e-mail — la dirección electrónica (I)
adequate adecuado, -a (10-1)
adolescence la adolescencia (10-1)
adolescent el / la adolescente (10-1)
to **adopt** adoptar (8-2)
advance el avance (6-2)
advice el consejo (3-2)
to **advise** aconsejar (3-2)
aerobics ejercicios aeróbicos (3-2)
aerosol el aerosol (9-2)
to **affect** afectar (9-2)
affectionate cariñoso, -a (4-1)
afraid:
to be — (of) tener miedo (de) (I)
African africano, -a (8-2)
after después de (I)
afternoon:
at one (o'clock) in the afternoon a la una de la tarde (I)

Good —. Buenas tardes. (I)
in the — de la tarde (I)
this — esta tarde (I)
afterwards después (I)
again otra vez (I)
against contra (II, 1-2), en contra de (5-2)
age la edad (3-1)
agitated agitado, -a (II)
ago hace + *time expression* (I)
agree:
I —. Estoy de acuerdo. (I)
I don't —. No estoy de acuerdo. (I)
Agreed. De acuerdo. (II)
air conditioner el aire acondicionado (II)
airline la línea aérea (II)
airplane el avión (I)
airport el aeropuerto (II)
aisle el pasillo (II)
alarm clock el despertador (I)
alien el / la extraterrestre (II)
alive vivo, -a (II)
all todos, -as (I)
allergy la alergia (3-1)
almost casi (I, II)
alone solo, -a (I)
along por (II, II)
already ya (I)
also también (I)
always siempre (I)
am:
I — (yo) soy (I)
I — not (yo) no soy (I)
ambitious ambicioso, -a (6-1)
ambulance la ambulancia (II)
among entre (II)
amusement park el parque de diversiones (I)
amusing divertido, -a (I)
ancestor el antepasado, la antepasada (8-2)

and y (I)

— **you?** ¿Y a ti? *fam.* (I);
¿Y tú? *fam.* (I);
¿Y usted (Ud.)? *formal* (I)

angry enojado, -a (II)

to **get —** enojarse (II)

animal el animal (I)

ankle el tobillo (II)

anniversary el aniversario (II)

another otro, -a (I)

to **announce** anunciar (II)

announcement el anuncio (II)

announcer el locutor, la
locutora (II)

to **answer** contestar (II)

ant la hormiga (II)

antibiotic el antibiótico (3-1)

antique antiguo, -a (II)

any algunos, -as (II),
cualquier, -a (7-2)

anyone alguien (II)

Anything else? ¿Algo más? (I)

apartment el apartamento (I)

— **building** el edificio de
apartamentos (II)

to **appear** aparecer (zc) (1-1, 7-2)

to **applaud** aplaudir (II)

applause el aplauso (2-2)

apple la manzana (I)

— **juice** el jugo de manzana (I)

to **apply for a job** presentarse
(5-1)

to **apply (the law)** aplicar
(las leyes) (10-1)

to **approach** acercarse a (1-1)

appropriate apropiado, -a (3-1)

approximately
aproximadamente (II)

April abril (I)

aqueduct el acueducto (8-1)

Arab el / la árabe (8-1)

arch el arco (8-1)

archaeologist el arqueólogo,

la arqueóloga (7-1)

architect el arquitecto, la
arquitecta (II, 6-1)

architecture la arquitectura
(8-1)

Are you...? ¿Eres...? (I)

arm el brazo (I)

around por (II, II); alrededor de
(II)

to **arrest** arrestar (II)

arrival la llegada (II)

to **arrive late** llegar tarde (II)

art class la clase de arte (I)

article el artículo (II)

artist el artista, la artista (II)

artistic artístico, -a (I)

arts las artes (II)

martial — las artes marciales
(II)

as como (I), al igual que (7-2), a
medida que (10-2)

— **a child** de niño (II);
de pequeño (II)

— **a main dish** de plato
principal (I)

— **far as, up to** hasta (II)

— **soon as** en cuanto,
tan pronto como (9-1)

— **though it were** como si
fuera (6-2)

as much / many + *noun* + as
tantos, -as + *noun* + como

as + *adj.* + as tan + *adj.* + como
(II)

to **ask for** pedir (e → i) (I)

to **—forgiveness** pedir perdón
(4-2)

— **help** pedir ayuda (II)

to **ask a question** hacer una
pregunta (II)

asleep dormido, -a (II)

aspiration la aspiración (10-2)

aspirin la aspirina (3-1)

astronomer el astrónomo, la
astrónoma (7-2)

to **assimilate** asimilar(se) (8-1)

assist atender (5-1)

to **assure** asegurar (10-2)

at:

— **dawn** al amanecer (1-1)

— **dusk** al anochecer (1-1)

— **eight (o'clock)** a las ocho
(I)

— **eight (o'clock) at night** a
las ocho de la noche (I)

— **eight (o'clock) in the
evening** a las ocho de la
noche (I)

— **eight (o'clock) in the
morning** a las ocho
de la mañana (I)

— **home** en casa (I)

— **one (o'clock)** a la una (I)

— **one (o'clock) in the
afternoon** a la una
de la tarde (I)

— **the beginning** al principio
(1-2)

— **the end** al final (II)

— **what time?** ¿A qué hora? (I)

ATM el cajero automático (II)

atmosphere la atmósfera (9-2)

attempt el intento (7-2)

to **attend** asistir a (II)

attentive atento, -a (II)

athlete el / la atleta (II)

attraction(s) la atracción, *pl.*
las atracciones (I)

audience el público (II)

audition la audición, *pl.* las
audiciones (II)

auditorium el auditorio (II)

August agosto (I)

aunt la tía (I)

aunt(s) and uncle(s) los tíos (I)

authority la autoridad (10-1)

autumn el otoño (I)
avenue la avenida (II)
avocado el aguacate (II)
to avoid evitar (3-1)
awards ceremony la entrega
de premios (2-1)

B ....

baby el / la bebé, bebé (II)
babysitter el niñero, la niñera
(5-1)
back la espalda (II)
to back (each other) apoyarse
(4-1)
background el fondo (2-1)
backpack la mochila (I)
bacon el tocino (I)
bad malo, -a (I); mal (I)
badly mal (I)
bag la bolsa (I)
baked al horno (II)
balanced equilibrado, -a (3-1)
balcony el balcón, pl. los
balcones (8-1)
bald eagle el águila calva, pl.
las águilas calvas (9-2)
ball la pelota (II)
balloon el globo (I)
banana el plátano (I)
band (musical) la banda (II),
el conjunto (2-2)
bandage la venda (II)
bank el banco (II)
banker el banquero, la
banquera (6-2)
bargain la ganga (II)
to bargain regatear (II)
baseball:
to play — jugar al béisbol (I)
basement el sótano (I)
basket la cesta (II)
basketball:
to play — jugar al basquétbol
(I)
bathroom el baño (I)
battery la pila (9-1)
battle la batalla (8-2)
to be ser (I); estar (I)
He / She is / They are...
(years old). Tiene(n)... años. (I)

How old is / are...? ¿Cuántos
años tiene(n)...? (I)
to — + present participle estar
+ present participle (I)
to — a member ser miembro
(II)
to — able to poder (o → ue) (I)
to — about tratarse de (II)
to — acquainted with
conocer (I)
to — afraid (of) tener miedo
(de) (I)
to — based on estar basado, -a
en (II)
to — born nacer (II)
to — cold tener frío (I)
to — correct tener razón (I)
to — delighted alegrarse (4-1)
to — exhausted caerse de
sueño (3-2)
to — formed by componerse
de (8-2)
to — going to + verb ir a + inf.
(I)
to — guilty tener la culpa
(4-2)
to — in a good / bad mood
estar de buen / mal humor (3-2)
to — in charge of encargarse
(5-1), estar a cargo de (9-1)
to — in fashion estar de moda
(II)
to — in love with estar
enamorado, -a de (II)
to — involved in dedicarse a
(6-1)
to — jealous tener celos (4-1)
to — located quedar (I, II)
to — mistaken estar
equivocado, -a (4-2)
to — moved emocionarse (1-2)
to — online estar en línea (I)

to — **proud of** estar orgulloso, -a de (1-2)

to — **scared (of)** tener miedo (de) (I)

to — **sitting** sentado, -a (2-1)

to — **sleepy** tener sueño (I), caerse de sueño (3-2)

to — **standing** parado, -a (2-1)

to — **subject to** estar sujeto, -a a (10-1)

to — **sure** estar seguro, -a (II)

to — **surprised** sorprenderse (4-1)

to — **useful** servir (I)

to — **warm** tener calor (I)

to **become** convertirse (en) (7-2)

to — **aware of** tomar conciencia de (9-2)

to **become (a profession)** hacerse (profesión) (6-1)

beach la playa (I)

to **benefit** beneficiar (5-2)

beans los frijoles (II)

bear el oso (I)

to **beat** batir (II), vencer (1-2)

beautiful bello, -a (II), hermoso, -a (1-1)

beauty salon el salón de belleza, *pl.* los salones de belleza (II)

because porque (I), ya que (7-1)

— **of** a causa de (II)

to **become** ponerse (II), volverse (ue) (2-1)

to — **friends again** reconciliarse (4-2)

to — **the champion** salir campeón / campeona (1-2)

bed la cama (I)

to make the — hacer la cama (I)

bedroom el dormitorio (I)

beefsteak el bistec (I)

before antes de (I), anteriormente (8-1), ante (10-2)

to **begin** empezar (e → ie) (I)

to **behave well / badly** portarse bien / mal (II)

behavior el comportamiento (4-2)

behind detrás de (I)

belief la creencia (7-2)

belt el cinturón, *pl.* los cinturones (II)

benefits los beneficios (II, 5-1)

best:

the — el / la mejor, los / las mejores (I)

better than mejor(es) que (I)

between entre (II)

bicycle:

to ride a — montar en bicicleta (I)

bilingual bilingüe (II)

bill la cuenta (I)

binder:

three-ring — la carpeta de argollas (I)

binoculars los binoculares (1-1)

bird el pájaro (I), el ave (9-2)

birthday el cumpleaños (I)

Happy —! ¡Feliz cumpleaños! (I)

black hair el pelo negro (I)

block la cuadra (II)

blocks los bloques (II)

blond hair el pelo rubio (I)

blood la sangre (II)

blouse la blusa (I)

blow dryer el secador (II)

blue azul (I)

to **board** abordar (II)

boat el barco (I)

sail— el bote de vela (II)

boating:

to go — pasear en bote (I)

to **boil** hervir (e → ie) (II)

bone el hueso (II)

bonfire la fogata (II)

book el libro (I)

bookbag la mochila (I)

bookshelf el estante (I)

bookstore la librería (I)

boots las botas (I)

to **bore** aburrir (I)

it / they bore(s) me me aburre(n) (I)

to get bored aburrirse (II)

boring aburrido, -a (I)

to **borrow (from)** pedir prestado, -a (a) (II)

boss el jefe, la jefa (6-1)

both los dos, las dos (I), ambos (10-1)

to **bother** molestar (II)

bottle la botella (I)

to **bowl** jugar a los bolos (II)

box la caja (I)

boy el chico (I)

young — el niño (I)

boyfriend el novio (I)

bracelet la pulsera (I)

brand la marca (II)

brave valiente (II)

bread el pan (I)

to **break** romper (I); romperse (II)

breakfast el desayuno (I)

for — en el desayuno (I)

to **breathe** respirar (3-2)

bridge el puente (II)

bright *(color)* vivo, -a (II)

to **bring** traer (I), llevar (I)

I will — **you...** Le traigo... (I)

Will you — **me... ?** ¿Me trae... ? (I)

broth el caldo (II)

brother el hermano (I)

brothers; brother(s) and sister(s) los hermanos (I)

brown marrón (I)

— **(chestnut) hair** el pelo castaño (I)

brush el cepillo (II), el pincel (2-1)

   tooth— el cepillo de dientes (II)

   to brush (one's teeth) cepillarse (los dientes) (II)

to **build** construir (i → y) (5-2)

to **burn a CD** grabar un disco compacto (I)

to **burn (oneself), to burn up** quemar(se) (II)

bus el autobús, *pl.* los autobuses (I)

business los negocios (II), la empresa (6-1)

   —man el hombre de negocios (II, 6-1)

   —woman la mujer de negocios (II, 6-1)

busy ocupado, -a (I)

but pero (I), sino (7-2)

butter la mantequilla (I)

to **buy** comprar (I)

   — souvenirs comprar recuerdos (I)

by por (II, II)

   — + *vehicle* en + *vehicle* (I)

   — hand a mano (II)

C ....

café el café (I)

cake el pastel (I)

calcium el calcio (3-1)

to **call:**

   to — on the phone llamar por teléfono (II)

to **calculate** calcular (7-1)

calculator la calculadora (I)

calm tranquilo, -a (II)

camera la cámara (I)

   digital — la cámara digital (I)

camp el campamento (I)

campaign la campaña (5-2)

can la lata (I)

can:

   I — (yo) puedo (I)

   you — (tú) puedes (I)

candy los dulces (I)

canned enlatado, -a (II)

cap la gorra (I)

to **capture** capturar (II)

car el coche (I)

carbohydrate el carbohidrato (3-1)

card la tarjeta (I)

   credit — la tarjeta de crédito (II)

post— la tarjeta postal (II)

cardboard el cartón (I)

career la carrera (II)

careful cuidadoso, -a (6-1)

carrots las zanahorias (I)

to carry llevar (I)

   — out cumplir con (5-1)

cartoon el programa de dibujos animados (I)

cash el dinero en efectivo (II)

   to cash a check cobrar un cheque (II)

cash register la caja (II)

cashier el cajero, la cajera (II)

cast el yeso (II)

castle el castillo (II)

cat el gato (I)

to **catch** atrapar (9-2)

cathedral la catedral (II)

cattle la res (II)

cause la causa (II), el motivo (10-1)

CD:

   to burn a — grabar un disco compacto (I)

to **celebrate** celebrar (I)

center, downtown el centro (I, II)

centigrade degree el grado centígrado (3-1)

centimeter el centímetro (7-1)

century el siglo (2-1)

cereal el cereal (I)

ceremony la ceremonia (1-2)

certain:

   it is — es cierto (II)

certificate el certificado (1-2)

chain la cadena (I)

chair la silla (I)

   wheel— la silla de ruedas (II)

challenge el reto (8-2)

champion el campeón, la campeona, *pl.* los campeones (II)

championship el campeonato (II)

to **change** cambiar (II)

   to — one's mind cambiar de opinión (4-1)

   channel *(TV)* el canal (I)

to **chat** charlar (II)

chat rooms los salones de chat (II)

cheap barato, -a (I)

check:

   to cash a — cobrar un cheque (II)

   traveler's — el cheque de viajero (II)

personal — el cheque personal (II)

to **check (luggage)** facturar (el equipaje) (II)

to **check out** sacar (II)

cheerleader el animador, la animadora (II)

chemical químico, -a (9-1)

cherry la cereza (II)

chess el ajedrez (II)

chest el pecho (3-1)

chicken el pollo (I)

childhood la niñez (10-1)

childish infantil (I)

children los hijos (I); los niños (I)

to **chop** picar (II)

chore:

household **—** el quehacer (de la casa) (I)

chorus, choir el coro (II)

to **choose** escoger (II)

Christian cristiano, -a (8-1)

church la iglesia (I)

Protestant **—** el templo (I)

circle el círculo (7-1)

citizen el ciudadano, la ciudadana (5-2)

citizenship la ciudadanía (5-2)

city la ciudad (I)

civilization la civilización (7-1)

class la clase (I)

classical clásico, -a (2-2)

classified ad el anuncio clasificado (5-1)

classroom la sala de clases (I)

clean limpio, -a (I)

to **clean the bathroom** limpiar el baño (I)

cleaning la limpieza (9-2)

client el / la cliente (5-1)

to **climb (a rock or mountain)** escalar (1-1)

clock el reloj (I)

to **close** cerrar (II)

close (to) cerca (de) (I)

closed cerrado, -a (II)

closes se cierra (II)

closet el armario (I)

clothing store la tienda de ropa (I)

club el club, *pl.* los clubes (II)

athletic **—** el club atlético (II)

coach el entrenador, la entrenadora (II)

coat el abrigo (I)

coffee el café (I)

coin la moneda (II)

cold:

It's **—.** Hace frío. (I)

to be **—** tener frío (I)

to **collaborate** colaborar (4-2)

to **collect** recoger (I)

to **collect** coleccionar (II)

collection la colección, *pl.* las colecciones (II)

to **collide with** chocar con (II)

cologne el agua de colonia (II)

colony la colonia (8-2)

color:

What **— ... ?** ¿De qué color ... ? (I)

— s los colores (I)

comb el peine (II)

to **come** venir (I)

comedy la comedia (I)

comfortable cómodo, -a (II)

comical cómico, -a (I)

commentary el comentario (II)

to **communicate** comunicarse (I, 6-2)

I **—** (yo) me comunico (I)

you **—** (tú) te comunicas (I)

community la comunidad (I)

— center el centro de la comunidad (5-2)

compact disc el disco compacto (I)

to burn a **—** grabar un disco compacto (I)

company la compañía (5-1)

compass la brújula (1-1)

to **compete** competir (e → i) (II)

competition la competencia (II)

to **complain** quejarse (3-2)

complicated complicado, -a (I, II)

composition la composición, *pl.* las composiciones (I)

to **compute** calcular (7-1)

computer la computadora (I)

— graphics los gráficos (I)

— keyboard el teclado (I)

— mouse el ratón (I)

— screen la pantalla (I)

— science la computación (5-10)

— s / technology la tecnología (I)

laptop **—** la computadora portátil (I)

to use the **—** usar la computadora (I)

conceited vanidoso, -a (4-1)

to **concentrate** concentrarse (3-2)

concert el concierto (I)

conflict el conflicto (4-2)

to **confront** enfrentarse (8-2)

to **congratulate** felicitar (II)

Congratulations! ¡Felicidades! (II), ¡Felicitaciones! (1-2)

to **conquer** conquistar (8-1)

conquest la conquista (8-1)

conservation la preservación (9-2)

to **conserve** conservar (II)

considerate considerado, -a (4-1)

construction la construcción (8-1)

— project el proyecto de construcción (I)

to **contain** contener (3-1)

container el recipiente (9-1)

contest el concurso (II)

  beauty — el concurso de belleza (II)

to **contribute** contribuir (u → y) (7-2)

cook el cocinero, la cocinera (6-1)

to **cook** cocinar (I)

cookie la galleta (I)

cooking oil el aceite (II)

corn el maíz (II)

corner la esquina (II)

correct:

  to be — tener razón (I)

to **cost** costar (o → ue) (I)

  How much does (do)... —? ¿Cuánto cuesta(n)? (I)

cotton el algodón (II)

cough la tos (3-1)

counselor el consejero, la consejera (5-1)

to **count on** contar con (4-1)

country el país (I)

countryside el campo (I)

course:

  to take a — tomar un curso (I)

  — of studies el programa de estudios (II)

cousin la prima, el primo (I)

  — s los primos (I)

to **cover** cubrir (7-1)

cramp el calambre (3-2)

to **crash into** chocar con (II)

to **create** crear (I)

  to — a Web page crear una página Web (II)

crime el crimen (II)

  — movie la película policíaca (I)

criminal el / la criminal (II)

critic el crítico, la crítica (II)

to **criticize** criticar (4-2)

to **cross** cruzar (II)

crunches los abdominales (3)

crutches las muletas (II)

to **cry** llorar (II)

cup la taza (I)

to **cure** curar (6-2)

curtains las cortinas (I)

custom la costumbre (II)

customs la aduana (II)

customs officer el aduanero, la aduanera (II)

to **cut** cortar (I, II)

  to — oneself cortarse (II)

  to — one's hair cortarse el pelo (II)

  to — the lawn cortar el césped (I)

cut-paper decorations el papel picado (I)

D ....

to **damage** dañar (9-1)

dance el baile (I), la danza (2-2)

to **dance** bailar (I)

dancer el bailarín, la bailarina (II)

dangerous peligroso, -a (II)

to **dare** atreverse (4-2)

daring atrevido, -a (I)

dark oscuro, -a (II)

date:

  What is the —? ¿Cuál es la fecha? (I)

date la cita (II)

date of birth la fecha de nacimiento (5-1)

daughter la hija (I)

day el día (I)

  every — todos los días (I); cada día (I)

  What — is today? ¿Qué día es hoy? (I)

day-care center la guardería infantil (II)

dead muerto, -a (II)

December diciembre (I)

to **decide** decidir (I)

to **decorate** decorar (I)

decorations las decoraciones (I)

to **decrease** disminuir (9-2)

dedicated dedicado, -a (5-1)

delay el retraso (II)

delicious delicioso, -a (I)

delighted encantado, -a (I)

to **deliver** repartir (5-1)

delivery person el repartidor, la repartidora (5-1)

demand la demanda (6-2)

to **demand** exigir (3-2)

democratic democrático, -a (10-2)

demonstration la manifestación (5-2)

dentist el / la dentista (II)

department store el almacén, *pl.* los almacenes (I)

departure gate la puerta de embarque (II)

to **depend on** depender de (9-1)

deodorant el desodorante (II)

descendants la descendencia (8-2)

desert el desierto (II, 1-1)

design el diseño (7-1)

to **design** diseñar (6-1)

designer el diseñador, la diseñadora (II, 6-1)

desk el pupitre (I); el escritorio (I)

despite aunque (3-1), a pesar de (10-2)

dessert el postre (I)

  for — de postre (I)

to **destroy** destruir (i → y) (II)

destruction la destrucción (II)

to **detain** detener (10-2)

detective el / la detective (II)

to **develop** desarrollar (3-2)

development el desarrollo (6-2)

diameter el diámetro (7-1)

dictionary el diccionario (I)

to **die** morirse (II)

Did you like it? ¿Te gustó? (I)

diet la dieta (3-1)

difference of opinion la diferencia de opinión (4-2)

difficult difícil (I)

digital camera la cámara digital (I)

to **diminish** disminuir (9-2)

dining room el comedor (I)

dinner la cena (I)

dinosaur el dinosaurio (II)

diploma el certificado (1-2)

direct directo, -a (II)

direction la dirección, *pl.* las direcciones (II)

dirty sucio, -a (I)

to **disappear** desaparecer (zc) (6-2)

disaster:

  It was a —. Fue un desastre. (I)

discount store la tienda de descuentos (I)

discouraged desanimado, -a (1-2)

to **discover** descubrir (6-2)

to **discriminate** discriminar (10-1)

to **discuss** discutir (II)

dish el plato (I)

  as a main — de plato principal (I)

  main — el plato principal (I)

diskette el disquete (I)

disobedient desobediente (II)

distance la distancia (7-1)

to **do** hacer (I)

  — *(command)* haz (I)

  — you like to ... ? ¿Te gusta ... ? (I)

  I — (yo) hago (I)

  to — a project hacer un proyecto (II)

  to — a search hacer una búsqueda (II)

  to — gymnastics hacer gimnasia (II)

  to — push ups hacer flexiones (3-2)

  you — (tú) haces (I)

  What did you —? ¿Qué hiciste? (I)

doctor el médico, la médica (II)

doctor's / dentist's office el consultorio (II)

document el documento (I)

dog el perro (I)

  to feed the — dar de comer al perro (I)

doll la muñeca (II)

to **dominate** dominar (8-1)

to **donate** donar (5-2)

Don't eat. No comas. (II)

Don't leave, Don't let No dejes (II)

Don't speak. No hables. (II)

Don't write. No escribas. (II)

door la puerta (I)

to **doubt** dudar (II, 7-1)

to **download** bajar (información) (I)

drama el drama (I)

to **draw** dibujar (I)

dress el vestido (I)

  — code el código de vestimenta (10-1)

dresser la cómoda (I)

to **drink** beber (I), tomar (3-1)

drinks las bebidas (I)

to **drive** manejar (II)

driver el conductor, la conductora (II)

driver's license el permiso de manejar (II)

drum el tambor (2-2)

dry seco, -a (II)

to **dry** secarse (II)

due to ya que (7-1), debido a (10-2)

during durante (I)

to **dust** quitar el polvo (I)

duty el deber (10-1)

DVD player el lector DVD (I)

E ·

e-mail:
 — address la dirección electrónica (I)
 to write — escribir por correo electrónico (I)
ear el oído (3-1)
early temprano (I)
to **earn** *(money)* ganar (II)
Earth la Tierra (II, 7-2)
earthquake el terremoto (II)
earrings los aretes (I)
easy fácil (I)
to **eat** comer (I)
eating habit el hábito alimenticio (3-1)
eclipse el eclipse (7-2)
ecological ecológico, -a (II)
economical económico, -a (II, 9-1)
editor el redactor, la redactora (6-1)
to **educate** educar (5-2)
educational program el programa educativo (I)
efficient eficiente (II, 6-1)
eggs los huevos (I)
eight ocho (I)
eight hundred ochocientos, -as (I)
eighteen dieciocho (I)
eighth octavo, -a (I)
eighty ochenta (I)
either tampoco (I)
 I don't (like to) — a mí tampoco (I)
elbow el codo (II)
electricity la electricidad (II, 9-1)
elegant elegante (II)
elevator el ascensor (II)
eleven once (I)

to **eliminate** eliminar (II, 2-1)
else:
 Anything —? ¿Algo más? (I)
 What —? ¿Qué más? (I)
emergency room la sala de emergencia (II)
empire el imperio (8-2)
employee el empleado, la empleada (II)
empty vacío, -a (3-1)
to **encourage** fomentar (9-1)
to **end** terminar (I)
endangered (en) peligro de extinción (II)
to **endure** aguantar (3-2)
energy la energía (II, 3-1)
 — source la fuente de energía (6-2)
engineer el ingeniero, la ingeniera (II, 6-1)
English class la clase de inglés (I)
to **enjoy** disfrutar de (II), gozar (de) (10-1)
enormous enorme (II)
enough bastante (I), suficiente (9-1)
Enough! ¡Basta! (II)
to **enter** entrar (I)
enterprising emprendedor, -a (6-1)
enthusiasm el entusiasmo (2-2)
entrance la entrada (II)
environment el medio ambiente (II, 5-2)
equality la igualdad (10-1)
to **escape** escaparse (II)
especially especialmente (I)
establish establecer (sz) (8-2)
ethnic group el grupo étnico (8-1)
European europeo, -a (8-2)
even when aunque (3-1)
evening:
 Good —. Buenas noches. (I)

 in the — de la noche (I)
 this — esta noche (I)
every day cada día (I), todos los días (I)
everyone todo el mundo (II)
evidence la evidencia (7-1)
exactly en punto (II)
to **exaggerate** exagerar (2-2)
to **examine, to check** examinar (II)
to **excavate** excavar (7-1)
excessive excesivo, -a (9-2)
exchange el intercambio (8-2)
to **exchange** intercambiar (10-2)
excited entusiasmado, -a, emocionado, -a (II), animado, -a (1-2)
to **exchange** cambiar (II)
excursion, short trip la excursión, *pl.* las excursiones (II)
Excuse me. Perdón. (I)
to **exercise** hacer ejercicio (I)
to **exhaust** agotar(se) (9-1)
to **exist** existir (7-1)
exit la salida (II)
exit departure (II)
to **expel** expulsar (8-1)
expensive caro, -a (I)
experience la experiencia (I)
to **explain** explicar (II)
explanation la explicación (4-2)
to **exploit** explotar (9-2)
explosion la explosión, *pl.* las explosiones (II)
to **express (oneself)** expresar(se) (2-1)
to **extend** prolongar (6-2)
extinction:
 in danger of — en peligro de extinción (9-2)
extracurricular extracurricular
 — activities las actividades extracurriculares (II)
eye el ojo (I)

F ·························

face la cara (II)

to face enfrentarse (8-2)

face-to-face cara a cara (I)

factory la fábrica (6-2)

failure el fracaso (II)

fair justo, -a (5-2)

to fall caerse (II)

   I — (yo) me caigo (II)

   to — asleep dormirse (II)

   to — in love (with)

   enamorarse (de) (II)

   you — (tú) te caes (II)

fall el otoño (I)

famous famoso, -a (II), (2-1)

fan el aficionado, la aficionada (II)

fantastic fantástico, -a (I)

far (from) lejos (de) (I)

farmer el agricultor, la agricultora (II)

to fascinate fascinar (II)

fascinating fascinante (I)

fast rápidamente (I)

father el padre (papá) (I)

favorite favorito, -a (I)

to fear temer (4-1)

feather la pluma (9-2)

February febrero (I)

to feed the dog dar de comer al perro (I)

to feel sentirse (e → ie) (II)

   to — awful sentirse fatal (3-2)

feeling el sentimiento (2-1)

fever la fiebre (3-1)

fewer:

   — ...than menos... que (I)

   — than... menos de... (I)

fiber la fibra (3-1)

field el campo (6-2)

fifteen quince (I)

fifth quinto, -a (I)

fifty cincuenta (I)

fight la pelea (4-2)

to fight luchar (II), (8-2), pelearse (II)

figure la figura (2-1)

to fill (the tank) llenar (el tanque) (II)

film la película (I)

final último, -a (II)

finance las finanzas (6-1)

to find encontrar (o →ue) (II)

   — out averiguar (6-1), enterarse (6-2)

finger el dedo (I)

to finish terminar (I)

fire el incendio (II); el fuego (II)

firefighter el bombero, la bombera (II)

firewood la leña (II)

fireworks los fuegos artificiales (II)

firm la compañía (5-1)

first primer (primero), -a (I)

fish el pescado (I); el pez, pl. los peces (II)

   to go —ing ir de pesca (I)

to fit:

   It / They —(s) me well / poorly. Me queda(n) bien / mal. (I)

five cinco (I)

five hundred quinientos, -as (I)

to fix (one's hair) arreglarse (el pelo) (II)

flag la bandera (I)

flashlight la linterna (1-1)

flavorful sabroso, -a (I)

to flex flexionar (3-2)

flexible flexible (5-1)

flight el vuelo (II)

flight attendant el / la auxiliar de vuelo (II)

flood la inundación, pl. las inundaciones (II)

floor el piso (I)

   ground — la planta baja (I)

   second — el primer piso (I)

   third — el segundo piso (I)

flour la harina (II)

flower la flor, pl. las flores (I)

flu la gripe (3-1)

fly la mosca (II)

folder la carpeta (I)

to follow seguir (e → i) (II)

following siguiente (II)

food la comida (I), los alimentos (3-1)

food stand el puesto (II)

foot el pie (I)

football:

   to play — jugar al fútbol americano (I)

for para (I)

   — breakfast en el desayuno (I)

   — lunch en el almuerzo (I)

   — me para mí (I)

   — you para ti (I)

for (how long) por (II, II)

   — example por ejemplo (II)

   — the ... time por ... vez (II)

forbidden:

   It is — . Se prohíbe. (II)

to force obligar (10-1)

foreground el primer plano (2-1)

forest el bosque (II), (1-1)

to forget about olvidarse de (II)

   don't — no te olvides de (II)

to forgive perdonar (4-2)

fork el tenedor (I)

fortunately afortunadamente (II)

forty cuarenta (I)

to found fundar (8-1)

fountain la fuente (II)

four cuatro (I)

four hundred cuatrocientos, -as (I)

fourteen catorce (I)

fourth cuarto, -a (I)

free gratuito, -a (10-1), libre (10-2)

free time el tiempo libre (I), el ocio (6-2)

French fries las papas fritas (I)

frequently frecuentemente (II)

fresh fresco, -a (II)

Friday viernes (I)

fried frito, -a (II)

friendly simpático, -a (I)

friendship la amistad (4-1)

frightened asustado, -a (II)

from de (I); desde (II)

— **now on** de hoy en adelante (6-2)

Where are you —? ¿De dónde eres? (I)

frozen congelado, -a (II)

fruit salad la ensalada de frutas (I)

frying pan la sartén (II)

full lleno, -a (3-1)

— **time** a tiempo completo (5-1)

fun divertido, -a (I)

function la función (7-1)

to **function, to work** funcionar (II, 10-1)

fundamental fundamental (10-2)

to **fundraise** juntar fondos (5-2)

funny gracioso, -a (I); cómico, -a (I)

furious furioso, -a (II)

furniture los muebles (II)

future el futuro (II)

G ....

gadget el aparato (6-2)

game el partido (I)

game show el programa de concursos (I)

garage el garaje (I)

garden el jardín (I)

garlic el ajo (II)

gasoline la gasolina (II)

to **gather** recoger (I)

gathering la reunión, *pl.* las reuniones (II)

gel el gel (II)

gene, genes el gene, *pl.* los genes (6-2)

generally generalmente (I)

generous generoso, -a (II)

genetics la genética (6-2)

geometric(a) geométrico, -a (7-1)

gesture el gesto (2-2)

to **get** obtener (1-2)

to — **a good grade** sacar una buena nota (II)

to — **along well / badly** llevarse bien / mal (II)

to — **dressed** vestirse (e → i) (II)

to — **lost** perderse (1-1)

to — **married** casarse (con) (II)

to — **ready** prepararse (II)

to — **rid of** deshacerse de (9-1)

to — **up** levantarse (II)

gift el regalo (I)

gift certificate el cupón de regalo, *pl.* los cupones de regalo (II)

girl la chica (I)

young — la niña (I)

girlfriend la novia (I)

to **give** dar (I); regalar (II)

to — **a speech** dar un discurso (II)

to — **a ticket** poner una multa (II)

glass el vaso (I); el vidrio (I)

global warming el recalentamiento global (9-2)

gloves los guantes (I)

to **go** ir (I); pasar (II)

Let's —! ¡Vamos! (I)

to be —ing to + *verb* ir a + *inf.* (I)

to — **to bed** acostarse (o → ue) (II)

to — **boating** pasear en bote (I)

to — **camping** ir de cámping (I)

to — **crazy** volverse loco (II)

to — **down** bajar (II)

to — **fishing** ir de pesca (I)

to — **on foot** ir a pie (II)

to — **on vacation** ir de vacaciones (I)

to — **out** salir (I)

to — **shopping** ir de compras (I)

to — **to school** ir a la escuela (I)

to — **up** subir (II)

goal *(in sports)* el gol (II), la meta (1-2)

to score a — meter un gol (II)

god, goddess el dios, la diosa (7-2)

going to con destino a (II)

gold el oro (II)

golf:

— **club** el palo de golf (II)

to **play —** jugar al golf (I)

good bueno (buen), -a (I)

— **afternoon.** Buenas tardes. (I)

— **evening.** Buenas noches. (I)

— **gracious** caramba (II)

— **morning.** Buenos días. (I)

Good-bye! ¡Adiós! (I)

good-looking guapo, -a (I)

gossipy chismoso, -a (4-1)

to **govern** gobernar (8-1)

government el gobierno (9-1)

grade *(in school)* la nota (II)

  to get a good — sacar una buena nota (II)

to **graduate** graduarse (u → ú) (II, 6-1)

graduation la graduación, *pl.* las graduaciones (II)

grandfather el abuelo (I)

grandmother la abuela (I)

grandparents los abuelos (I)

grapes las uvas (I)

grate la reja (8-1)

gray gris (I)

  — hair el pelo canoso (I)

greasy grasoso, -a (II)

Great! ¡Genial! (I)

green verde (I)

  — beans las judías verdes (I)

  — house effect el efecto invernadero (9-2)

to greet saludar(se) (II)

to **grill** asar (II)

grill la parrilla (II)

grilled asado, -a (II)

ground floor la planta baja (I)

ground, floor el suelo (II)

to **grow** crecer (9-1)

grown-ups los mayores (II)

guarantee la garantía (10-2)

to **guarantee** garantizar (5-2)

guide el / la guía (II)

guidebook la guía (II)

guilty culpable (10-2)

guitar:

to play the — tocar la guitarra (I)

gym el gimnasio (I)

gymnastics la gimnasia (II)

H ....

hail granizo (1-1)

—hail caer granizo (1-1)

hair el pelo (I)

  black — el pelo negro (I)

  blond — el pelo rubio (I)

  brown (chestnut) — el pelo castaño (I)

  gray — el pelo canoso (I)

hair stylist el peluquero, la peluquera (6-1)

half media, -o (I)

  — past y media *(in telling time)* (I)

ham and cheese sandwich el sándwich de jamón y queso (I)

hamburger la hamburguesa (I)

hand la mano (I)

  to shake —s darse la mano (II)

handicrafts la artesanía (II)

happiness la felicidad (10-1)

happy contento, -a (I); alegre (II)

  — birthday! ¡Feliz cumpleaños! (I)

harmony armonía (4-2)

hardworking trabajador, -ora (I)

to **have** tener (I)

  I — to... tengo que + *inf.* (I)

  to — a barbecue hacer una parrillada (II)

  to — a birthday cumplir años (II)

  to — a cold estar resfriado, -a (3-1)

  to — a good / bad time pasarlo bien / mal (1-1)

  to — a picnic hacer un picnic (II)

  to — fun divertirse (e → ie) (II)

  to — in common tener en común (4-1)

  to — just... acabar de + *inf.* (I)

  to — lunch almorzar (o → ue) (II)

to **have** haber *(as an auxiliary verb)* (II)

he él (I)

he / she is es (I)

He / She is / They are... (years old). Tiene(n) ... años. (I)

head la cabeza (I)

health:

  for one's — para la salud (I)

  to maintain one's — para mantener la salud (I)

healthy saludable (3-1)

to **hear** oír (II)

heart el corazón (3-2)

heat la calefacción (II)

to **heat** calentar (e → ie) (II)

height estatura (3-1), el alto (7-1)

Hello! ¡Hola! (I)

to **help** ayudar (I), atender (5-1)

  How can I — you? ¿En qué puedo servirle? (I)

help la ayuda (II)

her su, sus *possessive adj.* (I); la *dir. obj. pron.* (I); le *ind. obj. pron.* (I)

here aquí (I)

heritage la herencia (8-2)

hero el héroe (II)

heroine la heroína (II)

Hey! ¡Oye! (I)

to **hide (oneself)** esconder(se) (II)

high alto, -a (II)

high school el colegio (II)

highway la carretera (II)

hill la colina (II)

him lo *dir. obj. pron.* (I); le *ind. obj. pron.* (I)

his su, sus (I)

historical histórico, -a (II)

hockey el hockey (II)

to **hold a position** desempeñar un cargo (6-1)

hole el agujero (9-2)

holiday el — festivo (II)

home la casa (I)

  at — en casa (I)

  — office el despacho (I)

  (to) — a casa (I)

home la casa (I)

  — for the elderly el hogar de ancianos (5-2)

homeless people la gente sin hogar (5-2)

homework la tarea (I)

honest honesto, -a (4-1)

to **hope (for)** esperar (4-1)

horrible horrible (I)

horror movie la película de horror (I)

horseback:

  to ride — montar a caballo (I)

hospital el hospital (I)

hospitality la hospitalidad (6-2)

hot caliente (II)

  — dog el perrito caliente (I)

  It's —. Hace calor. (I)

hotel el hotel (I)

hour:

  in the ... — en la ... hora *(class period)* (I)

house la casa (I)

household:

  —-appliance store la tienda de electrodomésticos (I)

  — chore el quehacer (de la casa) (I)

housing la vivienda (6-2)

how!

  — + *adj.!* ¡Qué + *adj.*! (I)

  — awful! ¡Qué asco! (I)

How? ¿Cómo? (I)

  — are you? ¿Cómo está Ud.? *formal* (I); ¿Cómo estás? *fam.* (I); ¿Qué tal? *fam.* (I)

  — can I help you? ¿En qué puedo servirle? (I)

  — do you go to...? ¿Cómo se va...? (II)

  — do you make ...? ¿Cómo se hace ...? (II)

  — do you say... ? ¿Cómo se dice... ? (I)

  — does it (do they) fit (you)? ¿Cómo te queda(n)? (I)

  — does it seem to you? ¿Qué te parece? (II)

  — is ... spelled? ¿Cómo se escribe ...? (I)

  — is (it)...? ¿Qué tal es...? (II)

  — long...? ¿Cuánto tiempo hace que...? (II)

  — many? ¿Cuántos, -as? (I)

  — much does (do) ... cost? ¿Cuánto cuesta(n) ... ? (I)

  — old is / are ... ? ¿Cuántos años tiene(n) ... ? (I)

  — was it (for you)? ¿Cómo lo pasaste? (I)

however sin embargo (1-2)

to **hug** abrazar(se) (II)

hundred:

  one — cien (I)

hungry:

  I'm —. Tengo hambre. (I)

hunting la caza (9-2)

hurricane el huracán, *pl.* los huracanes (II)

to **hurt** doler (o → ue) (I, II)

to **hurt oneself** lastimarse (II)

hurry prisa (II)

  to be in a — tener prisa (II)

husband el esposo (I)

I . . . .

I yo (I)

  — am soy (I)

  — am not no soy (I)

  — do too a mí también (I)

  — don't either a mí tampoco (I)

  — don't think so. Creo que no. (I)

  — forgot se me olvidó (II)

  — have seen he visto (II)

  — 'll do as I please haré lo que me dé la gana (6-1)

  — stay at home. Me quedo en casa. (I)

  — think ... Creo que ... (I)

  — think so. Creo que sí. (I)

  — will bring you ... Le traigo ... (I)

  — wish ojalá (4-1)

  — would like Me gustaría (I); quisiera (I)

  — would be interested ... Me interesaría ... (5-2)

  — would love to ... Me encantaría ... (5-2)

  —'m hungry. Tengo hambre. (I)

  —'m sorry. Lo siento. (I)

  —'m thirsty. Tengo sed. (I)

ice el hielo (9-2)

ice cream el helado (I)

iced tea el té helado (I)

I.D. card el carnet de identidad (II)

to **identify oneself with** identificarse con (2-2)

if si (I)

to **ignore** ignorar (4-2)

illness la enfermedad (6-2)

image la imagen (2-1)

immediately inmediatamente (II)

  impatient impaciente (I)

important importante (I)
impress impresionar (1-1)
impressive impresionante (I)
to **improve** mejorar (II, 4-2)
in en (I)
  — addition to además de (6-1)
  — danger of extinction (en) peligro de extinción (II)
  — favor of a favor de (5-2)
  — front of delante de (I)
  — general por lo general (II)
  — love with enamorado, -a de (II)
  — my opinion para mí (I)
  — other words o sea que (7-2)
  — order to para + *inf.* (I)
  — that way de ese modo (10-1)
  — the ... hour en la ... hora (class period) (I)
  — the middle of en medio de (II)
  — your opinion para ti (I)
include incluir (3-1)
to **increase** aumentar (6-2)
incredible increíble (I)
industry industria (6-2)
inequity la desigualdad (10-2)
inexpensive barato, -a (I)
inexplicable inexplicable (7-1)
influence la influencia (8-1)
to **influence** influir (i → y) (2-1)
information la información (I)
  — technology la informática (6-2)
ingredient el ingrediente (II)
inhabitant el / la habitante (7-2)
inhuman inhumano, -a (10-1)
injection, shot la inyección, *pl.* las inyecciones (II)
injured herido, -a (II)
injured person el herido, la herida (II)
injustice la injusticia (10-1)

innocent inocente (10-2)
insect repellent el repelente de insectos (1-1)
inside dentro de (II)
to **insist** insistir en (II)
to **inspect** registrar (II)
to **inspire** inspirar (2-1)
instead of en vez de (10-1), en lugar de (10-2)
to **integrate** integrarse (8-1)
intelligent inteligente (I)
interest el interés (II)
to **interest** interesar (I)
  it / they interest(s) me me interesa(n) (I)
interesting interesante (I)
to **interpret** interpretar (2-2)
interpretation la interpretación (2-2)
intersection el cruce de calles (II)
interview la entrevista (II, 5-1)
  — program el programa de entrevistas (I)
to **interview** entrevistar (II)
intimate íntimo, -a (4-1)
to **invade** invadir (8-1)
to **invent** inventar (6-2)
invention el invento (6-2)
to **investigate** investigar (II)
iron el hierro (3-1)
is es (I)
  he / she — es (I)
  it — true es cierto (II)
  it la, lo *dir. obj. pron.* (I)
  — depends depende (II)
  — fits (they fit) me well / poorly. Me queda(n) bien / mal. (I)
  — has been... Hace + *time* + que... (II)
  — is ... Son las *(in telling time)* (I)

  — is forbidden... Se prohíbe... (II)
  — is impossible for me... Me es imposible... (5-2)
  — is made of... Está hecho, -a de... (II)
  — is one o'clock. Es la una. (I)
  — is the ... of ... Es el *(number)* de *(month) (in telling the date)* (I)
  — is the first of ... Es el primero de *(month)*. (I)
  — seems to me me parece que (II)
  — was fue (I)
  —was not me! ¡Yo no fui! (4-2)
  — was a disaster. Fue un desastre. (I)
  —'s a ... es un / una ... (I)
  —'s cold. Hace frío. (I)
  —'s hot. Hace calor. (I)
  —'s necessary. Es necesario. (I)
  —'s raining. Llueve. (I)
  —'s snowing. Nieva. (I)
  —'s sunny. Hace sol. (I)
it / he / she will be ser: será (II)
itinerary el itinerario (II)

J

jacket la chaqueta (I)
January enero (I)
jealous celoso, -a (4-1)
jeans los jeans (I)
jetski la moto acuática (II)
jewelry (gold, silver) las joyas (de oro, de plata) (II)
jewelry store la joyería (I)
Jew(ish) judío, -a (8-1)
job el trabajo (I)
  — **application** la solicitud de empleo (5-1)
to **join** juntarse (II)
judge el juez, la jueza, *pl.* los jueces (II, 6-1)
to **judge** juzgar (10-2)
juice:
  apple — el jugo de manzana (I)
  orange — el jugo de naranja (I)
July julio (I)
to **jump (rope)** saltar (a la cuerda) (II)
June junio (I)
junk food la comida basura (3-1)
jury el jurado (10-2)
just:
  to have — ... acabar de + *inf.* (I)
justice la justicia (10-2)

K

to **keep (a secret)** guardar un secreto (4-1)
to **keep on (doing)** seguir (+ present participle) (5-1)
ketchup la salsa de tomate (II)
key la llave (II)
key chain el llavero (I)
keyboard (computer) el teclado (I)
to **kill** matar (II)
kind:
  What — **of ... ?** ¿Qué clase de ... ? (I)
kind amable (4-1)
king el rey (II)
to **kiss** besar(se) (II)
kitchen la cocina (I)
knee la rodilla (II)
knife el cuchillo (I)
to **know** saber (I); conocer (I, II)
  I — **(yo)** conozco (I)
  I — **(how to)** (yo) sé (I)
  you — (tú) conoces (I)
  you — **(how to)** (tú) sabes (I)
knowledge los conocimientos (5-1)

L

laboratory el laboratorio (I)
lack la falta (9-2)
ladder la escalera (II)
lake el lago (I)
lamp la lámpara (I)
language el idioma (II)
land la tierra (8-2)
landscape el paisaje (1-1)
language la lengua (8-2)
laptop computer la computadora portátil (I)
large grande (I)
last último, -a (II)
last:
  — **night** anoche (I)
  — **week** la semana pasada (I)
  — **year** el año pasado (I)
to **last** durar (I)
late tarde (I)
to **arrive** — llegar tarde (II)
later:
  See you — ¡Hasta luego!; ¡Nos vemos! (I)
to **laugh** reírse (e → í) (II)
law *(study of)* el derecho (II)
law la ley (II), (5-2)
lawyer el abogado, la abogada (II, 6-1)
lazy perezoso, -a (I)
leading man el galán (II)
league la liga (II)
to **learn** aprender (a) (I)
leather el cuero (II)
to **leave** salir (I)
to **leave** dejar (II)
  don't — no dejes (II)
  to— footprints dejar huellas (8-1)
Leave me alone. Déjame en paz. (II)

left:
  to the — (of) a la izquierda (de) (I)
leg la pierna (I)
legend la leyenda (7-2)
lemonade la limonada (I)
length el largo (7-1)
less:
  — ... than menos ... que (I)
  — than menos de (I)
to let dejar (II)
  don't — no dejes (II)
Let's go! ¡Vamos! (I)
Let's see ... A ver ... (I)
letter la carta (I, II)
  to mail a — echar una carta (II)
lettuce la lechuga (I)
level el nivel (3-1)
liberty la libertad (10-1)
library la biblioteca (I)
to lie mentir (e → ie) (II)
life la vida (II)
lifeguard el / la salvavida (5-1)
to lift weights levantar pesas (I)
to light encender
light *(color)* claro, -a (II)
light la luz, *pl.* las luces (I)
to light encender (e → ie) (II)
lightning el relámpago (1-1)
like como (I)
to like:
  Did you — it? ¿Te gustó? (I)
  Do you — to ...? ¿Te gusta ... ? (I)
  He / She doesn't — ... No le gusta ... (I)
  He / She —s ... Le gusta ... (I); A él / ella le gusta(n) ... (I)
  I don't — to ... (A mí) no me gusta ... (I)
  I don't — to ... at all. (A mí) no me gusta nada ... (I)

I — ... Me gusta ... (I)
I — to ... (A mí) me gusta ... (I)
I — to ... a lot (A mí) me gusta mucho ... (I)
  — to ... better (A mí) me gusta más ... (I)
I —d it. Me gustó. (I)
I would — Me gustaría (I); quisiera (I)
What do you — better (prefer) to do? ¿Qué te gusta hacer más? (I)
What do you — to do? ¿Qué te gusta hacer? (I)
What would you — ? Qué desean (Uds.)? (I)
Would you —? ¿Te gustaría? (I)
You — ... Te gusta ... (I)
likely probable (7-1)
likewise igualmente (I)
to limit limitar (9-1)
lips los labios (II)
to listen to music escuchar música (I)
little:
  a — un poco (de) (I)
to live vivir (I)
living vivo, -a (II)
living room la sala (I)
locker el armario (I, II, 10-1)
long largo, -a (I)
to look:
  to — (at) mirar (I)
  to — for buscar (I)
  to — like parecerse a (2-2)
loose flojo, -a (II)
to lose perder (e → ie) (II)
  —one's balance perder el equilibrio (1-1)
lot:
  a — mucho, -a (I)
to love encantar (I)

He / She —s ... A él / ella le encanta(n) ... (I)
I / You — ... Me / Te encanta(n)... (I)
love el amor (II)
loving cariñoso, -a (4-1)
low bajo, -a (II)
luggage el equipaje (II)
  to check — facturar el equipaje (II)
lunch el almuerzo (I)
  for — en el almuerzo (I)
lyrics la letra (2-2)

M ·

machine máquina (6-2)
madam (la) señora (Sra.) (I)
magazines:
  to read — leer revistas (I)
majority la mayoría (6-2)
mail:
  — carrier el cartero, la cartera (II)
  — box el buzón, *pl.* los buzones (II)
  to — a letter echar una carta (II)
main:
  — character el personaje principal (II)
  — dish el plato principal (I)
  as a — de plato principal (I)
to **maintain one's health** para mantener la salud (I)
to **make:**
  — *(command)* haz (I)
  to — a living ganarse la vida (II)
  to — an effort hacer un esfuerzo (1-2)
  to — decisions tomar decisiones (6-1)
  to — the bed hacer la cama (I)
  to — noise hacer ruido (II)
  to — peace with hacer las paces (4-2)
  You are making me nervous. Me estás poniendo nervioso, -a. (II)
make-up el maquillaje (II)
mall el centro comercial (I)
man el hombre (I)
  older — el anciano (I)
business— el hombre de negocios (II)
manager el / la gerente (II, 5-1)
manner la manera (II)

manners los modales (II)
many muchos, -as (I)
  How —? ¿Cuántos, -as? (I)
March marzo (I)
march la marcha (5-2)
mark *(in school)* la nota (II)
  to get a good — sacar una buena nota (II)
market el mercado (II)
marketing el mercadeo (6-2)
married casado, -a (6-1)
marvel la maravilla (8-1)
match el fósforo (II)
match el partido (I)
materials los materiales (II)
mathematics class la clase de matemáticas (I)
matter el asunto (10-1)
mature maduro, -a (6-1)
May mayo (I)
maybe quizás (I)
mayonnaise la mayonesa (II)
me me *ind. obj. pron* (I)
  for — para mí (I), me (I)
  it matters / they matter to
    — me importa(n) (II)
  it seems to — me parece que (II)
  — too a mí también (I)
  to — me (I)
  with — conmigo (I)
meal la comida (I)
to **mean:**
  It —s ... Quiere decir ... (I)
  What does ... —? ¿Qué quiere decir ... ? (I)
to **measure** medir (i) (7-1)
meat la carne (I)
mechanic el mecánico, la mecánica (II)
medal la medalla (2-1)
media los medios de comunicación (6-2)

medicine la medicina (II)
medium mediano, -a (II)
meddlesome entrometido, -a (4-1)
to **meet** reunirse (u → ú) (II)
meeting la reunión, *pl.* las reuniones (II), el encuentro (8-2)
melody la melodía (2-2)
melon el melón, *pl.* los melones (II)
to **melt** derretir (9-2)
member el miembro (II)
  to be a — ser miembro (II)
to **memorize** aprender de memoria (II)
menu el menú (I)
merchandise la mercancía (8-2)
messenger el mensajero, la mensajera (5-1)
messy desordenado, -a (I)
microphone el micrófono (2-2)
microwave el microondas (II)
military *(adj.)* militar (II)
milk la leche (I)
million un millón (II)
  —s of millones de (II)
mine mío, -a, -os, -as (II)
mirror el espejo (I)
Miss (la) señorita (Srta.) (I)
missing:
  to be — faltar (I)
mission la misión (8-2)
missionary el misionario, la misionaria (8-2)
to **mistreat** maltratar (10-1)
mistreatment el maltrato (10-1)
to **mistrust** desconfiar (4-1)
misunderstanding el malentendido (4-2)
to **mix** mezclar (II)
mixing la mezcla (8-2)
moment:
  a — un momento (I)

Monday lunes (I)
  on —s los lunes (I)
money el dinero (I)
money exchange la casa de cambio (II)
monkey el mono (I)
month el mes (I)
monument el monumento (I)
moon la Luna (II)
more:
  — ... than más ... que (I)
  — or less más o menos (I)
  — than más de (I)
morning:
  Good —. Buenos días. (I)
  in the — de la mañana (I)
mosque la mezquita (I)
mother la madre (mamá) (I)
mountain range sierra (1-1)
mountains las montañas (I)
mouse (computer) el ratón (I)
mouth la boca (I)
to move moverse (o → ue) (II), andar (1-1), mudarse (6-1)
movement el movimiento (2-1)
movie la película (I)
  action — la película de acción (II)
  — theater el cine (I)
  to see a — ver una película (I)
to mow the lawn cortar el césped (I)
Mr. (el) señor (Sr.) (I)
Mrs. (la) señora (Sra.) (I)
much:
  so — tanto (I)
mural el mural (2-1)
muscle el músculo (II)
museum el museo (I)
music:
  to listen to — escuchar música (I)
  —al program el programa musical (I)

musician el músico, la música (II)
Muslim el musulmán, la musulmana ((8-1)
must deber (I)
  one — hay que (I)
mustard la mostaza (II)
my mi (I); mis (I)
  — name is ... Me llamo ... (I)
mysterious misterioso, -a (7-1)
myth el mito (7-2)
mystery la película policíaca (I), el misterio (7-1)

N ....

name:
  My — is ... Me llamo ... (I)
  What is your —? ¿Cómo te llamas? (I)
  What's his / her —? ¿Cómo se llama? (I)
nails las uñas (II)
napkin la servilleta (I)
narrow estrecho, -a (II)
native el / la indígena (8-2)
naughty travieso, -a (II)
national park el parque nacional (I)
natural preserve la reserva natural (9-2)
natural resource el recurso natural (9-1)
nature la naturaleza (II, 1-1)
near cerca (de) (I)
neat ordenado, -a (I)
necessary:
  It's —. Es necesario. (I)
neck el cuello (II)
necklace el collar (I)
to need
  I — necesito (I)
  I — ... Me falta(n) ... (I)
  you — necesitas (I)
neighbor el vecino, la vecina (II)
neighborhood el barrio (I)
neither ... nor ni ... ni (I)
nervous nervioso, -a (II)
never nunca (I)
new nuevo, -a (I)
news program el programa de noticias (I)
newscast el noticiero (II)
newspaper el periódico (I)
newsstand el quiosco (II)
next siguiente (II), próximo (6-1)
  — to al lado de (I)

nice simpático, -a (I), amable (4-1)

night:
  at — de la noche (I)
  last — anoche (I)

night table la mesita (I)

nine nueve (I)

nine hundred novecientos, -as (I)

nineteen diecinueve (I)

ninety noventa (I)

ninth noveno, -a (I)

No way! ¡Qué va! (4-2)

nobody nadie (II)

noise el ruido (II)

none ningún, ninguno, -a (II)

nose la nariz, *pl.* las narices (I)

not:
  — yet no...todavía (II)
  — ... or ni ... ni (I)

notebook el cuaderno (I)

nothing nada (I)

November noviembre (I)

now ahora (I)

nurse el enfermero, la enfermera (II)

nutrition la alimentación (3-1)

nutritious nutritivo, -a (3-1)

O

obedient obediente (II)

obey obedecer to (II), hacer caso (4-2)

observatry el observatorio (7-1)

observe observar to (II)

to **obtain** conseguir (e → i) (II), obtener (1-2)

to **occupy** ocupar (8-1)

to **occur** ocurrir (II), suceder (1-1)

o'clock:
  at eight — a las ocho (I)
  at one — a la una (I)

October octubre (I)

odor el olor (II)

of de (I)
  — course por supuesto (I)

What is it made —? ¿De qué está hecho, -a? (II)

to **offend** ofender (II)

to **offer** ofrecer (II)

office (home) el despacho (I)

office la oficina (II)

offspring la descendencia (8-2)

often a menudo (I)

Oh! What a shame / pity! ¡Ay! ¡Qué pena! (I)

oil el petróleo (9-1)
  — spill el derrame de petróleo (9-2)

okay regular (I)

old viejo, -a (I); antiguo, -a (II)
  He / She is / They are ...
  years —. Tiene(n) ... años. (I)
  How — is / are ... ? ¿Cuántos años tiene(n) ... ? (I)
  —er mayor, *pl.* mayores (I)
  —er man el anciano (I)
  —er people los ancianos (I)
  —er woman la anciana (I)

on en (I)
  — Mondays, on Tuesdays ... los lunes, los martes ... (I)

— the grill a parrilla (II)
— time a tiempo (II)
— top of encima de (I)
— weekends los fines de semana (I)

once there una vez allí (1-1)

one uno (un), -a (I)
  at — (o'clock) a la una (I)
  — hundred cien (I)
  — must hay que (I)

onion la cebolla (I)

online en la Red (I)
  to be — estar en línea (I)

only sólo (I), único, -a (8-1)

to **open** abrir (I)

open abierto, -a (II)

opens se abre (II)

opinion:
  in my — para mí (I)

opportunity la oportunidad (II)

or o (I)

orange anaranjado, -a (I)
  — juice el jugo de naranja (I)

orchestra la orquesta (II)

to **order** pedir (e → i) (I)

to **organize** organizar (5-2)

origin el origen (7-2)

other otro, -a (I)

others los / las demás (I)

our nuestro(s), -a(s) (I)

outcome el resultado (8-2)

outdoors al aire libre (II)

outer space el espacio (II)

outrageous exagerado, -a (II)

outside fuera (de) (II)

oval el óvalo (7-1)

oven el horno (II)

to **overwork** explotar (9-2)

own propio, -a (I)

owner el dueño, la dueña (II, 5-1)

ozone layer la capa de ozono (9-2)

P

to **pack the suitcase** hacer la
maleta (II)
pain el dolor (II)
to **paint (one's nails)** pintarse
(las uñas) (II)
painter el pintor, la pintora (II)
painting el cuadro (I), la
pintura (2-1)
palace el palacio (II)
palette la paleta (2-1)
pants los pantalones (I)
paper:
  sheet of — la hoja de papel (I)
parade el desfile (II)
paramedic el paramédico, la
paramédica (II)
parents los padres (I)
park el parque (I)
  amusement — el parque de
  diversiones (I)
  national — el parque nacional
  (I)
part time a tiempo parcial (5-1)
participant el / la participante
(1-2)
to **participate (in)** participar (en)
(II)
party la fiesta (I)
surprise — la fiesta de sorpresa
(II)
to **pass** pasar (II)
passenger el pasajero, la
pasajera (II)
passport el pasaporte (II)
pastel *(colors)* pastel *adj.* (II)
pastime el pasatiempo (II)
pastries los pasteles (I)
patience la paciencia (II)
patient paciente (I)
  to be — tener paciencia (II)
to **pay (for)** pagar (por) (I)

to **pay attention** prestar atención
(II)
  — to hacer caso (4-2)
peace la paz (II), (10-1)
peaceful pacífico, -a (10-2)
peach el durazno (II)
peas los guisantes (I)
pedestrian el peatón, *pl.* los
peatones (II)
to **peel** pelar (II)
pen el bolígrafo (I)
pencil el lápiz, *pl.* los lápices (I)
  — sharpener el sacapuntas,
  pl. los sacapuntas (I)
people la gente (I), el pueblo
(7-1)
  older — los ancianos (I)
pepper la pimienta (I)
to **perform** realizar (2-2), actuar
(2-2), cumplir con (5-1)
perfume el perfume (I)
period la época (8-1)
to **permit, to allow** permitir (II)
person la persona (I)
pesticide el pesticida (9-1)
pharmacy la farmacia (II)
phenomenal fenomenal (II)
phenomenon el fenómeno (7-1)
phone:
  to talk on the — hablar por
  teléfono (I)
photo la foto (I)
  to take —s sacar fotos (I)
photographer el fotógrafo, la
fotógrafa (II)
photography la fotografía (II)
physical education class la
clase de educación física (I)
piano lesson (class) la lección
de piano (I)
picnic el picnic (II)
piece el pedazo (II)
pills las pastillas (II)

pilot el / la piloto (II)
piñata la piñata (I)
pineapple la piña (II)
pink rosado, -a (I)
pizza la pizza (I)
place el lugar (I)
to **place** poner (I)
to **plan** pensar (e → ie) (I)
plant la planta (II)
to **plant** sembrar (5-2)
plastic el plástico (I)
plate el plato (I)
play la obra de teatro (I)
to **play** jugar (a) (u → ue) *(games,
sports)* (I); tocar *(an instrument)*
(I)
  to — baseball jugar al béisbol
  (I)
  to — basketball jugar al
  básquetbol (I)
  to — football jugar al fútbol
  americano (I)
  to — golf jugar al golf (I)
  to — soccer jugar al fútbol (I)
  to — sports practicar deportes
  (I)
  to — tennis jugar al tenis (I)
  to — the guitar tocar la
  guitarra (I)
  to — the role of hacer el
  papel de (II)
  to — video games jugar
  videojuegos (I)
  to — volleyball jugar al
  vóleibol (I)
playground el patio de recreo
(II)
player el jugador, la jugadora (II)
plaza la plaza (II)
pleasant agradable (5-1)
to **please very much** encantar (I)
pleased to meet you mucho
gusto (I)

plot el argumento (II)
poem el poema (2-2)
poet el / la poeta (2-2)
point of view el punto de vista (10-2)
poison el veneno (9-1)
police officer el / la policía (II)
to **polish (one's nails)** pintarse (las uñas) (II)
polite cortés, *pl.* corteses (II)
politician el político, la política (II)
to **pollute** contaminar (6-2)
polluted contaminado, -a (II, 9-1)
pollution la contaminación (II, 9-1)
pool la piscina (I)
poor pobre (I)
— **thing** pobrecito, -a (II)
population la población (8-1)
pork el cerdo (II)
— **chop** la chuleta de cerdo (II)
portrait el retrato (2-1)
position el puesto (5-1)
possession la posesión, *pl.* las posesiones (I)
post office el correo (II)
poster el cartel (I)
pot la olla (II)
potatoes las papas (I)
pottery la cerámica (2-1)
poverty la pobreza (10-1)
power el poder (8-2)
powerful poderoso, -a (8-2)
practical práctico, -a (I)
practice la práctica (II)
to **predict** predecir (6-2)
to **prefer** preferir (e → ie) (I)
I — (yo) prefiero (I)
I — **to ...** (a mí) me gusta más ... (I)
you — (tú) prefieres (I)

to **prepare** preparar (I)
to **prescribe** recetar (II)
prescription la receta (II)
present el regalo (I)
presentation la presentación, *pl.* las presentaciones (I)
presenter el presentador, la presentadora (II)
to **preserve** conservar (9-1)
press la prensa (10-2)
pretty bonito, -a (I)
price el precio (I)
principal *(of a school)* el director, la directora (II)
primary school la escuela primaria (I)
prize el premio (II)
problem el problema (I)
to **produce** producir (9-2)
product el producto (6-2)
profession la profesión, *pl.* las profesiones (II)
program el programa (I)
programmer el programador, la programadora (6-1)
project el proyecto (II)
to **prolong** prolongar (6-2)
to **promote** promover (ue) (9-1)
proposal la propuesta (10-2)
to **propose** proponer (10-2)
proof la evidencia (7-1)
protein la proteína (3-1)
Protestant church el templo (I)
to **protect** proteger (II), (5-2)
protection la protección (9-1)
provided that con tal que (9-2)
punctual puntual (II, 5-1)
to **punish** castigar (9-1)
punishment el castigo (10-2)
pure puro, -a (II)
purple morado, -a (I)
purpose el fin, *pl.* los fines (10-2)

purse el bolso (I)
to **pursue a career** seguir una carrera (II), (6-1)
to **put** poner (I), colocar (9-1)
— *(command)* pon (I)
I — (yo) pongo (I)
to — **on** *(clothing, make-up, etc.)* ponerse (II)
to — **out** *(fire)* apagar (II)
you — (tú) pones (I)
pyramid la pirámide

Q . . . .

quality cualidad (4-1)
quarter past y cuarto (I)
queen la reina (II)
question la pregunta (II)
to ask a — hacer una pregunta (II)
quickly rápidamente (I)

R

rabbit el conejo (7-2)

race la carrera (II, 1-2), la raza (8-2)

rain la lluvia (II)

to rain llover (o → ue) (II)

It's —ing. Llueve. (I)

rather bastante (I)

to reach alcanzar (1-2), llegar a (10-2)

— an agreement ponerse de acuerdo (4-2)

to react reaccionar (4-2)

to read magazines leer revistas (I)

ready listo, -a (II)

realistic realista (I)

reality program el programa de la vida real (I)

to realize darse cuenta de (1-2)

Really? ¿Verdad? (I); ¿De veras? (I)

really en realidad (II)

reason la razón (10-1)

to rebel rebelarse (8-2)

receptionist el recepcionista, la recepcionista (5-1)

to receive recibir (I)

recently recientemente (II)

reception desk la recepción (II)

recipe la receta (II)

to recommend recomendar (e → ie) (II)

to reconquer reconquistar (8-1)

to record grabar (II)

recreation center el centro recreative (5-2)

rectangle el rectángulo (7-1)

to recycle reciclar (I)

recycling center el centro de reciclaje (I)

red rojo, -a (I)

— haired pelirrojo, -a (I)

to reduce reducir (zc) (II), (6-2)

reference la referencia (5-1)

refrigerator el refrigerador (II)

refuge el refugio (1-1)

to register inscribirse (1-2)

registration la inscripción (1-2)

rehabilitation center el centro de rehabilitación (5-2)

rehearsal el ensayo (II)

to rehearse ensayar (II)

relatives los parientes (II)

to relax descansar (I), relajar (3-2)

to remember recordar (o → ue) (II)

to rent alquilar (II)

to repair reparar (5-1)

to repeat repetir (e → i) (II)

to replace reemplazar (6-2)

report el informe (I)

reporter el reportero, la reportera (II)

to represent representar (2-1)

representative el / la representante (1-2)

to request solicitar (5-1)

requirement el requisito (5-1)

rescue el rescate (9-2)

to rescue rescatar (II)

reservation la reservación, pl. las reservaciones (II)

reserved reservado, -a (I)

to resolve resolver (o → ue) (4-2)

respect el respeto (10-1)

to respect respetar (II)

responsibility la responsabilidad (5-2)

responsible responsible (5-1)

to rest descansar (I)

restaurant el restaurante (I)

result el resultado (8-2)

to result resultar (II)

to return regresar (I, II)

to — a book devolver (o → ue) (un libro) (II)

review la reseña (2-2)

to revolt rebelarse (8-2)

rhythm el ritmo, el compás (2-2)

rice el arroz (I)

rich rico, -a (I)

to ride:

to — a bicycle montar en bicicleta (I)

to — horseback montar a caballo (I)

right:

to the — (of) a la derecha (de) (I)

— away en seguida (II)

rights los derechos (5-2)

ring el anillo (I)

river el río (I)

road la calle (I)

to rob robar (II)

rock la piedra (II), la roca (1-1)

role el papel (II)

to play the — of hacer el papel de (II)

Roman romano, -a (8-1)

romantic movie la película romántica (I)

room el cuarto (I); la habitación, pl. las habitaciones (II)

double occupancy — la habitación doble (II)

single occupancy — la habitación individual (II)

to straighten up the — arreglar el cuarto (I)

rope la cuerda (II)

round redondo, -a (7-1)

round-trip ida y vuelta (II)

ruins las ruinas (II, 7-1)

rug la alfombra (I)

rule la regla (II), la ley (5-2)

to rule gobernar (8-1)

to run correr (I)

to — out agotar(se) (9-1)

S

sack la bolsa (I)
sacred sagrado, -a (7-2)
sad triste (I)
to sail navegar (II)
sail la vela (II)
salad la ensalada (I)
  fruit — la ensalada de frutas (I)
salary el salario (II, 5-1)
sale la liquidación, *pl.* las liquidaciones (II)
salesperson el dependiente, la dependienta (I)
salsa la salsa (II)
salt la sal (I)
same mismo, -a (I)
sandwich:
  ham and cheese — el sándwich de jamón y queso (I)
satisfactory satisfactorio, -a (10-1)
Saturday sábado (I)
sausage la salchicha (I)
to save ahorrar (II, 6-1)
to save salvar (II)
to say decir (I)
  How do you —?¿Cómo se dice? (I)
  to — good-bye despedirse (e → i) de (II)
  You — ... Se dice ... (I)
  You don't —! ¡No me digas! (I)
to scare asustar (1-1)
scared:
  to be — (of) tener miedo (de) (I)
scene la escena (II)
schedule el horario (I)
science:
  — class la clase de ciencias naturales (I)
  — fiction movie la película de ciencia ficción (I)

scientist el científico, la científica (II, 6-1)
scissors las tijeras (II)
to score (a goal) meter un gol (II)
score el tanteo (II)
to scream gritar (II)
screen:
  computer — la pantalla (I)
to scuba dive bucear (I)
sculpture escultura (2-1)
sculptor el escultor, la escultora (2-1)
secret el secreto (4-1)
sea el mar (I)
seal la foca (9-2)
to search (for) buscar (I)
search la búsqueda (II)
  to do a — hacer una búsqueda (II)
  to — *(luggage)* registrar (II)
season la estación, *pl.* las estaciones (I)
seat el asiento (II)
second segundo, -a (I)
  — floor el primer piso (I)
secretary el secretario, la secretaria (II)
security checkpoint la inspección, *pl.* las inspecciones de seguridad (II)
to see ver (I)
  Let's — A ver ... (I)
  — you later! ¡Nos vemos!; Hasta luego. (I)
  — you tomorrow. Hasta mañana. (I)
  to — a movie ver una película (I)
to seem like parecerse a (2-2)
self-confidence confianza en sí mismo, -a (3-2)
self-portrait el autorretrato (2-1)

selfish egoísta (4-1)
to sell vender (I)
to send enviar (I, II)
to separate separar (I)
September septiembre (I)
serious serio, -a (I), grave (9-1)
to serve servir (e → i) (I)
service el servicio (6-2)
  — station la estación de servicio (II)
to set (sun) ponerse (el sol) (7-2)
  to set the table poner la mesa (I)
seven siete (I)
seven hundred setecientos, -as (I)
seventeen diecisiete (I)
seventh séptimo, -a (I)
seventy setenta (I)
shadow la sombra (7-2)
shake hands dar(se) la mano (II)
shame:
  What a —! ¡Qué lástima! (II)
shampoo el champú (II)
to share compartir (I)
to shave afeitarse (II)
she ella (I)
sheet of paper la hoja de papel (I)
shelf el estante (I)
shellfish los mariscos (II)
shelter el refugio (1-1)
to shine brillar (7-2)
ship el barco (I)
shirt la camisa (I)
  T— la camiseta (I)
shoe store la zapatería (I)
shoes los zapatos (I)
shoe size el número (II)
short bajo, -a *(stature);* corto, -a *(length)* (I)
shortage la escasez (9-1)
shorts los pantalones cortos (I)

should deber (I)

shoulder el hombro (II)

show el programa (I), el espectáculo (2-2)

to **show +** *movie or TV program* dar (I); mostrar (ue) (2-1)

shower la ducha (II)

shrimp el camarón, *pl.* los camarones (II)

shy reservado, -a (I)

sick enfermo, -a (I)

sierra la sierra (1-1)

sign el letrero (II); la señal (II)

  stop — la señal de parada (II)

silk seda (II)

silly tonto, -a (I)

silver la plata (II)

similarity la semejanza (8-2)

since desde (II)

sincere sincero, -a (4-1)

to **sing** cantar (I)

singer el / la cantante (II)

single soltero, -a (6-1)

sink el fregadero (II)

sir (el) señor (Sr.) (I)

sister la hermana (I)

site:

  Web — el sitio Web (I)

six seis (I)

six hundred seiscientos, -as (I)

sixteen dieciséis (I)

sixth sexto, -a (I)

sixty sesenta (I)

size la talla (II)

to **skate** patinar (I)

to **skateboard** montar en monopatín (I)

skates los patines (II)

to **ski** esquiar (I)

skill la habilidad (5-1)

skin la piel (9-2)

to **skip (a meal)** saltar (una comida) (3-1)

skirt la falda (I)

sky el cielo (II)

to **sleep** dormir (I)

to **fall asleep** dormirse (II)

sleeping bag el saco de dormir (1-1)

sleepy:

  to be — tener sueño (I)

slice el pedazo (II)

slide la diapositiva (I)

slowly lentamente (II); despacio (II)

small pequeño, -a (I)

to **smile** sonreír (e → í) (II)

smoke el humo (II)

snack la merienda (3-1)

to **sneeze** estornudar (3-1)

to **snorkel** bucear (I)

to **snow:** nevar (e → ie) (II)

  It's —ing. Nieva. (I)

solar solar (II)

soldier el / la soldado (8-2)

to **solve** resolver (o → ue) (II)

so tan (II), de modo que (10-2)

  so + *adj.* tan + *adj.* (II)

  so much tanto (I)

  so-so regular (I)

  so that de modo que (10-2)

soap el jabón (II)

soap opera la telenovela (I)

soccer:

  to play — jugar al fútbol (I)

sociable sociable (I)

social service el servicio social (5-2)

social studies class la clase de ciencias sociales (I)

society la sociedad (5-2)

socks los calcetines (I)

soft drink el refresco (I)

software el software (I)

solid-colored de sólo un color (II)

to **solve** resolver (o → ue) (7-2)

some unos, -as (I)

some algún, alguno, -a (II)

  some day algún día (II)

someone alguien (II)

something algo (I)

sometimes a veces (I)

son el hijo (I)

  —s; —(s) and daughter(s) los hijos (I)

song la canción, *pl.* las canciones (I,II)

soon pronto (II)

sorry:

  I'm —. Lo siento. (I)

sound (stereo) system el equipo de sonido (I)

to **sound like** sonar (ue) a (2-2)

soup:

  vegetable — la sopa de verduras (I)

soup kitchen el comedor de beneficencia (5-2)

source la fuente (II)

  — of inspiration la fuente de inspiración (2-1)

souvenirs los recuerdos (I)

  to buy — comprar recuerdos (I)

spaceship la nave espacial (7-1)

spaghetti los espaguetis (I)

Spanish class la clase de español (I)

special especial (II)

  special effects los efectos especiales (II)

  special event el evento especial (II)

  species la especie (9-2)

speech el discurso (II)

to **spell:**

  How is ... spelled? ¿Cómo se escribe ... ? (I)

  It's spelled ... Se escribe ... (I)

to **spend** gastar (II)
  to — time with friends pasar tiempo con amigos (I)
spicy picante (II)
to **spill** tirar (II)
  don't — no tires (II)
spoiled consentido, -a (II)
spoon la cuchara (I)
sports:
  — equipment el equipo deportivo (II)
  —-minded deportista (I)
  — program el programa deportivo (I)
  to play — practicar deportes (I)
spring la primavera (I)
stadium el estadio (I)
stage el escenario (2-2)
stairs, stairway la escalera (I)
stamp el sello (II)
to **stand:**
  — out destacarse (2-2)
  — up pararse (2-2)
stapler la grapadora (II)
star:
  movie — la estrella (del cine) (II)
to **start** empezar (e → ie) (I); comenzar (e → ie) (II)
state el estado (10-1)
statue la estatua (II)
to **stay:** quedarse (II)
  I — at home. Me quedo en casa. (I)
steak la carne de res (II)
to **steal** robar (II)
step el paso (2-2)
stepbrother el hermanastro (I)
stepfather el padrastro (I)
stepmother la madrastra (I)
stepsister la hermanastra (I)
stereo system el equipo de sonido (I)

still todavía (II)
still life la naturaleza muerta (2-1)
to **stitch** *(surgically)* dar puntadas (II)
stitches las puntadas (II)
stomach el estómago (I)
to **stop** parar (II), detener (9-2)
  — doing something dejar de (1-1)
stoplight el semáforo (II)
to **stop over** hacer escala (II)
stopover la escala (II)
store la tienda (I)
  book— la librería (I)
  clothing — la tienda de ropa (I)
  department — el almacén, *pl.* los almacenes (I)
  discount — la tienda de descuentos (I)
  household-appliance — la tienda de electrodomésticos (I)
  jewelry — la joyería (I)
  shoe — la zapatería (I)
stories:
  to write — escribir cuentos (I)
storm la tormenta (II)
story el piso (I)
stove la estufa (II)
to **straighten up the room** arreglar el cuarto (I)
straight derecho (II)
strange extraño, -a (7-1)
strategy la estrategia (6-2)
strawberries las fresas (I)
street la calle (I)
strength la fuerza (3-2)
stress el estrés (3-2)
stressed out estresado, -a (3-2)
to **stetch** estirar (3-2)
to **stroll** dar un paseo (1-1)
strong fuerte (3-1)
student el / la estudiante (I)
studious estudioso, -a (I)

to **study** estudiar (I)
stupendous estupendo, -a (II)
stupid tonto, -a (I)
style el estilo (II)
subject el tema (2-1)
subway el metro (II)
success el éxito (II)
  to be —ful tener éxito (II)
suddenly de repente (II)
to **suffer** sufrir (10-1)
sugar el azúcar (I)
to **suggest** sugerir (e → ie) (II), proponer (10-2)
suit el traje (I)
suitcase la maleta (II)
summer el verano (I)
to **sunbathe** tomar el sol (I)
Sunday domingo (I)
sunglasses los anteojos de sol (I)
sunny:
  It's —. Hace sol. (I)
supermarket el supermercado (II)
supplies los materiales (II)
support el apoya (10-1)
to **support (each other)** apoyarse (4-1)
sure seguro, -a (II)
to **surf the Web** navegar en la Red (I)
surprise la sorpresa (II)
suspicious sospechoso, -a (10-2)
structure la estructura (7-1)
sweater el suéter (I)
sweatshirt la sudadera (I)
sweet dulce (II)
to **swim** nadar (I)
swimming la natación (II)
swimsuit el traje de baño (I)
symbol el símbolo (7-2)
synagogue la sinagoga (I)
synthetic fabric la tela sintética (II)
syrup el jarabe (3-1)

T •

T-shirt la camiseta (I)

table la mesa (I)

  to set the — poner la mesa (I)

to take llevar (I), tomar (3-1)

  to — a bath bañarse (II)

  to — a course tomar un curso (I)

  to — a shower ducharse (II)

  to — a tour hacer una gira (II)

  to — a trip hacer un viaje (II)

  to — a walk dar una caminata (II), dar un paseo (1-1)

  to — away quitar (II)

  to — care of cuidar a (II)

  to — into account tener en cuenta (6-2)

  to — lessons tomar lecciones (II)

  to — out the trash sacar la basura (I)

  to — photos sacar fotos (I)

  to — place tener lugar (1-2)

  to — shelter refugiarse (1-1)

talented talentoso, -a (I)

to talk hablar (I)

  to — on the phone hablar por teléfono (I)

tall alto, -a (I)

tank el tanque (II)

taste el sabor (II)

to taste probar (o → ue) (II)

tasty sabroso, -a (I); rico, -a (I)

tea el té (I)

  iced — el té helado (I)

to teach enseñar (I)

teacher el profesor, la profesora (I)

teaching la enseñanza (10-1)

team el equipo (II)

to tear romperse (II)

technical school la escuela

técnica (II)

technician el técnico, la técnica (II)

technological tecnológico, -a (6-2)

technology / computers la tecnología (I)

technology / computer class la clase de tecnología (I)

teddy bear el oso de peluche (II)

teeth los dientes (II)

  to brush one's — cepillarse los dientes (II)

television:

  to watch — ver la tele (I)

television set el televisor (I)

to tell decir (I)

  — me dime (I)

  to — jokes contar (chistes) (o → ue) (II)

  to — the truth decir la verdad (II)

temple el templo (I)

ten diez (I)

tennis:

  to play — jugar al tenis (I)

tent la tienda de acampar (1-1)

tennis racket la raqueta de tenis (II)

tenth décimo, -a (I)

thank you gracias (I)

that que (I); ese, esa (I)

  —'s why por eso (I)

that one (over there) aquel, aquella (II)

the el, la (I) los, las (I)

  — best el / la mejor, los / las mejores (I)

  — worst el / la peor, los / las peores (I)

theater el teatro (I)

  movie — el cine (I)

their su, sus (I)

them las, los *dir. obj. pron.* (I), les *ind. obj. pron.* (I)

then entonces (I)

then luego (II)

theory la teoría (7-2)

there allí (I)

  — is / are hay (I); haya *(subjunctive)* (II)

  — was hubo (II)

  — was / — were había (II)

  — will be habrá (II)

therefore por eso (I), así que (6-1), por lo tanto (6-1)

these estos, estas (I)

they ellos, ellas (I)

they died se murieron (II)

thief el ladrón, la ladrona, *pl.* los ladrones (II)

thing la cosa (I)

to think pensar (e → ie) (I), opinar (10-2)

  I don't — so. Creo que no. (I)

  I — ... Creo que ... (I)

  I — so. Creo que sí. (I)

  to — of one's self pensar en sí mismo, -a (4-2)

  What do you — (about it)? ¿Qué te parece? (I)

third tercer (tercero), -a (I)

third floor el segundo piso (I)

thirsty:

  I'm —. Tengo sed. (I)

thirteen trece (I)

thirty treinta (I); y media *(in telling time)* (I)

thirty-one treinta y uno (I)

this este, esta (I)

  — afternoon esta tarde (I)

  — evening esta noche (I)

  — way así (1-1)

  — weekend este fin de semana (I)

What is — ? ¿Qué es esto? (I)

those esos, esas (I)

those (over there) aquellos, aquellas (II)

thought el pensamiento (10-1)

thousand:

  a — mil (I)

threat la amenaza (9-2)

to **threaten** amenazar (9-1)

three tres (I)

three hundred trescientos, -as (I)

three-ring binder la carpeta de argollas (I)

through por (II), a través de (2-1)

to **throw** arrojar(se) (7-2)

  to—away tirar (II), echar (9-1)

thunder el trueno (1-1)

Thursday jueves (I)

ticket el boleto (I), la entrada (2-2)

ticket la multa (II)

tie la corbata (I); el empate (II)

tight apretado, -a (II)

tile el azulejo (8-1)

time la época (8-1)

time:

  At what —? ¿A qué hora? (I)

  free — el tiempo libre (I)

  on — a tiempo (II)

  to spend — with friends pasar tiempo con amigos (I)

  What — is it? ¿Qué hora es? (I)

timid tímido, -a (II)

tip la propina (II)

tired cansado, -a (I)

to **a** *prep.* (I)

  in order — para + *inf.* (I)

  — the a la, al (I)

  — the left (of) a la izquierda (de) (I)

  — the right (of) a la derecha (de) (I)

toast el pan tostado (I)

today hoy (I)

together juntos, -as (4-1)

tolerance la tolerancia (10-1)

to **tolerate** aguantar (3-2)

tomatoes los tomates (I)

tomorrow mañana (I)

  See you —. Hasta mañana. (I)

ton la tonelada (7-1)

too también (I); demasiado (I)

  I do (like to) — a mí también (I)

  me — a mí también (I)

toothbrush el cepillo de dientes (II)

toothpaste la pasta dental (II)

top:

  on — of encima de (I)

touching emocionante (I)

tourist el / la turista (II)

toward hacia (1-1)

towel la toalla (II)

tower la torre (8-1)

town el pueblo (II)

toy el juguete (I)

to **trace** trazar (7-1)

traffic el tráfico (II)

trail el sendero (II)

train el tren (I)

  electric — el tren eléctrico (II)

to **train** entrenarse (2-1)

training el entrenamiento (1-2)

trainer el entrenador, la entrenadora (II)

to **translate** traducir (zc) (6-1)

translator el traductor, la traductora (6-1)

transparent tape la cinta adhesiva (II)

to **trap** atrapar (9-2)

to **travel** viajar (I)

  travel agency la agencia de viajes (II)

  travel agent el / la agente de viajes (II)

to **treat** tratar (10-1)

tree el árbol (I)

tremendous tremendo, -a (I)

trial el juicio (10-2)

triangle el triángulo (7-1)

tricycle el triciclo (II)

trip el viaje (I)

to **trip (over)** tropezar (e → ie) (con) (II)

trophy el trofeo (1-2)

tropical rain forest la selva tropical (II), (9-2)

truck el camión, *pl.* los camiones (II)

trumpet la trompeta (2-2)

trust la confianza (4-1)

to **trust** confiar (i → í) (4-1)

truth la verdad (II)

to **try on** probarse (o → ue) (II)

to **try to** tratar de (II)

Tuesday martes (I)

  on —s los martes (I)

turkey el pavo (II)

to **turn** doblar (II)

  to — in entregar (II)

  to — in homework on time entregar la tarea a tiempo (II)

  to — into convertirse en (7-2)

  to — off apagar (II)

  to — on encender (e → ie) (II)

  to — out resultar (II)

turtle la tortuga (II)

TV channel el canal (I)

twelve doce (I)

twenty veinte (I)

twenty-one veintiuno (veintiún) (I)

to **twist** torcerse (o → ue) (II)

two dos (I)

two hundred doscientos, -as (I)

typical típico, -a (II)

U

Ugh! ¡Uf! (I)

ugly feo, -a (I)

uncle el tío (I)

uncles; uncle(s) and aunt(s) los tíos (I)

underneath debajo de (I)

to **understand** comprender (I); entender (e → ie) (II)

understanding comprensivo, -a (4-1)

unemployment el desempleo (10-2)

unfair injusto, -a (5-2)

unfortunately desafortunadamente (1-2)

unity la unidad (8-1)

universe el universo (7-2)

university la universidad (II)

unforgettable inolvidable (I)

unknown desconocido, -a (8-2)

unless a menos que (9-2)

unlikely improbable (7-1)

until hasta (II)

upon arriving al llegar (8-2)

us:

 (to / for) — nos *ind. obj. pron.* (I)

to **usually do something** soler (ue) (5-1)

use el uso (6-2)

to **use:**

 to — a stationary bike hacer bicicleta (3-2)

 to — a treadmill hacer cinta (3-2)

 to — the computer usar la computadora (I)

 What's it —d for? ¿Para qué sirve? (I)

used usado, -a (I)

useful:

 to be — servir (I)

 is — for sirve para (I)

V

vacation:

 to go on — ir de vacaciones (I)

to **vacuum** pasar la aspiradora (I)

vain vanidoso, -a (4-1)

valley el valle (II), (1-1)

value el valor (10-2)

variety la variedad (8-2)

various varios, -as (II)

VCR la videocasetera (I)

vegetable soup la sopa de verduras (I)

vendor el vendedor, la vendedora (II)

very muy (I)

 — well muy bien (I)

veterinarian el veterinario, la veterinaria (II)

via satellite via satélite (6-2)

victim la víctima (II)

video games:

 to play — jugar videojuegos (I)

videocassette el video (I)

to **videotape** hacer un video (I)

vinegar el vinagre (II)

to **violate** violar (10-2)

violence la violencia (II)

violent violento, -a (I)

virtual reality la realidad virtual (6-2)

to **visit** visitar (I)

 to — chat rooms visitar salones de chat (I)

vitamin la vitamina (3-1)

voice la voz, *pl.* las voces (II)

volleyball:

 to play — jugar al vóleibol (I)

volunteer el voluntario, la voluntaria (I)

 — work el trabajo voluntario (I)

to **vote** votar (10-1)

W

to **wait** esperar (II)

waiter, waitress el camarero, la camarera (I)

to **wake up** despertarse (e → ie) (II)

to **walk** caminar (I), andar (1-1)

 to take a — dar una caminata (II)

wall la pared (I)

wallet la cartera (I)

to **want** querer (e → ie) (I)

 I — (yo) quiero (I)

 you — (tú) quieres (I)

war la guerra (II, 8-2)

warm:

 to be — tener calor (I)

was fue (I)

to **wash** lavar (I)

 to — the car lavar el coche (I)

 to — the clothes lavar la ropa (I)

 to — the dishes lavar los platos (I)

 to — one's face lavarse la cara (II)

waste el desperdicio (9-1)

to **waste** desperdiciar (9-1)

wastepaper basket la papelera (I)

watch el reloj pulsera (I)

 to watch television ver la tele (I)

water el agua (I)

watermelon la sandía (II)

waterskiing el esquí acuático (II)

way la manera (II, 3-1), el modo (10-2)

we nosotros, -as (I)

weak débil (3-2)

wealth la riqueza (8-2)

to **wear** llevar (I)

weapon el arma, *pl.* las armas (8-2)

weather el clima (9-2)

What's the — like? ¿Qué tiempo hace? (I)

Web:

to surf the — navegar en la Red (I)

— page la página Web (I)

— site el sitio Web (I)

Wednesday miércoles (I)

wedding la boda (II)

week la semana (I)

last — la semana pasada (I)

weekend:

on —s los fines de semana (I)

this — este fin de semana (I)

to weigh pesar (7-1)

weight el peso (3-1)

welcome bienvenido, -a (II)

well bien (I); pues ... *(to indicate pause)* (I)

very — muy bien (I)

—behaved bien educado, -a (II)

wet mojado, -a (II)

whale la ballena

What? ¿Cuál? (I)

— a shame! ¡Qué lástima! (II)

— are you like? ¿Cómo eres? (I)

(At) — time? ¿A qué hora? (I)

— color ... ? ¿De qué color ... ? (I)

— day is today? ¿Qué día es hoy? (I)

— did you do? ¿Qué hiciste? (I)

— do you like better (prefer) to do? ¿Qué te gusta hacer más? (I)

— do you like to do? ¿Qué te gusta hacer? (I)

— do you think (about it)?

¿Qué te parece? (I, II)

— does ... mean? ¿Qué quiere decir ... ? (I)

— else? ¿Qué más? (I)

— happened to you? ¿Qué te pasó? (I, II)

— is she / he like? ¿Cómo es? (I)

— is the date? ¿Cuál es la fecha? (I)

— is this? ¿Qué es esto? (I)

— is your name? ¿Cómo te llamas? (I)

— kind of ... ? ¿Qué clase de... ? (I)

— time is it? ¿Qué hora es? (I)

— would you like? ¿Qué desean (Uds.)? (I)

— 's happening? ¿Qué pasa? (I)

— 's his / her name? ¿Cómo se llama? (I)

— 's it (used) for? ¿Para qué sirve? (I)

— 's the weather like? ¿Qué tiempo hace? (I)

what!:

— a good / nice idea! ¡Qué buena idea! (I)

— a shame / pity! ¡Qué pena! (I)

what lo que (II)

When? ¿Cuándo? (I)

Where? ¿Dónde? (I)

— are you from? ¿De dónde eres? (I)

(To) —? ¿Adónde? (I)

whether si (I)

Which? ¿Cuál? (I)

while mientras (que) (II)

once in a — de vez en cuando (II)

white blanco, -a (I)

who que (I)

Who? ¿Quién? (I)

Why? ¿Por qué? (I)

wide ancho, -a (II)

width el ancho (7-1)

wife la esposa (I)

wild salvaje (9-2)

Will you bring me ... ? ¿Me trae ... ? (I)

window la ventana (I)

window *(airplane)* la ventanilla (II)

windsurf el surf de vela (II)

winter el invierno (I)

with con (I)

— me conmigo (I)

— my / your friends con mis / tus amigos (I)

— respect to en cuanto a (10-1)

— whom? ¿Con quién? (I)

— you contigo (I)

What do you serve it —? ¿Con qué se sirve? (II)

without sin (I)

— a doubt sin duda (II)

witness el / la testigo (10-2)

woman la mujer (I)

older woman la anciana (I)

business— la mujer de negocios (II)

wonder la maravilla (8-1)

wonderful estupendo, -a (II), maravilloso, -a (8-1)

wood el bosque (1-1)

wool la lana (II)

word la palabra (II)

work el trabajo (I)

— of art la obra de arte (2-1)

volunteer — el trabajo voluntario (I)

to work trabajar (I)

workshop el taller (2-1)

world el mundo (II)

worldwide mundial (10-2)

to **worry** preocuparse (3-2)

worse than peor(es) que (I)

worst:

  the — el / la peor, los / las peores (I)

Would you like? ¿Te gustaría? (I)

wrist la muñeca (II)

to write:

  to — e-mail escribir por correo electrónico (I)

  to — stories escribir cuentos (I)

writer el escritor, la escritora (II, 2-2)

writing la escritura (7-2)

X ····························

X-ray la radiografía (II)

Y ····························

yard el jardín (I)

year el año (I)

  He / She is / They are … —s old. Tiene(n) … años. (I)

  last — el año pasado (I)

yellow amarillo, -a (I)

yes sí (I)

yesterday ayer (I)

yoga el yoga (3-2)

yogurt el yogur (I)

you *fam. sing.* tú (I); *formal sing.* usted (Ud.) (I); *fam. pl.* vosotros, -as (I); *formal pl.* ustedes (Uds.) (I); *fam. after prep.* ti (I); *sing. ind. obj. pron* te (I), *pl. fam. ind. obj. pron.* os (I), *ind. obj. pron.* le, les (I)

  And —? ¿Y a ti? (I)

  for — para ti (I)

it matters (it's important),

they matter to — te importa(n) (II)

to / for — *fam. pl.* os (I)

to / for — *fam. sing.* te (I)

with — contigo (I)

— can se puede (II)

— don't say! ¡No me digas! (I)

— have seen has visto (II)

— know conocen (II)

— look (good) te ves (bien) (II)

— say … Se dice … (I)

young joven (I)

— boy / girl el niño, la niña (I)

— man el joven (I)

— people los jóvenes (II)

— woman la joven (I)

—er menor, *pl.* menores (I)

your *fam.* tu (I); *fam.* tus, vuestro(s), -a(s) (I); *formal* su, sus (I)

yours tuyo, -a, -os, -as (II)

yuck! ¡Uf !(I)

Z ····························

zero cero (I)

zoo el zoológico (I)

Índice

Structures are most often presented first in *A primera vista*, where they are practiced lexically. They are then explained later in a *Gramática* section or a *¿Recuerdas?* or *Nota*. Lightface numbers refer to the pages where structures are initially presented or, after explanation, where student reminders occur. **Boldface numbers** refer to pages where structures are explained or are otherwise highlighted.

Acknowledgments

Cover Design Tamada Brown & Associates

Program Graphic Development Herman Adler Design

Maps Mapping Specialists

Technical Illustration/Additional Graphics Design Five Creatives; Roberta Warshaw

Illustrations Wilkinson Studios Artists: Seitu Hayden **pp. 37, 39, 87, 118, 119, 128, 164,181, 188, 218, 225, 257, 418.** Reggie Holladay **pp. 24, 25, 28, 50, 78, 79, 130, 131, 234, 265, 281, 285, 286, 298, 299, 304, 309, 356, 357, 409;** Tim Jones **pp. 27, 160, 183, 206, 207, 220, 373, 390, 391;** Judy Love **pp. 372, 395, 462.** Tom McKee **pp. 28, 47, 80, 89, 127, 136, 142, 174, 175, 210, 211, 222, 229, 262, 280, 326.**

Photography Front and back covers: (background) The Image Bank; (inset) James Blair/Houles P. Blair/National Geographic.

Photographers who contributed to the studio/location photography: Bill Burlingham, Burlingham Photography and John Morrison, Morrison Photography.

Frontmatter vi: Flash! Light/Stock • Boston; **vii:** Beryl Goldberg; **ix:** Claudia Uribe/Estock Photo; **x- xii:** Beryl Goldberg; **xiii:** Albert Lorenz; **xv:** Hubert Stadler/Corbis; **xvi:** Dana White/PhotoEdit; **xvii:** George Mattei/Envision; **xviii:** (bg.) Jose Fuste Raga/Corbis, (i.) Minden Pictures; **xix:** (i.) John Elk Photography; **xx:** (bg.) Steve Kaufman/Corbis, (i.) Taxi/Getty Images; **xxii:** (bg.) Stone/Getty Images; (i.) The Image Bank/Getty Images; **xxiv:** Ed Simpson/Getty Images; **xxvi:** Dennis Degnan/Corbis; **xxviii:** (bg.) Michelle Chaplow/Corbis, (i.) AFP/Corbis; **xxix:** The Image Works; **xxx:** (bg.) John Elk Photography, (i.) John Elk Photography; **xxxi:** (i.) John Elk Photography; **xxxii–xxxiii:** Ed Young/CORBIS.

Para Empezar p. 0: Ulriche Welsch; **p. 1:** (t.) Beryl Goldberg, (b.) Bob Daemmrich/The Image Works; **p. 2:** (l.) Michael Newman/PhotoEdit; (r.) Richard Hutchings/PhotoEdit; **p. 4:** Michelle D. Bridwell/PhotoEdit; **p. 6:** (l.) LWA-Dann Tardiff/Corbis, (r.) Tom & Dee Ann McCarthy/Corbis; **p. 8:** (b.r.) Tony Freeman/PhotoEdit; (l.) Beryl Goldberg, (t.r.) David-Young-Wolff/PhotoEdit; **p. 11:** Michael Kevin Daly/Corbis; **p. 14:** PhotoDisc; **p. 15:** David Frazier/The Image Works, (t.) Spenser Ainsley/The Image Works.

Capítulo 1 p. 16: Joe Viesti/The Viesti Collection, Inc; **p. 18:** (b.r.) NHLI/Getty Images, (l.) Joe McBride/Corbis, (t.r.) Brian Drake/SportsChrome; **p. 20:** (bg.) Anna Zuckerman -Vdovenko/Index Stock Imagery; (i.) used by permission of Museo de Arte Comteporáneo de la Universidad de Chile; **p. 22:** (b.c) Pearson photo archive, (b.l.) Pearson photo archive; (b.r.) David Young-Wolff/PhotoEdit; (m.r.) Pearson photo archive; (t.l.) Pearson photo archive; (t.r.) Daniel Rivademar/Odyssey/Chicago; **p. 23:** (b.l.) Tom Stewart/Corbis, (b.r.) PhotoNetworkStock, (m.c.) Galen Rowell/Corbis, (t.l.) PhotoNetworkStock, (t.r.) Galen Rowell/Corbis; **p. 26:** Pearson photo archive, (b.r.) Corbis; **p. 27:** Stock • Boston; **p. 29:** Photo Researchers, Inc.; **p. 30:** Photo Researchers, Inc.; **p. 34:** Photo Researchers, Inc.; **p. 35:** Odyssey/Chicago; **p. 41:**Odyssey/Chicago; **p. 45:** (b.r.) Michael Groen, (m.r.) Associated Press, AP, (t.r.) Associated Press, AP; **p. 48:** (b. r.) Roberto Reyes Ang; (b.c) Bridgeman Art Library, (b.l.) Odyssey/Chicago; **p. 51:** (t.b) © Jimmy Dorantes/Latin Focus.com; **p. 54:** Robert Frerck/Odyssey/Chicago; **p. 55:** Gianni Dagli Orti/Corbis; **p. 57:** Photo Researchers, Inc.

Capítulo 2 p. 62: (b.) José Antonio Velásquez, (t.) Pablo Picasso/Art Resource, NY; **p. 64:** (b.c) Sepp Seitz/Woodfin Camp and Associates, (l.) Richard Hutchings/PhotoEdit, (r.) Tony Freeman/PhotoEdit; **p. 66:** (bg.) Pablo Corral/Corbis, (i.) Artists Rights Society/Art Resource, NY; **p. 68:** (m.l.) Bob Daemmrich/Stock • Boston, (t.l.) Alfonso Fernández, (b.l.) Artists Rights Society/Art Resource, NY; **p. 69:** (b.r.) Fundació Joan Miró, Baracelona/Fundació Joan Miró, Baracelona, (t.l.) Fundació Joan Miró, Baracelona/Corbis, (t.r.) Artists Rights Society/Art Resource, NY; **p. 70:** Dina Bursztyn; **p. 71:** (b.) Pablo Corral V/Corbis, (m.l.) Oswaldo Guayasamín/Picture Search, (t.l.) Carlos Enriquez:/Art Resource, NY, (t.r.) Getty Images, Inc.; **p. 73:** (b.r.) Diego Velázquez De Silva/Art Resource, NY, (t.r.) Alfonso Fernández; **p. 74:** (b.) Peggy Guggenheim Collection Venice/Dagli Orti (A)/TheArtArchive, (t.) The Museum of Modern Art/Licensed by SCALA/Art Resource, NY. Given anonymously. ©2002 Kingdom of Spain, Gala-Salvador Dalí Foundation/Artists Rights Society/Art Resource, NY; **p. 75:** The Museum of Modern Art/Licensed by SCALA/Art Resource, NY; **p. 77:** Remedios Varo/Artist Rights Society; **p. 78:** (b.) Museo Nacional de Historia, Castillo de Chapultepec, Mexico City, D.F., Mexico/Art Resource, NY; **p. 80:** (b.r.) Pepón Osorio; **p. 81:** Picture Search; **p. 82:** (b.) Robert Fried/Stock • Boston, (t.l.) Photofest; **p. 83:** (b.l.) Carol Rosegg/Associated Press, AP, (r.) Bob Daemmrich Photography, Inc.; (t.l.) Ed Bock/Corbis, (t.r.) E. Bordis/Estock Photo; **p. 84:** (t.r.) Facundo Cabral; **p. 85:** (m.r.) AFP/Corbis; **p. 86:** Courtesy Don Francisco; **p. 91:** David Young-Wolff/PhotoEdit; **p. 93:** (b.r.) © 1980–2003, W. Chasan - All rights reserved. Todos Los Derechos Reservados, (t.r.) Kenneth Ehlers/ImageState/International Stock; **p. 94:** (b.) Claudia Uribe/Estock Photo/Estock Photo, (c.) Francisco Goya/Art Resource, NY, (l.) Francisco Goya; **p. 95:** (b.) Index Stock Imagery, (c.) Francisco Goya/Bridgeman Art Library, (t.) Francisco Goya/Art Resource, NY; **p. 96:** (l.) Fernando Botero, (r.) Salvador Dalí/Salvador Dalí Museum,St. Petersburg, FL; **p. 97:** Bob Daemmrich/Stock • Boston; **p. 101:** Dana White/PhotoEdit; **p. 102:** Spencer Grant/PhotoEdit; **p. 103:** Andrea Renault/Globe Photos.

Capítulo 3 p. 108: Michelle D. Bridwell/PhotoEdit; **p. 110:** (t.l.) HIRB/Index Stock Imagery, (t.r.) Michael Newman/PhotoEdit; **pp. 112-113:** (bg.) Corbis; **p. 112:** (b.c) Christie's Images/Corbis; **p. 120:** Owen Franken/Corbis; **p. 124:** (t.) Helen Norman/Corbis, (b.) Royalty Free Corbis; **p. 132:** ©David Young-Wolff/PhotoEdit; **p. 133** (b.) John Alves/Mystic Wanderer Images, (t.) ©Michael Newman/PhotoEdit; **p. 134:** ©David Young-Wolff/PhotoEdit; **p. 135:** Zephyr Pictures/Index Stock Imagery; **p. 140:** (m.l.) National

Geographic Society, (b.) ©John Neubauer/PhotoEdit; **p. 141:** (m.r.) ©Erich Lessing/Art Resource, NY, (t.r.) ©Macduff Everton Corbis, (b.r.) ©Erich Lessing/Art Resource, NY; **p. 143:** ©Michael Newman/PhotoEdit; **p. 147:** Dorling Kindersley; **p. 148:** (t.) EyeWire/ Getty Images, (b.) ©Michael Prince/Corbis.

Capítulo 4 p. 154: (t.l.) ©David Young-Wolf/PhotoEdit, (m.c.) Robert Frerck/Pearson photo archive, (t.r.) ©David Young-Wolff/PhotoEdit; **158-159:** (bg.) Robert Essel/Corbis, (b.c.) Pablo Picasso/Art Resource NY; **p. 161:** (t.r.) Robert Fried/DDB Stock Photo, (t.l.) Bob Daemmrich/Stock • Boston, (b.r.) David Simson/Stock • Boston, (b.l.) David Simson/Stock • Boston; **p. 162:** (t.c.) Royalty-Free/Corbis, (b.c) Royalty-Free/Corbis; **p. 167:** ©Royalty-Free/Corbis; **p. 169:** Esbin-Anderson/PhotoNetworkStock; **p. 170:** (b.r.) Ryan McVay/Getty Images, Inc.; **p. 172:** ©Bob Daemmnch/Stock • Boston; **p. 177:** ©Myrleen Ferguson Cate/PhotoEdit; **p. 179:** (b.r.) Univision, (r.) Carmen Lomas Garza, photo by Wolfgang Dietz; **p. 183:** (b.l.) Sergio Barrenechea/Associated Press, EFE; **p. 185:** RF Corbis; **p. 186:** Diego Rivera/Art Resource, NY; **p. 187:** (b.) ©Tony Freeman/PhotoEdit, (b.l.) Kelly-Mooney Photography/Corbis, (t.r.) ©Bill Ross/Corbis; **p. 189:** Corbis; **p. 192:** ©Kurt Stier/Corbis; **p. 193:** Latin Focus.com.; **p. 194:** Pablo Picasso/Art Resource, NY; **p. 195:** (b.r.) ©A. Ramey/PhotoEdit.

Capítulo 5 p. 200: (t.l.) Steve Skjold/PhotoEdit, (t.r.) Aaron Haupt/Stock • Boston; **p. 202:** (b.l.) David Young-Wolff/PhotoEdit, (t.) Jeff Greenberg/PhotoEdit, (b.r.) James Shaffer/PhotoEdit; **p. 204-205:** (bg.) Stephen Frisch/Stock • Boston, (b.c) Tamayo Rufino/Art Resource, NY; **p. 212:** Robert Frerck/Odyssey/Chicago; **p. 213:** Mug Shots /Corbis; **p. 215:** ©Archivo Icongrafico, S. A. /Corbis; **p. 216:** Corbis; **p. 217:** ©Michael Newman/PhotoEdit; **p. 219:** Diego Rivera/Detriot Institute of the Arts; **p. 223:** (r.) ©Tony Freeman/PhotoEdit, (l.) ©Michael Newman/PhotoEdit; **p. 226:** (t.) Don Smetzer/Getty Images, Inc.; **p. 227:** ©Bob Daemench/Stock • Boston; **p. 228:** ©Dwayne Newton/PhotoEdit; **p. 230** (t.) ©Spencer Grant/PhotoEdit; **p. 231:** Guillermo Arias/Associated Press, AP; **p. 232** (r.) Ed Bailey/Associated Press, AP, (t.r.) Jorge Jaramillo/AP/World Wide Photos, (l.) ©Farrell Grehan/CORBIS Corbis; **p. 233** (b.r.) Associated Press, AP Associated Press, AP, (b.l.) ©AFP/CORBIS Corbis; **p. 235** ©Charles Gupton Corbis; **p. 241** Isaac Hernandez/ MercuryPress.com.

Capítulo 6 p. 246: (t.l.) Bob Daemmrich/The Image Works, (t.r.) Corbis; **p. 248:** (t.c.) Photodisc/Getty Images, (t.l.) Corbis, (t.r.) Danny Lehman/Corbis; **p. 250:** (bg.) Roger Ressmeyer/Corbis, (i.) Roberto Matta/Art Resource, NY; **p. 254:** (b.l.) Esbin-Anderson/The Image Works, (t.l.) David Young Wolff/PhotoEdit, (t.r.) Bob Daemmrich/The Image Works; **p. 255:** (t.l.) Stock • Boston, (t.r.) Vincent DeWitt/Stock • Boston; **p. 257:** Bob Daemmrich/Stock • Boston; **p. 260:** Photo Library International/Corbis; **p. 262:** Courtesy of the Library of Congress; **p. 266:** (b.l.) Getty Images, (b.r.) Bill Aron/PhotoEdit, (b.r.) Michael Newman/PhotoEdit, (t.r.) George B. Diebold/Corbis; **p. 267:** (b.l.) Sonya Dawes/The Image Works, (b.r.) Stone/Getty Images, (t.c.) Corbis, (t.l.) David Young-Wolff/PhotoEdit, (t.r.) Chinch Gryniewicz/Corbis; **p. 268:** (b.c) RM/Corbis, (m.r.) John Madere/Corbis, (t.l.) Ed Kashi/Corbis; **p. 270:** Peter Menzel/Stock • Boston; **p. 271:** Kraft Brooks/SYGMA/Corbis; **p. 274:** Kent News & Pictures/Corbis; **p. 275:** Corbis; **p. 276:** Larry Lawfer/Index Stock Imagery; **p. 277:** NMPFT/Topham/The Image Works; **p. 278:** (b.c) Randy Faris/Corbis, (b.l.) Sergio Pitamitz/Corbis; **p. 278:** (b.r.) Jan Butchofsky-Houser/Corbis; **p. 279:** (b.) Joseph Sohm; Visons of America/Corbis, (m.r.) Joseph Sohm; Visons of America/Corbis; **p. 287:** Paul Barton/Corbis;

Capítulo 7 p. 292: (c.) Jane Tyska/Stock • Boston, (l.) Jane Tyska/Stock • Boston, (r.) Danny Lehman/Corbis; **p. 294:** (c.) Darrell Gulin/Dembinsky Photo Assoc., (l.) Rod Planck/Dembinsky Photo Assoc., (r.) Adam Jones/Dembinsky Photo Assoc.; **p. 296:** (bg.) Peter Menzel/Stock • Boston, (i.) Charles & Josette Lenars/Corbis; **p. 300:** (b.) Bill Bachmann/PhotoEdit, (t.) D.Donne Bryant/DDB Stock Photo; **p. 301:** (b.) Chris Lisle/Corbis, (t.) Buddy Mays/TravelStock; **p. 311:** Bill Bachmann/ PhotoEdit; **p. 314:** Charles & Josette Lenars/Corbis, Larry Dunmire/PhotoNetworkStock; **p. 315:** Larry Dunmire/ PhotoNetworkStock, Gianni Dagli Orti/Corbis, PhotoNetworkStock; **p. 321:** John Neubauer/PhotoEdit; **p. 322:** (l.) Roger Ressmeyer/Corbis, (r.) Barbara Alper/Stock • Boston; **p. 323:** Vo Trung Dung/Corbis; **p. 324:** (b.l.) Corbis, (b.r.) Corbis; **p. 325:** (m.r.) Charles & Josette Lenars/Corbis, (t.r.) Corbis; **p. 327:** LA VENTA/SYGMA/Corbis; **p. 330:** Francis G. Mayer/Corbis; **p. 333:** The Granger Collection, New York.

Capítulo 8 p. 338: Patrick Ward/Stock • Boston; **p. 340:** (t.c.) Robert Frerck/Stone/Getty Images, (t.l.) Mark Antman/The Image Works, (t.r.) Carl & Ann Purcell/Corbis; **p. 342:** (bg.) Stock • Boston, (i.) Joaquín Sorolla y Bastida/No credit provided; **p. 344:** (m.l.) Patrick Ward/Corbis, (m.r.) Paul Almasy/Corbis; **p. 345:** (l.) Stephanie Colasanti/Corbis, (m.l.) Dallas & John Heaton/Stock • Boston, (m.r.) Age Fotostock, (r.) Deveria, Eugene (1808-1865) ©Giraudon /Art Resource, NY; **p. 346:** (b.l.) Andrea Pistolesi/Image Bank/Getty Images, (bg.) Paul Almasy/Corbis, (m.c.) John and Lisa Merrill/Corbis; **p. 347:** (b.r.) Stephanie Maze/Corbis, (m.r.) Beryl Goldberg, (t.l.) D. Donne Bryant/DDB Stock Photo; **p. 348:** (b.r.) Charlie Waite/Stone/Getty Images; **p. 349:** (m.l.) Macduff Everton/Corbis, (m.r.) Charles Kennard/Stock • Boston; **p. 350:** Chad Ehlers/Index Stock Imagery; **p. 353:** Michael Newman/PhotoEdit, (m.r.) Richard Bickel/Corbis, **p. 355:** (m.r.) Hulton Archive/Getty Images, (t.r.) Spencer Grant/PhotoEdit; **p. 358:** (m.r.) Monica Stevenson/Foodpix/Getty Images, (t.c.) Tony Freeman/PhotoEdit; **p. 359:** (m.r.) Bill Bachmann/PhotoEdit, (t.r.) Paul Barton/Corbis; **p. 360:** Giraudon/Art Resource, NY; **p. 361:** (b.r.) Snark /Art Resource, NY, (t.r.) Michel Zabe/Art Resource, NY; **p. 362:** Steve Skjold/PhotoEdit, (b.r.) Bob Daemmrich/The Image Works; **p. 363:** Douglas Faulkner/Corbis; **p. 365:** Jeff Greenberg/PhotoEdit; **p. 366:** Myrleen Ferguson/PhotoEdit; **p. 367:** Rudi Von Briel/PhotoEdit; **p. 368:** David Young-Wolff/PhotoEdit; **p. 370:** Philip James Corwin/Corbis; **p. 371:** (b.c) John Elk III/Stock • Boston, (b.l.) Richard Cummins/Corbis, (t.r.) Richard Cummins/Corbis; **p. 377:** (b.r.) D. Donne Bryant/DDB Stock Photo, (t.r.) Charles & Josette Lenars/Corbis; **p. 378:** Hulton Archive/Getty Images; **p. 379:** George Mattei/Envision.

Capítulo 9 p. 384: (t.l.) Sergio Dorantes/Corbis, (t.r.) Contifoto/Corbis Sygma/Corbis; **p. 386:** (b.) Buddy Mays/Corbis, (t.l.) Stephen Frink/Corbis, (t.r.) Corbis; **p. 388:** (bg.) Michael & Patrica Fogden/CORBIS/Corbis, (i.) Banco de México Trust Schalkwijk/Art Resource, NY/Art Resource, NY; **p. 392:** HIRB/Index Stock Imagery; **p. 393:** (t.l.) Robert Fried/Stock • Boston, (t.r.) Bob